Gottlieb Christian Crusius, Henry Smith

A complete Greek and English lexicon for the poems of Homer and the Homeridae

Illustrating the domestic, religious, political, and military condition of the heroic age and explaining the most difficult passages

Gottlieb Christian Crusius, Henry Smith

A complete Greek and English lexicon for the poems of Homer and the Homeridae
Illustrating the domestic, religious, political, and military condition of the heroic age and explaining the most difficult passages

ISBN/EAN: 9783741112409

Manufactured in Europe, USA, Canada, Australia, Japa

Cover: Foto ©Andreas Hilbeck / pixelio.de

Manufactured and distributed by brebook publishing software (www.brebook.com)

Gottlieb Christian Crusius, Henry Smith

A complete Greek and English lexicon for the poems of Homer and the Homeridae

A complete
Greek and English lexicon
for the poems of
Homer
and the Homeridae
by
G. Ch. Crusius

Translated from the German
with corrections and additions
by
Henry Smith

Revised and edited
by
Thomas Kerchever Arnold.

New edition

London
Rivingtons
Oxford-Cambridge
1874

PREFACE

TO

THE FIRST ENGLISH EDITION.

A SECOND edition of Crusius's Homeric Lexicon, considerably improved by the author, was very carefully reviewed by *Dr. Ameis*, of Mühlhausen, in the "Jahrbücher für Philologie und Pädagogik" for 1843. The substance of Dr. Ameis's valuable remarks was introduced into the *third* edition, which was published in 1848, after Crusius's death, by Dr. Kühner, who availed himself of some manuscript criticisms by another scholar, whose name is not mentioned.

The American translation by Professor Smith nearly anticipated the improvements of the third edition by embodying the remarks of Ameis. This translation I have carefully revised, and the far larger portion of the work has been compared with the third German edition. The additions of the American editor were enclosed in crotchets: these I have removed, wherever I found that Crusius or his German editor had adopted the correction or addition suggested by Dr. Ameis. I have also added, occasionally, the derivations of rare words as given by *Lobeck, Döderlein*, or *Lucas;* and have frequently substituted Cowper's translations for those of Voss, which often, especially in the case of happy compounds, lose all their felicitous precision by being turned into English. I have also added, here and there, the explanations of the most recent editors, *Dübner* on the Iliad, *Fäsi* on the Odyssey. In carrying the work through the press, I have removed a very considerable number of false references (some of which still remain in the third German edition), and several erroneous interpretations, occasioned by a misapprehension of the German original, which a reference to the passage, as it stands in the poet himself, would have enabled the learned translator to avoid. Upon the whole, however, he has executed a difficult task successfully; and well deserves the thanks of English, as well as of American students.

T. K. A.

AUTHOR'S PREFACE.

Notwithstanding the great number of excellent helps which have been published, for a series of years past, in illustration of the Homeric poems, there has still, so far as my acquaintance extends, appeared no complete Lexicon, presenting within a moderate compass, to the numerous readers, and especially to the young readers of these poems, every thing necessary for understanding them. In my apprehension, a Lexicon of a particular author, although designed only for schools, should not contain simply an alphabetic series of words with their definitions, but should also particularly notice peculiarities of expression, and those passages which in point of construction or the signification of words, are difficult to be understood, or admit of different interpretations; it should also embrace, in connexion with the words, and especially with the proper names, the requisite explanations from mythology, geography, antiquities, and other auxiliary sciences, and thus form, as it were, a repertory of every thing needful for understanding the author. To what extent I have attempted to attain this object, will be seen by noticing the contents of this Lexicon. First, then, it contains all the words found in the Iliad and Odyssey, in the hymns, and other small poems. Secondly, especial attention is paid to the explanation of difficult passages; and, as far as space permitted, differing views, when existing, have been noticed. Thirdly, it contains all the proper names, accompanied by the necessary mythological and geographical explanations.

Before speaking further of the plan of this work, it is proper, perhaps, that I should justify myself in applying to it the expression, "A complete Lexicon."

The most copious Lexicon of Homer we possess, is the work of *Damm*, which appeared in 1765, under the title: "Novum Lexicon Græcum etymologicum et reale, cui pro basi substratæ sunt concordantiæ Homericæ et Pindaricæ." It embraces, as is well known, in addition to the Pindaric vocabulary, all the words to be found in the Iliad and Odyssey, with a careful citation of the passages in which they occur. In the last edition it has been improved, in point of convenience, by an alphabetical arrangement; and by the copious additions of Prof. Rost of Gotha, it has been brought nearer to the present standard of Greek scholarship. Although that carefully-executed work is not to be brought into comparison with the present, in respect to its extent and peculiar design, yet it does not contain the whole wealth of the Homeric language, since all the words and proper names peculiar to the hymns are wanting. That we should find in it omissions of single words, even in the Iliad and Odyssey, as ἄμαθος, ἀμπείρω, ἀναπείρω, Δύμη, Ἑλικάων, ἐκτάδιος, ἐλάσσων, πολύρρηνος, ῥυσός, φώκη, etc. was certainly, considering the compass of the work, to be expected. A still older work, "W. Seberi Argus Homericus s. Index Vocabulorum in omnia Homeri Poëmata," is a mere catalogue of the Homeric forms of words, without explanation. Important as this work is for the study of Homer, it has contributed no advantage to my undertaking, except that of enabling me by a comparison, to determine whether any word had been omitted. And even this comparison it was necessary to make with great caution, since the text of Homer has undergone many alterations since the publication of the work. Among the remaining Lexicons, I may mention that of Koës, which has appeared however only in the sample of the letter A; and the separately-published Lexicons of the Iliad and Odyssey, by *Lünemann*. How defective these books are, is known to every scholar who has examined them. In the definitions of the words, little more is to be found than in any general Lexicon; and small attention is paid to the explanation of difficult passages, and to the proper names of mythology and geography. That, finally, general Lexicons do not possess this completeness, is obvious from the fact, that proper names are for the most part excluded, and when introduced, commonly lack particular explanation. The Lexicon of Passow, however, forms an exception to these remarks*, because this distinguished Greek scholar directed his particular attention to the Homeric vocabulary. With a deep conviction of the value of the service which its lamented author has rendered to the poems of Homer, I gratefully acknowledge the solid information I have often derived from his excellent work. That, however, in many difficult passages of these poems, a satisfactory explanation is wanting, and that many mythological and geographical articles are either not introduced, or lack an explanation sufficient for understanding the poet, will have been remarked by those who have used the work.

With these remarks, it is proper I should indicate more specifically the plan which I have followed in the composition of this Lexicon.

The demand which may properly be made in a Lexicon of a single author, in regard to Grammar, I hope, in accordance with the plan of the work, to have met. In the case of substantives and adjectives, the Epic and poetic forms of the cases are annexed, commonly with a reference to the ordinary forms. The verb demanded particular attention. Here, I have given not only the main tenses, but also in

---

* I need not say, that this applies in a still higher degree to the admirable Lexicon of Liddell and Scott.—T. K. A.

addition the Epic and poetical forms. Difficult forms of persons and tenses, which the younger student would not easily trace, I have, after the example of other Lexicons, introduced into the alphabetic series, and referred to their ground form. For the further information of students, I have referred to the large Grammar of Thiersch, to the intermediate one of Buttmann, which is commonly used in the schools, and to that of Rost, as well as to the recently-published Grammar of my valued colleague, Dr. Kühner [in the 3rd Ed. to his School Grammar]. The large Grammar of Buttmann is rarely quoted, and only when the intermediate one affords no information on the topic in hand. In connexion with the common forms, the poetical forms are also given. Finally, I have thought it expedient, according to the derivation of the Grammars, to place the different forms of a root under the form which is in use as the Present, cf. ἀκακίζω, ἀραρίσκω, δατέομαι, &c.

In addition to the Etymology, in the case of derivative words, those which occur only in the poets are designated as poetic, and if found only in Epic writers, as Epic. For these references, I gratefully acknowledge my obligation to the Lexicon of Rost. To quantity, sufficient attention has, as a general principle, been paid, to mark the long syllables. A more extended explanation is given when the quantity admits of a doubt.

In regard to the definition of words, and to the numbering of the significations, a careful examination will show, that I have endeavoured to follow a natural arrangement. That I should, in a majority of words, agree with other Lexicons, results from the nature of the case; and I gratefully acknowledge, that in this point I am much indebted to the labours of Passow and Rost. It has been an especial aim, in the arrangement of the significations, to render the examination of them easy. For this reason, the main definitions, as well as those modifications of signification which a word receives in various connexions, are printed in spaced type [in this Ed. in Italics]; and the peculiar significations of the middle voice are distinguished from those of the active. In difficult words, I have not only compared the modern commentators and translators, but have also consulted the Scholia of the old Grammarians, the Commentary of Eustathius, and the Lexicon of Apollonius. Not unfrequently has the translation of Voss been cited verbatim, when it appeared important in the explanation of a word or passage. What degree of attention has been paid to the illustration of the domestic, religious, political, and military condition of the heroic age, will be seen by an examination of individual words, as βασιλεύς, δῆμος, of the mythological articles, of the names of clothes, weapons, &c. Finally, an equal degree of care has been bestowed upon the syntactic use of verbs in reference to cases and prepositions, and upon the explanation of the particles. In this connexion, justice requires that I should acknowledge my indebtedness to the Grammar of Dr. Kühner,

supply the place of a commentary, it appears to me necessary, not only to indicate the passages explained, but also to indicate those in which a word occurs in a peculiar signification or connexion. This desideratum I have endeavoured to supply, and have also marked the so-called ἅπαξ εἰρημένα with †. In order to distinguish the language of the hymns from that of the Iliad and Odyssey, an asterisk (*) is prefixed to the words which occur only in the hymns and other small poems. If to an article *Il. or *Od. is annexed, it shows that the word occurs only in the Iliad or Odyssey

As I have mentioned, as a second peculiarity of this Lexicon, the explanation of difficult passages, I may add a word upon this point. A careful examination of the book will show that not many difficult passages occur, for which there is not offered at least one translation ; in passages which admit of different explanations, the opposing views are always cited, with the grounds upon which they rest. The passages which have received a more detailed explanation, have been arranged in a special register, at the end of the preface, with a reference to the word under which the explanation is given, because, in many passages, it might be sought under different words.

The mythological and geographical proper names have been introduced into the alphabetical series, partly because the verbal explanation of them is found in appellatives in use ; and partly because the different accentuation of the proper name and appellative, is rendered more distinct by juxtaposition.

In the case of proper names which do not occur as appellatives, the definitions are given, for which I am indebted principally to Hermann, Diss. de Mythol. Græcorum Antiquissima, and De Historiæ Græcæ Primordiis (Opus. II. 1827). I have thus endeavoured to remove a ground of complaint which has reached me from various respectable quarters, in regard to my Lexicon of Greek proper names[*]. That the mythological and geographical explanations have not been borrowed from that work, but have been for the most part written for the purpose of illustrating the Homeric poems, will be seen by a comparison of the two works. For the mythological articles, I have consulted especially M. G. Hermann's Handbuch der Mythologie aus Homer und Hesiod, E. L. Cammann's Vorschule zu der Iliade, and D. E. Jacobi's Handwörterbuch der griechischen und römischen Mythologie. Upon the principal works which have appeared on the Homeric Geography, as those of Schönemann, Voss, Uckert, G. F. Grotefend, Völcker, as well as upon other writings which treat of this subject, as Mannert's Geographie der Griechen und Römer, Ottfried Müller's Geschichte hellen. Stämme, I. Bd., etc., I have bestowed a careful attention, although the plan of the work allowed only the more important points to be noticed.

[*] Griechisch-Deutches Wörterbuch der mythologischen und geographischen Eigennamen, nebst beigefügter kurzer Erklärung und Angabe der Sylbenlänge, etc. Hanover, 1832.

From what has been said, it will be inferred, that I have spared no pains in consulting all the helps for the explanation of Homer, within the compass of my acquaintance. The text which I have had principally in my eye is that of Wolf; in connexion with which, however, I have referred to the editions of Heyne, Bothe, and Spitzner; and in the hymns to Ilgen, Hermann, and Frauke. For definitions and explanations, materials have been drawn, not merely from the above sources, but also from the observations of Köppen, Heinrichs, Nitzsch, Nägelsbach, and from particular works on the Homeric language, as Buttmann's Lexilogus, Lehrs de Aristarchi Studiis Homericis, etc.; and I acknowledge with sincere gratitude the information I have derived from them. The work of Dr. Gräfenhan, Grammat. Dialectici Epicæ, Vol. I. L. 1, which will present an accurate and fundamental view of the phenomena of the Epic dialect, came into my hands whilst the last sheet was in the press; some more important matters from this work I have given in an appendix.

To what extent, in the execution of the work, I have succeeded in filling out the plan, which has been sketched, must be left to the candid decision of those who are qualified to judge. The more deep my conviction is of having often fallen short of my aim, the more thankful shall I be to receive any corrections or hints for improvement.

Finally, it will be the highest reward I can receive for the labour bestowed upon it, should intelligent teachers judge as favorably in regard to the utility of the book, as one sharp-sighted student of the Homeric poems has already expressed himself. I refer to Dr. Grotefend, the director of the Lyceum in this city, to whose inspection the plan of the undertaking, and a part of the work itself, was submitted.

G. CH. CRUSIUS.

Hanover, Nov. 1835.

INDEX OF DIFFICULT PASSAGES.

(VID. PREFACE.)

			Page				Page
Il. 1, 170	see	ἀφύσσω	80	Il. 11, 635	see	πυθμήν	364
566		χραισμέω	437	671		Πύλος	365
580		εἴπερ	125	12, 36		καναχίζω	226
2, 218		συνέχω	386	107		ἔχω	184
303		χθιζός	435	177		λάϊνεος	257
318		ἀρίζηλος	67	340		ἑτώχατο	163
356 }		δρμημα	313	433		ἔχω	184
590 }				13, 130		προθέλυμνος	357
701		ἡμιτελής	193	132		ψαύω	440
3, 100		ἀρχή	70	137		συμφερτός	384
180		εἴποτε	125	257		κατάγνυμι	229
205		ἀγγελίη	3	346		τεύχω	396
4, 214		ἄγνυμι	5	359		ἐπαλλάσσω	147
5, 384		ἐπιτίθημι	160	543		ἐάφθη	118
397		πυλός	365	707		τάμνω	389
487		ἀλίσκομαι	27	14, 35		πρόκροσσος	358
770		ἠεροειδής	190	40		πτήσσω	363
6, 168		γράφω	96	209		ἀνεῖσα	45
7, 239		ταλαύρινος	389	419		ἐάφθη	118
298		ἀγών	8	499		φή	422
336		ἐξάγω	143	15, 80		εἶμι	125
8, 328		νευρή	291	252		ἀίω	21
378		γηθέω	93	16, 216		ψαύω	440
9, 46		εἰ δέ	122	371		ἄγνυμι	5
235		ἔχω	184	422		θοός	204
378		κάρ	226	507		λείπω	260
506		φθάνω	422	667		καθαίρω	221
567		κασίγνητος	227	17, 42		ἀδήριτος	8
10, 224		πρό	356	213		ἰνδάλλομαι	215
351		οὖρον	319	297		αὐλός	76
391		ἄγω	7	18, 570		Δίνος	264
11, 51		κοσμέω	247	592		ἀσκέω	71
243		ΕΙΔΩ	122	19, 140		κλοτοπεύω	243

INDEX OF DIFFICULT PASSAGES.

		Page			Page
Il. 19, 183	see ἀπαρέσκω	58	Od. 7, 107	see καιρόεις	222
209	ἰείη	210	123	θειλόπεδον	199
402	ἑώμεν	184	8, 187	πάχετος	330
21, 126	ὑπαΐσσω	410	351	ἐγγυάω	118
172	μεσοπαλής	278	9, 135	πίαρ	342
22, 254	ἐπιδίδωμι	153	459	ῥαίω	367
356	προτιόσσομαι	361	10, 124	πείρω	332
483	ἀπουρίζω	61	86	κέλευθος	236
23, 30	ὀρεχθέω	311	11, 597	κραταιΐς	249
574	δικάζω	110	614	ἐγκατατίθημι	119
760	κανών	226	14, 521	ἀμοιβάς	33
762	σηνίον	342	15, 78	ἀγλαΐη	5
24, 58	γυνή	96	404	τροπή	405
79	Μέλας πόντος	274	16, 114	χαλεπαίνω	431
			17, 232	ἀποτρίβω	61
Od. 1, 130	λίς	265	268	ὑπεροπλίζομαι	412
234	βάλλω	84	18, 192	κάλλος	224
2, 33	ὀνίνημι	308	19, 203	ἴσκω	217
89	εἰμι	125	229	λάω	260
203	ἴσος	218	565	ἐλέφας	134
206	ἐριδαίνω	166	20, 302	Σαρδάνιον	372
3, 269	πεδάω	331	21, 71	μῦθος	287
4, 208	ἐπικλώθω	155	22, 31	ἴσκω	217
353	ἐφετμή	181	143	ῥώξ	371
5, 248	ἀράσσω	64	304	πτώσσω	364
252	ἴκρια	213	322	ἀράομαι	63
	σταμίν	380	348	ἔοικα	147
300	μή	281	23, 191	πάχετος	330
6, 201	διερός	110			
242	δέατ'	100	H. Merc. 75	πλανοδίη	344
265	ἐπίστιον	159	427	κραίνω	249
7, 86	ἐρείδω	164	H. Cer. 280	κατενήνοθεν	233
87	θριγκός	205	H. 26 7	κρύπτω	252

ABBREVIATIONS.

absol.	signifies	absolute.	Ion.	signifies	Ionic.
accus.	,,	accusative.	iterat.	,,	iterative.
act.	,,	active.	κ. τ. λ.	,,	καὶ τὰ λοιπά = etc.
adj.	,,	adjective	Lex.	,,	Lexicon.
adv.	,,	adverb.	Buttm. Lex.		Buttmann's Lexilogus
Æol.	,,	Æolic.	metaph.	,,	metaphorical.
aor.	,,	aorist.	mid.	,,	middle.
Apd.	,,	Apollodorus.	neut.	,,	neuter.
Apoll. or Ap		Apollonii Lex. Homericum.	Od.	,,	Odyssey.
			optat.	,,	optative.
Att.	,,	Attic.	partcp.	,,	participle.
Batr.	,,	Batrachomyomachia.	pass.	,,	passive.
comm.	,,	common, commonly.	perf.	,,	perfect.
compar.	,,	comparative.	plupf.	,,	pluperfect.
conj.	,,	conjunction.	plur.	,,	plural.
dat.	,,	dative.	poet.	,,	poetic.
depon.	,,	deponent.	signif.	,,	signification, signifies.
Dor.	,,	Doric.	sing.	,,	singular.
Ep.	,,	Epic.	subj.	,,	subjunctive.
epith.	,,	epithet.	V.	,,	Vaier or Voss.
fem.	,,	feminine.	=	,,	equivalent to.
fut.	,,	future.	†	,,	ἅπαξ εἰρημένον.
gen.	,,	genitive.	?	,,	doubtful.
h.	,,	hymn.	*	,,	only in the hymns.
Il.	,,	Iliad.	*Il.	,,	only in the Iliad.
imperat.	,,	imperative.	*Od.	,,	only in the Odyssey.
imperf.	,,	imperfect.	[ ]	,,	additions by the Translators, or by the English Editor.
infin.	,,	infinitive.			
intrans.	,,	intransitive.			

Cp. = Cowper.
Db. = Dübner.
Död. = Döderlein.
Füs. = Füsi.

Note.—To save space "Il." has been omitted; so that references to which "Od." is not prefixed, are all of them from the *Iliad*.

HOMERIC LEXICON.

A.

A, the first letter of the Gr. alphabet; as a numeral *one;* in Homer therefore the sign of the first Rhapsody. The 24 Rhapsodies (or *books*), both of the Iliad and Odyssey, are distinguished by the 24 letters of the Gr. alphabet.

α, in composition, is 1) *a privative* (before a vowel commonly ἀν), the English *in-* or *un-,* denoting a *negation* of the idea; sometimes also giving it a *bad* sense; ἄδηλος, *in*-visible, ἄπαις, child-*less*, ἄβουλος, *ill*-advised, ἀναίτιος, *in*-nocent. 2) *a copulative* [answering to the adv. ἅμα], indicates primarily a connexion of two objects, also mly conveying the notion of *equality, collection,* and *intensity;* ἄλοχος (λέχος), *bedfellow, wife;* ἀτάλαντος, *equiponderant;* ἀθρόος (θρέω), *assembled, crowded together.* 3) *a intensive,* strengthening the adj. with which it is compounded and answering to the adv. ἄγαν, ἄβρομος, *loud-roaring;* ἀσπερχής, *very impetuous.* This *intensive* a is found in but very few compounds [if at all] and is denied by many Gram. 4) *a euphonic* is prefixed for mere sound's sake to many words beginning with two consonants ; ἀβληχρός for βληχρός ; ἀστεροπή for στεροπή.

ἄ, interj., an exclamation denoting *displeasure, pity, astonishment; oh! ah!* ἆ δειλέ, *ah wretch!* 11, 441.

ἀδᾱ́τος, ον, poet. (ἀάω), 1) *inviolable* = *what one does not dare to violate ;* epith. of the waters of the Styx, 14, 271. 2) = *what one cannot violate, cannot injure,* &c.; as an ep. of a contest, Od. 21, 91. 22, 5. According to Buttm. Lexil. p. 4, the waters of the Styx are called *inviolable,* because the gods swore by them an oath *not to be broken ;* and in the Od. the contest is called *inviolable,* i. e. *that which may not be spoken against,* hence *honorable, distinguished ;* but Passow translates the word *irrevocable,* i. e. a contest whose result is decisive. The old Gram. suppose either a double a privative, or an a intensive, and explain ἀδᾱ́τος by πολυβλαβής, *very injurious.*

ἀαγής, ές (ἄγνυμι), *not to be broken, difficult to break, strong,* ῥόπαλον, Od. 11, 575.†

ἀάομαι, depon. mid. see ἀάω.

ἄαπτος, ον, poet. (ἅπτομαι), *not to be touched, unapproachable, invincible,* epith. of the strong hands of the gods and heroes, 1, 567. 7, 309.

ἀάσχετος, ον, Ep. for ἄσχετος.

ἀάω, poet. ($\smile \smile \_$), aor. 1. act. ἄασα. contr. ἆσα, aor. mid. ἀασάμην, 3. sing. ἄσατο, aor. pass. ἀάσθην. Of pres. only 3 sing. mid. ἀᾶται. 1) Act. trans. *to injure, to harm,* with acc. ἦ ῥά τιν' ἤδη βασιλήων τῇδ' ἄτῃ ἄασας ; hast thou ever before injured any king by such misfortune ? i. e. brought him into such misfortune ? 8, 236. *b)* Especially *to injure in the understanding, to infatuate, to befool, to mislead, to delude,* with and without φρένας : οἴνῳ, to stupify his mind with wine, Od. 21, 297. ἄασαν μ' ἕταροι, my companions befooled me, Od. 10, 68 [in this passage it is, *have wronged* or *injured* me]; and δαίμονος αἶσα, Od. 11, 61 ; hence pass. *to be deluded, infatuated, blinded, to fall into disaster,* 16, 685. Ἄτη, ἣ πρῶτον ἀάσθην, Ate, by whom I was first infatuated, 19, 136. ἀασθεὶς φρεσίν, Od. 21, 301. II) Mid. [exclusively in ref. to the *mind*] *to delude oneself, to let oneself be deceived, to mistake, to err, to act foolishly,* 9, 116 ; also ἀάσατο μέγα θυμῷ, he was utterly infatuated in mind, 11, 340. *b)* As dep. mid. with acc. *to lead astray,* 19, 91.

Ἀβακέω (βάζω), poet. aor. ἀβάκησα, properly, *to be without speech;* gener. *to be uninformed, to be ignorant, to be unsuspicious,* Od. 4, 249.†

Ἄβαντες, οἱ, the *Abantes,* the earliest inhabitants of the island of Euboea, who went to Troy under Elephenor the son of Chalcodon ; probably a colony from the Pelop. Argos which emigrated to Eubœa under king Abas ; according to Strabo they came from Thrace, 2, 536.

Ἀβαρβαρέη, ἡ (from ἀ and βάρβαρος native), a fountain nymph, mother of Æsepus and Pedasus by Bucolion, 6, 22.

Ἀβάς, αντος, ὁ (from ἀ and βαίνω not going away, Nabito, Herm.), a Trojan, son of *Eurydamas,* killed by Diomedes, 5, 148.

Ἄβιοι, οἱ, the *Abii,* nomadic Scythians in the north of Europe, accord. to Strabo, VII. p. 360, on the Ister, 13. 6.† (prop. *poor, needy,* from α and βίος : Wolf and Heyne have marked it as a proper name ; it was previously explained as an adjective.)

[ἄβιος, ον, see Ἄβιοι.]

*ἀβλαβέως, poet. for ἀβλαβῶς, adv. (ἀβλαβής), *harmlessly, without harm,* h. Merc. 83.

*ἀβλαβίη, ἡ, poet. for ἀβλάβεια (βλά-

B

πτω), *inviolability.* 2) *harmlessness, innocence;* in the plur. ἀβλαβίαι νόοιο, h. Merc. 393.

Ἄβληρος, ὁ, a Trojan. killed by Antilochus, son of Nestor, 6, 32.

ἀβλής, ῆτος, ὁ, ἡ, poet. (βάλλω), *not discharged, unshot,* epith. of an unused arrow, 4, 117. †

ἄβλητος, ον, poet. (βάλλω), *not hit, unhurt,* 4, 540. †

ἀβληχρός, ή, όν (a euphon. and βληχρός), *weak, powerless, gentle;* χείρ, the feeble hand of Venus, 5, 337; τεῖχος, a weak wall, 8, 178; θάνατος. a gentle death, Od. 11, 135. [Cf. ἁμαλός and μαλακός. Buttm. Lex. 194.]

ἄβρομος, ον (a intens. and βρόμος according to Apoll. Lex.), *loud-shouting, very clamorous.* Epith of the Trojans, 13, 41.† Passow with Eustath. makes a euphon. and translates *clamorous.* Buttm. makes a copulative, and translates *shouting together.*

ἀβροτάζω, poet. (prob. from aor. 2 ἀμβροτεῖν, Epic for ἁμαρτεῖν), *to miss,* τινός any one: found only in aor. 1 subj. μήπως ἀβροτάξομεν (ep. for ἀβροτάξωμεν) ἀλλήλοιϊν, lest we miss one another, 10, 65. † See Thiersch. § 232. Buttm. Lex. p. 82.

ἅβροτος, η, ον, later ος, ον, poet. (βροτός) = ἄμβροτος, *immortal, divine, holy.* νύξ ἀβρότη, *sacred night,* because it is a gift of the gods, 14, 78. (The meaning *without men* is doubtful. See Buttm. Lex. p. 83.)

Ἄβυδος, ἡ, *Abydos,* a city in the Trojan dominion opposite the Hellespont. opposite Sestos, now *Avido,* 2, 836. Hence the adv. Ἀβυδόθεν, *from A.,* and Ἀβυδόθι, *in* or *at A.*

ἀγάασθαι, see ἄγαμαι.

ἀγαγον, see ἄγω.

ἀγάζομαι, pres. not used by Homer, but supplies the tenses assigned to ἄγαμαι.

ἀγαθός, ή, όν, *good, excellent, strong,* distinguished of its kind. a) Spoken of persons, espec. of physical force and bravery; often with accus. of the limiting word, βοὴν ἀγαθός, good in the battle-cry (see βοή), epith. of leaders. β) Of birth, *noble, high-born* (opposed to χέρης), Od. 15, 324. b) Of things and states, εἰς ἀγαθὰ εἰπεῖν, μυθεῖσθαι, to speak for good, 0, 102. 23. 305. (cf. φρονέω) πείθεσθαι εἰς ἀγαθόν, 11, 789. ἀγαθὰ φρονεῖν, to be *well-intentioned, right-minded,* 6, 162. Neut. pl. subst. ἀγαθά, Od. 14, 441. Irreg. comp. ἀμείνων, βελτίων, κρείσσων, λωΐων, superl. ἄριστος, βέλτιστος, κράτιστος, λώϊστος, etc. [Lobeck doubts the relationship between ἀγαθός and ἄγαμαι, which Butim. approves of. Path. Serm. Græc. p. 363.]

Ἀγάθων, ωνος, ὁ (amplif. of ἀγαθός), son of Priam and Hecuba, 24, 249.

ἀγαίομαι, Ep. form of ἄγαμαι, only in pres. in the sing. *to be indignant, to be angry,* Od. 20, 16.†

ἀγακλεής, ές, poet. (ἄγαν, κλέος), gen. έος, *very illustrious, famous, glorious,* generally of men; once of Hephæstus (Vulcan), * 11. 21, 379.

Ἀγακλέης, contr. ῆς, ῆος, ὁ, a Myrmidon, father of Epigeus, *11. 16, 571.

ἀγακλειτός, ή, όν = ἀγακλεής, poet. *very celebrated, famous, glorious,* generally of men. b) Of things: only ἀγακλειτὴ ἑκατόμβη, a glorious hecatomb, Od. 3, 59.

ἀγακλυτός, όν, poet. (κλυτός), prop. of which one hears much, *far-famed, most glorious,* generally of men. b) Of things: only ἀγακλυτὰ δώματα, Od. 3, 388. 428.

* ἀγαλλίς, ίδος, ἡ, a bulbous-rooted flower *of the Iris tribe,* perhaps the *swordlily,* h. Cer. 7. 226.

ἀγάλλομαι, mid. only pres. *to glory or exult in, to be proud of* any thing, with the dat. generally in the partcp. spoken of men: ἵπποισιν καὶ ὀχεσφιν, proud of horses and chariots, 12. 114. Of gods: of the Thriæ, h. Merc. 553. Of Pan: φρένα μολπαῖς, to be proud in heart of the songs, h. 18, 24. Of mares: πώλοισιν, exulting in their foals, 20, 222. Of birds: πτερύγεσσι, exulting in their wings, 2, 462. Of ships (met.): Διὸς οὔρῳ, to exult in the fair wind of Zeus, i. e. to be favoured with a fair wind, Od. 5. 176. b) With a partcp. of Hector: ἀνάλλεται ἔχων τεύχεα, he exults in arms, 17, 473.

ἄγαλμα, ατος, τό (ἀγάλλω), prop. what contributes to splendour, or serves for ornament [= καλλώπισμα, πᾶν ἐφ᾽ ᾧ τις ἀγάλλεται], *an ornament, a jewel,* 4, 144. Od. 4, 602. Spoken especially of votive offerings to the gods, *a glorious* or *acceptable offering.* Of the Trojan horse, ἄγαλμα θεῶν, Od. 8, 509. Of a bullock adorned as a victim, Od. 3, 438. [The meaning *image,* etc. is post-Homeric.]

ἄγαμαι, dep. mid. a collateral Ep. form of ἀγάομαι and ἀγαίομαι, fut. ἀγάσομαι, (Wolf νεμεσήσεαι, Od. 1, 389). aor. 1. Ep. ἠγασάμην, ἠγασσάμην. (Fr. ἄγαμαι only 1 sing. pres. fr. ἀγάομαι 2 pl. pres. ἀγάασθε Ep. for ἀγᾶσθε. Inf. pres. ἀγάασθαι for ἀγᾶσθαι, 2 pl. impf. ἠγάασθε for ἠγᾶσθε.) 1) *to esteem,* in a good sense, *to admire, to venerate,* with acc. 3, 181; μῦθον, 7, 404; without acc. *to wonder,* Od. 23, 175; with partcp. 3. 224. 2) *to consider as too great;* in a bad sense, *to envy, to grudge* (in which signif. Hom. uses the pres. ἀγάομαι and ἀγαίομαι), with the dat. of pers. spoken of (especially of the gods, 17, 71), and acc. of the thing: τὰ μέν που μέλλεν ἀγάσσεσθαι θεὸς αὐτός, but this must even a god have envied [if it had happened: and therefore it did not happen. F.], Od. 4, 181; and with inf. νῦν μοι ἀγᾶσθε, θεοί, βροτὸν ἄνδρα παρεῖναι, now ye envy me, ye gods, that a mortal man is with me, Od. 5, 119. 8, 565. 3) *to be offended with, to be angry at,* with acc. κακὰ ἔργα, Od. 2, 67; κότῳ to be offended, to regard with anger, 14, 111.

Ἀγαμεμνονίδης, ου, ὁ, son of Agamemnon = Orestes, Od. 1, 32.

Ἀγαμέμνων. 3 Ἀγγελίης.

Ἀγαμέμνων, ονος, ὁ (fr. ἄγαν and μένω most constant), son of Atreus, grandson of Pelops, king of Mycenæ, the most powerful of the Grecian kings before Troy. He was, it is true, commander in chief; still his power was not so great that he could issue unconditional commands. He was also distinguished by his bodily stature, 2, 478; and personal bravery, 11; but was sometimes wanting in decision and circumspection. Hurried away by passion, he insulted the priest Chryses, and when obliged to restore his daughter, he caused Brisëïs to be taken by violence from the tent of Achilles, whose anger he was able to appease only by personal apology, 9. According to Od. 1, 300, and 11, 410 sq., Ægisthus, who had seduced his wife Clytæmnestra, in conjunction with his paramour murdered him when he returned from Troy. His daughters are named in 9, 287. Hence adj. Ἀγαμεμνόνεος, έη, έον, belonging to Α.

Ἀγαμήδη, ἡ, daughter of Augēas, king of Elis, wife of Mulius. She was acquainted with all the medicinal herbs which the earth produces, 11, 740.

Ἀγαμήδης, ους, ὁ (fr. ἄγαν and μῆδος counsel, son of Erginus king of Orchomenus and brother of Trophonius, architect of the temple of Apollo at Delphi, h. in Ap. 296.

ἄγαμος, ον (γάμος), unmarried, 3. 40.†

ἀγάννιφος, ον, poet. (νίφω), very snowy, covered with snow, epith. of Olympus, whose summit according to the statement of travellers is never free from snow, *1, 426. 18, 186.

ἀγανός, ή, όν, poet. (γάνος, γάνυμαι, 1) gentle, mild, lovely. ἔπεα, 2, 180; βασιλεύς, Od. 2, 230. ἀγανὰ βέλεα, the gentle arrows of Apollo and Artemis (Diana), since sudden, gentle death (in opposition to death produced by long sickness) was ascribed in the case of men to Apollo, and of women to Artemis, Od. 3, 280. 15, 411. See Apollo and Artemis. 2) Active, rendering mild, propitiatory, agreeable, welcome, δῶρα, 9, 113; εὐχωλή, a grateful vow, 9, 499. Od. 13, 357.

ἀγανοφροσύνη, ἡ (φρήν), mildness, gentleness, 24, 772. Od. 11, 203.

ἀγανόφρων, ον, gen. ονος, poet. (φρήν), of a gentle disposition, mildly disposed, 20, 467.

ἀγάομαι, Ep. form of ἄγαμαι, q. v.

ἀγαπάζω and ἀγαπάζομαι as dep. mid. = ἀγαπάω, only in the pres. 24, 464. Od. 7, 33. 16, 17.

ἀγαπάω (akin to ἄγαμαι), aor. ἠγάπησα, poet. ἀγάπησα, 1) to receive kindly, to treat with kindness or attention, with acc. spoken generally of men, Od. 16, 17. 23, 214; of a god: θεὸν ὧδε βροτοὺς ἀγαπαζέμεν ἄντην, that a god should thus openly favour mortals, 24, 464. 2) to be content, to be satisfied, οὐκ ἀγαπᾷς, ὃ (= ὅτι) ἔκηλος δαίνυσαι; art thou not content, that

ἀγαπάζομαι, dep. mid.: its partcp. stands in an absolute sense with φιλέω and κυνέω. οὐκ ἀγαπαζόμενοι φιλέουσ', do not cordially entertain, Od. 7, 33. welcome, 21, 224.

ἀγαπήνωρ, ορος, ὁ (ἀνήρ), manhood-loving, manly, bold, brave, epith. of heroes, 8, 114, Od. 7. 170.

Ἀγαπήνωρ, ορος, ὁ, son of Ancæus, grandson of Lycurgus, king and commander of the Arcadians. According to a later tradition, he was carried by a storm to Cyprus upon his return, 2, 610. Comp. Apd. 3, 10. 8.

ἀγαπητός, ή, όν (ἀγαπάω), beloved, dear, epith. of an only son, Od. 2, 365. Il. 6, 401; thence ἀγαπητῶς, with love, cheerfully, willingly, Batr.

ἀγάρροος, ον, poet. (ῥέω), strong-flowing, rapid, epith. of the Hellespont, 2, 845; of the sea, h. Cer. 34.

Ἀγασθένης, εος, ὁ (adj. ἀγασθενής, very strong), son of Augeas, king of Elis, father of Polyxenus, 2, 624.

ἀγάστονος, ον, poet. (στένω), properly, strong-sighing; then loud-roaring, deep-roaring; epith. of Amphitrite, Od. 12, 97. h. Ap. 94.

Ἀγάστροφος, ὁ (from στρέφω turning himself often), son of Pæon, a Trojan, killed by Diomedes, 11, 338.

* **ἀγατός**, όν, poet. for ἀγαστός, admired, neut. as adv. h. Ap. 515.

Ἀγαύη, ἡ, daughter of Nereus and Doris, 18, 42; (In Wolf and Spitzner Ἀγαυή, cf. A. Gräfenhan Gr. dial. Ep. p. 58.)

ἀγαυός, ή, όν (ἄγαμαι), admirable, wonderful, glorious, excellent, noble, generally epith. of kings and heroes; also of the Hippomolgi, 13, 5; of birth, μνηστῆρες ἀγαυοί, noble suitors; of the Phæaces: πομπῆες ἀγαυοί, excellent conductors, Od. 13, 71; and of Proserpine, Od. 11, 213. Superl. ἀγαυότατος, Od. 15, 229.

ἀγγελίη, ἡ (ἄγγελος), a message, an embassy, news, tidings. ἀγγελίη τινός, a message from or about any one, 15, 640; and ἀγγελίην πατρὸς φέρειν, to bring tidings of the father, Od. 1, 408. ἀγγελίην ἐλθεῖν, to come on an embassy, i. e. to bring a message, as an ambassador, 11, 140. In the last passage and some others, the old grammarians incorrectly suppose a subst. ὁ ἀγγελίης = ἄγγελος; but the best modern critics suppose an accus. or a gen. sing. of the fem. ἀγγελίη, cf. Buttm. Lex. (in voc.) Thiersch § 268, 2. Spitzner Il. 13, 252. ἀγγελίην ἐπὶ (Wolf. ἔπι) Τυδῆ στεῖλαν, they sent Tydeus on an embassy, 4, 384. ἤλυθε σεῦ ἕνεκ' ἀγγελίης (gen. caus.), connect thus, ἠλ. ἀγγ. σεῦ ἕνεκα, he came on account of a message on your behalf, 3, 205. ἠέ τευ ἀγγελίης μετ' ἐμ' ἤλυθες; or comest thou to me on account of some message? 13, 252. ἀγγελίης οἴχνεσκε, he was wont to go on account of a message, i. e. to carry messages, 15, 640.

ἀννελίης, ὁ. Ion. for ἀγγελίας, ου, ὁ, ac-

Ἀγγελιώτης. 4 Ἀγῑνέω.

see ἀγγελίη; cf. Rost. ausf. Lex. who defends the view of the ancients, *a messenger, an ambassador*. ἠλ. σεῦ ἕνεκ' ἀγγ. he came as an ambassador on thine account, 3, 206; cf. 13, 252. 11, 640. 15, 640. 4, 384.

* ἀγγελιώτης, ου, ὁ=ἄγγελος, *a messenger*, h. in Merc. 296. Comp. ἔριθος.

ἀγγέλλω (ἄγω), fut. ἀγγελέω, Ep. for ἀγγελῶ, aor. ἤγγειλα, aor. mid. ἠγγειλάμην, *to bear a message, to give information, to bear tidings*; often absol. 8, 398. 409; with the dat. of the pers. Od. 4, 24. 2) *to announce, recount, report*; with accus. of the thing, ἐσθλά, 10, 448; ἔπος, 17, 701; θέμιστας, h. Ap. 391; also of the person, τινά, to give intelligence of any one, Od. 14, 120. 122; and with inf. κήρυκες ἀγγελλόντων παῖδας πρωθήβας λέξασθαι, let the heralds proclaim that the adult youth are to post themselves for their watch, &c. 8, 517; comp. Od. 16, 350.

ἄγγελος, ὁ, ἡ, *a messenger, an ambassador*, whether male or female: *heralds* are called Διὸς ἄγγελοι, messengers of Zeus, 1, 334; Ὄσσα, 2, 93; also birds by whose flight divination was performed, 24, 292. 296.

ἄγγος, εος, τό, *a vessel* for wine, milk, etc. 2, 471. Od. 2, 289; *a jar, pail*, &c.

ἄγε, ἄγετε, properly imperat. fr. ἄγω, *bear*; then, as interject. *up! on! come on! quick!* Often strengthened: ἀλλ' ἄγε, ἄγε δή, *up, then! on, then!* comm. with imperat. also with the 1 and 2 pl. subj. ἄγε δὴ τραπείομεν, 3, 441. ἄγε δὴ στέωμεν, 11, 348; and ἄγετε περιφραζώμεθα, Od. 1, 76; and with the 1 sing. Od. 20, 296; once only with imperat. 3 plur. 2, 437 ἀλλ' ἄγε—ἀγειρόντων. On εἰ δ' ἄγε, *up, then!* see εἰ.

ἀγείρω (ἄγω), aor. ἤγειρα, Ep. ἄγειρα, perf. pass. ἀγήγερμαι, aor. 1. pass. ἠγέρθην. Peculiar Ep. forms: 3 pl. plupf. ἀγηγέρατο, 3 pl. aor. ἤγερθεν for ἠγέρθησαν, aor. sync. 2 mid. ἀγέρμην, part. ἀγρόμενος. 1) Active, *to collect, to assemble*; spoken of men, with accus. λαόν, 2, 438; ἀγορήν, to call an assembly, Od. 2, 28. b) Of things: *to collect, δημόθεν ἄλφιτα καὶ οἶνον*, Od. 19, 197; πύρνα, to collect by begging pieces of wheaten bread, Od. 17, 362. II) Mid. with the sync. aor. 2 and aor. 1 pass. *to assemble, to come together*; περὶ αὐτόν, 4, 211. ἐς ἀγορὴν ἀγέροντο, they came to the assembly, 18, 245. b) Trop. in the aor. pass. ὅτε δὴ ἄμπνυτο καὶ ἐς φρένα θυμὸς ἀγέρθη, when now he respired and life was collected into the heart, i. e. when he came to himself, 22, 475. Od. 5, 458. ἀψορρόν οἱ θυμὸς ἐνὶ στήθεσσιν ἀγέρθη, courage (hope) returned to his breast, 4, 152. μάχην ἤγειρας, 13, 778, belongs to ἐγείρω, q. v. Of like import are the poet. forms ἠγερέθονται, ἠγερέθοντο, and ἠγερέθεσθαι accord. to Arist. for ἠγερέεσθαι.

ἀγελαῖος, αίη, αῖον (ἀγέλη), *belonging to a herd, grazing in herds*. Il. and Od. epith. of cattle.

Ἀγέλᾱος, Ion. Ἀγέλεως, ὁ (fr. ἄγω and λαός leader of the people), 1) son of *Phradmon*, a Trojan, whom Diomédês slew before Troy, 8, 257. 2) a Greek slain by Hector, 11, 302. 3) son of *Damastor*, a suitor of Penelopê, slain by Ulysses, Od. 22, 293.

* ἀγέλαστος, ον (γελάω), *without laughing, sad*, h. Cer. 200; hence ἡ Ἀγέλαστος πέτρη, the mourning rock at Eleusis in Attica; Apd. In Od. 8, 307, in some editions ἀγέλαστα stands for γελαστά.

Ἀγελείη, ἡ, poet. (ἄγω, λεία), *the collector of booty*, epith. of Minerva as the protectress of heroes, Il. and Od.

ἀγέλη, ἡ (ἄγω), *herd, crowd*, with and without βοῶν and ἵππων, 19, 281.

ἀγεληδόν, adv. (ἀγέλη), *in herds, in crowds*, 16, 160.†

ἀγέληφι, poet. dat. for ἀγέλῃ, *in the herd*. Further see Thiersch Gr. § 177, 20. [See also Buttm. § 56, note 9.)

ἀγέμεν, poet. for ἄγειν.

ἄγεν, Ep. for ἐάγησαν, see ἄγνυμι.

ἀγέραστος, ον (γέρας), *without a present as a token of honour, unrewarded*, 1, 119.†

ἀγερίθομαι, Ep. form, fr. ἀγείρω, more correctly ἠγερέθομαι, which see.

ἄγερθεν, poet. for ἠγέρθησαν, see ἀγείρω.

ἀγέρωχος, ον, *proud, honour-loving, ambitious, noble-minded*, epith of the Trojans, Mysians, and Rhodians, 2, 654. 10, 430; and of Periclymenus, Od. 11, 286. Used, according to the Gram., by Homer in a good sense; later, *insolent, overbearing*; further, see Buttm. Lex. The derivation is uncertain; prob. fr. a n. 3, γέρας, ἔχω (hence = *richly-gifted*); cf. τιμάοχος.

ἄγη, ἡ (ἄγαμαι), *awe, admiration, veneration*, 21, 221. Od. 3, 227.

ἄγη, Ep. = ἐάγη, see ἄγνυμι.

ἀγηγέραθ'= ἀγηγέρατο, see ἀγείρω.

ἀγηνορίη, ἡ (ἀγήνωρ), *manliness, lofty courage, bravery*; spoken generally of men; of beasts, *boldness, strength*, 12, 46. 2) *arrogance, pride, insolence*; in the plur. ἀγηνορίῃσιν ἐνιέναι τινά, to inspire any one with arrogance, *Il. 9, 700.

ἀγήνωρ, ορος, ὁ, ἡ, poet. (ἄγαν; ἀνήρ), *very brave, courageous, bold*, epith. of heroes; also θυμός, 9, 398. 2) In a bad sense, *arrogant, proud, insolent*, μνηστῆρες, Od. 1, 144; and spoken of Achilles, 9, 699; θυμός, 2, 276.

Ἀγήνωρ, ορος, ὁ, son of *Antênôr* and *Theânô*, one of the bravest Trojan heroes, who contended even with Achilles, 11, 59.

ἀγήραος, ον, contr. ἀγήρως, ων (γῆρας), *not growing old, ever young*; often in connexion with ἀθάνατος, 8, 539; *imperishable, eternal*; spoken of the ægis of Zeus, 2, 447. Hom. has both forms; the contr. 12, 323. 17, 444. Od. 5, 218.

ἀγήρως, ων=ἀγήραος, ον, see ἀγήραος.

ἀγητός, ή, όν (ἄγαμαι), *admired, admirable, distinguished, glorious*; with accus. εἶδος ἀγητός, glorious in form, 5, 778. 24, 376; φρένας, Od. 14, 177.

ἀγῑνέω (a protracted form of ἄγω), fut. ἀγινήσω, h. Ap. 57; *to lead, to drive; to*

Ἀγκάζομαι.

bring, to fetch; spoken of things, like ἄγω: ὕλην, 24, 784. Od. 17, 294.

ἀγκάζομαι, depon. mid. (ἀγκάς), *to take up in the arms;* with accus. νεκρὸν ἀπὸ χθονός, to take up a dead body from the earth, 17, 722. †

Ἀγκαῖος, ὁ (lit. embracing with the arms, fr. ἀγκαί). 1) son of *Lycurgus* and *Eurynome,* father of Agapēnor, king of Arcadia, 2, 609. 2) an Ætolian from Pleurŏn, a powerful wrestler who was vanquished by Nestor in the funeral games in honour of Amarynceus, 23, 635.

* **ἀγκαλέω,** Ep. for ἀνακαλέω, *to call upon, to invoke;* hence ἀγκαλέουσιν, as Herm. reads for καλέουσιν, h. in Ap. 373.

ἀγκαλίς, ίδος, ἡ, prop. a dimin. of ἀγκάλη, *the arm;* only in the plur. *the arms;* dat. ἐν ἀγκαλίδεσσι φέρειν, to bear in the arms, *Il. 18, 555. 22, 503.

* **ἄγκαλος,** ὁ=ἀγκαλίς, h. Merc. 82.

ἀγκάς, adv. (prop. accus. from the obsolete ἀγκή), *with* or *in the arms,* in connexion with ἔχειν, λάζεσθαι, μάρπτειν, 5, 371. 23, 711. Od. 7, 252.

ἄγκιστρον, τό (ἄγκος), *a barb, a fish-hook,* *Od. 4, 369. 12, 322.

ἀγκλίνας, poet. for ἀνακλίνας, part. aor. from ἀνακλίνω.

ἀγκοίνη, ἡ, poet. (ἀγκών), *the elbow;* plur. *the arms,* only in the dat. ἐν ἀγκοίνῃσί τινος ἰαύειν, to rest in the arms of any one, 14, 213. Od. 11, 261.

ἄγκος, εος, τό, prop. a curve, hence *the elbow, the arm.* λαβεῖν τινα κατ' ἄγκεα, to take any body in one's arms, h. in Merc. 159. Comp. Herm. Commonly, 2) a *mountain-glen;* a glen, *dale,* 20, 490. Od. 4, 337.

ἀγκρεμάσασα, see ἀνακρεμάννυμι.

ἀγκυλομήτης, εω, ὁ, ἡ, poet. (μῆτις), *that has crafty* (lit. *crooked*) *designs, wily, politic, artful,* epith. of Κρόνος (Saturn), because he overreached his father Uranus, 2, 205. 319. h. in Ven. 22.

ἀγκύλος, η, ον (ἀγκη), *bent, curved, crooked,* epith. of the bow, 5, 209; and of the round-wheeled chariot, 6, 30.

ἀγκυλότοξος, ον, poet. (τόξον), *furnished* or *armed with bent bow,* epith. of the Pæonians, *Il. 2, 848.

ἀγκυλοχείλης, ου, ὁ, poet. (χεῖλος), *having a hooked bill* or *beak,* epith. of birds of prey, 16, 428. Od. 19, 538.

ἀγκυλοχήλης, ου, ὁ, poet. (χηλή), *having crooked claws,* Batr. 296.

ἀγκών, ῶνος, ὁ, prop. the angle formed by bending the arm, *the elbow,* 5, 582. 2) ἀγκὼν τείχεος, the salient (or jutting) angle of the wall, 16, 702.

* **ἀγλαόθειρος,** ον, poet. (ἔθειρα), *having beautiful hair, bright-haired,* epith. of Pan, h. in Pan. 5.

ἀγλαΐζω, poet. (ἀγλαός), *to make splendid* or *glittering;* in Hom. only in mid. fut. infin. ἀγλαΐεῖσθαι, *to exult in, to be proud of* a thing; with the dat. σέ φημι διαμπερὲς ἀγλαΐεῖσθαι, I declare that thou shalt glory in them perpetually (i. e. all

ἀγλαΐη, ἡ, poet. (ἀγλαός). 1) every thing possessing external splendour, *beauty, blooming appearance, ornament;* a) in a good sense, spoken of Penelope: ἀγλαΐην ἐμοὶ θεοὶ ὤλεσαν, the gods have destroyed my bloom, Od. 18, 180. Ἀμφότερον, κῦδος τε καὶ ἀγλαΐην καὶ ὄνειαρ δειπνήσαντας ἴμεν, sc. ἐστί. [Here it seems to denote the *joyous look* opp. to *an exhausted jaded one:* κῦδος καὶ ἀγλαΐη form *one* complex notion.] Both strength with a joyous countenance and refreshment are ensured to those who travel after taking food. They feel both more of spirit and joyous alacrity and more refreshment, etc. Voss]. Od. 15, 78; of a spirited horse, ἀγλαΐηφι πεποιθώς, trusting to his beauty, 6, 510; therefore *b*) In a bad sense, *ostentation, pride, vanity;* also in the plur. of the goatherd, Melantheus : ἀγλαΐας φορέειν, to exhibit pride, Od. 17, 244; and of a dog kept for display, Od. 17, 310. 2) In the plur. *festive joy, festivity,* h. Merc. 476.

Ἀγλαΐη, ἡ, *Aglaia,* wife of Charopus, mother of Nireus, 2, 672.

ἀγλαΐηφι, poet. dat. from ἀγλαΐη.

* **ἀγλαόδωρος,** ον, poet. (δῶρον), *with splendid gifts,* or *splendid in gifts,* epith of Ceres, h. in Cer. 54. 192.

ἀγλαόκαρπος, ον, poet. (καρπός), *with splendid fruits, fruit-distributing;* δένδρεα, Od. 7, 155; epith. of Cer., h. Cer. 4. 2) *having beautiful hands* [lit. *wrists*]; ἑταῖραι, h. in Cer. 23.

ἀγλαός, ή, όν, poet. (ἀγάλλω), *glittering, splendid, beautiful;* in a literal sense: ὕδωρ, sparkling water, Od. 3, 424; metaph. ἄποινα, splendid ransom, 1, 23 ; εὖχος, 7, 203. Often spoken of men: *distinguished, excellent, glorious ;* of Paris: κέρᾳ ἀγλαέ, who makest a display with the bow, 11, 385; in a bad sense. See also κέρας.

ἀγνοιέω, poet. for ἀγνοέω (νοέω), aor. ἠγνοίησα, Ep. iterative form, ἀγνώσασκε, Ion. for ἀγνοήσασκε, (incorrectly written ἀγνώσασκε, Od. 23, 95), *not to know, not to perceive,* mly with a negative, οὐκ ἠγνοίησε, she did not fail to observe, 1, 537. In Od. 24, 218, for αἴ κέ μ' ἐπιγνοίη —ἦε κεν ἀγνοίησι, we should undoubtedly read with Thiersch. § 216, 49. the subj. ἀγνοιῆσι. The subj. is required by πειρήσῃ and φράσσ.; hence we must also read ἐπιγνώῃ for ἐπιγνοίη.

ἁγνός, ή, όν, *pure, chaste, holy,* epith. of Artemis and Proserpine, Od. 5, 123. 11, 386; once ἁγνὴ ἑορτή, a holy feast, Od. 21, 259 ; ἄλσος, h. in Merc. 187. Hence adv. ἁγνῶς, Ap. 121.

* **ἄγνος,** ἡ and ὁ, a kind of willow-tree, the *chaste-tree* [vitex agnuscastus], h. Merc. 410.

ἄγνυμι, fut. ἄξω, aor. 1. ἦξα, Ep. ἔαξα, aor. 2 pass. ἐάγην, Ep. ἄγην (ᾰ once ᾱ), *to break, to break in pieces,* with accus. πολλοὶ ἵπποι ἄξαντ' λιπὸν ἅρματ' ἀνάκτων, many horses having broken left behind

Ἀγνώς. 6 Ἀγρονόμος.

(ἄξαντε, dual. with plur. since the poet thinks of the horses as in pairs, see Buttm. § 33. note 8. Kühner II, § 427); ὕλην, to break or dash down the forest, spoken of a rushing boar, 12, 148. 2) Pass. *to be broken, to break*, ἐάγη ξίφος, the sword broke, 16, 769. τοῦ δ' ἐξελκομένοιο πάλιν, ἄγεν (poet for ἐάγησαν) ὀξέες ὄγκοι, when he drew it back (Machaon, the arrow), the sharp barbs were broken: others,—the barbs were bent back. The meaning *to bend* cannot be sustained; and the Scholia explain it: κατεάγησαν, ἐκλάσθησαν. The connexion also requires this translation. (Machaon comes to the wounded Menelaus, and draws the arrow out of his girdle; the barbs break off and remain behind; he therefore takes off his belt in order to extract the broken points.)

ἀγνώς, ῶτος, ὁ, ἡ (γνῶμι), *unknown*, Od. 5, 79.

*ἀγνῶς, adv. from ἀγνός, *purely*, h. Ap.

ἀγνώσασκε, iterative form of the aor. 1 from ἀγνοέω, Od. 23, 95. The orthography ἀγνώσσασκε is false. (See Thiersch. Gr. § 210, 22.)

ἄγνωστος, ον (γνωστός), 1) *unknown, unrecognized*, τινί, Od. 2, 175. 2) *unknowable, not to be recognized*. σ'... ἄγνωστον τεύξω πάντεσσι, I will make thee incapable of being known by any man (disguise thee), *Od. 13, 191. 397.

ἄγονος, ον (γόνος), unhw. n, 3, 40.†

ἀγοράασθε, see ἀγοράομαι.

ἀγοράομαι, depon. mid. (ἀγορή), aor. ἠγορησάμην, 3 pl. impf. ἠγορόωντο, Ep. for ἠγορῶντο, 1) *to meet in assembly, to hold an assembly, to deliberate*, 4, 1. 2) *to speak in an assembly, to speak* in general, τινί with any one; often in connexion with μετέειπεν, 1, 73.

ἀγορεύω (ἀγορή), fut. εὔσω, aor. 1 ἠγόρευσα, properly *to hold an assembly*. ἀγορὰς ἀγορεύειν, *to deliberate*, 2, 787; then, *to speak in an assembly*, to harangue, ἐν Δαναοῖσι, ἐνὶ Τρώεσσι, 1, 109. 7, 361. 8, 525. 2) Generally, *to speak, to announce*, τί τινι: θεοπροπίας, the will of the gods, 1, 385. ἔπεα πρὸς ἀλλήλους, to speak words one to another, 3, 155. μήτι φόβονδ' ἀγόρευε, advise not to flight, 5, 252. πρῆξιν ἀγορεύειν, to speak of an enterprise, Od. 3, 82.

ἀγορή, ἡ (ἀγείρω), 1) *an assembly*, especially *a popular assembly*, in distinction to βουλή an assembly of the princes, 2, 51—33. Od. 3, 127. ἀγορὴν ποιεῖσθαι, τίθεσθαι, to hold an assembly, 8, 2. Od. 9, 171; καθίζειν, Od. 2, 69; λύειν, *to dismiss an assembly*, 1, 305. Od. 2, 69. 2) the business in an assembly, *discourse, deliberation, counsel*; e. pec. in the plur. ἔχειν τινὰ ἀγοράων, to restrain any one from speaking, 2, 275. εἰδὼς ἀγορέων, skilled in speaking (debate), 9, 441. 3) *the place of holding an assembly, market-place*, a certain place in towns where the higher classes sat upon stone seats, Od. 6, 266. Il. 18, 504; in the camp of the Greeks it was close by Agamemnon's tent: in Troy it was upon the highest citadel, παρὰ Πριάμοιο θύρῃσιν, 2, 788. 7, 545. 4) *market*, the place of sale, Ep. 14, 5.

ἀγορῆθεν, adv. *from the assembly*, Il. and Od.

ἀγορήνδε, adv. *to the assembly*, Il. and Od.

ἀγορητής, οῦ, ὁ (ἀγορή), *an orator, speaker*, connected with βουληφόρος, Il. and Od.

ἀγορητύς, ύος, ἡ (ἀγορή), *the talent of speaking, eloquence*, Od. 8, 168.†

*ἄγος, εος, τό, Ion. for ἅγος (ἅζω). *reverence, awe, pious fear*, θεῶν, h. Cer. 479. So Wolf. and Herm. for ἄχος.

ἀγός, οῦ, ὁ (ἄγω), Ep. *leader*, Κρητῶν, *Il.

ἀγοστός, ὁ (ἄγνυμι), prop. *the bent in*, hence the *bent-hand; the palm* or *hollow of the hand*, always ἕλε γαῖαν ἀγοστῷ, he grasped the earth with his hand, *11, 425. 13, 508. [∾ ἄγκος, ἀγκάλη. L. and S.]

ἄγραυλος, ον (αὐλή), *dwelling, sleeping*, or *lying in the fields* or *country*, ποιμένες, 18, 162; βόες, πόριες, cattle, calves living in pastures, 24, 81. Od. 10, 410.

ἄγρει, pl. ἀγρεῖτε, prop. imperat. from ἀγρέω, Æolic for αἱρέω, liter. *seize!* then like ἄγε, *up! on! quick!* pl. Od. 20, 149.

ἄγρη, ἡ, *the chase, the act of catching;* of fish, Od. 12, 330. 2) what is caught, *the game taken, prey*, Od. 22, 306.

ἄγριος, η, ον (ἀγρός), in Hom. only once -ος fem. Od. 9, 119; elsewhere of two endings, 3, 24. 19, 88; *living in the country* (in opposition to a town), *wild, unrestrained*; αἴξ, σῦς: and neut. plur. τὰ ἄγρια, every thing wild, *game*, 5, 33. 2) Spoken often of men: *wild, rude, fierce, cruel;* ἄγριος Κύκλωψ, Od. 2, 19; of the passions: χόλος ἄγριος, fierce anger, 4, 23; θυμός, 9, 629. ἄγρια εἰδέναι, to be cruel, savage.

Ἄγριος, ὁ, son of *Portha*on and *Euryte* in Calydon, brother of Œneus and Alcathous. His sons wrested the royal authority from Œneus and gave it to their father; they were however slain by Diomedes, 14, 117. According to Apd. 1. 8. 6. he was the father of Thersites.

ἀγριόφωνος, ον (φωνή), *having a harsh, rough, uncouth voice* or *pronunciation*, ['men of barbarous speech,' *Cp.*] epith. of the Sinties of Lemnos, Od. 8, 294.†

ἀγρόθεν and ἀγρόθε, adv. *from the country*, *Od. 13, 268.

ἀγροιώτης, ου, ὁ, poet. *a man from the country, inhabiting the country*. ἀνέρες ἀγροιῶται, rustic men, 11, 549; βουκόλοι, rural herdsmen, Od. 11, 293.

ἀγρόμενος, see ἀγείρω.

ἀγρόνδε, adv. *to the fields, to the country*. *Od.

ἀγρονόμος, ον (νέμω), prop. *pasturing* or *dwelling in the country*. ἀγρονόμοι νύμφαι, rural nymphs. Od. 6, 106.†

Ἀγρός. 7 Ἀγω.

ἀγρός, οῦ, ὁ, cultivated land, *a field*, pl. possessions of lands, fields, as opposed to houses, Od. 4, 757. Il. 23, 832; *country*, as opposed to town, also a *country villa* or *estate*, Od. 24, 205. πολυδένδρος ἀγρός, an estate abounding in trees, a *well-wooded* estate, Od. 23, 139. ἐπ' ἀγροῦ, in the fields, Od. 5, 489, in opposition to the town: in the country, Od. 1, 185.

ἀγρότερος, η, ον, poet. for ἄγριος, living in the fields, *wild*, as ἡμίονοι, ἔλαφοι, 2, 852. 21, 486. 2) *field-loving*, the *huntress* = ἀγραία, epith. of Artemis (Diana), 21, 471. (The verse is doubtful.)

ἀγρότης, ου, ὁ (ἀγρός), *countryman, an inhabitant of the country*, Od. 16, 218.†

ἀγρώσσω (ἄγρη), a collat. form fr. ἀγρεύω, *to hunt, to catch*, ἰχθῦς, Od. 5, 53.†

ἄγρωστις, ιος, ἡ (ἀγρός), that which grows in the fields, *grass, pasturage*, Od. 6, 90.† [Intpp. ad Theoph. make the *agrostis=triticum repens*.]

ἀγυιά, ἡ (ἄγω), once ἄγυια, 20, 254, *a way, a street* in towns, 6, 391. b) *road, path,* σκιόωντο πᾶσαι ἀγυιαί, all the paths or *roads* were darkened (growing dark): a picture descriptive of nightfall, Od. (Hom. never has the nom. sing. see Rost. Gr. § 32. p. 86.)

ἄγυρις, ιος, ἡ, Æol. for ἀγορά, *an assembly, a multitude*, ἀνδρῶν, Od. 3, 31; νεκύων, the multitude of the dead, 16, 661. ἐν νηῶν ἀγύρει, among the multitude of ships, 24, 141.

ἀγυρτάζω (ἀγύρτης), *to collect by begging*, χρήματα, Od. 19, 284.†

ἀγχέμαχος, ον (μάχομαι), *fighting in close combat, close-fighting*, epith. of brave warriors who fight with the lance or sword, *13, 5. 16, 248.

ἄγχι, adv. 1) *near*, in place; often with a following gen. ἄγχι θαλάσσης, 9, 43; also with gen. preceding Ἕκτορος ἄγχι, 8, 117. b) With dat. which however is generally better taken as dependent on the verb; ἄγχι παρίστατο ποιμένι λαῶν, 5, 570. 6, 405. 2) in time: *soon, forthwith*. ἄγχι μάλα, very soon, Od. 19, 301: (comp. ἆσσον, superl. ἄγχιστα and ἀγχοτάτω.)

ἀγχίαλος, ον (ἅλς), also ἀγχιάλη, h. Ap. 32, *near the sea, situated on the coast*, epith. of a maritime town, 2, 640. 697.

Ἀγχίαλος, ὁ, 1) a Greek, whom Hector slew, 5, 609. 2) father of Mentes, friend of Ulysses and king of the Taphians, Od. 1, 180. 3) a noble Phæacian, Od. 8, 112.

ἀγχιβαθής, ές (βάθος), gen. έος, *near the deep*, genr. *deep*; θάλασσα, Od. 5, 413 ; † [deep to the very shore, L. and S.]

ἀγχίθεος, ον (θεός), *near to the gods, similar to them*, epith. of the Phæacians, on account of their happy mode of life, or accord. to Nitzsch *nearly related to the gods*, *Od. 5, 35; cf. h. Ven. 201.

ἀγχιμαχητής, οῦ, ὁ = ἀγχέμαχος, *who fights in close combat, a close-fighting warrior*, 2, 604. 8, 173.

ἀγχίμολος, ον (μολεῖν), prop. *coming near;* only in neut. as adv. of place.

ἀγχίμολόν οἱ ἦλθε, he came near to him, 4, 529. ἐξ ἀγχιμόλοιο (sc. τόπου) 'ἐιν, to see from near, 24, 352. 3) Of time, *soon*. ἀγχίμολον μετ' αὐτόν, soon after him, Od. 17, 336; or perhaps of place: close behind him.

ἀγχίνοος, ον (νόος), prop. having a mind that is always ready: quickly apprehending, *intelligent, acute*, Od. 13, 331.†

Ἀγχίσης, εω, ὁ (very similar fr. ἄγχι and ἴσος, Pariliuus Herm.), 1) son of Capys and the nymph *Themis*, father of Æneas and king of Dardanus on Ida. Aphroditē (Venus) loved him and bore Æneas to him, 2, 819. 20, 239. h. in Ven. 45. Hom. mentions Hippodameia as his eldest daughter, 13, 429. 2) father of Echepolos, which see.

Ἀγχισιάδης, ου, ὁ, son of Anchises= Æneas, 17, 754.

ἄγχιστα, see ἄγχιστος.

ἀγχιστῖνος, ίνη, ινον (lengthened fr. ἄγχιστος), *near, crowded together*. ἀγχιστῖνοι ἔπιπτον νεκροί, 17, 361. Od. αἱ ἀγχιστῖναι ἐπ' ἀλλήλῃσι κέχυνται, 5, 141. This passage is differently explained. Heyne and Voss understand it of the slain sheep; cf. Schol. Vill. and Od. 22, 389. Damm, of the sheep huddling together from fear of the lion.

ἄγχιστος, η, ον (superl. from ἄγχι), *the nearest*; in Hom. only neut. sing. ἄγχιστον, very near. ὅθι τ' ἄγχιστον πέλεν αὐτῷ, where it was nearest to him [i. e. on the side that was next to him], Od. 5, 280. Often the neut. ἄγχιστα, with gen. 20, 18; tropically, spoken of a great similarity, ἄγχιστα αὐτῷ ἐῴκει, he very closely resembled him, 2, 58. Od. 6, 152. ἄγχιστα ἐΐσκειν τινά τινι, Od. 6, 151.

ἀγχόθι adv. = ἀγχοῦ, *near*, with. gen. ἀγχόθι δειρῆς, 14, 412. Od. 13, 103.

*ἀγχοτάτω, superl. of ἀγχοῦ, *very near*; with gen. h. Apol. 18.

ἀγχοῦ, adv. (prop. gen. from the obsolete ἀγχός), *near*. ἀγχοῦ ἵστασθαι, to approach, 2, 172. 2) With gen. ἀγχοῦ δὲ ξύμβληντο πυλάων νεκρὸν ἄγοντι, near the gates they met, etc. 24, 709 Od. 6, 5.

ἄγχω, *to choke, to strangle;* with accus. ἄγχε μιν ἱμὰς ὑπὸ δειρήν, the thong under his neck choked him, 3, 371.†

ἄγω, fut. ἄξω, aor. 2 ἤγαγον, aor. 2 mid. ἠγαγόμην, Ep. ἀγαγόμην (rarely aor. 1 ἦξα, part. ἄξας, Batr. 115. 119. Ep. imper. aor. 2. ἄξετε and inf. ἀξέμεν, 24, 663; aor. 1. mid. ἠξάμην, 8, 505. 545; ἄξασθε, ἄξαντο). 1) Primary meaning, *to lead, to convey, to carry;* spoken for the most part of things living (as φέρειν, of lifeless things, Od. 4, 622); therefore 1) Of living objects, both men and brutes, *to lead, to carry away, to bring;* according to the accompanying prep. and adv. with the accus., also τινά τινι, to conduct any one to any one, Od. 14, 386; also in a cnariot, ἤγον (ἵπποι) Μαχάονα, 11, 598; also of brutes: *to bring or convey an ox*, and ἑκατόμβην, a hecatomb (because it consisted of cattle, 1, 99) Especially *a*) Spoken of

Ἀγών.   8   Ἀδίκως.

carrying away by violence, τέκνα, γυναίκας, 9, 594; also τινὰ ἐν νήεσσιν, 4, 239. b) More rarely of inanimate things, οἶνον (by ship), 7, 467; ὅστεα οἴκαδε. 7, 335; λαίλαπα, to bring a tempest, 4, 278; φόρτον, Od. 14, 296. c) Trop. κλέος τινὸς ἄγειν, to carry, i. e. to spread any one's fame, Od. 5, 311; πένθος τινί, to occasion grief to any one, Batr. 49. 2) to lead, to conduct; spoken of the commander: λαόν, 10, 79; λόχον, to lay or set an ambuscade, 4, 392. Od. 14, 469; of gods: τὸν δ᾽ ἄγε Μοῖρα κακὴ θανάτοιο τέλοσδε, Fate led him to death, 13, 602. ἄγε νείκος Ἀθήνη, Minerva led the battle, 11, 721; also absolute, κῆρες ἄγον μέλανος θανάτοιο, the Fates of black death led, 2, 834. 11, 332. 3) Trop. πολλῇσιν μ᾽ ἄτῃσι παρὲκ νόον ἤγαγεν Ἕκτωρ, Hector led me foolishly into great misfortune, 10, 391. So Heyne. Others (Köppen) construe, νόον παρεξήγαγε, and take the dative as dat. of the means: by forceful delusion Hector misled my mind, 10, 391. The part. ἄγων often stands with verbs of motion. στῆσε δ᾽ ἄγων, 2, 558. ἔβαν ἄγοντες, 1, 391. II) Mid. to lead, carry, or take away for oneself; with accus. λαὸν ὑπὸ τεῖχος, the people to the wall, 4, 407; γυναῖκα οἴκαδε, 3, 93; Trop. διὰ στόμα τι, to carry any thing in the mouth, 14, 91. 2) to conduct home; γυναῖκα πρὸς δώματα, to conduct a wife home, 16, 189; without δώματα, Od. 14, 211; to marry a wife, 2, 659. Also spoken of the father who brings the son a wife, Od. 4, 59: and of the bridemen, Od. 8, 28.

ἀγών, ῶνος, ὁ (ἄγω), 1) assembly, place of assembly, a) the assembly, the circle of spectators, 24, 1. θεῖος ἀγών, assembly of the gods, 18, 376; where it may also mean the place of assembling, as αἴτε μοι εὐχόμεναι θεῖον δύσονται ἀγῶνα, who supplicating for me shall go into the divine assembly, or (according to V.) into the sacred place, 7, 298; (prob. the company of female suppliants, or according to others the temple itself as the abode of the gods.) b) place of collection, rendezvous, station; νεῶν, of the ships, 15, 428. 2) the place of combat in public games, both for the combatants and spectators, 8, 258. 448. 685. Od. 8, 200.

ἀδαημονίη, ἡ (δαήμων), ignorance, inexperience, Od. 24, 244.† [For the reading ἀδαημοσύνη, see Bothe in loc. and Buttm. Lexil. p. 31. Am. Ed.]

ἀδαήμων, ον, gen. ονος, poet. (δαήμων), ignorant; inexperienced; with gen. μάχης. Il. πληγῶν, unacquainted with blows, Od. 17, 283.

ἀδάκρυτος, ον (δακρύω), without tears, fearless, not weeping, 1, 415. Od. 24, 61; ὄσσε, Od. 4, 186.

Ἀδάμας, αντος, ὁ (= ἀδάμαστος), son of the Trojan Ἀσίως, killed by Μηρίόνης, 12, 140.

ἀδάμαστος, ον (δαμάω), unconquerable, inflexible, unyielding; epith. of Pluto, 9, 158.†

ἀδδεής, ές, poet. for ἀδεής, fearless, always κύον ἀδδεές, 8, 423.

ἀδδηκώς, poet. for ἀδηκώς, see ἀδέω.

ἀδδην, poet. for ἄδην.

ἀδεής, ές, poet. ἀδειής and ἀδδεής (δέος), fearless, bold, insolent, impudent, ἀδευής, 7, 117; κύον ἀδδεές, a term of reproach, 8, 423. Od. 19, 91.

ἀδελφειός and ἀδελφεός, ὁ, Ep. for ἀδελφός (δελφύς), brother ἀδελφειός, 5, 21. 6, 61.

ἀδευκής, ές, gen. έος, Ep. (δεῦκος), prop. not sweet, bitter, sour; metaph. φῆμις, disagreeable prating, Od. 6, 273. [Amaram famam, malum rumorem; so Barnes and Bothe. Am. Ed. ὄλεθρος, πότμος, *Od. 4, 489. 10, 245.

ἀδεύητος, ον (δεύω), undressed, βοέη, *Od. 20, 2. 142.

ἈΔΕΩ, pres. obsolete; only the optat. aor. ἀδήσειε, and part. perf. ἀδδηκότες Ep. also ἀδήσειε and ἀδηκότες (from ἄδην), to be satiated, to be disgusted. μὴ ξεῖνος δείπνῳ ἀδδήσειεν, that the stranger might not be disgusted (incommoded) at his meal, Od. 1, 134; twice, καμάτῳ ἀδδηκότες ἠδὲ καὶ ὕπνῳ, oppressed by labour and sleep, 10, 98. Od. 12, 281. καμάτῳ ἀδδηκότες αἰνῷ, fatigued with severe labour, 10, 312. 399. Some of the Schol. derive it from ἄδος (ἆ), and therefore double the δ; according to several ancient Gram. and Buttm. Lexil. p. 24, α is long in ἄδος, and the doubling not necessary; but Lobeck has proved that the α is short: ad Buttm. Ausf. Gr. 2, 99. Spitzn. returns to the double δ.

ἄδην, poet. ἄδδην. adv., prop. accus. of an old subst. ἄδη, sufficiently, enough, to satiety, as ἔδμεναι, 5, 203. 2) Metaph. with gen. οἵ μιν ἄδην ἐλόωσι πολέμοιο, who shall pursue him to satiety in war (to make him feel wearied and disgusted with war), 13, 315; cf. 19, 423. ἀλλ᾽ ἔτι μίν φημι ἄδην ἐλάαν κακότητος, I think I shall yet reduce him to misery enough, Od. 5, 290. The gen. is correctly explained as a gen. of place; Buttm. Lexil. p. 27, rejects the orthography ἄδδην, [and the notion of its being an acc. ἄδην· ἐλαύνειν=probe exercitare: to give him enough of war.]

ἀδήριτος, ον (δηρίω), uncontested, unfought. ἀλλ᾽ οὐ μὰν ἔτι δηρὸν ἀπείρητος πόνος ἔσται, οὐδέ τ᾽ ἀδήριτος, ἤτ᾽ ἀλκῆς, ἤτε φόβοιο, but this labour (battle) shall not much longer be unattempted, and unfought, whether it be for victory or for flight, 17, 42.† (The gen. accord. to Eustath. and Schol. A. depends upon ἀπείρητος by hyperbaton, the governing word in Greek being frequently separated from the governed by intervening words, cf. Spitzner and Schol. A. τὸ δὲ ἑξῆς ἀπείρητος πόνος ἔσται ἤτ᾽ ἀλκῆς ἤτε φόβοιο, οἷον πειρασόμεθα ἤτοι ἀνδρείας ἢ φυγῆς. Heyne and Köppen incorrectly construe: πόνος ἀλκῆς ἤτε φόβοιο, the contest of force or flight.)

*ἀδίκως, adv. (from ἄδικος), unjustly, unrighteously, h. Merc. 316.

* ἀδικέω (ἄδικος), fut. ήσω, to do wrong, to insult, h. Cer. 367; part. ἀδικήσας.

ἀδινός, ή, όν, poet. (ἄδην), abundant, hence 1') closely pressing, thronged, crowded; spoken of sheep and goats, 1, 92. 4, 320; of bees, 2, 87. 2) thick, closely encompassed, κῆρ, prop. the heart, closely encompassed by the entrails or thick flesh, 16, 481. Od. 19, 516. 3) strong, vehement, loud, γόος, 18, 316; ὄψ, h. Cer. 67; Σειρῆνες, the loud-voiced Sirens, Od. 23, 326. The neut. plur. and sing. often as adv., as ἀδινὸν στοναχῆσαι, to groan aloud, 18, 124. ἀδινὰ κλαίειν, to weep passionately or aloud, 24, 510. Comp. ἀδινώτερον κλαίειν, Od. 16, 216.

ἀδινῶς, adv. strongly, heavily, deeply; ἀνενείκασθαι, to sigh deeply, or groan heavily (with deep-drawn breath), [Lexil. p. 105.] 19, 314.†

ἀδμής, ῆτος, ὁ, ἡ, poet. (δαμάω), 1) unbroken, untamed; of animals which have not yet come under the yoke, ἡμίονοι, Od. 4, 637. 2) single, unmarried, παρθένος, *Od. 6, 109. 228.

*'Αδμήτη, ἡ, daughter of Oceanus and Tethys, h. in Cer. 421.

ἄδμητος, η, ον = ἀδμής no. 1, untamed, βοῦς, 10, 292. Od. 3, 383. 2) παρθένος, h. Ven. 82.

Ἄδμητος, ὁ, son of Pheres, king of Pherae in Thessalia, husband of Alcestis, father of Eumēlus, 2, 713.

ἅδον, see ἀνδάνω.

ἄδος, εος, τό (ἄδην), satiety; and then the consequent weariness, dislike to what one is doing, disgust. ἄδος τέ μιν ἵκετο θυμόν, weariness (or disgust) has come upon his soul, 11, 88.†

*ἄδοτος, ον (δίδωμι), ungifted, h. in Merc. 573.

'Αδρήστεια, ἡ, Adrastēa, a city in Mysia on the Propontis, named from its founder Adrastus. The region round the town was afterwards called τὸ τῆς 'Αδραστείας πεδίον, 2, 828.

'Αδρήστη, ἡ, Ion. for 'Αδράστη (from α and διδράσκω : not to be escaped), a noble handmaid of Helen, Od. 4, 123.

'Αδρηστίνη, ἡ, daughter of Adrastus = Αἰγιαλέα, 5, 412.

Ἄδρηστος, ὁ, Ion. or *Ἄδραστος, Adrastus, 1) son of Talaus, king of Argos, father of Argea, Hippodamea, Delpylē, and Ægialeus. Driven from this city by Amphiarāus, he fled to Sicyon, where he succeeded his grandfather Polybus in the government. He received the fugitive Polynīces, gave him in marriage his daughter Argea, and put in motion the expedition against Thebes, 2, 572. 14, 121. He also received the exiled Tydeus and gave him a daughter in marriage, 14, 121. 2) son of the soothsayer Merops and brother of Amphius, leader of the Trojan allies from Adrastea and Apæsus, 2, 830; slain with his brother by Diomedes, 11, 328 seq. 3) a Trojan conquered by Menelaus in battle, who was about to yield to his prayers and spare his life, when Agamemnon killed him, 6, 37 seq. 4) a Trojan slain by Patroclus, 16, 694.

ἁδροτής, ῆτος, ἡ, perfect maturity, the perfection of the adult body, physical strength, manly vigour; connected with ἥβῃ, *16, 857. 22, 363; and with μένος, 24, 6. (The reading ἀνδροτῆτα is properly rejected by Wolf.)

ἄδυτος, ον (δύω), adj. unapproachable, that may not be entered; hence as subst. τὸ ἄδυτον, and in h. Merc. 247, also ὁ ἄδυτος (sc. χῶρος), the innermost part of a temple, which only priests could enter, the sanctuary; and mly the holy place, temple, 5, 448. 512.

*ᾄδω, Att. for ἀείδω; hence fut. ᾄσομαι, h. 5. 2.

*ἀδώρητος, ον (δωρέομαι), ungifted, without receiving any present, h. Merc. 168.

ἀεθλεύω, Ep. and Ion. for ἀθλεύω (ἆθλος), only pres., which form Spitzn. has adopted in 24, 734, to contend for a prize, to combat [' to cope with him in manly games' Cp.], 4, 389; ἐπί τινι, in honour of some one, 23, 274. 2) to labour, to suffer, to endure; πρὸ ἄνακτος ἀμειλίχου, labouring for a cruel master, or in the sight of, etc. 24, 734. In the last signif. Homer generally uses ἀθλέω, q. v. *Il.

ἀέθλιον, τό, Ep. for ἄθλιον (ἆθλος), 1) a prize. ἀέθλια ποσσὶ ἀρέσθαι, to bear away the prizes in the race, 9, 124. 266. ἀέθλια ἀνελέσθαι, 23, 823; also ἀνελεῖν, 23, 736. 2) = ἀέθλος, prize-fight, contest, combat, Od. 24, 169. 3) the armour of combat, weapons, Od. 21, 62; (only in the Ep. form.)

ἄεθλον, τό, Ep. and Ion. for ἆθλον, 1) a prize, reward of a combat, 22, 163; plur. 23, 259; to go for the prizes, to be sent to the race, 11, 700; mly a reward, present, 23, 620. 2) In the plur. = ἄεθλος, a combat. ἐπεντύνεσθαι ἄεθλα, Od. 24, 89.

ἄεθλος, ὁ, Ep. and Ion. for ἆθλος, 1) a contest, combat, 16, 590. Od. 8, 131. 2) combat in war, every thing one suffers, fatigue, labour, want. μογεῖν ἀέθλους, to endure troubles, Od. 4, 170. (Hom. uses only the Ep. form, except ἆθλος, Od. 8. 160.)

ἀεθλοφόρος, ον, Ep. and Ion. for ἀθλοφόρος (φέρω), prize-bringing, victorious (in the race); ἵπποι, 9, 124. The Ep. form only in *Il. 22, 22. 162.

ἀεί, adv. Ion. and poet. αἰεί and αἰέν, always, continually, for ever, ever. θεοὶ αἰὲν ἐόντες, the eternal gods, 1, 290. It stands often for emphasis' sake with other words of equivalent import, as ἀσκελὲς αἰεί, etc. The com. form occurs but seldom in Hom. 12, 211: in other cases always αἰεί, and αἰέν when a short ultimate is required, 1, 520; hence Od. 1, 341 must be read αἰέν; see Herm. h. Ven. 202.

ἀείδω, Ep. and Ion. for ᾄδω, fut. ἀείσομαι, Att. ᾄσομαι, 5, 2. 1) Intrans.

Ἀεικείη. 10 Ἀελπτέω.

to sing, absol. 2, 598; τινί, to any one, Od. 1, 325; παρά τινι, before any one, Od. 1, 154. *b*) Spoken of birds, Od. 19, 519; of the bowstring, *to twang,* Od. 21, 411. 2) Trans. *to celebrate, to sing,* μῆνιν, 1, 1; κλέα ἀνδρῶν, 9, 189; παιήονα, 1, 473. Mid. as dep. *to celebrate in song, to hymn,* Ἥφαιστον, h. 17, 1. 20, 1; *a prop. short, but long at the beginning of a verse, and when it occurs in a quadrisyllabic form at its close.* Herm. reads ἀείσεο as Ep. imperat. aor. 2, for ἀείδεο, in h. 17. 1. Buttm. ausfür. Sprachl. § 96. Anm. 10. rejects the form ἀείδεο also in h. 20. 1.

ἀεικείη, poet. for αἰκία (εἰκός), *abuse, insult, indignity, outrage,* 24, 19; plur. ἀεικείας φαίνειν, to exhibit insolence, Od. 20, 309.

ἀεικέλιος, η, ον, also ος, ον, poet. for αἰκέλιος (εἰκός), 1) *unseemly, improper, unjust, shameful, contemptible;* ἀλαωτύς, Od. 9, 503; ἄλγος, horrible pain, Od. 14, 32; στρατός, a contemptible, i. e. small troop, 14, 82. 2) In reference to external form, *mean, ugly, disgusting,* Od. 6, 142; πήρη, δίφρος, Od. 17, 357. 20, 259; = ἀεικής, q. v.

ἀεικελίως, adv. poet. for αἰκελίως, *unsuitably, disgracefully, horribly.* *Od. 8, 231. 16, 109.

ἀεικής, ές, gen. έος, poet. for αἰκής = ἀεικέλιος, *unseemly, shameful, contemptible;* νόος, Od. 20, 366; λοιγός, πότμος, cruel suffering, end, 1, 341; ἔργον, an unseemly deed; often in the plur. μισθός, pitiful wages, 12, 435. The neut. with the inf. οὐ οἱ ἀεικές—τεθνάμεν, it is not disgraceful for him to die defending his country, 15, 496; and absolute, ἀεικέα μερμηρίζειν, to meditate mischief, Od. 4, 533. 2) Spoken of external form, *ugly, disgusting,* πήρη, Od. 13, 437. The neut. plur. as adv. ἀεικέα ἔσσο, thou wert shamefully clad, Od. 16, 199.

ἀεικίζω, poet. for αἰκίζω (ἀεικής), fut. ἀεικίσω, Ep. and Att. ἀεικιῶ, aor. 1. ἀείκισα, poet. ἀείκισσα, aor. mid. ἀεικισάμην, aor. 1 pass. ἀεικίσθην, *to treat unbecomingly, to abuse, to insult, or dishonour;* with accus. νεκρόν, a dead body, by leaving it unburied, or in any other way, 16, 545. 22, 256; ξεῖνον, to treat a stranger improperly, 18, 222. 2) Mid. = act. 16, 559.

ἀειράσας, see ἀείρω.

ἀείρω, poet. for αἴρω, aor. ἤειρα and Ep. ἄειρα, aor. mid. ἀειράμην and ἠράμην (ἤρατο, ἠράμεθα), with moods from aor. 2 ἀρόμην, subj. ἄρωμαι, optat. ἀροίμην, inf. ἀρέσθαι, aor. 1 pass. ἀέρθην. Ep. for ἤρθην, poet. 3 pl. ἄερθεν for ἀέρθησαν, ἀερθείς, and ἀρθείς, 3 sing. plupf. pass. ἄωρτο, Ep. form ἠερεθόνται. 1) Active, 1) *to lift up, to elevate, to raise aloft;* with an accus. λᾶαν, a stone, 7, 268; ἔγχος ἄντα τινός, to raise a spear against any one, 8, 424; also with ὑψόσε, to lift up high, 10, 465; hence aor. pass. to be lifted, κῆρες πρὸς οὐρανὸν ἄερθεν, 8, 74. ἐφύπερθεν ἀερθεὶς δύνον (being raised up=) raising myself

up above him, I turned it round and round, Od. 9, 383 (of Ulysses boring out the eye of Polyphemus); spoken of the eagle: ἐς αἰθέρα ἀέρθη, was borne, i. e. mounted to the sky, Od. 19, 540; and in the plupf. pass. μάχαιρα ἄωρτο, the knife was suspended, hung, 3, 272. 2) to lift, i. e. *to take up, to bring,* δέπας, οἶνον τινί, 6, 264. 3) to lift, i. e. *to take away, to carry away,* σῖτον ἐκ κανέου, Od. 17, 335; νεκρὸν ὑπὲκ Τρώων, 17, 589; ἐκ βελέων, 16, 678; spoken of ships: ἄχθος, to bear away a cargo, Od. 3, 312. II) Mid. 1) *to rise, to raise oneself;* spoken of running horses: ὑψόσ' ἀειρέσθην, 23, 501; of a ship: πρύμνη ἀείρετο, the stern rose, Od. 13, 85. 2) to take up for oneself, i. e. *to bear away, to take, to receive, to obtain.* πέπλον, ἕλκος; ἀέθλια πόσσιν, to win prizes in the race, 9, 124; so κῦδος, κλέος, νίκην; and strengthened, οἱ αὐτῷ κῦδος, to acquire glory for himself, 10, 307. The dat. expresses, *for another* (his advantage or disadvantage), Od. 1, 240; but also ἦ γάρ κέ σφι μάλα μέγα κῦδος ἄροιο, truly, thou wouldst acquire with them very great glory, 9, 303; [cf. 4, 95;] as ἐνὶ Τρώεσσι, 16, 84; πρὸς Δαναῶν, 16, 84. 3) *to take upon oneself, to bear,* τί, Od. 4, 107. 1, 390.

ἀεκαζόμενος, η, ον (ἀέκων), acting reluctantly, constrained, forced, often strengthened by πολλά, 6, 458. Od. 13, 277. (Only partcp.)

ἀεκήλιος, ον, Ep. for ἀεικέλιος. ἀεκήλια ἔργα, unseemly deeds, 18, 77.†

ἀέκητι, adv. (ἀέκων), *in spite of, against the will of;* often with the gen. Ἀργείων ἀέκητι, against the will of the Greeks, 11. 666. θεῶν ἀέκητι, in spite of the gods, 12, 8. Od. 8, 663.

ἀέκων, ουσα, ον (ἕκων), Ep. for ἄκων, *not willing, reluctant, against one's will, without design.* δέκοντος ἐμεῖο, against my will, 1, 301. σε βίῃ ἀέκοντος ἀπηύρα νῆα, he took the ship from thee by force, against thy will, Od. 4, 646; see ἀπαυράω. The other form occurs only in, οὐκ ἀέκοντε πετέσθην, viz. ἵππω, not reluctant flew the steeds, 5, 366. and often.

ἄελλα, ἡ (ἔλλω, εἴλω), [less probably ἄω], *a tempest, whirlwind, hurricane,* when several winds meet; often in the plur. χειμέριαι ἄελλαι, winter storms, 2, 293. ἄελλαι παντοίων ἀνέμων, tempests of all the winds, Od. 5, 292. 304; and in comparison: he battled ἶσος ἀέλλῃ, like the hurricane, 12, 40.

ἀελλής, ές (ἄελλα), *excited by the storm, tempest-driven, impetuous,* κόνισαλος, 3, 13.† (According to Buttm. ausf. Gr. § 41, 9. 15, more correctly ἀελλῆς for ἀελλήεις, like τιμῆς).

ἀελλόπους, οδος, ὁ, ἡ. Ep.ἀελλοπός (πούς), *storm-footed, rapid as the wind,* epith. of Iris, only in the Ep. form, *Il. 8, 409. 21, 77. 159; of steeds, h. Ven. 218.

[ἀελπής, see ἀελπτής.]

ἀελπτέω (ἄελπτος), *not to hope, to despair,* ἀελπτέοντες, 7, 310;† which must

Ἀελπτής. 11 Ἄημι.

be read with the Synizesis (before Wolf, falsely written ἀέλπονταες; Eustath. read ἀελπέοντες, which, according to Lobeck on Phrynicus, p. 575, is correct.)

ἀελπτής, ἐς (ἔλπομαι), gen. ος, *unhoped, unexpected*, Od. 5. 408. † Before Wolf, ἀελπέα, which Lobeck defends. Phryn. p. 570.

* ἀέλπτος, ον (ἔλπομαι), *unhoped, unexpected*, h. Ap. 91.

ἀενάων, ουσα, ον (ἀεί, νάω), *ever-flowing*. ἀενάοντο ὕδατα, perennial waters, Od. 13, 109 ; † (the first a long.)

ἀέξω, orig. form, later contr. αὔξω, Epig. 13, 3; prop. ἀΓέξω with the digamma; only in the pres. and imperf. without augment. I) Act. 1) *to increase, to nourish, to bring up, to augment;* οἶνον, to cause wine to grow (the rain), Od. 9, 111 ; κράτος, μένος, θυμόν, to augment power, courage, 12, 214 ; πένθος ἐνὶ στήθεσσι, to nourish grief in the heart, 7, 139 ; υἱόν, to rear a son, Od. 13, 360. Spoken of the gods : ἔργον, to bless the work, to give it success, Od. 15, 372. II) Mid. *to increase, to grow, to grow up;* Τηλέμαχος ἀέξετο, Telemachus grew up, Od. 22, 426. h. Merc. 408. κῦμα ἀέξετο, the wave arose, Od. 10, 93. χόλος ἐν στήθεσσιν ἀέξεται, anger waxes in the breast, 18, 110. Metaph. ἦμαρ ἀέξεται, *the day waxes* ['till the morning brightened into noon' Cp.], 8, 66. Od. 9, 56.

ἀεργίη, ἡ (ἀεργός), *inactivity, idleness*, only Od. 24, 251. †

ἀεργός, όν, contr. ἀργός (ἔργον), *inactive, lazy, idle*. The antithesis of πολλὰ ἐοργώς, 9, 320. Od. 19, 27.

ἀερέθομαι, see ἠερέθομαι.

ἀερθείς, see ἀείρω.

ἀέρθεν, see ἀείρω.

ἀερσίπους, ὁ, ἡ, gen. οδος, contr. ἀρσίπους, h. Ven. 212 ; (πούς) [in Hom. only plur.], *foot-raising, high-stepping*, epith. of ἵπποι, * Il. 3, 327.

ἄεσα and ἆσα (ἀέσαμεν, ἄσαμεν, ἄεσαν), infin. ἀέσαι, aor. 1, from obsol. 'ΑΕΩ, related to ἄημι, properly to breathe in sleep, *to sleep*, Od. 3, 490 ; νύκτας, Od. 19, 342 ; (the first ă. but by augment ā.)

* Od. [satiandi notionem habet ἄεσα, dormiendi vero ἀέσαι. Lob. Techn. 153.]

ἀεσιφροσύνη, ἡ, Ep. (ἀεσίφρων), *levity, thoughtlessness, folly*, in the pl. Od.15,470.†

ἀεσίφρων, ον, gen. ονος (ἀάω, φρήν), *disordered in mind, silly, thoughtless, simple*. The antithesis is ἔμπεδος, 20, 183 ; θυμός. Od. 21, 303 ; (prop. for ἀασίφρων. Buttm. Lexil. p. 7.) [Gr Syn. 111.]

'ΑΕΩ, see ἄεσα.

ἀζαλέος, η, ον (ἄζω), poet. *dried, dry, arid*, δρῦς, 11, 494 ; ὕλη, dry wood, Od. 9, 234. ἀζαλέη βῶς, dried bull's hide, i. e. a shield prepared of bull's hide, 7, 239 ; ὄρος, a dry mountain, i. e. upon which there is much dry wood, that is easily set on fire, 20, 491.

* ἀζαίνω, poet. for ἀζαίνω, *to dry up;* mid. *to wither* ἀζάνεται δένδρεα, h. in Ven. 271.

* 'Ἀζανίς, ίδος, ἡ, *Azanian,* ἡ—κούρη, the Azanian maiden=Corōnis, mother of Æsculapius by Apollo, because the family of her lover was from Azania, i. e. Arcadia, h. in Ap. 209; Wolf and Ilgen. But the Ep. and Ion.form is 'Ἀζηνίς ; hence Herm. substitutes 'Ἀτλαντίδα for the common reading 'Ἀζαντίδα ; the explanation is however obscure. See Herm. and Franke in loc.

'Ἀζείδης, αο, ὁ, son of Azeus=Actor, 2, 513.

'Ἀζεύς, έως, ὁ, son of *Clymenus*, brother of Erginus, Stratius, and father of *Actor*, Pausan. 9. 37. 2.

ἄζη, ἡ (ἄζω), prop. *dryness, aridity ;* then *soil contracted by drought*. σάκος πεπαλαγμένον ἄζῃ, a shield discoloured by dirt, Od. 22, 184. †.

ἀζηχής, ές, gen. έος,*continual, unceasing, incessant*, ὀδύνη, 15, 25 ; ὀρυμαγδός, 17, 741. The neut. ἀζηχές as adv. *unceasingly*, μεμακυῖαι, 4, 435 ; φαγεῖν, Od. 18, 3. (The Gram. derive it from ἀ and διέχω, so that ἀζηχής stands for ἀδιεχής by a change of δ into ζ; accord. to Rost, prop. dry, then *solid, perpetual*, from ἄζα. [Lob. Path. 336, prefers the former der.)]

ἄζομαι, mid. (act. ἄζω, Hes. op.), *to dry, to wither.* αἴγειρος ἀζομένη κεῖται, the poplar lies withering, ['exposed to parching airs,' Cp.] 4. 487. †

ἄζομαι, poet. depon. only pres. and impf. 1) *to stand in awe of* any one, with an accus. espy of gods and venerable personages, *to reverence, venerate, honour* any one, 'Ἀπόλλωνα, 1, 21 ; μητέρα, Od. 17, 401. 2) Intrans. *to fear, to dread*, with an infin. ἅζετο Διὶ λείβειν οἶνον, he feared to pour a libation of wine to Jupiter, 6, 266 ; and with μή : ἅζετο μὴ Νυκτὶ ἀποθύμια ἕρδοι, he dreaded to do any thing displeasing to Night, 14, 261.

'Ἀηδών, όνος, ἡ (prop. Ep. for ἀείδων, the songstress, the nightingale). *Aëdōn*, daughter of *Pandareus*, wife of *Zethus* king of Thebes, mother of Itylus. From envy towards her sister-in-law Niobe, she meditated the murder of her eldest son, but by mistake slew her own son. Having been changed into a nightingale by Zeus, she thenceforth bewailed him, Od. 19, 518. According to a later fable she was the wife of the artist Polytechnus in Colophon, cf. Anton. Lib. 11.

* ἀήθεια, ἡ (ἦθος), *unusualness, strangeness, novel condition* or *circumstances*, Batr. 72.

ἀηθέσσω, poet. for ἀηθέω (ἀήθης), *to be unaccustomed*, with gen., spoken of horses : ἀηθέσσον ἔτι νεκρῶν, they were as yet unaccustomed to the [sight of] dead bodies, 10, 493. †

ἄημι, Ep. (ἄεω), infin. ἄηναι, poet. ἀήμεναι, partcp. ἀείς, impf. 3 sing. ἄη, partcp. pass. ἀήμενος, imperf. mid. ἄητο (retaining always the η), *to breathe, to blow, to storm;* spoken of wind : Θρῄκηθεν ἄητον, 9, 5. ἄη Ζέφυρος, Od. 14, 458. Pres. partcp. λέων ὑόμενος καὶ ἀήμενος, a lion which goes through rain and wind, Od. 6, 131.

Ἀήρ. 12 Ἀθρέω.

II) Mid. only in a trop. signif. δίχα δέ σφιν ἐνὶ φρεσὶ θυμὸς ἄητο, the heart within their breasts was agitated in two different directions, i. e. they were irresolute, [Bothe, "the heart i, their bosom breathed discord;" and Cowper, "each breathing discord,"] 21, 386; but also: περί τ' ἀμφίτε κάλλος ἄητο, beauty breathed around, h. in Cer. 277.

ἀήρ, ἠέρος, Ion. and Ep for ἀέρος, ἡ, the lower, thick air, in distinction from the pure upper air, αἰθήρ, the atmosphere, 14, 288. 2) vapour, fog, clouds, mist, by which any thing thing is hidden from the view. ἐκάλυψε ἠέρι πολλῇ, 3, 381. 8, 50; and περὶ δ' ἠέρα πουλὺν ἔχευεν, she poured much mist around, 5, 776. 3) obscurity, darkness, 5, 864. Od. 8, 562. [Lexil. p. 37.]

ἀήσυλος, ον, poet. for αἴσυλος. ἀήσυλα ἔργα, impious deeds, 5, 876.†

ἀήτης, ου, ὁ (ἄημι), a blowing, a blast, spoken of vehement wind, often in connexion with ἀνέμοιο, ἀνέμων, 15, 626; also plur. ἀῆται ἀργαλέων ἀνέμων, blasts of dreadful winds, 14, 254. Od. 4, 567. b) Absol. for ἄνεμος, Od. 9, 139.

ἄητος, ον, poet. (ἄημι), stormy, boisterous. θάρσος ἄητον ἔχουσα, full of stormy boldness, used of Minerva, 21, 395.† (The derivation from ἄημι i. q. πνέω, according to Eustath. appears most natural, when we compare this with v. 386, θυμὸς ἄητο; the other explanations of the Schol. ἀκόρεστος from ἀΩ to satiate, or μέγιστος, have less weight; the last is approved by Buttm. Lex. p. 45. He regards it as identical with αἴητος, and from its supposed relationship to αἰνός, gives it the idea, prodigious, astonishing.)

ἀθάνατος, ον, also ος, η, ον, 10, 404. (θάνατος and αἰ, 1) immortal, spoken particularly of the gods, who alone are called ἀθάνατοι, 4, 394; also of what belongs to the gods, eternal, imperishable, αἰγίς, 2, 447; ὄμοι, Od. 4, 79. 2) endless, enduring, in reference to men; κακόν, Od. 12, 118.

ἄθαπτος, ον (θάπτω), unburied, 22, 386. Od. 11, 54.

ἀθεεί, adv., poet. (θεός), without god, without the will or direction of god, Od. 18, 352.†

ἀθεμίστιος, ον (θέμις), lawless, unjust, impious, Od. 18, 141; spoken of the Cyclops Polyphēmus: ἀθεμίστια εἰδέναι, to be versed in impiety, *Od. 9, 189. 428.

ἀθεμίστος, ον (θέμις [pl. θέμιστες]), prop. knowing no laws or civil institutions, lawless, uncivilized; spoken of the Cyclopes, Od. 9, 106. cf. v. 112; mly unrighteous, unjust, 9, 63. Od. 17, 363.

ἀθερίζω, only pres. and imperf. to slight, to despise, to disdain; with accus. 1, 261; connected with ἀναίνομαι, Od. 8, 212; (fr. θέρω, θεραπεύω; according to Ap. fr. ἀθήρ, ἔρος, chaff.)

ἀθέσφατος, ον (θέσφατος), prop. not to be expressed even by a god, ineffable, immeasurable, unspeakably great: θάλασσα, Od. 7, 273; γαῖα, h. 14, 4; ὄμβρος, immense rain, 3, 4; νύξ, endless night, Od. 11, 372. 15, 392.

Ἀθῆναι, αἱ, Ep. also ἡ Ἀθήνη, Od. 7, 80: Athenæ, capital of Attica, originally only a fortress established by Cecrops and called Κεκροπία; afterwards enlarged by Theseus, and called by the name of its tutelary goddess Atheuæ 2, 546. h. Ap. 30.

Ἀθηναίη, ἡ = Ἀθήνη.

Ἀθηναῖος, ὁ, an Athenian, 2, 546.

Ἀθήνη, ἡ. Ep. also Ἀθηναίη, [Athēnē, the Roman] Minerva, daughter of Zeus, according to Hom. without mother; he calls her Τριτογένεια, q. v.; according to a later fable, sprung from the head of Zeus, h. in Ap. 308; in Min. κή, 5; (hence Ἀθήνη, according to Herm. Nelacia, the unsuckled.) She is the symbol of wisdom united with power, and every thing stands under her protection, the performance of which requires reflection and spirit. Especially is she, 1) the tutelary divinity of cities at peace; every thing which gives prosperity to cities is her work; she therefore equally with Hephæstus (Vulcan) presides over every art, Od. 23, 160; and especially over female labours, Od. 2, 116. 6, 233. 2) she also protects cities in war against external foes; hence fortresses and walls are under her protection, and she is called ἐρυσίπτολις, Ἀλαλκομενηΐς. Thus she becomes also the goddess of war, but only of that war which is conducted with wisdom and profit, comp. Ἄρης; hence she is called ληΐτις, ἀγέλεια, λαοσσόος, etc. In this character she conducts battles, shelters heroes who in war unite bravery with discretion, 5, 333. 837. 21, 406. Hence also she is called Παλλάς, the spearbrandisher, and Hom. often writes Παλλὰς Ἀθηναίη or Ἀθήνη, 1, 200. 4, 78.

ἀθερηλοιγός, ὁ (ἀθήρ, λοιγός), Ep. for ἀθερηλοιγός, the destroyer of corn-beards: Tiresias so calls the winnowing-shovel, by which the grain is separated from the beards or chaff, in the oracle on the future fate of Ulysses, *Od. 11, 128. Od. 23, 275.

ἀθλέω (ἄθλος), aor. 1. ἄθλησα, prop. = ἀθλεύω, to contend for a prize; mly to toil, to endure, to suffer; only used in partcp. aor. ἀθλήσαντε πολίσσαμεν, which we built with much labour, 7, 453. 15, 30.

ἀθλητήρ, ῆρος, ὁ (ἀθλέω), Ep. for ἀθλητής, a combatant, a prize-fighter, Od. 8, 164.†

ἄθλος, ὁ, prose form for ἄεθλος, a contest, a prize-combat, Od. 8, 160.†

ἀθλοφόρος, ον, com. form for Ep. ἀεθλοφόρος, q. v.

Ἀθόως, Ep. for Ἄθως, q. v.

ἀθρέω, Ep. and Ion. for ἀθρέω, aor. ἤθρησα, to regard with fixed look, to see, to look, to gaze at, Od. 12, 232; εἴς τι, 10, 11; and with accus. τινά, to behold, to observe any one, 12, 391. [Wyttenb. a demortuo quodam θρέω traductum putat. Lob. Techn. 153.]

ἀθρόος. 13 **Αἴας.**

ἀθρόος, όη, όον, *collected, multitudinous, together, crowded.* ἀθρόοι ἴομεν, let us go together, 2, 439; also strengthened by πᾶς: ἀθρόοι ἦλθον ἅπαντες, they came all together in a body, Od. 3, 34. ἀθρόα πάντ' ἀπέτισε, he atoned for all at once, Od. 1, 43; comp. 22, 271. Hom. has only the plur.

ἄθυμος, ον (θυμός), *spiritless, dejected,* Od. 10, 463. †

ἄθυρμα, ατος, τό (ἀθύρω), *play, amusement, a plaything,* a toy, Od. 18, 323. ποιεῖν ἀθύρματα, to make playthings ['to build plaything-walls,' Cp.]; spoken of a boy making sand-heaps, 15, 363; mly *sport, amusement,* spoken of the lyre, h. Merc. 32; *trinket, ornament,* Od. 15, 415. 18, 323.

ἀθύρω, only pres. *to play, to amuse oneself;* spoken of children, 15, 364; like *ludere,* of a song, h. 18, 15; with accus. λαῖφος ἀθύρων, playing with the covering, h. in Merc. 152. 2) Mid. on the lyre, h. in Merc. 485.

Ἄθως, ω, ὁ, Ep. Ἀθόως, όω, a very high mountain, or rather point, of the promontory *Actê,* on the south-west coast of the Strymonic gulf, now *Monte Santo,* or *Agios Oros,* 14, 229. h. Ap. 33.

αἰ, conjunct. Æol. and Ep. for εἰ, always in connexion with κέ, αἲ κε and αἴ κεν, for the Att. ἐάν, *if, in case, if perchance, if perhaps.* It stands 1) In the protasis of conditional sentences with the *subjunctive,* but only when a hope, wish, anxious desire, etc. is expressed, *if perchance, in case.* αἲ κέν μοι—Ἀθήνη κῦδος ὀρέξῃ ἀμφοτέρω κτεῖναι, κ. τ. λ., if perchance Minerva should accord me the glory, etc., 5, 260; so likewise 11, 797. Od. 8, 496. 12, 53. *b*) With the *optative,* more rarely and for the most in dependent discourse: ἠνώγει Πρίαμος—εἰπεῖν, αἴ κέ περ ὕμμι φίλον καὶ ἡδὺ γένοιτο, μῦθον Ἀλεξάνδροιο, if perchance it might be agreeable to you, 7, 387. In other places Wolf and Thiersch read instead of the optat. the subjunct., as 5, 279. 24, 687: in Od. 13, 389, Thiersch (without reason) would read αἴθε for αἴ κε. 2) In indirect questions, after verbs of seeing, trying, proving, etc, with subjunct. *whether perchance, if perhaps.* ὄφρα ἴδητ', αἴ κ' ὔμμιν ὑπέρσχῃ χεῖρα Κρονίων, whether Kronos will protect you with his hand, 4, 249. 1, 207. Often before αἴ κε some such word as σκοπῶν, πειρώμενος, may be supplied, ὀτρυνέω ἀνιστήμεναι (πειρώμενος), αἴ κ' ἐθέλησιν ἰθεῖν, 10, 55; cf. 11, 796. Od. 1, 379. 2, 144. 3) In *a wish* (where for emphasis' sake it is always written αἴ) it never stands alone, but always in connexion with γάρ and γὰρ δή, *if but, would that,* always with the *optative,* which leaves it undetermined whether the wish is possible or impossible. αἲ γὰρ τοῦτο γένοιτο, would that this might be so, Od. 8, 339. αἲ γὰρ αὔτως εἴη, would that it might but be so, 4, 189; hence also of a wish whose fulfilment is impossible: αἲ γάρ—ἡβώμι, ὡς, would that I were bu still so young as, etc. 7, 132; rarely with infin. αἲ γὰρ—ἐχέμεν, Od. 7, 312, where according to the ancients ἐθέλοις is to be supplied (comp. however Rost, Gr. § 125. Anm. 3. Kühner, Gr. § 306, Rem 11, d.). In like manner Od. 24, 380.

αἶα, ἡ (properly γαῖα with the soft pronunciation), used only in the nom. gen. and accus. sing. *the earth, the land.* πᾶσαν ἐπ' αἶαν, over the whole earth; often πατρὶς αἶα, one's country; one's fatherland, 2, 162.

Αἶα, ἡ, pr. n. *Æa,* a mythic country, which is placed in the east, as the abode of *Æetes* in the Argonautic expedition (in the earliest fable prob. the Taurica Chersonesus, later Colchis, where was found a town Æa), and as the abode of Circê in the west; see Αἰαίη. Hom. has not this word as pr. n.

Αἰαίη, ἡ (Αἶα), 1) The *Ææan,* an appellation of Circe as an inhabitant of the *Ææan island,* Od. 9, 32. 2) νῆσος, the *Ææan island,* the abode of *Circe,* a mythic island, which, according to the most current and probable view, lies in the west, north of the Læstrygonians, above Sicily, whither Ulysses sailed from Æa with a north wind. According to another view the island of Circe lay in the far-north-east, and is identical with the abode of Æetes, Strabo, 1. p. 45. The older Scholiasts understand by it the promontory of *Circeii* in Italy, and suppose that it was formerly an island, Od. 10, 135. It is difficult to explain the remark of Homer, Od. 12, 3, that here is the abode of Eos and the rising of Helios. The most probable explanation is, that Ulysses, after his return from the gloomy underworld, has here arrived at regions illuminated by day-light. According to Völcker, Hom. Geog. p 31, and Weidasch, Eos and Helios are to be here regarded as gods; as such, like other deities, they have several abodes, cf. 14, 259—61.

Αἰακίδης, ου, ὁ, son of Æacus = *Peleus,* 10, 15. 2) grandson of Æacus = *Achilles,* 11, 805.

Αἰακός, ὁ (according to Herm. *Malivortus, averter of evil,* from αἰ and ἄκος), son of *Zeus* and *Ægina,* the just king of the island of Ægina, father of Peleus and Telamon by Endeïs, and of Phocus by the nymph Psammathe, 21, 189.

Αἴας, αντος, ὁ (according to Herm. *Vulturnus, the impetuous,* from ἀΐσσω, but, according to Eustath, *the pitiable,* from αἰ, αἰάζω), *Ajax* 1) ὁ Ὀιλῆος and ὁ Λοκρός, son of *Oileus,* leader of the Locrians, smaller of stature than the Telamonian Ajax, but a good lancer, 2, 530. His impudent boasting against Poseidôn he expiated by his death, Od. 4, 449. He was also hated by Athênê, because, according to a later fable, he had violated Cassandra in her temple in Troy. 2) ὁ Τελαμώνιος, son of *Telamon,* king of Salamis, brother of Teucer, next to Achilles the bravest of the Greeks; he even ventured upon

Αἰγαγέη. 14 **Αἰγύπτιος.**

a single combat with Hector, 7, 182. He contended with Ulysses for the arms of Achilles, and slew himself in a fit of madness, when he failed to obtain them, Od. 11, 544.

Αἰγαγέη, ἡ, Hom. h. in Ap. 40, a conjectural reading of Ilgene's for Αἰσαγέη. He derives it from αἴξ and γῆ, and understands by it the promontory Αἰγᾶν in Æolis; according to Hermann the change is unnecessary.

Αἰγαί, αἱ, 1) αἱ Ἀχαϊκαί, a little town in Achaia, on the Crathis, with a temple of Poseidôn, not far from Helicē, 8, 203. h. Ap. 32. 2) a city on the island Eubœa, on the west coast, also having a temple of Poseidôn, 13, 21. Od. 5, 381; or an island near Eubœa, according to Strabo, p. 386, and Steph. B.; or, according to Voss, a rocky island between Tenos and Chios; comp. Eustath. 13, 21. Plin. IV. 12. Other ancient commentators understood in this place also the Achaian Ægæ. (Αἰγαί plur. fr. αἰγά=αἴξ, the dashing of the waves.)

Αἰγαίων, ωνος, ὁ (the stormy, fr. αἴξ a storm), a hundred-handed sea-giant, so called among men, but among the gods *Briareus*. According to Apd. 1, 1, son of Uranus and Gæa. Thetis called him to the help of Zeus when the gods threatened to bind him, 1, 403.

αἰγανέη, ἡ (αἴξ), *a javelin, a hunting-spear*, prop. that used for hunting wild goats. [Coraes, on Plut. T. V. 343, derives it from ἀκή. Lob. Path. 186.]

Αἰγείδης, ου, son of Ægeus=*Theseus*, 1, 265.

αἴγειος, είη, ειον, poet. also αἴγεος (αἴξ), *of goats, relating to goats;* hence τυρός, goat's-milk cheese, 11, 639. 2) *made of goat's skin;* ἀσκος, a goat-skin bottle. 3, 247. κυνέη αἰγείη, a helmet of goat-skin, Od. 24, 231.

αἴγειρος, ἡ, *the poplar*, perhaps *black-poplar, aspen, populus nigra,* Linn., 4, 482; as a tree of the under-world, Od. 10, 510.

αἴγεος, έη, εον, poet. for αἴγειος, Od, 9, 196.

Αἰγιάλεια, ἡ, daughter of Adrastus, wife of Diomēdes, king of Argos, 5, 412; according to others, daughter of Ægialeus, grand-daughter of Adrastus. According to later fable she lived in adulterous intercourse with Comētes son of Sthenēlus, and caused her husband on his return to be expelled with violence; vid. Diomedes.

αἰγιαλός, ὁ (prob. from ἀἴξ and ἅλς a place where the sea beats), *a coast, a shore, beach*, Il. and Od.

Αἰγιαλός, ὁ (the coast-land), the part of the Peloponnesus from the Corinthian isthmus to the borders of Elis, or the later *Achaia*, according to the fable named from *Ægialeus*, son of Inachus, 2, 575; cf. Apd. 2, 11.

Αἰγίαλος, a little town and territory of the Henēti, in Paphlagonia, 2, 855.

αἰγίβοτος, ον (αἴξ, βόσκω), *goat-pastur-ing, goat-nourishing;* epith. of the island Ithaca, Od. 4, 606. As subst. *goat-pasture,* Od. 13, 246.

αἰγίλιψ, ιπος, ὁ ἡ (λείπω), prop. abandoned of goats, *high, steep, inaccessible;* epith. of πέτρη, *II. 9, 15.

Αἰγίλιψ, ιπος, ἡ, pr. n. of a place in Acarnania, built upon a rock, according to Strabo, IX. p. 452; according to others in Ithaca, or a little island near Epirus, 2, 633.

Αἴγινα, ἡ (according to Herm. *Quassatia*), *Ægina,* an island of the Saronic gulf, originally Œnōne and Œsopia, which received its name from Ægina the daughter of Asopus; now *Engia;* 2, 562. (Αἰγίνῃ, h. in Ap. 31.)

Αἴγιον, τό, *Ægium,* one of the chief towns in Achaia, later the rendezvous of the Achaian league; now *Vostizza,* 2, 574.

αἰγίοχος, ὁ (ἔχω), *the ægis-bearer, ægis-brandisher;* epith. of Zeus, Il. and Od.

*αἰγιπόδης, ου, ὁ (πούς), *goat-footed;* epith. of Pan. h. 19, 2.

αἰγίς, ίδος, ἡ (either fr. αἴξ, *goat*, because in ancient times goat-skin was used in constructing armour, or, in more strict accordance with Homeric usage, fr. ἀἴξ, *a storm*, because the brandishing of it excited confusion), *the ægis,* the shield of Zeus, emblem of powerful protection. Hephæstus made it of metal, 15, 308. It was similar to other shields of heroes, and upon it were terrific images, the Gorgo, surrounded by Eris, Alcē, and Iocē. By its movement Zeus excited terrour and confusion. Apollo and Athēnē (Minerva) also sometimes bore it, 15, 308. 2, 448. The ægis however served not only to excite terrour, but also for protection, 21, 400. 18, 204. 24, 40. It is described 5, 738. cf. 2, 448.

Αἴγισθος, ὁ, *Ægisthus,* son of Thyestes by his daughter Pelopea. He seduced Clytæmnestra the wife of Agamemnon, and slew him on his return from Troy, Od. 11, 409. He reigned twelve years over the wealthy Mycenæ, till at length he was slain by Orestes, Od. 1, 35. (According to mythology he was suckled by a goat; hence his name: αἴξ θάω, θῆσαι, Æl. V. H. 12, 42.)

αἴγλη, ἡ (akin to ἀγάλλω), *splendour, brightness,* of the sun and moon, Od. 4, 45; of brass, 2, 458; and generally, *light,* Od. 6, 45.

αἰγλήεις, εσσα, εν (αἴγλην), *glittering, brilliant, shining, bright;* epith. of Olympus, Il. and Od. The neut. as adv. h. 31, 11.

αἰγυπιός, ὁ, a large bird of prey, prob. *the Lammergeyer, a vulture,* fr. αἴξ and γύψ, 17, 466. Od. 16, 217.

Αἰγύπτιος, ίη, ιον, *Egyptian* (always to be pronounced in Hom. as a trisyllable, 9, 382). 2) Subst. *an Egyptian,* Od. 4, 83.

Αἰγύπτιος, ὁ, father of Antiphus and Eurynomus, an old man in Ithaca, who opened the assembly convened by Telemachus, Od. 2, 15.

Αἴγυπτος. 15 Αἰδώς.

Αἴγυπτος, ἡ, 1) As fem. *Egypt*, a country in North Africa. Od. 17, 448. 2) ὁ ποταμός, *the Nile*, which had in Hom. the same name with the country, Od. 4, 351. 355. 14, 257. 258.

αἰδεῖο for αἰδέο, see αἰδέομαι.

αἰδέομαι, poet. αἰδομαι, dep. fut. -έσομαι, poet. -σσ, aor. 1. mid. Ep. ᾐδεσάμην and αἰδεσσάμην, and aor. pass. with like signif. *to be abashed, to dread, to be ashamed*; only in a moral sense, in reference to gods and venerable persons, etc. 1) Absol. with infin. αἰδεσθεν ἀνήνασθαι, they were ashamed to refuse it, 7, 93; also with μήπως, 17, 95. 2) With accus. of the pers. *to stand in awe of any one, to venerate, to reverence, to honour*, 1, 23; spoken also of things, μέλαθρον, to honour the roof, i. e. to respect the rites of hospitality, 9, 640. (αἰδόμαι only in the pres.)

ἀϊδηλος, ον (a and ἰδεῖν), prop. *making invisible*, hence *devouring, destructive*; epith. of fire, of Arēs, and of Athēnē, II. of the suitors, Od. 16, 29. (cf. Buttm. Lex. p. 50.

ἀϊδήλως, adv. *in a destructive manner*, 21, 220.†

Ἀΐδης (‾), ao, ὁ, Ep. for Ἅιδης, Ep. gen. Ἀΐδεω trisyllabic, Od. 10, 512; (from a and ἰδεῖν, *Nelucus*, the invisible.) In Hom. always the name of a person, except in Il. 23, 244; *Hades, Pluto*, son of Kronos (Saturn) and Rhea, third brother of Zeus, received, at the division, the under-world, 15, 187. He was ruler of the realm of shades and of the dead, hence Ζεὺς καταχθόνιος; his wife was Persephōnē. He was a powerful, inexorable god, yet Herāclēs (Hercules) bore off his dog Cerberus from the lower world, and even wounded the god, 5, 395. His abode was *Hades* (δῶμ᾽ Ἀΐδαο, Ἀΐδος δόμοι). According to the universal imagination of later antiquity, Hades was beneath the earth, or in the interior of it. Even in Hom. we find unquestionable traces of this notion, cf. 20, 63 seq. Od. 5, 185. 20, 81. In other passages however the fancy of the poet places it only on the other side of the ocean, which separates it from the illuminated portion of the earth, Od. 10, 509. 11, 156; without distinctly fixing it beneath the earth as he does Tartarus, 8, 16. He describes it as a region spacious and dark, with mountains, woods, and waters, like the earth, Od. 10, 509 seq. Il. 8, 16. The entrance to the nether world was furnished with strong gates, which Cerberus watched, 8, 366. Od. 11, 622. Four rivers flowed through the realm of shades: the Acherōn, Pyriphlegēthon, Cocȳtus, and Styx, Od. 10, 513. All men after death were obliged to enter the lower world; still before burial they could not pass the river, but flitted about as shadows, see ψυχή. The shades have no memory, and only recollect after they have drunk blood (Od. 11, 56. 153); with which, however, the representation in Od. 24, 10 seq. seems at variance. The entrance to the under-world Hom. places in the west, near the gloom of the Cimmerians. Here, with him, the entrance to Hades is northward and Elysium southward (Od. 11, init.), comp. Völcker, Hom. Geogr. § 70. p. 136 seq. Concerning the situation of the lower world C. F. Grotefend has the following remark, in the Allgem. Geogr. Ephemer. B. XLVIII. 3 St. 1815, p. 258. As the earth's circuit on its upper surface had the form of a gradually declining shell, the same was imagined also to be true on the side turned from heaven, and that it was covered with a vaulted arch in a manner similar to the upper world. This nether and shade-inhabited surface was called ἀϊδής, because it had no communication with the upper world. Cf., in regard to the vaulted roof, the dreadful abode of the Titans, Τάρταρος, 8, 13. 481, and 14, 279. Kindred forms of Ἀΐδης are, by metaplasm: gen. Ἀΐδος, dat. Ἀΐδι; and the lengthened form Ἀϊδωνεύς, dat. Ἀϊδωνῆϊ. To go into the lower world is expressed by: πύλας Ἀΐδαο περήσειν, 23, 71; εἰς Ἀΐδαο δόμους or δόμον (also Ἀΐδαο δῶμα, Od. 12, 21), ἰέναι, καταδῦναι, etc.; and εἰς Ἀΐδαο alone (sc. δῶμα, etc.], 8, 367; also simply Ἀϊδόσδε. To be in the lower world: εἶναι εἰν Ἀΐδαο δόμοισιν, 22, 52; and without δόμοις Od. 11, 211.

* ἀΐδιος, ίη, ιον, for ἀείδιος (ἀεί), *eternal, everlasting*, h. 29, 3.

αἰδοῖα, τά, *the pudenda*, 13, 568.† prop. plur. from

αἰδοῖος, η, ον (αἰδώς), 1) Act. *having shame, modest, bashful, discreet, chaste*; ἄλοχος, 6, 250; ἀλήτης, a bashful beggar, Od. 17, 578. 2) Pass. *inspiring shame*, etc.; hence *estimable, venerable, honourable, reverend*; often united with δεινός; often ἄλοχος, 6, 250; παρθένος, 2, 514; ἑκυρός, 3, 172: and spoken only of persons, βασιλεύς, 4, 402; ξεῖνος, 19, 254. Compar. αἰδοιότερος.

αἰδοίως, adv. *honorably*, ἀποπέμπειν, Od. 19, 243.†

αἴδομαι. poet. for αἰδέομαι, q. v.

Ἀΐδος, Ἀΐδι, Ep. gen. and dat. by a metaplasm, vid. Thiersch § 181, 45. Buttm. § 56. note 8. Rost § 47. c. Often in the construction Ἀΐδος εἴσω, 6, 284; sc. δόμον, and εἰς Ἀΐδος, 13, 415; in full, 19, 322; εἰν Ἀΐδος, sc. δόμῳ, 24, 593; hence the adv. Ἀϊδόσδε, to Hades, 7, 330; (the formula εἰς Ἀϊδόσδε, Od. 10, 502, is changed by Wolf into εἰς Ἀΐδος δέ.)

ἀϊδρείη, ἡ (ἄϊδρις), *ignorance, inexperience, imprudence;* only in plur. Od. 10, 231. 11, 272. *Od.

ἄϊδρις, ιος, ι, Ep. dat. ἀϊδρεῖ (ἴδρις), *ignorant, unintelligent, inexperienced*, 3, 219; with gen. χώρου, Od. 10, 282.

Ἀϊδωνεύς, ῆος, ὁ, poet. lengthened form of Ἀΐδης, nom. 20, 61; dat. 5, 190.

αἰδώς, όος, contr. οῦς, ἡ, 1) *the feeling of shame* which one has in view of doing any thing wrong, *shame;* αἰδοῖ εἴκων, from [yielding to] shame, 10, 238 ἴσχε

Αἰεί. 16 Αἰθίοπες.

αἰδὼς καὶ δέος, shame and fear restrained, 15, 657. αἰδῶ θέσθ' ἐνὶ θυμῷ, have shame in (your) mind, 15, 561. b) the *diffidence, respect, awe, reverence* of the younger before the elder, the inferior before the superior. οὐ μέν σε χρὴ αἰδοῦς, there is no need of diffidence, Od. 3, 14. 24. 8, 480. 17, 347. 2) that which inspires shame; hence a) *shame, disgrace;* αἰδώς, 'Αργεῖοι, it is a shame, a disgrace, 5, 787. 8, 228. 13, 122. b) the *pudendum;* τὰ δ' αἰδῶ ἀμφικαλύπτει, sc. εἵματα, 2, 262.

αἰεί and αἰέν, Ion. and poet. for ἀεί, q. v.

αἰειγενέτης, ἀο, ὁ (γίγνομαι), *eternal, everlasting, immortal;* epith. of the gods, Il. and Od.

αἰετός, ὁ (ἄημι), Ep. for ἀετός, *eagle*, so called from his rustling flight, Linn. *faleo aquila.* The eagle is of a black or brown colour and the strongest and most rapid of birds, 21, 253; for this reason especially the messenger of Zeus, 24, 310. 292. As a prophetic bird, the eagle, on account of his lofty flight and his symbolical acts, was peculiarly significant, 12, 200. Od. 19, 545; vid. Nitzsch on Od. 2, 146.

αἰζήϊος, lengthened Ep. form fr. αἰζηός, 17, 520. Od. 12, 83.

ἀΐζηλος, ον, according to Hesych. and Etym. Magn.=ἀΐδηλος, *invisible*, with a change of the δ into ζ after the Æolic mode; prob. the correct reading in 2, 318, for ἀρίζηλος, according to Buttm. Lexil. p. 52, but see Nägelsbach Anm. p. 134. τὸν μὲν ἀΐζηλον θῆκεν θεός, the god made him again invisible, according to Clc. de Div. 2, 30, *idem abdidit et duro firmavit tegmina saxo.* The connexion certainly favours this reading, since it demands an antithesis to ὅσπερ ἐφηνέν, but Spitzner has retained ἀρίζηλον, as the only reading of the Cdd.

αἰζηός, ὁ, lengthened αἰζήϊος (perhaps from a intens. and ζέω, ζάω [Död. from αἴθω)], prop. to bubble up, *lively, active, hot, vigorous*, 16, 716. h. Ap. 449. As subst. in the pl. *youth, men*, with idea of strength and activity; αἰζηοὶ θαλεροί, 3, 26.

Αἰήτης, ἄο, ὁ, fr. αἴα, *Tellurinus*, according to Herm.), son of Helios (Sol) and Perse, brother of Circe, father of Medēa, the crafty king of Æa, to whom Jason went in his expedition after the golden fleece, Od. 10, 137. 12, 70.

αἴητος, ον (ἄημι), Ep. for ἄητος (like ἀιετός); hence πέλωρ αἴητον, the noisy monster; πνευστικός Hesych., 18, 410.† This epith. seems suitable for Hephæstus from the great noise connected with his occupation, cf. v. 409. The other explanations: (μέγας Eustath.) *great of* Buttm. and (συρώδης Hesych.) *sooty* of Voss, seem less satisfactory; see Buttm. Lex. p. 47.

αἰθαλόεις, εσσα, εν (αἴθαλος), *sooty, black from smoke, soot-black*, μέλαθρον, 2, 415; μέγαρον, Od. 22, 239. αἰθαλόεσσα κόνις, sooty dust, i. e. ashes united with dust, or generally, dust, 18, 23.

αἴθε, Dor. and Ep. for εἴθε, a particle expressing a wish, *would that, oh that but.* 1) With the optat. when it is uncertain whether the wish is of possible or impossible accomplishment: αἴθε σέο φέρτερος εἴην, oh that I were stronger than thou, 16, 722. αἴθε τελευτήσειεν ἅπαντα, would that he might accomplish it all, Od. 7, 331. 2) In connexion with ὤφελον, ες, ε, with an infin. following, to indicate a wish which cannot be accomplished; a) Spoken of the present: αἴθ' ὄφελες παρα νηυσὶν ἀδάκρυτος ἦσθαι, would that thou mightest sit here at the ships tearless, 1. 415. b) Of the past: αἴθ' ἅμα πάντες ὠφέλετε πεφάσθαι, would that ye had all been slain together, 24, 253. The form εἴθε is rare in Hom. Od. 2, 32.

Αἴθη, ἡ, *Bay*, name of a steed of Agamemnon, 23, 295; adj. αἴθός, ή, όν, fire-coloured.

αἰθήρ, έρος, ὁ, in Hom. also ἡ. 16, 365 1) *the pure, upper air*, in distinction from the lower, ἀήρ, 14, 288 ; and which is often hidden from our eyes by clouds; hence οὐρανόθεν ὑπερράγη ἄσπετος αἰθήρ, from heaven the infinite ether downward bursts, or opens [breaks up, clears off. Am. Ed], 8, 558; cf. 15, 20. Because Olympus extends its summit into the ether, it is represented as the abode of the gods; hence of Zeus it is said, αἰθέρι ναίων, dwelling in ether, 2, 412. Od. 15, 523. 2) In general, *clear, bright weather, serenity of the sky*,=αἴθρη, 16, 365. ὡς δ' ὅτ' ἀπ' Οὐλύμπου νέφος ἔρχεται οὐρανὸν εἴσω αἰθέρος ἐκ δίης, as when from Olympus a cloud comes over heaven after a serene sky; where ἐκ is translated by *after*, signifying time, cf. Spitzn. in loc.

Αἴθικες, Æthikes, a people of Thessalia, dwelling on Pindus, but afterwards on the borders of Epirus, 2, 744. Strabo, IX. p. 429.

Αἰθιοπεύς, ῆος, ὁ, an assumed ep. form of Αἰθίοψ, for the accus. plur. Αἰθιοπῆας, 1, 423.

Αἰθίοπες, οἱ, sing. Αἰθίοψ, οπος, ὁ, ep. form Αἰθιοπεύς (prop. *the imbrowned*, from αἴθω and ὤψ), *the Æthiopians;* in Hom. they are represented as dwelling on Oceanus, 1, 423. 23, 206; as being the remotest people of the earth (ἔσχατοι), and as being separated into two divisions, dwelling partly in the east and partly in the west, Od. 1, 23, 24. They are neighbours of the Egyptians and Erembians, Od. 4, 83. The manifold opinions of commentators cannot be all cited here. The old geographers place them in the south, and consider the Nile or the Red Sea as the dividing line, Strabo, II. p. 103. Two classes of Æthiopians are mentioned by Herodotus, 7, 70. Voss supposes the Æthiopians occupied the entire margin of the light-side (south). The poet imagined the Æthiopians to be in the south, without possessing any very accurate knowledge. He considers them as dwelling *easterly* and

Αἰθόμενος.   17   **Αἱμασία.**

westerly, because on account of the great heat (as Nitzsch on Od. 1, 22, remarks) they could not live in the direct south itself. He regards them therefore as being partly in Lybia and partly in the remoter parts of Asia, perhaps as far as Phœnicia, cf. Od. 4, 84. G. F. Grotefend, Geogr. Ephem. B 48. St. 3, correctly remarks: —The Æthiopians dwelling in the remotest south belong to both hemispheres. As far as historical geography extends dwell busy, active men, Od 6, 8. Nearer the margin of the earth dwell the fabulous nations, the Æthiopians, the Phæaces, the Pygmies, etc. In regard to the epith. ἀμύμονες, the blameless, and in regard to the journeys of the gods to them, I will only cite a remark from Völcker, Hom. Geog. § 47: —The Æthiopians are with Hom. a general name for the last inhabitants of the earth, the most remote people he knew of; to whom he might send the gods, in order to gain time for events which according to his plan must occur. The epithet ἀμύμονες rests perhaps on a similar ground with that on which certain Scythians are elsewhere denominated the most just among men (the Abii), viz., a confused notion of the innocence and justice of semi-savage nations that are but little known, which has in all ages been cherished, when an opposite opinion, a belief in their utter ferocity and wildness, has not yet been formed. See Völck. Hom. Geogr. § 46, 47.

αἰθόμενος, η, ον, prop. partcp. mid. (αἴθω), *burning, flaming*, with πῦρ, 6, 182; δαλός, 13, 320; δαίς, Od. 1, 428.

αἴθουσα, ἡ (prop. partcp. act. from αἴθω, sc. στοά, because the sun shone into it), *porch, gallery, piazza, portico*, which extended along the house on both sides of the door, Od. 4, 297. Il. 6, 243. Above, the portico was covered by the projecting roof of the house, which was supported by pillars; towards the court it was open, so that the sun could shine in; through this porch was the passage from the court to the vestibule πρόδομος. Such porches were also attached to the out-buildings, 9, 468. Od. 8, 57. Their main design was to afford a place in which to enjoy the sun; the chariots were placed in them, Od. 4, 24; strangers were allowed to sleep in them, Od. 3, 399. In Od. 4, 302 [cf. 15, 5], the αἴθουσα is included in the πρόδομος δόμων, see Cammann Hom. Vorsch. p. 325.

αἰθοψ, οπος. ὁ ἡ (αἴθω, ὤψ), prop. of *fiery look*; then, *sparkling, shining, gleaming, beaming*; χαλκός; οἶνος, the sparkling wine, 4, 259; not ruddy, see Od. 12, 19, where it stands connected with ἐρυθρός; καπνός, the dark smoke, Od. 10, 152.

αἴθρη, ἡ (αἰθήρ [for tne same r. as ἀήρ, αἰθήρ, αὔρα. Lob. Path. 58]), *pure, clear air, fair weather*, 17, 646. Od. 6, 44.

Αἴθρη, ἡ, Ion. for Αἴθρα, Æthra, daughter of Pittheus, wife of Ægeus, to whom she bore Theseus. Castor and Pollux, when they rescued Helen from Theseus, made her prisoner; she followed Helen to Troy, 3, 144.

αἰθρηγενέτης, ου, ὁ, Od. 5, 296; and αἰθρηγενής, ές (γίγνομαι), epith. of *Boreas*, 15, 171. 19, 356; *ether-born, produced in pure* or *cold air*; correctly passive Eustath., for compounds in γενής have always such a signification. The other explanation *cold-producing*, or, according to Voss, *clear-blowing* ['*cloud dispelling*,' Cp.] is against the analogy of the language.

* αἴθριος, ον (αἰθήρ), *clear, fair, serene*; epith. of Zephyr, h. in Ap. 433.

αἴθρος, ὁ (αἴθρη), *morning-cold, frost, rime*, Od. 14, 318.†

αἴθυια, ἡ, a *water-fowl* (V. Diver), *fulica mergus* ['*sea-mew*,' Cp.], *Od. 5, 337 and 353.

αἴθω, whence comes αἰθόμενος, q. v.

αἴθων, ωνος, ὁ (αἴθω), prop. *burning, fiery*, 1) Of colour, *shining, sparkling, flashing, gleaming, beaming*; of iron, 4, 485. 7, 473; spoken of brass and vessels made of it, 9, 123. 2) Metaph. spoken of larger animals; *fiery, fierce, spirited*; as λέων, 10, 24; ἵπποι, 2, 839; ταῦρος, 16, 488. Od. 18, 371, and αἰετός, 15, 690. The old grammarians referred it to the disposition; modern commentators, *fiery-red, red*, but it cannot well denote a common and regular colour, but describes rather the *shining hide*, plumage, &c. of smooth-coated or well-fed animals: the shining steeds, the sparkling lion, eagles, the fiery bull.

Αἴθων, ωνος, ὁ, 1) the name which *Ulysses* adopted before he discovered himself to Penelope, Od. 19, 183. 2) the steed of Hector, = *Bay* or *Fiery*, 8, 185.

αἴκ' for αἴκε, see αἰ.

αἰκή, ἡ (¯ ¯ ¯ from ἀΐσσω), an Ep. form or ἆξις, *a vehement rush. an attack, impetus*; only in the plur. τόξων αἰκαί, a discharge of bows, V. Il. 15, 709.†

* ἄϊκτος, ον (ἱκνέομαι), *inaccessible, unapproachable*, h. Merc. 346; accord. to Herm. conject. for ὅδ' ἐκτός.

ἀϊκῶς, Ep. for ἀεικῶς, *in an unseemly manner*, 22, 336.†

αἷμα, ατος, τό, 1) *blood*, with Hom. the seat of life, Od. 3, 455; hence the shades were obliged to drink blood before they could recover the power of recollection, Od. 11, 50. 97 seq. γαστὴρ ἐμπλείη κνίσσης τε καὶ αἵματος, a stomach filled with fat and blood, as food, Od. 18, 118; cf. v. 45. 2) *bloodshed, slaughter*, with ἀνδροκτασίη and κυδοιμός, 11, 164. φόνος τε καὶ αἷμα, 19, 214. 3) Like *sanguis*; *blood, consanguinity, race*, 6, 211. εἶναι αἵματος ἀγαθοῖο, to be of noble blood, Od. 4, 611 (perhaps from αἴω = ἄημι).

αἱμασία, ἡ [usually explained]: *thornbush*, for hedging a field or garden; mly a fence [prob. a *dry-wall* loosely put together: αἱμασίας λέγειν = to *collect* and pile up stones, etc. to make a *dry-wall*, a

Αἱματόεις. 18 Αἰολίη νῆσος.

fence.] *Od. 18, 359. 24, 224; see Buttm. Lex. p. 76, 8. [der. from αἷμος, *point,* doubtful.]

αἱματόεις, εσσα, εν (αἷμα), *bloody, sprinkled with blood, blood-red, blood-stained,* 5, 82. Od. 22, 405; σμῶδιξ, a bloody wheal ['whelk,' *Cp.*], 2, 267. 2) Transl. *bloody, of days, wars,* etc. [ἥματα, πόλεμος, 9, 326. 650.

Αἱμονίδης, ου, ὁ, *Hæmonides,* son of Hæmon=*Mæon,* 4, 394.

Αἱμονίδης, ου, ὁ, son of Æmon=*Laerkés* of Tuessalia, 17, 467.

αἱμοφόρυκτος, ον (φορύσσω), *stained* or *sprinkled with blood,* κρέα. Od. 20, 348.†

αἱμύλιος, ον (αἱμύλος), Ep. prop.*stealing into the soul, flattering, wheedling, deceptive,* λόγοι. Od. 1, 56. †h. Merc. 317; (prob. from αἷμος, a point ; hence, pointed, penetrating. [Lob. thinks that αἱμύλος itself came from αἱμύλλω, which the ancients derived from ἅμα or αἷμων, *scitus.*])

* αἱμυλομήτης, ου, ὁ (μῆτις), *flattering, cunning,* h. in Merc. 13.

αἷμων, ονος, ὁ, Ep. = δαίμων, δαήμων, *acquainted with, experienced;* with gen. θήρης, 5, 49.† Geist dispp. Hom. IV. 1, derives it from ἀϊω, *audio, sentio,* and therefore writes αἴμων.

Αἴμων, ονος, ὁ, 1) a hero of Pylus, 4, 296. 2) father of Mæon, q. v.

αἰνά, neut. plur. from αἰνός, q. v.

αἰναρέτης, ου, ὁ (ἀρετή) [male fortis], *brave to others' harm (fearfully* or *hurtfully brave);* only in voc. αἰναρέτη, of Achilles, 16, 31.†

Αἰνείας, αο, and Αἰνείω, 5, 334 ; (the *praised,* from αἰνέω, but acc. to h. in Ven. 198, from αἰνός), *Æneas,* son of Anchises and Aphroditê, a descendant of Tros, consequently related to Priam, king of the Dardanians, 2, 280 seq. 20, 215. He was, it is true, a brave hero; still he does not mingle much in the war. In the battle with Diomedes, Aphroditê (Venus) saved him, 5, 311 ; and in that with Achilles, Poseidon, 20, 178. According to Hom. Æneas remains in Troy, 20, 307; later traditions speak of him as having migrated to Italy.

αἰνέω (αἷνος), fut. αἰνήσω, Ep. for αἰνέσω, aor. 1. ἤνησα, for ἤνεσα, *to praise, to commend, to approve;* spoken of persons and things, with accus. Il. and Od. μή με μάλα αἴνες μήτε νείκεε, neither praise nor blame me, i. e. be silent about it, 10. 249.

αἰνίζομαι, depon. Ep. form fr. αἰνέω, *to praise,* 13, 374. Od. 8, 487.

Αἶνος, ὁ, a Pæonian slain by Achilles, 21, 210.

αἰνόθεν, adv. poet. (αἰνός), i. e. ἐκ τοῦ αἰνοῦ; only αἰνόθεν αἰνῶς, *most horribly, from bad to worse;* a periphrastic superl. like οἰόθεν οἷος, 7, 97.†

αἰνόμορος, ον, poet. (μόρος), *ill-fated, miserable, unfortunate,* 22, 480. Od. 9, 53.

αἰνοπαθής, ές, gen. έος (πάσχω), *dreadfully suffering, deeply afflicted* ['sad mourner as I am.' *Cp.*] Od. 18, 201.†

αἶνος, ὁ, Ep. 1) *discourse, narrative:* elsewhere μῦθος, Od. 14, 508. 2) *a commendatory discourse, praise, approbation,* 23, 795. τί με χρὴ μητέρος αἶνον, what need is there of my mother's praise, i. e. that I should praise her. Buttm. Lexil. p. 59, thinks it is distinguished from μῦθος, discourse generally, by indicating *a speech full of meaning, skilfully framed.* [Lob. says B. was too hasty in inferring the existence of αἴνω, *laudo,* Techn. 123.]

Αἶνος, ἡ, *Ænus,* a town in Thrace, at the mouth of the Hebrus, previously Πολτυοβρία, i. e. the town of Poltys according to Strabo, VII.; hence adv. Αἰνόθεν, from Ænus, 4, 520.

αἰνός, ή, όν, Ep. and Ion. for δεινός, *dreadful, frightful, terrific, great;* spoken of every thing which by its greatness, producing fearful and especially sad effects, excites our astonishment and terrour ; of the gods : *terrible,* i. e. cruel, stern; Zeus, 4, 25 ; Athênê, 8, 423 ; of other objects; of battle : 3, 20. Od. 8, 519; of passions: 4, 169, 7, 215. αἰνότατος λόχος, a most dreadful ambuscade, Od. 4, 441. ἐν αἰνῆσιν νεκάδεσσιν, in the horrible heaps of the dead, 5, 885. Neut. plur. αἰνὰ πάσχειν, *to* suffer dreadful things, 22, 431. Often as adv. αἰνὰ ὀλοφύρεσθαι, to lament greatly, Od. 22, 447. αἰνὰ τεκοῦσα, bearing for misfortune, 1, 414: Schol. ἐπὶ κακῷ. Superl. αἰνότατος, η, ον, 4, 25. (The derivation is obscure. Damm derives it from the interjection αἶ, contr. from αἰανός; Buttm. Lexil. derives it from a root αἴω, from which by means of the ending νός (as δεινός from δεῖσαι) αἰνός is formed.)

αἴνυμαι, dep. Ep. (for ἄρνυμαι fr. αἴρω [Lob. supposes a radical verb αἴνω, *capio,* whence αἴνυμαι and ἀναίνομαι, *repudiare,* Techn. 124]), only pres. and impf. without augm. *to take, to take away, to seize;* with accus. τεύχεα ἀπ' ὤμων, 11, 580 ; ὅστρον, 15, 459; with gen. τυρῶν αἰνύμενος, taking some of the cheeses, Od. 9, 223 ; metaph. πόθος αἴνυταί με, longing desire seizes me, Od. 14, 144.

αἰνῶς, adv. (αἰνός), *terribly, frightfully,* τείρεσθαι, 5, 352 ; and my *greatly, exceedingly,* φιλεῖν, ἐοικέναι, τέρπεσθαι, also of wretchedness, *miserably,* Od. 17, 24.

αἴξ, αἰγός, ἡ (ἀίσσω), dat. plur. αἴγεσιν, 10, 486, *goat;* ἄγριος, wild goat, 4, 105. and Od.

αἴξασκον, ες, ε, Iter. aor. 1. fr. ἀΐσσω.

Αἰολίδης, ου, ὁ, son of Æolus=*Sisyphus,* 6, 154; Cretheus, Od. 11, 237.

Αἰολίη νῆσος, ἡ, the *Æolian island,* the abode of Æolus, son of Hippotas, ruler of the winds ; a mythic island, surrounded by a brazen, impregnable wall, in the west of the Hom. Geog., Od 10, 1. 25. The ancients made it one of the Lipari islands, and Strabo *Strongyle,* the largest of them, now *Stromboli,* formerly famed for its volcanic eruptions. Since, however, Ulysses sailed without obstruction

Αἰολίς.

with a west wind to Ithaca in the east, and was driven directly back by the tempest, the moderns have, with greater probability, placed it immediately beyond the southern point of Sicily, between Sicily and Africa. Völcker, Hom. Geog. finds it in one of the Argades ; Voss, on the other hand, explains the epithet πλωτή to mean *floating*, and gives it a double location, once east of Trinacria, and once west of Atlas ; see πλωτός.

* Αἰολίς, ἴδος, ἡ, *Æolian*, Ep. 4.

Αἰολίων, ωνος, ὁ, son of Æolus=*Macar*, h. in Ap. 37.

Αἰόλλω, poet. (αἰόλος), *to move rapidly hither and thither, to turn often*; e. g. γαστέρα, *to turn* the stomach (breast) of an animal in roasting it, Od. 20, 27.†

αἰολοθώρηξ, κος, ὁ (θώραξ), *having a flexible cuirass or coat of mail* (rapid or active in his cuirass, V.); or, having a variegated, richly adorned cuirass, Köp., 4. 489.† see αἰόλος [and Buttm. Lex. 12].

αἰολομίτρης, ου, ὁ (μίτρα), *having a flexible belt* (active in the belt, V.); or, with a variegated belt, 5, 707.† see αἰόλος.

αἰολόπωλος (πῶλος), *with rapid steeds*, 3, 185.† and h. 3, 138; or, with piebald steeds, see αἰόλος.

αἰόλος, η, ον (prob. related to ἄελλα, fr. ἔλλω, εἴλω), *moving or turning rapidly, moveable, active;* spoken of animals: πόδας αἰόλος ἵππος, the light-footed courser, 19, 404. αἰόλος ὄφις, the lithe or writhing serpent, 12, 208. σφῆκες μέσον αἰόλοι, wasps moveable in the middle, 12, 161. ('Ring-streaked' cannot be reconciled with μέσον). αἰόλος οἶστρος, the flitting gad-fly, Od. 22. 300. αἰόλαι εὐλαί, swarming worms, 22, 509; spoken of arms, *easily moved, rapid*; τεύχεα, arms which can be easily handled (*light, wieldy*), 5, 295 ; σάκος, 7. 222. This is the true meaning in the Hom. poems, as the derivation shows, see Buttm. Lexil. p. 63. 2) later it had the signif. *changeful of hue, gleaming, variegated*, since rapid motion gives objects this appearance; αἰόλον ὄστρακον, the variegated shell of the turtle, h. Merc. 33. (Some annotators adopt this signif. in the case of the wasps, arms, etc. but Hom. for this uses ποικίλος.)

Αἴολος, ὁ (*the rapid*, adj. αἰόλος), 1) son of Hellen and the nymph Osreis, or of Zeus ; king of Thessaly, father of Cretheus, Sisyphus, Athamas, etc. 6, 154. 2) son of Hippotes and Melanippe, according to Humer; or, according to Diod. 4, 311, son of Poseidon and Arne, great-grandson of Hippotes, king of the Æolian island. He is represented as a friend of the gods and as the disperser of the winds. He lived with his twelve children, six sons and six daughters, in blissful abundance, Od. 10, 5—9. He entertained hospitably the wandering Ulysses, and even gave him the winds enclosed in a bag; and Od. 10, 25 seq. (see Völck. Hom. Geogr. p. 115.)

Αἱρέω.

Αἴπεια, ἡ, *Æpēa*, a maritime town in Messenia ; according to Strabo, the later *Thuria*; or, according to Paus., *Corone*, 9, 152.

αἰπεινός, ή, όν, poet. (a form of αἰπύς), *high, loftily situated, eminent ;* espec. epith. of towns situated upon mountains, Γονόεσσα, 2, 573 ; "Ιλιος, 13, 773 ; κάρηνα, lofty summits. 2, 869. Od. 6, 123.

αἰπήεις, εσσα, εν (poet. form of αἰπύς), *lying high, lofty*, Πήδασος, 21, 87.†

αἰπόλιον, τό (αἰπόλος), *a herd of goats;* mly αἰπόλια αἰγῶν, 2, 474; alone, Od. 17, 213. 20, 174.

αἰπόλος, ὁ (αἴξ and πολέω), prop. *goat-pasturing*, ἀνήρ, 2, 474. As subst. *goat-herd*, generally with αἰγῶν, Od. 17, 247.

αἰπός, ή, όν, Ep. form of αἰπύς, e. g. πόλις, 13, 625. Od. 3, 130. αἰπὰ ῥέεθρα, 8, 369.

Αἴπυ, τό (adj. αἰπύ), *Æpy*, a town in Elis on the borders of Messenia, prob. the later Αἰπιόν; according to Strab. VIII. p. 349, *Margalia* on the Selleis, 2, 592. h. in Ap. 423.

αἰπύς, εῖα, ύ, poet. forms are αἰπεινός, αἰπήεις, αἰπός; 1) *high, loftily situated, eminent;* spoken of mountains and towns, ὄρος, πτολίεθρον, Ἴλιον αἰπύ, τεῖχος, Il. ; βρόχος, a high depending cord, 11, 278. 2) Metaph. *deep, dreadful, difficult*, ὄλεθρος, dreadful destruction, 6, 57. According to Nitzsch, Od. 1, 11, αἰπ. ὄλεθ. is 'deep destruction in which it is easy to plunge;' [an epith. of death, where the discourse relates to escape from great danger, Nitzsch in loc. ;] φόνος, dreadful slaughter, 17, 365. Od. 4, 843 ; χόλος, 15. 223. αἰπὺς πόνος, 11, 601. αἰπύ οἱ ἐσσεῖται, hard will it be for him, 13, 317.

Αἴπυτος, ὁ, *Æpytus*, son of Elatus, king of Phæsana in Arcadia. His monument was on the declivity of the Cyllenian mountain ; from this, Αἰπύτιος, ον, the Æpytian; τύμβος, 2, 604. cf. Paus. 8, 16, 2. [Αἰπύτιος, ον, see Αἴπυτος.]

αἱρέω, fut. αἱρήσω, aor. 2. act. εἷλον, Ep. ἕλον and ἕλεσκον, fut. mid. αἱρήσομαι, aor. mid. εἱλόμην, Ep. ἑλόμην, 1) *to take, to catch, to grasp, to seize ;* with accus.. e. g. ζωόν τινα, to take one alive, 6, 38 ; *by what*, with gen. τινά κομῆς, to take one by the hair, 1, 197 ; χειρός, by the hand, 1, 323. 4, 542 ; *with what*, with dat. χαλκὸν ὀδοῦσιν, to hold the brass with the teeth ; χερσὶ δόρυ, γαῖαν ἀγοστῷ ; but, καθαρὰ χροῒ εἵμαθ' ἑλοῦσα, having taken or put clean attire upon her body, Od. 17, 58 ; metaph. χόλος αἱρεῖ με, anger seizes me, 4, 23. In like manner ἵμερος, δέος, λήθη, ὕπνος. 2) *to take away*, τί ἀπ' ἀπήνης, from the carriage, 24, 579 ; ἀχλὺν ἀπ' ὀφθαλμῶν, the cloud from the eyes, 5, 127 ; with two accus. τὸν ἄτη φρένας εἷλε, confusion took away his senses, 16, 805. *b*) Espec. in war, *a*) Of things, *to take, to capture*, πόλιν, νῆας,

Αἶρος. 20 **Αἴσυλος.**

*ε*ίay, τινά, 4, 457, and often [spoken of enemies meeting in battle, it has always this meaning, unless accompanied by ζωόν or something equivalent in the context]; Am. Ed. *to take, to seize,* ζωόν τινα, 6, 38, II) Mid. 1) *to take for oneself, to seize,* ἔγχος, δόρυ, 3, 338. 10, 31; the connected preposition to govern the translation τόξα ἀπὸ πασσάλου, to take down the bow from the hook or peg, 5, 210; ἀπ᾿ ὤμων τεύχεα, 7, 122; ἐκ δίφροιο, to take out of the chariot, 10, 501. 2) *to take, to obtain, to procure, to receive*; τί, 18, 500; δόρπον, Od. 14, 347. Metaph. ὕπνου δῶρον, to enjoy the gift of sleep, 7, 482; ἄλκιμον ἦτορ, to take bold heart, 5, 529; ὅρκον τινός, to take an oath from any one, Od. 4, 746; also τινί, 22, 119. 3) *to select, to choose,* τέμενος, γυναῖκας, 9, 578. Od. 9, 334.

Ἆρος, ὁ (ῑ) from a and Ἶρος, a sportive play upon the name Irus : *noi-Irus, unhappy Irus,* Od. 18, 73.†

αἴρω, contr. for ἀείρω, q. v. Hom. has of the common form only the pres. act, in εἴδοντο νέκυν αἴροντας, 17, 724; the aor. 1. mid. ἠράμεθα, ἤρατο; of the aor. 2. the indic. without augm. ἀρόμην, and the other moods ἄρωμαι, ἀροίμην, ἀρέσθαι, see ἀείρω.

Ἀΐς, obsolete nom. of Ἀΐδης, q. v.

αἶσα, ἡ, Ep. (from αἴω, akin to δαίω), 1) *share,* in general, which one has of a thing : ληΐδος, a share of the booty, 18, 327. Od. 5, 40. Hence, *that which is fitting, justice, propriety.* κατ᾿ αἶσαν, according to right, or propriety with justice (= good reason); often with εἰπεῖν. ἐν καρδὸς αἴσῃ, see κάρ. 2) the assigned *lot of life, fate, destiny,* which the gods accord to men, *fortune* or *misfortune,* 1, 416. Often in Hom. αἶσά μοι, with infin. following, εἰ δέ μοι αἶσα τεθνάμεναι, if it is my lot to die, 24, 224. cf. 16, 707. Od. 5, 113. ἔτι γάρ μοι ἐλπίδος αἶσα, I have still some hope, Od. 16, 101. 19, 84; κακὴ αἶσα, evil fate, 5, 209; com. in a bad signif. 3) *the fateful decree of a god;* Διός, of Zeus, 9, 608. ὑπὲρ Διὸς αἶσαν, against the decree of Zeus, 17, 321. δαίμονος αἶσα κακή, Od. 11, 61.

Αἶσα, ἡ, the goddess of *Fate,* like Μοῖρα, who at birth assigns to every one his lot, 20, 127. Od. 7, 197. The poet thus personifies *eternal, unchangeable, governing fate,* the inviolable law of nature, without however giving a form to the deity.

Αἰσαγέης ὄρος, τό, an unknown mountain in Asia Minor, near Clarus, h. Ap. 40; see Αἰγαγέη.

Αἴσηπος, ὁ, *Æsepus,* 1) a river in Asia Minor, which falls into the Propontis near Cyzicus, 2, 825. 12, 21. 2) son of Bucolion, a Trojan, slain by Euryalus, 6, 21.

ἀΐσθω, Ep. (ἄημι), only pres. part. and imperf. *to breathe out* (= ἀποπνέω), θυμόν, *16, 468. 20, 403.

αἴσιμος, ον, Ep. (αἶσα), and ος, η, ον, 1) *fitting, right, proper, just.* φρένας αἰσίμη ἦσθα, thou wert sound in mind, Od.

23, 14. αἴσιμα ἔργα ἀνθρώπων, the just works of men, piety, Od. 14, 84. Often the neut. αἴσιμα with παρειπεῖν, to advise that which is suitable, 6, 62. αἴσιμα πίνειν, to drink moderately, Od. 21, 294. φρεσὶν αἴσιμα εἰδέναι, to know in mind that which is right, i. e. *to be just, well disposed,* 15, 207. αἴσιμα πάντα τίνειν, to pay every thing just, to make all due amends, Od. 8, 348. 2) *destined by fate,* only αἴσιμον ἦμαρ, the day of fate ; and in the construction, αἴσιμον ἦεν, it was destined by fate, 9, 245. Od. 15, 239.

αἴσιος, ον, Ep. (αἶσα), *sent by fate, auspicious;* only in a good sense : αἴσ. ὁδοιπόρος, a traveller sent for good, 24, 376.†

ἀΐσσω (ᾱ and ῑ), aor. 1. act. ἤϊξα, subj. ἀΐξω. partcp. ἀΐξας, aor. pass. ἠΐχθην, infin. ἀϊχθῆναι, 1) Intrans. *to move rapidly, to hasten, to run, to rush, to spring.* Spoken of things animate and inanimate ; of gods : of Athênê, ἤϊξεν ἐπὶ χθόνα, she sprang to the earth, 4, 78 ; often βῆ ἀΐξασα, rushing she went, 2, 167 ; of men, mostly in a hostile sense : *to rush upon, to attack impetuously,* ἔγχεϊ, with the lance ; φασγάνῳ, ἵπποις, the sword, the chariot ; of the flitting motion of the shades in the under world : τοὶ δὲ σκιαὶ ἀΐσσουσιν, Od. 10, 495 ; of animals : οἱ ἵπποι μάλ᾿ ὦκα ἤϊξαν πεδίονδε, swiftly rushed the steeds to the plain, Od. 15, 183 ; of wild boars, 12, 147 ; of birds : *to fly, to soar,* πρὸς οὐρανόν, 23, 868 ; ὑπὲρ ἄστεος, 24, 320. Od. 15, 164. *b)* Spoken of inanimate things ; of missiles : δούρατα ἐκ χειρῶν ἤϊξαν, the spears flew from the hands, 5, 657 ; of smoke : ἀπὸ χθονός, to rise from the earth. Metaph. of the soul : ὡς δ᾿ ὅτ᾿ ἂν (ὅταν) ἀΐξῃ νόος ἀνέρος, as when darts a man's thought, 15, 80. 2) Pass. as depon. ἐκ χειρῶν ἡνία ἠΐχθησαν, the reins flew from his hands, 16, 404.

ἄϊστος, ον, Ep. (ἰδεῖν), prop. that of which nothing is known, *unseen, unknown, vanished, annihilated,* 14, 258. ἄϊστον ποιεῖν τινα, to make one invisible, used of Ulysses, because it was not known whether he would return, Od. 1, 235.

ἀϊστόω, poet. (ἄϊστος), fut. ώσω, aor. optat. ἀϊστώσειαν, and aor. pass. ἀϊστώθην, *to make invisible, to destroy,* Od. 20. 79. Hence pass. *to be destroyed, to vanish,* *Od. 10, 259.

αἰσυητήρ, ῆρος, ὁ, poet. (related to αἰσυμνήτης), *princely, regal, royal,* κοῦρος, 24, 347.† Instead of this word, whose signif. and derivation were unknown even to the ancients, the edition of Spitzner has αἰσυμνητήρ.

Αἰσυήτης, ου, ὁ (αἰσυητηρ), a Trojan, father of Alcathous, 2, 793. 13, 427.

αἰσυλοεργός, όν, *practising wickedness,* 5, 403.† (Thus Spitzner, as the reading of Aristarchus for ὀβριμοεργός.)

αἴσυλος, ον (prob. from αἶσα), Ep. *unjust, impious, improper.* αἴσυλα ῥέζειν, to practise impiety, 5, 403 ; μυθήσασθαι, to speak impious things, Il. ; εἰδέναι, h. Merc. 164.

Αἰσύμη. 21 Ἀκάμας.

Αἰσύμη, ἡ, a city in Thrace, 8, 304. Αἰσύμηθεν, from Æsymê.

αἰσυμνητήρ, ῆρος, ὁ=αἰσυμνήτης, 24, 347; and the ancients explain it here by βασιλικός, royal. Cf. αἰσυητήρ.

αἰσυμνήτης, ου, ὁ, poet. (αἰσυμνάω), he who adjudges to persons what is due; the *arbiter* or *judge* of a *contest*, Od. 3, 258.†

Αἴσυμνος, ὁ, a Greek, 11, 303.

αἴσχιστος, η, ον, superl. and αἰσχίων, compar. of αἰσχρός.

αἶσχος, εος, τό, *shame, indignity, insult;* in the plur. τὰ αἴσχεα, shameful deeds, 3, 342. Od. 1, 229. ὃς ἤδη νέμεσίν τε καὶ αἴσχεα πόλλ' ἀνθρώπων, one who felt the blame and many taunts of men, i. e. so felt them as to give no occasion for them, 6, 351.

αἰσχρός, ή, όν (αἶσχος), compar. αἰσχίων, ιον, superl. αἴσχιστος, η, ον, 1) *ugly, deformed;* in a physical sense, αἴσχιστος ἀνὴρ ὑπὸ Ἴλιον ἦλθεν, the ugliest man who came to Troy (under its walls), 2, 216. h. Ap. 197. 2) *shameful, disgraceful, insulting;* αἰσχρὰ ἔπεα, *abusive,* insulting words, 3, 38. The neut. followed by infin. 2, 119.

αἰσχρῶς, adv., *shamefully, insultingly,* 23, 473. Od. 18, 321.

αἰσχύνω (αἶσχος), aor. 1 ᾔσχυνα, perf. pass. ᾔσχυμμαι, I) Act. 1) *to make ugly, to deform, to disfigure;* with accus. πρόσωπον, 18, 24. νέκυς ᾐσχυμμένος, a corpse, i. e. *treated with indignity, dishonoured* (mutilated), 18, 180. 2) Metaph. *to insult, to dishonour, to disgrace,* γένος. λέχος, *to dishonour a man's bed,* Od. 8, 269. 11) Mid. *to be ashamed;* absolute, Od. 18, 12; τί, *to shrink from any thing with shame;* to fear any thing, Od. 21, 323.

Αἴσων, ονος, ὁ, (according to Herm. *Opportunus,* from αἶσα), son of Cretheus and Tyro, grandson of Æolus I., father of Jason, king of Iolcus, in Thessaly. According to a later tradition Medea renewed his youth, Od. 11, 259.

αἰτέω, fut. αἰτήσω, aor. infin. αἰτῆσαι, h. Ven. 225, *to ask, to beg, to demand;* absol. Od. 18, 49: with accus. of the pers. and thing, αἰτεῖν τι, 5, 358; τινά, Od. 17, 365; also both, τινὰ δόρυ, *to ask any one* for a spear, 22, 295; τινί, for any one, κούρησ' αἰτήσουσα τέλος θαλεροῖο γάμοιο, *to solicit youthful nuptials* for the damsels, Od. 20, 74. *b*) With infin. following, 6, 176.

αἰτιάασθαι, Ep. form for αἰτιᾶσθαι, see αἰτιάομαι.

αἰτιάομαι (αἰτία), depon. mid. 3 sing., optat. αἰτιόῳτο, Ep. for αἰτιῷτο, 3 pl. impf. ᾐτιόωντο, Ep. for ᾐτιῶντο, *to blame, to accuse;* with accus. 11, 78. Od. 20, 135; also with two accus. when the thing is expressed by a neut. pron., Od. 1, 32.

αἰτίζω, Ep. (αἰτέω), *to ask earnestly, to beg;* absol. Od. 4, 651. 17, 228; with accus. of the thing, Od. 17, 222, and of the person, Od. 17, 346.

αἴτιος, ίη, ιον (αἰτία), having the blame of any thing, *guilty, blameworthy;* used in Hom. only in a bad sense. οὔτι μοι αἴτιοί εἰσιν, they have in no respect wronged me, 1, 153. Od. 1, 348.

αἰτιόῳτο, Ep. for αἰτιῷτο, 3 sing. optat. pres. from αἰτιάομαι.

Αἰτώλιος, ίη, ιον, *Ætolian,* 4, 399.

Αἰτωλοί, οἱ, the *Ætolians,* inhabitants of Ætolia, in Greece, between Acarnania and Thessaly, which received its name from Ætôlus, son of Endymion, 2, 638.

αἰχμάζω (αἰχμή), fut. άσω, Ep. άσσω, *to brandish the lance;* constr. with αἰχμάς, †, 324.†

αἰχμή, ἡ (ἀκμή or ἀΐσσω), prop. *the point of the lance,* χαλκείη, 4, 461; mly *the lance, the spear.*

αἰχμητά, ὁ, Ep. and Æol. for αἰχμητής. 5, 197.

αἰχμητής, οῦ, ὁ, a *lancer, a spearman,* hence g. t. for *warrior,* 1, 152, and often. 2) As adj. *warlike,* 1, 846; ἀνήρ, 3, 49.

αἶψα, adv. *quickly, directly, immediately.* αἶψα δ' ἔπειτα, immediately thereupon; αἶψα δέ in the narration of a fact, 2, 664. Od. 2, 6; and αἶψά τε in general propositions, 19, 221; see Herm. ad Hymn. in Cer. 485.

αἰψηρός, ή, όν (αἶψα), *hasty, quick.* αἰψηρὸς κόρος γόοιο, quick is the satiety of grief (one is quickly sated with grief, V.) λῦσεν ἀγορὴν αἰψηρήν for αἶψα, he quickly dispersed the assembly; or with V. the busy council, 19, 276. Od. 2, 257. Nitzsch ad loc. translates: the stirring, the quickly moving assembly.

ἀΐω, poet. only pres. and impf. without augm. ἄϊον, *to observe, to perceive,* like *sentire;* mly *to hear,* with gen., seldom with accus. φθογγῆς, to hear the voice, 16, 508; πληγῆς, to feel the blow, 11, 532; or, rather, to hear the lash (i. e. the crack of the whip); φίλον ἄϊον ἦτορ, 15, 252, I felt my heart, (viz. its pulsation, because ἦτορ occurs for the most part in a physical sense.) Others: I knew it in my mind. Voss and Bothe: for I was breathing out my life, (with the Schol. ἀπέπνεον, so that ἀΐω=ἀω, ἄημι.)

αἰών, ῶνος, ὁ, comm. ἡ, 1) *duration, long time.* 2) *an age, life,* connected with ψυχή: αἰῶνος ἀμερδεσθαι, to be bereaved of life, 22, 58; ἀπ' αἰῶνος ὀλέσθαι, to perish from life, 24, 725. *b*) Spoken of animals: αἰῶνα ἐκτορέειν, to pierce the life, h. Merc. 42; (according to Ruhnken, the spinal marrow), also plur. δι' αἰῶνας τορεῖν, spoken of cattle, h. Merc. 119.

ἀκάκητα, Ep. for ἀκακήτης, ου, ὁ=ἄκακος (κακός), who is free from evil, *from guile,* &c. *the bearer of happiness, the deliverer from evil,* epith. of Mercury, 16, 185. Od. 24, 10.

ἀκαλαῤῥείτης, αο, ὁ (ἀκαλός =ἥκαλος, *still*], ῥέω), *gently-flowing, softly flowing,* epith. of Oceanus, 7, 422, and Od.

ἀκάμας, αντος, ὁ, ἡ (κάμνω), *unwearied, untiring,* epith. of Sol, of the Sperchius, and of the wild boar, 18, 239. 484. 16, 176. *Il.

Ἀκάμας, αντος, ὁ, 1) son of Antenor

'Ακάματος.

and Theāno, leader of the Dardanians, slain by Meriōnes, 2, 823. 16, 342. 2) son of Eussōrus, leader of the Thracians, slain by the Telamonian Ajax, 2, 844. 6, 8. 3) son of Asius, 12, 140.

ἀκάματος, ον=ἀκάμας, untiring, never-resting, epithet of fire, 5, 4. Od 20, 123.

ἄκανθα, ἡ (ἀκή), thorn, thistle, Od. 5, 328.†

*'Ακάστη, ἡ (greatly distinguished, from a intens. and κέκασμαι), daughter of Oceanus and Thetis, h. Cer. 421.

'Άκαστος, king of Dulichium, Od. 14, 336.

ἀκαχείατο, see ἀκαχίζω.
ἀκαχεῖν, see ἀκαχίζω.
ἀκαχήμενος, see ἀκαχίζω.
ἀκαχήσω, see ἀκαχίζω.
ἀκαχίζω, Ep. and Ion. ('ΑΧΩ) aor. 2 ἤκαχον, whence again fut. ἀκαχήσω, aor. 1 ἤκάχησα, mid. ἀκαχίζομαι, kindred form of ἄχομαι or ἄχνυμαι, aor. ἠκαχόμην, perf. ἀκάχημαι and ἀκήχεμαι, 3 pl. ἀκηχέδαται (perhaps ἀκηχέαται is preferable), 17, 637; 3 pl. plupf. ἀκαχείατο for ἀκάχηντο; infin. perf. ἀκάχησθαι. partcp. ἀκαχήμενος, fem. ἀκηχεμένη (the accent on perf. ind. and partcp. is drawn back: see Buttm. § 111, note 2; also a partcp. pres. ἀχέων, ουσα. 1) Act. to trouble, to afflict; with accus. Od. 16, 432. 2) Mid. to trouble oneself, to grieve, to be grieved, θυμῷ, 6, 488; τῷ μήτι θανὼν ἀκαχίζευ, grieve not that thou art dead, Od. 11, 486; in the perf. to be troubled, sad, often absolute with θυμόν and ἦτορ: θεοὶ δ' ἀκαχείατο θυμόν, were troubled at heart, 12, 179. b) With gen. and dat. of the object; ἵππων, about the steeds, 11, 702. ὅ μοι πυκινῶς ἀκάχηται, who is deeply troubled about me, Od. 23, 360.

ἀκαχμένος, η, ον, Ep. sharpened, pointed, epith of the lance, 11.: of the axe, Od. 5, 235; of the sword, Od. 22, 80; (prop. partcp. perf. pass. from theme 'ΑΚΩ, acuo, for ἀκαγμένος with Att. redupl.)

ἀκάχοιτο, see ἀκαχίζω.
ἀκείομαι, Ep. for ἀκέομαι; but ἀκειά-μενοι, a false reading for ἀκειώμενοι, from ἀκέομαι.

ἀκέομαι, Depon. Ep. mid. ἀκείομαι (ἀκήν [hence originally =to quiet]), aor. 1 ἠκεσάμην, imper. ἄκεσσαι, 1) to heal, to cure; with acc. ἕλκεα, wounds, 16, 29; also τινά, any one, 5, 448; metaph. to calm, to allay, to help, δίψαν, to allay thirst, 22, 2; absol. 13, 115. Od. 10, 69. 2) to repair, to restore, νῆας, Od. 14, 383.

ἀκερσεκόμης, ου, ὁ (κείρω, κόμη), un-shorn, having long hair, epith. of Apollo, 20, 39.†

'Ἀκεσσαμενός, ὁ (partcp. ἀκεσάμενος), father of Peribœa, king of Thrace, founder of the city Akesamenæ, 21, 142.

ἀκεστός, ή, όν (ἀκέομαι), curable, that may be calmed, φρένες, 13, 115.†

ἀκέων, ἔουσα, dual ἀκέοντε, silent, still, quiet [cf. ἀκήν]. ἀκέων is for the most part used as an adv. without distinction of gender or number, 4, 22. 8, 459. Od.

21, 89; the feminine however ἀκέουσα occurs 1, 565, and once the dual ἀκέοντε, Od. 14, 195 (prob. from a and χάω for ἄκαος, Ion. ἀκέων, Buttm. Lexil. p. 27 [Cf. Död. Hom. Gloss. 130]).

ἀκήδεστος, ον (κηδέω), uncared for, neglected; spoken of the dead unburied, 6, 60.†

ἀκηδέστως, adv. in a cruel, pitiless manner, remorselessly, *11. 22, 465. 24, 417.

ἀκηδέω (κῆδος), aor. 1 ἀκήδεσα, to neg-lect, to slight, to disregard; with gen. *11. 14, 427. 23, 70.

ἀκηδής, ές, gen. έος (κηδέω), without care, 1) Act. free from care, at ease, 21, 123; spoken of the gods, 24, 526; negli-gent, Od. 17, 319. 2) Pass. uncared for, neglected, disregarded, as Od. 6, 26. 19, 18. 20, 130. 11. 21, 123; of a corpse: un-buried, 24, 554. Od. 24, 187.

ἀκήλητος, ον (κηλέω), not to be charmed, stubborn, unbending, νόος, Od, 10, 329.†

ἄκημα, ατος, τό (ἀκέομαι), a remedy, an alleviation, relief, ὀδυνάων, 15, 394.

ἀκήν, adv. (prop. acc. from obs. ἀκή [=ἡσυχία, Hesych. ἀκᾷ, calmly, Pind. Död. 130. According to Buttm. adv. from acc. ἀκέαν, Ion. ἀκέην· ἄκαος (χάω) non hiscens]), quietly, silently, still; often πάντες ἀκὴν ἐγένοντο σιωπῇ, all were quiet and silent, 3, 95; ἀκὴν ἔσαν, Od. 2, 82.

ἀκηράσιος, ον, poet. (κεράννυμι), un-mixed, unadulterated, pure, οἶνος, Od. 9, 205;† untouched, unmown, λειμών, h. Merc. 72.

ἀκήρατος, ον (κεράννυμι), unmixed, pure, ὕδωρ, 24, 300. 2) Metaph. unin-jured, unwasted, κλῆρος, 15, 498. Od. 17, 532.

ἀκήριος, ον (κήρ), without misfortune, uninjured, unharmed, *Od. 12, 98. 23, 328. b) Act. innocuous, ῥάβδος, h. Merc. 530.

ἀκήριος, ον (κῆρ), without heart, 1) In physical signif. lifeless, dead, 11, 392. 2) Metaph. heartless, spiritless, cowardly, 7, 100; δέος (heartless fear, Cp.), 5, 812. 11.

ἀπηχέδαται, see ἀκαχίζω.
ἀκηχεμένη, see ἀκαχίζω.

ἀκιδνός, η, ον, only compar. ἀκιδνότερος, weak, inferior, insignificant, Od. 18, 130; with εἶδος, in appearance, *Od.5, 217. 8, 169.

ἄκικυς, υος, ὁ, ἡ, Ep. (κίκυς), without power, weak, feeble, *Od. 9, 515. 21, 131; (according to Thiersch, § 199, 5, from a and κίω, unable to go.)

ἀκίχητος, ον, poet. (κιχάνω), not to be attained, unattainable. ἀκίχητα διώκειν, to pursue what is unattainable, 17, 75.

ἄκλαυστος, ον, later form for ἄκλαυτος, Od. 11, 54, 72; [in some editions.]

ἄκλαυτος, ον (κλαίω), 1) unwept, un-lamented; spoken of one dead, 22, 386. 2) Act. without tears, tearless, Od. 4, 494. Voss: unwept.

ἀκλεής, έος, ὁ, ἡ, poet. (κλέος), ἀκλειής and ἀκληής, without fame ; fameless, in-glorious; accus. sing. ἀκλεία, for ἀκλεέα, Od. 4, 728; plur. nom. ἀκλεεῖς, poet.

Άκλειής. 23 Άκρητος.

strengthened for ἀκλεεῖς, 12, 318. In ἀκλεές αὔτως, the neut. prob. is as adv. 7, 100 ; Buttm. [who allows that ἀκλεές may =ἀκλεέες], Lex. p. 296.
ἀκλειής, see ἀκλεής.
ἀκλειώς, adv. ingloriously, 22, 304. Od. 2, 241.
ἀκληεῖς, poet. for ἀκλεεῖς, see ἀκλεής.
ἄκληρος, ον (κλῆρος), without lot, without possessions, hence 1) poor, needy, Od. 11, 489.† 2) unallotted, undivided, wild, γαῖα, h. Ven. 123.
ἀκμή, ή (ἀκή), edge. ἐπὶ ξυροῦ ἀκμῆς, on a razor's edge,ωἵστατοι [" in balance hangs, pois'd on a razor's edge," Cp.], i. e. it is on the point of decision (an adage), 10, 173.†
ἄκμηνος, ον, fasting, with σίτοιο or πόσιος, without meat, or drink, *19, 163, 346. (ἀκμή [ἄκμη Lob. Path. 193] is said to be Æol. =νηστεία.)
ἀκμηνός, όν ([=ὁ ἀκμάζων] ἀκμή), full grown, grown up, Od. 23, 191.†
ἀκμής, ῆτος, ὁ, ή (κάμνω), unwearied, vigorous, fresh, *11, 802. 15, 697.
* ἄκμητος, ον=ἀκμής, h. Ap. 520.
ἀκμόθετον, τό (τίθημι) the place where the anvil is placed, anvil-block, stithy, 18, 410. Od. 8, 274.
ἄκμων, ονος, ὁ (κάμνω), an anvil, 15, 19. Od. 8, 274.
ἄκνηστις, ιος, ή (ἄκανος), the back-bone, the spine, Od. 10, 161.†
ἀκοίτης, ου, ὁ (a copulat. and κοίτη), bed-fellow, husband, 11. and Od.
ἄκοιτις, ιος, ἡ, bed-fellow, wife, Il. ἀκοίτις, accus. plur. Od. 10, 7.
ἄκολος, ὁ (κόλον), a morsel, a crumb, Od. 17, 222.†
* ἀκόλυμβος, ον (κόλυμβος), who cannot swim, Batr. 157.
ἀκομιστίη, ἡ (κομίζω), want of tending or care, privation, Od. 21, 284.†
ἀκοντίζω (ἄκων), aor. ἀκόντισα and ἀκόντισσα, prop. to hurl the javelin, but mly to cast, δουρί, ἔγχεϊ; also with accus. αἰχμάς, to hurl lances. The object aimed at stands in the gen. τινός, at any one; also κατά τι, ἐπί τινι, and εἰς τινα, 4, 490. 16, 358. Od. 22, 282; later also, τινά, to hit or pierce any one with a lance, Batr. 209.
* ἀκόντιον, τό (dimin. of ἄκων), a dart, a javelin, h. Merc. 460.
ἀκοντιστής, οῦ, ὁ, poet. (ἀκοντίζω), lancer, dartsman, spearman, Il. and Od.
ἀκοντιστύς, ύος, ἡ, Ep. for ἀκόντισις (ἀκοντίζω), the act of casting spears, a contest with spears (i. e. as a martial find a remedy when the evil is done, 9, 250.
ἄκοσμος, ον (κόσμος), without order, indecent, unbecoming, ἔπεα, 2, 213.†
ἀκοστάω or ἀκοστέω, aor. 1 ἀκόστησα, 6, 506. 15, 263; in the phrase: ἵππος ἀκοστήσας ἐπὶ φάτνῃ, full fed at the manger. The best derivation is from ἀκοστή, =κριθή, barley [as being bearded, ἀκή]; hence, to consume barley, to be fed with barley, cf. Buttm. Lex. p. 72.
ἀκουάζω, h. Merc. 428; and ἀκουάζομαι, dep. mid. Ep. form of ἀκούω, to hear; with gen. Od. 9, 7. πρῶτω γὰρ καὶ δαιτὸς ἀκουάζεσθον ἐμεῖο, for ye are the first to hear from me of a feast, i. e. are first invited, 4, 343.
ἀκουή, ή (ἀκούω). Ep. for ἀκοή, properly, hearing; a sound (as heard), spoken of the crash of a tree when felled: ἔκαθεν δέ τε γίγνετ᾽ ἀκουή, there is hearing from afar, i. e. the sound, or crash of it is heard at a distance, 16, 634; others give here the signif. echo, noise. 2) that which is heard, information, μετὰ πατρὸς ἀκουὴν ἱεσέσθαι, to go in quest of intelligence of his father, Od. 2, 308 ; βῆναι, Od. 4, 701. 5, 19.
ἄκουρος, ον (κοῦρος), without son, childless, Od. 7, 64.†
* ἀκουστός, ή, όν, heard, audible, h. Merc. 512.
ἀκούω, fut. ἀκούσομαι, aor. 1 ἤκουσα, 1) to hear, with the gen. of the person heard; ἀοιδοῦ ; the thing generally in accus. μῦθον, the discourse, and τί τινος, any thing from any one (ex aliquo), Od. 12, 389 ; but also in gen. μυκηθμοῦ ἤκουσα, I heard the roar or bellowing, Od. 12, 265. The person about whom any thing is heard is mly put in the gen. Od. 1, 287. 289, rarely in accus. and with περί τινος, Od. 19, 204. 2) to hearken to any one, to listen, spoken of the gods; comm. with gen., rarely with dat., which is prop. dat. commod. ἀνέρι κηδομένῳ, to hearken to a suffering man; of subjects, to obey, Od. 7, 11. 3) The pres. in the signif. of the past, have heard, know (cf. Gr. p. 766, g), Od. 3, 193. 4, 688. The mid. as depon. τινός, to hear, 4, 331.
ἀκράαντος, ον, poet. (κραιαίνω), unfinished, unaccomplished, ἔργον, 2, 138; spoken of a prophecy: unfulfilled, not to be fulfilled, Od. 2, 202. 19, 565.
ἀκραής, ές, gen. έος (ἄκρος, ἄημι), prop. high-blowing, strong-blowing, brisk, fresh, epith. of a favorable wind, *Od. 2, 421. 14, 253.

Ἄκρις. 24 Ἀλάομαι.

libation of pure wine, because, in compacts, unmixed wine was offered to the gods, 2, 341. 4, 159.
ἀκρίς, ίδος, ἡ, *a locust*, 21, 12.†
ἄκρις, ιος, ἡ, Ion. and Ep. for ἄκρη, *point, summit, peak*; always in the plur. accus. δι' ἄκριας, through (amongst) the mountain tops, Od. 10, 281; nom. plur. h. Cer. 383.
Ἀκρίσιος, ὁ (*unjudged*, from α and κρίνω, *Inseparatinus*, Herm.), son of Abas and Ocelia, great grandson of Danaus, father of Danaë. He expelled his brother Prœtus; after his return they divided the kingdom, so that Acrisius reigned in Argos, and Prœtus in Tiryns, Apd. 2, 21.
Ἀκρισιώνη, ἡ, daughter of Acrisius = Danae, 14, 319.
ἀκριτόμυθος, ον (μῦθος), *speaking in a confused manner, prating* or *babbling foolishly*, ὄνειροι, senseless dreams, or hard of explanation, Od. 19, 560. Il. 2, 246.
ἄκριτος, ον (κριτός), 1) *not separated, confused*, τύμβος, a common grave, in which the multitude were thrown indiscriminately, 7, 337; μῦθοι, confused discourse, prating, 2, 796. ἄκριτα πόλλ' ἀγορεύειν, Od. 8, 505. 2) *undecided, unadjusted*, νείκεα, unadjusted contentions, 14, 205. 304. 3) not to be decided, *enduring, perpetual*; ἄχος, 3, 412; adv. ἄκριτον, endlessly. πενθήμεναι, Od. 18, 174.
ἀκριτόφυλλος, ον (φύλλον), *thickly leaved, covered with foliage, thickly wooded*, ὄρος, 2, 868.†
ἀκροκελαινιάω, Ep. (κελαινός), only partcp. ἀκροκελαινιόων, Ep. for ἀκροκελαινιῶν, *becoming black on the surface, dark-flowing*, epith. of a river, 21, 249.†
ἀκρόκομος, ον, poet. (κόμη), *having hair on the crown, crown-haired*, epith. of the Thracians, because they wore the hair bound in a knot on the crown, or wore hair on the crown only, 4, 533.†
ἄκρον, τό (neut. from ἄκρος), *the extreme, the summit, the point*; Ἴδης, the summit of Ida, 16, 292; Ἀθηνέων, the promontory [head-land, *Cp.*] of Athens, *Od. 3, 278; ποδός, Batr. 253.
Ἀκρόνεως, ὁ, a Phæacian, Od. 8, 111.
ἀκρόπολις, ιος, ἡ (πόλις), the upper city, *a citadel, a fortress*, *Od. 8, 494. 505; in the Il. ἄκρη πόλις, 6, 88.
ἀκροπόλος, ον, Ep. (πολέω), *being high, high-soaring, lofty*, epith. of mountains, 5, 523. Od. 19, 205.
ἀκρόπορος, ον, Ep. (πείρω), *penetrating with the point, sharp-pointed*, ὀβελοί, Od. 3, 463.†
ἄκρος, η, ον (ἀκή), superl. ἀκρότατος, η, ον, *extreme, highest, ending in a point*; in Hom. only in a physical sense: ἐπ' ἄκρῳ χείλει ἐφεστηώτες, standing on the extreme brink, 12, 51; ἄκρη χείρ, the end of the hand, 5, 336. ἐς πόδας ἄκρους, to the extremities (toes) of the feet, 16, 640. The neut. ἄκρον, as adv. 20, 229.
ἀκρωτήριον, τό (ἄκρος), *the extremity of

a thing; hence ἀκρωτήρια πρύμνης, the top of a ship's poop, h. 33, 10.
Ἀκταίη, ἡ (ἀκτή), prop. she who dwells on the coast, a Nereid, 18, 41.
ἀκτή, ἡ (ἄγνυμι), prop. fem. of ἀκτός, *broken, crushed*), 1) Poet. *corn bruised* or *ground in the mill*, comm. with ἱεροῦ ἀλφίτου or Δημητέρος, 13, 322. Od. 2, 355; see ἄλφιτον. 2) the place where the waves break, *shore, coast*, 11. and Od.
ἀκτήμων, ονος, ὁ, ἡ (κτῆμα), *without possessions, poor, needy*; with gen. χρυσοῖο, in gold, *9, 126. 268.
*ἀκτήρ, ἤρος=ἀκτίν, a now rejected reading, h. 32, 6.
ἀκτίς, ἶνος, ἡ, dat. ἀκτίνεσσιν and ἀκτῖσιν, Od. 5, 479. 11, 16; *a ray, a beam*, with Ἠελίοιο.
*ἄκτιτος, ον (κτίζω), poet. for ἄκτιστος, *untilled, waste*, h. Ven. 123.
Ἀκτορίδης, ου, ὁ, a descendant of Actor =*Echecles*, 16, 189.
Ἀκτορίς, ίδος, ἡ, a female servant of Penelope, Od. 23, 228.
Ἀκτορίων, ωνος, ὁ, son of Actor. τὼ Ἀκτορίωνε, the sons of Actor, *Eurytus* and *Cteatus*, who from their mother were also called the *Molïones*, 2, 621; see Μολίων.
Ἄκτωρ, ορος, ὁ (from ἄγω *leader*), 1) son of Deion, in Phocis, and Diomede, husband of Aegina, father of Menœtius, grandfather of Patroclus, 11, 785. Apd. 1, 9. 4. 2) son of Phorbas and Hyrminē, brother of Augeas, husband of Molionē, father of Eurytus and Cteatus, 11, 785. Apd. 3) son of Azeus, father of Astyocheë, grandfather of Ascalaphus and Ialmenus of Orchomenus, 2, 513.
ἄκυλος, ἡ, *the edible acorn*, fruit of the evergreen-oak (ilex), Od. 10, 242.†
ἀκωκή, ἡ (ἀκή), *point, edge*, ἔγχεος, δουρός, Il. and Od.
ἄκων, οντος, ὁ, *a javelin, a dart, a spear*. ἔρκος ἀκόντων, see ἕρκος.
ἄκων, ουσα, ον (ᾱ contr. from ἀέκων q. v.) only in τῷ δ' οὐκ ἀέκοντε πετέσθην, Il. and Od.
ἅλαδε, adv. *into the sea, to the sea*, also εἰς ἅλαδε.
ἀλάλημαι, Ep. perf. with pres. signif. from ἀλάομαι, q. v.
ἀλαλητός, ὁ (ἀλαλή), mly *a loud cry, a battle-cry, a shout of victory*, 4, 436. Od. 24, 463; but also *a cry of distress*, 21, 10.
ἄλαλκε, ἀλαλκών, ἀλαλκεῖν, see ἀλέξω.
Ἀλαλκομενηΐς, ίδος, epith. of Athene, probably from the town *Alalcomenæ*, in Bœotia, where she had a temple; according to others, from ἀλαλκεῖν, *the protectress*, 4, 8. 5, 908.
ἀλαλύκτημαι, *to toss oneself around restlessly, to be agitated with anxiety, to be in anguish*, 94† (prop. perf. from ἀλυκτέω, with pres. signif.).
*ἀλάμπετος, ον (λάμπω), *without brightness, dark*, h. 32, 5.
ἀλάομαι, depon. mid. impf. ἠλώμην, aor. 1 ἠλήθην, Ep. ἀλήθην, perf. ἀλάλη-

Ἀλαός. — Ἀλείσιον.

μαι, infin. ἀλάλησθαι, part. ἀλαλήμενος, *to wander about without aim, to rove, to stray, to roam;* with the prep. κατά, ἐπί, περί τι, 6, 201. Od. 4, 91. The perfect infin. and partcp. ἀλαλήμενος have the accent retracted on account of its pres. signif. 23, 74. Od. 11, 167. 14, 122.

ἀλαός, όν (λάω), *not seeing, blind,* ˈprop. ˇˇˇ, Od. 8, 195; but in μάντιος ἀλαοῦ, Od. 10, 493. 12, 267, ˉˉˉ;) cf. Thiersch. Gram. § 190, 22. *Od.

ἀλαοσκοπιή, ἡ (σκοπίη), lit. *a blind look-out; a useless watch,* ∾ ἥν ἔχειν, [ˈ*to look in vain,*ˈ Cp.] 13, 10. ἀλαοσκοπίη is an incorrect reading 10, 515.

ἀλαόω, poet. (ἀλαός), aor. ἀλάωσα, *to make blind, to blind.* τινὰ ὀφθαλμοῦ, to blind one's eye, *Od. 1, 69. 9, 516.

ἀλαπαδνός, ή, όν ˈἀλαπάζωι, poet. compar. ἀλαπαδνότερος, 4, 305; *easy to vanquish.* σθένος οὐκ ἀλαπαδνόν, insuperable strength, 5, 783; spoken of cattle, Od. 18, 373. 2) *powerless, weak, unwarlike,* 2, 675; μῦθος, h. Merc. 334.

ἀλαπάζω, poet. (λαπάζω), fut. ἀλαπάξω, aor. ἀλάπαξα without augm.; prop. *to empty, to exhaust;* πόλιν, to plunder a city, to sack, 2, 367, and often. 2) *to overpower, to vanquish, to destroy,* φάλαγγας, στίχας, Od. 17, 424. 19, 80; absol. Il. 12, 67:—then *to ruin, to reduce to distress,* Od. 17, 424.

ἀλαστέω, poet. (ἄλαστος), partcp. aor. ἀλαστήσας, prop. not to forget a thing; but mly, *to be displeased, to be angry,* *12, 163. 15, 21.

Ἀλαστορίδης, ου, ὁ, son of Alastor = Tros.

ἄλαστος, ον (λήθω or λάζομαι), *not to be forgotten, intolerable, immeasurable,* πένθος, 24. 105; ἄχος, Od. 4, 108. ἄλαστον ὀδύρεσθαι, to lament unceasingly, Od. 2) not to be forgotten or forgiven, *abominable, accursed,* 22, 261. Achilles applies the term to Hector: thou whose treatment of Patroclus I can never forget, 22, 261.

Ἀλάστωρ, ορος, ὁ (one burdened with the guilt of blood, or who does not forget to take vengeance), 1) father of Tros, 20, 463. 2) a companion of Sarpēdōn from Lycia, slain by Ulysses, 5, 677. 3) a Greek, who bore the wounded Teucer from the battle, 8, 333. 13, 422. 4) an Epean, 4, 295. 7, 333.

ἀλαωτύς, ύος, ἡ, poet. (ἀλαόω), a *blinding, a bereaving of sight,* Od. 9, 503.†

ἀλγέω (ἄλγος), fut. ἀλγήσω, 1) *to feel pain, to be distressed by pain,* primarily of the body; ὀδύνῃσι, 12, 206; with accus. κεφαλήν, Batr. 193. 2) Spoken of the mind: *to be troubled, to be pained,* Od. 12, 27.

ἀλγίων, ον, compar., ἄλγιστος, superl. of ἀλγεινός, q. v.

ἄλγος, εος, τό, *pain, suffering,* primarily of the body; then of the mind, *trouble, distress;* comm. in plur. ἄλγεα πάσχειν, to endure sufferings, pain, distress; spoken of the sufferings of war, 2, 667. 9, 321; by sea, Od. 1, 4.

ἀλδαίνω, poet. (ἀλδω), aor. 2 ἤλδανον, *to nourish, to make great, to enlarge,* τί τινι. μέλε' ἤλδανε ποιμένι λαῶν, she dilated the limbs of the shepherd of the people, Od. 18, 70. 24, 768.

ἀλδήσκω, Ep. (ἀλδαίνω), *to grow, to grow up;* spoken of a harvest, 23, 599.†

ἀλέασθαι, see ἀλέομαι.

ἀλεγεινός, ή, όν, poet. for ἀλγεινός (ἄλγος), irreg. compar. ἀλγίων, ον, superl. ἄλγιστος, η, ον, *painful, sad, oppressive, burdensome,* 2, 787. Od. 3, 206. 2) *difficult, hard;* with infin. ἵπποι ἀλεγεινοὶ δαμῆναι, hard to break, to be subdued, 10, 402; spoken of a mule: ἀλγίστη δαμάσασθαι, 23, 655. The compar. occurs only in the neut. ἀλγίον, mly in the signif. *the worse, so much the worse,* 13, 278. Od. 4, 292; where some [without reason] regard it as used for the positive.

Ἀλεγηνορίδης, ου, ὁ, son of Alegēnōr = Promachus, [14, 503.]

ἀλεγίζω, poet. (ἀλέγω), only in pres. and imperf *to trouble oneself about a thing, to care for;* with gen. and always with a negat. οὐκ ἀλεγίζειν τινός, 1, 160. 8, 477; once absol. *15, 106.

ἀλεγύνω (=ἀλέγω), *to trouble oneself about;* with accus. always with δαῖτα, to prepare a meal, *Od. 1, 374. 2, 139; δολοφροσύνην, to practise deceit, h. Merc. 361; ἀγλαΐας, h. Merc. 476; absol. h. Merc. 557.

ἀλέγω, poet. (a, λέγω), only pres.; kindred forms ἀλεγίζω and ἀλεγύνω, prop. to compute, to reckon together; hence, *to value, to esteem, to be careful;* comm. with negat. absol. 11, 389; absol. κύνες οὐκ ἀλέγουσαι, careless sluts, spoken of Penelopē's maidens [but without the coarse meaning that the words would have in English], Od. 19, 154. *a*) With gen. of the person: *to trouble oneself about one, to care for him,* 8, 483. Od. 9, 115. 275. *b*) With accus. of the thing: ὄπιν θεῶν, to regard the vengeance of the gods, 16, 388; νηῶν ὅπλα, to keep, to secure the tackle of ships, Od. 6, 268. *c*) With a partcp. spoken of the *Litæ* (Prayers): αἱ—μετόπισθ' Ἄτης ἀλέγουσι κιοῦσαι, who walk behind Atē carefully, steadily, 9, 504.

ἀλεείνω, Ep. form of ἀλέομαι (ἀλέη), only pres. and imperf. *to escape, to shun, to flee;* with accus. absol. κερδοσύνῃ ἀλέεινεν, with craft (craftily) he turned away, avoided me, Od. 4, 251. *b*) With infin. κτείνειν, ἀλεξέμεναι ἀλέεινεν, 6, 167. 13, 356.

ἀλεή, ἡ, poet. (ἄλη), *the act of avoiding, escaping,* 22, 301.†

ἀλέη, ἡ (ἄλω), *warmth, the heat of the sun,* Od. 17, 23.

ἄλειαρ, ατος, τό, poet. (ἀλέω), prop. that which has been ground, *flour, wheaten flour;* in plur. Od. 20, 108.†

ἀλείς, εἶσα, έν, partcp. aor. pass. from εἴλω.

Ἀλείσιον, τό (λεῖος), *Alesium,* a place in Elis, no longer in existence in the time

'Αλείσιον. of Strabo, who however mentions a region near Olympia called τὸ 'Αλείσιον, 2, 617.

'Αλείσιον κολώνη, ἡ, either a hill near Alesium, or a monument of Alesius, who according to Eustath. on 2, 617, was a son of Scillus, suitor of Hippodameia, 11, 757.

ἄλεισον, τό (prob. from λεῖος, not smoothly wrought, wrought *in relief; embossed*), *a goblet*, always costly, and mostly of gold, 11, 774; and Od. 3, 53.

ἀλείτης, ου, ὁ, poet. (ἀλιταίνω), *a sinner, a seducer, a vile wretch*; spoken of Paris, and of the suitors of Penelope, 3, 28. Od. 20, 121.

ἄλειφαρ, ατος, τό (ἀλείφω), *salve, unguent, balsam*, with which the dead were anointed before burning, 18, 351. Od. 3, 408.

ἀλείφω (λίπος), aor. ἤλειψα, aor. mid. ἠλειψάμην, 1) Act. *to anoint*, for the most part with λίπ' ἐλαίῳ, olive oil, 18, 350; also λίπ' alone, Od. 6, 227, see λίπα; spoken particularly of anointing after the bath, Od. 19, 505; κηρὸν ἐπ' ὠσίν, to rub wax upon the ears, Od. 12, 200 2) Mid. *to anoint oneself*, with λίπ' ἐλαίῳ, and with accus. χρόα, to anoint one's body, 14, 175.

'Αλεκτρυών, όνος, ὁ (=ἀλέκτωρ), father of the Argonaut Leïtus, 17, 602; 'Αλέκτωρ, Apd. 1, 9. 16.

*ἀλέκτωρ, ορος, ὁ (α, λέγω), prop. the sleepless, *the cock*, Batr. 193.

'Αλέκτωρ, ορος, ὁ, son of Pelops and Hegesandra, whose daughter Iphiloché married Megapenthes, son of Menelaus, Od. 4, 10.

ἀλέκω, assumed theme of ἀλέξω.

ἄλεν, Dor. and Ep. for ἐάλησαν, see εἴλω.

ἀλέν, neut. partcp. aor. pass. from εἴλω.

'Αλέξανδρος, ὁ (man-repelling, from ἀλέξω and ἀνήρ), an honorary name of Paris son of Priam, because according to the Schol. when a shepherd, he often bravely defended himself against robbers, 3, 16 [this is improbable].

ἀλεξάνεμος, ον (ἄνεμος), *wind-repelling*, epith. of a thick mantle, Od. 14, 529.†

ἀλέξασθαι, ἀλεξάμενος, see ἀλέξω.

ἀλεξέω furnishes tenses to ἀλέξω.

ἀλεξητήρ, ῆρος, ὁ (ἀλέξω), *repeller, defender, helper*, μάχης, a repeller of the battle (from others), protector in battle, 20, 396.†

ἀλεξίκακος, ον (κακός), *averting evil, repelling misfortune*, epith. of Nestor, 10, 20.†

ἀλέξω, (theme ΑΛΕΚ), infin. ἀλεξέμεναι, fut. ἀλεξήσω, aor. 1 optat. ἀλεξήσειεν, Od. 3, 346 ; Ep. aor. 2 ἤλαλκον, infin. ἀλαλκεῖν, partcp. ἀλαλκών (from theme ΑΛΚΩ), whence an Ep. fut. ἀλαλκήσει, Od. 10, 288, where Wolf reads ἀλάλκῃσι; mid. aor. subj. ἀλεξώμεσθα, infin. ἀλέξασθαι, 1) Act. *to ward off, to avert*, τί τινι, any thing from any one; κακὸν ἦμαρ Δαναοῖσιν, the evil day from the Greeks, 9, 251 ; νήεσσι πῦρ, 9, 347.

5) With dat. only: *to defend* any one, *in help*, 3, 9. 5, 779. 2) Mid. *to repel from oneself*, τινά, any one, 13, 475. Od. 18, 62; absol. *to defend oneself*, 11, 348. Od. 9, 57.

ἀλέομαι and ἀλεύομαι, Ep. and poet. (ἄλη), kindred form ἀλεείνω, aor. 1 ἠλευάμην and ἀλευάμην, subj. ἀλέηται, optat. ἀλέαιτο, imper. ἀλέασθε, infin. ἀλεύασθαι and ἀλέασθαι, partcp. ἀλευάμενος, *to shun, avoid, flee*; with accus. ἔγχεα, μῆνιν, and absol. 5, 28. b) With infin. ὄφρα καὶ ἄλλος ἀλεύεται (Ep. for ἀλεύηται), ἠπεροπεύειν, that another also may shrink from deceiving. Od. 14, 400. Il. 23, 340.

ἄλεται, Ep. with shortened mood-vowel for ἄληται; subj. aor. where elsewhere we find ἄλεται, 11, 192 ; see ἅλλομαι.

ἀλετρεύω (ἄλετος), *to grind*; with accus. καρπόν, Od. 7, 104.†

ἀλετρίς, ίδος, ἡ (ἀλέω), *grinding, γυνή*, a grinding woman, the female slave who grinds the corn, Od. 20, 105.†

ἀλεύομαι=ἀλέομαι, q. v.

ἀλέω, aor. 1 ἤλεσα, Ep. ἄλεσσα, *to grind*, Od. 20, 109. † in Tmesi.

ἀλεωρή, ἡ (ἀλέομαι), poet. *the act of avoiding, retreating, flight*, 24, 216. 2) *defence, protection*; spoken of the cuirass, 12, 57. 15, 533.

ἄλη, ἡ, *the act of wandering* or *roaming about*, *Od. 10, 464. 21, 284.

ἀληθείη, ἡ (ἀληθής), *truth*; only ἀληθείην μυθεῖσθαι, καταλέγειν, 24, 407. Od. 11, 507.

ἀληθείς, see ἀλέομαι.

*ἀληθεύω (ἀληθής), fut. σω, *to speak the truth, to be sincere*. Batr. 14.

ἀληθής, ές (λήθω), *undisguised, sincere, true, upright*, γυνή, 12, 433. 2) *true*, often neut. plur. ἀληθέα εἰπεῖν, Il. and Od.

'Αλήϊον πεδίον, τό, the Aleïan plain in Asia Minor, where Bellerophontes, hated by the gods, wandered solitarily about, 6, 201. According to a later tradition, proud of having slain Chimæra, he here attempted to soar upon Pegasus to the abode of the gods; he was however thrown, and perished from grief. According to Herod. it was near the city Mallus in Cilicia, between the rivers Pyramus and Sinarus, Hdt. 6, 85. (Signif. prob. from ἄλη, the field of wandering, or from λήϊον, harvestless, uncultivated.)

ἀλήϊος, ον (λήϊον), without possessions, poor, *destitute of an estate*, *9, 125. 267.

ἄληκτος, ον, Ep. ἄλληκτος (λήγω), *unceasing, endless, incessant*, θυμός, 9, 636; νότος, Od. 12, 325. The neut. sing. as adv. incessantly, πολεμίζειν, 11, 12. Hom. has only the Ep. form.

ἀλήμεναι, Ep for ἀλῆναι, see εἴλω.

ἀλήμων, ονος, ὁ (ἀλάομαι), *wandering about*, Od. 19, 74 ; subst. *a vagrant*, *Od. 17, 376.

ἀλῆναι, see εἴλω.

ἄληται (ἅληται ed. Wolf), 3 sing. aor. 2 subj. from ἅλλομαι, 21, 536.

Ἀλητεύω. 27 Ἀλιτήμων.

ἀλητεύω (ἀλήτης), only pres. *to wander about, to roam;* often in Od., comm. spoken of vagrants, *to beg*, Od. 14, 126. 16, 101; but also of hunters, Od. 12, 330.

ἀλήτης, ου, ὁ, *a vagrant, a beggar*, *Od. 14, 124.

Ἀλθαία, ἡ, daughter of Thestius and Erythemis, sister of Leda, wife of Œnius of Calydon, who bore to him Meleager, Deïanira, etc. The post-Homeric legends state that she slew Meleager by burning the fire-brand upon which, according to the prediction of the Parcæ his life depended, because in a contest concerning the prize in the Calydonian chase, he slew her two brothers, v, 555.

ἄλθομαι, Ep. mid. *to heal* (intrans.), *to be healed, to get well*, 5, 417.† (ἄλθω, akin to ἀλο, to make grow.)

ἁλιαής, ἐς (ἄημι), gen. έος, *blowing over* or *on the sea*, epith. of a favorable wind, Od. 4, 361.†

Ἁλίαρτος, ὁ (situated on the sea, from ἅλς and ἄρω), *Haliartus*, a town in Bœotia, on the shore of the lake Copaïs, now *Mazi*, 2, 503; also ἡ, Diod.

ἀλίαστος, ον, poet. (λιάζομαι), *unbending, not to be stayed, incessant, immense*, μάχη, πόλεμος, ὅμαδος. The neut. as adv. ἀλίαστον ὀδύρεσθαι, to lament incessantly, 24, 549. *11.

*ἀλιγείτων, ον, poet. (γείτων), *near the sea*, Ep. 4.

ἀλίγκιος, ον (ἧλιξ), prop. of equal age, but generally, *like, equal, similar,* τινί, 6, 401. Od. 8, 174.

ἁλιεύς, ῆος, ὁ (ἅλς), *a fisherman*, Od. 12, 251. 22, 384, and mly, 1) *a seaman, a sailor*, Od. 24, 418; as adj. ἐρέται ἁλιῆες, rowers on the sea, Od. 16, 349. *Od.

Ἁλιζῶνες, οἱ, sing. Ἁλιζών, ῶνος, ὁ (encircled by the sea, from ἅλς and ζώνη), the *Halizones*, a people on the Euxine, in Bithynia, neighbours of the Paphlagonians, 2, 856. Steph. According to Strabo, prob. the later Chalybians, who in his time were called Chaldæi. Eustath. and Strabo also cite the nom. Ἀλίζωνος. (They must not be confounded with Ἀλαζῶνες, a nomadic people in Scythia.)

Ἁλίη, ἡ (fem. of ἅλιος), daughter of Nereus and Doris, 18, 40.

Ἁλιθέρσης, ου, ὁ, son of Mastōr, a faithful friend of Ulysses in Ithaca, Od. 2, 157. 17, 68.

ἁλιμυρήεις, εσσα, εν, poet. (μύρω), *flowing into the sea, rushing seaward*, ποταμός, 21, 190. Od. 5, 460.

ἅλιος, ίη, ιον (ἅλς), *belonging to the sea, dwelling in the sea;* γέρων ἅλιος, the old man of the sea=*Nereus*, 1, 556; ἅλιαι θεαί, sea-goddesses, 24, 84: ἀθάναται ἅλιαι, 18, 84; also ἅλιαι alone, 18, 432. 2) *fruitless, idle, vain,* βέλος, μῦθος, ὁδός, ὅρκιον, 11. and Od. (The second signif. is comm. derived from ἄλη, but unnecessarily[?]. since the earliest language connected with the sea the idea of unfruit- fulness.) [Related to ἄλη, ἀλαός (*blind*, lit. *bereaved*), ἠλός Död.}

Ἅλιος, ὁ, 1) a Lycian, 5, 678. 2) son of Alcinous, Od. 8, 119.

ἁλιοτρεφής, ές, poet. (τρέφω), gen. έος, *nourished in the sea, sea-fattened;* epith. of seals, Od. 4, 442.†

ἁλιόω (ἅλιος), aor. ἁλίωσα, without augm. *to make vain, to frustrate, to render void,* νόον Διός, Od. 5, 104; βέλος, to shoot an arrow without effect, 16, 737.

ἁλίπλοος, ον (πλέω), *whelmed in the sea*. τείχεα ἁλίπλοα θεῖναι, to sink the walls into the sea, 12, 26.†

ἁλιπόρφυρος, ον (πορφύρα), *coloured with the purple of the murex, sea-purple, dark-purple,* ἠλάκατα, φάρεα, *Od. 6, 53. 13, 108.

ἅλις, adv. (ἁλής), 1) *in heaps, in multitudes, in crowds, in swarms*, 2, 90. Od. 13, 136. Hom. never has a seq. gen. 2) *sufficiently, enough*, 14, 121. ἢ οὐχ ἅλις, is it not enough I with a seq. ὅτι or ὡς, 5, 349. 23, 670. ὅθι ἔκειτο ἅλις εὐῶδες ἔλαιον, where there was fragrant oil in abundance, Od. 2, 339.

ἁλίσκομαι (in the act. obsol. theme Ἁλο-), fut. ἁλώσομαι only Batr. 286, aor. 2 ἑάλων, ἥλων only Od. 22, 230, subj. ἁλώω Ep. for ἁλῶ, optat. ἁλοίην, Ep. ἁλώην, 9, 592, infin. ἁλῶναι, partcp. ἁλούς (ἁλόντε with ἁ, 5, 487), 1) *to be caught, taken, captured;* spoken of men and cities, 2) Metaph. θανάτῳ ἁλῶναι, to be snatched away by death, 21, 281. Od. 5, 312; hence also alone *to be killed*, 12, 172. 14, 61. 17, 506. Od. 18, 265. * μήπως, ὡς ἀψῖσι λίνου ἁλόντε πανάγρου—κύρμα γένησθε, lest ye, as if caught in the meshes of a net, should become a prey, 5, 487. (According to Buttm. Gr. Grm. § 33, 3, 1, the dual stands here as an abbreviated form of the plur.; it is more satisfactorily explained on the ground that the discourse relates to two objects, viz.: Hector, and the remainder of the people (see v. 485); or with the Schol.: ye and the women.) [To avoid the anomalous ᾱ in ἁλόντε, Bothe proposes to read ἁλύοντε, from ἀλύω, *trepide erro*.]

ἀλιταίνω, poet. aor. 2 ἤλιτον once, 9, 375; aor. mid. ἀλιτόμην, infin. ἀλιτέσθαι, with like signif. *to do wrong, to sin;* always with accus. τινά, to sin against any one, 9, 375. 19, 265; ἀθανάτους, Od. 4, 378; Διὸς ἐφετμάς, to violate the commands of Zeus, 24, 570.

ἀλιτήμενος, η, ον, an Ep. perf. partcp. with accent of pres. for ἠλιτημένος from ἀλιταίνω with active signif. *doing wrong, sinning:* with dat. θεοῖς, against the gods, Od. 4, 807.† According to Rost Vollst. Lexik. under ἀλιταίνω, the dat. in this passage indicates the person in whose estimation the predicate is not true of the subject: 'for he is no sinner in the eyes of the gods.'

ἀλιτήμων, ονος, ὁ (ἀλιταίνω), *sinning, wicked.* *24. 157. 186.

Ἀλιτρός. 28 Ἀλλά.

ἀλιτρός, ὁ, contr. for ἀλιτηρός, *a wicked man, a sinner,* 8, 361; δαίμοσιν, against the gods, 23, 595; also in a softer sigulf. *knave, rogue,* Od. 5, 182.

Ἀλκάθοος, ὁ (quick in defence, from ἀλκή and θόος), son of Asyêtês; he was the husband of Hippodameia the sister of Æneas, and had brought him up; Idomeneus slew him, 12, 93. 13. [427.] 465.

Ἀλκάνδρη, ἡ, wife of Polybus, in the Egyptian Thebæ, with whom Menelaus lodged, Od. 4, 126.

Ἀλκανδρος, ὁ (man-repelling, from ἀλκή and ἀνήρ), a Lycian, slain by Ulysses, 5, 678.

ἄλκαρ, τό (ἀλκή), gen. and dat. obsol. *defence, protection, bulwark;* with gen. Ἀχαιῶν, of the Achaians, 11, 823; and dat. Τρώεσσι, for the Trojans, 5, 644; but γήραος ἄλκαρ, a protection against age, h. Ap. 193. °Il.

ἀλκή, ἡ, with metaplast. dat. ἀλκί, also ἀλκῇ, Od. 24, 509. 1) *strength, physical power,* 3, 45. 6, 263. Od. 22, 237. 2) *defence, protection, help,* ὅ τοι ἐκ Διὸς οὐχ ἕπετ᾽ ἀλκή, that help from Zeus follows thee not, 8, 140. 14, 786. Od. 12, 120. 3) the power to defend, whether of body or mind, *strength, courage, boldness,* 2, 234. ἐπιειμένος ἀλκήν, clothed with courage, 7, 164. μνῄσασθαι θουρίδος ἀλκῆς, to remember, think of impetuous courage, 5, 718. 4) Personified as a goddess and represented on the ægis, 5, 740.

°ἀλκήεις, εσσα, εν, poet. (ἀλκή), *defending, courageous, brave, bold,* h. 26, 3.

Ἄλκηστις, ιος, ἡ, *Alcestis,* daughter of Pelias and Anaxibia, wife of Admêtus, king of Pheræ in Thessaly. By a decree of the Fates, according to later mythology, Admetus was to be delivered from death, if some one should die for him. Alcestis laid down her life for him, but Persephônê sent her back, 2, 715.

ἀλκί, Ep. dat. of ἀλκή, from the obsol. root, ἄλξ; always ἀλκὶ πεποιθώς, trusting to his strength, 5, 299.

Ἀλκιμέδων, οντος, ὁ (meditating defence, from ἀλκή and μέδων), son of Laerces, leader of the Myrmidons under Achilles, after the death of Patroclus, his charioteer, 16, 197.

Ἀλκιμίδης, ου, ὁ, son of Alcimus = *Mentor,* Od. 21, 235.

ἄλκιμος, ον (ἀλκή), *strong,* ἔγχος, δόρυ. 2) Spoken of warriors, *courageous, brave;* also of animals, 20, 169.

Ἄλκιμος, ὁ, 1) father of Mentor. 2) a Myrmidon, friend of Achilles, 19, 392.

Ἀλκίνοος, ὁ (of a spirited disposition, from νόος), son of Nausithous, grandson of Poseidôn, king of the Phæaces in Scheria, by whom Ulysses, having suffered shipwreck, was hospitably received, Od. 6, 12 seq. 8, 118.

Ἀλκίππη, ἡ, a female slave of Helen in Sparta, Od. 4, 124.

Ἀλκμαίων, ονος, ὁ (from ἀλκή and μαίομαι striving for defence), son of Amphiaraus and Eriphŷlê, brother of Amphilŏchus, and leader of the Epigŏni against Thebes, Od. 15, 248. According to later mythology, when Amphiaraus, betrayed by his wife, was obliged to go to the Theban war, he directed him, in case of his death, to slay his mother. He did it, and was on this account persecuted by the Furies, till at last he found rest in an island of the Achelôus.

Ἀλκμάων, ονος, ὁ, Ep. for Ἀλκμαίων, son of Thestôr, a Greek, slain by Sarpedôn before Troy, 12, 394.

Ἀλκμήνη, ἡ, daughter of Electryôn, king of Mycenæ, wife of Amphitryôn in Thebes, mother of Heracles by Zeus, and of Iphicles by Amphitryon. Hêrê hated her, delayed the birth of Heracles and accelerated that of Eurystheus, that the latter might have the dominion over the former, 14, 323. 19, 119. Od. 11, 266.

ἀλκτήρ, ἦρος, ὁ (ἀλκή), *defender, helper,* ἀρῆς, averter of a curse, i. e. of calamity, injury, death, 14, 485. 18, 100; spoken of a javelin: κυνῶν καὶ ἀνδρῶν, a defence against dogs and men, Od. 14, 531. 21, 340.

Ἀλκυόνη, ἡ, a name of *Cleopatra* wife of Meleager; so named from *Alcyone,* daughter of Æolus, who after the death of her husband Ceÿx, plunged into the sea, and was changed by Thetis into a kingfisher. The point of comparison would then consist only in this, that Marpessa, like Alcyonê, separated from her husband wept. More naturally and probably, Heyne and Spitzner understand by ἀλκυών the kingfisher (see ἀλκυών), 9, 562.

Ἀλκυών, όνος, ἡ, as prop. name = Ἀλκυόνη, 9, 563, ed. Wolf.

ἀλκυών, όνος, ἡ, Ion. for ἀλκυών, the *sea-kingfisher,* alcedo (from ἅλς and κύειν, because it was thought to brood in the sea). Heyne and Spitzner write 9, 563 ἀλκυόνος instead of Ἀλκ. because Hom. knew nothing of the transformation of Alcyonê. They therefore refer the words πολυπενθέος οἶτος ἔχουσα to the tender wailings of the kingfisher, which is often mentioned by the poets. These form a good point of comparison for the sad voice and tender complaints of Marpessa, separated by Apollo from her beloved.

ἄλκω, obsol. root of ἀλαλκεῖν, ἀλέξω.

ἀλλά, conj. (prop. neut. from ἄλλος), *but, still, yet, however, notwithstanding;* it indicates in general a greater or less opposition in the thought. It is used: 1) For connecting with the foregoing an entirely opposite idea, the first being quite set aside. It then often follows a negative proposition, = *but,* 1, 94: it indicates the antithesis after οὐδέ, 2, 754. 2) For annexing a different thought of such a character, that the force of the preceding clause is but partially removed. This takes place both after affirmative and negative clauses, and is translated by *but, however, still, yet;* and the antithesis is prepared by μέν

Ἀλλεγεν. ἦτοι, γέ, etc. 1, 24. 16, 240. The antithesis also often consists in a hypothetic protasis, εἰ—ἀλλά, 1, 281; εἴπερ—ἀλλά, 8, 154; εἴπερ τε,—ἀλλά τε, 1, 82. 3) To mark an exception, after a negative clause. After οὔτις ἄλλος, ἀλλά is translated *than*, 21, 275. Od. 3, 377; also after οὔτι ἄλλος, Od. 8, 311 seq. cf. 12, 403 seq. 4) It stands at the beginning of a clause adverbially, to indicate the transition to a different thought; hence in exhortations, exclamations, etc. ἀλλ' ἄγε, ἀλλ' ἄγε δή, *but come on! but up now!* 5) It is often connected with other particles: ἀλλ' ἄρα, *but indeed*, after a negative; ἀλλά γάρ, *but certainly, still indeed* (prop. each particle retains its original signif., the first marking the antithesis, the second the reason; still the antithesis must often be supplied from the connexion); ἀλλ' οὐ γάρ, *but—not*, Od. 14, 334. 19, 591; ἀλλ' ἦτοι, *but yet* [*at profecto; at videlicet.* Klotz]; ἀλλὰ καὶ ὥς, *but even thus;* ἀλλ' οὐδ' ὥς, *but not even thus.*

ἄλλεγεν, ἀλλέξαι, Ep. for ἀνέλεγεν, ἀναλέξαι from ἀναλέγω.

ἄλλῃ, adv. (prop. dat. sing. from ἄλλος), 1) *in another way. elsewhere*, 13, 49; *in another manner*, φρονεῖν, h. Ap. 169. 2) *away to some other place, elsewhere;* that my reward is going away, i. e. to another, 1, 120; τρέπειν τι, 5, 187. 3) *otherwise*, 15, 51.

ἄλληκτος, ον, Ep. for ἄληκτος, q. v.

ἀλλήλων (from ἄλλοι, ἄλλων, prop. ἀλλάλλων), only in gen. dat. accus. of plur. and dual (the nom. is from the signif impossible). *one another, mutually, reciprocally.* ἴδμεν δ' ἀλλήλων γενεήν, we know each other's race, 20, 203; ἀλλήλοιϊν Ep. for ἀλλήλοιυ as gen. 10, 65.

ἀλλόγνωτος, ον (γιγνώσκω), *known to others*, hence *strange to us, foreign*, δῆμος, Od. 2, 366.†

ἀλλοδαπός, ή, όν (either lengthened from ἄλλος, or contracted with ἔδαφος [no. Cf. Lexil. under ἐχθοδοπῆσαι]), *from another land, strange, foreign*, Od. 14, 231. 2) Subst. *a stranger.* 3, 48.

ἀλλοειδής, ές (εἶδος), *of a different form, of different appearance*, Od. 13, 194.† (ἀλλοειδέα is to be read as trisyllabic.)

ἄλλοθεν, adv. (ἄλλος), *from another place, from a different place*, Od. 3, 318; often ἄλλοθεν ἄλλος, which, like the Latin *alius aliunde*, expresses a double clause, see ἄλλος; *one from one place, another from another*, 2, 75. Od. 9, 401.

ἄλλοθι, adv. (ἄλλος), *elsewhere*, sometimes with gen. ἄλλοθι γαίης, elsewhere upon earth, i. e. in a strange land, Od. 2, 131; πάτρης (elsewhere than in one's country=), far from one's country, *Od. 17, 318.

ἀλλόθροος, ον (θρόος), *sounding differently, speaking in a foreign tongue*, *Od. 1, 183. 3, 302.

ἀλλοῖος, η, ον (ἄλλος), *of different quality, differently formed*, 4, 258; always with the idea of comparison, ἀλλοῖός μοι ἐφάνης ἠὲ πάροιθεν, thou appearest to me now a different person from what thou didst before, Od. 16, 161.

ἄλλομαι, aor 1 ἡλάμην, only Batr. 252, comm. aor. 2 ἡλόμην, of which only subj. ἄληται, Ep. ἄλεται (ἄλεται Wolf, cf. Spitz. on 11, 192), Ep. 2 and 3 sing. of sync. aor. 2 ἆλσο, ἆλτο, partcp. ἄλμενος, 1) *to leap*, ἐξ ὀχέων, from the chariot, 11. εἰς ἵππους. 2) Spoken of any vehement motion, *to rush, to run*, ἐπί τινι, upon any one, 13, 611; *to fly*, spoken of an arrow, 4, 125.

ἀλλοπρόσαλλος (πρός, ἄλλος), *turning from one to another, alternately with both parties, fickle, inconstant*, epith. of Arēs, 5, 831. 889. *Il.

ἄλλος, η, ον, 1) *another*, with gen. ἄλλος Ἀχαιῶν; it seems to stand pleonastically with πλήσιος, ἕκαστος, 4, 81. 16, 697; ἄλλος μέν, ἄλλος δέ, *the one, the other.* 2) οἱ ἄλλοι and ἄλλοι, *the rest*, 2, 1. 17, 280. τὰ ἄλλα, contr. τἆλλα, better τἄλλα (cf. Buttm. Gram. § 29. note 2), the rest, cætera, 1, 465. 3) *another*, i. e. different, not like the preceding, 13, 64. Od. 2, 93; with ἀλλά following, 21, 275; or εἰ μή, h. Cer. 78; hence 4) Poet.= ἀλλότριος, *strange, foreign*, Od. 23, 274. 5) τὰ ἄλλα, and τὸ ἄλλο, *in other respects, besides*, 23, 454. 6) Hom. often connects ἄλλος with another case, or with an adv. of the same root, so that, like the Lat. *alius*, it contains a double clause: ἄλλος δ' ἄλλῳ ἔρεζε θεῶν, one sacrificed to one, another to another of the immortal gods, 2, 400. cf. 2, 304. Od. 14, 228. 7) Sometimes ἄλλος, like the French *autre*, is apparently superfluous, marking something diverse from the thing mentioned. It may often be translated, *on the other hand*, 21, 22. Od. 1, 132. 2, 412.

ἄλλοσε, adv. (ἄλλος), *to another place, in another place*, *Od. 23, 184. 204.

ἄλλοτε, adv. (ὅτε). 1) *another time, once, formerly.* 2) Often ἄλλοτε—ἄλλοτε, or ὅτε μέν—ἄλλοτε δέ, 11, 566; *at one time—at another, now—then, now—now*. 3) In connexion with ἄλλος: ἄλλοτε ἄλλῳ Ζεὺς ἀγαθόν τε κακόν τε διδοῖ, Zeus gives good and evil now to one, now to another, Od. 4, 237.

ἀλλότριος, η, ον (ἄλλος), 1) *strange*, i. e. belonging to another. βίοτος, ἀλλοτρίων χαρίσασθαι, to be liberal with others' property, Od. 17, 452; οἱ δ' ἤδη γναθμοῖσι γελοίων ἀλλοτρίοισι, they laughed now with strange jaws, i. e. either *immoderately* (sparing their jaws in laughing as little as if they belonged to others), or with *distorted* countenance, i. e. with a *forced, unnatural* laugh, Od. 20, 347. 2) *strange*, i. e. from another land, φώς, a foreigner, Od. 18, 218;=hostile, ὅ, 214. Od. 16, 102.

ἄλλοφος, ον, Ep. for ἄλοφος.

ἀλλοφρονέω (φρονέω), prop. to be of another opinion, hence 1) *to be thinking of something else, to be in thought*, Od. 10, 374. 2) *to lose one's wits* or

Ἀλλυδις. 30 *Ἀλφηστής*

one's *senses, to be senseless,* 23, 698, only partcp.

ἄλλυδις, Ep. adv. (ἄλλος), *to another place;* with ἄλλος added, διά τ' ἔτρεσεν ἄλλυδις ἄλλος, they fled one to one place, another to another, 11, 486. 17. 729.

ἄλλυδις ἄλλῃ, one in this way, another in that, Od. 5, 71. τοῦ κακοῦ τρέπεται χρώς ἄλλυδις ἄλλῃ, the colour of the dastard changes now in this way, now in that, 13, 279.

ἀλλύεσκεν, poet. for ἀνελύεσκεν, literat. imperf. fr. ἀναλύω.

ἄλλως, adv. (ἄλλος), 1) *otherwise, in another manner,* 5, 218; sometimes in a good sense, *otherwise,* i. e. better, 11, 391. 14, 53. 19, 401. Od. 8, 176. 20, 211. 2) *otherwise* (than we believe [than as it should be]), i. e. *rainly, in vain,* 23, 144. 3) *without aim, without object,* Od. 14, 124. 4) in another view, *in other respects, for the rest, besides,* ὁ δ' ἀγήνωρ ἐστὶ καὶ ἄλλως, 9, 695. Od. 17, 577. 21, 87.

ἅλμα, ατος, τό (ἅλλομαι), *the act of leaping, springing,* *Od. 8, 103. 129.

ἅλμη, ἡ (ἅλς), 1) *salt water, brine,* esply of the sea, Od. 5, 53. 2) *the dirt* from dried *spray,* *Od. 6, 137.

ἁλμυρός, ή, όν (ἅλμη), *salt, briny;* only with ὕδωρ, salt water, the briny flood, *Od. 4, 511.

ἀλογέω (λόγος), without care, *to take no heed, to disregard, to despise,* 15, 162.†

ἀλόθεν, adv. ἅλς, *from the sea;* ἐξ ἁλόθεν, from the sea, 21, 335.

ἀλοιάω, poet. for ἀλοάω (ἀλωή), *to beat, to strike;* with acc. γαῖαν χερσίν, 9, 568.†

ἀλοιφή, ἡ (ἀλείφω), what is used for anointing, *fat, ointment,* to make any thing supple, 17, 390; also oil for the human body, Od. 6, 220. 2) *fat,* esply *hog's fat,* connected with the flesh, 9, 208. Od. 8, 476.

'Αλόπη, ἡ, a town in Phthiōtis (Thessaly), near Larissa, under the dominion of Achilles, 2, 682 (otherwise unknown).

"Αλος, ἡ, a town in Achaia Phthiōtis (Thessaly) on mount Othrys, not far from Pharsālus, belonging to Achilles' realm, 2, 682. (Better "Αλος, as Dem. Strab. from ἅλς, named from the salt-pits.)

ἁλοσύδνη, ἡ, *one living in the sea,* name of *Thetis,* 10, 607. 2) pr. n. appellation of *Amphitrītē,* Od. 4, 404 (from ἅλς and ὕδνης, nourished from the sea; or poet. for ἀλοσύνη, from ἅλς and σύω=σεύομαι, with epenthetic δ, moving in the sea).

ἄλοφος, ον, Ep. ἄλλοφος (λόφος), *without crest,* 10, 258.†

ἄλοχος, ἡ (λέχος), *bed-fellow, wife.* 2) *concubine,* 9, 336. Od. 4, 623.

ἀλόω, Ep. for ἀλάου, imper. pres from ἀλάομαι, Od.

ἀλόωνται, see ἀλάομαι, Od.

ἅλς, ἁλός, ὁ, *salt,* sing. only Ion. and poet. 9, 214; comm. plur. ἅλες; εἴδαρ ἄλεσσι μεμιγμένον, food seasoned with salt, Od. 11, 123. 23, 270. οὐδ' ἅλα δοίης, prov., thou wouldst not give even a grain of salt, i. e. not the smallest portion, Od.

17, 455. 2) ἡ ἅλς, poet. *the briny deep,* the sea, 1, 141; and often opposed to γῆ, Od. [The latter is the primary idea; cf. Od. 11, 122. 123. Am. Ed.]

ἅλσο, Ep. syncop. 2 sing. aor. 2 of ἅλλομαι.

ἅλσος, εος, τό (ἅλδω), *a sacred grove,* or wood, and nly a region consecrated to a deity, 2, 506.

'Άλτης, αο and εω, ὁ, a king of the Leleges of Pedasus, father of Laothoë, 21, 85. 86. 22, 51.

ἅλτο, Ep. syncop. 3 sing. aor. 2 from ἅλλομαι.

'Αλύβας, αντος, ἡ, a town of uncertain situation, according to Eustath. the later *Metapontium,* in Lower Italy, according to others='Αλύβη, Od. 24, 304.

'Αλύβη, ἡ, a town on the Pontus Euxinus, whence silver comes, 2, 858. According to Strabo the later Chalybes dwelt here, from whom the Greeks first procured their metals.

ἀλυσκάζω, only pres. and imperf. poet, lengthened form fr. ἀλύσκω, 1) *to avoid, to flee;* with accus. ὕβριν, Od. 17, 581. 2) Absol. *to flee,* νόσφιν πολέμοιο, from the war, 5, 253. 6, 443.

ἀλυσκάνω, poet. form of ἀλύσκω in the imperf. Od. 22, 330.†

ἀλύσκω (ἀλεύομαι), poet. form, fut. ἀλύξω, aor. ἤλυξα, *to avoid, to escape, to shun;* with accus. ὄλεθρον, to escape destruction, 10, 371; θάνατον, Od. 2, 353. ἤλυξα ἑταίρους, I had withdrawn myself from my companions, Od. 12, 335. 2) Absol. *to fly, to escape,* προτὶ ἄστυ, to the city, 10, 348. Od. 22, 460.

*ἀλύσσω (Ep. form from ἀλύω), *to be beside oneself,* only of dogs which have tasted blood, *to be fierce,* 22, 70.†

ἄλυτος, ον (λύω), *indissoluble,* πέδαι, 13, 37; πεῖραρ, 13, 360; δεσμοί, Od. 8, 275.

ἀλύω, poet. (akin to ἄλη, *to be beside oneself,* a) from pain, *to be greatly distressed,* 5, 352. 24, 12. Od. 9, 398. b) from joy : ἢ ἀλύεις, ὅτι "Ἶρον ἐνίκησας, art thou beside thyself, that thou hast conquered Irus, Od. 18, 333 (ὔ, once ῦ, Od. 9, 398).

ἀλφάνω, poet. ἤλφον, optat. ἄλφοι, prop. to find; in Hom. *to gain, to procure,* τινί τι, as μυρίον ὦνον, a prodigious price, Od. 15, 453; βίοτον πολύν, Od. 17, 250. 20, 383 : ἑκατόμβοιον, 21, 79.

'Αλφειός, ὁ, *Alphēus,* a river in Elis, which rises in Arcadia, and flows into the Ionian sea near Pitanē, now *Alfeo,* 2, 592. 2) *the river-god,* 5, 545. Od. 3, 489.

ἀλφεσίβοιος, η, ον (ἀλφεῖν, βοῦς), prop. *cattle finding,* epith. of virgins who have many suitors that bring cattle as presents (ἕδνα), to purchase them from their parents; hence *much-wooed,* 18, 593.†

ἀλφηστής, οῦ, ὁ (ἀλφεῖν), *the inventor, the finder;* adj. in the Od. ἄνδρες ἀλφησταί, *inventive, gainful men* (accord. to Eustath. epith. of man, who thus distinguishes himself from the beasts; or better with Nitzsch on Od. 1, 349, indus-

Άλφι. 81 Άματροχίη.

trious, intent upon gain, and therefore also inventive), *Od. 1, 349, h. Ap. 458.

ἄλφι, τό, indeclin. poet. shorter form for ἄλφιτον, h. Cer. 208.

ἄλφιτον, τό (ἀλφεῖν), *uncooked* or *parched barley*, because this was the earliest general food, reduced by a hand-mill to meal or a coarse powder; hence sing. ἀλφίτου ἱεροῦ ἀκτή, the ground or crushed meal of the sacred barley [a periphrasis for ἄλφιτα or ἄρτον, Schol.], Od. 14, 429. 11, 631, and μυλήφατον ἀλφ., Od. 2, 355. Oftener in the plur. ἄλφιτα, *barley-flour*, from which bread, cakes, porridge, etc. were prepared, 11, 631. Od. 10, 234. Also in sacrifices it was sprinkled on the flesh, Od. 2, 290.

ἄλφοι, see ἀλφαίνω.

Ἀλωεύς, ῆος, ὁ (thresher, from ἀλωή), son of Poseidōn and Canacē, husband of Iphimedeia, father of the Alōides, Otus, and Ephialtes, 5, 386.

ἀλωή, ἡ (ἀλοάω), poet. *a threshing-floor*, a level place in the field for threshing grain, 5, 499. 20, 496. 2) a cultivated piece of ground, sown with grain or planted with trees, *fruit-garden, vineyard, corn-field*, 9, 534. Od, 1, 193.

ἀλώη, Ep. for ἀλῷ, 3 sing. subj. aor. 2, but ἀλῴη, Ep. for ἀλοίη, 3 sing optat. from ἀλίσκομαι.

ἀλώμενος, partcp. pres. from ἀλάομαι.

ἀλώμεναι, Ep. for ἀλῶναι, see ἀλίσκομαι.

ἀλώω, Ep. for ἀλῶ, see ἀλίσκομαι.

ἄμ, abbrev. for ἀνά, before β, π, φ: ἂμ πεδίον, ἂμ φόνον.

ἅμα, 1) adv. *at once*: with τε—καί. *at once—and; both—and*, 1, 417. 8, 64, &c. 2) prep. with dat. *a*) of time; *at the same time with; together with*, ἅμα δ' ἠελίῳ καταδύντι, together with the setting sun, 1, 592. *b*) of persons: *together with, in company with, along with;* ἅμα λαῷ θωρηχθῆναι, to arm with the people. *c*) Of equality, or similarity, prop. *together with;* then, *like*. ἅμα πνοιῇς ἀνέμοιο, like the blasts of wind (i. e. keeping pace with them), 16, 149. Od. 1, 98.

Ἀμαζόνες, αἱ (from ἀ and μάζος, breast-less), *the Amazons*, warlike women of mythic antiquity, who allowed no man among them, and amputated the right breast in infancy, to allow a freer use of the bow. Their abode, according to most poets, was on the river Thermōdon, in Cappadocia, or in Scythia, on the Palus Mæōtis. According to 6, 186, they invaded Lycia, but were destroyed by Bellerophontēs, and according to 3, 189, they also attacked Phrygia in the kingdom of Priam. Obscure traditions of armed Scythian women were probably the origin of this fable.

Ἀμάθεια, ἡ (living in the downs, from ἄμαθος), daughter of Nereus and Doris, 19, 48.

ἄμαθος. ἡ, poet. = ψάμαθος, *sand, dust*, 5, 586.† Plur. the dunes on the sea-coast, h. in Ap. 439.

ἀμαθύνω (ἄμαθος), *to reduce to dust, to destroy, πόλιν*, 9, 593. 2) *to conceal* [in the sand], κόνιν, h. Merc. 140.

ἀμαιμάκετος, η, ον, *very great, monstrous, prodigious*, epith. of Chimæra, and of a mast, 6, 179. Od. 14, 311 (of uncertain derivation, comm. from ἀ and μῆκος, or, according to Passow, from ἄμαχος, μαίμαχος, with reduplic. *invincible*, cf. δαίδαλος.)

ἀμαλδύνω (ἀμαλός), aor. ἠμάλδυνα, prop. *to render soft;* hence *to destroy, to demolish;* τεῖχος, *to tear down a wall*, *7, 463. 12, 18.

ἀμαλλοδετήρ, ῆρος, ὁ (ἄμαλλα, δέω), *the sheaf-binder*, *18, 553, 554.

ἀμαλός, ή, όν, Ep. for ἀπαλός, *tender, weak*, 22, 310. Od. 20, 14.

ἄμαξα, ἡ, Ep. and Ion. for ἅμαξα (ἄγω), *wagon*, in distinction from the two-wheeled war-chariot, ἅρμα, 7, 426. Od. 9, 241. 2) The *Wagon*, a constellation in the northern sky, a name of the Great Bear in the heavens [compare the name Charles's Wain]; see Ἄρκτος, 18, 487. Od. 5, 273.

ἀμαξιτός, ἡ (ἅμαξα), sc. ὁδός, *a wagon-road, a street*, 22, 146. †h. Cer. 177.

ἀμάρη, ἡ, *a channel for water, a ditch*, 21, 259.†

ἁμαρτάνω, fut. ἁμαρτήσομαι, aor. ἥμαρτον, Ep. also ἤμβροτον (by metathesis, changing a into o, with β epenthetic, and a change of the breathing,) 1) *to fail, to miss*, not to hit the mark, τινός, any one; spoken e»ply of missiles, 10, 372; hence 2) metaph. *to fail, to err, to deviate;* νοήματος ἐσθλοῦ. she swerved not from a noble mind, Od. 7, 292. οὐχ ἡμάρτανε μύθων, he mistook not the words, i. e. he always selected the right words, Od. 11, 511; also absol. *to fail, err, mistake*, 9, 501. Od. 21, 155. 3) *to fall of what one has, to lose, to be deprived of*, ὑπωπῆς, Od. 9, 512. 4) *to make a failure in any thing;* δώρων, failed not to bring gifts, 24, 68.

ἁμαρτῇ or **ἀμαρτῆ**, adv. (ἅμα, ἀράω), *together, at the same time*, 5, 656. Od. 22, 81. Others write ἀμαρτῇ or ὁμαρτῇ.

ἁμαρτοεπής, ές, Ep. (ἔπος), *missing the proper words, idly prating*, 13, 824.†

*ἁμαρυγή, ἡ** (μαίρω), poet. for μαρμαρυγή, *the glimmering, flashing, gleaming* of the eyes, h. Merc. 45.

Ἀμαρυγκείδης, ου, ὁ, son of Amarynceus = *Diores*, 2, 622. 4, 517.

Ἀμαρυγκεύς, ῆος, ὁ (ἀμαρύσσω), son of Alector, a brave warrior who went from Thessaly to Elis, and aided Augeas against Heraclēs. As a reward, Augeas shared with him the throne. His funeral is mentioned 23, 631. .

*ἀμαρύσσω, fut. ξω, *to shine, to gleam*, ἀπὸ βλεφάρων, h. Merc. 278. 415.

ἀματροχάω, poet. (τρέχω), only partcp. pres. ἀματροχόων, Ep. for ἀματροχῶν, *running with*, Od. 15, 451.†

ἀματροχίη, ἡ, Ep. (τρέχω), *the running together of chariots* [a clash of chariots, Cp.], 23, 422.†

C 4

'Αμιυρός. 32 Άμήχανος.

άμαυρός, ή, όν, poet. (μαίρω), not shining, dark, indistinct, είδωλον, *Od. 4, 824. 835.
άμάχητι, adv. (μάχη), without battle, without contest, 21, 437.†
άμάω (άμα), aor. άμησα, Ep. for ήμησα, aor. mid. άμησάμενος, prop. to gather; hence 1) Act. to mow, to reap; absol, 18, 551; with accus. 24, 451. Od. 9, 135. 2) to collect for oneself; with accus. γάλα έν ταλάροισι, the milk curd in baskets, Od. 9, 217.
άμβαίνω, άμβάλλω, and other words with άμβ; see άναβαίνω. άναβάλλω, etc.
άμβατός, όν, poet. for άναβατός.
άμβλήδην, see άναβλήδην.
άμβολαδήν. adv. see άναβολαδήν.
άμβροσίη, ή (prop. fem. from άμβρόσιος, sc. according to the ancients έδωδή), ambrosia, 1) the food of the gods, which was agreeable in taste, and secured Immortality, Od. 5, 93. 199. 9, 359. 2) the oil of the gods, with which the immortals anointed themselves, 14, 170; cf. 172. 3) used as food for the horses of Hērē, 5, 777, and Od. 4, 445. Eidothea gives ambrosia to Menelaus to remove a disagreeable smell. According to Buttm. Lexil. 79, it is a subst. and signifies immortality, for the gods eat immortality, they anoint themselves with it, and it is also the food of their steeds.
άμβρόσιος, η, ον, (βροτός) immortal, of divine nature. νύμφη, h. Merc. 230. 2) Spoken of what belongs to the gods; ambrosial, divine, as χαίται, πέδιλα, έλαιον. 1, 529. 3) Of what comes fro˘ the gods : divine, sacred, as νύξ, ύπνος, 2, 19, 57.
άμβροτος, ον (βροτός)=άμβρόσιος, immortal, divine, θεός, 20, 358; and spoken of whatever belongs to the gods: ambrosial, αίμα, 5, 539; κρήδεμνον. Od. 5, 347. 2) divine, sacred, and generally excellent, lovely; spoken of whatever comes from the gods. νύξ, Od. 11, 330.
άμέγαρτος, ον (μεγαίρω), prop. not to be envied; hence 1) Spoken of things: sad, dreadful, severe, πόνος, 2, 420; αύτμή άνέμων, Od. 11, 400. 2) Of persons, as epith. of contempt; wicked, vile, miserable, Od. 17, 219 (cf. Buttm. Lexil. p. 407).
άμείβοντες, see άμείβω.
άμείβω. fut. άμείψω, fut. mid. άμείψομαι, aor. 1 ήμειψάμην. I) Act. to alternate, to change, to exchange, a) Intrans. only in partcp. οί άμείβοντες, the alternating, i. e. the rafters, 23, 712. b) Comm. trans. to change. to exchange ; with accus. έντεα, 17, 192; τί τινος, one thing for another; τεύχεα χρύσεα χαλκείων πρός τινα, to exchange golden weapons for brazen with any one, 6, 235; γόνυ γουνός, one knee with the other, i. e. to walk slowly 11, 547. II) Mid. to change for oneself, to exchange; hence 1) to interchange, to alternate ; in partcp. άμειβόμενος, alternating, 1, 604. 9, 471. άμείβεσθαι κατά οίκους, to change by houses, i.e. to go from house to house, Od. 1, 375.

b) Often έπέεσσι, μύθοισι τινά, to alternate with words with any one, i. e. to reply. 2) Spoken of place : to exchange, to leave ; with accus. ψυχή άμείβεται έρκος όδόντων, the soul passes over the wall of the teeth, i. e. the lips, 9, 409; and spoken of drink, which goes over the lips into the mouth, Od. 10, 328. 3) to requite, to compensate ; δώροισι. to requite with presents. i. e. to make compensatory gifts, Od. 24, 285.
άμείλικτος, ον (μειλίσσω), not gentle, harsh, inexorable, όψ, *11, 137; also h. Cer. 260.
άμείλιχος, ον=άμείλικτος, 'Αίδης, 9, 159; ήτορ, v. 572.
άμείνων, ον, gen. ονος, irreg. compar. of άγαθός ; spoken of persons : braver, more valiant; of things : better, more profitable, 1, 116 (prob. originally more pleasant, from a root related to the Latin posit. amœnus ; see Kühner I. § 325. 2).
άμέλγω, only pres and imperf. to milk, μήλα, Od. 9, 238. Mid. όίες άμελγόμεναι γάλα, sheep yielding milk, 4, 434.
άμελέω (μέλει), aor. άμέλησα, Ep. for ήμέλ. to be free from trouble, to neglect, to forget, with gen. always with ner. κασιγνήτοιο, not to forget a brother, *8, 330 13, 419.
άμεναι, Ep. for άέμεναι, Infin. pres. see 'ΑΩ.
άμενηνός, όν (μένος), without power, weak, feeble, epith. of the wounded and dead. 5, 887. Od. 10, 521 ; of dreams, Od. 19, 562. h. Ven. 189.
άμενηνόω (άμενηνός), aor. άμενήνωσα, to render weak. inefficacious ; with accus. αίχμήν, to make the lance inefficacious, 13, 562.†
άμέρδω (fr. άμείρω, cf. κείρω, κέρδος), aor. act. ήμερσα, Ep. άμερσα, aor. pass. άμέρθην, prop. to deprive of a share ; but mly, to deprive, to bereave ; with accus. of the person : τόν όμοίιον άμέρσαι, to rob an equal, i. e. one having equal claims, 16, 53. b) With accus. of the person and gen. of the thing: τινά όφθαλμών. to deprive any one of eyes, Od. 8, 64 ; pass. αίώνος, 22, 58 ; δαιτός, Od. 21, 290. 2) to blind, to obscure ; with accus. αύγή άμερδεν όσσε, the brightness blinded their eyes, 13. 340. καπνός άμέρδει καλά έντεα, the smoke injured the beautiful weapons, Od. 19, 18.
άμέτρητος, ον (μετρέω), immeasurable, prodigious, πόνος, *Od. 19, 512. 23, 249.
άμετροεπής, ές, immoderate in words, endlessly prating, loquacious, 2, 212.†
άμητήρ, ήρος, ό (άμάω), mower, reaper, 11, 67.†
άμητος, ό (άμάω), the act of mowing or reaping, the harvest, 19, 223. †(ά).
*άμηχανής, ές, poet. for άμήχανος, h Merc. 447.
άμηχανίη, ή (άμήχανος), embarrassment, hesitation, perplexity, despair [inopia consilii], Od. 9, 295.†
άμήχανος, ον (μηχανή), without means, i. e. 1) helpless, unfortunate, at a loss

Ἀμισώδαρος. 33 **Ἀμύκλαι.**

τινός, about any one, Od. 19, 363. 2) Pass. against which there is no expedient; spoken of things: *difficult, impossible*; ὄνειροι, inexplicable dreams, Od. 19, 560; ἔργα, deeds not to be averted, *irremediable evils* (Eustath. δεινά), 8, 130. b) Of persons: *not to be subdued, impracticable, unyielding, hard-hearted*, absol. 16, 29; but ἀμήχανός ἐσσι παραρρητοῖσι πιθέσθαι, *thou art not easily brought* to obey exhortations, 13, 726.

Ἀμισώδαρος, ὁ, king of Caria, father of Atymnius, 16, 328.

ἀμιτροχίτωνες, οἱ, poet. epith. of the Lycians, 16, 419†; either, *without a girdle* ['*uncinctured,*' Cp.], (from a priv. μίτρα and χιτών, those who wear no girdle under the cuirass, cf. μίτρα,) or *having the girdle joined to the cuirass* (from a copulat. μίτ. and χιτ.).

ἀμιχθαλόεις, εσσα, εν, poet. (μίγνυμι), *inaccessible, inhospitable*, epith. of Lemnos, 24, 753. †h. Ap. 36 (prob. lengthened from ἄμικτος, and not from μίγνυμι and ἅλς).

ἄμμε, ἄμμες, ἄμμι, Æol. and Ep. for ἡμᾶς, ἡμεῖς, etc.

ἀμμίξας, poet. for ἀναμίξας.

ἀμμορίη, ἡ, Ep. for ἀμοιρία (μόρος), *misfortune, misery*, Od. 20, 76.†

ἄμμορος, ον, Ep. for ἄμορος (μόρος), 1) *not participating, not enjoying*, with gen. λοετρῶν Ὠκεανοῖο, excluded from bathing in the ocean; spoken of the Great Bear, which is always visible to the Greeks. 18, 489. Od. 5, 275. 2) From μόρος, i. q. μοίρη, *unfortunate, miserable*, 6, 408. 24, 773.

ἀμνίον or ἄμνιον, τό (αἷμα), *a vessel for receiving the blood of victims, a sacrificial bowl*, Od. 3, 444.†

Ἀμνῖσός, ὁ, a haven in Crete, at the river *Amnisus*, north from Cnosus, founded by Minos, Od. 19, 188.

ἀμογητί, adv. (μογέω), *without trouble, easily*, 11, 637.†

*ἀμόγητος, ον (μογέω), *unwearied*, h. 7, 3.

ἀμόθεν, adv. Ep. (ἀμός, poet. =τίς) *from some place or other, from some part or other*. τῶν ἀμόθεν εἰπὲ καὶ ἡμῖν, begin where you please and tell to us also something of them, Od. 1, 10.† Schol. Τῶν περὶ τὸν Ὀδυσσέα ὁπόθεν θέλεις πράξεων ἀπό τινος μέρους ἀρξαμένη διηγοῦ ἡμῖν.

ἀμοιβάς, άδος, ἡ, poet. fem. of ἀμοιβαῖος (ἀμοιβή), *serving for a change*. χλαῖνα, ἥ οἱ παρεκέσκετ' (=παρέκειτ') ἀμοιβάς, a mantle which lay by him (*was laid by*) for a change, Od. 14, 521.† Others read παρεχέσκετ' ἀμοιβάς, and explain it as accus. plur. of ἀμοιβή.

ἀμοιβή, ἡ (ἀμείβω), *return, recompense, compensation* or *indemnity, restitution, requital*; in a good and bad signif. χαρίεσσα ἀμοιβὴ ἑκατόμβης, a gracious return for the hecatomb, Od. 3, 59. τίειν βοῶν ἀμοιβήν, to make restitution (compensation) for the cattle, Od. 12, 382. *Od.

ἀμοιβηδίς, adv. Ep. (ἀμοιβή), *changing* *alternately, successively*, 18, 506. Od. 18, 310.

ἀμοιβός, ὁ (ἀμείβω), *that exchanges with another that relieves him, a substitute*, οἱ ἦλθον ἀμοιβοί, who came to relieve others, 13, 793 †[in requital of former aid from Priam, Eustath.].

ἀμολγός, ὁ (ἀμέλγω=turgeo), *milking, milking-time*; with Hom. always νυκτὸς ἀμολγῷ, at the hour of milking. The milking-time of the night is twofold, one at evening, as 22, 317; the other in the morning, as Od. 4, 841; therefore: *evening* and *morning twilight*; and mly, *the darkness of the night*, 11, 173. Buttm. in Lex. p. 89, with Eustath. 15, 324, with great probability regards ἀμολγός as an old Achaian word meaning ἀκμή, and translates it, *in the dead* or *depth of the night*. [D. makes μολγός with prothetic a related to μολύνειν, μελαίνειν, p. 244.]

Ἀμοπάων, ονος, ὁ (ἅμα, ὀπάων, companion), son of Polyæmōn, a Trojan slain by Teucer, 8, 276.

ἀμός (al. ἁμός), ή, όν, Æol. and Ep.= ἡμέτερος, *our*. ἁμός, ή, όν is adopted by Spitzner on the authority of Apoll. de pron. and Etym. Mag. cf. Spitzner ad 6, 414.

ἄμοτον, adv. (from ἄμεναι, ΑΩ), *insatiably, incessantly, restlessly, continually, unceasingly*, 4, 440 (μέμαα). 13, 46. Od. 6, 83 (τανύεσθαι). [The ancients derived it from μότον, *lint*.]

ἀμπ. Ep. abbrev. for ἀναπ.; as ἀμπείρας for ἀναπείρας.

ἀμπελόεις, εσσα, εν (ἄμπελος), once ἀμπελόεις as fem. 2, 561, *full of vines, abounding in grapes, vine-clad*; epith. of countries and towns, 3, 184.

ἄμπελος, ἡ, *a vine*, *Od. 9, 110. h. 6, 39.

ἀμπεπαλών, Ep. for ἀναπεπαλών, see ἀναπάλλω.

ἀμπερές, adv. only in tmesis, διὰ δ' ἀμπερές, Od. 21, 422; for διαμπερές, q. v.

ἀμπέχω (ἀμφί, ἔχω), impf. ἄμπεχον, *to embrace, to surround, to cover*; only ἄλμη, ἥ οἱ νῶτα καὶ εὐρέας ἀμπεχεν ὤμους, the brine, which covered his back and broad shoulders, Od. 6, 225.†

ἀμπήδησε, see ἀναπηδάω.

ἀμπνεῦσαι, see ἀναπνέω.

ἄμπνυε, see ἀναπνέω.

ἀμπνύνθη, see ἀναπνέω.

ἄμπνυτο, see ἀπνύω.

ἄμπυξ, υκος, ἡ (ἀμπέχω), *a head-band* or *fillet*, a female ornament, 22, 469.†

ἄμυδις, adv. Æol. from ἅμα, *together*; spoken of time, Od. 12, 415. 2) *together, in a crowd*, of place, 10, 300; καθίζειν, to sit down together, Od. 4, 659.

Ἀμυδών, ῶνος, ἡ, a town in Pæonia, on the Axius, 2, 849.

Ἀμυθάων, ονος, ὁ, 1) son of Cretheus and Tyro, brother of Æson, husband of Idomenē, father of Bias and Melampus; he is said to have founded Pylus in Messenia, Od. 11, 259. 2) 17, 348, the reading of Bothe for Ἀπισάων + Cdd.

Ἀμύκλαι, αἱ, a town in Laconia, on the

C 5

Άμύμων. 'Αμφί.

Εurōtas, residence of Tyndareus, famed for the worship of Apollo, now *Slavo-Chorion*, 2, 584.

ἀμύμων ["""], gen. ονος (μῶμος, censure, with a change of ω into υ; after Æol. dial.), *blameless, irreproachable*, an honorary epith. of persons in reference to birth, rank, or form, without regard to moral worth: *noble, high-born*, and thus even the adulterer Ægisthus is called, Od. 1, 29. *b*) Spoken also of things,= *excellent, glorious*, οἶκος, μῆτις, 10, 19; νῆσος, Od. 1, 232. 9, 414. 12, 261.

ἀμύντωρ, ορος, ὁ (ἀμύνω), *defender, helper, protector*, 13, 284. Od. 2, 326.

'Αμύντωρ, ορος, ὁ, 1) son of Ormenus, 10, 266. 2) Probably another, 9, 447. 10, 266.

ἀμύνω (μύνη), ἀμυνῶ, aor. ἤμυνα, ἠμυνάμην, Ep. infin. pres. ἀμυνέμεναι for ἀμύνειν. 1) Act. *to avert, to ward off*; rarely τί τινος, something from some one, λοιγὸν Δαναοῖσιν, destruction from the Greeks, 1, 341; ἀστεῖ νηλεὲς ἦμαρ, to remove the day of destruction from the city, 11, 588. *b*) More rarely τί τινος; Κῆράς τινος, to repel the Fates from any one, 4, 11; Τρῶας νεῶν, the Trojans from the ships, 15, 731; also the gen. alone, νηῶν, to defend the ships, 13, 109: περί τινος, to fight for any one, i. e. avenge him, 17, 182; sometimes without dat. of person, φόνον κακόν, 9, 599. 13, 783. Od. 22, 208; absol. 13, 312. 678. *c*) Oftener the dat. stands alone : to fight for any one, i. e. *to help, to assist* him, 5, 486. 6, 262. 2) Mid. *to avert, to remove* from oneself, with accus. νηλεὲς ἦμαρ, 11, 484. *b*) *to defend oneself, to fight for oneself*, often absol. and with gen. τινός, and with περί τινος. to fight for any one, to defend him ; νηῶν, to defend the ships, 12, 179 ; σφῶν αὐτῶν, 12, 155, or περὶ πάτρης, to fight for one's country, 12, 243.

ἀμύσσω, fut. ἀμύξω, *to scratch, to tear, to lacerate*; c. accus. στήθεα χερσίν, to tear the skin from the breast with the hands, i. e. nails, 19, 284; metaph. θυμὸν ἀμύξεις, thou wilt tear (distress) thy heart, spoken of one in anger, 1, 243. *II.

ἀμφαγαπάω (ἀγαπάζω), poet. form, *to embrace with love, to treat with affection, to receive hospitably* ; with accus. Od. 14, 381. 2) Mid. as depon. 16, 192 ; h. Cer. 291.

* ἀμφαγαπάω = ἀμφαγαπάζω; whence ἀμφαγάπησα, h. Cer. 439.

ἀμφαγερέθομαι, better ἀμφηγερέθομαι, q. v.

ἀμφαγείρομαι (ἀγείρω), aor. 2 ἀμφαγέροντο, *to collect, to gather* (intrans.), τινά, about any one, 18, 37.†

ἀμφαβά, adv. see ἀμφαδός.

ἀμφαδίην, adv. see ἀμφάδιος.

ἀμφάδιος, η, ον, Ep. for ἀμφάδιος (ἀναφαίνω), *open, manifest, public*, γάμος, a real marriage, Od. 6, 288 ; comm. accus. ἀμφαδίην, as adv. *publicly, unconcealed*, 7, 196. 13, 356.

ἀμφαδός, όν, Ep. for ἀναφαδός (ἀναφαίνω), *open, public, notorious*. ἀμφαδὰ ἔργα γένοιτο, the thing should be manifest [i. e. his secret be disclosed], Od. 19, 391; comm. neut. sing. ἀμφαδόν, as adv. in opposit. to λάθρη, 7, 243 ; to δόλῳ, Od. 1, 296. 11, 120; to κρυφηδόν, Od. 14, 330. 19, 299.

ἀμφαΐσσομαι (ἀΐσσω), *to rush up from all sides* ; spoken of the mane of horses with dat. ἀμφὶ δὲ χαῖται ὤμοις ἀΐσσονται, the mane floated about their shoulders, *6, 510. 15, 267, only in tmesis.

ἀμφαλείφω (ἀλείφω), infin. aor. ἀλείψαι, only in tmesis, *to anoint round about*, 24, 582.†

ἀμφαραβέω (ἀραβέω), aor. ἀράβησα, *to rattle, to resound round about*; spoken of arms, 21, 408.†

* ἀμφανέειν, poet. for ἀναφανεῖν, see ἀναφαίνω.

ἀμφασίη, ἡ, Ep. for ἀφασίη, *speechlessness*, comm. with ἐπέων, prob. a pleonasm. δὴν δέ μιν ἀμφασίη ἐπέων λάβε, for a long time speechlessness held him, 17, 695. Od. 4, 704.

ἀμφαϋτέω (αὐτέω), *to resound all around*, only in tmesis, 12, 160.† (ῦ).

ἀμφαφάω (ἀφάω), partcp. pres. ἀμφαφόων, Ep. for ἀμφαφάων, infin. pres. mid. ἀμφαφάασθαι for ἀμφαφάεσθαι, *to handle all about, to feel all over;* with accus. λόχον, spoken of the Troj. horse, Od. 4, 277. 8, 196 ; τόξον, to handle the bow, Od. 19, 586. 2) Mid. as depon. ᾗ μάλα δὴ μαλακώτερος ἀμφαφάασθαι, indeed, far easier is Hector now to handle, 22, 373.

ἀμφεποτᾶτο, see ἀμφιποτάομαι.

ἀμφέπω = ἀμφιέπω.

ἀμφέρχομαι, depon. (ἔρχομαι), aor. ἀμφήλυθον, *to go around*, with accus. any thing ; metaph. only in Hom. μὲ ἀμφήλυθε αὐτή, a cry surrounded me, Od. 6, 122, and κνίσσης αὐτμή, the fume of the fat surrounded me, Od. 12, 369. *Od.

ἀμφέχανε, from ἀμφιχαίνω.

ἀμφέχυτ' for ἀμφέχυτο, see ἀμφιχέω.

ἀμφήκης, ἐς (ἀκή), gen. έος, *sharp on both sides, double-edged*, epith. of the sword, 10, 256. Od. 16, 80.

ἀμφήλυθε, see ἀμφέρχομαι.

ἀμφήμαι (ἧμαι), *to sit round about*, only in tmesis. ἀμφὶ δ' ἑταῖροι εἴατο, 15, 10.†

ἀμφηρεφής, ἐς (ἐρέφω), gen. έος, *covered all around* (or, *at both ends*), *well covered*, epith. of the quiver, 1, 45.†

ἀμφήριστος, ον (ἐρίζω), *contested on both sides, undecided*. 2) *equal in fight* ; ἀμφ. τιθέναι τινά, to place one upon an equality (in the race), 23, 382.†

ἀμφί, a) Adv. *round about, around*, 4, 328. Od. 2, 153; it is often separated from the verb in compos. by a particle, and is to be taken in tmesis: ἀμφὶ περί, as adv. 21, 10. B) Prepos. with three cases : *round about, around*, like περί, except that ἀμφί, rather Ion. and poet., expresses prop. enclosing on two sides : 1) With gen. *about, on account of, for the sake of*, to indicate the object about which the action is performed. ἀμφὶ πίδακος μά-

Ἀμφίαλος. 35 Ἀμφίδασυς.

χεσθαι, to fight for a fountain, 16, 825; metaph. ἀμφὶ φιλότητος ἀείδειν, to sing about (of) love, Od. 8, 267. 2) With dat. a) Of place, *around, upon, about*, with the idea of rest: τελαμὼν ἀμφὶ στήθεσσιν, 2, 388. 3, 328. ἤριπε δ᾽ ἀμφ᾽ αὐτῷ, he sank upon it, 4, 493 ; also mly spoken of nearness in place, 12, 175. τὴν κτεῖνε ἀμφ᾽ ἐμοί, at my side, near me, Od. 11, 422. Il. 9, 470. ἀμφ᾽ ὀβελοῖσιν κρέα πείρειν, in the construct. praegn. to pierce the flesh with the spits, so that it is on them round about, 2, 427; in like manner, στῆσαι τρίποδα ἀμφὶ πυρί, Od. 8, 434. ἀμφ᾽ ὀχέεσσι βαλεῖν κύκλα, to put the wheels upon the chariots, 5, 722. b) Indicating the cause; *about*, on account of, ἀμφὶ νέκυϊ μάχεσθαι, 16, 565. ἀμφὶ γυναικὶ ἄλγεα πάσχειν, 3, 157. 3) With accus. a) Of place, with the idea of motion about, to, or into; *about, to, along, around in*; ἀμφὶ ῥέεθρα, along the waves, 2, 461. ἀμφὶ ἄστυ ἔρδειν ἱρά, round about in the city, 11, 706. Of persons: οἱ ἀμφ᾽ Ἀτρείωνα βασιλῆες, the princes about Atrides. 2, 445. cf. δ, 781. In Hom., however, the chief person is included in the sense; οἱ ἀμφὶ Πρίαμον, Priam and his followers, 3, 146. b) Indicating *cause, occupation*, about an object, μνήσασθαι ἀμφί τινα, to mention about any one, h. 6, 1. In Hom. ἀμφί sometimes stands after the dependent cases. In composition with verbs it has the same signif. and sometimes also, *on both sides*.

ἀμφίαλος, ον (ἅλς), *surrounded by the sea, sea-girt*, epith. of Ithaca, *Od. 1, 386. 395.

Ἀμφίαλος, ὁ, a Phaeacian, Od. 8, 114. 128.

Ἀμφιάραος, ὁ (from ἀμφί and ἀράομαι, prayed for by both sides), son of Oïcles or of Apollo, husband of Eriphȳlē, father of Alcmæōn and Amphilŏchus, a noted prophet and king of Argos. He took part in the Calydonian chase, in the Argonautic expedition, and in the Theban war. Because, as prophet, he knew that he should perish before Thebes, he concealed himself; but was betrayed by his wife for a necklace. He was swallowed with his chariot, in the Theban war, by the earth. Subsequently he had a temple at Orōpus, Od. 15, 244.

ἀμφιάχω (ἰάχω), partcp. perf. ἀμφιαχυῖα, *to cry round about, to scream*, v. a. 2, 316.†

ἀμφιβαίνω (βαίνω), perf. ἀμφιβέβηκα, 1) *to go around, to travel around*; with accus. ἠέλιος μέσον οὐρανὸν ἀμφιβεβήκει, but when the sun had travelled round the midst of heaven, i. e. had reached the midst of heaven, 8, 68; spoken of gods : Χρύσην, to walk about Chrysē as tutelary god, i. e. to protect, 1, 37. Od. 9, 198. 2) Mly *to surround, to encircle*, esply in the perf. νεφέλη μιν ἀμφιβεβήκειν, Od. 12, 74 ; with dat. 16, 66; metaph. πύνος φρένας ἀμφιβέβηκεν, trouble has occupied thy heart, 6, 355.

ἀμφιβάλλω (βάλλω), aor. 2 ἀμφέβαλον, fut. mid. ἀμφιβαλεῦμαι, Ep. for ἀμφιβαλοῦμαι, aor. 2 ἀμφιβαλόμην, 1) Act. *to cast about, to put on*, one thing upon another, τί τινι : ὤμοισιν αἰγίδα, to cast the ægis over the shoulders, 18, 204. b) Spoken of putting on clothing, It takes two accus., but in this case the prepos. is always separated from the verb; φᾶρός τινα, 23, 588; χιτῶνά τινα, Od. 3, 467; with dat. of person only in ἀμφὶ δέ μοι ῥάκος βάλον, Od. 14, 342 ; metaph. κρατερὸν μένος ἀμφιβάλλειν, to equip oneself with great strength, 17, 742. c) *to embrace, to clasp, to throw around*, in full χεῖρας γούνασι, throw the hands (arms) about any one's knees, Od. 7, 142; ἀλλήλους, 23, 97. ὡς οἱ χεῖρες ἐχάνδανον ἀμφιβαλόντι, as much as the hands of him grasping held, i. e. *as much as* he could hold *with both hands*, Od. 17, 344; hence mly, *to surround, to enclose*. 2) Mid. *to cast about oneself, to put on*, with reference to the subject, τί τινα: ὤμοισιν ξίφος, to hang the sword over one's shoulders, 2, 45; νήριν, Od. 17, 197.

ἀμφίβασις, ιος, ἡ (βαίνω), *the act of going around, of encircling* [espec. for a defence, as of a corpse, cf. Passow, s. v. and ἀμφιβαίνω], 5, 623.†

*ἀμφίβιος, ον (βίος), living both in water and on land, *amphibious*; νομή, a double abode, Batr. 59.

ἀμφίβροτος, η, ον (βροτός), *encompassing the man, protecting the man*, always ἀμφιβρότη ἀσπίς, *2, 389. 11, 32.

ἀμφιβρύχω, see βρυχάομαι.

Ἀμφιγένεια, ἡ, a town in Messenia, prob. the later Ἀμφεια, 2, 593. Steph. after Strab. in Elis.

*ἀμφιγηθέω (γηθέω), partcp. perf. ἀμφιγηθώς, *to rejoice around*, i. e. greatly, h. Ap. 273.

Ἀμφιγυήεις, ὁ (γυιός), *lame in both feet, halting*, epith. of Hephæstus, 1, 607. 14, 239.

ἀμφίγυος, ον, Ep. (γυῖον), prop. having limbs on both sides, epith. of the spear, probably *furnished with iron at both ends* for fighting and sticking in the earth. According to others, *double-cutting, wounding with both ends*, or to be handled with both hands, 13, 147. Od. 16, 474. [But *Herm.* (with *Död.*) supposes it a pike for *cutting and thrusting*, its head being furnished, at about the middle of each side, with a *sharp curved blade*.]

ἀμφιδαίω, Ep. (δαίω), perf. ἀμφιδέδηε, *to kindle around*, in the perf. intrans. *to burn around*; only metaph. πόλεμος ἄστυ ἀμφιδέδηε, the contest burned around the city, *8, 329; μάχη, 12, 35.

Ἀμφιδάμας, αντος, ὁ (from ἀμφί and δαμάω, subduing round about), a hero from Scandia in Cythēra, table-friend of Molus, 10, 269. 2) father of Clysonōmus from Opus, 23, 87.

ἀμφιδασυς, εια, υ (δασύς), *rough round about, roughly bordered*, epith. of the ægis surrounded with tassels, θύσανοι. (Others, *woolly, shaggy all over, impenetrable,* cf. Schol. and Passow.] 15, 309.†

ἀμφιδινέω (δινέω), perf. pass. ἀμφιδεδίνημαι, *to turn or put around,* κολεὸν νεοπρίστου ἐλέφαντος ἀμφιδεδίνηται, the scabbard is encompassed with polished ivory [rather a scabbard *of polished ivory encloses it*], Od. 8, 405; also spoken of metal: ᾧ πέρι χεῦμα κασσιτέρου ἀμφιδεδίνηται, around which there runs a (casting=) plate of tin, 23, 562.

ἀμφιδρυφής, ές, poet. (δρύπτω), gen. έος, *lacerated all around,* ἄλοχος, a wife who tears the skin from her cheeks from grief at the death of her husband, 2, 700.†

ἀμφίδρυφος, ον=ἀμφιδρυφής, 11, 393.†

ἀμφίδυμος, ον (δύω [the verb: rather from δύο, *two:* cf. δίδυμος, τρίδυμος, *tergeminus,* &c. Lob. Path. 165]), *accessible all around,* or *having a double entrance,* epith. of a haven, Od. 4, 847.

ἀμφιελαύνω (ἐλαύνω), only in tmesis, *to draw* or *trace round about,* Il. τεῖχος πόλει, a wall about a city, Od. 6, 9.

ἀμφιέλισσος, ον, poet. (ἐλίσσω), *impelled onward on both sides, double-oared,* epith. of ships, 2, 165. It occurs only in the fem. ἀμφιέλισσα; for which reason, according to Rost Vollst. Lex., the Gramm. falsely assumed an adj. ἀμφιέλισσος, η, ον. Rost also prefers, after the use of the later Epic writers, the signif. *swaying from this side to that, unsteady.*

ἀμφιέννυμι (ἔννυμι), fut. ἀμφιέσω, aor. Ep. ἀμφίεσα (σσ), aor. mid. ἀμφιεσάμην (σσ), 1) Act. *to put around, to put on,* εἵματα, clothes (upon another), Od. 5, 167. 264. 2) Mid. *to put upon oneself,* anything, with accus. χιτῶνας, Od. 23, 142. cf. 14, 178.

ἀμφιέπω and ἀμφέπω (ἕπω), only impf. poet. *to be around any thing, to surround;* with accus. τὴν πρύμνην πῦρ ἀμφεπεν, the flame surrounded the stern, 16, 124. Od. 8, 437. 2) *to be engaged about* any thing, *to prepare, to attend to;* with accus. τινά, 5, 667; βοὸς κρέα, to dress ox-flesh, 17, 778; στίχας, to arrange the ranks, 2, 525. The partcp. is often absol. in the sense of an adv.: *earnestly, carefully, busily,* 19, 392. Od. 3, 118.

ἀμφιεύω (εὕω), *to singe round about,* only in tmesis, Od. 9, 389.†

ἀμφιζάνω (ἱζάνω), *to sit round about* [to *settle upon*]; χιτῶνι, upon his tunic, 18, 25.†

ἀμφιθαλής, ές, poet. (θάλλω), gen. έος, *blooming, flourishing on both sides;* spoken of a child whose parents are both living (a child of blooming parents, V.), 22, 496.†

Ἀμφιθέη, ἡ (on both sides of divine origin), mother of Anticlēa, wife of Autolycus, and grandmother of Ulysses, Od. 19, 416.

ἀμφίθετος, ον, poet. (τίθημι), *that may be placed on either end;* φιάλη, either,

with Aristarchus, a goblet that can be placed on either end, or having handles on both sides; *a double goblet,* *23, 270. 616.

ἀμφιθέω (θέω), *to run around;* with accus. μητέρα, about the mother, Od. 10, 413.†

Ἀμφιθόη (Θοός), daughter of Nereus and of Doris, 18, 42.

ἀμφικαλύπτω (καλύπτω), fut. ἀμφικαλύψω, ἀμφεκάλυψα, 1) Act. *to cover round about, to conceal;* with accus. prim. spoken of clothes, 2, 262: of the arm: ὀστέα, 23, 91. δόμος ἀμφεκάλυψέν με, the house concealed me, received me, Od. 4, 618; πόλις ἵππον, Od. 8, 511. b) Metaph. ἔρως φρένας ἀμφεκάλυψε, love obscured my mind, 3, 442. θάνατός μιν ἀμφ., death embraced him, 5, 68. 2) *to surround, to put around,* to cover as with a veil; τί τινι, to put any thing around one, to cover him with it: ῥάκος κεφαλῇ, Od. 14, 349; σάκος τινί, to place a shield before any one (for protection), 8, 331; ὄρος πόλει, to put a mountain over the city, Od. 8, 569; νύκτα μάχῃ, to draw the veil of night around the battle, 5, 507.

ἀμφικεάζω (κεάζω), aor. ἐκέασα, Ep. σσ, *to hew on all sides, to split;* τὸ μέλαν δρυός, Od. 14, 12.†

Ἀμφίκλος, ὁ (famed round about, fr. κλέος), a Trojan, slain by Achilles, 16, 313.

ἀμφίκομος, ον (κόμη), *having hair all around, thick-leaved,* epith. of a tree, 17, 677.†

ἀμφικονέβω, only by tmesis, see κονάβέω.

ἀμφικύπελλος, ον (κύπελλον), always with τὸ δέπας, the *double goblet,* according to Aristot. Hist. An. 9, 40; a goblet which formed a cup on both ends, 1, 584; see Eustath. and Buttm. Lexil. p. 93.

ἀμφιλαχαίνω (λαχαίνω), *to dig round about,* φυτόν, Od. 24, 242.†

Ἀμφιλόχος, ὁ, son of Amphiaraus and Eriphylē, a prophet of Argos, who took part in the expedition of the Epigoni against Thebes, and then in the Trojan war. After his return, he founded with Mopsus the town of Mallus in Cilicia, and was killed in a duel with Mopsus, Od. 15, 248.

ἀμφιλύκη, ἡ (from the obsol. λύξ, akin to λευκός), only in connexion with νύξ; *the twilight, the gray of the morning,* 7, 433.†

ἀμφιμαίομαι, depon. (μαίομαι), aor. impf. ἀμφιμάσασθε, *to touch round about, to wipe off;* τραπέζας σπόγγοις, Od. 20, 152.†

ἀμφιμάσασθε, see ἀμφιμαίομαι.

ἀμφιμάχομαι, depon. mid. (μάχομαι), *to fight about* a place, *to assail;* with accus. Ἴλιον, μιν, to attack, 6, 461. 9, 412. 2) With gen. *to fight* for any one, to defend him, νέκυος, 18, 20; τείχεος, 15, 391. *11.

Ἀμφίμαχος, ὁ (from μάχομαι, *fighting round about*), 1) son of Cteatus, grandson of Actor, leader of the Epeans from Elis, 2, 260. Hector slew him, 13, 187. 2) son of Nomion, leader of the Carians, slain by Achilles, 2, 870.

Ἀμφιμέδων, οντος, ὁ (from μέδων, *ruling round about*), son of Melaneus, suitor of Penelope, whom Telemachus slew, Od. 24, 103.

ἀμφιμέλας, αινα, αν (μέλας), *black round about*, always with φρένες, prob. from the nature of the diaphragm, which is situated in the inmost darkness of the body; *the darkly-enveloped diaphragm* (*the black diaphragm, heart*). Others explain it, *angry, gloomy*, 1, 103. Od. 4, 661.

ἀμφιμέμυκε, from the following.

ἀμφιμυκάομαι, depon. (μυκάομαι), aor. ἀμφέμυκον, perf. ἀμφιμέμυκα, *to bellow all around, to low, to resound, to echo*. δάπεδον ἀμφιμέμυκεν, Od. 10, 227; in tmesis spoken of the gates: *to creak*, 12, 460.

ἀμφινέμομαι, mid. (νέμω), prop. *to pasture round about, to dwell; to inhabit*; with accus. 2, 521. Od. 19, 132.

Ἀμφινόμη, ἡ (*pasturing round about*), daughter of Nereus and Doris, 18, 44.

Ἀμφίνομος, ὁ, son of Nisus from Dulichium, a suitor of Penelope, slain by Telemachus, Od. 16, 394.

Ἀμφίος, ὁ (from ἀμφί *going about*), 1) son of Selagus of Pæsus, an ally of the Trojans, slain by the Telamonian Ajax, 5, 612. 2) son of Merops, brother of Adrastus, leader of the Trojans, 2, 830 (with lengthened ι).

ἀμφιξέω (ξέω), aor. ἀμφέξεσα, *to scrape round about, to polish*, Od. 23, 196 †

ἀμφιπέλομαι, depon. mid. poet (πέλω), *to move around* any one, *to surround* him; with dat. ἀοιδὴ ἀκουόντεσσι ἀμφιπέλεται, *the song resounded around the hearers*, Od. 1, 352.†

ἀμφιπένομαι, depon. mid. (πένομαι), *to be occupied about* any one; with accus. Od. 15, 467; hence comm. in a good signif. *to tend* [e. g. a *wounded* man], *to take care of, to wait upon*, 4, 220 [to *take charge* of]; in a bad sense *to assail, to fall upon* [of *dogs* setting to work to devour a *corpse*], 23, 184.

ἀμφιπεριστέφω (στέφω), *to wreathe round*; only in mid. with dat. metaph. χάρις οὐκ ἀμφιπεριστέφεται ἐπέεσσιν, *grace is not entwined with his words*, i. e. his words are not crowned with grace. Od. 8, 175.†

ἀμφιπεριστρωφάω, poet. (στρωφάω a collateral form of στρέφω), *to turn round about*; with accus. ἵππους, *to drive the horses about, or round and round*, 8, 348.†

*ἀμφιπεριφθινύθω, poet. (φθινύθω), *to perish round about, to dry up* (of *dark*), h. Ven. 272.

ἀμφιπεσοῦσα, see ἀμφιπίπτω.

ἀμφιπίπτω, poet. (πίπτω), aor. 2 ἀμφέπεσον, *to fall round* = *to fall* or *throw oneself upon, to embrace*, τινά, any one; of a wife who in anguish throws herself upon her dead husband, Od. 8, 523.†

ἀμφιπολεύω (ἀμφίπολος), *to be occupied about* an object, *to support, to attend to, to tend, to take care of; to wait upon*; with accus. ὄρχατον (an *orchard*), Od. 24, 244; βίον, *to protect my life* [spoken by Penelopê of Ulysses], Od. 18, 254. 19, 127. '2) Intrans. *to be about* any one, *to serve* him. Od. 20, 78. *Od.

ἀμφίπολος, ἡ (πέλω), prop. an adj. *busied about* any one; with Hom. always subst. fem. *handmaid, maiden, female companion*, in distinction from a female slave; also ἀμφίπολος ταμίη, 24, 302.

ἀμφιπονέομαι, Ep.=ἀμφιπένομαι, fut. ἀμφιπονήσομαι, *to be busy about* any one, τινά, 23, 681; spoken of things, *to take care* or *charge of*, τί, 23, 159; τάφον, Od. 20, 307.

ἀμφιποτάομαι, depon. mid. (ποτάομαι), poet. form, *to fly round about*; with accus. τέκνα, *to flutter round the young*, 2, 315.†

ἀμφίρρυτος, η, ον, Ep. ἀμφίρυτος (ῥέω), *having a current all around, sea-girt*, epith. of *islands*, *Od. 1, 50. 98. only in Ep. form.

ἀμφίς (ἀμφί), poet. I) Adv. 1) *about, round about, on both sides*. βαθὺς δέ τε Τάρταρος ἀμφίς, 8, 481. ἀμφὶς εἶναι, *to be (stand, dwell, &c.) about* (a person), *to dwell*, 9, 464. 24, 488. ἀμφὶς ἔχειν, *to clasp about, spoken of bonds*. Od. 8, 340. 2) *upon, on both sides*. ζυγὸν ἀμφὶς ἔχειν, *to have the yoke on both sides, to have it on*, Od. 3, 486. ὀλίγη ἦν ἀμφὶς ἄρουρα, *a little ground was on both sides* (of the armies), i. e. *between*, 3, 115. 3) *apart*. γαῖαν καὶ οὐρανὸν ἀμφὶς ἔχειν, *to hold earth and heaven apart*, Od. 1, 54. τὼ μὲν ζυγὸν ἀμφὶς ἐέργει, them (the cattle) *the yoke keeps apart*, 13, 706. ἀμφὶς ἀγῆναι, *to break in two*, 11, 559. 4) *separate, remote*. ἀμφὶς εἶναι, Od. 19, 221; hence often=*each for himself*, Od. 22, 57. ἀμφὶς φρονεῖν, φράζεσθαι, *to think differently, to be of different sentiments*, 2, 13. 11) Prepos. like ἀμφί, comm. after its dependent case, 1) With gen. *about*. ἅρματος ἀμφὶς ἰδεῖν, *to look over* a chariot [i. e. to see whether it is fit for use], 2, 384. *b) far from*. ἀμφὶς φυλόπιδος, Od. 16, 267. ἀμφὶς ὁδοῦ, *out of the road*, Od. 19, 221. 2) With dat. ἄξονι ἀμφίς, *about the axle-tree*, 5, 723. 3) With accus. Κρόνον ἀμφίς, *about Cronos* (Saturn), 14, 203. εἴρεσθαι ἀμφὶς ἕκαστα, *to ask about every thing*, i. e. each thing separately, one thing after another, Od. 19, 46.

ἀμφιστεφανόω (στέφανος), *to wreathe around, like winding a garland*; pass. *to be wound round, like a garland*; trop. ὅμιλος ἀμφιστεφάνωτο, *the crowd had collected in a circle*, h. Ven. 120.

ἀμφιστεφής, ές, *placed about in a*

Ἀμφιστέφω. 38 *Ἄν.

circle, 11, 40, an old reading for ἀμφιστρεφής, q. v.

[ἀμφιστέφω, 18, 205, explained by Damm as a case of tmesis; see στέφω.]

ἀμφίστημι (ἴστημι), aor. 2 ἀμφέστην, trans. *to place around.* 2) Intrans. in mid. and aor. 2 act. *to stand around*; absol. 18, 233. 24, 712; with accus. ἀμφίστασθαι ἄστυ, *to invest the city*, 18, 233. Od. 8, 5. (Hom. only intrans.)

ἀμφιστρατάομαι (στρατός), *to invest with an army, to beleaguer*; with accus. πόλιν, 11, 713.†

ἀμφιστρεφής, ές, poet. (στρέφω), gen. έος, turned to different sides [of the *three* heads of a dragon, Schol. ἀλλήλαις περιπεπλεγμέναι=] *interlaced, intertwined*, 11, 40.†

ἀμφιτίθημι (τίθημι), aor. 1 ἀφῆθκα, aor. 2 mid. ἀμφεθέμην, aor. pass. partcp. ἀμφιτεθείς, 1) Act. *to place around, to put around* or *on*; κεφαλῇ κυνέην, to put a helmet on the head; hence pass. κυνέη ἀμφιτεθεῖσα, 10, 271. 2) Mid. *to put upon oneself*; with accus. ξίφος, Od. 21, 431.

ἀμφιτρέμω (τρέμω), *to tremble all over*, 21, 507. †in tmesis.

Ἀμφιτρίτη, ἡ (according to Herm. *Amfractus*, broken in every part), daughter of Nereus, [and accord. to later mythology] wife of Poseidôn, who ruled with him the Mediterranean sea. She bore to him Tritôn, Od. 5, 422. 12, 60.

Ἀμφιτρύων, ωνος (molesting all around, from τρύω), son of Alcæus and Hipponoê, husband of Alcmênê, father of Iphiclês and foster father of Heraclês. He reigned first in Tiryns and later in Thebes, 5, 392. (ι comm. without position.)

*ἀμφιτρομέω, φοβέω=ἀμφιτρέμω, *to tremble all over, to be very much afraid*, τινός, on account of any one, Od. 4, 820.†

*ἀμφιφαείνω, Ep. form for ἀμφιφαίνω, *to shine about*, τινά, h. Ap. 202.

ἀμφίφαλος, ον (φάλος), *furnished with knobs* or *studs round about*, according to the comm. explanation; accord. to Köppen, *having a strong crest*; or accord. to Buttm. Lexil. 523, *whose φάλος stretched from the crest backwards as well as forwards*; epith. of the helmet, *5, 743. 7, 41; see φάλος.

ἀμφιφοβέω (φοβέω), aor. pass. ἀμφεφοβήθην, *to terrify all round.* 2) Pass. *to be terrified all round, to fly from*, τινά, 16, 290.†

ἀμφιφορεύς, ῆος, ὁ (φέρω), a large vessel which is carried by both sides, *a two-handled vase* for wine, honey, Od. 2, 290. 2) *an urn*, 23, 99.

ἀμφιφράζεσθαι, mid. (φράζω), *to consider on both sides, to weigh well*, 18, 254.†

ἀμφιχαίνω (χαίνω), aor. 2 ἀμφέχανον, *to yawn around, to swallow with greediness*, τινά, 23, 79.†

ἀμφιχέω (χέω), aor. 1 act. Ep. ἀμφέχευα, Ep. syncop. aor. 2 mid. ἀμφεχύμην (3 sing. ἀμφέχυτο), aor. 1 pass. ἀμφεχύθην, 1) Act. prop. *to pour around*; metaph. *to spread around*; ἠέρα τινί, obscurity, mist around any one, 17, 270. 2) Mid. and aor. 1 pass. *to be diffused* or *shed round, to be poured about, to surround*; with accus. trop. θείη μιν ἀμφέχυτο ὀμφή, a divine voice sounded around him, 2, 41. τὴν ἄχος ἀμφεχύθη, distress poured itself over her, Od. 4, 716. 2) Spoken of persons, *to embrace*; with accus. Od. 16, 214; absol. Od. 22, 498.

ἀμφιχυθείς, see ἀμφιχέω.

ἀμφίχυτος, ον, (χέω) *poured around*; τεῖχος, a wall cast up all around, an earth mound, 20, 145.

Ἀμφίων, ίονος (part. ἀμφιών walking around), 1) son of Jasius and Persephónê (according to Eustath.), father of Chloris, king of Orchomenus in Bœotia, Od. 11, 285. 2) son of Zeus and Antiopê, brother of Zethus, distinguished for his skill in song and in performing on the harp. When he was surrounding Thebes with a wall, the stones joined themselves together at the sound of his lyre. His wife Niobê bore him several children, Od. 11, 262. Homer distinguishes the two, though later tradition often confounds them, cf. O. Müller, Gesch. hell. Stämme I. S. 231. 3) a leader of the Epeans, 13, 692.

ἀμφότερος, η, ον (ἄμφω), *both*. Of the sing in Hom. only the neut. as adv. ἀμφότερον βασιλεύς τ' ἀγαθὸς κρατερός τ' αἰχμητής, both at once, a good king and a brave spearman, 3, 179; often in the dual and plur. 5, 156. 17, 395.

Ἀμφότερος, ὁ, a Trojan slain by Patroclеs, 16, 415.

ἀμφοτέρωθεν, adv. *from both sides, on both sides*, 5, 726. Od. 7, 113.

ἀμφοτέρωσε, adv. *towards both sides*, in both directions, γεγωνέμεν, *8, 223.

ἀμφουδίς, adv. (prob. from ἀμφίς and οὖδας), *from the ground*; κάρη ἀείρειν, to raise the head from the ground, Od. 17, 237.†

ἀμφράσσαιτο, see ἀναφράζομαι.

ἄμφω, τώ, τά, τώ, gen. ἀμφοῖν, *both*; spoken of single persons, and also of two parties, as 2, 124. Hom. has only the nom. and accus. Sometimes indecl. h. Cer. 13.

ἄμφωτος, ον (οὖς), *two-eared, two-handled*, ἄλεισον, Od. 22, 10.†

ἀμφῶν, Ep. for ἀμάσιεν, see ἀμάω.

ἀμώμητος, ον (μωμέομαι), *irreproachable, blameless*, 12, 109.†

ἄν, a particle, Ep. and enclit. κέ, before a vowel κέν (κέ is prop. only a dialectic variation of ἄν, and in use generally agrees with it, although it does not indicate the conditional relation so distinctly, and hence admits a more frequent use.—These particles indicate a conditional proposition or sentence, i. e. they show that the predicate of the sentence is not true absolutely, but is to be considered as depending upon certain circumstances or conditions. The English language has no word perfectly equivalent to ἄν (though it may sometimes be translated by *perhaps*, *possibly*, Lat. *forte*), but expresses its meaning by the mood of the verb (*may*, *can*, *might*, *could*, etc. write). It cannot therefore stand in sentences which express an unconditional affirmation, but only in the following cases: I) With the indicat. 1) With the indicat. pres. and perf. ἄν cannot stand, because that which is represented as actually passing or past can be subjected to no condition. The same, according to Herm. de partic. ἄν holds true of κέ; and the passages in which κέ is connected with these tenses are changed by him, e. g. τῷ καί κέ τις εὔχεται ἀνήρ—λιπέσθαι, where, according to Cod. Vrat., τέ is to be read for κέ, 14, 484; δῶρον δ', ὅ ττι κέ μοι δοῦναι φίλον ἦτορ ἀνώγει, where we must read ἀνώγῃ, Od. 1, 316; τάδε κ' αὐτὸς οἴσαι, where Herm. reads γ' αὐτός, Od. 3, 255; ὅτε κέν ποτ'—ζώννυνταί τε νέοι, καὶ ἐπεντύνονται ἄεθλα, Od. 24, 87, where we must with Thiersch, Gr. Gram. § 322, 11, read ὅτε περ, or take ζώννυνται as subjunct. and read ἐπεντύνωνται. According to Rost, however, κέ may accompany the indicat. pres. wherever the discourse relates to things which are to be derived from others as natural consequences, as 14, 484. Od. 3, 255. 2) With the fut. indicat. we frequently find the Ep. κέ (rarely ἄν), when the proposition expressed in the fut. is dependent upon a condition; εἰ δ' Ὀδυσσεὺς ἔλθοι—αἶψά κε—βίας ἀποτίσεται ἀνδρῶν, Od. 17, 540. cf. 22, 66. Commonly, however, the conditional clause is wanting; εἰρέαι, ὁππόθεν εἰμέν· ἐγὼ δέ κέ τοι καταλέξω, I will (if thou wilt hear) tell thee, Od. 3, 80, cf. 4, 176. 7, 273. 22, 42. 3) It stands with the indicat. of the histor. tenses (impf. plupf. and aor.), a) to indicate that the proposition would prove true, or would have proved true, only on a certain condition; but as that condition has not been, or cannot be fulfilled, so the proposition has not proved, or will not prove true; καὶ νύ κ' ἔτι πλείονας Λυκίων κτάνε—Ὀδυσσεύς, εἰ μὴ ἄρ' ὀξὺ νόησε Ἕκτωρ, and now would Ulysses have slain still more Lycians, if Hector had not immediately observed it, 5, 679. The condition is often wanting, and must be supplied from the context. ἦ τέ κεν ἤδη λάϊνον ἕσσο χιτῶνα, indeed, thou wouldst be already clothed with a tunic of stone, 3, 56. b) To denote repetition in past time, the action being represented by ἄν as conditional, viz. as repeated only in certain cases. In Hom., however, this use is exceedingly rare, Od. 2, 104 (19, 149. 24, 139); ἔνθα κ ε ν ἠματίη ὑφαίνεσκεν μέγαν ἱστόν, she was wont to weave (because we believed her, cf. v. 103), where Wolf needlessly reads καί. μάλιστα δέ κ' αὐτὸς ἀνέγνω, 13, 734, chiefly himself is wont to experience it, where some take κ' as καί abbrev. and Herm. de part. ἄν, for δέ κ' proposes δέ τ'. Likewise οἵ κε τάχιστα ἔκρινεν, Ο‛l. 18, 263, where Herm. would

read οἵ τε. A peculiar case is Od. 4, 546. ἦ γάρ μιν ζωόν γε κιχήσεαι ἢ κεν Ὀρέστης κτείνεν ὑποφθάμενος. Nitzsch on this passage says: This aor. with κέν is to be compared with no other sentence of this form; ἢ κεν are closely connected, and the whole is equivalent to κιχήσεαι· εἰ δὲ μή, κτεῖνεν, or otherwise Orestes has slain him, cf. Rost, Gram. p. 587, and Thiersch, § 353, 1. II) With the subjunct. ἄν serves to define more closely the idea expressed by it. The subj. expresses a *supposed notion* (*res cogitata*), but with reference to a future *decision*; the ἄν indicates the external circumstances and relations upon which the decision depends. 1) In the Epic language the subjunct. with ἄν stands instead of the fut. indicat.; with a certain difference, however, the indicat. fut. representing the future event as already decided; the subjunct. on the other hand representing the future event as one which it is possible may sooner or later occur. τάχ' ἄν ποτε θυμὸν ὀλέσσῃ, he will, it is probable, soon lose his life, 1, 205. οὐκ ἄν τοι χραίσμῃ κίθαρις, thy harp would not [I deem] then avail thee, 3, 54. 2) In dependent clauses, in connexion with conjunctions and pronouns, to represent the event as conditional, i. e. as depending upon circumstances; ὄφρα ἴδητ' αἴ κ' ὔμμιν ὑπέρσχῃ χεῖρα Κρονίων, whether—would protect you, 4, 249. In like manner, εἴ κε, ἤ κε; ἐπεί κε, ἐπεὶ ἄν; ὅτε κεν, ὅτ' ἄν, ὁπότε κεν, etc., ὃς ἄν or κε, οἷος ἄν; comp. the several conjunctions and the relative. III) With the optative, ἄν expresses the fact that the supposition expressed by this mood is conditional; εἰ καὶ ἐγώ σε βάλοιμι—αἶψά κε—εὖχος ἐμοὶ δοίης, thou wouldst confer renown upon me, 16, 625; hence it stands, 1) To express an undetermined possibility. κείνοισι δ' ἂν οὔτις—μαχέοιτο, no one wo...d be able to contend, 1, 271. 2) The ἄν with the optat. often stands as a softer mode of expressing a command or entreaty, 2, 250, and with οὐ in the question οὐκ ἂν ἐρύσαιο; couldst thou not hold him back? instead of hold him back, restrain him, 5, 456. 3) In interrogative sentences, where the optative can be generally translated by *can* or *could*. On the optat. with ἄν in dependent clauses, e. g. with relative pronouns, see under the relative and conjunctions. IV) ἄν with the infin. and partcp. expresses also a condition, which will be clearly seen by resolving these forms of the verb into clauses expressed by the finite verb, 9, 684. V) Repetition of ἄν and κε. Hom. never repeats ἄν, but he unites 1) ἄν with κε to give greater stress to the condition, 11, 187. 13, 127. In other cases the reading is doubtful, as Od. 6, 259, where Nitzsch would read καί for κέν. 2) The repetition of κε is rare, Od. 4, 733. VI) ἄν is properly short; however, it seems long in 8, 21. 406.

άν, 1) Poet. abbrev. for ἀνά (better ἀν), before ν, τ; becomes before labials ἀμ, before palatals ἀγ. 2) Poet. abbrev. for ἄνα, i. e. ἀνέστη, he arose, 3, 268. cf. ἄνα.

ἀνά, abbrev. ἀν, ἀμ, ἀγ, 1) Preposition. *up, upon, on,* opposed to κατά, comm. with accus. Ep. also with gen. and dat. 1) With gen. only in the phrase ἀνὰ νηὸς βαίνειν, to go on shipboard, Od. 2, 416. 9, 177. 15, 284; where, however, according to Rost, Gr. p. 495, it is better to assume a tmesis, so that the gen. appears to depend upon ἀναβαίνειν. 2) With dat., *on, upon,* ἀνὰ σκήπτρῳ, upon the sceptre, 1, 15. ἀνὰ ὤμῳ, Od. 11, 128. ἀνὰ χερσίν, on the hands, h. Cer. 286. 3) With accus. *a)* Of place: to indicate a direction to a higher object, *up, upon;* τιθέναι τι ἀνὰ μυρίκην, 10, 466, ἀναβαίνειν ἀνὰ ῥωγάς, to ascend the steps, Od. 22, 143; to denote extension, *through, throughout, along.* ἀνὰ νῶτα, along the back, 13, 547. ἀνὰ δῶμα, through the house, 4, 670; in like manner, ἀνὰ στρατόν, μάχην, ὅμιλον: ἀνὰ στόμα ἔχειν, to have in the mouth, 2, 250. φρονέειν ἀνὰ θυμόν, to revolve in the mind, 2, 36. πᾶσαν ἀν' ἰθύν, in every undertaking, Od. 4, 434. ἀν' ἰθύν, upwards, Od. 8, 377. *b)* Of time, only ἀνὰ νύκτα, through the night, 14, 80. *c)* Of number, *to, up to.* ἀνὰ εἴκοσι μέτρα χεῦεν, Od. 9, 209. II) Adv. *thereon, thereupon.* ἀνὰ βότρυες ἦσαν, grapes were thereon, 18. 562. It stands pleonastically with a verb compounded with ἀνά, 23, 709. In composition it has the same signification, and besides it indicates direction towards the point of starting, *back again* [the Lat. *re-* denoting repetition, e. g. ἀναφράζομαι].

ἄνα is 1) A prepos. with retracted accent, and stands as interj. for ἀνάστηθι: *up then;* comm. ἀλλ' ἄνα, 6, 331. 2) A vocat. from ἄναξ, only in the construct. ὦ ἄνα, Ζεῦ ἄνα.

ἀναβαίνω, Ep. ἀμβαίνω (βαίνω), aor. 1 ἀνέβησα, aor. 2 ἀνέβην, aor. 1 mid. ἀνεβησάμην (once partcp. ἀναβησάμενοι, transit. Od. 15, 475), 1) Trans. in aor. 1 act. *to lead up, to cause to ascend*=τινά. any one (into a ship, to *put* a person *on board*, &c. 1, 144), once in the mid. νὼ ἀναβησάμενοι, after they had *put* us on board, Od. 15, 475. II) Intrans. in the aor. 2 act. *to ascend, to go up;* with accus. οὐρανόν, to mount to heaven, 1, 497; ὑπερῷα, to ascend to the upper apartments, Od. 23, 1; more frequently with εἰς, ἐπί τι; once with dat. νεκροῖς, to pass over the dead bodies, 10, 493; most generally, a) *to ascend the ship (go on board, embark),* often with the omission of νῆα (twice with gen. νηός, Od. 2, 416. 9, 177; see ἀνά). β) *to ascend upon land, to land,* Od. 14, 353. γ) *to put to sea, to go from the shore to sea, to sail away,* ἀπὸ Κρήτης, Od. 14, 252; esply ἐς Τροίην, to sail from Greece to Troy, Od. 1, 210. *b)* Metaph. φάτις ἀνθρώπους ἀναβαίνει, fame spreads among men, Od. 6, 29.

ἀναβάλλω, Ep. ἀμβάλλω (βάλλω), 1) prop. *to throw up.* 2) *to throw back,* hence *to put off, to delay,* ἄεθλον, Od. 19, 584. II) Mid. *to lift oneself,* hence *to begin;* with infinit. ἀείδειν, to begin to sing, Od. 1, 155. 8, 256 (according to the old Gramm. from the strong elevation of the voice). 2) *to put off, defer, delay* (with reference to the subject). μηδ' ἔτι ἔργον ἀμβαλλώμεθα, let us no longer delay our work, 2, 436.

ἀνάβατος, ον, Ep. ἄμβατος (ἀναβαίνω), *that may be ascended, easy of ascent,* 6, 434. Od 11, 316.

ἀναβέβρυχε. 3 sing. perf., the pres. does not occur, 17, 54.† in connex. with ὕδωρ: *the water gushes* or *spouts forth.* Some Gramm. assume in the pres. ἀναβρύχω or ἀναβρύζω; others, as Buttm. Lex. 206, trace it by comparison with ὑπόβρυχα (*under water*) to ἀναβρέχω, whence the reading ἀναβέβροχεν; others again to the root βρυχάομαι, from which occurs the perf. βέβρυχα, but with ῡ.

'Αναβησίνεως, ὁ (that travels by ship), a Phaeacian, Od. 8, 113.

ἀναβληδήν, Ep. ἀμβληδήν (ἀναβάλλομαι 1), *rising* with a sudden impulse, *vehemently,* γοᾶν, 22, 476.† [to lament with vehement outcry, Passow; *alte petitis suspiriis,* Heyne; cf. ἀναβολάδην].

ἀνάβλησις, ιος, ἡ (βάλλω), *a delaying, procrastination,* κακοῦ, *2, 380. 24, 655.

ἀναβολάδην, Ep. ἀμβολάδην (ἀναβάλλω), *throwing up, boiling up.* λέβης ζεῖ ἀμβολάδην, the cauldron boils bubbling up, 21, 364.†

ἀναβράχω (βράχω), only Ep. aor. ἀνέβραχον, *to rattle, to crash, to creak;* spoken of arms, 19, 13; of doors, Od. 21, 48.

ἀναβρόχω, occurring only in the optat. aor. 1 ἀναβρόξειε, and in the partcp. aor. 2 pass. ἀναβροχέν, *to swallow up again, to absorb;* of Charybdis: ὅτε ἀναβρόξειε θαλάσσης ὕδωρ, when she swallows up again the sea-water, Od. 12, 240; and ὕδωρ ἀπολέσκεν ἀναβροχέν, the water being absorbed and swallowed up again, disappeared, Od. 11, 586. cf. Buttm. Lex. 201. *Od.

ἀναβρύχω, see ἀναβέβρυχε.

ἀναγιγνώσκω (γιγνώσκω), only aor. 2 ἀνέγνων, *to know accurately, to perceive clearly,* with accus. τινά, Od. 4, 250. γόνον, Od. 1, 216. Il. 13, 734; σήματα, Od. 19, 250. 23, 206; absol. *to perceive clearly,* 13, 734.

ἀναγκαίη, ἡ (prop. fem. from ἀναγκαῖος), Ep. *compulsion, necessity,* dat. ἀναγκαίῃ, *by force,* 4, 300. Od. 19, 73.

ἀναγκαῖος, αίη, αῖον (ἀνάγκη), *compulsory, urgent, coercive, necessary;* μῦθος, a compulsory word, i. e. a decree, an authoritative sentence, Od. 17, 399. ἦμαρ ἀναγκαῖον, the day of force, of slavery, 16, 836, = δούλιον ἦμαρ. 2) *of necessity,* or *compulsion, by compulsion,* πολεμισταί, Od. 24, 499.

ἀνάγκη, ἡ (ἀνάγω), *force, compulsion,*

Άναγνάμπτω. 41 Άνακέλομαι.

violence, necessity, often in the dat. ἀνάγκῃ, from necessity, *on compulsion, forced*, ἀείδειν, πολεμίζειν; also act. *with violence, vehemently*: ἰσχύειν, κελεύειν, ὑπ' ἀνάγκης, by force, Od. 19, 156.

ἀναγνάμπτω (γνάμπτω), aor. 1 ἀνέγναμψα, aor. 1 pass. ἀνεγνάμφθην, *to bend back*; δεσμόν, to loose the bond, Od. 14, 348; pass. αἰχμὴ ἀνεγνάμφθη, the point was bent back, 3, 348. 7, 259.

ἀνάγω (ἄγω) fut. ἀνάξω, aor. 2 act. ἀνήγαγον, 1) *to lead up, to lead to a high place*, from the sea-coast into the country, τινά, Od. 4, 534, or into the high seas, thus often spoken of the voyage to Troy; to take any one to sea, γυναῖκα ἐξ ἀπίης γαίης, 3, 48; Ἑλένην, 6, 292; λαὸν ἐνθάδε (to Troy), 9, 338; also mly of sea-voyages, 13, 627. *b*) *to conduct home*, γυναῖκα δόμονδε, Od. 3, 272; often, mly, *to conduct to, to bring*, spoken of persons and things: δῶρα, to bring presents, 8, 203; τινὰ ἐς μέσσον, Od. 18, 89. 2) Mid. prop. to conduct oneself up, *to put out to sea, to sail away*. τοὶ δ' ἀνάγοντο, they sailed back, 1, 478. Od. 19, 202.

ἀναδέδρομα, see ἀνατρέχω.

ἀναδέρκω, Ep. (δέρκω), aor. 2 ἀνέδρακον, *to look up, to look upwards*; ὀφθαλμοῖσιν, to open the eyes again, 14, 436.†

ἀναδέσμη, ἡ (δέω), *a fillet, a head-band*, of females, 22, 469.†

ἀναδέχομαι, depon. mid. (δέχομαι), aor. 1 ἀνεδεξάμην, aor. sync. ἀνεδέγμην, *to take up*, σάκος, 5, 619. 2) *to take upon oneself, to bear, to endure*, ὀϊζύν, Od. 17, 563.

*ἀναδίδωμι (δίδωμι), aor. 1 ἀνέδωκα, *to proffer, to present, to give*, with accus. h. Merc. 111.

*ἀναδύνω (δύνω)=ἀναδύομαι, Batr. 90.

ἀναδύω (δύω), only mid. and aor. 2 ἀνέδυν, infinit. ἀναδῦναι, aor. 1 mid. ἀνεδυσάμην [ἀνεδύσετο or ἀνεδύσατο, Buttm. § 96. note 9], intrans. *to emerge, to come forth out of*; with gen. ἁλός, from the sea, 1, 359; and with accus. κῦμα, v. 496, to emerge from the wave. 2) *to withdraw* [towards the interior of a crowd]; ἐς ὅμιλον, to retreat into the crowd, 7, 218; and with accus. πόλεμον, to avoid the war, 13, 225; absol. Od. 9, 377. (ἀνδύεται poet. for ἀναδύεται.)

ἀναέεδνος, ον (ἔδνον), 1) *ungifted*, i. e. for whom the bridegroom presents no gifts to the parents, 9, 146. 2) *without dowry*, with whom the bridegroom receives nothing from the parents, 13, 366. This explanation is, however, justly rejected by Spitzner on 9, 146. *il.

ἀναείρω (ἀείρω), aor. 1 ἀνάειρα Ep. for ἀνήειρα. 1) *to raise, to lift up*; with accus. χεῖρας ἀθανατοῖσι, to lift up the hands to the gods, 7, 130; τινά=*to throw* a man, spoken of wrestlers striving to lift up and throw each other. 2) *to lift, to bear away* (as a prize), δύω τάλαντα, 23, 614; κρητῆρα, 23, 582.

ἀναθηλέω, Ep. (θηλή), fut. ἀναθηλήσω, *to become verdant again, to bloom, bud or sprout out again*, 1, 236.†

ἀνάθημα, τό (τίθημι), that which is put up, esply *a votive offering to a deity* which is put up in a temple [not Homeric]. 2) any present of value; hence, *ornament, decoration*. Thus H. calls dancing and singing ἀναθήματα δαιτός, embellishments of the feast or table ['enlivening sequel of the banquet's joys,' Cp.], Od. 1, 152. 21, 430.

ἀναθρώσκω (θρώσκω), *to spring* or *leap up, to bound off*. ὕψι ἀναθρώσκειν, to bound up into the air, spoken of a descending rock, 13, 140.†

ἀναιδείη, ἡ (ἀναιδής), *shamelessness, impudence, effrontery*. ἀναιδείην ἐπιειμένος, clothed in impudence, 1, 149. ἐπιβῆναι ἀναιδείης, to have given oneself up to wantonness [' *to have overpassed the bounds of modesty*,' Cp.], Od. 22, 424.

ἀναιδής, ές (αἰδέομαι), *shameless, impudent*, as the suitors of Penelope. 2) *ungovernable, dreadful*, as κυδοιμός, 5, 593; λᾶας, the terrible or monstrous stone, 14, 521. Od. 11, 597.

ἀναίμων, ον (αἷμα), gen. ονος, *bloodless, without blood*, spoken of the gods, 5, 342.†

ἀναιμωτί, adv. *without bloodshed*, 17, 363. Od. 18, 149.

ἀναίνομαι, aor. 1 ἠνηνάμην, Ep. ἀνηνάμην, (fm ἀνά and αἶνος, Död.) [according to Buttm. r, ἀν or ἀνα (=no) with termin. αίνω], *to deny, to refuse, to reject*; with accus. δῶρα, to spurn gifts, 9, 679; ἔργον ἀεικές, a shameful act, Od. 3, 265; δόσιν, Od. 4, 651. 10, 18; τινά, to reject any one, Od. 8, 212; with infin. *to deny*, ὁ δ' ἀναίνετο μηδὲν ἑλέσθαι, said that he had not received any thing, 18, 500, also *to refuse to do* [λοιγὸν ἀμῦναι], cf. 450; absol. 7, 93. 9, 510.

ἀναιρέω (αἱρέω), aor. 2 ἀνεῖλον, and its partcp. ἀνελών, fut. mid. ἀναιρήσομαι, aor. 2 ἀνειλόμην, Ep. ἀνέλ.. 1) *to lift up, to take away, to remove*; βοῦν ἀπὸ χθονός, to lift an ox from the earth, Od. 3, 453; ἄεθλια, to bear off prizes, 23, 736; πολλά, to receive much, said of a beggar, Od. 18, 16. 2) Mid. oftener, *to take up for oneself, to receive, to bear away*; κούρην, to take a child in the arms, 16, 8; οὐλοχύτας, to take the sacred barley, 2, 410; ἐπιφροσύνας, to assume reason, to become prudent, Od. 19, 22. [εἴ σ' ἀνελοίμην=if I were to take you (hire you), of a daylabourer, Od. 18, 357.]

ἀναΐσσω (ἀΐσσω), aor. 1 ἀνήϊξα, *to leap up, to rise suddenly* from a sitting posture, 3, 216. Od. 1, 410. πηγαὶ ἀναΐσσουσι, the fountains gush forth, 22, 148; once with accus. ἅρμα, to leap (upon=) into the chariot, 24, 440.

ἀναίτιος, ον (αἰτία), *without guilt, blameless*. ἀναίτιον αἰτιᾶσθαι, to impeach a guiltless individual, 11, 653. Od. 20, 135.

ἀνακαίω (καίω), *to kindle*, πῦρ, *Od. 7, 13. 9, 251.

*ἀνακεκλόμεναι, see ἀνακέλομαι.

*ἀνακέλομαι, poet. (κέλομαι), aor. 2 with redupl. ἀνεκεκλόμην, *to call upon, to invoke*, τινά, h. Pan. 18, 5.

Ἀνακεράννυμι. 42 Ἄναξ.

ἀνακεράννυμι (κεράω), aor. ἀνεκέρασα, Ep. σσ, *to mix again; κρητῆρα οἴνου, to mix the mingling vessel again full of wine*, Od. 3, 390† [to *mingle wine again in the replenished bowl*, cf. 339].

ἀνακηκίω (κηκίω), *to spout* or *bubble up; to gush forth*, of sweat [oozing forth] and blood, *7, 262. 13, 705.

ἀνακλῖνω (κλίνω), aor. 1 ἀνέκλῖνα, partcp. ἀγκλίνας Ep. for ἀνακλίνας, aor. 1 pass. ἀνεκλίνθην, 1) *to incline, to lean back, to cause to rest; τόξον ποτὶ γαίῃ*, to let the bow rest (against =) upon the earth, 4, 113. The Schol. refers the action of ἀγκ. in 4, 113, to the subject, ἐπήρεισεν ἑαυτόν. Am. Ed.] πρός τι, Od. 18, 103; pass. aor. *to lean oneself back*. spoken of persons rowing and of persons sleeping. ἀνακλινθεὶς πέσων ὕπτιος, leaning back he sank supine, Od. 9, 371. 2) *to lean back = to push back, to open*, opposed to ἐπιθεῖναι; θύρην, to open the door, Od. 22, 156; so also νέφος, 5, 571; λόχον [i. e. the *wooden horse*, filled with concealed warriors], Od. 11, 525.

*ἀνακλύζω (κλύζω), *to wash*, or *dash up*, Ep. 3.

ἀνακοντίζω (ἀκοντίζω), *to spout out, to dart forth, to gush out*, spoken of blood, 5, 113.†

ἀνακόπτω (κόπτω), *to strike (dash* or *drive) back, to undo*, ὀχῆας, the bolts, Od. 21, 47.†

ἀνακράζω (κράζω), aor. 2 ἀνέκραγον, *to cry out, to speak (my thoughts) aloud, to prate garrulously*, Od. 14, 467.†

ἀνακρεμάννυμι (κρεμάννυμι), aor. 1 ἀνεκρέμασα, partcp. ἀγκρεμάσας, *to hang up; τὶ πασσάλῳ*, to hang up any thing upon a hook or peg, Od. 1, 440. h. Ap. 8.

*ἀνακτορίη, ἡ (ἀνάκτωρ), *rule, command*, the direction of steeds, h. Ap. 234.

ἀνακτόριος, ίη, ιον (ἀνάκτωρ), *belonging to the master*, Od. 15, 397.†

ἀνακυμβαλιάζω (κύμβαλον), *to be overturned with a rattling noise*. δίφροι ἀνακυμβαλίαζον, the o'ertumbled chariots rang (*Cp*.], 16, 379.†

ἀναλέγω and ἀλλέγω (λέγω), aor. 1 ἀνέλεξα, infin. ἀλλέξαι, Ep. for ἀναλέξαι, *to gather, to collect*, ἔντεα, 11, 755; ὀστέα, 21, 321. *11.

ἀναλκείη, ἡ (ἀλκή), *feebleness, weakness, cowardice*, always in the plur. 6, 74, *11.

ἀναλκίς, ιδος, ὁ ἡ (ἀλκή), *powerless, weak, cowardly*, comm. connected with ἀπτόλεμος, accus. ἀνάλκιδα and ἄναλκιν once, Od. 3, 375.

ἄναλτος, ον (ἄλθω) [ἄλδω = αὐξάνω; whence ἀλτόν = τὸ πολύ. Hes. Cf. admitus, Lob. Techn. 74]. not to be satiated, *insatiable*, γαστήρ, Od. 17, 228. 18, 114. *Od.

ἀναλύω and ἀλλύω (λύω), Ep. iterative impf. ἀλλύεσκεν, aor. 1 ἀνέλυσα, *to loose, to unravel; ἱστόν*, to unravel or undo the web, Od. 2, 109. 19, 150; τινὰ ἐκ δεσμῶν, to deliver any one from bonds, Od. 12, 100; πρυμνήσια, Od. 9, 178. 2) Mid. *to loose for oneself; τινὰ ἐς φάος*, to bring any one to the light, h. Merc. 258. (ν elsewhere short in the pres, but in Od. 2, 110, long through the accent.)

ἀναμαιμάω (μαιμάω), *to rage through;* with accus. πῦρ ἀναμαιμάει ἄγκεα, the fire rages through the valleys, 20, 490.†

ἀναμάσσω (μάσσω), fut. ξω, prop. *to rub on, to anoint*, hence ὃ (viz. μέγα ἔργον) σῇ κεφαλῇ ἀναμάξεις, according to Damm: *facinus, quod capiti tuo allines ut maculam mortiferam*, i. e. which thou shalt expiate with thy head, Od. 19, 92.† Eustath. derives the metaph. from the wiping of the sword upon the head of a slain warrior, to show that he deserved death. Several modern annotators, however, suppose that the word ἀναμάσσειν properly signifies, *to wipe off, to cleanse*. and thus stands simply for *to expiate*, as in English, to wash away a crime (according to Bothe), or in French, *se laver d'un crime* (Dugas Montbel).

ἀναμένω, poet. ἀναμίμνω (μένω), aor. 1 ἀνέμεινα, *to expect, to await*, τί, Ἠῶ δῖαν, Od. 19, 342.†

ἀναμετρέω (μετρέω), *to re-measure, to measure back;* Χάρυβδιν, to measure back my course again to Charybdis, Od. 12, 428.†

*ἀναμηλόω (μηλόω), partcp. aor. ἀναμηλώσας, prop. to examine with the probe; according to Ruhnken's conjec. for ἀναπηλήσας, h. Merc. 41.

ἀναμίγνυμι, poet. ἀναμίσγω (μίγνυμι), aor. 1 ἀνέμιξα, partcp. ἀμμίξας, *to mix up, to mingle together; κρί λευκόν*, to mix therewith white barley, Od. 4, 41; τί τινι, 24, 529. Od. 10, 536.

ἀναμιμνήσκω (μιμνήσκω), aor. 1 ἀνέμνησα, *to remind*, τινά τι, any one of any thing, Od. 3, 211.†

ἀναμίμνω (μίμνω), poet. for ἀναμένω, *to await*, with the accus. 2) Absolut. *to wait, to persist*, *16, 363.

ἀναμίσγω = ἀναμίγνυμι, Od.

ἀναμορμύρω (μορμύρω), Ep. iterative impf. ἀνεμορμύρεσκε, *to roar, to rebellow*, spoken of Charybdis, Od. 12, 238.†

ἀνανέομαι, Ep. ἀννέομαι, depon. mid. (νέομαι), *to rise, to ascend*, spoken of the sun, Od. 10, 192.†

ἀνανεύω (νεύω), aor. ἀνένευσα, prop. to throw the head up and move it back, the token amongst the Greeks of refusal, opposed to κατανεύω; hence, to refuse by a nod, *to deny, to refuse*, absol. 6, 311; with accus. 16, 250; with inlin. 16, 252; ὀφρύσι, to shake my brows [*Cp*.], *to forbid by a sign with the eye-brows*, Od. 9, 468.

*ἀνανέω (νέω), aor. ἀνένευσα, *to swim up, to recover*, like *emergere*, Batr. 223.

ἄναντα, adv. *upwards*, up hill, 23, 116.†

ἄναξ, ακτος, ὁ (from ἀνά, as πέριξ from περί), dat. four Ep. ἀνάκτεσιν, 15, 557; voc. ἄνα, spoken only of gods. 1) Prop. every *ruler, master, lord*, the master of a family, οἴκοιο, Od. 1, 397; master of slaves, 24, 734. Od. 4, 87. 10, 559. 2) esply, *sovereign, king*. a) Spoken of all

Ἀναξηραίνω. 43 **Ἀνασείω.**

gods; esply of Apollo, 1, 36. 75. b) Of earthly princes and kings, prop. the chief of a nation (cf. βασιλεύς). Thus Hom. calls all heroes; but Agamemnon, as commander-in-chief, he calls ἄναξ ἀνδρῶν, Il. once spoken of Orsilochus, ἄναξ ἀνδρεσσιν, 5, 546. [But also Euphētēs, 15, 532; Eumēius, 23, 288 (Am. Ed.).] c) Of other noble and principal men, as Tiresias, Od. 11, 143; of the sons of kings, Od. 17, 186.

ἀναξηραίνω (ξηραίνω), aor. 1 ἀνεξήρανα, whence Ep. subj. ἀνξηράνῃ for ἀνξηρήνῃ, to dry up, ἀλωήν, a seed-plot (garden, orchard), 21, 347.†

ἀνοίγεσκον, see ἀνοίγω.

ἀναπάλλω (πάλλω), partcp. aor. 2 ἀμπαλών, Ep. for ἀναπεπαλών, Ep. aor. sync. 3 sing. ἀνέπαλτο, 1) to swing upward or backward; often ἔγχος ἀμπεπαλὼν προΐει, prop. having swung back the spear (to give it more force), he hurled it; he hurled the uplifted spear, 3, 355 and often. 2) Pass. mid. together with the Ep. aor. sync. mid. to leap up, to spring up, ἀναπάλλεται ἰχθύς, 23, 692; of Achilles, to leap up (for joy), 20, 424; spoken of a wounded horse, ἀλγήσας ἀνέπαλτο, he sprang up for pain, 8, 85. That the form ἀνέπαλτο belongs to ἀναπάλλω, and not to ἀνεφάλλομαι, is proved by Spitzner in Excurs. XVI. z. Il.

ἀναπαύω (παύω), aor. 1 ἀνέπαυσα, to cause to cease, to let rest, τινά τινος, any one from a thing; ἔργων, from labour, 17, 550.†

*ἀναπείθω (πείθω), aor. ἀνέπεισα, to persuade, to prevail upon; with accus. Batr. 122.

ἀναπείρω, Ep. ἀμπείρω (πείρω), aor. 1 partcp. ἀμπείρας, to pierce with a spit, to transpierce or transfix, to spit, σπλάγχνα, the entrails, 2, 426.†

ἀναπεπταμένος, η, ον, see ἀναπετάννυμι.

ἀναπετάννυμι (πετάω), aor. 1 ἀνεπέτασα, Ep. σσ, perf. pass. ἀναπέπταμαι, to spread out, to unfold, to expand, ἱστία, the sails, 1, 480. Od. 4, 783; pass. said of foldingcoors: ἀναπεπταμένας σανίδας ἔχον, they held open the folding-doors, 12, 122.

ἀναπηδάω (πεδάω), aor. 1 ἀνεπήδησα, Ep. ἀμπήδησα, to l. ap up, to stand up, ἐκ λόχου, from ambuscade, 11, 379.†

*ἀναπηλέω = ἀναπάλλω, aor. partcp. ἀναπηλήσας, to swing upwards, Hom. h. in Merc. 41, where Wolf after Ruhnken has ἀναμηλώσας, q. v.

ἀναπίμπλημι (πίμπλημι), fut. ἀναπλήσω, aor. 1 ἀνέπλησα, to fill to the brim, to fill up; metaph. πολέμοιο, rest from war, *11, 801.

ἀναπνέω (πνέω), aor. 1 ἀνέπνευσα, infin. ἀμπνεῦσαι, Ep. for ἀναπνεῦσαι, imper. aor. syncop. 2 ἄμπνυε, aor. 1 pass. ἀμπνύνθη, and aor. syncop. mid. ἄμπνυτο, Ep. for ἀνέπνυτο, to respire, to take breath, to rest, to recover oneself; κακότητος from suffering, 11, 382; πόνοιο, 15, 235. In like signif. the aor. 1 pass. and aor. sync. mid. ὁ δ᾽ ἀμπνύνθη καὶ ἀνέδρακεν ὀφθαλμοῖσιν, he breathed again, and opened his eyes, 14, 436. ὅτε δή ῥ᾽ ἄμπνυτο καὶ ἐς φρένα θυμὸς ἀγέρθη, when he breathed again, and life returned to his breast, Od. 5, 458. cf. 11, 359.

ἀνάποινος, ον (ποίνη), without ransom, unransomed, 1, 99.†

ἀναπρήθω (πρήθω), aor. ἀνέπρησα, prop. to light up; to cause to blaze up; to burst out [orig. = to spirtle, to fizz, Buttm.]; in Hom. only δάκρυα, to shed a flood of tears (cf. Buttm. Lex. p. 484), 9, 433. Od. 2, 81. Others: to shed hot tears. Död. considers it a syncopated form of ἀναπεράω, p. 8.

ἀνάπτω (ἅπτω), aor. ἀνῆψα, perf. pass. and imperat. ἀνήφθω, to hang up, to attach, to affix; πείρατα, to attach the ropes to the mast, Od. 9, 137; ἐξ αὐτοῦ sc. ἱστοῦ, which according to the Schol. is to be supplied from ἱστοπέδη, Od. 12, 51. 162; ἀγάλματα, to hang up, suspend, votive offerings (in a temple) Od. 3, 274. Metaph. μῶμον, to impute fault, blame, Od. 2, 84. *Od.

ἀνάπυστος, ον (ἀναπυνθάνομαι), sought out, known, Od. 11, 274.†

ἀναρπάζω (ἁρπάζω), aor. 1 ἀνήρπασα, partcp. ἀναρπάξας, to snatch up, to bear away upwards, to pull out, ἔγχος, 22, 276; hence, to hurry away; τινὰ ἀπὸ μάχης, to drag a man out of the battle, 16, 436; spoken esply of a tempest, Od. 4, 515. 5, 419.

ἀναῤῥήγνυμι (ῥήγνυμι), aor. 1 ἀνέρρηξα, to tear up, to tear in pieces, with accus. βοὸς βοείην, the skin of the ox; spoken of a lion which seizes an ox, 18, 582; γαῖαν, 20, 63. 2) to break through, to destroy, τεῖχος, 7, 461. *Il.

ἀναρρῑπτέω = ἀναρρίπτω, only pres. and impf. Od. 13, 78.†

ἀναρρίπτω, also ἀναρριπτέω (ῥίπτω), aor. ἀνέρριψα, to throw up, to cast upward; ἅλα πηδῷ, to fling up the brine with the oar (to indicate hard rowing), Od. 7, 328; and without πηδῷ, Od. 10, 30.

ἀναῤῥοιβδέω (ῥοιβδέω), aor. ἀνεῤῥοίβ-

ἀνασεύω (σεύω), Ep. syncop. aor. mid. ἀνέσσυτο, *to spring up; αἶμα ἀνέσσυτο,* the blood spouted up, 11, 458.†

ἀνασπάω (σπάω), aor. mid. ἀνεσπάσάμην, *to draw up.* Mid. to draw up for oneself, *to draw out; ἔγχος ἐκ χροός,* to draw out the spear from the body, 13, 274.†

ἄνασσα, ἡ (ἄναξ), *queen, mistress,* only three times; spoken of Dêmêtêr, 14, 326; of Athênê, Od. 3, 380; and of a mortal, Od. 6, 149.

ἀνάσσω (ἄναξ), fut. ἀνάξω, infin. aor. 1 mid. ἀνάξασθαι, 1) *to rule, to reign, to be sovereign;* spoken both of men and gods, comm. with dat. 1, 180; less often with gen. Τενέδοιο, Ἀργείων, 1, 38; with prep. μετ' ἀθανάτοισιν, to rule among the immortals, 4, 61;—ἐν Βουδείῳ, to reign in Budêum, to have the royal power, 16, 572; with gen. and dat. together: Τρώεσσιν τιμῆς τῆς Πριάμου. to rule the Trojans with the power of Priam, 20, 180. Od. 24, 30. Pass. *to be ruled,* τινί, by any one, Od. 4, 177; once in the mid. τρὶς ἀνάξασθαι γένε' ἀνδρῶν, to reign through three generations, Od. 3, 245. The accus. does not depend upon ἀνάξασθαι, but is accus. denoting the length of time, cf. Nitzsch ad loc.

ἀνασταδόν, adv. (ἵστημι). *standing upright,* *9, 671. 23, 469.

ἀναστεναχίζω = ἀναστενάχω, poet. *to groan aloud,* νειόθεν ἐκ κραδίης, deeply from the breast, 10, 9.† ed. Wolf, where others read ἀνεστονάχιζε.

ἀναστενάχω (στενάχω), *to sigh out,* to groan aloud, *to lament,* τινά, for any one, 23, 211. Mid. to sigh aloud; intrans. *18, 315.

ἀναστοναχίζω = ἀναστεναχίζω, the earlier reading, cf. Spitzner Excurs. III.

ἀναστρέφω (στρέφω), aor. 1 ἀνέστρεψα, prop. *to turn about, to turn around, to overturn,* 23, 436. 2) Mid. *to turn oneself around, to ramble about, versari.* γαῖαν ἀναστρέφομαι, I tarry, or dwell, in a land, Od. 13, 326.

ἀναστρωφάω, poet. form of ἀναστρέφω, e. g. τόξον πάντῃ, to turn the bow in every direction, Od. 21, 394.†

(ἀνασχέθω), assumed pres. for the Ep. aor. 2 ἀνέσχεθον, see ἀνέχω.

ἀνεσχέμεν, see ἀνέχω.

ἀνάσχεο, for ἀνάσχου, see ἀνέχω.

ἀνάσχετος, ον, Ep. ἀνσχετος (ἀνέχω), *that may be endured, to be borne, tolerable,* Od. 2, 63.†

ἀνασχών, see ἀνέχω.

ἀνατέλλω (τέλλω), aor. 1 ἀνέτειλα, *to cause to come up; ἀμβροσίην ἵπποις,* to cause ambrosia to spring up for the steeds, 5, 777.†

ἀνατίθημι (τίθημι), fut. ἀναθήσω, *to place* or *set up, to hang up;* only metaph. ἐλεγχείην τινί, to make a charge upon or against any one, 22, 100.†

ἀνάτλημι (ΤΛΑ'Ω), pres. obsolete aor. 2 ἀνέτλην, *to take upon oneself, to bear, to endure,* κῆδεα, Od. 14, 47; φάρμακον, to endure the magic draught, viz. to withstand its strength, *Od. 10, 327; πολλά, h. 14, 6.

ἀνατολή, ἡ (ἀνατέλλω), poet. ἀντολή, *the rising* of the sun; in the plur. Od. 12, 4.†

ἀνατρέπω (τρέπω), *to overturn;* only in the mid. aor. 2 ἀνετραπόμην, *to fall over, to fall backwards,* *6, 64. 14, 447.

ἀνατρέχω (τρέχω), aor. 2 ἀνέδραμον, perf. ἀναδέδρομα, 1) *to run up, to spring up. to rise up;* ἐγκέφαλος παρ' αὐλὸν ἀνέδραμεν ἐξ ὠτειλῆς, the brain gushed from the wound upon the haft-hole (of the spear), i. e. the socket of the spearhead (L. and S.), 17, 297 [see also αὐλός]; πυκναὶ σμώδιγγες ἀνέδραμον, frequent weals rose up from blows, 23, 717; trop. ἀναδέδρομε πέτρη, the rock *runs up, rises up.* Od. 5, 412. 10, 4; and spoken of Achilles: ἀνέδραμεν ἔρνεϊ ἶσος, he ran up (shot up) like a shoot, 18, 56. 2) *to run back,* with αὖθις, ὀπίσω, 5, 599; ὣκ ἀπέλεθρον, 11, 354.

ἄναυδος, ον (αὐδή), *without voice, speechless,* *Od. 5, 466. 10, 378.

ἀναφαίνω (φαίνω), aor. 1 ἀνέφηνα, 1) *to cause to shine, to make bright* or *clear.* ἀμοιβηδὶς δ' ἀνέφαινον δμωαί, the maids kindled the fire by turns (viz. to produce light), Od. 18, 310; comm. metaph. *to cause to appear, to disclose, to discover, to show,* θεοπροπίας, divine mysteries, 1, 87, ποδῶν ἀρετήν, 20, 411; τινά, to discover any one, to make him known, Od. 4, 254; ἐπεσβολίας, to show loquacity, Od. 4, 159. II) Mid. and pass. *to shine forth, to show oneself.* ἀναφαίνεται ἀστὴρ ἐκ νεφέων, a constellation, a star, shines forth from the clouds, 11. 62; also metaph. ὄλεθρος ἀναφ., destruction appears, 11, 174; πατρὶς ἄρουρα, Od. 10, 29.

ἀναφαδά, adv. = ἀναφανδόν, *Od. 5, 221.

ἀναφανδόν (ἀναφαίνω), *visibly, openly,* *16, 178.

ἀναφέρω (φέρω), aor. 1 ἀνένεικα, aor. mid. ἀνενεικάμην, 1) *to bring up, to fetch up;* Κέρβερον ἐξ Ἀΐδαο, Od. 11, 625. 2) Mid. *to fetch up from oneself,* sc. breath. ἀδινῶς ἀνενείκατο, he drew a deep breath, *a deep sigh,* 19, 314 (according to the Schol. he groaned out deeply; who supplies the ellipsis with στεναγμόν), cf. Buttm. Lex. p. 105.

ἀναφλύω (φλύω), *to gush up, to bubble up, to boil,* as boiling water, 21, 361.†

ἀναφράζομαι (φράζομαι), aor. 1 ἀνεφρασάμην, optat. ἀμφράσσαιτο, Ep. for ἀνεφρ., *to observe again,* or *to recognise,* οὐλήν, the scar, Od. 19, 391.†

ἀναχάζομαι, mid. (χάζομαι), aor. 1 ἀνεχασάμην, partcp. Ep. ἀναχασσάμενος, *to retreat, to retire,* Od. 7, 280. 11, 97; in the Il. mly, out of the battle; comm. with ἄψ, ὀπίσω, 11, 461.

ἀναχωρέω (χωρέω), fut. ἤσω, *to give way, to retire,* often absol. with ἄψ, 3, 35. 4, 305; πόλινδε, 10, 210; ἐκ μεγάροιο, Od. 17, 461. ἀνεχώρησαν μεγάροιο μνηστῆνδε,

they withdrew to a recess of the palace, Od. 22, 270.
ἀναψύχω (ψύχω), aor. 1 pass. ἀνεψύχθην, to revive by a cool breeze, to refresh, ἀνθρώπους, the men (by Zephyrus), Od. 4, 568; φίλον ἦτορ, to refresh themselves, 13, 84; ἕλκος, to cool a (chafed and burning) wound, 5, 795. Pass. to be refreshed, to revive. ἀνέψυχθεν φίλον ἦτορ, 10, 575.
ἀνδάνω, Ion. and poet. imperf. ἥνδανον and ἐήνδανον, aor. 2 ἅδον for ἔαδον, and εὔαδον with the digamma, perf. 2 ἔαδε, to please, to gratify, to be agreeable; with dat. of the pers. ἅδε Ἔκτορι μῦθος, the word pleased Hector, 12, 80. 18, 510. Od. 3, 150; with two datives. 1, 24; with infin. οὐδ' Αἴαντι ἥνδανε θυμῷ ἐστάμεν, it pleased not Ajax in his heart [θυμῷ, local dat.] to stand, 15, 674; ἑαδὼς μῦθος, a pleasing, agreeable address, 9, 173. Od. 18, 422.
ἄνδιχα, adv. (ἀνά and δίχα), in two parts, in twain, asunder; κεάζειν, to split asunder, 16, 412; δάσασθαι, 18, 511.
ἀνδράγρια, τά (ἀνήρ, ἄγρα), spoils taken from an enemy slain, βροτόεντ', the gory spoils [Cp.], 14, 509.†
Ἀνδραιμονίδης, ου, ὁ, son of Andræmon = Thoas, 7, 168.
Ἀνδραίμων, ονος, ὁ, husband of Gorgō daughter of Œneus, and father of Thoas, who after Œneus reigned in Calydōn in Ætolia, 2, 638.
ἀνδραχάς, adv. (ἀνήρ), i. q. κατ' ἄνδρας, man by man. Od, 13, 14.†
ἀνδραπόδεσσι, metaplastic dat. plur. from ἀνδράποδον.
ἀνδράποδον, τό, a slave; only in dat. ἀνδραπόδεσσι, as if from ἀνδράπους, 7, 475.† cf. Thiersch, Gram. § 197, 60. [According to Doederl. from ἀνήρ and ἀποδόσθαι to sell, al. ἀνήρ, πούς.]
ἀνδραχθής, ές (ἀνήρ, ἄχθος), poet. gen. έος, man-burdening, as heavy as a man can carry: χερμάδια, huge stones [a strong man's burden each, Cp.], Od. 10, 121.†
ἀνδρειφόντης, ου, ὁ (φονεύω), man-slaying, epith. of Arēs, *2, 651.
ἄνδρεσσι, Ep. for ἀνδράσι.
ἀνδρόκμητος, ον (κάμνω), made or wrought by men; τύμβος, 11, 371.†
ἀνδροκτασίη, ἡ, Ep. (κτείνω), homicide, slaughter, carnage, esply in battle; comm. in the plur. the slaughter of a single man, 23, 86.
Ἀνδρομάχη, daughter of Eëtiōn, king of the Cilician Thebæ, wife of Hector, 6, 422. Her father and seven brothers were slain by Achilles. She was tenderly attached to her husband. According to a later tradition, she became, after Hector's death, the wife of Neoptolemus.
ἀνδρόμεος, έη, εον (ἀνήρ), belonging to a man, manly, human; κρέας, αἷμα, χρώς, human flesh, blood, skin; ὅμιλος, the crowd of men, 11, 538.
ἀνδρότης, ἡ, a false reading for ἀδροτής.
ἀνδροφάγος, ον (φαγεῖν), man-devouring, cannibal, epith. of Polyphēmus, Od. 10, 200.†

ἀνδροφόνος, ον, poet. (φονεύω), man slaying, epith. of Arēs and Hector, 4, 441. 1, 242; φάρμακον, a destructive drug, a deadly poison, Od. 1, 261.
ἀνδύεται, poet. for ἀναδύεται.
ἀνεγείρω (ἐγείρω), aor. 1 ἀνέγειρα, to awaken, τινὰ ἐξ ὕπνου, any one from sleep, 10, 138. Trop. to arouse, to cheer, τινὰ μειλιχίοις ἐπέεσσι, any one with soothing words, Od. 10, 172.
ἀνέγνων, see ἀναγινώσκω.
ἀνεδέγμεθα, see ἀναδέχομαι.
ἀνέδραμον, see ἀνατρέχω.
ἀνείργω, Ep. for ἀνείργω (εἴργω), imperf. ἀνέεργον, to press back, to restrain, φάλαγγας, μάχην. *3, 77. 7, 55; with ἐξοπίσω, h. Merc. 211.
ἀνείω, a pres. assumed by the Gramm. for the aor. forms ἀνέσαντες and ἀνέσαιμι; but see ἀνεῖσα.
ἄνειμι (εἶμι), partcp. ἀνιών, imperf. ἀνήϊον 1) to ascend, to arise, ἐς περιωπήν, Od. 10, 146. ἠελίου ἀνιόντος, the sun arising, 8, 536. Od. 1, 24 [here = the east]. 2) to return, ἐκ πολέμου, 6, 480; ἐξ Αἰθιόπων, Od. 5, 282; to return home by ship, Od. 10, 332. 3) Mly ἐς τινά, to approach any one, adire aliquem, to ask a favour, 22, 492.
ἀνείμων, ον (εἷμα), gen. ονος, without clothing, destitute of clothing. Od. 3, 348.†
ἀνείρομαι (εἴρομαι), poet. for ἀνέρομαι, only pres. and imperf. to ask, to inquire, to interrogate; with accus. of person, also with double accus. ὅ μ' ἀνείρεαι, ἠδὲ μεταλλᾷς, about which thou questionest me and inquirest, 3, 177.
ἀνεῖσα (εἷσα), a defective aor. 1, of which only the 1 sing. optat. ἀνέσαιμι and partcp. ἀνέσαντες occur: to place upon. ἐς δίφρον ἀνέσαντες ἄγον, they placed him upon the chariot and bore him, 13, 657. εἰ κείνω γε—εἰς εὐνὴν ἀνέσαιμι, If I could but bring them to the marriage-bed, 14, 209. (The Gramm. derive these forms from the obsol. pres. ἀνέζω. Eustath. ad Il. 14, 209, explains both by ἀναθεῖναι; hence with Thiersch, Gram. § 226. Anm., it must be derived from the defective aor. εἷσα. The derivation of the aor. ἀνέσαιμι from ἀνίημι, according to Buttm., Gram. § 108, 4, is inadmissible, as no where else does an aor. 1 optat. of this form occur. [See, however, Krüger Zweiter Theil, § 38, 1, 6. p. 97, and under εἷσα.]
ἀνεκτός, όν (ἔχω), to be borne, sufferable, endurable; in H. mly with negat. ἔργα, οὐδ' ἔτι ἀνεκτά, 1, 573. Od. 20, 223. οὐκέτ' ἀνεκτῶς, no longer tolerable, 8, 355.
ἀνελθών, partcp. aor. 2 from ἀνέρχομαι.
ἀνέλκω (ἕλκω), to draw upward, to draw up; τόξου πῆχυν, to draw up the curve of the bow, in order to shoot [cf. τόξον], 11, 375. 13, 583; but also νευρήν, to draw the bow-string, Od. 21, 128. 150; σταθμόν, 12, 434. 2) Mid. to draw out for oneself; τρίχας, to tear one's hair, 22, 77; ἔγχος, to draw forth the lance from the body of an enemy, Od. 22, 97.

Άνελών. 46 Άνεω.

άνελών, see άναιρέω.
άνεμος, ό (άημι). *a blowing, a breeze, wind.* H. mentions only four winds: Eurus, Notus, Zephyrus, and Boreas, Od. 5, 295.
άνεμοσκεπής, ές, poet. (σκέπας), gen. έος, *guarding against the wind, warding off the wind*, epith. of the mantle, 16, 224.†
άνεμοτρεφής, ές, poet. (τρέφω), gen. έος, *nourished by wind, storm-nursed.* It occurs twice: κύμα, a wave excited by the wind, 15, 625; έγχος, a spear whose handle is taken from a tree which has been exposed to the wind, and thus become firm in fibre, 11, 256.
Άνεμώλεια, ή, see Άνεμώρεια.
άνεμώλιος, ιον (άνεμος), *windy;* only trop. *useless, idle, unprofitable, vain.* άνεμώλια βάζειν, to prate idle words, 4, 355. Od. 4, 837.
Άνεμώρεια, ή, later Άνεμώλεια, a town in Phocis near Delphi, that derived its name from the strong winds which swept it from Parnassus, 2, 521.
άνενείκατο, see άναφέρω.
άνέπαλτο, see άναπάλλω.
άνερείπομαι, depon. mid. (έρείπω [utsφάλλειν, *ad casum dare*, άνασφάλλειν, *resurgere*, eodem modo έρείψαι *est dejicere*, άνερείψαι, *sustollere*, *et in altum levare*. Lob. Tech. 44]), aor. 1 άνερειψάμην, *to snatch up, to bear away, upwards, to carry off;* with accus. spoken esply of the Harpies and of a tempest, Od. 1, 241. 4, 727; once of the gods, 20, 234 (to assume a pres. άνερείπτω is not necessary, cf. Buttm., Gr. Gram. p. 131).
άνερύω (έρύω), *to draw up, to hoist,* ιστία, the sails, Od. 9, 77, in tmesis.
άνέρχομαι (έρχομαι), aor. 2 άνήλυθον, *to go up, to ascend,* ές σκοπιήν, a watchtower, a place of observation, Od. 10, 97; trop. spoken of a young tree: *to grow up, to shoot up*, Od. 6, 163. 167. 2) *to come back, to return,* with which άψ and αύθις stand, 4, 392. 6, 187.
άνερωτάω (έρωτάω), imperf. άνηρώτων, *to question, to ask again,* Od. 4, 251.†
άνέσαιμι, see άνείσα.
άνεσαν, see άνίημι.
άνέσαντες, see άνείσα.
άνέσει, Ep. for άνήσει, see άνίημι.
άνέσσυτο, see άνασεύω.
άνέστιος, ον (εστία), *without a hearth, without a home,* 0, 63.†
άνευ, adv. with gen. *without, apart from;* spoken of persons and things. άνευ θεού, without god, without the will or influence of a god, Od. 2, 372. άνευ έμέθεν, without my wish and knowledge, 15, 232. 2) *far from, remote from.* άνευ δηίων, far from the enemy, 16, 239.
άνευθε, and before a vowel άνευθεν (άνευ), *far, remote, far off,* absol. often with partcp. ών, ούσα, όν, far-distant; κιών, *going away,* 1, 35; according to Plat. άποχωρών. 2) With gen. like άνευ, *without, apart, from.* άνευθε θεού, without god, without divine co-operation, 5, 185. άνευθεν έμείο, 16, 80. *b) remote,*

far from. άνευθε πατρός τε φίλων τε, 21, 78. Od. 10, 554.
άνέφελος, ον (νεφέλη), *unclouded, cloudless,* Od. 6, 44.† (ā)
άνέχω (έχω), 3 sing. indicat. pres. άνέχησι, Od. 19, 111; fut. άνέξω, aor. 2 άνέσχον, poet. άνέσχεθον, fut. mid. άνέξομαι and άνασχήσομαι, Ep. infin. άνσχήσεσθαι, aor. 2 mid. άνεσχόμην, Ep. imperat. άνσχεο and άνάσχεο. 1) Act. *to hold up, to raise, to lift up,* with accus. κεφαλήν, Od. 17, 291 ; often χείρας θεοίς άνέχ., to raise the hands to the gods in prayer; once to lift the hands for a pugilistic combat, Od. 18, 89; comm. the mid. σκήπτρον θεοΐσι, to raise the sceptre to the gods (in swearing), 7, 412, hence trop. *to maintain; εύδικίας, to maintain righteousness, justice,* Od. 19, 111. *r) to hold back, to check, to restrain,* ίππους, 23, 426. 3) Intrans. *to project, to arise, emerge.* αίχμή άνέσχεν, the spear's head projected, 17, 310; *to emerge* from the water, Od. 5, 320. II) Mid. 1) Prop. *to hold oneself up, to keep erect,* not to fall, esply spoken of the wounded, 5, 285; hence metaph , *a) to bear, to endure,* comm. with accus. κήδεα, κακά, once with gen. δουλοσύνης άνέχεσθαι, *to endure slavery,* Od. 22, 423; In the dependent clause stands for the most part a partcp. as with verbs of suffering : ούκ άνέξομαί σε άλγε' έχοντα for έχειν, I will not suffer thee to endure, etc. 5, 895. παρά σοίγ' άνεχοίμην ήμενος, I could bear to sit by thee, Od. 4, 595. ξείνους άνέχεσθαι, to suffer strangers among, Od. 7, 32 ; hence, *to receive hospitably,* Od. 17, 13. *b)* Absol. *to hold out, to restrain oneself;* often τέτλαθι καί άνάσχεο, bear up and command thyself, 1, 586. 5, 382. 2) *to hold up, to elevate,* like άνέχειν (when the discourse relates to things belonging to us), with accus. σκήπτρον, the sceptre, to swear, 10, 321 ; δούρατα, to raise the spear for hurling, 11, 593. 12, 138; χείρας, to raise the hands to smite oneself for grief, 22, 34; and for joy, Od. 18, 100. The partcp. pres. άνασχόμενος stands often absol. *to rise, to raise oneself* (for striking), where from the preceding something may be sometimes supplied, as ξίφος, 3, 362. It is not necessary, however, with Eustath., to supply χείρα at 23, 666. Od. 14, 25. 18, 95. (In Od. 24, 8, άνά τ' άλλήλησιν έχονται, άνά is a prepos. with the dat.: they hold one by another, i. e. hang together.

άνεψιός, ό, *a sister's son;* and mly a kinsman by blood, *a cousin*, *9, 464 (with ι lengthened 15, 554).
άνέω, obsol. theme of άνίημι.
άνεω, usually written άνεω, as if from an obsol. adj. άνανος, άνάος, άνεως (from άω, άύω), and regarded as a nom. plur. Att. decl. *noiseless, still, silent:* but its use with the *sing.* (and with reference to a *fem.* noun) in Od. 23, 93, ή δ' άνεω δήν ήστο is against this supposition. It occurs usually only with the plur. έγέ-

'Ανήγαγον. 47 Ανίη.

νέσθε, έγένοντο, ήσαν. According to Buttm. Lex. p. 107, it is, as even Aristarchus supposed, an adv. like ούτω, and should therefore be written άνεω without ι.

ανήγαγον, see ανάγω.
ανήη, Ep. for άνῇ, see ανίημι.
ανήκεστος, ον (ακέομαι), not to be healed, incurable, intolerable, χόλος, άλγος, *5, 394. 15, 217.
ανηκουστέω (ακούω), aor. ανηκούστησα, not to hearken to, not to obey, τινός, any one, *15, 230.
ανήμελκτος, ον, poet. (αμέλγω), unmilked, Od. 9, 439.†
ανήνοθε, Ep. ('ΑΝΕΘΩ), 3 sing. perf. 2, which occurs partly in the signif. of the present to mark a concluded action, and partly in narration as a preterite, to issue forth, to spring up. αἷμ' ἔτι θερμὸν ἀνήνοθεν ἐξ ὠτειλῆς, the blood still warm gushed from the wound, 11, 266; and κνίσση ανήνοθεν, the smoke of the fat rolls upward, Od. 17, 270. (It is comm. referred to ανθέω, see Thiersch, Gram. § 232, 20, but, according to Buttm. Lex. p. 134, the theme is άνθω, ανέθω, lengthened by redupl.)
ανήνυστος, ον (ανύω), not to be accomplished, unaccomplished, έργον, Od. 16, 111.
ανήνωρ, ορος, ὁ (ανήρ), not a man, unmanly, cowardly, *Od. 10, 340, 341.
ανήρ, gen. ανέρος and ανδρός, dat. pl. ανδράσι and ανδρεσσι, a man, as opposed to a woman, 17, 435; also with the idea of bravery, ανέρες έστε, φίλοι, be men, 5, 529, cf. αναξ ανδρών. 2) man, in opposition to a god, πατήρ ανδρών τε θεών τε. 3) man, in opposition to a youth; and, 4) a husband, 19, 291. Od. 11, 327. Very common is the junction of this word with another subst. or adj. as ανήρ βασιλεύς, ανήρ ήρως, ανήρ Αργείος, by which the expression becomes more honorable. (α is prop. short, but in the arsis and in the trisyllabic cases always long.)
ανήροτος, ον (αρόω), unploughed, uncultivated, *Od. 9, 109. 123.
ανήθω, see ανάπτω.
Άνθεια, ἡ, a town in Messenia, according to Strab. the later Thuria, 9, 151.
Ανθεμίδης, ου, ὁ, Ep. for Ανθεμιωνιάδης, son of Anthemiōn, 4, 488.
Ανθεμίων, ωνος, ὁ, father of Simoeisius in Troy, 4, 473.
ανθεμόεις, εσσα, εν (άνθεμον), flowery, blooming, epith. of meadows, 2, 467. 2)

ανθέριξ, ικος, ὁ (αθήρ), the beard on the ear of corn; an ear of corn, 20, 227.†
ανθέω, aor. 1 ήνθησα, infin. ανθήσαι, to shoot up, to grow up; in this prob. prim. signif. it is found in Od. 11, 320. †h. Ap. 139.
Άνθηδών, ονος, ἡ, a town in Bœotia, on the coast, with a port, 2, 508.
ανθινός, ή, όν (άνθος), of flowers, flowery. εἶδαρ άνθινον, food from flowers, Od. 9, 84.† Thus Hom. calls the fruit of the lotus, which the Lotophagi ate; prob. merely a poet. designation of a vegetable diet formed from blossoms; others explain it metaph. delicate.
ανθίστημι (ίστημι), aor. 2 αντέστην, trans. to place opposite. 2) Intrans. aor. 2 and mid. to oppose oneself to, to resist, τινί, any one, 20, 70; absol. 16, 305. *11.
άνθος, εος, τό (ανά), prop. the shooting bud, τέρεν άνθεα, Od. 9, 449; comm. a blossom, a flower, 2, 89. 9, 542; trop. ήβης άνθος, the bloom of youth, 13, 484; κουρήϊον, h. Cer. 108.
ανθρακιή, ἡ (άνθραξ [which Lob. thinks may be related to αίθω: he compares candeo, carbo]), a heap of coals, 9, 213.†
άνθρωπος, ὁ, man, as a race, and as an individual, in distinction from gods and brutes; also the dead are called άνθρωποι, Od. 4, 565.
'ΑΝΘΩ, assumed theme of ανήνοθε.
ανιάζω (ανία), trans. to excite disgust, to weary, with accus. 23, 721; to distress, to afflict, Od. 19, 323. 2) Intrans. to be displeased, to be weary. to be tired, of a thing, Od. 4, 460. 598; then to be grieved, to grieve oneself, with dat. κτεάτεσσιν, about his possessions, 18, 300. (ι either long or short in H.)
ανιάω (ανία), Ion. and Ep. ανιήσω, partcp. aor. pass. ανιηθείς = ανιάζω, to weary, to vex, with accus. Od. 2, 115. Pass. to be burdened. οὐ γάρ τίς τοι ανιάται παρεόντι, no one is burdened by thy presence, Od. 15, 335; esply and often, ανιηθείς, absol. dejected, disgusted, troubled. ["Η μήν καί πόνος εστίν ανιηθ. κ.τ.λ. (1) nimirum laboribus fungimur, ut moleste ferentes redire velimus. Lehrs. The toil is undoubtedly one for returning home, from weariness and disgust; or (as Felton translates it) truly the labour is such that one might justly wish to return, being worn out by the long-continued fatigue of the war, 2, 291. (2) N. presses the aor. partcp. perpessos diuturnæ man-

'Ανιηθείς.   'Ανοστάς.

eure.' Cp.]: thus Scylla is called, *Od. 12, 221. (ι always long.)

ἀνιηθείς, see ἀνιάω.

ἀνίημι (ἴημι), fut. ἀνιήσω, once ἀνέσει, Od. 18, 265, aor. 1 ἀνῆκα and ἀνῆκα, aor. 2 only 3 plur. ἄνεσαν, subj. ἀνίῃ for ἀνῇ, optat. ἀνείην, partcp. plur. ἀνέντες. I) Act. *to send up, to let ascend*. ἀήτας Ὠκεανός ἀνίησιν, Oceanus sends up the blasts of Zephyr, Od. 4, 568; ὕδωρ, *to cast up water*, opposed to ἀναροιβδεῖν, spoken of Charybdis, Od. 12, 105. (Here also have been cited ἀνέσαντες, ἀνέσαιμι, *to place upon*, see ἀνείσα.) 2) Comm. *to let loose*, hence a) *to let go, to leave.* ὕπνος ἀνῆκεν ἐμέ, sleep left me, 2, 71. δεσμῶν τινὰ ἀν., to free any one from bonds, Od. 8, 359; to liberate, as opposed to ἀλῶναι, Od. 18, 265; according to others, *to send home*. b) *to loosen, to open*, πύλας, the gates, 21, 587 (i. e. by undoing the bars of the gates which secured them on the inside). c) Esply, *to let loose upon any one, to send upon, to set upon*. σοὶ δ' ἐπὶ τοῦτον ἀνῆκεν 'Αθήνη, *tibi hunc immisit*, 5, 405; and ἄφρονα τοῦτον, v. 761; hence mly *to excite, to urge, to incite*, Ζεὺς—ἀνῆκεν, 15, 691; τοῖσιν (for them, for their aid) Θρασυμήδεα δῖον ἀνῆκεν, 17, 705; often with infin. Μοῦσα ἀοιδὸν ἀνῆκεν ἀείδειν, the muse excited the bard to sing, Od. 8, 73. σὲ δ' ἐνθάδε θυμὸς ἀνῆκεν ἀνασχεῖν, 6, 236. 7, 25. II) Mid. *to loosen for oneself, to open*; with accus. κόλπον, to bare the bosom, 22, 80; αἶγας, to draw the skin from the goats, to flay them, Od. 2, 300. (ι short, but used long if the metre requires it.)

ἀνιηρός, ή, όν (ἀνία), *burdensome, troublesome, sad*; πτωχός, a troublesome beggar; compar. ἀνιηρέστερος, Od. 2, 190.

ἀνιπτόπους, ποδος, ὁ, ἡ (νίπτω, πούς), *with unwashed feet*, 16, 235. †epith. of the Σελλοί, the priests of Zeus at Dodona, to indicate their rough mode of life; as they probably lived like a kind of monks, destitute of every convenience.

ἄνιπτος, ον (νίπτω), *unwashed*, 6, 266.†

ἀνίστημι (ἵστημι), fut. ἀναστήσω, Ep. ἀνστήσω, aor. 1 ἀνέστησα, imper. ἀνστῆσον, Ep. for ἀνάστησον, aor. 2 ἀνέστην; dual ἀνστήτην, Ep. for ἀνεστήτην, partcp. ἀνστάς, for ἀναστάς. I) Trans. in the pres. imperf. and aor. 1 act. *to cause to rise*, with accus. of the person sitting, *to chase away, to scatter*, 1, 191; γέροντα χειρός, to raise the old man by the hand, 24, 515; *to wake out of sleep*, κήρυκα, the herald, 24, 689; to wake to life the dead, 24, 551. 756; from an abode, i. e. *to cause to emigrate*, Od. 6, 7; metaph. *to excite, to instigate*, esply to combat, τινί, against any one, 7, 116. 10, 176. II) Intrans. in the aor. 2 perf. act. and mid. *to get up, to arise*, from a seat, in order to speak, τινί, to any one, 1, 58. v. 205; ἐξ ἑδέων, 1, 533; from an encampment, 10, 55. 2) *to rise* from rest for combat, 2, 694; τινί, against any one, 23, 635. Od. 18, 334; to

arise again, spoken of the wounded and dead, 15, 287. 21, 56.

ἀνίσχω (ἴσχω), a form of ἀνέχω, *to lift up*, χεῖρας θεοῖσι, 8, 347; mid. *to command oneself, to endure*, 7, 110.

ἀνιχνεύω (ἰχνεύω), *to trace out, to track*, 20, 192.†

ἀννεῖται, poet. for ἀνανεῖται, see ἀνανέομαι. Od.

ἀνεξηραίνω, poet. for ἀναξηραίνω.

ἀνοήμων, ον (νοήμων), *without reason, senseless, imprudent*, *Od. 2, 270. 17, 273.

ἀνόητος, ον (νοέω), *unobserved, unperceived* [*not to be comprehended, wonderful*], h. Merc. 80.

ἀνοίγνυμι, poet. ἀνοίγω and ἀναοίγω (οἴγνυμι), imperf. ἀνέῳγεν and ἀνῷγεν, and Ep. iterative ἀναοίγεσκον, 24, 455; *to open, to unlock, to undo*, θύρας, the doors, Od.: κληῖδα, to open, thrust back the bolt, 24, 455, see κληίς; ἀπὸ χηλοῦ πῶμα, to remove the cover from a chest, 16, 221.

ἀνόλεθρος, ον (ὄλεθρος), *not destroyed, snatched from destruction, unslain*, 13, 761.†

ἀνομαι, see ἄνω.

ἄνοος, ον (νόος), *thoughtless, senseless, devoid of mind*, 21, 441.†

ἀνοπαία, or ἀνόπαια according to Aristarchus, Od. 1, 320; ὄρνις ὡς ἀνοπαία διέπτατο, an ancient word about whose meaning the Gramm. are at variance. Most probably ἀνοπαία is an adverb. =ἀνωφερές, *she flew away upwards*; as Empedocles, according to Eustathius, employed it (καρπαλίμως δ' ἀνόπαιον). Herodian likewise explains it as an adverb, for ἀοράτως, *invisibly* (from α and ὄπω = ὄπτομαι). Others, as Aristarchus, write ἀνόπαια, and regard it as a kind of eagle, like the sea-eagle; others again write ἀν' ὀπαῖα, from ὀπαῖον, the aperture for smoke; hence Voss, 'quick through the aperture for smoke she flew.' So also Nitzsch.

ἀνορούω (ὀρούω), aor. 1 ἀνόρουσα, without augm. *to arise suddenly, to spring up, to ascend*, ἐκ θρόνων and ἐξ ὕπνου, from the seats, from sleep; ἐς δίφρον, to spring upon the chariot, 11, 273; and spoken of the sun: 'Ἠέλιος ἀνόρουσεν ἐς οὐρανόν, the sun mounted quickly up the sky, Od. 3, 1.

ἀνόστιμος, ον (νόστιμος), *without return, who cannot return*; ἀνόστιμον τιθέναι, to prevent a person's return, Od. 4, 182.†

ἄνοστος, ον (νόστος), *without return, not returning*, Od. 24, 528.†

ἄνουσος, ον (νοῦσος), *without sickness, in health, well*, Od. 14, 255.†

ἀνούτατος, ον (οὐτάω), *not wounded*, distinguished from ἄβλητος; esply not wounded with the sword, *unclouen*, 4, 540.†

ἀνουτητί, adv. *unwounded*, 22, 371.†

ἀνστάς, ἀνστήσων, ἀνστήσων, ἀνστήτην, abbrev. Ep. for ἀναστάς, etc. from ἀνίστημι.

Άνστρέψειαν. 49 Άντιβολέω.

άνστρέψειαν, poet. for άναστρέψειαν, Il.
άνσχεθέειν, άνσχεω, poet. for άνασχεθεῖν, άνάσχου, from άνέχω.
άνσχετος, poet. for άνάσχετος. Od.
άντα (άντί, 1) *against, opposite*, face to face, esply with μάχεσθαι. στῆ άντα σχομένη, she stood, with her face turned towards him, Od. 6, 141; metaph. θεοῖσι άντα ἐώκει, he resembled the gods, face to face, i. e. plainly, 24, 630. άντα τιτυσκόμενος, *straight* before him *at* the object, Od. 21, 48. II) Prep. with gen. *opposite, before.* 'Ηλιδος άντα, opposite Elis, 2, 626. άντ' Αίαντος έείσατο, against Ajax, 15, 415. άντα παρειάων σχέσθαι κρήδεμνα, to hold a veil before the cheeks, Od. 1, 334. άντα σέθεν, *before thee,* in thy presence, Od. 4, 115. *b*) Esply in a hostile sense, *against*; άντα Διὸς πολεμίζειν, to fight against Zeus, 8, 428. cf. v. 424.

άντάξιος, ον (άξιος), prop. standing in equipoise, *equal in worth, equivalent*; with the gen. ιητρὸς άνὴρ πολλῶν άντάξιος άλλων, worth as much as many others, 11, 514; hence the neut. οὐκ ἐμοὶ ψυχῆς άντάξιον, not an equivalent to me for life, 9, 401. *II.

*άνταποδίδωμι (δίδωμι), aor. 2 άνταποδοῦναι, *to give again, to give back, to restore,* Batr. 187.

άντάω (άντα), imperf. ήντεον, fut. άντήσω, aor. ήντησα. The pres. άντάω does not occur in H.=άντιάω, 1) With gen. *to meet* any one (designedly), 16, 423; spoken of things: *to happen upon, to engage in,* to partake of; as μάχης, δαίτης, ὀπωπῆς, to meet the sight, to see, Od. 3, 97. 2) With dat. *to meet* any one (by chance), to fall in with any one, 6, 339; absol. 4, 375.

'Αντεια, ἡ, *Antēa,* daughter of king Iobates in Lycia, wife of Prœtus; in the tragic poets *Sthenoboia,* 6, 160.

άντέχω (έχω), imper. aor. 2 mid. άντίσχεσθε, *to hold against, to hold before*; mid. *to hold before oneself,* τί τινος, something against any thing; τραπέξας ἰῶν, to oppose the table to the arrows, Od. 22, 74.†

άντην, adv. (άντί [*Lob.* thinks it an *adverbial acc.*, like πέραν, fm άντη; which Hermann reads in Soph. El. 175 in the sense of a *prayer*]), 1) *opposite, against,* άντην ἵστασθαι, to place oneself in opposition, 11, 590. 2) *directly forwards, ex adverso*; ἔρχεσθαι, to go forward, 8, 399. άντην βαλλόμενος, hit, wounded in the breast, 12, 152. 3) *in the face of, openly, visibly.* άντην εἰσιδεῖν, to look in the face. άντην άγαστάξειν, to love visibly, 24, 464. όμοιωθήμεναι άντην, visibly to compare, to vie, with any one, 1, 187. Od. 3, 120. In the last phrase some give it the signif. *placed before,* i. e. in direct comparison with others [as Passow, with reason]; θεῷ ἐναλίγκιος άντην, very similar, Od. 2, 5.

'Αντηνορίδης, ao, ὁ, son of Antenor, 3, 123.

'Αντήνωρ, ορος, ὁ (contending with a man, conf. άντιάνειρα), son of Æsyetes and Cleomestra, husband of Theano, father of Agenor, Acamas, etc.; one of the wisest of the Trojan princes, who advised in vain the surrender of Helen and the restoration of her effects. According to a later tradition, he emigrated, after the destruction of Troy, to Italy, and built there Padua, 3, 184. 7, 347.

άντί, prepos. with gen. 1) Of place: *opposite, against,* άντὶ όφθαλμοῖιν, before the eyes, Od. 4, 115. Wolf, however, has άντα, as in 15, 415, and in other places άντί for άντία, cf. 8, 233. 21, 481. 2) Commonly spoken of an equivalent, a comparison: *in place of, instead, for.* άντὶ πολλῶν λαῶν ἐστὶν άνήρ, one man is equal to many, 9, 116. άντὶ κασιγνήτου ξεῖνος τέτυκται, a guest is instead of, i. e. equal to, like a brother, Od. 8, 546. τῶνδ' άντί, 23, 650; separated from the word governed, 21, 75.

άντία, adv. prop. neut. plur. from άντίος.

άντιάνειρα, ἡ (άνήρ), fem. occurring only in the nom. and accus. plur.: *manlike, masculine,* epith. of the Amazons, *II. (Masc. άντιάνωρ is not used.)

άντιάω, Ep. άντιόω, for άντιῶ (άντί), aor. 1 ήντίασα; poet. form άντάω and άντομαι, *to go against, to meet.* 1) With gen. of the person: *to meet* any one, chiefly from design, both with a good intention, as Od. 24, 56, and with a bad: *to go against in battle, to attack,* 7, 231. *b*) Spoken of things: πολέμοιο, μάχης, to go against the war, the battle, to engage in it, 13, 215. 20, 125; of the gods: *to accept, to receive, to enjoy,* the gods being regarded as present and participating; ἑκατόμβης, ἱρῶν, to accept of a hecatomb, of victims, 1, 67. Od. 1, 25. 3, 436. 2) With the dat. *to meet any one by accident, to fall in with,* Od. 18, 147; ἐμῷ μένει, 6, 127. 3) With accus. *to go to,* in order to prepare; ἐμὴν λάχος άντιόωσα, preparing my couch, only 1, 31. II) Mid. as depon. *to take part,* with gen. γάμου, in the wedding, 24, 62.

άντιβίην, adv. (βίη), prop. accus. fem. from άντίβιος, *contending against, face to face, in a hostile manner;* ἐρίζειν τινί, to contend perversely with any one. 1, 278; ἐπέρχεσθαί τινι, to rush upon any one, 5, 220. *II.

άντίβιος, η, ον (βίος), prop. using force against any one, *contentious, hostile*; only dat. άντιβίοισιν ἐπέσσι, Il. and Od. The neut. άντίβιον as adv. *against*; μάχεσθαί τινι, to fight against any one, 3, 435.

άντιβολέω (άντιβολή), aor. άντεβόλησα, 11, 809, *to go against, to approach. a*) With gen. of the thing: *purposely to approach,* to take part in; μάχης, τάφου, the battle, the funeral solemnity, 4, 342. Od. 4, 547. *b*) With the dat. *to meet by chance,* to fall in with; comm. spoken of the pers. 7, 114; rarely of things; φόνῳ, to be present at the slaughter, Od. 11, 416. 24, 87. (Buttm. Lex. p. 122, rejects άντεβόλησα.)

ἀντίθεος, η, ον (θεός), godlike, divine, mly distinguished, comm. epith. of heroes, in reference to descent, strength, and physical advantages; also of the companions of Ulysses, Od. 4, 571; sometimes of nations, 12, 408. Od. 6, 241; rarely of women. ἀντιθέη ἄλοχος, Od. 11, 117. 13, 378; of Polyphemus, Od. 1, 70; and of the suitors, Od. 14, 18.

ἀντίθυρος, ον (θύρα), opposite the door; hence, κατ' ἀντίθυρον κλισίης, Od. 16,159.†

Ἀντίκλεια, ἡ, daughter of Autolycus, wife of Laertes, mother of Ulysses and Ctimĕnē; she died from grief for her absent son, 11, 85. 15, 362.

Ἀντίκλος, ὁ, a Greek who was with Ulysses in the wooden horse before Troy, Od. 4, 286.

ἀντικρύ, adv. (prob. from ἀντικρούω), 1) directly opposite, against; like ἄντην, e. g. μάχεσθαι, 5, 130. 819; ἀπόφημι, to say face to face, to one's face, openly, 7, 362; with gen. 8, 301. 2) directly through, straight forward; ἀντικρὺ δι' ὤμου, straight through the shoulder, 4, 481; hence also throughout, entirely, διαμᾶν, 3, 359. (ἀντικρύς is not Homeric. ν is origin. anceps, but in H. always long, except 5, 130.)

Ἀντίλοχος, ὁ (opposing the ambuscade), eldest son of Nestor and Eurydĭcē; according to Od. 3, 452 (of Anaxibia, Apd). He accompanied his father to Troy, distinguished himself by brave deeds, and was beloved by Achilles, 23, 556. At the funeral games of Patroclus he received, in chariot-racing, the second prize; in running, the last, 18, 623 sqq. He was killed before Troy by Memnon, king of the Æthiopians, Od. 4, 188.

Ἀντίμαχος, ὁ (fighting against), a Trojan, father of Hippolochus, Pisander, and Hippomachus, who insisted most strenuously that Helen should not be surrendered, 11, 122 sqq.

Ἀντίνοος, ὁ, son of Eupīthes, the most impudent among the suitors. He hurled the stool at Ulysses, excited Irus against him, and was slain by him, Od. 4, 660. 18, 46. 22, 15 sqq.

ἀντίον, adv. see ἀντίος.

Ἀντιόπη, ἡ, daughter of Asōpus, mother of Amphion and Zethus, Od. 11, 260. According to Apd. daughter of Nycteus.

ἀντίος, η, ον (ἀντί), against, opposite, towards, in both a good and bad signif. ἀντίος ἔστη, he stood opposite, i. e. before him; ἦλθεν, he came towards. Il. b) Comm. with gen. ὅστις τοῦγ' ἀντίος ἔλθοι, whoever should come towards it, 5, 301; rarely with dat. 7, 20. 20, 22. 2) The neut. sing. ἀντίον, and plur. ἀντία, often stand as adv., 1) towards, against, before, with gen. ἀντίον ἰέναι τινός, to go against any one. 5, 256; ἀντι' Ἀλεξάνδροιο, 3, 425; ἀντία (before) δεσποίνης φάσθαι, Od. 15, 377. 2) In a hostile signif. against. ἀντίον εἰπεῖν, to contradict, 1, 230. στήμεναι ἀντία τινός, to withstand any one, 22, 253. μάχεσθαι ἀντία τινός,

20, 88. Od. 1, 79, with gen. (In ἀντίον αὐδᾶν τινά, to speak against, i. e. to answer any one the accus. depends upon αὐδᾶν; in like manner with εἰπεῖν.)

ἀντιόω. Ep. for ἀντιῶ, see ἀντιάω.

ἀντιπεραῖος, η, ον (ἀντιπεράς), lying opposite, esply beyond the sea. τὰ ἀντιπεραῖα, the opposite coast, 2, 635.†

ἀντιόχεσθε, see ἀντέχω.

*ἀντίτομος, ον (τέμνω), cut against; the neut. τὸ ἀντίτομον, an antidote, chiefly from roots, h. Cer. 229.

ἀντιτορέω (τορέω), aor. 1 ἀντετόρησα, to perforate, to pierce through; spoken of a spear: with gen. χροός, 5, 337. 2) to break through, with accus. δόμον, 10, 267. h Merc. 178. (ἀντιτορήσων is the reading of Herm. for αὐτοπρεπὴς ὡς, v. 86; ὁδόν, to accomplish the way.)

ἄντιτος, ον, poet. for ἀνάτιτος (τίω), requited again. ἄντιτα ἔργα, deeds of recompense or vengeance, Od. 17, 51. τότ' ἄντιτα ἔργα γένοιτο παιδὸς ἐμοῦ, then would there be deeds of vengeance for my son, 24, 213.

Ἀντιφάτης, αο, ὁ, in the accus. Ἀντιφάτῃ, Od. 10, 116. (1) a Trojan slain by Leonteus, 12, 191.] 2) son of Melampus, father of Oicles, Od, 15, 242. 3) king of the savage, gigantic Læstrygones, who devoured one of the scouts of Ulysses. According to the Schol. a son of Poseidōn, Od. 10, 111 sqq.

ἀντιφερίζω (φέρω), to put oneself against, to compare oneself, τινί, with any one, *21, 357; τί, in any thing, 488.

ἀντιφέρω (φέρω), only in the mid. to put oneself against, to oppose oneself; absol. μάχῃ, 5, 701. Od. 16, 238; prop. τινί, Il. and Od. by a common Græcism. ἀργαλέος Ὀλύμπιος ἀντιφέρεσθαι, it is hard to oppose Olympian [Zeus], 1, 589; with accus. of the thing and dat. of the pers. μένος τινί, one's strength to any one, i. e. to measure strength with any one, 21, 482.

Ἀντίφονος (reciprocally slaying), a younger son of Priam, 24, 250.

Ἄντιφος, ὁ, 1) son of Priam and Hecuba, whom, together with Isus, Achilles bore off, and liberated for a ransom, 4, 490. Agamemnon slew him, 11, 101. 2, son of Pylæmēnes and the nymph Gygæa, a Mæonian and ally of the Trojans, 2, 864. 3) son of Thessalus, leader of the Greeks from Nisyrus and the Calydnian islands, 2, 678. 4) a friend of Ulysses of Ithaca, Od. 17, 68. [5) son of Ægyptius in Ithaca. He accompanied Ulysses to Troy, and was devoured by the Cyclops, Od. 2, 19 seq.]

ἄντλος, ὁ, the bilge-water in a ship's hold; also, the ship's hold itself, Od. 12, 411. 15, 479.

ἀντολή, ἡ, see ἀνατολή.

ἄντομαι, poet. form fr. ἀντάω, only in the mid. pres. and imperf.; prop. to meet; ἀλλήλοισιν ἐν πολέμῳ, to meet one another in battle. 15, 698. Trop. διπλόος ἤντετο θώρηξ, the double cuirass met, i. e.

Ἄντρον.   51   **Ἀοιδή.**

was fastened together [the edges of the cuirass met, so as to lie double one over the other, Döderl.]; according to others, stood in the way, 4, 133. 2) Mly, *to meet, to fall in with*, 2, 595; and with dat. 11, 237.

ἄντρον, τό, *a cave, grotto, cavern*, *Od. 9, 216, and often.

Ἀντρών. ῶνος, ὁ (Ἄντρων, h. Cer. 491), a town in Thessaly on Œta, prob. a place full of caves. 2, 697.

ἄντυξ, ῦγος, ἡ, prop. any *curve* or *circle*; hence, 1) *the rim* or *margin of the shield*, a metallic hoop covered with leather, 6, 118; also *the shield* itself, 14, 412. 2) *the seat-rim*, a margin which extended around upon the two semicircles of the chariot-seat, and terminated in a knob to which the reins were fastened, 5, 262. E. mentions two ἄντυγες, 20, 500. 5, 728; either because the chariot-seat consisted of two semicircles, or because a rim extended around above and below. 3) *a circle*, the path of the planets, h. 7, 8.

ἄνυσις, ιος, ἡ (ἀνύω), *accomplishment, fulfilment, end, completion*. ἄνυσις δ' οὐκ ἔσσεται αὐτῶν, there will be no accomplishment of them, i. e. they will not attain it, 2, 347. οὐκ ἀνυσίν τινα δήομεν, we shall find no end, i. e. we shall effect nothing, Od. 4, 544.

ἀνύω (ἄνω), fut. ἀνύσω, aor. 1 ἤνυσα, fut. mid. ἀνύσομαι, Ep. σσ, 1) *to accomplish, to bring to an end*; with accus., *a) ἔργον*, to finish a work, Od. 5, 243. *b)* to make way. ὅσσον τε νηῦς ἤνυσεν, as much as a ship traversed, sc. ὁδοῦ, Od. 4, 357. cf. 15, 294. *c) to destroy, to consume*, spoken of fire, Od. 21, 71. 2) With partcp. [and negat.] *to achieve nothing*. οὐκ ἀνύω φθονέουσα, by envious resistance I effect nothing, 4, 56. In Od. 10, 373, σὺ γὰρ οἴω, ἀνύσσεσθαι τάδε ἔργα, the Schol. explain the fut. mid. by ἀνυσθῆναι, I do not think these things will be effected. Passow regards it as mid., in which case we must supply ἡμᾶς (a and υ always short).

ἄνω (ᾰ), imperf. ἤνον, akin to ἀνύω, *to finish, to accomplish* ; ὁδόν, to accomplish a journey, Od. 3, 496. Pass. *to be accomplished*, spoken of time ; νὺξ ἄνεται, the night is coming to an end, 10, 251. (Related to the adv. ἄνω, and theme of ἀνύω ; ᾰ long, except 16, 473.)

ἄνω, adv. (ἀνά), *up, upwards, above, over*, Od. 11, 596; spoken of the cardinal points : *northward*, 24, 544.

ἄνωγα, Ep. old perf. without augm. with the signif. of a pres., *I command, bid, order, incite, prompt*; often in connexion with ἐποτρύνω, κέλομαι, very often θυμὸς ἀνώγει or ἀνωγέ με, my mind prompts me, i. e. I desire, with accus. of the pers. and infin. pres. or aor., 2, 280; with dat. only, 10, 531. 16, 339. 20, 139. Of this perf. occur only : ἄνωγας, ἄνωγε, ἄνωγμεν, subj. ἀνώγῃ, optat. ἀνώγοις, imper. ἄνωγε (comm. ἄνωχθι, ἀνωγέτω and ἀνώχθω), ἀνώγετε and ἄνωχθε, infin.

ἀνωγέμεν for ἀνωγέναι, plupf. ἠνώγεα, ἠνώγει, ἠνώγειν. This perf. passes over into the flexion of the pres.; hence, a pres. ἀνώγει, ἀνώγετον [a pres. ἀνώγω defended by Spitzn. ad 18, 90]; 3 perf. ἄνωγε or ἄνωγεν, imperf. ἤνωγον and ἄνωγον, hence fut. ἀνώξω, aor. 1 ἤνωξα, Od. 10, 531. (Buttm. Lex. p. 185, assigns it to an old theme ἄγγω, related to ἀγγέλλω; according to others, an old perf. from ἀνάσσω.)

ἀνώγεεν, see ἀνοίγνυμι.

(ἀνωγέω), obsol. pres. from which is derived the imperf. ἠνώγεον, 7, 394, for which Bentley reads ἤνωγον : Spitz. ἠνώγειν.

ἀνώγω, Ep. fut. ἀνώξω, *to command, to bid*. a new pres. formed from ἄνωγα, q. v.

ἀνωθέω (ὠθέω), aor. part. ἀνώσας, *to push up* or *off*, sc. ναῦν, impelling the ship from land into the high sea, Od. 15, 552.†

ἀνωϊστί, adv. (οἴομαι), *unexpectedly*, Od. 4, 92.†

ἀνώϊστος, ον (οἴομαι), *unexpected, unapprehended, unsuspected*, 21, 39. †Epigr. 14, 1.

ἀνώνυμος, ον (ὄνομα), *nameless, unnamed*, Od. 8, 552.†

ἀνώομαι=ἀνύομαι, a senseless reading in h. Ap. 209, for which μνωόμενος has been proposed, and for which Herm. proposes ἀγαιόμενος.

ἀνωχθι, ἄνωχθε, see ἄνωγα.

ἄξασθε, ἄξαντο, see ἄγω.

ἄξετε, see ἄγω.

ἀξίνη, ἡ (perhaps from ἄγνυμι), *an axe, the battle-axe*, of which the Hom. heroes made use only in exigencies, 13, 612. 15, 711. (ῐ)

ἄξιος, ίη, ιον (ἄγω), prop. equiponderant; hence, 1) *of equal value*; with gen. λέβης βοὸς ἄξιος, a cauldron equal in value to an ox, 23, 885. οὐδ' ἑνὸς ἄξιοί εἰμεν Ἕκτορος, we are not equal to the single Hector, 8, 234. σοὶ δ' ἄξιον ἔσται ἀμειβῆς, viz. δῶρον, it will be to thee worth a recompense, i. e. will bring thee a like present, Od. 1, 318. 2) absol. *worthy, suitable, agreeable*. ἄξια ἄποινα, suitable ransom, 6, 46; ὦνος, Od. 15, 429.

Ἀξιός, ὁ, a river in Macedonia, which flows into the Thermaic gulf, now *Vistrizza*, 2, 849.

ἄξυλος, ον (ξύλον), *without wood*. 2) *not deprived of wood*; ὕλη, an uncut, dense forest, 11, 155.†

Ἄξυλος, ὁ, son of Teuthras from Arisbe in Thrace, slain by Diomedes, 6, 12. (υ is here long.)

ἄξων, ονος, ἡ (ἄγω), *the axle-tree* in a chariot, of iron, brass, or ash-wood; also the entire *wheel*; ὑπὸ δ' ἄξοσι φῶτες ἔπιπτον, the men fell under the wheels. *16, 378.

ἀοιδή, ἡ, later contr. ᾠδή h. Cer. (ἀείδω), 1) *song*, primarily, the gift of song, the art of song, 2, 595. Od. 1, 328. *b)* the act of *singing*, which was comm. accompanied by the harp, Od. 1, 421. 17, 605

D 2

Άοιδιάω. 52 Άπαμείβομαι.

2) *song, poem* which was sung. στονόεσσα ἀοιδή, an elegy, 24, 721. 3) the subject of the song: *story, report, tradition*, Od. 8, 580. 24, 200.

ἀοιδιάω (ἀοιδή), Ep. form fr. ἀείδω, *to sing,* *Od. 5, 61. 10, 227.

ἀοίδιμος, ον (ἀοιδή), *sung, celebrated in song;* in a good sense, h. Ap. 299; in a bad sense, hence *infamous.* 6, 358.†

ἀοιδός, ὁ (ἀείδω), *a singer* and *poet, a bard;* prop. an adj., hence ἀοιδὸς ἀνήρ. The Epic minstrel, in the heroic age, was highly honoured, and kings and sovereigns derived pleasure from his art. Indeed he was often their friend, as one was commissioned by Agamemnon to guard his wife, Od. 3, 267. He was, like the μάντις, inspired by a deity, and hence holy and inviolable; he was αὐτοδίδακτος: no one taught him his art (Od. 22, 347), but a god bestowed upon him the gift. It was the Muses chiefly who inspired him and aided his memory, Od. 8, 73.

ἀολλής, ές (related to εἴλω and ἔλλω), *gathered together, all together, crowded;* always in the plur. οἱ δ' ἅμα ἀΐστώθησαν ἀολλέες, they all disappeared together, Od. 10, 259; spoken esply of armies: ἀολλέες ὑπέμειναν, in thick array they maintained their ground, 5, 498.

ἀολλίζω (ἀολλής), aor. ἀόλλισα, aor. 1 pass. ἀολλίσθην, *to bring together, to assemble;* with accus. 6, 287. Pass. *to be assembled, to assemble,* 15, 588. *11.

ἄορ, ἄορος, τό (ἀείρω), prop. any weapon which one bears: *the sword,* which was suspended from a belt; with ὀξύ, 21, 173. Od. 11, 24; ταννῆκες, 14, 385. cf. ξίφος. (a in the dissyllabic cases is always long; in the trisyllabic, long in the arsis and short in the thesis.)

ἄορες, οἱ, only in accus. plur. ἄορας, Od. 17, 222.† of doubtful signification. This word is mentioned among several presents. Eustath. and Apollod. explain it to mean *women* [γυναῖκας], considering it a metathesis for ὄαρας; others explain it to mean *tripods,* or *cauldrons,* λέβητες (with handles for hanging). Prob. it is, with Hesych., to be regarded as only a heterogeneous form for ἄορα, *swords;* as some of the Gramm. also read; cf. Thiersch, Gram. § 197, 60.

ἀορτήρ, ῆρος, ὁ (ἀείρω), prop. a belt of any kind from which something hangs, but esply *a sword-belt* = τελαμών, the band from which the sword was suspended, 11, 31. Od. 11, 609. 2) *a thong* from which the wallet hung, Od. 17, 198.

ἀοσσητήρ, ῆρος, ὁ (ἀοσσέω), *a helper, deliverer, defender, protector,* 15, 254. Od. 4, 165.

ἄουτος, ον (οὐτάω), *unwounded, uninjured,* 18, 536.†

ἀπαγγέλλω (ἀγγέλλω), iterat. impf. ἀπαγγέλλεσκον, aor. 1 ἀπήγγειλα, *to bear a message, to announce, to relate,* τινί τι, any thing to any one; with πάλιν, *to report, to bring back information,* Od. 9, 95.

ἀπάγχω (ἄγχω), *to throttle, to strangle,* with accus. Od. 19, 230.†

ἀπάγω (ἄγω), fut. ἀπάξω, aor. 2 ἀπήγαγον, *to bear away, to carry away, to lead away, to conduct,* with accus. Od. 4, 289; often with οἴκαδε, Od. 16, 370; with αὖτις, πατρίδα γαῖαν, *to take back, to convey home,* 15, 706; υἱὸν εἰς Ὀπόεντα, 18, 326. 2) *to bring,* βοῦς, Od. 18, 278.

ἀπαείρω (ἀείρω), Ep. for ἀπαίρω, *to lift up, to bear away.* 2) *to take oneself away, to go away, to depart,* with gen. πόλιος, from the city, 21, 563.†

ἀπαί, poet. for ἀπό.

ἀπαίνυμαι, depon. (αἴνυμαι), Ep. impf. ἀπαίνυντο, *to take away, to take;* with accus. τεύχεα, κῦδος, Il.; νόστον, Od. 12, 419. τί τινος, ἡμισύ τ' ἀρετῆς ἀποαίνυται Ζεὺς ἀνέρος, Zeus takes half of the strength from a man, Od. 17, 322.

Ἀπαισός, ἡ (Παισός, ἡ, 5, 612), a town in Asia Minor, 2, 828.

ἀπαΐσσω (ἀΐσσω), aor. partcp. ἀπαΐξας, *to spring* or *leap down, to hasten down;* with gen. κρημνοῦ, from the rock, 21, 234.†

ἀπαιτίζω (αἰτίζω), poet. form of ἀπαιτέω, *to demand back, to reclaim,* χρήματα, Od. 2, 78.†

ἀπάλαλκε, ἀπαλάλκοι, see ἀπαλέξω.

ἀπάλαμνος, ον, poet. (παλάμη), for ἀπάλαμος, prop. without a hand, hence *helpless, awkward;* ἀνήρ, an irresolute man, 5, 597.†

ἀπαλέξω (ἀλέξω), fut. ξήσω, aor. 1 optat. ἀπαλεξήσαιμι and Ep aor. 2 ἀπάλαλκον, *to ward off, to repel, to hold back,* τινά, Od. 4, 766; τινά τινος, any one from another, 24, 371; with the gen. of the thing, κακότητος, *to hold back any one from destruction, to spare him,* 17, 364; κύνας κεφαλῆς, 22, 348.

ἀπάλθομαι, Ep. (ἀλθέω), fut. ἀπαλθήσομαι, *to heal entirely,* ἕλκεα, *wounds,* *8, 405. 419.

ἀπαλοιάω (ἀλοάω), Ep. aor. 1 ἀπηλοίησα, prop. *to thresh out,* then *to beat in pieces, to crush;* with accus. ὀστέα, 4, 522.†

ἀπαλός, ή, όν (prob. from ἅπτω), *soft* to the touch, *tender;* spoken chiefly of parts of the human body, δειρή, αὐχήν, ἦτορ, 11, 115. Neut. as adv. ἀπαλὸν γελᾶν, *to laugh gently,* Od. 14, 465.

ἀπαλοτρεφής, ές (τρέφω), gen. έος, *well-nursed, well-fattened,* σίαλος, 21, 363.†

*ἀπαλόχρως, ὁ, ἡ (χρώς), accus. plur. ἀπαλόχροας, *having tender skin,* h. Ven. 14.

ἀπαμάω (ἀμάω), aor. 1 ἀπήμησα, *to mow down, to cut off;* with acc. Od. 21, 301. †in tmesis.

*ἀπαμβλύνω (ἀμβλύνω), perf. pass. ἀπήμβλυμαι, *to blunt.* Pass. *to become blunt, to perish,* Ep. 12, 4.

ἀπαμβροτεῖν, see ἀφαμαρτάνω.

ἀπαμείβομαι (ἀμείβω), *to reply, to answer;* chiefly in partcp. ἀπαμειβόμενος προσέφη, Il. and Od.; τινά, Od. 400. 11, 347.

ἀπαμύνω

ἀπαμύνω (ἀμύνω), aor. ἀπήμυνα, to ward off, to hold back, to avert, τί τινι, any thing from any one; λοιγὸν ἡμῖν, to avert destruction from us, 1, 67; κακὸν ἦμαρ Αἰτωλοῖσιν, 9, 597. 2) Mid. a) to defend oneself: πόλις ἣ ἀπαμυναίμεσθα, in which we may defend ourselves, 15, 738. b) to repel from oneself, τινά, 24, 369. Od. 16, 72.

ἀπαναίνομαι, dep. mid. (ἀναίνομαι), aor. 1 ἀπηνηνάμην, to deny utterly, to refuse, to reject, 7, 183; with acc. Od. 10, 297.

ἀπάνευθε, only before a vowel ἀπάνευθεν (ἄνευθε), 1) Adv. far off or away; apart, ἀπάνευθε κιών, going away, 1, 35 [Nägelsbach shows that κιών is to be taken as aor., 'having withdrawn.' ἀποχωρήσας Plat.]; φεύγειν, 9, 478. 2) As prep. with gen. far from, away from, ἀπάνευθε νεῶν, 1, 45; τοκήων, Od. 9, 36; metaph. ἀπάνευθε θεῶν, without the knowledge or against the will of the gods, 1, 549.

ἀπάντῃ or ἀπάντη, adv. (ἅπας), in every direction, 11.; κύκλῳ ἀπάντῃ, all around; on every side, Od. 8, 278.

ἀπανύω (ἀνύω), aor. 1 ἀπήνυσα, to finish entirely; οἴκαδε, sc. τὴν ὁδόν, to accomplish the journey home, Od. 7, 326.†

ἅπαξ, adv. once, *Od. 12, 22b [once for all, at once, Od. 12, 350].

ἀπαράσσω (ἀράσσω), aor. 1 ἀπάραξα, to smite off (κάρη, 14, 497), to strike off or down, with the spear or sword; with accus. τρυφάλειαν, 13, 577; δόρυ ἀντικρύ, 16, 116; χαμᾶζε, to the earth, 14, 497. *ΙΙ.

ἀπαρέσκω (ἀρέσκω), only in the mid. to conciliate entirely, to gain over again. οὐ νεμεσητὸν, βασιλῆα ἄνδρ' ἀπαρέσσασθαι, It cannot be a just subject of censure, to conciliate again a royal personage, when one has been the first to act with passion [or, injustice], 19, 183.† Thus the ancients explained this clause, in harmony with the position of Achilles and Agamemnon (Sch. ἀπαρέσσασθαι, τουτέστι τῆς βλάβης ἀπαλλάξασθαι καὶ ἐξιλάσασθαι). So Damm and Voss. Heyne, considering this opposed to both the sense of the passage and the meaning of ἀπαρέσσασθαι = to be displeased, angry, as it occurs in later writers, refers βασιλῆα ἄνδρα to Achilles: "one must not take it ill if a royal personage is displeased." So Passow and Bothe. But (1) the testimony of Eustath. and the Schol. is adverse to this view; (2) ἀπό in composition often indicates only a strengthening, cf. ἀπειπεῖν, 9, 309; and (3) the apodosis, "we cannot censure a royal personage who is insulted, if he is angry at the insult," does not accord with the protasis, which exhorts Agamemnon to greater moderation. [Surely moderation is recommended, if the want of it justly offends.]

ἀπάρχομαι, depon. mid. (ἄρχω), aor. 1 ἀπηρξάμην, to begin, to commence; used only of the sacred act preceding a sacrifice, which consisted in cutting off some of the hairs from the forehead of the victim and casting them into the fire; hence τρίχας ἀπάρχεσθαι, to cut off the hair, and commence the sacrifice, by throwing it into the fire ['to give the forelock to the flames,' Cp.], 19, 254. Od. 14, 422; and absol. ἀπαρχόμενος, beginning the sacrifice, Od. 3, 446.

ἅπας, ἅπασα, ἅπαν (πᾶς), entire, all, whole, plur. all together. οἶκος ἅπας, the whole house, Od. 4, 616.

ἅπαστος, ον (πάομαι), that has not eaten, fasting, 19, 346. b) With gen. ἐδητύος ἠδὲ ποτῆτος, without taking meat (and =) or drink, Od. 4, 788.

ἀπατάω (ἀπάτη), fut. ἀπατήσω, aor. Ep. ἀπάτησα, to deceive, to mislead, to cheat, to defraud, τινά, any one, 9, 344. Od. 4, 348.

ἀπάτερθε, before a vowel ἀπάτερθεν, adv. (ἄτερ), separated, apart. 2) Prep. with gen. far from, far away from, 5, 445. *ΙΙ.

ἀπάτη, ἡ (ἀπαφεῖν [cf. ἀπαφίσκω]), deceit, deception, fraud, mly in a bad sense, connect. with κακή, 2, 114; also without a bad signif. an artifice, plur. Od. 13, 294.

ἀπατήλιος, ον (ἀπάτη), deceitful, deceptive, wily: -ια βάζει [fallacia loquitur], Od. 14, 127. 157; εἰδώς, practised in deceit, in wiles.

ἀπάτηλος, ον = ἀπατήλιος, 1, 526.† and h. 7, 13.

ἀπατιμάω (ἀτιμάω), aor. ἀπητίμησα, to dishonour, to insult grossly, τινά, 13, 113.†

(ἀπαυράω), Ep. in the pres. obsol. impf. sing. ἀπηύρων, ας, α, as aor. (ἀπηύρατο, Od 4, 646, is an anomalous reading) and partcp. aor. 1 ἀπούρας, to take away, to seize and bear away, to despoil, to rob. a) With double accus. τινά θυμόν, to take away a man's life; in like manner τεύχεα. b) With dat. of the pers. τινί τι, 17, 236. Od. 3, 192. Note.—That it is construed with gen. of pers. seems to be doubtful: 1, 430, τήν ῥα βίῃ ἀέκοντος ἀπηύρων, whom they took away by violence against his will. Here the gen. is absol. or dependent upon βίῃ (by violence offered one unwilling, cf. Od. 4, 646); and in Od. 18, 273, it is governed by ὅλβον. [Cf. however the passages cited by Spitzner ad Il. 15, 186; also Od. 19, 405, and 19, 89; ὅτ' Ἀχιλλῆος γέρας αὐτὸς ἀπηύρων. Am. Ed.] The aor. originally prob. sounded ἀπέfραν (as ἀπέδραν); partcp. ἀπόfρας, hence ἀπούρας; and the pres. ἀποfράω, ἀπαυράω. According to Buttm. (Lex. p. 144) it is related to ἀφρεῖν: according to others to αἱρέω. [So Lob., "non multum abest, quin ἀπαυρᾶν τί τινος latino auferre præmium ab aliquo, auferre aliquid insultum, par et simile esse putem." Lob. Techn. 136.]

(ἀπαφάω), obsol. pres., whence comes ἀπαφίσκω, q. v.

ἀπαφίσκω, Ep. ('ΑΦΩ [cf. ἀκαχίζομαι fm ἀχομαι, Lucus, and as to the meaning the Lat. palpare. Hence the notion is that of stroking down. To this ἀπάτη, -άω are related]), aor. ἤπαφον, infin. ἀπαφεῖν,

Ἀπέειπε. 54 Ἀπέχω.

mid. 3 sing aor. optat. ἀπάφοιτο 1) *to deceive, to cheat, to delude*, τινά, any one, Od. 11, 217. 2) Mid. same signif. with act. μήτις με βροτῶν ἀπάφοιτ' ἐπέεσσιν, lest some one of mortals should deceive me with words, *Od. 23, 216.
ἀπέειπε, see ἀπεῖπον.
ἀπέεργε, see ἀποέργω.
ἀπειλέω (related to the Dor. ἀπελλαί [Doric name for the *popular assembly*; whence ἀπελλάζειν. Of the same family as ἠπ-ύω, ἔπ-ος, ὀψ, Buttm., p. 177]), fut. ἀπειλήσω, prop. *to speak loud, to boast*, cf. 8, 150; hence 1) Mly in a bad sense, *to threaten, to menace*, τινί τι, any thing to any one; and instead of the accus. the infin. 1, 161. Od. 11, 313; ἀπειλάς, to utter threats, 16, 201. 2) In a good signif. *to boast, to vaunt* oneself, Od. 8, 383. b) *to vow, to promise*, 2', 863. 872. (Impf. dual ἀπειλήτην, Od. 11, 313. Cf. Thiersch, § 221, 83. Buttm., § 105, note 16.)
ἀπειλή, ἡ, always plur. [in H.] *boasting* (as the verb), *threatening*, 9, 244. Od. 13, 126. b) *vaunting*, a boastful promise, in a good sense, 20, 83.
ἀπειλητήρ, ῆρος, ὁ, *a boaster, a threatener*, 7, 96.†
ἄπειμι (εἰμί), fut. ἀπέσομαι, poet. σσ, impf. ἀπῆν, Ep. ἀπέην, plur. ἄπεσαν, *to be absent, to be distant*; absol. with gen. τινός, from any one, 17, 278. Od. 19, 169.
ἄπειμι (εἶμι), imper. ἄπιθι, partcp. ἀπιών, *to go forth, to go away, to depart*, chiefly in the partcp. The pres. in the signif. of the fut. Od. 17, 593.
ἀπεῖπον (εἰπεῖν), a defect. aor. 2, a supplement to ἀπόφημι; 3 sing. Ep. ἀπέειπε and ἀπόειπε, subj. ἀποείπω, optat. ἀποεί ποιμι. imper. ἀπόειπε and ἀπόειπε, infin. ἀποειπεῖν, ἀπειπέμεν. 1) In H. only, *to speak out, to utter, to announce*, κρατερῶς, 9, 432; with accus. μῦθον, ἀγγελίην, 7, 416. 9, 309: ἐφημοσύνην, Od. 16, 340. 2) *to refuse, to deny*, τί, any thing, 1. 515; hence also 3) *to denounce*, Od. 1, 91: and *to renounce*, μῆνιν, anger, 19, 35 [ἀπόειπε with gen. 3, 406, where now stands, accord. to Aristarchus correctly, ἀπόειπε, q. v.).
Ἀπειραίη, ἡ, the *Apiræan*, γρηΰς, Od. 7. 8. Eustath. derives it as Dor. from Ἤπειρος from the continent, or from Epirus, but against the quantity of the first syllable; cf. Ἀπείρηθεν.
ἀπειρέσιος, and ἀπερείσιος, poet. lengthened for ἄπειρος, *boundless, unbounded*, γαῖα. 2) Mly *infinite, immeasurably great* or *numerous*, ἄποινα, 1, 13; δίζύς, ἄνθρωποι.
Ἀπείρηθεν, adv. either *from the continent*, or *from Epirus*, Od. 7, 9; cf. Nitzsch in loc. The poet. intends perhaps by ἡ ἄπειρος or Ἀπείρη the unbounded region towards the north.
ἀπείρητος, η, ον, Ion. and Ep. for ἀπείρατος (πειράω). 1) *unattempted, untried, unessayed*, spoken of things, πόνος,

17, 41; cf. ἀδήριτος. 2) *unproved, untried*, said of persons, where one has no knowledge, Od. 2, 170; hence *inexperienced, unacquainted with*, φιλότητος, h. Ven. 133.
ἀπείριτος, ον, poet. for ἀπειρέσιος, *boundless*, πόντος, Od. 10, 195. *h. Ven. 120.
ἀπείρων, ονος, ὁ ἡ (πείρας), *illimitable, immeasurable*, γαῖα, δῆμος, δεσμοί, Od. 8, 340; ὕπνος, an infinitely long sleep, 24, 776. Od. 7, 286.
ἀπεκλανθάνω (λανθάνω), imper. aor. mid. ἀπεκλελάθεσθε; *to cause to forget entirely*. 2) Mid. *to forget entirely*; with gen. θάμβευς, forget astonishment, i. e. cease to wonder, Od. 24, 394.†
ἀπέλεθρος, ον (πέλεθρον), prop. *not to be measured by a πέλεθρον (=πλέθρον), immeasurable*, ἴς, 11. Od. 9, 538. Neut. as adv. ἀπέλεθρον, immeasurably far, to a great distance, 11, 354.
ἀπεμέω (ἀμέω), aor. 1 ἀπέμεσα, Ep. σσ, *to expectorate, to vomit forth*, with accus. αἷμα, 14, 437.†
ἀπεμνήσαντο, see ἀπομιμνήσκω.
ἀπεναρίζω, poet. (ἐναρίζω), prop. *to despoil a corpse of arms*; but mly *to despoil* with double accus. ἔντεα τινά, *12, 195. 15, 343; only in tmesis.
ἀπένεικα, see ἀποφέρω.
ἀπέπλω, see ἀποπλώω.
ἀπερείσιος, ον = ἀπειρέσιος, poet.
ἀπερύκω (ἐρύκω), fut. ἀπερύξω, *to restrain, to keep back, to repel*; with accus. 4, 542. Od. 18, 105.
ἀπέρχομαι (ἔρχομαι), aor. 2 ἀπῆλθον, perf. ἀπελήλυθα, *to go away, to depart*; with prep. and with gen. alone, πάτρης, οἴκου, 24, 766. Od. 2, 136.
ἀπερωεύς, έως, ὁ (ἐρωέω), one who restrains, *a hinderer, a baffler*, ἐμῶν μενέων, 8, 361.†
ἀπερωέω (ἐρωέω), aor. ἀπερώησα, prop. to flow back, but mly *to hasten away, to retire*; with gen. πολέμου, to retire from the conflict, 17, 723.†
ἄπεσαν, are ἄπειμι.
ἀπευθής, ές (πεύθομαι), 1) Pass. of which one has heard nothing, *unknown, unascertainable*, Od. 3, 88. 2) Act. that has heard nothing, *ignorant, uninformed*, Od. 3, 184.
ἀπεχθαίρω (ἐχθαίρω), aor. 1 ἀπέχθηρα. 1) *to hate bitterly*, with accus. 3, 415. 2) Trans. *to render odious, to make disgusting*, ὕπνον καὶ ἐδωδήν τινι, Od. 4, 105.
ἀπεχθάνομαι, mid. (ἐχθάνομαι), aor. 2 ἀπηχθόμην, *to become odious, to be hated*, τινί, 6, 140. 24, 27. (The pres. ἀπεχθάνεαι, Od. 2, 202, has likewise an intrans. signif.; ἀπηχθόμην is aor. A pres. ἀπέχθομαι is not known to H. Cf. Buttm., Gram. § 114. Rost. p. 238.
ἀπέχω (ἔχω), fut. ἀφέξω and ἀποσχήσω, Od. 19, 572; aor. 2 ἀπέσχον, fut. mid. ἀφέξομαι. aor. 2 mid. ἀπεσχόμην. I) Act. *to repel, remove, avert*. a) τί τινος, something from any thing, χεῖρας λοιμοῖο, 1, 97; νῆα νήσων, Od. 15, 33. b) *to avert*,

Ἀπηλεγέως. 55 Ἀπο.

τί τινι; πᾶσαν ἀεικείην χροΐ, every indignity from the body, I. e. to protect it against, 24, 19; χείρας μνηστήρων, Od. 20, 263. II) Mid. *to restrain oneself, to abstain* from a thing; with gen. πολέμου, from the war, 8, 35; ἀλλήλων, 14, 206; βοῶν, Od. 12, 321; *to spare any one,* Od. 19, 489. *b)* With accus. and gen. χείρας κακῶν, to restrain the hands from evil, Od. 22, 316.

ἀπηλεγέως, adv. (ἀλέγω), *recklessly, openly,* μῦθον ἀποειπεῖν, 9, 309. Od. 1, 373.

ἀπήμαντος, ον (πημαίνω), *uninjured, unharmed,* Od 19, 282.†

ἀπήμων, ον, gen. ονος (πῆμα), *without injury.* 1) Pass. *uninjured, unharmed,* 1, 415. 13, 761. 2) Act. *innocuous, harmless,* οὖρος, πομποί; hence ὕπνος, propitious sle-p, 14, 164; μῦθος, 12, 80.

ἀπήνη, ἡ, *a carriage, a wagon,* a four-wheeled vehicle, different from ἅρμα, chiefly for transporting freight,=ἅμαξα, 24, 324. Od. 6, 72. [" Synonyma sunt plurima : πήνα, Hes. Gallicumque benna. Γάπος, ὄχημα Τυρρηνοί, Hes. κανάνη (media longa), ἀμάνη, ἅμαξα, ἄγαννα: nec sciri potest unane horum omnium stirps fuerit, an specie similis re diversa." *Lob. Path.* 194.]

ἀπηνήναντο, see ἀπαναίνομαι.

ἀπηνής, ές, gen. έος (antithet. to ἐνηής) [" opp. προσηνής: nonnulli a prepositionibus deflexa putant, ut ab ὑπό, ὑπήνη διὰ τὸ ὑποκάτω εἶναι ἢ ὡς εἰρήνη, γαλήνη." *Lob. Path.* 194], *harsh, cruel, unfriendly, unyielding,* θυμός, μῦθος, νόος, 15, 94. Od. 18, 381.

ἀπήραξεν, see ἀπαράσσω.

ἀπηύρων, ας, α, see ἀπαυράω.

ἀπήωρος, ον (αἰωρέω), *hanging down, far-waving,* ἀπήωροι δ᾽ ἔσαν ὄζοι, Od. 12, 435.†

ἀπιθέω (πείθω), fut. ἀπιθήσω, aor. ἀπίθησα, *not to obey, to be disobedient,* τινί, always with a neg. οὐδ᾽ ἀπίθησε μύθῳ, he was not disobedient, i. e. he obeyed the word, 1, 220; with gen. h. Cer. 448.

ἀπινύσσω (πινυτός), *to be without sense, without consciousness,* κῆρ, 15, 10. *b) to be silly, foolish,* Od. 6, 258.

ἄπιος, η, ον (from ἀπό, as ἀντίος from ἀντί), *remote, distant.* τηλόθεν ἐξ ἀπίης γαίης, from far, from the distant land, 1, 270. Od. 7, 25. (The old Gramm. take it incorrectly as a proper name, and derive it from Apis, the name of an old king who reigned in Peloponnesus. They understood by it *Peloponnesus.* This appellation is however post-Homeric, and the two words are moreover distinguished by the quantity; ἄπιος has ᾰ, and Ἄπιος has ᾱ; see Buttm., Lex. p. 134.

Ἀπισάων, ονος, ὁ, 1) son of Phausius, a Trojan, 11, 578. 2) son of Hippasus, a Pæonian, 17, 348.

ἀπιστέω (ἄπιστος), *to disbelieve, to distrust,* with accus. Od. 13, 357.†

ἄπιστος, ον (πίστις), 1) *perfidious,*

faithless. *3, 106. 24, 63. 2) *incredulous, mistrustful,* κῆρ, Od. 14, 150. 391.

ἀπίσχω, poet. =ἀπέχω, Od. 11, 95.†

*ἄπληστος, ον (πίμπλημι), *insatiable, immense,* χόλος, h. Cer. 83 ; thus correctly with Herm. for ἄπληητος.

ἁπλοῖς, ίδος, ἡ, *simple, single,* χλαῖνα, 24, 230. Od. 24, 276. (The opposite of διπλοῖς, it being wrapped but once round the body; cf. διπλοῖς.)

*ἁπλόω (ἁπλοῦς), aor. ἥπλωσα, *to spread, to unfold,* οὐρήν, Batr. 74 (86).

ἄπνευστος, ον (πνέω), *without breath, breathless, swooning,* Od. 5, 456.†

ἀπό, Ep. ἀπαί, 1) Prep. with gen. *from.* 1) Spoken of *space,* a) To indicate distance from a place or object, with verbs of motion, often with the subordinate idea of elevation : *down from,* ἀφ᾽ ἵππων ἄλτο χαμᾶζε, down from the chariot, 11. ἀφ᾽ ἵππων, ἀπὸ νεῶν μάχεσθαι, to attack from the chariots, from the ships, 15, 386 ; ἅψασθαι βρόχον ἀπὸ μελάθρου, to suspend the cord from a beam, Od. 11, 278 ; pleonast. ἀπ᾽ οὐρανόθεν. *b)* To denote departure or origin from a place without regard to distance, *from.* ἵπποι ποταμοῦ ἀπὸ Σελλήεντος, horses from the river Selleīs, 12, 97. ἀπὸ πύργου, 22, 447. *c)* To denote distance from a place or object with verbs of rest. μένειν ἀπὸ ἧς ἀλόχοιο, to remain far from his spouse, 2, 292 ; ἀπ᾽ Ἄργεος, 12, 70 ; and pleonast. ἀπὸ Τροίηθεν, 24, 492; metaph. ἀπὸ σκοποῦ καὶ ἀπὸ δόξης μυθεῖσθαι, to speak wide from the mark and expectation, i. e. against them, Od. 11, 344. ἀπὸ θυμοῦ εἶναι, to be far from the heart, i. e. hated, 1, 562. 2) Of *time,* to indicate departure from a given point, *after, since* ; ἀπὸ δείπνου, 8, 54. 3) In other relations in which a departure from something is conceivable ; *a)* Of *origin.* οὐκ ἀπὸ δρυὸς οὐδ᾽ ἀπὸ πέτρης ἐστί, he springs neither from the oak nor the rock, i. e. proverbial, he is not of uncertain origin, Od. 19, 163. *b)* Of the *whole,* in reference to its parts, or that which belongs to them. κάλλος ἀπὸ Χαρίτων, Od. αἶσα ἀπὸ ληΐδος, a share in the spoil, Od. 5, 40. ἄνδρες ἀπὸ νηός, h. 12, 6. *c)* Of *the cause.* ἀπὸ σπουδῆς, from seriousness. seriously, 12, 233. *d)* Of the *means* and *instrument.* ἀπὸ βιοῖο πέφνεν, with the bow, 24, 605. 11) As *adv.* without case, poet. *from, away, far, without,* when it is for the most part to be connected with the verb. πάλιν δ᾽ ἀπὸ χαλκὸς ὄρουσε βλημένου, 21, 594; in like manner, 11. 845. Od. 16, 40. III) In composition with verbs it signifies *dis-, de-, re-, un-, in-,* etc., *away, off,* etc., and indicates separation, departure, cessation, completion, requital, want.

ἄπο (with retracted accent), thus written when it stands after the subst. it governs. θεῶν ἄπο κάλλος ἔχουσα, h. Ven. 77. Further, many Gramm. accent thus the word in the signif. *far from ;* this accentuation was, however, rejected

D 4

Ἀποαίνυμαι.   56   Ἀποθαυμάζω.

by Aristarchus and Herodian as needless, cf. Schol. Ven. Il. 18, 64. In Wolf's H. it is found only Od. 15, 517.
ἀποαίνυμαι, poet. for ἀπαίνυμαι.
ἀποαιρέομαι, poet. for ἀφαιρέομαι.
ἀποβαίνω (βαίνω), fut. ἀποβήσομαι, aor. 2 ἀπέβην, Ep. aor. 1 mid. ἀπεβήσατο, and ἀπεβήσετο = ἀπέβη. 1) *to go away, to depart,* ἐκ πολέμοιο, 17, 189; also μετ' ἀθανάτους, 21, 298; πρὸς Ὄλυμπον, Od. 1, 319. 2) *to descend, to alight,* ἐξ ἵππων, from the chariot, 3, 265; and gen. alone, 17, 480; ἐπὶ χθόνα, 11, 619.
ἀποβάλλω (βάλλω), only in tmesis, aor. 2 ἀπέβαλον, *to cast away;* with accus. χλαῖναν, to throw away the cloak. 2) *to let fall,* δάκρυ παρειῶν, tears from the cheeks, Od. 4, 198; νῆας ἐκ πόντον, to cause the ships to run into the sea, Od. 4, 358.
ἀπόβλητος, ον (βάλλω), *to be cast away, despicable, worthless,* ἔπεα, δῶρα, 2, 361. 3, 65.
ἀποβλύζω (βλύζω), *to belch, to eructate, to vomit forth,* οἶνον, 9, 491.†
ἀποβρίζω, poet. (βρίζω), partcp. aor. ἀποβρίξας, *to sleep one's fill,* Od. 9, 151. 12, 7.
ἀπογυιόω (γυιόω), subj. aor. ἀπογυιώσω, *to lame entirely,* and mly *to weaken, to enfeeble,* 6, 265.†
ἀπογυμνόω (γυμνόω), partcp. aor. pass. ἀπογυμνωθείς, *to lay bare,* esply to despoil of arms, Od. 10, 301.†
ἀποδαίομαι, obsol. pres. which furnishes the tenses to ἀποδαίομαι.
ἀποδαίομαι, poet. (δαίω), fut. ἀποδάσομαι, Ep. σσ, aor. ἀπεδασάμην, *to share with others;* τινί τι, *to divide any thing with any one,* 17, 231. 24, 595.
ἀποδειδίσσομαι, poet. (δειδίσσομαι), *to frighten away or back;* with accus. 12, 52.†
ἀποδειροτομέω (δειροτομέω), fut. ήσω, *to cut the throat, to cut off the head, to kill,* τινά, 18, 336. Od. 14, 35.
ἀποδέχομαι, depon. mid. (δέχομαι), aor. 1 ἀπεδεξάμην, *to take, to receive,* with accus. ἄποινα, 1, 95.†
ἀποδιδράσκω (διδράσκω), aor. 2 ἀπέδραν, *to run away,* ἵο ᾖ; ἐκ νηός, Od. 16, 65; νηός, 17, 516.
ἀποδίδωμι (δίδωμι), fut. ἀποδώσω, aor. 1 ἀπέδωκα, aor. 2 optat. ἀποδοίην, infin. ἀποδοῦναι, 1) *to give out, to restore, to return,* τί τινι, something to any one; spoken chiefly of things which one is under obligation to give back; hence, 2) *to repay, to requite;* θρέπτρα τοκεῦσιν, to repay to parents their dues for rearing, i. e. to make returns of gratitude and duty, 4, 478. 17, 302; πᾶσαν λώβην, to expiate the whole insult, 9, 387.
ἀποδίεμαι, poet. (δίεμαι), *to drive back, to drive away;* τινὰ ἐκ μάχης, to drive any one from the fight, 5, 763.† (ἀπόδ. with ᾱ, cf. δίεμαι.
ἀποδοχμόω (δοχμόω), aor. 1 ἀπέδοχμωσα, *to bend sideways, to bend to one side;* αὐχένα, the neck, Od. 9, 372.†

ἀποδράς, see ἀποδιδράσκω.
ἀποδρύπτω (δρύπτω), aor. 1 ἀπέδρυψα, aor. 1 pass. ἀπεδρύφθην, *to tear off, to scratch, to excoriate, to lacerate;* with accus. Od. 17, 480; ἔνθα κ' ἀπὸ ῥινοὺς δρύφθη, here would his skin have been lacerated. Od. 5, 426.
ἀποδρύφω = ἀποδρύπτω, in ἵνα μή μιν ἀποδρύφοι ἑλκυστάζων, lest by dragging he should lacerate him, 23, 187.† (Pres. optat. accord. to Buttm., Gram. § 92. Anm. 13; or, according to Passow, optat. aor. 2 from ἀποδρύπτω.)
ἀποδύνω, poet. for ἀποδύομαι; only in the impf. ἀπέδυνε βοείην, he put off the ox-hide, Od. 22, 364.†
ἀποδύω (δύω), fut. ἀποδύσω, aor. 1 ἀπέδυσα, aor. 2 ἀπέδυν, aor. 1 mid. ἀπεδυσάμην, 1) Trans. pres. act., also fut. and aor. *to pull off, to strip off,* with accus. εἵματα, the clothes from any one; esply spoken of stripping off the arms of dead warriors, τεύχεα, 4, 532. 2) Intrans. mid. and aor. 2 *to put off from oneself, to lay off;* εἵματα, to put off one's clothes, Od. 5, 343. 349.
ἀποείκω, poet. for ἀπείκω (εἴκω). *to retire from, to leave;* with gen. θεῶν ἀπόεικε κελεύθου, leave the way of the immortals; adopted by Wolf, 3, 406, for ἀπόεικε, after Aristarchus [cf. ἀπέοικον]. The ancients understood by κέλευθος θεῶν, the path by which the gods go to Olympus (Schol. Ven. A. τῆς εἰς τὰς θεὰς ὁδοῦ εἶκε καὶ παρεχώρει μὴ βαδίζουσα εἰς αὐτούς). The following verse does not accord with the metaph. signif. *commerce, intercourse of the gods,* as translated by Voss.
ἀποεῖπον = ἀπεῖπον.
ἀποεργάθω, poet. for ἀπείργω; only impf. ἀποέργαθον, *to separate, to divert, to remove,* τινὰ τινος, 21, 599; ῥάκεα σύλης, he removed the rags from the wound, Od. 21, 221.
ἀπόεργω. Ep. for ἀπείργω, imperf. ἀπόεργον, *to keep off, to separate, to divide,* τί τινος. ὅθι κληῒς ἀποέργει αὐχένα τε στῆθός τε, where the clavicle separates the neck and breast, 8, 326; τινὰ τινος, to drive one from a thing, 24, 238; with accus. alone, Od. 3, 296. ἀποεργμένη, h. Ven. 17, is a perf. pass. partcp. without redupl.; cf. Buttm., Gram. under εἴργω.
ἀπόερσε, a defect. Ep. aor. 1 indic., subj. ἀπόερσῃ. optat. ἀποέρσειε, 6, 348. 21, 283. 329, *to tear away, to hurry off, to sweep off;* with accus. (It is mly derived from ἀπέρδω, with a causative signif. Buttm., in Lex. p. 156, with more probability derives it from ἀπείρω) [*to wash away, to sweep away,* 21, 283: considering ἔρδω a *causative* of ῥέω, and related to ἄρδω. ὅν ῥά τ' ἔναυλος ἀπόερσῃ, *whom the torrent has washed away,* 21, 329 : Μή μιν ἀποέρσειε...... ποταμός, lest the flood should wash him away. So 6, 348: ἔνθα με κῦμ' ἀπόερσε, *there the wave would have washed me away.* So Lob.].
ἀποθαυμάζω (θαυμάζω), aor. ἀπεθαύ-

ἀπόθεστος.

μασα, *to be greatly astonished at*; with accus. Od. 6, 49.†

ἀπόθεστος, ον, poet. (ἀποτίθημι), *abjectus, despised*, κύων ['*a poor unheeded cast-off*,' Cp.], Od. 17, 296.† Some derive it from θέσσασθαι, *to wish*; hence: *not wished for, disregarded*.

ἀποθνήσκω (θνήσκω), partcp. perf. ἀποτεθνηώς, *to die away, to die*; in the perf. *to be dead*, 22, 432.

ἀποθορών, see ἀποθρώσκω.

ἀποθρώσκω (θρώσκω), aor. 2 ἀπέθορον, *to leap down, to spring away*; with gen. νηός, *to leap down* from the ship, 2, 702. 16, 748. 2) *to rise*, or *ascend* (*lightly*) from any thirg; of smoke, γαίης, Od. 1, 58.

ἀποθύμιος, ον (θυμός), prop. *remote from the heart, disagreeable, odious*. ἀποθύμια ἔρδειν τινί, *to displease any one*, 14, 261.†

ἀποικίζω (οἰκίζω), aor. 1 ἀπῴκισα, *to cause to emigrate, to settle, to transplant, to another abode*, τινὰ ἐς νῆσον, Od. 12, 135.†

ἄποινα, τά (from α and ποίνη), *the ransom*, by which freedom is purchased for a prisoner, 1, 13. 111; or the price a prisoner gives for life and liberty, 2, 230. 6, 46. 2) mly *requital, compensation*, 9, 120. (Used only in the plur.)

ἀποίσω, see ἀποφέρω.

ἀποίχομαι, depon. mid. (οἴχομαι), *to be absent, to be at a distance*, Od. 4, 109; πολέμοιο, *to keep aloof from the war*, 11, 408. 2) *to remove oneself, to go away*, τινός, 19, 342.

ἀποκαίνυμαι, depon. mid. poet. (καίνυμαι), *to surpass, to vanquish*; τινά τινι, any one in something, *Od. 8, 127. 219.

ἀποκαίω (καίω), optat. aor. ἀποκῆαι, *to burn up, to consume*; with accus. 21, 336.† (In tmesis.)

ἀποκαπύω (καπύω), aor. ἀπεκάπυσα, *to breathe out, to gasp away*, ψυχήν, 22, 467.† (In tmesis.)

ἀποκείρω (κείρω), Ep. aor. 1 ἀπέκερσα, aor. 1 mid. ἀπεκειράμην. prop. *to shear off*; then *to cut off, to cut through*, with accus. τένοντα, the sinews, 10, 456. 14, 466. 2) Mid. *to cut off* for oneself; χαίτην, *to cut off* one's hair, as a token of grief, 23, 141. *Il.

ἀποκηδέω (κηδέω), partcp. aor. ἀποκηδήσας, *to be negligent, to be careless, inattentive*. αἴ κ' ἀποκηδήσαντε φερώμεθα χεῖρον ἄεθλον, if we from being negligent should carry off a smaller prize, 23, 413.† The dual is here used with the plur. because the speaker (Antilochus) has in mind himself and his steeds.

ἀποκινέω (κινέω), aor. 1 ἀπεκίνησα, Ep. iterative, ἀποκινήσασκε, *to remove, to drive away, to take away*; with accus. δέπας τραπέζης, *to remove the goblet from the table*. 11, 636; τινὰ θυράων, *to drive any one from the door*, Od. 22, 107.

*ἀποκλέπτω (κλέπτω), fut. κλέψω, *to steal away, to purloin*, h. Merc. 522.

ἀποκλίνω (κλίνω), *to bend away, to turn*

57

Ἀπολήγω.

aside, to drive back; with accus. βοῦς εἰς αὔλιν, h. Ven. 169; trop. ἄλλῃ ἀποκλίνειν, *to turn in another direction*, i. e. *to give the dream another turn* (= interpretation), Od. 19, 556.†

ἀποκόπτω (κόπτω), fut. ἀποκόψω, aor. 1 ἀπέκοψα, *to cut away, to cut off*; with accus. αὐχένα, τένοντας, 11, 146. Od. 3. 449; παρήορον, *to separate a mate-horse* by severing the thong with which it was attached ['*the side-rein*,' Cp.], 16, 474.

ἀποκοσμέω (κοσμέω), *to put in order by taking away*; hence, *to clear away*, ἔντεα δαιτός, *the furniture of a feast*, Od. 7, 232.†

ἀποκρεμάννυμι (κρεμάω), aor. 1 ἀπεκρέμασα, *to let any thing hang down, to droop* (trans.); ἡ ὄρνις αὐχέν' ἀπεκρέμασεν, *the bird* [ἧε *head reclined*' [Cp.], 23, 879.†

ἀποκρίνω (κρίνω), in the partcp. aor. 1 ἀποκρινθείς, *to separate, to sunder*. τὼ οἱ, ἀποκρινθέντε ἐναντίω ὁρμηθήτην, these, separated (from their friends), rushed against him, 5, 12.†

ἀποκρύπτω (κρύπτω), aor. 1 ἀπέκρυψα, *to conceal, to hide*, τινί τι, any thing from any one; τινὰ νόσφι θανάτοιο, *to hide any one from death*, i. e. *to rescue him from death*, 18, 465.

ἀποκτάμεν, ἀποκτάμεναι, see ἀποκτείνω.

ἀποκτείνω (κτείνω), aor. 1 ἀπέκτεινα, aor. 2 ἀπέκτανον, Ep. ἀπέκταν, ας, α, infin. ἀποκτάμεν for ἀποκτάναι, aor. 2 mid. with pass. signif. ἀπεκτάμην, partcp. ἀποκτάμενος, *to kill, to slaughter, to slay*, τινὰ χάλκῳ, any one with the brass [weapon], Il. and Od. ἀπέκτατο πιστὸς ἑταῖρος, his faithful companion was slain, 15, 435. (On ἀπεκτάμην, see Buttm., § 110, 7.)

ἀπολάμπω (λάμπω),*to shine forth, to flash back, to be reflected*. τινός, from a thing: ὡς αἰχμῆς ἀπέλαμπε, so flashed back [the splendour] from the spear, 22, 319. 2) Mid. χάρις δ' ἀπελάμπετο πολλή, *grace was reflected* afar, 14, 183. Od. 18, 298. h. Ven. 175.

ἀπολείβω (λείβω), *to let drop*, mid. *to drop, to distil*, τινός, *from any thing*. ὀθονέων ἀπολείβεται ὑγρὸν ἔλαιον, the liquid oil trickled from the close-woven linen, i. e. it was so thick that the oil did not penetrate it; or, according to Voss, it was so glossy that oil seemed to be flowing down [so Cp., '*bright as with oil*,' &c.], Od. 7, 107.† πλοκάμων, h. 23, 3.

ἀπολείπω (λείπω), 1) *to leave behind to leave remaining*, οὐδ' ἀπέλειπεν ἔγκατα, he left not the entrails remaining, Od. 9, 292. 2) *to abandon*; spoken of place, δόμον, 12, 169. 3) Intrans. *to go from, to go out, to fail*, Od. 7, 117.

ἀπολέσκετο, see ἀπόλλυμι.

ἀπολήγω (λήγω), fut. ἀπολήξω, aor. 1 ἀπέληξα, *to leave off, to cease, to desist*; with gen. μάχης, *to quit the battle*; εἰρεσίης, *to desist from rowing*, Od. 12, 224. b) With partcp. οὐδ' ἀπολήγει χαλκῷ δῃῶν, he does not cease cutting

'Απολιχμάω. 58 Άπονάω.

down with his sword, 17, 565. cf. Od. 19, 166. c) Absol. *to cease, to pass away*, 6, 149.

ἀπολιχμάω (λιχμάω), *to lick off, to suck*, in H. only in the mid. οἵ σ' ὠτειλήν αἷμ' ἀπολιχμήσονται, which will suck the blood from the wound, 21, 123.†

ἀπολλήξῃς, ἀπολλήξειαν, Ep. for ἀπολήξῃς, ἀπολήξειαν, see ἀπολήγω.

ἀπόλλῦμι (ὄλλυμι), fut. ἀπολέσω, Ep. σσ, aor. 1 ἀπώλεσα and ἀπόλεσσα, mid. aor. 2 ἀπωλόμην, 3 plur. ἀπόλοντο, perf. 2 ἀπόλωλα, 1) In the act. trans. *to destroy, to kill, to slay*; spoken chiefly of slaughter in battle; with accus. 1, 268. 5, 758: also of things: *to raze*, Ἴλιον, 5, 648. 2) *to lose, to suffer the loss of*; often θυμόν, to lose life. ἀπολ. νόστιμον ἦμαρ, to lose the day of return, Od. 1, 354; βίοτον, οἶκον, Od. 2, 49. 4, 95. II) Mid. and also 2 perf. has an intrans. signif. : *to perish, to die, to be lost, undone, to fall* (in battle); often with dat. ὀλέθρῳ, Od. 3, 87; more rarely with accus. αἰπὺν ὄλεθρον, to die a cruel death, Od. 9, 303; κακὸν μόρον, by an evil fate, Od. 1, 166: ὑπό τινι, to perish by some one, Od. 3, 235. 2) *to disappear, to vanish, to fail*, καρπὸς ἀπόλλυται, the fruit disappears, Od. 7, 117. ὕδωρ ἀπολέσκετο, the water vanished (Cp.), Od. 11, 586. ἀπὸ νέ σφισιν ὕπνος ὄλωλεν, their sleep is lost, it has left them, 10, 186. οὐ γὰρ σφῷν γε γένος ἀπόλωλε τοκήων, for the race of your fathers is not lost, i. e. you are not of unknown descent; or, with Nitzsch, you are not degenerate, the nobility of your ancestry is not lost in you, Od. 4, 62. cf. 19, 163.

Ἀπόλλων, ωνος, ὁ (prob. from ἀπόλλυμι, the destroyer), *Apollo*, son of Zeus and Latona, brother of Artemis; accord. to 4, 101, born in Lycia (see Λυκηγενής), or according to later mythology, in Delos, h. in Ap. 27; with long, flowing hair, and of eternal beauty and youth. In H. he is distinguished from Helios, and appears, 1) As *a god inflicting punishment*, and as such carries a bow and arrows (hence the epith. ἀργυρότοξος, κλυτότοξος, ἕκατος, etc.). He slays with his arrows men who die not by a violent, but by a sudden natural death; just as the sudden death of women is ascribed to Artemis, Od. 11, 318. 15, 410. He slays also in anger; he sends pestilence and contagion upon men, 1, 42. 2) As *the god of prophecy*; his oracle is represented as being in the rocky Pytho, 9, 405; he communicates the gift of foreseeing future events, 1, 72. 3) As *the god of song and the lyre*; he communicates to bards the knowledge of the past, Od. 8, 488; and enlivens by the music of the lyre the feasts of the gods, 1, 602. 4) Finally, he is mentioned by H. as *the protector of herds*; he fed the mares of Eumēlus, 2, 766; and pastured the herds of Laomedon, 21, 448. In the Iliad he is always on the side of the Trojans, and is worshipped as the tutelary deity in Troy and on the coast of Asia (Chrysē, Cilla). 4, 509; see the appellations Σμινθεύς, Φοῖβος, (Ἀπόλλων has prop. ἅ; in the quadrisyllabic cases also α.)

ἀπολούω (λούω), aor. 1 ἀπέλουσα, fut. mid. ἀπολούσομαι, aor. 1 mid. ἀπελουσάμην, *to wash off, to wash*; with double accus. Πάτροκλον βρότον αἱματόεντα, to wash away the clotted gore from Patroclus, 18, 345. 2) Mid. *to wash oneself*; ἄλμην ὤμοιιν, to wash the brine from the shoulders, Od. 6, 219; with double accus. 23, 41.

ἀπολυμαίνομαι, mid. *to purify oneself*, chiefly in a religious sense, to cleanse oneself by bathing before a sacrifice, when any one by some act, as e. g. touching a dead body, had become unclean, *1, 313, 314. 2) *to destroy*, whence ἀπολυμαντήρ, ῆρος, ὁ, *a destroyer, a spoiler*. δαιτῶν ἀπολ., the spoiler of feasts, *a disturber*; the beggar Irus is thus called, Od. 17, 220. 377. It is explained by the Schol.: ὁ τὰ καθάρματα ἀποφερόμενος τῶν εὐωχιῶν, one who consumes the fragments of a feast, *platelicker* (Voss, *fragment-eater*). This explanation agrees with the signif. of ἀπολυμαίνεσθαι occurring in H., and deserves therefore the preference over the explanation of modern lexicons, viz., *a disturber of feasts*.

ἀπολύω (λύω), aor. 1 ἀπέλυσα, fut. mid. ἀπολύσομαι, 1) *to loose, to unbind*, τί τινος; ἱμάντα κορώνης, to loose the thong from the ring, Od. 21, 46; τοίχους τρόπιος, Od. 12, 420. 2) *to free, to liberate*; in the Il. to liberate any one for a ransom, 1, 95. 6, 427. II) Mid. *to ransom, to redeem*, τινὰ χρυσοῦ, any one for gold, 22, 50. (ῡ)

ἀπομηνίω (μηνίω), fut. ἀπομηνίσω, aor. 1 ἀπεμήνισα, *to cherish wrath, to persevere in anger*, τινί, 2, 772. 7, 230. Od. 16, 378. (ῑ in the pres., ῑ in the fut. and aor.

ἀπομιμνήσκομαι, mid. (μιμνήσκω), aor. ἀπεμνησάμην, *to remember*, in 24, 428.† τινί is dat. commod.: to bethink oneself in favour of any one.

ἀπόμνυμι and ἀπομνύω (ὄμνυμι). imperf. ἀπώμνυν, and 3 plur. ἀπώμνυον, aor. 1 ἀπώμοσα, *to swear*, to take an oath that something has not happened or shall not happen, ὅρκον, Od. 2, 377. 10, 381; *to assure on oath* that one will not do or has not done something, *to abjure* (antith. to ἐπόμνυμι), *Od. 10, 345. 18, 58.

ἀπομόργνυμι (ὀμόργνυμι), aor. 1 mid. ἀπομορξάμην, 1) *to wipe off, to dry up*; with accus. αἷμα, blood, 5, 798. 16, 414. 2) Mid. *to wipe oneself*; παρειὰς χερσί, to wipe the cheeks with the hands, Od. 18, 200; δάκρυ, 2, 269. Od. 17, 304.

ἀπομυθέομαι, depon. mid. (μυθέομαι), *to dissuade, to warn against*, τινί τι, 9, 109.†

ἀπονάω, poet. (νάω=ναίω), obsol. pres. aor. 1 ἀπένασσα, Ep. σσ (aor. 1 mid. ἀπενασάμην, prop. to cause any one to dwell

Ἀπονέομαι.   Ἀποπροαιρέω.

in another place, *to transplant, to cause to emigrate*, and mly, *to send away*, with the accus. κούρην ἄψ, to send back the damsel, 16, 86. 2) Mid. *to change one's residence, to emigrate*; Δουλίχιόνδε, to remove to Dulichium, 2, 629; Ὑπερησίηνδε, Od. 15, 254.

ἀπονέομαι, depon. (νέομαι), only pres. and imperf. *to go away, to return, to go back*; ἐκ μάχης, 16, 252; προτὶ ἄστυ, to the city, 12, 74; ἐπὶ νῆας, to the ships, 15, 305; ἐς πατρός, sc. δόμον, Od. 2, 195. (ᾱ)

ἀπόνηθ', ἀπονήμενος, see ἀπονίνημι.

ἀπονίζω (νίζω), in the pres. and imperf. used for ἀπονίπτω. 1) *to wash off or away*; with accus. Od. 23, 75. 2) Mid. *to wash oneself from*; with accus. ἱδρῶ θαλάσσῃ, to wash oneself from sweat in the sea, 10, 572. (In ἀπενίζοντο, ε is used as long.)

ἀπονίνημι (ὀνίνημι), *to profit from*; in H. only Mid. ἀπονίναμαι, fut. ἀπονήσομαι, aor. 2 Att. ἀπωνήμην, Ep. ἀπονήμην, optat. 2 sing. ἀπόναιο, partcp. ἀπονήμενος, *to use, enjoy, to have advantage*, τινός, of any thing. οἷος τῆς ἀρετῆς ἀπονήσεται, he will enjoy his bravery alone, 11, 763. οὐδὲ—ἧς ἥβης ἀπόνηθ' (for ἀπώνητο, he had no advantage from his youth, 17, 25; also obsol. οὐδ' ἀπόνητο, he had no advantage, profit (viz., from raising the dog), Od. 17, 293; (Theseus from the seduction of Ariadne), Od. 11, 324; (Ulysses from his son), Od. 16, 120.

ἀπονίπτω (νίπτω), a later form for νίζω; the pres. mid. once Od. 18, 179; aor. 1 ἀπένιψα, aor. 1 mid. ἀπενιψάμην, *to wash away, to cleanse by washing*; with accus. βρότον ἐξ ὠτειλέων, to wash away the blood from wounds, Od. 24, 189. 2) Mid. *to wash oneself* (sibi); with accus. χρῶτα, the body, Od. 18, 172.

ἀπονοστέω (νοστέω), fut. ἀπονοστήσω, *to come back, to return home*; also with ἄψ, 1, 60. Od. 13, 6, and often.

ἀπόνοσφι, before a vowel ἀπόνοσφιν (νόσφι), adv. *separately, apart, afar*, βῆναι, 11, 555; εἶναι, 15, 548. ἀπόνοσφι κατίσχεσθαι, 2, 233. ἀπόνοσφι τραπέσθαι, to turn oneself aside, Od. 5, 350. 2) Prep. *far from, remote from*; with gen. (which mly precedes), ἐμεῦ, far from me, 1, 541; φίλων ἀπόνοσφιν, Od. 5, 113.

*ἀπονοσφίζω (νοσφίζω), Ep. σσ, *to separate, to divide*, τινά δόμων, h. in Cer. 158. Pass. *to be deprived of*, θεῶν ἐδωδῆς, h. Merc. 562.

ἀποξέω (ξέω), aor. 1 ἀπέξεσα, *to shave off*, hence *to cut off*; with accus. χεῖρα, =ἀποκόπτω, 5, 81.†

ἀποξύνω (ὀξύνω), aor. 1 ἀπέξυνα, *to sharpen, to point*; with accus. ἐρετμά, oars, Od. 6, 269. 9, 326. In both passages the connexion plainly requires the signif. *to smooth*, for which reason Buttm., Lexil. p. 70. would read ἀποξύσωσιν for ἀποξύνουσιν, and ἀποξῦσαι for ἀποξῦναι.

ἀποξύω (ξύω)=ἀποξέω, aor. 1 ἀπέξυσα, *to shave off, to polish*; γῆρας, to strip off old age, i. e. to become young, a fig. borrowed from serpents that cast their skins, 9, 446.†

ἀποπαπταίνω (παπταίνω), fut. ἀποπαπτανέω, Ep. for ἀποπαπτανῶ, *to look around* (as if to fly), *to look around fearfully*, 14, 101.†

ἀποπαύω (παύω), aor. 1 ἀπέπαυσα, fut. mid. ἀποπαύσομαι, 1) *to cause to cease, to stop, to restrain*, τινά, any one, 18, 267; τινός, from a thing; πολέμου, 11, 323; also with accus. and infin. τινὰ ἀλητεύειν, to stop one from begging, Od. 18, 114. 2) Mid. *to cease, to abstain from*, πολέμου, 1, 422. Od. 1, 340; where now ἀποπαύε stands instead of ἀποπαύεο.

ἀποπέμπω (πέμπω), fut. ἀποπέμψω, Ep. ἀππέμψει, Od. 15, 83; aor. ἀπέπεμψα, *to send away, to send off, to let go*; with accus. 2) *to send back*, δῶρα, Od. 17, 76.

ἀποπέσσησι, see ἀποπίπτω.

ἀποπέτομαι (πέτομαι), aor. 2 ἀπεπτάμην, partcp. ἀποπτάμενος, *to fly away, to fly back*; spoken of an arrow, 13, 857; of the god of dreams, ἀποπτάμενος ᾤχετο, he vanished in flight, 2, 71; of the soul, Od. 11, 222.

ἀποπίπτω (πίπτω), aor. 2 ἀπέπεσον, *to fall down, to sink down*, 14, 351; spoken of the bats, ἐκ πέτρης, to fall down from the rock, Od. 24, 7.

ἀποπλάζω (πλάζω), only aor. pass. ἀποπλάγχθην, partcp. ἀποπλαγχθείς, in the act. *to cause to wander or err*. Pass. *to wander, to be struck back* [fin an object aimed at], Od. 8, 573; νήσου, to be driven from the island, Od. 12, 285; ἀπὸ θώρηκος πολλὸν ἀποπλαγχθείς, ἑκὰς ἔπτατο διστός, from the cuirass *'wide wand'ring'* (Cp.) flew the arrow away, 13, 592. ἡ μὲν ἀποπλαγχθεῖσα (τρυφάλεια) χαμαὶ πέσε, springing far away the helmet fell to the ground, 13, 578.

ἀποπλείω, poet. for ἀποπλέω (πλέω), *to sail away, to set sail*, οἴκαδε, 9, 418. Od. 8, 501.

ἀποπλύνω (πλύνω), *to wash away or off*; with accus. only the iterat. imperf. λάϊγγας ποτὶ χέρσον ἀποπλύνεσκε, the sea washed the stones to the beach, Od. 6, 95.†

ἀποπλώω, Ion. for ἀποπλέω; to which the Ep. aor. 2 ἀπέπλω belongs Od. 14, 339.†

ἀποπνέω, Ep. ἀποπνείω (πνέω), *to breathe out, to exhale*; with accus. πυρὸς μένος, to breathe out the strength of fire, said of the Chimæra, 6, 182; πικρὸν ἁλὸς ὀδμήν, to exhale the disagreeable odour of the sea, Od. 4, 406. 2) *to expire*; θυμόν, to breathe forth the life, i. e., to die, 4, 524. 13, 654; and without θυμόν, Batr. 100.

*ἀποπνίγω (πνίγω), aor. 1 ἀπέπνιξα, *to choke outright, to strangle*, τινά, Batr. 119.

ἀποπρό (πρό), 1) Adv. *far away*, φέρειν, 16, 669. 2) Prep. with gen. *apart, far from*, νεῶν, 7, 343. (In composition it strengthens ἀπό.)

ἀποπροαιρέω (αἱρέω), partcp. aor. 2

ἀποπροελών, to take away, to take off, τινός, any thing; σίτου, Od. 17, 457.†
ἀποπροέηκε, see ἀποπροΐημι.
ἀποπροελών, see ἀποπροαιρέω.
ἀπόπροθεν, adv. from far, from a distance [remote, far away], 10, 209. Od. 6, 218.
ἀπόπροθι, adv. ἀποπρό, in the distance, far away, 10, 410. Od. 4, 757.
ἀποπροΐημι (ἵημι), aor. 1 Ion. ἀποπροέηκα, to send far away, to send forth, to despatch, τινὰ πόλινδε, any one to the city, Od. 14, 26; ἰόν, to shoot an arrow, Od. 22, 82. 2) to let fall, ξίφος χαμᾶζε, Od. 22, 327. (ˇ ˉ ˘ ˘ ˉ).
ἀποπροτέμνω (τέμνω), partcp. aor. 2 ἀποπροταμών, to cut off from, to carve from; with gen. νώτου [' carving forth a portion from the loins of a huge brawn,' Cp.], Od. 8, 475.†
ἀποπτάμενος, see ἀποπέτομαι.
ἀποπτύω (υ in the pres. ῠ or ῡ) (πτύω), to spit out, to vomit forth, to throw, cast up, τί, any thing, 23, 781; said of the sea-wave, ἁλὸς ἄχνην [' scatter wide the spray,' Cp.], 4, 426.
ἀπόρθητος, ον (πορθέω), not pillaged, not razed, unsacked, πόλις, 12, 11.†
ἀπόρνυμι (ὄρνυμι), to excite from a place, only mid. to rush forth from a place; Λυκίηθεν, to come from Lycia, 5, 105.†
ἀπορούω (ὀρούω), aor. 1 ἀπόρουσα, to leap down, to hasten down, from a chariot, 5, 20, 836. 2) to recoil [21, 593: πάλιν δ' ἀπὸ χαλκὸς ὄρουσεν, ' with a swift recoil back flew the spear,' Cp.; of a person], to spring back, 21, 251. Od. 22, 95.
ἀποῤῥαίω (ῥαίω), aor. 1 ἀπόῤῥαισα, prop. to break off. 2) to tear away, τινά τι, any thing from any one [οὐ ... κτήματα, to rob you of your property], Od. 1, 404; τινὰ ἦτορ, to deprive of life, Od. 16, 428.
ἀποῤῥήγνυμι (ῥήγνυμι), aor. 1 ἀπέῤῥηξα, to break off, to tear away; with accus. δεσμόν, his halter, spoken of a horse, 6, 507; κορυφὴν ὄρεος, Od. 9, 481; θαιρούς, to break [burst, Cp.] the hinges (of a gate), 12, 459.
ἀποῤῥιγέω (ῥιγέω), perf. 2 †ἀπέῤῥῑγα; prop. I shudder with cold; hence fig. I shudder to do any thing; I shrink from doing it; dare not do it; c. infin. Od. 2, 52.† (The perf. with pres. signif.)
ἀποῤῥίπτω (ῥίπτω), aor. 1 ἀπέῤῥιψα, to throw away, to cast off; with accus. καλύπτρην, a veil, 22, 406; metaph. μῆνιν, to lay aside anger, 9, 517; μηνιθμόν, *16, 282.
ἀποῤῥώξ, ῶγος, ὁ, ἡ (ῥήγνυμι), prop. adj. torn off, steep, abrupt. ἀκταὶ ἀποῤῥῶγες, the rugged shores. Od. 13, 98. 2) ἡ as subst. a portion torn off, a fragment, a branch; spoken of a river, Στυγὸς ὕδατος ἀπορρώξ, an arm of the Stygian water, 2, 755; of Cocȳtus, Od. 10, 514; also spoken of excellent wine, ἀμβροσίης καὶ νέκταρος, an efflux of ambrosia and nectar. Od. 9, 359.

ἀποσύομαι (σεύω), only in Ep. sync. aor. 2 mid. ἀπεσσύμην, to haste away, to rush away or off; with gen. δώματος, from the house, 9, 390; ἐκ μυχόν, Od. 9, 236. (υ short; σ doubled with augm.)
ἀποσκεδάννυμι (σκεδάννυμι), aor. 1 ἀπεσκέδασα, to scatter, to disperse, to drive asunder; with accus. ψυχάς, Od. 11, 385; βασιλῆας, 19, 309; metaph. κήδεα θυμοῦ, to dismiss cares from the mind [' scatter wide thy cares, Cp.]; to dispel, Od. 8, 149.
ἀποσκίδνημι, poet. form from ἀποσκεδάννυμι; in H. only mid. ἀποσκίδναμαι, to disperse, 23, 4.†
ἀποσκυδμαίνω (σκυδμαίνω), (intrans.), to be very angry, to be vehemently enraged, τινί, against any one, 24, 65.†
ἀποσπένδω (σπένδω), to pour out, chiefly to pour out wine at sacrifices, and upon taking oaths, in honour of the gods, to pour out a drink-offering, to offer a libation, *Od. 3, 394. 14, 331.
ἀποσταδά, adv. = ἀποσταδόν, Od. 6, 143.†
ἀποσταδόν, adv. (ἀφίστημι), absent, at a distance, μάρνασθαι, 15, 556.†
ἀποστείχω (στείχω), aor. 2 ἀπέστιχον, to go away, to depart, Il.; οἴκαδε, to return home, Od. 11, 132; ἀνὰ νῆσον, Od. 12, 143.
ἀποστίλβω (στίλβω), to gleam, to sparkle, to emit brightness. λίθοι—ἀποστίλβοντες ἀλείφατος, stones, shining as with oil; we must be here supplied (for H. uses this expression to indicate great brightness), Od. 3, 408.†
ἀποστρέφω (στρέφω), fut. ἀποστρέψω, aor. 1 ἀπέστρεψα, Ep. iterat. ἀποστρέψασκε, 1) Trans. to turn away, to turn back; πόδας καὶ χεῖρας (in order to tie them behind), Od. 22, 173; to reverse, ἴχνια, h. Merc. 76. b) to cause to turn, to make to return; with accus. 15, 62. 22, 197; to draw off any one from any thing, τινὰ πολέμοιο, 12, 249 (where Spitzner reads ἀποστρέψειες for ἀποτρέψειες). ἀποστρέψοντας ἑταίρους, sc. αὐτόν, friends to call him back, 10, 355. 2) [According to some interpreters it is] intrans. in Od. 11, 597, ἀποστρέψασκε=it rolled back (of a stone). (But in this sense, as Nitzsch observes, we should at least expect ὑποστρέφειν, and it is prob. trans. See κραταιίς.]
ἀποστρέψασκε, see ἀποστρέφω.
ἀποστυφελίζω (στυφελίζω), aor. 1 ἀπεστυφέλιξα, to drive back by force, to repel, τινά τινος, 16, 703. τρὶς νεκροῦ ἀπεστυφέλιξαν, thrice they drove him back (repulsed him) from the dead body, *18, 158.
*ἀποσυρίζω (συρίζω), to pipe out, to whistle, h. Merc. 280.
ἀποσφάλλω (σφάλλω), aor. 1 ἀπέσφηλα, to lead from the right road, to cause to stray; τινά, any one, Od. 3, 320; metaph τινὰ πόνοιο, to cause any one to fail of the object of his labour [' to frustrate his labours,' Cp.], 5, 567.
ἀποσχίζω (σχίζω), aor. 1 ἀπέσχισα, to

'Αποτάμνω. 61 'Αποφθινύθω.

split off, to split asunder, to cleave; with accus. πέτρην, Od. 4, 507.† In tmesis.

ἀποτάμνω (Ion. for ἀποτέμνω), aor. 2 ἀπέταμον, *to cut off, to cut asunder,* στομάχους, 3, 392 [ῥῖνα, οὔατα, &c.]; ἵππω παρηορίας, 8, 67. 2) Mid. *to cut off any thing for oneself,* κρέα, 22, 347; hence *to drive away,* βοῦς, h. Merc. 74.

ἀποτηλοῦ, adv. (τηλοῦ), *far in the distance, remote,* Od. 9, 117.†

ἀποτίθημι (τίθημι), aor. 1 ἀπέθηκα, aor. 2 mid. ἀπεθέμην, subj. ἀποθείομαι Ep. for ἀποθῶμαι, infin. ἀποθέσθαι, 1) *to lay aside, to lay up, to put up;* with accus. δέπας ἐπὶ χηλῷ, 16, 254. 2) Mid. *to lay down* or *aside, to put off,* τί, any thing; φύσας ὅπλα τε πάντα, 18, 409; τεύχεα, to lay down one's arms, 3, 89; metaph. ἀνιήν, to lay aside objurgation, 5, 492.

*ἀποτιμάω (τιμάω), fut. ἀποτιμήσω, *not to honour, to slight;* with accus., h. Merc. 35.

ἀποτίνυμαι, poet. for ἀποτίνομαι. πολέων ποινήν, to take vengeance for many [a Grecian slain, Cp], 16, 398; τινά τινος, to cause one to atone for any thing, Od. 2, 73.

ἀποτίνω (τίω), fut. ἀποτίσω, aor. 1 ἀπέτισα, fut. mid. ἀποτίσομαι, aor. 1 ἀπετισάμην. I) Act. prop. *to pay back, to requite,* τὶ τριπλῇ, 1, 128; πολλά τινι, Od. 2, 132; a) Esply in a bad sense, *to pay the penalty, to atone* for any thing, τινί τι: τιμήν τινι, *to make compensation,* and *satisfaction* to any one, 3, 286; πᾶσαν ὑπερβασίην τινί, to requite [take vengeance upon] one for transgression, Od. 13, 193; Πατρόκλοιο ἕλωρα, to pay the penalty for Patroclus slain, 18, 93. σύν τε μεγάλῳ ἀπέτισαν σὺν σφῆσιν κεφαλῆσι, and then shall they make full satisfaction, even with their own heads, etc. (aor. for fut.) 4, 161. b) In a good sense, *to repay, to make good,* κομιδήν τινι, 8, 186; εὐεργεσίας, Od. 22, 235. cf. Od. 2, 132. II) Mid. 1) *to exact compensation, satisfaction,* etc.; with accus. of the thing, ποινὴν ἑτάρων, to require satisfaction, i. e., to take vengeance for his companions, Od. 23, 312; and mly *to punish,* βίας, Od. 16, 255. 3, 216; with accus. of the pers. τινά, to cause any one to make atonement, or to punish him, Od. 24, 480; absol. Od. 1, 268.

ἀποτίω = ἀποτίνω, not occurring in the pres.

ἀποτμήγω, Ep. form of ἀποτέμνω, aor. 1 ἀπότμηξα, *to cut* or *lop off, to cleave away;* with accus. χεῖρας ξίφει, 11, 146; κεφαλήν, Od. 10, 440; spoken of rivers κλιτῦς, to sweep away many a declivity [Cp.], 16, 390; metaph. τινὰ τινος, *to cut off,* or intercept any one from a thing, λαοῦ, 10, 364. 22, 456.

ἄποτμος, ον (πότμος), *unfortunate, wretched,* 24, 388. Superl. ἀποτμότατος, Od. 1, 219.

ἀποτρέπω (τρέπω), fut. ἀποτρέψω, aor. 2 ἀπέτραπον, aor. 2 mid. ἀπετραπόμην, 1) *to turn away, to turn aside, to divert, to drive away,* τινά, 15, 276; λαόν, 11, 758; πολέμοιο, to dissuade any one from war, 12, 249. 2) Mid. *to turn away, to turn back;* with αὖτις, 10, 200. 12, 329.

ἀποτρίβω (τρίβω), fut. ἀποτρίψω, *to rub off, to wipe off.* πολλά οἱ ἀμφὶ κάρη σφέλα — πλευραὶ ἀποτρίψουσι βαλλομένοιο, i. e., the ribs of him pelted at shall drive back (lit. rub off) many stools thrown at his head, i. e., many stools thrown at his head shall at least hit his ribs, Od. 17, 232.† Some read πλευράς, and take σφέλα in the nom., less in accordance with the poetic language. [Others refer ἀμφὶ κάρη to the *throwers*: 'many stools whirled round the head,' &c.]

ἀπότροπος, ον (τρέπω), *turned away, separated, far from men,* Od 14, 372.

ἀποτρωπάω, poet. form of ἀποτρέπω, *to turn away;* τινά, 20, 119; τί, Od. 16, 405. 2) Mid. *to turn oneself away,* τινός, from a thing; τόξου ταννυστύος, to withdraw or shrink from straining the bow, Od. 21, 112; with infin. *to delay, to hesitate,* δακέειν ἀπετρωπῶντο λεόντων, 18, 585.

ἀπούρας, a solitary partcp. aor. 1 from an obsol. root, which in signification belongs to ἀπαυράω, *to take away,* q. v. [Either an anomaly for ἀπουρήσας, as ἔχραισμον from χραισμεῖν; or a regular or syncopated form of a barytone, ἀποαϝείρας.—ἀπαυράν arising from *elision,* ἀπαυρᾶν from *contraction*; for οαυ=ωυ (as in ἑωυτοῦ) or ου, the a falling away, Död. p. 18]

ἀπουρίζω, fut. ἀπουρίσω, only 22, 489.† ἄλλοι γὰρ οἱ ἀπουρίσσουσιν ἀρούρας; according to the common explanation, Ion. for ἀφορίζω, they will *remove the boundaries of his fields,* and so *lessen* them; or, according to Buttm., Lexil. p. 146, related to ἀπαυράω (they will take his fields from him), who also prefers the other reading ἀπουρήσσουσιν.

*ἀποφαίνω (φαίνω), aor. 1 ἀπέφηνα, *to disclose, to bring to light, to make known, to manifest,* Batr. 143.

ἀποφέρω (φέρω), fut. ἀποίσω, aor.¹ 1 ἀνένεικα, *to bear away, to bring away;* with accus. spoken of horses, ἀπό τινος, 5, 256. 2) *to carry from one place to another, to convey;* τεύχεά τινι, Od. 16, 360; τινὰ Κόωνδε, of ships, 14, 255; μῦθον τινί, to report tidings to any one, 10, 337.

*ἀποφεύγω (φεύγω), *to flee away, to escape,* with accus. Batr.

ἀπόφημι (φημί), *to announce;* with ἀντικρύ, to declare directly, 7, 362, Ep. 2) Mid. in like manner: ἀπόφασθε ἀγγελίην, 9, 422. To this is assigned the aor. ἀπεῖπον, q. v.

ἀποφθίω (φθίω), imperf. ἀπέφθιθον, poet.=ἀποφθίνω, *to perish,* Od. 5, 110. 133. 7, 251. (Buttm. Gram. § 114, rejects the reading ἀπέφθιθον, and prefers ἀπέφθιθεν for ἀπεφθίθησαν, as aor. pass. from φθίω, cf. Rost, Gram. p. 334.)

ἀποφθινύθω, poet. (φθινύθω), intrans. *to perish, to die,* 5, 643. 2) Trans. θυμόν, *to lose life,* 16, 540. ª 11.

Άποφθί'νω. 62 *Άρα.

άποφθί'νω, poet. (φθίνω), only aor. sync. mid. άπεφθίμην, impf. άποφθίσθω, 8, 429, optat. άποφθί'μην for άποφθιοίμην, Od. 10, 51; partcp. άποφθίμενος, aor. 1 pass. άπεφθίθην; hence 3 plur. άπέφθιθεν, Od. 23, 331 [conf. also άποφθίθω], *to perish, to die*, 3, 322; λυγρώ όλέθρω, Od. 15, 268; λυγαλέω θανάτω, Od. 15, 358; ήδ πεσών —άποφθίμην—ήδ άκέων τλαίην, whether I falling from the ship should perish in the sea, Od. 10, 51.

άποφώλιος, ον, poet. accord. to the Schol.=μάταιος, prop. *idle, vain, empty, worthless*. Od. 14, 212; spoken of the mind, νόον άποφώλιος, Od. 8, 177; ούκ άποφώλια εϊδώς, not knowing worthless things, not weak of understanding, Od. 5, 182. 2) *fruitless, unproductive*; εύναί άθανάτων, Od. 11, 249. (The deriv. is uncertain; according to some from φωλεός, according to others from άπό and όφελος.)

άποχάζομαι, depon. mid. (χάζομαι), *to yield, to retire*, βόθρου, Od. 11, 95.†

άποχέω (χέω), Ep. aor. άπέχευα, *to pour out, to spill*, είδατα έραζε, *Od. 22, 20. 85, in tmesis.

άποψύχω (ψύχω), partcp. aor. pass. άποψυχθείς, 1) *to breathe out, to be breathless, to swoon*, Od. 24, 348. *b*) *to become cool*. 2) Mid. *to let* (a thing) *dry; to dry for oneself*; with accus. τοι δ' ίδρω άπεψύχοντο χιτώνων, they dried the sweat of the garments ('*their tunics sweat-imbued—They ventilated*,' Cp.], 11, 621. 22, 1; ίδρώ άποψυχθείς, 21, 561.

*άπρεπέως, poet. for άπρεπώς, adv. (πρέπω), *in an unbecoming manner, indecorously*, h. Merc. 272.

άπρηκτος, ον (πράσσω) 1) *undone, unaccomplished, vain, unproductive, fruitless*; άπρηκτον πόλεμον πολεμίζειν, 2, 121; άπρηκτοι έριδες, idle contentions, 2, 376. 2) Pass. *not to be managed, severe, incurable, unavoidable*. όδύναι, Od. 2, 49; άνίη, Od. 12, 223. The neut. as adv. άπρηκτον νέεσθαι, to return without effecting one's purpose, 14, 221.

άπριάτην, adv. (πρίαμαι), *unbought, unransomed, gratuitously*, 1, 99. Od. 14, 317.

άπροτίμαστος, ον, Ep. for άπρόσμαστος (μάσσω), *untouched, undefiled, pure*, 19, 263.†

άπτερος, ον (πτερόν), *unwinged, without wings*; only in the phrase τή δ' άπτερος έπλετο μύθος ['*nor his words flew wing'd away*,'Cp.], i. e., what he said did not escape her; she noted it, although words easily fly away (πτερόεντα), Od. 17, 57. 19, 29.

άπτήν, άπτήνος, ό, ή (πτηνός), *unfeathered, unfledged, callow*, νεοσσός, 9, 323.†

άπτοεπής, ές (πτοέω, έπος), *fearless* or *undaunted* in *speaking*, bold, 8, 209.† According to others, άπτοεπής from άπτεσθαι, assailing with words, cf. 1, 582.

άπτόλεμος, ον, poet. (πόλεμος), *unwarlike, cowardly*, *2, 201.

άπτω, aor. 1 ήψα, aor. 1 mid. ήψάμην and άψάμην, aor. pass. Ep. έάφθη, q. v.

1) Act. *to attach, to fasten, to join*; with accus. only εύστρεφές έντερον οίός, Od. 21. 408. II) Mid. *to join for oneself*; βρόχον άφ' ύψηλοίο μελάθρου, to make the noose fast to the lofty roof, Od. 11, 277; *to attach oneself to, to stick to, to hit*. τόφρα μάλ' άμφοτέρων βέλε' ήπτετο, so long the weapons hit both sides, 8, 67. 11, 85, and mly *to touch, to grasp, to lay hold of, to clasp, to seize*: with gen. άψασθαι γούνων, νηών, χειρών, κεφαλής; κύων συός άπτεται κατόπισθε, ίσχία τε γλουτούς τε, a dog seizes the boar from behind, by the hips and loins, 8, 339. Thus Eustath. explains the passage in accordance with connexion, assuming that to the genit. an accus. of nearer definition is annexed, and supplying κατά with ίσχία, etc. Others construct ίσχία τε γλουτούς τε, with έλισσόμενόν τε δονεύει: metaph. βρώμης ήδέ ποτήτος, to touch food and drink, Od. 10, 379.

άπτω, fut. mid. άψομαι, *to inflame, to kindle, to light*; only mid. *to take fire, to blaze up*; ότε δή τάχ' ό μοχλός—έν πυρί μέλλεν άψεσθαι, when now the ¢take 'should soon have flamed' (Cp.) in the fire, Od. 9, 379.

άπύργωτος,ον (πυργόω), *without towers, unfortified*, Θήβη, Od. 11, 263.†

άπυρος, ον (πύρ), *without fire, not having come in contact with fire, unsoiled by fire*: spoken of cauldrons and tripods as yet new, 9, 122. 23, 267; or, with others, *not to be used on the fire*, but e. g. for mixing wine.

άπύρωτος, ον=άπυρος, φιάλη, a vessel not yet touched by fire, 23, 270.†

άπυστος, ον (πυνθάνομαι), 1) Pass. of which nothing is heard, *unknown, unheard of*, Od. 1, 242. 2) Act. who has heard of nothing, *ignorant, uninformed*, Od. 5, 127; with gen. μύθων, Od. 4, 675.

άπωθέω (ώθέω), fut. 1 άπώσω, aor. 1 άπωσα, Ep. άπέωσα, fut. mid. άπώσομαι, aor. 1 mid. άπωσάμην, *to thrust away, to drive* or *push away*; with accus. Τρώας, 8, 206; κακά νηών, misfortune from the ships, 15. 503; πόλεμον νηών, 16, 251; θυράων λίθον, Od. 9, 394.

άρα, particle Ep, also άρ and enclit. ρά (ΑΡΩ). [All the forms occur before consonants; before vowels άρ' and ρ'; ρα may also stand before a vowel with the digamma.] This particle, which never stands as the first word of a sentence, but which occupies an early place in it, expresses, in accordance with its derivation from ΑΡΩ, to suit, to be adapted, a close connexion, *exactly, just*, hence *only, thereupon*. 1) A most intimate con-

’Αραβέω. 63 ’Αραρίσκω.

nexion between two ideas or thoughts: a) After relatives, in correlative clauses, of place, time, and manner. Άτρείδης δ' άρα χείρα—την βάλεν, ή ρ' έχε τόξον, precisely the hand with which, 13, 594. τῇ ρα, just there, just where, 14, 404. 11, 149; εὖτ' ἄρα, ὅτ' ἄρα, just as; τότ' ἄρα, exactly then. b) After a demonstrative pronoun, when by it an object previously named is referred to, or something already stated in general is repeated and more exactly explained, just, exactly, then; e. g. 4, 499—501, υἱὸν Πριάμοιο νόθον βάλε Δημοκόωντα— τόν ρ' Ὀδυσεὺς—βάλε, him then, and v. 488. τοῖον ἄρα—ἐξενάριξεν Αἴας (as a recapitulation of the whole narration), cf. 13, 170 —177; τόν ρα—νύξε; so ταῦτ' ἄρα, just these; with demonstrat. adv. τῷ ἄρα, just therefore, ἔνθ' ἄρα, just then or there, ὣς ἄρα, just so, and the frequent ἤ ρα and ὥς ἄρ' ἔφη. Hence c) In sequences, οὗτοι ἄρ'—ἦσαν, these then were, 2, 760; τοὔνεκ' ἄρα, on this account then: here belongs the construction with interrogatives, τίς τ' ἄρ, τῶν—ἦν, now then, who of these, etc., 2, 761. Hence 2) It is also employed in clauses where a previous mistake is indicated, or information upon some unthought of point communicated, then, therefore. νηλέες οὐκ ἄρα σοίγε πατὴρ ἦν ἱππότα Πηλεύς, not therefore was, 16, 33. cf. 9, 316. Od. 13, 209. 17, 454; also in explanatory and illustrative clauses. ὅτι ρα, ἐπεί ρα, because namely, 1, 56. 13, 416. 3) It indicates the direct progress of actions and events: hence it serves a) To connect actions and states which in point of time succeed one another, and of which the one seems to proceed from the other, then, thereupon, 1, 68. 306. 464; hence frequently in connexion with αἶψα, αὐτίκα, καρπαλίμως; further, ἐπεί ρα, ὅτε ρα, as soon as, 14, 641; and in both protasis and apodosis, ὅτε δή ρα—δή ρα τότε, then forthwith, 11, 780. b) bly in enumerating several consecutive events, 5, 592. With negat. οὐδ' ἄρα, it signifies, according to Nägelsbach, a) und not once, Od. 9, 92. b) and immediately not (no longer), Od. 4, 716; cf. Nägelsbach, Excurs. III. p. 191. Kühner, Gram. § 630.

ἀραβέω (ἄραβος), aor. 1 ἀράβησα, to rattle, to resound; spoken of the arms of a falling warrior. ἀράβησε τεύχε' ἐπ' αὐτῷ, 4, 504. 5, 42, and often.

ἄραβος, ὁ (ἀράσσω [and the other verba pulsandi, ῥάω, ῥαβάσσω. Lob. Path. 285]), noise, rattling; ὀδόντων, chattering of the teeth, 10, 375.†

Ἀραιθυρέη, ἡ, a town and territory in Argolis, accord. to Strabo the later Phlius, between Sicyon and Argos, which took its name from the daughter of Aras; or rather the signif. is from ἀραιός and θυρέα, a narrow pass, 2, 571.

ἀραιός, ή, όν, thin, small, narrow, κνῆμαι, 18.411; γλῶσσαι, 16, 161, εἴσοδος, the narrow entrance of a port, Od. 10, 90. 2) delicate, weak, unwarlike; spoken of the hand of Aphroditē, 5, 525.

ἀράομαι, depon. mid. (ἀρά), fut. ἀρήσομαι, aor. 1 ἠρησάμην, to pray, to address supplications to the gods; with dat. Ἀπόλλωνι, 1, 35. 2) to wish, yet only when one's wish is expressed aloud; with infin. 4, 143. Od. 1, 163; with ἕως and optat. Od. 19, 367. b) to wish present, to invoke; with accus. ἐπεί—ἀρήσετ' Ἐρινὺς, when the mother shall invoke the Erinnyes, Od. 2, 135. Once ἀρήμεναι for ἀρᾶν, infin. act., but according to Buttm., Gram. § 114, aor. 2 pass. of the root ἄρομαι, in accordance with the connexion: πολλάκι που μέλλεις ἀρήμεναι, thou wilt oft have prayed, Od. 22, 322.

ἀραρίσκω, poet. (th. ΑΡΩ [cf. εἱλελίζω, ἀκαχίζω, ἀπαφίσκω]), aor. 1 act. ἦρσα, infin. ἄρσαι, aor. 2 act. ἤραρον. Ep. ἄραρον, partcp. ἀραρών, perf. ἄρηρα, partcp. ἀρηρώς, fem. ἀραρυῖα, pluperf. ἀρήρειν, aor. 1 pass. only 3 plur. ἄρθεν, 16, 211, Ep. aor. 2 mid. only partcp. ἄρμενος. (The pres. ἀραρίσκω, Od. 14, 23, has been formed from the aor. 2 act.) I) Trans. in the aor. 1 and 2 act. (The last twice intrans. 16, 214. Od. 4, 777.) To join, hence 1) to annex, to bind, to fit to, to secure, to prepare, τί, any thing; τινί, with or of something; κέρα, to bind the horns, 4, 110. οἱ δ' ἐπεὶ ἀλλήλους ἄραρον δόεσσι, when with their shields they had locked themselves together, 12, 105; and pass. μᾶλλον δὲ στίχες ἄρθεν (Ep. for ἄρθησαν), the ranks pressed more closely together, 16, 211. b) τί τινι, to fasten or attach one thing to another; ἰκρία σταμίνεσσιν, Od. 5, 252; ἄγγεσιν ἄπαντα, to preserve, to put up every thing in vessels, Od. 2, 289; πίθλα πώδεσσιν, Od. 14, 23; hence mly to construct, to prepare, to build, τί τινι, any thing of or from a thing; τοῖχον λίθοισι, to build a wall of stones, 16, 212 (in which sense also the perf. ἄρηρεν stands, Od, 5, 248; which is, however, according to the Schol. only a false reading for ἄρασσεν, cf. Nitzsch ad loc.). Metaph. μνηστήρσιν θάνατον, to prepare death for the suitors, Od. 16, 169. 2) to provide, to furnish, τί τινι; πώμασιν ἀμφορέας, Od. 2, 353; νῆα ἐρέτῃσιν, Od. 3, 280; metaph. ἤραρε θυμὸν ἐδωδῇ, he furnished, i. e. refreshed his heart with food, Od. 5, 95. 3) to suit any thing to any one, to make agreeable, only 1, 136. γέρας ἄρσαντες κατὰ θυμόν, suiting a present to my mind, i. e., selecting one, etc. II) Intrans. in the perf. and plupf. 1) to be joined together, to stand in close array, and mly to fit, to be suited to, to sit close. Τρῶες ἀρηρότες, the Trojans in close array, 13, 800; and so aor. 2, 16, 214. ζωστὴρ ἀρηρώς, a close-fitting girdle, 4, 134; mly with dat. θώρηξ γυάλοισι ἀρηρώς, a cuirass joined together, constructed of plates, 15, 530. cf. Od. 6, 267; to suit, τινί, any thing. δοῦρα παλάμηφιν ἀρήρει, 3, 338. κυνέη ἑκατὸν πολίων πρυλέεσσ' ἀραρυῖα, 5, 744. πύλαι

*Άραρον. 64 "Αργος.

πύκα στιβαρώς άραρυΐαι, 12, 454; σανίδης, Od. 2, 344; rarely with prepos. έν άρμονίησιν άρήρη, the timbers hold fast in the joints, Od. 5, 361. cf. άρμονίη. πίθοι ποτί τοίχον άρηρότες, vessels arranged against the wall (fitted to the wall), Od. 2, 342; metaph. σύ φρεσίν ήσιν άρηρώς, not firm in understanding, Od. 10, 553. 2) fitted out, well furnished; σκολόπεσσι, with fishes, 12, 56. ζώνη έκατόν θυσάνοις άραρυΐα, 14, 181. cf. Od. 2, 267. 3) Metaph. to be befitting, agreeable, pleasant. μύθος, δ—πάσιν ήραρεν, which was pleasing to all, Od. 4, 777, aor. 2 here intrans. III) Mid. only the partcp. aor. 2 sync. as adj. άρμενος, η, ον, fitted to, attached to; with dat. έπίκριον άρμενον τώ ίστώ, the sail-yard attached to the mast, Od. 5, 254; with έν: τροχός άρμενος έν παλάμησιν, a wheel suited to the hands, 18, 600; πέλεκυς, Od. 5, 234.

άραρον, see άραρίσκω.

άράσσω [see άραβος], fut. ξω, to strike, to knock, to beat; in our editions of H. found only in tmesis, άπαράσσω and συναράσσω [and once έξαράσσω, Od. 12, 422], q. v. In Od. 5, 248, Bothe, instead of the reading άρηρεν of Eustath., has adopted the reading of the Codd. άρασσεν. He reads, therefore, καί ήρμοσεν άλλήλοισιν γόμφοισιν δ' άρα τήνγε καί άρμονίησιν άρασσεν. Also Nitzsch, Bd. II. p. 36, approves this as the only true reading, because άρηρεν is always elsewhere used intransitively, and ήραρεν with ήρμοσεν is tautological; cf. Apoll. Rhod. II. 614. Άρασσεν stands for συνήρασσεν, belongs prop. to γόμφοισιν, and is by zeugma to be referred to άρμονίησιν also. Bothe translates the verse: 'he hammered (fastened) together the raft with nails and joints.'

άράχνιον, τό (άράχνη), a spider's web, Od. 8, 280. 16, 35. *Od.

άργαλέος, έη, έον, heavy, difficult, troublesome, oppressive, that which can hardly be borne; more rarely, which is difficult to accomplish, έργον, άνεμος, μνηστύς, Od. 2, 199; mly with dat. of pers. and infin. άργαλέον μοι πάσι μάχεσθαι, hard it is for me to contend with all, 20, 356; more rarely, άργαλέος γάρ 'Ολύμπιος άντιφέρεσθαι, hard is it to oppose the Olympian Zeus, 1, 589, and Od. 4, 397 (prob. from α Intens. and έργον; or, according to some, from άλγος, with an exchange of λ for ρ).

Άργεάδης, ου, ό, son of Argeus=Polymelus, 16, 417.

Άργεΐος, είη, είον (Άργος), of Argos, Argive. Ήρη Άργείη, the Argive Here, 4, 8; Ελένη, the Peloponnesian, 2, 161; cf. 'Αργος, h. 3. 2) Subst. a man of Argos, primarily an inhabitant of the city of Argos. b) an inhabitant of the Argive territory; and, because this was the principal people before Troy, a denomination of all the Greeks, 2, 352.

Άργειφόντης, ου, ό (Άργος, φονεύς), the Argicide, an appellation of Hermes, because he slew the guardian of Io the many-eyed Argus, 2. 103. Od. 1, 38. [Άργος (propter oculorum splendorem=) Micuus. See note, end of Άργός.]

άργεννός, ή, όν, poet. for άργός, white, shining, δίες, but also όθόναι, silver-coloured veil, 3, 141 [hence the islands 'Αργεννούσαι and the promontory 'Αργεννον=Capo Bianco, Lob. Path. 188].

άργεστής, άο, ό (άργός) epith. of Notus, prob. rapid, or raising white foam (like albus Notus, Hor., [=rapidus, vehemens: ταχύς, Apoll., for in H. (mistaken by Horace) Notus does not disperse, but collect the clouds. Luc. p. 181]), 11, 306 21, 334. As an adj. it is, according to the Gramm., oxytone, άργεστής; as prop. name, paroxytone, cf. Spitzner ad II. 11, 306.

άργέτι, άργέτα, poet. for άργήτι, άργήτα, see άργής.

άργής, ήτος, ό, ή, white, clear, shining, beaming [Lucas would construe it quick-flashing, to combine both rapidity and brightness. It is an epithet, not of άστεροπή (fulgur), but of κεραυνός (fulmen), the lightning that strikes], mly spoken of lightning: but also of έανός. άργής δημός, white fat, 11, 817. 21, 127 (poet. shortened dat. and accus. άργέτι, άργέτα, 11, 817. 21, 127).

άργικέραυνος, ου, ό (κεραυνός), having a blaze of white lightning. darting, glowing lightning, epith. of Zeus; subst. the hurler of lightning (Voss), *20, 16.

άργινόεις, εσσα, εν (άργός), white, shining, epith. of the towns Camirus and Lycastus, from the white limestone mountains, 2, 647. 656; ούρεα, h. Ap. 18, 12.

άργιόδους, οντος, ό, ή (όδούς), white-toothed, white-tusked, epith. of boars and dogs, 10, 264. Od. 8, 60.

άργίπους, ποδος, ό, ή (πούς), swift-footed, epith. of dogs, 24, 211.† of horses, h. in Ven. 212. See note on 'Αργειφόντης.

Άργισσα, ή, a place in Thessalia Pelasgiotis, on the Peneus, the later Argura, 2, 737.

άργμα, τος, τό (άργω), the first-fruits, the firstlings, the portions of the victim cut off and burnt in honour of the gods, Od. 14, 446.†

Άργος, ό, pr. name of a dog, Od. 17, 292; see adj. άργός.

Άργος, εος, τό, 1) Argos (Argi), chief city in Argolis, on the Inachus, now Argo, in the time of the Trojan war the residence of Diomedes, 2, 559. It had the epithets 'Αχαιϊκόν, Ίασον, 'Ιππόβοτον. 2) the Argolic plain, the realm in which Agamemnon ruled, having his residence in Mycenae, 1, 30. 2, 108. 3) It signif. also the entire Peloponnesus, Argos being the chief city of the Achaians and the most powerful kingdom in the Peloponnesus; hence, in connexion with Hellas, it stands for all Greece, Od. 1, 344. 4, 726. 4) τό Πελασγικόν, a town in Thessaly, under the dominion of Achilles, according to some the later Larissa, not

Ἀργός. 65 Ἀρή.

extant in the time of Strabo, 2, 681. (ἄργος, τό, signifies, accord. to Strab., *plain*, and is peculiarly a name of Pelasgian towns, as Λάρισσα, see Müller I. § 125.)

ἀργός, ή, όν (related to ἄργυρος [see Hermann's note in 'Αργειφόντης]), *shining, gleaming, white*, epith. of a goose, Od. 15. 161; and of victims shining with fat (*nitidus*), 23, 30. 2) *rapid, fleet*, often epith. of dogs, πόδας ἀργοί, 18, 578. Od. 2, 11; and without πόδας, 1, 50. (According to the Schol. and some modern commentators, it signifies *white dogs*, see Köppen; the connexion, however, refutes this signif., since the reference is to the entire race. The signif. *swift-footed*, some derive from ἔργον and the intens. α, ἀεργός, contr. ἀργός, *without toil, swift-running*. The true derivation is that, being primarily used of light, it signifies *glimmering, shining* (Herm. *micuus*); then of the running of dogs, *fleet*, since swiftness in running produces a glimmering appearance: see Nitzsch in Anm. to Od. 2, 11.)

Ἀργόσδε, to Argos.

ἀργύρεος, έη, εον (ἄργυρος), *silver, adorned with silver*, often used of articles belonging to the gods and to the rich, 1, 49. 5, 727. Od. 4, 53.

ἀργυροδίνης, ου (δίνη), *silver-whirling, having silver eddies*, epith. of rivers, *2, 752. 21, 8.

ἀργυρόηλος, ον (ἦλος), *adorned with silver nails* or *studs*, ξίφος, θρόνος, 3, 334. Od. 7, 162.

ἀργυρόπεζα, ἡ (πέζα), *silver-footed*, metaph. for shining, epith. of Thetis, *1, 538.

ἄργυρος, ὁ (related to ἀργός), *silver*. H. mentions it very often, and names as its source the town Alybe in the country of the Halizones (cf. Ἀλύβη). We find mention of vessels of massive silver, e. g., a *mixing vase* (Od. 9, 203), *cauldrons, goblets, cups*, etc., Od. 1, 137. 4, 53. In other places the articles seem only plated or washed with silver, e. g., the handles of the swords, 11, 31. Od. 8, 404; the door-posts in the palace of Alcinous, Od. 8, 89; or inlaid with silver, e. g., a seat, Od. 19, 56; the bed of Ulysses, Od. 23, 200.

ἀργυρότοξος, ον (τόξον), *having a silver bow, god of the silver bow*, epith. of Apollo, 2, 766. Od. 7, 64; also as subst. 1, 37.

Ἀργυφέη, ἡ, an unknown town in Elis, h. Ap. 422; where Ilgen would read Ἀμφιγένεια.

ἀργύφεος, έη, εον, poet. (ἄργυρος [Vocalis (ε) exstruaecus additae exemplum certum sed unicum praebet ἀργύφεος: quod propter consonae mutationem cum ξυλόφιον et ξυλήριον conferri posset, nisi utrumque mendi speciem praeberet. Lob. Path. 299]), *silver-shining, silver-white*; σπέος, 18, 50; φάρος, robe, Od. 5, 230. [In Hes. Theog. 574, ἀργυφής of a garment.]

ἄργυφος, ον = ἀργύφεος, epith. of sheep 29. 621. Od. 10, 85.

Ἀργώ, οῦς, ἡ, *Argo*, the ship of the Argonauts, named either from the builder Argos, or from ἀργός, swift, Od. 12, 70.

ἀρδμός, ὁ (ἄρδω), *a place where cattle are watered, a watering-place, a drinking-place*, 18, 521. Od. 13, 247.

*ἄρδω, fut. ἄρσω, *to give drink, to water*, h. 8, 3. Mid. *to water oneself, to drink*, h in Ap. 263.

ἀρειή, ἡ (ἀρά), *cursing, imprecation, threatening, menacing*, 17, 431; 20, 109 (ᾱ).

Ἀρέθουσα, ἡ (ἄρι, θέω), that runs briskly), a fountain on the west side of the island Ithaca, Od. 13, 408.

Ἄρειος, ον (Ἄρης), mly Ἀρήϊος in H., *devoted to Arês*. τεῖχος Ἄρειον, the wall of Arês, i. e., Thebes.

ἀρείων, ἄρειον, *better, stronger, superior, braver*; a compar. which from the meaning is assigned to ἀγαθός, related to ἀρι or Ἄρης; accus. sing. ἀρείω, for ἀρείονα, Od. 3, 250; nom. plur. ἀρείους, for ἀρείονες, Od. 2, 477.

Ἀρείων, ονος, ὁ, the steed of Adrastus, to which he owed his deliverance before Thebes, 23, 346. Ἀρίων, Apd.

ἄρεκτος, ον, Ep. for ἄρρεκτος (ῥέζω), *not done, unaccomplished*, 19, 150.†

ἀρέσαι, ἀρέσασθαι, see ἀρέσκω.

ἀρέσκω (th. ἀρέω), fut. ἀρέσω, aor. 1 act. ἤρεσα, mid. fut. ἀρέσομαι, Ep. σσ, aor. 1 ἠρεσάμην, Ep. σσ, 1) Act. in H. trans. *to make good, to compensate, to requite, to make satisfaction*, 9, 120. 2) Mid. oftener, *to make good for oneself, to compensate* or *requite for oneself*. ταῦτα ἀρεσσόμεθα, these things will we settle, 4, 362. 6, 526. Od. 22, 55; said of persons: *to propitiate, to conciliate, to appease*, τινά, Od. 8, 402; τινί, by a thing; τινὰ δώροισιν, *to propitiate any one by presents*, 9, 112. Od. 8, 396, 415.

ἀρετάω (ἀρετή), *to prosper, to flourish, to succeed*, Od. 8, 329. λαοὶ ἀρετῶσι, the people flourish, Od. 19, 144.

Ἀρετάων, ονος, ὁ, a Trojan who was slain by Teucer, 6, 31.

ἀρετή, ἡ, *worth, ability, excellence*, any thing by which one distinguishes himself. In H. it means esply, 1) In gods, *glory*, 9, 498. 2) In men, *strength, courage, bravery, activity of body*; also external advantages, *fortune, beauty, honour*, etc. ἀμείνων παντοίας ἀρετάς, ἠμὲν πόδας, ἠδὲ μάχεσθαι, superior in every virtue, both in running and fighting, 15, 642; *fortune*, spoken of Ulysses, Od. 13, 44; *strength*, Od. 18. 133. 3) In women, *excellence, beauty, fortune*, Od. 2, 206. 18, 250. (The moral idea of virtue is not known to H. It is derived from ἄρω or from Ἄρης, or, accord. to Nitzsch on Od. 3, 57, from ἀρέω, any thing which is pleasing.)

ἀρή, ἡ, Ion. for ἀρά, *prayer, supplication, petition*, 15, 378. 23, 199, ἀράων ἀίουσα. Od. 4, 767; mly in a bad sense, *imprecation, malediction*. ἐξαίσιος ἀρή,

Άρήγω.

cruel imprecation, 15, 598; hence 2) the *destruction, evil*, or *misfortune* imprecated, 12, 334. Od. 2, 59. 24, 489, ἀρήν καὶ λοιγὸν ἀμῦναι. [14, 485, ἀρῆς ἀλκτῆρα γενέσθαι (cædis vindicem, *Heyne*), one *who averts from himself the curse of unrevenged blood*, i. e., by killing the slayer of his near relation. *Lob.*] (According to Heyne, 12, 334, the word in the first signif. has a, in the second, ᾱ; but, according to Passow, the quantity depends upon the position in the verse.)

ἀρήγω (related to ἀρκέω), fut. ἀρήξω, *to help, to assist, to come to aid*, τινί, any one; often in the Il. also with dat. instrum.: ἔπεσιν καὶ χερσίν, to help with word and deed. 1, 77. 2) *to repel*, with accus. ὄλεθρον, Batr. 280.

ἀρηγών, όνος, ὁ, ἡ, *a helper*; as fem. *4, 7.

Ἀρηΐθοος, ον (θοός), *fleet as Arês, rapid in the battle*, *4, 280.

Ἀρηΐθοος, ὁ, pr. n. 1) husband of Philomelê, grandfather of Menesthius, king of Arnê in Bœotia, with the appellation of club bearer, 7, 9. cf. v. 137 seq. Lycurgus surprised him on his return from Arcadia in an ambuscade, and slew him, v. 141 seq. His grave was shown in Arcadia, Paus. 2) father of Menesthius, 7. 8; for the ὅν, v. 9, relates to 'Ἀρηϊθόοιο ἄνακτος, see Heyne. 3) a Thracian, charioteer of Rhigmus, slain by Achilles, 20, 486.

Ἀρήϊος, ον, Ion. for ἄρειος, *devoted to Arês, warlike, brave, martial*; spoken often of persons; more rarely of things: τεύχεα, ἔντεα, weapons of Arês, 6, 340. Od. 16, 284.

Ἀρηϊκτάμενος, η, ον (κτείνω), *slain by Arês, fallen in battle*, 22, 72.†

Ἀρηΐλυκος, ὁ (λύκος, a wolf like Arês), 1) father of Prothoênôr, q. v. 2) a Trojan, slain by Penthous, 26, 308.

Ἀρηΐφατος, ον (ΦΕΝΩ, πέφαμαι). *slain by Arês, killed in battle*, 19, 31. Od. 11, 41.

Ἀρηΐφιλος, *beloved by Arês, warlike, brave*, epith. of the Achaians, 6, 73.

ἀρήμεναι, see ἀράομαι.

ἀρημένος, η, ον (ᾱ), an Ep. partcp. perf. pass. of doubtful derivation; explained by the Schol. by βεβλαμμένος, *burdened, oppressed, tormented*. γήραϊ λυγρῷ ἀρημένος, 18, 435; oftener in the Od. ὕπνῳ καὶ καμάτῳ ἀρημένοις, oppressed with sleep and fatigue, Od. 6, 2. (Accord. to Thiersch, Gram. § 232, p. 385, from ἀρέω, related to βαρύς; according to others, to ἀραιός.)

(ἀρήν, ὁ,) in nom. obsol.; from this the syncop. cases ἀρνός, ἀρνί, ἄρνα, plur. ἄρνες, dat. ἀρνάσι, Ep. ἀρνέσσι, prop. *a male sheep, a ram*, Od. 4, 65; but particularly *a young sheep, a lamb* (from ῥήν, with euphon. prefix a, hence ἀρήν, ἀρρήν, ἀρσήν).

ἀρηρομένος, η, ον, see ἀρόω.

Ἀρήνη, ἡ, a town in Elis, on the river Minyeius, according to Strabo, VIII. 346,

prob the later *Samicon*, which, perhaps, was the fortress of Arenê; but accord. to another passage of Strabo, VIII. 348, the later *Erana*, in Messenia: cf. Paus. 4, 2. 3 2, 591. 11, 723.

Ἄρης, gen. Ἄρεος, Ep. Ἄρηος, dat. Ἄρει, Ἄρεϊ, Ep. Ἄρηϊ, accus. Ep. Ἄρη, Ἄρην, Ἄρηα, 5, 909, vocat. Ἄρες, *Arês*, son of Zeus and Hêrê, god of war and of the fierce tumult of battle; the symbol of stormy, impetuous bravery, in contradistinction from Athênê. He is represented as the brother of Eris (Discord). Deimos (Terror) and Phobos (Flight) are his sons, 4, 440. 13, 280. 15, 119. He delights only in war and bloodshed (ἆτος πολέμοιο, μιαιφόνος, βροτολοιγός, etc.): he knows in his bravery neither plan nor moderation (θοός, θοῦρος, ὄβριμος). He has his abode chiefly among the rude, warlike nations, the Thracians, the Phlegyes, and the Ephyri, 13, 301; and in the Il. is sometimes on the side of the Trojans, sometimes on that of the Greeks (ἀλλοπρόσαλλος). Arês is large and handsome in appearance; his body covers 7 plethra; he cries as loudly as 10,000 men, upon being wounded by Diomêdês, 5, 860. Of his earlier fortunes, the confinement in which he was held by Otus and Ephialtês, and from which he was delivered by Hermês, and his intrigues with Aphroditê, are mentioned by H., 5, 385. Od. 8, 267 seq. 2) As an appellat. it stands for *war, battle, slaughter, destruction, arms*, when, however, the personification is not entirely lost sight of: συνάγειν Ἄρηα, to begin the battle, 2, 381; and ἔριδα Ἄρηος, 14, 149; ἐγείρειν ὀξὺν Ἄρηα, 2, 440; *weapons*, for ἔγχος, 13, 444. (The first syllable short; in the arsis, however, it is long, cf. 5, 31.)

ἀρητήρ, ῆρος, ὁ (ἀράομαι), prop. one who prays; then *a priest*, since he prays for the people, *1, 11. 5, 78.

Ἀρήτη, ἡ (ᾱ), daughter of Rhexênôr, wife of Alcinous in Phæacia, Od. 7, 64—77.

Ἀρητιάδης, ου, ὁ (ᾱ), son of Arêtus, Od. 16, 395. (The first a short.)

ἀρητός, ή, όν, Ion. for ἀρατός (ἀράομαι), *wished for, prayed for*. 2) In H. in a bad sense, *imprecated, accursed, dreadful*, γόος, 17, 37.

Ἄρητος, ὁ, 1) son of Nestor, Od. 3, 414. 2) son of Priam, slain by Automedon, 17, 494.

ἄρθεν, Ep. for ἤρθησαν, see ἀραρίσκω.

ἀρθμέω (ἀρθμός), aor. 1 partcp. ἀρθμήσας, *to join*. 2) Intrans. *to be united together*. διέτμαγεν ἐν φιλότητι ἀρθμήσαντε, they parted from each other united in friendship [' *they parted friends,*' Cp.]. 7, 302.†

ἄρθμιος, η, ον (ἀρθμός), *united in friendship, friendly; at peace with* any one, τινί, Od. 16, 427.†

ἀρθμός, ὁ (ἄρω), union, intimacy, friendship, h. Merc. 524.

ἀρι-, an inseparable particle, like ἐρι,

Ἀριάδνη. 67 **Ἀρκέω.**

which heightens the meaning, prob. related to ἀρείων.

Ἀριάδνη, ἡ (Herm. *Roborina*), daughter of Minos and Pasiphaë, who helped Theseus out of the labyrinth. She followed him, but was slain on the island Dia (Naxos) by Artĕmis. By '*the testimony of Dionysus*' (Διονύσου μαρτυρίησιν), commentators understand that Ariadnē received the embraces of Theseus in a grove of the island which was sacred to that god, and was therefore slain, Od. 11, 321 seq. Il. 18, 592.

ἀρίγνωτος, η, ον (γνωτός), *much distinguished, easily known,* ἀρίγνωτοί τε θεοί, 13, 72. Od. 6, 108. 2) In the iron. sense, *well known,* noted, *notorious,* Od. 17, 375. (˘ ˘ ¯ ˘ and ˘ ¯ ˘ ˘, Od. 17.)

ἀριδείκετος, ον (δείκνυμι), *much pointed out, hence, greatly distinguished, very famous;* chiefly as superl. with gen. ἀνδρῶν, λαῶν, 11, 248. Od. 8, 382.

ἀρίζηλος, ον, also ἀριζήλη, 18, 219 (from ἀρι and ζῆλος=δῆλος, with the digamma, which prob. before δ passed over into σ); *very clear, very manifest, very brilliant,* αὐγή, 22, 25; φωνή, a clear voice; spoken of a miraculous phenomenon: τὸν (sc. δράκοντα) ἀρίζηλον θῆκε θεός, the god made him visible, or, according to others, *significant,* i. e., a prodigy, 2, 319. cf. Buttm., Lex. p. 53 sqq., and ἄζηλος.

ἀριζήλως, *clearly, entirely,* Od. 12, 453.†

ἀριθμέω (ἀριθμός), fut. ήσω, infin. aor. 1 pass. ἀριθμηθήμεναι for ἀριθμηθῆναι, *to count, to reckon up, to count together, to enumerate;* with accus. Od. 4, 411. 10, 204. εἴπερ γάρ κ' ἐθέλοιμεν—ἀριθμηθήμεναι ἄμφω, if we both, Achaians and Trojans, should be counted, 2, 124.

ἀριθμός, ὁ (ἄρω), *number, amount, multitude,* *Od. 4, 451. 11, 449.

Ἄριμα, τά, sc. ὄρη, *the mountains of the Arimi;* or, as a people, Ἄριμοι οἱ, *the Arimi,* 2, 783. εἰν Ἀρίμοις most commentators take as mountains, see Τυφωεύς. This chain of mountains has been located in Mysia, Lydia, Cilicia, and Syria; since, in the imagination of the poets, a giant inspired by Zeus lies buried where there are earthquakes and volcanic fire. Strab., XIII. p. 606, prefers Mysia; here, at any rate, was a region exhibiting traces of volcanic fire, and which was therefore called ἡ Κατακεκαυμένη.

ἀριπρεπής, ές, gen. έος (πρέπω), *exceedingly prominent, very distinguished, magnificent, glorious, splendid,* spoken of men, beasts, and things; with dat. ἀριπρεπὴς Τρώεσσιν, distinguished among the Trojans, 6, 477.

Ἀρίσβας, αντος, ὁ, father of Liocritus, perhaps a Theban, 17, 345.

Ἀρίσβη, ἡ, a town in Troas, not far from Abydos, 2, 836. Adv. Ἀρίσβηθεν, from Arisbē, 11, 96.

*ἀρίσημος, ον (σῆμα), *very distinguished,* noted, h. in Merc. 12.

ἀριστερός, ή, όν, *left;* ὦμος, the left shoulder. ἐπ' ἀριστερά, upon the left; μάχης, 5, 355; στρατοῦ, 13, 326; χειρός, on the left hand. 2) Metaph. spoken of omens, *sinister, inauspicious,* because to the Greek diviner, who looked towards the north, the left hand indicated misfortune, 12, 240. Od. 20, 242. [σκαιός is not used in this sense. Död.]

ἀριστερόφιν, adv. or Ep. accus. with suffix φιν (cf. Rost, Dial. § 23, b), ἀριστερός, *upon the left side, left; only* with prepos. ἐπ' ἀριστερόφιν, 13, 309. 17, 116.

ἀριστεύς, ῆος, ὁ (ἄριστος), *the best, the most excellent,* sing. 17, 203; in H. chiefly plur., οἱ ἀριστῆες, the chiefs, chieftains, leaders, 2, 404.

ἀριστεύω (ἀριστεύς), *to be first, to be most excellent, to distinguish oneself, to excel,* τινός, any one, 6, 461; τινί, in a thing, βουλῇ, in counsel, 11, 627; also ἐν μάχῃ, 11, 409; and with the infin. 6, 460.

ἄριστον, τό, *breakfast, prandium,* taken in H. soon after sunrise, 24, 124. Od. 16, 2 (ά).

ἄριστος, η, ον (superl. of ἀγαθός from ἀρείων), *the best, most excellent, most distinguished,* in H. spoken only of external advantages, and esply of warlike power. Ἀργείων οἱ ἄριστοι, the noblest of the Argives: often connected with the accus., εἶδος ἀρίστη, most excellent in form, 2, 715. ἵπποι ἄριστοι, 2, 763 (contr. with article ὥριστος for ὁ ἄριστος, 11, 288; see Thiersch, Gram. § 165, 1.)

ἀρισφαλής, ές, gen. έος (σφάλλω), *very slippery,* οὐδός, Od. 17, 196 †

ἀριφραδέως, adv. *very clearly,* Od. 23, 225.†

ἀριφραδής, ές, gen. έος (φράζομαι), *easily distinguishable, very plain or clear, very observable,* 23, 240; σῆμα, Od. 11, 126. 23, 73.

Ἀρκαδίη, ἡ (prop. fem. from Ἀρκάδιος), *Arcadia,* a district in the middle of the Peloponnesus, 2, 603.

Ἀρκάς, άδος, ὁ (ά), an *Arcadian,* an inhabitant of Arcadia, 2, 611.

Ἀρκεισιάδης, ου, ὁ (ά), son of Arcesius =Laertes, Od. 4, 755.

Ἀρκείσιος, ὁ, *Arcesius,* son of Zeus and Euryodia, husband of Chalcomedūsa, father of Laertes, Od. 16, 118. 120. (According to Eustath. ad loc. he received the name because he was suckled by a bear.)

Ἀρκεσίλαος, ὁ (from ἀρκέω and λαός, defender of the people), son of Lycus, leader of the Boeotians in the Trojan war, sailed to Troy with ten ships, and was slain by Hector, 2, 495. 15, 329.

ἀρκέω, fut. ἀρκέσω, aor. 1 ἤρκεσα, 1) *to avert, to hold back, to remove,* τινί τι, something from any one; ὄλεθρον τινί, 6, 16, and ἀπό τινος, 13, 440. 2) With dat. only, *to defend, protect, help* any one, 15, 529. Od. 16, 261; and without cases, *to profit, to avail, to be of use;* οὐδ' ἤρκεσε

ἄρκιος, η, ον (ἀρκέω), *helping, advantageous, sufficient,* μισθός, 10, 304. 2) on which one may depend, *sure, certain, safe* (Ap. ἕτοιμον), οὔ οἱ ἄρκιον ἐσσεῖται, with infin. 2, 393 [*there shall be nothing on which he can rely* (which can *give* him a well-grounded hope of escaping the dogs and birds). νῦν ἄρκιον ἢ ἀπολέσθαι ἠὲ σαωθῆναι, now we may rely upon it (i. e., it is *certain*) that we shall either perish or be saved. Buttm., Lex. p. 163]. 15, 502. (Accord. to Buttm. the last is the primary meaning, and the only one in H.; hence μισθὸς ἄρκιος, a sure, definite reward.)

ἄρκτος, ὁ. ἡ, 1) *a bear*, Od. 11, 611. h. Ven. 71. 2) Ἄρκτος, pr. n. *the Great Bear* or *the Wain*, a constellation in the northern heavens, which embraces seven stars, and towards which Ulysses directed his course, Od. 5, 273. It is very near the polar star, and to the inhabitants of the northern hemisphere never sets, 18, 485 seq. Od. 5, 273. According to a later fable, it was Callisto metamorphosed to a bear.

ἅρμα, ατος, τό (ἄρω), *a chariot,* esply *the war-chariot;* the plur. often stands for the sing. 2) *the chariot and team,* 4, 306. 10, 322. Often ἵπποι καὶ ἅρματα, 5, 199. The war-chariots of the Hom. heroes had but one axle-tree (ἄξων) and two wheels (τροχοί), 5, 838. 6, 42. From the middle of the chariot and out of the axle-tree proceeded the pole (ὁ ῥυμός), which was single. The felloes (ἡ ἴτυς) of the wheels, 4, 486, were surrounded by iron or brazen tires (ἐπίσσωτρα). The hole of the nave, and the nave itself (αἱ πλῆμναι), were guarded with metal, and to this the spokes (κνῆμαι) were attached. Upon the axle-tree was placed a body or seat (ὁ δίφρος), which was circular before and behind, and had an opening for the convenience of ascending and alighting. At the fore-end of the pole was a hole, in which a pin (ὁ ἕστωρ) was inserted to keep the yoke from slipping (cf. τὸ ζυγόν). Two horses were commonly attached to one chariot; sometimes a third was added, which was bound to one of the pole-horses with a thong, and was called παρήορος. In single passages mention is made of a chariot with four horses, 8, 185. In the chariot were always two warriors, one who fought with the spear, ὁ παραιβάτης, and another acting as charioteer (ὁ ἡνίοχος). The chariot was chiefly used in the first onset, in order to force the enemy to sudden flight, 11, 711. 761. This, of course, could happen only on level ground. In battle itself, the warriors leapt from the chariot and fought on foot: cf. the several words, and esply ἵππος, παραιβάτης, ἡνίοχος.

Ἅρμα, ατος, τό, a village in Bœotia, not far from Tanagra, where Amphiaräus and his chariot were swallowed up by the earth, 2, 499.

ἁρματοπηγός, όν (πήγνυμι), *that makes chariots;* ἀνήρ, chariot-maker, 4, 485.†

ἁρματροχιή, ἡ (τροχός), *a wheel-rut*, 23, 505.†

ἅρμενος, ον, see ἀραρίσκω.

ἁρμόζω (ἄρω), aor. 1 ἥρμοσα, 1) *to join together, to fit together, to unite,* τί τινι; spoken of naval architecture. ἥρμοσσε ἀλλήλοισιν sc. πάντα, he joined together, Od. 5, 247. 2) Intrans. *to fit, to suit;* of the cuirass. ἥρμοσε αὐτῷ, it fitted him, 3, 333. 17, 210. II) Mid. *to join together for oneself, to construct,* σχεδίην χαλκῷ, Od. 5, 162.

Ἁρμονίδης, ου, ὁ (ξ), a Trojan artist, father of Phereclus, 5, 60.

ἁρμονίη, ἡ (ἁρμόζω), prop. *a joining together, a joint,* or *cramp,* Od. 5, 248. 361. 2) Trop. *an alliance between men, compact, agreement,* 22, 255.

*Ἁρμονίη, ἡ, daughter of Arês and Aphroditê, wife of Cadmus, h. Ap. 195.

Ἁρναῖος, ὁ, name of the beggar Irus, which he had received from his mother, Od. 18, 5.

ἀρνειός, ὁ (prop. adj. from ἀρνός), ἀρνειὸς δίς, the male sheep; subst. *a ram,* 2, 550. Od. 1, 25.

ἀρνέομαι, depon. mid. aor. 1 ἠρνησάμην, *to deny, to refuse, to reject;* with accus. ἔπος, to refuse a request, 14, 212; γάμον, Od. 1, 249. 2) Absol. *to say no, to refuse, to deny,* 14, 191; ἀμφί τινι, h. Merc. 390.

ἀρνευτήρ, ῆρος, ὁ, *a tumbler,* 16, 742. 2) *a diver,* who plunges head first into the water, 12, 385. Od. 12, 413 (prob. from ἀρήν). [The distinction in signif. is without ground, and, whether the comparison is with a diver (δύτης), or with a tumbler (κυβιστήρ), it is always the same.]

Ἄρνη, ἡ, a town in Bœotia, 2, 507; abode of the mace-bearer Areīthous, 7, 8. According to Strabo, it is the later *Acræphiôn;* according to Pausanias, *Chæroneia;* others think it was swallowed by the lake Copais, Strabo, IX. p. 413. Thucydides, 1, 60, makes it built 60 years after the taking of Troy, by the Bœotians, who, having before been expelled by the Pelasgians, fled to Arnê in Thessaly, and then again expelled the Pelasgians. Perhaps they only rebuilt the Bœotian town.

ἀρνός, ἀρνί, etc., from the obsol. ἀρήν, q. v.

ἄρνυμαι, depon. mid. (from αἴρω, Ep. only pres. and imperf., *to seek to obtain what one does not yet possess, to obtain for oneself, to procure, to acquire, to gain;* with the accus. of the thing and dat. of the pers., τιμήν τινι, to obtain satisfaction for any one, 1, 159; βοείην, to gain an ox-hide as a prize, 22, 160. 2) to strive to retain what one has, *conservare, to defend, to maintain,* πατρὸς κλέος, 6, 446; ψυχήν, to deliver his life, Od. 1, 5.

Ἀροίμην.

ἀροίμην, ἄροιο, ἄροιτο, see ἀρείω.
ἄροσις, ιος, ἡ (ἀρόω), arable ground, plough-land, 9, 580. Od. 9, 134.
ἀροτήρ, ῆρος, ὁ (ἀρόω), a ploughman, an agriculturist, 18, 542.
ἄροτος, ὁ (ἀρόω), ploughing, tilling, in the plur. tillage, Od. 9, 122.†
ἄροτρον, τό (ἀρόω), a plough, aratrum, 10, 353. Od. 13, 32.
ἄρουρα, ἡ (ἀρόω), arable land, seeded land, land under tillage, 6, 195. 2) land in general, 3, 115. πατρὶς ἄρουρα, country. Od. 1, 407. 3) the whole earth, ἐπὶ ζείδωρον ἄρουραν, 8, 486. Od. 3, 3.
* Ἄρουρα, ἡ, as pr. n.=Γαῖα, 2, 548 [and in Wolf, in Od. 11, 309].
ἀρόω, 3 plur. pres. ἀρόωσι, Ep. for ἀροῦσι, fut. ἀρόσω, partcp. perf. pass. ἀρηρομένος, to plough, to till, to cultivate, Od. 9, 108. νειὸς ἀρηρομένη, a ploughed fallow, a well-tilled fallow, 18, 548.
ἁρπάζω, fut. ἁρπάξω, aor. 1 ἥρπαξα and ἥρπασα, to tear away, to carry away, to plunder, to rob, said often of animals of prey, 9, 556; τινά, to ravish or bear off any one, 3, 444; πήληκα ἀπό τινος, to wrest or seize away one's helmet, 13, 528. 2) to grasp suddenly, to seize, λᾶαν, 12, 445 (prob. from the th. ἅρπω).
ἁρπακτήρ, ῆρος, ὁ (ἁρπάζω), a robber, a ravisher, 24, 262.†
ἁρπαλέος, η, ον, seizing, rapacious; trop. enticing, attractive; accord. to others, pass. eagerly sought, κέρδεα ἁρπαλέα (hoarded gains, V.), Od. 8, 164.
ἁρπαλέως, adv. eagerly, greedily, ἦσθε, Od. 6, 250. 14, 110.
* Ἁρπαλίων, ωνος, ὁ, son of Πυλαιμένης, king of the Paphlagonians, slain by Meriones, 13, 641 seq.
ἅρπη (ἅρπω [cf. sarpo and ὄρπη, which Hesych. says was an instrumentum falcatum. Lob. Techn. 259]), a swift bird of prey, with a clear voice, prob. the sea-eagle, falco ossifragus, Linn.; according to V., an eagle, 19, 350.†
* Ἅρπυια, ἡ (ἅρπω), plur. αἱ Ἅρπυιαι, prop. which robs, which seizes away; H. mentions first the harpy Ποδάργη, 16, 150, which bore the steeds of Achilles to Zephyr. In the Od. they appear in the plur. as spirits of the tempest (personified storms), as indistinct mythic rapacious beings. When any one disappeared, so that it was not known what was become of him, it was said the harpies had borne him off, Od. 1, 241. 20, 77. Accord. to Hes., h. 267, they are the daughters of Thaumas and Electra. Later writers gave them the body of a bird with the face of a maiden, Apd. 1, 2, 6.
ἄρρηκτος, ον (ῥήγνυμι), not to be broken, indissoluble, τεῖχος, δεσμοί, πεῖραρ, 13, 360. Od. 8, 275. 2) Metaph. indestructible, 2, 490.
ἄρρητος, ον (ῥέω), unspoken, not uttered, ἔπος, Od. 14, 466.†
ἄρσην, εν, gen. ενος, Ion. for ἄρρην, masculine, vigorous, strong, θεός, 8, 7; βοῦς, 7, 315; ὄϊες, Od. 9, 425.

Ἀρτύνω.

* Ἀρσίνοος, ὁ (kindly disposed), father of Hecamede, a distinguished citizen of Tenedos, 11, 626.
ἀρσίπους, οδος, ὁ ἡ, see ἀερσίπους.
* Ἀρτακίη, ἡ, a fountain in the country of the Laestrygones, Od. 10, 108. A fountain of the same name is mentioned in the Argonautic story, near Cyzicus.
ἀρτεμής, ές (ἄρτιος), uninjured, unharmed, sound, 5, 515. Od. 13, 43.
* Ἄρτεμις, ιδος, ἡ (accord. to Herm. Sospita, or = ἀρτεμής, the inviolate), Artemis (Diana), daughter of Zeus and Latona, sister of Apollo, goddess of the chase; spoken of in connexion with the island Ortygia, Od. 5, 123. She is the symbol of immaculate virginity, of youthful beauty, and excels in height and elegance of stature all the nymphs, Od. 6, 102. Her love for the chase led her continually to the mountains and forests. She slew women with her arrows, as Apollo did men; hence the sudden and easy death of women was ascribed to her, 6, 205. She is always on the side of the Trojans. Her appellations are, ἰοχέαιρα, κελαδεινή, ἀγροτέρη, q. v.
* Ἀρτεπίβουλος, ὁ (ἄρτος and ἐπιβουλεύω), one that lies in wait for bread, Artepibûlus, name of a mouse, Batr. 264.
ἄρτι, 1) in H., in compos., it signifies perfectly, exactly, as if from ἄρτιος. 2) now, at once, at this moment, 19, 56. 21, 288, where Wolf more correctly reads ἄρτι.
ἀρτιεπής, ές, gen. έος (ἄρτιος, ἔπος), speaking excellently, skilled in speaking, 22, 281.†
ἄρτιος, η, ον (ἄρω), suiting, fitting, exactly agreeing, coinciding; only neut. plur. ἄρτια βάζειν, to speak to the point, 14, 92. οἱ φρεσὶν ἄρτια ᾔδη, he thought things agreeing with him, i. e., he was of like sentiments, 5, 326. This appears to be a more correct explanation than 'he found him wise of mind,' cf. Od. 19, 248.
ἀρτίπος, Ep. for ἀρτίπους, ποδος, ὁ ἡ (πούς), having straight, well-formed feet, swift of foot, epith. of Ἄρης and of Ἄτη, 9, 505.
ἀρτίφρων, ονος, ὁ ἡ (φρήν), perfect in understanding, very intelligent, Od. 24, 260.†
ἄρτος, ὁ, bread, esply wheaten bread, * Od. 17, 343. Batr. 35.
* Ἀρτοφάγος, ὁ (φαγεῖν), Bread-eater, name of a mouse, Batr. 214.
† ἄρτυμα, ατος, τό (ἀρτύω), which serves to prepare food, seasoning, a condiment, Batr. 41.
ἀρτύνω and ἀρτύω (ἄρω), fut. ἀρτυνέω, aor. 1 ἤρτυνα, aor. 1 pass. ἀρτύνθην, aor. 1 mid. ἠρτυνάμην, 1) to join together, to annex, to arrange; σφέας αὐτούς, to form themselves in close array, 12, 86; σφέας αὐτοὺς συργηδόν, to arrange themselves in the form of a tower, i. e., in a parallelogram, 12, 43. 2) Mly to prepare, to make ready, to put in order, to dress (a line, phalanx, &c.), ὑσμίνην, 15, 303; λόχον,

Ἀρτύω. 70 Ἄσιος.

Od. 14, 469. ἀρτυνθη μάχη, the fight began, 11, 216; esply spoken of every thing for which craft and cunning are requisite, *to devise, contrive*, &c., δόλον, ψεύδεα, θάνατόν τινι, Od. 24, 153. II) *to join, to prepare, to arrange for oneself. a helper, a defender, a favourer*, τινί, 8, ἐρετμὰ τροποῖς ἐν δερματίνοισιν*, to fasten the oars in leathern thongs, Od. 4, 782; metaph. βουλήν, *to arrange, to deliver counsel or advice*, 2, 55; *according to others, to cause to assemble in council.*
ἀρτύω=ἀρτύνω, only pres. and imperf., 18, 379. Od. 11, 439.

Ἀρύβας, αντος, ὁ, a Phœnician from Sidon, Od. 15, 326.

ἀρχέκακος, ον (κακός), *beginning evil*; νῆες, the woe-commencing ships of Paris, 5, 63.†

Ἀρχέλοχος, ὁ, son of Antenor, a Trojan, slain by Ajax, 2, 823. 14, 465.

Ἀρχεπτόλεμος, ὁ, son of Iphitus, charioteer of Hector, 8, 128.

ἀρχεύω, poet. (ἄρχω), *to lead, to command*, with dat. 5, 200.

ἀρχή, ἡ, *commencement, beginning, cause, occasion*. εἵνεκ' ἐμῆς ἔριδος καὶ Ἀλεξάνδρου ἕνεκ' ἀρχῆς, i. e., ἕνεκα ἐμῆς καὶ ἕνεκα Ἀλ. ἀρχῆς ἔριδος, on account of my quarrel, and on account of Paris the cause of it; or, accord. to the Venet. Schol , on account of the beginning of Paris, 3, 100 ; hence it is said of him, ἥτ' ἔπλετο νείκεος ἀρχή, 22, 116 ; of Patroclus, 11, 604. φόνου ἀρχή, Od. 21, 4. 2) the point of commencement, ἐξ ἀρχῆς, from the beginning, i. e., *always, of old*, Od. 2, 254.

ἀρχός, ὁ, *leader, commander, chief*, also ἀρχὸς ἀνήρ. ἀρχοὶ μνηστήρων, Od. 4, 653 ; a commander of the ship, h. 6, 25.

ἄρχω, fut. ἄρξω, aor. 1 ἦρξα, I) Active, *to be first*, to do any thing first, when another is to follow; esply, *to precede, to lead the way*, rarely with partcp., ἦρχε κιών, 3, 417 ; hence, a) Mly *to commence, to begin, to prepare* ; with gen. μάχης, μύθοιο, δαιτὸς θεοῖς, to regulate a banquet for the gods, 15, 95 ; with infin. ἦρχε νέεσθαι, he went forth first, 2, 84 ; and with the partcp. ἦρχον χαλεπαίνων, I was first angry, 2, 378. 2) to be first, as leader, *to lead, to command, to rule*; mly with gen., rarely with dat. 2, 805. Od. 14, 230 ; or with ἐν, 13, 690; once intrans. according to Schol. like κρατεῖν : *to have the advantage, to conquer*. σέο ἕξεται ὅττι κεν ἄρχῃ, it will depend upon thee what prevails (in counsel) : Voss, however, what he proposes (Bothe, *quodcunque prior dixerit*), 9, 102. II) Mid. *to commence, to begin*, without reference to others ; with gen. μύθων, Od. 7, 233. Il. 9, 97 ; μολπῆς, Od. 6, 101 ; also, ἔκ τινος, Od. 23, 199 ; also with infin. 7, 824. 2) In religious acts, see ἀπάρχεσθαι, *to offer any thing as a sacrifice*, πάντοθεν μελέων, i. e., to begin by cutting off the limbs on all sides, Od. 14, 428.

ἈΡΩ, poet., an obsol. pres.; see ἀραρίσκω.

ἀρωγή, ἡ (ἀρήγω), *help, aid, protection* [favour], 4, 408. ἐπ' ἀρωγῇ τινι, out of favour to either party [with partiality], 23, 574.

ἀρωγός, όν, *helping*, in H. only subst. *a helper, a defender, a favourer*, τινί, 8, 205. Od. and ἐπὶ ψευδέσσιν, a helper to liars [cf. ψευδής], 4, 235 ; in an assembly, 18, 502 [=*patronus*, in judicio. H.].

ἄσαι, contr. for ἄάσαι, from ἀάω. 2) Infin. aor. 1, from ἄω, *to satiate*, 11, 574.

ἄσαμι, see ἄω.

Ἀσαῖος, ὁ, a Greek slain by Hector, 11, 301.

ἄσαμεν, see ἄεσα.

ἀσάμινθος, ἡ, Ep. *a bathing-tub*, 10, 576, and Od. [ωσμήχειν*, to wash, rub*. Densey. Död. " Multa pro desperatis relinquenda.—ἀσάμινθος, quo non solum *lubrum* sed *cista* et πᾶν τὸ κοῖλον significatur." Lob. Path. 369.]

ἄσατο, see ἀάω.

ἀσασθαι, see ἄω.

ἄσβεστος, ον, also ἀσβέστη 16, 123 (σβέννυμι); *unquenchable, inextinguishable*, φλόξ, mly metaph. *unceasing, immense, infinite*; γέλως, βοή, κλέος, Od. 4, 584.

[Ἄσβεστος, ὁ, a demon, καμίνῳ δηλητήρ, Epig. 14, 9 ; in Barnes Ἀσβολος.]

ἄσε, contr. for ἄασε, see ἀάω.

ἀσήμαντος, ον (σημαίνω), prop. *unmarked*, then, *without a keeper, unwatched*, μῆλα, 10. 485.†

ἄσθμα, ατος, τό (ἄω), *difficult respiration, a gasping, painful breathing* 15, 10. ἀργαλέῳ ἔχετ' ἄσθματι, he was oppressed with a dreadful difficulty of breathing, *16, 109.

ἀσθμαίνω (ἄσθμα), *to breathe with difficulty, to respire heavily*, spoken of one dreaming, 10, 496; *to gasp for breath*, spoken of one running, 10, 377 ; *to rattle in the throat*, spoken of the dying, 5, 585. 21, 182.

Ἀσιάδης, ου, ὁ, son of Asius, 12, 140. (The first a long.)

Ἀσίης, Ion. for Ἀσίας, gen. ao, εω, ω. son of Cotys, grandson of Manes, king of Lydia, 2, 461. Ἀσίω ἐν λειμῶνι, ed. Wolf, upon the meadow of Asias. Ἀσίῳ, according to the Schol. and Etymol. Mag. Steph., gen. for Ἀσίον, from Ἀσίας, who, according to Herud., 4, 45, gave name to a district in Lydia. It was a fruitful region on the Caӱstrus, which by eminence was called λειμών and Ἀσία. (In Strabo, XIV. p. 650, Ἀσίῳ stands as adj., and Herm., on h. Ap. 250, and Spitzner think this alone correct ; so that this region takes its name from ἄσις (slime) : cf. Mannert's Geograph. VI. 2, p. 15. From the necessity of the metre, Ἀσίω has ā.)

Ἀσίνη, ἡ, a town in Argolis, west from Hermionê, under the dominion of Diomêdês, 2, 560.

ἀσινής, ές (σίνομαι), *uninjured, unharmed*, Od. 11, 110. 12, 137.

Ἄσιος, ὁ, 1) son of Dymas, brother of

Ἄσιος. 71 Ἀσπαστός.

Hecuba, a Phrygian, slain by Ajax, 16, 717. 2) son of Hyrtacus from Arisbe, an ally of the Trojans, slain by Idomeneus, 2. 835. 13, 384. 17, 582.

Ἄσιος, η, ον, of Asia, hence Ἀσίῳ ἐν λειμῶνι, ed. Spitzner: see Ἀσίης.

ἄσις, ιος, ἡ, slime, filth, 21, 321.†

ἄσιτος, ον (σῖτος), without eating, fasting, spoken of Penelopê, Od. 4, 788.†

Ἀσκάλαφος, ὁ, son of Arês and Astyóchê, brother of Ialmenus, king of the Minyæ in Orchomenus, an Argonaut and a hero in the Trojan war; he was slain by Deïphŏbus, 2, 511; and 15, 110. (ἀσκάλαφος, the night-owl.)

Ἀσκανίη, ἡ, a town and territory on the Ascanian lake, on the borders of Phrygia and Mysia, upon the authority of Strabo. He understands therefore 2, 862, of the borders of Phrygia, and 13, 792, of the borders of Mysia. Steph. calls it incorrectly a town of Troas.

Ἀσκάνιος, ὁ, 1) a Phrygian, an ally of the Trojans from Ascania, 2, 862. 2) son of Hippotion, a Mysian and ally of the Trojans, 13, 793.

ἀσκεθής, poet. for ἀσκηθής. a false reading, Od. 14, 255 [defended by Bothe].

ἀσκελέως, adv. from ἀσκελής, continually, unceasingly. ἀσκ. ἀεὶ μενεαίνειν, 19, 68.†

ἀσκελής, ές (from a intens. and σκέλλω to dry up, Schol. σκληρός), very dry, withered, lean, powerless, Od. 10, 463. 2) Metaph. hard, obstinate, perpetual, pertinacious. So the neut. ἀσκελές as adv. κεχόλωται, Od. 1, 68. κλαίειν, Od. 4, 543. (According to others, better no. 1. from ἀ and σκέλος, without legs, powerless.)

ἀσκέω, imperf. ἤσκουν, 3 sing. before a vowel ἤσκειν for ἤσκεεν, aor. 1 ἤσκησα, perf. pass. ἤσκημαι, 1) In H. in the orig. signif.: to work skilfully, to elaborate; with accus. εἴρια, 3, 388; eply to work or do any thing professionally; κέρα, 4, 110. ἅρμα χρυσῷ εὖ ἤσκηται, the chariot is well adorned with gold, 10, 438; very often in the partcp. with another verb: θρόνον τεύξει ἀσκήσας, working as an artist he will make a seat. 14, 240. Batr. 125. 2) to put in order, to arrange skilfully, to clean; χιτῶνα, Od. 1, 439. χορὸν Δαίδαλος ἤσκησεν Ἀριάδνῃ, Dædalus composed or invented a dance for Ariadnê, 18, 592. Thus Voss, Damm, and Köppen. It is explained by διδάσκειν χορόν. But ἀσκεῖν always indicates professional work; hence better, to construct a dance. The allusion is to an artificial work of Dædalus; and, at a later day, a relief of white marble, called the choral dance of Ariadne, was shown in Gnossus. So Heinrichs in loc., Siebel on Paus. 9, 40. 2.

ἀσκηθής, ές (ἀσκέω [ἀσκηθής fm ἀσκάστος (the στ being softened into θ, as in ἀγαθός fm ἀγαστός), σκάζω, σκαιός. Död. Pott compares the Ga-l, sgad.—(scatheless?)]), prop. taken care of; hence, unharmed, uninjured, 16, 247; often spoken of a happy return, Od. 5, 26. 144. (For ἀσκεθέες, Od. 14, 255, Wolf has correctly adopted ἀσκηθέες, to be pronounced ἀσκηθείς.)

ἀσκητός, όν (ἀσκέω), carefully wrought, skilfully prepared; νῆμα, fine-spun varn, Od. 4, 134; artificially wrought, λέχος, *Od. 23, 189.

Ἀσκληπιάδης, ου, ὁ, son of Æsculapius =Machaon, 4, 204.

Ἀσκληπιός, ὁ, Æsculapius, in the Il. not yet a divinity, but an excellent physician, father of Podalirius and Machaôn, prince of Trikka and Ithômê in Thessaly, 2, 732. It is not determined whether he is meant in the Od. 4, 232, under the name Παιήων; in the Il. he is distinguished from the physician of the gods. In later writers, son of Apollo and Corônis or Arsinoê, god of the healing art, Hom. h. 15. († by poet. licence, 2, 731.)

ἄσκοπος, ον (σκοπός), prop. not hitting the mark; hence, inconsiderate, thoughtless, careless, 24, 157. 186.

ἀσκός, ὁ, a skin-bottle, for holding wine, 3, 247. Od. 9, 196; a skin-sack of Æolus, Od. 10, 19.

ἄσμενος, ον (prop. for ἡσμένος [for ἡσάμενος (cf. ἤσατο δ᾽ αἰνῶς, κ.τ.λ.), he rejoiced, Od. 9, 353), ἀδέω new theme fm ἀδεῖν. Syncope (1) aspirates an initial spiritus lenis, ἡέλιος, ἥλιος; (2) softens an initial spiritus asper. Thus ἥλατο, ἁλόμενος become ἄλτο, ἄλμενος. Död.], fr. ἥδομαι), pleased, joyful, glad. φύγεν ἄσμενος ἐκ θανάτοιο, glad to have escaped death, 20, 350. Od. 9, 63. ἐμοὶ δέ κεν ἀσμένῳ εἴη, it would be pleasing to me, 14, 108.

ἀσπάζομαι, depon. mid. (σπάω), prop. to welcome any one, by extending him the hand and drawing him towards oneself, to receive kindly, to embrace, to salute, τινὰ χερσίν, with the hands, Od. 3, 35; δεξιῇ ἐπέεσσί τε, 10, 542.

ἀσπαίρω (σπαίρω), to palpitate, to struggle, chiefly spoken of dying men and beasts, 3, 293. 12, 203; ποδεσσί, with the feet, Od. 22. 473; once spoken of the heart, 13, 443.

ἄσπαρτος, ον (σπείρω), unsown, not sown, *Od. 9, 100. 123.

ἀσπάσιος, η, ον (ἀσπάζομαι), also ος, ον, Od. 23, 233. 1) welcome, desired, dear, agreeable. τῷ δ᾽ ἀσπάσιος γένετ᾽ ἐλθών, 10, 36. Od. 5, 394, ἀσπάσιον τόγε θεοὶ κακότητος ἔλυσαν, to his joy the gods delivered him, Od. 5, 397. 2) joyful, glad, content, Od. 23, 238 [here more properly belongs Od. 5, 397; cf. Passow, and Crusius, ed. 1, s. v.].

ἀσπασίως, adv. gladly, willingly, joyfully; γόνυ κάμψειν, gladly to bow the knee, i. e., to supplicate, 7, 118. 11, 327; ἰδεῖν, Od. 4, 523.

ἀσπαστός, ον=ἀσπάσιος, welcome, desired, Od. 23, 239. The neut. ἀσπαστόν, as adv. ὡς Ὀδυσῆ (i. e., Ὀδυσῆϊ) ἀσπαστὸν ἐείσατο γαῖα καὶ ὕλη, so desir-

Ἄσπερμος. 72 Ἄστρον.

able to Ulysses appeared the land and the forest, Od. 5, 398. 8, 295.

ἄσπερμος, ον (σπέρμα), without seed, *without offspring, childless*, 20, 303.†

ἀσπερχές (σπέρχω and a intens.), *hastily, very warmly, vehemently, impetuously*; esply μενεαίνειν, 4, 32. Od. 1, 20; πεχολῶσθαι, 16, 61.

ἄσπετος, ον (ἐσπεῖν, i. q., εἰπεῖν), prop. *unspeakable, ineffable.* ἄσπετα πολλά, unspeakably many, 11, 704. ὅσσα τάδ' ἄσπετα πολλά, how manifold are these immense numbers. Od. 4, 75; hence, 2) Mly, *unspeakably great, infinite, immense;* ὕλη, also οὖδας, ῥόος, κλέος, ἀλκή. The neut. ἄσπετον, adv. τρεῖτε ἄσπετον, you tremble greatly, 17, 322. 3) φωνὴ ἄσπετος, h. Ven. 238, Passow explains as 'a noiseless voice,' contrary to the Gr. *usus loquendi*: the emendation of Hermann is excellent: φωνῇ τρεῖ ἄσπετον, cf. Herm. ad loc.

ἀσπιδιώτης, ου, ὁ (ἀσπίς), a *shield-bearer, armed with a shield,* always with ἀνήρ, *2, 554.

ἀσπίς, ίδος, ἡ (prob. from στίζω), *the round shield,* cf. σάκος and λαισήϊον. The shield was commonly prepared of bull's hide, having several coats of it one over another (βοείη and ταυρείη). The shield of the Telamonian Ajax had seven layers of leather, and over them an eighth of brass, 7, 222. 12, 294. Other shields again had merely metal plates, as that of Achilles, 20, 270. It was perfectly round (εὔκυκλος), and so large that it covered almost the entire body (ἀμφιβρότη). In the middle it had an arched elevation, 20, 275; in the middle of this is a boss (ὀμφαλός), hence ὀμφαλόεσσα, 6, 118. Inwardly there were handles (κάνονες) and a leathern strap (τελαμών), by which, out of battle, it was carried on the back.

ἀσπιστής, οῦ, ὁ (ἀσπίς), *bearing a shield, armed with a shield,* only in gen. plur. ἀσπιστάων, *4 90. 5, 577.

Ἀσπληδών, όνος, ἡ, a town in Bœotia, on the river Melas, in the realm of the Minyæ, 2, 511; also Σπληδών, Strabo.

ἀσπουδί, adv (σπουδή), *without zeal, without pains, without toil,* 8, 112; without spirited resistance, in a *cowardly* way, 22, 304.

ἄσσα, Ion. for ἅτινα, see ὅστις.

ἄσσα, Ion. for τινά, ὁποῖ' ἄσσα, Od. 19, 218.† (ἄσσα for ἅσσα, 10, 409, is doubtful; cf. Spitzner.)

Ἀσσάρακος, ὁ, son of Tros and Callirrhöe, grandson of Ericthonius, father of Capys, grandfather of Anchises, 20, 232 seq.

ἆσσον, adv. compar. to ἄγχι, *nearer*; often with ἰέναι, ἱκέσθαι, to approach; sometimes with gen. 14, 247; αἵματος, Od. 11, 89.

ἀσσοτέρω, adv., a later compar. from ἆσσον, *nearer*; with gen., and also with prep. καθίζειν παραὶ πυρί, to seat oneself nearer the fire, *Od. 17, 572.

ἀστάχυς, υος, ὁ=στάχυς, with a euphon., *an ear of corn,* 2, 148.†

ἀστεμφέως, adv. (ἀστεμφής), *immoveably, firmly*; ἔχειν, to hold fast, Od. 4, 419, 459.

ἀστεμφής, ές (στέμβω [=κινῶ· ἀστεμφής, ἀκίνητος. Lob. thinks στέμβειν=*proculcare, proterere*, fm στείβειν· so that ἀστεμφής (c. a pleonast.)=στιπτός, *inculcatus, spissus, compactus;* theu *firmus, immobilis.* Cf. στιβαρός: et *stipulum apud veteres firmum dicebatur.* Fest. *Lob. Techn.* 33]), *immoveable, firm, unshaken,* βουλή, *2, 344. †Neut. ἀστεμφές, as adv., ἔχειν τι, to hold any thing immoveable, 3, 219.

Ἀστέριον, τό, a place near Magnesia, not far from the mountain Titanus in Thessaly, 2, 735.

Ἀστερίς, ίδος, ἡ (star-island), a little island in the Ionian sea, on the south-east entrance of the sound between Cephallenia and Ithaca, Od. 4, 846. Ἀστερία, ἡ, Strabo, X. p. 457. It has been sought in vain by the moderns; accord. to Dodwell the island *Daccalio,* accord. to W. Gell the promontory *Chelia;* cf. Nitzsch ad loc.

ἀστερόεις, εσσα, εν, Ep. (ἀστήρ), 1) *starry, abounding in stars,* οὐρανός. 2) *star-like, sparkling, shining;* θώρηξ, 16, 134; δόμος, 18, 370.

Ἀστεροπαῖος, ὁ (ἀστεροπή), son of Pelagon, grandson of the river-god Axius, leader of the Pæonians, slain by Achilles, 12, 102. 21, 137 seq.

ἀστεροπή, poet. for ἀστραπή [~ στράφω. Hesych. explains στροπή, στροφή, στοπρία by ἀστραπή, *igneus vortex, quem fulmen facit.* Lucret. 6, 397. *Lob. Tech.* 41], *lightning, a flash of lightning,* *10, 154.

ἀστεροπητής, οῦ, ὁ, *the hurler of lightning, the thunderer,* appellat. of Zeus, *1, 154.

ἀστήρ, έρος, ὁ, dat. plur. ἀστράσι or ἀστρασι (Buttm. approves the first, Gram., § 47, N. 3.), *a star, a constellation,* 22, 307. Od. 13, 93. ἀστὴρ ὀπωρινός, *the autumnal star* [the dog-star], 5, 5; mly a *meteor*, 4, 75 (a *fire-ball*, Köp.).

ἀστός, ὁ (ἄστυ), *a citizen,* 11, 242. Od. 13, 192.

ἀστράγαλος, ὁ [οἷον ἀστράβαλες ἐναλλαγῇ τοῦ β. Eust. 1289, 59. στρέφεσθαι=στρέφεσθαι. Et. Magn. *strigare.* στράγξ, στραγγουρία (urina *tortuosa,* Plin.). στραγγαλίζειν (= συστρέφειν, Hesych.). στραβός, ἀστραπή fm στράφω. *Lob. Techn.* 54], 1) *the neck-joint, a vertebra,* 14, 466; also plur. *a joint: ἐκ δέ οἱ αὐχὴν ἀστραγάλων ἐάγη,* his neck was luxed from the joint, Od. 10, 560. 2) *the ankle-bone,* the bone at the ankle, *talus,* from which dice were made; hence, 3) a kind of die, in the plur. *the game of dice,* 23, 88.

ἀστράπτω (στράπτω), partcp. aor. ἀστράψας, *to lighten, to hurl lightning,* ἐπιδέξια, *2, 353.

ἄστρον, τό, *a constellation; a star* only in plur. 5, 555. Od. 12, 312.

Ἄστυ. 73 **Ἀταρπιτός.**

ἄστυ, εος, τό, *a town, a city*, in H. spoken both of large and small towns, with the name in the gen. Ζελείης, Ἰλίου πόλις καὶ ἄστυ, 17, 144 (where, accord. to the Schol., πόλις is to be understood the social union of citizens. πολίτεια; and by ἄστυ, the walls and houses. τεῖχος καὶ δόμοι); plur. *abodes, habitations* in general, Od. 1, 3. Adv. ἄστυδε, *to the city*, 18, 255.

Ἀστύαλος, ὁ (ἅλς), a Trojan, slain by Polypœtes, 6, 29.

Ἀστυάναξ, ακτος, ὁ (ἄναξ, *defender of the city*), appellat. of Scamandrius, son of Hector, which the Trojans gave him, 6, 403.

ἀστυβοώτης, ου, ὁ (βοάω), *crying through the city*, epith. of the herald, 24, 701.†

Ἀστυνόμη, ἡ (νέμω, *city-swaying*), daughter of Chryses (Χρυσηΐς), born at Chrysa. Achilles took her captive in the Hypoplacian Thebes, whither her father had sent her for protection from the enemy. Agamemnon received her as his share of the booty, but was obliged to restore her to her father to avert the wrath of Apollo, 1, 370. [The name, however, is not found in the *text* of H.]

Ἀστύνοος, ὁ (νόος), a leader of the Trojans, slain by Diomēdēs, 5, 144. 2) son of Protiaon, a Trojan, slain by Neoptolemus, 15, 455.

Ἀστυόχεια, Ep. for Ἀστυόχη (ἔχω, *protecting the city*), 1) daughter of Actor, mother of Ascalaphus and Ialmenus by Arēs, 2, 513. 2) daughter of Phylas of Ephyra, mother of Tleptolemus by Heraclēs, 2, 658. According to Pindar, Od. 7, 41, *Astydamia*.

[Ἀστυόχη, 2, 513; see Ἀστυόχεια, no. 1.]

Ἀστύπυλος, ὁ (πύλη), a Pæonian, slain by Achilles, 21, 209.

ἀσύφηλος, ον, *unworthy, vile, insulting*. ὥς μ' ἀσύφηλον ἔρεξεν, that he treated me shamefully, 9, 697. (Eustath., however, ἀσύφηλον αὐτὸν ἐν Ἀργ. ῥέξαι, ὃ ἐστι, θεῖναι, ποιῆσαι, to make any one vile; but in H. ῥέζειν always means, 'to do, to do *to*, to perform.') οὔπω σεῦ ἄκουσα κακὸν ἔπος οὐδ' ἀσύφηλον, I have not yet heard from thee an evil or unworthy word, 24, 767. *Il. (The derivation is uncertain, according to Eustath., prob from ἄσοφος, lengthened ἀσύφηλος. Æol. ἀσύφηλος, accord. to others from αἴσυλος).

ἀσφαλέως, adv. (ἀσφαλής), *continually, unceasingly*, 13, 145; metaph. *securely, safely, prudently*, ἀγορεύειν, Od. 8, 171. (V. *speaking to the point*.)

ἀσφαλής, ἐς (σφάλλω), *not tottering, immoveable, standing firm*, Od. 6, 42 [θεῶν ἕδος ἀσφαλές, *the immoveable seat of the gods;* elsewhere only] the neut. ἀσφαλές, as adv. *perpetually, continually*, 15, 683.

Ἀσφαλίων, ονος, ὁ, a servant of Menelaus, Od. 4, 216.

ἀσφάραγος, ὁ (φάρυγξ), *the throat, the gullet*, 22, 328.†

ἀσφοδελός, όν (ἀσφόδελος, *the asphodel), producing asphodel*. ἀσφοδελὸς λειμών, the asphodel-meadow in the nether world, where the shades of heroes abide, Od. 11, 539. b. Merc. 221. (The asphodel is a lily form plant, the bulb on whose roots was used as food by poor people, Hes. Op. 4.)

ἀσχαλάω, 3 sing pres. ἀσχαλᾷς for ἀσχαλᾷ, *to be vexed, sad, dejected, indignant*, τινός, about any thing, Od. 19, 159. 534; with partcp. 2, 293. 24. 403. οἵ πού με μάλ' ἀσχαλόωσι μένοντες, *who are probably waiting for me very unwillingly; are much vexed at having to wait for me so long*, Od. 1, 304 (according to Doederl. related to ἄχος, as ἴσχω with ἔχω).

ἀσχαλόω, see ἀσχαλάω.

ἀσχάλλω = ἀσχαλάω. Od. 2, 193.†

ἄσχετος, ον (σχεῖν), Ep. ἀάσχετος, 1) *not to be held in, ungovernable, irresistible*, μένος, 5, 892; but μένος ἄσχετος, ungovernable in strength or anger, Od. 2, 85 2) *not to be endured, insupportable*, πένθος, 16, 549.

Ἀσωπός (ἅσις, *slime-river*), a river in Bœotia which falls into the Euripus, now *Asopo*, 2, 572. 2) the river-god, son of Oceanus and Tethys, father of Ægīna, Antiŏpē, Od. 11, 260.

ἀτάλαντος, ον (τάλαντον), prop. like in weight, *equal to, like*, τινί, 2, 627; Διὶ μῆτιν, equal in wisdom to Zeus, 2, 169; θεόφιν, Od. 3, 110.

ἀταλάφρων, ονος, ὁ, ἡ (φρονέω), *having a child-like mind*, hence my *tender*, παῖς, 6, 400.†

ἀτάλλω (ἀταλός), *to skip like a child*, hence 1) *to leap joyfully, to gambol;* spoken of sea animals, ἐκ κευθμῶν, leaping from the clefts, 13, 27. 2) Trans. ἀτιτάλλω, *to nourish, to bring up, to foster*, Ep. Hom. 4, 2. Pass. *to increase, to grow up*, h. in Merc. 400.

ἀταλός, ή, όν (related to ἀπαλός), *childlike, tender, juvenile*, παθενικαί, Od. 11, 39. Il. 20, 222. ἀταλὰ φρονεῖν, to cherish youthful, joyful feelings, *to be blithe* or *gay of heart*, 18, 567. cf. h. Cer. 24.

ἀτάρ, conjunct. chiefly poet. = αὐτάρ, *but, yet, however*, like δέ; it always begins the clause: 1) It denotes nly an unexpected, a surprising antithesis, 3, 268. 270; often with the voc. 6, 429; Ἕκτορ, ἀτὰρ σοῦ ἔφης, Hector, but thou saidst, 22, 331; after an antecedent μέν, 6, 84. 86. 2) It expresses a sudden transition, chiefly in the apodosis after ἐπειδή. αὐτὰρ ἐπειδὴ Τρῶας ἐνόησαν, ἀτὰρ ἐγένετο ἰαχή, but when they perceived the Trojans, *then* arose a cry, 12, 144. 3) It is often connected with other particles: ἀτάρ τε, 4, 484; ἀτὰρ δή, 23, 871; ἀτὰρ μὲν νῦν γε, Od. 18, 123.

ἀταρβής, ές (τάρβος), *undismayed, fearless*, appellat. of Phobos, 13, 299.†

ἀτάρβητος, ον (ταρβέω) = ἀταρβής· νόος, 3, 63.†

ἀταρπιτός, ἡ, Ion. for ἀτραπιτός, *a path*, 18, 565. Od. 17, 234.

E

'Αταρπός. 74 Ατλας.

ἀταρπός, ἡ, Ion. for ἀτραπός (fr. τρέπω), prop. ὀδός, *a way from which one cannot wander; a path, a footway*, 17, 743. Od. 14, 1.

ἀταρτηρός, ή, όν (prob. from ἀτηρός, with a repetition of the first letters), *injurious, hostile*, Ἴλιαδ 1, 223; Μέντωρ, Od. 2, 243.

ἀτασθαλίη, ἡ (ἀτάσθαλος), *indiscretion, impiety, insolence, arrogance;* always in the plur. 4, 409. Od. 1. 7.

ἀτασθάλλω (ἀτάσθαλος), *to be indiscreet, insolent, arrogant;* only partep. *Od. 18, 57. 19, 88.

ἀτάσθαλος, ον (ἄτη), *indiscreet, insolent, arrogant, presumptuous, infatuated;* spoken of men and actions, 22, 418. Od. 16, 86; often in the neut. plur. ἀτάσθαλα μηχανᾶσθαι, ῥέζειν, *to practise wickedness*, 11, 695; and esply spoken of the suitors in the Odyss., Od. 3, 207. 17, 588. (According to Etym. Mag. from ἄτη and θάλλω [fm ἀταστός, verbal of a form ἀτάζειν, fm ἀτέω († ἄω, noceo), *Död.* who thinks ἀτασθλός was syncopated fm ἀταστλός, as ἰμάσθλη fm ἰμαστέλη, θύσθλα fm θύσταλα, &c. p. 163]).

ἄτε (prop. accus. plur. from ὅστε), *as, like, like as*, 11, 779. 32, 127.† Thus Damm. According to Lehrs de Aristarch. stud. p. 162 seq. it never stands thus in H., but is to be taken as neut. plur.

ἀτειρής, ἐς (τείρω), *not to be worn out, indestructible, firm, lasting;* spoken of brass and iron, 5, 292. 2) Metaph. *indefatigable, unconquerable;* of men, 15, 697; μένος, Od. 11, 270; of the voice, 17, 555; and of the heart, κραδίη, πέλεκυς ὣς ἐστιν ἀτειρής, thy heart is unyielding, like an axe, 3, 60.

ἀτέλεστος, ον (τελέω), *unfinished, unended, unaccomplished*, Od. 8, 571. ἀτ. τιθέναι πόνον (in connexion with ἄλλος), to make the labour unaccomplished, i. e., to render nugatory, 4, 57; hence *vain, fruitless*, ὀδός, Od. 2, 273. 2) without ending, *without ceasing*, ἔδειν, Od. 16, 111.

ἀτελεύτητος, ον (τελευτάω), *unaccomplished, unfulfilled*, 1, 527; ἔργον, *4, 175.

ἀτελής, ἐς (τέλος), *without end;* pass. *unfinished*, Od. 17, 546.† 2) *uninitiated;* with gen. ἱερῶν, h. in Cer. 481.

ἀτέμβω, *to injure, to violate;* with accus. ξείνους, Od. 20, 294. 21, 311: metaph. *to deceive*, θυμόν, Od. 2, 90. Pass. *to be deprived of, to be bereft*, τινός, of any thing; ἴσης, of an equal share, 11, 705. Od. 9, 42. ἀτέμβονται νεότητος, they are bereft of youthful vigour, 23, 445.

ἀτέοντες, see ἀτέω.

ἄτερ, poet. prep. with gen. *without*, πολέμου, 4, 376. 2) *apart, far from* ἄλλων, 1, 498.

ἀτέραμνος, ον (τείρω), *unsoftened, hard, stern, inexorable*, κῆρ, Od. 23, 127† [opp. of τέρην, Lob.].

ἀτερπής, ἐς (τέρπω), *joyless, sad, disagreeable*, λιμός, 19, 354; χῶρος, Od. 7, 279.

ἄτερπος, ον = ἀτερπής, 6, 285.†

ἀτέω (ἄτη), *to act blindly, fool-hardily;* only in partep. 20, 332† [ἀτέων only as partep. in Hdt. *infatuated*].

ἄτη, ἡ (ἀάω [ἄειν, *to hurt, harm;* ἄομαι ἀατός, ἀάτη, ἀΓάτα, Pind. Pyth. 3, 28; 4, 24 ἀνάτα]), 1) Mly *injury, destruction, evil*, 2, 111. 9, 237; partic. *mental disturbance, confusion*, 16, 805; also *indiscretion*, 1, 412: *blindness, folly*, in which crime is perpetrated, 19, 88 Od. 15, 233. 2) *wickedness*, the base act itself, Ἀλεξάνδρου, 6, 356. Od. 12, 372; also *misfortune, punishment*, which one incurs by crime, Od. 4, 261; with the subordinate idea of *guilt, blood-guiltiness*, 24, 480.

Ἄτη, ἡ, *Até*, as a goddess, daughter of Zeus, who seduces men to indiscreet actions, and thereby brings evil upon them. She has soft feet, with which she does not touch the earth (ἁπαλοὶ πόδες), but rushes rapidly (ἀρτίπος) over the heads of men, and accomplishes the resolutions of Zeus and Fate; she leads Zeus himself into an illusion, and is by him hurled from heaven, 19, 91—130, and 9, 505.

ἀτίζω (τίω), *to value little, not to regard, to be careless;* only partep. 20, 166 † ἀτιμάζω=ἀτιμάω, only pres. and impf. Od. In the Il. only Ep. iterative, impf. ἀτιμάζεσκον, 9, 450.

ἀτιμάω (τιμάω), Ep. fut. (ἀτιμήσω), aor. 1 ἠτίμησα, *not to honour, not to value, to disregard, to despise;* with accus. mly of persons; also ἔργον μάχης, 6, 522; μῦθον, 14, 127; chiefly in the Il.

ἀτίμητος, ον (τιμή), *not valued, not regarded, despised*, 9, 648.†

ἀτιμίη, ἡ (τιμή), *dishonour, insult, infamy, contempt;* in plur. ἀτιμίῃσιν ἰάλλειν τινά, to bring any one into contempt, Od. 13, 142.†

ἄτιμος, ον (τιμή), compar. ἀτιμότερος, 16, 90; superl. ἀτιμότατος, 1) *unhonoured, dishonoured, despised*, 1, 171. 2) *not valued, without payment*. τοῦ νῦν οἶκον ἄτιμον ἔδεις, thou consumest his possessions without recompense, Od. 16, 451. (Accord. to Eustath. either ἀτιμώρητον, unavenged, or adv. ἀτίμως, i. e., δωρεάν.)

ἀτιτάλλω, Ep. (ἀταλός), aor. 1 ἀτίτηλα, *to rear, to nourish, to bring up;* with accus. spoken of children, 14, 202. 24, 60; and of brutes, *to feed*, 5, 271. Od. 14, 41.

ἄτιτος, ον (τίω), *unpaid, unexpiated, unavenged*, 13, 414. ἵνα μή τι κασιγνήτοιο ποινὴ δηρὸν ἄτιτος ἔῃ, that the punishment for my brother may not be long unpaid, 14, 484. Because ἄτιτος has here ἴ, Clark proposes δηρὸν ἔῃ ἄτιτος; cf. Spitzner ad loc.

Ἄτλας, αντος, ὁ (from τλῆναι and ἁ intens. the *supporter*), a god, who "knows the depths of the sea, and holds the pillars which keep heaven and earth

*Άτλητος. 75 Αύδάω.

apart (ἀμφίς)," Od. 1, 52. His origin is not mentioned by H.; he is the father of Calypso [and of Maia. h. 17, 1]. Perhaps the original idea is that of a mountain upon whose summits the heavens rest. Whether H. intended the mountain in Libya, or another in the west, is uncertain. Accord. to Hesiod, Th. 507—519, he is a doomed Titan, who as a punishment bears up the vault of heaven.

ἄτλητος, ον (τλῆμι), not to be borne, insupportable, ἄχος, πένθος, *9, 3. 19, 367.

ἄτος, ον, contr. for ἄατος, poet. (ἄω), insatiable; with gen πολέμοιο, in battle, μάχης, δόλων ἠδὲ πόνοιο, 11, 430. Od. 13, 293.

ἀτραπιτός, ἡ (τρέπω) = ἀταρπός, a path, Od. 13, 195.†

Ἀτρείδης, ου, ὁ, son of Atreus, often plur. οἱ Ἀτρείδαι, the Atridae, Agamemnon and Menelaus.

Ἀτρείων, ωνος, ὁ = Ἀτρείδης.

ἀτρεκέως, adv. (ἀτρεκής), exactly, truly, agreeably to truth, ἀγορεύειν, καταλέγειν; once with μαντεύσθαι, Od. 17, 154.

ἀτρεκής, ές, exact, correct, true; the neut. ἀτρεκές, as adv. truly, strictly, 5, 208. δεκὰς ἀτρεκές, exactly a decade, Od. 16, 245 (prob. from τρέω, not trembling, not from τρέχω [the insertion of the κ sound is found in σφε-σ-ως = σφώος: Hesych. gives ἅα συστροφὴ ὕδατος. Cf. aqua. Lob.]).

ἀτρέμα, before a vowel ἀτρέμας, adv. (τρέμω), without trembling, immoveable, quiet, still. ἀτρέμας ἧσο, 2, 200. ἔχειν ἀτρέμα τι, to hold any thing still, 15, 318 (without σ only in this place); Od. 13, 92.

Ἀτρεύς, ῆος, ὁ, son of Pelops and Hippodamia, brother of Thyestes, king of Mycenae, accord. to H. father of Agamemnon and Menelaus by Aerōpē (accord. to Aeschyl. grandfather and fosterfather). [A later tradition represents that] he quarrelled with his brother Thyestes, and placed his sons before him to eat. His famous sceptre Thyestes inherited, 6, 106 (from ἀ and τρέω, the unterrified).

ἄτριπτος, ον (τρίβω), prop. unworn, spoken of hands, not hardened, unexercised, Od. 21, 151.†

ἄτρομος, ον (τρέμω), not trembling, fearless, unterrified, μένος, θυμός, *5, 125. 16, 163.

ἀτρύγετος, ον (τρυγάω), where is nothing to be harvested, unfruitful, barren; epith. of the sea in distinction from the earth, which is called πολυφορβος, 1, 316; and once of the ether, 17, 425. h. Cer. 67. [Herodianus, E. M. 167, 29: ἀπὸ τοῦ ἀτρύτος ἀτρύτος (ut ἀτίετος) καὶ πλεονασμῷ τοῦ γ' ἀτρύγετος. ap. Lob. Path. 145.]

Ἀτρυτώνη (τρύω), the unwearied, the indefatigable, the invincible, epith. of Athēnē (lengthened from ἀτρύτη), 2, 137.

ἄττα, a term of affection used by a younger in addressing an older person, good father (related to ἄττα, πάππα), 9, 607. Od. 16, 31.

ἀτύζομαι (related to ἀτάω [and so to ἄεω, nocere, Död, who, however, derives it from ἀντύειν, a collateral form of ἀντέειν, as ἀχεύειν, ἀχέειν)], aor. 1 pass. ἀτυχθείς, to be amazed, to be confounded, to be terrified, bewildered, 1) Absol. ἀτυζομένη δὲ ἔοικας, you appear like one confounded, 15, 96. ἀτυζομένη (sc. ὥστε) ἀπολέσθαι, shocked to death, 22, 474 [prae dolore mente captam ut periculum mortis esset. Heyne]. 2) With accus. πατρὸς ὄψιν, to be terrified at the sight of, 6, 463. 3) Often to fly terrified, πεδίοιο, through the plain, 18, 7: spoken of steeds, 6, 38. (The act. ἀτύζω, to confound, is first found in Ap. Rh.)

Ἀτυμνιάδης, ου, ὁ, son of Atymnius = Mydōn, 5, 581.

Ἀτύμνιος, ὁ, 1) father of Mydōn, a Trojan, 5. 581. 2) son of Amisodarus of Caria, who was slain by Antilōchus, 16, 317 seq.

αὖ, adv. the original signif. relates to place: back, backwards, as still in the verb, αὐερύειν; then metaph. 1) Of time: again, once more, νῦν αὖ, δεύτερον αὖ; also to indicate a repetition, 1, 540. 2) on the other hand, on the contrary, but, to indicate an antithesis to the preceding, mly connected with δέ (δ' αὖ), 4, 417. Od. 3, 485. αὖ often = δέ, 11, 367; hence often after a preceding μέν, 11, 17. 19, 108 seq. 3) likewise, further, moreover, to facilitate the progress of the narration, 3, 200. Od. 4, 211.

αὐαίνω (αὔω), Ep. for αὐαίνω, to dry, to dry up, to wither, partcp. aor. 1 αὐανθέν, dried, seasoned, Od. 9, 321.†

αὐγάζομαι, mid. (αὐγή), prop. I am enlightened; hence, to see clearly, to perceive, to distinguish, τί, any thing, 23, 458.† (The act. αὐγάζω, to enlighten.)

Αὐγειαί, αἱ, 1) a town in Laconia, near Gythium; later, accord. to Strabo, Αἴγειαι, 2, 583. 2) a town in Locris, 2, 532.

Αὐγείας, ου, ὁ (the shining), epith. for Αὐγέας, son of Phorbas and Hyrminē, or of Elius or Helius, king of Ephȳra in Elis, an Argonaut, father of Agasthenēs, Phyleus, and Agamēdē, 11, 740. H. mentions him in a contest with Neleus; he is chiefly known by his herd of three thousand cattle, whose stall was not cleaned in thirty years; Heraclēs accomplished this labour in one day, Apd. 2, 5. 5.

αὐγή, ἡ, light, a beam of light, splendour, brilliancy; spoken chiefly of the sun. ὑπ' αὐγὰς Ἡελίοιο φοιτᾶν, ζώειν, to walk, to live under the beams of the sun, Od. 2, 181. 15, 349; also spoken of lightning and of fire, 13, 244. Od. 6, 308.

Αὐγηϊάδης, ου, ὁ, Ep. for Αὐγειάδης, son of Augeas = Agasthenēs. 2, 624.

αὐδάω, impf. ηὔδων, aor. 1 ηὔδησα, to discourse, to speak; τινά, to address any

Αὐδή. 76 Αὐτάγρετος.

one; often ἀντίον αὐδᾶν τινά, to answer any one; with double accus. ἔπος τινὰ ἀντίον αὐδᾶν, 5, 170. μεγάλα αὐδᾶν, to utter impious words, Od. 4, 505.

αὐδή, ἡ (ἄω), speech, language, voice; spoken of men, and prop. of the sound and strength of the voice; once of the twittering of a swallow, Od. 21, 411.

αὐδήεις, εσσα, εν (αὐδή), endowed with human voice, speaking, melodious; spoken prop. of men, Od. 5, 334. cf. Il. 19, 407. If a deity receives this appellation, it is thereby indicated that he employs a human voice. Thus Circé, Od. 10, 136; Calypso, Od. 12, 449.

αὐερύω (ἐρύω), aor. 1 αὐέρυσα, to draw back; with accus. νευρήν (in order to shoot), 8, 325; chiefly absol. to draw back the neck of the victim whose throat is to be cut, 1, 459 seq. 2) to draw out again, στήλας, 12, 261.

αὖθ', i. e. αὖτε, before a spiritus asper, 2, 540.

αὖθι. adv. contr. for αὐτόθι, 1) Of place [=ἐν τῇ αὐτῇ χώρᾳ, in the same place where one already is (even, just, precisely), there]: on the spot, there, here, 1, 492. 3, 244. 7, 100. ἐζόμενος κατ' αὖθι, 13, 653 (where κατά belongs to ἔζεσθαι), cf. Od. 21, 55; in like manner κατ' αὖθι λίπεν, 24, 470. 2) Of time: at once, instantly, Od. 18, 339.

αὐίαχος, ον, crying together, shouting aloud, epith. of the Trojans, 13, 41.† (Eustath. makes it from ἁ intens. and ἰαχή, between which an Æol. digamma, for euphony's sake, is inserted, whence arose ν; others say, not crying, contrary to the custom of the Trojans: since H. represents the Greeks as advancing to battle in silence, the Trojans shouting).

αὔλειος, η, ον (αὐλή), belonging to the court or yard before a house. αἱ αὔλειαι θύραι, the doors of the court; either the doors which lead from the street into the front yard, or from the vestibule into the front yard. οὐδός αὔλειος, the threshold of the court door, *Od. 1, 104.

αὐλή. ἡ (ἄω), the court, an open, airy place which surrounded the house. It was encircled by a wall, paved, and furnished with a double door, Od. 9, 184. In the court were situated the stables for cattle, and in the centre stood the altar of Zeus ἑρκεῖος. From the court one entered the πρόδομος. In the αὐλή was often the place for family meeting, and also the court for the cattle, 4, 344. Achilles had a similar court about his tent, 24, 452. 2) the fence encircling the court, 5, 138. Od. 14, 5. 3) Sometimes the entire dwelling, Od. 4, 72. cf. Od. 1, 425.

αὐλίζομαι, depon. (αὔλις), prop. to spend the night in the court; to be enclosed, spoken of cattle and swine, Od. 12, 265. 14, 412. *Od.

*αὔλιον, τό (αὐλή), a fold, a grotto, a hut, a dwelling, h. Merc. 103.

αὖλις, ιδος, ἡ, a place of stopping, esply to spend the night, a camp, a lodge, h. Merc. 71. αὖλιν θέσθαι, to pitch a camp, 9, 232; spoken of birds. αὖλιν ἐσιέμεναι, betaking themselves to rest, Od. 22, 473.

Αὐλίς, ίδος, ἡ, a village in Bœotia, with a large and small haven, where the fleet of the Greeks assembled to sail against Troy, now Vuthi, 2, 496.

αὐλός, ὁ (ἄω, to blow), a wind-instrument, which, partly from the mouth-piece necessary to it, and partly from its strong, deep tone, we may conclude to have been similar to our hautboy or clarionet, a flute, a pipe. It was made of cane, wood, bone, or metal, 10, 13. 18, 495. h. Merc. 451. Voss, Od. 10, 10, reads αὐλῷ for αὐλῇ. There were many kinds, cf. Eustath. on Il. 18, 495, and esply Bottiger in Wieland's Attic Museum, B. I. H. 1, S. 330 seq. 2) any hollow body, perforated to admit something: the hole of the spear, into which the shaft was introduced. ἐγκέφαλος παρ' αὐλὸν ἀνέδραμεν ἐξ ὠτειλῆς, then gushed forth the brain by the socket (others, more improbably, in a stream). περόνη τέτυκτο αὐλοῖσιν διδύμοισι, the clasp was (of the spear) from the wound, 17, 297, made with double holes; in which the hooks caught, Od. 19, 227; metaph. αὐλὸς παχύς, a thick jet of blood (ἡ ἀναφορά τοῦ αἵματος, Eustath.), Od. 22, 18.

αὐλών, ῶνος, ὁ (αὐλός), a mountain-defile, a valley, h. in Merc. 95.

αὐλῶπις, ιδος. ἡ (ὤψ), epith. of a helmet, τρυφάλεια. accord. to Hesych. furnished with a visor, 5, 182. According to the Schol., having a socket in which the crest was inserted. *Il.

αὖος, η, ον, Att. αὖος (ἄω, αὔω), dried, dry, hardened. ξύλα, βοέη [δένδρεα ἀπώλαι, περίκηλα. The neut. sing. αὖον, as adv. hollow; spoken of a dull, dead sound, as if it were produced by dry bodies, [opp. to the ringing sound of metal]. 12, 160; αὖον ἄϋσεν, 13, 44. [Cf. σκληρὸν ἐβρόντησεν, Hes. Th. 839; aridus sonus, Lucr. 6, 119. "Epitheton in corporibus siccis mutuatum, quæ collisa inter se fragorem edunt." Lob.]

ἄϋπνος, ον (ὕπνος), without sleep, sleepless, νύκτες, ἀνήρ, 9, 325. Od. 10, 84.

αὔρη, ἡ, Ion. for αὔρα (ἄω, αὔω [ἄημι]), a breath, a breeze, air, ὀπωρίνη, h. Merc. 147; esply the cool air from water, or of the morning, Od. 5, 469.

αὔριον, adv. (αὔρη, prop. neut. of αὔριος [αὔριον, sync. fm ἀξέριον: ἤέριος, early in the morning. Cf. demain=de mane: and Germ. Morgen, morgen. Död.]), the morrow, 8, 535. Od. 11, 351.

αὐσταλέος, η, ον, poet. (αὔω, αὐστός), prop. dried up, withered, dirty, filthy, Od. 19, 327.†

αὐτάγρετος, ον (ἀγρέω), poet. for αὐθαίρετος, self-chosen, at one's option, voluntary, Od. 16, 148;† with infin. h Merc. 474.

Αὖταρ. 77 Αὐτός.

αὖταρ, conj. (from αὖτ' ἄρ'),=ἀτάρ, *but, still, however, furthermore*; like ἀτάρ used at the beginning of a sentence, to indicate an antithesis, 1, 133; or to mark a sudden transition, 1, 488. 3, 315. 20, 38. αὖταρ ἄρα, 2, 103.

αὖτε, adv. poet. (from αὖ and τε)=αὖ, *again*, 1, 202. 578. 2) *but, on the other hand*, also used to mark an antithesis or a transition, or instead of δέ after μέν, 3, 241. Od. 22, 6.

αὐτέω (ἀΰω), *to cry, to shout*, 20, 50; spoken of things: *to resound, to sound*, 12, 160. [Cf. αὖον αὔτεῖν in αὖος.] 2) With accus. τινά, to call any one, *11, 258.

αὐτή, ή (ἀΰω), *a cry, a loud shout*, eply *the battle-cry*, with πτόλεμος, 6, 328; and *the battle* itself, 11, 802. ἵκετ' αὐτή, 11, 466; ed. Spitz. (where Wolf reads ἵκετο φωνή).

αὐτῆμαρ, adv. (ἦμαρ), *on the same day*, 1, 81. Od. 3, 311.

αὐτίκα, adv. (αὐτός), *at once, instantly, on the spot*; often αὐτίκα νῦν and μάλ' αὐτίκα, also αὐτίκ' ἄρα, αὐτίκ' ἐπεί, as soon as; αὐτίκ' ἔπειτα, then directly; with partcp. αὐτίκ' ἰόντι, the moment thou art gone, Od. 2, 367. 17, 327.

αὖτις, adv. Ion. for αὖθις (lengthened fr. αὖ), *again, back*. πάλιν αὖτις φέρειν, to carry back again, 5, 257; often with verbs: αὖτις ἰέναι, to go again. 2) *hereafter, at a subsequent time*, 1, 140. 3, 440.

αὐτμή, ή (ἄω), *a breath, air, wind*, spoken of the breath of men, 9, 609; of the wind of the bellows, 18. 471; of the wind, Od. 11, 400, 407. 2) *fume, vapour, smoke*, 14, 174. Od. 12, 369; *heat, flame*, Od. 9, 389.

αὐτμήν, ένος, ὁ, poet.=αὐτμή, 23, 765. Od. 3, 289.

αὐτοδίδακτος, ον (διδάσκω), *self-taught, self-educated*, Od. 22, 347.†

αὐτόδιον, adv. (lit. *on the same way*), *on the spot, at once*. Od. 8, 449.† (Either fm ὁδός, or only lengthened fm αὐτός, as μαψίδιος fm μάψ.)

αὐτόετες, adv. (ἔτος), *in the same year, in one year*, Od. 3, 322.†

αὐτόθεν, adv. (αὐτός), *from the same place, from here, from there*; mly with prep.: αὐτόθεν ἐξ ἑδρέων, directly from the seats, 20, 77. Od. 13, 56.

αὐτόθι, adv. poet. and Ion. (αὐτός), *in the same place, here, there*, 3, 428. Od. 4, 302.

*Αὐτοκάνης ὄρος, τό, a promontory in Æolis near Phocæa in Asia, h. in Ap. 35. Ilgen would read 'Ακροκάνης, and refers it to the promontory Κάνη of Strabo. Herm. thinks the reading is not to be changed, and that perhaps we are to understand by it a part of the promontory.

αὐτοκασιγνήτη, ή, *an own sister*, Od. 10, 137.†

αὐτοκασίγνητος, ὁ, *an own brother*, *Il. 3, 238.

Αὐτόλυκος, ὁ (λύκος), son of Hermês (Mercury) and Chiônê or Philônis, father of Anticlêa, grandfather of Ulysses. He had his residence on Parnassus, and was noted for dissimulation and cunning, Od. 19, 394 seq. He bore off the famous helmet of Amyntôr from Eleôn, 10, 267; and gave to his grandson the name of Ulysses, Od. 19, 459.

αὐτόματος, η. ον (μέμαα), *acting from one's own motion, spontaneous, self-moved, of his (its) own accord*; αὐτόματος ἦλθε, 2. 408. 5, 749: spoken esply of the wonderful tripods of Hêphæstus (Vulcan), which moved themselves, *18, 376.

Αὐτομέδων, οντος, ὁ (μέδων), son of Diôrês, charioteer of Achilles from Scyrus, 9, 209. 17, 429.

Αὐτονόη. ή, a handmaid of Penelôpê, Od. 18, 182.

Αὐτόνοος, ὁ, 1) A Greek slain by Hector, 11, 301. 2) a Trojan whom Patroclus slew, 16, 694.

αὐτονυχί, adv. (νύξ), *in the same night*, 8, 197.†

*αὐτοπρεπής, ές (πρέπω), a doubtful reading in h. Merc. 86. This word yields here no sense. Wolf adopts the reading of the Cdd. Paris and Mosc.: ὁδὸν αὐτοτροπήσας, which is equally unsatisfactory. The conjecture of Hermann accords best with the connexion: ὁδὸν ἀντιτορήσων, about to pass over a way.

αὐτός, ή, ό (from αὖ—τος), prop. *again he*, then *the same; he, she, it*. I) *the same, self*, and spoken of all three persons which are indicated by the verb; the personal pronouns are, however, often connected with it; in the third person it stands alone. It gives prominence and distinctness to an object, and occurs in many senses: 1) In the Hom. language, αὐτός frequently indicates an antithesis to a person or thing. Thus the body, in distinction from the soul, is called αὐτός: αὐτούς, bodies, in opposition to souls, 1, 4; αὐτός, the prince, in distinction from his subjects, 6, 4; αὐτοί, men, in distinction from the ships, 7, 338. b) *even*, to render the connected noun emphatic, 6, 451; in designations of place, *precisely, exactly*, 13, 614; esply with σύν: αὐτῇ σὺν φόρμιγγι, together with the lyre, 9, 194: and without σύν: αὐτῇ γαίῃ αὐτῇ τε θαλάσσῃ, 8, 24. 2) *self, of oneself, of one's own accord*, 17, 254. οἱ δὲ καὶ αὐτοὶ πανέσθων, Od. 2, 168. b) *self*, i. e. without another, *alone*, 2, 233. 8, 99. 13, 729. Od. 1, 53. 15, 310. 3) Often in connexion with the personal pronouns, but always separated in the oblique cases: ἐμέθεν αὐτῆς, οἱ αὐτῷ, σὺ αὐτόν, etc.; the pron. once stands after, as αὐτόν μιν, Od. 4, 244. Also αὐτός alone stands for the pron. of the first and second persons: αὐτός for ἐγὼ αὐτός, 13, 252; περὶ αὐτοῦ, i. e. ἐμαυτοῦ, Od. 21, 249. 4) Often in the gen. αὐτοῦ, αὐτῶν, etc. is put for emphasis' sake with the possessive pronoun. τὰ σ' αὐτῆς ἔργα, thine own works, 6, 490; αὐτῶν σφετέρῃσιν ἀτασθαλίῃσιν ὄλοντο, by their own folly Od. 1, 7. 5) *the same, the very*

E 3

Αὐτοσταδίη. 78 Ἀφαμαρτοεπής.

same, for ὁ αὐτός, often in H., 12, 225. Od. 8, 107. II) he, she, it, esply in the oblique cases. αὐτόν is regarded by the Grammarians as enclitic when it signifies barely him. In 12, 204, the Schol. retain the enclisis [and read κόψε γάρ αὐτον]; the moderns reject it: cf. Thiersch, § 205, 11. Anm. III) With the article, ὁ αὐτός, ἡ αὐτή, τὸ αὐτό, the same, the very same; still rare in H. τὼ δ' αὐτώ, 1, 338; τὴν αὐτὴν ὁδόν, 6, 391. IV) In composition it signifies 1) self-originated, not formed by human instrumentality. 2) mixed with nothing; αὐτόξυλος, merely of wood. 3) personally, of one's own power.

αὐτοσταδίη, ἡ (ἵστημι), close combat, where man fights with man (with the sword or spear), 13, 325.†

αὐτοσχεδά, adv.=αὐτοσχεδόν, 16, 319 †

αὐτοσχεδίη, ἡ (prop. fem. from αὐτοσχέδιος, very near), in H., a combat where man contends with man,=αὐτοσταδίη, a close combat, mêlée [mingled battle, hand to hand, Cp.]; only in the dat. and accus. αὐτοσχεδίῃ μίξαι χεῖράς τε μένος τε, to mingle hands and strength in close fight, to mingle battle, 15, 510. αὐτοσχεδίην πλήττειν τινά, to strike any one close at hand, i. e. with the sword, 12, 192. 2) ἐξ αὐτοσχεδίης, suddenly, without premeditation, h. Merc. 55.

αὐτοσχεδόν, adv. once αὐτοσχεδά (σχεδόν), very near, close at hand, cominus; μάχεσθαι, to fight man to man; οὐτάζεσθαί τινα, to wound any on- in close fight, i. e. with the sword, 7, 273.

αὐτοτροπήσας, see αὐτοπρεπής.

αὐτοῦ, adv. (prop. gen. from αὐτός), in the same place, there, here; often with another word: αὐτοῦ ἐνὶ Τροίῃ, 2, 237; αὐτοῦ ἔνθα, just there, 8, 207; κεῖθι αὐτοῦ. h. Ap. 374; αὐτοῦ ἀγρῶν, Od. 4, 639. 2) on the spot, directly, 15, 349.

αὐτόφι, αὐτόφιν, Ep. gen. and dat. sing. and plur. from αὐτός, always with prep. ἀπ' αὐτόφιν, ἐπ' αὐτόφιν, παρ' αὐτόφιν, 11, 44. 12, 302.

Αὐτόφονος, ὁ, a Theban, father of Polyphontes, 4, 395.

αὐτοχόωνος, ον, Ep. for αὐτόχωνος contr. from αὐτοχόανος (χοάνη), barely cast, rough cast, not smoothed by filing and polishing, epith. of the discus, 23, 826. † (Others: whole cast, not hollow.)

αὕτως or αὔτως (the old Gramm. distinguish αὕτως, idly, and αὔτως for οὕτως, thus; cf. Schol. on Il. 1, 133; Etym. Mag. Buttmann, Lex. would take αὕτως every where as a form of οὕτως. Herm. de pron. αὐτός, Opusc. I. p. 338, and Thiersch, Gram. § 198, 5, consider αὕτως more as the true form, and as an adv. from αὐτός, with the Æol. accent, which last we may regard as most correct. Wolf follows them in the Il., but αὔτως stands still in the Od.) It signifies prop. 1) even so, just so, thus; hoc ipso modo. αὕτως ὥστε γυναῖκα, 22, 125. Od. 14, 143; hence, Ep. ὡς δ' αὕτως,

later ὡσαύτως, in the same way, 3, 339. Od. 3, 64. 2) even thus still, as yet, in reference to a past state, 18, 338; λάβῃς, λευκὸς ἔτ' αὔτως, 23, 267; or, even so, even thus, in reference to a present state: ἀλλά καὶ αὕτως ἀντίον εἶμ' αὐτῶν, but even thus I will go against them, 5, 255. 18, 198; often καὶ αὕτως, even thus, nevertheless, i. e. without reward, 9, 598; hence, 3) only thus, nothing more; all nisi. ἀλλ' αὕτως ἄχθος ἀρούρης, but a mere burden of the earth. Od. 20, 379; often in connexion with adv., μὰψ αὕτως, ἀκλεὴς αὕτως, etc.; hence also, in vain, to no purpose. αὕτως ῥ' ἀνέεσσ' ἐριδαίνομεν, we contend with words to no purpose, 2, 342; without reason, 6, 55.

αὐχένιος, η, ον, belonging to the neck. τένοντες αὐχένιοι, the sinews of the neck. Od. 3, 450.†

*αὐχέω (from αὐχή, related to εὐχή), to vaunt oneself, to boast, ἐπί τινι, Batr. 57.

αὐχήν, ἕνος. ὁ, the neck, spoken of men, 5, 147. 161; of brutes, 5, 657.

αὐχμέω (αὐχμιῇς [Död. derives αὐχμός fm αὐστός, αὐκτός; as αἰχμή fm αΐσσειν, δραχμή fm δράσσειν]), prop. to be dry, withered; to look squalid, rough; squalere. γήρας λυγρὸν ἔχεις αὐχμεῖς τε κακῶς, Od. 24, 250.†

*αὐχμήεις, ἐσσα, εν (αὐχμή), dry, dusty, dirty, squalidus, h. 18, 6.

I. αὔω, Ep. for αὔσω, prob. to make dry; hence, to kindle, to light, Od. 5, 490.†

II. αὔω, aor. 1 ἤϋσα and ἄϋσα (ὔ), to cry, to shout aloud; often with the adv. μακρόν, μέγα, δεινόν. b) Spoken of inanimate things: to sound, to resound, 13, 409; αὖον, 441. 2) Trans. to call, τινά, any one, rarely 11, 461. 13, 477. (αὔω, dissyllabic in pres. and imperf. but in the further flexion with ῡ̄.)

ἀφαιρέω, and poet. ἀποαιρέω, 1, 275 (αἱρέω), fut. ἀφαιρήσω, aor. ἀφεῖλον, partcp. ἀφελών, fut. mid. ἀφαιρήσομαι, aor. 2 mid. ἀφειλόμην and ἀφελόμην, 1) to take away, to take from, τινί τι, Od. 11, 455. 2) Mid. more frequent, to take away any thing for oneself, to bear off; always with the idea of one's own advantage, τι, any thing, νόστον, νίκην. 16, 82. 690. The pers. from whom something is taken stands in the dat., accus, and rarely gen.: to take away any thing from any one, to deprive him of a thing; τινὰ κούρην, 1, 275; τινὶ ψῆρας, 1, 161. Od. 1, 9; πολλῶν θυμόν, to deprive many of life, 5, 673. Od. 22, 219.

ἀφαλος, ον, without a crest-cone; i. e. the metal boss or socket, into which the crest is inserted, 10, 258.†

ἀφαμαρτάνω (ἁμαρτάνω), aor. 2 ἀφάμαρτον and ἀπήμβροτον, 16, 466, to miss, not to hit, τινός, any one, said esply of arrows, spears, etc., 8, 119. 2) to lose what one possessed, to be bereft or deprived of a thing, with gen. 6, 411.

ἀφαμαρτοεπής, ές (ἔπος),=ἁμαρτοεπής, who misses his point in speaking, loquacious, 3, 215 †

Ἀφανδάνω. 79 Ἀφραδέω.

ἀφανδάνω (ἀνδάνω), *not to please, to displease*, Od. 16, 387.

ἄφαντος, ον (φαίνω), *invisible, not seen, vanished, destroyed, forgotten,* *6, 60. 20, 303.

ἄφαρ, adv. poet. (either from ἄπτω, or from ἀπό and ἄρα: cf. Thiersch, § 198, 3. Anm.): originally it signified an immediate consequence; hence, 1) *directly, immediately, quickly, suddenly*, 19, 405. In certain phrases, as 'it is better,' it means *directly, forthwith, in promptu*, i. e. the advantage accrues immediately after the act, Od. 2, 169. Il. 17, 417. 2) Often without the idea of immediate consequence, *then, thereupon*, 11, 418. Od. 2, 95; ἄφαρ αὐτίκα, then immediately, 23, 593. 3) *continually, constantly*, according to Damm, only 23, 375.

Ἀφαρεύς, ῆος, ὁ, son of Calētōr, slain by Æneas, 13, 541.

ἀφαρπάζω (ἁρπάζω), aor. 1 ἀφάρπαξα, *to tear away*, κόρυθα κρατός, the helmet from the head, 13, 189.†

ἀφάρτερος, η. ον (compar. fr. adv. ἄφαρ), *quicker, fleeter,* ἵπποι, 23, 311.†

ἀφαυρός, ή, όν, *weak, powerless, feeble,* παῖς, 7, 235; oftener in compar. ἀφαυρότερος, and superl. ἀφαυρότατος (fr. αὔω, ἀφαύω, or fr. ταῦρος with a intens.).

ἀφάω (ἀφή), *to feel, to touch, to examine,* ἀσπίδα, 6, 322; †only partcp. pres. ἀφόωντα, Ep. from ἀφῶντα; ἀφόωντα, ed. Wolf; ἀφόωντα, Spitzn., which last, according to Cd. Venet. and Apoll. Lexic. alone is correct: cf. Spitzner ad loc.

Ἀφειδας, αντος, ὁ (from ἀ and φείδω, unsparing), son of Polyphēmōn from Alybas, father of Eperitus, for whom Ulysses gave himself out, Od. 24, 305.

ἀφείη, see ἀφίημι.

ἀφενος, τό, *abundance, wealth, riches,* in connexion with πλοῦτος, 1, 171. Od. 14, 99. (Apoll. and Schol. think it from ἀπό and ἑνός, prop. ἡ ἀφ' ἑνὸς ἐνιαυτοῦ περίουσα, the products of a year.)

ἀφέξω and ἀφέξομαι, see ἀπέχω.

* **ἀφῆλιξ, ικος** (ἧλιξ), *beyond the years of youth, growing old*, h. in Cer. 140.

ἀφῆμαι (ἧμαι), *to sit apart, separate*, only partcp. pres., 15, 106.†

ἀφήτωρ, ορος. ὁ (ἀφίημι), *the hurler, he that shoots arrows*, appellat. of Apollo, 9. 404.† (Some derive it from φάω, and regard it as = ὁμοφήτωρ, the diviner.)

ἄφθιτος, ον (φθίω), *not destroyed, imperishable, everlasting*, mly spoken of what belongs to the gods, 2, 46. Od. 9, 133.

* **ἄφθογγος, ον** (φθόγγος), *soundless, voiceless, dumb*, h. Cer. 198.

ἄφθονος, ον, *without envy*, 1) Act. *not envious, benevolent, giving freely*, h. 30, 16. 2) Pass. *not penurious, abundant, in abundance*, h. in Ap. 536.

ἀφίημι (ἵημι), 3 plur. imperf. ἀφίουν, as if from ἀφιέω, fut. ἀφήσω, aor. 1 ἀφῆκα and ἀφῆκα, aor. 2 dual and plur. subj. ἀφέη Ep. for ἀφῇ, optat. ἀφείην, I) *to send away, to dismiss, to let go*, τινά, any one, in a good and bad signif., 1, 25 ; ζωόν τινα, *to let one go alive*, 20, 464: spoken chiefly of missile weapons: *to cast, to discharge, to hurl*, as δόρυ, ἔγχος and ἰοπαυνόν, 8, 133; mly *to cast away*; ἄνθος, to cast the flower, said of grape-vines just setting for fruit, Od. 7, 126; metaph. δίψαν, *to remove thirst*, 11, 642; μένος, to lose the strength, 13, 444. 16. 613, etc.; in Pass.: τοῦ δέ τε πολλοὶ ἀπὸ σπινθῆρες ἵενται, from it (the star) many sparks were emitted, 4, 77. II) Mid. *to send oneself away from anything*; hence, *to let go off, to let loose*; with gen. δειρῆς οὔπω ἀφίετο πήχεε, *she did not loosen her arms from his neck*, Od. 23, 240. (ι prop. short, long only by augm.; once, however, without this reason, Od. 22, 231.)

ἀφικάνω, poet. (ἱκάνω), only pres. and imperf. = ἀφικνέομαι, *to go to, to come to, to reach;* mly with accus., once with πρός, 6, 386.

ἀφικνέομαι, depon. mid. (ἱκνέομαι), fut. ἀφίξομαι, aor. ἀφικόμην, perf. ἀφῖγμαι, Od. 6, 297; *to go to, to come to, to reach*, to go to a person or a place; mly with accus. νῆας, to the ships, more rarely with εἰς, ἐπί, κατά, and ὑπό and πρός τι, Od. 6, 297; metaph. *to overtake, to affect*. ἄλγος ἀφίκετό με, 18, 395.

ἀφίστημι (ἵστημι), aor. 2 ἀπέστην, perf. ἀφέστηκα, syncop. form in dual and plur. ἀφέσταστι, partcp. ἀφεσταώς, 3 plur. pluperf. ἀφέστασαν, aor. mid. ἀπεστησάμην. 1) Trans. *to put away*, not used in H. 2) Intrans. in aor. 2, perf. and pluperf., like the mid. *to stand apart, to stand aloof, to remove*, 4, 340. Od. 11, 544; *to be removed*, τινός, from a thing, 23, 517. b) In the mid. *to weigh out for oneself*, in order to pay; once, δείδω, μὴ τὸ χθιζὸν ἀποστήσωνται χρεῖος, I fear, lest they should pay back to us the debt of yesterday, i. e. requite evil for evil, 13, 745.

ἄφλαστον, τό, *the curved stern of a vessel*, with its decorations, 15, 716.† (In the Schol. on Ap. Rh., σανίδιον κατὰ τὴν πρύμνην.)

ἀφλοισμός, ὁ (related to ἀφρός), *foam, the froth of one enraged*, 15, 607.† (Others more improb. ψόφος ὀδόντων, gnashing of teeth.)

ἀφνειός, ον (ἄφενος), *rich, wealthy, opulent*, with gen. βιότοιο, in the means of living, 5, 544; χρυσοῖο, Od. 1, 165. The compar. ἀφνειότερος and superl. ἀφνειότατος, 20, 220.

ἀφοπλίζω (ὁπλίζω), *to disarm*, only mid. *to disarm oneself*, with ἔντεα, to lay aside one's arms, 23, 26.†

ἀφορμάω (ὁρμάω), in H. only depon. pass. ἀφορμάομαι, in aor. pass. ἀφωρμήθην, *to rush away, to hasten away*, ναῦφιν, 2, 794; hence absolute, *to go away, to depart*, Od. 2, 376.

ἀφόωντα, or ἀφῶντα, see ἀφάω.

ἀφραδέω (ἀφραδής), *to be imprudent*,

Ἀφραδής.   **Ἀχαιίς.**

indiscreet, to speak or act inconsiderately, Od. 9, 294. Il. 9, 32.

ἀφραδής, ές (φράζομαι), *inconsiderate, irrational, imprudent*, μνηστῆρες. Od. 2, 282. νεκροὶ ἀφραδέες, the unreflecting, senseless dead, Od. 11, 476; adv. ἀφραδέως, *thoughtlessly, indiscreetly*, 3, 436.

ἀφραδίη, ἡ (φράζομαι), *inconsideration, imprudence, carelessness, folly*; often in the plur. 5, 649; νόοιο, 10, 122. 16, 354. 2) *ignorance, inexperience*, πολέμοιο, 2, 368.

*ἀφράδμων, ον = ἀφραδής, h. in Cer. 257.

ἀφραίνω, poet. (φρήν), *to be irrational, indiscreet, foolish*, 2, 257. Od. 20, 360.

*ἄφραστος, ον (φράζομαι), *not observed, unknown*, ἔργα, h. Merc. 80; *not to be discovered, invisible*, στίβος, h. Merc. 353. Compar. ἀφραστότερος, Epigr. 14.

ἀφρέω (ἀφρός), *to foam, to froth*. ἵπποι ἄφρεον στήθεα, upon the breast, 11, 282.†
(ἄφρεον with synizesis.)

ἀφρήτωρ, ορος, ὁ (φρήτρη), *without society, without tribe, without connexions, unsocial*, 9, 63.†

Ἀφροδίτη, ἡ, daughter of Zeus and Dionē, 5, 348; or, according to a later tradition, born from the foam of the sea (ἀφρός), h. in Ven., wife of Hēphæstus (*Vulcan*), and paramour of Arēs (*Mars*) (Od. 8, 276), goddess of sensual love and of marriage, of pleasure and of beauty, 5, 429. Od. 20, 74. She is represented as exceedingly attractive and beautiful, 3, 396; distinguished by her smiling look (φιλομμειδής), but tender and unfitted for war. She is beautifully adorned (χρυσείη), the Graces themselves having furnished her clothing, 5, 338, and these constitute her society. She always carries a magic girdle, with which she subdues both gods and men, 14, 214 seq. With this girdle Hērē inspires Zeus with great love for herself. Aphroditē was on the side of the Trojans; she had given occasion to the war, 5, 349 seq. Æneas was her son, 5, 313. She had splendid temples in Cyprus and in Cytherē. 2) Metaph. like Ἄρης, it signifies *love, the enjoyments of love*, Od. 22, 444.

ἀφρονέω (ἄφρων), *to be foolish, or to act irrationally, foolishly*, only partcp. pres., 15, 104.†

ἀφρός, ὁ, *foam*, of water, 5, 599; of a raging lion, *20, 168.

ἀφροσύνη, ἡ (ἄφρων), *want of reason, senselessness, indiscretion, folly*, Il. in plur. Od. 16, 278. 24, 457.

ἄφρων, ον (φρήν), *irrational, senseless, indiscreet, inconsiderate, foolish* (antith. to ἐπίφρων), Od. 23, 12; *rash, raging*, spoken of Arēs and Athēnē, 5, 761. 875.

ἄφυλλος, ον (φύλλον), *leafless, deprived of leaves*, 2, 425.†

ἀφυσγετός, ὁ (ἀφύω), *slime, mud, filth*, which a river bears with it, 11, 495.†

ἀφύσσω, fut. ἀφύξω, aor. 1 ἤφυσα and poet. σσ, aor. mid. ἀφυσσάμην, Ep. σσ, 1) *to draw off*, apply from a larger vessel to a smaller, οἶνον ἀπό and ἐκ κρητῆρος, 1, 598. Od. 9, 9; ἐν ἀμφιφορεῦσιν. Od. 2, 349; with gen. alone, pass. πολλὸς δὲ πίθων ἠφύσσετο οἶνος, much wine was drawn from the vessels. Od. 23, 305. 2) Metaph. πλοῦτον, *to accumulate riches*, as if to draw up in full draughts. The passage 1, 170, οὐδέ σ' ὀίω ἐνθάδ' ἄτιμος ἐών, ἄφενος καὶ πλοῦτον ἀφύξειν, is explained in different ways; 1) In the ancients we find a twofold explanation. Some (Eustath. and Schol Venet.) supposed an hyberbaton, and connected ἐνθάδ' ἄτιμος ἐών with εἶμι Φθίηνδε, v. 169, so that the former words refer to Achilles. Others (Schol. Venet.) supposed the nom. stands for gen., and referred these words to Agamemnon. 2) In the modern annotators we find a threefold explanation: a) The first is connected with that of Eustath., but differs in constructing ἐνθάδε with ἀφύξειν, viz., 'I do not believe, since I am dishonoured (without reward), that you will here accumulate riches.' Ruhkopf and Stadelmann p. 62, prefer this, partly because the nom. ἄτιμος ἐών stands in close connexion with ὀίω, partly because it agrees with the connexion, since Achilles thinks that Agamemnon will make little progress without his help. b) The second explanation (Clarke and Köppen) refers ἄτιμος ἐών, on account of v. 175, to Agamemnon, and constructs, οὐκ ὀίω σε, ἄτιμος ἐών (for ἄτιμον ἐόντα)—ἀφύξειν. Reference is made to 2, 351, for a similar anacoluthon. 3) Both explanations, the one on account of the hyperbaton, and the other on account of the harsh anacoluthon, are justly rejected by almost all modern critics. They either make σ' a dat. σοί (cf. Wolf. Vorles. 1. p. 102, and Spitzner, Excurs. XIII. § 3), or they read with Bentley σοὶ ὀίω, because οἱ is not elided in σοί (cf. Voss Anm. p. 6. Bothe and Thiersch, § 338, 10). They read consequently, οὐδέ σοι ὀίω ἐνθάδ', ἄτιμος ἐών, etc., i. e. 'I have no mind whilst I am dishonoured, to gather riches for you here. With this explanation the words connect far better with the preceding νῦν δ' εἶμι Φθίηνδ', and the reply of Agamemnon turns mainly on t is threat of Achilles. II) Mid. 1) *to draw off or out for oneself, to pour out or in*; with accus. οἶνον ἐκ κρητῆρος, 3, 259; and ἀπὸ κρητῆρος, 10, 579. 2) Metaph. *to heap up*, ἀμφὶ δὲ φύλλα ἠφυσάμην, Od. 7, 285. On διὰ δ' ἔντερα χαλκὸς ἤφυσε, see διαφύσσω.

Ἀχαιαί, αἱ, *Achaian or Achæan women*, fem. of Ἀχαιοί, Od. 2, 119.

Ἀχαιιάς, άδος, ἡ, Ep. for Ἀχαιάς, *Achaian*, or Ἀχαιαν; as subst. an *Achaian* or *Achæan woman*, 5, 422.

Ἀχαιικός, ή, όν, Ep for Ἀχαικός, *Achaian* or *Achæan*; λαός, the Achaian or Achæan people, 13, 141; Ἄργος, 9, 141.

Ἀχαιίς, ίδος, ἡ, *Achaian* or *Achæan*, with or without γαῖα, the Achaian land,

Ἀχαιοί. 81 **Ἀχρεῖον.**

esply the dominion of Achilles in Thessaly, 1, 254; see Ἀχαιοί. 2) Subaud. γυνή, *an Achaian woman*, 2, 235; in contempt, 9, 395.

Ἀχαιοί, οἱ, nom. sing. Ἀχαιός, ὁ, *the Achaians* or *Achæans*, the most powerful of the Grecian tribes in the time of the Trojan war, whose main residence was in Thessalia, 2, 684; but who also had possessions in Peloponnesus as far as to Messene, chiefly in Argos, 5, 114. The Danai and Myrmidons were branches of this tribe. Perhaps they had spread themselves also to Ithaca. Od. 1, 90; and to Crete, Od. 19, 138. Tradition says they derived their name from Achæus, son of Xuthus, grandson of Hellen, Apd. 1, 7. 3. The entire Greeks are often so called in H. from the main tribe, 1, 2. Od. 1, 90.

ἄχαρις, ὁ (χάρις), *disagreeable, joyless*; in compar. ἀχαρίστερος, Od. 20, 392.†

ἀχάριστος, ον (χαρίζομαι), *disagreeable, displeasing*, Od. 8, 236† [δόρπον ἀχαρίστερον, '*a sadder feast*,' Cp.].

*ἀχειρής, ές (χείρ), *without hands*, epith. of the crabs, Batr. 300.

Ἀχελώϊος, ὁ, Ep. for Ἀχελῷος, a river between Ætolia and Acarnania, which flows into the Ionic sea; now *Aspro-Potamo*, 21, 194. 2) a river in Phrygia, which rises in the mountain Sipylus, 24, 616.

ἄχερδος, ἡ, more rarely ὁ, *a wild, thorny bush*, suitable for hedging; *thornbush, thorn, the hawthorn*, Od. 14, 10.†

ἀχερωΐς, ίδος, ἡ, *the white poplar, the silver poplar, populus alba*, Linn.; 13, 389. 16, 482; prob. from Ἀχέρων, because it was believed that Heraclês brought it from the under-world. *Il.

Ἀχέρων, οντος, ὁ (as if ὁ ἄχεα ῥέων, the river of woe), *Acherôn*, a river of the under-world, into which Pyriphlegethôn and Cocytus flow, Od. 10, 513. *Od.

ἀχεύω (ἄχος), *to be sad, afflicted, troubled*, only partcp. with accus. θυμόν, in heart, 5, 869; τινός, about any one, Od. 16, 139; and with εὕνεκα, Od. 21, 318.

ἀχέω = ἀχεύω, also only partcp. τινός, about any one, 18, 446; and with ἕνεκα, 20, 293.

ἄχθομαι (ἄχθος), 1) *to be laden, freighted*. νηῦς ἤχθετο τοῖσι, the ship was laden, Od. 15, 457. b) Metaph. to be burthened or oppressed, ὀδύνῃσι, oppressed with pains, 13, 354; with accus. ἄχθομαι ἕλκος, I am pained by the wound, 5, 361. 2) Esply spoken of mental states: *to be oppressed, pained, sad, indignant, vexed, grieved*; with κῆρ, 11, 274. 400; ἤχθετο δαμναμένους Τρώεσιν, he grieved to see them conquered by the Trojans, 13, 352 (ἤχθετο in Od. 14, 366. 19, 337, belongs to ἔχθομαι).'

ἄχθος, εος, τό (related to ἄχω), *load, burden*. ἄχθος ἀρούρης, burden of the earth, proverbially spoken of a worthless man, 18, 104. Od. 20, 379.

Ἀχιλλεύς, ῆος, ὁ, also Ἀχιλεύς (when required by the metre), son of Peleus and Thetis, king of the Myrmidons and Hellênes in Thessalia, the braves: hero before Troy. He was educated by Phœnix; son of Amyntor, who also accompanied him to Troy, 9, 448; in music and the healing art he was instructed by Chiron, 11. 832. His friend is Patroclus; his son, Neoptolemus, who resided in Scyros, 19, 326—333; and whom Ulysses brought to Troy, to engage in the contest, Od. 11, 509. Achilles is the hero of H.: great physical power, a great mind, violent passions, but also a feeling heart, are his characteristics. Insulted by Agamemnon, he forgets himself in his wrath; he finally gives ear to his mother, but does not fight for the Greeks till the death of Patroclus, 19, 321. According to H. he died in battle, Od. 24, 430. 5, 310. (The name is derived from ἄχος and λαός, the people's grief, Apd. *Molestinus*, Herm.)

ἀχλύς, ύος, ἡ, *obscurity, darkness, cloud*, esply *the darkness of death, the night of death*; spoken of fainting, 5, 696 [κατὰ δ' ὀφθαλμῶν κέχυτ' ἀχλ., '*sickly mists*,' Cp.]; of death, Od. 22, 88 (υ is long in nom. and accus.).

ἀχλύω (ἀχλύς), aor. ἤχλῦσα, *to become dark, to darken* or *cloud*, spoken of the sea, Od. 12, 405.†

ἄχνη, ἡ, Ion. for ἄχνα (related to χνόη), prop. what is abraded from the surface of a body; hence 1) *chaff*, 5, 499. 2) *foam* of the sea, 4, 426. Od. 5, 403.

ἄχνυμαι, Ep. depon. only pres. and imperf. ἄχος, *to feel pain, to be afflicted, sad, troubled*; often with accus. θυμόν, κῆρ ἐνὶ θυμῷ, and with gen. caus. τινός, about any one, Od. 14, 376; and περί τινι, h. Cer. 77; also περὶ ἄχνυτο, 14, 38; once spoken of lions, 18, 320; cf. ἀκαχίζω.

ἄχολος, ον (χολή), *without bile, without anger*. 2) *which expels anger, anger-quelling*, φάρμακον, Od. 4, 221.†

ἄχομαι, mid. *to be sad, to be afflicted*, Od. 18, 256. 19, 129.

ἄχος, εος, τό (a word derived from the natural ejaculation of one in pain, as ah!), *pain, grief, sadness, affliction, trouble*; always spoken of the mind: ἐμοὶ δ' ἄχος, it pains me, 5, 759; with gen. about any one, ἐμοὶ ἄχος σέθεν ἔσσεται, I shall have pain on thy account, 4, 169: also in plur. ἄχεα, *sufferings, pains*, 6, 413. Od. 19, 167.

ἀχρεῖον, adv. (prop. neut. of adj. ἀχρεῖος, ον), *unprofitably, uselessly, aimlessly*, only twice: 1) ἀχρεῖον ἰδών, 2, 269, looking foolish or confused, spoken of Thersites, who looked confounded or embarrassed when he received blows from Ulysses. Voss translates, 'with a wry look;' and with this agrees the explanation of Wolf in Vories. zu Il. p. 44. "But it is uncertain," says Wolf, "whether Thersites does this from pain or

E 5

'Άχρημοσύνη. 82 Βαθύθριξ.

purposely, to excite the pity of the Greeks. The latter agrees well with his character." 2) άχρείον έγέλασσεν, Od. 18, 163, she laughed without cause, she uttered a forced laugh; spoken of Penelope, who, notwithstanding her inward trouble, wished to appear cheerful to the suitors. Here again άχρεΐον expresses something artificial, unnatural (έπίπλαστον, υποκεκριμένον, Schol. Α.), *Usteri.*
άχρημοσύνη, ή (άχρήμων), *poverty, want, penury,* Od. 17, 502.†
* άχρηστος, ον (χρηστός), *profitless, vain,* neut. as adv. Batr. 70.
άχρι, before a vowel άχρις (related to άκρος), adv. 1) Of place: *at the extreme, on the surface,* 17, 599. *b) to the extreme, entirely,* 4, 522. 2) Of time: *until,* with gen. άχρι μάλα κνέφαος, till late at night, Od. 18, 369.
άχυρμιή, ή (άχυρον), prop, the place where the chaff falls, *a chaff-heap,* 5, 502.†
ΑΧΩ, see άκαχίζω.
άψ, adv. of place: *backwards, back,* often with a verb: άψ όράν, ιδεϊν. 2) Of time: *again,* 5, 505.
'Αψευδής (from ά and ψεύδος, not deceitful), daughter of Nereus and Doris, 18, 46.
αψίς, ίδος, ή, Ion. for άψίς (άπτω), *a knot, a mesh.* άψίδες λίνου, the meshes of the net, 5, 487.†
άψόρρον, adv. see άψορρος.
άψόρροος, ον (ρέω), *back-flowing,* epith. of Oceanus, which like a river encircles the earth and flows back into itself, 18, 399. Od. 20, 65.
άψορρος, ον (prop, abbreviated from άψόρροος), *retreating back,* άψορροι έκίομεν, άπονέοντο, 3, 313. Oftener the neut. sing. άψορρον as adv. *back,* with βαίνειν, άπονέεσθαι. *b) again,* 4, 152.
άψος, εος, τό (άπτω), *connexion, articulation,* esply of the limbs, *a joint.* λύθεν δε οί άψεα πάντα, all her limbs [joints] were loosed (i. e. in slumber), Od. 4, 794. 18, 189.
ΑΩ, theme of άημι.
ΑΩ, theme of άεσα and άσα, q. v.
ΑΩ (ά), pres. infin. άμεναι for άέμεναι, infin. fut. άσειν, aor. 1 άσα, infin. άσαι, infin. fut. άσεσθαι, aor. 1 άσασθαι; I) *to satiate,* τινά, any one: with gen. mat. άσαι Άρηα αίματος, Ares with blood, 5, 289; ίππους όρόμου, 18, 281; metaph. spoken of the spear: ίεμένη χροός άμεναι άνδρομέοιο, lusting to sate itself with human flesh, 21, 70. II) Mid. *to satiate onself;* ήτορ σίτοιο, to refresh the heart with food, 19, 307; έώμεν or έωμεν (19, 402) is assigned to this verb as subj. for άωμεν, see άωμεν.
άωρ, see άορες.
άωρος, ον (ώρα), *untimely, unformed;* hence *ugly, deformed* (Schol. άπρεπής), πόδες, spoken of Scylla, Od. 12, 89.†
άωρτο, 2 sing, pluperf. pass. from άείρω.
άωτέω (expanded form fr. άω), originally *to snore;* then *to sleep,* spoken esply of a deep sleep; in H. always with ύπνον. 10, 159. Od. 10, 548; see Buttm. Lex. p. 182.
άωτον, τό and ό άωτος (in H. the gend. is indeterminate; Pindar has only άωτος; later poets have also τό άωτον from άημι), prop, *a flock,* or *lock* of wool, έύστροφος οίός άωτος, the well-twisted wool of the sheep, spoken of a sling, 13, 599, 716; so also Od. 1, 443; spoken of the woolly skin of a sheep, Od. 9, 434; once spoken of the finest linen: λίνοιο λεπτόν άωτον, the delicate nap or down of the linen, 9, 661; metaph. *the best, the most beautiful,* inasmuch as the woolly surface of cloths tests their beauty and newness. Cf. Buttm. Lex. p. 182. According to the old Schol. it signifies *a flower,* then metaph. like άνθος, *the bloom,* i. e., *the finest, the most beautiful* (still the signif. *flower* is nowhere found in the poets).

B.

B, the second letter of the Greek alphabet; hence the index of the second rhapsody.
βάδην, adv. (βαίνω), *step by step, slowly,* antith. to running, 13, 516.†
* βαδίζω (βάδος), fut. ίσω, *to step, to go, to travel,* h. Merc. 210.
βάζω, fut. βάξω, perf. pass. βέβακται, *to prate, to speak, to talk;* with accus. άνεμώλια, μεταμώνια, to prate idle things; πεπνυμένα, άρτια, to speak discreetly, to the point, Od. 8, 240. δίχα βάζειν, to speak differently, Od. 3, 127; with double accus. βάζειν τινά τι, to say any thing to any one, 9, 59; and pass. έπος βέβακται, Od. 8, 408.
βάθιστος, η, ον, superl. for βαθύς.
* βάθος, εος, τό (βαθύς), *depth,* λίμνης, Batr. 86.
βαθυδίνήεις, εσσα, εν (δίνη), *deep-whirling, having deep whirlpools,* only twice, 21, 15. 603; elsewhere the following.
βαθυδίνης, ου, ό (δίνη), *deep-whirling, deep-eddying, having deep whirlpools,* epith. of Oceanus and of rivers, 20, 73 Od.
βαθύζωνος, ον (ζώνη), *deep-girdled,* i. e. girdled close under the breast, so that the garment might hang in full folds down to the feet, because this took place only on festal days; hence in general: *splendidly clothed,* or *beautifully girdled,* epith. of the Trojan women, 9, 594. Od. 3, 154. [According to Passow, *low-girdled,* not girdled close under the breast, but above the hips.]
* βαθύθριξ, τριχος, ό, ή (θρίξ), with thick hair, *thick-woolled, thick-fleeced,* spoken of sheep, h. Ap. 412.

Βαθυκλήρος.   83   Βάλλω.

* βαθύκληρος, ον (κλῆρος), *rich in land, having great estates*, Ep. 16, 4.

Βαθυκλῆς, ῆος, ὁ, son of Chalcon, a Myrmidon, slain by Glaucus, 16, 594.

βαθύκολπος, ον (κόλπος), *deep-bosomed*, either literally from their full bosoms, or from the folds of the dress; hence, *splendidly-clothed*, epith. of the Trojan women, 18, 122; and of the nymphs, h. Ven. 258.

βαθυλείμος, ον (λειμών), *having rich meadows, having deep grass*, epith. of a town, 9, 151. 293.

βαθυλήϊος, ον (λήϊον), *having high grain, fruitful, τέμενος*, 18, 550.†

βαθύνω (βαθύς), *to make deep, to deepen, to excavate*; with accus. χῶρον, 23, 421.†

βαθυρρείτης, αο, ὁ (ῥέω) = βαθύρροος, 21, 195.†

βαθύρροος, ον (ῥέω), *deep-flowing*, epith. of Oceanus, 14, 314. Od. 11, 13.

βαθύς, εῖα, and Ep. βαθέη, βαθύ, superl. βάθιστος, 1) *deep* or *high*, according to the position of the speaker; τάφρος, ἄμαθος, Τάρταρος, ἠϊών, lofty coast [or, perhaps, having deep sand], 2, 92; metaph. of the soul: φρὴν βαθεῖα, the inmost soul, 19, 125. 2) *deep*, with the idea of *thick, dark*, ὕλη, 5, 555; also metaph. ἀήρ, the thick air, Od. 1, 144; λαῖλαψ, the strong tempest, 11, 306. 3) *deep* in length, or extending inward, ἄγκος, 20, 489; hence αὐλή, a deep court (V. with lofty enclosure), 5, 142.

* βαθύσκιος, ον (σκιά), *deep-shaded*, h. Merc. 229.

* βαθύστερνυς, ον (στέρνον), *high-breasted, wide-arched*; and *mly broad*, ala. frag. Hom. 23.

βαθύσχοινος, ον (σχοῖνος), *deeply over-grown with rushes, rushy*, epith. of Asopus ['*to the reedy banks of the Asopus*,' Cp.], 4, 383. h. 8, 5.

* βαθύτριχα, see βαθύθριξ.

βαίνω, fut. βήσομαι, aor. 1 trans. ἔβησα, aor. 2 ἔβην, Ep. βῆν, 3 plur. ἔβησαν, Ep. βῆσαν, ἔβαν, βάν, subj. βῶ, Ep. βείω, optat. βαίην, infin. βήμεναι and βῆναι, partcp. βάς, βᾶσα, βάν, perf. βέβηκα, also the sync. forms βεβάᾱσι, infin. βεβάμεν, partcp. βεβαώς, βεβαυῖα, pluperf. ἐβεβήκειν, syncop. 3 plur. βέβασαν, also Ep. aor. mid. ἐβήσετο, more rarely ἐβήσατο = ἔβη. According to Buttm., Gr. Gram., ἐβήσατο is correct only when used in a causative sense for ἔβησε. N.B. The form βέβηκα, rare in H., has only the signif. *to have gone*; the sync. forms βίβαα, that of the pres. *to go*, and the pluperf. mostly an aorist sense. (The ground form is ΒΑΩ, Ep. forms βιβάω, βίβημι, βιβάσθω.) 1) Intrans. *to go*, and 1) *to walk, to step, to proceed*, spoken of men and beasts, the direction ot the motion being indicated sometimes by the prep. εἰς, ἐν, ἐπί, κατά, μετά, πρός, etc., and sometimes by the accus. merely: εἰς δίφρον, 5, 837; also δίφρον, πόδας, 3, 262. Od. 3, 162; ἐπὶ νηός, to

ἐπὶ νηυσίν, to sail away in ships, 2, 351 [also ἐν νηυσίν, 2, 510]; ἐπί τινα, *to go to* any one, 2, 18: ἀμφί τινι, to go about any one (to defend him), 5, 299; μετ' ἴχνια τινος, to follow one's steps, Od. 3, 30. b) In a hostile sense: *to rush upon* any one, with ἐπί, μετά and accus., also ἐπί τινι, 16, 751. 2) With partcp. of another verb, by which the kind of motion is determined: ἔβη φεύγων, he fled; ἔβη ἀΐξασα, see ἀίσσω; the partcp. fut. denotes the aim: ἔβη ἐξεναρίξων, he went to slay, 11, 101; ἀγγελέων, Od. 4, 28. 3) With infin. following: *to set out, to proceed, to begin*. βῆ δ᾽ ἰέναι, he set out to go, quickly he went, 4, 199; so also βῆ θέειν, ἐλάαν. 4) Metaph. spoken of inanimate things: ἐννέα ἐνιαυτοὶ βεβάᾱσι, nine years have passed away, 2, 134. πῇ ὅρκια βήσεται ἡμῖν, whither will our oaths go, i. e., what will become of our oaths, 2, 339. ἰκμὰς ἔβη, the moisture (of the bull's hide) vanished, 17, 392. II) Trans. in aor. 1, only poet. and Ion. act. ἔβησα, 1) *to cause to go, to conduct, to cause to mount or alight*. φῶτας βῆσεν ἀφ᾽ ἵππων, 16, 810; but ἀμφοτέρους ἐξ ἵππων βῆσε κακῶς ἀέκοντας, he hurled both down from the chariot, unwilling as they were, 5, 164. βῆσαι ἵππους, 11, 756.

* Βάκχειος, είη, ειον, relating to Bacchus or to his orgies, *drunken, intoxicated, frantic*, Βάκχειος Διόνυσος, hymn. 18, 46.

βάλανος, ἡ, *an acorn*, fruit of the oak, *Od. 10, 242. 13, 409.

Βαλίος, ὁ (adj. βαλιός, spotted [for tasse, i. q. αἰόλος, Lob.]), Piebald, a horse of Achilles, 16, 149.

βάλλω [primitive βέλ-ω in βέλος], fut. βαλέω, aor. 2 ἔβαλον, perf. βέβληκα, pluperf. βεβλήκειν (often in the sense of the aor., 5, 66. 73, 661), perf. pass. βέβλημαι, Ep. also βεβόλημαι, yet with the difference that the former is used literally of body, the latter metaph. of mind, 9, 3; pluperf. βεβλήμην, 3 plur. βεβλήατο for βέβληντο. Of an aor. syne. mid. with pass. signif. occur ἔβλητο, infin. βλῆσθαι, partcp. βλήμενος, subj. βλήεται for βλήηται, optat. (βλείμην) βλεῖο, etc 1) Act. *to cast, to throw, to hurl*, λύματα εἰς ἅλα, 1, 314; spoken of all kinds of missile weapons: ἰόν, Od. 20, 62; hence, *to shoot, to hit, to wound*, τινά, or τί τινι, e. g. τινά δουρί, any one with the spear, 5, 73; δίστῷ, 5, 393; στῆθος χερμαδίῳ, 14, 410; τινά λάεσσιν, 3, 80: also τινά τί τινι, 11, 583; still the dat. is mly wanting; τινὰ στῆθος, to hit any one in the breast, 4, 480; also absol. *to hit*, in opposition to ἁμαρτάνω, to miss, 11, 351. 13, 10; as a consequence, *to prostrate, to lay* a person *low, to slay*, τινὰ ἐν κονίῃσι, 8, 156. cf. 4, 173. 5, 17; metaph. ἄχεϊ, πένθεϊ βεβολημένος, hit, wounded by pain, sorrow, 9, 3. Od. 10, 247. b) *to cast*; spoken of a strong motion: *to drive*; e. g. ἑτέρωσε χάσμα, to

Βαμβαίνω. 84 Βασιλεύς.

ἑτέρωσε ὄμματα, to turn away the eyes, Od. 16, 179; spoken of ships, νῆας ἐς πόντον, to urge the ships into the sea, Od. 4, 359; νέας πρὸς πέτρας, Od. 12, 71. 2) to hit, spoken of touching a surface, to besprinkle, to bespatter, to bestrew. ῥαθάμιγγες ἔβαλλον ἄντυγα, the drops besprinkled the chariot-rim, 11, 536. 20, 501; of dust, τινά, 23, 502. κτύπος οὔατα βάλλει, the noise strikes the ear, 10, 535. τόπον ἀκτῖσι βάλλει ἥλιος, the sun irradiates the place, Od. 5, 479. 3) to cast away, to let fall, to lose; δάκρυ, to shed tears. 4) In a weaker sense, to put, to put on, to annex, to put off, τὶ ἐν χερσίν τινος, 5, 574; κύκλα ἀμφ' ὀχέεσσι, 5, 722; φιλότητα μετ' ἀμφοτέροισι, to establish friendship between the two, 4, 16; ὕπνον ἐπὶ βλεφάροισι, to let fall, Od. 1, 364. b) Oftener of clothing and weapons: to put on. 5) to fall, to flow, to run, spoken of a river, εἰς ἅλα, 11, 722; of steeds: περὶ τέρμα, about the goal, 23, 462. II) Mid. 1) to hit, to touch for oneself; χρόα λουτροῖς, to cleanse one's limbs in the bath, h. Cer. 50. 2) to cast any thing about oneself, to put on; ἀμφὶ ὤμοισιν ξίφος, to suspend, 3, 334; αἰγίδα, 5, 738; metaph. ἐν θυμῷ χόλον τινί, to cherish anger against any one in the heart, 14, 50; μετά, or ἐν φρεσίν, ἐν θυμῷ, to lay any thing to heart, to consider, to ponder, νοστόν, 9, 435. 611. Od. 11, 428; more rarely, to lay up, to preserve in the heart, 15, 566; absolute, ἐτέρως ἐβάλοντο; they determined otherwise, Od. 1, 234; where Nitzsch with Spitzner prefers ἐτέρωσ' ἐβάλοντο, the reading of other manuscripts: ἐβόλοντο for ἐβούλοντο, is approved by Thiersch, Gram. § 168, 12, and Buttm., Lexil. p. 199. [For the pass. signif. of the 2 aor. sync. mid. see Buttm., § 110, 7.]

βαμβαίνω (related to βάζω), to stammer, to shudder for fear, to chatter with the teeth, 10, 375.†

βάν, Ep. for ἔβαν, see βαίνω.

βάπτω. 1) to dip, to immerse, with accus. πέλεκυν εἰν ὕδατι (to harden it), Od. 9, 392.† 2) to tinge, to colour, Batr. 221.

βαρβαρόφωνος, ον (φωνή), speaking a foreign tongue, rude of speech, epith. of the Carians, 2. 867.† (Voss, 'with a barbarous utterance,' since the Carians as Pelasgians spoke Greek, but their pronunciation was uncouth.)

βάρδιστος, η, ον. Ep. for βράδιστος, superl. see βραδύς.

ΒΑΡΕΩ = βαρύθω, only used in the Ep. partcp. βεβαρηώς, burdened, heavy. οἴνῳ βεβαρηότες, drunken with wine, *Od. 3, 139. 19, 122.

* βάρος, τό, weight, load, Batr. 91.

* βαρύβρομος, ον (βρέμω), heavily thundering, crashing, fr. 78.

βαρύθω (βαρύς), to be loaded, burdened, incommoded. βαρύθει μοι ὦμος ὑπ' αὐτοῦ, my shoulder is distressed by the wound, 16, 519.†

βαρύνω (βαρύς), aor. 1 ἐβάρυνα, aor. 1 pass. ἐβαρύνθην, also Ep. perf. βεβαρηώς (see ΒΑΡΕΩ), to load, to burden, to oppress, with accus. τινά, 5, 664. Pass. βαρύνεσθαι γυῖα, χεῖρα, to he distressed, lame in the limbs, in the hand, 19, 165. 20, 480. κάρη πήληκι βαρυνθέν, the head burdened with the helmet, *8. 308.

βαρύς, εῖα, ύ, 1) heavy, great, strong. βαρεῖαι χεῖρες, 1, 89. b) heavy, i. e., heavily pressing, severe, troublesome, oppressive; ὀδύναι, great pains; so also ἄτη, ἔρις, etc. 2) Spoken of sound. φθόγγος, Od. 9, 237; esply the neut. sing. and plur. βαρύ and βαρέα, as adv. with στενάχειν, to groan heavily, aloud, 8, 334.

βαρυστενάχων, ουσα, ον (στενάχω), sighing, groaning heavily, *4, 153.

* βαρύφθογγος, ον (φθογγή), deep-voiced, loud-roaring, λέων, h. Ven. 160.

βασίλεια, ἡ, fem. of βασιλεύς, queen, princess, *Od. 7, 241.

βασιλεύς, ῆος, ὁ, 1) ruler, king, sovereign, and mly commander, leader, 1, 9. In the heroic age, βασιλεύς was the designation of the chief of any community or district, who owed his authority to his valour his wealth, or his intelligence. As all bodily and mental endowments were considered a direct gift of the deity, so also was the regal dignity; hence he was called διογενής, διοτρεφής. The duties and employments of the king, 2, 197. Od. 1, 386 (δίκη βασιλήων), were 1) He assembled the public council, and led in debate, 2, 50. 9, 33. Od. 2, 26. 2) He was leader of the nation to war. 3) He was obliged to decide upon right and wrong, 16, 542. Od. 19, 110. 4) It was his place to present the solemn sacrifices, 2, 402. 412. [Cf. Jahrbüch. Jahn und Klotz, März 1843, p. 255.] His power was limited; he could decide nothing without consulting the most respectable men of the nation (βουλὴ γερόντων), and, in important cases, the general assembly of the people (ἀγορά). His prerogatives (γέρας) were 1) The presidency on public occasions, and a larger portion at feasts, 8, 162. 2) A distinct portion of land (τέμενος). 3) [Tributes or] gifts established by custom (θέμιστες), 9, 156. The ensigns of regal dignity were the sceptre (σκῆπτρον) and the service of heralds (κήρυκες): cf. Cammann Vorschule z. Hom. p. 277 seq. Helbig. die sittlich. Zustände des griech. Heldenalters, Leipz. 1839, p. 277 seq. II) a prince, a king's son; also, all of the nobility who had possessions, great or small, Od. 1, 394. 8, 41. 390. III) lord, master of a family, 18, 556. From this word comes the Ep. compar. βασιλεύτερος, a greater king, more royal, and superl. βασιλεύτατος, the greatest king, 9, 69. (Prob. from βαίνω in the trans. sense, and λαός, that conducts the people to war.) [The royal dignity, even in the heroic age, was hereditary: cf. Ph.

Βασιλεύω. 85 Βιάζω.

Humpert. de Civitat. Hom. Bonnæ, 1839, p. 4—11.]
βασιλεύω (βασιλεύς), *to be king, to rule, to reign,* ὑπὸ Πλάκῳ, 6, 425. 2) *to rule over* any one, *to govern,* with dat. 2, 206; [esply] once with gen. [to be queen] Πύλου, Od. 11, 285 [cf. Il. 6, 425].
βασιλήϊας, ίη, ήϊον, Ion. for βασίλειος (βασιλεύς), *royal, princely, γένος,* Od. 16, 401.†
βασιληΐς, ίδος, ἡ (fem. adj. to βασιληΐως), τιμή, the royal dignity, 6, 193.†
βάσκε, only in connexion with ἴθι, βάσκ' ἴθι, go, hence *away, haste,* 2, 8. The imper. of an Ep. form of βαίνω, which occurs in compos. In the infin. ἐπιβάσκω, q. v.
βαστάζω, fut. σω, *to lift up, to elevate, to raise,* with accus. λᾶαν, τόξον, Od. 11, 593. 21, 405. 2) *to bear,* τὶ νώτοισι, upon the back, Batr. 78.
βάτην, for ἐβήτην, see βαίνω.
Βατίεια, ἡ (prob. from βάτος, thornhill), a hill before the Scæan gate of Troy, by tradition the sepulchral mound of Myrinna, q. v. 2, 813.
* βατοδρόπος, ον (δρέπω), *plucking or extirpating brambles,* h. Merc. 190.
βάτος, ἡ, *a bramble, a thorn-bush,* Od. 24, 230.†
* βατραχομυομαχία, ἡ, *battle of the frogs and mice,* a well-known mockheroic poem, incorrectly ascribed to H.
* βάτραχος, ὁ, *a frog,* Batr.
βεβάασι, βεβάμεν, βέβασαν, βεβαώς, see βαίνω.
βεβαρηώς, see βαρέω.
βεβίηκε, see βιάω.
βεβλήαται, βεβλήατο, see βάλλω.
βεβολήατο, see βάλλω.
βεβρώθω, Ep. form for βιβρώσκω (theme ΒΡΟΩ with epenth. θ), *to consume, to devour,* εἰ δὲ σύγ' — ὠμὸν βεβρώθοις Πρίαμον Πριάμοιό τε παῖδας, if thou couldst devour Priam and his sons raw [alive], 4, 35.† (According to Buttm. Gram., βεβρώθοις belongs to a peculiar verb with strengthened sense βεβρώθω (from ΒΡΟΩ, with epenth. θ): cf. Rost, p. 284.)
βεβρωκώς, βεβρώσεται, see βιβρώσκω.
βέη, βείομαι, see βέομαι.
βείω, Ep. for βῶ, see βαίνω.
βέλεμνον, τό, poet.=βέλος, only in the plur. *a missile,* arrows or spears, *15, 184. 22, 206.
Βελλεροφόντης, ου, ὁ (from Βέλλερος and φονή), the slayer of Bellerus, an appellation of Hipponous, son of Glaucus, who slew unintentionally Bellerus, prince of the Corinthians, 6, 155; see Ἱππόνοος. [The tradition in regard to Bellerus is post-Homeric.]
* βελόνη, ἡ (βέλος), *a needle, a point,* Batr. 130.
βέλος, εος, τό (βάλλω), 1) *a missile weapon, telum,* esply, *a javelin, an arrow,* and mly whatever is hurled at an enemy, *a stone,* Od. 9, 493; poet. the gentle arrows of Apollo and Artemis, to indicate a sudden death, see Apollo and Artemis; but also of plague, 1, 51. 2) the *direction or stroke* of a missile weapon, 8, 513; hence, ἐκ βελέων τινά ἕλκειν, to draw any one from the track of missile weapons, 4, 465. 3) Metaph. spoken of the pangs of parturition, 11, 269.
βέλτερος, η, ον, [related to βόλεσθαι, velle, according to some], poet. irreg. compar. of ἀγαθός. *better, more excellent,* prob. related to βάλλω.
βελτίων, ον, irreg. compar. of ἀγαθός. Od. 17, 18. † Earlier reading for βέλτερον.
βένθος, εος, τό, Ep. for βάθος, τό, *deep, depth,* esply of the sea, 11. θαλάσσης πάσης βένθεα εἰδέναι, to know the depths of the sea, i. e, to possess great intelligence, in contradistinction from the physical strength of Atlas, who bore the pillars of heaven, Od. 1, 53; cf. 4, 386. βένθεα ὕλης, the depths of the forest, Od. 17, 316; βένθοσδε, Od. 9, 51.
βέομαι and βείομαι (ΒΕΙΩ), 2 sing. βέη, 1 plur. βιόμεσθα, h. Ap. 528; βεόμεσθα, an Ep. pres. with fut. signif.: *I will go, I will walk,* οὔτε Διὸς βέομαι φρεσίν, I will not walk (conduct) according to the mind of Zeus [i. e. I will not obey him], 15, 194; *I will live,* 16, 852. 22, 431 (either an Ep. fut. like κείω, or a subj. used as a fut. from βάω, βαίνω, Buttm., Gr. Gram. § 114. Thiersch, Gram. § 223, 88. Rost, p. 284).
βέρεθρον, τό, Ep. for βάραθρον, *abyss, gulf,* spoken of Tartarus, 8, 14; and of Scylla, Od. 12, 94.
βῆ, poet. for ἔβη, see βαίνω.
βηλός, ὁ (prob. from ΒΑΩ), *a threshold,* poet. dwelling-house, *1, 591. 15, 23.
* βῆμα, τό (βαίνω), *a step, a pace, a footstep,* h. Merc. 222. 345.
βήμεν, βήμεναι, see βαίνω.
Βῆσα, ἡ, a town of the Locrians, 2. 532; according to Strabo Βῆσσα, and only a forest valley.
βήσαμεν, βῆσε, see βαίνω.
βήσετο, see βαίνω.
βῆσσα, ἡ (βαίνω), *a ravine, a forest valley,* H. mly οὔρεος ἐν βήσσῃς, in the glades of the mountain; alone 18, 588. Od. 19, 435. h. Ap. 284.
βητάρμων, ονος, ὁ (ἁρμός), *a dancer,* prop. one who takes steps after measured time, *Od. 8, 250. 383.
βιάζω, Ep. earlier form, βιάω (βία), whence perf. act. βεβίηκα, pres. mid. 3 plur. βιόωνται for βιῶνται, Od. 11, 503; 3 plur. optat. βιῷατο Ep. for βιῷντο, 11, 467; imperf. 3 plur. βιόωντο, Ep. for ἐβιῶντο, Od. 23, 9; fut. mid. βιήσομαι, aor. mid. ἐβιησάμην (βιάζω in the act. occurs in H. as pres. only Od. 12, 297; elsewhere H. employs βιάζομαι in the pres. and imperf. as depon. mid. These tenses are pass. in 15, 727. 16, 102). 1) Act. *to subdue, to overpower, to oppress, to force,* τινά, Od. 12, 297; metaph. ἄχος βεβίηκεν Ἀχαιούς, pain oppressed the Achaians, 10, 145; hence pass. βιάζεσθαι

βελέεσσιν, to be harassed by weapons, 11, 576. II) Mid. more freq. as dep. *to overcome, to subdue*, τινά, 22, 229. Od. 21, 343: τινά ψεύδεσι, to vanquish any one by deceit, to overreach him, 23, 576; with double accus. τινά μισθόν, to wrest from one his hire, 21, 451.

βίαιος, η, ον (βίη), *violent, acting by violence*, ἔργα, Od. 2, 236. † Κῆρες, h. 7, 17.

βιαίως, adv. *violently, forcibly,* *Od. 2, 237.

Βίας, αντος, ὁ, 1) son of Amythaon and Idomene from Pylos, brother of Melampus. He courted Pero, the daughter of Neleus; and, after Melampus had procured for Neleus the cattle of Iphiclus, he received her as a wife. His sons are Talous, Perialces, etc. Apd. 1, 9. 11. Whether the companion of Nestor mentioned Il. 4, 296, is brother of Melampus, accord. to Od. 15, 225 seq. is uncertain. 2) an Athenian, 13, 691. 3) a Trojan, 20, 460.

βιάω, Ep. form for βιάζω, q. v.

βιβάς, ᾶσα, άν, partcp from the obsol. **βίβημι,** a form of βαίνω, mly μακρὰ βιβάς, long-striding, with ὕψι, 13, 371.

βιβάσθων, ουσα, ον, partcp. from the obsol. βιβάσθω = βαίνω, always with ἀκρά, taking long strides, *Il.

βιβάω, Ep. form of βαίνω, *to stride*. πέλωρα βιβᾷ, he strode prodigiously, h. Merc. 225; imperf. ἐβίβασκεν, h. Ap. 133; also partcp. βιβῶν, βιβῶσα, 3, 22. Od. 11, 539.

βιβρώσκω (fut. βρώσω), aor. 2 ἔβρων, ep. h. Ap. 127; perf. βέβρωκα, fut. pass. βεβρώσομαι, *to eat, to devour, to consume*, with accus. 22, 94; and with gen. Od. 22, 403. χρήματα κακῶς βεβρώσεται, the property will be riotously consumed (Ep. form βεβρώθω).

βίη, ἡ, Ep. for βία, Ep. dat. βίηφι, 1) *strength, force*, spoken chiefly of bodily power, rarely of mental, 3, 45; also of brutes and inanimate things, ἀνέμων; H. often used it periphrastically of distinguished men, like μένος, σθένος, etc., e. g. Πριάμοιο βίη, the force of Priam = the powerful Priam, 3, 105; so Διομήδεος, and with an adj. Ἡρακληείη, the power of Heraclês, 2, 665. 11, 699. 2) *violence*, mly in plur. *violent acts*, 5, 521. Od. 15, 329.

Βιήνωρ, ορος, ὁ, Ep. for Βιάνωρ, a Trojan, slain by Agamemnon, 11, 92.

*Βιοθάλμιος, ον (θάλλω), *in the vigour of life, in the bloom of vigorous life*, h. Ven. 190.

βίος, ὁ, *life, life-time,* *Od. 15, 491; and Batr.

βιός, ὁ, *a bow,* = τόξον, Il. and Od.

βιοτή, ἡ = βίοτος, *life*, Od. 4, 585.†

*Βιότης, ητος, ἡ = βίοτος, h. 7, 10.

βίοτος, ὁ (βιόω), *life*, as μοῖρα βιότοιο, the measure of life, 4, 170. 2) the means of living, *bona vitae, property*, ἀλλότριος, another's property, Od. 1, 160. 377.

βιάω (βίος), aor. 2 ἐβίων, infin. βιῶναι,

aor. 1 mid. ἐβιωσάμην. 1) *to live,* spoken of men and beasts. 2) *to restore life, to save life.* σὺ γάρ μ' ἐβιώσαο, thou hast saved my life, only Od. 8, 468. Οn βιώμεσθα, h. Ap. 528. see βέομαι.

βιῴατο, βιώωνται, βιώωντο, see βιάζω.

*βλαβερός, ή, όν (βλάπτω), *injurious, hurtful,* h. Merc. 36.

βλάβω [as πείρειν is imperfectly reduplicated in πρέπειν, so βέλειν, βαλεῖν in βλάβειν. Död.], th. of βλάπτω, obsol. except in βλάβεται, see βλάπτω.

*βλαισός, ή, όν, *crooked, bent outwards,* spoken chiefly of the feet, crooked-legged, Batr. 299.

βλάπτω (βλάβω), aor. 1 ἔβλαψα, perf. pass. βέβλαμμαι, aor. 1 pass. ἐβλάφθην. aor. 2 pass. ἐβλάβην, 23, 461 (from βλάβω only βλάβεται occurs), 1) *to impede* in running, *to obstruct, to hinder,* with accus., Od. 13, 22; τινὰ κελεύθου, to hinder one from returning, Od. 1, 195; γούνατα, to lame any one's knees, 7, 271; hence, pass. βλάβεται γούνατα, 19, 166. βλάβεν (for ἐβλάβησαν) ἅρματα καὶ ἵππω, chariots and horses were hindered, remained behind, 23, 545. βέλεμνα Διόθεν βλαφθέντα, arrows obstructed by Zeus, or rendered ineffectual, 15, 489. βλαφθῆναι ἐνὶ ὄζῳ, to be held in a branch, to be entangled, 6, 39; ἐν ἀσπίδι, 15, 647; κατὰ κλόνον, to be impeded in the tumult of battle, 16, 331. 2) Metaph. *to confuse, to astound, to mislead,* φρένας, 15, 724. Od. 14, 178; also without φρένας, 9, 507. Od. 21, 294; and βλαφθείς, 9, 512; hence: βλάβεται ἀγορητής, the orator is confused, 19, 82. 2) *to injure, to hurt,* Batr. 180; in H. only βεβλαμμένος ἦτορ, wounded in heart, once 16, 660; still others, more correctly, βεβλημένος. See Spitzner ad loc.

βλεῖο, see βάλλω.

βλεμεαίνω, *to feel one's strength, to be arrogant, to be proud,* always with σθένεϊ, of one's strength, *8, 337. 2) In the Batr. 275, *to desire earnestly, to strive for, to threaten.* [Död. connects it with the roots βαλ-, βολ-, βλεφ-, &c., and makes it mean *looking courageous, having a spirited look.* Hesych. gives ζαβλεμέως = μεγάλως, πεποιθώς, and Panyas, fr. vI., has ἀβλεμέως πίνειν, *fortiter bibens.* Later writers give it a neg. meaning, ἀβλεμέως, ἀφροντίστως.]

*βλέπω, *to see;* with accus. ὄμμους, Batr. 67.

βλέφαρον, τό (βλέπω), *the eyelid,* in plur. 10, 26. Od. 5, 271, dual Od. 17, 490.

βλήεται, Ep. for βλήηται, see βάλλω.

βλήμενος, η, ον, see βάλλω.

βλῆτρον, τό (βάλλω), *a cramp* or *nail.* ξυστὸν κολλητὸν βλήτροισιν, a pike fastened with cramps (rings) or nails, 15, 678.† (less probably, *joint.*)

βληχή, ἡ, a word derived from the sound. *the bleating* of sheep, οἰῶν, Od. 12, 266.†

βλοσυρός, ή, όν, *honourable, manly;*

Βλοσυρῶπις. 87 Βοίδειον.

terrific, savage (δεινός, σεμνός, Eustath.), ὀφρύσι, πρόσωπα, *7, 212. 15, 608.

Βλοσυρῶπις, ἡ (ὤψ), *of frightful look*, epith. of Gorgo, 11, 36.†

βλωθρός, ή, όν (βλώσκω), *growing up, shooting up, slender*, spoken of trees, 13, 390. Od. 24, 234.

βλώσκω, poet. (for μλώσκω, from μέλω), aor. 2 ἔμολον, perf. μέμβλωκα (for μέμλωκα), *to go, to come*, spoken of ships, 15, 720; also metaph., chiefly of time, 24, 781. Od. 17, 190.

βοάγριον, τό (βοῦς—ἄγριος), *a shield* formed of the wild ox-hide, 12, 22. Od. 16, 296 [either fm βοῦς ἄγριος (Et. Magn. ἐξ ἀγρίων βοῶν γενόμενα), or fm βοῦς, ἀγρεύω. Apoll. τὰ τῶν βοῶν ἀγρεύματα, *boûm exuviæ: de bove captum*, i. e. *scutum corio bubulo tectum*.

Βοάγριος, ὁ, a stream in Locris near Thronium, which in Strabo's time was called Μάνης, the raging, 2, 533.

βοάω (βοή), fut. βοήσω, aor. 1 ἐβόησα, partcp. βοήσας, Ion. contr. βώσας, 12, 337; Ep. pres. indic. βοάᾳ for βοᾷ, βοόωσιν for βοῶσιν, partcp. βοόων for βοῶν, etc. 1) *to call aloud, to cry*, spoken chiefly of heroes; of animals: of the cock, *to crow*, Batr. 193; of inanimate things: *to resound, to roar, to re-echo*. κῦμα βοάᾳ ποτὶ χέρσον, the wave roared upon the land, 14, 394; ἠϊόνες βοόωσιν (poet. for βοῶσιν), 17, 265.

βοή, fem. from the following.

βόειος, η, ον, and **βόεος,** η, ον (βοῦς), *relating to cattle, made of ox-hide*. ἡ βοείη and ἡ βοέη, subaud. δορά, *ox-hide*, 11, 843; then a) *a shield covered with ox-hide*, 5, 512 (as 10, 155, ῥινὸν βέος). b) *a thong*, h. Ap. 487. 503.

βοεύς, ῆος, ὁ, *a thong of ox-hide* attached to the sails, Od. 2, 426. 15, 291. h. Ap. 407.

βοή, ἡ, *a cry, a loud call*, also *a cry of grief, lamentation*, Od. 14, 265; eaply *the battle-cry, the tumult of battle*, βοὴν ἀγαθός, a common epith. of distinguished heroes, in reference to their loud voice of command, good in the battle-cry [or in the battle itself, Passow]. 2) Metaph. spoken of the *sound* of instruments, 18, 495; of the *noise, tumult* of the sea, Od. 24, 48.

Βοηθοΐδης, ου, ὁ, son of Boethous = *Eteoneus*, Od. 4, 31.

βοηθόος, ον (θέω), *hastening to the tumult of battle, swift in battle*, spoken of heroes, 13, 477; ἅρμα, 17, 481.

βοηλασίη, ἡ (ἐλαύνω), *the driving off of cattle, the plunder of cattle*, the common kind of robbery in the Homeric age; and mly *plundering, robbery*, 11, 672.†

βοητύς, ύος, ἡ, Ion. for βόησις, *the act of calling, crying, clamour*, Od. 1, 369.†

βοθρός, ὁ (related to βάθος), *a hole, ditch, pit*, 17, 58. Od. 11, 25.

Βοίβη, ἡ, a town in Pelasgiotis, in Thessalia, not far from Pheræ; now *Bio*, 713; hence: **Βοιβηΐς,** ίδος, ἡ, *Bæbean*;

ἡ λίμνη, the Bœbean lake, near the town thus called, Il. 1. c.

Βοιώτιος, ίη, ιον, *a Bœotian*, an inhabitant of Bœotia, a district in Hellas which derived its name from Bæotus, o from its rich pastures, 4, 294.

(βολέω), obs. theme of βεβόλημαι, see βάλλω.

βολή, ἡ, *a cast, the act of throwing*, metaph. as βέλος, αἱ βολαὶ ὀφθαλμῶν, the glance of the eyes, *Od. 4, 150.

βόλομαι, Ep. for βούλομαι, q. v.

βομβέω (from βόμβος), fut. ήσω, *to give a hollow sound, to rattle*, spoken only of falling bodies, 11. and Od.

βοόων, Ep. for βοῶν, see βοάω.

***βορβοροκοίτης,** *mud-lier*, name of a frog (from βόρβορος, slime, and κοίτη, bed), Batr. 229.

Βορέης, αο, ὁ, Ep. for Βορέας, gen. Βορέω, 23, 692; 1) *the north wind*, or, more exactly, the *north-north-east*. 2) *Boreas*, as a mythic personage, son of Astræus and Eos, Hes. Th. 379; he dwelt in Thrace, 9, 5. He is sire of the mares of Erichthonius, 20, 205. (Βορέης. 9, 5.)

βόσις, ιος, ἡ (βόσκω), *food, pasture*, 19, 268.†

βόσκω, fut. βοσκήσω, 1) *to pasture, to drive to the pasture*, spoken of a herdsman, βοῦς, 15, 548 [cf. Spitzner ad 16, 150]. 2) *to feed, to nourish*, primarily of animals, but also of men, τινά, Od. 14, 325; and γαστέρα, to fill the stomach, Od. 17, 228. 559. II) Mid. *to pasture* or *feed oneself, to graze*, spoken of animals, κατά τι, 5, 162 [also absol. Od. 12, 355]. 2) *to crop, to feed upon*; with accus. ποίην, h. Merc. 232. cf. 559.

βοτάνη, ἡ (βόσκω), *pasture, food, grass*, 13, 493. Od. 10, 411.

βοτήρ, ῆρος, ὁ (βόσκω), *a herdsman*, Od. 15, 504.†

***βοτής,** οῦ, ὁ=βοτήρ, Epigr. 11, 1.

βοτός, ή, όν (βόσκω), *pastured, fed*; τὰ βοτά, every thing which is pastured, cattle, 18, 521.†

βοτρυδόν, adv. (βότρυς), *in clusters, like grapes*, νένονται, 2, 89; said of bees.†

βότρυς, υος, ἡ, *the grape, a cluster of grapes*, 18, 562.† h. 6, 40.

βοῦ (βοῦς), often in composition indicates that which is very great, prodigious, e. g., βούβρωστις, etc.

βούβοτος, ον (βόσκω), *grazed by cattle*, Od. 13, 246.†

βούβρωστις, ἡ (βοῦς, βιβρώσκω), prop. *bulimy, voracious hunger*, and mly *hunger, poverty, want*, 24, 532.†

βουβών, ῶνος, ὁ, *the groin, the pudendum, the thigh*, 4, 492.†

βουγάϊος, ὁ (γαίω), one who is proud of his strength, *a boaster*, only as a term of reproach, 13, 824. Od. 18, 79.

Βούδειον, τό (ἡ Βούδεια, Steph.), 16, 572; a town of uncertain position, prob. a town in Magnesia, according to Steph., or in Phthiotis, according to Venet. Schol.

Βουκολέω. 88 Βρίζω.

βουκολέω (βουκόλος), *to pasture cattle;* with accus. of βοῦς, 21, 448. 2) Mid. *to feed, to graze,* 20, 221.

Βουκολίδης, ov, ὁ, son of Bucolus = Sphelus, 15. 338.

* βουκολίη, ἡ, *a herd of cattle,* h. Merc. 498.

Βουκολίων, ωνος, ὁ, eldest son of Laomedon, husband of Abarbarea, 6, 22.

βουκόλος, ὁ, *a herdsman* (from βοῦς and the obsol. κολέω), with ἀνήρ, 13, 571. Od. 11, 293.

βουλευτής, οῦ, ὁ (βουλεύω), *counsellor, senator;* as adj. γέροντες, the old men of the council, 6, 114.†

βουλεύω (βουλή), fut. σω, aor. 1 σα, and aor. 1 mid. σάμην, 1) *to hold a council, to consult, to deliberate,* absol. 2, 347; often with βουλήν, to give counsel, 9, 75; 10, 147; to hold a council, to deliberate, 10, 415; τινί, to counsel any one, to consult for any one, 9, 94. 2) *to plot, to decide upon, to purpose,* with accus. ὄλεθρον, φύξιν, κέρδεα, ὁδὸν φρεσίν, Od. 1, 141; and with dat. of the pers. τί τινι, to purpose any thing against any one, with infin. following, 9, 458; also περί τινος, Od. 16, 234; ἐς μίαν, sc. βουλήν, to take like counsel, to be unanimous, harmonious, 2, 379. II) Mid. *to advise oneself, to form a resolution, to decide, to purpose;* with accus. ἀπάτην, 2, 114; βουλεύειν τινά, h. Merc. 167, is false Greek; hence H. connects ἐμέ and σέ with ἐπιβήσομαι, cf. Franke ad loc.

βουλή, ἡ, *counsel* which one imparts, *advice,* 2, 55. 10, 147. 2) *purpose, will, resolution,* esply of the gods, 12, 234. Od. 8, 82. 3) *a council* or *assembly,* as βουλὴ γερόντων, the assembly of the elders, in distinction from ἀγορά, q. v. 2, 143. 194.

βουληφόρος, ον (φέρω), *giving counsel, who deliberates,* epith. of sovereigns in the Il. and of the ἀγορά in Od. 9, 112.

βούλομαι, Ep. βόλομαι (only βόλεται, 11. 319; βόλεσθε, Od. 16, 387), fut. βουλήσομαι, h. Ap. 264. 1) *to will, to wish* (according to Buttmann, Lex, βούλομαι is distinguished from ἐθέλω, the latter expressing a mere wish, or proclivity, whereas the former expresses an active willing, with purpose; still in H. βούλομαι also stands for ἐθέλω); with accus. τί, any thing, 3, 41; mly with infin. or with accus. and infin. 1, 117. Od. 16, 387. Ζεὺς Τρώεσσιν ἐβούλετο κῦδος ὀρέξαι, Zeus wished to bestow glory upon the Trojans, 11, 79. cf. 319. 2) τί τινι, without infin. *to grant, to purpose, to accord* any thing to any one, Τρώεσσιν βούλετο νίκην, said only of the gods, because with them to will and to accomplish are identical, 7, 21. 2) *to wish rather, to prefer;* with ἤ or ἤπερ following: βούλομ' ἐγὼ λαὸν σόον ἔμμεναι ἢ ἀπολέσθαι, I would rather that the people should be safe than that they should perish, 1, 117. 11, 319. Od. 3, 232; sometimes also without ἤ, 1, 112.

βουλυτός, ἡ (λύω), subaudit. καιρός, the time when the cattle are unyoked; this took place at sunset; in H. only adv. βουλυτόνδε, at evening, 6, 779. Od. 9, 58.

βουπλήξ, ῆγος ἡ (πλήσσω), prop. adj. goading the oxen; in H. subst. *an ox-goad,* stimulus, 16, 135.†

Βουπράσιον, τό, a town in Elis, on the borders of Achaia; in the time of Strabo, a territory in addition had this name (perhaps from πράσον, a leek), 2, 615.

βοῦς, βοός, ὁ and ἡ, dat. plur. βουσί, Ep. βόεσσι, *a bull, an ox, a cow;* also βοῦς ἄρσην and ταῦρος βοῦς, 17, 389. 2) ἡ, subaud. ἀσπίς, *a shield covered with ox-hide,* 7, 238 (where the Dor. accus. βῶν is found), 12, 105.

βουφονέω (βουφόνος), *to slaughter cattle,* 7, 466.†

* βουφόνος, ον (φονεύω), *slaughtering* or *sacrificing cattle.* h. Merc. 436.

βοῶπις, ιδος, ἡ (βοῦς, ὤψ), *ox-eyed,* i. e. *large-eyed* ['ample-eyed,' Cp.], epith. of distinguished women, 3, 144, and of the majestic Hêrê, 1, 551.

Βοώτης, ου, ὁ = βούτης, *the herdsman,* in H. the constellation of *Arcturus,* near the Great Bear; so named by the Ionians, who made the Great Bear a wagon, Od. 5, 272.

βραδύς, εῖα, ύ, compar. βραδύτερος and βράσσων, superl. βράδιστος, and by metathesis βάρδιστος, 23, 310. 530; *slow, sluggish;* spoken also of the mind, *dull, stupid,* νοός, 10, 226.

βραδυτής, ῆτος, ἡ (βραδύς), *slowness, sluggishness,* 19, 411. [†]

βράσσων, ον, compar. of βραδύς, 10, 226.

βραχίων, ίονος, ὁ, *the arm; πρυμνός,* the upper part of the arm, *the shoulder,* plur. Od. 18, 69.

βράχω, a word derived from the sound it describes, *to crash, to rattle, to creak, to resound,* spoken chiefly of inanimate things; of the rattling of armour, 4, 420; of the creaking of a chariot, 5, 835; of the resounding of the earth, 21, 387; and of the roaring of a river, 21, 9. 2) Of living beings: *to cry, to roar;* of the wounded Arês, 5, 863; of a horse, 16, 468 (where Spitzner, however with probability, understands the noise of his fall).

* βρέγμα, ατος, τό, *the upper part of the head, the skull,* Batr. 231.

βρέμω, *fremo, to murmur, to roar, to resound,* spoken of the sea, 4, 425; in like manner the mid. βρέμομαι, 2, 209; and of the wind, 14, 399.

βρέφος, τό, *the embryo in the womb,* 23, 266.† later an infant (related to τρέφω).

βρεχμός, ὁ = βρέγμα, *the upper part of the head,* 5, 586.†

Βριάρεως, ὁ, a hundred-handed giant, see Αἰγαίων *(the strong).*

βριαρός, ή, όν (βριάω), *strong, stout,* epith. of the helmet, *11, 375.

βρίζω, poet. (related to βρίθω), *to feel heavy;* mly *to be drowsy, to be inactive* 4, 223.†

Βριήπῠος. 89 Βῶρος.

βριήπῠος, ον (ἀπύω), crying aloud, loud-voiced ['brazen-throated,' Cp.], epith. of Arês, 13, 521.†

βρῐθοσύνη, ἡ (βριθύς), heaviness, burden, loud, weight, 5, 839. 12, 460.

βρῐθύς, εῖα, ύ (βρίθω), heavy, weighty, always epith. of the spear, ἔγχος, Il. and Od.

βρί̆θω, fut. βρίσω, h. Cer. 456; aor. 1 ἔβρισα, perf. 2 βέβρῐθα, with pres. signif. and mid. 1) to be heavy, to be burdened, weighed down, τινί and τινός, σταφυλῇσι μέγα βρίθουσα ἀλωή, κ vineyard heavily laden with grapes, 18, 561. βεβρίθει (subaud. ναῦς) σάκεσσι καὶ ἔγχεσιν, Od. 16, 474, cf. 19, 112. ταρσοὶ μὲν τυρῶν βρίθον, Od. 9, 219. 15, 334; also mid. μήκων καρπῷ βριθομένη, a poppy loaded with fruit, 8, 307; and with the idea of an oppressive surcharge, ὑπὸ λαίλαπι πᾶσα βέβρῐθε χθών, the whole earth is burdened with the tempestuous rain, 16, 384; metaph. ἔρις βεβριθυῖα (for βαρεῖα), 21, 385. 2) to have preponderance, to be superior, to surpass, in aor. 1 ἐδύνω βρίσας (prevailing by bridal gifts), Od. 6, 159; spoken of an overpowering multitude: to press hard, to prevail, 12, 346. 17, 233. 512.

* βρῐ́μη, ἡ, rage, anger, noise, h. 28, 10.

* βρῐσάρματος, ον (ἅρμα), chariot-loading, epith. of Arês, h. 7, 1. cf. 5, 839.

Βρῑσηίς, ίδος, ἡ, daughter of Brises, Hippodamia, a female slave of Achilles, who had slain her husband Mynes and her brothers. 19, 291—300. Agamemnon took her from him, 2, 689 sqq.

Βρί̆σης, εος, Ep. ῆος, ὁ, son of Ardys, king of the Leleges in Pedasus, or a priest in Lyrnessus, 2, 689. 1, 392.

βρομέω (βρόμος), to hum, spoken of gnats, 16, 642.†

βρόμος, ὁ (βρέμω), roaring, crackling, spoken of fire, 14, 396.† 2) Of the loud sound of flutes, h. Merc. 452. h. 26, 10.

βρονταώ (βροντή), aor. 1 ἐβρόντησα, to thunder, always spoken of Zeus, θ, 133. Od. 12, 415.

βροντή, ἡ, thunder, Διός, 13, 796; Ζηνός, Od. 20, 121.

βρότεος, ον, Ep. for βρότειος (βρότος), mortal, human, φωνή, Od. 19, 545.† h. Ven. 47.

βροτόεις, εσσα, εν (βρότος), sprinkled with blood, bloody; ἔναρα, bloody spoils, 6, 481; once βροτόεντ᾽ ἀνδράγρια, *14, 509.

βροτολοιγός, όν (λοιγός), man-destroying, man-slaying, epith. of Arês ['homicidal Mars,' Cp.], often in Il.; once Od. 8, 115.

βροτός, ὁ, ἡ, mortal, prop. adj. βροτὸς ἀνήρ, 5, 604; often as subst. a mortal, a man, and ἡ βροτός, a mortal woman, Od. 5, 334 (related to μόρος).

βρότος, ὁ, the blood which is flowing from a wound, or which has already coagulated, gore, always with αἱματόεις; 7, 425; μέλας, Od. 24, 189 (Æol. from ῥέω, ῥότος).

βροτόω, to make bloody; βεβροτωμένα τεύχεα, arms defiled with blood ['armour gore-distained,' Cp.], Od. 11, 41.†

βρόχος, ὁ, a noose, a knot, for suspending, *Od. 11, 278. 22, 472.

* βρύκω, ξω, to bite, to tear by biting, prop. to gnash with the teeth, Epigr. 14, 13.

Βρυσειαί, Ep. for Βρῡσεαί, an old town in Laconia, south of Sparta, 2, 583 (perhaps from βρύσις, ἡ, welling up).

βρῠχάομαι, depon. mid. perf. βέβρυχα, to roar, to howl; H. has only the perf. and pluperf. with pres. signif.; spoken of the shriek of one falling with a mortal wound, 13, 393. 16, 486 (not 'gnashing the teeth'); and of the noise of waves, 17, 264. Od. 5, 412. 12, 242.

βρύω, to overflow, with reference to an internal force swelling and bursting; to be swollen, distended. ἔρνος ἄνθεϊ βρύει, bursts into flower, 17, 56.†

βρώμη, ἡ, poet. for βρῶμα, food, connected with ποτής, *Od. 10, 177. h. Cer. 394.

βρῶσις, ιος, ἡ (βιβρώσκω), the act of eating food, in distinction from πόσις, 19, 210. Od. 1, 191.

* Βρωτός, ή, όν, adj. verb. (βιβρώσκω), eaten, edible, Batr. 30.

βρωτύς, ύος, ἡ = βρῶσις, 19, 205. Od. 18, 407.

βύβλινος, η, ον, made of papyrus, ὅπλον νεός, Od. 21, 391.† According to Eustath, not here the Egyptian paper-plant, from the inner bark of which ropes were made, but either hemp or tree-bark. Voss translates 'from the bark of the byblus.'

* βυθός, ὁ, depth, abyss, Batr. 119.

βύκτης, ου, ὁ (βύω: or, more probably, βύζω), blowing, blustering, roaring, rude, ἄνεμοι, Od. 10, 20.† (ἠχητικοί, Schol.)

* βύρσα, ἡ, skin, hide, Batr. 127.

βυσσοδομεύω (δομέω), prim. to build in the depths; hence metaph. to meditate, to purpose any thing secretly; only in a bad sense, κακὰ φρεσί, to purpose evil secretly in the heart, Od. 8, 273. 17, 66; μύθους ἐνὶ φρεσί, Od. 4, 676. *Od.

βυσσός, ὁ = βυθός, depth, 24, 80.†

βύω, fut. βύσω, perf. pass. βέβυσμαι, to stop up, to fill up, τινός, with any thing; τάλαρος νήματος βεβυσμένος, a basket filled with yarn, Od. 4, 134.†

βῶλος, ἡ (prob. from βάλλω), a clod, a lump of earth, Od. 18, 374. †

βωμός, ὁ (βαίνω), an elevation, a support upon which something is placed, a pedestal, a base of a statue, Od. 7, 100; a stand for a chariot, 8, 441. 2) Esply an altar, often ἱεροί or θεῶν βωμοί. βωμός is distinguished from ἐσχάρα by having steps or an ἀνάβασις. Cf. Nitzsch on Od. 2, p. 15.

[βῶν, 7, 238, see βοῦς, and cf. Buttm., Gram. § 50, note 2.]

Βῶρος, ὁ, 1) son of Perieres, husband of Polydora, daughter of Peleus, 16, 177;

cf. Apd. 3, 13. 2) father of Phæstus, from Tarne in Lydia, 5, 44 βώσαντι, see βοάω.
βωστρέω, to call, to call to, for help, τινά, Od. 12, 124.† [from βοάω lengthened, like ἐλαστρέω].
βωτιάνειρα, ἡ (βόσκω, ἀνήρ), man-nourishing, nurse of heroes, epith. of Phthia, 1, 155 †
βώτωρ, ορος, ὁ, Ep (βόσκω), herdsman, connected with ἀνήρ, 12, 302. Od. 14, 102.

Γ.

Γ, the third letter of the Greek alphabet, and hence the sign of the third rhapsody.
γαῖα, ἡ, like αἶα, poet. for γῆ (which form rarely occurs in H., 21, 63. Od. 11, 67, etc.), 1) the earth, the ground, the land, in distinction from the heavens or the sea, 8, 16. 46, 479. 2) land, region, often with πατρίς, father-land, country; in the plur. also often spoken of islands, Od. 8, 284. 3) earth, ground, 2, 699. 15, 715; also dust. ὑμεῖς πάντες ὕδωρ καὶ γαῖα γένοισθε, may you become earth, dust [' rot where ye sit,' Cp.], 7, 99; hence also κωφὴ γαῖα, spoken of Hector's corpse, 24, 54.
Γαῖα, ἡ, pr. n. Gæa (Tellus), wife of Uranus (Cœlus), mother of the Cyclôpes, Titans, etc. h. 30, 17; μήτηρ πάντων.
Γαιήϊος, η, ον (γαῖα), springing from Gæa. Γαιήϊος υἱός, son of Gæa = Tityus, Od. 7, 324.
γαιήοχος, ον (ἔχω), earth-holding, earth-embracing, epith. of Poseidôn; earth-quakes being, on the one hand, ascribed to him (see ἐνοσίχθων), and he could, on the other, hold together and secure the earth (Voss. earth-girdling, not, however, with perfect propriety, since ἔχειν is in H. never equivalent to cingere, and Poseidôn is god only of the Mediterranean sea); later, earth-defending. Cf. Cammanns, Vorsch. p. 173. Il. 9, 183. Od. 1, 68.
γαίω, only partcp. pres. to be proud of any thing, to exult in, always with κύδεϊ, one's strength: epith. of Zeus, Arês, etc. *1, 405 (an old theme, to be seen in many derivatives, as γάνυμαι, γηθέω, etc.).
γάλα, γάλακτος, τό, milk, λευκόν, 4, 434. Od. 4, 88.
γαλαθηνός, όν (θῆσθαι), milk-sucking; hence young, tender, νεβροί, *Od. 4, 336.
*Γαλαξαύρη, ἡ, a nymph, companion of Persephonê, h. Cer. 423.
Γαλάτεια, ἡ, daughter of Nereus and Doris, 18, 45.
* γαλέη, ἡ, a weasel, a marten, Batr. 5.
γαλήνη, ἡ, quiet, rest, serenity, a calm, esply spoken of the sea. γαλήνη νηνεμίη,

a windless calm, Od. 5, 392. 2) the quiet surface of the sea. ἐλαύνειν γαλήνηρ [' to brush the placid flood,' Cp.; to sail over calm seas], *Od. 7, 319.
γάλοως, gen. γάλοω, ἡ, nom. pl. γάλοῳ, sister-in-law, husband's sister, *3, 122.
γαμβρός, ὁ (γαμός), any one related by marriage: hence 1) son-in-law, most freq. 2) brother-in-law, sister's husband, 5, 474. 13, 464.
γαμέω (γάμος), fut. γαμέσω and γαμέω, 9, 391; aor. 1 ἔγημα, fut. mid. γαμέσομαι, poet. σσ, 3, 394; aor. 1 ἐγημάμην, 1) Spoken of the man, to take a wife, to marry, τινά, also ἄλοχον, 9, 390; also in a mere physical signif., Od. 1, 36. 2) Mid. spoken of the woman, to get married, to marry, τινί, 9, 394. b) Of the parents, to give in marriage, to marry, γυναῖκα τινί, 9, 394.
γάμος, ὁ, a marriage, 1) As a festal day, a wedding. γάμον τεύχειν, ἀρτύειν, to prepare the nuptial solemnity, Od. 1, 277. 4, 770; esply nuptial feast, 19, 299. Od. 1, 226 (in distinction from εἰλαπίνη). Od. 4, 3. 3) nuptials, wedlock, Od. 18, 272. 11. 13, 382.
γαμφηλαί, αἱ (related to γνάμπτω), the jaw-bones, the cheeks, only plur. *13, 200.
γαμψῶνυξ, υχος, ὁ, ἡ (ὄνυξ), with crooked claws, epith. of birds of prey, αἰγυπιοί, 16, 428. Od. 16, 217.
γανάω (γάνος), to gleam, to glitter, to shine, only partep. pres. γανόωντες, γανόωσαι, Ep. for γανῶντες, γανῶσαι, prim. spoken of polished metals, 13, 265; of garden-beds: πρασιαὶ γανόωσαι, splendid beds, Od. 7, 128; of a flower, h. Cer. 10.
γάνυμαι, depon. mid. (γαίω), fut. γανύ-σομαι, Ep. σσ, to be glad, to be delighted, to rejoice in, with dat. ἀνδρὶ οὐ γανύσσε-ται, 14, 504; also γάνυται φρένα, he is glad at heart, 13, 493. Od. 12, 43.
Γανυμήδης, εος, ὁ, accus. εα and ην, son of king Tros in Troy, great-grandson of Dardanus, the most beautiful youth of his time; he was borne off by Zeus, through the instrumentality of an eagle, and chosen by him as cup-bearer instead of Hebe, 5, 266; and 20, 232 (of cheerful disposition).
γάρ, conj. (γέ, ἄρα), for, since, because, employed in assigning a reason. This particle, which never stands at the beginning of a sentence, unites properly the signif. of γέ and ἄρα, and is used in introducing a proof, an explanation, a supplement, and a consequence. It can only be translated for, although, with the exception of the Hom. γάρ τε, it never annexes a clause so closely to the preceding. 1) In introducing a proof and explanations: for, because, namely. The explanatory signif. is esply preponderant, when a demonstrative pronoun or subst. precedes, 1, 9. 12, 55. 8, 148. As a peculiarity of the Greek language, note the following : a) Very common is it for the explanatory clause with γάρ to precede

Γάργαρον.   91   Γελάω.

the clause to be explained, in which case it must be translated *indeed*, or *since*, 1, 423. 7, 73. The following clause is introduced by τῷ: πολλοὶ γάρ τεθνᾶσιν Ἀχαιοί — τῷ σε χρὴ — παῦσαι, 7, 328. Most frequently it follows an address, Od. 1, 337. 10, 174. 190. 226. *b*) Often the clause to be proved must be supplied from the connexion, 11, 408. Od. 10, 501. 2) In introducing a supplement or consequence; here belongs γάρ, *a*) In exclamatory and optative clauses: αἲ γάρ, εἰ γάρ, q. v. *b*) In questions: τίς γάρ, for who; πῶς γάρ, 1, 122. 10, 424. 18, 182. 3) In connexion with other particles: ἀλλὰ γάρ, *at enim, sed enim*, in which use the proving clause sometimes follows, but is mly omitted, 7, 242. Od. 14, 355; γὰρ δή, for indeed, 2, 301. Od. 5, 23; γὰρ οὖν, for now; γάρ ῥα, for certainly; γάρ τε, for, 1, 81; γάρ τοι, for certainly: οὐ μὲν γάρ, for certainly not, 24, 66. cf. Rost, p. 706. Kühner, § 692. (καὶ γάρ, for indeed, 3, 188. 4, 43; καὶ γάρ ῥα, for indeed now, 1, 113.]

Γάργαρον, τό, the southern point of Mount Ida in Troas, on which stood a temple of Zeus, 8, 48. 14, 292. (As appellat. *multitude, fulness*.)

γαστήρ, έρος, contr. γαστρός, ἡ, *the belly, the paunch*, venter; *the womb*, 6, 58. 2) Chiefly *the stomach*; hence, *appetite, greediness*. βόσκειν γαστέρα, to fill the stomach, Od. 17, 228. Batr. 57; but γαστέρι νέκυν πενθῆσαι, to mourn for one dead with the stomach, i. e., by fasting, 19, 223. 3) *stomach, a stomach-sausage*, a stomach filled with minced meat, Od. 18, 44.

γάστρη, ἡ, *the belly*, a round belly of a vessel, 18, 348. Od. 8, 437.

γαυλός, ὁ [but γαῦλος, ship], *a milkpail, a pail*, Od. 9, 223.†

* γαυρόω (related to γαίω), *to make proud*. mid. *to conduct proudly, to pride oneself*, Batr. 267.

(γάω), obsol. theme fr. which the Ep. perf. γέγαα for γέγονα is derived, see γίγνομαι.

γδουπέω, poet. for δουπέω = δουπέω.

γέ, an enclitic particle, marking the emphatic character of an idea, and giving it prominence. It stands always after the word to which it gives force. It can sometimes be translated by *truly, indeed, still, at least*; but can mly be expressed only by emphasis of voice. γέ serves consequently 1) To give prominence to an idea, whether in amplification or limitation. In this case it cannot mly be translated, but is to be indicated by stress of voice: χόλον γε. 1, 81; ὄφρ᾽ εὖ εἰδῶ, εἰ ἐτεόν γ᾽ Ἰθάκην τήνδ᾽ ἱκόμεθα, Od. 24, 259. Very frequently it stands with personal and demonstrative pronouns: ἔγωγε, σύγε. Also twice in one sentence, 5, 286. 22, 266. εἰ σύγε σῷ θυμῷ ἐθέλοις· κέλομαι γὰρ ἔγωγε, 23, 854. cf. 15, 48. On the use of γέ with the pronoun, the following is to be noted: *a*) When in disjunctive clauses the pronoun is placed in antithesis to itself, or to a substantive separated from it, γέ is found in the second member: εἰπέ μοι, ἠὲ ἑκὼν ὑποδάμνασαι, ἢ σέ γε λαοὶ ἐχθαίρουσ᾽, whether *thou* of thine own accord art overcome (dost willingly suffer it), or whether *thee* the people hate, etc. Od. 3, 214. cf. Il. 2, 237. 10, 481. 12, 239. In this case the pronoun is for us often superfluous. *b*) γέ is attached to a pronoun in order to recall with emphasis a preceding idea. For us in this case the pronoun is often superfluous: πατὴρ δ᾽ ἐμὸς ἄλλοθι γαίης, ζώει ὅγ᾽ ἢ τέθνηκεν, Od. 2, 131. cf. 3, 89. Il. 10, 504. The last is true also in adversative sentences. 2) γέ assumes rather the character of a conjunction, and serves to give prominence to the proof or supplement of a clause, and has either an adversative or concessive signif., Od. 19, 86. It is then often connected with relatives and conjunctions, and can be translated by *indeed, at least, certainly, namely*. *a*) With relatives, as ὅς γε, ὅστις γε, οἷός γε, 5, 303. Od. 1, 229. *b*) With conjunctions, εἴγε, *if indeed, since, si quidem*, Od. 9, 529. Il. 1, 393; εἰ μή γε, Od. 10, 343; ὅτε — γε, Od. 2, 31; ὅτε — μή — γε, Il. 13, 319; πρίν γε, οὐ πρίν γε, namely not before; also repeated, πρίν γε, πρίν γε, 5, 288; ἐπεί — γε, *quandoquidem*, 1, 259. 3) οὐδέ — γε, μηδέ — γε, at least not, 14, 221. γέ with a preceding negat. can mly be translated *never*, 1, 261. Od. 4, 291. γέ μέν has an adversat. signif.: *but*, at, Il. 2, 703. Od. 5, 206. Cf. Kühner, § 596. Thiersch, § 303.

γέγαα, γεγάασι, γεγαώς. See γίγνομαι.

γέγηθα, perf. of γηθέω.

γέγωνα, poet. perf. with pres. signif. of which the 3 sing. is also imperf. with aor. signif., partcp. γεγωνώς, infin. γεγωνέμεν, plupf. ἐγεγώνει. From a pres. γεγωνέω, derived from this perf., the following forms occur: infin. γεγωνεῖν, imperf. ἐγεγώνευν, Od. 9, 47; *to call audibly, to cry, to proclaim*. ὅσον τε γέγωνε βοήσας, as far as he crying called audibly, i. e. as far as his voice reached, Od. 5, 400. Il. 12, 337; τινί, to call to any one, 8, 227; also μετὰ θεοῖς, Od. 12, 370.

γεγωνέω. See γέγωνα.

γείνομαι (obsol. theme ΓΕΝΩ), aor. 1 ἐγεινάμην, 1) In the pres. only Ep. and pass. *to be born, to be begotten*. οἱ γεινόμενοι, those who are born, 10, 71. Od. 4, 208. 2) Aor. 1 mid. *to bear, to beget*, spoken both of mother and father, 5, 800. ἐπὴν γείνεαι αὐτός, when thou hast begotten them (men), Od. 20, 202 (this is subj. aor. 1, with shortened mood-vowel, γείνηαι).

γείτων, ονος, ὁ, *neighbour*, Od. 4, 16; as adj. *neighbouring*, Od. 9, 48. Batr. 67.

γελαστός, ή, όν (γελάω), *laughed at, laughable, ridiculous*, ἔργα, Od. 8, 307.† Cf. ἀγέλαστος.

γελάω, contr. γελῶ, and Ep. γελόω,

Γελοιάω. 92 Γερήνιος.

partcp. γελώωντες and γελώοντες, Od. 18, 111; Ep. form γελοιάω, aor. 1 ἐγέλασα, poet. σσ, 1) *to laugh*, ἐπί τινι, at any thing, 2, 270; μάλα ἡδύ, very heartily, 11, 378; δακρυόεν, tearfully, 6, 484; χείλεσιν, with the lips, i. e. apparently, 15, 102; see ἀχρεῖον, ἀλλοτρίοις γναθμοῖς, see the adj. 2) Spoken of inanimate things; ἐγέλασσε δὲ πᾶσα περὶ χθὼν χαλκοῦ ὑπὸ στεροπῆς, laughed round about, i. e. the whole earth gleamed with the brightness of the brass, 19, 362. Cf. h. in Cer. 14.

γελοιάω, Ep. form from γελάω, aor. 1 ἐγελοίησα, h. Ven. 49; whence γελοιών, 3 plur. imperf. and partcp. γελοιῶντες (γελοιῶντες), Od. 20, 390.

γελοιίος, η, ον, Ep. for γέλοιος (γέλως), *laughable, ridiculous*, 2, 215.†

γελοιῶντες, Od. 20, 390; either poet. for γελώοντες, or read with Buttm. γελοιόωντες, and derive from γελοιάω.

γέλος, ὁ, Æ 1. for γέλως; γέλον for γέλω stood before Wolf, Od. 20, 346.

γελάω, γελόωντες, see γελάω.

γελόωντες, see γελάω.

γέλως, ωτος, ὁ, dat. γέλῳ for γέλωτι, Od. 18, 100; accus. γέλῳ for γέλωτα and γέλων, Od. 18, 350. 20, 346; *a laugh, laughter* (more correctly in the dat. γέλῳ; Buttm. Gram. § 56, note 6. Thiersch Gram. § 188. Kühner Gram. I. § 295, 1).

γενεή, ἡ, Ion. for γενεά, 1) *birth, family, race, descent*, 6, 145. 151. 21, 153. γενεῆς καὶ αἵματος, of race and blood, 6, 211. γενεῆ τινος and ἐκ τινος, 21, 157. γενεὴν Διὸς εὔχομαι εἶναι, 21, 187. Of steeds: *race, stock, breed*, 5, 208. 265; hence with τόκος, race and birth, 7, 128. 15, 141; hence, *a*) *birth-place*, 20, 340; and with πατρὶς ἄρουρα, Od. 1, 407; also of the eagle's eyrie, Od. 15, 175. *b*) *race, stock, family*, esply *noble descent*, 20, 306. Od. 4, 27. αὐτῷ γὰρ γενεὴν ἄγχιστα ἐῴκειν, 14, 474. *c*) *offspring, descendant*, as with Spitzner it is perhaps to be understood in 21, 191. 2) *race*, i. e. all who belong to a species, spoken of men, esply those who are contemporary (æquales), 6, 146; and in like manner, φύλλων γενεή, the race (crop) of leaves (*folia uno eodemque vere prognata*); hence also, *a*) *the age of man, a generation*, which accord. to Hdt. was 33 years, so that three generations amounted to 100 years, 1, 250. Od. 14, 325. *b*) *age* in general; γενεῇ ὁπλότερος, 2. 707; ὁπλότατος, 9, 58; πρότερος, 15, 166. Cf. Spitzner, Excurs. IX. § 2. p. 7.

γενέθλη, ἡ (γένος), 1) *birth, generation, race, stock*, of men: εἶναι γενέθλης or ἐκ γενέθλης, Od. 4, 232; of horses: *stock*, 5, 270. 2) *place of origin, origin*, ἀργύρου, 2, 657. 3) *offspring, descendant*, h. Ap. 135. Cf. Spitzner Excurs. IX. § 3. p. 12.

γενειάς, άδος, ἡ, *beard*, Od. 16, 176.†

γένειον, τό (prob. from γένος), *the chin*. γενείου ἅπτεσθαι, 10, 454. Od.

γενειάω (γένειον), aor. ἐγενείησα, *to become bearded, to obtain a beard, to arrive at manhood*, *Od. 18, 176. 269.

γένεσις, ιος, ἡ (ΓΕΝΩ), *generation,*

creation, origin, spoken only of Oceanus: θεῶν γένεσις, *14, 201.

γενετή, ἡ, poet. for γενεή, *birth*. ἐκ γενετῆς, from birth, 24, 535. Od. 18, 6. h. Merc. 440.

γενναῖος, η, ον (from γέννα, ἡ, Ep. for γένος), *suited to one's descent, inbred, natural*. οὐ μοι γενναῖον, 5, 253.†

γένος, τό (ΓΕΝΩ), 1) *race, birth, descent*, 6, 209; hence γένος (accus. absol.) εἶναι ἐκ τινος, to spring from any one, 5, 544. γένος βασιλήων εἶναι, to spring from kings, Od. 4, 63; hence also *place of birth, country*, Od. 15, 267. 24. 269. Esply, *a*) *race, family, kindred*, Od. 8, 583. 15, 533. *b*) *offspring, descendant*, 19, 122; so also with adj. θεῖον γένος, 6, 180. 9, 538. 2) *race*, as the collective body of individuals in a species: ἡμιθέων ἀνδρῶν, race of demi-gods, 12, 23, h. 31, 18; also βοῶν γένος, Od. 20, 212. 3) *race*, in reference to time. *the age of man*, Od. 3. 248; mly *age*; γένει ὕστερος, younger in age, 3, 215.

γέντο, 3 sing. aor. of a theme elsewhere absol.; accord. to some, Æol. for ἕλετο, ἕλτο, as κέντο for κέλετο, *he seized, he grasped*, with accus. 5, 25. 8, 43. Cf. Buttm. Gram. § 114. Rost Gram. § 82, IV. 6.

γένυς, υος, ἡ, accus. plur. γένυας, contr. γένυς. Od. 11, 320; *the cheek-bone, the jaw*, both of men and brutes, 11, 416.

ΓΕΝΩ, theme of γίγνομαι.

γεραιός, ή, όν (γηραιός, not found in H.), *old, aged*, esply *venerable by age*; subst. ὁ γεραιός, *an old man, a venerable sage*; αἱ γεραιαί, *the aged women, matrons*, 6. 87. Comp. γεραίτερος, η, ον.

γεραίρω (γέρας), prop. to distinguish by a gift: and generally, *to honour, to distinguish*. τινὰ ῥώτοισιν, any one with back-pieces, 7, 321. Od. 14, 441.

Γεραιστός, ὁ, *Geræstus* a promontory and port in Eubœa, orig. a temple and grove of Poseidôn, now *Cabo Mantelo* or *Lion*, the town is called *Gerestro*, Od. 3, 177.

γέρανος, ἡ, *a crane*, *2, 460. 3, 3.

γεραρός, ή, όν (γεραίρω), *honorable, venerable*, epith. of heroes. Compar. γεραρώτερος, η, ον, *3, 170. 211.

γέρας, αος, τό, plur. Ep. γέρα for γέραα, gen. γεράων, related to γῆρας, 1) *a present, a reward*, *a*) a gift to distinguish any one, e. g. a larger portion of meat and wine, Od. 4, 66; or a part of the spoil, Od. 7, 10. Cf. Il. 1, 118; also spoken of gods, 4, 49. *b*) any act performed to honour any one, as to cut the hair in honour of [or mourning for] the dead, Od. 4, 197. Il. 16, 457. 2) *office, prerogative, dignity, power*, as τὸ γὰρ γέρας γερόντων, this is the office of the aged men (viz. to sit in council), 4, 32?. Od. 11. 184.

*γεράσμιος, ον (γέρας), *honouring, conferring honour*, h. Merc. 122.

Γερήνιος, ὁ, *the Gerenian*, epith. of Nestor, from the town *Gerenia* (Γερηνία,

Γέρον. 93 Γίγνομαι.

Paus. 3, 21), or *Gerenon* (Γέρηνον, τό, Eust.), in Messenia, where Nestor was educated, whilst Heracles destroyed Pylus, 2, 336.

γέρον, see γέρων.

γερούσιος, η, ον, *belonging to old men, appertaining to old men* as members of the council : ὅρκος, an oath which they swore, 22, 119. γερούσιος οἶνος, wine of honour, a larger portion of wine by which the eldest were honoured at the table of the king, 4, 259. Od. 13, 7—9.

γέρων, οντος, ὁ, voc. γέρον, *an old man, an elder ;* οἱ γέροντες, the eldest of the nation, who were distinguished by their experience and respectability of character, and whose counsel was first asked by the king, 2, 83. 4, 344. Cf. βουλή and βασιλεύς. 2) As adj. in neut. γέρον σάκος, an old shield, Od. 22, 184.

γεύω, *to cause to taste,* in H. only mid. γεύομαι, fut. γεύσομαι, aor. 1 ἐγευσάμην, *to taste,* τινός: προικὸς Ἀχαιῶν, Od. 17, 413. 2) Metaph. *to make a trial, to try, to taste, to feel,* mly spoken of fighting: χειρῶν, to try the fists, Od. 20, 181; so also ὀϊστοῦ, ἀκωκῆς. γευσόμεθα ἀλλήλων ἐγχείῃσιν, we will try one another with spears, 20, 258.

γέφυρα, ἡ, *a dam, a dyke, a levee, a wall of earth,* to prevent the overflowing of a river: τὸν δ᾿ οὔτ᾿ ἄρ τε γέφυραι ἐεργμέναι ἰσχανόωσι, the well-fortified dykes do not restrain it, 5, 88, 89. (Voss and Köppen, *bridges,* a signif. not found in H. ; see ἔργω and 17, 797.) 2) the interval between two armies, which like a dyke separates them : *battle-field.* Thus modern critics explain πολέμοιο γέφυρα and γέφυραι, 4, 371. The sing. is found only 8, 553. The ancients more correctly understood by it the spaces between the ranks, in which one could best flee. Between the hostile armies there was no space. Cf. Wolf's Vorles. II. p. 269.

γεφῡρόω (γέφυρα), aor. 1 γεφύρωσα, *to make a dam, to dam up,* with accus. ποταμόν, to dam up a river, in that a fallen tree checks the current, 21, 245 ; κέλευθον, to make a way or passage, *15, 357.

γῆ, ἡ, contr. γέα=γαῖα, in H. as pr. n. 3, 104. 15, 36.

* γηγενής, έος, ὁ, ἡ (γένος), *earth-born, son of the earth,* epith. of the giants, Batr. 7.

γηθέω (γαίω), fut. ήσω, aor. γήθησα, perf. γέγηθα, with pres. signif. *to rejoice, to be glad, joyful,* with φρένα, θυμῷ, absol. often with partcp. τώγε ἰδὼν γήθησεν, 1, 330.—νῦν δή που Ἀχιλλῆος κῆρ γηθεῖ, φόνον—Ἀχαιῶν δερκομένῳ for δερκομένου, now indeed the heart of Achilles rejoices, as he beholds the slaughter of the Achaians, 14, 140 (cf. Rost, p. 643, Anm. 2. Kühner, § 587, c. Anm. 1). *b*) With accus. of that at which one rejoices, 9, 77 : εἰ νῶϊ—Ἕκτωρ γηθήσει προφανεῖσα, whether Hector will rejoice over us when we appear, etc. 8, 377, 378. (προφανεῖσα is dual fem. gen. according to the reading of Aristarch. ; others read προφανεῖσα and refer it to ἰδωμαι.) Cf. Spitzner.

γηθοσύνη, ἡ (γηθέω), *joy, gladness,* *13, 29. 21, 390; plur. h. Cer. 437.

γηθόσυνος, η, ον (γηθέω), *joyful, glad, cheerful,* τινί, about any thing, 13, 82. Od. 5, 269.

(γήθω), obsol. theme of γηθέω.

γηράς, see γηράω.

γῆρας, αος, τό, dat. γήραϊ and γήρᾳ (Thier., § 189, 18), *age, old age,* 5, 153 Od. 2, 16.

γηράω and γηράσκω, aor. 2 ἐγήρα (like ἔβα), 7, 148 ; partcp. γηράς, 17, 197. 1) *to grow old, to become aged.* 2) Metaph. spoken of fruits, *to become old, to ripen,* Od. 7, 120.

γῆρυς, νος, ἡ, *a voice, a call,* 4, 437.†

*γηρύω (γῆρυς [Död. supposes it allied to γέρω, *resembling,* but not *related* to, κέρω (=*to cry, queri*). Hence intens. γράζειν, γρύζειν, *grunnire* (*grunt*): hence γηρύεσθαι =*fabulari,* opp. to the earnest and important ἀγορεύειν, ἀγοράσθαι, p. 197])), *to utter a sound* or *voice.* 2) Mid. *to sing,* h. in Merc. 426.

Γίγαντες, οἱ, sing. Γίγας, αντος, ὁ (from ΓΑΩ *Genitales,* Herm.), a savage race and odious to the gods, in the region of Hyperia, hence in the neighbourhood of Trinacria, or perhaps in Epirus, which Zeus destroyed on account of their crimes, Od. 7, 59. 206. 10, 120. According to Od. 7, 206, they were related to the Phæaces, and sprung from Poseidôn. 2) According to Hes. Th. 105, monstrous giants with serpent-legs, sons of Uranus and Gæa, who endeavoured to storm Olympus, but were vanquished by the lightnings of Zeus, Batr. 7. Apd. 1, 6. 1.

γίγνομαι (γένω), fut. γενήσομαι, aor. 2 ἐγενόμην, perf. γέγονα, Ep. (γέγαα), 3 plur. γεγάασι (anomal. 2 plur. γεγάατε, Batr. 143, for which Thiersch, § 217, reads γέγαστε), partcp. γεγαώς, infin. γεγάμεν, *to be born, to come into being, to become, to happen.* The aor. 2, *I came,* takes the place of the aor. of εἰμί. *I was ;* in the perf. *to be by birth,* and mly *to be.* 1) Spoken of men : *to be born, to become.* ἐξ ἐμέθεν γεγαῶτα, sprung from me, 9, 456. Od. 4, 112. In the aor. 2, *to be,* Od. 6, 201. The perf. often with pres. signif. ὁπλότεροι γεγάασι, they are younger, 4, 325. Od. 13, 160. 2) Of inanimate things : *to arise, to come into being, to happen.* γίγνεται ἄνθεα, the flowers arise, come into being, 2, 468. τάδε οὐκ εὔνοντο, this did not happen, 3, 176. *b*) Of mental states: ἄχος γένετο αὐτῷ, he was pained. ποθή Δαναοῖσι γένετο, desire seized the Greeks, 11, 471. 3) With predicate following : *a*) Subst. *to become something* ; χάρμα τινί, a rejoicing to any one, 6, 82. φάος τινὶ γίγνεσθαι, to become a light to, 8, 282 ; μέλπηθρά τινι, 18, 179 ; proverbial, ὕδωρ καὶ γαῖαν, to become water and earth, i. e., to be destroyed, 7, 99. πάντα γίγνεσθαι, to be

Γιγνώσκω. 94 Γναμπτός.

:ome every thing, Od. 4, 418: cf. 458. *b*) With adj. τοῖσι πόλεμος γλυκίων γένετο, 2, 453. 4) With prep. and adv. ἐπὶ νηυσίν, to be at the ships, 8, 180. ὅπως ὄχ' ἄριστα γένοιτο, 3, 110.
γιγνώσκω, fut. γνώσομαι, aor. 2 ἔγνων, partcp. γνούς, subj. γνῶ and γνώω, optat. γνοίην, imper. γνῶθι, infin. γνῶναι and γνώμεναι, 1) *to observe, to perceive, to apprehend, to discover, to recognize, to become acquainted with*, τινά, 5, 815; ἀσπίδι, by the shield, 5, 182; in a bad sense: εὖ νύ τις αὐτὸν γνώσεται, many a one will then become well acquainted with him [i. e., will fall by his hands], 18, 270; sometimes with gen. γνῶ χωομένοιο, he observed that he was angry, 4, 357. Od. 21, 36. 23, 109. 2) *to know, to understand*, βουλήν, 20, 20. ὄρνιθας γνῶναι, to understand the flight of birds, Od. 2, 159. It is followed by ὅτι, also ὅ, *quod*, 8, 140; ὡς and εἰ, 21, 266.
γλάγος, εος, τό, Ep. for γάλα, *milk*, *2, 471. 16, 643.
γλακτοφάγος, ον (φαγεῖν), contr. for γαλακτοφάγος, *milk-eating*, epith. of the Hippomolgi, 13, 6; later, name of a Scythian tribe.
Γλαύκη, ἡ, daughter of Nereus and Doris, 18, 39.
γλαυκιάω (γλαυκός), *to look about with sparkling eyes*, spoken of lions, only partcp. pres. γλαυκιόων, of fiery look, 20, 172.†
γλαυκός, ή, όν (λάω, γλαύσσω [in Ap. Rhod. 1, 1281, δια-γλαύσσουσι] = γελαύσσω; whence γλαυκός, as λευκός fm λεύσσω, *Död.: who makes to shine* the primary meaning of γελᾶν]; prop *shining, bright*, accord. to the derivat.; epith. of the eyes of lions, cats, hence *bluish-grey, blue, clear* ('dark,' Voss), only of the sea, 16, 34.† [Vox γλαυκός splendoris vim qualicunque colori adjunctam notat, *Luc.*]
Γλαῦκος, ὁ, *Glaucus*, 1) son of Sisyphus and Meropē, father of Bellerophontes, with the appellation Ποτνιεύς, because he dwelt in Potniæ in Bœotia. Aphroditē inspired his mares with such fury that they tore him in pieces, 6, 154. 2) son of Hippolochus and grandson of Bellerophontes, leader of the Lycians, friend of Diomēdēs, 2, 876. Cf. 6, 119 seq.
γλαυκῶπις, ιδος, ἡ (ὤψ), accus. γλαυκώπιδα and γλαυκῶπιν, Od. 1, 156; epith. of Athēnē, either *with sparkling eyes*, as cats and owls, *bright-eyed, with beaming* or *fiery eyes*, cf. 1, 200: or *having lightbrown, hazel eyes, clear-eyed*, having special reference, however, to her piercing look (Schol. Venet. ἀπὸ τῆς πρὸς τὴν πρόσοψιν τῶν ὀφθαλμῶν καταπλήξεως), ('blue-eyed,' Voss), 2, 166. 2) Substantive, *the clear-eyed*, 5, 406. Cf. Nitzsch on Od. 1, 44; and Cammann, p. 187.
Γλαφύραι, αἱ, a town in Thessalia, otherwise unknown, 2, 712.

γλαφυρός, ή, όν (γλάφω), *excavated, hollow, arched*, epith. of grottoes, ships, and of the φόρμιγξ, πέτρη, 2, 88; also λιμήν, a deep, spacious harbour, Od. 12, 305.
γλήνη, ἡ (λάω [accord. to Död. fm γελαίνειν, *inus.*, whence γελανής. Pind. Cf. τραπής, τρηπής, &c., fm τετραίνειν, περαίνειν]), 1) *the sight of the eye, the pupil of the eye*, 14, 494. Od. 2) *a puppet* (maiden), from the diminished image in the pupil of the eye; in contempt, κακὴ γλήνη, timorous puppet! 8, 164.
γλῆνος, εος, τό (λάω [also referred to inus. γελαίνειν, *Död.*]), *an ornament, any thing precious*, 24, 192.†
* γληχών, ῶνος, ἡ, Ion. for βληχών, *penny-royal*, h. in Cer 209.
Γλίσσας, αντος, ἡ (Γλίσσας and Γλισσᾶς, Paus.), an old town in Bœotia near Thebes, on Mount Hypaton, in ruins in the time of Pausanias, 2, 504.
γλουτός, ὁ, *the buttock, the seat*, *Il. in plur. 8, 340.
γλυκερός, ή, όν = γλυκύς, compar. γλυκερώτερος, *sweet*, Il. Od.
γλυκύθυμος, ον (θυμός), *of mild disposition, sweet-tempered*, 20, 467.†
* γλυκυμείλιχος, ον (μείλιχος), *sweetly flattering, sweetly caressing*, h. 5, 19.
γλυκύς, εῖα, ύ, compar. γλυκίων, *sweet, having an agreeable taste*, νέκταρ, 1, 598; metaph. *lovely, agreeable*, ὕπνος, πόλεμος, ἵμερος, αἰών, Od. 5, 152.
* γλύφανον, τό (γλύφω), *a carver's knife, a chisel, an auger*, h. Merc. 41.
γλυφίς, ίδος, ἡ (γλύφω), *a notch* cut in the arrow to fit it to the bow-string, 4, 122. Od. 21, 419.
* γλύφω, fut. ψω, *to excavate, to hollow out*, Batr.
γλῶσσα, ἡ, *the tongue* of men and animals; γλώσσας τάμνειν, to cut up the tongues of victims, Od. 3, 332. 341. (The tongues at the end of the sacrificial feast were offered esply to Hermēs, i. e., they were cut up, laid on the fire, and burned: cf. Athen. I. 14.) 2) *dialect, language*, 2, 804. γλῶσσ' ἐμέμικτο, the language was mixed, 4, 438. h. Ven. 113.
γλωχίς or γλωχίν, ῖνος, ἡ (γλῶξ), prop. any projecting, tongue-formed point; the end of the yoke-strap, 24, 274.† (On the ending, see Buttm., Gram. § 41, 2.)
γναθμός, ὁ (γνάω, κνάω), *the jaw* of men and beasts; proverbial: πάντας ὀδόντας γναθμῶν ἐξελαύνειν, to knock all the teeth from the jaws, Od. 18, 29; and ἀλλοτρίοις γναθμοῖς γελᾶν, Od.; see ἀλλότριος.
* γνάθος, ἡ = γναθμός, Ep. 14, 13; the common prose form.
γναμπτός, ή, όν (γνάμπτω), *curved, crooked*, ἄγκιστρον, Od. 4, 369; γόνυ, 11, 416. 2) *flexible, supple*, spoken of the limbs of animate beings; metaph. γναμπτὸν νόημα, a placable disposition, 24, 41.

Γνάμπτω. 95 Γουνός.

γνάμπτω, aor. 1 γνάμψα, *to bend, to curve*. ἐν γόνυ γνάμψα, 23, 731.†

γνήσιος, η, ον (sync. from γενήσιος), *belonging to the race, genuine, pure, regular*; υἱός in opposition to νόθος, 11, 102. Od. 14, 202.

γνύξ, adv. (γόνυ), *with bent knee*, always γνὺξ ἐριπών, to sink upon the knees, *5, 68.

γνώ, γνώμεναι, γνώομεν, see γιγνώσκω.

γνώριμος, ον (γιγνώσκω), *known, an acquaintance*, Od. 16, 9.†

γνωτός, ή, όν (γνῶναι), *known, noted*. γνωτὸν δέ, καὶ ὃς μάλα νήπιός ἐστιν, it is known even to him, who is very simple, for ἐκείνῳ, ὅς, 7, 401. 2) *related, a relative by blood*, of any degree, 3, 174 ; hence also for *brother*, 15, 336. 17, 35.

γνώω, γνώωσι, see γιγνώσκω.

γοάω, Ep. γοάω, infin. pres. Ep. γοήμεναι, fut. γοήσομαι, aor. 2 γόον, 6, 500; γοάασκεν, iterat. imperf., 1) *to lament, to mourn, to complain*, often in particp. 2) With accus. *to bewail, to mourn*, πότμον τινός. Of the mid. only the fut. occurs, 21, 124. (γοήμεναι is, Buttm., Gram., § 105, note 16, an Infin. pres.)

γόμφος, ὁ, *a peg of wood, a nail, a pin*, Od. 5, 248. † Here, nails with which Ulysses fastened the vessel or raft together.

* γονεύς, έως, ὁ, *a procreator, a father*, plur. *parents*, h. Cer. 241.

γονή. ἡ (γένω), *that which is begotten, a child, offspring, progeny*, 24, 539. Od. 4, 755.

γόνος, ὁ (γένω), 1) *race, origin*=γένος, Od. 1, 216. 4, 207. h. Ven. 104. 2) *What is begotten, child, descendant*, 5, 635; and often.

Γονόεσσα, ἡ, Ep. for Γονοῦσα, *Gonoussa*, a fortified village, or a promontory between Pellene and Ægira in Achaia, 2, 573. Cf. Paus. 5, 18. 2.

γόνυ, τό, gen. γούνατος and γουνός, nom. plur. γούνατα and γοῦνα, gen. γούνων, dat. γούνασι (γούνασσι) and γούνεσσι, 9, 488. 1) *the knee*. γόνυ κάμπτειν, to bend the knee, i. e., *to rest, to sit*, 7, 118. ἐπὶ γοῦνα ἕζεσθαι, *to seat oneself upon the knees*, 14, 437. The ancients considered the knees as the chief seat of physical power, hence γούνατά τινος λύειν, to loose one's knees, to lame him, to prostrate him, to slay him, 5, 176. εἴσοκέ μοι φίλα γούνατα ὀρώρῃ, whilst my knees move, i. e., as long as I am strong, 9, 610. Od. 18, 133. ὥς τοι γούναθ' ἵκοιτο, that your knees might obey you, 4, 314. 2) In humble supplication, it was customary to embrace the knees; hence ἅψασθαι γούνων, 1, 512; γοῦνα λαβεῖν, Od. 6, 147; γούνατά τινος ἱκάνεσθαι, Od. 3, 92; ἀνὰ γοῦνα κύειν, 8, 371. Hence also, ἐν γούνασι θεῶν κεῖται, it lies in the lap of the gods, it depends on their will. 17, 514. Od. 1, 267; accord. to Nitzsch, 'in the power of the gods,' since the early language indicated this by the term *knee*.

γόον, Ep. for ἔγοον, see γοάω.

γόος, ὁ (γοάω), *wailing, lamentation, complaint*, always connected with weeping, τινός, for any one, Od. 4, 113; chiefly lamentation for one dead, 18, 316.

γοάω, see γοάω.

Γόργειος, η, ον (Γοργώ), *of Gorgo, belonging to Gorgo, Gorgon*. Γοργείη κεφαλή, the Gorgon head, 5, 741. Od. 11, 634.

Γοργυθίων, ωνος, ὁ, son of Priam and Castianira from Æsyme ; Teucer slew him, 8, 302.

Γοργώ, ἡ, gen. Γοργοῦς (the terrible, related to ὀργή). *Gorgo*, a frightful monster, whose head is mentioned chiefly as exciting terrour. Medusa is mly understood by it, one of the three Gorgones mentioned by Hesiod, whose look was petrifying, 8, 349. 11, 36. H. places her in the lower world, Od. 11, 634. Hesiod and later writers mention three : *Stheno, Euryale*, and *Medusa*, daughters of Phorcys and Ceto, who had serpents for hair. According to Hesiod, they dwell far west on Oceanus ; accord. to later writers, in the Gorgon isles.

Γόρτυς, υνος, ἡ (Γόρτυνα, ἡ, Strab.), *Gortyna*, chief city of the island of Crete, near its centre, on the river Lethæus, subsequently famed for its splendid edifices and two ports ; the ruins are near the modern Me-sara, 2, 646. Od. 3, 294. (On the nom. Γόρτυν, see Buttm., Gram. § 41.)

γοῦν (γε, οὖν), *at least, hence*, only twice, in the Il. 5, 258. 16, 30. Accord. to Thiersch, § 329, 1. Anm. and Spitzner on 5, 258, γοῦν is not Homeric; hence the latter has adopted γ' οὖν after the Cod. Venet.

γουνάζομαι, depon. mid. (γόνυ), fut. γουνάσομαι, prop. *to embrace any one's knees;* hence, *to supplicate at one's feet, to supplicate earnestly*, τινά, 1, 427 ; ὑπέρ τινος, for any one, 15, 665; πρός τινος and τινός, to conjure by any one, Od. 11, 68. 13, 324 ; but γούνων γουνάζεσθαι, to embrace one's knees, 22, 345 (Ep. form γουνόομαι).

γούνατα, γούνασι and γούνεσσι, see γόνυ.

Γουνεύς, ὁ (field-man, γουνός), leader of the Arcadians before Troy, 2, 747.

γουνόομαι, Ep. for γουνάζομαι, 1) *to supplicate*, with accus. 9, 583. πολλὰ θεοὺς γουνούμενος, Od. 4, 443. 2) *to vow in supplicating*, Od. 10, 521. Cf. v. 526.

γουνός, ὁ (γόνος), *a cultivated field, a fruitful field, a fertile place*, rarely alone, Od. 11, 193; mly γουνὸς ἀλωῆς, a fertile field, 18, 97. Od. 1, 193; also Ἀθηνάων, Od. 11, 323. (Others say the signif. *fruitful field* conflicts with γουνὸς Ἀθηνάων : for Attica was stony and not fertile. They cite as akin to it γόνυ, γῶνος, according to which it would signify prop. *projecting angle;* and then mly *elevation*.')

γραῖα, ἡ (γραῖος), an aged female, an old woman, Od. 1, 438.†

Γραῖα, ἡ, a very ancient town in Bœotia, near Orōpus; accord. to Pausan. the later *Tanagra*, 2, 498.

γραπτύς, ύος, ἡ, a scratch, an injury, e. g., by thorns. γραπτῦς for γραπτύας, Od. 24, 229.†

γράφω, aor. 1 ἔγραψα, to scratch, to engrave, with accus. γράψας ἐν πίνακι θυμοφθόρα πολλά, after he had inscribed upon the tablet many fatal signs, 6, 168 (a kind of picture-writing or hieroglyphics; for H.'s heroes were not acquainted with alphabetic writing, cf. Wolf, Proleg. p. lxxxi; and also σήματα); spoken of the spear's head: to graze, to injure, ὀστέον, 17, 599.

Γρήνικος, ὁ, Ion. for Γράνικος, a river in the Lesser Mysia, now *Ustvola*, 12, 31; afterwards famed by the battle of Alexander the Great (from Γρᾶς, the conductor of a colony, and νίκη, Strab. xiii. 582).

γρηΰς, ἡ, Ep. also γρηός, Ion. for γραῦς. dat. γρηΐ, voc. γρηΰ and γρηΰ, an aged female, an old woman. (γρηΰς is incorrect; see Thiersch, Gram. § 181, 46, c.)

* γρουνός, ὁ = γυνός, fire-brand, Fr. 67.

γύαλον, τό (prob. related to κοῖλος), a hollow, an arch; θώρηκος, the swell of the cuirass. 5, 99. This piece of armour consisted of two curved plates, one of which covered the breast, the other the back; these were joined at the sides by hooks or thongs, see Pausan. 10, 26. 2; hence, θώρηξ γυάλοισιν ἀρηρώς, a cuirass fitted together from convex plates, *15, 530. 2) ravine, valley, h. Ap. 336. h. 25, 5.

Γυγαίη λίμνη, ἡ, 1) the *Gygæan lake*, a lake in Lydia, at Mount Tmolus, not far from the Caystrus, later Κολόη, 20, 391. 2) the nymph of the lake, mother of Mesthles and Antiphus, 2, 865 (from γύγης, a water-fowl).

* γυιάτιδος, Epig. 15, 13; a corrupt word, for which Herm proposes ἀγυιάτη.

γυῖον, τό, a limb, chiefly a hand, foot, knee; always in the plur. τὰ γυῖα, limbs; ποδῶν γυῖα, the feet, 13, 512; hence, γυῖα λύειν, to loose the limbs, 7, 6; ἐλαφρὰ θεῖναι, to render the limbs light, 5, 122; ἐκ δέος εἵλετο γυίων, Od. 6, 140. 2) the body, the lap, h. Merc. 20.

γυιόω (γυιός), γυιώσω, to lame, to enfeeble, ἵππους, 8, 402. 416.†

γυμνός, ή, όν. naked, bare; mly without arms, unarmed, 16, 815; also spoken of things: γυμνὸν τόξον, the bared bow, i. e. the bow taken from its case, Od. 11, 607; γυμνὸς ὀϊστός, the bared arrow (taken from the quiver), Od. 21, 417.

γυμνόω (γυμνός), fut. ώσω, only aor. I pass. ἐγυμνώθην. 1) to lay bare, to uncover; in the pass. to strip oneself, to deprive oneself, with gen. ῥακέων, to free oneself from the rags, Od. 22, 1. 2) Chiefly spoken of warriors, who are spoiled of their arms, 12, 428; and τεῖχος ἐγυμνώθη, the wall was laid bare, i. e., open to attack, 12, 399.

γυναικεῖος, είη, εῖον (γυνή), female, belonging to women. γυναικεῖαι βουλαί, Od. 11, 437.†

γυναιμανής, ές, gen. έος (μαίνομαι), woman-mad, extravagantly fond of women (amorous, V.), epith. of Paris, *3, 39. 13. 769.

γύναιος, α, ον = γυναικεῖος. γύναια δῶρα, presents to a woman, *Od. 11, 521. 15, 247.

γυνή, ἡ, gen. γυναικός. 1) a woman, a female, in distinction from a man, 15, 683, without reference to rank or age; therefore often in Od. a maid; also in a contemptuous signif.: γυναικὸς ἄρ' ἀντὶ τέτυξο, thou art become a woman, 8, 163. Often in connexion with subst. which have the force of adj. γυνὴ ταμίη, ἀλετρίς, etc. 2) a wife, a cons rt, 6, 160. 8, 57. 3) a mistress of a family, a mistress, Od. 4) a mortal woman, in distinction from a goddess, 14, 315. Od. 10, 228. In γυναῖκα θήσατο μαζόν, 24, 58, according to the Schol. γυναῖκα stands for γυναικεῖον, or this construction can be explained by the fig. καθ' ὅλον καὶ μέρος. Cf. Thiersch, Gram. § 273.

Γύραι, αἱ (sc. πέτραι, the *Gyræan rocks*), where the Locrian Ajax suffered shipwreck; accord. to Eustath. near Myconus, or, more correctly, near the promontory Caphareus of Euboea, Od 4, 500; cf. Quint. Sm. 570 (from γυρός), whence adj. Γυραῖος, αίη, αῖον, *Gyræan*; hence Γυραίη πέτρη, Od. 4, 507.

γυρός, ή, όν, round, curved, crooked. γυρὸς ἐν ὤμοισιν, round-shouldered, hump-backed, Od. 19, 246.†

Γυρτιάδης, ου, ὁ, son of Gyrtius = Hyrtius, 14, 512.

Γυρτώνη, ἡ (Γυρτών, ῶνος, Strab.), a town in Pelasgiôtis (Thessalia), on the declivity of Olympus, on the Penēus, now *Salambria*, 2, 738.

γύψ, γυπός, ἡ, dat. plur. γύπεσσι, the vulture, Il. and Od. 11, 578.

γωρυτός, ὁ, bow-case, Od. 21, 54 (related to χωρέω, equivalent to θήκη, ὡς χωροῦσι τὸ ῥυτόν, Eustath.).

Δ.

Δ, the fourth letter of the alphabet, hence the sign of the fourth rhapsody.

δα, an inseparable prefix, which strengthens the signif., according to some derived from διά, very, exceedingly.

δαείω, Ep. for δαῶ, see ΔΑΩ.

(δάζομαι), obsol. theme, from which are formed the fut. and aor. of δαίω.

δαήμεναι, Ep. for δαῆναι, see ΔΑΩ.

δαήμων, ον, gen. ονος (δαῆναι), know-

δαῆναι. 97 **Δαιτρόν.**

ing. intelligent, acquainted with, expert, skilful, with gen. ἄθλων, Od. 8, 159; ὀρχηθμοῖο, v. 263; ἐν πάντεσσ' ἔργοισι, Il. 23, 671.

δαῆναι, see **ΔΑΩ.**

δαήρ, *έρος,* ὁ, voc. δᾶερ, *brother-in-law,* husband's brother. (On the word see Buttm., Gram. § 45, 5. note 1, and gen. plur. δαέρων, dissyllabic, 24, 769.) *Il.

δάηται, see **δαίω.**

δαί, Ep. dat. see δαίς, 13, 286.

δαιδάλεος, *η, ον* (δαίδαλος), *artfully, skilfully made; beautifully wrought; artfully adorned;* spoken of weapons or furniture which are inlaid or adorned with metal or wood: ἔντεα, θρόνος, ζωστήρ, and other productions of art; in Od. 1, 131, δαιδάλεον belongs to θρόνον. Cf. Nitzsch on the verse, p. 99.

δαιδάλλω (δαίδαλος), *to work artfully, to adorn skilfully, to ornament, to inlay;* to adorn with gold, silver, and ivory, λέχος χρυσῷ, ἀργύρῳ, Od. 23, 200; σάκος, Il. 18, 479.

δαίδαλον, *τό,* subst. *a work of art, embroidery,* sing. Od. 19, 227; plur. τὰ δαίδαλα, *works of art,* Il. 5, 60; pictures inwrought with metal-work and embroidery, 14, 179 (prob. from δάω, δάλλω, δαιδάλλω).

Δαίδαλος, *ὁ,* prop. *the artist,* is a collective name, and indicates a series of Attic and Cretan artists, who, at the beginning of the arts, gave life and motion to statues. H. calls him ὁ Κνώσσιος, from Knosos (Gnossus) in Crete, and as the inventor of an artificial dance which he wrought for Ariadnê, 18, 592; cf. ἀσκέω and χορός. Accord. to Attic tradition, he was the son of Eupalamus in Athens, father of Icarus. He fled on account of the murder of his nephew Talus to Crete, and built there the labyrinth; thence he went to Sicily, Apd. 3, 15, 8.

δαίζω, poet. (δαίω), fut. ξω, aor. ἐδάϊξα, perf. pass. δεδαϊγμένος, 1) *to divide, to share, to separate into parts,* Od. 14, 434; with accus. often *to tear in pieces. to split, to cut in pieces.* χιτῶνα χαλκῷ, 2, 416; κόμην, to tear out the hair, 18, 27; hence δεδαϊγμένος ἦτορ, pierced through at the heart, 17, 535. *b)* Metaph. ἐδαίζετο θυμὸς ἐνὶ στήθεσσιν, the heart in their breast was torn (by disquiet and pain), 9, 8; but ὤρμαινε δαϊζόμενος κατὰ θυμὸν διχθάδι', with ἤ, ἤ following, he deliberated upon it doubly divided in mind, i. e., he was balancing between two purposes, 14, 20. ἔχων δεδαϊγμένον ἦτορ, having a torn (troubled) heart, Od. 13, 320. 2) *to cut or hew down, to cleave, to slay,* ἵππους τε καὶ ἀνέρας, 11, 497. Pass. often χαλκῷ δεδαϊγμένος, hewn down with the sword, 18, 236. 22, 72.

δαϊστάμενος, *η, ον* (δαΐς, κτείνω), *slain in battle,* *21, 146. 301.

δαιμόνιος, *ίη, ον* (δαίμων), prop. proceeding from a demon or divinity, *divine,* νύξ, h. Merc. 98. 2) Spoken of every thing which according to the belief of the old world indicated a higher power, which excited astonishment, and thus fear; *astonishing, admirable.* H. uses it only in the vocative as a word of address to men, to express astonishment, horrour, etc. at a strange action or speech; *strange, wonderful,* sometimes in a good sense, *my (good) friend,* as 2, 190. 6, 407. Od. 14, 443; sometimes in reproach, *wretch, wretched (cruel, wicked) man,* 1, 561. 4, 31.

δαίμων, ονος, ὁ, ἡ, 1) any *divine being,* believed to be efficient in the production of events which were regarded as above ordinary human capability and power, and which yet could be ascribed to no particular divinity, 5, 438; we are not, however, to associate the later demons with those of H.; *a demon, a divinity.* The demon guides the fate of men, Od. 16, 64; he sends them happiness, is their tutelary spirit, Od. 21, 201; but he also allots misfortunes, sends sickness, Od. 5, 396. κακὸς δαίμων, Od. 10, 64. δαίμονος αἶσα κακή, Od. 11, 61; hence often used for *fate, happiness, misfortune.* τοὶ δαίμονα δώσω, I will give the demon to thee, i. e., death, 8, 166. πρὸς δαίμονα, against destiny, 17, 98. σὺν δαίμονι, with divine aid, 11, 792. 2) *deity, god, goddess,* spoken of definitely named divine persons, Aphroditê, 3, 420. h. 18, 22; and in the plur. *gods,* 1, 122. 6, 115.

δαίνυ' for ἐδαίνυσο, see δαίνυμι.

δαίνυμι, Ep. (δαίω), fut. δαίσω, aor. 1 mid. ἐδαισάμην, Ep. forms: 3 sing. optat. mid. δαινῦτο (for νιτο), 24, 665; 3 plur. δαινύατο, Od. 18, 248; imperf. mid. 2 sing. δαίνυ' for ἐδαίνυσο, 24, 63; 1) Act. prop. *to distribute, to give one his portion,* spoken only of a host: δαιτά τινι, to give any one food, 9, 70; τάφον, γάμον, a funeral feast, a marriage feast, Od. 3, 309 4, 3. Il. 19, 299. 2) Mid. *to eat, to feast,* spoken of the guests; often absolutely, but also with accus. δαῖτα, to consume a feast; in like manner εἰλαπίνην, κρέα; and of the gods, ἑκατόμβας, 9, 535.

δαΐς, ἴδος, ἡ (δαίω), 1) *a brand, a torch, a flambeau,* only plur. Od. 1, 428. 2) *war, battle,* only in the apocopat. dat. δαΐ. 13, 286. 14, 387.

δαίς, τός, ἡ (δαίω), *a meal, a feast, an entertainment, a sacrificial feast,* often in H. spoken of men and gods. δαὶς ἐΐση, an equally distributed feast, πίειρα 19, 179. 2) Of the food of wild beasts, 24, 43. but not often [Aristarchus, according to Lehrs, p. 96, placed the comma before βροτῶν, so as to connect it with δαῖτα, which would bring the signif. to no. 1].

δαίτη, ἡ, poet. for δαίς, 10, 217. Od. 3, 44. 7, 50.

δαίτηθεν, adv. *from the feast,* Od. 10, 216.

δαιτρεύω (δαιτρός), fut. σω, prop. *to divide into equal portions, to distribute,* spoken of booty, 11, 688. 2) *to cut off, to curve,* Od. 14, 433.

δαιτρόν, *τό* (δαίω), *that which is distributed*

F

Δαιτρός. 98 Δαμάω.

tributed, a portion; πίνειν, to drink a given portion, 4, 262.†

δαιτρός, ὁ (δαίω). one who distributes, a carver, a distributer, chiefly of meat at a feast in small pieces, because the hands were used in eating, *Od. 4, 57, 17, 331.

δαιτροσύνη, ἡ, carving, helping or distributing meat at table, Od. 16, 253.†

δαιτυμών, όνος, ἡ (δαιτύς), mly a companion at table. 1) one who is invited, a guest, a feaster, Od. 8, 66. 2) an ordinary companion at table, once, *Od. 4, 621 ; see Nitzsch on the verse.

δαιτύς, ύος, ἡ, Ep. for δαίς, a meal, an entertainment, 22, 496.†

Δαίτωρ, ορος, ὁ, a Trojan slain by Teucer, 8, 275.

δαΐφρων, ονος, ὁ, ἡ, signifies 1) (from δαΐς, φρήν), thinking of battle, eager for battle, warlike, 2, 23; thus in the Iliad, except 24, 325 (a book mly regarded as of later date). 2) (from δαῆναι), wise, intelligent, experienced; so always in the Od. 15, 356, 8, 373 ; according to Buttm., Lex. p. 209. Nitzsch, on Od. 1, 48, derives it simply from δαῆναι in the signif. to have proved, tried ; consequently spoken of a warrior: proved, tried ; and of one in peace : experienced, intelligent [cf. G. Hermann, Opusc. VII. p. 250].

δαίω, the ground meaning of the root ΔΑ is perhaps to divide, to cut up, to destroy. There occur:
1) δαίω, poet., in the act. only pres. and imperf., perf. 2 δέδηα, aor. 2 mid. 3 sing. subj. δάηται=καίω. 1) Trans. in the act. = καίω [δαίειν = to set on fire; καίειν to destroy by fire, to burn. Död.], to kindle, to inflame, to set on fire; with accus. πῦρ, φλόγα, 9, 211; also δαῖέ οἱ ἐκ κόρυθος—πῦρ, she (Athēnē) kindled a flame upon his helmet, 5, 4. cf. v. 7. 2) Mid. perf. 2 δέδηα, intransit. to burn, to burst into flames, to flame, as δαιδμενον σέλας, 8, 75; metaph. ὄσσε δαίεται, his eyes sparkle, spoken of the lion, Od. 6, 132; of Hector, 12, 466. πόλεμος δέδηε, the war is enkindled, rages, 20, 18. ἔρις, στέφανος πολέμοιο, ὄσσα δεδήει, the report was enkindled, i. e. spread rapidly, 2, 93 ; οἰμωγή δέδηε, arose, Od. 20, 353.

2) δαίομαι, poet. (only mid. in H. in the signif. to divide, act. δαίζω), fut. δάσομαι, Ep. σσ, aor. 1 ἐδασάμην, Ep. σσ, perf. δέδασμαι (δεδαίαται, Od. 1, 23), also a form δατέομαι. 1) Reflex. (for oneself), to divide, to distribute, to share, τί τινι ; in the pres. κρέα μνηστῆρσι, Od. 17, 332. 13, 140 ; often in the fut. and aor. πάντα ἄνδιχα, to divide all into two parts, 18, 511; also κτήματα, μοίρας, πατρῷία: likewise, b) to tear in pieces, 23, 21. Od. 18, 87. 2) Pass. to be divided, in the perf. 1, 125; spoken of the Ethiopians : διχθὰ δεδαίαται, Od. 1, 23. δαίεται ἦτορ, my heart is torn, Od. 1, 48.

δάκνω, aor. 2 ἔδακον, infin. Ep. δακέειν, to bite, to sting, spoken of dogs and gnats, *7, 572; of a mouse, Batr. 47; metaph.

δάκε φρένας Ἕκτορι μῦθος, the discourse wounded Hector's heart, 5, 493 (in the aor. 2 in Il.; pres. in Batr.).

δάκρυ, τό, poet. for δάκρυον, tears: in nom. and accus. sing. and dat. plur. δάκρυσι.

δακρυόεις, εσσα, εν (δάκρυον), tearful, 1) Act. weeping abundantly, shedding tears, 6, 455. The neut. as adv. δακρυόεν γελᾶν, to laugh with tears in the eyes, 6, 484. 2) worthy of tears, lamentable, τό-λεμος, μάχη, 5, 737.

δάκρυον, τό (poet. δάκρυ), a tear; δακρυόφιν, Ep. gen. 17, 696. Od. 4, 705; often δάκρυα, χέειν, λείβειν, βάλλειν.

δακρυπλώω (πλώω), to flow in tears, spoken of an intoxicated man, whose eyes overflow, Od. 19, 122.†

δακρυχέω, shedding tears, weeping; only in partcp. pres., Il. and Od.

δακρύω, aor. 1 ἐδάκρυσα, perf. pass. δεδάκρυμαι, intrans. to weep, to shed tears; in perf. pass. to be in tears, 16, 7. δε-δάκρυνται ὄσσε, eyes were full of tears, Od 20, 204 ; παρειαί, v. 353.

*δάκτυλος, ὁ, a finger, a toe, Batr. 45.

δαλός, ὁ (δαίω), (titio) a brand, a firebrand, 13, 320, and Od. 5, 488.

δαμάζω=δαμάω, as pres. not used in H.; but aor. 1 pass. ἐδαμάσθην, 19, 9. 16, 816.

δάμαρ, αρτος, ἡ, poet. (δαμάω), a wife, a consort ; prop. domita, in distinction from ἀδμής, 3, 122. Od. 4, 126.

Δάμασος, ὁ, a Trojan, 12, 183.

Δαμαστορίδης, ου, ὁ, son of Damastor =the Lydian Tlepolemus, 16, 416. 2) the suitor Agelaus, Od. 22, 293.

Δαμάστωρ, ορος, ὁ (the tamer), father of Agelaus in Ithaca, Od.

δαμάω, fut. δαμάσω, poet. σσ, Ep. δαμάω, thus δαμάᾳ, δαμόωσιν, aor. 1 ἐδά-μασα, poet. σσ, fut. mid. δαμάσομαι, poet. σσ, aor. 1 mid. ἐδαμασάμην, poet. σσ, subj. 3 sing. δαμάσσεται for δαμά-σηται, 11, 478; perf. pass. δέδμημαι, aor. 1 pass. ἐδμήθην and ἐδαμάσθην, aor. 2 pass. ἐδάμην, 3 plur. δάμεν for ἐδάμησαν, subj. δαμείω, Ep. for δαμῶ, optat. δαμείην, infin. δαμῆναι, Ep. δαμήμεναι, fut. 3 pass. δεδμήσομαι, h. Ap. 543: ground signif. 1) to subdue, hence 1) Spoken of animals : to tame, to bring under the yoke, for travelling or agriculture, 10, 403. 2) Of maidens: to bring under the yoke of wedlock, to marry, to espouse, s u b i g e r e, τινὰ ἀνδρί, 18, 432. On Od. 3, 269, see πεδάω ; also without reference to marriage : to violate, to defile, 3, 301. 3) Mly to subdue, to conquer, to vanquish, spoken of fate, Od. 11, 398. Il. 16, 434. 816. 18, 119 ; τινὰ πληγῇσιν, Od. 4, 244. 18, 54; also by prayers : ἐμῷ θῆμῳ (cf. vinci precibus), 9, 158. Esply a) to conquer in battle, στίχας, often in pass. τινί, ὑπό τινι, or χερσίν τινος, 3, 429. 2, 860; hence also to kill, 1, 61. 11, 98, and often. b) to bring into subjection, to subject, τί τινι, 6, 159: and pass. often : ἦ τοι πολλοὶ δεδμήατο κοῦροι, truly

Δαμείω. 99 Δατέομαι.

many youths are subject to thee, 3, 183. 5, 878. Od. 3, 304. c) Metaph. spoken of states and inanimate objects: *to subdue, to overpower, to exhaust*; of sleep, 10, 2; of wine, Od. 9, 454; of passions, 6, 74. 14, 316; of the waves of the sea: to be exhausted, Od. 8, 231. II) Mid. like the act. except with a reference to the subject, 5, 278. 10, 210. δαμάσασθαι φρένας οἴνῳ, to stupify the mind with wine, Od. 9, 454. (Other forms are δαμνάω, δάμνημι.)

δαμείω, δάμεν, δαμήμεναι, ser δαμάω.

δαμνάω = δαμάω, of which occurs only 3 sing. prs. δαμνᾷ, Od. 11, 221; 3 sing. impf. ἐδαμνα and δάμνα, iterat. fr. δάμνασκε, h. Ven. 252; and 2 sing. pres. mid. δαμνᾷ for δάμνασαι, 14, 199; cf. Spitzner.

δάμνημι, pass. δάμναμαι, Ep. (like ἵστημι) = δαμνάω, *to subdue, to overpower*. Besides the pres. act. H. uses the pres. and imperf. pass. The mid. only Od. 14, 488. h. Ven. 17.

δαμώωσιν, Ep. for δαμῶσιν, see δαμάω.

Δανάη, ἡ, daughter of Acrisius, mother of Perseus by Zeus, 14, 319; see Περσεύς.

Δαναοί, οἱ, *the Danai*, prop. the subjects of king Danaus of Argos; in H. 1) the inhabitants of the kingdom of Argos = Ἀργεῖοι, the subjects of king Agamemnon. 2) Often the Hellenes in general, because Agamemnon was the principal leader, 1, 42, 56, and Od. (Danaus, son of Belus, father of fifty daughters, contended with his brother Ægyptus concerning the kingdom of Egypt, fled to Greece, and founded Argos, about 1500 B.C. Apd. 2, 1. 4. According to Ottfr. Müller, Gesch. hell. St. 1. p. 109, Danaus is only a mythic personification of the stock. He derives the name from δανός, dry, and thinks that originally τὸ δανάον Ἄργος was used in the same sense as τὸ δίψιον.)

δανός, ἡ, όν (δαίω) *dried, dry, withered*, ξύλα, Od. 15, 322.† δανὰ ξύλα, *fire-wood*, [δανός *combustible; fit for burning*. Död.]

δάος, τό (δαίω) = δαλός, *a pine torch, a fire-brand*, *a torch*, 24, 647. Od. 4, 300, and often.

δάπεδον, τό (δα, Dor. for γῆ or for διά), *ground, earth*, Od. 11, 577. 2) Mly the *floor* of a chamber, *the house-floor*, 4, 2; chiefly Od.

δάπτω, and with reduplicat. δαρδάπτω, fut. δάψω, *to tear in pieces, to lacerate*, spoken of wild beasts, 11, 481; metaph. of a spear: χρόα, to tear the skin, 13, 831; and of fire: *to consume*, *23, 183.

Δαρδανίδης, ου, ὁ, a son or descendant of Dardanus = Priam, 3, 303; *Anchises*, h. in Ven. 178. [2) = *Ilus*, 11, 166.]

Δαρδανίη, ἡ, *Dardania*, 1) an old city in Asia Minor, on the Hellespont, at the foot of Ida, which was founded by the old king Dardanus, and whose residence it was, 20, 216; distinct from Ilium of Strab., XIII. p. 590; and from the Æol.

town ἡ Δάρδανος, which lay further south, 110 stadia from the mouth of the Rhodius, which falls into the Hellespont, Strab., XIII. 595. 2) sc. γῆ, a small district above Troas on the Hellespont which Æneas ruled. H. mentions only the inhabitants, the Dardanians, i. e., Δάρδανοι, q. v.; according to Strab., XIII. v. 561, p. 596, from Zeleia to Scepsis.

Δαρδάνιος, ίη, ιον, *Dardanian*, proceeding or named from Dardanus. αἱ Δαρδάνιαι πύλαι, the Dardanian gate, 5, 789 = αἱ Σκαιαί, q. v. 2) Subst. the *Dardani*, i. q. Δάρδανοι, q. v.

Δαρδανίς, ίδος, ἡ, *Dardanian*, also *Trojan*, as subst. *a Trojan woman*, 18, 122. 339.

Δαρδανίων, ωνος, ὁ, prop. a descendant of Dardanus, in the plur. = Δάρδανοι, e. g. Τρῶες καὶ Δαρδανίωνες. 7, 414.

Δάρδανος, οἱ, sing. 2, 701, the *Dardanians*, prop. the inhabitants of Dardania, the subjects of Æneas; they were the more ancient stock, hence the poet joins Τρῶες καὶ Δαρδανίωνες, 3, 456. 7, 348.

Δάρδανος, ὁ, son of Zeus and Electra, brother of Jasius from Arcadia; he emigrated to Samothrace, and thence to Asia Minor, where he founded the town Dardania. His wife Batia, daughter of Teucer, bore him Ilus and Ericthonius, 20, 215. 303. Apd. 3, 12. 1. 2) son of Bias, a Trojan, whom Achilles slew, 20, 460. 3) Adj. = Δαρδάνιος: Δάρδανος ἀνήρ, 16, 807.

δαρδάπτω, a strengthened form of δάπτω, *to tear in pieces*, 11, 479; metaph. κτήματα, Od. 14, 92; χρήματα, to squander property, Od. 16, 315.

Δάρης, ητος, ὁ, a priest of Hephæstus in Troy, father of Phegeus and Idæus, 5, 9. seq.

δαρθάνω, aor. ἔδαρθον, Ep. ἔδραθον, *to sleep*, only aor. Od. 20, 143.†

δασασκέτω, δάσασθαι, δάσομαι, see δαίω.

δάσκιος, ον, poet. (δα, σκιά), *very shady, deeply shaded*, ὕλη, Il. Od. and h.

δασμός, ὁ (δαίω), *division, distribution*, 1, 166. + h. in Cer. 86.

δασπλῆτις, ἡ, *difficult of approach, dreadful, terrible*, epith. of the furies. Od. 15, 234.† (From δα and πελάω, not πλήσσω. Thiersch, Gram. § 199, 5. Cf. τειχεσιπλήτης.) [= δαιδὸ πελάτις, δαισπελάτις (cf. κραταίπεδον, κράσπεδον), *that brings a torch near; approaching with a torch; torch-bearing.* Död.].

δασύμαλλος, ον (μαλλός), *having thick wool, thick-woolled*, Od. 9, 425.†

δασύς, εῖα, ύ, *rough, thickly planted, hairy*, ῥῶπες, δέρμα, *Od. 14, 49. 51.

δατέομαι (δαίω), Ep. form in pres. and impf. for δαίομαι, 1) *to divide, to distribute*, ληΐδα, 9, 138; metaph. μένος Ἄρηος δατέονται, they divided among one another the fury of Ares, i. e., they fought on both sides with equal rage, 18, 264. χθόνα ποσσὶ δατεῦντο, they divided the ground with their feet, i. e., passed over it in steps, 23, 121. b) *to allot to*

Δαυλίς. 100 Διδίσκομαι.

oneself, i. e., to receive, spoken of the gods, who are pleased with the savour of sacrifices, 8, 550. *c*) Mly *to distribute*, κρέα, Od. 1, 112. 2) *to lacerate, to crush*, 20, 394.†

Δαυλίς, ίδος, ή, a town in Phocis, upon an elevation not far from Delphi, the scene of the old fable of Tereus, Progne, and Philomele, 2, 520 (from δαυλός, thickly overgrown).

δάφνη, η, *laurel*, Od. 9, 183. † h. Ap. 396.

δαφοινεός, όν = δαφοινός. είμα δαφοινεόν αίματι, 18, 538.†

δαφοινός, όν (δα, φοινός), *blood red, very red, dark-red, fire-coloured*, spoken of lions, serpents, and jackals, *II. h. Ap. 304.

ΔΑΩ, Ep. th. of διδάσκω, with the signif. *to teach* and *to learn*; from this theme the following forms occur in H.: aor. 2 act. δέδαε, perf. partcp. δεδαώς. aor. 2 pass. έδάην, subj δαώ, Ep δαείω, infin. δαήναι, Ep. δαήμεναι, whence fut. δαήσομαι, perf. act. δεδάηκα, and perf. pass. partcp. δεδαημένος, h. Merc. 483; and an infin. pres. (as if fr. δέδαα) δεδάασθαι. 1) The signif. *to teach* has only the aor. 2 act. δέδαε, with double accus. τινά τι, Od. 6, 233. 8, 448; and with infin. Od. 20, 72. 2) To the signif. *to learn, to know, to experience*, belong the remaining forms Thus aor. 2 pass. with accus. 6, 150; once with gen. πολέμοιο δαήμεναι, to be acquainted with war, 21, 487; τινός, to become acquainted with, Od. 19, 325; partcp. perf. act. δεδαώς, *having learned, instructed*, έκ θεών, Od. 17, 519; and δεδάηκα άεθλον, has learned [is acquainted with] κ combat, Od. 8, 134. ού δεδαηκότες άλκήν, not acquainted with conflict, defence, Od. 2, 61. Pres. mid. *to teach oneself, to become acquainted with*. δεδάασθαι γυναίκας, to inform oneself about the women, Od. 16, 316. (To the same theme belong also the Ep. forms δώω and δέατο.)

δέ, conj. *but, on the other hand, on the contrary*. This conj., which, like the Lat. *autem*, may indicate every kind of opposition, has either an adversative or conjunctive force. I) Adversative, 1) Most commonly in the case of opposed notions, of which the first has μέν, see μέν; also μέν, μέν, and δέ, δέ, succeed each other. *b*) δέ often stands also without a preceding μέν, when the speaker would not give a pre-intimation of the antithesis, or where the first member forms but a weak antithesis. In the last case it is found also with the repetition of the same or of an equivalent word, ὡς 'Αχιλεύς θάμβησεν—θάμβησαν δέ καί άλλοι, 24, 484 ; οί δέ καί αύτοί άλγε' έχουσιν, Od. 1, 33. II. 14, 9. 12. From the last use of δέ without μέν has 2) the conjunctive force of this particle developed itself. Here it can mly be translated by *and*, but must often be omitted in translating. This takes place

a) When a transition is made from one subject to another: cf. 1, 43—49. *b*) When it connects sentences of which the latter may be regarded as standing in a subordinate relation, in which case δέ often expresses a reason, and stands for γάρ. It can then be translated by *since, for, because* [or omitted]: άλλά πίθεσθ' άμφω δέ νεωτέρω έστόν έμείο, 1, 259. 520. cf. 2, 26. 9, 496. 3) It often stands in the apodosis, and has both an adversative and conjunctive force. *a*) The adversative δέ, on the other hand, on my part, *again*. a) After a hypothetical protasis: εί δέ κε μή δώωσιν, έγώ δέ κεν αύτός έλωμαι. I myself on the other hand, etc. 1. 137. 12, 215. β) After a comparative or relative protasis: οίη περ φύλλων γενεή, τοίη δέ καί άνδρών, 6. 146. Od. 7, 108. *b*) The conjunctive δέ annexes the apodosis to the protasis as if a relation, not of subordination but of equality, existed between them ; thus, after a temporal protasis with έπεί, έπειδή, όφρα, όπότε, έως, 1, 57. 16, 199. 21, 53. 4) In connexion with other particles: *a*) καί δέ, also on the other hand, but also, in H. 23, 80. Od. 16, 418. *b*) δέ δή, but still, but now, 7, 94. *c*) δέ τε, and also 1, 404; but also, Od. 1, 53. 4, 379 [also separated, as 9, 519]. δέ never stands at the beginning of a sentence, but takes the second, and often the third place.

δέ, inseparable enclitic particle, which is annexed 1) To nouns, to indicate the direction whither. It stands mly with the accus. κλισίηνδε, Θρήκηνδε, οίκόνδε. In 'Αϊδόσδε it is connected with the gen. because the accus. is to be supplied, see 'Αϊδης. More rarely we find it with adj. as ὅνδε δόμονδε, to his house. 2) To pronouns, to strengthen their demonstrative force; as ὅδε, τοιόσδε, etc. (The last probably originated from δή.)

δέατ' for δέατο. Ep. the only form of an obsol. verb δέαμαι, Od. 6, 242.† πρόσθεν μοι άεικέλιος δέατ' είναι, before he appeared ugly to me. (According to Buttm., Lex. p. 216, from aor. 2 δαήναι, to see, whence pass. δέαμαι for δάαμαι, *to appear*. Before Wolf the reading here was δόατ', and was referred to δοάζομαι, q. v.)

δέγμενος, see δέχομαι.

δέδαα, δεδάασι, δεδάηκα, δεδαημένος, δεδαώς, see ΔΑΩ.

δεδαίαται, see δαίω 2.

δεδαϊγμένος, see δαίζω.

δίδασται, see δαίω 2.

δέδηε, δεδήει, see δαίω.

δίδια, Ep. δείδια, in the plur. after the analogy of verbs in μι, without union-vowel, δείδιμεν, δείδιτε, δεδίασι, imperat. δείδιθι, etc. Perf. from the old th. δίω with pres. signif. *I fear*, instead of the later pres. δείδω, see δίω.

1) δεδίσκομαι and δειδίσκομαι, only pres. and impf. Ep. form (from δείκνυμι), *to greet, to welcome*, τινά, δεξιτερή χειρί Od. 20, 197; δεϊται, to greet with the

*Δεδίσκομαι, cup, i. e., to drink to, Od. 18, 121; absol. Od. 3, 41 (from δέκομαι, δίσκομαι, with reduplicat. δεδίσκομαι).
11) *δεδίσκομαι, a form of δειδίσσομαι, h. Merc. 103.
δεδίσσομαι, poet. δειδίσσομαι, q. v.
δεδμήατο, see δαμάω.
δεδμημένος, 1) Perf. partcp. from δαμάω, 10, 2. 2) From δέμω, to build, 6, 245.
δεδοκημένος, Ep. partcp. perf. pass. from the Ion. δέκομαι for δέχομαι, watching, lying in wait, 15, 730.†
δέδορκα, see δέρκομαι.
δεδραγμένος, see δράσσω.
δέελος, η, ον, Ep. for δῆλος, 10, 466.†
δεῖ (from δέω), it is necessary, it is fitting; in H. Il. 9, 337; † elsewhere always χρή: see δέω.
δείδεκτο and δειδέχατο, Ep. strengthened form for δέδεκτο, δεδέχατο: see δείκνυμι.
δειδήμων, ον, gen. ονος (δείδω), fearful, cowardly, timid, 3, 56.†
δείδια, etc., see δείδω and δίω.
δειδίσκομαι, see δεδίσκομαι II.
δειδίσσομαι, Ep. and δεδίσκομαι, only h. Merc. 163; depon. mid. (δείδω), fut. δειδίξομαι, infin. aor. 1 δειδίξασθαι, 1) Trans. to terrify, to frighten, to frighten away, τινά, any one, 4, 184; τινὰ ἀπὸ νεκροῦ, any one from a corpse, 18, 164. 2) Intrans. to fear, to be dismayed, 2, 190.
δείδοικα, see δείδω.
δείδω, only 1 sing. pres. (formed from the Ep. perf. δείδια), fut. δείσομαι, aor. 1 ἔδεισα, Ep. ἔδδεισα, partcp. δείσας, perf. δέδοικα, Ep. δείδοικα (also the Ep. δέδια, δείδια, etc.), with pres. signif. 1) Intrans. to fear, to be anxious, to be alarmed, often absol.; only περί τινι, for any one, 10, 240. h. Cer. 246; also with μή, that, following, δείδω, μή τι πάθῃσιν, 11, 470; rarely with infin. δείσαν ὑποδέχθαι, 7, 93. 2) Trans. to fear, to dread, τινά or τί, very often θεούς, Od. 14, 389 On the orthography ἔδδεισα, more correctly ἔδεισα, see Buttm., Gram. p. 274, margin. note. Kühner, p. 120.
δειελιαω (δείελος), only aor. 1 partcp. δειελιήσας, to await the evening, to wait till evening. σὺ δ' ἔρχεο δειελιήσας, Od. 17, 599.† (Accord. to Clarke and Buttm. Lex. p. 229, to take an afternoon's repast, which, however, the ancient Gramm., oi παλαιοί, according to Eustath. rejected. The latter explains it, ἕως δείλης διατρίψας ἐνταῦθα.)
δείελος, ον (δείλη), belonging to the declining day, relating to afternoon and evening. δείελον ἦμαρ, evening, Od. 17, 606. ὁ δείελος ὀψὲ δύων, sc. ἥλιος, the late evening: the late-setting sun of evening, 21, 232.
δεικανάομαι, depon. mid. only pres. and imperf. δεικανόωντο (δείκνυμι), to offer the hand in greeting; and mly to welcome, to salute, to receive, ἐπέεσσι, δέπασσιν, Od. 18, 111. Il. 15, 86.
δείκνυμι, th. ΔΕΚΩ, aor. 1 δεῖξα, aor.

mid. ἐδειξάμην, h. Merc. 367; perf. mid. δείδεγμαι, Ep. for δέδεγμαι, 3 plur. δειδέχαται, 3 sing. pluperf. δείδεκτο, and 3 plur. δειδέχατο, 1) Prop. to present the hand; hence a) to show, to point out, to indicate, τί τινι, spoken of the gods: σῆμα, τέρας, to let a sign or prodigy be seen, Od. 3, 174. Il. 13, 244; ἔργα, h. 31, 19. b) to advertise, to inform, 19, 332. 2) Mid. a) to point to, εἰς τι, h. Merc. 367. b) to show, τί τινι, 23, 701. c) to greet, to welcome, 9, 196. Od. 4, 59; perf. and pluperf. mid. with pres. signif. δεπάεσσιν (dat. instrum.) δειδέχατ' ἀλλήλους, they greeted one another with cups, i. e., they drank to one another, 4, 4; κυπέλλοις, 9, 671. cf. 9, 224; μύθοισι, Od. 7, 72; see Buttm., Gramm., under δείκνυμι, p. 274.
δείλη, ἡ (contr. from δείελη, sc. ὥρα), the declining day, the latter part of the afternoon, and the early part of the evening, 21, 111.† as the connexion with ἠώς and μέσον ἦμαρ shows. (According to Buttm., Lexil. p. 225, from εἴλη, heat, prop. the time in which the heat extends itself, afternoon; δείλη has the same relation to εἴλη, as διώκω to ἰώκω.)
δείλομαι (δείλη), to incline towards evening, accord. to Aristarch. δείλετο for δύσετο, Od. 7, 289.†
δειλός, ή, όν (δείδω), fearful, cowardly, timid, opposed to ἄλκιμος, 13, 278; hence in H. weak, contemptible, miserable, bad, 1, 293; δειλαὶ δειλῶν ἐγγύαι, Od. 8, 351. On this passage cf. ἐγγυάω. 2) wretched, unfortunate, miserable, poor. In the address: ἆ δειλέ, ἆ δειλοί, Od. 14, 361. Il. 11, 816.
δεῖμα, ατος, τό (δείδω), fear, terrour, fright, 5, 682.†
*δειμαίνω, ανῶ, to be afraid, h. in Ap. 404.
*δειμαλέος, η, ον, frightful, dreadful, ὅπλον, Batr. 289.
δείματο, see δέμω.
δείμομεν, Ep. for δείμωμεν, see δέμω.
Δεῖμος, ὁ (app. δειμός), Terrour, in the Il. as a personified, mythic being, servant and charloteer of Arēs, like Phobos, 4, 440. 11, 37. 15, 119. According to Hes. the son of Arēs.
δεινός, ή, όν (δείδω), frightful, terrible, awful, terrific, αἰγίς, πέλωρον, chiefly neut. as adv. δεινὸν αὔειν, to shout terribly, 11, 10; δέρκεσθαι, 3, 342. 2) In a milder signif. applied to that which by its greatness and power inspires awe and admiration: aweful, sublime, venerable, in connexion with αἰδοῖος, 3, 172. 18, 394. Od. 8, 22.
δεῖος, ους, τό, poet. for δέος, 15, 4; only in gen.
δειπνέω (δεῖπνον), aor. ἐδείπνησα, pluperf. δεδειπνήκει, Od. 17, 359; to break-fast, to take the morning meal, 19, 334, and often Od.; later, to take the principal meal; so even in h. Ap. 497.
δείπνηστος, ὁ (δειπνέω), the time of breakfast, meal-time, Od. 17, 170. (Ac-

Δειπνίζω. 102 **Δέπας.**

cording to the Schol. the Gramm. make a distinction: δείπνηστος, *meal-time;* δειπνηστός, the meal itself.

δειπνίζω (δειπνέω), aor. 1 ἐδείπνισα, only partcp. δειπνίσσας, *to entertain, to give a meal to any one*, with accus. *Od. 4, 535. 11, 411.

δεῖπνον, τό. in H. *breakfast*, or, more correctly, the principal meal, which was taken by those not in service about noon; in distinction from δόρπος, 8, 53. 10, 578. Od. 15, 316. An army going to battle took this meal at day-break, 2, 381; mly *meal, repast, entertainment*, Od. 17, 176; spoken of horses : *food*, 2, 383. (According to Nitzsch on Od. 1, 124, it is in H. everywhere the *principal meal* ; according to Voss on h. Cer. 128, it is prop. *an early meal*, which as a feast indeed might last till towards evening ; in H. it seems every where to signify *meal* in general.)

* δειράς, άδος, ἡ (δειρή), *the ridge of a mountain, a mountain-chain*, h. Ap. 281.

δειρή, ἡ, *the neck*, of men and beasts, 3, 396.

δειροτομέω (τέμνω), fut. ήσω, *to cut off the neck, to behead*, 21, 89. Od. 22, 349.

δείρας, see δέρω.

Δεισήνωρ, ορος, ὁ, a Lycian, 17, 217.

(δείω), assumed th. of δείδω.

δέκα, oi, αἰ, τά, indecl. *ten* (from δάκω, δείκνυμι, the ten fingers), often for an indefinite number.

δεκάκις, adv. *ten times*, 9, 379.†

δεκάς, άδος, ἡ, *a decade. the number ten*, 2, 126. Od. 16, 245.

δέκατος, η, ον (δέκα), *tenth* ; often as a round number, 1, 54.

δεκάχιλοι, αι, α, *ten thousand* (only in H.), 5, 860.†

δέκτης, ου, ὁ (δέχομαι), prop. a receiver ; then *a beggar*, Od. 4, 248.†

δέκτο, see δέχομαι.

* δέλτος, ἡ, *a writing-tablet, a table*, Batr. 2, in the plur.

* Δέλφειος, η, ον (Δελφοί), *Delphian*, βωμός, h. in Ap. 496 ; doubtful. Herm. conjectures αὐτίκ' ἄρ' ἀφνειός for αὐτὸς Δέλφειος.

δελφίν, see δελφίς.

* Δελφί́νιος, ὁ, the *Delphian*, appell. of Apollo, either from the name of the serpent slain by him, or because he, upon a dolphin, or changed into a dolphin, led the Cretan colony which emigrated to Delphi, h. in Ap. 493, see Paus. 1, 19, 1.

δελφίς, ῖνος, ὁ, more correctly δελφίν, *a dolphin* (see Buttm., Gram. § 41, note 1), 21, 22. Od. 12, 96.

* Δελφοί ῶν, οἱ, *Delphi*, a famous oracle in Phocis, first found h. 27, 14 ; in H. elsewhere Πυθώ, q. v.

δέμας, τό, defect. (δέμω), *the form of the body, the stature, a body, the external shape*, mly spoken of men with φυή, 1, 115; and with εἶδος, 24, 376; twice of animals, Od. 10, 240. 17, 307 ; and mly *body*, νεκρόν, Ba:r. 106. 2) As adv. like *instar, in form, in the likeness of.* δέμας πυρός, 'like fire, 11, 596. 13, 673. (In H. only in accus., e. g. μικρός, ἄριστος δέμας.)

δέμνιον, τό (δέμω), always in the plur., *a bedstead*, Od. 4, 297. 1, 277, and often; in Il. only 24, 644 ; and mly *a bed, a couch*.

δέμω, aor. 1 ἔδειμα, perf. pass. δέδμημαι, aor. 1 mid. ἐδειμάμην, 1) *to build, to construct* : with accus. πύργον, τεῖχος, ἔρκος ἀλωῆς, h. Merc. 87. θάλαμοι πλησίοι ἀλλήλων δεδμημένοι. 6, 245. 249. 2) Mid. *to build for oneself*, οἴκους, Od. 6, 9 (the imperf. only Od. 23, 192 ; pres. h. Merc. 87).

δενδίλλω, only partcp. to wink with the eyes: accord. to the Schol. to give to understand by a side look ; mly *to give the wink*, εἴς τινα, 9, 180.†

δένδρεον, τό, Ion. for δένδρον, *a tree*; in H. always the Ion. form (δενδρέῳ, δενδρέων, 3, 152. Od. 19, 520, are disyllabic).

δενδρήεις, εσσα, εν (δένδρον), *wooded, woody, covered with trees*, *Od. 1, 51. h. Ap. 221.

Δεξαμένη, ἡ, daughter of Nereus and Doris, 18, 44 (on the contrary, δεξαμενή, *the fish-pool*).

Δεξιάδης, ου, ὁ, son of Dexias = Iphinous, 7, 15.

* δεξίαομαι, depon. mid. (δεξιά), *to welcome with the right hand*, h. 5, 16.

δεξιή, ἡ (sc. χείρ, origin. fem. of δεξιός), *the right hand*, as a mark of salutation or promise, 10, 542. 2) *a promise, an agreement, a contract*, 2, 341. 4, 159.

δεξιός, ή, όν, 1) *right, on the right hand* ; μαζός, the right breast, 4, 481 ; ὦμος, Od. ; ἐπὶ δεξιά, *on the right, to the right*, opposed to ἐπ' ἀριστερά, 7, 238. 2) *propitious, auspicious, lucky*, chiefly spoken of the flight of birds and of other omens in divination. To the Greek diviner, who faced the north, auspicious omens came on the right from the east, inauspicious on the left from the west, 12, 239; hence ὄρνις δεξιός = αἴσιος, 13. 821. Od. 15, 160 ; hence ἐνδέξιος, ἐπιδέξιος· According to Buttm., Lex. p. 291, it never signifies in H. *ingenious, dexterous*. (δεξιός, from δέκω, related to δέχομαι and δείκνυμι.)

δεξιόφιν, adv. (δεξιός), *ἐπὶ δεξιόφιν*, *on the right, at the right*, 13, 308.†

δεξιτερός, ἡ, όν, poet. (lengthened from δεξιός), Ep. dat. δεξιτερῆφι, *at* or *on the right*. δεξιτερῇ χείρ, 7, 108. Od. 1, 121; and δεξιτερή alone, the right hand, 1, 501.

δέξο, see δέχομαι.

δέος, ους, τό Ep. δεῖος, of which only gen. δείους (δείω), *fear, alarm*, often with χλωρόν, ἀκήριον. 2) *cause of fear.* οὔ τοι ἔπι δέος, thou hast no cause of fear, i. e., thou hast nothing here to fear (cf. Nägelsbach), 1, 515; and with infin. σοὶ οὐ δέος ἔστ' ἀπολέσθαι, 12, 246.

δέπας, αος, τό. plur. nom. δέπα, dat. plur. δεπάεσσι, δέπασσιν. *a goblet, a cup*, mly of gold, or silver with a golden rim, Od. 15, 116. Also connected with ἀμφικύπελλον, q. v. Mly it is a drinking-cup.

Δέρκομαι. 103 Δέχομαι.

yet sometimes a larger cup in which the mixing took place, 11, 632.

δέρκομαι. depon. iterat. imperf. δερκέσκετο, perf. δέδορκα, aor. 2 έδρακον, 1) *to look, to see, to look on;* often άμϕὺ δερκομένου ἐπὶ χθονί, so long as I see the light on the earth, i. e., as long as I live, 1, 88; δεινόν, to look terribly. The perf. with pres. signif. πῦρ ὀϕθαλμοῖσι δεδορκώς, flashing fire from the eyes, Od. 19, 446. 2) Trans. *to see, to perceive, to behold,* with accus. 14, 141.

δέρμα, ατος, τό (δέρω), *the pelt, the skin, a hide,* mly of beasts, once of men, 16, 341. 2) a prepared skin, *leather, a skin-bottle,* Od. 2, 291.

δερμάτινος, η, ον, *leathern,* τροπαί, *Od. 4, 782. 8, 53.

δέρον, for ἔδερον, see δέρω.

δέρτρον, τό (δέρω), *the peritoneum* or *omentum,* a membrane covering the bowels. δέρτρον ἔσω δύνειν, i. e. εἰς δέρτρον. to penetrate to the caul, spoken of the vultures of Tityus, Od. 11, 579.†

δέρω, aor. 1 ἔδειρα, *to draw off the skin, to flay,* with accus. βοῦν, 2, 422; μῆλα, Od. 10, 533.

δέσμα, ατος, τό, poet. for δεσμός (δέω), only in the plur. δέσματα, *bonds, fetters,* Od. 1, 204. 8, 278. 2) the band with which the hair of the higher classes of women was confined, *a fillet,* 22, 468.

* **δεσμεύω** (δέσμη), *to bind, to fetter,* 6, 17.

δεσμός, ὁ (δέω), in the plur. δεσμοί, Il. and Od.; also δεσμά, τά, h. Ap. 129. h. 7, 13; *fetter, bond,* 5, 391; of a horse: *the halter,* 6, 507; *a cable,* Od. 13, 100; *the door-thong,* Od. 21, 241.

* **δεσπόζω** (related to δεσμός), fut. σω, *to rule, to command,* τινός, h. Cer. 366.

δέσποινα, ἡ, *a female sovereign, a mistress,* also ἄλοχος, γυνὴ δέσποινα, *Od. 3, 403. 7, 347.

* **δεσπόσυνος,** ον, *belonging to the master of a family,* λέχος. h. Cer. 144.

δετή, ἡ (prop. fem. from δετός, sc. λαμπάς), a bundle of pine-sticks tied together, *a torch,* 11, 554. 17, 663.

δευήσεσθαι, see δεύω.

Δευκαλίδης, ον, ὁ, Ep. for Δευκαλιωνίδης, son of Deucalion=*Idomeneus,* 12, 117.

Δευκαλίων, ωνος, ὁ, son of Minos and Pasiphaë, father of Idomeneus, an Argonaut and Calydonian hunter, 13, 452. Ulysses (Odysseus) names him to Penelope as his father, Od. 19, 180. 2) a Trojan, slain by Achilles, 20, 478.

δεῦρο, adv. of place, *here, hither,* mly with verbs of motion, 1, 153. Od. 4, 384. 2) As a particle of exhortation, *up! on! here! δεῦρ' ἄγε,* come on! δεῦρ' ἴθι. come hither! 3, 130. (With the plur. δεῦτε.) Instead of δεῦρο, 3, 240, Spitzner and Dindorf have adopted δεύρω, after Herodian and the Schol. Cf. Thiersch, Gram. § 147, 5.

δεύτατος, η, ον, *the last,* superl. of δεύτερος, 19, 51. Od. 1, 286.

δεῦτε, adv. *here, hither,* etc., like δεῦρο, always with the plur.: δεῦτε ϕίλοι, δεῦτ' ἄγετε, 7, 350; ἴομεν, 14, 128. (From δεῦρ' ἴτε, contr. : so Buttm.)

δεύτερος, η, ον, superl. δεύτατος, η, ον, *the second,* 1) In respect of rank and order, spoken of one inferior in combat, 23, 265. 498. 2) In respect to time: δεύτερος ἦλθε, he came as the second, i. e., *later,* 10, 368; with gen. ἐμεῖο δεύτερος, later than I, after me, outliving me, 23, 248. The neut. often as adv. δεύτερον, for the second time, *secondly, again,* connected with αὖ and αὖτε, and plur. δεύτερα, 23, 538.

I) **δεύω** (only pres. and imperf. act. and pass.), *to moisten, to wet,* with accus. γαῖαν, παρειάς, 13, 655. Od. 8, 522; dat. δάκρυσι, with tears, Od. 7, 260. Pass. Il. 9, 570. 2) *to fill,* ἄγγεα, the vessels, 2, 471.

II) **δεύω,** prop. δεϜ, with digamma, Ep. for δέω (cf. δεῖ), of the act. only aor. 1 ἐδεύησε and δήσε for ἐδέησε, *to want, to fail.* ἐδεύησεν δ' οἰήιον ἄκρον ἱκέσθαι, it failed to reach the extremity of the rudder, Od. 9, 540. (483.) δῆσεν ἐμεῖο (without digamma), he lacked me, 18, 100. More mly, 2) Mid. δεύομαι, fut. δευήσομαι, *to want, to be destitute, to need,* τινός, 2, 128. Od. 6, 192; θυμοῦ, to be deprived of life, 3, 294. οὐ δευέσθαι πολέμοιο, not to lack battle, i. e., to have enough to combat, [οὐδαμοῦ οἶμαι ἀπολεμήτους εἶναι Eust.] 13, 310. Others, as Heyne, explain it without necessity, 'to be inferior' ['no where so much to need battle, i. e., aid, as upon the left;' so Clarke and Bothe]. 3) *to be wanting* in a thing, *to be inferior.* μάχης πολλὸν ἐδεύεο, thou wert far inferior in battle, with gen. of person. ἄλλα πάντα δεύεαι Ἀργείων, in all other things thou art inferior to the Argives, 23, 484.

δέχαται, see δέχομαι.

δέχθαι, see δέχομαι.

δέχομαι, depon. mid. fut. δέξομαι, aor. 1 ἐδεξάμην, perf. δέδεγμαι, pluperf. ἐδεδέγμην or ἐδέγμην, partcp. δεδεγμένος or δέγμενος, fut. 3 δεδέξομαι=δέξομαι, Ep. sync. aor. ἐδέγμην; from this δέκατο and δέκτο. imper. δέξο, infin. δέχθαι. Thiersch, § 218, 59, 60. Rost, Gram. p. 291, and Dial. 51. (Here belongs as an Ep. perf. δεδοκημένος from δέκομαι, 15, 730, watching, lurking.) 1) *to take, to receive, to accept,* what is presented, with accus. ἄποινα, δέπας, and in various regards. *a)* Spoken of the gods: ἱρά, to receive the victims, 2, 420. *b) to receive hospitably, to entertain,* τινά, 18, 331. Od. 19, 316. *c)* to receive as an infliction, *to bear, to suffer,* μῦθον, Od. 20, 271; κῆρα, to suffer fate, 18, 115. Mly παρά τινος, to receive from one, 24, 429; oftener τινός alone, 7, 400; and with dat. δέχεσθαί τι τινί, to take any thing from any one, 2, 186. Od. 15, 282; but χρυσὸν ἀνδρὸς ἐδέξατο, she received gold for her husband [i. e. she betrayed him], Od. 11,

Δεψέω. 104 Δηίφοβος.

327. 2) to receive, τινά, a) In a hostile sense, to await, to expect. In H. in this signif. only the perf. δέδεγμαι or δέγμαι, with pres. signif. and pluperf. as imperf. έδεδέγμην or έδέγμην, partcp. δεδεγμένος and δέγμενος, fut. δεδέξομαι; often with dat. instrum.: έγχεί, δουρί, τόξοισι: τόνδε—δεδέξομαι δουρί, 5, 238; spoken of a hunter standing at his station, 4, 107; also of the boar: ἀνδρῶν καὶ κυνῶν κολοσυρτὸν δέχαται, they await the tumult of the men and dogs, 12. 147. b) Mly to wait, to await, with ὁππότε, εἰσόκε, 2, 794. 10, 62; with accus. and infin. only Od. 9. 513. 12, 230. 3) Intrans. or pass. once to follow, like excipere: ὥς μοι δέχεται κακὸν ἐκ κακοῦ, thus one misfortune after another follows me, 19, 290.

δεψέω (δέφω), fut. ήσω, partcp. aor. 1 δεψήσας, prop. to prepare hides, to soften, κηρόν, Od. 12, 48.†

δέω, infin. pres. δεῖν, h 6. in Dion. 12, fut. δήσω, aor. ἔδησα and δῆσα, aor. 1 mid. ἐδησάμην, Ep. iterat. δησάσκετο, 24, 15, perf. pass. δέδεμαι, Ep. form δίδημι, from this δίδη, 11, 105. 1) to bind, to fetter, to fasten; τινὰ δεσμῷ, or ἐν δεσμῷ, to bind one with fetters, 10. 443. 5, 386. χαλκέῳ ἐν κεράμῳ δέδετο, he lay bound in a brazen prison, 5, 387; with ἐκ τινος, παρά τινι and τι, to fasten to any thing; metaph. πῶς ἂν ἐγώ σε δέοιμι, how could I bind thee, i. e. hold thee to thy word, Od. 8, 352 (Nitzsch, however, takes it in lit. signif.). 2) to restrain, to hinder; μένος καὶ χεῖρας δῆσαι, 11. 73; τινὰ κελεύθου, to hinder any one from a journey, Od. 4, 380. 469. II) to bind on any thing for oneself (sibi), ὑπὸ ποσσὶ πέδιλα, 2, 44; περί and παρά τι, 8, 26. 17, 290; ὅπλα ἀνὰ νῆα, Od. 2, 430.

δέω, aor. 1 δῆσα, see δεύω.

δή, adv. (prop. abbrev. from ἤδη), already, now, just, certainly, indeed. It is never found at the beginning of a clause, except in the Ep. constructions δὴ τότε, δὴ γάρ, but as subordinate gives strength to another word. The orig. signif. is 1) temporal, 1) already, just, now, spoken of the immediate present in distinction from the past or the future, καὶ δή, and now, 1, 161; δὴ νῦν, just now. Od. 2, 25; μὴ δή, ne jam, after verbs of fearing, 14, 44. 2) already, at last, still, in numbering, 2, 134. 24, 107; καὶ δή, and already, 1. 161. 15, 251; ὣς δή, as already, 17, 328; γὰρ δή, for already, 17, 546. 3) Esply is δή connected with adv. of time, to express that now something becomes a reality, as νῦν δή, now then, Ep. δὴ νῦν, esply in the apodosis τότε δή, then at last, or δὴ τότε, ὀψὲ δή; in the protasis ὅτε δή, ὁπότε δή, when now, etc. From this last use has arisen II) The determinative signif. [its conclusive and therefore exclusive force] by which δή defines precisely the degree and measure of an idea; just, exactly, only, now. 1) With verbs, esply with the imper. ἄγε δή, come then, 3, 411; φράζεσθον δή, consider only,

6, 306. Often with μή: μὴ δή—ἔλπεο, only do not hope [= huc tantum te rogo, ne—], 20, 200. 2) With adj. ὠκύμορος δή μοι ἔσσεαι, 18, 95; esply with superl. κράτιστοι δή, 1, 266. 3) With pronouns, it either marks the prominence of the word: ἐκεῖνος δή, he now [exclusion, he and no other]; or recalls a foregoing subject, τοῦπερ δὴ θυγάτηρ, his daughter now, 6, 398. 4) With indefinite pronouns, it heightens the indefiniteness: ἄλλοι δή, others, whoever they may be [whom you please], 1, 295. 5) With particles, a) just, exactly, now, a) With conjunctions: ὡς δή, ἵνα δή, that, that now: ὡς δή, that however [with ὄφελον, utinam]. Od. 1, 217. β) With particles of explanation: γὰρ δή, Ep. δὴ γάρ, mly with temporal signif; ὡς δή, mostly ironical, 1, 110. γ) ἀλλὰ δή, but now. δ) With interrogative particles [= modo, the speaker wishing that his question, if nothing else, may be answered. N.]: πῆ δή. 2, 339; ποῦ δή. b) certainly, truly, assuredly: ἦ δή, ἦ μάλα δή, καὶ δή, δὴ που, assuredly indeed; δὴ αὖτε, now again. which also by crasis form δηὖτε; incorrect therefore is δ' αὖτε, 1, 340. 7, 448.

δηθά=δήν, abbrev. δήθ', 2, 435; adv. long, a long time; δηθὰ μάλα, very long.

δηθύνω (δηθά), to delay, to loiter, to linger, 1, 27, and Od. 12, 121.

Δηϊκόων, ωντος, ὁ, son of Pergasus. a Trojan, slain by Agamemnon, 5, 534 (Ep. from Δηϊκάων for Δηϊκάωων, from δηΐς= δαΐς and κάω=κτείνω, slaying in battle).

Δηϊοπίτης. ου, ὁ, son of Priam, slain by Ulysses (Odysseus), 11, 420.

δήϊος, η, ον, Ion. for δάϊος (δαΐς), hostile. destructive, ἀνήρ, πόλεμος; πῦρ. consuming fire, 6, 331. 2) Subst. as enemy. 2, 544. (ἴ; sometimes disyllabic, ηι with synizesis, 2, 415. 544. cf. Spitzner Pros § 6, 5, d.) *II.

δηϊοτής, ῆτος, ἡ (δήϊος), the tumult of war, battle, contention; often Il. mly, slaughter, massacre, Od. 12, 257.

Δηΐοχος, ὁ, a Greek. 15, 341.

δηϊόω, contr. δῃόω (δήϊος), fut. δηώσω, aor. ἐδήωσα, aor pass. ἐδηώθην, prop. to treat in a hostile manner; to desolate, to destroy, to cut down, to slaughter, to tear in pieces, with accus. and dat. instrum. ἔγχεί, χαλκῷ· ἀλλήλων ἀμφὶ στήθεσσι ἀσπίδας, to destroy the shields about each other's breasts, 5, 452; ἔλαφον, to tear in pieces a stag, 16, 158; περί τινος, to fight about any one, 16, 195, (δηϊόω is often resolved like verbs in αω: δηϊόων, δηϊόωεν, etc.; the contr. form is found according to the necessity of the metre, δῃοῦν δῃώσουσιν.)

Δηΐπυλος, ὁ, a companion of Sthenelus, 5, 325.

Δηΐπυρος, ὁ, a Grecian hero, slain by Helenus, 13 576.

Δηΐφοβος, ὁ, son of Priam and Hecuba, one of the first heroes among the Trojans, 12, 94. 13, 413. In Od. 4, 276, he ap-

Δηλέομαι. 105 Δῆνεα.

companied Helen to the hollow horse, and according to a late tradition became her husband after the death of Paris.

δηλέομαι, depon. mid. (δαίω), fut. δηλήσομαι, aor. 1 ἐδηλησάμην, 1) to destroy, in opposition to ὀνινάναι, h. Merc. 541; to harm, to injure, with accus. ῥίνον, Od. 22, 278; Ἀχαιοὺς ὑπὲρ ὅρκια, to injure the Achaians contrary to the oaths, 4, 67. 72; to slay, Od. 11, 401. b) Of inanimate things : to destroy, to lay waste, καρπόν, 1, 156; ὅρκια ὑπερβασίῃ, to violate the oaths by transgression, 3, 107. 2) Intrans. to do injury, to do wrong, 14, 102; ὑπὲρ ὅρκια, to do wrong contrary to treaty, 4, 236. 271 (It is unnecessary to supply Ἀχαιούς, as 4, 67).

δήλημα, τό (δηλέομαι), injury, destruction, δηλήματα νηῶν, said of the winds (abstr. for concr.), Od. 12, 286.†

δηλήμων, ον, (δηλέομαι) gen. ονος, injurious, destructive, 24, 33. Subst. destroyer, βροτῶν δηλήμων, the destroyer of mortals, Od. 18, 85. 116.

*δηλητήρ, ῆρος, ὁ (δηλέομαι), destroyer, Ep. 15, 8.

*Δηλιάς, άδος, ἡ, Delian, belonging to the island Delos, h. Ap. 157.

Δῆλος, ἡ, Delos, a little island of the Aegean sea, which belonged to the Cyclades, with a town of the same name, birth-place of Apollo and Artemis, originally Ὀρτυγία, Od. 6, 162. h. in Ap. 16, 61 (prob. from δῆλος, visible, because Zeus caused it suddenly to emerge, when Latona was persecuted by Hērē).

δῆλος, η, ον (Ep. δέελος, (Il. 466.†), visible, plain, manifest, Od. 20, 333.†

Δημήτηρ, gen. τερος and τρος, accus. μήτερα and Δήμητρα (prob. γῆ and μήτηρ, mother earth). Dēmētēr (Ceres), daughter of Kronus and Gaea (Tellus), sister of Zeus, mother of Persephonē by Zeus, the symbol of productive fruitfulness; hence, the tutelary deity of agriculture, and through this of civil order and law, 5, 500. She had a temple in Pyrasus in Thessalia, 2, 696. She loved Iasion, and by him bore Plutus, Od. 5, 125. Esply h. in Cer.

δημιοεργός, όν, Ep. for δημιουργός (ἔργον), prop. working for the public benefit; holding a public office; profitable to the commonwealth. Thus H., Od. 17, 383, characterizes seers, physicians, architects, bards, and Od. 19, 135, public heralds ; metaph. ὀρθρος, the morning that calls forth the population to work, h. Merc. 98.

δήμιος, ον (δῆμος), relating to the people, pertaining to the commonwealth, public, οἶκος, Od. 20, 264; πρῆξις, a public affair, opposed to ἰδίη, Od. 3, 82; αἰσυμνῆται, Od. 8, 259. δήμιόν τι ἀγορεύειν, to speak any thing for the public good, Od. 2, 32; the neut. plur. δήμια πίνειν, adv. to drink at the public cost, 17, 250. According to Nitzsch on Od. 1, 226, wine which stood as a common stock in the tent of the chief leader, cf. 9, 71.

δημιουργός, see δημιοεργός.

δημοβόρος, ον (βορά), devouring the people, i. e. that consumes the property of the people, βασιλεύς, 1, 231.†

δημογέρων, οντος, ὁ (γέρων), an elder, one who for age and birth is honoured by the people, 3, 149; [Död. considers it a sort of popular tribune, or counsellor] the prince himself, 11, 372. *II.

δημόθεν, adv. from the people, at the public expense, Od. 19, 197.†

Δημοκόων, ωντος, ὁ, son of Priam and of a female slave from Abydos, slain by Odysseus (Ulysses), 4, 499.

Δημολέων, οντος, ὁ, son of Antenor and Theanō, slain by Achilles, 20, 395.

Δημοπτόλεμος, ὁ, a suitor of Penelōpē, Od. 22, 242.

δῆμος, ὁ, 1) the people, a community, 2, 547. Od. 1, 237, governed by one king or by several chiefs. In the heroic age, every community or district was independent ; states, properly so called, did not exist; at the extent, smaller communities only attached themselves to a larger. Thus, among the Phaeaces there were twelve princes; Alcinous was the thirteenth. As divisions of the people, H. mentions tribes and families (φῦλα and φρῆτραι). Further, he distinguishes 1) kings (ἄνακτες, βασιλῆες), 2) the chief men (γέροντες), and 3) the free citizens (δῆμος), who were by no means proper subjects of the king, but only obeyed him when the public good required it. Hence δήμου ἀνήρ, a man of the people, 2, 198; and as adj. δῆμος ἰών, perhaps for δήμιος, a man of the people, 12, 213. 2) the country, the territory, which a people occupied, often with gen. ἐν δήμῳ Ἰθάκης, Λυκίης, Φαιήκων; metaph. Ὀνείρων, the land of dreams, Od. 24, 12. κατὰ δῆμων, in the land, Od. 4, 167 [also (3) the country opp. the city, Od. 11, 14, Κιμμερίων ἀνδρῶν δῆμός τε πόλις τε. Död.] (prob. from δέμω, culture; according to Rost from th. ΔΑΜ, δαμάω, the subject folk. And so Död. cf. δέδμητο δὲ λαὸς ὑπ' αὐτῷ).

δημός, ὁ, fat, grease (prop. of the caul), of beasts, Il. and Od.; and of men, 8, 380.

Δημοῦχος, ὁ, son of Philētōr, a Trojan slain by Achilles, 20, 457.

*Δημοφόων, ωντος, ὁ, Ep. for Δημοφῶν (from φάω), brightest of the people, cf. Etym. Mag.), son of Keleus and Metanira, whom Dēmētēr educated in Eleusis, h. in Cer. 234.

δήν (related to δή), long, a long time οὐδὲ δὴν ἦν, he lived not long. 6, 131 (before the δ the vowel always becomes long).

δηναιός, ή, όν (δήν), long-lasting, long-lived, 5, 407.†

δῆνεα, τά (related to δάω), resolutions,

F 5

Δήποτε. 106 Διακλάω.

purposes, designs, thoughts; ήπια, gentle thoughts, 4, 361 ; in a bad signif., artifices, plans, wiles, όλοφώϊα, Od. 10, 289 (Hesych. assumes τὸ δῆνος as sing.).

δήποτε, δήπου, in H. only separated see δή.

δηριάομαι, depon. mid. poet. (δῆρις), pres. infin. δηριάασθαι, Ep. for δηριάσθαι, imperf. 3 plur. δηριόωντο, Ep. for έδηριώντο (also aor. from δηρίομαι), to contend, to fight, with arms, Od. 8, 78; περὶ νεκροῦ, about a dead body, 17, 134; with words : άμφί τινι, 12, 421.

δηρίομαι, depon. aor. 1 mid. δηρϊσάμην, and aor. pass. εδηρίνθην, only in aor. In H. to contend, to fight, δηρίσαντο επέεσσι, Od. 8, 76.† τὼ περὶ Κεβριόναο δ,ρινθήτην, they fought about Kebriones, 16, 756.†

δῆρις, ιος, ή, contention, fighting, combat, battle, 17, 158. Od. 24, 515.

δηρός, ή, όν (δήν) = δηναιός, long, longlived. δηρὸν χρόνον, a long time, 14, 206. h. Cer. 282; the neut. δηρόν as adv. long, ἐπὶ δηρόν, for a long time, 9, 415.

δήσε. Ep. for ἔδησε from δέω, but also for έδησε from δέω, to want, see δεύω.

δήω, Ep. fut. without the tense characteristic, from ΔΑΩ, there occur δήεις, δήομεν, δήετε, I shall find; with accus. οὐκέτι δήετε τέκμωρ Ἰλίου, you will not accomplish the destruction of Troy, 9, 418. 685 ; άλσος, Od. 6, 291. (According to others, pres. with fut. signif.)

*Δηώ, οῦς, ἡ, a name of Deméter (Ceres), h. in Cer. 492. (The deriv. uncertain; prob. from δήω, to find; see Spanhem. Call. in Cer. 133.)

Δία, see Ζεύς.

Δία, ἡ, the island Naxos, near Crete: ἐν Δίῃ, Od. 11, 325. It was called divine, because it was sacred to Dionysus (Bacchus.) See 'Αριάδνη.

διά, 1) Prepos. with gen. and dat., ground signif. through. 1) With gen. α) Of place : a) To indicate a motion which goes through an object and out again, διά ὤμου ἦλθεν ἔγχος, through the shoulder. ἔθυσεν διὰ προμάχων, 17, 281. For greater exactness of idea, H. connects διά with ἐκ and πρό, see διέκ and διαπρό. β) Of motion in place, without the connected idea of emerging : through, διὰ νήσου ἰών, Od. 12, 335. b) Of the manner, prop. post-Homeric; only ἐπρεπε καὶ διὰ πάντων, before all, 12, 104. 2) With accus. a) Of place, to denote extension through an object; only poet. διά δώματα, διὰ ρήσσας, 11. 6) Of time, to indicate extension through a period : διά νύκτα, through the night [by night], 2, 57 [in some passages, as here, the two ideas of time and place are combined, see Passow]. c) Of cause, means, etc. a) The cause : through, on account of, δι' ἀτασθαλίας, Od. 23, 67. β) The means : through, διὰ μαντοσύνην, 1, 72; Ἀθηναίης διὰ βουλάς, 15, 71. II) Adv. without case : through, esply in the compounds διαπρό, διάκ. q. v. III) In compos. it

denotes 1) A motion through anything. 2) Completion and intenseness : very, entirely. 3) Separation [often like diin English]: apart, asunder. 4) Mutual operation : with one another. 5) A mingling in colours and materials : διάλευκος, mixed with white (διά prop.`` ``, but sometimes long in the beginning of a verse, 3, 357. 4, 135. 11, 436).

διαβαίνω (βαίνω), aor. 2 διέβην, partcp. διαβάς, 1) Intrans. to place the feet apart, to stride, εὖ διαβάς ['parting wide his feet for vantage' sake. Cp.], 12, 458. 2) Trans. to go through, to cross, to pass over; with accus. τάφρον, to cross the ditch, 10, 198 ; and absol. εἰς Ἤλιδα, to cross to Elis, Od. 4, 635.

διαγιγνώσκω (γιγνώσκω), aor. 2 infin. διαγνῶναι, to distinguish, to discriminate, to inspect closely, τινά, 7, 424 ; ὀστέα, 23, 240. *11.

διαγλάφω (γλάφω), aor. 1 partcp. διαγλάψας, to dig out, to hollow out, εὐνάς, Od. 4, 438.†

διάγω (ἄγω), aor. 2 διήγαγον, 1) to conduct through, to transport, τινά (by ship), Od. 20, 187.† 2) to spend a period of time, to live, αἰῶνα, h. 19, 7.

διαδαίομαι (δαίω), Ion. to divide, to distribute, διὰ ταῦρα δασάσκετο, 9, 333;† see διαδατέομαι.

διαδάπτω (δάπτω), aor. 1 ἔδαψα, to tear in pieces, to lacerate, χρόα, *5, 858. 21, 398.

διαδατέομαι, Ep. (δατέομαι), to distribute, διὰ κτῆσιν δατέοντο, 5, 158 †

διαδέρκομαι, depon. (δέρκομαι), aor. 2 διέδρακον, to look through, to see through, with accus. 14, 344.†

διαδηλέομαι, depon. mid. (δηλέομαι), to injure severely, to lacerate. ὀλίγου σε κύνες διεδηλήσαντο, the dogs had nearly torn thee to pieces, Od. 14, 37.†

διδει, see διάημι.

διαείδομαι, Ep. mid. (εἴδω), fut. διαείσομαι, 1) to let be seen, to show clearly, ἀρετήν, 8, 535. 2) to show oneself clearly, ἀρετῆ διαείδεται, 13, 277.

διαειπεῖν, poet. for διειπεῖν, q. v.

διάημι, Ep. (ἄημι), from the form διάω, 3 sing. imperf. διάει, to blow through, with accus. *Od. 5, 478. 19, 440.

διαθειόω (θειόω), to fumigate with brimstone, δῶμα, Od. 22, 494.†

διαθρύπτω (θρύπτω), aor. 2 pass. διετρύφην, to break in pieces. ξίφος διατρυφέν, 3, 363.†

διαίνω, aor. 1 ἐδίηνα, to moisten, to wet, with accus , 21, 202. 22, 495. Pass. διαίνετο ἄξων, *13, 30.

διαιρέω (αἱρέω), aor. 2 διεῖλον, poet. δίελον, to take apart, to separate, with accus. only in tmesis, 20, 280.†

διακεάζω (κεάζω), aor. ἐκέασα, poet. σσ. to split apart, to split, ξύλα, in tmesis, Od. 15, 322.†

διακείρω (κείρω), aor. 1 infin. διακέρσαι, prop. to cut apart or in pieces; metaph. to destroy, to render void, ἔπος, 8, 8.†

διακλάω (κλάω), aor. 1 διέκλασα, poet.

Διακοιοανέω. 107 Διαπρύσιον.

σσ, *to break in pieces*, with accus. τόξον, 5, 216.†

διακοιρανέω, formerly πολέας διακοιρανέοντο, 4, 230; now, more correctly, πολέας διὰ κοιρανέοντα, see κοιρανέω.

διακοσμέω (κοσμέω), fut. ήσω, *to arrange separately, to divide, to place*, τινά, 2, 476; διακοσμηθῆναι ἐς δεκάδας, to be divided into decades, 2, 126. διὰ τρίχα κοσμηθέντες, distributed into three parts, 2, 665. 2) Mid. *to arrange throughout, to adorn*, with accus. μέγαρον, Od. 22, 457.

διακριδόν, adv. (διακρίνω), *distinctly, clearly, decidedly*, ἄριστος, 12, 103. 15, 108.

διακρίνω (κρίνω), fut. Ep. διακρινέω, Ior διακρινῶ, aor διέκρῖνα, aor. 1 pass. διεκρίθην and διεκρίνθην, optat. 2 plur. διακρινθεῖτε, infin. Ep. διακρινθήμεναι, partcp. διακρινθείς, 1) *to separate from one another, to put asunder*, with accus. αἰπόλια, 2, 475; *to part*, spoken esply of combatants: μένος ἀνδρῶν, 2, 387. cf. 7, 292; metaph. *to distinguish*, σῆμα, Od. 8, 195; hence pass. with fut. infin. mid., Od. 18, 149, *to be separated, to separate*, 2, 815; of combatants: *to separate, to withdraw from each other*, i. e. to end the contest, to become reconciled, 3, 98. οὐ γὰρ ἀναιμωτί γε διακρινέεσθαι οἴω μνηστῆρας καὶ κείνον, I do not think the suitors and he will separate without blood, Od. 18, 149. 20, 180.

διάκτορος, ὁ, *a messenger*, appell. of Hermês as messenger of the gods (in the Iliad this office is commonly discharged by Iris, cf. 2, 786), connected with Ἀργειφόντης, 2, 103; with Ἑρμῆς, Od. 12, 390. 15, 319; and often alone in the hymns. (Mly derived from διάγω: ὃς διάγει τὰς ἀγγελίας τῶν θεῶν, cf. Eustath. on 2, 103. Buttin. Lex., p. 230, derives it from an old theme διάκω, διώκω, intrans. *I run*, so that it is = διάκονος. Nitzsch, on Od. 1, 84, prefers the derivation from διάγω, and explains it: *the conductor:* [and so Död. cf. Ἑρμ. ἡγεμόνιος, σομπαῖος, ἐνόδιος, &c.: *qui erranti comiter monstrat viam*. His conducting the shades across the Styx is post-Homeric.]

διαλέγομαι (λέγω), Ep. aor. 1 διελεξάμην, *to separate* (in thought), *to revolve, to ponder any thing, to reflect upon*. τίη μοι ταῦτα διελέξατο θυμός; why did my heart ponder these things? *11, 407. 17, 97.

διαμάω (ἀμάω), fut. ήσω, *to mow through, to cut through*, with accus., χιτῶνα [ripp'd wide his vest. Cp.], *3, 359. 7, 253.

διαμελειστί, adv. (μελεϊστί), *limb from limb, piecemeal*, τάμνειν, *Od. 9, 291. 18, 339.

διαμετρέω (μετρέω), *to measure through, to measure off*, χῶρον, 3, 315.†

διαμετρητός, ή, όν (μετρέω), *measured off, measured*, χῶρος, 3, 344.†

*διαμήδομαι = μήδομαι, Ep. 4, 12, doubtf.

διαμοιράομαι, dep. mid. (μοιράω), *to divide into parts, to separate*. ἔπταχα πάντα διεμοιρᾶτο, divided them all into seven pieces, Od. 14, 434;† in the following, τὴν ἴαν—θῆκεν, supply μοῖραν.

διαμπερές, adv. 1) *through and through, entirely through*, 5, 284. Od. 5, 480; with gen. 12, 429. 20, 362. κλήρῳ νῦν πεπάλαχθε διαμπερές, cast lots throughout, 7, 171. 2) Spoken of time: *continually, unceasingly*. αἰεὶ διαμπερές, ἤματα πάντα διαμπερές, 15, 70. 16, 99 (from διά, ἀνά, and πέρας, with epenthetic μ).

διάνδιχα, adv. (διά, ἀνά, δίχα), *in two ways, in two parts*; μερμηρίζειν, to be of two opinions, to hesitate, to ponder anxiously, 1, 198. 13, 455; with ἤ, ἤ following: σοὶ διάνδιχα δῶκε, he hath given to you in a divided manner, i. e. but one of two things, 9, 37. Schol. διρρημένως.

διανύω (ἀνύω), fut. ὔσω, aor. διήνυσα, *to complete entirely, to finish*; ὁδόν, to finish a way or journey, h. Cer. 380. κακότητα διήνυσεν ἀγορεύων, he finished narrating his sufferings, i. e. he recounted his sufferings to the end, *Od. 17, 517.†

διαπείρω (πείρω), *to pierce through*, 16, 405.† in tmesis.

διαπέρθω (πέρθω), fut. διαπέρσω, aor. 1 διέπερσα, aor. 2 διέπραθον, infin. διαπραθεῖν, Ep. for διεπραθεῖν, aor. 2 mid. διεπραθόμην, *to destroy utterly, to lay waste, to ravage*, with accus. πόλιν, ἄστυ. 2) Mid. only aor. 2, *to perish*, Od. 15, 384.

διαπέταμαι, depon. mid. (πέταμαι), aor. 2 διεπτάμην, *to fly through*, spoken of missiles, 5, 99; absol. *to fly away*, 15, 83. Od. 1, 320.

*διαπλέκω, (πλέκω), fut. ξω, *to interweave, to entangle, to weave together*, h. in Merc. 80.

διαπλήσσω (πλήσσω), *to break in pieces, to split*, with accus. δρῦς, 23, 120.† Thus Wolf; where others read διαρρήσσοντες or διαπλίσσοντες.

διαπορθέω, poet. = διαπέρθω, from which partcp. aor. 1 διαπορθήσας, 2, 691.†

διαπραθεῖν, see διαπέρθω.

*διαπρέπω (πρέπω), *to be prominent, to be visible*, h. Merc. 351.

διαπρήσσω (πρήσσω), Ion. for πράσσω), *to bring to an end, to accomplish, to finish*, with accus. κέλευθον, Od. 2, 213; also without κέλευθον, they marched through the plain, 2, 785; with partcp. ἤματα διήπρησσον πολεμίζων, I spent days in fighting, 9, 326. ἅπαντα οὔτι διαπρήξαιμι λέγων ἐμὰ κήδεα, if I were to recount to you my sufferings for a year, I should not get through them all, Od. 14, 197.

διαπρό (πρό), *through and out, entirely through*, Wolf in the Il. διαπρό, in the Od. διὰ πρό, 5, 66. Od. 22, 295; cf. Spitzner, Excurs. XIV. on Il.

*διαπρύσιον, adv. *passing through*, spoken of place: πρῶν πεδίοιο διαπρύσιον τετυχηκώς, a hill extending far into the

F 6

*Διαπρύσιος.   Διαχέω.

plain, 17, 748. 2) *piercing, loud* of sound, ήΰσεν, 8, 227. h. Ven. 80; prop. neut. from
*διαπρύσιος, ον, *passing through, penetrating, piercing*, h. Ven. 19; κεραϊστής, h. Merc. 336 (prob. Æol. from περάω).
διαπτοιέω (πτοέω), *to frighten away, to scare*, with accus. γυναίκας, Od. 18, 340.†
*διαπυρπαλαμάω, see πυρπαλαμάω.
διαρπάζω (άρπάζω), *to tear in pieces, to lacerate*, spoken of wolves: μῆλα, 16, 355.
διαρραίω (ραίω), fut. σω, aor. 1 infin. διαρραίσαι, *to break in pieces entirely, to destroy utterly;* with accus. of inanimate things: πόλιν, οἶκον, *to destroy;* of men, 9, 78. 2) Mid. fut. διαρραίσομαι, with pass. signif. τάχα δ' ἅμμε διαρραίσεσθαι όἴω, quickly I think, we shall both be destroyed, 24, 355. (So the Schol. διαφθαρήσεσθαι ; Damm and Voss take the infin. fut. in an act. signif. and supply αυτόν.)
διαρρήγνυμι (ρήγνυμι), *to break through, to break in pieces;* with accus. only mid. διαρρήξασθαι έπάλξεις to break through the breastworks, 12, 308.†
*διαρρήδην, adv. (διαρρηθῆναι), *with clear words, distinctly*, h. Merc. 313.
διαρρίπτω (ρίπτω), *to throw through, to shoot through*, only Ep. imperf. 3 sing. διαρρίπτασκεν ὀιστόν, Od. 19, 575.†
διασεύω (σεύω), only 3 sing. Ep. aor. 2 mid. διέσσυτο, with accus. λαόν, to hurry through the people, 2, 450 ; often with gen. τάφροιο, through the ditch, 10, 194; spoken of missiles, with gen. στέρνοιο, 15, 542 ; ἐκ μεγάροιο, Od. 4, 37.
διασκεδάννυμι (σκεδάννυμι), fut. σκεδάσω (ᾷ), aor. διεσκέδασα, *to scatter*, with accus. δούρατα, Od. 5, 370; to destroy, νῆα, Od. 7, 275 ; metaph. ἀγλαΐας τινί, to dissipate one's arrogance, Od. 17, 244.
διασκίδνημι (σκίδνημι), poet. form from διασκεδάννυμι, *to scatter*, νέφεα, 5, 526.†
διασκοπιάομαι, depon. mid. (σκοπιάζω), *to look down around from an elevation, to watch, to observe*, with accus. έκαστα, *10, 388. 17, 252.
διασχίζω (σχίζω), aor. 1 διέσχισα, aor. 1 pass. διεσχίσθην, *to split asunder, to tear in pieces*, with accus. ίστία, Od. 9, 71. Pass. 16, 316.
διατάμνω, Ep. for διατέμνω, and aor. 2 διέταμον, *to cut through*, 17, 522. 618, in tmesis ; Ep. form διατμήγω.
διατελευτάω (τελευτάω), *to finish entirely*, to accomplish fully, with accus. 19, 90.†
*διατίθημι (τίθημι), aor. 1 διέθηκε, *to place apart, to put, to place, to lay*, θεμείλια. h. Ap. 254. 294.
διατινάσσω (τινάσσω), aor. 1 διετίναξα, *to shake apart, to dash in pieces*, with accus. σχεδίην, Od. 5, 363.† in tmesis.
διατμήγω (τμήγω), Ep. for διατέμνω, aor. 1 διέτμηξα, aor. 2 διέτμαγον, aor. 2 pass. διετμάγην, 1) *to cut through, to cut in pieces;* κηροίο τροχὸν τυτθά, Od. 12, 174 ; δόρυ χαλκῷ, Od. 8, 507 ; metaph.

νηχόμενός λαίτμα διέτμαγον, swimming I cut through the deep. Od. 7, 276. cf. 5, 409. 2) Mly, *to separate, to scatter*, 'Αχαιούς, 21, 3 ; νῆας, Od. 3, 291. Pass. 1) *to be cut in pieces, to be divided*. σανίδες διέτμαγεν, Ep. for διετμάγησαν, 12, 462. 2) *to separate, to scatter*, 16, 354 ; *to part*, 1. 531. 7, 302. cf. άρθμέω.
διατρέχω (τρέχω), aor. 2 διέδραμον, *to run through*, with accus. κέλευθα, ύδωρ, *Od. 3, 177. 5, 100.
διατρέω (τρέω), aor. 1 διέτρεσα, *to run away from fear, to scatter*, *11, 481. 486.
διατρίβω (τρίβω), aor. 1 διέτριψα, *to rub or bruise in pieces*, with accus. ρίζαν. 11. 847. 2) Spoken of time: prop. subaud. χρόνον, *to spend time*, and as intrans. *to linger, to delay*, τινός, about any thing: όδοίο, a journey, Od. 2, 404 ; hence, 3) *to procrastinate, to check, to hinder*, with accus. Od. 2, 265 ; χόλον, 4, 42 ; so μητρὸς γάμον, Od. 20, 341 ; with double accus. διατρίβει 'Αχαιούς γάμον, to put off the Achaians about the marriage, Od. 2, 204.
διάτριχα, adv. *in three ways, in three parts ;* Wolf always writes διὰ τρίχα, it is only in h. Cer. 86, that διάτριχα is found; cf. Spitz. on Il. 2, 655.
διατρύγιος, ον (τρύγη), όρχος, Od. 24, 342,† a vineyard whose grapes ripen at different times (διά), Eustath., or where grain is sown between the rows of vines. The first is correct.
διατρυφέν, see διαθρύπτω.
διαφαίνομαι (φαίνω), only mid. *to shine through, to be visible, to appear*, with gen. νεκύων, between the dead, 8, 491 ; spoken of a glowing body, *to sparkle, to shine brightly*, Od. 9, 379.
*διαφέρω (φέρω), only fut. mid. διοισομαι, *to bear apart;* mid. *to differ, to contend, to be at variance*, h. Merc. 255.†
διαφθείρω (φθείρω), fut. διαφθέρσω, perf. 2 διέφθορα, 1) *to destroy utterly, to desolate*, with accus. πόλιν, 13, 625. 2) The second perf. intrans. *to perish*, like perii : μαινόμενε — διέφθορας, thou art rushing to destruction, 15, 128. (Schol. διέφθαρσαι.)
διαφορέω (φορέω), a form of φέρω, *to disperse, to spread abroad*, κλέος, Od. 19, 333.†
διαφράζω (φράζω), only Ep. aor. 2 διεπέφραδον, *to speak clearly, to show distinctly*, τινί τι, 18, 9. Od. 6, 47.
διαφύσσω (φύσσω), aor. 1 διήφυσα, Ep. διάφυσσα, 1) Prop. *to draw through, to draw out* any thing from a vessel to the bottom, with accus. οἶνον, Od. 16, 110. 2) Metaph. *to pierce, to cut through, to lacerate*, cf. Virg. Æn. II. 600, *haurire;* διήφυσε σαρκός, he (the boar) tore the flesh, Od. 19. 450 ; so also in tmesis, διά τ' έντερα χαλκὸς ήφυσε, the brass [weapon] cut through the entrails, 13, 507.
διαχέω, Ep. διαχεύω (χέω), only aor. 1 3 plur. διέχευαν, *to pour out, to diffuse*. 2) In H. only : *to divide, to carve, to distribute*, spoken of slain victims, with accus. 7, 316. Od. 3, 456.

Διάω. 109 Διερός.

διάω, more correctly διαάω, see διάημι.
*διδάσκαλος, ό, ή, a teacher, a female teacher, h. Merc. 556.
διδάσκω (δάω), aor. 1 act. έδίδαξα, Ep. έδιδάσκησα, h. Cer. 144; perf. pass. δεδίδαγμαι, to teach, to instruct. a) With accus. of the thing: πάντα, 9, 442. b) With accus. of the pers. τινά, 11, 832. c) With double accus. τινά τι, to teach a man any thing, 23, 307. Od. 8, 481; for accus. the infin. όμως έργα έργάζεσθαι, to teach the maids to perform work, Od. 1, 384. 22, 422; hence, pass. to be instructed, to learn, τι πρός τινος, to learn any thing from any one, 11, 831; and partcp. with gen. διδασκόμενος πολέμοιο [a learner yet of martial feats. Cp.], 16, 811.
δίδημι. Ep. form, from δέω, to bind; from which, δίδη, 3 imperf. for έδίδη, 11, 105.†
διδοῖ, διδοῖσθα, see δίδωμι.
διδυμάων, ονος, ό (δίδυμος), a twinbrother, only in dual and plur. connected with παῖς, and alone, 5, 548.
δίδυμος, η, ov, double, twofold, αὐλοί, Od. 19, 227. 2) twins, in plur. 23, 641. (prob. from δίς)
δίδωμι, fut. δώσω, aor. 1 έδωκα, and δῶκα, only in indicat. sing. aor. 2 act. (έδων), only in plur. indicat. έδομεν. etc. and in the subj., optat., imperat., perf. pass. δέδομαι. H. has: 1) Also forms from διδόω, pres. διδοῖς and διδοῖσθα, 19, 270; (incorrectly διδοισθα,) διδοῖ, imperf. δίδου for έδίδου, and fut. διδώσομεν, Od. 13, 358; infin. διδώσειν, Od. 24, 314. 2) Forms with lengthened stem-vowel: pres. imperat. δίδωθι, Od. 3, 380; infin. διδοῦναι for διδόναι (not aor. 2, 24, 425. 3) The Iterat. forms of aor. 2, δόσκον, δόσκε, Od. 19, 76. 1) to give, to present, to bestow, τινί τι, 1, 123; in reference to the gods, to offer to devote, θεοῖσι έκατόμβας, 7, 450; spoken of the gods, to grant, to accord, εὖχος, νίκην, κῦδος, often of evils: to decree, to inflict, άλγεα, κήδεα, 1, 96. Od. 7, 242. b) With accus. the pers. τινά τινι, to give over, to deliver, νέκυν πυρί, κυσίν, 17, 127; τινά όδύνησιν, άχέεσσι, 5, 397; esply of parents, who give their daughters in marriage to a man: θυγατέρα άνδρί, 6, 192. 11, 226. c) An infin. is often added, which serves as a further limitation of the sentence: δῶκε τεύχεα 'Ερευθαλίωνι φορῆναι, he gave arms to Ereuthalion to bear, 7, 149; and with the infin. pass. πολεμόνδε φέρεσθαι, 11, 798. cf. 23, 183. 2) With accus. and infin. to give, to grant, to let, to permit, αὐτὸν πρηνέα δὸς πεσέειν, 1-t him fall prone, 6, 307. 3) Pass. only once: σύ τοι δέδοται πολεμήϊα έργα, the works of war are not accorded to thee, 5, 428.
δίε, see δίω.
διείργω, Ep. for διείργω (έέργω), to separate, to keep apart, with accus. τοὺς διέργον έπάλξιες, 12, 424.†
διάδραμον, see διατρέχω.

διειπον (εῖπον), a defect. aor. 2, of which occur only imper. δίειπε, infin. διαειπέμεν, Ep. for διειπεῖν, prop. to speak through, to finish speaking; then, to speak clearly, distinctly, with dat. of the person, 10, 425. διαειπέμεν άλλήλοισιν, to converse fully with each other, Od. 4, 215.
διείρομαι, poet, and Ion. (έρομαι), only pres. to question strictly, to interrogate strictly, τί, 1, 550; and τινά τι, any one about any thing, 15, 93. Od. 4, 292.
διέκ (διά, έκ), entirely, through; Wolf in the Il. correctly, διέκ, 15, 124; but in Od. δι' έκ. Od. 17, 61. 10, 388. cf. Spitzner Excurs. XVIII.
διελαύνω (έλαύνω), aor. 1 διήλασα, 1) Trans. to drive through, τί τινος; ίππους τάφροιο, 10, 564; to thrust through, έγχος λαπάρης, a spear through the loins, 16, 318; δόρυ άσπίδος, 13, 161. 2) Intrans. to pass through, to hurry through, with accus. όρη, h. Merc. 96.
διελθέμεν, see διέρχομαι.
δίεμαι, mid. (ΔΙΗΜΙ), like τίθεμαι, in H. there occur of the pres. 3 plur δίενται, subj. δίηται, δίωνται, optat. δίοιτο (cf. τίθοιτο), infin. δίεσθαι, 1) Intrans. to become terrified, to fly, spoken of horses : δίενται πεδίοιο, they fly through the plain, 23, 475; of lions: σταθμοῖο δίεσθαι, to let himself be driven from the enclosure, 12, 304. 2) Oftener trans. [as causative] to terrify, to chase away, to drive, with accus. 7, 197; θηλυς, 12, 276; ξεῖνον άπὸ μεγάροιο, Od. 20, 343; ίππους προτὶ άστυ, to drive the steeds to the city, 15, 681; spoken of a dog: κνώδαλον, ὅ, ττι δίοιτο, Od. 17, 317. (Rem. δίεμαι together with the above cited forms belongs to the act. ΔΙΗΜΙ, which has the trans. signif. to chase, to terrify, of which the 3 plur. imperf. ένδίεσαν still occurs. The mid. means either to let oneself be driven, or it has the signif. of the act. with a weak reflexive sense; δίω on the contrary is always intrans. and signifies to fear [but 11, 22, 251 τρὶς περὶ άστυ ... δίον, fled, with var. lect. δίες. [Död.].
διέξειμι (έξειμι), to pass through any thing. τῇ έμελλε διεξίμεναι πεδίονδε, there he was about to pass out into the plain, 6, 393.†
διεξερέομαι (έρέομαι, Ep. form, from εἴρομαι), to question closely, to scrutinize, τινά τι, 10, 432.†
διεπέφραδε, see διαφράζω.
διέπραθον, see διαπέρθω.
διέπτατο, see διαπέταμαι.
διέπω (έπω), impert. δίεπον and δίεπον, 1) to manage, to direct, to administer, τί, e. g. πόλεμον, to prosecute the war, 1, 166. Od. 12, 16. 2) to arrange, to put in order, to command, στρατόν, 2, 207; άνέρας σκηπανίῳ, to drive away the men with a staff, 24, 247.
διερέσσω (έρέσσω), aor. διήρεσα, poet. σα, to row through, χερσί, with the hands, *Od. 12, 444. 14, 351.
διερός, ή, όν, only twice in the Od. and a word of doubtful signif. The ancients

διέρχομαι. 110 **δικασπόλος.**

explained it, *wet, moist*; metaph. *fresh, lively, living.* (Eustath. after Aristarch. ζώς, σπουδαίος, and derived it from διαίνω); hence, διερὸς βροτός, a vigorous (living) mortal, Od. 6, 201. (Others read here δυερός from δύη, unhappy.) διερῷ ποδὶ φευγέμεν, to fly with swift foot, Od. 9, 43. Nitzsch on Od. 6, 201, takes as the prop. signif. *liquid, flowing, liquidus;* metaph. *active, moveable.* He construes the sentence thus : οὗτος ἀνήρ, ὅς κεν ἵκηται φέρων δηϊοτῆτα, οὐκ ἔστι διερὸς βρ. οὐδὲ γένηται, and paraphrases it, 'neither now nor ever shall that man move actively and well, who penetrates with hostile force into the land of the Phæaces.' Voss, 'there moves not yet a mortal man, nor shall there ever be one, who,' etc. Lehrs de Aristarch. stud. p. 59 [and so Död], derives διερός from δίεμαι (cf. στυγερός), and explains it, Od. 9, 43, by *fugax*; but Od. 6, 201, act. *fugalor.* '*Non est istε vir fugator homo, i. e. non is est, quem fugere opus sit.*'

διέρχομαι (ἔρχομαι), fut. διελεύσομαι, aor. 2 διῆλθον, infin. Ep. διελθέμεν, *to go through, to pass through, to traverse,* with accus. πῶΰ, the flock, 3, 198 ; ἄστυ, 6, 392 ; with gen. μεγάροιο, Od. 6, 304. 2) *to pass through, to pierce,* spoken of missiles, with gen. χροός, to pierce through the skin, 20, 100 ; absol. 23, 876. 3) Metaph. *to go over, to reflect upon,* μετὰ φρεσί τι, h. Ven. 277.

διέσσυτο, see διασεύω.

διέτμαγεν, see διατμήγω.

διέχω (ἔχω), aor. 2 διέσχον, only intrans. *to go through, to penetrate, to pierce,* to pass through a body and come forth on the opposite side, spoken of an arrow : διὰ δ' ἔπτατο ὀϊστός, ἀντικρὺ δὲ διέσχε, the arrow flew through and came forth on the other side, 5, 100 ; so also 11, 253. 20, 416. In like manner δι' ὤμου ἔγχος ἔσχεν, 13, 520.

δίζημαι, Ep. depon. mid., fut. διζήσομαι, Od. 16, 239 (from δίζω), *to seek out, to search for,* τινά, 4, 88; or with εἴπου. 2) *to seek to procure, to be at pains, to strive;* absol. ἕκαστος μνάσθω ἐδνοισιν διζήμενος, let each one woo, striving with presents, Od. 16, 391 ; νόστον τινί, to seek to accomplish one's return, Od. 23, 253 ; and with accus. alone, Od. 11, 100. (An Ion. word, with η retained.)

δίζυξ, υγος, ὁ, ἡ (ζυγόν), pl. δίζυγες, *harnessed in pairs,* or *two abreast,* ἵπποι, *5, 195. 10, 473.

δίζω, only imperf. δίζε, *to doubt, to be doubtful, to be uncertain,* with ἤ, 16, 713.†

διηκόσιοι, αι, α, Ep. for διακόσιοι, *two hundred,* Il.

διηνεκής, ές (διανέκω, i. q. διαφέρω), *continuous, uninterrupted, continuus,* the adj. spoken only of place : *far-extending, long, great,* ῥάβδοι, 12, 297 ; νῶτος. 7, 321 ; ῥίζαι διηνεκέες, 12, 134; ἀτραπιτοί, far-extending ways, Od. 13, 195 ; ἄλξ, the continuous or long furrow, Od. 18, 375. The adv. διηνεκέως with

ἀγορεύειν, *to recount at large,* in the natural order, Od. 7, 241. 12, 56.

διήρεσα, see διερέσσω.

διῆται, see δίεμαι.

διίημι (ἵημι), *to send through, to throw through, to discharge,* with gen. only in tmesis. διὰ δ' ἧκε σιδήρου, *Od. 21, 328.

διϊκνέομαι, depon. mid. (ἰκνέομαι), fut. διίξομαι, aor. διϊκόμην, *to go through;* only metaph. *to narrate at length,* πάντα, *9, 61. 19, 186.

Διϊπετής, ές (Διὸς, πίπτω), *fallen from Zeus,* i. e. *from the air, descending from heaven,* an appell. of rivers, because they are swollen by rain, 17, 263 ; and of Αἰγύπτος (Nile), Od. 4, 477. Later also οἰωνοί, h. in Ven. 4 (the second ι long).

δίϊστημι (ἵστημι), only intrans. aor. 2 διέστην, dual διαστήτην, and pres. mid. διίσταμαι, 1) *to open, to divide itself, to separate,* 12, 86 ; θάλασσα, the sea divided, 13, 29. 2) Metaph. *to differ, to quarrel.* ἐξ οὗ—διαστήτην ἐρίσαντε, they quarrelled and were alienated, *1, 6.

[**Δίφιλος** = Διΐ φίλος, thus Freytag and others, 1, 74. cf. Jahr. J. und K., p. 258]

δικάζω (δίκη), fut. δικάσω, aor. 1 ἐδίκασα, Ep. σσ, 1) Act. spoken of a judge : *to judge, to pronounce sentence, to decide* between two parties, with dat. τινί; Τρωσί τε καὶ Δαναοῖσι δικαζέτω, let him decide the controversy between the Trojans and Greeks, 8, 431. τοῖσιν (σκήπτροις) ἔπειτ' ἤϊσσον ἀμοιβηδὶς δὲ δίκαζον, with these they (γέροντες) arose and in turn delivered their sentence, 18, 506. ἐς μέσον ἀμφοτέροισι δικάσσατε, decide (ye princes), between the two, according to equity. Thus speaks Menelaus, 23, 574, when Antilochus, at the games of Patroclus, received the second prize, which was prop. due to Eumēlus. Menelaus now also lays claim to it, because Antilochus had artfully impeded his chariot, v. 579. εἰ δ' ἄγε, ἐγὼν αὐτὸς δικάσω, come on, said he at last, I myself will deliver a judgement; he then proposes that Antilochus should swear that he did not intentionally impede his chariot, Od. 11, 547; spoken of gods : κρυπτάδια, *to take secret resolutions,* 1, 542. 2) Mid. of the parties : *to go to law, to bring a matter before a court,* Od. 11, 545. 12, 440.

δίκαιος, η, ον (δίκη), *just, righteous, practising justice,* one who fulfils what right demands towards gods and men ; thus Chirōn, 11, 832 ; the Abii, 13, 6. 19, 181 ; on the other hand, the suitors are οὐδὲ δίκαιοι, Od. 2, 282, as also the Cyclōps, Od. 8, 575 (because they violated the universally sacred rites of hospitality). Compar. δικαιότερος, and superl. δικαιότατος.

δικαίως, adv. *justly, in a becoming manner,* μνάσθω, Od. 14, 90.†

δικασπόλος, ὁ (πολέω), *a judge, one who dispenses justice,* 1, 238 ; with ἀνήρ, Od. 11, 186.

Δικάρηνος. 111 Διόσκουροι.

*δικάρηνος, ον (κάρηνον), two-headed, Batr. 300.
*δικέρως, ωτος, ὁ (κέρας), two-horned, epith. of Pan, h. 18, 2.
δίκη, ἡ, 1) Originally, usage, custom, right, that which is introduced by custom, ἥν ἐστὶ δίκη βασιλήων, Od. 4, 691; θεῶν, Od. 19, 43. αὕτη δίκη ἐστὶ βροτῶν, this is the lot of mortals, Od. 11, 218; δμώων, Od. 14, 59. 2) right, justice, a cause or suit. δίκας ἐπιδευὲς ἔχειν, to lack justice, 19, 180. δίκην ἐξελαύνειν, to expel, to pervert justice, 16, 388; τίειν, Od. 14, 84. εἰπεῖν δίκην, to speak justice, to pronounce (spoken of a judge), 18, 508. b) In the plur. δίκαι, the administration of justice, 16, 542. Od. 11, 570. 3) cause, suit; διδόναι καὶ λαμβάνειν, to give and receive right, i. e. to submit a cause and receive a decision, h. Merc. 312.
δικλίς, ίδος, ἡ (κλίνω), bent double, double, folding, epith. of [two-leaved] doors, πύλαι, θύραι, 12, 455. Od. 2, 345.
δίκτυον, τό, a fishing-net, Od. 22, 386.†
δινέω and δινέω (δίνη), (δινεύω only pres. and imperf. iterat. δινεύεσκεν), from δινέω also aor. 1 pass. δινηθείς. 1) Act. to turn in a circle or vortex, to whirl, to move around, σόλον, 23, 840; ζεύγεα, to drive around. 18, 543; μοχλόν, to twirl the stake, Od. 9, 388. 2) Intrans. to turn oneself in a circle, spoken of dancers, 18, 494; metaph. to wander about, to move around, κατὰ μέσσον, 4, 541; παρὰ θῖνα, 24, 12; κατὰ οἶκον, Od. 19, 67; in like manner in pass. ὅσσα δινεύοθην, the eyes rolled around, 17, 680; to walk about, Od. 9, 153. ἐπὶ ἄστεα δινηθῆναι, Od. 16, 63.
δίνη, ἡ, a vortex, a whirlpool, in a river, *21, 11. 132.
δινήεις, εσσα, εν (δίνη), whirling, full of whirlpools, epith. of a river, 2, 877. Od. 11, 242.
δινωτός, ή, όν (δινόω), prop. turned in a circle; in H. turned round, formed round (well-turned), λέχεα, 3, 391; κλισίη, Od. 19, 56. ἀσπὶς ῥινοῖσι βοῶν καὶ νώροπι χαλκῷ δινωτή, a curved or arched shield made of bull's hide and glittering brass, 13, 407.
Διογενής. έος, ὁ, ἡ (γένος), sprung from Zeus, Jore-born, a common epith. of heroes and kings, because they receive their dignity from Zeus, the king of kings, cf. 1, 337. Od. 2, 352.
Διόθεν, adv. (Διός), from Zeus, according to the will of Zeus, 15, 489. 24, 194.
διοϊστεύω (διστεύω), fut. σω, to shoot an arrow through, τινός, any thing, Od. 19, 578. 21, 76. 97. 2) Absol. to shoot an arrow, Od. 12, 102.
διοίσομαι, κες διαφέρω.
δίοιτο, see δίεμαι.
*διοιχνέω (οἰχνέω), to go through, to walk about, h. 8, 10.
Διοκλῆς, ἧος, ὁ, 1) son of Orsilochus, grandson of Alpheus, father of Crethôn and Orsilochus, king of Pherœ in Messenia, 5, 542. Telemachus spent the night with him, Od. 3, 488; prob. a

vassal of Agamemnon, cf. 9, 151. 2) one of the princes of Eleusis, whom Dêmêtêr taught the ceremonies of the sacred service, h. Cer. 473 (but v. 153 Διόκλου).
διόλλυμι (ὄλλυμι), perf. II. διόλωλα, trans. to destroy utterly. 2) Mid. and perf. II. intrans. to perish utterly. οὐδ' ἔτι καλῶς οἶκος ἐμὸς διόλωλε, and my house is no longer ruined with any show of decency, i. e. formerly ye did it with moderation, but now without any regard to decency, Od. 2, 64.†
Διομήδη, ἡ, daughter of Phorbus, slave of Achilles, 9, 665.
Διομήδης, εος, ὁ, accus. η, and εα, son of Tydeus and Deipylê, husband of Ægialea, king of Argos, 5, 412. He took part in the second expedition against Thebes, 4, 406; and went to Troy with 80 ships, 2, 568. He was among the bravest in the army, and performed many exploits, which H. celebrates in the fifth book (Διομήδους ἀριστεία). He exchanged armour with the Lycian Glaucus, an hereditary guest, 6, 230. According to H., he returned happily to Argos, Od. 3, 180; according to later tradition, he directed his course, after his return, to lower Italy, where he built the town Arpi.
Δῖον, τό, a town in Eubœa, on the promontory Kenæon, 2, 538.
Διόνυσος, Ep. Διώνυσος, ὁ, son of Zeus and Semelê, god of wine and joy, 14, 325; h. 6, 56. H. was acquainted with the insult offered him in Thrace. Him, the drunken divinity, the Thracian Lycurgus would not tolerate, so that he fled to Thetis into the sea, 6, 132, seq. According to Od. 11, 325, the poet was also acquainted with his love for Ariadnê. (The word according to Voss, signifies the god of Nysa, or, according to Herm., Torculus, from διά and an old verb, from which ὄνυξ is derived.)
διοπτεύω (ὀπτεύω), to observe closely, to look about, 10, 451.†
διοπτήρ, ἧρος, ὁ, a spy, a scout, 10, 562.†
διορύσσω (ὀρύσσω), partcp. aor. 1 διορύξας, to dig through; τάφρον, to open a ditch or furrow, Od. 21, 120.†
δῖος, δῖα, δῖον (from Διὸς for δῖος), prop. sprung from Zeus, prob. 9, 538; then generally. divine, exalted, great, glorious, excellent. 1) As epith. of the gods, only in fem. δῖα θεά, glorious goddess, 10, 290; often δῖα θεάων, most exalted of goddesses, δῖα Χάρυβδις, Od. 12, 104. 2) Of distinguished men, not heroes merely, but others; noble, excellent, δῖος ὑφορβός, Od. 14, 48; of entire people: δῖοι Ἀχαιοί, δῖοι ἑταῖροι (Σαρπηδόνος), 5, 692. 3) Of noble animals: of horses; ἵππος, 8, 185. 4) Of inanimate things, as the earth, sea, cities (cf. ἱερός), since they are under the divine influence or derive their origin from gods, Od. 5, 261. 11, 16, 365.
Δῖος, ὁ, son of Priam, 24, 251.
*Διόσκουροι, οἱ, sons of Zeus, chiefly

Διοτρεφής. 112 Δμωή.

Cástōr and Polydeukēs (*Pollux*), only divided, Διὸς κούροι, h. 16, and 33, 1. 9.

Διοτρεφής, ές (τρέφω), *nourished by Zeus*, epith. of kings, see Διογενής, and of Scamandrus, 21, 223; ἄνθρωποι, Od. 5, 378.

δίπλαξ, ακος, ἡ, *laid double, laid twofold, in double layers*, δημός, 23, 243. 2) As subst. ἡ, *a double mantle*, a mantle that can be wrapt around double, cf. Od. 13, 224. Il. 10, 134; others say, a garment of double texture, the ground being white, the figures purple, or generally, of double texture, 3, 126. 22, 441; in full ἡ δίπλαξ χιτών, Od. 19, 241.

διπλόος, η, ον, contr. only in fem. διπλῆ, *double, two-fold*, θώρηξ, 4, 133; χλαῖνα, a double mantle, 10, 134. Od. 19, 226.

δίπτυχος, ον (πτύσσω), *double-folded, laid double*, λώπη, a double garment, Od. 13, 224. Also neut. plur. δίπτυχα ποιεῖν, *to lay double*, i. e. to lay the flesh or thigh pieces of the victims upon a layer of fat, and upon this to place still another, 1, 461. Od. 3, 458.

Δίς, ὁ, obs. nom. of the oblique cases Διός, Διί, Δία, of Ζεύς, q. v.

δίς, adv. *twice, double*, Od. 9, 491.†

δισθανής, ές (θανεῖν), *twice dead*, Od. 12, 22.†

δισκέω (δίσκος), *to cast the discus*. δίσκῳ ἐδίσκεον ἀλλήλοισιν, among one another, Od. 8, 188.†

δίσκος, ὁ (δικεῖν), *the discus, the quoit*, a round flat stone, with a hole and thong in the middle with which to hurl it. It was as early as H.'s time a common sport, to cast this, 2, 774. Od. 4, 626; he who cast it furthest receiving the prize, esply Od. 8, 186; δίσκου οὖρα, 23, 431. It is distinct from the σόλος, q. v.

δίσκουρα, τά (οὖρον), *the distance to which the discus was cast*. ἐς δίσκουρα λέλειπτο, he was left a quoit's cast behind, 23, 523.† cf. οὖρον.

*διττός, ἡ, όν (Ep. δισσός), *two-fold, double*, Batr. 61.

διφάω, *to seek out, to trace;* τήθεα, to seek oysters, spoken of a diver, 16, 747.†

δίφρος, ὁ (for διφόρος), 1) Prop. the *chariot-seat*, for two persons, the *double seat* in the war-chariot for the charioteer and the warrior, 5, 160. 23, 132. It was round, partly open for mounting, and hung upon straps, 5, 727; sometimes in the Il. it signifies the *war-chariot* itself; *a travelling-carriage* with two seats, Od. 3, 324. 2) Mly, *a seat*, a chair, and, as it seems, a low one, 3, 424. Od. 1, 717.

δίχα, adv. 1) *divided into two parts: double*. δίχα πάντα ἠρίθμεον, in two bands, Od. 10, 203. 2) Metaph. *of two sorts, in two ways, different*, 18, 510; θυμὸν ἔχειν, to have different sentiments, 20, 32; βάζειν, Od. 3, 127.

διχθά, adv. poet. for δίχα, *two-fold*, etc. τοὶ διχθὰ δεδαίαται, Od. 1, 23. διχθὰ κραδίη μέμονε, my heart is divided, 16, 435.

διχθάδιος, η, ον, *two-fold, double*, Κῆρες, 9, 411; neut. as adv. 14, 21.

*διχόμηνος, ον (μήν), *in the middle of the month*, at the time of the full moon, h. 32, 11.

δίψα, ἡ, *thirst*, 11, 642.

*διψαλέος, η, ον, poet. (δίψα), *thirsty*, Batr. 9.

διψάω (δίψα), *to thirst, to be thirsty*, Od. 11, 584.†

δίω, Ep. ground form of δείδω. From this occur: imperf. ἔδιον, Ep. δίον, 3 sing. δίε, perf. δέδια and δείδια, with pres. signif. pl δέδιμεν, δέδιτε, δεδίασι, imper. δέδιθι, infin. δεδίμεν, partcp. δεδιώς, 3 plur. pluperf. ἐδεδίσαν, and from this an imperf. δείδια, 18, 34. [24, 358.] 1) Intrans. *to fear, to be fearful*, περὶ γὰρ δίε νηυσὶν Ἀχαιῶν, he feared greatly for the ships of the Achaians, 9, 433. 11, 557; ποιμένι λαῶν, in like manner in the perf. δέδια = δείδοικα, see δείδω. 2) *to flee, to run*, περὶ ἄστυ, only at 22, 251 [with var. lect. δίες. Död.]. The middle forms δίενται, δίηται, etc. belong to δίεμαι, q. v.

διωθέω (ὠθέω), aor. διῶσα, *to push apart, to tear asunder*, 21, 244.†

διώκω (δίω), only pres. and imper. I) Active, *to cause to run;* hence, 1) *to drive away, to drive forward, to expel*, with accus. διώκω δ' οὔτιν' ἔγωγε, I drive no one forth, Od. 18, 409; ἅρμα καὶ ἵππους, 8, 439; sometimes absol. to drive, 23, 344. 424; spoken of a ship driven by winds or oars, Od. 5, 332; hence pass. ἡ δὲ νηῦς ἤλυθε, ῥίμφα διωκομένη, the ship approached rapidly propelled, Od. 13, 162. 2) *to pursue, to follow*, in opposition to φεύγω; τινά, 5, 672; absol. 5, 223. 8, 107; metaph. *to strive after, to seek to obtain*, ἀκίχητα, 17, 175. 3) Intrans. *to run swiftly, to hasten*, h. Merc. 350. cf. 5, 213. 23, 344. II) Mid. *to drive before me*, τινὰ πεδίοιο, through the plain, 21, 602; δόμοιο. Od. 18, 8.

Διώνη, ἡ, mother of Aphrodītē by Zeus, 5, 370. h. Ap 93. Accord. to Hes. Th. 353, daughter of Oceanus and Tethys; or, Apd. 1. 3, daughter of Uranus (Cœlus).

Διώνυσος, ὁ, Ep. for Διόνυσος.

Διώρης, εος, ὁ, 1) son of Amarynkeus, leader of the Epēi, slain before Troy by Peirus, 2, 622. 4, 518. 2) father of Automedōn companion in arms of Achilles, 17, 429.

δμηθείς, δμηθήτω, see δαμάω.

δμῆσις, ιος, ἡ (δαμάω), *the act of subduing, taming, curbing*. ἵππων ἐχέμεν δμῆσίν τε μένος τε, to hold the curbing and the force of steeds [l. e. to be able to restrain or to urge on against the enemy], 17, 476.

δμήτειρα, ἡ, *a female subduer, conqueror*, epith. of Night [*resistless conqueror of all*. Cp.], 14, 259;† prop. from *δμητήρ, ῆρος, ὁ, *a subduer, conqueror, victor*, h. 21, 5.

Δμήτωρ, ορος, ὁ, a fictitious character, feigned by Odysseus (Ulysses), son of Jason, king of Cyprus, Od. 17, 443.

δμωή, ἡ, prop. one subdued; hence, a

Δμώς. 113 Δόλοψ.

slave (female), spoken primarily of those free-born and reduced to slavery by war (distinct from δούλη), 18, 28. cf. 9, 658. b) Mly. a female slave, a maid-servant, only plur. also δμωαὶ γυναῖκες, 6, 323. They were employed at all kinds of house-work. They were obliged to clean the house, grind the corn, bake, weave, etc.

δμώς, ωός, ὁ (δαμάω), [from δμής (L.). Död. supposes a dialectic δομᾶν· δμώς by metath. fm δομητός, domitus,] prop. one conquered; hence, a slave, primarily by capture in war (see δοῦλος), Od. 1, 398. b) Mly, a slave, a servant, a bond-man, often in the plur. δμῶες ἄνδρες. The male slaves were obliged to do the heavier house-work, to split wood, to look to the cattle, to take care of the flocks, and to till the ground. In the Iliad only 19, 333; often in Od. Accord. to Nitzsch on Od. 4, 10, δμώς, a slave in general, whether born such, purchased, or taken in war.

δνοπαλίζω (δονέω), fut. ξω, to shake hither and thither, to hurl down, with accus. ἀνὴρ ἄνδρ' ἐδνοπάλιζεν, 4, 472; ῥάκεα, to fling (cast, wrap) his tatters round him, Od. 14, 512.

δνοφερός, ή, όν (δνόφος = νέφος), dusky, dark, black, νύξ, Od. 13, 269; ὕδωρ, 9, 15. 16, 4.

δοάσσατο, defect. aor. 1 mid., of which the 3 sing. subj. occurs δοάσσεται (for δοάσσηται), to appear, to seem. ὧδε δέ οἱ φρονέοντι δοάσσατο κέρδιον εἶναι, thus it appeared to him, on reflection, to be better, 13, 458. Od. 5, 474. ὡς ἄν τοι πλήμνη γε δοάσσεται ἄκρον ἱκέσθαι κύκλου, that the nave of the wheel may seem to graze the surface (the exterior part of the goal), 23, 339. (A shortened form fr. δοιάζω; it is according to Buttman, Lex., p. 212, more correctly derived from δέαται, it seems (with vowel-change of o for e) (q. v.).

δοιή, ή, doubt, uncertainty. ἐν δοιῇ (εἶναι), to be in doubt, 9, 230.†

δοιός, ή, όν, two-fold [in later poets (δ. γάμος, Cuil.), but in H. always two. Död.]. only dual δοιώ, and plur. δοιοί, αί, ά = δύω, two, both, 5, 7. 28. The neut. plur. δοιά as adv. in two ways, of two kinds, Od. 2, 46. The dual δοιώ is indecl., 24, 648.

δοκεύω (δέκομαι), to endeavour to seize, with accus., spoken of a dog following a wild animal: ἰσχία γλουτούς τε [close-threatening flank or haunch. Cp.], 8, 340; hence to watch, to lie in wait for, τινά, 13, 545. 16, 313; mly to observe. Ὠρίωνα, of the Great Bear, 18, 488. Od. 5, 274; δεδοκημένος, see δέχομαι.

δοκέω, aor. 1 ἐδόκησα Ep. for ἔδοξα, h. Merc. 208. 1) Trans. to be of opinion, to think, to believe. δοκέω νικήσειν Ἕκτορα, I believe I shall conquer Hector, 7, 192. 2) Intrans. to appear, to seem; with dat. of the pers. πέπλος οἱ δοκέει χαριέστατος εἶναι, 6, 90; ὥς μοι δοκεῖ εἶναι ἄριστα, as it seems to me to be best, 9, 103; more rarely with infin. fut. 6, 338; δόκησε σφίσι θυμὸς ὣς ἔμεναι, their feelings seemed to be such, Od. 10, 415.

δοκός, ή, a beam, esply of the roof, 17, 744. Od. 19, 38.

δόλιος, η, ον (δόλος), crafty, deceitful, sly, artful, spoken only of things, ἄρεα, τέχνη; κύκλος, the crafty circle which the hunters draw around a wild animal, *Od. 4, 792. Adv. δολίως, craftily, Batr. 93.

Δολίος, ὁ, a slave of Laertēs in Ithaca, father of Melanthius and Melanthô, Od. 4, 735.

δολίχαυλος, ον (αὐλός), having a long tube, long-tubed; αἰγανέη, a hunting-spear with a long tube into which the iron head of the spear was introduced, or simply long-shafted. Od. 9, 156.†

δολιχεγχής, ές (ἔγχος), armed with a long spear, Παίονες, 21, 155.†

δολιχήρετμος; ον (ἐρετμός), having long oars, long-oared, νῆες, Od. 1, 499; spoken of people: using long oars, sea-faring, maritime, Φαίηκες, *Od. 8, 191

δολιχόδειρος, ον, Ep. δουλιχόδειρος.

δολιχός, ή, όν, long, spoken of space: ἔγχεα, δόρυ. 2) Of time: long, lasting, νόσος, νύξ; of space and time together: πλόος, Od. 3, 169. Neut. as adv. δολιχόν, 10, 52.

*Δολιχός. ὁ (accord. to Voss l. c. to be written Δόλιχος), pr. n. of a prince in Eleusis, h. in Cer. 155.

δολιχόσκιος, ον (σκιά), long-shadowing, casting a long shadow, epith. of a spear, Il. and Od.

δολόεις, εσσα, εν, poet. (δόλος), crafty, cunning, insidious, artful, Κίρκη, Od. 9, 32; metaph. spoken of bonds, δέσματα, Od. 8, 281.

δολομήτης, ου, ὁ = δολόμητις, only in voc. δολομῆτα. 1, 540.†

δολόμητις, ι (μῆτις), full of artful plots, perfidious, artful, epith. of Ægisthus and Clytemnestra, *Od. 1, 300. 11, 422.

Δόλοπες, οἱ, see Δόλοψ.

Δολοπίων, ίονος. ὁ, father of Hypsēnōr, a Trojan, priest of Scamander, 5, 77. (fr. δόλοψ.)

δόλος, ὁ (δέλεαρ), 1) Prop. a bait, to take fish, Od. 12, 252; hence, any trap or stratagem, to take or deceive any one, spoken of the Trojan horse, Od. 8, 494; and of the net-work in which Hêphæstus confined Arês, Od. 8, 276. δόλος ξύλινος, a mouse-trap, Batr. 116. 2) In general: cunning, deceit, an artful plot, a stratagem, often in the plur. δόλοι, tricks, wiles, 6, 187.

*δολοφραδής. ές (φράζω), of crafty mind, cunning, h Merc. 282.

δολοφρονέων, ουσα, ον (φρονέω), devising deception, plotting fraud, crafty-minded, only partcp. Il. and Od.

δολοφροσύνη, ή, thought of treachery, meditated deception, fraud, plur. artifices, 19, 97. 112. h Merc. 361.

Δόλοψ, οπος, ὁ, 1) a Dolopian. The Dolopes were a powerful tribe in Thes-

Δόλων. 114 Δράγμα.

salia, on the river Enīpeus, 9, 484; later on Pindus. II) As masc. prop. nom. 1) son of Lampus, grandson of Laomedōn, a Trojan slain by Menelaus, 15, 525 seq. (δόλοψ, a spy.) 2) son of Clytius, a Greek, 11, 302.

Δόλων, ωνος, ὁ, son of Eumēdēs, a Trojan, who attempted to penetrate, as a spy, the camp of the Greeks, but was taken and slain by Diomēdēs and Odysseus (Ulysses), 10, 314 seq. (from δόλος, cunning).

δόμονδε, adv. *to one's home, homeward;* also ὅνδε δόμονδε, 16, 445; † often Od.

δόμος, ὁ (δέμω), prop. what is built, a *building;* hence, 1) *a house, dwelling,* spoken of the temples of the gods, 6, 242 ['Ερεχθῆος πυκινὸν δόμον, the firm house of Erectheus = the temple of Athēnē, Od. 7, 81, cf. Nitzsch ad loc.]; of the dwellings of men; also the compass of all the buildings, 6, 242; in this case mly plur.; also of brutes, as pens of sheep, and nests of bees, 12, 301. 169. 2) *a chamber, an apartment,* esply that of the men, 1, 255. 22, 291.

δονακεύς, ῆος, ὁ (δόναξ), *a reed-bed, a place full of rushes,* 18, 576. †

δόναξ, ακος, ὁ (δονέω), 1) *a reed, δόνακες,* reed-stalks, Od. 14, 474. h. Merc. 47. 2) that which is made of reed, *an arrow,* 11, 584.

δονέω, aor. 1 ἐδόνησα, fut. mid. δονήσεται, *to put in motion, to agitate, to drive hither and thither,* with accus. spoken of the wind which agitates the trees, 17, 55; and drives the clouds, 12, 157; of the gad-fly: οἶστρος βόας ἐδόνησεν, it drove about the cattle, Od. 22, 300. Mid. fut. with pass. signif. h. Ap. 270.

δόξα, ἡ (δοκέω), *opinion, notion, expectation.* ἀπὸ δόξης, contrary to expectation, 10, 324. Od. 11, 344.

δορός, ὁ (δέρω), *a leathern bottle,* *Od. 2, 354. 380.

δορπέω (δόρπον), fut. δορπήσω, *to sup, to take the evening meal,* Od. 15, 302.

δόρπον, τό, *the evening meal, supper,* ἅμα ἠελίῳ καταδύντι, 19, 207. 24, 2; and mly, *a meal;* in plur. δόρπα, 8, 503. Od. 4, 213.

δόρυ, τό, gen. Ep. δούρατος and δουρός, dat. δούρατι, δουρί, accus. δόρυ, dual δοῦρε, plur. δούρατα, δοῦρα, gen. δούρων, dat. δούρασι and δούρεσσι (H. never uses the common form δόρατος), 1) *wood, the trunk of a tree,* Od. 6, 167. 2) Mly *a beam, timber;* δόρυ νήϊον and δοῦρα νεῶν, ship-timber, 2, 135. 3) every thing made of wood, *a spear-handle,* δόρυ μείλινον, an ashen spear-handle, cf. ἔγχος, mly *a spear, lance, javelin;* the Hom. heroes bore in battle and generally elsewhere two spears, 11, 43. Od. 1, 256; and hence poet. *war, battle,* δουρὶ πάλιν νέρθαι, to ravage a city by war, 16, 708.

Δόρυκλος, ὁ, son of Priam, slain by the Telamonian Ajax, 11, 489.

*δορυσθενής, ές (σθένος), *powerful with the spear,* h. Mart. 3.

δόσις, ιος, ἡ (δίδωμι), *a present, a gift,* 10, 213. Od. 6, 208.

*δότειρα, ἡ, *a giver* (female), *a donor,* Ep. 7, 1; fem. from

δοτήρ, ῆρος, ὁ, poet. (δίδωμι), *a giver, a donor, bestower,* σίτοιο, 19, 44. †h. 7, 9.

δαύλειος, η, ον (δοῦλος), *slavish, servile,* Od. 24, 252. †

δούλη, ἡ, *a female slave, a maid-servant,* prop. one born in slavery, fem. of δοῦλος, 3, 409. Od. 4, 12.

δούλιος, η, ον (δοῦλος), *slavish, servile,* only δούλιον ἦμαρ, the day of slavery, 6, 463.

Δουλίχιον, τό, an island in the Ionian sea, south-east from Ithaca, which according to H. belonged to the Echīnades, and was inhabited by Epeans; from it the warrior Meges went to Troy; according to Strabo, the island *Dolichē;* according to a tradition of the modern Greeks, a sunken island *Cacaba,* 2, 625; Δουλιχιόνδε, adv. to Dulichium, Od. 14, 397. Δουλιχιεύς, ῆος, ὁ, an inhabitant of Dulichium.

δουλιχόδειρος, ον, Ep for δολιχόδειρος (δειρή), *having a long neck, long-necked,* epith. of the swan, 2, 460. 15, 692.

δουλοσύνη, ἡ, *slavery, servitude, bondage,* Od. 22, 423. †

δουπέω, poet. (δοῦπος), aor. 1 ἐδούπησα and ἐγδούπησα, perf. 2 δέδουπα, 1) *to make a noise, to make a heavy sound,* esply spoken of falling in battle, often δούπησε πεσών, he gave a hollow sound in falling. 2) absol. *to sound, to fall,* 13, 426. 23, 679.

δοῦπος, ὁ, *noise, a dull or heavy sound.* δοῦπος ἀκόντων, the clash of spears: ποδῶν, the sound of feet, Od. 16, 10; spoken of the noise of the sea, Od 5, 401; of the rushing of mountain torrents, 4, 455.

δουράτεος, η, ον (δόρυ), *wooden, made of wood,* ἵππος, Od. 8, 493. 512. h. Merc. 521.

δουρηνεκής, ές (ἐνεγκεῖν), only neut. as adv. *as far as a spear is cast, a spear's cast off,* 10, 357. †

δουρικλειτός, όν (κλειτός), *famed in hurling the spear, famed with the spear,* epith. of heroes, 5, 578. Od. 15, 52.

δουρικλυτός, όν (κλυτός) = δουρικλειτός, 2, 645. Od. 17, 71; and often.

δουρικτητός, ή, όν (κτάομαι), *captured with the spear, taken in war,* 9, 343. †

δουρός, δουρί, see δόρυ.

δουροδόκη, ἡ (δέχομαι), a place for keeping spears, *an armoury for spears,* Od. 1, 128. †

δόχμιος, η, ον (δοχμή), *transverse, across, oblique,* neut. plur. as adv. πάραντά τε δόχμιά τ' ἦλθον, sidewise and obliquely through, 23, 116. †

δοχμός, ή, όν, *oblique, sidewise;* δοχμὼ ἀΐσσοντε, 12, 148. †

*δοχμόω, *to bend, to incline to the side,* in the pass. h. Merc. 146.

δράγμα, ατος, τό (δράσσω), what one can grasp with the hand, *a handful, a bundle of corn,* as much as the reaper

Δαγμεύω. 115 Δρύναμις.

grasps in cutting. δράγματα ταρφέα πίπτει, handful after handful falls, 11, 69; or as much as the labourer embraces to bind, a sheaf, 18, 552.

δραγμεύω (δράγμα), to collect the ears of grain into sheaves, to bind in bundles, 18, 555.†

δραίνω (δράω), to wish to do any thing, 10, 96.†

*δράκαινα, ή. a female dragon, fem. of δράκων, h. in Ap. 300.

*Δράκανον, τό, a town and promontory on the island Icaria, h. 26, 1.

Δρακίος, ὁ, a leader of the Epei, 13, 692.

δράκων, οντος, ὁ, a dragon, a large serpent, 2, 308; in H., as with us, dragons belong to the class of fabulous animals, cf. 11, 39. Od. 4, 457 (prob. from δέρκομαι).

*δράξ, ακός, ὁ (δράσσω), a handful, Batr. 240.

δράσσω, depon. mid. δράσσομαι, perf. δέδραγμαι, to grasp, to seize, to collect, with gen. only partcp. δεδραγμένος κόνιος, grasping the dust with the hand, *13, 393. 16, 486. (The act. only in later writers.)

δρατός, ή, όν, metathesis for δαρτός (δέρω), flayed, skinned, σώματα, 23, 169.†

δράω, pres. subj. δρώωσι, optat. δρώοιμι, to be active; esply to serve, to wait upon, *Od. 15, 317. 324.

ΔΡΑΩ, obsol. theme of διδράσκω.

ΔΡΕΜΩ, obsol. theme; see τρέχω.

δρεπάνη, ή (δρέπω), a sickle, 18, 551.†

δρέπανον, τό = δρεπάνη, Od. 18, 368.†

δρέπω, to break off, to pluck, with accus. ἄνθεα, h. Cer. 425; mly Od. 12, 357. b. Cer. 429.

*δρησοσύνη, ή, service, worship, ἱερῶν, h. Cer. 476.

Δρῆσος, ὁ, a Trojan, slain by Euryalus, 6, 20.

δρηστήρ, ῆρος, ὁ, Ion. for δραστήρ (δράω), a servant; fem. δρήστειρα, ή, a female servant, *Od. 10, 349. 16, 248.

δρηστοσύνη, ή, activity, assiduity in serving, Od. 15, 321.†

δριμύς, εῖα, ύ, sharp, biting, pungent, prop. spoken of taste, then metaph. βέλος, the piercing arrow (spoken of the shooting pangs of parturition), 11, 270; fierce, violent, χόλος, 18, 322; δριμεῖα μάχη, the fierce battle, 15, 696; μένος, Od. 24, 319.

δρίος [= δρυΐος, D.], in the plur. τὰ δρία, Hes. underwood, thicket, forest. δρίος ὕλης, Od. 14, 353.† (The gender in the sing. is uncertain, since besides the nom. sing. in H. and the plur. in Hes. no cases occur.)

δρόμος, ὁ (ΔΡΕΜΩ, δέδρομα), 1) the act of running, a race, 18, 281. 23, 758. 2) a race-course, a race-ground, Od. 4, 605; and, in general, level surface, Batr. 96.

Δρυάς, άδος, ή (δρῦς), a Dryad, a wood-nymph, who lived and died with her own peculiar tree.

Δρυάς, αντος, ὁ, 1) one of the Lapithae, a friend of Peirithous, 1, 263. 2) father of king Lycurgus, 6, 130.

δρυΐνος, η, ον, of oak, of oaken wood, Od. 21, 43.†

δρυμός, ὁ, plur. τὰ δρυμά, an oak wood, and mly, a wood, a forest, only in plur. 11, 118. Od. 10, 150. 197.

δρύοχος, ὁ (ἔχω), plur. δρύοχοι, according to Eustath. and the Schol. the oaken props or stays, standing in two rows, on which the ship rested, whilst being built, that it might not be injured by the wet sand. Damm and Passow incorrectly define it to be the oaken ribs fastened in the keel of a ship to which the remaining wood-work is attached, Od. 19, 574.† Odysseus (Ulysses) compares the axes placed in a row to them.

Δρύοψ, πος, ὁ, 1) son of Priam, slain by Achilles, 20, 455. 2) son of Apollo, father of Dryope, h. in Pan. 34.

δρύπτω, aor. 1 ἔδρυψα, aor. mid. ἐδρυψάμην, 1) to scratch, to tear off, to lacerate; βραχίονα ἀπὸ μυώνων, to tear the arm from the muscles, 16, 324. 2) Mid. to tear oneself, παρειάς, Od. 2, 153.

δρῦς, δρυός, ή, an oak, it was sacred to Zeus, Od. 14, 328. As an adage: οὐ πως νῦν ἔστιν ἀπὸ δρυὸς οὐδ' ἀπὸ πέτρης ὀαρίζειν, it behoves not now to chat together (as) from an oak or a rock, i. e. to talk familiarly about indifferent things, 22, 126; οὐκ ἀπὸ δρυὸς οὐδ' ἀπὸ πέτρης ἐσσί, thou art neither from the oak nor from the rock, i. e. thou art not of doubtful descent, Od. 19, 163.

δρυτόμος, ον, poet. for δρυοτόμος (τέμνω), felling oaks, cutting oaks, *11, 86. 16, 633.

δρώοιμι, δρώωσι, see δράω.

δῦ, Ep. for ἔδυ, see δύω.

δυάω (δύη), to render unhappy, to plunge into wretchedness, ἀνθρώπους, Od. 20, 195.† (δυόωσι, Ep. for δυῶσι.)

δύη, ή, wretchedness, misery, misfortune. δύης ἐπὶ πῆμα γενέσθαι, to sink in the depths of misery, *Od. 14, 338. (Prop. from δύω, immersion.)

*δυήπαθος, ον (πάσχω), suffering misery, miserable, h. Merc. 468.

Δύμας, αντος, ὁ, 1) father of Asius and Hecuba in Phrygia, 16, 718. a) a Phaeacian, Od. 6, 22.

δύναμαι, see δύω.

Δύμη, ή, Dyma, a town in Achaia, on the sea, at an earlier period, Στράτος, Il.; now Caminitza, h. in Ap. 425.

(δῦμι), obsol. form from δύω.

δύναμαι, depon. mid. fut. δυνήσομαι, aor. 1 ἐδυνησάμην and ἐδυνάσθην, to be able, to have power, to be in a condition to do any thing, absol. and often with infin. b) With accus. Ζεὺς δύναται ἄπαντα, Zeus has all power, can do all things, Od. 4, 237. c) μέγα δύνασθαι, to be very powerful, Od. 1, 275. (υ is long in the partcp. by the arsis, Od. 1, 275.)

Δυναμένη, ή (the mighty), a Nereid, 18, 43.

δύναμις, ιος, ή, power, ability, might, force; esply bodily power. ὅση δύναμις πάρεστιν, as far as my power extends,

Δύνω. 116 Δύω.

8, 294; πὰρ δύναμιν, beyond my power, 13, 787.

δύνω, a form of δύω, only in the indicat. pres. and imperf. mid. δύομαι, 8, 43; see δύω.

δύο or δύω, with dual and plur., *two*, in H. indecl. τῶν δύο μοιράων, 10, 253. δύω κανόνεσσ' ἀραρυῖα, 13, 107. δύω δ' ἄνδρες ἐνείκεον, 18, 498. σὺν δύο, two together, 10, 224.

δυοκαίδεκα and δυώδεκα, poet. for δώδεκα, indecl. *twelve*, Il. and Od.

δυς, an inseparable particle denoting *aversion, difficulty, weariness, misfortune*, etc. like the English *in-, un-, mis-,* etc.; to words having a good signif. it gives an opposite sense, and (sometimes) in words of a bad signif. it strengthens the sense.

δυσαής, ές, poet. (ἄημι), *blowing adversely, blowing violently, blustering*, epith. of the wind and chiefly of Zephyr, 23, 200; gen. δυσαήων for δυσαέων, Od. 13, 99.

δυσάμμορος, ον (ἄμμορος), *very unfortunate, ill-fated*, *22, 428. 485.

δυσαριστοτόκεια (ἄριστος, τίκτω), one who had borne, to her misfortune, a most brave son, *an unhappy mother of a hero*, so Thetis calls herself, 18, 54.

δύσβωλος, ον (βῶλος), *having a bad soil, unfruitful*, Ep. 7.

δύσεο, δύσετο, see δύω.

δύσζηλος ον (ζῆλος), *irascible, choleric*. Od. 7, 307. 2) *dangerously rivalling*, τινί, Ep. 8, 2.

δυσηλεγής, ές (λέγω), *laying in a hard bed* [= ἀλεγεινός (fm. ἀλγεῖν, ἀλέγειν), *afflictive, causing grief*], epith. of war and of death, 20, 154. Od. 22, 325 (others say from ἀλέγω, *regarding no one*).

δυσηχής, ές (ἠχέω), *sounding dreadfully, terribly*, epith. of war, prop. spoken of the clash of arms, 2, 686. 2) *having an evil sound*, in whose very name lies an evil foreboding, *frightful, abominable*, epith. of death, *16, 442. 18, 464; τινί, h. Ap. 64.

δυσθαλπής, ές (θάλπω) *ill at warming, badly warming, cold*, χειμών, 17, 549.†

δυσθῡμαίνω (θυμός), *to be vexed, to be angry*, h. Cer. 363.

δυσκέλαδος, ον (κέλαδος), *sounding dreadfully, resounding*, φόβος, 16, 357.†

δυσκηδής, ές (κῆδος), *anxious, melancholy, sad*, νύξ, Od. 5, 466.†

δυσκλεής, ές (κλέος), *without fame, inglorious*, poet. accus. δυσκλέα for δυσκλεία, 2, 115. 9, 22.

δύσκον, see δύω.

δυσμενέων, ουσα, ον (μένος). *ill-disposed*, in partcp. masc. sing. and plur. *Od.

δυσμενής, ές (μένος), *adverse, hostile, evil-disposed*, 3, 51, and often; and subst. *an enemy*, 10, 193.

δυσμήτηρ, ερος, ἡ (μήτηρ), *an evil mother, a bad mother*, Od. 23, 97.†

δύσμορος, ον (μόρος), *having an evil lot, unfortunate, wretched*, Il. and Od.

Δύσπαρις, ιος, ὁ, *unfortunate Paris, odious Paris* [*curst Paris* Cp.], *3, 39. 13, 769.

δυσπέμφελος, ον (πέμπω), *dangerous to cross, boisterous, stormy*, πόντος, 16, 748.†

δυσπονής, ές (πόνος), *laborious, toilsome, wearisome*, Od. 5, 493.†

δύστηνος, ον (στένω), *groaning heavily, sighing deeply, wretched, miserable*; subst. δυστήνων παῖδες, the children of wretched parents, 6, 127.

*δυστλήμων, ον (τλῆμων), *much-suffering, wretched*, h. Ap. 53.

δυσχείμερος, ον (χεῖμα), *having a severe winter, wintry, stormy*, epith of Dodona, 2, 750. 16, 234.

δυσώνυμος, ον (ὄνυμα, Æol. for ὄνομα), *having a bad name*; hence, *odious, hated, abominable*, as μοῖρα, 12, 116; ἠώς, Od. 19, 571.

δυσωρέομαι. depon. mid. (fr. ὦρος for οὖρος), fut. ἠσομαι, *to have an anxious night-watch, to watch without rest*, spoken of dogs which watch the sheep: περὶ μῆλα, 10, 183.† Spitzner, instead of the mid. δυσωρήσονται (for which Thiersch. § 346, 10, requires δυσωρήσωνται) has restored from Apoll. Lex. the acl. δυσωρήσωσι, which also analogy (cf. ἀωρέω) recommends.

δυσωρέω, act. ed. Spitz. cf. δυσωρέομαι (the final remark).

δύω, aor. 2 ἔδυν, sing. 3 δῦ for ἔδυ. Ep. iterat. δύσκον, subj. δύω, infin. δῦναι. Ep. δύμεναι, partcp. δύς, perf. δέδυκα, mid. pres. δύομαι, fut. δύσομαι, aor. 1 ἐδυσάμην, with the Ep. forms ἐδύσετο, ἐδύσετο, imper. δύσεο (characteristic of aor. 1, and termination of aor. 2). The partcp. δυσόμενος Od. 1, 24, is by some commentators considered future, as in the Epic poets the fut. is used to indicate that also which commonly takes place, but it is better to consider it partcp. of aor. 2, cf. Rost. Gr. p. 408. 6th Ed. Krüg. Flexionslehre, p. 115, top. Of the pres. only the partcp. δύνω occurs, 21, 232. The form δύνω = δύομαι. All these forms have the intrans. signif. *to go in*, hence, 1) Spoken of the relations of place: *a*) Of places and regions: *to go into, to enter, to penetrate into, to plunge into*, with accus. πόλιν, to go into the city; τεῖχος, 15, 345. δῦναι στίας, Od. 13, 366; πόντον, to plunge into the sea, 15, 19; γαῖαν, to go under the earth, 6, 19; δόμον Ἄϊδος εἴσω, 3, 322; νέφεα δῦναι (spoken of the stars), 11. 63; often πόλεμον, μάχην, ὅμιλον, to go into the war, the battle, the crowd; δύεσθαι θεῖν ἀγῶνα, to enter an assembly of the gods, 18, 376; with prep. βέλος εἰς ἐγκέφαλον δῦ, the arrow penetrated into the brain. 8, 85; ἐς πόντον; uncommon: δύσαν εἰς Αἴαντα, he pressed upon Ajax (to shelter himself under his shield), 8, 271. *b*) Metaph of human conditions: κάματος γυῖα δέδυκεν, fatigue entered the limbs, 5, 811. ὀδύναι δῦνον μένος Ἀτρείδαο, Il. 268. δῦ μιν Ἄρης Ares, i. e. martial fury, entered him, 17, 210; also with double accus. Od. 20, 286. 2) Spoken of clothes and arms, with accus. apparently trans.

Δύω. [117 *Δώτιον.

to put on, to clothe oneself in; δύνειν and δύεσθαι, δῦναι, δύσασθαι τεύχεα, ἔντεα, κυνέην, to put on a helmet, 5, 845; χιτῶνα, to put on a tunic, 18, 416. 23, 61. *b*) Also with added dat. τεύχεα ὤμοιιν, to put the arms about one's shoulders, 16, 64. ἔντεα χροΐ, 9, 596; and with prepos. ἐν: ὅπλοισιν ἐνὶ ἐδύτην, 10, 254; ἐν τεύχεσσι δύοντο, Od. 24, 496; also εἰς τεύχεα, Od. 22, 201; metaph. δύεσθαι ἀλκήν, to gird oneself with strength (*to put on one's might*, Cp.), 9, 231. 3) Absol. *to penetrate, to soak into*, δύνει ἀλοιφή, 17, 392; πᾶν δ' εἴσω ξίφος, 16, 340. Esply spoken of the sun and stars: *to set*; *to go down*, often ἠέλιος δ' ἄρ ἔδυ, δύσετο δ' ἠέλιος, and Βοώτης ὀψὲ δύων, and δυσομένου Ὑπερίονος, Hyperion beginning to set, Od. 1, 24. (δύω is short in the pres and imperf. act. and mid. in the remaining tenses long, as also in δύνω; hence δύω is long only in subj. aor. 2, as 6, 340. 7, 193, etc.)

δύω, see δύο.

δυώδεκα, poet. for δώδεκα, q. v.

δυωδεκάβοιος, ον, poet. (βοῦς), *worth twelve oxen*, 23. 703.†

δυωδέκατος, η, ον, Ep. for δωδέκατος, *the twelfth*, ἠώς, 1, 493.

δυωκαιεικοσίμετρος, ον (μέτρον), *containing two-and-twenty measures*, τρίπους [*of twenty and two measures*. Cp.], 23, 264.†

δυωκαιεικοσίπηχυς, υ (πῆχυς), *two-and-twenty cubits long*, ξυστόν, 15, 678.†

δῶ, τό, abbrev. Ep. form for δῶμα, *a house*, used only in the nom. and accus. 1, 426. Od. 1, 176 [prob. the primitive word, Buttm. Gram. § 57, note 3.—See note on κρῖ].

δώδεκα, indecl. *twelve*, poet. also δυοκαίδεκα and δυώδεκα, Il. and Od. The number 12, like 9, used often in H. as a round number.

δωδέκατος, η, ον, *the twelfth*, poet. δυοδέκατος and δυωδέκατος, 24, 781.

Δωδωναῖος, αίη, αῖον, Dodonian, an appellation of Zeus, from the celebrated oracle at Dôdôna. Achilles called upon him as god of the Pelasgians, to whom also the Myrmidons belonged, 16, 233.

Δωδώνη, ἡ, according to Schol. Ven. a town in Molossis, in Epirus, on mount Tomarus. At an earlier day it belonged to Thesprôtia; and according to H. Il. 2, 750, the Perrhæbi came from its vicinity, Hdt. also was acquainted with it, 7, 185. It was the oldest and most noted oracle of Greece. Tradition says that Deucaliôn first built here a temple to Zeus, to which subsequently, according to Hdt. 2, 55, a pigeon flew from the oracle at Thebes in Egypt, which spoke with a human voice and commanded the inhabitants to establish here an oracle of Zeus. Strabo, more correctly, denies its Egyptian origin, and calls it an establishment of the Pelasgians, cf. Πελασγικέ, 16, 233. The temple was situated on mount Tomarus.

The priests (Σελλοί) communicated oracles sometimes from the rustling of the sacred oak (cf. Od. 14, 327), sometimes from the sound of a brazen caldron moved by the wind. It was, according to Pouqueville, near the place now called Proskynisis. (According to Strabo, there was a second Dôdôna in Perrhæbis, near Scotussa.) The name is said to have been derived from the sound of the caldron Δώδω.

δώη and δώῃσι, Ep. for δῷ, see δίδωμι.

δῶμα, ατος, τό (δέμω), 1) *a house, a dwelling*, often in plur. δώματα; spoken of men and gods, δῶμ' Ἀΐδαο, 15, 251. 2) *a single apartment of a house, a room, an apartment*, esply that of the men, i. q. μέγαρον, often in the Od.

δωρέομαι, depon. mid. (δῶρον), aor. ἐδωρησάμην, *to bestow, to present*, with accus. ἵππους, 10, 557.†

δωρητός, ή, όν (δωρέομαι), *presented with gifts*, that may be propitiated with presents, 9, 526.†

Δωριεύς, έος, ὁ, plur. Δωριέες, *the Dorians*, one of the main branches of the Hellênes, deriving their name from Dorus, son of Helen. They resided at first about the Olympus, but removed subsequently to the district of Dôris, and after the Trojan war to Peloponnesus and Asia Minor. Hom. Od. 19, 177, speaks of Dorians in Crete, and calls them τριχάϊκες, the trebly-divided [*with waving locks*. Död. vid.], according to the Schol. because they dwelt in Euboea, Crete, and Peloponnesus, or, more correctly, because they inhabited three cities.

Δώριον, τό, *Dôrium*, a place in western Messênia or Elis, where the bard Thamyris in a contest with the Muses lost his sight, 2, 594. According to Strab. VIII. p. 350, it is unknown; some think it a district or a mountain; others suppose it to be *Oluris* in Messenia. According to Pausan. 8, 33, 7, who says its ruins were near a fountain, it was situated on the Neda near Andania; according to Gell it was in the vicinity of the modern Sidero Castro.

Δωρίς, ίδος, ἡ, daughter of Nêreus and Dôris, 18, 45.

δῶρον, τό, *a gift, a present*, a) δῶρα θεῶν, either presents which are made to them, *votive offerings*, 3, 54. 8, 203; or which are received from them, 20, 268. δῶρα Ἀφροδίτης, the gifts of Aphroditê, i. e. beauty, and the pleasures of love, 3, 54. Ὕπνου δῶρον, the gift of sleep, 7, 482. *b*) In reference to men, 17, 225. Od. 1, 311: esply *gifts of hospitality*, which friends mutually gave, Od. 4, 589. 600.

*Δώς, ἡ (the giver), a name of Dêmêtêr, h. Cer. 122, ed. Herm.; Δηώ, Wolf.

δωτήρ, ῆρος, ὁ, *a giver*; δωτῆρες ἑάων, Od. 8, 325.†

δωτίνη, ἡ, *a gift, a present* = δῶρον, Il. and Od.

*Δώτιον πεδίον, τό, the *Dotian plain*.

Δωτώ.

a plain surrounded by mountains between Magnēsia, Phthiōtis, and the Pelasgian plain near Ossa, h. 15, 5.

Δωτώ, οῦς, ἡ, a Nereid, 18, 43.

δώτωρ, ορος, ὁ, a giver, a bestower. Hermēs is called δώτωρ ἑάων, Od. 9, 335. h. 16, 12.

δώωσι, see δίδωμι.

E.

E, the fifth letter of the Greek alphabet, and therefore the sign of the fifth book or rhapsody.

ἐᾶ, 1) Ep. for ἦν, see εἰμί. 2) For εἶα, see ἐάω.

ἔα, see ἐάω.

ἐάγην, see ἄγνυμι.

ἔαδα, see ἁνδάνω.

ἐάλη, see εἴλω.

1) ἑανός, ἡ, όν, Ep. (prob. from ἕω, ἕννυμι, as στέφανος from στέφω), 1) As adj. with ᾰ, prop. that may easily be put on, flexible, soft (fine, V.); πέπλος, a light, soft robe, 5, 734. 6, 385. ἑανῷ λιτί, 18. 352; and κασσίτερος, thin-beaten, flexible tin, 18, 613.

II) ἑανός, as subst. always with ᾱ, once εἱανός, 16, 9; a robe, a garment, of goddesses and distinguished women: νεκτάρεος ἑανός, 3, 389. 14, 178. 21, 507. This word, which occurs only in the Il., varies in the quantity of its penultima. As an adj. it has ᾰ, and Buttm. would derive it from ἑάω, so that originally it signifies yielding, pliant. As subst. it has always ᾱ and is masc., cf. 21, 507. (Later ἑανόν.) The significations fine, thin, shining, splendid, are derived by mere conjecture from the Hom. passages.

ἔαξα, see ἄγνυμι.

ἔαρ, ἔαρος, τό, poet. gen. εἴαρος, h. Cer. 174; and ἦρος, h. Cer. 455; spring, 6, 148. ἔαρ νέον ἱσταμένον, the newly beginning spring, Od. 19, 519.

ἐαρινός, ἡ, όν, poet. εἰαρινός, q. v.

ἔασιν, Ep. for εἰσί, 3 plur. pres. from ἦμαι.

ἐάφθη (Wolf), more correctly, ἰάφθη (Spitz. aft. Aristarch. and Tyrann.), Ep. 3 sing. aor. 1 pass. only twice, ἐπὶ δ' ἀσπὶς ἐάφθη καὶ κόρυς, 13, 543; and ἐπ' αὐτῷ δ' ἀσπὶς ἑ. κ. κ. 14, 419, prob. from ἅπτω for ἥφθη, with the syllab. augm. ἐάφθη = ἥφθη (al. inflictum erat; al. aptum, alligatum erat). I substitute Spitzner's explanation: "loco priore gutture Apharei Æneæ cuspide perrupto caput in alteram partem reclinatum fuisse tradit, galea ergo et clypeus, utpote loro subnexo retenti, ei sunt juncti et in eandem vergunt partem. Quare non adjicit αὐτῷ... Hector vero Ajacis saxo percussus resupinus cadit, eique adjuncti tenentur clypeus et galea." Excurs. xxiv. Buttm., Lex., p. 242, would, with the old Grammarians, without probability, derive it from ἕπομαι, as an aor. 1 pass.

ἐάω, Ep. εἰάω, fut. ἐάσω, aor. 1 εἴασα, Ep. ἔᾰσα, 1) to let, i. e. to permit, to allow, to suffer, absol. 17, 449; with infin. and accus. τούσδε δ' ἔα φθινύθειν, let those perish, 2, 346. τὰ προτετύχθαι ἐάσομεν, we will let that be past and gone [will renounce vain musings on the past, Cp.], 18, 112. οὐκ ἐάν, not to suffer, i. e. to hinder, to forbid, Od. 19, 25. 2) to let go, to let depart, to leave, to give up, with accus. χόλον, 9, 260; ἵππους, to lead steeds, 4, 226; τινά, to let any one go, 4, 42; also, to leave any one, 5, 148; and often. 3) to intermit, to forbear, to cease, with infin. κλάψαι, 24, 71; also with accus. Od. 14, 444 (α is short in the pres. and imperf., before σ long: H. uses iu the pres. and imperf. partly the contract. forms ἐῷ, ἐᾷ, ἐῶμι, and partly the Ep. forms ἐάᾳ, ἐᾷ and ἔα, monosyllabic, 5, 256).

ἑάων, gen. plur. from ἐΰς, q. v.

ἑβδόματος, η, ον, poet for ἕβδομος, 7, 248.

ἕβδομος, η, ον (ἑπτά), the seventh, Il. and Od.

ἔβλητο, Ep. see βάλλω.

ἐγγεγάασι, see ἐγγίγνομαι.

ἐγγείνομαι (γείνομαι), in the pres. obsol., only aor. 1 ἐνεγεινάμην, to engender within, with accus. εὐλὰς ἐγγείνωνται, 3 plur. subj. aor. 1, 19, 26.†

ἐγγίγνομαι (γίγνομαι), Ep. perf. only 3 plur. ἐγγεγάασιν, to be born in, perf. to be in, to live in; with dat. τοὶ ἐγγεγάασιν Ἰλίῳ, who dwell in Troy, 4, 41. 6, 193.

ἐγγυαλίζω (γύαλον), fut. ἐγγυαλίξω, aor. 1 ἐγγυάλιξα, prop. to give into the hand, hence to give up, to communicate, to bestow, τί τινι; σκῆπτρόν τινι, 9, 99; τιμήν, κῦδος, κέρδος; τινά τινι, to give any one to one, Od. 16, 66.

ἐγγυάω (ἐγγύη), fut. ήσω, to give up any thing as a pledge, hence to become security, mid. to be bail, to be surety. δειλαί τοι δειλῶν γε καὶ ἐγγύαι ἐγγυάασθαι, Od. 8, 351.† Among the various explanations of this passage (in the Schol.), the connexion seems best suited by the following construction: ἐγγύαι τῶν δειλῶν (i. e. ὑπὲρ τῶν δειλῶν, Eustath.) καὶ δειλαί εἰσ' ἐγγυάασθαι, i. e. sureties for the worthless give a worthless security. Or, with Passow, 'for the worthless it is of no avail to become surety.' So, in effect, Baumgarten-Crusius in Jahrbüch für Philol. IX. 4, p. 436: 'Such sureties,' says he, 'are generally as bad as the persons for whom they are undertaken.' Nitzsch [observing that δειλός is weak, powerless] refers δειλῶν to Hēphæstus, and explains: δειλὴν ἐγγύην ἐγγυᾶται ὁ πρὸς δειλὸν ἐγγυώμενος, he who gives security to a weak person gives a weak security [the reason follows: thus how could I (Hēphæstus) make you (Poseidōn) responsible, if Arēs should refuse to pay? lame suitor, lame security Cp.].

ἐγγύη. ἡ (γυῖον), *surety* by delivering a pledge; and mly *security, surety, τινός*, for any one, Od. 8. 351.†

ἐγγύθεν, adv. (ἐγγύς), 1) Of place: *from near, near*, e. g. ἔρχεσθαι, ἱστασθαι; with dat. ὁ γάρ οἱ ἐγγύθεν ἦεν, he was near him, 17, 554. 2) Of time: *near, soon*, 18, 133.

ἐγγύθι, adv. (ἐγγύς), 1) Of place: *near*, sometimes with gen. Πριάμοιο, 6, 317. 2) Of time: *near, soon*, 10, 251; with dat. 22, 300.

ἐγγύς, adv. 1) of place: *near, near by*, either without a case or with gen.; also with infin. following, 11, 340. 2) Of time: *near, soon*, 22, 453. Od. 10, 86.

ἐγδούπησαν, see δουπέω.

ἐγείρω, aor. 1 ἤγειρα, mid. aor. sync. ἠγρόμην, Ep. ἐγρόμην, infin. ἐγρέσθαι, aud with pres. accent ἐγρέσθαι. Od. 13, 124; perf. 2 ἐγρήγορα: here belong the forms ἐγρήγορθε, ἐγρηγόρθαι, ἐγρηγόρθασι, 1) Act. 1) *to wake, to awaken*, τινὰ ἐξ ὕπνου, 5, 413; and alone, 10, 146. 2) *to arouse, to excite, to animate, to encourage*, τινά, 5, 208. 15, 242; often Ἄρηα, to excite Arês, i. e. the battle, 11.; and πόλεμον, φύλοπιν, πόνον, μάχην, also θυμόν, μένος, to excite the spirit. II) Mid. together with the sync. aor 2 and perf. 2, *to be awake, to watch*, 2, 41 ; ἀμφὶ πυρήν, 7, 434. The perf. 2, *I am awake* (imper. ἐγρήγορθε for ἐγρηγόρατε, infin. ἐγρηγόρθαι ἐγρηγόρθαι), 10, 67 (as if from ἐγρηγορμαι), and 3 plur. perf. ἐγρηγόρθασι, 10, 419; which extraordinary form either comes through ἐγρηγόρθαι, or has sprung from a theme ἐγερέθω abbrev. ἐγέρθω, and from this ἐγρήγορθαι); see Buttm. Gram. p. 277. Rost Dial. 75. D. Anm. 1.

ἔγκατα, τά, the interior, *the entrails*; only plur. 11, 176. Od.; dat. plur. ἔγκασι, 11, 438.

ἐγκατατήγνυμι (πήγνυμι), aor. 1 ἐγκατέπηξα, *to infix, to fasten in*; ξίφος κουλεῷ, to thrust the sword into the scabbard, Od. 11, 98.†

ἐγκατατίθημι (τίθημι), only mid. aor. 2 3 sing. ἐγκάτθετο, and imperat. ἐγκάτθεο, *to lay down upon for oneself, to place in, to conceal*; ἱμάντα κόλπῳ, to hide the girdle in the bosom, as an amulet (not 'to put on around'), 14, 219. 223; thus Voss and the Schol.: inetaph. τὴν ἄτην θυμῷ, to weigh the punishment in one's heart, Od. 23, 223. Extraordinary is τελαμῶνα ᾗ ἐγκάτθετο τέχνῃ, Od. 11, 614; prop. he laid the sword-belt upon his art, i. e. he applied to it his art. According to Eustath. a periphrasis for ἐτεχνήσατο, because it was not prepared easily and quickly, but with toil. Others explain it [better], *ἐνεθόησεν*, he invented, devised [conceived, Fäsi] it, etc. This explanation is preferred by Nitzsch. The reading of the Schol. Harl. is easier: ὃς κεῖνα τελαμῶνι ἐφ᾽ ἐγκάτθετο τέχνην, he laid out [ex-pended all the resources of] his art upon it. So Schneider in Lex.

ἔγκειμαι (κεῖμαι), fut. ἐγκείσομαι, *to lie in*, with dat. ἱματίοις, to lie in garments, spoken of one dead, 22, 513.†

Ἐγκέλαδος, ὁ (the roaring), one of the hundred-handed giants who stormed heaven, Batr. 285.

ἐγκεράννυμι (κεράννυμι), aor. 1 ἐνεκέρασα, *to mix in, to mingle, to dilute*, οἶνον, 8, 189. Od. 20, 223.

ἐγκέφαλος, ὁ (κεφαλή), prop. adj., which is in the head; subst *the brain* (subaud μυελός, marrow), 11. and Od. χόλος δ᾽ εἰς ἐγκέφαλον δῦ, Il. 8, 85.

ἐγκιθαρίζω (κιθαρίζω), *to play to any one on the guitar* or *harp*, h. Ap. 201. Merc. 17.

ἐγκλιδόν, adv. (κλίνω), '*bending, inclining*, h. 23.

ἐγκλίνω (κλίνω), perf. pass. ἐγκέκλιμαι, *to bend, to incline to*. 2) *to lean upon*, hence metaph. πόνος ὕμμι ἐγκέκλιται, the labour rests upon you, 6, 77.†

ἐγκονέω (κονέω), *to be diligent, quick*, esply in service, only partcp. στόρεσαν λέχος ἐγκονέουσαι, they quickly prepared the bed, 24, 648. Od. 7, 340.

ἐγκοσμέω (κοσμέω), *to arrange in*, τί τινι; τεύχεα νηΐ, to arrange the tackling and furniture in a ship, Od. 15, 218.†

ἐγκρύπτω (κρύπτω), aor. 1 ἐνέκρυψα, *to hide in, to conceal*; δαλὸν σποδιῇ, Od. 5, 488.† (Buttm. for the sake of position would read here ἐγκρύψε for ἐνέκρυψε, cf Ausf. Gr. § 7, p. 38.), h. Merc. 416.

ἐγκυκάω, see κυκάω.

ἐγκυρέω, Ion. and poet. (κυρέω), aor. 1 ἐνέκυρσα, *to fall into, to fall upon* any thing, with dat. φάλαγξι, upon the phalanxes, 13, 145.†

ἐγρέμαχος, ον (μάχη), *exciting battle* [*battle-rousing*]; fem. ἐγρεμάχη, epith. of Athênê, h. Cer. 424.

ἔγρεο, see ἐγείρω.

ἐγρηγόρθαι, ἐγρηγόρθασι, ἐγρήγορθε, Ep. perf. forms: see ἐγείρω.

ἐγρηγορόων, Ep. for ἐγρηγορῶν, from ἐγρηγοράω, *watching, waking*, a newly formed pres. from the peri. ἐγρήγορα, Od. 20, 6.†

ἐγρηγορτί, adv. (ἐγρήγορα), *awake*, 10, 182.†

ἐγρήσσω (from ἐγείρω, ἐγείρω), *to watch, to be awake*, only pres. 11, 551. Od. 20, 33.

ἔγρομαι, a pres. form assumed without reason for the infin. ἐγρέσθαι, Od. 13, 124, which the Gramm. and Wolf accent ἐγρέσθαι, see ἐγείρω.

ἐγχείη, ἡ, Ep. for ἔγχος, *a spear, a lance*, 3, 345. [The signif. 'battle with spears,' is unnecessary, cf. Jahrb. J. und K., p. 259. Am. Ed.]

ἐγχείῃ, Ep. for ἐγχέῃ, see ἐγχέω.

ἐγχέλυς, νος, ἡ, *an eel*, plur. ἐγχέλυες, Ep. for ἐγχέλεις, 21, 203. 353.

ἐγχεσίμωρος, ον, *skilled in the use of the spear*, epith. of brave warriors, 2, 692. Od. 3, 188. (The ancients themselves did not know the derivation,

Ἐγχέσπαλος. 120 Ἐεικοσάβοιος.

They explain it: οἱ περὶ τὰ δόρατα μεμορημένοι, and derive it from μόρος, μοίρα, whose fate it is to bear the spear; others from μῶλος, battle, changing λ into ρ; others from μωρός, raging with the spear. If we compare ἰόμωροι and ὑλακόμωροι, we may infer that the word indicates *skill*.)

ἐγχέσπαλος, ον (πάλλω), *wielding the spear*, epith. of warriors, *2, 131.

ἐγχέω (χέω), 3 sing. subj. ἐγχείῃ, Ep. for ἐγχέῃ, aor. 1 act ἐνέχευα, 3 plur. ἐνέχεαν, mid. ἐνεχευάμην, 1) *to pour in*, with accus. ὕδωρ, οἶνον, 18, 347. οἶνον δεπάεσσι, to pour wine into the goblets, Od. 9, 10. *b*) *to pour in*, spoken of things dry; ἄλφιτα δοροῖσιν, Od. 2, 354. 2) Mid. *to pour in for oneself* (sibi), ὕδωρ), Od. 19, 387: often in tmesis.

ἔγχος, εος, τό. *a spear, a javelin*. The spear consisted of a long wooden shaft (δόρυ), which was pointed with brass (αἰχμή), 6, 319. Commonly it was six feet and more long; that of Hector was eleven cubits (ἐνδεκάπηχυ). The shaft was commonly made of ash, cf. μελίη. The lower end of the shaft (σαυρωτήρ) was also pointed with brass, that, when the bearer wished to rest, it might easily penetrate the ear h, 10, 152. 22, 224. The spear was used both in thrusting and hurling. Hence warriors went into battle with two, that they might have a second when the first had been fruitlessly hurled or been broken, 3, 18. 12, 298. cf. Köpke Kriegswes. der Griechen, p. 115.

ἐγχρίμπτω (χρίμπτω), aor. 1 act. ἐγχρίμψα, aor. 1 pass. only partcp. ἐγχριμφθείς, 1) *to force on, to push on, to drive on*; once intrans. *to press on.* τῷ σὺ μάλ' ἐγχρίμψας ἐλάαν σχεδὸν ἅρμα καὶ ἵππους, pressing on to this (the goal) drive the chariot and horses near, 23, 314. Mly pass. 1) αἰχμὴ ὀστέῳ ἐγχριμφθεῖσα, the point driven to the bone, 5, 662. ἀσπίδ' ἐνιχριμφθείς, dashed down with the shield, 7, 272. 2) Absol. *to crowd in, to push close on.* νωλεμὲς ἐγχρίμπτοντο, 17, 413; with dat. πύλῃσιν, to the gates, *17, 405.

ἐγώ, and Ep. before a vowel ἐγών, gen. Ep. ἐμέο, ἐμεῖο, ἐμεῦ, μεῦ, ἐμέθεν, I, gen. *of me*; also strengthened ἔγωγε; μ' for μοι in μ' οἴῳ, Od. 4, 367; cf. Gram. and on the plur. see ἡμεῖς.

ἐδάην, see ΔΑΩ.

ἐδανός, ή, όν, *pleasing, agreeable, delicious*, an epith. of oil in 14, 172.† h. Ven. 63. (The ancients derived it from ἐδύς, ἥδομαι.)

ἔδαφος, τό (ἕδος), *a seat, basis, bottom*, upon which any thing rests, νηός, Od. 5, 249.†

ἔδδεισα, Ep. for ἔδεισα, see δείδω.

ἐδέδμητο, see δέμω.

ἐδείδιμεν, ἐδείδισαν, see δείδω, δίω.

ἔδεκτο, see δέχομαι.

*ἔδεσμα, ατος, τό (ἔδω), *food, victuals*, Batr. 31.

ἐδήδοται, ἐδηδώς, see ἔδω

ἐδητύς, ύος, ἡ (ἔδω). *food, victuals*, often with πόσις, 9, 92. Od. 1, 150. 3, 67.

ἔδμεναι, Ep. for ἐδέμεναι, from ἔδω.

ἔδνον, τό, only in the plur. τὰ ἔδνα, Ion. ἔεδνα, *bridal presents*, in different senses: 1) presents which the suitor gives the bride: the common use. *b*) presents which the suitor gives to the father of the bride, and with which he in a manner purchases her, 16, 178. Od. 8, 318. 2) the dowry or outfit which the father gives the bride; according to Nitzsch, a part of the bridal presents, Od. 1, 277. 2, 196 (in the Il. always ἔδνα, in the Od. also ἔεδνα).

ἐδνοπαλίζειν, see ὀνοπαλίζω.

ἐδνόω, Ep. ἐεδνόω (ἔδνα), *to promise for presents*, only in mid. aor. 1 ἐεδνωσάμην, to betroth a daughter. θύγατρα, spoken of a father who marries his daughter, Od 2, 53.†

ἐδνωτής, Ep. ἐεδνωτής, οῦ, ὁ (ἔδνα), the one who affiances. *the bride's father, a father-in-law*, 13, 382;† only in the Ep. form.

ἔδομαι, see ἔδω, ἐσθίω.

ἔδος, εος, τό (ἔζομαι), 1) *the act of sitting.* οὐχ ἔδος ἐστί, it is no time to sit, 11, 648. 23, 205. 2) *a seat*, 1, 534. 581. 3) *a residence, an abode*, spoken of Olympus: ἀθανάτων ἔδος, the abode of the immortals, 8, 456; and metaph. the place on which any thing rests, *ground, basis.* ἔδος Θήβης, and periphrastically, ἔδος Οὐλύμποιο, 24, 144; situation, Od. 13, 344.

ἐδράθον, Ep. for ἔδαρθον, see δαρθάνω.

ἔδραμον, see τρέχω.

ἕδρη, ἡ, Ion. and Ep. for ἕδρα (ἔδος), 1) *a seat*, 19, 77. 2) the place where one sits, *the seat of honour.* τίειν τινὰ ἕδρῃ, to honour one with a chief seat, 8, 162. cf. 12, 311.

ἑδριάομαι, depon mid. (ἕδρα,) infin. ἑδριάασθαι Ep. for ἑδριᾶσθαι, imperf. ἑδριόωντο Ep. resol. for ἑδριῶντο, *to seat oneself, to sit down*, 10, 198. Od. 3, 35.

ἔδυν and ἔδυν, see δύω.

ἔδω (Ep. for ἐσθίω), Ep. infin. ἔδμεναι, fut. ἔδομαι, 4, 237; perf. act. ἔδηδα. partcp. ἐδηδώς, perf. pass. ἐδήδομαι (as aor. ἔφαγον), iterat. imperf. ἔδεσκε, 1) *to eat*, with accus. Δημήτερος ἀκτήν, 13, 322; with gen. Od. 9, 102; also spoken of brutes: *to eat, to devour.* 2) *to waste, to consume*, οἶκον, κτήματα. Od. metaph. καμάτῳ καὶ ἄλγεσι θυμόν, the heart with labour and care, Od. 9, 75. cf. 24, 129. (For ἔδω in the pres. ἐσθίω, ἔσθω also occurs.)

ἐδωδή, ἡ (ἔδω), *food, nourishment*, food for horses, 8, 504. Od. 3, 70.

ἑέ, poet. for ἕ, *himself, herself, itself*. see οὗ.

ἔεδνα, τά, ἐεδνόω, ἐεδνωτής, Ep. for ἔδνα, ἐδνόω, ἐδνωτής, q. v.

ἐεικοσάβοιος, ον, Ep. for εἰκοσ. (βοῦς), *worth twenty oxen.* τιμὴν ἐεικοσάβοιον ἄγειν, to bring a recompense of twenty oxen, Od. 22, 57. Neut. plur. *Od. 1, 431.

Ἐείκοσι.

εείκοσι, and before a vowel δείκοσιν, Ep. for εἴκοσι.
εείκόσορος, ον. Ep. for εἰκόσ., *having twenty ranks of rowers*, Od. 9, 322,† a rare form for εἰκοσήρης like τριήρης.
εείκοστός, ή, όν, Ep. for εἰκοστός, *the twentieth*.
εείλεον, Ep. for εἴλεον, see εἰλέω.
εείσάμενος, εεισάμην, see ΕΙΔΩ.
εεισάσθην, 15, 544, see εἶμι.
εέλδομαι, εέλδωρ, see ἔλδομαι, ἔλδωρ.
εέλμεθα, εελμένος, see εἴλω.
εέλπομαι, see ἔλπομαι.
εέλσαι, see εἴλω.
εεργάθω, see ἐργάθω.
εέργνῡμι, Ep. form of ἔργω, *to shut up*, κατὰ συφεοῖσιν ἐέργνυ, Od. 10, 238;† see ἔργω.
εέργω, see ἔργω.
εερμένος, see εἴρω.
εέρση, εερσήεις, Ep. for ἔρση, ἐρσήεις.
εέρτο, see εἴρω.
εέρχατο, see ἔργω.
εέσσατο, see ἔννυμι.
εέσσυατο, see εἶσα.
εέστο, see ἔννυμι.
ἔζομαι, depon. mid. (ʹΕΔΩ, ΕΩ), only pres. and imperf. without augm. *to seat oneself, to sit*, mly with ἔν τινι, rarely ἔς τι, Od. 4, 51; with ἐπί τινι and τι; metaph. κῆρες ἐπὶ χθονὶ—ἐζέσθην. the fates (of the Achaians) (in the balance) settled to the earth [*sunk low; subsided*. Cp.], 8, 74. (There is no act. ἔζω, from which it is common to derive the tenses εἶσα, εἰσάμην, ἔσσομαι, see εἶσα.)
ἔηκε, Ep. for ἧκε, see ἵημι.
ἔην, Ep. for ἦν, see εἰμί.
ἐήνδανε, see ἀνδάνω.
ἔηος, gen. masc. as if from ἐΰς, see ἐΰς.
ἔης, gen. Ep. for ἧς, but ἐῆς from ἑός.
ἔησθα, see εἰμί.
ἔησι, see εἰμί.
ἐθ', abbrev. for ἔτι.
ἔθειρα, ἡ, prop. *the hair of the head*, h. 7, 4, in the ll. only plur.; spoken of the mane of horses, 8, 42; or of the horsehair crest, *16, 795 (related to ἐθείρω).
ἐθείρω (θέρω), *to attend, to take care of, to cultivate*, ἀλωήν, 21. 347.†
ἐθελοντήρ, ῆρος, ὁ, Ep. for ἐθελοντής (ἐθέλω), *one who acts voluntarily, a volunteer*, Od. 2. 292.†
ἐθέλω, fut. ἐθελήσω, imperf. ἤθελον and ἔθελον, iterative ἐθέλεσκον, 1) *to will* (see βούλομαι), *to wish*, often with infin., or accus. with infin.; the imperat. with negat. serves the purpose of the spoken of animals: *a swarm, a flock, a herd*, of bees, geese, pigs, 2, 469. 459.

ἔθορον, see θρώσκω.
ἔθος, ους, τό, Att. for ἦθος, *habit, custom*, Batr. 34.
ἔθρεψα, see τρέφω.
ἔθω, from which we have the Ep. partcp. ἔθων, *accustomed*, 9, 540. 16, 260; mly perf. 2 εἴωθα, Ion. ἔωθα, partcp. εἰωθώς, *to be wont, to be accustomed*, with infin. The partcp. perf. is used absol. for *accustomed, customary*. μᾶλλον ὑφ᾽ ἡνιόχῳ εἰωθότι ἅρμα οἴσετον, they will draw the chariot better under the accustomed charioteer, 5, 231.

εἰ, conj. Ep. and Dor., also αἰ, 1) *if*, in the protasis of a conditional sentence. According to the relation of the condition to the conviction of the speaker, it stands 1) With the indicat. in all tenses when the condition is represented as something certain or without doubt, with pres., 1, 178; preter., 1, 290; fut., 1. 294. The apodosis is either in the indicat. of all tenses (also imperat. 1, 173), or in the optat. with ἄν, 1, 293. 6, 129. 2) With the subjunct. when the condition is represented as a mere supposition to be decided, *in case that, allow that*, mly εἰ κε, αἰ κε and εἰ—ἄν, in prose ἐάν. With the subjunct. εἰ also stands in the Ep. language alone, eaply εἴπερ, εἴ γ᾽ οὖν, καὶ εἰ, Od. 12, 96. 14, 373. Il. 12, 223. The apodosis is either in the indicat. with one of the principal tenses (or imperat.), or in the subjunct. aor. and pres., 1, 137; or in the optat. with ἄν, 4, 97. 3) With the optat. when the condition is represented as a mere supposition without regard to reality, a simple conjecture. Τρῶες μέγα κεν κεχαροίατο, εἰ τάδε πάντα πυθοίατο, the Trojans would rejoice, if they should learn all this, 1, 257. The apodosis stands in the optat. with ἄν, and sometimes also in the indicat., 10, 223. 4) With the indicat. of the historical tenses, when the reality of the condition is denied or rejected. The apodosis then stands, *a*) Mly in the indicat. hist. tenses with ἄν, so that the reality of the conclusion is also denied. καί νύ κ᾽ ἔτι πλέονας κτάνε Ὀδυσσεύς, εἰ μὴ ἄρ᾽ ὀξὺ νόησε Ἕκτωρ, and Odysseus (Ulysses) would have slain still more, if Hector had not quickly perceived it, 5, 679. Od. 4, 363. *b*) Or in the optat. with ἄν, the apodosis being merely indicated as possible, 2, 80. 5, 311. II) *if but, would*

Είαμενή. 122 Είδω.

supplied. The subjunct. or optat. may follow, 11, 797. 10, 55; on the general construction of εἰ, cf. Gr. 1281, sqq. 1361, sqq. [§ 851, sqq. § 877, sqq.]. IV) εἰ mly begins the sentence, so that other particles follow, as εἰ γάρ, εἰ δέ, εἰ καί, εἰ μή, etc., which see under their own articles. It follows in καὶ εἰ, even if; οὐδ' εἰ, not (even) if; ὡς εἰ, as if, see ὡσεί.

είάμενή or είαμενή, ή, a low moist place about rivers and swamps, *a low ground, a marsh, meadow, pasture*, *4, 483. 15, 631. It is mly derived from ἧμαι, *sedere*, hence είαμενή (εἴαται) for ἡμένη. Spitzner writes είαμενή, because both the deriv. and the best Gramm. require the spiritus asper.

εἰ—ἄν stands in H. for the Ep. εἰ κε, αἴ κε, when it is separated by particles, as εἰ δ' ἄν, εἴπερ ἄν, 3, 288. Of the contracted forms ἐάν and ἤν, only the last is found in H., cf. εἰ, I. 2.

είανός. Ep. for ίανός, 16, 9.†

είαρ, ρος, τό, poet. for ἔαρ, q. v.

είαρινός, ή, όν, Ep. for ἐαρινός (ἔαρ), *relating to spring, vernal*. ὥρη είαρινή, spring-time. ἄνθεα είαρινά, vernal flowers, 2, 89. Od. 18, 367.

είασα. είασκον, see ἐάω.

εἴαται, εἴατο, Ep. for ἧνται, ἧντο, see ἧμαι.

εἴατο, Ep for ἧντο, see εἰμί, I am.

εἴβω, Ep. for λείβω, *to drop*, always εἴβειν δάκρυον, to shed tears. *Od. 4, 153.

εἰ γάρ, 1) *for if*, in hypothet. sentences, 13, 276. 17, 156. Od. 18, 366. 2) *O that, if but*, a particle of wishing, with optat., 8, 538. 17, 561; more mly αἰ γάρ, q. v.

εἴγε, conj. 1) *if at least, if indeed, si quidem*, spoken of things which one may reasonably suppose; mly it is separated by other words. εἰ δύνασαί γε, 1, 393. 18, 427. It is found only once united: εἴγε μὲν είδείης, Od. 5, 206.

εἰ γοῦν, *even if, although*, 5, 258 † Thiersch, § 329. 1, rejects γοῦν as unhomeric, and reads εἴ γ' οὖν, which Spitzner adopts, see γέ.

εἰ δ' ἄγει, *come on then! up then!* in connexion with νῦν, δή, μήν, with imperat. and with δεῦρο, 17, 685; also with subj. or fut., Od. 9, 37; also with plur. following. 6, 376; and itself in the plur. εἰ δ' ἄγετ'—πειρηθῶμεν, 17, 381. There is a partial ellipsis of the protasis: εἰ δὲ βούλει, ἄγε.

είδάλιμος, η, ον (εἶδος), *handsome, beautiful in form, comely*. Od. 24, 279.†

είδαρ, ατος, τό, Ep. for ἔδαρ (ἔδω), *food*, food for horses, 5, 369; *bait* for fish, Od. 12, 252.

εἰ δέ, 1) *but if, and if*, in complete sentences, see εἰ. 2) εἰ δέ is sometimes used elliptically as an antithesis, in which case the verb must be supplied from the connexion. εἰ δὲ καὶ αὐτοί (sc. φεύξονται), φευγόντων, but if they will fly, let them fly, 9, 46. cf. 262. Il. 21, 487.

είδέω, 1) For εἰδῶ, subj. of οἶδα. 2)

An assumed theme for some forms of εἴδω and οἶδα, see ΕΙΔΩ.

είδήσέμεν, Ep. for είδήσειν, see ΕΙΔΩ.

εἰ δή, of a thing assumed to be *granted* or *undoubted*, with indic.: seldom with subj. as 1, 293 (where some make ὑπείξομαι, subj.), cf. 21, 463. 1) *if indeed, si quidem jam; if now truly, if really*, 13, 111. 18, 120. 24, 57. Od. 22, 359. 2) *whether really*, in questions, Od. 1, 207. 17, 484.

Είδοθέη, ή, Ep. for Είδοθέα, daughter of Proteus, who instructed Menelaus on the island of Pharos, how he could seize her father and compel him to prophesy, Od. 4, 365 seq. (from εἶδος and θέη, a divine form: in Eurip. Θεονόη.)

εἴδομαι, εἴδον, see ΕΙΔΩ.

εἶδος, εος, τό (ΕΙΔΩ), *the appearance, the form, mien*, spoken often of the human form in connexion with φυή, δέμας, 2, 58. 24, 376; of a dog, Od. 17, 308.

ΕΙΔΩ, ΙΔΩ, *to see, to know*, in the pres. act. obsol. The tenses in use are,

A) The aor. act. εἶδον, Ep. ἴδον, infin. ἰδεῖν, Ep. ἰδέειν, partcp. ἰδών, subj. ἴδω, and Ep. ἴδωμι, optat. ἴδοιμι, and the aor. mid. είδόμην and Ep. ἰδόμην, imperf. ἰδοῦ, infin. ἰδέσθαι, subj. ἴδωμαι, they signify *to see, to perceive, to behold, to observe*, and belong as aor. to ὁράω and ὁράσθαι, q. v. Remarkable is: οὐκ ἴδε χάριν αὐτῆς (sc. ἀλόχου), he did not enjoy her *grace* or *favour*; spoken of a warrior slain shortly after his marriage, 11, 243. Thus Eustath. explains it: οὐκ ἐχάρη ἐπὶ τῇ συμβιώσει αὐτῆς οὐδ' ἐπὶ τῇ τεκνοποιήσει. Others, 'he saw not her loveliness;' and Köppen understands by χάρις, thanks, gratitude, in reference to πολλὰ δ' ἔδωκε. Here belong the Ep. and Ion. mid. and pass. εἴδομαι, aor. 1 είσάμην, and ἐεισάμην, partcp. είσάμενος, and ἐεισάμενος, 1) *to be seen*; hence, *to appear, to seem*, 8, 559; εἴδεται ἧμαρ, 13, 98; τό τοι κῆρ εἴδεται εἶναι, that seems death to thee, 1, 228. 2, 215. 2) *to be like, to resemble*, with dat. ἐείσατο φθογγὴν Πολίτῃ, he resembled Polites in voice, 2, 791. 20, 81.

B) Perf. οἶδα, 2 οἶσθα, and οἶδας, Od. 1, 337; † plur. ἴδμεν, ἴστε, ἴσασι, subj. είδῶ, Ep. ἰδέω, 14, 235; plur. εἴδομεν for εἴδωμεν, εἴδετε, Ep. for εἰδῆτε, είδωσι, optat. είδείην, imperat. ἴσθι, infin. ἴδμεναι and ἴδμεν, Ep. for εἰδέναι, partcp. εἰδώς, υἶα, ός: from this always the fem. ἰδυίησιν πραπίδεσσιν, pluperf. ᾔδεα Ep. for ᾔδειν, 2 Ep. ἠείδης, ἠείδεις, ᾐδησθα for ᾔδεις, 3 ᾔείδη, ᾐείδει, Od. 9, 206; ᾔδεεν, ᾐδεε, ᾔδε, Ep. for ᾔδει, 3 plur. ἴσαν for ᾔσαν, 18, 405; fut. εἴσομαι, more rarely poet. εἰδήσω, infin. είδησέμεν, Od. 6, 257. 7, 327; all with the signif. *to know* (prop. to have perceived), *to understand, to recognise, to become acquainted with*, often connected with σάφα, also with φρεσί, ἐνὶ φρεσί, κατὶ φρένα, κατὰ θυμόν, in mind: primarily with accus. or infin. οἶδε νοῆσαι, χάρυν

Είδωλον.   123   Είλίπους.

τινὶ εἰδέναι, to feel gratitude (to be grateful) to any one, 14, 235. The dependent clause follows with the partcp. or with ὡς, ὅτι, ὅπως, more rarely the relat. ὅ, for ὅτι, 18, 197; in cases of doubt with εἰ, whether, or with ἦ, ἤ, 10, 342; also with only one ἤ, Od. 4, 109. 2) to understand, to be conversant with, πολεμήϊα ἔργα, 11, 719; also μήδεα, in like manner ἤπια δήνεα, to cherish gentle thoughts or sentiments, 4, 361; hence mly, to be disposed, as, ἄρτια, αἴσιμα, etc. 3) The partcp. often as adj.: γυναῖκες ἀμύμονα ἔργα εἰδυῖαι, women skilled in excellent works, 9, 270, cf. 3, 202. As adj. mly the partcp. with gen. εὖ εἰδὼς τόξων, well skilled (expert) in the bow (= archery), 2, 718; in like manner μάχης, πολέμου, etc. The gen. however is also found with the finite verb, 12, 229. 15, 412. The fut. εἰδησέμεν signifies also, to become acquainted with, Od. 6, 257.

εἴδωλον, τό (εἶδος), a form, an image. 2) a shadowy form, an illusive image or phantom, which has the exact form of the object (person) it is to represent, 5, 449; esply in pl. the shades of the dead, 23, 72. Od. 1, 476.

εἴεν, see εἰμί.

εἶθαρ, adv. poet. (εὐθύς), immediately, forthwith, *5, 337.

εἴθε, adv. if but, oh that, with optat. Od. 2, 33; more mly αἴθε, q. v.

εἰ καί, 1) if even, with indic. and optat. εἰ ἐτίαμ; in most cases καί refers to a word standing near, 16, 623. Od. 6, 310. 7, 194. 2) although, where it may be compared with the Lat. etiamsi, etsi, in so far as it refers to the whole concessive clause, 23, 832. Od. 11, 356. 18, 375. 3) whether also, in indirect questions, 2, 367. From this is to be distinguished καὶ εἰ, q. v. cf. Spitzner Excurs. XXIII. on Il. p. 7.

εἴ κε, εἴ κεν, if, Ep. = ἐάν, see εἰ I. 2. and αἴ κε.

εἴκελος, η, ον (εἴκω), like, similar, τινί, H. oftener ἴκελος.

εἰκοσάκις, adv. twenty times, 9, 379.†

εἴκοσι, indecl. Ep. ἐείκοσι, before a vowel ἐείκοσιν, twenty. In H. εἴκοσι never except in composition takes ν, but ι before a vowel is elided, εἴκοσ', Od. 2, 212.

[εἰκοσίμετρος, containing twenty measures, so Villoison and Clarke. 23, 264.]

εἰκοσινήριτος, ον (νήριτος), full twentyfold. The derivation is doubtful: according to Damm, the second factor is νήριτος, without dispute: but it is far better to explain the word with Eustath and the Schol. = πρὸς εἴκοσιν ἐριστὰ ἤτοι ἐρίζοντα καὶ ἰσάζοντα. ἄποινα, a twenty-fold ransom, 22, 349, a ransom competing with twenty (others), or equal to them [εἰκοσπλασίονα, εἰκοσάκις ἐξισούμενα τῇ τοῦ σώματος σωτηρίᾳ. Schol. A.].

εἰκοστός, ή, όν, Ep. ἐεικοστός, the twentieth.

ἔϊκτο, ἔϊκτον, ἐΐκτην, see ἔοικα.

εἰκυῖα, see ἔοικα.

ΕΙΚΩ, as pres. obsol.: from which only the 3 sing. imperf. occurs: σφίσιν εἶκε, it seemed good to them, 18, 520;† on the contrary, the perf ἔοικα, often, q. v.

εἴκω, fut. εἴξω, aor. εἶξα, Ep. iterat. 3 sing. εἴξασκε, 1) to yield, to retreat, also with ὀπίσσω, backwards; τινί, from any one; with gen. of place: εἴκειν πολέμου, to retreat from the battle, 5, 348; and with both: χάρμης Ἀργείοις, to retreat out of the battle from the Greeks, 4, 509; also from civility, 24, 100. Od. 2, 14; hence b) Metaph. to yield, to be inferior, τινί τι, to any one in any thing, 22, 459; also with dat. εἴκειν πόδεσσι, to be inferior in swiftness of foot, in running, Od. 14, 221. c) Also of the body: to yield, ὅπῃ εἴξειε μάλιστα, where it could not withstand (the lance), i. e. might be wounded, 22, 321. 2) to yield, to give way to, to follow, with dat. ὕβρει, arrogance, αἰδοῖ, ὀκνῳ: ᾧ θυμῷ εἶξας, following his inclination, 9, 598. 3) Apparently trans. εἶξαι ἡνία ἵππῳ, prop. to yield to the horse in respect to the reins, i. e. to give him loose reins, 23, 337, cf. 1. b.

εἰλαπινάζω (εἰλαπίνη), to feast, to be present at a feast, only pres. Il. and Od. from which

εἰλαπιναστής, οῦ, ὁ, a guest, one who feasts, 17, 577.†

εἰλαπίνη, ἡ, a splendid feast, a banquet, a sacrificial feast, Od. 11, 415. 1, 226 (prob. from πίνειν κατ' εἶλαρ).

εἶλαρ, ἀος, τό (εἴλω), prop. covering, then a protection, a defence, spoken of a wall: νεῶν τε καὶ αὐτῶν, a protection for the ships and for ourselves, 7, 338; of a rudder: κύματος εἶλαρ, against the waves, Od. 5, 257.

εἰλάτινος, η, ον, Ep. for ἐλάτινος, of fir, of fir-wood; Il. and Od.

εἵλε, see αἱρέω.

Εἰλείθυιαι, αἱ, the goddesses who preside over child birth, according to 11, 270, daughters of Hḗrē goddess of marriage, who send indeed bitter pangs, but also help women in labour, and aid the birth; *plur. 19, 119; but sing. 19, 103. 16, 187. The discourse is clearly of one, Od. 19, 188, who had a temple at Amnisus in Crete. According to Hes. Th. 922, there is but one, daughter of Zeus and Hḗrē, Apd. 1, 3. 1. In later writers she is the same with Artémis (from Ἐλεύθω, she who comes, Venilia Herm.).

Εἰλέσιον, τό, a place in Bœotia, near Tanagra, 2, 499. (According to Strabo, Εἰλέσιον, from ἕλος, swamp.)

εἰλέω, see εἴλω.

εἰλήλουθα εἰληλούθμεν, see ἔρχομαι.

εἰλίπους, οδος, ὁ, ἡ (εἴλω), dragging or trailing heavily the feet, with a trailing or lumbering gait, epith. of cattle, from their unsteady gait, esply with the hinder feet: only dat. and accus. plur. (Buttmann, Lex. p. 265, would translate it 'stampffüssig,' having feet suited for threshing (heavy-footed).)

Εἰλίσσω. 124 Εἰμί.

εἰλίσσω, Ep. for ἑλίσσω.
εἶλον and εἱλόμην, see αἱρέω.
εἰλύαται, see εἰλύω.
εἴλυμα, τό (εἰλύω), a veil, covering, clothing, Od. 6, 179.†
εἰλυφάζω, to whirl, to roll, with accus. φλόγα, 20, 492.†
εἰλυφάω = εἰλυφάζω, partcp. pres. εἰλυφόων for εἰλυφῶν, whirling, rolling. 11, 156.†
εἰλύω, Ep. for εἰλύω, perf. pass. εἴλυμαι. 3 plur. εἰλύαται for εἴλυνται, partcp. pass. εἰλυμένος, to wind about, to envelope, to veil, to wrap up, to cover, with accus. τινά ψαμάθοισιν, any one with sand, 21, 319 :† or prop. the compound κατειλύω. Of the pass. only the perf. αἵματι καὶ κονίῃσιν εἴλυτο, he was covered with blond and dust. 16, 640. Mly partcp. εἰλυμένος ὤμους νεφέλῃ, the shoulders enveloped in cloud, 5, 186; χαλκῷ, 18, 522; σάκεσι, Od. 14, 479. (ν always long, except in εἰλύαται.)
εἴλω in the pass.. εἰλέω in the act. Ep. for εἰλέω (th. ϜΕΛΩ), aor. 1 infin. ἔλσαι and ἐέλσαι, partcp. ἔλσας, perf. pass. ἔελμαι, partcp. ἐελμένος, aor. 2 pass. ἐάλην (like ἐστάλην from στέλλω), 3 plur. ἄλεν for ἄλησαν, infin. ἀλῆναι and ἀλήμεναι, partcp. ἀλείς, εἶσα, ἔν, all purely Epic forms. 1) Act. 1) to press, to thrust, to drive to straits, esply an enemy in war; with an accus. and the prep. κατά, ἐπί, or simply the dat. olisol.. 8, 215; κατὰ πρύμνας ἔλσαι, 1, 409; Τρῶας κατὰ ἄστυ, 21, 225; and with the mere dat. θαλάσσῃ ἔλσαι Ἀχαιούς, to drive the Achaians to the sea, 18, 294; also θῆρας ὁμοῦ εἰλεῦντα κατὰ λειμῶνα, driving the wild beasts over the meadow, Od. 11, 573; hence metaph. of a storm: τινά, to drive any one along, Od. 19, 200; in the Od. also to strike: ἐπεί οἱ νῆα κεραυνῷ Ζεὺς ἔλσας ἐκέασσε, when Zeus striking with lightning dashed in pieces his ship, Od. 5, 131. 7, 250. 2) to drive together, to shut up. Ἀχαιοὺς Τρῶες ἐπὶ πρύμνῃσιν, 18, 447; ἐν μέσσοισι, 11, 413; ἐνὶ σπῆϊ, to shut up in a cave, Od. 12, 210; ἐν στείνει, Od. 22, 460. Pass. to be pressed, to be driven, κατὰ ἄστυ ἐέλμεθα, 24, 662. cf. 18, 287; hence, of Arês: Διὸς βουλῇσιν ἐελμένος, pressed by the counsels of Zeus, 13, 524; hence also, b) to hold back, to check, τινά, 2, 294. II) Mid. and aor. pass. to be crowded together, to be shut in, to crowd together, ἀμφὶ Διομήδεα. 5, 782; spoken esply of persons beleaguered: ἀνδρῶν εἰλομένων, when men are besieged, 5, 203; esply in the aor. pass. οἱ δὴ εἰς ἄστυ ἄλεν, they crowded together into the city, 22, 12; Ἀργείους ἐκέλευσα ἀλήμεναι ἐνθάδε, to assemble, 5, 823; ἐν ἄστυ, 16, 714; ἐπὶ πρύμνῃσιν, 18, 76. 286. Hence ἀλὲν ὕδωρ, collected water, 23, 420. b) to bend oneself together, to gather oneself (bodily) up. τῇ ὕπο ϝᾶς ἄλεν, under this (the shield) he drew himself entirely up, i. e. he concealed himself, 3, 408. 20, 278.

ἧστο ἀλείς, he sat bent together, 16, 403; also of a lion gathering himself to spring on the prey, 20, 168; so also a warrior: Ἀχιλῆα ἀλεὶς μένεν, he awaited Achilles on the alert, 21, 571. cf. 22, 308. Od. 24, 538.
εἷμα, ατος, τό (ἕννυμι), a garment, clothing, dress in general, spoken of all kinds of clothes; hence often plur. εἵματα, the entire dress, Od. 2, 3. 6, 214.
εἷμαι, see ἕννυμι.
εἵμαρται, εἵμαρτο, see μείρομαι.
εἰ μέν, with εἰ δέ, often serves to mark an antithetic relation between two conditions. Sometimes the apodosis is wanting. e. g. εἰ μὲν δώσουσι γέρας (sc. καλῶς ἔξει, well and good), εἰ δέ κε μὴ δώωσιν, 1, 135.
εἰμέν, Ep. and Ion. for ἐσμέν, see εἰμί.
εἱμένος, see ἕννυμι.
εἰ μή, 1) if not, unless, nisi, in conditional clauses, where the whole clause is intended to be denied, see μή, 2, 156. 261. 2) except, without a verb, mly after ἄλλος. Od. 12, 326. 17, 383.
εἰμί (th. ἔω), H. forms: pres. 2 sing. ἐσσί and εἰς, 1 plur. εἰμέν, 3 plur. ἔασι, subj. ἔω and εἵω (εἴῃς, εἴῃ, not in ed. Wolf), opiat. εἴην, also ἔοις, ἔοι, infin. ἔμμεναι, ἔμμεναι, ἔμεν, ἔμμεν, partcp. ἐών (ὄντας, ὄντες, Od.), imperf. 1 sing. ἔα, ἦα, ἔην, ἔον, ἔσκον, 2 ἔησθα, ἦσθα, 3 ἔην, ἦεν, ἦεν, ἔσκε, 2 dual ἤστην, 3 plur. ἔσαν (εἴατο, Od. 20, 106, where others read εἴατο), fut. ἔσομαι, Ep. ἔσσομαι. 3 sing. ἐσσεῖται, etc. On the inclination of the accent. see Thiersch Gram. § 62. (Gr. 76, 82. Jelf. i. § 62, 63. Buttm. § 4, 2]. 1) As a verb of existence (in which case no inclination takes place), 1) to be, to exist, to have being. τὰ ἐόντα τά τ' ἐσσόμενα, the present and the future, 1, 70; chiefly in the signif. to live. σὺ δὴ ἦν, he did not long live, 6, 131. ἔτι εἰσί, they are still alive, Od. 15, 433. Hence the gods are often denominated αἰὲν ἐόντες, the ever-living, and οἱ ἐσσόμενοι, posterity; with an adv. Κουρήτεσσι κακῶς ἦν, it fared badly, went ill with, 9, 551. διαγνῶναι χαλεπῶς ἦν, it was hard to distinguish, 7, 424. 2) ἔστι with a following infin., it is possible, it is permitted, one can: often with negat. πὰρ δύναμιν οὐκ ἔστι πολεμίζειν, a man cannot fight beyond his strength, 13, 787. οὔπως ἔστιν καταβήμεναι, it is not possible to descend. 12, 65. cf. 357. The person is in the dat.; still also with accus. and infin., 14, 63. Od. 2, 318. 3) ἔστι with the dat. of the pers, it is to me, i. e. I have, I possess. εἰσίν μοι παῖδες, I have sons, 10, 170. II) As copula: 1) to be, mly connected with the subst. and adj.; also with adverbs. ἐκέων, ἀρήν, ἐγγύς, etc. 2) With gen. it indicates possession, property, descent. αἵματος εἰς ἀγαθοῖο, thou art of good blood. Od. 4, 611; material: εἷμα ἔσαν μέλανος κυάνοιο, the stripes were of dark steel, 11, 24. 3) With dat. οὐ κατηφείη καὶ ὄνειδος ἔσσεται, 17, 557;

also in the constr. ἐμοὶ δέ κεν ἀσμένῳ εἴη, it would be grateful to me, 14, 108. 4) Freq. with prepos. ἐκ πατρὸς ἀγαθοῦ, to spring from a noble father, 14, 113. 5) εἶναι is frequently omitted, e. g. 3, 391. 10, 437. 113. On εἴην in 15, 82, see εἰμι, at the close.

εἶμι (th. ἴω), pres. subj. ἴω, ἴῃσθα and ἴῃς, 3 ἴῃσι, ἴῃ, 1 plur. ἴομεν, Ep. for ἴωμεν, 3 ἴωσι, optat. 1 sing. εἴην, 15, 82; 3 ἴοι, εἴη and ἰείη, 19, 209; infin. ἴμεναι, ἴμμεναι, 20, 365; cf. Thiersch § 229; ἴμεν, ἰέναι, partcp. ἰών, imperf. Ep. ἦϊα, ἤϊον, 2 ἤϊες and ἴες, 3 ἤϊεν, ἤϊε, ἦεν, ἦε, ἴεν, ἴε, 3 ἴτην, 1 plur. ἤομεν, Od. 3, ἤϊον and ἤϊσαν, ἴσαν. Finally, in Ep. fut. mid. εἴσομαι, and aor. 1 εἰσάμην, to which may be added the pres. ἵεμαι. The pres. is even in H. used as a fut., 10, 55, though it is found in him as a pres. also. 1) to go, to come, to travel, to journey; frequently, according to the connexion, a) to go away, to return; often limited by adverbs: ἆσσον, αὖτις, ἐπί, ἐς, ἀνά, μετά, ἰέναι, ἀντία and ἀντίον τινός, to go against any one, 5, 256; ἐπί τινα, to go to any one, 10, 55. b) With accus. ὁδὸν ἰέναι, to go a journey, Od. 10, 103; with gen. of the place, ἰὼν πεδίοιο, going through the plain, 5, 597. c) With partcp. fut. it expresses an action which one is going or intending to perform. εἶσι μαχησόμενος, he goes to fight, 17, 147; also with infin., 15, 544. 2) Metaph. a) to fly, spoken of birds and insects, 17, 756. 2, 87. b) Of inanimate things : to go, to travel; ἐπὶ νηὸς ἰέναι, in a ship, Od.; spoken of an axe and spear: πέλεκυς εἶσι διὰ δουρός, the axe goes through the plank, 3, 61. Spoken of food, 19, 209; of clouds, smoke, tempest, 4, 278. 21, 522; and of time: (ἔτος) εἶσι τέταρτον, the fourth year will come to an end, Od. 2, 89, so Eustath., Voss : but Nitzsch, 'the fourth year will come,' in which case, in v. 106, τρίετες is to be changed into δίετες, and in v. 107, τέτρατον into δὴ τρίτον. II) Mid. in the same signif. ἐς περιωπὴν, to ascend to a place of observation, 14, 8. διαπρὸ δὲ εἴσατο καὶ τῆς, it went entirely through this also (μίτρη), 4, 138. 13, 191 (iota is short, but in ἴομεν sometimes long for metre's sake), see ἵεμαι.—N. B. 15, 80 seq. ὡς δ᾽ ὅτ᾽ ἂν ἀΐξῃ νόος ἀνέρος, ὅστ᾽ ἐπὶ πολλὴν γαῖαν ἐληλουθὼς—νοήσῃ ἐνθ᾽ εἴην ἢ ἔνθα, cf. ἀΐσσω. Some of the ancients take εἴην, or, by another reading, ἤην, as 1 sing. imperf. of εἰμί (I was); others read ἔει or ἤειν as 3 sing. imperf. of εἰμί (ibam): others again, εἴην as 3 sing. optat. from εἶμι or εἰμί: Voss leaves it undecided from which verb he takes it. Hermann, in the essay de leg. quibusd. substituerib. serm. Hom. (Op. II. 57), prefers the reading ἤην (hic fui et illic), which certainly suits ἐληλουθὼς well. Still, as ἤην occurs nowhere else as 1 pers., and as ἔνθα ἢ ἔνθα mly indicates motion, it is most probably to be regarded with Spitzner as optat. of εἶμι, εἴην (cf. 24, 139. Od. 14, 496), should I go here or there [secum cogitat, huc iverim an illuc]? The last mentioned critic, since the first pers. does not accord well with the Epic diction, thinks the reading εἴη more agreeable to the Hom. form of speech. Cf. Spitzner on the passage.

εἰν, poet. for ἐν, in.

εἰνάετες, adv. (ἐννέα, ἔτος), nine years long, from adj. εἰναετής, of nine years, Il., and Od. 3, 118.

εἰνάκις. adv., poet. for ἐννάκις, nine times, Od. 14, 230.

εἰνάλιος, η, ον, Ep. for ἐνάλιος, in the sea, of the sea; κήτος, a monster of the sea, Od. 443; κορώνη, the sea-crow, *Od. 5, 67.

εἰνάνυχες, adv. (ἐννέα νύξ), nine nights long, 9, 470.†

εἰνατέρες, αἱ, wives of brothers, sisters-in-law, *6, 378. 22, 473. (Sing. obsolete.)

εἴνατος, η, ον, Ep. for ἔνατος, q. v.

εἴνεκα, Ep. for ἕνεκα, q. v.

εἰνί, Ep. for ἐν.

εἰνόδιος, η, ον, Ep. for ἐνόδιος (ὁδός), on the way, 16, 260.†

εἰνοσίφυλλος, ον (ἔνοσις, φύλλον), leaf-shaking, clothed with foliage; forest-clad (Cp.), epith. of mountains [there stands, his boughs waving the mountain Neritus sublime. Cp.], 2, 632. Od. 9, 22.

εἴξασκε, see εἴκω.

εἷο, Ep. gen. for οὗ, his.

εἰνοκυίαι, see ἔοικα.

εἶπα, 1. q. εἶπον, q. v.

εἰπέμεναι, εἰπέμεν, see εἶπον.

εἴπερ, 1) if indeed, if really; if, in hypothetical sentences, when the two members are harmonious. The indic. subj. and optat. follow (see εἰ). εἰ τελέει περ, 8, 415. 16, 118. 24, 667. Od. 1, 188. εἴπερ γάρ κ᾽ ἐθέλῃσιν Ὀλύμπιος—ἐξ ἑδέων στυφελίξαι, 1, 580. In this passage, the apodosis is wanting, according to the interpretation of Wolf and Spitzner, viz. 'he is able to do so.' Voss, on the other hand, places the comma after Ὀλύμπιος ἀστεροπητής, and takes the words ἐξ ἑδέων στυφελίξαι (optat.), as apodosis, for 'if the Olymp. thunderer should will, he could hurl us,' etc. 2) even if, although, when the members are antith., 1, 81. 4, 38, 261. 8, 153.

εἴποθεν, more correctly εἴ ποθεν, if from any where, whether from any where, Od. 1, 115. 11, 9, 380.

εἴ ποθι, if any where, *Od. 12, 96.

εἶπον, Ep. ἔειπον, iterat. εἴπεσκον, subj εἴπω, 2 sing. εἴπῃσθα, optat. εἴποιμι, infin. εἰπεῖν, partcp. εἰπών. The imperat. εἰπέ, εἴπατε, Od. 3, 407; also the poet. form ἔσπετε, to say, to speak, τί τινι, any thing to any one: also, εἰπεῖν τινα, to address any one, 12, 210. 17, 237; εὖ εἰπεῖν τινα, to speak well of one, Od. 1, 302; (from ἔπω, prop. to recount; in use, it is the aor. of φημί.)

εἴποτε, more correctly εἴ ποτε, 1) if ever, if at any time, with indicat., 1, 39.

G 3

Εἴ που.   Εἰς.

394; with subj., 1, 340. 2) *whether ever, if ever*, in indirect questions with optat., 2, 97. 3) The Hom. formula εἴποτ' ἔην γε is variously explained. Most critics take it as an expression of a sad remembrance of what formerly existed; δαήρ αὖτε ἐμὸς ἔσκε, εἴ ποτ' ἔην γε, 3, 180. Thiersch § 329, 3, 'he was also my brother-in-law, if indeed he ever was so' [which is hardly credible]. Wolf likewise remarks in Vorles. zu Il. II. p. 202: " It expresses tender sensibility connected with dejection and regret: 'once he was.'" So Eustath. understands it; he says, 'it is as if she would say, οὐκ ἔστι, ἀλλὰ ποτὲ ἦν,' cf. Herm. ad Viger. p. 916: "*Cujus formulæ, quæ perdifficilis explicatu est, hic videtur sensus esse; si unquam fuit, quod nunc est non amplius, i. e. si recte dici potest fuisse, quod illi sui factum est dissimile, ut fuisse unquam vix credas. Est enim hæc loquutio dolentium, non esse quid amplius; ut vim ejus Germanice (Anglice) sic exprimas,*" but, alas! no longer so. Schütz in Hoogeveen Doct. Part. in Epit. red. p. 630, incorrectly considers it as an optat. 'ah would he were so still.' Besides 3, 180, this formula stands in 11, 761. 24, 428. Od. 15, 268. 19, 315.

εἴ που, *if perhaps (perchance, haply), if by any means*, Od. 4, 193.

εἴ πως, *if perchance, if in any way*, 13, 807.

Εἰραφιώτης, ου, ὁ, voc. Εἰραφιῶτα, appellat. of Dionȳsos. Hom. h. 26, 2. (The derivation is uncertain; perhaps from ἐν and ῥάπτω, sowed into the thigh. Schwenk in Zeitschr. für Alterthumsw. No. 151, 1835, derives it from ἔαρ and φίω = φύω, and translates, *spring-born*.)

εἴργω = ἐέργω, see ἔργω.

εἴρερος, ὁ (εἴρω, to bind), *captivity, servitude*, or *a female slave*, cf. Nitzsch, Od. 8, 529.†

*Εἰρεσίαι, αἱ, a town in Hestiæotis (Thessalia), h. in Apoll. 32. Others read, Πειρεσίαι; Ilgen understands by Εἰρεσίαι, the island *Irrhesia* of Pliny.

εἰρεσίη, ἡ (ἐρέσσω), *the act of rowing*, *Od. 10, 78. 11, 640.

Εἰρεσιώνη, ἡ (εἶρος), 1) An olive branch wound with wool and hung with fruits, a kind of harvest garland, which on the festivals Πυανέψια and Θαργήλια was carried around by boys with singing and then hung upon the house-door. 2) the *song* on such an occasion; and then mly *a song*, to solicit charity, Ep. 15.

Εἰρέτρια, ἡ, Ion. for Ἐρέτρια; an important town in the island of Eubœa, near Palæo Castro, 2, 537.

εἴρη, ἡ, an *assembly, a place of assembling*, plur., 18, 531.† (According to Schol. = ἀγορά, from ἐρεῖν) or from εἴρω, *sero*, keeping locked (the sacred gates, V.).

εἰρήμαι, see εἴρω.

εἰρήνη, ἡ, *peace*, Od. 24, 486. ἐπ' εἰρήνης. In peace, 2, 797. Od. 24, 486 (prob. from εἴρω, *sero*).

εἴριον, τό. Ep. for ἔριον, q. v.

εἰροκόμος, ον (κομέω), *working wool, carding wool*, 3, 387.†

εἴρομαι, Ion. and Ep. depon. mid., Infin. εἴρεσθαι, imperf. εἰρόμην, fut. εἰρήσομαι. 1) *to ask*, τινά, any one or after any one, 1, 553. 6, 239; τί, after any thing, 0, 416; and τινά τι, any one about any thing, Od. 7, 237; also ἀμφί τι, Od. 11, 570. 2) *to say*, cf. εἴρω. (Ep. forms ἐρέω. ἐρέομαι, ἔρομαι, q. v.)

εἰροπόκος, ον (πόκος), *woolly, covered with wool*, epith. of sheep, 5, 337. Od. 9, 443.

εἶρος, τό, Ep. for ἔρος, *wool*, *Od. 4, 135. 9, 226.

εἴρυαται, see ἐρύομαι.

εἰρύομαι and εἰρύω, Ep. for ἐρύομαι, and ἐρύω, q. v.

εἴρω, port. (theme FEP, *sero*), only partcp. perf. ἐερμένος, pluperf. ἔερτο, *to arrange in a row, to fasten together, to bind*; ὅρμος ἡλέκτροισιν ἐερμένος, a necklace joined or strung with amber, Od. 18, 296. h. Ap. 104; and ἔερτο, Od. 15, 460.

εἴρω, fut. ἐρέω, Ep. for ἐρῶ, perf. pass. εἴρημαι, 3 pluperf. pass. εἴρητο, fut. 3 εἰρήσομαι (a.r. 1 pass. ῥηθείς, from the theme ΡΕΩ). The pres. is Ep. and occurs only in the 1 sing., Od. 2, 162. The common form of the fut. h Cer. 406. 1) *to speak, to say, to tell*, τί, 4, 363; οὐ μέν τοι μέλεος εἰρήσεται αἶνος, not empty praise shall be spoken to thee, 23, 795; τινί τι, any thing to any one, 1, 297. 2) *to speak to, to communicate, to announce*, ἔπος, 1, 419; φόως ἐρέουσα, (about) to announce the light, 2, 49. II) Mid. *to say*, like the act., 1, 513. Od. 11, 542; *mly to ask*. prop. 'I cause to be told me,' conf. εἴρομαι. (These forms from εἴρω belong in use to φημί, q. v. The Ep. fut. ἐρέω, *I will say*, must not be confounded with the pres. ἐρέω, *I ask*.)

εἰρωτάω, Ion. and Ep. for ἐρωτάω, only pres. *to ask, to interrogate*, τινά τι, one about any thing, *Od. 4, 347. 17, 138.

εἰς, Ion. and Ep. ἐς, 1) Prep. with accus., ground signif. *into, to whither!* (cf. ἐν), to indicate a motion into the interior of an object, 1) Spoken of space: *a)* Of a local object, *into, to*; οἴχεσθαι ἐς Θήβην, 1, 366; εἰς ἅλα; esply of persons, with the implied idea of residence, εἰς Ἀγαμέμνονα, 7, 312; ἐς Μενέλαον. Od. 3, 317; with verbs of seeing: εἰς ὦπα ἰδέσθαι, to look (into) in the face. *b)* Of quantity: εἰς δεκάδας ἀριθμείσθαι, to be counted into decades, 2, 124. 2) Of time: *a)* In assigning a limit, *till, until*: ἐς ἠέλιον καταδύντα; in like manner ἐς τί ἔτι, till how long, 5, 465. *b)* In indicating continuance of time, for: ἐς ἐνιαυτόν, for a year, a year long, Od. 4, 86; ἐς θέρος, in the summer, Od. 14, 384. 3) Of cause, manner, etc.: *a)* The aim, εἰπεῖν εἰς ἀγαθόν, for good, 9, 102. *b)* Way and manner, ἐς μίαν βουλεύειν, harmoniously, 2, 379. *c)* A reference, εἰς φύσιν, Batr. 52. Remark 1) εἰς is often found with verbs signifying rest, instead of the prep. ἐν with the dat. It is a constructio praegnans by which the verb at the same time embraces the idea of motion : ἐφάνη λῖς εἰς ὁδόν, 15, 276 ; ἐς θρόνους ἕζοντο, Od. 4, 51. Rem. 2) εἰς stands apparently with the gen. by an ellipsis: εἰς Ἀΐδαο, subaud. δόμον; εἰς Αἰγύπτοιο (ὕδωρ), Od. 4, 581. II) Adv.; in this signif. it occurs but rarely. τὼ δ᾽ εἰς ἀμφοτέρω Διομήδεος ἅρματα βήτην, 5, 115. III) In compos. It has the general signif. *into, to*.

εἷς, μία, ἕν, gen. ἑνός. μιᾶς, ἑνός, ορ.; with super., 12, 243, also with art. ἡ μία, 2ͺ, 272 ; an Ep. form of εἷς is ἰός. q. v.

εἷσα (theme ἙΩ), an Ep. defect. Imperf. εἷσον, partcp ἕσας, ἕσασα, aor. 1 mid. ἐσάμην and ἐέσσατο, 1) *to seat, to cause to sit*, ἐν κλισμοῖσι, ἐς θρόνον, ἐπὶ θρόνου, 2) *to place, to lay, to bring into a place*, δῆμον ἐν Σχερίῃ, Od. 6, 8; σκοπόν, to place a watcher, 23, 359; λόχον, to lay an ambuscade, 4, 392. Od. 4, 531 ; τινὰ ἐπὶ νηός, h. 7, 10; and so mid. ἐέσσατο, Od. 14, 295; (what is wanting is supplied by ἱδρύω, see Buttm. Gram. § 108.)

εἰσαγείρω, poet. ἐσαγείρω (ἀγείρω), 1) *to collect into*, with accus. ἑρέτας ἐς νῆα, 1, 142. 2) Mid. *to assemble* (themselves) *in*, Od. 14, 248. b) Metaph. with accus. θυμόν, to recover spirit, 15, 240. 21, 417.

εἰσάγω, poet. ἐσάγω (ἄγω), aor. 2 εἰσήγαγον, *to lead into, to introduce*, with accus. Λαοδίκην ἐσάγουσα. leading in Laodikê, 6, 252. (The Schol. takes ἐσάγουσα intrans. and Voss. renders 'going to Laodike'), with double accus. ἑταίρους Κρήτην, to conduct his companions to Crete, Od. 3, 191 ; conf. Od. 4, 43 ; metaph. ποταμῶν μένος, 12, 18.

εἰσαθρέω, poet. ἐσαθρ. (ἀθρέω), *to behold, to discern in the midst*, τινά, 3, 450.†

εἰσακούω, poet. ἐσακούω (ἀκούω), aor. ἐσάκουσα, without augm. *to hearken to, to understand*, absol. 8, 97.† φωνήν, h. in Cer. 248.

εἰσάλλομαι, depon. mid. (ἅλλομαι), aor. 1 ἐσήλατο, and aor. 2 ἐσάλτο, *to spring upon, to leap upon*, with accus. τεῖχος, πύλας, to storm a wall, the gates, *12, 438. 466.

εἰσάμην, Ep. 1) Aor. 1 mid. of εἴδω. 2) Aor. 1 mid. of εἶμι.

εἰσαναβαίνω (βαίνω), aor. 2 εἰσανέβην, infin. εἰσαναβῆναι, *to mount up, to ascend, to go up to*, with accus. Ἴλιον, Λάχος, and εἰς ὑπερῷα, Od. 19, 602.

εἰσανάγω (ἄγω), *to lead into* ; τινὰ εὕερον, any one into slavery, Od. 8, 529; cf. πέρσος.

εἰσανείδον, def. aor. (ΕΙΔΩ), *to look up to any thing*, with accus. οὐρανόν, *16, 232. 24, 307.

εἰσάνειμι (εἶμι), *to ascend upon, to mount*. with accus. spoken of the sun, οὐρανόν, 7, 423.†

εἰσάντα, Ep. ἔσαντα (ἄντα), *opposite*, over against. ἔσαντα ἰδεῖν, to look into the face, 17, 334 ; εἰσαντα only Od. 5, 217.

εἰσαφικάνω, poet. form of εἰσαφικνέομαι, 14, 230. Od. 22, 99.

εἰσαφικνέομαι, depon. mid. (ἱκνέομαι), only aor. εἰσαφικόμην, *to go to a place, to arrive at*, with accus. Ἴλιον, Il. ; also τινά, Od. 13, 404.

εἰσβαίνω, poet. ἐσβαίνω (βαίνω), aor. 1 ἐσέβησα, aor. 2 εἰσέβην, 1) Trans. *to introduce, to bring in*, ἑκατόμβην, 1, 310.† 2) Intrans. *to enter, to go on board*, esply of a ship, Od. 9, 103. 179.

εἰσδέρκομαι, depon. (δέρκομαι), aor. ἐσέδρακον, *to look at, to perceive, to behold*, with accus., Il. and Od. only aor.

εἰσδύω, poet. ἐσδύω (δύω), only mid. ἐσδύομαι, *to go into, to enter*. ἀκοντιστὺν ἐσδύσεαι, thou wilt enter the battle fought with spears, 23, 622.†

εἰσεῖδον (ΕΙΔΩ). Ep. ἐσεῖδον, defect. aor. of εἰσοράω, *to look upon, to behold*.

εἴσειμι (εἶμι). *to go in, to come to*, μετ᾽ ἀνέρας. Od 18, 184; with accus. οὐκ Ἀχιλῆος ὀφθαλμοὺς εἴσειμι, I will not come before the eyes of Achilles, 24, 463.

εἰσελαύνω, Ep. ἐσελάω (ἐλαύνω), aor. 1 εἰσέλασα, *to drive into*, ἵππους, 15, 385; absol. εἰσελάων, the herdsman driving in, Od. 10, 83. 2) Intrans. *to steer into*, prop. subaud. ναῦν, Od. 13, 113.

εἰσερύω (ἐρύω), *to draw into*; with accus. νῆα σπέος, to draw the ship into a grotto, Od. 12, 317.†

εἰσέρχομαι, poet. ἐσέρχομαι (ἔρχομαι), fut. ἐσελεύσομαι, aor. 2 εἰσῆλθον, poet. εἰσήλυθον, *to go into, to come into, to enter*, with accus. Μυκήνας, πόλιν, also οἰκόνδε, 6, 3υ5 ; metaph. μένος ἀνδρας ἐσέρχεται, strength enters the men, 17, 157. Od. 15, 407.

εἴσθα, for εἶς, see εἶμι.

εἰσθρώσκω (θρώσκω), aor. 2 ἔσθορον, Ep. for εἰσέθορον, *to leap into*, only absol., *12, 462. 21, 18.

εἰσίεμεναι, see εἰσίημι.

εἰσίζομαι, poet. ἐσίζομαι (ἵζομαι), *to seat oneself in* ; λόχον, to place oneself in an ambuscade, 13, 285.†

εἰσίημι (ἵημι), *to send in*, mid. *to betake ones lf to*. αὖλιν ἐσιέμεναι, partcp. pres. betaking oneself to a resting-place, Od. 22, 470.† Others take it as partcp. pres. mid. of εἴσειμι (εἶμι) : and this is probably the more correct view.

εἰσίθμη, ἡ (εἴσειμι), *entrance*, Od. 6, 264.

εἰσκαλέω, poet. ἐσκαλέω, *to call in*, mid. *to call to oneself*; only in tmesis, ἐς δ᾽ ἄλοχον ἐκαλέσσατο, 24, 193.†

εἰσκαταβαίνω, Ep. ἐσκαταβαίνω (βαίνω), *to descend into* any thing, with accus. ὄργατον, Od. 24, 222.†

εἴσκω, Ep. lengthened from ἴσκω (ἴσος), 1) *to make similar, to render like*. αὐτὸν ἤϊσκεν δέκτῃ. he made himself like a beggar, Od 4, 247. 13, 313. 2) *to esteem like, to compare to*, τινά τινι, 3, 197. Τυδεΐδη αὐτὸν πάντα ἐΐσκω, 1

εἰσμαίομαι.

consider him in all respects like Tydides, 5, 181. τάδε νυκτὶ ἔοικε, Od. 26, 362; to compare, τινά τινι, 3, 197. Od. 6, 152. 8, 159. 3) to regard as, to judge, to suppose, absol. Od. 4, 148. and with accus. and infin., Od. 11, 363. ἦ ἄρα δή τι εἴσκομεν ἄξιον εἶναι τρεῖς ἑνὸς ἀντὶ πεφάσθαι, we judge it now sufficient that three have been slain instead of one, 13, 446. 21, 332.

εἰσμαίομαι (μαίομαι), aor. 1 ἐσεμασάμην, Ep. σσ, to affect, to distress, only metaph. μάλα με ἐσεμάσσατο θυμόν, he greatly distressed my heart, *17, 564. 20, 425.

εἰσνοέω (νοέω), aor. 1 εἰσενόησα, to remark, to perceive, τινά, Il. and Od.; ἴχνια, h. Merc. 218.

εἴσοδος, ἡ (ὁδός), entrance, access, Od. 10, 90.†

εἰσοιχνέω (οἰχνέω), to go into, with accus. νῆσον, *Od. 6, 157. 9, 120.

εἴσόκε, before a vowel εἰσόκεν (εἰς ὅ κε). 1) till, until, mly with the subjunc. which expresses an expected end, 2, 332. 446. b) With indicat. fut. 21, 134. Od. 8, 318. Il. 3, 409 (in this passage better subjunc. aor. with shortened mood vowel). c) With optat. 15, 70. Od. 22, 444. 2) as long as, with subjunc., 9, 609. 10, 89.

εἴσομαι, 1) Ep. fut. mid. of οἶδα, see ΕΙΔΩ. 2) Ep. fut mid. of εἶμι.

*εἰσοπίσω, adv. (ὀπίσω), for the future, in future, h. Ven. 104.

εἰσοράω (ὁράω), partcp. εἰσορόων, Ep. for εἰσορῶν, fut. εἰσόψομαι. aor. 2 εἰσεῖδον, mid. infin. pres. εἰσοράασθαι, Ep. for εἰσορᾶσθαι. to look upon, to behold, to regard, with accus. 1) With the idea of veneration. εἰσορᾶν τινα ὡς θεόν, to look upon any one as a god, i. e. to venerate, 12, 312; οr ἶσα θεῷ, Od. 15, 520. 2) Mid. like the act., Od. 3, 246.

ἶσος, ἴση, ἶσον (ἴ), Ep. lengthened from ἶσος, used however only in the fem., like, aequalis. in the following constructions: 1) δαῖς ἐΐση, an evenly divided feast, a common feast, spoken esply of sacrificial feasts in which each one receives an equal portion, 1, 468, and often. 2) νῆες ἐΐσαι, the even-floating ships. i. e. built alike strong on both sides, so as to preserve their equipoise in sailing, 1, 306. 3) ἀσπὶς πάντοσ᾽ ἐΐση, the every where equal shield, i. e. extending alike from the centre to all sides, hence entirely round, 3, 347. 4) φρένες ἔνδον ἐΐσαι, an equable mind, a mind remaining the same in all circumstances, Od. 11, 337. 14, 178. [5) ἵπποι ἐΐσαι (σταφύλῃ ἐπὶ νώτον), 2, 765.]

εἰσόψομαι, fut. of εἰσοράω.

εἰσπέτομαι (πέτομαι), aor. εἰσπτάμην, to fly into, with accus. πιτρην. 21, 494.†

εἰσφέρω (φέρω). 1) to bring in, to carry in, with accus. esply Od. 7, 6. 2) Mid. to bear away with oneself, to sweep away. spoken of a river; with accus. πεύκας, 11, 495.

εἰσφορέω, a form of εἰσφέρω, *Od. 6, 91. 19, 32

εἰσχέω (χέω), to pour in, 2) Mid. to pour oneself in, to rush into; only aor. sync. mid. ἐσέχυντο κατὰ πύλας, they rushed into the gates, *12, 470. 2L 610

εἴσω, Ep. ἔσω. 24, 155. 184. 199. Od. 7, 58; adv. (from εἰς). 1) to, into, inwards, εἰσεῖν, Od 3, 47. εἴσω ἀσπίδ᾽ ἔαξε, he broke in the shield, 7, 270; a) often with accus., which mly follows and depends upon the verb: Ἴλιον εἴσω, Οὐρανὸν εἴσω, etc. Only 24, 155. 184. 199. ἔσω precedes. b) With gen. only Od. 8, 290. 2) within, inside, perhaps Od. 7, 13.

εἴσωπός, ὀν (ὤψ), in the sight of, having in view; with gen. εἴσωποὶ ἐγένοντο νεῶν, they were in sight of the ships, 15, 653.†

εἶται, see ἕννυμι.

εἴτε—εἴτε, conj whether—or, be it this —or that, in indirect double interrogation: a) With indic., 1, 65. Od. 3, 90. b) With subj., 12, 239; εἴτε is also followed by ἢ καί, 2, 349.

εἴτε for εἴητε, see εἰμί.

εἴω, Ep. for ἐάω, 4, 55; but εἴω, see εἰμί.

εἴωθα, see ἔθω.

εἴων, see ἐάω.

εἵως, Ep. for ἕως, q. v.

ἐκ, before a vowel ἐξ, prepos. with gen. General signif. is from, out of, in contradistinction from ἐν. 1) Of place: in denoting removal from the interior or immediate vicinity of a place, out, out of, away from, esply with verbs of motion, ἰέναι, ἔρχεσθαι, etc. ἐκ νηῶν, from the ships. 6, 213. b) In denoting distance with verbs of rest, without, only Ep ἐκ βελέων, without the reach of weapons, 11, 163. With verbs of standing, sitting, hanging, etc., ἐκ stands to indicate the idea of consequent motion or distance contained in the verb. ἐκ δίφρου γουνάζεσθαι, down from the chariot, 11. 130. αὐτόθεν ἐκ δίφροιο καθήμενος, Od. 21, 420. ἐκ πασσαλόφι κρέμασεν φόρμιγγα, he hung from (upon) the hook, Od. 8, 67. 2) Of time: a) Spoken of direct departure from a point of time, from, esply ἐξ οὗ, from which time, since; and ἐκ τοῦ or ἐκ τοῦδε, from this time, 1. 493. ἐξ ἀρχῆς, from the beginning, at first. b) Spoken of the direct consequence, after. ἐξ αἰθέρος, 16, 365. 3) Spoken of cause, manner, etc.: a) Of origin. εἶναι, γίγνεσθαι ἔκ τινος, to spring from any one, 15, 187. b) Of the whole in reference to its parts. ἐκ πολέων πίσυρες, 15, 680. c) Of the author or agent, with pass and intrans. verbs, Ep. and Ion. like ὑπό, by. ἐφίληθεν ἐκ Διός, 2, 669. ἀπολέσθαι ἔκ τινος, 18. 107. d) Of the cause, ἐκ θεόφιν πολεμίζειν, to fight at the instigation of the gods, 17, 101. cf. 5, 384. ἐκ θυμοῦ φιλεῖν, to love from the heart,

9, 186. e) Of suitableness, *after, according to*. ὀνομάζειν ἐκ γενεῆς, (=) by the name of, after his family (by his hereditary name. Cp.], 10, 68. 4) ἐκ is often separated by some words from its gen., 11, 109; it is also in Epic writers placed after the gen., 1, 125; ἐκ after the subst. receives the accent; also when it is emphatic, 5, 865. See also the articles, διέκ, παρέκ, ὑπέκ. II) Adv. ἐκ is also used in its orig. signif. as an adv. of place: ἐκ δ' ἀργύρεον τελαμῶνα, and thereon (attached to it), 18, 480; and often in tmesis, 1, 436. 13, 394. III) In compos. ἐκ = out (of), away from, utterly; expressing separation, origin, completion.

Ἐκάβη, ἡ, *Hecuba*, daughter of Dymas, king of Phrygia, sister of Asius and wife of Priam, 16, 718; in later writers, daughter of Kisseus.

Ἑκάεργος, ὁ (ἔργον), *working at a distance, far shooting*; according to Nitzsch, *throwing from a distance*, epith. of Apollo, because he slew with arrows, = ἑκηβόλος, as adj. 5, 439. 2) As subst. *the far-shooter*, 1, 147, and Od. 8, 323.

ἐκάην, aor. 2 pass. of καίω.

ἔκαθεν, adv. (ἑκάς), *from far, from a distance*, also = ἑκάς, Od. 17, 25.

ἐκάθιζον, see καθίζω, Od. 16, 408.

Ἐκαμήδη, daughter of Arsinous of Tenedos, whom Nestor received as a slave, 11, 624.

ἑκάς, adv. (ἐκ), *far, at a distance, far from*; often as prep. with gen. 5, 791; and often with ἀπό, 18, 256. Compar. ἑκαστέρω, superl. ἑκαστάτω, *at the farthest*, 10, 113.†

ἑκαστέρω, adv. compar. of ἑκάς, Od. 7, 321.†

ἑκαστόθι, *to each* or *every*, Od. 3, 8.†

ἕκαστος, η, ον, *each (one), every one*, as a collective adj. frequently with the plur. 1, 606. 10, 215; more rarely in the plur. Od. 9, 164. 24, 417. It also stands in the sing. in apposition, after a noun or pronoun plur. for the purpose of more exact definition, when the latter might rather stand in the relation of a gen. οἱ δὲ αλλήρον ἐσημήναντο ἕκαστος, each one of them, 7, 175. πᾶσιν ἐπίστιόν ἐστιν ἑκάστῳ, Od. 6, 265.

ἑκάτερθε, before a vowel ἑκάτερθεν (ἑκάτερος), *on both sides*; also with gen. ὀφίλον, 3, 340.

Ἑκάτη, ἡ, *Hecate*, daughter of Perses or Perseus and Asteris, grand-daughter of Kolus and Phœbē, to whom Zeus gave the power to operate every where. She presided over purifications, wealth, honour, and all prosperity, h. in Cer. 25. 52. Hes. Th. 409. There was a cave sacred to her in Zerinthus in Samothrace, Steph. At a later day she was confounded with Artēmis, and worshipt as presiding over the magic art (prob. from ἕκατος, the far-working).

ἑκατηβελέτης, αο, ὁ, Ep. for ἑκηβόλος, 1, 75. †h. Ap. 137.

ἑκατηβόλος, ον (βάλλω), *far-throwing, far shooting*, or, *hitting from a distance*, epith. of Apollo, 5, 444; of Artēmis, h. 8, 6. As subst. 15, 231.

ἑκατόγχειρος, ον(χείρ), *hundred-handed*, epith. of Briareus, 1, 402.†

ἑκατόζυγος, ον, Ep. for ἑκατόζυγος (ζυγόν), *having a hundred benches of rowers, hundred-oared*, 20, 247.†

ἑκατόμβη, ἡ (βοῦς), *a hetacomb*, prop. a sacrifice of an hundred oxen; but mly, *a solemn sacrifice, a festal sacrifice*, e. g. of twelve oxen, 6, 93. 115; of eighty-one oxen, Od. 3, 59; also of other animals, Od. 1, 25.

ἑκατόμβοιος, ον (βοῦς), *worth a hundred oxen*, τεύχεα, *2, 449. 6, 236.

ἑκατόμπεδος, ον (πούς), *a hundred feet long*, 23, 164.† (Others ἑκατόμποδος).

ἑκατόμπολις, ι (πόλις), *having a hundred cities*, Κρήτη, 2, 649.†

ἑκατόμπυλος, ον (πύλη), *having a hundred gates, hundred-gated*, epith. of the Egyptian Thebes, 9, 383 †

ἑκατόν, indcl. *a hundred*, Il. and Od.

ἕκατος, ὁ, (ἑκάς), *far-shooting*, epith. of Apollo, 7, 83. 2) As subst. *the far-shooter*, 1, 385; cf. ἑκάεργος, ἑκηβόλος.

ἐκβαίνω (βαίνω), aor. 1 ἐξέβησα, aor. 2 ἐξέβην, 1) Intrans. *to descend, to alight, to disembark*, from a ship, 3, 113; πέτρης, to descend from a rock, 4, 107. 2) Trans. in the aor. 1 and fut. act. *to disembark, to put out*, with accus. Od. 24, 301. Il. 1, 438.

ἐκβάλλω (βάλλω), aor. 2 ἐξέβαλον, Ep. ἔκβαλλον, 1) *to cast out* of the ship, Od. 15, 481; τινὰ δίφρου, to hurl or dash a man down from his chariot, 5, 39. 2) *to strike* or *knock out*, i. e. to cause any thing to fall, τί τινι, and with gen. βιὸν χειρός, to strike the bow from the hand, 14, 419. 15, 468; also ἔκτοσε χειρός, Od. 14, 277; δοῦρα, to fell trees, Od. 5, 243. 3) *to let fall*; δάκρυα, Od. 19, 362; metaph. ἔπος, 18, 324. Od. 4, 503.

ἔκβασις, ιος, ἡ (βαίνω), *an exit, the act of coming from* or *out of*, *a landing-place*; ἁλός, a landing-place from the sea, Od. 5, 403.

ἐκβιώσκω, poet. (βλώσκω), aor. 2 ἐξέμολον, poet. ἔκμολον, *to go out*, 11, 604.†

ἐκγεγάμεν, see ἐκγίγνομαι.

ἐκγεγάοντα, see ἐκγίγνομαι.

ἐκγεγαώς, ἐκγεγαυῖα, see ἐκγίγνομαι.

ἐκγελάω (γελάω), aor. ἐξεγέλασα, poet. σε, *to laugh out, to laugh aloud*, Od. 16, 354. Il. 6, 471.

ἐκγίγνομαι, depon. mid. (γίγνομαι), aor. 2 ἐξεγενόμην, Ep. perf. ἐκγέγαα, from this the infin. Ep. ἐκγεγάμεν, partcp. Ep. ἐκγεγαώς, via. from which comes an Ep. fut. ἐκγεγάοντα, without σ, h. Ven. 198. Buttm. p. 272, note. 1) *to be born* or *begotten of*, τινός, any one, 5, 637. 20, 231; with dat. Πορθεῖ, 14, 115. 2) In the perf. *to spring from, to descend from*, τινός, any one, 5, 248. Od. 10, 138.

ἔκγονος, ον (ἐκγίγνομαι), *begotten* or

Ἐκδέχομαι. 130 Ἐκμείρομαι.

born of any one, as subst. *a descendant, progeny*, Il. and Od. ἡ ἔκγονος, *a daughter*. Od. 11, 235.

ἐκδέχομαι, depon. mid. (δέχομαι), *to take from, to receive in succession*, τί τινι, any thing from one, 13, 710.†

ἐκδέω (δέω), aor. ἐξέδησα, *to bind, to fasten*, with the accus. σανίδας, to fasten the door (with the thong), i. e. to lock it, Od. 22, 174; with gen. δρῦς ἡμιόνων, to attach the (felled) oaks to the mules (for them to drag home). [Not, *bound them on the mules*. Cp.], 23, 121.

ἔκδηλος, ον (δῆλος), *very clear, very manifest, distinguished*, μετὰ πᾶσιν, amongst all, 5, 2.†

ἐκδιαβαίνω (βαίνω), partcp. aor. 2 ἐκδιαβάντες, *to go entirely through* any thing, with accus. τάφρον, a trench, 10, 198.†

ἐκδίδωμι (δίδωμι), aor. 2 imperf. ἔκδοτε, *to give out, to give up, to deliver again*, with accus. κτήματα, 3, 459.†

*ἔνδικος, ον (δίκη), *administering justice, taking vengeance, punishing*, Batr. 96.

ἐκδύνω, Ep. for ἐκδύομαι, Od. 1, 437.

ἐκδύω (δύω), aor. 1 ἐξέδυσα, aor. 2 ἐξέδυν, partcp. ἐκδύς, 1) Trans. in the fut. and aor. 1, *to strip off*, τινὰ χιτῶνα, the tunic from any one. Od. 14, 341. 2) Mid. with aor. 2 intrans. *to put off, to lay aside*, τεύχεα, 3, 114. *b*) *to go out*, with gen. μεγάροιο, of the house, Od. 22, 234; metaph. *to escape*, with accus. ὄλεθρον, 16, 99; for ἐκδύμεν (Ep. infin. aor. 2, accord. to Wolf), read ἐκδῦμεν, i. e. ἐκδυίμεν, optat. aor. 2, conf. Buttm. Lex. p. 424. Thiersch § 231, 101.

ἐκεῖθι, adv. *there, in that very place*, Od. 17, 10.†

ἐκεῖνος, η, ο, Ep. κεῖνος (ἐκεῖ), *he, she, it, that person*, with pron. κεῖνος ὅγε, that person there, 3, 391; with subst. without art. κεῖνος ἀνήρ. *b*) Also δεικτικῶς, for adv. there: κεῖνος Ἄρης, 5, 604. Od. 18, 239; the dative κείνῃ as adv., Od. 13, 111. Voss on Aratus 75, decides that it must be κεῖνος when the preceding word is most important, 7, 77; on the other hand ἐκεῖνος, 9, 646. and var. lec.] 24, 90.

ἐκέκαστο, see καίνυμαι.
ἐκέκλετο, see κέλομαι.
ἐκέκλιτο, see κλίνω.

ἔκηα, see καίω.

ἐκηβολίη, ἡ (βάλλω), *skill in shooting, or hitting at a distance*; plur. 5, 54.†

ἐκηβόλος, ον (βάλλω), *far-shooting, far-hitting*, as ἑκατηβόλος, epith. of Apollo, 1, 14. 2) As subst. *the far-shooter*, 1, 96. 110.

ἕκηλος, ον, 5, 759; and εὔκηλος, prop. ἐFεκηλος, 1, 554. Od. 3, 263. 1) *quiet*, Od. 21, 259; *free from care, at ease*, 5, 759. h. Merc. 480. 2) *unmolested, unhindered*. ἕκηλος ἐρρέτω, let him go unhindered to ruin, 9, 376. cf. 6, 70. 17, 340. 3) Metaph. spoken of a resting, fruitless field, b. Cer. 431. (According

to Buttm. Lex. p. 284, prob. related to ἑκών, ἕκητι, with the adj. ending ηλος [related to ἀκήν, ἀκά, ἀκαλός (= ἥσυχος, Hesych.), ἦκα, Lob. Path. 109. Död. 134].

ἕκητι, prep. with gen. *on account of, by means of*; esply of the gods: *by the will of, by the favour of* Ἑρμείαο, *Od. 15, 319. 19, 86.

ἐκθνῄσκω (θνῄσκω), only aor. 2, *to die*. γέλῳ ἔκθανον, they died with laughter. i. e. laughed long and loud, Od. 18, 100.†

ἔκθορον, see ἐκθρῴσκω.

ἐκθρῴσκω (θρῴσκω), aor. 2 ἐξέθορον, Ep. ἔκθορον, *to leap from, to spring out*, with gen. προμάχων, 15, 573. Od. 10, 207; metaph. κραδίη μοι ἔξω στηθέων ἐκθρῴσκει, my heart leaps from my breast, i. e. beats violently, 10, 95.

ἐκκαθαίρω (καθαίρω), *to purify, to clear out*, with accus. οὔρους. 2, 153.†

ἐκκαιδεκάδωρος, ον (δῶρον), *sixteen palms long*, κέρα, 4, 109.†

ἐκκαλέω (καλέω), aor. 1 act. partcp. ἐκκαλέσας, 24, 582. aor. 1 mid. ἐκκαλεσσάμενος, *to call forth*, τινά. Mid. *to call to oneself*, Od. 24, 1.

ἐκκαλύπτω (καλύπτω), partcp. aor. mid. ἐκκαλυψάμενος, *to uncover, to unveil*; mid. *to uncover oneself*, Od. 10, 279, in tmesis.

ἐκκατιδών, old reading for ἐκ κατιδών, 4, 508.

ἐκκίω (κίω), *to go out*, Od. 24, 492; † in tmesis.

ἐκκλέπτω (κλέπτω), *to steal away, to take away privately*, with accus. *to lead off privately*, Ἄρηα, 5, 390.†

ἐκκυλίω (κυλίω), only aor. pass. ἐξεκυλίσθην, *to roll out, to fling off*; pass. *to be rolled from, to tumble from*, ἐκ δίφροιο. *6, 42. 23, 394.

ἐκλανθάνω, ἐκλήθω (λήθω), Ep. aor. 2 act. ἐκλέλαθον, and aor. 2 mid. ἐξελαθόμην, Ep. ἐκλελαθόμην with redupl. 1) Act. *to cause to forget*. τινά τι: Μοῦσα αὐτὸν ἐκλέλαθον κιθαριστύν, they caused him to forget his harp-playing, i. e. they took away from him the art of playing on the harp, 2, 600; also τινα τινος, Ἥρης ἐκλελαθοῦσα, h. Ven. 40. 2) Mid. *to forget*, with. gen. ἀλκῆς, 16, 602; and with the infin. Od. 10, 557.

ἐκλέλαθον, see ἐκλανθάνω.

ἐκληθάνω, poet. for ἐκλανθάνω, Od. 7, 221.†

ἔκλησις, ιος, ἡ (λήθω), *the act of forgetting, forgetfulness*, Od. 24, 485.†

ἐκλύω (λύω), fut. mid. ἐκλύσομαι, *to loose, to release*. 2) Mid. = act. τινὰ κακῶν, to release any one from toils, Od. 10. 286 †

ἐκμάσσατο, see ἐκμαίομαι.

*ἐκμαίομαι, depon. mid. (μαίομαι), aor. 1 ἐκμάσσατο *to ἐξεμάσ. to invent, to discover*, with accus. τέχνην, h. Merc. 511.

ἐκμείρομαι (μείρομαι), perf. ἐξέμμορα, *to participate chiefly in, to obtain* a *chief share of*, with gen. θεῶν τιμῆς, Od. 5, 335.†

Ἐκμολεῖν. 131 Ἐκτανύω.

ἐκμολεῖν, see ἐκβλώσκω.
ἐκμυζάω (μυζάω), partcp. aor. 1 ἐκμυζήσας, to suck out, with accus. αἷμα, 4, 218.†
ἔκπαγλος, ον (ἐκπλήσσω), exciting astonishment or terrour; terrific, frightful, awful, spoken of men, 18, 170; of things: χειμών, Od. 14, 522; ἔπεα, 15, 198. The accus. neut. ἔκπαγλον and ἔκπαγλα, as adv. dreadfully, terribly, as κοτεῖσθαι, and mly, vehemently, exceedingly, φιλεῖν.
ἐκπάγλως, adv. = ἔκπαγλον, Il. and Od.
ἐκπαιφάσσω, poet. (παιφάσσω), to leap furiously forth, 5. 803.†
ἔκπαλθ' for ἔκπαλτο, see ἐκπάλλω.
ἐκπάλλω (πάλλω), only sync aor. 2 mid. ἔκπαλτο. to gush out. μυελὸς σφονδυλίων ἔκπαλτο, the marrow gushed forth from the vertebræ, 20, 483.†
ἐκπατάσσω (πατάσσω), partcp. perf. pass. ἐκπεπαταγμένος, to push out, metaph. = ἐκπλήσσω, to terrify, to astound, pass., Od. 18, 327.†
ἐκπέμπω (πέμπω), 1) to send out or forth, 24, 681; κειμήλια ἄνδρας ἐς ἀλλοδαπούς, 24, 381; τινά, Od. 16, 3. b) to bring away, spoken of things: θεμείλια πύργων καὶ λάων, removed the foundation of blocks and stones, 12, 28. 2) Mid. to send away from oneself, to dismiss, τινὰ δόμου, any one from the house, Od. 20, 361.
ἐκπέποται, see ἐκπίνω.
ἐκπεράω (περάω), aor. 1 ἐξεπέρησα, to go through, to pierce through, with accus. λαῖτμα μέγα, to pass through the great deep, Od. 7, 35. 9, 323; absol. spoken of arrows and spears, 13, 652.
ἐκπέρθω (πέρθω), fut. ἐκπέρσω, aor. ἐξέπερσα, Ep. ἔκπερσα, to sack, to destroy, with accus. πόλιν, Ἴλιον, *1, 164; and often.
ἐκπεσέειν, see ἐκπίπτω.
*ἐκπέτομαι. depon. mid. (πέτομαι), aor. 2 ἐξέπτην (from the form ἵπταμαι), to fly out, Batr. 223.
ἐκπεύθομαι. Ep. for ἐκπυνθάνομαι.
ἐκπεφυυῖαι. see ἐκφύω.
ἐκπίνω (πίνω), aor. 2 ἔκπιον, Ep. for ἐξέπιον, perf. pass. ἐκπέπομαι, to empty, to exhaust, *Od. 9, 353. 22, 56.
ἐκπίπτω (πίπτω), aor 2 ἐξέπεσον, Ep. ἔκπεσον, infin. Ep. ἐκπεσέειν, to fall out, with gen. δίφρου, of the chariot, ἵππων, and with the dat. of pers. τόξον οἱ ἔκπεσε χειρός, from the hand, 8, 329. δάκρυ οἱ ἔκπεσε, 2, 266.
ἐκπλήσσω (πλήσσω), aor. pass. ἐξεπλήγην and ἐκπλήγην, Ep. for ἐξεπλάγην. 1) Act. to strike out, to cast out, metaph. any one (as by a blow), to stun, to terrify or amaze, τινά, Od. 18, 231. 2) Pass. intrans. to be amazed or confounded, to be stunned, to be awe-struck. 18, 225, with accus. ἐκ γὰρ πλήγη φρένας, he was amazed in mind, 16, 403.
ἐκποτέομαι, Ep. for ἐκπέτομαι (πέτομαι), to fly away, to fly down, spoken of snow, with gen. Διός, from Zeus, 19, 357.†

ἐκπρεπής, ές, gen. έος (πρέπω), distinguished, excellent, eminent, ἐν πολλοῖσι, 2, 483.†
ἐκπροκαλέω (καλέω), aor. ἐκπροὐκαλεσάμην, Ep. σσ, to call out or forth, mid. to call to oneself, τινὰ μεγάρων, from the house, Od. 2, 400 † h. Ap. 111.
ἐκπρολείπω (λείπω), partcp. aor. 2 ἐκπρολιπών, to leave (by going forth), with accus. λόχον, their ambush (the cavity of the wooden horse), Od. 8, 515.†
ἐκπτύω (πτύω), aor. 1 ἐξέπτυσα, to spit out, στόματος ἅλμην, Od. 5, 322.†
ἐκπυνθάνομαι (πυνθάνομαι), aor. 2 ἐξεπυθόμην, only infin. to seek, to ascertain, to enquire, with ἤ, ᾖ following. *10, 308. 320, in tmesis.
ἐκρέμω, imperf from κρέμαμαι.
ἐκρέω (ῥέω), to flow out, only in tmesis, 13, 655. Od. 9, 290.
ἐκρήγνυμι (ῥήγνυμι), aor. 1 ἐξέρρηξα, to break out, to tear out or up, with accus. νευρήν, 15, 469; with gen. ὕδωρ ἀλὲν ἐξέρρηξεν ὁδοῖο, the pent up water had torn away a part of the road, *23, 421.
ἐκσαόω (σαόω, Ep. for σώζω), aor. 1 ἐξεσάωσα. to rescue, to deliver, τινά, 4, 12; τινὰ θαλάσσης, from the sea, Od. 4, 501.
ἐκσεύω (σεύω), to drive out, only mid. ἐκσεύομαι, aor. sync. 3 sing. ἐξέσσυτο, aor. 1 pass. ἐξεσσύθην to hasten out, to hurry away, with gen. πυλέων, out of the gates, 7, 1. φάρυγος ἐξέσσυτο οἶνος, the wine gushed from his throat, Od. 9, 373; metaph. βλεφάρων ἐξέσσυτο ὕπνος, sleep fled away from the eyes, Od. 12, 366. 2) Spoken of the spear's head: to come out, to emerge, in the aor. pass. 5, 293.
ἐκσπάω (σπάω), aor. 1 mid. ἐξεσπασάμην, poet. σσ, 1) Act. to draw out, with accus., 5. 859. 2) Mid. to draw out (with reference to the subject), ἔγχος στέρνοιο, his spear from his breast, *4, 530. 7, 255.
ἐκστρέφω (στρέφω), aor. 1 ἐξέστρεψα, to turn out, to tear out, with accus. ἔρνος βόθρου, the plant from the trench, 17, 58.†
ἔκτα, see κτείνω.
ἐκτάδιος, ίη, ιον (ἐκτείνω), extended, spread out, wide, χλαῖνα, 10, 134.†
ἔκταθεν, see κτείνω.
ἔκταμε, see ἐκτάμνω.
ἐκτάμνω, Ep. for ἐκτέμνω (τάμνω), aor. 2 ἐξέταμον, Ep. ἔκταμον, 1) to cut out, with accus. μηρούς. the thigh-bones (of the victims), 2, 423; ὀϊστὸν μηροῦ, an arrow from the thigh (spoken of the physician), 11, 515. 829. 2) to cut down, to fell; of trees, timbers, αἴγειρον, 4, 486; ῥόπαλον, Od. 9, 320; and of the boar, ὕλην, 12, 149.
ἔκταν, Ep. for ἔκτασαν, see κτείνω.
ἐκτανύω (τανύω, Ep. for τείνω), aor. 1 ἐξετάνυσα, Ep. σσ, aor. 1 pass. ἐξετανύσθην, 1) to stretch out, to extend on the ground, τινά. 11, 844; ἐν κόνι, 24, 18. Spoken of the wind: ἐπὶ γαίῃ, to cast to the ground, 17, 58; pass. to be stretched out, to be prostrated, to lie, 7, 271.

G 6

ἐκτελείω, Ep. for ἐκτελέω.
ἐκτελέω, Ep. ἐκτελείω (τελέω), fut. ἐκτελῶ, Ep. ἐκτελέω, aor. 1 ἐξετέλεσα, Ep. σσ, perf. pass. ἐκτετέλεσμαι, aor. pass. ἐξετελέσθην. 1) *to finish, to complete*, with accus. ἔργον, ἄεθλον, φᾶρος, Od. 2, 98: in the pass. spoken of time, Od. 11, 294. 2) *to finish, to fulfil, to perform*, spoken of the gods. γάμον, Od. 4, 7; τινὶ γόνον, to give offspring to any one, 9, 493; *to perform, to fulfil*, ὑπόσχεσιν, ἀπειλάς, ἐέλδωρ. Il. and Od.

ἐκτίθημι (τίθημι), aor. 2 partcp. ἐκθείς, *to put out, to place out*, λάχος, Od. 23, 179.†

ἐκτινάσσω (τινάσσω), *to thrust out, to dash out*, only aor. 1 pass. ἐκ δ' ἐτίναχθεν ὀδόντες, 16, 348.†

ἔκτοθεν, adv. Ep. for ἔκτοσθεν, *from without, without, apart from*, *Od. 1. 132; but ἔκτοθεν αὐλῆς, Od. 9, 338, is without in the court.

ἔκτοθι, adv. (ἐκτός), *out of, without*, with gen. *15, 391, 22, 439.

*ἐκτορέω (τορέω), *to thrust out*, with accus. αἰῶνα, to take away life, h. Merc. 42.

Ἑκτορίδης, ου, ὁ, son of Hector = Astyanax, 6, 401.

ἐκτός, adv. (ἐκ), *out of, without*, εἶναι, 4, 151; ἐκτὸς ἀπὸ κλισίης, 10, 151; mly with gen. *out of, far from*, τείχεος, Il. and Od.

ἔκτος, η. ον (ἕξ), *the sixth*, Il. and Od.
ἔκτοσε, adv. *out of, without*, with gen. Od. 14, 277.†

ἔκτοσθε, before a vowel ἔκτοσθεν, Ep. ἔκτοθεν (ἐκτός), *from without, without*, also as prep. *on the outside of*, with gen. 9, 552, conf. ἔκτοθεν.

*ἐκτρέφω (τρέφω), aor. 1 mid. ἐξεθρεψάμην, *to bring up, to nourish*; mid. *to rear for oneself*, τινά, h. Cer. 221. Batr. 30

ἔκτυπα, see κτυπέω.

*ἐκτυφλόω (τυφλόω), *to blind utterly*, Batr. 241.

Ἕκτωρ, ορος, ὁ, *Hector*, son of Priam and Hecuba, husband of Andromachē and father of Astyanax, the bravest amongst the Trojan leaders and heroes, 2, 816. He bravely defended his country, and at last fell by Achilles, 24, 553. From this the adj. Ἑκτόρεος, έη, εον, appertaining to Hector. χιτών (from ἔχω, who held fast, who protected; Plat. Cratyl. p. 393 = ἄναξ).

ἐκυρή, ἡ, *a mother-in-law*, *22, 451. 24, 770.

ἐκυρός, ὁ, poet. *a father-in-law*, *3, 172. 24, 770.

ἐκφαίνω (φαίνω), fut. ἐκφανῶ, aor. 1 pass. ἐξεφάνθην, Ep. for ἐξεφάνθην, aor. 2 pass. ἐξεφάνην. 1) *to expose, to bring to view*, φόωςδε, to bring to light (spoken of the goddess of birth), 19, 104. 2) Mid. with aor. 1 and 2 pass. *to shine out, to appear, to gleam, to become visible*, 4, 468; ὄσσε δεινὸν ἐξεφάανθεν, terribly gleamed the eyes, 19, 17; with gen.

Χαρύβδιος, from Charybdis, Od. 12, 441.

ἐκφέρω (φέρω), fut. ἐξοίσω, 1) *to bear out, to bring out*, τινά and τί τινος. 5, 234. 23, 259; a) *to bear out*, esply spoken of the dead. 24, 786. b) *to bear away, of a prize*, ἄεθλον. 23, 785. c) *to bear away, to carry out*, κτῆμα, Od. 15, 470. 2) *to bring on*, μισθοῖο τέλος. the time of reward, 21, 450. 3) Intrans. sc. ἑαυτόν. *to outrun, to run before*, spoken of a race of men, and also of horses, 23, 376. 759.

ἐκφεύγω (φεύγω), aor. 2 ἐξέφυγον, Ep. ἐκφυγον, *to flee away, to escape*. 1) With gen. of place, ἁλός, out of the sea, Od. 23, 236; esply spoken of missile weapons: *to fly away*, 11. 380; χειρός, from the hand, 5, 18. 2) With accus. when it denotes escape from danger: *to avoid, to escape*, ὁρμήν, 9, 355; θάνατον, κῆρα, Il. and Od.

ἐκφημι (φημί), fut. ἐξερέω, aor. 2 ἐξεῖπον, *to speak out, to communicate, to announce*, τί τινι. Of φημί H. has only infin. pres. mid. ἐκφάσθαι ἔπος, *Od. 10, 246. 13. 308.

ἐκφθίνω (φθίνω), *to consume entirely, to destroy*: only 3 pluperf. pass. νηῶν ἐξέφθιτο οἶνος, the wine was consumed out of the ships, *Od. 9, 163. 12, 329.

ἐκφορέω (a form of ἐκφέρω), *to bear out*, Od. 22, 451. 24, 417. Mid. poet. *to press forth*, νηῶν, out of the ships, 17, 360.

ἔκφυγε, see ἐκφεύγω.

ἐκφύω (φύω), perf. ἐκπέφυκα, partcp. fem. ἐκπεφυυῖαι, *to beget, to cause to grow*. 2) Intrans. mid. aor. 2 and perf. act. *to spring* or *grow from*, with gen. ἑνὸς αὐχένος, from one neck, 11, 40.†

ἐκχέω, Ep. ἐκχεύω (χέω), aor. 1 mid. Ep. ἐκχευάμην, pluperf. pass. ἐξεκέχυμην, Ep. aor. sync. 2, ἐξέχυτο, and ἔκχυτο, partcp. ἐκχύμενος. 1) *to pour out*, οἶνον (for sacrifice), 3, 295. II) Mid. 1) Aor. 1 *to pour out for oneself, to shoot out*, ὀϊστούς. Od. 22, 3. 2) With Ep. aor. sync. 2 *to pour itself out, to stream forth*, 21, 300; metaph. spoken of things, 4, 526; of numerous men and animals streaming forth, 16. 259. ἱππόθεν, out of the horse. Od. 8, 515.

ἐκχύμενος, ἔκχυτο, see ἐκχέω.

ἑκών, ἑκοῦσα, ἑκόν, *voluntary, willing, without force*. 2) *purposely, of design, of set purpose*, 10, 372. Od. 4, 372.

ἐλάαν, see ἐλαύνω.

ἐλαίη, ἡ, *the olive-tree, the olive*, Il., esply in the Od. sacred to Athēnē, hence ἱερή. Od. 13, 372.

ἐλαίϊνος, η, ον, = ἐλαϊνός, *Od. 9, 320, 394.

ἐλαϊνός, ή, όν, *made of the olive-tree, of olive-wood*, 13, 612. Od. 5, 236.

ἔλαιον, τό (ἐλαίη), *oil, olive-oil*, mly anointing-oil, used after bathing and often perfumed, Od. 2, 339. Il. 23, 186; often λίπ' ἐλαίῳ, see λίπα.

ἔλασα, ἐλάσασκε, see ἐλαύνω.

Έλασος. 133 Έλεαίρω.

Έλασος, ὁ, a Trojan slain by Patroclus, 16, 696 (= the driver; from ἔλασις).

ἔλασσα, see ἐλαύνω.

ἐλάσσων, ον, gen. ονος (compar. of the poet. ἐλαχύς, and used as compar. of μικρός), *smaller, less, worse*, 10, 357.

ἐλαστρέω. Ion. for ἐλαύνω, *to drive*, with accus. ζεύγεα, teams, 18, 543.†

ἐλάτη, ἡ, *the pine*, or *red-fir, pinus abies*, Linn.: 5, 560. 2) that which is made of pine-wood: an oar, 7, 5. Od. 12, 172.

ἐλατήρ, ῆρος, ὁ (ἐλαύνω), *a driver*, esply of horses, *a charioteer*, *4, 145. 23, 369. 2) *one who drives away*, βοῶν, h. Merc. 14.

Ἐλατιωνίδης, αο. ὁ, poet. for Ἐλατίδης, son of Elatius = Ischys, h. Apoll. 210.

Ἔλατος, ὁ, 1) sovereign of the Lapithæ at Larissa in Thessaly, father of Kæneus (Cæneus) and Polyphēmus, also of Ischys. 2) An ally of the Trojans, slain by Agamemnōn, 6, 33. 3) a suitor of Pēnelopē, Od. 22, 267.

Ἐλατρεύς, έως, *a Phæacian*, Od. 8, 111 (the rower).

ἐλαύνω, poet. ἐλάω (Ep. ἐλόω), poet. imperf. ἔλων for ἔλαον, 24, 696; fut. ἐλάσω, Att. ἐλῶ (whence Ep. ἐλόωσι for ἐλῶσι, Od. 7, 319; infin. ἐλάαν for ἐλᾶν), aor. 1 ἤλάσα, poet. ἔλασα, σσ, Ep. iterat. aor. ἐλάσασκε, subj. Ep. 2 sing. ἐλάσῃσθα, aor. 1 mid. ἠλασάμην, Ep. σσ, perf. pass. ἐλήλαμαι, pluperf. ἠληλάμην and ἐληλάμην, 3 sing. ἐληλάδατο, Od. 7, 86; or more correctly ἐληλέατο, for the ἐρηρέδατ' of Wolf; conf. Thiersch 212, 35. Butim. § 103, p. 197. 1) Act. 1) *to drive, to put in motion*, spoken of men, brutes, and inanimate things, with accus. τινὰ ἐς μέσσον, 4, 299; of flocks: μῆλα ὑπὸ σπέος, 4, 279; εἰς σπέος, Od. 9, 337; particularly a) Of horses, chariots, ships, ἵππους, ἅρματα, νῆα, 5, 236. Od. 7, 109; hence: νηῦς ἐλαυνομένη, a sailing ship, Od. 13, 155. b) *to drive off*, of cattle seized as plunder, βοῦς. 1, 154. c) *to press, to urge as an enemy*: οἱ δέ μιν ἅδην ἐλόωσι, καὶ ἐσσύμενον. πολέμοιο, 13, 315 (cf. ἅδην, Spitzner ad loc. places a comma after ἐλόωσι, and connects consequently καὶ ἐσσύμενον with πολέμοιο). ἔτι μίν φημι ἅδην ἐλάαν κακότητος, Od. 5, 290 (cf. ἅδην). Metaph. χεὶρ ὀξείης ὀδύνῃσιν ἐλήλαται (Voss. 'my hand is tortured with sharp pangs'), 16, 518. 2) *to strike*, esply spoken of missile weapons: διὰ στήθεσφιν δόρυ, 8, 259; and pass. ὀϊστὸς διὰ ζωστῆρος ἐλήλατο, the arrow was driven through the girdle, 4, 135; ὤμῳ ἔνι, 5, 400; hence: *to strike, to smite, to cleave*, of other weapons: ἐλαύνειν τινὰ ξίφει, 11, 109; with double accus. τινὰ ξίφει κόρσην, to smite one with a sword on the temple, 13, 576. cf. 614; also οὐλήν, Od. 21, 219; mly b) *to strike*, τινὰ σκήπτρῳ, 2, 199; τέτρην. Od. 4, 507; χθόνα μετώπῳ, the earth with the forehead, Od. 22, 94. c) πόντον ἐλάτῃσιν, to strike the sea with oars, 7, 5; hence ἐλαύνοντες,

those rowing, Od. 13, 22. 3) *to drive*, metaph. a) Spoken of the working of brass, which is driven or beaten out by hammers: *to beat, to forge*, ἀσπίδα, 12, 296; πτύχας, 20, 270. b) *to draw or trace out*, τάφρον, 9, 349; hence: χάλκεοι τοῖχοι ἐληλάδατ', brazen walls were traced, Od. 7, 86 (where Wolf reads ἐρηρέδατο); ὄγμον, to mow a swath, 11, 68. c) κολῳὸν ἐλαύνειν, to excite a tumult, 1, 575. d) ἐλαύνειν δίκην, see ἐξελαύνω. 4) Intrans. *to travel, to go, to proceed*, spoken of chariots: μάστιξεν ἐλάαν, βῆ δ' ἐλάαν, 11.; of ships, Od. 3, 157. 12, 124. II) Mid. with reference to the subject, chiefly in the signif. number 1, *to drive away for oneself* with accus. Od. 4, 637; ἵππους ἐκ Τρώων, 10, 537; ῥύσια, 11, 674.

ἐλαφηβόλος, ον (βάλλω), *stag-slaying*; ἀνήρ, a stag-hunter, a deer-shooter, 18, 319.†

ἔλαφος, ὁ, ἡ, *a stag, a hind*. ἐλάφοιο κραδίην ἔχων, having the heart of a stag, i. e. cowardly, 1, 225. cf 13, 102.

ἐλαφρός, ή, όν, compar. ἐλαφρότερος, superl. ἐλαφρότατος (kindred to ἔλαφος), 1) *light* in motion, *agile, swift*, γυῖα, 5, 122. 13. 61; spoken of men, with accus. πόδας, Od. 1, 164; and with the infin. of horses: θείειν, swift (of a horse), Od. 3. 370. 2) *light* in weight, λᾶας, 12, 450; metaph. *light*, i. e. not burdensome or distressing, πόλεμος, 22, 287.

ἐλαφρῶς, adv. *lightly*, πλώειν, Od. 5, 240.†

ἐλάχιστος, η, ον, superl. of ἐλαχύς, *the smallest, the least*, h. Merc. 573.

ἔλαχον, see λαγχάνω.

ἐλαχύς, εῖα, ύ, *small, short, insignificant, worthless*; the positive occurs only in the fem. ἐλάχεια, as proparoxyt. Od. 9, 116. 10, 509. h. Ap. 197; and (as the reading of Zenodotus) Od. 9, 116. 10, 509, instead of λάχεια. Voss in his translation follows Zenodotus, and Bothe has adopted the same reading. See λάχεια.

ἐλάω, an old form for ἐλαύνω.

ἔλδομαι and oftener ἐέλδομαι, prop. ἐΡέλδομαι, poet. depon. only pres. and imperf. *to wish, to desire, to long for*, with gen. τινός, 14, 269. Od. 5, 210; and with accus. 5, 481; and with infin. τῷ τις καὶ μᾶλλον ἐέλδεται ἐξ ἔρον εἶναι (ἴημι), [things] of which men are more eager to satisfy their desire [things sought with keener appetite by most Than bloody war. Cp.], 13, 638. Od. 4, 162. 5. 219; once in pass, signif.: νῦν τοι δελδέσθω πόλεμος, κακός, now let evil war be desired by thee, 16, 494.

ἔλδωρ and ἐέλδωρ, τό, poet. *wish, desire, longing* (only in the Ep. form), 1, 41. Od. 17, 242.

ἔλε, Ep. for εἷλε, see αἱρέω.

ἐλεαίρω, a lengthened Ep. form of ἐλεέω, Ep. iterat. imper. ἐλεαίρεσκον, *to have compassion, to pity*, with accus. παῖδα, 6, 407; with κήδομαι, 2, 27. 11, 665.

ἐλεγχείη. 134 **Ἐλεφήνωρ.**

ἐλεγχείη, ἡ, Ep. (ἐλέγχω), reproach, blame, shame, ignominy, 11. and Od.

ἐλεγχής, ἐς, gen. ἐος, poet. (ἐλέγχω), superl. ἐλέγχιστος, covered with reproach, reprehensible, infamous, despised, 4, 242; superl. 2, 285. Od. 10, 72.

ἔλεγχος, τό. reproach, blame, ignominy, shame; ἔλεγχος ἔσσεται, 11, 315. ἡμῖν δ' ἂν ἐλέγχεα ταῦτα γένοιτο, to us this would be a reproach, Od. 21, 329; esply in personal addresses, to denote disgraceful cowardice; abstract for concrete, κάκ' ἐλέγχεα, cowardly dastards, 2, 235. 5, 787 (as in Lat. opprobria).

ἐλέγχω, aor. 1 ἤλεξα (prob. from λέγω), to put to shame; to disgrace, to dishonour, with accus. τινά, Od. 21, 424; hence to despise. μὴ σύγε μύθον ἐλέγχῃς μηδὲ πόδας, despise not their address, nor their journey, i. e. their mission [slight not their embassy, nor put to shame Their intercession. Cp.], 9, 522.

ἐλέειν, i. e. ἐλεῖν, see αἱρέω.

ἐλεεινός, ή, όν (ἔλεος), pitiable, deserving compassion, exciting pity, 24, 309. 2) pitiful, woeful, δάκρυον, 8, 331. 16, 219; compar. ἐλεεινότερος, 24, 504; superl. ἐλεεινότατος, Od 8, 530. The neut. sing. and plur. as adv. ἐλεεινά, pitiably, 2, 314.

ἐλεέω (ἔλεος), fut. ἐλεήσω, aor. ἠλέησα, poet. ἐλέησα, 1) to compassionate, to pity any one, τινά, and absol. to feel pity, 6, 484. 16, 431. 2) to regret, to lament, 17, 346. 352.

ἐλεήμων, ον, gen. ονος (ἐλεέω), compassionate, merciful, Od. 5, 191.†

ἐλεινός, ή, όν, Att. for ἐλεεινός, also h. Cer. 285.

ἐλεητύς, ύος, ἡ. Ep. for ἔλεος, compassion, pity, *Od. 14, 82. 17, 451.

ἔλεκτο, see λέγω.

ἐλελίζω, poet. (a strengthened form from ἑλίσσω), aor. 1 act. ἐλέλιξα, aor. 1 mid. ἐλελιξάμην, aor. 1 pass. ἐλελίχθην, Ep. sync. aor. 2 mid. 3 sing. ἐλέλικτο, 13, 558. 1) to put in a tremulous motion, to whirl, to roll, with accus. σχεδίην, Od. 5, 314; pass. Od. 12, 416; hence mly to cause to tremble, to shake, to agitate, Ὄλυμπον, 1, 530. 8, 199. Pass. to tremble, to shake, 12, 448; ἐλελίχθη γαῖα, 22, 448; ἐλελίζετο πέπλος, h. Cer. 183. 2) to turn suddenly, without the notion of repetition, spoken always of the sudden turning of warriors from flight against the enemy, 17, 278. Pass. 5, 497. 6, 106. 11, 588. II) Mid. to dart forward in spiral folds, winding in spiry volumes, spoken of a serpent, in aor. 1, 2, 316. 11, 39. 2) Like pass. to tremble, to shake, ἔγχος ἐλέλικτο, 13, 558.

Ἑλένη, ἡ, Helena, daughter of Zeus and Leda, sister of Kastōr and Polydeukēs (Castor, Pollux), and Klytæmnēstra (Clytemnestra), wife of Menelaus, mother of Hermionē, famed for her beauty. She was seduced by Paris son of Priam and conveyed to Troy, and thus became the cause of the Trojan war, 2,

161. 3, 91. 121, seq. After the destruction of Troy, she returned with Menelaus to Sparta, Od. 4, 184, seq. (prob. = ἑλάνη, the torch, i. e. cause of war.)

Ἔλενος, ὁ, Helenus, 1) son of Priam and Hekabē (Hecuba), a noted prophet, 6, 76. According to a later tradition, he alone of the sons of Priam survived; he went to Epirus, and after the death of Neoptolemus married Andromachē, Paus. 2) son of Œnopiōn, 5, 707.†

ἑλεόθρεπτος, ον (τρέφω), marsh-nourished, marsh-born, growing in marshes σέλινον, 2, 776.†

ἔλεος, ὁ, pity, compassion, 24, 44.†

ἐλεός, ὁ, the table upon which the cook carved the meat, a kitchen table, 9, 215. Od. 14, 432.

ἔλεσκον. see αἱρέω.

ἐλετός, ή, όν, that which one can seize, that may be taken. ἀνδρὸς ψυχὴ πάλιν ἐλθεῖν, οὔτε λεϊστή, οὔθ' ἑλετή, for οὔτε λεϊστόν, οὔθ' ἑλετὸν ψυχὴν πάλιν ἐλθεῖν, it is not to be obtained by booty or ga·n. that the soul of a man should return again, 9, 409.†

ἔλευ. Ep. for ἕλου, see αἱρέω.

ἐλεύθερος, η, ον (from ἐλεύθω), free; only ἐλεύθερον ἦμαρ, the day of freedom, i. e. freedom itself: opposed to δούλιον ἦμαρ, 6, 455. ἐλεύθερος κρητήρ, the mixing-cup of freedom, i. e. which is mingled in joy at regaining freedom, *6, 528.

†Ἐλευσινίδης, ao, ὁ, son of Eleusis = Keleos (Celeus).h. in Cer. 105 (with short ι).

[Ἐλευσίνιος, ία, ιον, Eleusinian, h. Cer. 267.]

*Ἐλευσίς, ῖνος, ἡ (ἔλευσις, arrival), a town and borough in Attica, belonging to the tribe Hippothoontis, having a temple of Dēmētēr, famed for the Eleusinian mysteries, which were celebrated by yearly processions from Athens; now Lepsina, h. in Cer. 97; Ἐλευσῖνος δῆμος, v. 490.

Ἐλευσίς, ῖνος, ὁ, father of Keleos (Celeus) and Triptolemus, founder of Eleusis, Apd. 1, 5. 2.

ἐλεφαίρομαι, depon. mid. (kindr. with ἔλκω), aor. 1 partcp. ἐλεφηράμενος, to deceive by empty hopes, and mly to deceive, to delude; spoken of dreams, Od. 19, 565 (with reference to ἐλέφας, q. v., v. 564, as a paronomasia), with accus. 23, 338.

ἐλέφας, αντος, ὁ, ivory, the tooth of an elephant; in H. only in this signif. Elephants themselves are not mentioned; ivory, however, was procured by commerce, and was valued as an ornament, 5, 583, together with gold and silver, Od. 4, 73. Deceitful dreams come through a gate of ivory, since ivory by its shining promises light, but deceives by its impenetrable opacity, cf. Schol. Od. 19, 560; see ἐλεφαίρομαι and ὄνειρος.

Ἐλεφήνωρ, ορος, ὁ, son of Chalcōdōn, sovereign of the Abantes before Troy, 2, 540. 4, 463.

Ἔλεψα. 135 Ἕλκω.

[ἔλεψα, aor. 1 of λέπω. q. v.]
Ἐλεών, ῶνος, ὁ, 1) a village in Bœotia, north-west of Tanagra, 2, 500. 10, 266; the Gramm. fix upon it as the residence of Amyntor, see Strab. IX. p. 439, upon Parnassus; others take it for Ἡλώνη. (Ἐλεών, see ἕλος, a marshy place.)
ἐληλάδατο see ἐλαύνω.
ἐλήλαται, ἐλήλατο. see ἐλαύνω.
ἐληλουθώς, see ἔρχομαι.
ἐλθέμεν, ἐλθέμεναι, see ἔρχομαι.
Ἐλικάων, ονος, ὁ, son of Antênôr and husband of Laodikê (Laodice), daughter of Priam, 3, 123.
Ἐλίκη, ἡ, a considerable town in Achaia, founded by Ion, with a splendid temple of Poseidôn. It was destroyed by an earthquake Olym. 101, 4. 11. 2, 575. 8, 203.
*ἑλικοβλέφαρος, ον (βλέφαρον), having moving eye-lashes, shooting lively glances, h. 5, 19.
*ἑλικτός, ή, όν (ἑλίσσω), wound, tortuous, curled, h. Merc. 192.
*Ἑλικών, ῶνος, ὁ, Helikôn (Helicon), a noted mountain in Bœotia, sacred to Apollo and the Muses, now, according to Wheeler, Licona. In H. h. in Nep. this mountain was also sacred to Poseidôn, Batr. 1.
Ἑλικώνιος, η, ον, Heliconian, of Helicon. 2) Subst. ὁ Ἑλικώνιος, an appellation of Poseidôn. Some commentators, 20, 404, derive it from the town Helicê in Achaia, where Poseidôn was worshipt, see Ἑλίκη, cf. Hdt. 1, 148. According to its form, more correctly derived from the mountain Helicon in Bœotia; see Ilgen, ad h. in Pos. 21, 3, and Paus. 9 29, 1.
ἑλικῶπις, ιδος, ἡ, see ἑλίκωψ.
ἑλίκωψ, ωπος, ὁ (ἑλίσσω), having glancing eyes, having rolling eyes, fiery-eyed; a mark of spirit and youthful fire. Voss: having gay, joyful looks, epith. of the Achaians, *1. 389. 3, 190; and a pecul. fem. ἑλικῶπις, 1, 98;† an epith. of the Muses, h. 33, 1. Wolf and Köppen prefer the deriv. from ἕλιξ, ἑλικός (ἑλικτός), with round arched eyes, Apoll. Lex. cf. (βοῶπις).
ἕλιξ, ικος, ὁ, ἡ, adj. twisted, bent, curved, as epith. of cattle, like camurus, crooked-horned. It is incorrectly referred to the legs: for it is mly connected with εἰλίποδες, 21, 448. Od. 1, 92.
ἕλιξ, ικος, ἡ, subst. prob. any thing twisted; particularly a bracelet, 18, 401.† h. in Ven. 87.
ἐλίσσετο, see λίσσομαι.
ἑλίσσω, poet. (ἕλιξ), imperf. εἱλισσόμην, 12, 49; aor. 1 act. ἕλιξας, aor. 1 mid. ἑλιξάμην, aor. partcp. pass. ἑλιχθείς, I) to roll, to twist, to whirl, to turn around, mid. ἑλισσόμενον περὶ δίνας, 21, 11. Esply a) Subaud. ἵππους: περὶ τέρματα, to guide round the goal, 23, 309. 466; in the aor. partcp. turned again, viz. from flight, 12, 74. II) Mid. 1) to wind oneself, to turn oneself, ἀμφί τι, h. 6, 40, and with accus. h. 32, 3, spoken of the serpent, περὶ χειῇ, 22, 95; of the fume of fat, to roll up in volumes, 1, 317; hence also to turn hither and thither, to run hither and thither, of Hêphæstus: περὶ φύσας, about his bellows, 18, 372; of a wild boar: διὰ βήσσας, 17, 283. cf. 8, 340. 12, 19. 2) Like the act. to roll, to whirl around, with accus. κεφαλὴν σφαιρηδόν, 13, 204.
ἑλκεσίπεπλος, ον (πέπλος), having a long trailing robe, epith. of the Trojan women, 6, 442. 22, 105.
ἑλκεχίτων, ον (χιτών), having a long chitôn or tunic, having a trailing tunic, epith. of the Iônians, 13, 665.†
ἑλκέω, poet form of ἕλκω, from which, besides the imperf. εἵλκεον, 17, 395, the fut. ἑλκήσω, a.r. 1 act. ἥλκησα, aor. 1 partcp. pass. ἑλκηθείς, accus. with the strengthened signif., 1) to drag, to draw along, with accus. νέκυν, 17, 395; as prisoners: ἑλκηθεῖσαι θύγατρες, 22, 62. Esply a) to tear, τινά (spoken of dogs, which tear a corpse), 17, 558. 22, 556. b) Mly to abuse, to dishonour, γυναῖκα, Od. 11, 580.
ἑλκηθμός, ὁ (ἑλκέω), a dragging, a drawing along, capture, 6, 465.†
ἕλκητον, see ἕλκω.
ἕλκος, εος, τό, a wound. ἕλκος ὕδρου, a wound from a serpent, *2, 723; often plur.
ἑλκυστάζω, poet. form of ἕλκω, to draw, to drag along, ouly partcp. pres. *23, 187. 24, 21.
ἑλκύω, a later form of ἕλκω, aor. Ep. ἕλκυσα, Batr. 235.
ἕλκω, poet. ἑλκέω, infin. pres. ἑλκέμεναι and ἑλκέμεν, poet. for ἕλκειν, only pres. and imperf. the last without augment in Il. and Od.; εἵλκεον, only h. Cer. 308. 1) to draw, to drag, to trail; to draw along, to drag along; spoken of things animate and inanimate, τινὰ ποδός, any one by the foot, 13, 383. Od. 16, 276; ἐκ δίφροιο, 16, 409; ὀϊστὸν ἐκ ζωστῆρος, 4, 213; also βέλος, ἔγχος; ἄροτρον νειοῖο, to draw the plough through the field, 10, 353; of mules, 17, 743. ᾧτε—νειὸν ἂν' ἕλκητον βόε οἴνοπε πηκτὸν ἄροτρον, Od. 13, 32 (the subj. after ᾧτε is prop. to be resolved by ἐάν, Rost, Gr. § 123, 2). Esply a) to draw, to pull; νευρὴν γλυφίδας τε, to draw the bow-string and arrow-notch (for shooting an arrow), Od. 21, 419. Il. 4, 122; conf. ἀνέλκω. b) to draw up, for weighing. ἕλκειν τάλαντα, to draw up the scales, 8, 72. 22, 212; ἱστία βοεύσιν, to draw up the sails, Od. 2, 246. 15, 291. c) to draw, to draw down; νῆας ἅλαδε, to launch the ships, 2, 152. 163; pass. 14, 100. d) Metaph. to draw after, to let follow, νύκτα, 8, 486. 2) to drag, Ἕκτορα περὶ σῆμα. 24, 52. 417. Mid. to draw (with reference to the subject), ξίφος, a sword, 1, 194; χαίτας ἐκ κεφαλῆς προθελύμνους, to draw out the hairs from the head with the roots, 10, 15; τόξον ἐπί τινι, to draw

Ἕλλαβε. 136 **Ἐμβαίνω.**

the bow at any one (viz. τόξου πῆχυν), 11, 583. ἐπισκύνιον, see the word, spoken of lions, 17, 136. 11. and Od.

ἕλλαβε, Ep. for ἔλαβε, see λαμβάνω.

Ἑλλάς, άδος, ἡ, 1) Originally, a town in Phthiôtis (Thessaly), according to tradition founded by Hellenus. Its situation is unknown. It belonged, together with Phthia, to the dominion of Achilles, and was the capital of the realm of the Æacidæ, 2, 683. 2) the territory of the town *Hellas*, between the Asôpus and Enipeus, and, in connexion with Phthia, the realm of Peleus, 9, 395. Od. 11, 496. 3) It indicates, in connexion with Argos, as there were the extremities of the country, all *Greece*, Od. 1, 344; cf. Nitzsch ad loc.

ἐλλεδανός, ὁ (ἑλλάς), *a straw band*, for binding sheaves, 18, 553.† h. Cer. 456.

ἐλλείπω (ἐν, λείπω), imperf. ἐψέλειπον *to leave behind in.* 2) Intrans. *to be behind*, to remain behind. h. Ap. 213.

Ἕλλην, ηνος, ὁ, plur. οἱ Ἕλληνες, *the Hellènes*, the main stock of the original inhabitants of Greece, who derived their name, according to tradition, from Hellèn, son of Deukaliôn (Deucalion); they dwelt first about Parnassus in Phocis, and subsequently emigrated into Thessaly, Apd. 1, 7. 3. In H. prop. the inhabitants of the city and territory of Hellas in Thessaly, who had become powerful by the spread of the Pelasgians. As the Hellènes, together with the Achaians, were the most powerful tribes before Troy, H. embraces all the Greeks under the name Πανέλληνες, 2, 510.

Ἑλλήσποντος, ὁ, *the sea of Hellê*, so called from Hellê, daughter of Athamas, who was drowned here; now the *straits of the Dardanelles*, or of *Gallipoli*, 2, 845.

ἐλλισάμην, see λίσσομαι.
ἐλλίσσετο, see λίσσομαι.
ἐλλιτάνευε, see λιτανεύω.

ἐλλός, ὁ, *a young stag, a fawn*, ποικίλος, Od. 19, 228.†

ἔλοιμι, see αἱρέω.
ἕλον, ἑλόμην, see αἱρέω.

ἕλος, εος, τό, *a marsh, a swamp, a meadow*, a moist place fit for pasturage. εἰαμενὴ ἕλεος, a low pasture, 4, 483. Od. 14, 474.

Ἕλος, ους, τό, 1) a town on the sea in Laconia, above Gythion, founded, according to tradition, by Hêlius son of Perseus, or rather named from its swamps. At a later period it was destroyed by the Spartans, and its inhabitants reduced to slavery, 2, 584. 2) a village or region in Elis on the river Alphêus, not known in the time of Strabo, 2, 594.

ἑλόωσι, see ἐλαύνω.

ἐλπίς, ίδος, ἡ, *hope*. ἔτι ἐλπίδος αἶσα, there is still some hope, Od. 16, 101. 19, 84. h. Cer. 37.

Ἑλπήνωρ, ορος, ὁ, voc. Ἑλπῆνορ, *a companion of Odysseus (Ulysses)*, who was transformed by Kirkê (Circé). Intoxi-

cated with wine, he fell asleep on Circê's roof, and during his sleep falling down broke his neck, Od. 10, 552. Odysseus (Ulysses) saw him in Hadês, Od. 11, 51.

ἔλπω, poet. 1) Act. *to excite hope, to cause to hope, to let hope*, τινί, any one, Od. 2, 91. 13, 380. Oftener 2) Mid. ἔλπομαι, Ep. ἐέλπομαι, perf. ἔολπα, pluperf. ἐώλπειν, with signif. of the pres. and imperf. *to hope*, and mly, *to expect, to think, to suppose*, 7, 199; and, in a bad sense, *to apprehend, to fear*, 13, 8; also absol. ἔλπομαι, 18, 194. It has a) An accus. νίκην, 13, 609. 15, 539. b) More mly an infin. 3, 112; or an accus. with an infin. οὐδ᾽ ἐμὲ νηΐδά γ᾽ οὕτως ἔλπομαι. γενέσθαι. I do not think I am born so simple, 7, 198; chiefly with an adjunct clause having a distinct subject, Od. 6, 297. According to the difference in sense we find the infin. pres., perf., fut. and aor., 9, 40. Od. 3, 375. 6, 297. Π. 15, 288. Often the pleon. θυμῷ, κατὰ θυμόν, ἐν στήθεσσιν, also θυμὸς ἔλπεται (imperf. without augm. with exception of Od. 9, 419).

ἐλπωρή, ἡ, poet. for ἐλπίς, *hope*, with infin., *Od. 2, 280. 6. 314.

ἔλσαι, infin. ἔλσας, see εἴλω.

ἐλύω, Att. ἐλύω, only aor. 1 pass. ἐλύσθην, *to wind up, to crook, to coil*. pass. *to roll oneself, to crook or coil oneself up, to prostrate oneself*; προσάρεσεν ποδῶν, 24, 510. ὑπὸ γαστέρ᾽ ἐλυσθεὶς. curled up under the belly, Od. 9, 433. but ῥυμὸς ἐπὶ γαῖαν ἐλύσθη, the pole fell to the ground, 23, 393.

ἔλχ᾽ for ἔλκε, see ἕλκω.

ἙΛΩ, ἕλω, obsol theme of εἵλω.

ἙΛΩ, obsol. root of the aor. εἷλον, see αἱρέω.

ἕλων, Ep. for ἕλαον, see ἐλαύνω.

ἕλωρ, ωρος, τό (ἑλεῖν), *booty, spoil, prey*, spoken esply of unburied corpses, the prey (ἕλωρ καὶ κύρμα) of enemies, 5, 488. 684; or of birds and dogs, Od. 3, 271. 2) ἕλωρα (τὰ) Πατρόκλοιο, the prey of Patroclus, i. e. the penalty for his slaughter, 18, 93.

ἑλώριον, τό = ἕλωρ, *booty, prey*, plur. 1, 4.†

ἐμβαδόν, adv. (ἐμβαίνω), *on foot, by land*, 15, 505.†

ἐμβαίνω (βαίνω), aor. 2 ἐνέβην or ἔμβην subj. ἐμβῇ, ἐμβήῃ for ἐμβῇ, perf. ἐμβέβηκα, 3 plur. ἐμβέβασαν, partcp. ἐμβεβαώς, 1) Intrans. *to enter, to step into to embark, to go into, to mount*, νηΐ τινι ἐν νηΐ, in the ship, Il., and absol. 2, 6;9; ἵπποις καὶ ἅρμασι, into the chariot, 5, 199; metaph. μολυβδαίνῃ κατὰ βοὸς κέρας ἐμβεβαυῖα, a leaden ball fixed upon the horn of the ox, 24, 81. 2) *to tread or trample upon*, τινί, Od. 10, 164; also ἔμβητον, dash on! in the address of Antilochus to his horses, 23, 403 (upon the race-ground) 3) *to intervene, to approach*; ἀπ᾽ Οὐλύμποιο, 16, 94. 4) Trans. aor. I ἐνέβησα, *to bring in, to put in*, with accus. Od. 11, 4, in tmesis.

Ἐμβάλλω. 137 Ἔμπης.

ἐμβάλλω (βάλλω), aor. 2 ἐνέβαλον, Ep. ἔμβαλον, infin. ἐμβαλέειν, 1) to cast in, according to the context to hurl in, to lay on, to bring, to give, mly τί τινι, rarely ἔν τινι, πῦρ νηί, to cast fire into the ship, 15, 598; τινὰ πόντῳ, 14, 258; τὶ χερσίν, to give any thing into the hand, 14, 218; in a bad sense, 21, 47; τινὰ εὐνῇ, to conduct any one to the couch, 18, 85; κώπῃς, to lay hands on the oars (to row with all their might; ἐπκύμβερε remis]. subaud. χεῖρας, Od. 9, 489. 10. 129. 2) Metaph. of the soul: ἵμερον θυμῷ, to infuse a longing into the mind, 3, 139; μένος τινί, 10, 366; also with double dat., σθένος τινὶ καρδίῃ, θυμῷ, to inspire any one's heart with strength, with courage, 14, 151. II) Mid. to cast ἐν for oneself, κλήρους, 23, 352; metaph. τὶ θυμῷ, to lay any thing to heart, to expect, 10, 447, 23, 313.

ἐμβασιλεύω (βασιλεύω), to be king, to reign, τινί, over any one, 2, 572. Od. 15, 413.

*Ἐμβασίχυτρος, ὁ (χύτρα), Pot-explorer, name of a mouse, Batr. 137.

ἐμβίβασαν, see ἐμβαίνω.
ἐμβεβαώς, s-e ἐμβαίνω.
ἐμβῇ and ἐμβήῃ, see ἐμβαίνω.
ἔμβη, Ep. for ἐνέβη, see ἐμβαίνω.
ἐμβλάπτω, formerly 6, 39, now divided.
ἐμβρέμομαι, depon. mid. (βρέμω), to murmur, to roar in, with dat. ἱστίῳ, 15, 627.†

ἔμβρυον, τό (βρύω), prop. the unborn fruit of the womb, an embryo, 2) a new-born lamb, *Od. 9, 245. 309. 342.

ἔμαθεν, poet. for ἐμοῦ, see ἐγώ.
ἐμεῖο, Ep. for ἐμοῦ, see ἐγώ.
ἐμέμηκον, see μηκάομαι.
ἔμεν and ἔμεναι, see εἰμί.
ἔμεν and ἔμεναι, Ep. for εἶναι, see ἵημι.
ἐμέω, ἐμοῦ, Ep. for ἐμοῦ, see ἐγώ.
ἐμέω, to spit out, αἷμα. 15, 11.†
[ἐμήσατο, aor. 1 mid. of μήδομαι.]
ἔμικτο, see μίγνυμι.
ἔμμαθε, see μανθάνω.
ἐμμαπέως, poet. adv. immediately, directly, quickly, with ἀπόρουσε, 5, 836, and ὑπάκουσε, Od. 14, 485 (prob. from μαπέειν = μάρπτειν, to grasp, to clutch; others improb. from ἅμα τῷ ἔπει, with the word).

ἐμμεμαώς, υἷα, ός, Ep. μεμαώς, vehemently desirous, ardently striving, eager, vehement, *5, 142. 330. 240. 838 (see μέμαα).

ἔμμεν and ἔμμεναι, Ep. for εἶναι, see εἰμί.

ἐμμενές, adv. (neut. from ἐμμενής), steadfast, constant, perpetual, always ἐμμενὲς αἰεί, 10, 361. Od. 9, 386.

ἔμμορα, see μείρομαι.
ἔμμορος, ον (μόρος), partaking of, sharing in, with gen. τιμῆς, Od. 8, 480.† h. Cer. 481.

ἐμός, ἐμή, ἐμόν, adj. possess. (ἐμοῦ), mine, my, more rarely compounded with the article, τοὐμός, 8, 360. Strengthened by the gen. of αὐτός: ἐμὸν αὐτοῦ χρεῖος,

my own need. Od. 2, 45. h. Ap. 328. Often also objective: ἐμὴ ἀγγελίη, an embassy which concerns me, 20, 205.

ἐμπάζομαι, Ep. depon. only pres. and imperf. to trouble oneself about any thing, to care for any thing, with gen. θεοπροπίης, 16, 50†; often in the Od.; once with accus. ἱκέτας, Od. 16, 422 (prob. from ἔμπαιος).

ἔμπαιος, ον, Ep. adj. = ἔμπειρος, acquainted with, experienced in, *Od. 20, 379. 21, 400 (with shortened diphthong in Od. 20. 379).

*ἔμπαλιν, adv. (πάλιν), backwards, bark, h. Merc. 78.

ἐμπάσσω (πάσσω), aor. 1 ἐνέπασα, Ep. σσ, to sprinkle upon; in H. to inweave, with accus. 3, 126,† and in tmesis, 22, 441.

ἔμπεδος, ον (ἐν, πέδον), prop. standing in the earth; hence firm, immoveable, not to be shaken, τεῖχος, βίη, ἴς, μένος. τοῖσι ἔμπεδα κεῖται, sc. γέρα, their gifts lie still secure, 9, 335. 2) Of time: perpetual, constant, lasting, φυλακή, 8, 521; κομιδή, Od. 8, 453. 3) Metaph. firm, steadfast, constant, ἦτορ, φρένες, 6, 352. Od. 18, 215; spoken of Priam, 20, 183. The neut. sing. and plur. ἔμπεδον and ἔμπεδα, with the same signif., 1, firmly, steadfastly, μένειν. 2) perpetually, constantly, θέειν (to go on running), 13, 141. Od. 18, 113.

*ἐμπελάζω (πελάζω), fut. σω, intrans. to approach, δόμῳ, h. Merc. 523.

ἐμπεσεῖν, see ἐμπίπτω.

ἐμπήγνυμι, fut. πήξω, to stick or thrust into, to strike (only in tmesis), 5, 40. Od. 22, 83.

ἔμπης, Ep. and Ion. for ἔμπας (prop. ἐν πᾶσι), at all events, for all that (cf. toutefois). i. e. although, still, yet; hence often ἀλλ' ἔμπης, but still, 1, 562. Od. 4, 100; or with δέ preceding, Od. 3, 209; and following, 5, 191; strengthened, ἀλλὰ καὶ ἔμπης, but even so; but nevertheless, 2, 297. 19, 422; καὶ ἔμπης, Od. 5, 205; and so also in the passages, where according to some it signifies entirely, totally, at all, 14, 174. 19, 308. Od. 19, 302. Sometimes it stands also when, of two cases, one is indicated as preponderating. τόφρ' ὑμεῖς εὔχεσθε—σιγῇ ἐφ' ὑμείων, ἵνα μὴ Τρῶές γε πύθωνται, ἠὲ καὶ ἀμφαδίην, ἐπεὶ οὔτινα δείδιμεν ἔμπης, since, for all that [or, be that as it may], we fear no one (i. e. though they should hear), 7, 195; also in other cases: see 12, 236. 17, 632; hence with ref. to something unexpected: ἔμπης, μοι τοῖχοι, κτλ., why surely [strange as it is, the walls of the house] seem to me to shine like fire [= tamen ita est, quanquam non putabam initio], Herm. ad Vig. p. 782. So also Od. 19, 334. 2) Often connected with πέρ with a partcp. (tmesis). Νέστορα δ' οὐκ ἔλαθεν ἰαχή, πίνοντά περ ἔμπης, 14, 1. Properly ἔμπης belongs in sense to what precedes, as ὅμως is also constructed; the sense is: the cry still did not escape

Ἐμπίμπλημι. 138 Ἐν.

Nestor, although occupied with drinking, see 17, 229. Od. 11, 351. 15, 361. According to the Gramm., in 14, 174, and Od 18, 395, it signifies ὁμοίως, but incorrectly, see Spitzner ad loc.
ἐμπίμπλημι and ἐμπίπλημι (πίμπλημι), aor. 1 ἐνέπλησα, aor. 1 mid ἐνεπλησάμην, aor. 1 pass. ἐνεπλήσθην, infin. ἐνιπλησθῆναι, Ep. sync. aor. 2 mid. ἔμπληντο, 21, 607, and ἔμπληντο, Οd. 8, 16. 1) *to fill up, to fill full,* τί τινος, any thing with any thing; ῥέεθρα ὕδατος, 21, 311; θυμὸν ὀδυνάων, Od. 19, 117. 2) τινά, *to satiate* any one, Od. 17, 503; hence pass. aor. 1, υἱὸς ἐνιπλησθῆναι ὀφθαλμοῖς, to satiate myself with looking on my son; to gaze my fill, Od. 11, 452. Mid. *to fill oneself,* τινός, with any thing, 21, 607. Od. 7, 221; eoply Ep. aor. 2 mid., Od. 8, 16. 2) *to fill for oneself,* τι; spoken of the Cyclopes, μεγάλην ηδύν, Od. 9, 296 and with gen. μένεος θυμόν, 22, 312.
ἐμπίπτω (πίπτω), aor. ἐνέπεσον and ἔμπεσον, 1) *to fall in, to fall upon, to hit;* with dat. πῦρ ἔμπεσε νηυσίν, the fire fell into the ships, 16, 113, and ἐν ὕλῃ, 11, 155. ἐνέπεσε ζωστῆρι ὀϊστός, the arrow pierced into the girdle, 4, 134. 2) Metaph. spoken of men : *to rush in, to press in;* with dat. ὑσμίνῃ, into the battle, 11, 297 ; προμάχοισι, Od. 21, 526. b) Of the mind: χόλος ἔμπεσε θυμῷ, anger has entered the soul, 9, 436. 14, 207; and with double dat., 16, 206.
ἔμπλειος and ἐνίπλειος, η, ον, Ep. for ἔμπλεος (πλέος), *filled, full,* with gen. *Od. 14, 113; only in the Ep. form.
ἐμπληγδήν, adv. (ἐμπλήσσω), *rashly, inconsiderately,* Od. 20, 132.†
ἔμπλην, adv. (πλάω, πελάζω), *near, in the neighbourhood,* with gen., 2, 526.†
ἐμπλήσατο, see ἐμπίπλημι.
ἔμπληντο, ἔμπληντο, see ἐμπίμπλημι.
ἐμπλήσσω, see ἐνιπλήσσω.
ἐμπνύω, Ep. ἐμπνείω, aor. 1 ἐνέπνευσα and ἔμπνευσα, 1) *to breathe into* or *upon, to blow upon,* with dat. : μάλ' ἐμπνείοντε μεταφρένῳ, breathing on my back [of horses held immediately behind a person], 17, 502; with accus. ἱστίον, into the sail, spoken of wind, h. 6, 33. 2) Metaph. *to inspire, to give,* τί τινι, any thing to any one, spoken of the gods: μένος, θάρσος τινί, 10, 482. Od. 9, 381; with infin.. Od. 19, 138.
ἐμποιέω (ποιέω), fut. ήσω, *to make ... in,* with accus. 18, 490 ; ἐν πύργοις πύλας, gates in towers, 7, 438. 18, 400. 2) Mid. like act. h. Merc. 527.
ἐμπολάω (ἐμπολή), Ep. imperat. mid. ἐμπολόωντο, *to purchase;* mid. *to purchase for oneself,* with accus. βίοτον, Od. 15, 456.†
ἔμπορος (πόρος), any one who travels in another person's ship, *a sea-passenger, a traveller,* later ἐμβάτης, *Od. 2, 319. 24, 300.
ἐμπρήθω = ἐνιπρήθω, q. v.
ἐμπυριβήτης, ὁ (πῦρ, βαίνω), *going on the fire, pre-bestriding,* τρίπους, 23, 702.†

ἐμφορέω, poet. form of ἐμφέρω (φορέω), *to bring in,* only pass. *to be brought in,* with dat. κύμασιν ἐμφορέοντο, they were borne in upon the waves, *Od. 12, 419. 14, 309.
ἔμφυλος, ον (φῦλον), *belonging to the same race* or *tribe, native,* ἀνήρ, Od. 15, 273 †
ἐμφύω (φύω), aor. 1 ἐνέφυσα, aor. 2 ἐνέφυν, perf. (ἐμπέφυκα), only 3 plur. ἐμπεφύασι, partcp. fem. ἐμπεφυυῖα, 1) Trans pres. act. fut. and aor. 1 act. *to implant, to inspire, to infuse into,* τί τινι. θεός μοι ἐν φρεσὶν οἴμας παντοίας ἐνέφυσεν, a deity has breathed many melodies into my soul, Od. 22, 348. 2) Intrans. mid. and aor. 2 and perf. act. *to be produced in, to grow in;* with dat. τρίχες κραινῳ ἐμπεφύασι, the hairs grow upon the skull of the horses, 8, 84; hence metaph *to cling to, to fasten oneself to.* ὡς ἔχετ' ἐμπεφυυῖα, thus she held clinging fast, 1, 513; with double dat. ἐν τ' ἄρα οἱ φῦ χειρί for ἐνέφυ, held fast his hand, 6, 253, and often.
ἐν, poet. ἐνί, Ep. εἰν or εἰνί, I) Prep. with dat. ground signif. *in, on, upon, at.* 1) Used of place, ἐν signifies a) *being in a place.* ἐν γαίῃ, ἐν δώμασι; in like manner in geography, ἐν Ἄργεῖ, ἐν Τροίῃ. b) *being surrounded by* any thing. οὐρανὸς ἐν αἰθέρι καὶ νεφέλῃσι, 15, 192; often spoken of persons : *between, amidst, amongst,* of being in a crowd, ἐν ἀθανάτοις; hence *before, coram* (surrounded by a crowd of hearers). ἐν πᾶσιν, Od. 2, 194. 16, 378; metaph. of external and internal conditions in which one may be. ἐνὶ πτολέμῳ, ἐν φιλότητι, 4, 258. 7, 302. So also of persons in whose power any thing lies. δύναμις γὰρ ἐν ὑμῖν, the power is in you, Od. 10, 69. cf. 11. 7, 102. c) *being upon* another thing. ἔστη ἐν οὔρεσιν, upon the mountains. ἐν ἴπποις. d) *being in* or *by* another thing. ἐν οὐρανῷ, 8, 555. ἐν ποταμῷ, 18, 521. 2) Used as cause, instrument, means, it signifies a) *before, with.* ὁρᾶν, ἰδεῖν ἐν ὀφθαλμοῖς, to see before or with the eyes, 1, 587. Again : ἐν χερσὶ λαβεῖν, to take with the hands, 15, 229. cf. Od. 9, 164. b) Suitableness: *according to.* ἐν μοίρῃ, i. e. κατὰ μοῖραν. Od. 22, 54. ἐν καρὸς αἴσῃ, 9, 378. 3) Apparently ἐν often stands for εἰς with verbs of motion, since it includes at the same time the idea of the subsequent rest; thus ἐν γούνασι πίπτειν, to fall (and remain) upon the knees, 5, 370. Often βάλλειν ἐν κονίῃσι, ἐν τεύχεσσιν ἔδυνον, 23, 131. 4) Sometimes it stands with a gen., in which case a subst. is to be supplied. ἐν Ἀλκινόοιο, subaud. οἴκῳ, Od 10, 282; particularly εἰν Ἀΐδαο, 22, 389. 5) ἐν also stands after a subst., 18, 218 ; esply ἐνί, which then has the accent on the first syllable, 7, 221. II) Adverb ; ἐν is often an adv. of place without case : *therein, thereby, thereon,* Od. 1, 51. 2, 340, where it is sometimes explained as in tmesis

Ἐν.   139   Ἔνδον.

[mly connected with δέ, thus ἐν δέ; it then takes the adv. signif. *besides, moreover, together, with,* etc., Od. 5, 260].
III) In composition it has an adv. signif. and indicates the *resting* or *being* in or upon something.

ἕν, neut. of εἷς, *one*.

ἐναίρω, infin. pres. ἐναιρέμεν, aor. 1 mid. ἐνηράμην, 1) *to destroy, to kill,* τινά, in the II. always in battle with the adjunct τόξῳ, χαλκῷ; πολλοὶ δ' αὖ σοὶ Ἀχαιοὶ ἐναιρέμεν, many Achaians hast thou to slay, 6, 229. Mid. in the signif. of act. with reference to the subject with accus., 5, 43. 6, 32. Od. 24, 424, and metaph. μηκέτι χρόα καλὸν ἐναίρεο, destroy not thy beautiful skin, Od. 19, 263. (Buttm. Lexil. p. 109. Rem. derives it, not from ἐν and αἴρω, but from ἔνεροι, related to ἔναρα, ἐναρίζω, hence, prop. to send to the nether world.)

ἐναίσιμος, ον (αἴσιμος), prop. that which is in fate, 1) *indicating fate, prophetic, ominous, auspicious, fatalis, portentous*, 2, 353. ἐναίσιμα μυθήσασθαι, to utter words of fate (spoken of a soothsayer). Od. 2, 159; neut. sing. as adv. ἐναίσιμον ἐλθεῖν, to come seasonably, 6, 519. 2) *befitting, just, equitable,* δῶρον, ἀνήρ, φρένες.

ἐναλίγκιος, ον (ἀλέγκιος), *similar, like,* τινί, 5, 5; and τί, in any respect, θεοῖς, αὐδήν, Od. 1, 371; and often.

ἐνάλιος, Ep. εἰνάλιος, q. v.

*ἔναλος, ον (ἅλς) = ἐνάλιος, *in the sea,* h. Ap. 180.

ἐναμέλγω (ἀμέλγω), *to milk into,* with dat. Od. 9, 223.†

ἔναντα, adv. (ἄντα), *over against, opposite,* with gen . 20, 67.†

ἐναντίβιον, adv. from ἐναντίβιος (βία), *striving forcibly against,* and mly *against,* with μάχεσθαι, στῆναι, μεῖναι, II. and Od.

ἐναντίος, η, ον (ἀντίος), 1) *opposite, in front of,* 6, 247; with dat, 9, 190. Od. 10, 89; hence, *visible,* Od. 6, 329. 2) *against, in opposition to,* in a hostile sense, mly with gen. Ἀχαιῶν, 5, 497; [but sometimes in a friendly sense with gen. and vice versa in a hostile sense with dat. cf. 1, 534. (Nägelsb.), 15, 304. 20, 252. Od. 14, 278.] Frequently the accus. neut. ἐναντίον, adv. as with μάχεσθαι, μίμνειν, ἐλθεῖν, etc.

ἔναξε, aor. 1 from νάσσω.

ἔναρα, τά (ἐναίρω), *the arms* taken from a slain enemy, *spolia;* and mly *warspoils, booty.* ἔναρα βροτόεντα, bloody arms, *6, 68. 480. (Sing. not used.)

ἐναργής, ές, *visible, clear, manifest, plain,* spoken esply of the gods who appear to men in their real form: χαλεποὶ θεοὶ φαίνεσθαι ἐναργεῖς, terrible are the gods when they appear manifest, 20, 131. cf. Od. 7, 201. ἐναργὲς ὄνειρον, κ plain dream, Od. 4, 841; (some derive .t from ἀργός, ἀργής, *white, clear,* others from ἐν ἔργῳ.)

..ἀσηρώς, νία, ός (partep. perf. from

ἐνάρω), only as an adj., *filled in, fastened in,* Od. 5, 236.†

ἐναρίζω (ἔναρα), fut. ἐναρίξω, aor. 1 ἐνάριξα, prop. to strip a slain enemy, in H. with double accus. τινὰ ἔντεα, to despoil any one of his arms, 17, 187. 22, 323. 2) *to slay in battle,* 5, 155; and mly *to slay,* *1, 191.

ἐναρίθμιος, ον (ἀριθμός), *reckoned with, counted among, numbered with,* Od. 12, 65. 2) *esteemed,* ἐν βουλῇ, 2, 202.

ἔνατος, η, ον, and εἴνατος, *the ninth,* 2, 295. 313.

*ἔνασσαν. Ep. for ἔνασαν, see ναίω.

ἔναυλος, ὁ, poet. (αὐλός), 1) *a ravine,* formed by winter torrents, 16, 71; *the torrent* itself, 21, 283. 312. 2) *a valley,* h. Ven. 74, 124.

ἐνδείκνυμι (δείκνυμι), *to show, to manifest,* only mid. *to shew oneself to any one,* Πηλείδῃ ἐνδείξομαι, either with Voss: 'I will explain myself to Peleides,' or with the Schol.: ' I will defend myself,' (ἀπολογήσομαι), 19, 83.†

ἕνδεκα, indecl. (δέκα), *eleven,* II. and Od.

ἑνδεκάπηχυς, υ (πῆχυς), *eleven cubits long,* ἔγχος, *8, 494.

ἑνδέκατος, η, ον, *the eleventh,* ἡ ἑνδεκάτη, absol. subaud. ἡμέρα, Od. 2, 374.

ἐνδέξιος, η, ον (δεξιός), *on the right, on the right hand.* ἐνδέξια σήματα, omens on the right, i. e. auspicious, 9, 236; see δεξιός. Often as adv. ἐνδέξια, *on the right, to the right;* this direction was in all important cases observed as auspicious, 1, 597; in lots, 7, 184. Thus also Odysseus (Ulysses) begging, Od. 17, 365. 2) Later: *dexterous, skilful,* h. in Merc. 454.

ἐνδέω (δέω), aor. 1 ἐνέδησα, *to bind in* or *upon, to fasten, to fetter,* with accus. νευρήν, 15, 469; τί ἔν τινι, Od. 5, 260; metaph. Ζεὺς ἐνέδησέ με ἄτῃ, Zeus has entangled me in misfortune, 2, 111. 9, 18. (Conf. ἐφάπτω.)

*ἐνδιάομαι, depon. (ἔνδιος), *to be in the open air,* h. 32, 6.

ἐνδίημι, Ep. (δίημι), 3 plur. imperf. ἐνδίεσαν, for ἐνεδίεσαν, *to drive away, to pursue,* 18, 584 † conf δίεμαι.

ἔνδινα, τά, *the entrails, the intestines,* 23, 806.† (from ἔνδον), or, the parts concealed under the armour, a doubtful passage.

ἔνδιος, ον, *at mid-day;* ἔνδιος ἦλθε. Od. 4, 450 II. 11, 725. (From Δίς, obsol. root of Διός, the bright air; hence in reference to mid-day, the brightest part of the day, morning and evening being comparatively dusky, cf. εὔδιος, ἠέρι, ἠέριος.)

ἔνδοθεν, adv. (ἔνδον), *from within,* ὑπακούειν, Od. 4, 283. 20, 101. 2) *within, inside of,* with gen. αὐλῆς, 6, 247.

ἔνδοθι, adv. (ἔνδον), *within,* 6, 498, with θυμός, 1, 243. Od. 2, 315. 2) *within, inside of,* with gen. πύργων, 31, 18, 287.

ἔνδον, adv. (ἐν), *within, in, at home,* ἔνδον εἶναι, mly spoken of a dwelling,

'Ενδουπέω. 140 'Ενιαύσιος.

ένδουπέω, 10, 378. 13, 363. 2) With gen. Διὸς ἔνδον, in the abode of Zeus, 20, 13. 23, 200.
ἐνδουπέω (δουπέω), aor. 1 ἐνδούπησα, without augm. *to fall in with a noise, to make a heavy sound in. μέσσῳ ἐνδούπησα,* I dashed into the midst [of the waves]. *Od. 12, 443. 15, 479.
ἐνδυκέως, adv. *carefully, zealously, assiduously, faithfully, cordially,* in the Il. rarely δέχεσθαι, 23, 90. Often in the Od. with πέμπειν, λούειν; ἐνδ. ἐσθίειν, to eat eagerly, Od. 14, 109; (prob. fr. ἐν and δύω, conf. ἀτρεκής from τρέω.)
ἐνδύνω = ἐνδύομαι, only imperf. ἐν ἔδυνε, 2, 42. 10, 21.
ἐνδύω (δύω), aor. 1 ἐνέδυσα, aor. 2 ἐνέδυν, partcp. ἐνδύς, aor. 1 mid. ἐνεδυσάμην. 1) Trans. *to dress, to clothe,* τινά. Batr., 160. 2) Mid. with aor. 2 and perf. act. intrans. *to go in,* then, *to put on, to dress in,* with accus. χιτῶνα, 5, 736; χαλκόν, 11, 16.
ἐνέηκα, Ep. for ἐνῆκα, see ἐνίημι.
ἔνειμαι, see φέρω.
ἔνειμι (εἰμί), imperf. ἐνῆεν, 3 plur. ἔνεσαν, *to be in, to be at, to be within,* 1, 593. Od. 9, 164; with dat. ἐνείη μοι ἦτορ, if a brazen heart were within me, 2, 490.
ἕνεκα, Ep. εἵνεκα and ἕνεκεν (Od. 17, 288. 310), prep. *on account of, for the sake of, for, by means of,* with gen. placed sometimes before and sometimes after: ἕνεκ' ἀρητῆρος, 1, 94.
ΕΝΕΚΩ, obsol. root, from which several of the tenses of φέρω, are formed.
ἐνενήκοντα, Ep. ἐννήκοντα, indecl. *ninety,* 2, 602.
ἐνένιπον, see ἐνίπτω.
ἐνένιπτεν, see ἐνίπτω.
ἐνένισπον, see ἐνίσπω.
ἐνέπω and ἐννέπω, imper. ἔννεπε, optat. ἐνέποιμι, partcp. ἐνέπων, imperf. ἔνεπον and ἔννεπον, aor. ἐνισπον, infin. ἐνισπεῖν, subj. ἐνίσπω, optat. ἐνίσποιμι, fut. ἐνίψω, 7, 447. Od. 2, 137, and ἐνισπήσω, Od. 5, 98. 1) *to tell, to relate, to recount, to communicate,* τί τινι, any thing to any one, μῦθον, ὄνειρον, ὄλεθρον, 8, 412. 2, 80. ἄνδρα μοι ἔννεπε, announce to me the man, Od. 1, 1; μνηστήρων θάνατον, Od. 24, 414. 2) *to speak, to say, to talk,* absol. 2, 761. Od. 3, 93; πρὸς ἀλλήλους, 11, 643; (fr ἐν and ἔπω accord. to the old Gram.; Buttm. Lexil. p. 123, makes it only a strengthened form of εἰπεῖν, as ὀψ, ὀμφή, ἐνοπή, so ἔπω, ἔμπω, ἐνέπω.)
ἐνερείδω (ἐρείδω), aor. 1 ἐνέρεισα, *to push, thrust,* or *drive in,* μοχλὸν ὀφθαλμῷ, the stake into the eye, Od. 9, 383.†
ἔνερθε, before a vowel ἔνερθεν, also νέρθε, νέρθεν, adv. *from beneath,* 13, 75; *beneath:* οἱ ἔνερθε θεοί, the infernal gods, 14, 274. 2) With gen. beneath, ἔνερθε Αἴδεω, 8, 16; also ἀγκώνος ἔνερθε, 11, 234.
ἔνεροι, oi (prop. ἔνφεροι, *inferi*), the inhabitants *of the infernal world,* both the deities and the dead, 15, 188. h. Cer. 358. (From ἐν ἐνερ, *infer.*)

ἐνέρτερος, η, ον, compar. of ἔνεροι, *deeper, farther under.* ἐνέρτεροι Οὐρανιώνων, deeper than the children of Uranus, 5, 898.†
ἔνεσαν, Ep. see ἔνειμι.
ἐνεσίη, ἡ, Ep. ἐννεσίη (ἐνίημι), *suggestion, counsel,* command, plur. 5, 894.†
ἐνεστήρικτο, see ἐνστηρίζω.
ἐνετή, ἡ (ἐνίημι), *a buckle, a clasp,* = περόνη, 14, 180 †
Ἐνετοί, οἱ, *Heneti,* a people in Paphlagonia, who however are not afterwards mentioned, ?, 852. Tradition connects them with the Venetians in Italy and makes the last the descendants of the former Ἐνετοί. Strabo.
ἐνεύδω (εὕδω), *to sleep in,* with dat οἴκῳ, in the house, *Od. 3, 350. 20, 95.
ἐνεύναιος, ον (εὐνή), *lying in the bed;* τὸ ἐνεύναιον, *bedding, bed,* Od. 14, 51; plur. *beds,* *Od. 16, 35.
ἐνηείη, ἡ (ἐνηής), *gentleness, mildness, benevolence,* 17, 670.†
ἐνηής, ές, *gentle, mild, benevolent,* 17, 204. 23, 252. Od. 8, 200 (related to ἑός).
ἔνημαι (ἧμαι), *to sit in,* Od. 4, 272.†
ἐνήρατο, 3 sing. aor. mid. from ἐναίρω.
ἔνθα, adv. (ἐν), 1) Of place: *there, in that place, here;* also for relat. ὅθι, *where,* 1, 610. It more rarely expresses a motion, *hither, thither,* 13, 23. Od. 3, 295; with gen. h 18, 22. Often ἔνθα καὶ ἔνθα, here and there, hither and thither, 2, 462; thither and back, Od. 2, 213; in the length and breadth, 7, 156. 10, 264. Od. 7, 86. 2) Of time: *then,* at that time, now, 2, 155. Od. 1, 11; also ἔνθα δ' ἔπειτα, Od. 7, 196.
ἐνθάδε, adv. (ἔνθα), 1) *there, here,* 2, 296. Od. 2, 51. 2) *thither, hither,* 4, 179.
ἔνθεν, adv. (ἐν), 1) Spoken of place: *from hence, from thence.* ἔνθεν μὲν—ἔνθεν δέ, from this side—from that side, Od. 12, 235. ἔνθεν, ἔνθεν with gen. h. Merc. 226. α) Metaph. of descent: ἔνθα ἐμοὶ γένος, ὅθεν σοι, my race is derived from the same source whence thine is, 4, 58. b) For the relat. ὅθεν: οἶνος, ἔνθεν ἔπινον, of which they drank, Od. 4, 220; with ἔνθα preceding, Od. 5, 195. 2) Of time: *from this time, henceforth,* 13, 741.
ἐνθεῦτεν, adv. (ἔνθεν), *from hence, hence away,* *8, 527 9, 365.
ἔνθορε, see ἐνθρώσκω.
ἐνθρώσκω (θρώσκω), aor. 2 ἔνθορον, Ep. for ἐνέθορον, *to leap in, to spring among,* with dat. ὁμίλῳ, 15, 623; πόντῳ, 24, 79. λὰξ ἔνθορεν ἰσχίῳ, he dashed his heel against his thigh [*smote with his uplifted heel Ulysses' haunch.* Cp.], Od. 17 233.
ἐνθύμιος, ον (θυμός), *lying on the heart, causing anxiety.* μή τοι λίην ἐνθύμιος ἔστω, let him not be a great cause of anxiety to thee, Od. 13, 421.†
ἐνί, poet. for ἐν, also in composition, see ἐν.
ἐνιαύσιος, ον (ἐνιαυτός), *a year old,* σῦς, Od. 16, 454.†

Ἐνιαυτός.

ἐνιαυτός, ὁ, *a year.* Διὸς ἐνιαυτοί, the years of Zeus, so far as he regulates the course of time, 2, 134. cf. Od. 14, 93. Originally it meant any complete period of time, embracing particular phenomena, *a cycle,* hence ἔτος ἦλθε, περιπλομένων ἐνιαυτῶν, the year came in the revolutions of time, Od. 1. 16. τελεσφόρον εἰς ἐνιαυτόν, within (i. e. up to it, as its limit) the completed year [τελεσφόρος, *bringing an end, completing both other things and itself*], Od. 4, 86.

ἐνιαύω (ἰαύω), *to sleep in, to dwell in,* *Od. 9, 187. 15, 557.

ἐνιβάλλω, poet. for ἐμβάλλω.

ἐνιβλάπτω, old reading in 6, 39. 647; see βλάπτω.

ἐνίημι (ἵημι), fut. ἐνήσω, aor. 1 ἐνῆκα, Ep. ἐνέηκα, partcp. aor. 2 ἐνείς, 1) *to send in, to let in, to drive in,* spoken of persons; τινά, any into the war, 14, 131; πέλειαν (to introduce another), Od. 12, 65; metaph. with accus. of the pers. and dat. of the thing: τινὰ μᾶλλον ἀγηνορίησιν, to lead one deeper into his pride, i. e. to increase his haughtiness, 9, 700; πόνοισι, to plunge into troubles, 10, 89; ὁμοφροσύνῃσιν, Od. 15, 198. 2); *to put into,* according to the difference of the context: *to throw into, to thrust into,* mly τί τινι, rarely ἔν τινι; πῦρ νηυσίν, 12, 441; often ἐνιέναι νῆα πόντῳ, to launch, Od. 2, 295; also without νῆα, to put to sea, Od. 12, 401; metaph. of the mind: τινὶ ἀνάλκιδα θυμόν, to infuse into any one a timid spirit, 16, 656. τινὶ θάρσος ἐνὶ στήθεσσιν, 17, 579; τινὶ κότον, to excite anger in any one, 16, 449.

Ἐνιῆνες, οἱ. Ion. for Αἰνιᾶνες, sing. Ἐνιήν, the Æniänes, an ancient tribe, which dwelt first about Ossa, and afterwards in Epirus, between Othrys and Œta, 2, 749.

ἐνικλάω (κλάω), poet. for ἐγκλάω, *to break in pieces; metaph. to destroy, to make null,* with accus. *8, 408. 422.

Ἐνιπεύς, ῆος, ὁ, a river in Elis, which flowed into the Alphêus, now *Enipeo.* Od. 11, 238. Thus Strabo; but probably the river here mentioned is the *Thessalian Enipeus,* which flowed into the Apidänus, or rather the river god whose form Poseidön assumed, cf. Nitzsch ad Od 3, 4.

ἐνιπή, ἡ (ἐνίπτω). *a harsh address,* always in a bad signification, *blame, reproof, invective,* 4, 62; threatening, *insult,* Od. 20, 266; often strengthened by an adj., 5, 492. Od, 10, 448.

ἐνίπλειος, ον, poet. for ἔμπλειος, q. v.

ἐνιπλήσασθαι for ἐμπλήσασθαι, from ἐμπίμπλημι.

ἐνιπλήσσω (πλήσσω). Ep. for ἐμπλήσσω, aor. 1 ἐνέπληξα, partcp. ἐνιπλήξας, only intrans. *to fall into, to plunge into,* with dat. τάφρῳ, 12, 72. 15, 344; ἕρκει, to fall into a snare, see ἕρκος, Od. 22, 469.

ἐνιπρήθω (πρήθω), Ep. for ἐμπρήθω,

Ἐννεάχιλοι.

fut. ἐμπρήσω (9, 242) and ἐνιπρήσω, aor. 1 ἐνέπρησα, *to set on fire, to inflame, to burn up,* with accus. νῆας, νεκρούς: often strengthened with πυρὶ and πυρὸς αἰθομένοιο, 16, 82. 2) Spoken of wind, *to blow into, to swell out.* ἐν δ' ἄνεμος πρῆσεν ἱστίον. the wind blew into or swelled the middle of the sail, 1, 481 [πρήθω = (1) *to burn,* (2) *to spirtle, to pour out;* (*to blow*], Buttm. Lex. 486.

ἐνίπτω, poet. aor. 2 ἐνένιπον (incor. ἐνένιππον) and ἠνίπαπον (with redupl. like ἐρύκακον), prob. *to address harshly, to assail with harsh language, to chide, to blame* c. per-onæ accus.; not however always with the idea of abuse. κραδίην ἠνίπαπε μύθῳ, he excited his heart [of Ulysses rousing up his own courage: "*smiling on his breast reprov'd The mutinous inhabitant within.*" Cp.]; Od. 20, 17; often with a dat. χαλεπῷ μύθῳ χαλεποῖσι ὀνείδεσιν, 2, 245. 3, 438; also simply μύθῳ τινά, to reprove any one with words, 3, 427; and without μύθῳ, 24, 768. 15, 546. (H. has two aorists; ἐνένιπτεν, 15, 546. 552, is rejected by Buttm. Lex. p. 125, as contrary to the *usus loquendi,* he would read ἐνένιπεν, which Sptz. adopts; ἐνίσσω is a form of equivalent import. According to Ruhnken, the theme is ἴπος, a press; hence ἴπτω, ἐνίπτω, to press, to burden; see Thiersch, § 232, p. 389.)

ἐνισκίμπτω, Ep. for ἐνσκίμπτω (σκίμπτω), aor. 1 act. partcp. ἐνισκίμψας, aor. 1 pass. ἐνισκίμφθην, 1) *to fasten to, to fix,* τί τινι; οὔδει καρήατα, hanging their heads to the ground, 17, 437. Pass. *to be fastened in, to remain attached.* δόρυ οὔδει ἐνισκίμφθην, 16, 612. 17, 528.

ἐνισπε, ἐνισπεῖν, see ἐνέπω.

Ἐνίσπη, ἡ, a place in Arcadia, unknown even in the time of Strabo, 2, 606; cf. Paus. 8, 25, 7.

ἐνίσπω, poet. form of ἐνέπω, of which, however, H. has only single forms supplementary to ἐνέπω, viz. fut. ἐνίψω and ἐνισπήσω, aor. 2 ἔνισπες, etc. The aor. 2 ἐνένισπε, 23, 473, should be changed to ἐνένιπε, see Buttm. Lexil. p. 125; Spitzner has adopted ἐνένιπεν.

ἐνίσσω, poet. form of ἐνίπτω (as πίσσω of πέπτω] (=to *fall on* a man], *to assail, to chide,* with accus.; but absol. 15, 198. 22, 497; also partcp. pass. ἐνισσόμενος, Od. 24, 163.

ἐνιτρέφω, an old reading, 19, 326.

ἐνιχρίμπτω, poet. for ἐγχρίμπτω.

ἐννέα, indecl. *nine.* The number nine is often used by the poets as a round number, and as a triple triad; it seems to have been esteemed sacred, 2, 96. 6, 174. 16, 785.

ἐννεάβοιος, ον (βοῦς), *worth nine oxen,* τεύχεα, 6, 236.†

ἐννεακαίδεκα, indecl. *nineteen,* 24, 496.†

ἐννεάπηχυς, υ (πῆχυς), *nine cubits long,* 24, 270. Od. 11, 311.

ἐννεάχιλοι, αι, α, poet. for ἐννεάκις χίλιοι, *nine thousand,* *5, 860. 14, 148.

Ἔννεον 142 *Ἐντίθημι.*

ἔννεον, Ep. for ἔνεον, see νέω.
ἐννεόργυιος, ον (ὀργυιά), nine fathoms long, Od. 11, 312.† (in H. it is quadrisyllabic, and it is to be read ἐννεόργυιος).
ἐννέπω, poet. for ἐνέπω, q. v.
ἐννεσίη, ἡ, poet. for ἐνεσίη, q. v.
ἐννέωρος, ον (ὥρα), for nine years, nine years old, ἀλείφαρ, 18, 351. ἐννέωρος βασίλευε, he reigned during nine years, Od. 19, 179 (always trisyllabic, by synizesis of εω).
ἐννήκοντα, Ep. for ἐνενήκοντα, Od. 19, 174.†
ἐννῆμαρ, adv. (ἐννέα and ἦμαρ), for nine days, often in Il. and Od.
Ἔννομος, ὁ, 1) an ally of the Trojans from Mysia, mentioned as an augur, slain by Achilles, 2, 858. 17, 218. 2) A Trojan, slain by Odysseus (Ulysses), 11, 422.
Ἐννοσίγαιος, ὁ, poet. for ἐνοσίγαιος (ἔνοσις), the earth-shaker, appellation of Poseidôn, because earthquakes were ascribed to him: as subst. 7, 455 and 9, 183, see Ποσειδῶν. (ἔνοσις) related to ὄθομαι, so Buttm. Lex. p. 115 [No: he considers ἔνοσις related to ἔνω, ἐνόω with the meaning of to shake.]
ἔννυμι, poet. (ἘΩ), fut. ἕσω, poet. σσ, aor. 1 act. ἕσσα, aor. 1 mid. ἐσσάμην, Ep. ἐεσάμην, infin. ἕσασθαι, 24, 646; perf. pass. εἵμαι, partcp. εἱμένος, 3 plur. pluperf. εἴατο, 18, 596; also as if from ἕσμαι, 2 sing. perf. ἕσσαι, and pluperf. 2 sing. ἕσσο, 3 ἕστο and ἕεστο, 12, 464; 2 dual ἕσθην. Fundamental signif. 1) to clothe, to put on; with double accus. τινὰ εἵματα, χλαῖναν, 5, 904. Od. 15, 338. 2) Mid. and pass. to clothe oneself in, to attire oneself in, prop. spoken of clothes; with accus. φάρος, Od. 10, 543. χρύσεια εἵματα ἕσθην, they had attired themselves in golden clothing. 18, 517. χλαῖνας εὖ εἱμένοι, beautifully clad in mantles. Od. 15, 331. 2) Metaph. spoken of weapons: to put upon oneself (sibi), περὶ χροῒ χαλκόν, 14, 383; τεύχεα, 4, 432; also ἀσπίδας ἑσσάμενοι, covering themselves with shields, 14, 372; also εἱμένος ὤμοιϊν νεφέλην, 'his shoulders wrapt in cloud,' 15, 308; ἀή τέ κεν ἤδη λάϊνον ἕσσο χιτῶνα, already hadst thou been clothed with a tunic of stone, i. e. wouldst have been stoned,'3, 56.
ἐννύχιος, η, ον (νύξ), by night, nightly, nocturnal, 11, 683. Od. 3, 178.
ἔννυχος, η, ον = ἐννύχιος, 11, 716.†
ἐνοινοχοέω (χέω), to pour wine into, οἶνον, in the partcp., Od. 3, 472.†
ἐνοπή, ἡ (ἐνέπω), 1) a voice, a tone, Od. 10, 147; a sound, of inanimate things, αὐλῶν, συρίγγων, 10, 13. 2) a cry, esply a battle-cry, in connexion with κλαγγή, 3, 2; μάχη, 12, 35. b) a cry of lamentation, 24, 160.
Ἐνόπη, ἡ (appell. ἐνοπή), a town in Messênia, which Agamemnon promised to Achilles for a dowry, 9, 150; according to Paus. 3, 26, = Gerênia.
ἐνόρνυμι (ὄρνυμι), aor. 1 ἐνῶρσα, aor.

αγι... mid. only 3 sing. ἐνῶρτο, act. to excite in, to awaken in: with accus. rei and dat. of pers. σθένος τινί, to excite strength in any one, 2, 451; γόον τινί, 8, 499: αὐτοῖς φύζαν, 15, 62. Mid. to be excited in or among, to arise amongst. ἐνῶρτο γέλως θεοῖσιν, 1, 599. Od. 8, 326.
ἐνορούω (ὀρούω), aor. 1 ἐνόρουσα, to leap in or upon; with dat. to rush upon, to attack, Τρωσί, 16, 753; spoken of lions: αἴγεσιν, *10, 486.
ἔνορχος, ον (ὄρχις), not mutilated, not castrated, 23, 147.†
Ἐνοσίχθων, ονος, ὁ (ἔνοσις, χθών), earth-shaker, a name of Poseidôn, as adj. 7, 445. Subst. often 8, 208; see Ἐννοσίγαιος.
ἐνοσκίμπτω, see ἐνισκίμπτω.
ἐνοστάζω (στάζω), perf. pass. ἐνέσταικται, to instil; metaph. εἰ δή τοι σοῦ πατρὸς ἐνέστακται μένος, if the spirit of the father is implanted in (instilled into. Cp.) thee, Od. 2, 271.†
ἐνοστηρίζω (στηρίζω), to fasten in, only pass. ἐγχείη γαίῃ ἐνεστήρικτο, the spear remained fixed in the earth, 21, 168.†
ἐνοστρέφω (στρέφω), to turn in. Mid. to turn oneself in; with dat. μηροῖς ἰσχίῳ ἐνοστρέφεται, the thigh-bone turns in the socket, 5, 306.†
ἐντανύω (τανύω) = ἐντείνω, fut. ὀτανύσω, aor. 1 ἐντάνυσα, aor. 1 mid. ἐντανυσάμην, to stretch, to bend; with accus. βιόν, τόξον, νευρήν, Od. 19, 577. 587; pass. Od. 21, 92; mid. τόξον, to bend his bow, Od. 21, 403. *Od.
ἐνταῦθα, adv. (ἐν), hither; to this, 9, 601.†
ἐνταυθοῖ, adv. (ἐν), here, κεῖσο, 21, 122; ἧσο, Od. 18, 105. h. Ap. 363. Never hither. Cf. Herm. ad Arist. Nub. 813.
ἔντεα, τά, weapons, arms, 5, 220. ἔντεα Ἀρήϊα, 10, 407; chiefly the cuirass, 10, 34. 2) Mly utensils, furniture; δαιτός, the furniture of a feast, Od. 7, 23 : νηός, h. Ap. 489 (Ac ording to Buttm. Lex. p. 134, from ἔννυμι, prop. that which one puts on; the sing. is obsol.).
ἐντείνω (τείνω), perf. pass. ἐντέταμαι, 1) to stretch, to strain; perf. pass. to be strained or stretched in, to hang; with dat. δίφρος ἱμᾶσιν ἐντέταται, the chariot body hangs in braces, 5, 728. 2) to stretch upon or over, spoken of a helmet; ἱμᾶσιν. 'with many a thong, well braced within' (Cp.), 10, 263.
ἔντερον, τό (ἐντός), a gut, sing. only ἔντερον οἰός, a sheep's gut, Od. 21, 408. 2) Elsewhere plur. the bowels, the intestines, 10.
ἐντεσιεργός, όν (ἔντεα 2, ἔργον), working in harness, i. e. drawing, ἡμίονοι, 24, 277.†
ἐντεῦθεν, adv. thence, hence, Od. 17 568.†
ἐντίθημι (τίθημι), imperf. 3 sing. ἐνετίθει (τιθέω), aor. 1 ἐνέθηκα, aor. 2 infin. ἐνθέμεναι, Ep. for ἐνθεῖναι, mid. aor. 1 ἐνεθέμην, 3 sing. ἔνθετο, imperat. ἔνθεο; art. only in tmesis, to put in, to place in, to introduce, with accus, mly of in

animate things: κῆρε, 8, 70; νώτον διός, 9, 207. Mid. 1) *to put or place in, to introduce* (with reference to the subject), τί τινι: ἱστία νηΐ, to put the sails into the ship, Od. 11, 3; spoken of persons: τινὰ λεχέεσσι, to lay any one on the bed, 21, 124. *b)* Metaph. μή μοι πατέρας ὁμοίῃ ἔνθεο τιμῇ, place not our fathers in equal honour, i. e. do not confer equal honour upon them, 4, 410. 2) *to put into for oneself, to assume*, τί, chiefly, metaph. ἵλαον ἔνθεο θυμόν, assume a gentle spirit, 9, 369; χόλον θυμῷ, to conceive anger in his heart, 6, 326; κότον, Od. 11, 102; μῦθον θυμῷ, to take the word to heart, Od. 1, 361.

ἔντο, see ἕξημι.

ἐντός, adv. (ἐν), *therein, in*, 10, 10. Od. 2, 341. 2) Prep. with gen. *within*, λιμένος ἐντός, 1, 432, and often.

ἔντοσθε, and before a vowel ἔντοσθεν, adv. = ἐντός. *in, within*, absol. 10, 262. 2) With gen. 6, 364. Od. 1, 126.

ἐντρέπω (τρέπω), *to change, to turn about*, only pres. pass. οὐδέ νύ σοί περ ἐντρέπεται ἦτορ; even now is thy heart not changed? i. e. art thou not brought to a different purpose,—dost thou not relent? 15, 554. Od. 1, 60.

ἐντρέχω (τρέχω), *to turn in*; metaph. *to move in*. εἰ γυῖα ἐντρέχοι, 19, 385.†

ἐντροπαλίζομαι, depon. mid. Ep. (frequent, from ἐντρέπω), *to turn oneself often*, 6, 496; esply spoken of one who in a slow retreat from an enemy often looks back, *15, 547. 17, 109; always partcp. ἐντροπαλιζόμενος, oft *turning, or looking back*.

*ἐντροπίη, poet. (ἐντρέπω), *the act of turning, an artifice, a trick*, δόλιαι ἐντροπίαι, crafty artifices [slippery *turns*], h. Merc. 245.

ἐντύνω and ἐντύω (ἔντυα), aor. 1 partcp. ἐντύνας, aor. 1 mid. ἐντυνάμενος, *to equip, to prepare, to arrange, to furnish*, with accus. ἵππους, to make ready the horses, 5, 720; εὐνήν, to prepare the bed, Od. 23, 289; ἀοιδήν, to begin the song, Od. 12, 183; εὖ ἐντύνασα ἓ αὐτήν, having beautifully arrayed herself, 14, 162. Mid. 1) *to arm* or *prepare oneself*, Od. 6, 33; esply, *to adorn oneself*, Od. 12, 18. 2) *to prepare for oneself, to arrange for oneself*, with accus. δαῖτα, to prepare a feast for oneself, Od. 3, 83; ἄριστον, 24, 124; ἐντύω occurs only in the imperf. act.)

ἐντυπάς, adv. (τύπτω), *stretched upon the earth*, ἐντυπὰς ἐν χλαίνῃ κεκαλυμμένος, prostrate enveloped in a mantle, spoken of the sorrowing Priam, 24, 163.† (According to Voss '*so that only the form* (of the body appeared'). [Cp.: "*the hoary king sat mantled*, muffled close."]

ἐντύω, a form of ἐντύνω, q. v.

Ἐνυάλιος, ὁ (Ἐνυώ), *the warlike, the god of battle*, either as a name of Ἀρής, only in Il. as subst. 2, 651. 7, 166; or as an epith. 17, 211. (Eustath. derives it from ἐνύω = φονεύω, Hesych. πολε-

Ἐνυεύς, ῆος, ὁ, king of Scyrus, whom Achilles slew, 9, 668.

ἐνύπνιος, ον (ὕπνος), *occuring in sleep*, whence neut. as adv. ἐνύπνιον, in sleep, *in slumber*, θεῖός μοι ἐνύπνιον ἦλθεν ὄνειρος, a divine vision appeared to me in sleep, 2, 56. Od. 14, 495; cf. Thiersch, § 269; (ἐνύπνιον as a subst. a dream, a vision, in a later signif.)

Ἐνυώ, όος, ἡ, *Enyó*, the slaughtering goddess of war, companion of Ἀρής, 5, 333. 592: the *Bellona* of the Romans, (from ἐνύω = φονεύω, Herm. on the other hand ὕω, *Inundans*, cf. Ἐνυάλιος).

ἐνωπαδίως, adv. (ἐνωπή), *facing, in the presence of*, Od. 23, 94, Wolf.† Others read ἐνωπιδίως.

ἐνωπή, ἡ (ὤψ), *the countenance*, only in the dat. ἐνωπῇ, as adv. *in view of, openly*, *5, 374. 21, 510.

ἐνώπια, τά, *a wall of a house*, chiefly, the front walls, on both sides of the entrance. They were in part covered by the porch, and the chariots were generally placed against them, 8, 435. Od. 4, 42; as well as captured arms, 13, 261. They were characterized as παμφανόωντα, because they were upon the sunny side, or because they were adorned with metallic ornaments, Od. 4, 45; (prop. neut. plur. from ἐνώπιος, that which is before the eyes).

ἐνωπιδίως, see ἐνωπαδίως.

ἐνώψ, ῶπος, Ep. for ἐνωπή, *the countenance*, hence κατ' ἐνῶπα, in the face, a reading adopted by Spitzner, after Aristarchus, for κατένωπα, 15, 320.†

ἐξ, prep. before a vowel for ἐκ.

ἕξ, indecl. *six*. In composition ξ becomes κ before κ and π.

ἐξαγγέλλω (ἀγγέλλω), aor. 1 ἐξήγγειλα, *to proclaim, to publish, to disclose*, τί τινι, 5, 390.†

ἐξαγνυμι (ἄγνυμι), *to break out, to break in pieces*, with accus. ἐξ αὐχένα ἄξε βοός, *5, 161. 11, 175; (occurs only in tmesis).

ἐξαγορεύω (ἀγορεύω), *to speak out, to communicate, to publish*, with accus., Od. 11, 234.†

ἐξάγω (ἄγω), aor. 2 ἐξήγαγον, poet. ἐξάγαγον, *to lead out, to lead away, to bring out*, τινά, mly with gen. of place: τινὰ μάχης, ὁμίλου, πολέμοιο, 5, 35. 353; ἐκ μεγάροιο, Od. 8, 106; metaph. spoken of Ilithyia, the goddess presiding over births: τινὰ πρὸ φόωσδε, to bring any one to light, i. e. into the world, 16, 188. 2) Neut. *to go out, to march out*. τύμβον χεύομεν ἐξαγαγόντες, 7, 336 435. Thus Eustath. and Voss.: 'assembled without;' others: ἐξάγειν ἐκ πεδίου, to erect out of the plain, cf. Heyne; [so Bothe, *educentes ex campo tumulum*.]

ἐξάδιος, ὁ, one of the Lapithæ, at the marriage of Pirithous. 1, 264.

ἐξάετες (a form of ἐξέτης), adv. *for six years*, Od. 3, 115.†

ἐξαίνυμαι, depon. (αἴνυμαι), *to take*

Ἐξαίρετος. 144 **Ἐξάρχω.**

take away life, 4, 531, with double accus. 5, 155; and δῶρα, Od. 15, 206; (only pres. and imperf.)
ἐξαίρετος, ον (ἐξαιρέω), taken out, selected, chosen, distinguished, 2, 227. Od. 4, 643.
ἐξαιρέω (αἰρέω), aor. 2 ἐξεῖλον, poet. ἔξελον, infin. ἐξελεῖν, aor. mid. ἐξειλόμην, poet. ἐξελόμην, to take out, esply to choose, to select, κούρην τινί, for any one, 11, 627. 16, 56. Oftener mid. to take out for oneself, τί τινος, δίστὸν φαρέτρης, from the quiver, 8, 323; esply, a) to take away by force, to bereave, to despoil, 2, 690; and with ἐκ, 9, 331; frequently, θυμόν, φρένας, either with double accus. τινὰ θυμόν, to take away one's life, 15, 460. 17, 678; or with accus. and gen. τινὸς φρένας, 19. 137; μελέων θυμόν, Od. 11, 201; once τί τινι, 6, 234. b) to take out of several, i. e. to choose for oneself, 9, 272. Od. 14, 232.
ἐξαίρω (αἴρω), only mid. aor. 1. 3 sing. ἐξήρατο, to bear off for oneself, to secure, μισθούς, Od. 10, 84 with gen. Τροίης, to bear off as plunder from Troy, *Od. 5, 39
ἐξαίσιος, ον (αἴσιος), contravening right and justice, unrighteous, unjust, indecorous, wrong, ἀρή, 15, 598. οὔτε τινὰ ῥέξας ἐξαίσιον, nor ever wronging any man by an unjust act, Od. 4, 690. 2) exceeding the due measure, extraordinary. δείσας τινά, fearing him excessively, as adv. Od.17, 577.
ἐξαίσσω (ἀΐσσω), aor. 1 ἐξήιξα, aor. 1 pass. ἐξηΐχθην, intrans. to leap out, to rush forth, 12, 145; likewise pass. ἐκ δέ μοι ἔγχος ἤχθη παλάμηφιν, the spear flew from my hands, 3, 368.
ἔξαιτος, ον (αἴω = αἴνυμαι), taken out, selected, excellent οἶνος, 12, 320; ἐρέται, Od. 2, 307.
ἐξαίφνης, adv. (αἴφνης), suddenly, unexpectedly, *17, 738. 21, 14.
ἐξακέομαι, depon. mid. (ἀκέομαι), aor. 1 optat. ἐξακεσαίμην, to cure entirely, to heal thoroughly, to restore, 9, 507; metaph. to appease, to reconcile, χόλον, 4, 36. Od. 3, 145.
ἐξαλαόω (ἀλαόω), fut. ώσω, to blind entirely, to render blind, τινά, Od. 11, 103; ὀφθαλμόν, *Od. 9, 453. 504.
ἐξαλαπάζω (ἀλαπάζω), fut. ξω, aor. ἐξαλάπαξα, to empty, to depopulate, πόλιν, Od. 4, 176; chiefly in war: to sack, hence, to destroy, to raze, πόλιν, τεῖχος, νῆας, 20, 30.
ἐξαλέομαι, depon. mid. (ἀλέομαι), to avoid, to escape, 18, 586. in tmesis.†
ἐξάλλομαι, depon. mid. (ἄλλομαι), only part. aor. 2 sync. ἐξάλμενος, to leap out, to spring forth, with gen. προμάχων, from the front ranks, *17, 342. 23, 399.
*ἐξαλύω, poet. for ἐξαναλύσκω, to avoid, to escape, with acc. μόρον, h. 6. 51.
ἐξαναδύω (δύω), aor. 2 ἐξανέδυν, nartcp. ἐξαναδύς, to come forth, to emerge, ἁλός, from the sea. *Od. 4, 405. 5, 438; ἀφ' ὕδατος, Batr. 133.

*ἐξαναιρέω (αἰρέω), aor. 2 ἐξανεῖλον, to take out, to take away, with gen. h. in Cer. 255.
ἐξαναλύω (λύω), infin. aor.1 ἐξαναλῦσαι, to liberate completely, to set entirely free, to deliver, ἄνδρα θανάτοιο, from death, *16, 442. 22, 180.
ἐξαναφανδόν, adv. (ἀναφανδόν), openly, plainly, Od. 20, 48.†
*ἐξάνειμι (εἶμι), to ascend from. 2) to return, with gen. ἄγρης, h. 18, 15.
ἐξανίημι (ἵημι), to emit, to send forth, spoken of the bellows: αὐτμήν, 18, 471.
ἐξανύω (ἀνύω), aor. 1 ἐξήνυσα, to finish, to accomplish, to execute, βουλάς, 8. 370. 2) to slay (conficere), τινά, *11, 365. 20, 452
ἐξαπατάω (ἀπατάω), fut. ήσω, aor. 1 ἐξαπάτησα, without augm. to deceive, with accus. 9, 371. Od. 9, 414.
ἐξαπαφίσκω (ἀπαφίσκω), aor. 2 ἐξήπαφον, Od. 14, 379; aor. 1 ἐξαπάφησα, h. Ap. 376; aor. 2 mid. only optat. ἐξαπάφοιτο, 9, 376. 14, 160; to deceive, cheat, τινὰ μύθῳ, Od. l. c. Mid. = act. Διὸς νόον, to deceive the mind of Zeus, 14, 160; ἐπέεσσιν, 9, 376. The partcp. ἐξαπάφουσα as pres. is found in h. Ap. 379; it should prob. be written ἐξαναφοῦσα, as aor. 2; cf. h. Ven. 38.
ἐξαπίνης, adv. = ἐξαίφνης, suddenly, unexpectedly, 9, 6; and often.
*ἐξαπλόω (ἁπλόω), to unfold, to extend, δέμας, Batr. 106.
ἐξαποβαίνω (βαίνω), aor. 2 ἐξαπέβην, to go out of, to disembark, νηός, Od. 12, 306.†
ἐξαποδύνω (δύνω), to strip, to take off, εἵματα, Od. 5, 372;† cf. δύνω.
ἐξαπόλλυμι (ὄλλυμι), to destroy utterly; only intrans. aor. 2 mid. ἐξαπωλόμην, and perf. 2 ἐξαπόλωλα, to perish from, to vanish from, with gen. Ἰλίου, from Troy, 9, 60. ἐξαπόλωλε δόμων κειμήλια, the stores have vanished from the houses, 18, 290; ἠέλιος οὐρανοῦ, Od. 20, 357.
ἐξαπονέομαι, an old reading for ἐξ ἄπον, separated.
ἐξαπονίζω (νίζω), to wash off, to clean, πόδας τινί, Od. 19, 357.†
ἐξαποτίνω (τίνω), to expiate entirely, to atone f r, with accus. Ἐριννύας, 21, 412.†
ἐξάπτω (ἅπτω), aor. 1 ἐξῆψα, to append, to attach, with accus. and gen. πεῖσμα κίονος, the cable to a column or pillar, Od. 22, 466. Ἕκτορα ἵππων, 24, 51. Mid. to attach oneself to, 8, 20.
ἐξαράσσω (ἀράσσω), to strike out, to crush. ἐκ δέ οἱ ἱστὸν ἄραξε, Od. 12, 422;† in tmesis, cf. ἀράσσω.
ἐξαρπάζω (ἁρπάζω), aor. 1 ἐξήρπαξα, to snatch away, to bear off, with accus. and gen. of the place: τινὰ νηός, from the ship, Od. 12, 100; absol. to bear away, 3, 380. 20, 443.
ἔξαρχος, ον (ἄρχος), making a beginning; subst. a beginner. θρήνων, 24, 721.†
ἐξάρχω (ἄρχω), to begin, to commence, with gen. μολπῆς, ἐξάρχοντος (supply from the context ἀοιδοῦ), 18, 606. Od. 4, 19; γόοιο, 18, 51; with accus. βουλὰς

Ἐξαυδάω. 145 **Ἐξίημι.**

ἀγαθάς, to propose first salutary counsel, 2, 273; and χορούς, h. 27, 18. Mid. to begin, with gen. βουλῆς, Od. 12, 339.

ἐξαυδάω (αὐδάω), to speak out, to utter, connected with μὴ κεῦθε, 1, 363. 18, 74.

ἐξαῦτις, adv. (αὖτις), again, anew, 1, 223. 2) Of place: back, 5, 134. Od. 4, 213.

ἐξαφαιρέω (ἀφαιρέω), to take away, only mid. aor. 2 ἐξαφειλόμην, to take away for oneself; ψυχήν τινος, to take a man's life, Od. 22, 444.†

ἐξαφύω (ἀφύω), to draw out, to empty, to exhaust, οἶνον, Od. 14, 95.†

ἐξεῖδον (ΕΙΔΩ), Ep. ἐξιδον, defect. aor. of ἐξοράω, to see (out) μέγ' ἐξιδών, ὀφθαλμοῖσιν, he saw clearly with his eyes, 20, 342.†

ἐξείης, adv. (poet. for ἑξῆς), in course, in succession, in order, 1, 448. Od. 1, 145.

ἔξειμι (εἶμι), 2 sing. pres. Ep. ἔξεισθα, infin. ἐξίμεναι, imperf. ἐξῇει, to go out, θύραζε, 18, 448; with gen. μεγάρων, Od. 1, 374. h. Ap. 28.

ἐξεῖπον (εἶπον), defect. aor. 2 of ἐκφημι, to declare, to communicate, τινί τι 9, 61. 24, 654.

ἐξείρομαι, Ion. for ἐξέρομαι (εἴρομαι), to interrogate, to seek for, with accus. τινά, 5, 756; βουλήν, to ask counsel, only imperf. ἐξείρετο, 20, 15. Od. 13, 127.

ἐξεκυλίσθην, see ἐκκυλίω.

ἔξεισθα, see ἔξειμι.

ἐξελαύνω (ἐλαύνω), fut. ἐξελάσω, infin. ἐξελάαν (8, 527), aor. 1 act. ἐξήλασα, Ep. ἐξέλασσα, 1) to drive out, to drive away, to expel, spoken of men and brutes, with accus. τινὰ γαίης, to expel any one from the land, Od. 16, 381; τάφρου, 8, 255; μῆλα ἄντρου, Od. 9, 312; πάντας ὀδόντας γναθμῶν, to knock out every tooth from a man's jaws, Od. 18, 29; metaph. δίκην ἐξελαύνειν (subaud. ἀγορῆς), to expel or banish justice, 16, 388. 2) Intrans. to proceed, to drive, 11, 360.

ἐξελεῖν, see ἐξαιρέω.

ἐξέλκω (ἕλκω), to draw out, with gen. θαλάμης, Od. 5, 432. Pass. Il. 4, 214; see ἄγνυμι.

ἔξεμεν, Ep. for ἐξεῖναι, see ἐξίημι.

ἐξέμεν for ἐξεῖν, see ἔχω.

ἐξεμέω (ἐμέω), aor. 1 ἐξήμεσα, to vomit forth, to cast forth, spoken of Charybdis, *Od. 12, 237. 437.

ἐξέμμορε, see ἐκμείρομαι.

ἐξεναρίζω (ἐναρίζω), fut. ἴξω, and aor. 1. to strip the armour from the dead, with accus. τινὰ τεύχεα, 5, 151. 7, 146. 13, 619. 2) to kill, to slay, 4, 488. Od. 11, 272.

ἐξερεείνω, Ep. (ἐρεείνω), to seek after, to inquire after, to explore, 9, 672; πόρους ἁλός, Od. 12, 259; metaph. to try, κιθάραν [to elicit its tones], h. Merc. 483. Mid. like the act. τινὰ μύθῳ, 10, 81.

ἐξερείπω (ἐρείπω), aor. 2, only subj. ἐξερίπῃ and partcp. ἐξεριπών, prop. to cast down; in aor. 2 intrans. to fall, spoken of the oak, 14, 414 ; χαίτη ζεύγλης, the mane falling from the collar of the yoke, *17, 440. 19, 406.

ἐξερέομαι, depon. mid. Ep. form of ἐξείρομαι, to seek out, only pres. and imperf. ; see ἐξερέω.

1) ἐξερέω, Ep. for ἐξερῶ, fut. of ἐκφημι, to declare, to proclaim, 1, 204. ὧδε ἐξερέω, 1, 212. 8, 286. (It must not be confounded with the following word.)

11) ἐξερέω, Ep. for ἐρεείνω (ἐράω), only pres. 3 plur. ἐξερέουσι, subj. 3 sing. ἐξερέῃσι, optat. ἐξερέοις, partcp. ἐξερέων, to interrogate, to enquire after, to seek, with accus. ἕκαστα, Od. 14, 375; absol. Od. 3, 116: γόνον, to ask after a man's family, Od. 19, 166; to explore, to examine, κνημούς, Od. 4, 337. 17, 128 (like ἐξερεείνω, Od. 12, 259). Mid. as depon. ἐξερέομαι, to question, ἔκ τ' ἐρέοντο, 9, 671; and infin. ἐξερέεσθαι, subj. ἐξερέηται, Od. 1, 416; optat. ἐξερέοιτο, Od. 4, 119.

ἐξερύω (ἐρύω), aor. 1 ἐξείρυσα, poet. σσ and ἐξέρυσα, Ep. iterat. aor. ἐξερύσασκε, to draw out, to pull out, to tear out; with accus. and gen. βέλος ὤμου, the weapon from the shoulder, 5, 112; in like manner δόρυ μηροῦ, 5, 666; ἰχθύας θαλάσσης, Od. 22, 386; but τινὰ ποδός, to draw a man out by the foot, 10, 490; δίφρον ῥυμοῦ (by the pole), 10, 505; to tear out, μήδεα, Od. 18, 87.

ἐξέρχομαι, depon. (ἔρχομαι), only aor. 2 ἐξήλυθον and ἐξῆλθον, to go out, to come out, 9, 476. 576; with gen. κλισίης, out of the tent, 10, 140; μεγάροιο, Od. 21, 229.

ἐξερωέω (ἐρωέω), aor. 1 ἐξηρώησα, to spring out of the way, to run from the way, spoken of horses, 23, 468.†

ἐξεσίη, ἡ (ἐξίημι), embassy, mission; only ἐξεσίην ἐλθεῖν, to go on an embassy, to go any where as an ambassador, 24, 235. Od. 21, 20; see ἀγγελίην ἐλθεῖν.

ἐξέτης, ες, another form of ἐξαέτης (ἔτος), six years old, ἵππος, *23, 266. 655.

ἐξέτι (ἔτι), prep. with gen. since, from the time. ἐξέτι τοῦ ὅτε, from the time when, 9, 106. ἐξέτι τῶν πατρῶν, from the time of the fathers, Od. 8, 245. h. Merc. 508.

ἐξευρίσκω (εὑρίσκω), aor. 2 optat. ἐξεύροιμι, to find out, to discover, 18, 322.†

ἐξηγέομαι, depon. mid. (ἡγέομαι), to lead or conduct out, τινος, 2, 806.†

ἐξήκοντα, indecl. (ἕξ), sixty, 2, 584. Od. 14, 20.

ἐξήλασα, see ἐξελαύνω.

ἐξήλατος, ον (ἐξελαύνω), beaten, hammered out, ἀσπίς, 12, 295.†

ἐξῆμαρ, adv. (ἦμαρ), during six days, *Od. 10, 80.

ἐξημοιβός, όν (ἐξαμείβω), changed, for a change: εἵματα, garments for change, Od. 8, 249.†

ἐξηπάφον, see ἐξαπαφίσκω.

ἐξηράνθη, see ξηραίνω, II.

ἐξήρατο, see ἐξαίρω.

ἐξησκημαι, see ἐξασκέω.

ἑξῆς, poet. ἐξείης (ἔχω, ἔξω), in order, one after another, *Od. 4, 419. 580.

ἐξίημι (ἵημι), only infin. aor. 2 ἐξέμεν,

H

Ἐξῑθύ̄νω.   146   Ἔοικα.

Ep. for ἐξεῖναι, and aor. 2 mid. 3 plur. ἔξεντο in tmesis. Act. *to send out*, with accus. ἐς Ἀχαιούς, 11, 141. Mid. *to send out*, *to expel*, only in the common formula: ἐπεὶ πόσιος καὶ ἐδητύος ἐξ ἔρον ἕντο, after they had expelled the desire of food and drink, 1, 469. 2, 432.

ἐξῑθύ̄νω (ἰθύνω), *to make exactly straight* [to divide it aright. Cp.], δόρυ νήϊον, 15, 410.†

ἐξικνέομαι, depon. mid. (ἱκνέομαι), only aor. 2 ἐξικόμην, *to arrive at, to reach*, with accus. θώκους, 8, 439; *eply to reach at length*, with accus., Od. 13, 206. 11. 9, 479.

ἐξίμεναι, see ἔξειμι.

ἐξίσχω (ἴσχω = ἔχω), *to hold out;* with accus. and gen. of place: ἐξίσχει κεφαλὰς βερέθρου, she *protrudes* [Cp.] her heads out of the abyss (spoken of Scylla), Od. 12, 94.†

ἐξοίσω, see ἐκφέρω.

ἐξοιχνέω, poet. (a form of οἴχομαι), *to go out*, 3 plur. pres. ἐξοιχνεῦσι, 9, 384.†

ἐξοίχομαι (οἴχομαι), *to go out*, *to go away*, *to depart;* the pres. prop. with signification of perf. ἐς Ἀθηναίης, sc. δόμον, 6, 379. Od. 4, 665.

ἐξόλλυμι (ὄλλυμι), aor. 1 ἐξώλεσα, *to annihilate*, *to destroy utterly*, Od. 17, 597; φρένας τινί, to destroy a man's understanding (in tmesis), 7, 360. 12, 234.

*ἐξολολύζω (ἀλολύζω), *to howl out, to wail*, Batr. 101.

ἐξονομάζω (ὀνομάζω), prop. to call by name; *to name, to utter*, h. Merc. 59; and frequently ἔπος τ᾽ ἔφατ᾽, ἔκ τ᾽ ὀνόμαζεν, where it must be connected with ἔπος, to utter the word, like *eloqui verbum* (Voss, 'beginning he spake'), 1, 361. 3, 398, seq. [she said what she had to say and declared it fully, Nägelsb. ad Il. 1, 361].

ἐξονομαίνω (ὀνομαίνω), aor. 1 subj. ἐξονομήνῃς, and infin. ἐξονομῆναι, *to call by name*, with accus. ἄνθρα, 3, 166 ; γάμον, to name her marriage, Od. 6, 66. h. Ven. 253.

ἐξονομακλήδην, adv. (ὄνομα, καλέω), *mentioned by name, by name;* with ὀνομάζειν, 22, 415, and καλεῖν, Od. 4, 278.

ἐξόπιθεν, also ἐξόπιθε, adv. poet. for ἐξόπισθεν (ὄπισθεν), *from behind*, on the *back part*, *backwards*, 4, 298. 2) As prep. with gen. *behind*, κεράων, *17, 521.

ἐξοπίσω, adv. (ὀπίσω), 1) Of place: *backwards*, 11, 461; also prepos. with gen. *behind*, 17, 357. 2) Of time: *hereafter*, in future; only in Od. 4, 35. 13, 144.

*ἐξοργίζω (ὀργίζω), *to make angry, to exasperate*. Pass. *to become very angry*, Batr. 185.

ἐξορμάω (ὁρμάω), partcp. aor. 1 ἐξορμήσας, *to go forth, to rush* or *hurry forth*. μή σε λάθησιν κεῖσ᾽ ἐξορμήσασα sc. νηῦς, lest it (the vessel) unperceived by you rush thither, Od. 12, 221.†

ἐξορούω (ὀρούω), *to spring out, to leap out*, only in tmesis; spoken of the lot, 3, 325; of men, Od. 10, 47.

ἐξοφέλλω (ὀφέλλω), *to increase greatly, to augment*, with accus. ἐεδνα, Od. 15, 18.†

ἔξοχ᾽ for ἔξοχα, see ἔξοχος.

ἔξοχος (ἐξέχω), origin. *prominent*: metaph. *distinguished*, *excellent; spoken of men, 2, 188; of brutes, 2, 480; of a piece of land, τέμενος, 6, 194. 20, 184; often with gen. ἔξοχος Ἀργείων, *eminent among the Argives*, 3. 227; also with dat. ἔξοχον ἡρώεσσιν for ἐν ἡρώεσσιν, 2. 483. The neut. ἔξοχον and ἔξοχα as adv. *most, among all, before all*, 5, 61: ἐμοὶ δόσαν ἔξοχα, they gave it me by preference (before the rest), Od. 9, 551; often with gen. ἔξοχον ἄλλων, 9, 641; with superl. ἔξοχ᾽ ἄριστοι, by far the best, 9, 638. Od. 4, 629; also μέγ᾽ ἔξοχα, Od. 15, 227.

ἐξυπανίστημι (from ἐξ, ὑπό, ἀνά. ἵστημι), only in aor. 2, *to arise from a place under*. σμώδιξ μεταφρένου ἐξυπανέστη, a weal arose upon his back, 2, 267.†

*ἐξυφαίνω (ὑφαίνω), *to finish a web, to weave out*. Batr. 182.

ἔξω, adv. (ἐξ), *out, without*, Od. 10, 95. 2) *out of, away from*, 17, 265. Od. 12, 94; with gen. which, however, often depends at the same time upon the verb; στηθέων, 10, 94. ἔξω βῆτην μεγάροιο, Od. 22, 378.

ἔξω, see ἔχω.

ἐο. Ep. for οὗ, q. v.

ἐοῖ, Ep. for οἷ, see οὗ.

ἐοι, Ep. for εἴη, see εἰμί.

ἔοικα, ας, ε, perf. with pres. signif. (from ΕΙΚΩ, q. v.), 3 dual Ep. ἔϊκτον, partcp. ἐοικώς, once εἰκώς, 21, 254; fem. εἰκυῖα, once plur. ἐοικυῖαι, 18, 418; pluperf. ἐῴκειν, εις, ει, dual Ep. ἐΐκτην, 3 plur. ἐοίκεσαν, 13, 102. Also the Ep. pass. form ἔϊκτο, was like, 23, 107, and ἤϊκτο, Od. 4, 796. 1) *to be similar, to be like, to resemble*, τινί, any one, τί, in any thing; Μαχάονι πάντα, in all respects, 11, 613; δέμας γυναικί, Od. 4, 796; strengthened by ἄγχιστα [to resemble closely], εἰς ὦπα, 14, 174. Od. 1, 411; chiefly in partcp. νυκτὶ ἐοικώς, like night, 1, 47. cf. 3, 151, etc. 2) *to befit, to behove; to᾽ be proper, becoming, just;* always impers., except Od. 22. 348, where ἔοικα is pers., I ought, it behoves me. ἔοικα δέ τοι παρεείδειν. ὥστε θεῷ, it behoves me to sing before thee as before a god; cf. however, no. 3; often absol., as 1, 119; it takes the pers. in the dat., 9, 70. Only Od. 22, 196, ὥς σε ἔοικεν, seems to form an exception; supply, however, from the preceding passage, καταλέξασθαι; or it is constructed with an accus. and infin. οὗ σε ἔοικε, κακὸν ὡς, δειδίσσεσθαι, it does not become you to tremble like a coward, 2, 190. 234; or with an infin. simply: οὐκ ἔοικ᾽ ὀτρυνέμεν, 4, 286. The partcp. is often used as an adj. *becoming, suitable, fitting, deserved*. μῦθοι ἐοικότες, suitable speech, Od. 3, 134 (Voss: similar, i.e. to the discourse of Ulysses.

Έοιο.   147   Ἐπαλλάσσω.

ἐοικότα καταλέξαι, Od. 4, 239. ἐοικότι κεῖται ὀλέθρῳ, he lies in deserved death, i. e. he has his due punishment, Od. 1, 46; but εἰκυῖα ἄκοιτις, a fitting, i. e. dear spouse, 9, 399. 3) *to seem, to appear*; only ἔοικα δέ τοι παραείδειν, ὥστε θεῷ, I seem to thee as to a god to sing [*videor (mihi) tibi tanquam deo accinere*. Fäsi.], Od. 22, 348. (So Eustath.—Voss: thou listenest to my song like a god.) In this signif. ἔοικα is not elsewhere found in H., and therefore the former explanation seems preferable.
ἑοῖο, Ep. for ἑοῦ, see ἑός.
ἔοις, Ep. for εἴης, see εἰμί.
ἔολπα, perf. see ἔλπω.
ἔον, Ep. for ἦν, see εἰμί.
ἔοργα (ἔργω), see ἔρδω.
ἑορτή, ἡ, *a feast, a festival*, *Od. 20, 156. 21, 258.
ἑός, ἑή, ἑόν, Ep. for ὅς, ἥ, ὅν, pron. possess. (from οὗ), *his, her*, mostly without the article; this is found but rarely connected with it to strengthen it. τὸν ἑὸν τε Πόδαργον, 23, 295; τὰ ἃ δώματα, 15, 88. *b*) Strengthened by αὐτός: ἐὸν αὐτοῦ χρεῖος, his own need, Od. 1, 409. (The hiatus is mly found with it, cf. Od. 2, 247.)
ἐπαγάλλομαι, mid. (ἀγάλλω), *to be proud of* any thing, *to glory in* with dat. πολλῷ, 16, 91.†
ἐπαγγέλλω (ἀγγέλλω), aor. 1 ἐπήγγειλα, *to announce, to report*, εἴσω, Od. 4, 775.†
ἐπαγείρω (ἀγείρω), *to collect, to bring together*, with accus. 1, 126.†
ἐπᾶ γην, see πήγνυμι.
ἐπαγλαΐζομαι, depon. mid. (ἀγλαΐζω), *to pride oneself in* any thing, *to glory in*. οὐδέ ἔ φημι δηρὸν ἐπαγλαϊεῖσθαι (infin. fut.), I think he will not long exult in them, 18, 133.†
ἐπάγω (ἄγω), aor. 2 ἐπήγαγον, *to lead to, to bring to*, with accus. λίν, 11, 480. ὡς ἐπάγοντες ἴησαν. subaud. κύνας, as leading them they pressed on, i. e. as they pressed on to the chase, of absol. attacking, Od. 19, 445; metaph. *to induce, to cause*, in connexion with πεῖθω, Od. 14, 392.
ἐπαείρω, Ep. for ἐπαίρω (ἀείρω), aor. 1 ἐπήειρα, *to raise*, with accus. κεφαλήν, 10, 80; *to lift up upon, to lay upon*, with accus. and gen. of place; τινὰ ἀμαξάων, upon the carriages, 7, 426; κρατευτάων, *Il. 9, 214.
ἔπαθον, see πάσχω.
ἐπαιγίζω (αἰγίς), *to blow strongly upon, to rush upon*, spoken of wind, 2, 148. Od. 15, 293.
ἐπαινέω (αἰνέω), fut. Ep. ἐπαινήσω (1 plur. ἐπαινήσομεν, 16, 443), aor. ἐπῄνησα, *to praise, to approve, to pronounce good*; mly absol., but also with accus. μῦθον, 2, 335: and with dat. of the pers. Ἕκτορι, *to agree with Hector, 18, 312; and μῦθόν τινι, h. Merc. 457.
ἐπαινός, ἡ, όν (αἰνός), *very frightful, very terrible*; only fem. ἐπαινή as epith.

11, 47. According to others euphemistic for ἐπαινετή, *lauded, venerable*. The first explanation, as a strengthening of αἰνή (δεινή), deserves the preference; cf. Voss on h. Demet. 1. Buttm. Lex. p. 62, rejects ἐπαινή, and would read ἐπ' αἰνῇ, ἐπί being taken as an adv. = moreover, besides.
ἐπαΐσσω (ἀΐσσω), aor. 1 ἐπήϊξα, iterat aor. ἐπαΐξασκε, aor. 1 mid. ἐπηϊξάμην. *to rush upon, to assail*, often absol.; spoken of the wind, 2, 146; mly of battle. *o*) With gen. τινός, against any one, 5, 263. 323; never in the Od. *b*) With dat. τινί: Κίρκῃ ἐπαΐσσειν, to rush upon Kirkē (Circe), Od. 10, 295. 322; also with dat. instrum. ἔγχεϊ, δουρί, 5, 584; τινὶ μελίῃσι, Od. 14, 281. 3) With accus. transit. *to attack, to fall upon*, μόθον ἵππων, 7, 240. cf. 18, 159; τεῖχος, 12, 308; Ἕκτορα, 23, 64. II) Mid. *to move oneself quickly*; with gen. χεῖρες ὤμων, from the shoulders, 23, 628. *b*) With accus. ἐπαΐξασθαι ἄεθλον, to rush upon the prize, 23, 773.
ἐπαιτέω (αἰτέω), optat. aor. ἐπαιτήσειας, *to ask for in addition, to demand further*, with accus. 23, 593.†
ἐπαίτιος, ον (αἰτία), *that is guilty, that deserves to be complained of, culpable*. οὔτι μοι ὕμμες ἐπαίτιοι, I have no reason whatever to complain of you, 1, 335.†
ἐπακούω (ἀκούω), fut. ἐπακούσω and ἐπακούσομαι, h. Merc. 566; aor. ἐπήκουσα, Ep. without augm. *to listen to, to hearken to*, mly with accus. ἔπος, 2, 100; spoken of Hēlios, πάντα, 3, 277. Od. 11, 109; but also gen. βουλῆς, to hear the counsel, 2, 143. h. Merc. 566.
ἐπακτήρ, ἦρος, ὁ (ἐπάγω), *that goes upon a chase, a hunter*, Od. 19, 435. ἄνδρες ἐπακτῆρες, 17, 135.
ἐπαλάομαι, depon. pass. (ἀλάομαι), aor. partcp. ἐπαληθείς, *to wander over, to wander through, to reach in wandering*; with accus. Κύπρον, to wander to Cyprus, Od. 4, 83. πόλλ' ἐπαληθείς, after a long wandering, *Od. 4. 81. 15. 176.
ἐπαλαστέω (ἀλαστέω), aor. 1 partcp. ἐπαλαστήσας, *to be displeased at, to be angry*, Od. 1, 252.
ἐπαλείφω (ἀλείφω), aor. ἐπήλειψα, *to anoint, to besmear*, οὔατα πᾶσιν, *Od. 12, 47. 177, 200.
ἐπαλέξω (ἀλέξω), fut. ἐπαλεξήσω, *to ward off, to avert, to remove*, τί τινι, any thing from any one; Τρώεσσιν κακὸν ἦμαρ, 20, 315. 2) *to aid, to assist*, τινί, one, 8, 365. 11, 428. *Il.
ἐπαληθείς, see ἐπαλάομαι.
ἐπαλλάσσω (ἀλλάσσω), aor. 1 ἐπαλλάξας, 1) *to exchange, to alternate*. 2) *to entwine, to connect*, 13, 359.† ἔριδος κρατερῆς καὶ ὁμοιΐου πολέμοιο πεῖραρ ἐπαλλάξαντες ἐπ' ἀμφοτέροισι τάνυσσαν, the snare or cord of terrible contention and common war they drew alternately to both sides, i. e. they gave the victory now to the Trojans, now to the Greeks.

Ἐπάλμενος. **Ἐπαυρίσκω.**

of whom the former aids the Trojans, the latter the Greeks. This explanation which Heyne gives, has the difficulty that Zeus, who knows nothing of the undertaking of Poseidôn, must be regarded as contending with him; cf. Spitzner and Köppen. Hence it is better with the ancients to explain ἐπαλλάξαντες by συνάψαντες, συνδήσαντες, to connect, to entwine, to bind together, and to understand it as indicating a continual, unceasing battle. Thus Damm: *pugnae funem connectentes, ad utrosque intenderunt*. Köppen considers πεῖραρ πολ. = πείρατα πολ., see πεῖραρ, and translates: 'the issue of common war they stretched, alternating, over both,' cf. Il, 336. 14, 389. [The metaphor seems more satisfactorily taken from a cord, tied in a knot, whose two ends are drawn in opposite directions, to make the knot faster, cf. Jahrb. Jahn und Klötz, März 1843, p. 261. *Ed. Am.*]

ἐπάλμενος, see ἐφάλλομαι.

ἐπάλξις, ιος, ἡ (ἀλέξω), *a breast-work, a parapet*, esply the battlements of the city walls, behind which the besieged fight, *12, 258. 22, 3.

Ἐπάλτης, αα, ὁ, a Lycian slain by Patroclus, 16, 415. (Ἐπιάλτης.)

ἐπᾶλτο, see ἐφάλλομαι.

ἐπαμάομαι, depon. mid. (ἀμάω), aor. ἐπημησάμην, *to heap up, to heap together*, εὐνήν (of leaves), Od. 5, 482.†

ἐπαμείβω (ἀμείβω), fut. ἐπαμείψω, 1) *to exchange, to change*, τεύχεά τινι, arms with any one, 6, 230. 2) Mid. *to go alternately hither and thither*, with accus. νίκη ἐπαμείβεται ἄνδρας, victory alternates amongst men, 6, 339.

ἐπαμοιβαδίς, adv. (ἐπαμείβω), *alternately, mutually, reciprocally*. ἀλλήλοισιν ἔφυν ἐπαμοιβαδίς, they had grown mutually interlaced (the trees), Od. 5, 481.†

*ἐπαμοίβιος, ον = Ep. ἐπημοιβός, ἐπαμοίβια ἔργα, things of exchange, barter, h. Merc. 516.

ἐπαμύντωρ, ορος, ὁ (ἀμύντωρ), *a helper, a protector*, Od. 16, 263.†

ἐπαμύνω (ἀμύνω), aor. 1 ἐπήμυνα, infin. ἐπαμῦναι, *to come to aid, to help, to assist*, with dat. and absol. *6, 362. 8, 414.

ἐπανατίθημι (τίθημι), *to lay upon*, whence aor. 2 infin. Ep. ἐπανθέμεναι (for imperat.) σανίδας, shut the gates, 21, 535.† Wolf after Aristarchus has here introduced ἐπανθέμεναι instead of the former ἐπ' ἀψ θέμεναι.

ἐπανίστημι (ἵστημι), aor. 2 ἐπανέστην, *to cause to rise*; intrans. aor. 2 and perf. *to rise in addition*, 2, 85 †

*ἐπαντιάω (ἀντιάω), *to meet, to fall in with*, h. Ap. 152, in aor. 1.

ἐπαοιδή, ἡ, Ep. and Ion. for ἐπῳδή, prop. a magic song; then, *an incantation* for staunching blood, Od. 19, 457.†

ἐπαπειλέω (ἀπειλέω), aor. 1 ἐπηπείλησα, *to threaten in addition*, absol. 14, 45; τινί τι, to threaten a man with any thing, 1, 319; ἀπειλάς, Od. 13, 127.

ἐπαραρίσκω, poet. (ΑΡΩ), aor. 1 ἐπῆρσα, perf. ἐπάρηρα, Ion. for ἐνάραρα, 1) Trans. aor. 1, *to attach to, to fasten to;* θύρας σταθμοῖσιν, to fix the doors to the posts, 14, 167. 339. 2) Perf. and pluperf. intrans. *to be attached, to be infixed*, κληῖς ἐπαρήρει, 12, 456.

ἐπάρη, ἡ, Ion. for ἐπάρα (ἀρά), *an imprecation, a curse*, 9, 456.†

*παρήγω (ἀρήγω), infin. aor. 1 ἐπαρῆξαι, *to help, to aid*, τινί, 24, 39. Od. 13, 391.

ἐπαρήρει, ἐπαρηρώς, see ἐπαραρίσκω.

ἐπαρκέω (ἀρκέω), aor. 1 ἐπήρκεσα, *to ward off, to avert, to remove*, τινί τι, any thing from any one; ὄλεθρόν τινι, 2, 873; with accus. *to hinder* any thing, Od. 17, 568.

ἐπάρουρος, ον (ἄρουρα), *living in the country, being a rustic*, Od. 11, 489.†

ἐπαρτής, ἐς (ἀρτέω), *equipped, ready, prepared*, *Od. 8, 151. 14, 332.

*ἐπαρτύνω = ἐπαρτύω, h. in Cer. 128, in mid.

ἐπαρτύω (ἀρτύω), *to attach to, to fasten*, with accus. πῶμα, Od. 8, 447; metaph. πῆμα κακοῖο, to prepare punishment for crime, Od. 3, 152. 2) Mid. *to prepare for oneself*, δεῖπνον, h. in Cer. 128.

ἐπάρχομαι, mid. (ἄρχω), aor. 2 ἐπηρξάμην, prop. *to begin in addition*, in a religious signif.: to devote the first of a thing to the deity; always ἐπάρξασθαι δεπάεσσιν, spoken of libation; according to Buttm. Lex. p. 167, 'to pour out into the goblets for the purpose of libation,' so that in ἐπί the approach to each individual guest is indicated. Voss translates: 'to begin anew with goblets.' The word δεπάεσσι may be explained more correctly, 'into the goblets;' hence, to pour 'the first into the goblets' (for libation), since the goblets were already in the hands of the guests; cf. Nitzsch ad Od. 7, 183; and Köppen ad Il. 1, 471. 2) Mly, *to present, to offer*, with accus. νέκταρ, h. Ap. 125.

ἐπαρωγός, ὁ (ἀρωγός), *a helper, an aid*, Od. 11, 498.†

ἐπασκέω (ἀσκέω), perf. pass. ἐπήσκημαι, *to labour carefully in addition, to furnish with* any thing, with dat. αὐλὴ ἐπήσκηται τοίχῳ καὶ θριγκοῖσι, the court is surrounded with a wall and battlements, Od. 17, 266.†

ἐπασσύτερος, η, ον (ἆσσον), *near to each other, close upon one another, in quick succession;* sing. κῦμα ἐπασσύτερον ὄρνυται, wave upon wave arose, 4, 423; elsewhere plur., 8, 277. Od. 16, 366.

ἔπαυλος, ὁ (αὐλή), *a stall for cattle, a pen, for the night*, Od. 23, 358.†

ἐπαυρίσκω (ΑΥΡΩ), H. has of the mid. the pres. only, 13, 733. Of the act. only aor. 2 subj. ἐπαύρῃ, infin. ἐπαυρεῖν, Ep. ἐπαυρέμεν, fut. mid. ἐπαυρήσομαι, aor. ἐπηυρόμην, from which 2 sing. subj. ἐπαύρηαι and ἐπαύρῃ, and 3 plur. ἐπαύρωνται, 1) Act. 1) *to take to oneself, to obtain, to procure, to partake, to enjoy*, with gen. κτεάτων, 18, 302. Od. 17, 81.

Ἐπαφύσσω.   149   Ἔπειμι.

b) Frequently spoken of missiles; *to touch, to graze, to injure*, as it were tasting, with accus. χρόα, 11, 573. 13, 649. 15, 316; absol. 11, 391; and with gen. λίθου, to graze the stone (goal), 23, 340. II) Mid. 1) *to enjoy, to participate in*, in a good and bad signif. with gen. νόου, to enjoy intelligence, i. e. to enjoy the fruit of it, 13, 733; βασιλῆος, to learn to know their (bad) king [ironically: *that all may find much solace in their king*. Cp.]. 1, 410, 15, 17; and absol. οἴω μιν ἐπαυρήσεσθαι, I think he will soon feel it, or reap the fruits of it, 6, 353. *b*) With accus. *to receive*, to draw upon oneself, κακὸν καὶ μεῖζον, Od. 18, 107.

ἐπαφύσσω (ἀφύσσω), aor. ἐπήφυσα, *to pour upon* (*in addition*), Od. 19, 388 †

ἐπεγείρω (ἐγείρω), aor. sync. mid. ἐπέγρετο, partcp. ἐπαγρόμενος, 1) Act. *to awaken, to arouse*, with accus., Od. 22, 431. 2) Mid. *to wake up, to awake*, 10, 124. 14, 256; only aor. sync.

ἐπέγρετο, see ἐπεγείρω.
ἐπέδραμον, see ἐπιτρέχω.
ἐπέην, see ἔπειμι (εἰμί).

ἐπεί, Ep. also ἐπειή (ἐπεί), conj. used to indicate time and motive. 1) Of time: *as, when, after*, always spoken of the past, *a*) With the indicat. in asserting a fact, 1, 57. 458. *b*) With the subj. when the declaration is conditional [or *indefinite*], mly with ἄν or κε (ἐπεὶ ἄν, contr. ἐπήν). ἐπεὶ ἂν σύ γε πότμον ἐπίσπῃς, when thou shalt have met thy fate. Without ἄν with subj. only 15, 363. h. Ap. 158; cf. however Thiersch, § 324, 4. *c*) With optat. when the declaration indicates a frequently recurring case [*indefinite frequency*], 24, 14. The Ep. ἄν or κε is added when there is a condition, or the discourse is oblique, 9, 304. 19, 208. 24, 227; cf. Thiersch, § 324, 8. 2) Of a ground or motive: *as, because, since, inasmuch as, quoniam*, Ep. also ἐπειή, *a*) With indicat. ἄν is added when the clause is conditional. ἐπεὶ οὔ κεν ἀνιδρωτί γ' ἐτελέσθη, since it would not have been accomplished, 15, 228. *b*) In other cases the construction is as in no. 1. It can also often be translated by *for*, 3, 214. Sometimes, esply in address, ἐπεί stands where the protasis is wanting; we may supply, 'I will tell thee,' 3, 59. Od. 1, 231. 3, 103; or, 'let us fight,' 13, 68 (according to Voss, the apodosis is v. 73). 3) With other particles: ἐπεὶ ῥα, as soon as, since now. *b*) ἐπεὶ γε, since at least, since' (that is). *c*) ἐπεὶ οὖν, when then [referring a present action to the past from which it proceeds, &c.], *when once, when first* [with ref. to an action *to be related*, which depends upon this. Näg.], when therefore. *d*) ἐπεὶ περ, since indeed, since yet. ἐπεί is dissyllabic by synizesis, Od. 19, 314.

Ἐπειγεύς, ῆος, ὁ, son of Agacles, a Myrmidon, who, on account of the slaughter of his uncle, was obliged to fly from Budeum to Peleus, and who went with Achilles to Troy. He was slain by Hector, 16, 571, seq.

ἐπείγω, only pres. and imperf. I) Act. *to press, to urge, to pursue closely*, with accus., 12, 452; κεμάδα, to press, to pursue a roe, 10, 361; hence pass. ἐπείγεσθαι βελέεσσιν, to be pressed by weapons, 5, 622. 13, 511. *b*) *to drive, to urge on*, spoken esply of wind, 15, 382; νῆα, h. Ap. 408; and pass. Od. 13, 115; ἐρετμά, to move the oars, Od. 12, 205; hence, *to drive, to hasten*, ὦνον, Od. 15, 445. *c*) Intrans. *to press, to oppress, to urge*. ἀνάγκη ἐπείγει. 6, 85; γῆρας, 23, 623; cf. h. Ven. 231. II) Mid. *to urge* (*on*) *for oneself, to hasten*, γάμον, Od. 2, 97. 19, 142. *b*) *to press oneself*, spoken of the wind; hence, *to hasten, to make haste*, with infin., 2, 354. 6, 363. Frequently the partcp. ἐπειγόμενος stands as an adj. *hastening, rapid, quick*, 5, 902. *c*) With gen., hastening after any thing, *to long for, to desire*, ὁδοῖο, Od. 1, 309. 315. Ἄρηος, 19, 142; and with accus. and infin. ἠέλιον, δῦναι ἐπειγόμενος, wishing the sun might set, Od. 13, 30. (According to Buttm. Lex. p. 118, not a compound word.)

ἐπειδάν, conj. *as soon as, when, after*, 17. 285.† Thiersch, § 324, 1, rejects the word as not Homeric; and reads ἐπὴν δή.

ἐπειδή, conj. (ἐπεὶ δή), *since, as, when, after*. 1) Mly with indicat., and with preterite: ἐπειδὴ πρῶτα, since first, when once, *b*) With subj. ἐπειδὴ—δαμάσσεται (for δαμάσσηται), 11, 478. cf Spitzner 2) More rarely in assigning a reason, *since, because*, with indicat., 14, 65. In addresses, without apodosis, Od. 3, 211. 14, 149. ἐπεί has ε lengthened, 22, 379.)

ἐπεῖδον (εἶδον), defect. aor. 2 of ἐφοράω, *to look upon, to look at*, with accus., °22, 61; see ἐφοράω.

ἐπειή, Ep. for ἐπεὶ ἤ, always in the signif. *since, because*. According to Schol. Ven. ad Il. 1, 156, ἐπεὶ ἤ, would be more correct. This Thiersch, § 324. 2, approves, and Spitzner has adopted it.

ἐπείη, optat. pres. of ἔπειμι (εἰμί).
ἔπει κε, see ἐπεί.
(ἐπείκω), obsol. pres. of ἐπέοικε, q. v.

ἔπειμι (εἰμί), imperf. Ep. ἐπῆεν and ἐπέην, plur. ἔπεσαν, fut. Ep. ἐπέσσομαι, *to be at, to be upon, to be over*, absol. 5, 127. Od. 2, 344; with dat. loci. κάρη ὤμοισιν ἐπείη, may my head (no longer) remain on my shoulders, 2, 259; with dat. of pers. οἷσιν ἔπεστι κράτος, h. Cer. 150. 2) Of time: *to be after, to be left behind*, Od. 4, 756.

ἔπειμι (εἶμι), 3 sing. imperf. Ep. ἐπήϊεν, 3 plur. ἐπήϊσαν, Od. 11, 233, and ἐπῆσαν, Od. 19, 445; fut. ἐπείσομαι, aor. 1 mid. ἐπεισάμην, 21, 424. 1) *to go to, to come upon, to approach*, with accus. ἀγρόν, to go to the field, Od. 23, 359; metaph. πρίν μιν καὶ γῆρας ἔπεισιν, before old age comes upon her, 1, 29. 2) Esply in a hostile signif. *to rush upon, to attack*,

Ἐπειοί. 150 Ἐπεσβολίη.

to fall upon, with accus., 11, 367; with dat. 13, 482. 17, 741; and often without cases: ὁ ἐπιών, *the one attacking*, 5, 238; often ἐπ' ἀλλοισιν ἰόντες, marching against each other, 11.

Ἐπειοί, οἱ, *the Epêans*, the oldest inhabitants of Elis, who derived their name from Epêus, the son of Endymiôn, 2, 619; cf. Paus. 5, 1. 2.

Ἐπειός, ὁ, *Epêus*, son of Panôpeus, who, with the aid of Athênê, constructed the wooden horse, Od. 8, 493. He vanquished Euryalus in boxing, at the funeral games of Patroclus, but in casting the iron ball was conquered by Polypœtes, 23, 664, seq. 839.

ἐπεί—περ, conj. *since at least*, with indicat. always separated, see ἐπεί.

ἔπειτα, adv. (ἐπί, εἶτα), *thereafter, hereafter, afterwards, hereupon, thereupon, then*, marks 1) Primarily, the progress from one action to another in the narration. In future actions it signifies, *directly after*, Od. 2, 60; καὶ τότ' ἔπειτα, *and then at once*, 1, 426. It often follows πρῶτον, is connected with αὐτίκα, αἶψα; also ἔνθα, ἔπειτα. Sometimes it stands pleonastically, after a participle with a finite verb, 14, 223. 2) It often forms in the Epic language the apodosis, to render it emphatic: *a)* After a particle of time: ἐπειδὴ σφαίρῃ πειρήσαντο, ὠρχεῖσθην δὴ ἔπειτα, *then they danced*, Od. 8, 378; cf. 18. 545. *b)* After a particle of doubt or condition: εἰ μὲν δὴ νῦν τοῦτο φίλον,— Ἑρμείαν μὲν ἔπειτα — ὀτρύνομεν, *then will we send*, Od. 1, 84. 2. 273; so also in hypothetical clauses with ὅς κε, 1, 547. 2, 392. 3) *therefore*, (according to what you say), *then*, *a)* In a question, 9, 437. Od. 1, 65. *b)* In other clauses, 15, 49. 18, 357.

ἐπεκέκλετο, see ἐπικέλομαι.

ἐπέκερσα, see ἐπικείρω.

ἐπελαύνω (ἐλαύνω), aor. 1 ἐπήλασα, perf. pass. ἐπελήλαμαι, *to drive upon, to hammer out over*, spoken only of the working of metals, χαλκόν, 7, 223; of a shield: πολὺς ἐπελήλατο χαλκός, much brass was beaten out over it, 13, 804. 17, 493.

ἐπελήλατο, see ἐπελαύνω.

ἐπέλησε, see ἐπιλανθάνω.

ἐπεμβαίνω (βαίνω), partcp. perf. Ep. ἐπεμβεβαώς, *to go upon*, perf. *to stand upon*, with gen. οὐδοῦ, upon the threshold, 9, 582.†

ἐπενείκαι, see ἐπιφέρω.

ἐπένειμε, see ἐπινέμω.

ἐπενήνεον, see ἐπινηνέω.

ἐπενήνοθε (ἐνήνοθε), 3 sing. of an old Ep. perf. with pres. signif. which is also used as imperf. *to be or lie upon, to sit upon*, only four times; spoken of the head of Thersitês, as imperf. ψεδνὴ ἐπενήνοθε λάχνη, thin woolly hair was upon it, 2, 219; of a mantle: ἐπενήνοθε λάχνη, 10, 134; as pres. with accus. οἷα θεοὺς ἐπενήνοθεν αἰὲν ἐόντας, such as adheres to the gods, Od. 8, 365. h. Ven. 62. (Buttm.

Lex. p. 111, from ἔνθω or ἀνέθω, perf. with Att. redupl. ἀνήνοθα, see Thiersch, § 232)

ἐπεντανύω, Ep. form of ἐπεντείνω, *to stretch upon, to extend upon*, Od. 22, 467.†

ἐπεντύνω and ἐπεντύω (ἐντύω), *to equip, to put in order*, ἵππους, to harness the horses, 8, 374. Mid. *to put oneself in order, to prepare oneself*, ἄεθλα, for the contests, Od. 21, 89.

ἐπέοικα (ἔοικε), *it is becoming, it is befitting, it is proper*, with dat. pers. and infin. 4, 341: or accus. with infin., 1, 126. 10, 146. Ellipt. with accus. ὧν ἐπέοιχ' ἱκέτην ἀντιάσαντα (subaud. from the foregoing οὐ δεύεσθαι), which it is not becoming that an approaching suppliant should lack, Od. 6, 193. 14, 511. 2) *it is agreeable, it pleases*, 9, 392.

ἐπέπιθμεν, see πείθω.

ἐπέπληγον, see πλήσσω.

ἐπέπλως, see ἐπιπλώω.

ἐπεποίθει, see πείθω.

ἐπεπόνθει, see πάσχω.

ἐπέπταρε, see ἐπιπταίρω.

ἐπέπτατο, see ἐπιπέταμαι.

ἐπέπυστο, see πυνθάνομαι.

ἐπερείδω (ἐρείδω), aor. 1 ἐπέρεισα, *to stay upon, to lean upon, to thrust against*, with accus. ἔγχος ἐκ κενεῶνα, 5, 856; absol., 11, 235; metaph. ἱν' ἀπέλεθρον, to apply prodigious power, 7, 269. Od. 9, 538.

ἐπερέφω (ἐρέφω), *to roof over*, and hence, generally, *to build*, in tmesis, ἐπὶ νηὸν ἔρεψα, 1, 39.†

ἐπερρώσαντο, see ἐπιρρώομαι.

ἐπερύω (ἐρύω), aor. ἐπέρυσα. Ep. σσ, *to draw to, to draw towards*, θύρην κορώνῃ, (with the ring), Od. 1, 144 (see κορώνη). ἐπὶ στήλην ἐρύσαντες, *Od. 12, 16.

ἐπέρχομαι (ἔρχομαι), fut. ἐπελεύσομαι, aor. 2 ἐπῆλθον, Ep. ἐπήλυθον, perf. ἐπελήλυθα, 1) *to come to, to come on, to come near, to approach*, with dat. 12, 200; and absol. often indicating what was unexpected, Od. 9, 214; metaph. ἐπὶ κνέφας ἦλθε, darkness came on, 11, 194. Ἀχαιοὺς ἐπήλυθε νύξ, 8, 488. 9, 474; τοῖσιν ἐπήλυθε ὕπνος, sleep came upon them, Od. 5, 472. 12, 311; with the accus. esply when it contains the idea of *surprising* or *creeping upon insensibly*; ἐπήλυθέ μιν ὕπνος, Od. 4, 793. 10, 31; and of the spears: cutting the spear pressed upon the neck, 7, 262. 2) In a hostile signif. *to rush against any one, to fall upon, to attack*; without case, and with dat., 5, 220. Spoken of lions: βουσίν, 10, 485. 15, 630. 3) Of places: *to pass through, to go through*, like obire, with accus. ἄγκεα, to go through the valleys, 18, 321. Od. 16, 27.

ἐπεσβολίη, ἡ (ἔπος, βάλλω), words which one drops inconsiderately, *prattle, loquaciousness, idle discourse*. ἐπεσβολίας ἀναφαίνειν, to exhibit idle prattle (*to seem loquacious*, Cp.), Od. 4, 159† (not from ἔπεσι, but from ἔπεα and βάλλειν).

ἐπεσβόλος, ον (βάλλω), uttering idle, foolish words, loquacious (qui verba jacit); λωβητήρ (V. a troublesome prater), 2, 275.† According to Döderlein it is not to be explained by ἔπεα ἐκβάλλων, but by ἔπεσι βάλλων, i. e. ἰάπτων, verbis lacessens or feriens.
ἔπεσον, see πίπτω.
ἐπέσσον, see ἐφέπω.
ἐπέσσεται, see ἔπειμι (εἰμί).
ἐπέσσυται, see ἐπισεύω.
ἐπέστη, see ἐπίστημι.
ἐπέσχον, see ἐπέχω.
ἐπετήσιος, ον (ἔτος), annual, lasting a year, καρπός, Od. 7, 118.†
ἔπευ, Ion. for ἔπου, see ἔπομαι.
ἐπευφημέω (εὐφημέω), aor. ἐπευφήμησα, to assent, to speak approvingly. ἐπευφήμησαν αἰδεῖσθαι, κ.τ.λ., [their voice was to respect (him). Cp.], 1, 22.†
ἐπεύχομαι, depon. mid. (εὔχομαι), fut. ἐπεύξομαι, aor. 1 ἐπευξάμην, to pray, to supplicate a divinity, θεοῖς, Διί, 3, 350. Od. 14, 423. 2) to vaunt oneself, to boast, absol. and τινί, over any one, 11, 431.
ἔπεφνον, see ΦΕΝΩ.
ἐπέφραδον, see φράζω.
ἐπέχω (ἔχω), aor. 2 ἐπέσχον, partcp. ἐπισχών, aor. 2 mid. ἐπεσχόμην, Ep. 3 plur. pluperf. ἐπώχατο, q. v. 1) to hold on, to, upon, with dat. πόδας θρήνυϊ, to put the feet upon the stool, 14, 241. Od. 17, 410; hence: to hold out, to reach, to present, οἶνον, 9, 489; μαζὸν παιδί, 22, 83. 2) Intrans. to rush upon, to assail, τινί, Od. 19, 71. cf. Od. 22, 75. 3) to check, to restrain, to withhold, with accus. ῥέεθρα, 21, 244; and θυμὸν ἐνιπῆς, to restrain the mind from rebuke, Od. 20, 266; hence absol. to restrain oneself, to delay, 'Αντίνοος δ' ἔτ' ἐπεῖχε, Od. 21, 186. 4) to embrace, to occupy, to extend, with accus. ἑπτὰ πέλεθρα, 21, 407. ὁπόσσον ἐπέσχε πῦρ. as far as the fire extended, 23, 238. II) Mid. 1) to direct oneself to, to assail, like act. 2. Spoken of shooting with the bow, ἐπισχόμενος, aiming, Od. 22, 15. 2) Like act. 3, to restrain, to withhold, to hold up, with accus. ἑανῶν πτύχας, h. Cer. 176.
ἐπηβόλος, ον (βάλλω), that has attained any thing, partaking, possessing, with gen. νηός, ἐρετάων, Od. 2, 319.†
ἐπήγαγον, see ἐπάγω.
ἐπηγκενίδες, αἱ [long planks. Cp.], the long planks on the sides of a ship, which served to cover the ribs of the sides (σταμίνες) and extended from stem to stern. To prevent the pressure of water, Odysseus (Ulysses) covers these planks with osier hurdles (ῥίπεσσι οἰσυΐνῃσιν), Od. 5, 253, seq † (prob. from ἐνεγκεῖν = φέρειν, to extend oneself), see Nitzsch ad loc. and σταμίν.
ἐπήην, Ep. for ἐπῆν, see ἔπειμι (εἰμί).
ἐπηετανός, όν (ἔτος), 1) lasting a whole year, παρέχειν γάλα ἐπηετανόν, to give milk the whole year, Od. 4, 89; πλυνοί, Od. 6, 86. 2) sufficient for a whole year, abundant, superfluous, Od.

18, 360. 8, 233. The neut. ἐπηετανόν as adv. always in the year, Od. 7, 128; abundantly, in abundance, *Od. 7, 99. 10. 427.
ἐπήϊεν, see ἔπειμι (εἶμι).
ἐπῆλθον, and ἐπήλυθον, see ἐπέρχομαι.
*ἐπηλυσίη, ἡ, enchantment, fascination, h. Cer. 218, 220. Merc. 37.
ἐπημοιβός, όν (ἀμείβω), alternating, exchanging, corresponding; ὀχῆες, two bolts meeting each other, which one from each side of the door were fitted together, and held by a key, see κληΐς, 12, 456; χιτῶνες, clothes for a change, Od. 14, 513.
ἐπημύω, see ἠμύω.
ἐπήν, conj. Hom. for ἐπάν, see ἐπεί.
ἐπῄνεον, see ἐπαινέω.
ἐπῆξα, see πήγνυμι.
ἐπηπύω (ἠπύω), to call to joyfully, to applaud, with dat., 18, 502.†
ἐπήρατος, ον (ἐράω), beloved, lovely, charming, agreeable, spoken only of inanimate objects: δαίς, 9, 228; εἵματα, Od. 8, 366; mly of regions of Ithaca, Od. 4, 606.
ἐπήρετμος, ον (ἐρετμός), at the oar, rowing, ἑταῖροι, Od. 2, 403. 2) furnished with oars, νῆες, *Od. 4, 559.
ἐπηρεφής (ἐρέφω), covering over, standing over, overhanging, πέτραι, Od. 10, 131. 12, 59, κρημνοί, 12, 54 [overhanging precipices].
'Επήριτος, ὁ (disputed), son of Aphidas, from Alybas, whom Odysseus (Ulysses) pretended to be, Od. 24, 306.
ἐπῆρσε. see ἐπαραρίσκω.
ἐπῆσαν. see ἔπειμι (εἰμί).
ἐπητής, οῦ, ὁ (ἔπος), affable, humane, kind, benevolent, *Od. 13, 122. 18, 128.
ἐπήτριμος, ον (ἤτριον), prop. closewoven, hence; thickly over, close together, compact, πυρσοί, 18, 211; δράγματα ἐπήτριμα πίπτον, the sheaves fell close together, fell thick, 18, 552. 2) Of time: in quick succession, *19, 226.
ἐπητύς, ύος, ἡ (ἐπητής), friendly address, and mly kindness, benevolence, Od. 21, 306.†
ἐπί, I) Prepos. with gen., dat., and accus. Ground signif. at, upon, in manifold relations. A) With gen. a) To mark rest in a place: on, upon, in, at, near, esply with verbs of existence, rest, etc.: ἐπὶ μελίης ἐρεισθείς, 22, 225; and without a verb: ἐπὶ ὤμων, ἐπ' ἀγροῦ, ἐπὶ κρατὸς λιμένος, at the head of, Od. 13, 102; metaph. ἐπὶ ξυροῦ ἀκμῆς, 10, 173; see ἀκμή. b) To mark motion to an object, with verbs of motion: ἐρύειν νῆα ἐπ' ἠπείροιο, upon the land, 1, 485; βαίνειν ἐπὶ νηός. 2) Spoken of the time in or during which any thing happens. ἐπ' εἰρήνης, in time of peace, 2, 797; ἐπὶ προτέρων ἀνθρώπων, 5, 637. 3) To mark manner, cause, etc.: only σιγῇ ἐφ' ὑμείων, in silence by yourselves, i. e. for yourselves, 7, 195. B) With dative, 1) Spoken of place: a) To mark rest upon, at, or by an object: ἐπὶ χθονί, on the

Ἐπί.   152   Ἐπιβλής.

earth. 1, 68; ἐπί τινι καθῆσθαι. to sit by any one, Od. 2, 369; ἐπ' ἔργῳ, at the work. Od. 16, 111; also spoken of a conjunction, or concomitancy of things: ἐφ' ἕλκεϊ ἕλκος ἀρέσθαι, wound upon wound. 14, 130. cf. Od. 7, 120; ἐπὶ τῇσι, in addition to these, 9, 639; ἐπὶ τοῖς, to this, i. e. besides this, Od. 3, 113; ταχὺς ἔσκε θέειν ἐπὶ εἴδεϊ, together with, i. e. besides his beauty, Od. 7, 126. 17, 308. Hence also spoken of succession in time and place. ἐπὶ τῷδε ἀνέστη, with, i. e. after him, 7, 163. *b)* To mark motion to any thing, with verbs of motion, and that in a hostile signif.: *upon, against*, 1, 382. 3, 15. 2) Of time: ἐπὶ νυκτί, by night, 8, 529; ἐπ' ἤματι τῷδε, on this day, 13, 234; but ἐπ' ἤματι, by day, Od. 2, 284, and as adv. *daily*, Od. 14, 105. 3) Of manner, cause, etc.: *a)* To mark design, purpose: ἐπὶ δόρπῳ, for supper, Od. 18, 44; ἐπὶ χάρμῃ, 13, 104; ἐπὶ Πατρόκλῳ, for Patroclus, 23, 776; υἱὸν ἐπὶ κτεάτεσσι λιπέσθαι, to leave a son for his treasures [i. e. to inherit them], 5, 154. *b)* To mark the ground or motive: *about, at, for, on account of*; γελᾶν ἐπί τινι, 2, 270; μογεῖν, πάσχειν ἐπί τινι, 1, 162. 9, 492. *c)* To mark the price, or only, the condition: *for*; ἐπί τινι ἀθλεύειν, 23, 274; ἐπὶ μισθῷ for hire. ἐπὶ δώροις, for presents, 9, 162. *C)* With accus. 1) Of place: *a)* To mark direction or motion to an object: *to, towards, against*; ἐπὶ νῆας ἔρχεσθαι, ἔζεσθαι ἐπ' ἔρετμα, Od. 12, 171. *b)* To mark motion upon or over, or an extension, or spreading out upon: πλεῖν ἐπὶ οἴνοπα πόντον, Od. 1, 183. cf. 2, 370; ἐπ' ἐννέα κεῖτο πέλεθρα, Od. 11, 577; ἐπὶ γαῖαν, per terram, Od. 4, 417. cf. Od. 1, 299; ἐπὶ δεξιά, ἐπ' ἀριστερά, to the right, to the left. 2) Of time: *a)* In marking the limit: ἐπ' ἠῶ, till morning, Od. 7, 288. *b)* To mark continuance: *for, during*; ἐφ' ἡμέραν, 2, 299; ἐπὶ δηρόν, for a long time, 9, 415. In like manner to mark the measure: ὅσον ἔπι, as far as, 2, 616; ἐπὶ ἥμισυ πάσης, to the half of the entire ship, Od. 13, 114. 3) Of manner, cause, etc.: *a)* To mark design or purpose: ἐπὶ βοῦν ἴτω, for an ox, i. e. to fetch him, Od. 3, 421; στέλλειν ἐπ' ἀγγελίην, on an embassy, 4, 384; more rarely spoken of persons: ἐπ' Ὀδυσσῆα ἰέναι, Od. 5. 149. *b)* To mark conformity: ἐπὶ στάθμην, by the line, Od. 5, 245; ἐπ' ἴσα, 12, 436. *c)* To mark a respect in which any thing is true; ἄριστοι πᾶσαν ἐπ' ἰθύν, in every attack. 6, 79. II) As an adv. often found in H. in the signif. *then, moreover, besides, thereupon*, etc. 1, 458. 5, 705. Od. 3, 164. 285. It must often be connected with the verb. III) In composition with a verb it sometimes has the local significations of the adv. and sometimes it denotes a consequence in time, an accession, etc.

ἔπι, in anastrophe. 1) for ἔπι, when it follows the governed word. 2) for ἔπ-εστι, *it is present, it is there, there is, thou art*, Od. 14, 92; mly with dat. 1. 515. Od. 11, 307. Also with infin. following, οὐκ ἐπ' ἀνήρ—ἀρὴν ἀπὸ οἴκου ἀμύναι, there is no man to avert the evil from the house, Od. 2, 59.

ἐπιάλλω (ἰάλλω), aor. 1 ἐπίηλα, *to send to, to cast upon, to lead* or *bring to*. τί τινι; οὖρον Κῆρας τινί, Od. 2, 316: ἐπίηλεν τάδε ἔργα, he has brought about these things, *Od. 22, 49.

ἐπιάλμενος, see ἐφάλλομαι.

ἐπιανδάνω, poet. for ἐφανδάνω, q. v.

ἐπιαύω, another reading for ἐνιαύω, Od. 15, 557.

ἐπιάχω, poet. (ἰάχω), *to call to, to shout aloud to, to cheer, to applaud with shouts*, 7, 403. 13, 822. 2) Mly, *to cry out*, *5, 860. 14, 148 (only pres. and imperf.).

ἐπίβαθρον, τό (βαίνω), *the passage-money*, the price paid by a passenger (ἐπιβάτης) on ship-board, Od. 15, 449.†

ἐπιβαίνω (βαίνω), fut. ἐπιβήσω, aor. 1 ἐπέβησα, aor. 2 ἐπέβην. infin. Ep. ἐπιβήμεναι, fut. mid. ἐπιβήσομαι, aor. 1 ἐπεβησάμην (only the Ep. forms ἐπεβήσετο, ἐπιβήσεο). 1) Intrans. *to mount, to ascend, to step upon* or *into*. *a)* With gen. ἵππων δίφρου, 5, 46; 8, 44; πύργων, νεῶν, etc. again: πρόσσαιων, to mount the battlements, 12, 444; γαίης, to disembark, Od. 12. 282; metaph. of a corpse, to be laid upon the funeral pile, 4, 99. *b)* *to go to, to reach*, with gen. πόληος, to the city, 16, 396; with accus. rarely; Πιερίην ἐπιβᾶσα, over Pieria [not to P.], 14, 226. Od. 5, 50; often metaph. ἀναιδείης, to give oneself up to impudence, Od. 22, 424. εὐφροσύνης, Od. 23, 52; τέχνης, to try art. h. Merc. 166, 465. 2) Transit. only fut. and aor. 1 act. *to cause to mount, to cause to ascend*; τινὰ ἵππων, upon the chariot, 8, 129; hence: *to lead to, to place upon, to bring to*, πολλοὺς πυρῆς, 9, 546; τινὰ πάτρης, to send one to his country, Od. 7, 223; metaph. εὐκλείης, σαοφροσύνης. to elevate any one to renown, to bring one to understanding, 8, 285, Od. 23, 13.

ἐπιβάλλω (βάλλω), aor. 2 act. ἐπέβαλον, aor. 2 mid. ἐπεβαλόμην, 1) Act. *to cast upon, to lay upon*, with accus., 11, 846; ἐπιβάλλειν ἱμάσθλην, subaud. ἵπποις, to give the horses the lash, Od. 6, 320. *b)* Intrans. *to cast oneself upon, to go to*; ἡ δὲ Φεὰς ἐπέβαλλε, the ship sailed to Pheae. Od. 15, 297; h. Ap. 427. 2) Mid. *to cast upon for oneself*, κλήρους, Od. 14, 209. *b)* *to cast oneself upon a thing, to fall upon it, to seek* or *strive after*, with gen. ἐνάρων, 6, 68.

ἐπιβάσκω (βάσκω), poet. form of ἐπιβαίνω, with transit. signif.: κακῶν ἐπιβασκέμεν υἷας Ἀχαιῶν, to bring the sons of the Achaians into misfortunes, 2, 234.†

ἐπιβήμεναι, see ἐπιβαίνω.

ἐπιβήτωρ, ορος, ὁ, *one that mounts*, ἵππων, Od. 18, 263. 2) *a leaper* (spoken of the boar), *Od. 11, 131.

ἐπιβλής, ῆτος, ὁ (ἐπιβάλλω), prop. that

Ἐπιβοάω. 153 Ἐπιδιφριάς.

which is thrust forward; *a bolt or bar*, for fastening the door, 24, 453.†
ἐπιβοάω (βοάω), only fut. mid. ἐπιβώσομαι, Ion. for ἐπιβοήσομαι, *to cry to*.
2) Mid. *to call upon, to call to for aid*, with accus. θεούς, 10, 463. Od. 1, 378.
*ἐπιβόσκομαι (βόσκω), *to pasture upon, to feed upon*, τινί, Batr. 54.
ἐπιβουκόλος, ὁ (βουκόλος), *a herdsman*, always with βοῶν, *Od. 3, 422.
ἐπιβρέμω (βρέμω), *to roar against*, to kindle (trans.) with a roaring sound, πῦρ [*the wind roars through the fire*. Cp.] 17, 739.†
ἐπιβρίθω (βρίθω), aor. 1 ἐπέβρῑσα, *to fall heavily upon*. ὅτ' ἐπιβρίσῃ Διὸς ὄμβρος, when the rain of Zeus falls violently, 5, 91. 2) Metaph. *to press upon, to press heavily*, πόλεμος Τρώων, 7, 343. 12, 414; in a good sense : ὁππότε Διὸς ὧραι ἐπιβρίσειαν ὕπερθεν, when the hours of Zeus from above load (the vines) with fruit; *weigh down their boughs*, Od. 24, 344.
ἐπιβωσόμεθα, see ἐπιβοάομαι.
ἐπιβώτωρ, ορος, ὁ (βώτωρ), *a shepherd*, perhaps *chief-shepherd*, μήλων, Od. 13, 222.†
ἐπιγδουπέω, Ep. for ἐπιδουπέω, *to utter sounds around; to this is referred: ἐπὶ δ' ἐγδούπησαν [rolled sounds, as of thunder, around him], 11, 45.
ἐπιγίγνομαι (γίγνομαι), *to arise again, to come again*, spoken of time, 6, 148.
2) *to reach; ὅσον τ' ἐπὶ δουρὸς ἐρωὴ γίγνεται, *15, 358.
ἐπιγιγνώσκω (γιγνώσκω), aor. 2 ἐπέγνων, subj. 3 plur. Ep. ἐπιγνώωσι for ἐπιγνῶσι, optat. ἐπιγνοίη. *to recognize, to know again*, with accus. Od. 24, 217. 2) *to become acquainted with, to view* (the strife), *Od. 18, 30.
*ἐπιγναμπτός, ή, όν, *bent, curved, twisted*, h. Ven. 87.
ἐπιγνάμπτω (γνάμπτω), aor ἐπέγναμψα, *to curve, to bend around, to twist*, with accus. δόρυ, 21, 178; metaph. (*to bend the mind* =) *to influence, to prevail with, to persuade*, τινά, 2, 14; κῆρ, 1, 569; νόον ἐσθλῶν, to persuade the minds of the brave, *9, 514.
ἐπιγνοίη, see ἐπιγιγνώσκω.
ἐπιγνώωσι, see ἐπιγιγνώσκω.
ἐπιγουνίς, ίδος, ἡ (γόνυ), the part above the knee, *the thigh*. μεγάλην ἐπιγουνίδα θεῖτο, [so] he would get a bulky thigh [i. e. grow stouter], *Od. 17, 225.
ἐπιγραβδήν, adv. (ἐπιγράφω), *grazing [lightly inscribing] the surface; superficially, with a scratch*, 21, 166.†
ἐπιγράφω (γράφω), aor. 1 ἐπέγραψα, *to graze* or *scratch upon the surface*, with accus. χρόα, 4, 139; with double accus. τινὰ ταρσόν, *to graze* one the sole of the foot, 11, 388; hence, 2) ἐπιγράφειν κλῆρον, to mark a lot (by scratching upon it). 7, 187. (It is = σημαίνεσθαι, v. 175; the idea of writing is inadmissible.)
*ἐπιδαίομαι, depon. mid. (δαίω), *to communicate, to give*; ὅρκον, to take an oath upon *it*, h. Merc. 383 [Herm. prefers ἐπιδώσομαι ὅρκον].
'Ἐπίδαυρος, ἡ, a city in Argolis, on the Saronic gulf, with a temple of Aesculapius, now *Pidauro*, 2, 561.
ἐπιδέδρομε, see ἐπιτρέχω.
ἐπιδέξιος, ον (δεξιός), prop. *on the right*, only neut. plur. ἐπιδέξια, as adv. *on the right*. ὀρνυσθ' ἑξείης ἐπιδέξια, rise in order [to try the bow] from left to right, i. e. to the right beginning from him who occupies the seat of honour, at the mixing vessel, Od. 21, 141; see Buttm. Lex. p. 291. This direction was regarded as propitious, see δεξιός; hence αστράπτων ἐπιδέξια, lightening on the right (a sign of prosperity promised by the deity), 2, 353.
ἐπιδευής, ές, poet. for ἐπιδεής, *needing, wanting, lacking*, with gen. δαιτὸς ἐίσης οὐκ ἐπιδευεῖς, sc. ἐσμέν, we lack not a common meal, 9, 225. ἄλλης λώβης, οὐκ ἐπιδευεῖς, sc. ἐστέ, ye need no other wrong, 13, 622; absol. ὅς κ' ἐπιδευής, sc. ᾖ, who is needy, poor, 5, 481. 2) *inferior, deficient* (in), with gen. βίης, in power, Od. 21, 185; with double gen. βίης ἐπιδευέες εἰμὲν 'Ὀδυσσῆος, we are inferior in strength to Odysseus (Ulysses), Od. 21, 253; the neut as adv. ἐπιδευὲς ἔχειν δίκης, to lack justice, 19, 180.
ἐπιδεύομαι, depon. mid. (δεύομαι), *to fail in, to want, to lack*, with gen. χρυσοῦ, 2, 229; τούτων, Od. 15, 371. 2) *to be inferior, to be weaker*, with gen. μάχης, 23, 670; also with gen. of the pers. : πολλὸν κείνων ἐπιδεύεαι, thou art much inferior to them, 5, 636; and with double gen. μάχης Ἀχαιῶν, in battle to the Greeks, 24, 385.
ἐπιδημεύω (δημεύω), poet. for ἐπιδημέω, *to abide in the country, to be at home*, Od. 16, 28.†
ἐπιδήμιος, ον (δῆμος), *among the people, internal, domestic*, πόλεμος, 9, 64. b) *at home. present*, Od. 1, 194.
ἐπιδίδωμι (δίδωμι), fut. ἐπιδώσω, aor. 1 ἐπέδωκα, infin. aor. 2 ἐπιδοῦναι, *to give in addition, to add to*, τί τινι, 23, 559; to give as a dowry, θυγατρὶ μείλια, 9, 148. 290. 2) Mid. *to take thereto for oneself*, only ἐπιδώμεθα θεούς, let us take the gods to it (viz. as witnesses, supply from v. 255, μάρτυρους), 22, 254. (Schol. μαρτύρους ποιησώμεθα.) The derivation from ἰδέσθαι is improbable, although Voss. follows it: 'let us look up to the gods.'
ἐπιδινέω (δινέω), aor. partcp. ἐπιδινήσας, partcp. aor. pass. ἐπιδινηθείς, 1) Act. *to turn about, to whirl around in order to cast*, with accus. 3, 378. 7, 269. Pass. *to fly around in a circle*, spoken of an eagle, Od. 2, 151. 2) Mid. *to revolve any thing by oneself*; metaph. ἐμοὶ τόδε θυμὸς πόλλ' ἐπιδινεῖται, my mind often revolves this, i. e. the thought often occupies (haunts) my mind, Od. 20, 218.
ἐπιδιφριάς, άδος, ἡ (δίφρος), *the upper rim of the chariot-seat* = ἄντυξ, 10, 475.†

H 5

Ἐπιδίφριος. 154 Ἐπικερτομέω.

ἐπιδίφριος, ον (δίφρος), *lying upon the chariot-seat, being upon the chariot seat.* δῶρα ἐπιδίφρια τιθέναι, to lay the presents upon the chariot-seat, *Od. 15, 51. 75.

ἐπιδραμεῖν, ἐπιδραμέτην, see ἐπιτρέχω.

ἐπίδρομος, ον (ἐπιδραμεῖν), prop. whither one can run, *accessible, exposed to attack;* τεῖχος, a wall easy to storm or scale, 6, 434.†

ἐπιδόω (δύω), aor. 2 ἐπιδῦναι, *to set* only in tmesis. μὴ πρὶν ἐπ' ἠέλιον δῦναι, 2, 413 †

ἐπιδώμεθα, see ἐπιδίδωμι.

ἐπιείκελος, ον (εἴκελος), *similar, resembling,* τινί, always with ἀθανάτοισιν and θεοῖς, 4, 394, and Od. 15, 414.

ἐπιεικής, ές (ἔοικα), 1) *suitable, becoming, fitting, proper.* τύμβος ἐπιεικής τοῖος, a mound such as is fitting, 23, 246. Often the neut. either absol. ὡς ἐπιεικές, as is fitting, 8, 431; or with infin. ὅν κ' ἐπιεικὲς ἀκούειν, which (μῦθος) it is suitable to hear, 1, 547. cf. Od. 2, 207.

ἐπιεικτός, ή, όν (εἴκω), *yielding, giving way;* always with a negat. μένος οὐκ ἐπιεικτόν unyielding spirit, 5, 892; σθένος, invincible strength, 8, 32; πένθος, unceasing grief, 16, 549; hence, 2) With negat. *intolerable, evil,* like σχέτλιος. ἔργα οὐκ ἐπιεικτά (*not to be endured*), Od. 8, 307. The explanation 'not yielding,' i. e. having permanence, seems against the Hom. usus loquendi; cf. Nitzsch ad Od. 8. 307.

ἐπιειμένος, η, ον, see ἐπιέννυμι.

ἐπιείσομαι, see ἔπειμι (εἰμι).

ἐπιέλπομαι, depon. mid. only pres. (ἔλπω), *to hope,* with infin. 1, 545; with accus., Od. 21, 126.

ἐπιέννυμι, poet. for ἐφέννυμι (ἔννυμι), aor. 1 ἐπίεσσα, partcp. pass. ἐπιειμένος, 1) *to put on, to clothe, to put over;* with accus. χλαῖναν, to lay over, Od. 20, 143; metaph. in the partcp. perf. ἐπιειμένος, *clothed with;* with accus. ἐπιειμένος ἀναιδείην, clothed with impudence, 1, 149; ἀλκήν, with power, 7, 164. Od. 9, 214. 2) Mid. *to clothe oneself with,* νεφέλην, 14, 350; only in tmesis.

ἐπιζάφελος, ον, *vehement, violent;* χόλος, 9, 525; and the adv. ἐπιζαφελῶς, *vehemently, exceedingly,* 9, 516. Od. 6, 330. (The deriv. is uncertain; according to Apoll. from ζα and ὀφέλλειν.)

ἐπιῆλε, see ἐπιάλλω.

ἐπίηρα, only twice, in the phrase ἐπίηρα φέρειν τινί, *to be favorable to any one, to render oneself agreeable, to show kindness,* *1, 572. 578. Wolf. (Buttm. Lex. p. 335, supposes a tmesis, and writes separately, ἐπὶ ἦρα, cf. ἦρα.)

ἐπίηρανος, ον (ἄρω), *agreeable, welcome,* with dat., Od. 19, 343.† [Lex II. 341, 344.]

*ἐπίηρος, ον, *agreeable, grateful,* Frag. h. 56 † [Lex II. 338.]

ἐπιθαρσύνω (θαρσύνω), *to inspirit, to encourage, to embolden,* any one, with accus., 4, 183.†

ἐπιθεῖτε, see ἐπιτίθημι.

ἐπίθημα, τό, Ep. for ἐπίθεμα, that which is placed upon any thing, *a cover, a lid,* 24, 228.†

ἐπιθρέξας, see ἐπιτρέχω.

ἐπιθρώσκω (θρώσκω), *to leap upon;* with gen. νηός, the ship, 8, 515; with the dat τύμβῳ, upon the grave (by way of insult), 4, 177; without cases: τόσσον ἐπιθρώσκουσι, so far they leap (spoken of horses), *5, 772.

ἐπιθύω (θύω), aor. partcp. ἐπιθύσας, 1) *to rush upon, to attack,* 18, 175. Od. 16, 297. 2) *to desire earnestly,* h. Merc. 475. (Some derive it from ἰθύω, but this has always short υ; in both cases the υ is long; and ι is long by its position in the arsis.)

ἐπιΐστωρ, ορος. ὁ, ἡ (ἴστωρ), *acquainted with, experienced in;* with gen. μεγάλων ἔργων (*peritum,* i. e. *auctorem magnorum factorum,* Damm), Od. 21, 26 †

*ἐπικαίω (καίω), *to kindle upon, to light,* πῦρ, h. Ap. 49] ; in tmesis, 22, 170.

*ἐπικαμπύλος, ον (καμπύλος), *curved, bent,* h. Merc. 90.

ἐπίκαρ, adv. *on the head,* a different reading for ἐπὶ κάρ, 16, 392 ; see κάρ.

ἐπικάρσιος. η, ον (ἐπικάρ), prop. *head foremost, stooping forward.* αἱ νῆες ἐφέροντ' ἐπικάρσιαι, the ships were borne forward with depressed prow ['*their heads deep plunging.*' Cp.] (Voss, " with depressed masts"), Od. 9, 70 (according to Schol. 'careening, oblique, inclined').

Ἐπικάστη, ἡ, in the tragic poets Ἰοκάστη, daughter of Menœceus, and wife of king Laïus of Thebes, to whom she bore Œdipus. After he had ignorantly slain his father and solved the riddle of the Sphinx, he received as a prize his mother for a wife. When she discovered her relationship to him, she put an end to her life by hanging, Od. 11, 271.

ἐπίκειμαι, depon. mid. (κεῖμαι), fut. ἐπικείσομαι, *to lie upon;* spoken of doors, *to be joined to,* Od. 6, 19; metaph. ἐπικείσετ' ἀνάγκη, force will overpower 6, 458.

ἐπικείρω (κείρω), aor. 1 Ep. ἐπέκερσα, *to shear off, to cut off;* φάλαγγας, to cut down the squadrons, i. e. to penetrate, 16, 394. 2) Metaph. *to hinder, to render void;* μήδεα, *15, 467. 16, 120.

ἐπικελαδέω, poet. (κελαδέω), *to cry out, to cheer, to applaud,* only in tmesis. ἐπὶ δὲ Τρῶες κελάδησαν, *8, 542. 18, 310.

ἐπικέλλω, poet. (κέλλω), aor. ἐπέκελσα, 1) *to impel, to run into,* spoken only of ships ; νῆας, to run ships to the shore, Od. 9, 148. 2) Without accus. intrans. *to land, to lie on the strand;* Od. 9, 138 ; and of the ship, ἡ ἠπείρῳ ἐπέκελσεν, the ship ran upon the land, *Od. 13, 114.

ἐπικέλομαι, depon. mid. poet. (κέλομαι) aor. 2 Ep. ἐπεκελόμην, *to call to,* with accus. Ἐριννύς, 9, 454.†

ἐπικεράννυμι (κεράννυμι), aor. 1 infin. ἐπικρῆσαι, Ep. for ἐπικεράσαι, *to mingle with.* 2) *to mingle again;* οἶνον, to mix wine again, Od. 7, 164.†

ἐπικερτομέω (κερτομέω), *to insult, to*

Ἐπικεύθω. **Ἐπιληκέω.**

mock, to deride; only in the partcp. with προσέφης, 16, 744. Od. 22, 194. 2) In a milder signif. to jest with, to banter, 24, 649.
ἐπικεύθω (κεύθω). fut. ἐπικεύσω, to conceal, to hide, often with the negat., 8, 821 : μῦθον, Od. 4, 744.
ἐπικίδνημι, Ep. (κίδνημι, poet. form of σκεδάννυμι), pres. and imperf. mid. to strew over, to sprinkle upon. 2) to spread itself upon, to diffuse itself; with accus. ὕδωρ ἐπικίδναται αἶαν, the water spreads itself over the land, 2, 850; spoken of the morning light, *7, 451. 458.
ἐπικλείω, poet. (κλείω), to praise, to celebrate, with accus. ἀοιδήν, Od. 1, 351.† Or, with Nitzsch, to accompany with applause. The var. lec. ἐπικλύσω is preferred by Näg. ad Il. p. 230; and seems confirmed by Plato's ἐπιφρονέουσιν; but it wants MS. authority.
Ἐπικλῆς, ῆος, ὁ, a Lycian ally of the Trojans, slain by Telamonian Ajax, 12, 378.
ἐπίκλησις, ιος, ἡ (ἐπικαλέω), an appellation, a surname; only accus. absol. with the surname. τὸν ἐπίκλησιν Κορυνήτην κίκλησκον, 7, 138. Ἀστυάναξ, ὃν Τρῶες ἐπίκλησιν καλέουσι, 22, 506. Od. 5, 273. h. Ap. 386.
ἐπικλίνω (κλίνω), perf. pass. ἐπικέκλιμαι, to lean upon; pass. to be inclined. οὐδ' εὗρ' ἐπικεκλιμένας σανίδας, he found not the doors inclined, i. e. shut, 12, 121.†
ἐπίκλοπος, ον (κλέπτω), thievish, cunning, Od. 11, 364. 13, 291; also with gen. μύθων, crafty in words, 22, 281 ; τόξων, dextrous with the bow [rather, join θηητήρ καὶ ἐπίκλοπος, a right cunning examiner of the bow. Fäsi. It is ironical], Od. 21, 397.
*ἐπικλύζω (κλύζω), to inundate, to sprinkle. pass. κύμασι, Batr. 69.
ἐπικλύω (κλύω), to listen to, to understand, with accus., 23, 652 ; with gen. Od. 5, 150.
ἐπικλώθω (κλώθω), fut. ἐπικλώσω, aor. 1 act. ἐπέκλωσα, aor. 1 mid. ἐπεκλωσάμην, 1) to spin ; only metaph. ; prop. spoken of the Parcæ, who spin for every one his fate; then mly of the gods, to impart, to allot, to assign, τί τινι ; τινὶ ὄλβον, Od. 3, 208. 16, 64. ᾧτε Κρονίων ὄλβον ἐπικλώσει γαμέοντί τε γεινομένῳ τε, to whom the son of Kronus (Saturn) in his marriage and birth shall allot happiness, Od. 4, 208 (Eustath. reads instead of the fut. ἐπικλώσῃ, with more propriety). 2) Mid. as depon. spoken of the gods, to suspend ; ὄλεθρον ἀνθρώποις, destruction over men, Od. 8, 579 ; ὀίζύν, Od. 20, 196 ; and with infin. instead of accus. to allot,' to grant ; οἰκόνδε νέεσθαι, Od. 1, 17, and ζώειν, 24, 525 (in the Il. only once).
ἐπικόπτω (κόπτω), fut. ἐπικόψω, to strike upon from above; βοῦν, to strike upon the neck of the ox in order to kill it, to slay the ox, Od. 3, 443.†
ἐπικουρέω (ἐπίκουρος), fut. ἐπικουρήσω, to help, to aid, absol., 5, 614.†

only as subst. a helper, an assistant ; spoken of Arês, βροτῶν, h. 7, 9 ; and as fem., 21, 431. The plur. often used of the allies of the Trojans, 2, 130. 815. H. calls them frequently τηλεκλητοί, *9, 233.
ἐπικραίνω, Ep. lengthened ἐπικραιαίνω (κραίνω), aor. 1 ἐπέκρηνα, Ep. ἐπεκρήηνα, optat. ἐπικρήνειε, imperat. ἐπικρήηνον, 1) to finish, to fulfil, to accomplish, to grant, τινί τι ; ἐπικρήηνον, 1, 455 ; ἀρήν τινος, 15, 599 ; and absol. οὐ σφιν ἐπεκραίαινε, he did not grant it to them, 3, 302. 2) to rule to govern, θεούς, where Herm. would substitute οἴμους, h. Merc. 531 (from ἐπικραίνω. only ἐπικρήνειε, 15, 599, and pres. h. Merc. l. c.).
ἐπικρατέω (κρατέω), to hold the rule, to command, to govern, with dat. νήεσσιν, 10, 214, and absol., Od. 17, 320. 2) to have the mastery, to be victorious, to conquer, 14, 98.
ἐπικρατέως, adv. (ἐπικρατής), with great force, with might, *16, 81. 23, 863.
*ἐπικρέμαμαι, depon. mid. (κρέμαμαι), to hang upon, to hang over, to impend. πέτρη ἐπικρέμαται, h. in Ap. 284.
ἐπικρήηνον, Ep. see ἐπικραίνω.
ἐπικρήνειε, see ἐπικραίνω.
ἐπικρῆσαι, see ἐπικεράννυμι.
ἐπίκριον, τό (ἴκριον), a sail-yard, *Od. 5, 254. 318.
ἐπικυρέω (κυρέω), aor. ἐπέκυρσα, to fall upon any thing; to this is assigned ἐπὶ σώματι κύρσας, 3, 23 ; see κυρέω.
ἐπιλάμπω (λάμπω), aor. 1 ἐπέλαμψα, to shine upon. ἠέλιος ἐπέλαμψε, the sun shone thereon, 17, 650.† h. Merc. 141.
ἐπιλανθάνω and ἐπιλήθω (λήθω), aor. ἐπέλησα, fut. mid. ἐπιλήσομαι, aor. 2 mid. ἐπελαθόμην, 1) Act. to cause to forget; with gen. in aor. 1: ὁ ὕπνος ἀπέλησεν ἁπάντων, sleep caused a forgetfulness of every thing, Od. 20, 85. 2) Mid. to forget thereupon, any thing, with gen. Ἰθάκης, Od. 1, 57 ; and, generally, to forget, 7, 452 ; τέχνης, Od. 4, 455. The pres. ἐπιλανθάνω is not found in H., and from ἐπιλήθω only ἐπελήθετο, Od. 5, 324.
ἐπιλέγω (λέγω), to collect to or in addition ; only mid. in tmesis, ἐπὶ δὲ ξύλα πολλὰ λέγεσθε, 8, 507, and λέγοντο, v. 547.
ἐπιλείβω (λείβω), to pour upon, esply upon the flame in making libations of wine, Od. 3, 341 ; and in tmesis, 1, 463.
*ἐπιλέπω (λέπω), aor. ἐπέλεψα, to peel off, to strip off the bark, h. Merc. 109, where the reading is questioned [but without cause, Passow].
ἐπιλεύσσω (λεύσσω), to look upon, to see, τόσσον, 3, 12.†
ἐπιλήθομαι, see ἐπιλανθάνω.
ἐπιλήθος, ον (ἐπιλήθω), causing to forget, producing oblivion ; with gen. φάρμακον κακῶν ἐπιλήθον ἁπάντων, which caused an oblivion of all evils, Od. 4, 221.†
ἐπιληκέω (ληκέω), to make a noise upon, to clatter [to beat time whilst others dance, Passow, cf. Athenæus I. 13], Od.

'Επιλίγδην. 156 'Επίξυνος.

ἐπιλίγδην, adv. (λίγδην), scratching, grazing. 17, 599.†

ἐπιλλίζω (ἰλλίζω), to give the wink, to make a sign with the eyes, with dat., Od. 18, 11.† h. Merc. 387.

ἐπιλωβεύω (λωβεύω), to insult, to offer an affront to, Od. 2, 323.†

ἐπιμαίνομαι, depon. (μαίνομαι), aor. ἐπεμηνάμην, to be madly desirous of any thing, to desire vehemently; with dat. τῷ γυνὴ Προίτου ἐπεμήνατο, κρυπταδίῃ φιλότητι μιγήμεναι, for him the wife of Proetus passionately longed, that she might enjoy illicit love (according to Voss and the Schol. for ὥστε—μιγήμεναι); Köppen and Passow, by a forced construction, connect the sentence ἐπεμήνατο τῷ μιγήμεναι, 6, 160.†

ἐπιμαίομαι, depon. mid. (μαίομαι), fut. ἐπιμάσομαι, Ep. σσ, aor. 1 ἐπεμασάμην, Ep. σσ, 1) to touch, to handle, to feel, with accus. μάστιγι ἵππους, 17, 430. 5, 748; τινὰ ῥάβδῳ, Od. 13, 429. 16, 172. οἰῶν ἐπεμαίετο νῶτα, Od. 9, 441; spoken of a phy·ician, ἕλκος, to examine a wound, 4, 190; ξίφεος κώπην, to grasp the hilt of the sword, Od. 11, 530; χείρ, i. e. χειρί, not χεῖρ' as ed. Wolf. [cf. Eustath. and Bothe]. ἐπιμασσάμενος, grasping with the hand (viz. the sword), Od. 9, 301. cf. 19, 480; metaph. πυρὸς τέχνην, to essay the art of fire, h. Merc. 108. 2) With gen. to seek to attain, to desire, to strive after; σκοπέλου, to seek the rock, Od. 12, 220; and metaph. νόστου, Od. 5, 344; δώρων, 10, 401 (μαίομαι is used only in the pres. and imperf.; the other tenses are furnished by the obsol. μάομαι).

ἐπιμάρτυρος, ὁ (μάρτυρος), a witness on any occasion; spoken only of the gods, 7, 76. Od. 1, 273.

ἐπιμάσσομαι, see ἐπιμαίομαι.

ἐπίμαστος, ὁ (ἐπιμάομαι), prop. sought out, picked up; ἀλήτης, passively, a beggar picked-up on the road, Od. 20, 377.† The Schol. explains it actively, 'a beggar that picks up his living.'

ἐπιμειδάω (μειδάω), aor. partcp. ἐπιμειδήσας, to smile at or upon; always with προσέφη, 4, 356. 10, 400. Od. 22, 371.
*ἐπιμειδιάω = μειδάω, h. 9, 3.

ἐπιμέμφομαι, depon. mid. Ion. (μέμφομαι), to blame about, to reprove for, to reproach with, τινί τι, Od. 16, 97; with dat. of pers., Od. 16, 115. 2) to trouble oneself about, to be displeased with, to be angry; with gen. εὐχωλῆς, on account of a vow, 1, 65; and with ἕνεκα, 1, 94.

ἐπιμένω (μένω), aor. ἐπέμεινα, 1) to remain at, to tarry, to wait, ἐν μεγάροις, Od. 4, 587; ἐς αὔριον, Od. 11, 351; ἐπίμεινον, τεύχεα δύω, wait, that I may put on my armour, 6, 340; and with ἵνα, h. Cer. 160.

ἐπιμήδομαι, depon. mid. (μήδομαι), to plot, to devise, to contrive; δόλον τινί, an artifice against any one, Od. 4, 437.†

ἐπιμηνίω (μηνίω), to be angry, to be in a rage with, τινί. any one, 13, 460.†

ἐπιμιμνήσκω (μιμνήσκω), aor. 1 mid ἐπεμνησάμην, and aor. 1 pass. ἐπεμνήσθην, 1) to remind of. 2) Mid. with aor. pass. to remember, to think of, with gen. παῖδων, 15, 662; χάρμης, 17, 103. τοῦ ἐπιμνησθείς, remembering him, Od. 4. 189. (Only the mid. and partcp. aor. 1 pass.)

ἐπιμίμνω (μίμνω), poet. form fr. ἐπιμένω, to remain, to wait for, *Od. 14, 66. 15, 372.

ἐπιμίξ, adv. mixed, mingled together, pell-mell; spoken of warriors and horses confusedly blended together, 21, 16. 11, 525. Od. 11, 537. κτείνονται ἐπιμίξ, they were slain without distinction, 14, 60.

ἐπιμίσγω (μίσγω), Ep. form of ἐπιμίγνυμι, 1) Act. to mingle with. 2) Mid. which alone H. uses, to have intercourse with any one, to have commerce or communication with; with dat. Φαιήκεσσι, to come to the Phæacians, Od. 6, 241; in the Il. always spoken of battle. to meet, to mingle in fight; Τρώεσσι, with the Trojans, 10, 548; absol. to mingle in the battle, 5, 505.

ἐπιμνησαίμεθα, see ἐπιμιμνήσκω.

ἐπιμύζω (μύζω), aor. 1 ἐπέμυξα, to murmur or mutter at, to sigh from displeasure, *4, 20. 8, 251 (prop. to say μῦ to, always spoken of inarticulate sounds).

ἐπινέμω (νέμω), aor. 1 ἐπένειμα, to impart, to share, to distribute; with dat. σῖτον τραπέζῃ, to distribute the bread to the table, i. e. upon the table, 9, 216. 24, 625; spoken of persons: to distribute among several, Od. 20, 254.

ἐπινεύω (νεύω), aor. 1 ἐπένευσα, to give the nod to, to make a sign to, as an indication of command or of assent to a prayer, τινί, 9, 620. ὡς οἱ ὑπέστην πρῶτον, ἐμῷ δ' ἐπένευσα κάρητι, as I first promised him, and nodded with my head (to confirm the promise), 15, 75. h. in Cer. 169; and by tmesis, ἐπ' ὀφρύσι νεῦσε, 1, 528. Od. 16, 164; and mly to nod, κόρυθι, 22, 314.

ἐπινεφρίδιος, ον (νεφρός), at or upon the kidneys, 21, 204.†

ἐπινέω or ἐπινήθω (νέω), aor. 1 ἐπένησα, to spin, like ἐπικλώθω, used of the Parcæ. τινί τι, to allot any thing to any one. ἅσσα οἱ Αἶσα γεινομένῳ ἐπένησε λίνῳ, what Aisa spun in a thread for him at birth, i. e. what she allotted him, 20, 128; spoken of Moira, 24, 210. (H. does not use the pres.)

ἐπινηνέω, Ep. form (νηνέω, νήω), to heap upon, to lay upon; νεκροὺς πυρκαϊῆς, upon the funeral pile, *7, 428. 431.
*ἐπινήχομαι, depon. mid. Ep. form (νήχομαι), to swim upon, Batr.

ἐπινύσσεν, see πινύσσω.
*ἐπινώτιος, ον, lying on the back, Batr. 80.

ἐπίξυνος, ον, poet. for ἐπίκοινος (ξυνός), common, in common, ἐπίξυνῃ ἐν ἀρούρῃ [= κοινοὺς ὅρους ἐχούσῃ, Schol. Villois.], on the common boundary of a field, 12, 422.†

*ἐπιοινοχοεύω (οἰνοχοέω), to pour out wine, θεοῖς, h. Ven. 205.

*ἐπιόπτης, ου. ὁ. poet. for ἐπόπτης, ου, ὁ, a looker-on, a spectator, Ep. 12.

ἐπιορκέω (ἐπίορκος), fut. ἐπιορκήσω, to swear falsely, πρὸς δαίμονος, by a divinity, 19, 188.†

ἐπίορκος, ον (ὅρκος), swearing falsely, perjured. H. has only the neut. as subst. in the sing.: a false oath; as εἰ δέ τι τῶνδ' ἐπίορκον, sc. ἐστὶ, 19, 264; and ἐπίορκον ὀμνύναι, to swear a false oath, *10, 332. 19. 260.

ἐπιόσσομαι, depon. poet. (ὄσσομαι), to look at with the eyes; metaph. to consider, to observe; θάνατον ἑταίρων, 17, 381.†

ἐπίουρα, τά, see under οὖρον.

ἐπίουρος, ὁ (οὖρος), a spectator, a watch, an inspector, a keeper, like ἔφορος, with gen. ὑῶν ἐπίουρος, Od. 13, 405; with dat. Κρήτῃ, ruler over Crete, 13, 450.

ἐπιόψομαι, see ἐφοράω.

ἐπιπάσσω (πάσσω), to strew or sprinkle upon, with accus. φάρμακα, only in tmesis, *4, 219. 5, 401.

ἐπιπείθομαι, mid. (πείθομαι), fut ἐπιπείσομαι, prop. (to allow oneself) to be persuaded; to yield to persuasion, Od. 2, 103. 10. 406 : generally, to obey, to comply with, μύθῳ, 1, 565. 4, 412; with double dat. εἰ δέ μοι οὐκ ἐπέεσσ' ἐπιπείσεται, if he shall not obey my words, 15, 162. 178.

ἐπιπέλομαι, depon. mid. poet. (πέλομαι), to come to, to arrive; only the sync. partcp. ἐπιπλόμενον ἔτος, *Od. 7, 261. 14, 287; τινί, to any one, in tmesis, Od. 15, 408. 2) to reach, to extend, like ἐπιγίγνεσθαι, in tmesis, 10, 351.

ἐπιπέταμαι or ἐπιπέτομαι, depon. mid. (πέτομαι), aor. 2 ἐπεπτάμην, and from ἐπεπτόμην the infin. ἐπιπτέσθαι, to fly to, with dat. εἰπόντι ἐπέπτατο δεξιὸς ὄρνις, 13, 821. Od. 15, 160; and spoken of an arrow, καθ' ὅμιλον, 4, 126.

ἐπιπίλναμαι. depon. mid. poet. (πίλναμαι), a form of ἐπιπελάζω, to draw near, to approach. χιὼν ἐπιπίλναται [snow inundes. Cp.], Od. 6, 44.† (Only in the pres.)

ἐπιπλάζομαι (πλάζω), partcp. aor. 1 pass. ἐπιπλαγχθείς, to wander over, to stray about, with accus. πόντον, over the sea, Od. 8, 14.†

ἐπιπλέω (πλέω), to sail over, to navigate, with accus. ὑγρὰ κέλευθα, 1, 312; ἁλμυρὸν ὕδωρ, Od. 9, 227. (Only pres. and imperf. and in addition from the Ion. form ἐπιπλώω pres., aor. 1, and aor. 2, q. v.)

ἐπιπλήσσω (πλήσσω), fut. ἐπιπλήξω, to strike upon, with accus. τόξῳ, 10, 500 ; metaph. to reprove, to chide, to reproach, τινί, *12, 211. 23, 580.

ἐπιπλώω, Ion. and Ep. for ἐπιπλέω; from which partcp. pres. ἐπιπλώων, Od. 5, 284 ; 2 sing. aor. 2 ἐπέπλως, Od. 3, 15 ; partcp. ἐπιπλώς, 6, 291; and aor. 1 ἐπιπλώσας, 3, 47.

ἐπιπνέω, Ep. ἐπιπνείω (πνέω), aor. 1 ἐπέπνευσα, to blow upon, to breathe upon, to blow, absol. 5, 698; esply spoken of a favorable wind, with dat. νηΐ, to blow upon the ship, Od. 4. 357. 9, 139 (only the Ep. form ἐπιπνείω).

ἐπιποιμήν, ένος, ὁ, ἡ (ποιμήν), shepherd, shepherdess, as fem. Od. 12, 131.†

ἐπιπρέπω (πρέπω), to be prominent or conspicuous, to show or discover itself in, to appear in. οὐδέ τί τοι δούλειον ἐπιπρέπει, nothing servile appears in thee, Od. 24, 252.†

ἐπιπροέμεν, see ἐπιπροΐημι.

ἐπιπροϊάλλω (ἰάλλω), aor. 1 ἐπιπροΐηλα, to send forth to, with accus. θεούς, h. Cer. 327; spoken of things: to place before; τράπεζάν τινι. to place a table before any one, 11, 628.

ἐπιπροΐημι (προΐημι), aor. 1 3 sing. ἐπιπροέηκε, infin. aor. 2 ἐπιπροέμεν, Ep. for ἐπιπροεῖναι, to send away to, to send forth to, spoken of men, with accus. τινά, 9, 520; and dat. of the place: τινὰ νηυσίν, any one to the ships, 17, 708. 18, 58; but τινὰ νηυσὶν Ἴλιον εἴσω, to send any one in ships to Troy, 18, 439. b) Of missiles: to cast at, to throw or shoot at; ἰόν τινι, an arrow at any one, 4, 94. 2) Apparently intrans. to steer to, to sail to, sc. ναῦν: νήσοισιν, to the islands, Od. 15, 299. (ι in the middle syll. is short.)

*ἐπιπροχέω (χέω), to pour out at or upon any occasion, metaph. θρῆνον, to pour forth a lamentation, h. 18, 18.

ἐπιπταίρω (πταίρω), aor. 2 ἐπέπταρον, to sneeze at or upon; τινὶ ἐπέεσσιν, at any one's words, Od. 17, 545.† This was considered a propitious omen, b. Herm. 297.

ἐπιπτέσθαι, see ἐπιπέτομαι.

ἐπιπωλέομαι, depon. mid. (πωλέομαι), ο hire, to go over, to walk about, with accus. mly spoken of leaders : to inspect, with accus. στίχας ἀνδρῶν [' the warrior ranks Ranges.' Cp.], 3, 196. 4, 250; spoken also of warriors, in order to attack, στίχας ἔγχεί τε ἄορί τε, 11, 264. 540.

ἐπιρρέζω, poet. (ῥέζω), iterat. imperf. ἐπιρρέζεσκον, to sacrifice at or upon, Od. 17, 211.†

ἐπιρρέπω (ῥέπω), to incline towards, met. ἡμῖν ὄλεθρος ἐπιρρέπει, ' our own preponderating scale plunges us' (Cp.) into destruction, 14, 99.†

ἐπιρρέω (ῥέω), to flow to or upon, to run, spoken of a river: μὶν καθύπερθεν ἐπιρρέει, it flows upon it above, 2, 754; metaph. of men, to flow to, *11, 724.

ἐπιρρήσσω (ῥήσσω), to draw into, to push in, to thrust into ; ἐπιβλῆς, τὸν τρεῖς ἐπιρρήσσεσκον (iterat. imperf.), a bar, which three were wont to thrust in (to bar the door), *24, 454. 456.

ἐπιρρίπτω (ῥίπτω), aor. ἐπέρριψα, to cast upon. to throw to or against, δουρά τινι, a spear at any one, Od. 5, 310.†

ἐπίρροθος, ον, Ep. ἐπιτάρροθος, hastening to aid, helping, subst. helper, assistἀnί, with dat. 4, 390. 23, 770; see ἐπιτάρροθος (for ἐπιρρόθέω).

ἐπιρρώομαι, depon. mid. Ep. (ῥώομαι), aor. 1 ἐπερρωσάμην, 1) *to move rapidly or vehemently, at* or *about*, with dat. μύλαις δώδεκα ἐπερρώοντο γυναῖκες, twelve women moved vigorously (worked) at the mills, Od. 20, 107. 2) Spoken of the hair: *to roll* or *fall upon*. χαῖται ἐπερρώσαντο κρατὸς ἀπ' ἀθανάτοιο, the locks rolled forwards from his immortal head, 1, 529. cf. h. 26, 14; see ῥώομαι. By ἐπί is indicated that the motion of the hair follows the nod, Nägelsb.

ἐπισείω, Ep. ἐπισσείω (σείω), *to shake* or *brandish against*, τί τινι, spoken of Zeus: αἰγίδα πᾶσιν, to brandish the regis against all (to excite terrour), *4, 167. 15, 230 (only the Ep. form).

ἐπισεύω, Ep. ἐπισσεύω, for the most part poet. (σεύω), aor. 1 ἐπέσσευα, perf. pass. ἐπέσσυμαι, with pres. signif., pluperf. ἐπεσσύμην; which is also Ep. aor. 2. hence particp. with retracted accent, ἐπεσσύμενος. 1) Act. *to drive away, to put in motion*, with accus. δμῶας, to excite the servants against (me), Od. 14, 399; κῆτός τινι, to drive a sea-monster against one, Od. 5, 421. 2) Metaph. κακά τινι, to send evils upon any one, Od. 18, 256; ὀνείρατα, Od. 20, 87. II) Mid. and pass. esply perf. pass. as pres., and pluperf. as Ep. aor., prop. *to be driven on*. 1) *to hasten to, to rush to*, 2, 86; hence, ἐπεσσύμενος, hastening, ἀγορήνδε to the assembly, 2, 207; νομόνδε, 18, 575; with dat. τινί, to hasten to any one, Od. 4, 841; εἴς τινα, 13, 757; with gen. of place, πεδίοιο, through the plain, 14, 147; with accus. νῆα, to the ship, Od. 13, 19; δέμνια, Od. 6, 20; with infin. ὁ δ᾽ ἐπέσσυτο διώκειν, he made haste to pursue him, 21, 601; metaph. ἐπέσσυταί τοι θυμός, thy heart is driven, is prompted (to desire), 1, 173. 9, 42. b) In a hostile signif. *to rush upon, to attack*, often absol. and with dat., 5, 459. 584; with accus. τεῖχος ἐπεσσύμενος, 12, 143. 15, 395. (The gen. is unusual: τείχεος, 12, 388; depends upon βάλε: he cast him from the wall; cf. Spitzner; metaph. spoken of fire and water, 11, 737. Od. 5, 314. H. has only the Ep. form.)

ἐπίσκοπος, ὁ (σκοπέω), 1) *an observer, a spy, a scout*, with dat. νήεσσιν, against the ships, 10, 38. 342. 2) *overseer, commander, protector*, spoken of Hector, 24, 729. ἐπίσκοποι ἁρμονιάων, the defenders of covenants (of the gods), 22, 255; ὀδαίων, inspector of wares, Od. 8, 163.

ἐπισκύζομαι, depon. mid. (σκύζομαι), aor. 1 ἐπεσκυσάμην, *to be displeased, angry at* any thing, 9, 370; τινί, any one, Od. 7, 306.

ἐπισκύνιον, τό (σκύνιον), *the skin of the forehead*, above the cavity of the eyes, which moves in various passions, *supercilium, the brow*; hence metaph. like ὀφρύς, as a sign of anger, pride, spoken of lions: πᾶν δέ τ' ἐπισκύνιον κάτω ἕλ-κεται, he draws down his whole brow into frowns [*Cp*], 17, 136.†

ἐπισμυγερῶς, adv. (ἐπισμυγερός), as if scorched by flames (σμύχω, *uro*); hence *shamefully, miserably*, ἀπέτισεν, Od. 3, 195; ναυτίλλεται [*cum sua pernicie naviga verit*, cf. Barnes and Bothe], *Od. 4, 672.

ἐπίσπαστος, η, ον (ἐπισπάω), *drawn to oneself, attracted*. ἐπίσπαστον κακὸν ἔχειν, to have drawn an evil upon oneself, *Od. 18, 73. 24, 462.

ἐπισπεῖν, see ἐφέπω.

ἐπισπέρχω (σπέρχω), *to urge forward, to hasten on*, Od. 22, 451; with accus. κέντρῳ, to urge or spur on, sc. the steeds, 23, 430. 2) Intrans. *to urge oneself, to hurry forward rapidly*, ἄελλαι ἐπισπέρχουσι, Od. 5, 304.

ἐπισπέσθαι, ἐπισπόμενος, see ἐφέπω.

ἐπίσπω, see ἐφέπω.

ἐπισσείω, see ἐπισείω.

ἐπισσεύω, see ἐπισεύω.

ἐπίσσωτρον, τό, Ep. for ἐπίσωτρον.

ἐπισταδόν, adv. (ἐφίστημι), *proceeding to, going up to*, Od. 12, 392. 13, 54. οἱ δ᾽ ἄρα δόρπον ἐπισταδὸν ὡπλίζοντο, *Od. 16, 453; ἐπισταδόν is unnecessarily explained 'one after another;' Voss. 'busily.' The sense is, 'they went and prepared the evening meal.'

ἐπίσταμαι, depon. imperf. ἠπιστάμην, without augm. fut. ἐπιστήσομαι, 1) *to understand, to know, to be acquainted with*, with accus. ἔργα, 23, 705; ἔργα περικαλλέα, Od. 2, 117; spoken of women who are skilled in feminine works. 2) *to understand, to know how, to be able*; spoken both of the mind, as φρεσίν, 14, 92; θυμῷ, Od. 4, 730; and of the body, ᾗς χερσίν, 5, 60; with infin., 4, 404. ἠπίστατο μείλιχος εἶναι, he knew how to be mild to all, 17, 671. The partcp. pres. ἐπιστάμενος, η, ον, prop. understanding, mly as adj. *intelligent, practised, experienced*, often absol. of men and brutes, and also ἐπιστάμενοι πόδες, 18, 599. a) *skilful, dexterous*, mostly with infin. σάφα εἰπεῖν, 4, 404. b) With gen. ἐπιστάμενος πολέμοιο, acquainted with war, 2, 611, ed. Barnes; ἀοιδῆς, Od. 21, 406. c) With dat. ἐπιστάμενος ἄκοντι, sc. πολεμίζειν, 15, 282 (prob. Ion. for ἐφίσταμαι, to direct one's thought to any thing. cf. the Germ. *verstehen* and the Engl. *understand*). [Buttm. thinks it a simple vb.]

ἐπισταμένως, adv. *intelligently, skilfully, scientifically, dexterously*, 10, 265. Od. 20, 161.

ἐπιστάτης, ου, ὁ (ἐφίστημι), origin. one who approaches; only σὺς ἐπιστάτης, who approaches thee, a beggar, Od. 17, 455.† (Hesych. ἀπὸ τοῦ ἐφίστασθαι τῇ τραπέζῃ.)

*ἐπιστεναχίζω = ἐπιστενάχομαι, Batr. 73; but ἐπιστοναχίζω, ed. Frank.

ἐπιστενάχομαι, depon. mid. (στενάχω), *to groan at* or *over*, 4, 154.†

ἐπιστεφής, ές (ἐπιστέφω), *up to the brim, brimful*, with gen. only κρητῆρες

Ἐπιστέφω. 159 **Ἐπιτέτραπται.**

ἐπιστεφέας οἴνοιο, mixing-vessels brimful of wine, 8, 232. Od. 2, 431; see ἐπιστέφω.

ἐπιστέφω (στέφω), only in the mid. ἐπιστέφομαι, always κρητῆρας, ἐπεστέψαντο οἴνοιο, they filled the vessels full to the brim [they crowned the vessels with wine], 1, 470. 9, 175. Od. 1, 148, and elsewhere. The old Gramm. thus unanimously explain this, see Athen. XV. p. 674. I. 13 ; and also most modern, as Heyne, Voss; and Buttm. Lex. p. 291, who explains it, ' to fill so full that the liquor rises above the brim and forms a crown.' To fill the vessel thus full was a religious custom. To a use of garlands there is here no reference, as in Virg. Æn. 1, 723. The gen. with verbs of filling is common.

ἐπιστήμων, ον (ἐπίσταμαι), intelligent, experienced, acquainted with, Od. 16, 374.†

ἐπίστιον, τό (prop. neut. of ἐπίστιος, belonging to the hearth), subst. *a cover, a shed*, under which the ships drawn on shore stood supported by stakes; otherwise νεώριον; πᾶσιν ἐπίστιόν ἐστιν ἑκάστῳ, each one of all (the Phæaces) has here a shed, Od. 6, 265 ; cf. Nitzsch ad loc. Voss, incorrectly, 'they rest each one upon supporting props. The masc. ἑκάστῳ cannot refer to νῆες [in like manner Cowper, inaccurately, 'each stationed in her place.' *Am. Ed.*].

ἐπιστοναχέω (στοναχέω), = ἐπιστενάχομαι, from which aor. 1 ἐπεστονάχησα, *to roar*, spoken of the sea, 24, 79.†

*ἐπιστονοχίζω = ἐπιστεναχίζω, q. v.

ἐπιστρέφω (στρέφω), *to turn to, to turn towards*, with accus. only aor. 1 ἐπιστρέψας, 3, 370.† 2) Mid. *to turn oneself towards, to go, to penetrate*, h. 27, 10.

ἐπιστροφάδην, adv. (ἐπιστρέφω), *turning hither and thither, turning on all sides*; κτείνειν, to slay (to smite them) on all sides, 10, 483; τύπτειν, Od. 22, 308 (others, *fiercely*; Voss, *vigorously*; Schol. ἐνεργῶς).

ἐπίστροφος, ον (ἐπιστρέφω), prop. turning oneself to, *consorting with, holding intercourse with*; with gen. ἀνθρώπων, with men, Od, 1, 177.†

Ἐπίστροφος, ὁ, son of Iphitus, grandson of Naubolus, leader of the Phocians before Troy, 2, 517. 2) leader of the Halizonians, an ally of the Trojans, 2, 856. 3) son of Evēnos, brother of Mynes, slain by Achilles on the expedition against Lyrnessus, 2, 692.

ἐπιστρωφάω (στρωφάω), poet. form of ἐπιστρέφω, intrans. as ἐπιστρέφομαι, *to turn oneself to, to go into, to visit*; πώλεας πόληας, to go through cities, Voss, Od. 17, 486;† metaph. of cares, h. Merc. 44.

Ἐπίστωρ, ορος, ὁ, a Trojan, slain by Patroclus, 16, 695 (signif. = ἐπιστήμων).

ἐπισφύριον, τό (σφυρόν), prop. neut. of ἐπισφύριος), *an ankle-clasp*, a kind of hook or buckle, by which the greaves, consisting of two plates, were fastened: κνημῖδες ἐπισφυρίοις ἀραρυῖαι. According to others, *a covering for the ankle*, by which the plates were fastened ; hence Voss, ' plates fastened together with silver ankle-coverings,' *3, 331. 11, 18, etc.

*ἐπισχεδόν, adv. (σχεδόν), *near, almost*, h. Ap. 3.

ἐπισχερώ, adv. (σχερός), prop. connected together, *in a row, one after another, in order, like ἐφεξῆς*, with κτείνεσθαι, ἀναβαίνειν, *11, 668. 18, 68.

ἐπισχεσίη, ἡ (ἐπέχω), *a pretence, a pretext* ; with gen. οὐδέ τιν' ἄλλην μύθου ποιήσασθαι ἐπισχεσίην ἐδύνασθε, ἀλλ' ἐμὲ ἱέμεναι γῆμαι, you were able to make no other pretext for your resolution (or attempt) but wishing to marry me, Od. 21, 71.† (The ancients explain μύθου here by στάσις, uproar, noise, it being Æol. for μόθος, see μῦθος).

ἐπίσχεσις, ιος, ἡ (ἐπέχω), 1) *restraint, hindrance*. 2) *abstinence, moderation, temperance*, with infin. following, Od. 17, 451.†

ἐπίσχω (ἴσχω), form of ἐπέχω, 1) *to direct, to guide*, ἵππους, 17, 465. 2) *to hold up, to check*, Od. 20, 266 (according to the Schol., who explains ἐπίσχετε by κατάσχετε, as aor. 2 from ἐπέχω, q. v.).

ἐπίσωτρον, τό, Ep. ἐπίσσωτρον, *the tire*, the iron band encompassing the wooden circumference of a wheel (σῶτρον); only in the Ep. form, *5, 725. 11, 537. 23, 519.

ἐπιτάρροθος, ὁ, ἡ, *a helper, an assistant*, spoken of the gods; μάχης, in battle, 12, 180; also fem., 5, 808. 828. (From ἐπίρροθος, as ἀταρτηρός fr. ἀτηρός, see Thiersch, § 174. 7).

ἐπιτείνω (τείνω), *to stretch, to extend*; only in tmesis, 17, 736. Od. 11, 19.

ἐπιτέλλω (τέλλω), aor. 1 act. ἐπέτειλα, aor. 1 mid. ἐπετειλάμην, perf. pass. ἐπιτέταλμαι. 1) Act. *to end in addition* (cf. τέλλω in Schneider's Lex.), *to annex, to add* ; thus in tmesis, κρατερὸν δ' ἐπὶ μῦθον ἔτελλε [asperam ei vocem inmquam onus imposuit. Näg. Lob. 'Ρημ. 115], spoke in addition a harsh speech, 1, 25, 326. 16, 199. 2) *to commission, to order, to command, to impose, to bid*, τί τινι, πολλά τινι, 4, 229 ; μῦθόν τινι [but see above], 11, 486; often with only one of the two cases, συνθεσίας, to give commands to any one, 5, 320; often. absol. with infin. instead of accus., 4, 229. Hence pass. ἐμοὶ δ' ἐπὶ πάντ' ἐτέταλτο, every thing was entrusted to me, Od. 11, 524; with infin., 2, 643. 2) Mid. like act. *In commission, to command*, any one with infin., 2, 802. 10, 61 ; with accus. νόστος, ὃν ἐκ Τροίης ἐπετείλατο Ἀθήνη, the return which Athēnē had commanded from Troy, Od. 1, 327.

*ἐπιτερπής, ές (ἐπιτέρπω), *pleasurable, agreeable*, h. Ap. 413.

ἐπιτέρπω (τέρπω), 1) *to delight with, to charm*; only 2) Mid. *to delight in, to be charmed with*, ἔργοις, Od. 14, 228;† and with accus. θυμόν, ἦτορ, h. Ap. 146.' 204.

ἐπιτέτραπται, see ἐπιτρέπω.

ἐπιτετράφαται, see ἐπιτρέπω.
ἐπιηδές, adv. *enough, sufficiently, adequately*; in two passages: ἐς δ' ἐρέτας ἐπιηδὲς ἀγείρομεν, let us collect on board rowers enough, 1, 142. μνηστήρων σ' ἐπιηδὲς ἀριστῆες λοχόωσιν, in sufficient numbers the chief of the suitors lie in wait for thee, Od. 15, 28; later, with changed accent, ἐπιηδές. (According to Damm. from τείνω [So Död.: = μετ' ἐπιτάσεως, *intente*; *intently, earnestly*]: according to Buttm. Lex. p. 299, from ἐπὶ τάδε or τάδεσι; or, according to Passow, from τῆδες, a form of τῆτες).

*ἐπιτηρέω (τηρέω), aor. 1 partcp. ἐπιτηρήσας, *to wait for, to watch for*, νύκτα, h. Cer. 245.

ἐπιτίθημι (τίθημι), fut. ἐπιθήσω, aor. 1 ἐπέθηκα, aor. 2 optat. ἐπιθεῖτε, Ep. for ἐπιθείητε, infin. ἐπιθεῖναι, aor. 1 mid. ἐπεθήκατο, aor. 2 mid. ἐπέθετο, partcp. ἐπιθέμενος, *to place upon, to put upon*, I) *to put upon, to lay upon*, mly τινί τι; κρατὶ κυνέην, 11. rarely; τινὰ λεχέων, to lay any one upon the bed, 24, 589; φάρμακα, 4, 190; εἴδατα, to place food (upon the table), Od. 1, 140; spoken of sacrifices, Ποσειδάωνι ταύρων μῆρα, to offer the thighs of oxen to Poseidôn, Od. 3, 179; Ἀπόλλωνι, Od. 21, 267. b) Metaph. *to lay upon, to inflict*, ἄλγεα Τρωσί, 2, 40. πολλοὶ γὰρ δὴ τλήμεν ἐξ ἀνδρῶν, χαλέπ' ἄλγε' ἐπ' ἀλλήλοισι τιθέντες, many of us have suffered from [on account of] men, inflicting grievous pangs upon one another, says Dionê to Aphroditê, 5, 384. The Schol. unnecessarily connects ἐξ ἀνδρῶν and τιθέντες. The sense is, ' we have already suffered much because we have taken part in the affairs of men,' cf. v. 385, seq φωνήν, to inflict punishment, Od. 2, 102   2) *to put at* or *to, to attach, to add*, ἄλλα, 7, 364. 391; τινί τι; κορώνην, a curved end (to the bow), 4, 111; περόνην, Od. 19, 256. b) *to place before*, in order to close any thing, λίθον θύρησιν, Od. 13, 370; θύρας, to close the doors. 14, 169. Od. 22, 157; hence said of the Hours: ἡμὲν ἀνακλῖναι νέφος ἠδ' ἐπιθεῖναι, to put back the cloud and place it before, i. e. to open and shut, 5, 751. 8, 395; spoken of the Trojan horse, λόχον, Od. 11, 525.   c) Metaph. μύθῳ τέλος ἐπιθεῖναι, to put an end to the word, i. e. to fulfil the declaration, 19, 107. 20, 369; φρένα ἱεροῖσιν, to fix his heart upon, to direct his mind to the victims, 10, 16. II) Mid. *to put upon*, τί τινι; στεφάνην κεφαλῆφιν, 10, 31; χεῖρας στήθεσσίν τινος (his hands), 18, 317.

ἐπιτιμήτωρ, ορος, ὁ (τιμάω), *an avenger, one who inflicts punishment*, epith. of Zeus, ἐπιτιμήτωρ ἱκετάων τε ξείνων τε, Od. 9, 270.†

ἐπιτλῆναι (ΤΛΑΩ), only imper. aor. ἐπιτλήτω, absol. *to continue patient at* or *under*; with dat. μύθοισιν ἐμοῖσιν, my words, *19, 220. 23, 591.

ἐπιτολμάω (τολμάω), *to have courage*, *to dare, to take courage, to encourage oneself*, with infin., Od. 5, 353; absol. *to remain patient*, *Od. 17, 238.

ἐπίτονος, ον (τείνω), *stretched*, whence the subst. ὁ ἐπίτονος (subaud. ἱμάς), a rope with which the sail-yard is made fast to the mast, *the yard-rope*, Od. 12, 423.†

ἐπιτοξάζομαι, depon. mid. (τοξάζω), prop. to bend the bow at any one, *to shoot, to aim at* any one, with dat., 3, 79.†

ἐπιτραπέω, Ep. for ἐπιτρέπω, ἐπιτραπέουσι, 10, 421.†

ἐπιτρέπω (τρέπω), aor. 1 act. ἐπέτρεψα, aor. 2 act. ἐπέτραπον, aor. 2 mid. ἐπετραπόμην, perf. pass. ἐπιτέτραμμαι, 3 plur. Ion. and Ep. ἐπιτετράφαται, I) Act. 1) *to turn to, to give over to, to commit to, to thrust to*, τί τινι; οἰκόν τινι (to one's care), Od. 2, 226; without accus. expressed, aor. 2, τοῖσιν ἐπετράπομεν μάλιστα, to these we trusted most [sc. τὸ φυλάσσειν], 10, 59; instead of the accus. we have also the infin., 10, 116. 421. θεοῖς ἐπιτρέπειν τι, to leave to the gods, Od. 19, 502; hence pass. ᾧ ἐπιτετράφαται λαοί, to whom the people are entrusted, 2, 25; and spoken of the Hours: τῇς ἐπιτέτραπται οὐρανός, 5, 750. 2) *to turn to, to leave to, to yield to*, νίκην τινί, 21, 173; παισὶ κτήματα, to leave possessions to children, Od. 7, 149; and without accus. [expressed], οὐκ ἐπέτρεπε [sc. ἑαυτόν, cf. Nägelab. p. 313], γήραϊ, he yielded not to age, 10, 79. II) Mid. *to turn oneself to*. σοὶ θυμὸς ἐπετράπετο εἰρέσθαι, thy mind was inclined to ask, Od. 9, 12.

ἐπιτρέχω (τρέχω), aor. 2 ἐπέδραμον, partcp. aor. 1 ἐπιθρέξας, 13, 409;† perf. ἐπιδέδρομα, *to run to*, both to render aid and to attack. ἅρματα ἵπποις ἐπέτρεχον, the chariots rolled after the horses, 23, 504. 2) *to run over, to graze*, spoken of a spear, 13, 409. λευκὴ δ' ἐπιδέδρομεν αἴγλη, glittering splendour glances over it, Od. 6, 45. cf. Od. 20, 357.

ἐπιτροχάδην, adv. *running over cursorily, hastily, briefly* (but to the point); *in a summary way*, only ἀγορεύειν, 3, 213. Od. 18, 26.

ἐπιφέρω (φέρω), fut. ἐποίσω, *to bring to* or *upon*, only in a hostile signif.; χεῖράς τινι, to lay hands upon one, i. e. to attack him, Od. 16, 438; and βαρείας χεῖρας, 1, 89.

*ἐπιφθάνω (φθάνω), partcp. aor. 2 ἐπιφθάς, *to be beforehand, to anticipate*, Batr. 217.

ἐπιφθονέω (φθονέω), *to envy, to refuse enviously, to grudge, to forbid*, with dat. Od. 11, 149.

ἐπιφλέγω (φλέγω), *to kindle, to set fire to, to burn up*, with accus. ὕλην, νεκρόν, *2, 455. 23, 52.

*ἐπιφράζομαι (φράζομαι), aor. 1 ἐπεφρασάμην, Ep. σσ, and with like signif. aor. 1 pass. ἐπεφράσθην, Od. 5, 183. 1) *to think of, to meditate upon, to consider*, with accus. βουλήν, 2, 282. 13, 741;

'Επιφρονέω. 161 'Εποροὐω.

ἀbsol. 21, 410: mly *to observe, to perceive, to understand*, τι, 5, 665; in connexion with νοεῖν, Od. 8, 94. 533 ; *to recognize*, Od. 18, 94. 2) *to devise, to plan, to excogitate*, ὄλεθρόν τινι, Od. 15, 444; absol. οἶον δὴ τὸν μῦθον ἐπεφράσθης ἀγορεῦσαι! Od. 5, 183.
ἐπιφρονέω (ἐπίφρων), *to be thoughtful, intelligent, wise, discreet*, only partcp. pass., Od. 19, 385.†
ἐπιφροσύνη, ἡ (ἐπίφρων), *discretion, prudence, thoughtful care*, Od. 5, 437 ; in the plur. ἀνελέσθαι ἐπιφροσύνας, to assume a thoughtful care, *Od. 19, 22.
ἐπίφρων, ον (φρήν), *considerate, thoughtful, intelligent, wise, prudent*, spoken of persons, Od. 23, 12. ἐπίφρων βουλήν, prudent or wise in counsel, Od. 16, 242 ; of things, βουλή, a prudent counsel, Od. 3, 128. 19, 326.
***ἐπιφωνέω** (φωνέω), *to call to, to call* on any occasion, Fr. 12.
ἐπιχειρέω (χείρ), fut. ρήσω, *to lay hands upon, to seize*, with dat. δείπνῳ, *Od. 24, 386. 395.
ἐπιχεῦαι, see ἐπιχέω.
ἐπιχεῦαι (χέω), aor. 1 Ep. ἐπέχευα, infin. ἐπιχεῦαι, aor. 1 mid. ἐπεχευάμην, Ep. aor. sync. 2 mid. ἐπέχυντο, 1) *to pour upon or over*; χερσὶν ὕδωρ, water upon the hands, 24, 303. Od. 4. 212; χέρνιβα προχόῳ, water from the pitcher, Od, 1, 136 ; metaph. of sleep, in tmesis: μνηστήρεσσιν ὕπνον, Od. 2, 395; ἀνέμων ἀϋτμένα, to excite the breath of the winds, Od. 3, 289 ; δούρατα, to cast spears, 5, 618. b) Mid. a) *to pour upon for oneself*, spoken of things dry : *to pour upon, to heap upon*, ὕλην (as ballast), Od. 5, 257; χύσιν φύλλων, (an effusion =) a heap of leaves, Od. 5, 487. b) With Ep. sync. aor. 2, only metaph. of a multitude of men : *to pour upon, to rush to*, τοὶ δ' ἐπέχυντο, 15, 654. 16, 295.
ἐπιχθόνιος, ον (χθών), *living on the earth, earthly*, 1) As epith. of ἀνήρ, βροτός, ἄνθρωπος, 1, 266. 2, 553. 2) As subst. *an inhabitant of the earth*, h. 14, 2.
ἐπιχράω (χράω), *to attack, to fall upon, to assail*, with dat. of men and brutes, Τρώεσσιν, ἄρνεσσιν, 16. 352. 356. μηντέρι μοι μνηστῆρες ἐπέχραον, the suitors assailed my mother, i. e. pressed her with their suit, Od. 2, 50 (μοι is dat. ethicus used in the language of familiar discourse. Nitzsch.).
ἐπιχρίω (χρίω), aor. 1 ἐπέχρισα, 1) *to anoint, to besmear*, with accus. τόξον ἀλοιφῇ, Od. 21, 179 ; παρειάς, Od. 18, 172. 2) Mid. *to anoint oneself*, ἀλοιφῇ *Od. 18, 179.
ἐπιψαύω (ψαύω), *to touch upon the surface, to graze, to touch* ; metaph. *to feel* (slightly), ὅσσ' ὀλίγον περ ἐπιψαύῃ πραπίδεσσιν, who can feel though but a little with his heart, Od. 8, 547.†
ἐπιωγαί, αἱ (ἰωγή), places near the shore, where ships, secure from storms, could lie at anchor, *roads [sheltering coves*. Cp.], Od. 5, 404.†

ἐπιών, see ἔπειμι (εἶμι).
ἔπλε, Ep. for ἔπελε, see πέλω.
ἔπλεο or ἔπλευ, Ep. for ἐπέλου, and ἔπλετο, Ep. for ἐπέλετο, see πέλομαι.
ἔπλητο, see πελάζω.
ἐποίσω, fut. of ἐπιφέρω.
ἐποίχομαι (οἴχομαι). *In go to, to go, to come to*, 1) Absol., Od. 1, 143 ; limited, πάντοσε, 5, 508 : ἀνὰ στρατόν, 1, 383. 2) With accus. of persons and inanimate things, a) *to go to any one*, μνηστῆρας, Od. 1, 324. b) *to go about, to go through*, to inspect, spoken of a leader, 6, 81 ; στίχας ἀνδρῶν, 15, 279. πάσας ἐπῴχετο, he (went) up to them all (the seals), Od. 4, 451. c) *to fall upon* any one, *to attack*, with accus. οὐρῆας, spoken of Apollo, 1, 50 ; Κύπριν χαλκῷ (with a weapon), 5, 330 ; esply spoken of Apollo and Artemis : ἀγανοῖς βελέεσσιν (to pierce with gentle shafts. Cp.), Od. 11, 173. 15, 411; see 'Απόλλων. 3) Of things : *to go to any thing, to go about*, τί ; νηῶν ἴκρια, 15, 676 ; metaph. ἐποίχεσθαι ἔργον, to go to their work, to pursue or attend to it, 6, 492 ; δόρπον, Od. 13, 34 ; spoken of women : ἱστὸν ἐποίχεσθαι, to go about the loom, see ἱστόν, 1, 31.
ἔπομαι, mid. see ἔπω.
ἐπόμνυμι and **ἐπομνύω** (ὄμνυμι), imperf. ἐπώμνυον, fut. ἐπομοῦμαι, aor. ἐπώμοσα, *to swear by, to take an oath* of a thing; absol., Od. 15, 437 ; with accus. ὅρκον, with μήποτε and infin., 9, 132. 274 ; ἐπίορκον, a false oath, 10, 332.
ἐπομφάλιος, ον (ὀμφαλός), *at, upon the navel; on the boss*, spoken of a shield : βάλεν σάκος μέσσον ἐπομφάλιον, in the centre, on the boss, 7, 267.†
ἐποπίζομαι, depon. (ὀπίζομαι), *to honour, to reverence, to dread*, with accus. Διὸς μῆνιν, Od. 5, 146.† h. Ven. 291.
ἐποπτάω (ὀπτάω), *to roast upon, to roast*, ἔγκατα, Od. 12, 363.†
ἐποπτεύω (ὀπτεύω), *to look upon*, esply *to inspect, to superintend*, with accus. ἔργα ἐποπτεύεσκε, Od. 16, 140.†
(ἐπόπτομαι), pres. obsol., fut. ἐπόψομαι, see ἐφοράω.
ἐπορέγομαι, mid. (ὀρέγω), paricp. aor. ἐπορεξάμενος, *to extend oneself towards*, in order to attack, *to extend the spear* for a thrust, 5, 335,† subaud. ἔγχει, see ὀρέγω.
ἐπόρνυμι and **ἐπορνύω** (ὄρνυμι), imperf. ἐπώρνυε, aor. 1 ἐπῶρσα, imperat. ἔπορσον, Ep. aor. sync. mid. ἐπῶρτο, 1) *to excite, to awaken*, τί τινι ; μένος τινί, 20, 93. 2) *to urge on, to send to*, spoken of the gods: ὕπνον τινί, to send sleep upon any one, Od. 22, 429 ; οἶζύν, Od. 7, 271 ; μόρσιμον ἦμαρ, 15, 613. b) Frequently in a hostile signif. *to excite, to rouse against* any man, 5, 765 ; and with infin., 7, 42. II) Mid. together with Ep. aor. 2 and pluperf. *to rush against, to assail*; with dat. Ἀχιλῆϊ, against Achilles, 21, 324.
ἐπορούω (ὀρούω), aor. 1 ἐπόρουσα, *to leap upon, to spring upon, to rush upon*, any man, with dat. always in a hostile signif., 3, 379. 4, 172; and ἐν πόντῳ, h.

Ἔπορσον.

Ap. 400; with double dat. τινὶ δουρί (with the spear), 16, 320; metaph. spoken of sleep: αὐτῷ ὕπνος ἐπόρουσε, sleep fell upon him (with the notion of haste), Od. 23, 343. b) With the accus. ἅρμα, to leap upon the chariot, 17, 481.
ἔπορσον, see ἐπόρνυμι.
ἔπος, εος, τό, a word, and generally every thing expressed by speech; hence also, speech, narration, tradition, H. ἔπος καὶ μῦθος, discourse and narration, Od. 11, 561; in the plur. Od. 8, 91. According to the connexion it signifies a) a word pledged, a promise: διακέρσαι ἔπος, 8, 8. b) counsel, command, 9, 100. c) a response or oracle of a soothsayer, Od. 12, 266. d) narration, song of a bard, Od. 8, 91. 17, 519. e) word, in opposition to deed, 15, 234; hence ἔπεσιν καὶ χερσὶν ἀρήγειν, to help any man by word and deed, 1, 77. cf. Spitz. ad Il. 15, 234. f) the contents of discourse, matter, nearly = πρᾶγμα, thing, 11, 652. Od. 22, 289, in connexion with μῦθος, where ἔπος relates more to the substance of the narration, μῦθος to its intellectual form.
ἐποτρύνω (ὀτρύνω), aor. 1 ἐπώτρυνα, to incite, to urge on. 1) Spoken of persons, with accus. to encourage, to urge, to impel, to command; often θυμὸς ἐποτρύνει, and in connexion with ἀνώγει, mly with accus. and infin. following, ἑταίρους τάφρον διαβαινέμεν, to cross the trench, 12, 50; with dat. of the pers. and infin. only, 15, 258. Od. 10, 531. 2) Of things: to excite, to press, with accus. πόλεμόν τινι, to excite a contest against any man, Od. 22, 152; πομπήν, to ask urgently an escort, Od. 8, 30; but ἀγγελίας πολίεσσιν, to send embassies to the cities, Od. 24, 355. II) Mid. to press for oneself, to urge, πομπήν, Od. 8, 31.†
ἐπουράνιος, ίη, ιον (οὐρανός), in heaven, heavenly, epith. of the gods, 6, 129. Od. 17, 484.
ἐποχέομαι, mid. (ὀχέω), fut. ήσομαι, to ride upon, to travel, ἵπποις, 10, 330; ἵπποις καὶ ἅρμασι, to ride in chariots, *17, 449.
*ἐπόψιος, ον (ὄψις), to be looked at, conspicuous, remarkable, noted, h. Ap. 496 (old reading for ὑπόψιος, 3, 42).
ἐπόψομαι, see ἐφοράω.
ἔπραθον, see πέρθω.
ἑπτά, indecl. seven, often in Il. and Od.
ἑπταβόειος, ον (βόειος), made of seven layers of ox-hide, seven-hided, σάκος, *7, 220. 222.
ἑπταετής, ές (ἔτος), of seven years, only in neut. ἑπτάετες as adv. during seven years, *Od. 3, 305. 7, 259.
ἑπταπόδης, ου ὁ (πούς), seven feet long, θρῆνυς, 15, 729.†
*ἑπτάπορος, ον (πόρος), having seven courses, with seven paths, epith. of Pleiades, h. 7, 7.
Ἑπτάπορος, ὁ, a river of Mysia, 12, 20. According to Strab. XIII. p. 603, it is called Πολύπορος. It rises in the mountain Teunos, and falls, after manifold

Ἐπώνυμος.

windings, into the Sinus Adramyttēnus, at the village Celænæ.
ἑπτάπυλος, ον, seven-gated, having seven gates, epith. of the Bœotian Thebes, 4, 406. Od. 11, 263. cf. Apd. 3, 6. 6.
ἔπταρον, see πταίρω.
ἔπτατο, see πέτομαι.
ἕπτακα (ἑπτά), seven-fold; δαίζειν, to divide into seven parts, Od. 14, 434.†
ἙΠΩ, an obsol. theme from which come ἔπος, εἶπον, ἐνέπω and ἐννέπω, prop. to arrange; then, to speak, to say.
ἕπω, imperf. ἕπον, 1) Act. only Ep. to be about any thing, to be employed, to be busy, mly with prep. ἀμφί, μετά, περί; ἀμφ' Ὀδυσῆα Τρῶες ἕπον, the Trojans were engaged about Odysseus (Ulysses), i. e. they encompassed him, 11, 483; μετὰ Τυδέος υἱόν, to hasten to the son of Tydeus, 10, 516; περὶ τεύχεα, to busy oneself about the arms, 15, 555. In all these and other passages, a tmesis may be supposed. 2) Trans. with accus. to take care of, to clean, τεύχεα, 6, 321. II) Mid. ἕπομαι, imperf. εἱπόμην and Ep. ἑπόμην, fut. ἕψομαι, aor. 2 ἑσπόμην, imperat. Ep. σπεῖο, ἑσπέσθω, subj. ἕσπωμαι, optat. ἑσποίμην, infin. σπέσθαι, Od. 22, 324; ἕσπέσθαι, 5, 423; partcp. ἑσπόμενος, 12, 395. The first ε, in the subj., optat. infin., and partcp., is rejected by Becker, Thiersch, § 232, 56. Buttm. Gram. p. 280, and Spitz. Excurs. X. on Il., consider it correct and Epic, but reject the pres. ἕσπεται, Od. 4, 826; for which ἔρχεται must be read; signif. to follow. 1) Spoken of living beings: to go after, to accompany, with dat. chiefly of warriors who follow a leader, 2, 524. 675, seq., strengthened by ἅμα, 5, 551. Od. 11, 372; again, μετά τινι, 18, 234; also μετὰ κτίλον ἕσπετο, the flock followed the ram, 13, 492; again, σύν τινι. Od. 7, 304. b) Metaph. spoken of inanimate things: often of ships, Il.; of bridal presents: ὅσσα ἔοικε φίλης ἐπὶ παιδὸς ἕπεσθαι, as many as it is suitable to give with a dear daughter, Od. 1, 278. 2, 197. τρυφάλεια ἕσπετο ἅμα χειρί, the helmet followed the hand, i. e. he retained the helmet in his hand, 3, 376. ἐπάλξις ἕσπετο, the breast-work followed, i. e. fell down, 12, 398; metaph. to attach to, to be connected with, to follow, as κῦδος, τιμή, Ἄτη, 4, 415. 9, 573; ἔκ τινος, from, by means of, any man, 8, 140; to which meaning belongs h. Ven. 261. 2) to be able to follow, to come forth with, τινί, 16, 154. Od. 6, 319; metaph. spoken of the limbs and the bodily powers: γούνατα αὐτῷ ἕπεται, 4, 314; χεῖρες, Qd. 20, 237. 3) In a hostile signif. to pursue, τινί, 11, 165; ἀμφ' αὐτόν, 11, 474. 15, 257; only in Π. 4) In the imperat. equivalent to, to come. ἕπεο προτέρω, come nearer, 18, 387. Od. 5, 91.
*ἐπωλένιος, ον (ὠλένη), upon the elbows, in the arms, h. Merc. 433. 510.
ἐπώνυμος, ον (ὄνομα, ὄνυμα), deriving its name from, named after, having a sur-

Ἐπῶρτο. 163 Ἔργω.

name, from any particular occasion. Ἀλκυόνην καλέεσκον ἐπώνυμον, they named her Alcyonē with a surname (in reference to the sad fate of her mother), *i*, 562; the real name of a person containing a reference to character or fortune, Od. 7, 54. 19, 409. h. Ap. 373.

ἐπῶρτο, see ἐπόρνυμι.

ἐπώχατο, most probably 3 plur. pluperf. pass. from ἐπέχω, 12, 340.† πάσαι (πύλαι) ἐπώχατο, all the gates were closed (ἐπικεκλεισμέναι ἦσαν, Apoll. Hesych.). From ἐπέχω, perf. with change of vowel ὤχα (cf. συνόχωκα, ὀχεύς), perf. pass. ἐπωγμαι; ἐπέχειν τὰς πύλας, to shut the gates, is after the analogy of ἐπέχειν τὰ ὦτα, cf. Buţm. Gr. Gram. ἔχω; Rost, p. 308; Thiersch, § 232, 64; who however translates it: *to press*. Other explanations are *a*) 3 plur. pluperf. from ἐποίχω, with the reading ἐπώχατο, which cannot by any means signify 'to shut.' *b*) 3 plur. imperf. from ἐποίχομαι; with the reading πάσας ἐπώχατο, the Trojans ran to all, which does not accord with the connexion.

ἔραζε, adv. (ἔρα), *on the earth, to the earth*, with πίπτω and χέω, Il. and Od.

ἔραμαι, Ep. for ἐράω, depon. mid. aor. 1 ἠρασάμην, Ep. σσ, *to love, to love dearly*, with gen. frequently spoken of persons, 3, 446; of things: πολέμου, μάχης, 9, 64. 16, 208; δόρποιο, h. Cer. 129.

ἐραννός, ή, όν (ἐράω), *lovely, charming*, epith. of beautiful towns, 9, 531. Od. 7, 18.

ἔρανος, ὁ, *a meal*, to which each guest contributes his share, Od. 1, 226. 11, 415; *a pic-nic*. According to Nitzsch ad Od. 1, 226, ἔρανος, in the sense of a contribution to a common object, e. g. an entertainment, is not found in H., but it is to be taken in a general signif.: an entertainment of princes with a superior king; perhaps, *a friendly entertainment*.

ἐρατεινός, ή, όν (ἐράω), *lovely, agreeable, charming*, often spoken of countries, cities, rivers, also ἠνορέη, ὁμηλικίη, 3, 175. 6, 156; of persons, Od. 4, 13. 8, 230.

ἐρατίζω, Ep. form of ἐράω, *to desire vehemently*, with gen. χρειῶν ἐρατίζων, *11, 551. 17, 660.

ἐρατός, ή, όν (ἐράω), *beloved, lovely, agreeable*; δῶρ' Ἀφροδίτης, 3, 64.† Often in the hymns.

ἐργάζομαι, depon. mid. (ἔργον), augm. εἰργ. 1) *to work, to be active*, absol. Od. 14, 272. h Cer. 139; spoken of bellows, 18, 469. 2) Trans. *to perform, to do, to practise*, with accus. ἔργα, Od. 20, 72; ἔργα ἀεικέα, to practise shameful deeds, 24, 733; ἐναίσιμα, Od. 17, 321; also χρυσόν, to work gold, Od. 3, 435.

ἐργάθω, ἐεργάθω, poet. form of ἔργω, *to separate*. χρόα ἔργαθεν, 11, 437.† ἀπὸ δ' αὐχένος ὤμον ἐεργαθεν, 5, 147.†

*ἐργασίη, ἡ (ἐργάζομαι), *work, labour, activity*, h. Merc. 486.

*Ἐργῖνος, ὁ, son of Clymenus, king of Orchomenus, h. Ap. 297.

*ἔργμα, τό (ἘΡΓΩ), = ἔργον, *work, act, deed*, h. 27, 20. 32, 19.

ἔργον, τό (ἘΡΓΩ), 1) *work, deed, action*, often plur θέσκελα, ἀήσυλα ἔργα, ἔργα φιλοτήσια, the delights of love, Od. 11, 246; and in antithesis with μῦθος, βουλή, 9, 443. 2) *work, labour, business, occupation, trade*, limited by an adj. or subst. ἔργα γάμοιο, the works of marriage. ἔργα πολεμήϊα, works of war, 5, 428. 429. θαλάσσια ἔργα, seafaring business, 2, 614; fishing, Od. 5, 67; also spoken of animals, Od. 17, 313. Chiefly in the following special connexions: *a*) ἔργα ἀνδρῶν, works of men, i. e. agriculture, as the peculiar employment of men. Hence also ἔργον, labour in the field, Od. 14, 222; and ἔργα in the plur. *cultivated fields, estates*, 2, 751. Od. 14, 344; esply πίονα ἔργα, Od. 4, 318; and ἔργα πατρώϊα, Od. 2, 22; also ἔργα βοῶν, Od. 10, 98. *b*) ἔργα γυναικῶν, the works of women, i. e. partly the cares of housekeeping, but esply weaving, spinning, and other female labours of art, 9, 128. Od. 2, 117, cf. Od. 1, 356. *c*) In the Il. esply *the labours of war, fighting, battle, war*, 4, 470. cf. 539; also ἔργον μάχης, 6, 522. 3) the product of labour, *work*. ἔργα γυναικῶν, woven stuffs, 6, 289. ἔργα Ἡφαίστοιο, metallic products, Od. 4, 617. 4) Generally, *work, thing, matter, affair*, 1, 294; ἔργα δαιτός, 9, 228; ὅπως ἔσται τάδε ἔργα, how these things shall end, 4, 14; spoken of a great stone: μέγα ἔργον, a huge affair, 5, 303. 20, 286.

ἔργω, and mly ἐέργω, Ion. and Ep. for εἴργω, aor. 1 act. ἔρξα, perf. act. ἔεργμαι, 3 plur. Ep. ἔρχαται (without augm.), pluperf. 3 plur. ἐέρχατο and ἔρχατο, partcp. aor. pass. ἐρχθείς. The Attics distinguish between εἴργω, to exclude, and εἴργω, to include. H. has only the spirit. len. (εἴργω is found only 23, 72, ἐέργω, prop. ἐϜέργω is most common, a form of ἐέργνυμι, ἐργάθω.) Primary signif. *to separate*; according to the connexion: 1) *to include, to hem in, to confine*, with accus. ἐντὸς ἐέργειν, to include within, to limit, 2, 617. 845. 9, 404; δόμον, to shut up, Od. 7, 88; pass. with ἐν: ἐρχθέντ' ἐν ποταμῷ, confined in the river, 21, 282. Od. 10, 283. ἔνθα τε φρένες ἔρχαται, where the diaphragm is shut up, 16, 481. σάκεσσι ἔρχατο, 17, 354. γέφυραι ἐεργμέναι, confined, i. e. firmly fortified dams or dykes, 5, 89; see γέφυρα (*pontes sublicis firmati*, Heyne) 2) *to exclude, to separate, to prohibit, to remove*, 23, 72; with ἀπό: βέλος ἀπὸ χροός, 4, 130. ὅσον ἐκ νηῶν ἀπὸ πύργου τάφρος ἔεργεν, all the space from the ships onward, which the trench separated from the wall, 8, 213; cf. Spitz. [all the space from the ships to the wall and from the wall to the ditch, cf. Schol. and Heyne, ad loc.]; with the gen. alone: παιδός, 4, 131; ἀεργόμενοι

Ἔργω. 164 Ἐρείπω.

πολέμοιο, restrained from war, 13, 525. 3) Generally, *to press, to crowd,* λαὸν ἐπ' ἀριστερά, pressing the people to the left, or separating the people, i. e. touching the left side of the army, 12, 201; ἐπὶ νῆας, 16, 395; with ἐκτός, and gen., Od. 12, 219.

ἜΡΓΩ, obsol. pres. which furnishes tenses to ἔρδω or ῥέζω. q. v.

ἔρδω, poet. (ἘΡΓΩ), fut. ἔρξω, aor. ἔρξα, perf. ἔοργα, pluperf. ἐώργειν, 1) *to do, to make, to perform,* often absol., 4, 29; with accus. ἔργα, 10, 51. Od. 2, 236; with the dat. pers. τί τινι, 14, 261. Od. 14, 289; but more frequently with double accus. κακόν and κακά τινα, 3, 351. 9, 540; also εὖ ἔρξαι τινά, to benefit any man, 5, 630. 2) Esply *to offer, to sacrifice,* ἑκατόμβας, ἱερὰ θεοῖς, 2, 306 (ἔοργα and ἐώργειν are used in the signif. *to do,* cf. ῥέζω).

ἐρεβεννός, ή, όν (Ἔρεβος), *dark, gloomy,* νύξ, 5, 659; and ἀήρ, *5, 864.

Ἐρέβευσφι(ν), see Ἔρεβος.

ἐρέβινθος, ὁ, *a chick-pea,* perhaps *cicer arietinum,* Linn., 13, 589 †

Ἔρεβος, εος, τό, Ep. gen. Ἐρέβευς, Ἐρέβευσφι, *Erebus,* a gloomy place under the earth, between the upper world and the palace of Pluto, through which souls departing from the upper world pass to Pluto; *the nocturnal gloom of Hades,* but it is better to explain it, with Völcker and Nitzsch (Od. 10), the dark earth as the dwelling of the dead, and especially *the valley of death,* 8, 368. Od. 10, 528. 12, 81; Ἐρέβευσφι, 9, 572, appears corrupted from Ἐρέβεσφι, according to Thiersch, § 186, 4. Rost. Dial. 23, c.

Ἐρεβόσδε, adv. *to Erebus,* Od. 20, 356.†

ἐρείνω, poet. (ἔρομαι), *to ask, to interrogate,* with accus. pera. τινά, 6, 176; of the thing, γενεήν, 6, 145; and with double accus. τινά τι, Od. 1, 220. 4, 137; also ἀμφί τινι, after any man, Od. 24, 263. 2) *to try,* said of the lyre, h. Merc. 487. 3) *to say, to speak,* h. Merc. 313. Herm. reads ἐρέεινον for ἐρέεινεν and translates: *quum singula accurate disceptassent.* 11) Mid. as depon., Od. 17, 305. h. Merc. 313.

ἐρεθίζω (ἐρέθω), *to irritate, to provoke,* in a good signif. only: δμωάς, μητέρα, to excite to interest and curiosity, Od. 19, 45. b) Elsewhere in a bad signif. *to excite to anger, to irritate,* 1, 32; κερτομέοις, χαλεποῖς ἐπέεσσι, 5, 419. Od. 17, 395; and spoken of lions: κύνας τ' ἄνδρας τε, 17, 658.

ἐρέθω (kindred with ἔρις), poet. form of ἐρεθίζω, *to irritate, to anger,* with accus., 1, 519; and with infin., h. 7, 4, in the Od. spoken of cares: *to disquiet, to distress,* Od. 4, 813. πυκιναὶ δέ μοι ἀμφ' ἁδινὸν κῆρ ὀξεῖαι μελεδῶναι ὀδυρομένην ἐρέθουσιν, poignant cares thronging about my enveloped heart distress me grieving, Od. 19, 517 (μοί belongs to κῆρ).

ἐρείδω, aor. 1 ἔρεισα, aor. 1 mid. ἠρεισάμην, perf. pass. ἐρήρεισμαι, 3 plur.

Ion. ἐρηρέδαται, 3 sing. pluperf. ἠρήρειστο, aor. 1 pass. ἠρείσθην (augm. only in the aor. mid.). I) Act. 1) Trans. *to place firmly on, to lean upon, to fix firmly upon,* with accus. and prep. πρός, περί τι, ἐπί τινι and dat. alone. δόρυ πρὸς τεῖχος, 22, 112. Od. 8, 66; ἀσπίδ' ἐπὶ πύργῳ, 22, 97; pass. ἐπὶ μελίης ἐρεισθείς, leaned, supported upon his spear, 22, 225. ὁ δὲ θρόνοι περὶ τοῖχον ἐρηρέδατο, within were seats placed around the wall (others, fixed), Od. 7, 97. λᾶε ἀρηρέδαται δύο, 23, 329. χάλκεοι τοῖχοι ἐρηρέδατ' ἔνθα καὶ ἔνθα, brazen walls were erected on both sides, Od. 7, 86. According to Buttm. Gr. Gram. § 98, the reading ἐληλάδατ' or better ἐληλέατο, rejected by Wolf, is to be preferred, see ἐλαύνω. So also Voss: the walls extended); again: to put upon with violence, οὔδει ἐρείσθη, he was stretched upon the ground, 7, 145. 11, 144; οὔδει δέ σφιν χαῖται ἐρηρέδαται, their manes extended to the ground, 23, 284. b) *to thrust* any thing. *to press, to strike,* with the accus. since by pressure a moveable object is urged forward: ἀσπὶς ἀσπίδα ἔρειδε, κόρυς κόρυν, ἀνέρα δ' ἀνήρ, shield pressed shield, 13, 131 (said of pent-up troops); βελέεσσίν τινα, to press with missiles. 16, 108; hence pass. *to be thrust, to be pressed,* with διά: διὰ θώρηκος ἠρήρειστο ἔγχος, the spear penetrated the cuirass, 3, 358. 7, 252. 2) Intrans. *to lean upon, to press.* ἀλλήλῃσιν ἐρείδουσαι, pressing one upon another, i. e. quickly; according to Eustath. 'turning towards each other, so that one maid held the head, the other the feet of the dead,' Od. 22, 450; perhaps also intrans. βελέεσσιν, 16, 108. 11) Mid. *to support oneself upon, to lean upon,* with dat. σκήπτρῳ ἔγχει, 16, 108. II) Mid. gen. ἐρείσατο χειρὶ γαίης, with the hand upon the earth, 5, 309. 11, 355. 2) Absol. *to press, to exert oneself,* ἐρεισάμενος βάλε, 12, 457; and generally *to strive, to struggle,* 16, 736, of steeds, 23, 735. On ἐρηρέδαται, see Thiersch, § 212. 35. c. Buttm. p. 183.

ἐρείκω, aor. 2 ἤρικον, act. *to tear in pieces, to break up;* only mid. with aor. 2 intrans. *to tear, to break.* ἐρεικόμενος περὶ δουρί, spoken of the cuirass, 13, 441. ἤρικε κόρυς. *17, 295.

ἔρειο, Ep. for ἔρου, see ἔρομαι.

ἐρείομεν, Ep. for ἐρέωμεν, see ἔρέω.

ἐρείπω, poet. aor. 2 ἤριπον, perf. pass. ἐρήριμμαι, 3 sing. pluperf. ἐρέριπτο, Ep. shortened for ἐρήρ., 1) Trans. in the act. *to cast down, to demolish,* with the accus. τεῖχος, ἐπάλξεις, 12, 258. 15, 356. ἐρέριπτο τεῖχος Ἀχαιῶν, the wall of the Greeks was torn down, 14, 15. 2) Intrans. in aor. *to tumble down, to fall.* a) Mly spoken of men: ἐξ ὀχέων, ἐν κονίῃ, γνύξ; ἔστη γνὺξ ἐριπών, he sank on his knees, but still. held himself up (*sc.* *superiore parte corporis,* Damm], 5, 309. ἤριπε πρηνής, 5, 58. Od. 22, 296. b) Of trees: 16, 482. 13, 389. 21, 243.

Έρεμβοι. **Έριδαίνω.**

Έρεμβοί, οἱ, *the Erembi*, a people mentioned by H. after the Sidonians, Od. 4, 84. According to Hellanicus and most of the old Geogr. Strab. 16, p. 728, they were Troglodytæ (fr. ἔρα, *earth*, and ἐμβαίνειν), and dwelt east of Egypt, in Arabia. Others sought them in Cyprus; others still make them a branch of the Æthiopians, as Völcker Geogr. p. 89.

ἐρεμνός, ή, όν (kindred with ἔρεβος), *dark, black, gloomy,* γαῖα, Od. 24, 106. h. Merc. 427; more cly with the idea of dreadful, as αἰγίς, λαῖλαψ, νύξ, 4, 167.

ἔρεξα, see ῥέζω.

ἔρομαι, Ep. for εἴρομαι, whence imperf. ἐρέοντο, infin. ἐρέεσθαι, *to ask*.

ἐρέπτομαι, depon. mid. (kindred with ἐρείπω), *to graze, to eat, to feed upon, to browse*, always of brutes, λωτόν, κρῖ, πυρόν, 2, 776. 5, 196. 19, 553; δημόν (of a corpse), 21, 204; spoken of men who eat the uncooked fruit of the lotus, Od. 9, 97; always and only partcp.

ἐρέριπτο, see ἐρείπω.

ἐρεσίη, ἡ, see εἰρεσίη.

ἐρέσσω (akin to ἐρέθω), *to row*, always intrans., 9, 361. Od. 11, 78.

ἐρέτης, ου, ὁ (ἐρέσσω), *a rower*, only in the plur. Il. and Od.

Ἐρετμεύς, ῆος, ὁ (= ἐρέτης), a Phæacian, Od. 8, 112.

ἐρετμόν, τό (Ep. for ἐρετμός), *an oar*, εὐῆρες, in H. always as neut., Od. 11, 121. 12, 15. 23, 268; also in the plur., Od. 11, 125.

Ἐρέτρια, ἡ, see Εἰρέτρια.

ἐρεύγομαι, depon. mid. aor. 2 ἤρυγον, 1) Intrans. *to belch, to eject wind upwards from the stomach*, spoken of the Cyclops: ἐρεύγετο οἰνοβαρείων, *heavy with wine*, he belched, Od. 9, 374. b) Metaph. of the sea, *to dash up,* ἐρευγομένης ἁλός, 17, 265. κύματα ἐρεύγεται ἠπειρόνδε, the waves dashed (with a *roaring* sound) *roaring* upon the land, Od. 5, 403. 438. c) In the aor. 2, *to bellow*, spoken of an ox, only 20, 403. 404. 406. 2) Trans. with the accus. φόνον αἵματος, *to vomit forth the bloody gore*, 16, 162.

Ἐρευθαλίων, ωνος, ὁ, a noble Arcadian, who was slain by Nestor in a war of the Pylians and Arcadians, 7, 136. 4, 319 (= ἔρευθος).

ἐρεύθω, aor. ἔρευσα, *to redden, to dye or colour red;* γαῖαν αἵματα, *11, 394. 18, 329.

ἐρευνάω (kindred with ἐρέω), fut. ήσω, *to search for, to track,* spoken of dogs:

was not distinguished from Erichthonius; according to H. he was a son of *Earth*, educated by Athēnē in her temple, and, as the primitive hero of Athens, worshipt with the patron goddess of the city, 2, 547. Od. 7, 81. According to later tradition, son of Hēphæstus and *Earth* or Atthis, daughter of Cranaus, Apd. 3, 14. 6.

ἐρέχθω (kindr. with ἐρείκω), *to tear in pieces;* metaph. θυμὸν δάκρυσι καὶ στοναχῇσι, *to torture the mind with tears and sighs*, Od. 5, 83. Pass. h. Ap. 358. 2) *to hurry hither and thither*, spoken of a ship: ἐρέχθεσθαι ἀνέμοισι, *to be tossed* [*rocked*. Cp.] by the (tempestuous) winds, 23, 317.

ἐρέω, Ion. for ἐρῶ, see εἴρω, and φημί.

ἐρέω, Ep. pres. for εἴρομαι, *to ask, to seek*, whence partcp. ἐρέων, 7, 128; subj. ἐρείομεν, Ep. for ἐρέωμεν, 1, 62; optat. ἐρέοιμεν, Od. 4, 192.

ἐρῆμος, η, ον (Att. ἔρημος, ον, prob. from ΈΡΑ), *solitary, deserted*, spoken of places, 10, 520. Od. 3, 270; μῆλα, 5, 140.

ἐρηρέδαται, see ἐρείδω.

ἐρητύω (ἐρύω), aor. 1 ἐρήτῡσα, iterat. form ἐρητύσασκε, aor. 1 pass. ἐρητύθην, 3 plur. ἐρήτῡθεν, Ep. for ἐρητύθησαν, without augm. I) Act. *to restrain, to check, to repress*, with accus. φάλαγγας, λαόν, often with dat. instrum. ἀγανοῖς μειλιχίοις ἐπέεσσιν. Pass. ἐρήτυθεν καθ' ἕδρας, they were restrained (or *settled*) upon their seats, 2, 99. 211; cf. 8, 345. Od. 3, 155. b) Metaph. *to hold in check, to moderate, to restrain,* θυμόν, 1. 192. Pass. 9, 635. 462. 13, 280. II) Mid. as depon. with accus. λαόν, 15, 723 (υ long before σ when a long syllable follows, short when a short follows, cf. Spitz. Pros. § 52, 5).

ἐρι-, an inseparable particle, which, like ἀρι, is used only in composition, and strengthens the idea of the word, *very*.

ἐριαυχην, ενος, ὁ, ἡ (αὐχήν), *having a lofty neck, high-necked,* epith. of steeds, *10, 305. 11, 159.

ἐριβρεμέτης, ου, ὁ (βρέμω), *loud-thundering,* epith. of Zeus, 13, 624.†

*ἐρίβρομος, ον** (βρέμω), *loud-roaring, loud-thundering,* epith. of Dionȳsos, h. Bacch. 6, 36.

ἐρίβρυχος, ον (βρύχω), *loud-bellowing,* h. Merc. 116.

ἐριβῶλαξ, ακος, ὁ, ἡ, and **ἐρίβωλος, ον** (βῶλαξ), *having great clods* [*deep-soiled,* Cp.], an epith. of fertile regions: both

Ἐριδήσασθαι.

quarrel, with dat. and ἀντία τινός, Od. 1, 79; and μετά τινι, Od. 21, 310: primarily spoken of a contest with words, ἐπέεσσι, 2, 342. 1, 574; metaph. spoken of winds, ἀλλήλοιϊν, 16. 765. 2) *to fight, to struggle*, Od. 2, 206. ἐριδαίνομεν εἵνεκα τῆς ἀρετῆς [where τῆς is dpt on ἀρετῆς, Fäsi], we struggle on account of the virtue, viz of Penelopê, as Aristarchus rightly explains it, τῆς ταύτης ἀρετῆς, s. Nitzsch ad loc. who rejects the explanation of Thiersch, Gr. § 284, 20, ' for precedence,' and of Voss : ' to combat for the prize.' absol. *to combat. to contend*, ἐριδήσασθαι ποσσίν, in running, 23, 792.

ἐριδήσασθαι, see ἐριδαίνω.

ἐριδμαίνω (poet. form of ἐρίζω). *to irritate, to provoke*, with accus. σφῆκας, 16, 260.†

ἐρίδουπος, ον = ἐρίγδουπος.

ἐρίζω (ἔρις), aor. 1 mid. (ἐρίσσεται subj. aor. 1), 1) *to contend, to dispute, to quarrel*, τινί with any man, primarily spoken of a verbal contest, then generally of a hostile disposition, τινί, with any man, 1, 6. 6, 131. 13, 109 ; ἀντιβίην τινί, to contend face to face with any man, 1, 277; περὶ ἴσης, for justice [suo jure, Heyne], 12, 423. 2) *to combat, to contend, to vie*, τινί, with any man, 6, 131; the thing which the combat respects stands, *a*) In the accus. Ἀφροδίτη κάλλος, with Aphroditê in beauty, 9, 389. Od. 5, 213. *b*) περί τινος, as μύθων, concerning eloquence, τόξων, in archery, 15, 284. Od. 8, 225. *c*) In the dat. ποσί, δρηστοσύνῃ, 13. 325. Od. 15, 321. *d*) With infin. χερσὶ μαχήσασθαι, Od. 18, 38; absol. Νέστωρ οἷος ἔριζεν (sc. αὐτῷ), vied with him, 2, 555, Wolf. II) Mid. *to contend*, with double dat. with any man, about any thing, 5, 172. ἀνδρῶν κέν τίς μοι ἐρίσσεται (for ἐρίσηται) κτήμασιν, no one of men would vie with me in possessions, Od. 4, 80.

ἐρίηρες, οἱ, see ἐρίηρος.

ἐρίηρος, ον (ἄρω), plur., by metaplasm, ἐρίηρες, prop. very suitable, hence: *a*) (*greatly*) *attached, faithful, intimate, dear*, ἑταῖροι, 3, 47. Od. 9, 100. *b*) *pleasing, agreeable*, who pleases all, ἀοιδός, Od. 1, 346.

ἐριθηλής, ές (θάλλω), *very verdant, blooming, beautiful, luxuriant*, epith. of cultivated fields and trees, *5, 90. 10, 467. 17, 53.

ἔριθος, ὁ, ἡ *labourer, a hired reaper*, 18, 550. 560. 2) *a servant, a companion*, hence τλήμων γαστρὸς ἔριθος = crepitus ventris, h. Merc. 296.

ἐρικυδής, ές (κῦδος), *very distinguished, famous, glorious*; δῶρα θεῶν, 3, 65 : ἥβη, 11, 225 ; and often δαίς, 24, 802. Od. 3, 66.

ἐρίμυκος, ον (μυκάομαι), *loud bellowing*, epith. of cattle, 20, 497. Od. 15, 235.

ἐρινεός, ὁ, *the wild fig-tree, caprificus*, Od. 12, 103. 2) In the Il. it is also a proper name of a particular region near Troy; *the fig-hill*, according to Voss. Strabo, XIII. p. 597, calls it a strong place planted with fig-trees, from which the city was most accessible to the enemy, 6, 433. ἐρινεὸς ἠνεμόεις, here was the watch-tower, 22, 145.

Ἐρινύς, and Ἐρινύς, ὑος, ἡ, plur. αἱ Ἐρινύες, contr. Ἐρινῦς. 9.484; *the Erinnyes*, goddesses of vengeance (the Furies of the Romans), H. does not mention their number, form or names, the sing. stands 9, 571. 19, 87; mly plur., 9, 454, seq. They are the symbol of the scourging of a guilty conscience which follows every act of impiety, and especially of the curse which rests upon any wretch who violates the most sacred duties of humanity. They punish therefore the disobedience of children to parents, 9. 454. Od. 2, 135. 11, 280; violated duties towards parents, kindred, and suppliants, 15, 204. Od. 17, 475; perjury, 19, 260; and every slaughter, 9, 571. Since they punish the impious man here in life, they show themselves hostile to men, and prompt them also to wicked actions, 19, 87. Od. 15, 231. Thus in character they approach the Fates, and as goddesses of fate they do not permit men to learn too much of their future destiny, 19, 418. They dwell in Erebus, Od. 15, 234. Il. 9, 571; and they punish transgressors even after death, 19, 270. According to Hes. Th. 185. *Earth* (Gaia) bore them from drops of the blood of Uranus, and Apd. 1, 1. 3, mentions as their names : *Tisiphonê, Megaera*, and *Alectô*. 2) As appell. curses: τῆς μητρός, 21, 412 (ῡ in the nom. In the derived cases ῠ. Ἐρινύς prob derived from an Arcad. word ἐρινύω, to be angry, Paus. 8, 25. 4 ; or from ἐρίνω. ἐρεννάω, to track, hence the correct orthography is Ἐριννύς, adopted by Spitz.].

ἔριον, τό, Ion. and Ep. εἴριον (dim. from εἶρος), *wool*, often in the plur. τὰ εἴρια, 3, 388; ἔριον only Od. 4, 124.

ἐριούνης, ου, and ἐριούνιος, ὁ, *that brings prosperity*, according to Schol. from ἐρι and ὀνίνημι, *very useful*, epith. of Hermês, 20, 72; ἐριούνης only 20, 34 Od. 8. 322. 2) As pr. n. for Hermês, 24, 360. 440.

ἔρις, ἴδος, ἡ, accus. ἔριν and ἔριδα (the last most common ; ἔριν only in the Od.), 1) *contention, strife, discord*; μάχεσθαι, to contend in strife, i. e. with words, 1, 8 (so Wolf rightly), cf. 7, 210. 20, 66; in like manner ἔριδι ξυνελαύνειν, to bring into strife, 20, 134. ἔριν στῆσαι ἔν τιν, Od. 16, 292; particularly in the Il. spoken of war : *contest, battle*, 3, 7. 5, 732. ἔριδα ξυνάγειν Ἄρηος, 5, 861. ἔριδα προβάλλειν, 11, 529. 2) *combat, emulation, rivalry*; hence ἐξ ἔριδος, from rivalry, 7, 111. Od. 4. 343. ἔρις ἔργοιο, emulation in a work, Od. 18, 366. ἔριδα προφέρειν, to show rivalry, Od. 6, 92. ἔριδα προφέρεσθαι τινι ἄθλων, to propose a combat to any man, Od 8, 210.

Ἔρις, ιδος, ἡ, *Eris*, as a goddess, the author of fighting and contention, 4, 441; sister and wife of Arês, 5, 518. 20, 48.

Ἐρισθενής.

Accord. to Hes. Th. 223, she is the daughter of Night. She is mentioned 11, 3. 4. 18, 535. Later, the goddess of strife and discord.

ἐρισθενής, ές (σθένος), *very strong, all-powerful*, epith. of Zeus, 13, 54. Od. 8, 289.

ἔρισμα, ατος, τό (ἐρίζω), *the occasion of contention, the apple of discord, contention*, 4, 38.†

ἐρισταφυλος, ον (σταφυλή), *of large grapes*, οἶνος [*the vinous grape, large-cluster'd*. Cp.], *Od. 9, 111. 358.

*ἐρισφάραγος, ον (σφαραγέω), i. q. ἐρισμάραγος; *loud-sounding, loud-thundering*, epith. of Poseidôn, h. Merc. 187.

ἐρίτιμος, ον (τιμή), *highly-prized, precious, splendid, highly-honoured*, epith. of the ægis, 2, 447; and of gold, *9, 126.

ἔριφος, ὁ, ἡ, *a kid*, Il. and Od.

Ἐριφύλη, ἡ, daughter of Talaus and Lysimachê, wife of Amphiaräus. She suffered herself to be bribed by Polynices with the necklace of Harmonia, and persuaded her husband to take part in the expedition against Thebes, although as a prophet he foresaw his death. According to the direction of the father, her son Alcmæon put her to death, Od. 11, 326.

Ἐριχθόνιος, ὁ, son of Dardanus and Batia, father of Tros, distinguished for his wealth, as three thousand mares fed in his pastures, 20, 219, seq.

Ἐριῶπις, ιδος, ἡ, wife of Oïleus, 13, 697.

*ἑλίκωπις, ιδος, ἡ (ὤψ), *large-eyed*, Ep. 1, 2.

ἑρκεῖος, ον, Att. ἕρκειος, prop belonging to the court (ἕρκος), hence Ἑρκεῖος, ὁ, *house-protecting*, an epith. of Zeus, because as a tutelary deity he commonly had his altar in the front court, Od. 22, 335.†

ἑρκίον, τό (dimin. from ἕρκος), *an enclosure, a hedge, a wall*, αὐλῆς, 9, 476. Od. 18, 102.

ἕρκος, εος, τό (εἴργω), 1) *an enclosure, a hedge, a fence*, for the protection of fields and gardens, 5, 90; and especially about the court of the dwelling, Od. 21, 238; hence *the court, the front court*, Od. 2) *a cage, a net, a trap* to take birds; perhaps *a fowling-floor*, Od. 22, 489. 3) Metaph. *a protection, a defence*, spoken of the girdle and the shield: ἕρκος ἀκόντων, against javelins, 4, 137. 15, 645; βελέων, 5, 316; spoken even of

Ἑρμιόνη.

larity to a palisade, see Nitzsch ad Od. 1, 64.

ἕρμα, ατος, τό, I) (From the root ἔρδω, ἐρέδω, ἐρείδω), any thing which contributes to the support or strengthening of a body, *a prop, a stay, a post;* esply the shores upon which ships, when drawn out upon the land, rested, to prevent their rotting; later φάλαγγες, 1, 486. 2, 154; metaph. spoken *a*) Of men: ἕρμα πόληος, the support, the pillar of the city, 16, 549. Od. 23, 121; and *b*) Spoken of a pointed arrow: μελαινέων ἕρμ᾽ ὀδυνάων, the prop [or, as the *substratum*] of black pangs, upon which the pangs, as it were, rested, 4, 117 (Voss, 'the fountain of dark tortures;' Aristarchus rejects the verse).

II) (From εἴρω, to place in a row), only in the plur. ἕρματα, τά, every thing strung in a row, *an ear-ring, a pendant*, 14, 182. Od. 18, 297 (ἀνώτια, Schol.), cf. Buttm. Lex.

Ἑρμαῖος, η, ον, consecrated to Hermès; hence ὁ Ἑρμαῖος λόφος, *the hill of Hermês*, in Ithaca, behind the city, on the mountain Neïon, Od. 16, 471.

Ἑρμῆς, Ep. Ἑρμείας, ὁ, gen. Ἑρμείαο, Ἑρμείω, 15, 214; and Ἑρμέω, h. Merc. 413; dat. Ἑρμῇ, Ep. Ἑρμείᾳ, Ἑρμέῃ (ed. Spitz. Ἑρμέᾳ), 5, 390, and Ἑρμείῃ, h. 18, 36; accus. Ἑρμῆν, Ep. Ἑρμείαν, voc. Ἑρμῆ, Ep. Ἑρμεία, Hermês (*Mercurius*), son of Zeus and Maia, according to Od. 8, 335. 14, 435. He is a messenger of the gods, together with Iris, supporting, however, more the character of a protector and mediator, 24, 334. Od. 5, 28; hence διάκτορος. As ensigns, he bore the golden-winged shoes, Od. 5, 45, and the magic rod, the *caduceus*, with which he closed in sleep the eyes of men and opened them again, v. 47; whence χρυσόρραπις. He is the bestower of blessings, of prosperity, and of wealth acquired by traffic, whence ἐριούνιος, ἀκάκητα, σῶκος, 14, 491. Od. 15, 319. On account of his wisdom and cunning he is called εὔσκοπος, and he protects wise and crafty men, Od. 19, 397. He is mentioned in Od. 24, 1, as guide of departed souls into the under world. In the Hom. hymn an account is given of his birth, the invention of the seven-stringed lyre, and his first theft of cattle. (Signif. according to Damm, from εἴρω, to speak, for ἐρέας, one who communicates; more correctly, from εἴρω, perf.

'Ερμῆς. 168 Ἐρύκω.

that there was an entrance from here to the infernal world, 2, 560. Έρμιών, όνος, ἡ, Scyl. Polyb.

ἑρμίς or ἑρμίν, ἰνος, ὁ (ἕρμα), a support; eaply a bed-post, foot of the bedstead, *Od. 8, 278. 23, 198.

Ἕρμος, ὁ, Hermus, a river in Æolis (Asia), which rises in Phrygia, flows by Smyrna, and empties itself into the gulf of Smyrna between Temnos and Leuca; now Sarabad, 20, 392.

ἔρνος, εος, τό, a young scion, a shoot, a sprout, spoken of young trees which had run up to some height, 17, 53. Od. 6, 163; as a simile of Achilles, ἀνέδραμεν ἔρνεϊ ἴσος, 18, 56; Spoken of Telemachus, Od. 14, 175.

ἔρξω, see ἔρδω.

*ἐρόεις, εσσα, εν (ἔρος), lovely, amiable, h. Ven. 264. h. Merc. 31.

ΕΡΟΜΑΙ, Ep. form εἴρομαι, ἐρέομαι and ἐρέω; H. has only of the aor. ἠρόμην, subj. ἐρώμεθα, optat. ἔροιτο, and the infin. as pres. accented ἐρέσθαι (Att. ἐρέσθαι), to ask, τινά or τί, also with double accus., Od. 3, 243; and τινὰ περί τινος, any man concerning any man, Od. 1, 135. 405; ἀμφί τι, Od. 11, 572; ἀμφί τινι, Od. 19, 95.

ἔρος, ὁ, Ep. for ἔρως, q. v.

ἑρπετόν, τό (ἕρπω), in the Ep. language not merely that which creeps, but every thing which goes on feet, generally, a beast. ὅσσ' ἐπὶ γαῖαν ἑρπετὰ γίγνονται (Voss, 'every thing that lives and moves on the earth'), Od. 4, 418;† later, a creeping thing, a snake.

ἑρπύζω (from ἕρπω), to creep, to crawl, to move with difficulty, spoken of men who from trouble or great age crawl along, Od. 1, 193. 13, 220. 11. 23, 225.

ἕρπω, to creep, to crawl. εἷρπον ῥινοί, the skins crawled, spoken of a prodigy, Od. 12, 395; elsewhere, to creep about imperceptibly, Od. 17, 158. 2) Generally to go, to walk, to move, 17, 447. Od. 18, 131. h. Cer. 366.

ἐρράδαται, see ῥαίνω.

ἔρριγα, see ῥιγέω.

ἔρρω (kindred with ῥέω), fut. ἐρρήσω, h. Merc. 259. 1) to walk painfully, to walk unsteadily, to halt, spoken of the gait of Hephæstus, 18, 421. 2) to go about sad or wretched, to wander around, Od. 4, 367. h. Merc. 259; eaply to go or come to misfortune or injury, 8, 239. 9, 364. b) Often, to go to one's ruin, 9, 377; eaply in the imperat. an expression of disgust: ἔρρε, go to ruin, away with thee, begone, 8, 164. Od. 10, 72. ἔρρετε, 24, 239.

ἔρση, ἡ, Ep. always ἐέρση (prob. fr. ἄρδω), dew, 23, 598. Od. 13, 245; plur. ἐέρσαι αἵματι μυδαλέαι, dew-drops, impregnated with blood, 11, 53. These bloody dew-drops, which were regarded as a token of divine anger, proceed from certain butterflies, which after emerging from the chrysalis state emit a bloody fluid, which appears, often in considerable quantities, upon leaves, plants, and fences, see Wilms. Naturgesch. 2. p. 646. 2) ἔρσαι, Od. 9, 222, new-born lambs.

ἐρσήεις, εσσα, εν, Ep. ἐερσήεις, dewy, covered with dew. ἐρσήεις λωτός, 14, 348. b) Metaph. of a corpse: fresh, i. e. uncorrupted. ἐερσήεις κεῖται, 24, 419. ἐρσήεις, v. 757.

Ἐρύαλος, ὁ, a Trojan, slain by Patroclus, 16, 411. (Heyne from the Cdd. has Ἐρύλαος (from ἐρύω and λαός, deliverer of the people), with whom agree Spitz. and Buttm. Lex. p. 286, since the long α in Ἐρύαλος contravenes analogy).

ἐρύγμηλος, η, ον (ἐρυγεῖν), loud-bellowing, epith. of an ox, 18, 580.†

ἐρυγών, see ἐρεύγομαι.

ἐρυθαίνω, poet. for ἐρυθραίνω, to redden; only mid. to make oneself red, to blush, *10, 484. 21, 21.

Ἐρυθαῖνοι, οἱ (ὑψηλοί), a town in Paphlagonia, according to Eustath.; or, more correctly, with Strab., XII. p. 545, two hills on the sea, which in his time, from the red colour of the soil, were called Ἐρυθῖνοι, 2, 855.

Ἐρύθραι, αἱ, an old town of Bœotia, on Cithæron, in the region of Platæa, on the south bank of the Asôpus, 2, 499. According to Eustath. the Bœotian town should be written βαρυτόνως and the Ionian ὀξυτόνως; more correctly, however, should both be written βαρυτόνως. to distinguish them from the adj. ἐρυθρός; at present, we find Ἐρυθραί in Hdt., Thuc. etc.

ἐρυθρός, ή, όν, red, prop. dark-red, οἶνος, Od; νέκταρ, 19, 38; generally red, ruddy, χαλκός, 9, 365.

ἐρυκακέειν, ἐρύκακον, see ἐρύκω.

ἐρυκανάω, poet. form for ἐρύκω, to hold back. κεῖνον ἐρυκανόωσι, Od. 1, 199.†

ἐρυκάνω, poet. form for ἐρύκω, Od. 10, 429.†

ἐρύκω (poet. forms ἐρυκάνω, ἐρυκανάω), fut. ἐρύξω, aor. 1 ἔρυξα, aor. 2 ἠρύκακον, 5, 321. 20, 458: and ἐρύκακον, infin. ἐρυκακέειν, I) Act. to hold back, 1) to hold, to restrain, ἐνὶ μεγάροισι γυναῖκας, Od. 19, 16; eaply spoken of guests, τινά, 6, 217. Od. 1, 14; to hold fast, πότνος πολλοὺς ἐρύκει, 21, 39; γῆ, 21, 62. 2) to check, to hold in, to restrain, ἵππους, λαόν, 6, 80 (from flight); metaph. μένος, to check one's force, 8, 178; θυμόν, to restrain one's mind, i. e. will, Od. 11. 105. ἕτερός με θυμὸς ἐρύκει, another thought checks me, Od. 9, 302. 3) to hold back, to keep off, to repel; without case 11, 352; τινά τινος, e. g. μάχης, from battle, 18, 126; also τινί τι, like ἀλαλκεῖν; κακόν τινι, to avert evil from any man, 15, 450; λιμόν τινι, Od. 5, 166. 4) to hold back, i. e. to hold apart, to separate. ὀλίγος δ' ἔτι χῶρος ἐρύκει, 10, 161. II) to hold oneself back, to delay, Od. 4, 373. 17, 17. μή μοι ἐρύκεσθον, delay not, 23, 443. b) With accus. to delay any man, 12, 285.

Ἐρύλαος.

Ἐρύλᾱος, ὁ, a Trojan, 16, 411. ed. Spitz.; cf. Ἐρύαλος.

ἔρυμα, τό (ἐρύομαι), *protection, defence, covering,* χροός, spoken of the μίτρη, 4, 137.†

Ἐρύμανθος, ὁ, a mountain in Arcadia, on the borders of Elis, where Heracles slew the Erymanthian boar; now Χίρια, Od. 6, 103.

Ἐρύμας, αντος, ὁ, 1) a Trojan, slain by Idomeneus, 16, 345. 2) a Trojan, slain by Patroclus, 16, 415 (the protector).

ἐρυσάρματος, ον (ἅρμα), *chariot-drawing*, epith. of horses, 15, 354. 16, 370; only in the metaplastic plur. ἐρυσάρματες, ἐρυσάρματας.

ἐρυσίπτολις, ι (πόλις), *delivering the city, protecting the city,* as epith. of Athēnē, 6, 305.† h. 10, 1.

*ἐρυσμός, ὁ (a form of ἔρυμα), a protection, h. Cer. 230.

ἐρύω and εἰρύω, Ion. and poet. fut. act. ἐρύσω (Ep. σσ) and ἐρύω (with σ elided); whence 3 plur. ἐρύσουσι, 11, 454. 15, 351; aor. 1 act. ἔρυσα (Ep. σσ) and εἴρυσα, perf. pass. εἴρυμαι, whence 3 plur. εἴρυαται, 14, 75; pluperf. 3 plur. εἴρυατο, 15, 654; mid. fut. ἐρύσομαι, Ep. ἐρύομαι, aor. 1 mid. ἐρυσάμην (Ep. σσ) and εἰρυσάμην, pluperf. εἴρυτο, he had drawn, Od. 22, 90. H. also uses 1) From the form ΕΙΡΥΜΙ the mid. εἴρυμαι, ἔρυμαι, in the signif. *to deliver, to protect,* in single forms: 3 plur. pres. εἰρύαται for εἴρυνται, 1, 239; εἰρύαται, Od. 16, 463; imperf. εἴρυντο, 12, 454. 2) The forms with ῡ in the pres. and imperf. infin. ἔρυσθαι, εἴρυσθαι, ἔρῡτο, εἴρῡτο, and εἴρῡτο, are to be regarded as contracted forms from ἐρύομαι; εἰρύαται is long by the arsis, as ἐρύετο, 6, 403. In the signif. of the aor. stands ἔρῡτο, 5, 23. 538: cf. Rost's Gram. p. 302. Kühner, § 235 (ἐρύω has always ῠ short; only in the contr. imperf. ῡ). (The form ἐρύομαι always signifies *to deliver.*) 1) Act. 1) *to draw,* more closely defired by prepos. or adv. with accus. πάλιν ἐρύειν τινά, to draw a man back, 5, 836; ὀϊστὸν ἐξ ὤμοιο, 5, 110; νευρὴν ἐπί τινι, to draw the string (of the bow) against any man, 15, 464; esply νῆα εἰς ἅλα, 1, 141; on the other hand, ἠπειρόνδε, Od. 10, 403; ἐπ' ἠπείροιο, the ship upon land (to guard it against rotting), Od. 16, 359; pass. νῆες εἰρύαται ἐπὶ θινί, the ships are drawn up on the sea-shore, 4, 248. 14, 75. ὁδὸν εἰρύαται, according to the Schol. are drawn up upon the way, Od. 6, 265; cf. below, 3 *b.* 2) *to draw* with violence, hence *a) to snatch, to tear away,* ἔγχος ἐκ χειρός, 13, 598; ῥινὸν ἀπ' ὀστεόφιν, Od. 14, 134; κρόσσας πύργων, 12, 258; προκρόσσας, 14, 35; esply νεκρὸν ἐρύειν, sometimes, to snatch away the dead body, spoken of the friends of the slain, to save it from abuse, 5, 573. 17, 581; sometimes spoken of enemies, to tear away the dead body, to plunder or insult it, 17, 230. 419. 18, 450. *b) to draw, to drag,* τινὰ ποδός, Od. 17, 479; περὶ σῆμα, 24, 16; hence spoken of dogs: τινὰ πρὸ ἄστεος, any man before the city, 11, 454. 15, 351. II) Mid. 1) *to draw, to draw off, to draw out,* always with reference to the subject, *to oneself, after* or *for oneself;* μάχαιραν, to draw one's knife, 3, 271; φάσγανον, ξίφος; δόρυ ἐξ ὠτειλῆς, 21, 200; τόξον, to stretch the bow, in order to shoot, Od. 21, 125; νῆας, 14, 79. Od. 9, 194. ἐρύσαντό τε πάντα, they drew all off (from the ships, in order to eat), 1, 466, etc. 2) *to draw to oneself,* with violence; τινὰ μάχης, to snatch any man out of the battle, 5, 456; νεκρόν τιν, the dead, like the act., 17, 104. 18, 152. 14, 422. 18, 174; hence 3) *to snatch away,* viz. from danger, *to deliver, to rescue,* τινά, spoken of Apollo, who rescued Æneas from the enemy, 5, 344. 11, 363. Od. 22, 372. χρυσῷ ἐρύσασθαί τινα, to free for gold, to ransom, 22, 351 (the signif. of the Schol. 'to weigh,' is not necessary), hence, in general, *a) to deliver, to shelter, to protect,* ἔρυτο, 4, 186. ἔρυετο Ἴλιον, 6, 403. Λυκίην εἴρυτο, 16, 542. πύλας εἴρυντο, 12, 454. *b) to ward off, to restrain, to repel, to obstruct;* Κῆρα, 2, 859. ἣ (μίτρη) οἱ πλεῖστον ἔρυτο, which most effectually kept off from him (the spear), 4, 138. 5, 538. ὁδὸν εἰρύαται, they obstruct the way, Voss, Od. 6, 265. Metaph. Διὸς νόον, to restrain the will of Zeus, 8, 143; χόλον, to check anger, 24, 584. *c)* to draw any thing to oneself for preservation, protection, etc. *to guard, to keep, to protect,* to watch, θύρας, Od. 23, 229; ἄκοιτιν, Od. 3, 268. ἔτι μ' αὖτ' εἰρύαται, they watch me still (Telemachus, of the suitors), Od. 16, 463; metaph. φρεσὶν ἐρύεσθαί τι, to keep any thing in the heart, Od. 16, 459; to spy out, to explore, δήνεα θεῶν, Od. 23, 82. οἵτε θέμιστας πρὸς Διὸς εἰρύαται, who guard the laws from Zeus [i. e. received from Zeus, or with authority derived from Zeus], 1, 239. *d) to observe, to follow,* ἔπος, βουλάς, 1, 216. 21, 230.

ἔρχαται, ἔρχατο, see ἔργω.

ἐρχατάω, poet. form from εἴργω, *to enclose, to hem in;* only in the pass. σύες ἐρχατόωντο. Od. 14, 15.†

ἐρχθείς, see ἔργω.

ἔρχομαι, depon. defect. fut. ἐλεύσομαι, aor. ἦλθον, Ep. ἤλυθον, infin. ἐλθεῖν, Ep. ἐλθέμεναι, perf. Ep. εἰλήλουθα, 1 plur. εἰλήλουθμεν, 9, 49; partcp. εἰληλουθώς, ἐληλουθώς, 15, 81.† 1) *to come, to go,* and according to the context and the connected prep. and adv. *to arrive, to go away, to come back,* αὖτις, ἄψ, πάλιν ἐλθεῖν, 1, 425. *a)* Spoken of animate beings: of men and brutes; metaph. also of other motion: by ship, 13, 172. ἐπὶ πόντον ἔρχεσθαι, to go upon the sea, Od. 2, 265; to voyage, of ships, Od. 14, 334; hence, on the other hand, πεζὸς ἦλθε, he came on foot, by land, 5, 204. 17, 613; spoken of the flight of birds and bees, 2, 88. *b)* Spoken of inanimate

I

ἐρῷ. 170 **Ἔσθω.**

things: of the dead, 17, 161; of natural phenomena, 9, 6. 4, 276; of the change of time: ἦλθε κνέφας, φάος ἦλθε, 8, 500. 17, 615; θέρος, Od. 11, 192; of other objects: γέρας ἔρχεται ἄλλῃ, the reward goes elsewhere, 1, 120; esply of missiles, 7, 261; διὰ ἀσπίδος, 3, 357; metaph. of the state of the body and soul: κακὸν ἦλθε, θάνατος, 15, 450. Od. 13, 60; τὸν δ᾿ αἶψα περὶ φρένας ἤλυθ᾿ ἰωή, the voice reached his sense or intellect; made itself audible, 10, 139; ὀδύνη διὰ χροὸς ἦλθε, 11, 398; ἄχος ἀπὸ πραπίδων ἦλθε, 22, 43. 2) It is construed a) With the accus. of the place whither: κλισίην, in to the tent, 1, 322; εἰς κλισίην. b) With accus. of nearer specification: ὁδὸν ἐλθεῖν, to go a way, a journey, Od, 3, 316; and spoken of those who lie in ambuscade, 1, 151; according to some, "to go on a (military) expedition" (so Nkg.); αὐτὰ κέλευθα, to go the same ways, 12, 225. cf. Od. 9, 262; ἀγγελίην ἐλθεῖν, to go on an embassy, 11, 140; see ἀγγελίη. ἐξεσίην, 24, 235. c) With gen. of place: πεδίοιο, to go through the plain, 2, 801. d) With partcp. a) Fut. which indicates the purpose: ἔρχομαι ἔγχος οἰσόμενος, I go to bring the spear, 13, 256. β) With pres. partcp. or perf. which expresses the manner of coming: ἦλθε θέουσα, she came running, 11, 715; ἦλθε φθάμενος, 23, 779. αἱ κεν νέκυς ῃσχυμμένος ἔλθῃ, if the corpse come back disfigured, 18, 180. γ) The partcp. ἐλθών seems to be often used pleonastically, although it serves more completely to present the action: οὐ δύναμαι— μάχεσθαι ἐλθὼν δυσμενέεσσιν, I cannot go and fight with the enemy, 16, 521.

ἐρῷ, for ἔρωτι, see ἔρως.

ἐρῶ, Ep. ἐρέω, see εἴρω.

ἐρωδιός, ὁ, the common heron, ardea major, Linn., which builds its nest in marshes and sea-rushes. Köppen incorrectly supposes it to be the bittern, ardea stellaris, 10, 274.† It appears on the right (δεξιός), as ominous of good, and according to the Schol. was, especially for those who desired to execute some stratagem, a fortunate sign. Odysseus (Ulysses) and Diomêdês on their nocturnal visit as spies to the Trojan camp, could not see it, but only heard it, hence they concluded the enemy could not see themselves.

ἐρωέω (root ῥέω), fut. ἐρωήσω, aor. ἠρώησα, 1) to flow, to stream, to gush out. αἷμα περὶ δουρὶ ἐρωήσει, 1, 303. Od. 16, 441; metaph. of any violent motion, hence: 2) to leap, to run, ai (the steeds) δ᾿ ἠρώησαν ὀπίσσω, they ran back, 23, 433. 3) to hasten back, to cease, with gen. πολέμοιο, χάρμης, to cease from battle, 13, 776. 14, 101. 17, 422, h. Cer. 302; also absol. to retire, to withdraw. νέφος οὔποτ᾿ ἐρωεῖ, the cloud never retires, Od. 12, 75; to loiter, to tarry, 2, 179. 3) Once trans. to cause to retire, to repulse, τινὰ ἀπὸ νηῶν, 13, 57.

ἐρωή, ἡ, 1) any vehement motion, impulse, impetus, force, rushing, esply spoken of missiles: βελέων ἐρωή, the invasion [the dint, Cp.] of weapons, 4, 542. 17, 562; δούρατος, 11, 357; ὅσον τ᾿ ἐπὶ δουρὸς ἐρωὴ γίνεται, as far as the cast of a spear extends, 15, 358. λείπετο δουρὸς ἐρωήν, a spear's cast off, 23, 529. b) Metaph. of men: ὀφέλλει ἀνδρὸς ἐρωήν, the axe augments the power of the man, 3, 62; λιμυντῆρος, 13, 590. cf. 14, 488. 2) retreat, cessation, rest, πολέμων. *16, 302. 17, 761.

ἔρως, ωτος, ὁ, poet. ἔρος. Of the poet. form H. has ἔρος, ἔρῳ (more correctly ἔρω), Od. 18, 212; accus. ἔρον. The nom. ἔρως stands only in two passages, where position occurs, 3, 442. 14, 94; gen. ἔρωτος, Batr. 78; accus. ἔρωτα, h. Merc. 449; love, θεᾶς, to a goddess, 14, 315. Od. 18, 212; and generally, desire, longing, appetite, πόσιος καὶ ἐδητύος, 9, 92; γόου, 24, 227.

ἐρωτάω, Ion. and Ep. εἰρωτάω, to ask; hence imperf. ἠρώτα, Od. 15, 423.†

ἐς, Ep. and Ion. for εἰς, q. v. Also for the compounds beginning with ἐς, see under εἰς.

ἐσαγείρατο, see εἰσαγείρω.

ἐσάγω, ἐσαθρέω, see εἰσάγω, etc.

ἐσᾶλτο, see εἰσάλλομαι.

ἐσάντα, see εἰσάντα.

ἔσβη, see σβέννυμι.

ἐσδύσεαι, see εἰσδύω.

ἐσέδρακον, see εἰσδέρκομαι.

ἐσελεύσομαι, see εἰσέρχομαι.

ἐσεμάσσατο, see εἰσμαίομαι.

ἐσένυντο, see εἰσνέω.

ἐσήλατο, see εἰσάλλομαι.

ἔσθην, see ἕννυμι.

ἐσθής, ῆτος, ἡ (ἕννυμι), a garment, a robe, a dress, Od. 1, 165; mly collect. clothing. 2) cloth, carpeting, used for a bed, Od. 23, 290 (with digamma: vestis).

ἐσθίω, Ep. ἔσθω and ἔδω, only in the pres. and infin. ἤσθιε, ἤσθε, to eat, to consume, with accus. metaph. πάντας τὴν ἐσθίει (devours them all), 23, 182. οἶκος ἐσθίεται, the house, i. e. the property is being consumed, Od. 4, 318.

ἐσθλός, ή, όν, like ἀγαθός, good, valourous, brave, noble, excellent in its kind: a) Spoken of men and of every thing which concerns them: θηρητήρ, an excellent hunter, 5, 51; ἔν τινι, 15, 283. Esply in Il. a) Spoken of excellence in war, brave, in opposition to κακός, 2, 366. 5, 469. β) noble, of good descent, Od. 3, 553. b) Of things: φάρμακα, healing medicines, Od. 4, 228; τεύχεα, κτήματα, etc. c) good, favorable, propitious, ὄρνιθες, Od. 24, 311. 2) As subst. οἱ ἐσθλοί, the noble, the distinguished, often τὸ ἐσθλόν, good fortune, prosperity, in opposition to κακόν, 24, 530; τὰ ἐσθλά, prosperity, Od. 20, 56; possessions, valuables, Od. 10, 523.

ἔσθος, εος, τό (poet. for ἐσθής), a garment, cloth, 24, 94.

ἔσθω, poet form from ἐσθίω, to eat, to consume, mly of men, Od. 9, 479;

Ἐσιδεῖν. 171 Ἐτεόκρητες.

brutes, Od. 13, 409; metaph. κειμήλια, Od. 2, 73.
ἐσιδεῖν, see εἰσείδον.
ἐσιέμεναι, see εἴσίημι.
ἐσίζηται, see εἰσίζομαι.
ἔσκον, see εἰμί.
ἐσόψομαι, see εἰσοράω.
ἑσπέριος, η, ον (ἕσπερος), 1) Spoken of the time of day: *belonging to the evening, at evening,* Od. 2, 357; ἑσπέριος ἀνονεούμην, 21, 560. 2) Of a point of the compass: *western, belonging to the west,* ἑσπέριοι ἄνθρωποι, Od. 8, 29.
ἕσπερος, ὁ, plur. τὰ ἕσπερα, Od. 17, 191; the evening hours, *vesper, the evening,* Od. 1, 423. 4, 786. 2) Adj. *belonging to evening,* h. 18, 14; ἐσπλῃ ὁ ἕσπερος ἀστήρ, the evening star, 22, 318 (with digamma).
ἔσπετε, Ep. imperat. for εἴπατε, a poet. form with epenthetic σ, four times in the Iliad, only in the constr. ἔσπετε νῦν μοι Μοῦσαι, see εἶπον.
ἑσπόμην, see ἕπομαι.
ἕσσα, ἕσσαι, ἑσσάμενος, see ἕννυμι.
ἑσσεῖται, see εἰμί.
ἑσσύοντο, see σεύω.
ἐσσί, see εἰμί.
ἕσσο, see ἕννυμι.
ἕσσυμαι, see σεύω.
ἑσσύμενος, prop. partcp. perf. pass. from σεύω, as adj. *hasty, rapid, precipitate,* from which adv. ἐσσυμένως, *hastily, quickly, rapidly,* 3, 85; and Od. see σεύω.
ἑστάμεν, ἑστάμεναι, see ἵστημι.
ἕσταμεν, see ἵστημι.
ἕσταν, see ἵστημι.
ἕστασαν, 3 plur. pluperf., but ἕστασαν for ἕστησαν, see ἵστημι.
ἕστηκα, ἑστήκειν, see ἵστημι.
ἕστο, see ἕννυμι.
ἕστρωτο, see στρώννυμι.
ἕστωρ, ορος, ὁ, *the shaft-pin,* the pin or nail at the end of the pole, over which a ring (κρίκος) was put. Through this ring the yoke-straps were made fast, 24, 272.1 (Prob. from ἵημι, ἀπὸ τοῦ ἔσωσαι.)
ἐσχάρη, ἡ, Ep. ἐσχαρόφιν for ἐσχάρης, ἐσχάρῃ, Od. 5, 59. 7, 169; 1) *the hearth, the house-hearth* (a *fire-place* on the earth), primarily for affording warmth; hence Penelope worked by it with her maidens, Od. 6, 305. b) the place for sacrificing, Od. 14, 420; hence supplicants sought refuge in it, hence: καθέζετο ἐπ' ἐσχάρῃ ἐν κονίῃσι πὰρ πυρί, he seated himself on the hearth in the dust by the fire, Od. 7, 153; cf. v. 169. Dat. ἐπ' ἐσχαρόφιν, Od. 19, 389. 2) any *fire-place.* ὅσσαι Τρώων πυρὸς ἐσχάραι, as many fire-places as are in the camp of the Trojans, 10, 418 (perhaps more correctly: as many fire-hearths as there are of Trojans, i. e. as many Trojan heads of families).
ἐσχατάω (ἔσχατος), *to be last, to be at the end.* only partcp. pres. ἐσχατόων, ὅωσα, Ep. for ἐσχατῶν, ὧσα. δηίων

ἐσχατόων, last man of the enemy, i. e. one in the rear, 10. 206; also spoken of cities (a frontier town), *2, 508. 616. (According to Buttm. the correct form is ἐσχατόω.)
ἐσχατιή, ἡ, 1) *the extremity.* a) *the limit, the border, the end of a place,* νήσου, λιμένος, Od. 2, 391. 5, 238; Φθίης, the borders of Phthia, 9, 484. ἐσχατιὴ πολέμοιο, the end of the battle, the extreme limb of the action, either the extremity of the wing or the rear, 11, 524. 20, 328. b) Spoken of a place remote 'rom a town, eaply lying on the sea, Od. 14. 104. 2) *the most remote part,* thus ἀγροῦ, Od. 4, 517. 5, 489.
ἔσχατος, η, ον (prob. from ἔχω, ἔσχον), *the extreme, the last, the most remote,* spoken only of place: ἔσχατοι ἄλλων, 10, 434; and ἔσχατοι ἀνδρῶν, thus H. calls the Ethiopians, because they were conceived of as dwelling at the extremity of the earth's surface, Od. 1. 23. Neut. plur. as adv. ἔσχατα. at the end, 8, 225.
ἐσχατόω, see ἐσχατάω.
ἔσχον, ἐσχόμην, see ἔχω.
ἔσω, see εἴσω.
*ἑταιρεῖος, η, ον, *as a friend, belonging to friendship.* 2) *intimate,* φιλότης, h. Merc. 58.
ἑταίρη, ἡ, Ep. and Ion. ἑτάρη, only 4, 441; a *female companion, a female friend, a mistress,* metaph. spoken of flight: φόβου ἑταίρη, 9, 2; and of the lyre, δαιτὶ ἑταίρη, Od. 17, 271. h. Merc. 478.
ἑταιρίζω. Ep. ἑταρίζω (ἑταῖρος), aor. 1 ἑτάρισα, Ep. σσ, aor. 1 mid only optat. ἑταρίσσαιτο, *to join or associate oneself with any man, to be a companion,* τινί, 24, 335. h. Ven. 46. Mid. *to make any man a companion for oneself, to take as an associate,* τινά, 13, 456.
ἑταῖρος, ὁ, Ep. and Ion. ἕταρος, *a companion, an associate, an assistant, a helper, a comrade,* spoken generally of associates in war and travel, 1, 179. Od. 1, 5; with dat., 18, 251: prop. adj. hence: ἑταῖρος ἀνήρ, Od. 8, 584; metaph. a favorable wind is called ἐσθλὸς ἑταῖρος, a good companion, Od. 11, 7. 12, 149 (both forms used according to the necessities of the metre, prob. ἔτης, akin to ἕταρος).
ἑτάρη, ἡ and ἕταρος, ὁ, see ἑταίρη, ἑταῖρος.
ἐτέθηπεα, see ΘΑΦΩ.
Ἐτεοκλῆς, έους, Ep. ἧος, son of Œdipus and Epicaste (in H. not Iocaste), who agreed with his brother Polynices, that they should reign alternately, each a year. Eteocles did not fulfil this covenant; hence arose the Theban war. For Tydeus, who came to him as an ambassador of Polynices, he laid an ambuscade, 4, 375; whence the adj. Ἐτεοκλήειος, η, ον, *Eteoclean,* βίη Ἐτεοκληείη, the power of Eteocles, see βίη. 4. 386.
Ἐτεόκρητες, οἱ (from ἐτεός and Κρῆς, true Cretans), *the Eteocretans* (native

Ἐτεός. 172 Ἐτώσιος.

Cretans, Voss), one of the five tribes in Crete. They were the aboriginal inhabitants of the island, and not of Hellenian derivation. According to Strab. they lived in the south; their chief city was Praesus, Od. 19, 176.

ἐτεός, ή, όν, *true, real*, as adj. νεικεῖν πόλλ' ἐτεά, to utter many true reproaches 20, 255; elsewhere only the neut. sing. as adv. 1) *true, agreeable to truth*, μαντεύεσθαι. 2, 300; (Hesych. ἀληθὲς ἀγορεύειν, 15, 53. 2) *in truth, in reality*, and often in the Od. εἰ ἐτεόν γε, if indeed really, Od. ᾖ 122.

ἐτεραλκής, ές (ἀλκή), *in which the strength or power is attached to one of two parties; decisive* (ἑτεροκλινής). Δαναοῖσι μάχης ἑτεραλκέα νίκην δοῦναι, to give a decisive victory in battle to the Greeks (Voss, ' an alternating victory;' Köppen, 'shifting'), 7, 26. 8, 171. Od. 22, 236. δῆμος ἑτεραλκής, a decisive body, a superior force, i. e. which gives new courage to the others, 15, 738 (Voss, *changeful*).

ἑτερήμερος, ον (ἡμέρη), *changing with the day*. ζώουσ' ἑτερήμεροι, they live on alternate days, spoken of Kastôr and Polydeukês (Castor and Pollux), Od. 11, 303.†

ἕτερος, η, ον, ἑτέρῃφι, Ep. dat. fem. 1) *the other, one of two*, alter, 5, 258. 288; plur. ἕτεροι, the one part, alter utri, 20, 210. 7, 292. 378. In correlative clauses we have ἕτερος μέν, ἕτερος δέ, or ἄλλος, ἕτερος, 13, 731; also ὁ μέν, ἕτερος δέ, 22, 151; sometimes the first ἕτερος is wanting. 7, 420. 24, 528. ἑτέρῃ χειρί, with one hand, or ἑτέρῃ or ἑτέρηφιν alone, according to the connexion, with the right or left, 12, 452. 16, 734 b) In counting, *the second*, instead of δεύτερος. 16, 179; ἕτεροι δέ, 7, 420. 2) *the other, alius*, opposed to many, like ἄλλος; ἕτερα ἅρματα. sc. those of *the enemy*, 4, 306; ἕτερος, ἄλλος, 9, 313; ἕτεραι, ἄλλαι, Od. 9, 124.

ἑτέρσετο, see τερσαίνω.

ἑτέρωθεν, adv. *from the other side*, ἐπιάχειν, 13, 835. 2) Poet. for ἑτέραθι, *on the other side, opposite*, 3, 230. 6, 247. h. Merc. 366.

ἑτέρωθι, adv. *on the other side, elsewhere*, Od. 4, 531. Il. 5, 351; ἔνθεν—ἑτέρωθι, Od. 12, 235.

ἑτέρως, adv. *in another manner, otherwise*. νῦν δ' ἑτέρως ἐβάλοντο θεοί, Od. 1, 234.† H. has elsewhere only ἑτέρωσε, hence Spitz. de vers. heroic. p. 97 [and Observ. in Quint. Smyrn. p. 63], would read ἑτέρωσ', cf. βάλλω.

ἑτέρωσε, adv. *to another side, elsewhere, away*; νέκυν ἐρύειν, 4, 492; cf. 23, 231. ἑτέρωσε κάρη βάλλειν, 8, 306; φοβεῖσθαι, Od. 16, 163.

ἐντέταλτο, see ἐπιτέλλω.
ἐτετεύχατο, see τεύχω.
ἔτετμον, see ΤΕΜΩ.
ἐτέτμον, see τεύχω.

Ἐτεωνεύς, ῆος, ὁ, son of Boëthous, servant of Menelaus (θεράπων), Od. 4, 22. 15, 95. According to the Schol. he was a relative of Menelaus, his father being son of Argêus, and grandson of Pelops. (Eustath. signif. ὃν ἀληθεύων χρή.)

Ἐτεωνός, ὁ, a town in Bœotia, on the Asôpus, afterwards called, according to Strab., Σκάρφη, 2, 497.

ἔτης, ου, ὁ, only plur. *an acquaintance, a friend, a dependant*, always distinguished from relatives by blood or near kindred (ἑταῖροι, συνήθεις, App.), μιν κασίγνητοί τε ἔται τε, 6, 239. Od. 15, 273. ἔται καὶ ἀνεψιοί, 9, 464. ἔται καὶ ἑταῖροι. 7, 295. Nitzsch, ad Od. 4, 3, understands the *descendants* or rather the *retainers of the house* (prob. from ἔθος or ἐτός, ἐτεός).

ἐτήτυμος, ον (Ep. lengthened fr. ἔτυμος), *true, real, pure, genuine*, μῦθος, νόστος, Od. 3, 241. 23, 62. Esply the neut. as adv. ἐτήτυμον, *truly, really*, κείνου ὅδ' υἱὸς ἐτήτυμον, he is really his son, Od. 4, 157.

ἔτι, adv. 1) Spoken of the present: *still, even*, ἔτι καὶ νῦν, even now still, 1, 455. 2) Spoken of the future: *yet, still further, for the future*, 1, 96. Od. 4, 756. Often with the negat. οὐδ' ἔτι δὴν ἦν, and he lived not much longer, 6. 139. Od. 2, 63. 3) Enhancing the signif. with a compar. ἔτι μᾶλλον, still more, 14, 97. [Spoken also of past time, 2, 287. Od. 4, 7:6; *yet, even, when*]; (from εἰ, εἰμί, to be, cf. Thiersch, § 198, 4; ἔ in the arsis, 6, 139.)

ἔτλην, see τλῆναι.

ἑτοιμάζω (ἕτοιμος), fut. άσω, Ep. σσ. *to make ready, to prepare, to give as one's* γέρας, 1, 118. 19, 197. Mid. = act. Ἱρὸν Ἀθήνῃ, to present a victim to Athênê. 10, 571; ταύρους, Od. 13, 184.

ἕτοιμος, η, ον, Att. ἕτοιμος, *ready, prepared*, hence, 1) *real, accomplished, plain*. ἦ δὴ ταῦτα ἑτοῖμα τετεύχαται. these things indeed have really happened, i. e. are accomplished, 14, 53. ᾖ ᾖ ἄρ' ἑτοῖμα τέτυκτο, this was plain, was so, Od. 8, 364. b) that can be executed, *suitable, salutary*, μῆτις, 9, 425. Μῆτις 2) *ready, prepared, in readiness*, ὠνείατα 9, 91. αὐτίκα γάρ τοι ἔπειτα μεθ' Ἕκτορα πότμος ἑτοῖμος, decided, appointed, 18, 96 (prob. from ἐτός).

ἔτορον, see τορέω.

ἔτος, εος, τό, a *year*, distinguished from ἐνιαυτός, Od. 1, 16; in plur., ? 328. 11, 691.

ἔτραπον, see τρέπω.
ἐτράφην, ἔτραφον, see τρέφω.

ἔτυμος, η, ον (ἐτός), *true, pure, genuine*, only neut. plur. ἔτυμα, *truth*, in opposition to ψεύδεα, Od. 19, 203. 567. The sense. sing. ἔτυμον, as adv. *truly, agreeably to truth*, 10, 534. Od. 4, 140. 157. 2) *truth, really*, like ἐτεόν, 23, 440. Od. 22, 26.

ἐτώσιος, ον (ἐτός, *frustra*), *vain, ineffectual*. πάντα ἐτώσια τιθέναι, Od. 2,

256; hence: *profitless, idle*, ἄχθος, 18, 104. Esply neut. sing. as adv. *vainly, idly*, 3, 368. 14, 407.

εὖ and Ep. ἐΰ before two consonants, so that ν becomes long, adv. (prop. neut. from ἐΰς), *well, rightly, properly.* εὖ ἐρδειν, 5, 650; εὖ εἰπεῖν τινα, to *speak well of*. Od. 1, 302; esply with the notion: *skilfully, dexterously*, εὖ καὶ ἐπισταμένως, 10, 265; εὖ κρίνασθαι, Od. 4, 460. 2) *happily, fortunately.* εὖ οἴκαδ' ἱκέσθαι, 1, 19. Od. 3, 188. 3) Strengthening, as εὖ μάλα, *very, exceedingly*; with numerals: εὖ πάντες, all together, Od. 4, 294. (On the separation of the εὖ, see Thiersch, § 170, 7, 8, 9; Herm. ad h. Ap. 36.)

εὖ, Ion. and Ep. for οὗ, q. v.

εὐαγγέλιον, τό (ἄγγελος), *a present for a good message, a reward for joyful news*, *Od. 14, 152. 166.

εὐαγέως, poet. for εὐαγῶς (εὐαγής), purely, holily, h. Cer. 275. 370.

εὔαδε, see ἀνδάνω.

Εὐαιμονίδης, αο, ὁ, son of Euæmon = Eurypylus, 5, 76.

Εὐαίμων, ονος, ὁ, son of Ormenus, father of Eurypylus, brother of Amyntor, and great-grandson of Æolus, 2, 736.

εὐανθής, ές (ἄνθος), *very blooming, luxuriant*, λάχνη, Od. 11, 320;† χοροί, h. 30, 14.

Εὐάνθης, εος, ὁ, father of Maron, Od. 9, 197.

Εὔβοια, ἡ, *Eubœa*, an island of the Ægean sea, separated by the Euripus from Bœotia, now *Negroponte*. H. calls its inhabitants Abantes. It derived its name, according to the mythographers, from *Eubœa*, daughter of Asôpus, or rather, from its good pastures for cattle (εὖ βοῦς), 2, 535. Od. 3, 174.

εὔβοτος, ον (βόσκω), *having good pastures, good for pasturing*, Συρίη, Od. 15, 406.†

*εὔβους, συν (βοῦς), *abounding in cattle*, accus. εὔβουν, Herm. εὔβων, h. Ap. 54.

εὐγένειος, ον, Ep. ἠϋγένειος, *having a long beard, long maned* (Cp), λίς, λέων, only in the Ep. form, 11., Od. 4, 456.

εὐγενής, ές, Ep. ἠϋγενής and εὐηγενής (γένος), *nobly born, of good extraction*, *11, 427. 23, 81. In H. always εὐηγενής with η epenthetic, see Thiersch, § 166, 4; ἠϋγενής, only h. Ven. 94.

εὖγμα, ατος, τό (εὔχομαι), *boast*, κενὰ εὔγματα, Od. 22, 249.†

εὐγναμπτος, ον, Ep. ἐϋγναμπτος (γναμπτός), *well, beautifully bent*, in Ep. form; κληῖδες, Od. 18, 294.†

*εὐδαιμονίη, ἡ (δαίμων), *happiness, good fortune, felicity*, h. 10, 5.†

εὐδείελος, ον, epith. of Ithaca and of islands generally, most prob. signifying: *very plain, widely visible, conspicuous* (εὐπεριόριστος, App. Schol.), from δῆλος, resolved δέελος and δείελος, because islands, being bounded by the sea, stand out clearly to view; esply spoken of Ithaca, on account of its high shores,

*Od. 2, 167. 9, 21. 13, 212; of islands, Od. 13, 234; and Κρίση, h. Ap. 438. Thus Passow and Nitzsch ad Od. 9, 21. We have also the following derivations: 1) *situated in the west, western*, from δείλη, *evening*, but in the first place this word does not occur in the signif. *west*, and in the next place it is applicable, at the most, only to Ithaca, not to all islands. 2) Exposed to the *afternoon heat, sunny* (thus Voss in several places), from εὖ and εἴλη with δ inserted, cf. Eustath. ad Od. 9, 21. 3) *beautifully lighted, lying in the evening light*, according to Schol. ad Od 9, 21, from δείελος is far-fetched, see Buttm. Lex. p. 224.

εὐδικίη, ἡ (δίκη), *uprightness, the practice of uprightness;* in the plur. εὐδικίας ἀνέχειν, *to exercise justice*, prop. acts of justice [*to maintain justice*. Cp.], Od. 19, 111.†

εὔδμητος, ον, Ep. ἐΰδμητος (δέμω), *wellbuilt, beautifully built*, always in the Ep. form, except Od. 20, 302.

εὕδω, fut. εὑδήσω, aor. 1 εὕδησα. 1) *to sleep, to go to sleep*, with the accus. γλυκὺν ὕπνον εὕδειν, *to enjoy sweet sleep*, Od. 8, 445; spoken of death, 15, 482. 2) Metaph. *to rest, to cease*, spoken of the wind, 5, 524 (kindr. with ΆΩ, ΑΥ Ω).

Εὔδωρος, ὁ, son of Hermês and Polymêlê, was educated by his grandfather Phylas, king of Ephyra in Thesprotia; one of the five leaders of the Myrmidons, 16, 179, sec..; s· e Πολυμήλη.

εὐειδής, ές (εἶδος), *of handsome form, having a beautiful figure, beauteous*, γυνή, 3, 48.†

εὐηγεσίη, ἡ (εὐηγής), *good, noble conduct*, Od. 22, 374; in opposition to κακοεργίη. 2) *beneficence, kindness;* plur. εὐεργεσίας ἀποτίνειν, *to requite benefits*, *Od. 22, 235.

εὐεργής, ές (ἔργον), 1) Mly *wellwrought, beautifully built*, δίφρος, νηῦς, Il.; λώπη, Od. 13, 224; χρυσός, wellwrought gold, Od. 9, 202. 2) *well-done*, hence plur. εὐεργέα, benefits, Od. 4, 695. 22, 319.

εὐεργός, όν (ἔργον), *nobly acting, excellent*. καί ἡ ἀ' εὐεργὸς ἔησιν, *Od. 11, 434. 15, 422.

εὐερκής, ές (ἕρκος), *well-fenced, wellenclosed, well guarded*, αὐλή, 9, 472; θύραι, Od. 17, 267.

εὔζυγος, ον, Ep. ἐΰζυγος (ζυγός), *well yoked*, in H. spoken of ships: *having beautiful rowers' seats, well-furnished with rowers* = εὐήρετμος, *Od. 13, 116. 17, 288; others interpret, *well-planked; strong-built* (only in the Ep. form).

εὔζωνος, ον, Ep. ἐΰζωνος (ζώνη), *having a beautiful girdle, well-girded*, epith. of noble women, because the girdle about the breast gave a graceful form to the robe, 1, 429, and h. Cer.

εὐηγενής, ές, Ep. for εὐγενής, q. v.

εὐηγεσίη, ἡ (ἡγέομαι), *happy rule, good government*, Od. 19, 114.†

I 3

εὐηκής. **εὐηκής, ἐς (ἀκή), well-pointed, very** sharp, αἰχμή, 22, 319 †

Εὐηνίνη, ἡ, daughter of Evênus = Marpessa, 9, 557.

Εὐηνορίδης, ao, ὁ, son of Evenor = Leocritus, Od. 22, 294.

Εὔηνος, ὁ (= εὐήνιος, gentle), **Evenus,** 1) son of Arês and Dêmonicê, king of Ætolia, father of Marpessa. When Idas, son of Aphareus, bore off his daughter, he pursued him to the river Lycormas, and, as he could not overtake them, he plunged into it, and it received from him the name Evenus. Apollo likewise loved Marpessa, and wrested her from Idas, in the city Arenê in Messenia. Idas fought with him for her; Zeus at length separated them; and upon the free choice which he granted her, Marpessa chose Idas, 9, 557. 2) son of Selepius, king of Lyrnessus, father of Mynes and Epistrophus, 2, 693.

εὐήνωρ, ορος, ὁ, ἡ (ἀνήρ), prop. **manly,** in H. an epithet of wine and of iron; *strengthening the courage,* or *invigorating men,* *Od. 4, 622. 13, 19; or *befitting a man, heart-ennobling* [Cp.] (Voss, 'the spirit-strengthening wine and the man-ennobling brass ').

Εὐήνωρ, ορος, ὁ, father of Leocritus, Od. q. v.

εὐήρης, ες (ἄρω), well-joined, well-fitted, easy to handle or **use,** epith. of an oar, *Od. 11, 121 [*month-shaven, Cp.]. (The derivation from ἐρέσσω is incorrect.)

*εὐήρυτος, ον (ἀρύω), *easy to draw,* ὕδωρ, h. in Cer. 106.

εὐθαρσής, ές (θάρσος), of good courage, resolute, bold, h. 7, 9.

εὐθέμεθλος, ον, Ep. **ἠϋθέμεθλος, well-founded,** γαῖα, h. 30, 1.†

εὐθηνέω, to be in a flourishing condition, vigere; *to abound in, to be rich,* with dat. κτήνεσιν, h. 30, 10 (akin to τιθήνη).

εὔθριξ, τρίχος, ὁ, ἡ (θρίξ), having beautiful hair, having a beautiful mane; with flowing mane, epith. of steeds; only in the Ep. form **εὔτριχας,** *23, 13. 301. 351.

εὔθρονος, ον, Ep. **ἐΰθρονος (θρόνος), having a beautiful seat, well-throned,** epith. of Eôs; always Ep. form, 8, 565. Od. 6, 48.

εὔθυμος, ον (θυμός), 1) **having good courage.** 2) In H. **benevolent, kind,** Od. 14, 63.† Adv. **εὐθύμως, courageously,** Batr.

*εὐθύς and εὐθύ, adv. of place, *straight, directly,* εὐθὺ Πύλονδε, h. Merc. 342; **εὐθύς,** 355. In the Il. and Od. only the older form **ἰθύς, ἰθύ.**

εὔιππος, ον (ἵππος), having good steeds, epith. of Ischys, h. Ap. 210.

Εὔιππος, ὁ, a Trojan, slain by Patroclus, 16, 417.

εὐκαμπής, ές (κάμπτω), well-bent, beautifully curved, δρέπανον, κληῖς, *Od. 18, 368. 21, 6; τόξον, h. 27, 12.

εὔκαρπος, ον (καρπός), fruitful, abounding in fruits, γαῖα, h. 30, 5.

Εὔμαιος.

εὐέατος, ον, poet. for **εὐέαστος (ἐάζω), easy to spill, easily cleaved,** κέδρος, Od. 5, 60.†

εὔκηλος, ον, Æol. lengthened from **ἕκηλος,** prop. **ἐΐκηλος** (see **ἔκηλος). quiet,** l, 554. 2) **undisturbed,** 11, 371. Od. 14, 479

εὐκλεής, ές (κλέος), Ep. **εὐκλε-ής,** accus. plur. **εὐκλείας,** 10, 281. Od. 21, 331. **εὐκλεής,** 12, 318; **glorious, famous.** οὐ μὰν ἡμῖν **εὐκλεές,** it is not glorious for us, 17, 415; whence adv. **εὐκλεῶς,** Ep. **εὐκλειῶς, gloriously,** 22, 110.

εὔκλεια, ἡ, Ep. for **εὐκλεία, fame, glory,** Od. 14, 402. τινὰ εὐκλείης ἐπιβῆσαι, to elevate any man to fame, Voss [*to rouse him on glory's heights.* Cp.], Il. 8, 285.

εὐκλειής, ές and adv. **εὐκλειῶς,** poet. for **εὐκλεής** and **εὐκλεῶς.**

ἐϋκλήϊς, ίδος, ἡ (κληΐς), well-locked, θύρη, 24, 318.†

εὔκλωστος, ον (κλώθω), well-spun, well-woven, χιτών, h. Ap. 203.

εὐκνήμις, ΐδος, ὁ, ἡ, Ep. **ἐϋκνήμις (κνημίς), having beautiful greaves,** in the Il. epith of the Achæans; in the Od. also of ἑταῖροι, Od. 2, 402; always in the plur. and Ep. form, 1, 17.

εὔκομος, Ep. **ἐΰκομος, having beautiful hair, fair-haired,** epith. of noble women, Il. Od. h. Cer. 1.

εὐκόσμητος, ον (κοσμέω), beautifully adorned, h. Merc. 384.

εὔκοσμος, ον (κόσμος), well-arranged; only adv. **εὐκόσμως,** in (fitting) order. Od. 21, 123.†

εὔκραιρος, ον (κραῖρα), beautifully horned, spoken of cattle, h. Merc. 209.

ἐϋκτίμενος, η, ον (κτίμενος), well-built, well-inhabited, well-situated, truly an epith. of towns, islands, regions; spoken of houses, streets, and gardens, Od. 4, 476. Il. 6, 391. 20, 496. The common form **εὐκτιμένη,** h. Ap. 36, Herm. has rejected.

ἐΰκτιτος, ον, Ep. and Ion. for **εὔκτιστος (κτίζω), handsomely built,** Αἶσυ, 2, 592.† h. Ap. 423.

εὐκτός, ή, όν (εὔχομαι), wished, desired, 14, 98.†

εὔκυκλος, ον (κύκλος), well-rounded, in the Il. epith of the shield, 5, 797; in the Od. of the chariot, Od. 6, 58. 70; according to Eustath. to be referred to the wheels; **having beautiful wheels,** Voss [*strong-wheel'd.* Cp.]; κάνεον, Batr. 35.

εὐλείμων, ον, gen. **ονος (λειμών), having good meadows, abounding in meadows: meadowy** (convenient for pasturing, Voss), νῆσος, Od. 4. 607.†

εὐλή, ἡ (εἰλέω), *a worm, a maggot,* produced in dead bodies, etc., plur., *19, 26. 22, 509. 24, 414.

εὔληρα, τά, Ep. for the comm. **ἡνία, rein, check,** 23, 481;† (prob. from εἴλω, Schol. οἱονεὶ εἴληρα, ἀπὸ τοῦ περιειλεῖσθαι τοὺς ἱμάντας χερσὶ τῶν ἡνιόχων).

Εὔμαιος, the faithful swine-herd of Odysseus (Ulysses), son of Ctesius, king of the island Syria; he was stolen by a female Phœnician slave of his father,

*Εὐμελίη. 175 Εὔορμος.

and by the Phœnician sailors sold to Laertes, Od. 15, 402, seq. Odysseus (Ulysses) comes to him clad like a beggar, Od. 14, 1, seq. Telemachus lodged with him when he returned from Sparta. He conducted Odysseus (Ulysses) to the town, Od. 17, 201; and aided him in slaying the suitors, Od. 22, 267, seq. (prob. from εὖ and ΜΑΩ, the well-disposed).

*εὐμελίη, ἡ, poet. for εὐμέλεια, good singing, the reading preferred by Herm. for εὐμυλίη, in h. Merc. 325.

εὐμελίης, ου, ὁ, Ep. ἐὐμμελίης, q. v.

εὐμενέτης, ου, ὁ, poet. for εὐμενής, well-disposed, kind, affectionate (in opposition to δυσμενής), Od. 6, 185.†

εὐμενής, ές (μένος), well-disposed, benevolent, kind, ἦτορ, h. 21, 7.†

Εὐμήδης, εος, ὁ (very wise), father of Dolon, the rich herald of the Trojans, 10, 314.

*εὐμήκης, ες (μῆκος), very long, Batr. 130.

εὔμηλος, ον (μῆλον), having good or many sheep, abounding in sheep, Ὀρτυγίη, Od. 15, 406.† (V. 'good for sheep').

Εὔμηλος, ὁ, son of Admetus and Alcestis, who in eleven ships led the Thessalians from Pheræ, Boibē, and Iolcus, 2, 711. He possessed excellent horses, and would have won the prize in the funeral games of Patroclus, had not his chariot been broken, 23, 288, seq. Iphthimē, daughter of Icarius, is mentioned as his wife, Od. 4, 798.

ἐϋμμελίης, ὁ, Ep. for εὐμελίης, Ep. gen. ἐϋμμελίω for ἐϋμμελίαο (μελία [by assimilation for ἐΰσμελίης, fm. the orig. form σμελία, cf. σμίλαξ. σμῖλος, δένδρον· οἱ δὲ πρίνος. Hesych. Död.]), having a good ashen spear, skilled in the use of the spear, epith. of brave warriors, 17, 9; and esply of Priam, 4, 165. (The common form εὐμελίης does not occur in H.)

*εὐμολπέω (εὔμολπος), to sing sweetly, h. Merc. 478.

[Εὔμολπος, Eumolpus, a masc. proper name, h. Cer. 154, 475.]

*εὐμυλίη, ἡ, h. Merc. 325, an unknown word, for which Herm. would read εὐμελίη, Frank εὐελίη.

εὐνάζω = εὐνάω (εὐνή), fut. άσω, to cause to lie down, to lay down, Od. 4, 408. Mid. to lie down, to go to sleep, Od. 20, 1; παρά τινι, and with dat. alone, Od. 5, 119. h. Ven. 191; also spoken of brutes, *Od. 5, 65.

εὐναιετάων, ωσα, ον, well-inhabited, pleasant to live in, well-furnished; always in pass. signif. with πόλις, δόμοι, and μέγαρα, 2, 648. Od. 2, 400 (used only in the partcp.).

εὐναιόμενος, η, ον (ναίω), well-inhabited, populous; like εὐναιετάων with πόλις, πτολίεθρον, and Βούδειον, 16, 572; Σιδονίη, Od. 13, 285. There is no verb εὐναίω.

εὐνάω and εὐνάζω (εὐνή), fut. εὐνήσω, aor 1 pass. εὐνήθην 1) Act. to place in ambush, τινά, Od. 4, 440; mly to put to rest, to put to sleep; hence metaph. to quiet, to soothe = παύω, γόον, Od. 4, 758. 2) Mid. with aor. pass. to go to bed, to go to sleep, to sleep, εὐνηθῆναί τινι, with any one, 2, 821. 16, 176; and ἐν φιλότητι εὐνηθῆναι, 14, 360; metaph. spoken of storms: to be hushed, to be stilled, Od. 5, 384.

εὐνή, ἡ, Ep. gen. εὐνῆφι, 1) a couch, a bed, ἐξ εὐνῆφιν, 15, 580. Od. 2, 2, seq.; generally a place of rest, of the army, 10, 408; a lair of a wild beast, 11, 115; of cattle, Od. 14, 15; in the plur. εὐναί, the couches of Typhōeus, which some explain as the grave, 2, 783. b) a bed, i. e. a bedstead, the cushion for a bed, Od. 16, 34. c) the nuptial couch. εὐνῆς ἐπιβήμεναι, 9, 133; hence marriage, cohabitation. φιλότητι καὶ εὐνῇ μιγῆναι, to indulge the pleasures of love, 3, 445. 2) Plur. εὐναί, anchor-stones, i. e. stones used for anchors, which were either let down to hold the ship, or, as Nitzsch ad Od. 2, 418, p. 120, thinks, stones or masses of matter, with which the ship was attached to the strand when the water at the shore was too deep, see 14, 77; again, 1, 436. Od. 15, 498. 9, 137 [the above view is, however, retracted by Nitzsch, tom. III. p. 35].

εὐνῆθεν, adv. from the bed, Od. 20, 124.

Εὔνηος, ὁ, Ion. for Εὔνεως, son of Jason and Hypsipyle, in Lemnos, who sent wine to the Greeks in Troy, 7, 468; and exchanged a mixing-cup for Lycaon, 23, 747 (11om νηῦς, the good sailor, so named from his father).

εὔνητος, ον, Ep. ἐΰννητος (νέω), well-spun, beautifully woven, χιτών, πέπλος, 18, 596. Od. 7, 97; always in the Ep. form.

εὐνῆφι, εὐνῆφιν, see εὐνή.

εὖνις, ιος, ὁ, ἡ, bereft, deprived, with gen. υἱῶν, 22, 44; ψυχῆς, Od. 9, 524 (According to Eustath. from εἷς, ἑνός, whence ἕνις, εὖνις, cf. εὔηλος.)

ἐΰννητος, ον, Ep. for εὔνητος, q. v.

εὐνομίη, ἡ (νόμος), good observance of law, good morals, loyalty. Od. 17, 487;† in plur. good laws, h. 30, 11.

εὔξεστος, ον, Ep. ἐΰξεστος, η, ον (ξέω), well-smoothed, well-polished; spoken especially of any thing made of wood, and smoothed with a plane or any similar tool, especially of chariots, tables, bathing-tubs, oars, etc., 7, 5. Od. 4, 48: sometimes with two, and sometimes with three endings, see Thiersch, Gram. § 201, 16. In Od. 14, 225, ἄκοντες ἐΰξεστοι, it refers to the shaft, not, as Bothe supposes, to the point.

εὔξοος, ον, Ep. ἐΰξοος (ξέω), well-smoothed; like εὔξεστος, spoken of chariots, tables, and spear-shafts, 2, 390. 10, 373; but Od. 5, 237, σκέπαρνον ἐΰξοον, the well-whetted axe, which is explained by some as act. 'that hews well.'

εὔορμος, ον (ὅρμος), having good anchorage, or, with Nitzsch, 'having

*Εΰοχθος. Εὐρυάγυιος.

level shores,' λιμήν, 21, 23. Od. 4, 358.

*εὔοχθος, ον (perhaps from ὀχή), *fertile, fruitful*, γῆ, Ep. 7, 2.

*εὔπαις, δος, ὁ, ἡ (παῖς), *abounding in children, blessed with offspring*, h. 30, 5.

εὐπατέρεια, ἡ (πατήρ), *the daughter of a noble father* (V., 'of noble descent'), epith. of Helen and Tyro, 6, 292. Od. 11, 235.

Εὐπείθης, εος, ὁ (adj. εὐπειθής), father of the suitor Antinous of Ithaca; he wished to avenge the death of his son, whom Odysseus (Ulysses) had slain among the suitors, by a combat against him, but was slain by Laertes, Od. 1, 383. 24, 469, seq.

εὔπεπλος, ον (πέπλος), *having a beautiful mantle, handsomely clad, well-dressed*, epith. of noble women, 5, 424; Ναυσικάα, Od. 6, 49.

εὐπηγής, ές (πήγνυμι), Ep. for εὐπαγής, prop. pressed together; spoken of the physical frame, *well-knit, strong, firm*. ξεῖνος μέγας ἠδ' εὐπηγής, Od. 21, 334.†

εὔπηκτος, ον (πήγνυμι), *well-joined, firmly built*, epith. of buildings and tents, 2, 661. 9, 663. Od. 23, 41.

εὔπλειος, η, ον, Ep εὐπλεῖος (πλεῖος), *well-filled, entirely full*, πήρη, Od. 17, 467.†

εὐπλεκής, ές, Ep. ἐυπλεκής (πλέκω), *well-interwoven, beautifully entwined*, = εὔπλεκτος; θύσανοι, δίφροι, *2, 449. 23, 436; only in the Ep. form.

εὔπλεκτος, ον, Ep. ἐΰπλεκτος (πλέκω), *well, beautifully interwoven; well-twisted*, δίφρος, 23, 335, Ep. form; σειραί, strongly twisted cords, 23, 115, comm. form.

εὐπλοίη, ἡ, Ep. for εὔπλοια (πλέω), a *prosperous voyage or navigation*, 9, 362.†

εὐπλόκαμίς, ίδος, ἡ, Ep. form from εὐπλόκαμος, *having beautiful tresses; fair-hair'd*, only εὐπλοκαμίδες Ἀχαιαί, *Od. 2, 119. 19, 542.

εὐπλόκαμος, ον, Ep. ἐυπλόκαμος (πλόκαμος), *having beautiful tresses, fair-hair'd*, epith. of goddesses and of women, 6, 380. Od. 5, 125, seq.; only Ep. form.

εὐπλυνής, ές, Ep. ἐϋπλυνής (πλύνω), *well-washed, clean*, φᾶρος, Od. 8, 392. 425; only Ep. form.

εὐποίητος, ον and η, ον (ποιέω), *well-made, beautifully wrought*, spoken of works of every kind: *well-built*, πύλη, κλισίη; the fem. εὐποιητή, 5, 466. 16, 636; but εὐποίητος πυράγρη, Od. 3, 434; (Thiersch, § 201, 16.)

*εὐπόλεμος, ον (πόλεμος), *good in war, warlike*, h. 7, 4.

εὐπρήσσω (πρήσσω), *to make well, to arrange well*; whence ἐϋπρήσσεσκον, Od. 8, 259.† Eustath. reads, more correctly, ἐϋ πρήσσεσκον, see Thiersch, Gram. § 170, 7.

εὔπρηστος, ον (πρήθω), *strongly kindling, vehemently excited*, ἀϋτμή, from

the bellows (V. 'the glow-enkindling blast'), 18, 471.†

εὔπρυμνος, ον (πρύμνα), *having a well-built or beautifully adorned stern*, νῆες, 4, 248.†

εὔπυργος, ον (πύργος), *furnished with good towers*, epith. of fortified towns, 7, 71.†

εὔπωλος, ον (πῶλος), *having beautiful horses, abounding in horses, famed for horses*, epith. of Ilium, 5, 551. Od. 2, 18, often.

εὐράξ, adv. (εὖρος), *sidewise*, *11, 251. 15, 541.

εὐραφής, ές, Ep. ἐϋρραφής (ῥάπτω), *well-stitched, sewed fast*, δοροί (*skins close-seamed*. Cp.], *Od. 2, 354. 380; only Ep. form.

εὐρεής, ές, Ep. ἐϋρρεής, Ep. form of εὐρείτης; only in the gen. ἐϋρρεῖος, ποταμοῖο, contr. from ἐϋρρεέος, in *6, 508. 15, 265, and elsewhere; see the following.

εὐρείτης, ου, ὁ, Ep. ἐϋρρείτης, αο (ῥέω), *beautifully flowing, fair-flowing*, epith. of rivers, 6, 34. Od. 14, 257.

*Εὔριπος, ὁ, the *Euripus*, the strait between Euboea, Boeotia, and Attica; now the strait of *Egribos*, h. Ap. 222. (Prob. from εὖ and ῥίπτω.)

εὑρίσκω, fut. εὑρήσω, h. Merc. 302; aor. act. εὗρον, and aor. mid. εὑρόμην. 1) *to find what one seeks, to invent, to discover, to devise*; with accus. μῆχος, *to devise a means*, 2, 343; κακοῦ ἄκος, 9, 250 (see ἄκος); τέκμωρ Ἰλίου, *to find the end of Ilium, i. e. accomplish its destruction*, 7, 81. 9, 49; but τέκμωρ τι, *to find an expedient, a remedy*, Od. 4, 374. 2) *to find by chance, to light upon, to fall in with*, spoken of persons and things very often; with partcp. αὐτὸν ἥμενον, 5, 752. Mid. *to find out for oneself, to devise*. τέκμωρ, 16, 472; ὄνομα, Od. 19, 403; θανάτου λύσιν ἑταίροισιν, *to find deliverance from death for his companions*, Od. 9, 421. 2) *to find by chance or unawares*. οἵ τ' αὐτῷ κακὸν εὕρετο, *he drew evil upon himself*, Od. 21, 304.

εὖρος, ον, Ep. ἐΰρροος, *beautifully flowing, rapidly flowing*, epith. of rivers, *7, 329; 21, 130; always in the Ep. form.

Εὖρος, ὁ, the *Eurus*, or *south-east* wind, one of the four main winds of H., Od. 5, 295. 232. It is stormy, 2, 145. 16, 765; and as a warm wind it melts the snow, Od. 19, 206. (According to some, from αὔρα, according to others, kindred to ἠώς. cf. Buttm. Lex. p. 43, note 4.)

εὖρος, εος, τό (εὐρύς), *breadth, width*. Od. 11, 312.†

εὐρραφής, poet. for εὐραφής, q. v.
ἐϋρρεῖος, Ep. gen. see εὐρεής.
ἐϋρρείτης, ὁ, Ep. for εὐρείτης, q. v.
ἐΰρροος, Ep. for εὖρος, q. v.

εὐρυάγυιος, υια, υιον (ἀγυιά), *having broad streets, with spacious streets*, epith. of large cities, 2, 329. Od. 4, 246. 21, 230; also χθών εὐρυαγυία, h. Cer. 16; occurring only in the fem.

Εὐρυάδης, ου, ὁ, a suitor of Penelōpē, slain by Telemachus, Od. 22, 267.

Εὐρύαλος, ὁ, 1) son of Mecisteus; he went with his kinsman Diomēdēs to Troy, 2, 565; was one of the bravest heroes, 6, 20; he was also a powerful wrestler, but was conquered by Epeus, 23, 680. 2) a Phæacian, a victor in wrestling, who presented Odysseus (Ulysses) with a sword, Od. 8, 115.

Εὐρυβάτης, ου, ὁ, 1) a herald of Agamemnon, 1, 320. 9, 170. 2) a herald of Odysseus (Ulysses), who followed him to Troy, 2, 184. Od. 19, 247.

*εὐρυβίης, αο, ὁ, Ion. and Ep. for εὐρυβίας (βία), wide-ruling, having a wide sway, Κελεός, h. Cer. 295.

Εὐρυδάμας, αντος, ὁ, 1) a Trojan, father of Abas and Polyidus, who knew how to interpret dreams, 5, 149. 2) a suitor of Penelōpē of Ithaca, slain by Odysseus (Ulysses), Od. 18, 297. 22, 283.

Εὐρυδίκη, ἡ, daughter of Clymenus, wife of Nestor, Od. 3, 452.

Εὐρύκλεια, ἡ, daughter of Ops son of Pisenor; Laertes had purchased her at the price of twenty cattle, Od. 1, 429. 430. She brought up Odysseus (Ulysses), Od. 19, 482; then with Eurynome discharged the office of house-keeper and had the charge of the female slaves, Od. 22, 396. 23, 289. Her fidelity, attachment, and activity are often praised.

εὐρυκρείων, οντος, ὁ (κρείων), wide-ruling, epith. of Agamemnon and of Poseidōn, *1, 102. 355.

Εὐρύλοχος, ὁ, a companion and fellow-wanderer of Odysseus (Ulysses); he conducted a part of the crew to Circê, accompanied Odysseus (Ulysses) to the under-world, occasioned the slaughter of the sacred oxen of Helius, by which he drew death upon himself and his companions, Od. 10, 205. 11, 23.

Εὐρύμαχος, ὁ, son of Polybus, according to Od. 4, 629: he and Antinous were the most respectable amongst the suitors of Penelōpē; he was crafty and subtle, Od. 1, 399. 2, 177. He was slain by Odysseus (Ulysses), Od. 22, 69.

Εὐρυμέδουσα, ἡ, a female slave of Alcinous, king of Phæacia, who brought up Nausicaa, Od. 7, 8.

Εὐρυμέδων, οντος, ὁ, 1) father of Periboea, leader of the giants in Epirus, Od. 7, 58: cf. Pind. Pyth. VIII. 15—19. 2) son of Ptolemæus, the noble charioteer of Agamemnon, 4, 228. 3) a servant of Nestor, 8, 114. 11, 620.

εὐρυμέτωπος, ον (μέτωπον), broad-browed, always an epith. of cattle, 10, 292. Od. 3, 282.

Εὐρυμίδης, ου, ὁ, son of Eurymus = Telemus, a Cyclops, Od. 9, 509.

Εὐρυνόμη, ἡ, 1) daughter of Oceanus and Thetis, who received Hêphæstus when hurled from heaven into the sea, 18, 398, seq. According to Hes. Th. 98, she was the mother of the Graces; before Kronus, she with Ophian had the dominion of Olympus, Ap. Rh. 503. 2) the trusty stewardess of Odysseus (Ulysses), Od. 17, 490, seq. 19, 96.

Εὐρύνομος, ὁ, son of Ægyptius in Ithaca, a suitor of Penelōpē, Od. 2, 22. He is also mentioned in the contest with Odysseus (Ulysses), Od. 22, 242.

εὐρύνω (εὐρύς), aor. 1 εὔρυνα, to make broad, to widen, with ἀγῶνα, to enlarge the arena of combat, Od. 8, 260.†

εὐρυόδειος, α, ον (ὁδός), having broad roads, with wide ways (widely roamed over, V.), epith. of the earth, since it can be travelled over in all directions, only in fem. 16, 635. Od. 3, 453; and often.

εὐρύοπα, ὁ, Ep. for εὐρυόπης, as nom. 5, 265; as voc. 16, 241; a form of εὐρύωψ, whence the accus. εὐρύοπα, 1, 498. 8, 206; either (from ὤψ), wide-seeing, far-seeing, or (from ὄψ), wide-thundering, epith. of Zeus. The last signif. seems to contravene the Hom. usu loquendi, since ὄψ, though used to indicate the voices of men and beasts, is not applied to every loud noise. Eustath. and Hesych. give both explanations; Heyne, Wolf, Thiersch, § 151. 47. Anm. 2, decide in favour of the first signif. and Voss. ad h. Cer. 3, translates it the ruler of the world, see 13, 732. In h. Cer. 441, connected with βαρύκτυπος. [See Jahrb. von Jahn und Klotz. März 1843, p. 264.]

εὐρύπορος, ον (πόρος), prop. having broad ways, widely navigated, always an epith. of the sea, 15, 381. Od. 4, 432. 12, 2.

εὐρυπυλής, ές (πυλή), having wide gates, wide-gated, Ἄιδος δῶ, 23, 71. Od. 11, 571.

Εὐρύπυλος, ὁ, son of Euæmon, grandson of Ormenus, ruler of Ormenion in Thessaly, who sailed to Troy with forty ships, 2, 736; a brave warrior; he slew many Trojans, was wounded by Paris, and healed by Patroclus, 11, 841. In Pindar he is represented as the son of Poseidōn, king of Cyrene, and received the Argonauts in Lybia, cf. Müller, Orchom. p. 466. 2) son of Poseidōn and Astypalæa, father of Chalciopē, king of Cos, 2, 676. 3) son of Telephus and Astyochê, sister of Priam, king of Mysia. He was induced, by presents which Priam sent to his mother or wife, to go to the aid of Troy. He was slain by Neoptolemus, Od. 11, 520, seq. cf. Strab. p. 587.

εὐρυρέεθρος, ον (ῥέεθρον), flowing in a broad channel, wide-flowing, epith. of the Axius, 21, 141.†

εὐρυρέων, ουσα, ον (ῥέω), wide-flowing, epith. of the Axius, 2, 849. 16, 288; of the Xanthus, *21, 304.

εὐρύς, εῖα, ύ, gen. έος, είης, έος (Ep. accus. εὐρέα for εὐρύν, 6, 291. 18, 140); broad, wide, spacious, chiefly epith. of the heavens, the sea, countries, etc. [twice of cities, 2, 575. 18, 591]. εὐρέα νῶτα θαλάσσης, 2, 159. εὐρέας ὤμοι, 3,

I 5

227. τείχος εὐρύ, a thick wall, 12, 5. κλέος εὐρύ, a wide-spread report, Od. 23, 137. Cf. εὐρύτερος, 3, 194.

εὐρυσθενής, ές (σθένος), having a wide dominion, wide-ruling, epith. of Poseidôn, 7, 455. Od. 13, 140.

Εὐρυσθεύς, ῆος, ὁ, son of Sthenelus, and grandson of Perseus, king of Mycenæ; he was prematurely born, for Hêrê accelerated his birth, that he, and not Hêraclês might reign, according to an oath of Zeus in relation to the descendants of Perseus, 19, 100. 123, seq. Thus Eurystheus became master of Hêraclês and imposed upon him the well-known twelve labours, 15, 639. The last of these labours was to bring up the dog from hell, 8, 363. Od. 11, 617, seq.

Εὐρυτίδης, ου, ὁ, son of Eurytus = Iphitus, Od. 21, 14.

Εὐρυτίων, ωνος, ὁ, a Centaur, Od. 21, 295. cf. Apd. 2, 5. 4.

Εὔρυτος, ὁ, 1) son of Actor and Molione, brother of Cteatus, by tradition son of Poseidôn. Both marched to aid Augeas against the Pylians and Nestor, 11, 709, seq., and also against Hêraclês, who slew him in ambush, 2, 621. They were called Ἀκτορίωνε and Μολίονε, 11, 709. According to Apd. 2, 7. 2, they had together only one body, but two heads, four hands, as many feet, and possessed great strength. 2) son of Melaneus and Stratonice, king of Œchalia (in Thessaly, 2, 730; or in Messenia, Od. see Οἰχαλίη), father of Iole, of Iphitus, of Molion, etc., a famous archer. According to H. Apollo slew him, because he had challenged him to a contest in archery, Od. 8, 226, seq. Odysseus (Ulysses) received from his son Iphitus the bow of Eurytus, Od. 21, 32, seq. According to a late tradition Hêraclês slew him because he would not give him Iole, Apd. 2, 4. 8 (the bow-drawer, from ἐρύω).

*Εὐρυφάεσσα, ἡ, (the far-seeing), sister and wife of Hyperion, mother of Helius, of Sêlênê and Eôs, h. 31, 4.

εὐρυφυής, ές (φύω), wide-growing, epith. of barley, Od. 4, 604.†

εὐρύχορος, ον (χῶρος), having a broad space, roomy, spacious, extensive, epith. of cities and countries, 2, 498 (according to the Schol. Ep. shortened for εὐρύχωρος, see Thiersch, § 168, 10, and Nitzsch ad Od. 6, 4; with Passow we may derive it more simply from χορός, having broad dancing-places, hence generally, having broad plains).

εὐρύωψ, οπος, ὁ, see εὐρύοπα.

εὐρώεις, εσσα, εν (εὐρώς), mouldy, musty; and, since mould is generated only in the dark, confined places, it signif. generally, dark, gloomy, epith. of the under-world, 20, 65. Od. 10, 512. 23, 323. 24, 10 (improb. with Apoll. Hesych. poet. for εὐρύς).

Εὐρώπη, ἡ, Europa. 1) daughter of the Phœnician Agenor and of Telephassa. according to Apd. 3, 1. 1; H. calls her the daughter of Phœnix (if this is not an appel.), mother of Sarpedon and Minos by Zeus, who bore her off to Crete, in the form of a bull, 14, 321. Batr. 79. H. does not mention her name; it occurs first in Hdt. 1, 2. 2) the name of a division of the world, first mentioned in h. Ap. 251; in which place only northern Greece seems to be intended. (Signf. εὐρωπός = εὐρύς; hence εὐρώπη, ε-χάη, the extended, the far-stretching land; cf. Herm. ad h. Ap. l. c.)

ἰός, ἰό, Ep. ἠός, ἠό, gen. ἐῆος, accus. ἐῦν, 8, 303. Od. 18, 127; ἠῦν, 5, 628; neut. ἠύ, 17, 456. 20, 80: the form ἐῦ and εὖ in neut. only adv. 1) good, excellent, beautiful, glorious, spoken of persons and things, 2, 653. μάνος ἠύ, 17, 456. The gen. sing. ἐῆος, in the signif. of φίλος stands now correctly instead of ἐῆος, his, 1, 393, and 15, 138. 24, 422. 550, where it should even signify thine. 2) Generally plur. neut. ἐάων, as if from a nom. τὰ ἐά, good things, good, 24, 528; plainly neut. except θεοὶ δωτῆρες ἐάων, Od. 8, 325. 335. h. 17, 12 (see Buttm. § 35, 3. c. Thiersch. Gram. § 183, 10; on the other hand, Doederlein supplies from δόμος the kindred subst. δόσεων, cf. Kühner § 243, 3). [Cf. Jahrb. Jahn und Klotz, März 1843, pp. 264, 265.]

εὖσα, see εὕω.

εὔσσελμος, ον, Ep. ἐΰσσελμος (σέλμα well-furnished with oar-benches, or rowers, epith. of ships, 2, 170, and often. (It does not occur in the nom., cf. Spitz. ad Il. 16, 1.)

εὔσκαρθμος, ον, Ep. ἐΰσκαρθμος (σκαίρω), lightly bounding, easily leaping, epith. of horses, 13, 31.†

εὔσκοπος, ον, Ep. ἐΰσκοπος (σκοπέω), that takes good aim, good to hit, "Αρτεμις, Od. 11, 198. 2) (fr. σκοπέω,) seeing well, looking out sharply, epith. of Hermês, 24, 24. Od. 1, 38; only in the Ep. form.

ἐΰσσελμος, ον, Ep. for εὔσελμος, q. v.

'Εὔσσωρος, ὁ, Ep. Εὔσωρος, father of Acamas of Thrace, 6, 8.

εὐσταθής, ές, Ep. ἐϋσταθής (ἵστημι) standing firm, well-founded, μέγαρον 14, 374; θάλαμος, Od. 23, 178; always in the Ep. form.

εὐστέφανος, ον, Ep. ἐϋστέφανος (στέφανος), 1) beautifully crowned, Venus epith. of Artêmis, 21, 511; of Aphroditê and Mycenê, Od. 8, 267. 2, 126; of Dêmêtêr, h. Cer. 224; accord. to Apoll. Il. 21, 511, from στεφάνη, ψ————λ εἶδος. The back hair, to wit, was closed in a net, see ἀναδέσμη, and the fastened with a band (στεφάνη) behind. According to others it is to be interpreted of the girdle and = εὔζωνος strongly fortified, strongly walled, epith. of the city Thebe, 19, 99; στεφάνη (only in the Ep. form).

εὔστρεπτος, ον, Ep. ἐΰστρεπτος (στρέφω)

εὐστρεφής. 179 **Εὐχήνωρ.**

well-twined, *well-twisted*, spoken of leathern thongs, *Od. 2, 426. 15, 291.
εὐστρεφής, ές, Ep. ἐϋστρεφής, *well-wound, well-twisted*, spoken of cords, etc., Od. 9, 425. 10, 167; of a bow-string, 15, 463; of a gut-string, Od. 21, 408; always in the Ep. form.
εὔστροφος, ον, Ep. ἐϋστροφος (στρέφω), *well-wound, well-twisted;* οἰὸς ἄωτος, the well-twisted wool of the sheep, i. e. the string of the sling, *13, 599. 716, in the Ep. form.
*εὔστρωτος, ον (στρώννυμι), *well-spread, well-made*, λέχος, h. Ven. 158. Cer. 286.
εὖτε, Ep. 1) Conj. of time, for ὅτε (which arises from this by a rejection of the digamma), *at the time, when, as.* a) With Indic. 11, 735. The apodosis begins with ἔνθα τῆμος, δὴ τότε, καὶ τότε, etc., 6, 392. Od. 13, 93. *b*) In connexion with ἄν εὖτ' ἄν (see ὅτ' ἄν), *in case that, as soon as, as often as*, 1, 242. Od. 1, 192; once without ἄν, Od. 7, 202. c) With optat. h. 17, 8. 2) Adv. of comparison, for ἠύτε, *as when*, only once, 3, 10; and according to Aristarch., 19, 386; where Wolf and Spitz. write εὖτε; Buttm., Lex., would read ἠύτε, and Bothe has adopted the reading.
εὐτειχής, ές = εὐτείχεος.
εὐτείχεος, ον (τεῖχος), *having strong walls, well-walled,* Τροίη, Ἴλιος, 1, 129. A metaplast. accus. πόλιν εὐτείχεα, is found in 16, 57; which on account of the accent cannot be assigned to εὐτειχής (see however Thiersch, § 200, 20).
*εὐτείχητος, ον (τεῖχος) = εὐτείχεος, h. Ven. 112.
εὔτμητος, ον, Ep. ἐϋτμητος (τέμνω), *beautifully cut, well-cut*, always spoken of leathern articles, *7, 304. 10, 567; always in the Ep. form.
εὐτρεφής, ές, Ep. ἐϋτρεφής (τρέφω), *well-fed, fat*, *Od. 9, 425. 14, 530.
εὔτρητος, ον, Ep. ἐϋτρητος, *well-bored, well-pierced*, λοβοί, 14, 182; † Ep. form.
Εὔτρησις, ιος, ἡ, a village in Thespiæ, in Bœotia, with a temple of Apollo, who had an oracle there, 2, 502. According to Steph. it received its name from the many roads which traversed it.
ἰὔτριχας, see ἰϋθριξ.
εὔτροχος, ον, Ep. ἐϋτροχος (τροχός), *having good wheels, with beautiful wheels*, ἅρμα, ἄμαξα, 8, 438. Od. 6, 72; always in the Ep form.
εὔτυκτος, ον (τεύχω), *well-made, handsomely wrought, well-built*, κλισίη, 10, 566. Od. 4, 123; κυνέη, 3, 336; ἱμάσθλη, 8, 44.
*εὔυμνος, ον (ὕμνος), *abounding in hymns, much-praised*, h. Ap. 19, 207.
εὐφημέω (εὔφημος), fut. ήσω, *to use propitious words*, or *words of good omen*, or *to refrain from all words of bad omen*, especially in sacrifices and religious matters; hence generally *to be still, to be silent*, like *favete linguis*. εὐφημῆσαι κέλεσθε, command to be silent, 9, 171.†

Εὔφημος, ὁ, son of Trœsenus, an ally of the Trojans, leader of the Cicones, 2, 846.
*εὐφήμως, adv. (φήμη), *of good omen, propitiously; piously, religiously*, h. Ap. 171.
Εὐφήτης, ου, ὁ, king of Ephyræ, on the Selleis in Elis, 15, 532.
Εὔφορβος, ὁ, son of Panthous, one of the bravest Trojans; he wounded Patroclus, and was slain by Menelaus, 16, 806, seq. 17, 59. (Pythagoras affirmed that he was once this Euphorbus, cf. Diog. Laert. 8, 1. 4.) [Cf. also Horat. Carm. I. 28, 10.]
εὐφραδής, ές (φράζω), *speaking well, eloquent.* 2) *clear*, only adv. εὐφραδέως, *distinctly, eloquently;* γεγνυμένα ἀγορεύειν, Od. 19, 352.†
εὐφραίνω, Ep. ἐϋφραίνω (φρήν), fut. εὐφρανέω, aor. εὔφρηνα, 1) Act. *to delight, to gladden, to please*, τινά, 5, 688; τινὰ ἐνέεσσι, 24, 102; νόημα ἀνδρός, Od. 20, 82. 2) Mid. *to be delighted, to enjoy oneself*, Od. 2, 311 (both in the comm. and in the Ep. form, 7, 297).
εὐφρονέων, ουσα, ον, Ep. ἐϋφρονέων (φρονέω), *well-disposed, benevolent;* it denotes at once a kind disposition and intelligence, cf. Nitzsch, Od. 2, 160; only as particp. in the often repeated verse: ὅ σφιν ἐϋφρονέων ἀγορήσατο, etc., 1, 73, seq.
εὐφροσύνη, ή, Ep. ἐϋφροσύνη (εὔφρων), *gladness, joy, cheerfulness*, Od. 9, 6. 20, 8; in the plur. Od. 6, 156. *Od.
εὔφρων, ον, Ep. ἐΰφρων (φρήν), *joyful, gladsome, gay*, 15, 99; θυμός, Od. 17, 531. 2) Act. *gladdening, cheering*, οἶνος, 3, 246; in both forms.
εὐφυής, ές (φύω), *of beautiful growth, growing well*, πτελέη, 15, 243; μηροί, beautiful thighs, *4, 147.
εὔχαλκος, ον (χαλκός), *made of beautiful brass*, or *beautifully wrought of brass*, ὡς στεφάνη, ἀξίνη, 11.; λέβης, Od., handsomely adorned with brass, μελίη, κυνέη, 13, 612.
*εὐχερής, ές (χείρ), *managing any thing easily, dexterous*, Batr. 62.
εὐχετάομαι, poet. form for εὔχομαι, infin. εὐχετάασθαι, Ep. for εὐχητᾶσθαι, imperf. εὐχετόωντο, Ep. for εὐχετῶντο, 1) *to affirm any thing of oneself with confidence*, as τίνες ἔμμεναι εὐχετόωνται, Od. 1, 172; hence, 1) *to vaunt oneself, to boast*, ἐπέεσσι, 12, 391. 17, 19; ἐπί τινι, about any thing: Od. 22, 412. 2) In reference to the gods: *to pray, to supplicate*, with dat. Κρονίωνι, to Zeus, 9, 268; θεοῖσιν, 15, 369. Od. 12, 356; and generally, to show reverence, *to thank any man*, spoken of men only, in reference to a god, 11, 761. τῷ μέν τοι—, θεῷ ὡς, εὐχετοίμην, Od. 8, 467; see εὔχομαι.
εὐχή, ἡ, *a vow, a petition, a prayer*, only Od. 10, 526.†
Εὐχήνωρ, ορος, ὁ, son of the prophet Polyidus of Corinth, 13, 663; according

I 6

Εὔχομαι. 180 Ἐφέλκω.

to Paus. 1, 43, grandson of Polyidus (from εὖχος and ἀνήρ).

εὔχομαι, depon. mid. fut. εὔξομαι, aor. εὐξάμην; ground meaning, *to declare aloud, to affirm confidently;* hence, 1) *boastingly to affirm of oneself, to announce oneself,* often with infin. esply in reference to family: πατρὸς ἐξ ἀγαθοῦ γένος εὔχομαι εἶναι, 14, 113. Od. 1, 180 (in this there is contained not exactly the idea of boasting, but merely the declaration with a certain degree of complacency; since in that time every one boasted of that which he believed himself to be, see Nitzsch ad Od.); it stands elliptically: ἐκ Κρητάων γένος, εὔχομαι, viz. εἶναι, I boast descent from the Cretans, Od. 14, 199; often, *to boast, to vaunt, to brag,* 1, 91. 2, 597; αὔτως, 11, 388. 2) *to vow, to promise,* with infin., 18, 499; *to vow,* esply to the gods, τινί, and infin. εὔχετο Ἀπόλλωνι ῥέξειν ἑκατόμβην, 4, 119; and because benefits were in this way expected from the gods, 3) generally *to implore, to supplicate,* θεῷ, a god; and absol., 1, 87. 6, 240; also with dat. commod. αἴτε μοι εὐχόμεναι, praying for me, 7, 298. (H. never uses the augment.)

εὖχος, εος, τό, *glory, honour,* esply *military glory, victory;* often διδόναι εὖχός τινι, to give glory to any man, spoken both of the conquered, 5, 285. 654. 11, 445; and of the gods, 7, 81. 203; often in connexion with κλέος, νίκην; εὖχος ὀρέγειν, πορεῖν τινι, 13, 327. Od. 22, 7; cf. Spitz. ad Il. 15, 462; ἀρέσθαι, 11, 290. Passow explains it, *the object of supplication,* but most of the ancients *fame,* and this signif. is required in the Hom. use.

εὐχρόης, ές, a rare poet. form for εὔχροος (χρόα), *of a beautiful colour,* Od. 14, 24.†

εὐχωλή, ἡ (εὔχομαι), 1) *boasting, vaunting,* 8, 229; *exultation, the shout of victory,* in opposition to οἰμωγή, 4, 450. 864. *b)* the object on account of which one vaunts himself (cf. Wolf Vorles.). εὐχωλήν τινι καταλείπειν, 2, 160. 4, 173. 22, 433. 2) *a vow* made to the gods, 1, 65. 93; *prayer, supplication,* 9, 499. Od. 13, 357.

εὕω (kindred with αὔω), *to singe, to burn off;* mostly used of swine, from which the bristles were singed before roasting, Od. 2, 300. 14, 75. 426. σύες εὑόμενοι τανύοντο διὰ φλογός, the swine were stretched for singeing over the fire, 9, 468; and spoken also of the singeing of the eyebrows of the Cyclops, Od. 9, 389 (εὔω deserves the preference over εὕω, cf. Buttm. Gram., vol. ii. p. 140).

εὐώδης, ες (ὄζω, ὄδωδα), *odoriferous, sweet-scented, fragrant,* θάλαμος, 3, 382; ἔλαιον, Od. 2, 339.

εὐῶπις, ιδος ἡ, *having beautiful eyes, having a lovely countenance,* κούρη, *Od. 6, 113. 142. h. Cer. 334.

ἔφαγον, see ἐσθίω, ἔδω.

ἐφάλλομαι, depon. mid. (ἅλλομαι), aor. sync. 2 ἐπᾶλτο, partcp. ἐπάλμενος and ἐπιάλμενος, 1) *to spring upon, to leap upon;* ἵππων, the chariot, 7, 15; absol. κύσσε μιν ἐπιάλμενος, Od. 24, 320; esply 2) *to leap upon,* in a hostile signif., *to rush upon,* τινί, any man, 13, 643. 21, 140; and often absol. in the partcp., 7, 260. (H. uses only 3 sing. aor. ἐπᾶλτο and the partcp. aor. sync. ἐπάλμενος and ἐπιάλμενος, Passow.)

ἔφαλος, ον (ἅλς), *situated on the sea, maritime,* epith. of sea-board towns, *2, 538. 584.

ἔφαν, see φημί.

ἐφανδάνω, poet. ἐπιανδάνω (ἁνδάνω), *to please, to be agreeable.* ἡ βουλὴ θεοῖσιν ἐφήνδανε, 7, 45; also pres ἐπιανδάνει, 7, 407; and imperf. ἐπιήνδανε in the Od. often.

ἐφάπη, see φαίνω.

ἐφάπτω (ἅπτω), fut. ἐφάψω; only 3 sing. perf. pass. ἐφῆπται, and 3 pluperf. pass. ἐφῆπτο, and aor. 1 mid. ἐφηψάμην. I) Act. *to attach to, to fasten to;* hence pass. *to be attached to;* only in a metaph. signif. with dat. of pers. Τρώεσσι κήδε' ἐφῆπται, woes are attached to the Trojans, threaten them, 2, 15. 69: ὀλέθρου πείρατα, 12, 79. Od. 22, 33 (see πεῖραρ); ἀθανάτοισιν ἔρις καὶ νεῖκος, 21, 513. II) Mid. *to touch, to lay hold of, to attain:* with gen. ἐπὴν χείρεσσιν ἐφάψεαι (i. e. ἐφάψῃ) ἠπείροιο, as soon as thou shalt touch the land with thine hands, Od. 5, 348.

ἐφαρμόζω (ἁρμόζω), fut. όσω, intrans. *to fit, to be suitable, to suit,* τινί, 19, 385.†

ἐφέζομαι, depon. mid. (ἕζομαι), *to sit upon, to seat oneself upon,* with dat. δίφρῳ, δενδρέῳ, 3, 152; πατρὸς γούνεσιν, 21, 506. 2) *to seat oneself by,* Od. 17, 334 (only pres. and imperf.).

ἐφέηκα, see ἐφίημι.

ἐφείην, see ἐφίημι.

ἐφεῖσα (εἷσα), defect. aor. 1 infin. ἐφέσσαι, Ep. for ἐφέσαι, mid ἐφείσασθαι. imperat. ἔφεσσαι, Ep. for ἔφεσαι, partcp. ἐφεσσάμενος. Ep. for ἐφεσάμενος, infin. fut. ἐφέσσεσθαι, 9, 455; 1) Act. *to put upon, to lay* or *place upon.* καταστήσαι καὶ ἐφέσσαι τινά, to convey to and put ashore, Od. 13, 274. II) Mid. *to place any thing for oneself upon, to lay upon.* μήποτε γούνασιν οἷσιν ἐφέσσεσθαι φίλον υἱόν, 9, 455. ἐμὲ—γούνασιν οἷσιν ἐφεσσάμενος, Od. 16, 443. *b)* With gen. ἐφέσσαι με νηός, put me on board thy ship, Od. 15, 277. cf. 14, 295.

ἐφέλκω (ἕλκω), I) Act. *to draw towards, to entice, to allure,* hence pass. *to be enticed,* ῥείβροισιν ἐφελκόμενος, h. 18, 9. II) Mid. *to draw* or *drag to* or *after oneself;* with accus. ἐφέλκετο ἔγχος, he drew the spear along with him, 13, 597. metaph. ἐφέλκεται ἄνδρα σίδηρος, the sword attracts (excites) the hero, Od. 16, 294. 2) *to trail, to drag.* πόδες ἐφελκόμενοι, dragging feet, 23, 696.

Έφίννυμι. 181 Έφίστημι.

έφίννυμι, poet. έπιέννυμι, q. v.
έφέπω (poet. έπω), imperf. έφεπον, Ep. for έφεῖπον, fut. έφέψω, aor. έπέσπον, infin. έπισπεῖν, partcp. έπισπών, I) Act. primary signif. *to be behind*, hence 1) *to follow, to pursue, to drive*, τινά, 11, 177; absol., 15, 742: to attack, to assault, 20, 357. 494. *b*) *to drive before one*, ἵππους, 24. 326; and ἵππους τινί, to drive or impel one's horses against any man, 16, 724. 732. *c*) *to wander over* a place, *to go through, to run through* or *over*, κορυφάς όρέων, Od. 9, 121: πεδίον, the plain, 11, 496; ύσμίνης στόμα, to pass through the gorge of battle ['to urge the battle in the foremost ranks,' Passow], 20, 359. 2) *to follow any thing zealously, to prosecute, to pursue*, frequently: πότμον, θάνατον έπισπεῖν, to overtake or meet with death, i. e. to bring it on by one's own fault, 2, 359; in like manner οῖτον, όλέθριον ἧμαρ, Od. 3, 134. Il. 19, 294. II) Mid. **έφέπομαι**, aor. έφεσπόμην, infin. έπισπέσθαι, 1) *to follow, to pursue*, τινί, any man, 13, 495; έπισπέσθαι ποσίν, with the feet, to follow running, 14, 521. 2) *to obey, to hearken to*, θεοῦ όμφῇ, Od. 3, 215; έπισπόμενοι μένεῖ σφῷ, yielding to their impulse, Od. 14, 262. (Of the mid. H. uses only the aor.)
έφέσσαι, see έφεῖσα.
έφέσσαι, see έφεῖσα.
έφέστιος, ον (έστία), 1) *that is upon* or *at the hearth*. Esply of a suppliant who sits at the hearth. έμέ έφέστιον ἤγαγε δαίμων, a god led me to the hearth, Od. 7, 248. 2) *at one's own hearth, at home* (*settled, resident*); έφέστιοι όσσοι ἔασιν, *as many as are at home* (*are settled; reside*) in Troy; 2, 125. Thus the Schol., όσοι έστίας (τουτέστιν, οίκίας) αύτόθι (i. e. in the city of Troy) διανέμουσι. So also Eustath. and Hesych. Others say, 'whoever sit about the fire-places in the camp;' but cf. v. 130, and the other Hom. passages in which έφέστιος never refers to military life.—Od. 3, 324. ἧλθε—έφέστιος, Od. 23, 55.
έφετμή, ή (έφίημι), *command, commission, order, injunction*, 1, 484; esply in the plur., Il. In οί δ᾽ αίεί βούλοντο θεοί μεμνῆσθαι έφετμέων, Od. 4, 353, supply ήμᾶς: the gods would that we should always remember their commands; but the preterite is unsuitable, should we even with the Schol. render έφετμαί *prayers*. Hence Wolf, after Zenodotus, has included this verse in brackets, see Nitzsch ad loc.
έφευρίσκω (εύρίσκω), aor. έφεῦρον, 1) *to find, to meet with*, τινά, 2, 198, seq. 2) *to devise, to invent*, μῆτιν, Od. 19, 158 (where Wolf έθ᾽ εύρίσκω).
έφεψιάομαι, depon. mid. (έψιάομαι), *to insult, to deride, to mock at*, τινί, *Od. 19, 331. 370.
έφηγέομαι, depon. mid. (ήγέομαι), aor. έφηγησάμην, *to conduct any man any where, to lead on*, έπί στίχας ήγήσατο, he led on the ranks, 2, 687.† In tmesis.
έφημαι, depon. (ἧμαι), *to sit upon, to sit by*, with dat. θρόνῳ, Od. 6, 309; κληΐδεσσιν, *Od. 12. 215.
έφημέριος, η, ον (ήμέρα), *at a day, for a day, during the day*. ού κεν έφημέριός γε βάλοι δάκρυ, he could not shed a tear all day, i. e. through the (whole) day, Od. 4, 223. Mly at or for the day. έφημέρια φρονεῖν, to care only for the present day, not to trouble oneself about the future, *Od. 21, 85.
έφημοσύνη, ή = έφετμή, *commission, command*, 17, 697. Od. 16, 340.
έφησθα, see φημί.
έφθην, see φθάνω.
έφθιαθ᾽ for έφθίατο, see φθίω.
Έφιάλτης (the leaper upon; Alp), son of Αlōeus and Iphimedeia, brother of Otus, and by tradition son of Poseidōn. They were giants, of enormous size and strength; they heaped the mountains Ossa and Pelion the one upon the other, and attempted to storm heaven; Apollo slew them, Od. 11, 304—319. They held, 5, 385, Arēs for thirteen months a prisoner; Hermēs, however, delivered him, their step-mother Eriboea betraying the fact.
έφιζάνω (ίζάνω) = έφίζω, *to sit upon, to sit at*, δείπνῳ, 10, 578; metaph. spoken of sleep, *10, 26.
έφίζω (ίζω), only imperf. *to sit at*, esply *to sit upon*, *Od. 3, 411. 19, 55.
έφίημι (ἵημι), fut. έφήσω, aor. sing. έφήκα and έφηκα, of the aor. 2, the subj. έφίην, Ep. for έφῶ, optat. έφείην, imperat. έφες, fut. mid. έφήσομαι, I) Act. 1) *to send to, to despatch to*, spoken of persons, τινά τινι, *Ιριν Πριάμῳ, 24, 117; esply in a hostile signif. *to incite, to provoke, to instigate*, τινά, always with infin, ίχθοδοπήσαι, 1, 518; άείσαι, Od. 14, 464. 2) Spoken of inanimate things; *to cast against, to let fly at, to shoot against, to hurl*, of missiles, βέλεά τινι, 1, 51; λᾶαν, μελίην, 3, 12. 21, 170; hence also χεῖράς τινι, to lay hands on any man, 1, 567, seq. *b*) Metaph. κήδεά τινι, to send disasters upon any man, 1, 445; πότμον, 4, 396; νόστον τινί, to allot a (disastrous) return to any man, Od. 9, 38; spoken of Zeus. II) Mid. only *to commission, to command, to direct*, τινί τι, only fut., 23, 82; absol., 24, 300. Od. 13, 7 (ι is poet. long; only έφίει has ῑ, Od. 24, 180).
έφικνέομαι, depon. mid. (ίκνέομαι), aor. έφικόμην, *to attain, to arrive at, to hit or strike*, 13, 613.†
έφίστημι (ίστημι), perf. (έφέστηκα), 3 plur. έφεστᾶσι, infin. έφεστάμεν, partcp. (έφεστηκώς) έφεσταότος, pluperf. έφεστήκειν, 3 plur. έφεστάσαν, aor. 2 έφέστην, I) Trans. *to put* or *place upon*, H. only, II) Intrans. in the perf., pluperf., aor. 2, and mid. *to stand upon* or *in*, with dat. πύργῳ, 6, 373; έφίστη, 17, 609. 2) *to stand at* or *by*, κεφαλῆφιν, to stand at a man's head, 10, 496; θύρῃσιν, at the

ἐφόλκαιον. 182 **Ἐχέφρων.**

doors, Od. 1, 120; ἐφέστασαν ἀλλήλοισι, together, 13, 133; also παρά and ἐπί τινι, 12, 199; ἐπὶ χείλει, 12, 52; absol., Od. 22, 203. b) In a hostile signif. *to press upon, instare*, ἀλλήλοισιν, 15, 703. Batr. 284. Metaph. Κῆρες ἐφεστᾶσιν θανάτοιο μυρίαι, innumerable fates threaten, 12, 326. c) *to direct one's attention, to observe, to be busy at.* ἐπιστάντες κατέτρωξαν, Batr. 126. The pres. mid. *to place oneself at,* only once: θύρῃσιν ἐφίστατο, at the doors, 11, 644.

ἐφόλκαιον, τό (ἐφέλκω), πηδάλιον, Eust. *a helm, a rudder.* Thus Voss, Od. 14, 350; according to others, *a boat* = ἐφόλκιον.

ἐφομαρτέω (ὁμαρτέω), *to follow, to pursue*, absol., *8, 191. 12, 412. 23, 414; only imperf.

ἐφοπλίζω (ὁπλίζω), fut. ἐφοπλίσω, aor. ἐφώπλισα, partcp. ἐφοπλίσας, Ep. σσ, fut. mid. ἐφοπλίσομαι, 1) Act. *to prepare, to make ready*, with accus. δαῖτά τινι, a meal, 4, 344; ἅμαξαν καὶ ἡμιόνους, to harness the mules and carriage, Od. 6, 37; νῆα, to furnish out a ship, Od. 2, 295. 2) Mid. *to prepare any thing for oneself*, δόρπα, 8, 503. 9, 66.

ἐφοράω (ὁράω), fut. ἐπόψομαι, and Ep. ἐπιόψομαι, aor. ἐπεῖδον, 1) *to inspect closely, to look at, to survey,* with accus. spoken of the gods: ἀνθρώπους, to look upon men, Od. 13, 214; of Hēlius: πάντ' ἐφορᾷ καὶ ἐπακούει, 3, 277. Od. 11, 109. 12, 323; to visit, Κακοΐλιον, Od. 23, 19. 2) *to view*, in order to choose, *to look out, to select*, with accus. only in fut. in the Ep. form: ἐπιόψομαι, 9, 167. τάων (νεῶν) ἐγὼν ἐπιόψομαι, ἥτις ἀρίστη, from these I will select that which is best, Od. 2, 294.

ἐφορμάω (ὁρμάω), aor. ἐφώρμησα, aor. 1 pass. ἀφωρμήθην, 1) Act. *to urge against, to excite, to provoke against,* τί τινι, πόλεμόν τινι, war against any man, 3, 165; ἀνέμους, Od. 7, 272. II) Mid. with aor. pass. *to be urged on, to be excited* or *impelled*, esply with infin. ἐμοὶ αὐτῷ θυμὸς ἐφορμᾶται πολεμίζειν, my mind feels impelled (desires) to fight, 13, 74. Od. 1, 275. 4, 713; and without θυμός, Od. 21, 399; hence, 2) *to run to, to rush forth,* Od. 11, 206; esply in a hostile signif. *to rush upon, to attack, to assail,* ἔγχει, 17, 465; often absol., 20, 461. Od. 22, 300. b) *to make an attack upon, to assault*, trans. with an accus. ἔθνος ὀρνίθων, 15, 691. cf. 20, 461.

ἐφορμή, ἡ (ἐφορμάω), *a place for attacking, a passage, an entrance,* Od. 22, 130.†

ἐφυβρίζω (ὑβρίζω), *to treat with insolence, to insult about*, in the partcp., 9, 368.†

ἔφυδρος, ον (ὕδωρ), prop. *at* or *near the water.* 2) *moist, bringing rain*, epith. of Zephyr, Od. 14, 458.†

ἐφύπερθε and ἐφύπερθεν, adv. (ὕπερθε), *upon, above,* II. and Od. 2) *from above,* Od. 9, 383.

Ἐφύρη, ἡ, Att. Ἐφύρα, Ephyra, 1) the ancient name of Corinth, accord. to Paus. so called from Ephyra the daughter of Oceanus, see Κόρινθος. 6, 152. 2) an old Pelasgic town on the river Selleis in Elis, in the land of the Epēans, the abode of Augeias where (11, 741) many poisonous herbs grew, 2, 659; cf. Strab. VIII. p. 338, who also takes 15, 531. Od. l. 259. 2, 328, of Ephyra in Elis, cf. Ottf. Müllers Geschr. Hell. Stämme I. p. 273. 3) a very ancient town in Thesprotia, i. e. on the main-land opposite the Phaeaces; later *Cichyrus*. Mannert, Sickler, p. 42f; and Nitzsch ad Od. I. p. 45. explain Od. 1, 259. 2, 328, of the Thesprotian Ephyra, because Odysseus (Ulysses) on his return from Ephyra to Ithaca came to the Taphians who dwelt north of Ithaca. 4) a town in Thessaly, later *Crannon*, whence Ἐφυροι, q. v. (Ἐφύρα, prob. Æol. for Ἐφόρα = Ἐπωπή, *a watchtower.*)

Ἐφυροι, οἱ, the *Ephyri*, according to the Ven. Schol. Steph. and Strab. IX. p. 442, the inhabitants of Crannon in Thessaly (Pelasgiotis), which at an earlier period was called Ephyra, 13, 301.

ἔχαδον, see χανδάνω.

ἔχεα, see χέω.

ἐχέθυμος, ον (θυμός), *possessing intelligence*, or *checking one's desires.* οὐκ ἐχέθυμος, Od. 8, 320.†

Ἐχεκλῆς, ῆος, ὁ, son of Actor, husband of Polymēlē, ruler of the Myrmidons, 16, 189.

Ἔχεκλος, ὁ = Ἐχεκλῆς. 1) son of Agēnor, slain by Achilles, 20, 474. 2) a Trojan slain by Patroclus, 16, 694.

Ἐχέμμων, ονος, ὁ, Ep. Ἐχέμμων (Ἐχέμων, ed. Heyne), son of Priam, slain by Diomēdēs, 5, 160, seq.

Ἐχένηος, ὁ, one of the noble Phæaces. Od. 7, 155. 11, 342.

ἐχεπευκής, ἐς (πεύκη), *sharp, sharppointed, painful,* epith. of the arrow, 1, 51. 4, 129. (According to Buttm. Lex. p. 320, the ground signif. of πεύκη is not *bitterness,* but a *point*; the first is adopted by the ancients, see Eustath. See πεύκη.)

Ἐχέπωλος, ὁ (having steeds), 1) son of Thalysius, a Trojan, slain by Antilochus, 4, 458. 2) son of Anchises from Sicyon, who presented to Agamemnon the mare Æthe, because he would not go with him to Troy, 23, 296.

ἔχεσκον, see ἔχω.

Ἔχετος, ὁ, son of Euchēnor and Phlogea, a cruel king of Epirus, who cut off the noses and ears of strangers and cast them to the dogs, Od. 18, 85. According to the Schol. he blinded his daughter Metope and mutilated her lover Æchmodicus. Others make him the son of Buchetus and ruler of the Sicilians. cf. Od. 21, 308.

ἔχευα, ἐχευάμην, see χέω.

ἐχέφρων, ον, gen. ονος (φρήν), *having understanding, intelligent, prudent,* wise. 9, 341; epith. of Penelope (Voss. *chaste*) Od. 4, 111. 17, 390.

Ἐχέφρων. 183 Ἔχω.

Ἐχέφρων, ονος, ὁ, son of Nestor and Anaxibia or Eurydice, Od. 3, 413.
ἔχησθα, Ep. for ἔχῃς, see ἔχω.
ἐχθαίρω, poet. (ἔχθος), aor. ἤχθηρα, to hate, to be hostile to, with accus. opposed to φιλεῖν, Od. 4, 692. 15, 71. Il. 9, 452. 20, 306.
ἔχθιστος, η, ον, most hated, most odious, irreg. superl. of ἐχθρός, Il.
ἐχθοδοπέω (ἐχθοδοπός), aor. infin. ἐχθοδοπῆσαι, to proceed to act or to speak in a hostile manner, τινί, against any man, 1, 518.† (The derivation of ἐχθοδοπός is obscure; the grammarians derive it from ἔχθος and δοῦπος, to rush on with hostility, or = hostile-looking, ἐχθρός and ΟΠΤΩ; a derivation which Buttm. approves of: according to others it is only a lengthened form of ἐχθρός as ἀλλοδαπός.)
ἔχθομαι, poet. (ἔχθος), only pres. and imperf. to be odious, τινί, *Od. 4, 502. 756; ἤχθετο, Od. 14, 366. 19, 338.
ἔχθος, εος, τό, enmity, hatred, hostility, Od. 9, 277; plur. ἔχθεα λυγρά, grievous enmity, 3, 416. (Related either to ἄχθος, or ἔξω, ἐκτός.)
ἐχθρός, ή, όν (ἔχθος), hated, odious, spoken both of persons and things, τινί, 9, 312. Od. 14, 156; δῶρα, 9, 378. (Superl. ἔχθιστος.)
Ἐχῖναι, αἱ, νῆσοι, Ep. for Ἐχῑνάδες, the Echinades, a group of little islands in the Ionian sea, near the mouth of the Achelöus, on the coast of Ætolia and Acarnania. The nearest lay, according to Strab. X. p. 459, only five stadia, the most remote fifteen stadia from the coast, now Curzolari, 2, 625. Strabo reckons Dulichium amongst them. They acquired the name Hedgehog-islands (from ἐχῖνος), from their form; because they lay about the Achelous like the quills of a hedgehog, see Buttm. Lex. p. 364. According to Völcker Hom. Georg. p. 60, H. thought them on the coast of Elis, very near Samê and Zacynthus.
Ἐχίος, ὁ, 1) father of Mēkisteus, a Hellenian, 8, 333. 2) a Greek, slain by Polītes, 15, 339. 3) a Trojan, slain by Patroclus, 16, 416. (Ἐχίον, with a different accent from ἐχιον, adder's-bane.)
ἔχμα, ατος, τό (ἔχω). 1) any thing that holds back or obstructs, an obstruction, a hindrance, ἀμάρτη δ' ἐξ ἔχματα βάλλειν, to remove the rubbish from the channel, 21, 259; hence a) a bulwark, a defence, both for any thing: ἔχματα πύργων, 12, 260; and against any thing: ἔχμα ἐπηλυσίης, h. Merc. 37. b) a prop, a support, ἔχματα νηῶν, of stones, to hold firm the ships, according to the Schol. κρατήματα, 14, 410. (The transition from the sing. to the plur. is worthy of note.) 2) that which binds together, a bond, a chain, a fetter; ῥηγνύναι ἔχματα πέτρης, to burst the bonds of the rock, i. e. that which confined the stone to its bed of rock, 13, 139.
ἔχω, imperf. εἶχον, Ep. ἔχον, iterat. form imperf. ἔχεσκον, fut. ἔξω and

oftener σχήσω, aor. act. ἔσχον, infin. σχεῖν, Ep. σχέμεν, fut. mid. ἔξομαι and σχήσομαι, aor. mid. ἐσχόμην, 3 sing. σχέτο, without augm. only 7, 248. 21, 345; imperat. σχοῦ, infin. σχέσθαι, partcp. σχόμενος. An Ep. form of the aor. is ἐσχεθον, σχέθον, and from the aor. is formed a new pres. ἴσχω. Ground signif. to hold and to have. 1) Act. 1) Trans. to hold, to grasp, to hold fast, a) Primarily, to hold in the hands, χειρί or ἐν χειρί τι, 1, 14. 6, 319; μετὰ χερσίν, 11, 184. ἔχειν τινά τινος, to hold any man by any thing, χειρός, ποδός, by the hand, the foot, 4, 154. 11, 488. 16, 763. The direction is often indicated by an adv. or prep.: πρό τινος, ἐπί τινι, ἀντία ἀλλήλων, 5, 300. 569. ἔχειν τινί τι, to hold any thing to any man, 9, 209; metaph. φυλακάς, to keep watch, 9, 1; ἀλαοσκοπιήν, 13, 10; σκοπιήν, Od. 8, 302. b) to hold erect, to bear, to carry, κάρη ὑψοῦ, 6, 509; κάρη ὑπὲρ πασῶν, to erect the head above all, Od. 6, 107; κίονας, Od. 1. 53; hence metaph. to shelter, to protect, to preserve, 22, 322. 24, 730. c) to hold fast, to hold in, τινά, any man (by force or kindness), ἵππους, 4, 302; cf. 227, hence: ὀχῆες εἴχον πύλας, the bars held the doors fastened, 12, 456. 24, 453. metaph. ἔχει βέλος ὀξὺ γυναῖκα, held fast, pierced, 11, 269, ἐν φρεσίν, to retain, 3, 53. d) to hold up, to check, to restrain, to hold off (always, except 13, 51), in the fut. σχήσειν, 20, 27. 33, 720; ὀδύνας, 11, 848; τινά τινος, to repel or restrain any man from any thing, 2, 275. 13, 687. e) to hold out against, to withstand, esply an attacking enemy, 13, 51. Od. 1, 198, οὐδέ οἱ ἔσχεν ὀστέον, nor did his bone withstand, 16, 740. f) to keep towards, to direct, my ἵππους, νῆας, 3, 263; with ἐπί τινι, or adv. as πρόσθε, Πύλονδε, 11, 760; and absol. to sail any where, Od. 3, 182. 2) to have. a) to possess, spoken of every thing which belongs to any man as property, παράκοιτιν, 3, 53. cf. 13, 173. Od. 4, 569; hence pass. τοῦπερ θυγατήρ ἔχεθ' (ἔχετο) Ἕκτορι, whose daughter was had by Hector, i. e. married to Hector, 6, 398. b) Spoken of the gods, to hold, to inhabit, οὐρανόν, Ὄλυμπον, Od. 1, 67. 4, 756. αἴθη ἔχει κορυφήν, Od. 12, 76; also with the idea to have in power, to take care of, πατρώϊα ἔργα, Od. 2, 22. ἵππους ἔχων ἀτίταλλε, 24, 280. c) to have, to seize, to apprehend, spoken respecting any thing that appertains to soul or body; πόνον, ἄλγεα, μένος, 6, 525. 5, 895. 516. Often the condition stands as subject and the person as object, in the accus. Δία οὐκ ἔχεν ὕπνος, sleep held not Zeus, 2, 2. Ἀχαιοὺς ἔχε φύζα, 9, 2; hence pass. ἔχεσθαι ἀσθματι, to be seized with laborious breathing, 15, 10; in like manner: κακότητι, ἄλγεσι, Od. 6, 182. d) to have with oneself, to carry, to lead, spoken of things: σάκος ὤμῳ, εἷμα ἀμφ' ὤμοισιν; and according to the at bst. to cause, to

Ἔχω. 184 Ἔως.

make, spoken of a helmet; καναχὴν ἔχε, it emitted a sound, 16, 105. φόρμιγγες βοὴν εἶχον, the harps sounded, 18, 495; ὕβριν, to exhibit insolence, Od. 1, 368. The partcp. ἔχων often stands with another verb for greater exactness: τὸν ἔξαγε χειρὸς ἔχων, he led him out by the hand, 11, 188 : cf. 24, 280. 2) Intrans. 1) *to hold oneself*, to be in a place or condition. εὖ ἔχει, it is well, Od. 24, 245 ; *to maintain oneself, to persist*; mly limited by an adv. ἔχον (sc. οὕτως), ὥστε τάλαντα γυνή (sc. ἔχει), they held themselves, as a woman holds the balance (in equipoise); the first time intrans., the second trans., 12, 433. (Köppen from v. 436, supplies unnecessarily μάχην: 'they made the fight equal'). ἔξω, ὡς λίθος, Od. 19, 494. ἔχον ὡς σφιν πρῶτον ἀνήχθετο Ἴλιος, they were disposed, as at first, when Troy was odious to them, 24, 27. ἔχεν ἧ—ἐσᾶλτο, he held himself where he leaped in, 13, 679. οὐδ' οἱ ἔγχος ἔχ' ἀτρέμας, the spear remained not quiet, 13, 557; in opposition to ἐλέλικτο. 2) *to hold oneself, to tend to, to extend*; ὑψόσε, to extend upwards, Od. 19, 38. ὀδόντες ἔχον ἔνθα καὶ ἔνθα, projected here and there, 10, 263. ἔγχος ἔσχε δι' ὤμων, passed [as we say, *held right on*] through the shoulders, 14, 452. 3) *to be able, to be in a condition*, with infin. οὔπως ἔτι εἶχεν ὑποτρέσαι, he was no longer able to fly, 7, 217. 16, 110; without infin., 17, 354. II) Mid. *to hold oneself, to maintain oneself*, κρατερῶς, 16, 501. 17. 559; ἄντα σχομένη, holding herself opposite, i. e. opposite to him, Od. 6, 141. 2) *to hold oneself, to attach oneself, to hang on, to remain*, in a place: ἔγχος σχέτο ἐν τῇ ῥινῷ, 7, 248. πρὸς ἀλλήλοισι, ἔχονται, they hang to one another, Od. 5, 329; ἀνὰ δ' ἀλλήλῃσιν, up upon one another, Od. 24, 8; with gen. alone: πέτρης. upon the rock, Od. 5, 429 ; metaph. ἔσχετο φωνή, the voice faltered, 17, 696. *b*) Esply *to depend on* any man, τινός; σέο ἕξεται, it will depend upon thee, 9, 102; with infin., h. 30, 6; and ἔκ τινος, Od. 11, 346 ; hence *c*) *to be in any man's power, to be in a man's possession*. ἔντεα μετὰ Τρώεσσιν ἔχονται, 18, 130. 197; metaph. πείρατα νίκης ἔχονται ἐν θεοῖσιν, the event of victory is in the power of the gods, 7, 102. 3) *to withdraw oneself, to retire* [always aor. or fut. except 14, 129], with gen. αὐτῆς, 2, 98; μάχης, 3, 84; βίης, Od. 4, 422. 4) *to hold, to bear* for oneself, or with reference to the subject; with accus. ἀσπίδα πρόσθε, the shield before oneself, 12, 294; κρήδεμνα ἄντα παρειάων, Od. 1, 334. 21, 65, μένος καὶ χεῖρας σχήσεσθαι, like act. σχήσειν, 17, 638. cf. 12, 126. The following passage is differently explained; it belongs in signif. to no. 3, mid: οὐδ' ἔτι φασὶν σχήσεσθ' ἀλλ' ἐν νηυσὶ μελαίνῃσιν πεσέεσθαι, they say that they can no longer hold back, but will plunge into the dark ships, 9, 235. cf. 12,

106, 107. In both passages the Trojans are the subject. Thus Eustath. (ἤγουν ἐφέξειν ἑαυτοὺς, ἀλλὰ διώκοντας, ἐμπεσεῖσθαι ταῖς νηυσί), and Schol. Ven. and Voss. Another explanation, which Ruhkopf in Köpp. Anm. zu Il. 12, 105, gives, supplies ἡμᾶς to σχήσεσθαι, and refers it to the Greeks. They also quote Eustath. and the Schol. brev. ; but the connexion does not favour the interpretation. The case is different with 12, 125. 17, 639. cf. πίπτω.

ἐψιάομαι, depon. mid. (ἐψία), prop. *to play with small stones*; but generally *to play, to jest, to be pleased*, Od. 17, 530; *to be charmed*, with dat. μολπῇ καὶ φόρμιγγι, *Od. 21, 429.

ἔω, see εἰμί.
ἐῶ, ἰῶ, see ἐάω.
ἔωθα, see ἔθω.
ἑώκει, see ἔοικα.
ἐώπει, see ἔπω.

ἔωμεν, 19, 402 ; in ἐπεί χ' ἕωμεν πολέμοιο,† ed. Wolf; a rare form. Eustath. and the Gramm. explain it: πληρηθῶμεν, κορεσθῶμεν, and compare it to the formula ἐξ ἔρον ἕντο. They even derive it from a theme ἔω, i. e. πληρῶ, and consider it as subj. aor. 2 pass. Such an aor. pass. is contrary to all usus loquendi. Buttm. Lex. p. 25, and Gram. under ἄω, justly maintain that we must write either ἔωμεν or ἕωμεν. The first is the most simple. 1) ἔωμεν, Ep. for ὦμεν, 1 plur. aor. 2 subj. act. from ἵημι in the intrans. signif. *when we desist from war*, see ἵημι. 2) ἕωμεν, according to Buttm. Lex. p. 26, subj. pres. from *ΑΩ, *to satiate*, prop. ἄωμεν, and Ep. for metre's sake ἕωμεν; and on account of the spir. len. he reads ἐπεί κ' ἕωμεν, when we become sated with war; have had enough of the war. Spitz. Exc. 31, ad Il. defends the common deriv., and with the ancients adopts the forms ἔω, ἐάω, ἄω, ὤμεν and ἐώμεν, remarking that it is distinguished by the spir. asp. from ἐάω, ἄω.

ἐῶν, see εἰμί.
ἐῳνοχόει, see οἰνοχοέω.
ἐώργει, see ἔρδω.

ἕως, Ep. also εἵως, conj. of time. 1) To express simultaneous action, *as long as, whilst*, with indic. when the affirmation respects a reality ; in the apodosis prop. τέος, often simply δέ or τόφρα, 18, 15. 1, 193. 10, 507. Od. 12, 327. 2) In introducing a consequent, *up to, until*; *a*) With indicat., 11, 342. Od. 5, 123. *b*) With subj. and κέ, when a contemplated end is expressed, 3, 291. 24, 183. *c*) With optat. after a historical tense, Od. 5, 386. 9, 376 ; and with κέ, Od. 2, 78. 3) *in order that*, that, like ὄφρα, with optat., Od. 4, 800. 6, 80. 4) As adv. for τέως, *for a time, some time, in the mean time*, 12, 141. 13, 143. Od. 3, 126 ; prop. it then stands with an omission of the clause belonging to it, cf. Nitzsch ad Od. 3, 126. ἕως and εἵως change with the necessities of the metre; ἕως has its

Ἑῶοι. 185 Ζεύς.

natural quantity only once, Od. 2, 78; elsewhere it is either monosyllabic, as 17, 727; or to be pronounced as a trochee, like εἶος, as Thiersch, § 168, 10, would write it, 1, 193. 10, 507, and often.
ἕωσι, see εἰμί.
ἕωσι, see ἐάω.
ἑωσφόρος, ον (ἕως, φέρω), *bringing the morning* [*day's harbinger*, Cp.]; as a pr. n. Ἑωσφόρος, the morning star, 23, 226; † according to Hes. Th. 381, son of Astraeus and Eôs (in H. to be read as a trissyllable).

Z.

Z, the sixth letter of the Greek alphabet; and hence the index of the sixth rhapsody.

ζα-, an inseparable particle, a dialectic variety of δα, which in composition strengthens the notion of the simple word, as ζάθεος, ζάκοτος. It is mly derived from διά; more correctly, Hartung considers it a collateral form of ἄγα (ἄγαν).

ζαής, ές, gen. έος (ἄημι), *blowing violently, stormy*, ἄνεμος, 12, 157. Od. 5, 368. The heteroclit. accus. ζαῆν for ζαῆ (as Σωκράτην for Σωκράτη) is found in Od. 12, 313; see Thiersch, Gram. § 193. 35.

ζάθεος, έη, εον (θεός), *divine, very sacred, holy*, spoken of countries and places, inasmuch as they were supposed to be innabited by the gods, Κίλλα [*Cilla the divine*. Cp.], Νῖσα, Κρῖσα, *1, 38. 2, 520.

ζάκοτος, ον (κότος), *very angry, furious, violently enraged*, 3, 220.†

Ζάκυνθος, ή, an island in the Ionian sea, south of Samê, which, with Ithaca, Samê, and two small unknown islands, Ægilips and Crokyleia, constituted the Kephallenian kingdom, which was subject to Odysseus (Ulysses); now *Zante*, 2, 634. Because in this place the position before ζ ἰς neglected, Payne-Knight, in Proleg. Hom. p. 79, would read Δάκυνθος, see Thiersch, § 146. 8. ὑλήεσσα Ζάκυνθος, Od. 9, 24; but ὑλήεντι, agreeing with Ζάκυνθος, is feminine [see ὑλήεις], Od. 1, 246. 16, 123. The fact is, the first syllable can stand no where in heroic verse but at the close of a dactyl; hence the Epic poets could not prolong the preceding vowel.

*ζαμενής, ές (μένος), *very strong, very brave*; only in the superl. ζαμενέστατος, h. Merc. 307, as epith. of Apollo.

ζατρεφής, ές (τρέφω), gen. έος, *well-fed, fat, stout*, ταῦροι, 7, 223; αἶγες, Od. 14, 106; φῶκαι, Od. 4, 451.

ζαφλεγής, ές (φλέγω), gen. έος, prop. *brightly burning*; only metaph. *very ardent, spirited, lively*, spoken of men, 21, 465; and of horses, h. 7, 8.

ζαχρηής, ές, gen. έος, *pressing on ar-* *dently, blowing violently, impetuous*, spoken of winds, 5, 525; and of warriors, *12, 347. 13, 684. In the last passage, it is, with Heyne, Voss, and Spitzner, to be referred to the Greeks. (Undoubtedly Ion. for ζαχρηής from ζά and χράω; the reading ζαχρειής, as well as the derivation from χρειά, is unsuitable, see Thiersch, Gram. § 193. 35.)

ζάω, contract. ζῶ, *I live*; only partcp. pres. ζώντος, 1, 88; † see ζώω.

ζειά, ή, *spelt, farra*, according to Voss a species of wheat, cultivated like wheat, and better suited to the south than the north. It occurs only in the plur. and is spoken of as food for horses, Od. 4, 41. 604. This same spelt seems to be called ὄλυρα, 5, 196. Still Sprengel, Hist. rei Herbar., makes a distinction between ὄλυρα, *triticum Spelta*, and ζειά, *triticum Zea*, the last having grains like barley and larger ears.

ζείδωρος, ον (ζειά, δῶρον), *grain-giving, producing nourishment*, epith of the earth, 2, 548. Od. 3, 3. (The deriv. from ζάω, *life-giving*, according to Hesych. is contrary to analogy.)

Ζέλεια, ή, *Zeleia*, a town in Troas, at the foot of Ida, later belonging to Cyzicus, 2, 824. (From the neglect of position before this word, Payne-Knight, Proleg. Hom. p. 19, would read Δέλεια.) Cf. Ζάκυνθος, extr.

ζέσσεν, see ζέω.

ζεύγλη, ή (ζεύγνυμι), in H. distinguished from ζυγόν; the part of the yoke into which the heads of the harnessed animals were introduced; each yoke had therefore two ζεύγλαι; *the yoke-ring, the yoke-bow*, *17, 440. 19, 406.

ζεύγνυμι (the infin. pres. ζευγνύμεναι, ζευγνύμεν) and ζευγνύω, whence the imperf. ζεύγνυον for ζεύγν., 19, 343, aor. 1 ἔζευξα, Ep. ζεῦξα, aor. mid. ἐζευξάμην, perf. pass. ἔζευγμαι. 1) Act. 1) *to yoke together, to yoke, to harness*, with accus. ἵππους, βόας; sometimes with ὑφ' ἅρμασι, ὑπ' ἁμάξησιν, ὑπ' ἀπήνῃ or ὀχεσφίν, 23, 130. Od. 3, 478 6, 73. 2) *to join, to unite*, σανίδες ἐζευγμέναι, 18, 276. II) Mid. *to yoke or harness for oneself*, ἵππους, Od. 3, 192. 15, 145. 24, 281. (The form ζευγνύμεν, 16, 145, is worthy of note, with ῦ as infin. pres., but having every where else ῠ. Buttm, Herm., and Becker would write ζευγνύμεν, which the analogy ἔμεν, ἔμμεναι favours. Spitz., on the other hand, after the ancients, writes ζευγνύμεν. see Thiersch, § 231. 102. Buttm. Ausf. Gram. § 107. Anm. 30. p. 535. Rost. Gram. ζεύγνυμι.)

ζεῦγος, τό (ζεύγνυμι), *a yoke, a pair*, spoken of draught animals, 18, 543.†

Ζεύς, ὁ, vocat. Ζεῦ; the oblique cases are sometimes formed from ΔΙΣ, gen. Διός, dat. Διΐ, accus. Δία; sometimes from ΖΗΝ, gen. Ζηνός, dat. Ζηνί, accus. Ζῆνα (Ζῆν', 14, 265); *Zeus* (*Jupiter*), son of Cronus and Rhea, 15, 187; the most powerful amongst the gods, the father of

Ζεφυρίη. 186 Ζυγόν.

gods and men. 1) He is the ruler of the gods, who stand far below him in power and dignity. He convokes the assemblies of the gods, to deliberate on the concerns of his kingdom; yet durst no one of the gods oppose his settled resolution, 8, 12, seq. 19, 258. 2) He is, as god of the heavens, the governor of all natural phenomena. As such, he is throned in ether (αἰθέρι ναίων, ὑψίζυγος); he collects the clouds; hence, νεφεληγερέτης, κελαινεφής, gives rain and sunshine, and excites tempests. Thunder and lightning are the signs of his anger; by these he terrifies men, and gives them omens (hence τερπικέραυνος, ἀστεροπητής, ἀργικέραυνος, ἐρίγδουπος, ἐριβρεμέτης, etc.). 3) He also governs the fates of men (ταμίας); yet is he himself subject to the laws of Fate, 10, 71. Od. 6, 188. He is the author of royalty, the protector of magistrates, directs the assemblies of men, Od. 2, 69; the defender of house and hearth (ἑρκεῖος), Od. 22, 335; he is the patron of hospitality, protects guests and suppliants, hence, ξείνιος, Od. 9, 270. 6, 207; and ἱκετήσιος, Od. 13, 213. 4) His sister and wife is Hêrê, who often so opposes his will, that he threatens her with punishments, and even executes them, 15, 17, seq. 19, 95, seq. Not unfrequently he excites her just displeasure by the violation of nuptial fidelity, 14, 317, seq. 5) The form of Zeus is sublime, and inspires awe. With his head, which is surrounded with ambrosial locks, he gives assent or expresses his anger. The tokens of his power are thunderbolts and the ægis (αἰγίοχος). As the tutelary deity of the Pelasgians he is called Πελασγικός, and Δωδωναῖος, because he had an oracle at Dôdôna, see Δωδώνη. (In signif. Ζεύς is related to ζέω and ζάω, according to Herm. *Fervius*, live-giver, and Διός, fr. ΔΙΣ, prob. the upper air.)

Ζεφυρίη, ἡ, subaud. πνοή, *the west wind, the western breeze*, prop. a fem. from ζεφύριος, Od. 7, 119.† (The first syllable is here long by the arsis.)

Ζέφυρος, ὁ, 1) *Zephyrus, the evening or west wind*, one of the four main winds which H. mentions. It comes from the western ocean, Od. 4, 567; is opposed to Εὖρος, Od. 5, 332; still it blows with Boreas from Thrace, 9, 5; and unites with Notus on the Trojan plain. These apparent contradictions are most probably to be explained by the circumstance, that H. in the four main winds includes also the intermediate ones, cf. Nitzsch ad Od. 2, 419. It is often rough and violent (Od. 5, 295); brings snow, Od. 19, 206; and rain, Od. 14, 458; still its breath is also soft, Od. 7, 119; and breathes coolness upon the blessed in the Elysian fields. 2) It appears personified, 23, 200; and, as a deity, the wind-gods feast with him. To him the harpy Podarge bore the steeds of Achilles,

16, 150. According to Hes. Th. 379, he is the son of Astræus and Podargê.

ζέω, imperf. Ep. ζέε for ἔζει, 21, 365; aor. 1 ἔζεσα, Ep. συ, *to seethe, to boil, to bubble up, to be boiling hot*, spoken of water, 18, 349. 21, 365. Od. 10, 360; and λέβης ζεῖ, the cauldron boils, 21, 362.

Ζῆθος, ὁ, son of Zeus and Antiopê, brother of Amphīon, husband of Æoon, Od. 11, 262. 19, 523.

ζηλήμων, ον (ζηλάω), gen. ονος, *jealous, envious, unfavorable*, θεοί, Od. 5, 118.†

*ζηλοσύνη, ἡ, poet. for ζῆλος, *zeal*, 2) *jealousy, envy*, h. Ap. 100.†

*ζηλόω (ζῆλος), fut. ώσω, aor. 3 sing. optat. ζηλώσαι, 1) *to emulate, to imitate*, 2) *to be jealous, to envy*, absol. h. Cer. 168. 223.

(Ζήν), gen. Ζηνός, see Ζεύς.

*ζητεύω, poet. for ζητέω, *to seek*, with accus. h. Ap. 215. Merc. 392.

ζητέω, fut. ήσω, *to seek, to seek out, to search for, to trace*, τινά. 14, 258;† βόας, h. Merc. 22. 2) *to inquire, to ask for* any thing; with γόνος, Batr. 25.

ζόφος, ὁ, *darkness, obscurity*, hence, 1) *the obscurity* of the lower world. Ἐρεβόσδε ὑπὸ ζόφον, Od. 20, 356. *b*) *the realm of shades* itself, 15, 191. Od. 11, 57. h. Cer. 482. 2) *the dark*, shaded side of the earth, *the evening darkness, the west, evening*, in opposition to ἠώς, Od. 10, 190, seq. cf. 8, 29; πρὸς ζόφον, in antithesis to πρὸς ἠῶ τ᾽ ἠέλιόν τε, Od. 13, 241. Il. 12, 339. It is thus correctly explained by Heyne, Uckert, Grotefend. Nitzsch ad Od. 2, 146. Strabo and Voss interpret it incorrectly *midnight* (see Völcker's Hom. Geogr. § 27, p. 42). According to Buttm. Lex. p. 378, of the same family with δνόφος, νέφος.

ζυγόδεσμον, τό (δεσμός), *the yoke-band*, the leathern thong with which the yoke was bound to the pole, so that the animals did not draw by traces, but by the pole, 24, 270.† It is called ἐννεάπηχυ, nine cubits long, it being bound thrice around; cf. Köpke Kriegswesen der Griech. p. 137. (In H. it is neut., later also ὁ ζυγόδεσμος.)

ζυγόν, τό (ζεύγνυμι), Ep. gen. sing. ζυγόφιν, 24, 576. 1) *a yoke*, a transverse piece of wood attached to the pole, upon the two sides of which were two wooden bows or yokes (ζεύγλη and sometimes ζυγόν), into which the necks of the draught animals were introduced. In the middle, where it was attached to the tongue, it had an elevation (ὀμφαλός), 24, 269. 273. 5, 730. Od. 3, 486. It was furnished with rings (οἰήκεσσιν ἀραρός), 24, 269, for the reins, to prevent them from slipping, cf. λέπαδνον, ἔστωρ, κρίκος. eaply as ζυγὸν ἵππειον or ἵππων, mentioned 5, 799. 851. 2) *the bridge* or cross-bar, by which the two arms of the lyre were connected, and in which the pegs were inserted, 9, 187. h. Merc. 50. 3) Plur. *the rowers' seats* or *benches*, the transverse

Ζυγός.

beams in the middle space of vessels, which bound together the sides and formed seats for the rowers, Od. 9, 99. 13, 21. (The ground signification of ζυγόν is *uniting*, and especially a body which unites two others. In H. only neut.)

ζυγός, ὁ = ζυγόν, h. Cer. 217; in a metaph. signif. *a burden*.

ζωάγρια, τά (ζωός, ἀγρεύω), *a reward for the preservation of life*, prop. the present which the prisoner gives the victor for his life: ζωάγρια τίνειν, to pay this reward, 18, 407. ζωάγρια ὀφέλλειν τινί, to owe to any man the reward for saving life, i. e. to owe one's life to him, Od. 8, 462.

ζωγρέω (ζωός, ἀγρεύω), 1) *to take alive, to grant one's life*, with accus. (to a prisoner in war), 6, 46. 10, 378. 2) *to preserve in life, to reanimate*, θυμόν, 5, 698.

ζωή, ἡ (ζάω), *life*. 2) In H. *the support of life, sustenance, property*, like βίος, *Od. 14, 96. 16, 429.

ζῶμα τό (ζώννυμι), prop. *a broad band or girdle*, worn about the loins. Thus, the covering of the loins worn by wrestlers, *subligaculum*, 23, 683. With the Hom. warriors this band which was under the ζωστήρ, was connected with the cuirass, and since it was, as it were, a part of the cuirass, the latter is also called ζῶμα, which is otherwise called θώρηξ, 4, 187. 216. Thus Aristarchus, cf. Lehrs de Aristarch. stud. p. 125, and Voss. Others, as Heyne, understand by it, with Eustath., *the under garment or doublet*, of the Hom. warriors, which was confined by a girdle (ζωστήρ), Od. 14, 482 [see Heyne ad 11. 4, 132].

ζώνη, ἡ (ζώννυμι), 1) *a girdle, a zone, a waist-band*, chiefly of females, which they wore above the hips, so that the robe might fall in ample folds, 14, 181. Od. 5, 231. 10, 544; hence metaph. ζώνην λύειν, to loose the girdle, 11, 245. cf. h. Ven. 256. 2) Metaph. the part of the body where the girdle was worn, between the hips and the short ribs (ὁ περὶ τὸν γαστέρα τόπος), the smaller part of the body, *the waist*. Ἀρεὶ ζώνην ἴκελος, 2, 479; opposed to στέρνον; κατὰ ζώνην νύξε. he wounded him in the side or abdomen, 11, 234. Others (Wolf) interpret it in both passages of the girdle, as ζωστήρ, but this is clearly distinguished from it, 11, 236. Thus Voss, 'he wounded him in the girdle' [*he pierced the broider'd zone*. Cp.].

ζώννυμι. aor. ἔζωσα, aor. mid. ἐζωσάμην, iterat. imperf. ζωννύσκετο, 1) Act. *to gird*, esply *to gird for battle, to put on armour*, Od. 18, 76. II) Mid. *to gird oneself*, ζωστῆρι, 10, 78; ῥάκεσιν περὶ μήδεα. Od. 18, 67; absol. *to gird oneself, to equip oneself*, esply for battle, 11, 15. 23, 685. Od. 18, 30. *b*) With accus. χαλκόν, to put on the girdle, to gird on a weapon, 23, 130.

ζωός, ἡ, όν, *living, alive*, as ζωὸν ἑλεῖν τινα, 6, 50; ζώς, Ep. rare form for ζωός (from ζαός), 5, 887; accus. ζών, 16, 445.

ζωρός, όν (akin to ζωός), prob. *strong*; hence spoken of wine: *unmixed, undiluted, strong*. ζωρότερον κέραιε, mingle the wine stronger, i. e. mix less water with it, 9, 203.†

ζώς = ζωός, q. v.

[ζῶσμα = ζῶμα, but the form is rejected by Th. Magist. p. 411.]

ζωστήρ, ῆρος, ὁ (ζώννυμι), *the girdle, the waist belt* of warriors, which was worn around the body above the μίτρη and ζῶμα to protect the abdomen, so that it embraced the lower part of the cuirass, 4, 132, seq. 186, 215. 11, 236. It was probably made of leather and variegated (παναίολος, φοίνικι φαεινός, 7, 305), and covered with metal plates, 11, 237. It was confined by buckles or clasps, 4, 132. 2) *a girdle* with which the tunic (χιτών) was confined, Od. 14, 72.

ζώστρον, τό, *a girdle, a belt*, Od. 6, 38.†

ζώω, Ep. and Ion. for ζάω, *to live*, with accus. ζώειν ἀγαθὸν βίον, to lead a good [i. e. happy, tranquil (Cp.)] life, Od. 15, 491; and often in connexion with ὁρᾶν φάος Ἠελίοιο, 18, 61. H. has always, except ζῶντος, 1, 88, the form ζώω, arising from doubling the vowel of ζῶ, only in the pres. and imperf. ζώω, ζώεις, etc., partcp. ζώοντος, infin. ζώειν, ζωέμεναι, ζωέμεν, imperf. ἔζωον (see Thiersch, § 220. 74; Buttm. p. 284. Rost, p. 305).

H.

H, the seventh letter of the Greek alphabet, and therefore the sign of the seventh book.

ἤ, Ep. also ἠέ, a conjunction, indicating either exclusion or diversity. I) Exclusion: 1) In disjunctive sentences: ἤ, or; ἤ, ἤ, *either, or*; it not only expresses like *aut*, the necessary, but also like *vel*, an arbitrary exclusion, 1, 27. 138. Od. 14, 330. *b*) To indicate an equal weight in the opposing clauses, τέ is added: ἤτε, ἤτε = εἴτε, 11, 410. 17, 42. *c*) ἠμέν, ἠδέ, express not the disjunctive, but like τέ, τέ, the copulative signif.; prop. *as well, as*, 2, 789. 5, 128. Often to ἠδέ is annexed καί, 5, 128. Also ἠμὲν–καί, correl., 15, 664; ἠμὲν–δέ, 12, 428; or μὲν–ἠδέ, Od. 12, 168; τέ–ἠδέ, Od. 1, 12. Often also ἠδέ is used alone, 1, 334. 2) In disjunctive questions: *or, whether*. *a*) In direct questions, either double: ἤ, ἤ, utrum, an (in which case the first is not translated), Od. 1, 175. 6, 120; or single, Od. 1, 226. If a question has already preceded, ἤ, an serves to decide or to limit it: ἦ ἵνα ὕβριν ἴδη, peradventure to see, 1, 203. 5, 466. Od. 4, 710. *b*) In indirect questions, either single: *whether*, 8, 111. Od. 16, 138; or in the double question: ἤ, ἤ, *whether, or*, 1, 190. Od. 6, 142. Also the first ἤ is sometimes wanting, or its place supplied by εἰ. II) Diversity: *than*, *quam*. 1) After a comparative, and after such words as express an idea of comparison, as ἄλλος, οὐδεὶς ἄλλος; after βούλομαι, 1, 117. 2) It stands between two comparatives, when two qualities in one object are compared: πάντες κ' ἀρησαίατ' ἐλαφρότεροι πόδας εἶναι, ἤ ἀφνειότεροι χρυσοῖο, all would desire rather to be swift of foot than rich, Od. 1, 164 ['would desire to be swifter of foot than they now are, *rather* than richer,' in order either to escape or to ransom themselves, since to be richer would avail them nothing. *Fäsi*] 3) ἤ stands sometimes after a comparative, with the gen. of a demonstrative pronoun, so that the following clause may be regarded as an apposition to the pron., 15, 509. Od. 6, 182; cf. Kühner, § 622, seq. Thiersch, § 312, 352, note; ἤ οὐ and ἤ οὐκ are commonly to be pronounced with synizesis, 5, 349.

ἤ, adv. occurs in a two-fold signif. 1) In positive clauses it serves for confirmation and assurance: *certainly, truly, surely, verily*. It stands sometimes alone, 1, 229; mly however it is strengthened by other particles: ἤ δή, verily, of a truth, 1, 518; ἤ μάλα, certainly (very), 3, 204. Od. 16, 183; ἤ μάλα δή, most certainly; assuredly, 8, 102. Od. 1, 384; ἤ που, surely; ἤ τε, certainly. In like manner, ἤ νυ, ἤ που, when the affirmation at the same time contains a doubt, 3, 43. 22, 11; esply, ἤ μήν (μέν, μάν), a strengthened affirmation, most commonly used in an oath, *verily*, 2, 291; also with an infin. in dependent discourse: καί μοι ὀμοσσον, ἤ μέν μοι—ἀρήξειν, that thou wilt certainly (or assuredly) protect me, 1, 77. 14, 275. 2) In interrogations: num, where it cannot be translated into English; it includes at the same time an affirmation, mly in the following connexions: ἤ ἄρα δή, ἤ ῥα, ἤ ῥά νυ, ἤ νυ, ἤ νύ που. It stands without particles only when the party proposing the question, by a question immediately following conjecturally answers the first, in which case it may be rendered *perhaps, peradventure*: τί με ταῦτα λιλαίεαι ἠπεροπεύειν; ἤ πή μεάξεις, wilt thou peradventure lead me away, 3, 400. Od. 9, 405. 452.

ἤ, imperf. of εἰμί. 2) Imperf. of ἠμί.

ἤ, dat. fem. of the relat. pron. ὅς, ἤ, ὅ, in H. mly as an adv. (subaud. ὁδῷ or μερίδι). 1) *where, whither*, with τῇ, preceding, 13, 53. 2) *as, in what way*, ἤ θέμις ἐστί, as is right, 2, 73. 9, 33 According to Buttm. Lex. p. 535, ᾗ in H. has only a local signif. and in both passages must be written ἤ θέμις ἐστί, Od. 9, 268. 24, 286. With him agrees Thiersch, § 343, 7. Spitz. Excurs. II. Nitzsch ad Od. 3, 45, approves the ᾗ only when it stands with a gen., 9, 134. 276. Od. 9, 268.

ἦα, see εἰμί.

ἠβαιός, ή, όν, *little, small*, mly with negat. οὐ οἱ ἔνι φρένες οὐδ' ἠβαιαί, he has no understanding, not even a little, not the least, 14, 141. Od. 21, 288. Often the neut. ἠβαιόν as adv. *little*, Od. 9, 462; and with negat. οὐδ' ἠβαιόν, 2, 380.

ἠβάω (ἤβη), aor. ἤβησα, 1) *to be arrived at the age of puberty, to be in the bloom of one's life, to possess the full power of a man*. εἰθ' ὡς ἠβώοιμι, 7, 157. 11, 670. ἀνὴρ οὐδὲ μάλ' ἠβῶν, 12, 382. 2) Metaph. ἡμερὶς ἡβώωσα, a vigorous vine, Od. 5, 69. (H. has sometimes the contr. forms, ἡβῷμι, ἡβῶν, sometimes the forms with the vowel repeated after ω: ἠβώοντα, ἠβώοιμι.—ἠβώωσα, which Heyne would write ἠβώωσα, is correct; it is not a contraction but a repetition of the vowel, see Thiersch, § 220, 70.) [See also Buttm. § 105, note 10.]

ἤβη, *puberty, the age of manhood*, which was reckoned from the eighteenth year: hence mly *youth, the age of youth, the most powerful age of men*, 24, 348. Od. 10, 279. ἤβης ἱκέσθαι μέτρον, to arrive at the measure of youth, 11, 225; ἤβης ἄνθος ἔχειν, 13, 484; and generally *youthful vigour, manly vigour*, 23, 432. Od. 8, 181. h. 7, 9.

Ἤβη, ἡ, Hēbē, daughter of Zeus and Hērē, wife of Hēraclēs, Od. 11, 603. h. 14, 8; she appears as the cup-bearer of the gods, 4, 2; and as the handmaid of Hērē, 5, 722. She bathes Arēs her brother, 5, 905; later the goddess of youth.

ἠβητής, οῦ, ὁ (ἤβη), *a youth, a marriageable young man*, κοῦροι ἠβηταί, h. Merc. 56.

ἠβῷμι, see ἠβάω.

ἠβώοιμι, ἠβώοντα, ἠβώωσα, Ep. expanded forms from ἠβάω.

ἠγάασθε, see ἄγαμαι.

ἤγαγον, ἠγαγόμην, see ἄγω.

ἠγάθεος, η, ον (ἄγαν, θεός), *very divine, sacred, holy*, epith. of towns, countries, mountains, since they were regarded as under particular divine protection, 1, 252. Od. 2, 308. (Prob. fr. ἄγαν and θεῖος, or according to others fr. ἀγαθός; η is a poet. lengthening of α, see Buttm. Lex. p. 323.)

ἠγάσσατο, see ἄγαμαι.

ἡγεμονεύω (ἡγεμών), 1) *to go before, to point out*; τινι, to go before any man, Od. 3, 386; and absol., 5. 53. h. Ap. 437. Il. 15, 46; with accus. ὁδόν, to show the way, Od. 6, 261. 7, 30; and ὁδόν τιν. Od. 24, 225; metaph. ῥόον ὕδατι, to prepare a course for the water, 21, 258. 2) *to lead, to conduct, to command*, with gen., 2, 527. 552; once with dat., 2, 816; in this signif. mly in the Il.

ἡγεμών, όνος, 1) *a guide* upon the road, Od. 10, 505. 15, 310. 2) *a leader*,

ἡγέομαι. *a commander, a general*, 2, 265. 11, 746; often also ἀνὴρ ἡγεμών, 2, 365. 11, 746.

ἡγέομαι, depon. mid. (ἄγω), fut. **ἡγήσομαι**, aor. **ἡγησάμην**, 1) *to go before, to lead, to guide*, opposed to ἕπομαι, often absol., 9, 192. 12, 251, with dat. of pers., 22, 101; also πρόσθεν ἡγεῖσθαι, 24, 96. νήεσσι ἡγήσατο Ἴλιον εἴσω, he conducted the ships to Ilium (spoken of the prophet Calchas), 1, 71; ὁδόν τινι, to lead the way for a man = to show him it, Od. 10, 263; hence, ἡγεῖσθαί τινι πόλιν, to conduct any man to the town, Od. 6, 114; δόμον, Od. 7, 22; a rare construction is ἡμῖν ἡγείσθω ὀρχηθμοῖο (of a minstrel), let him lead us in the dance (*strike a dance*, Cp.], i. e. play for us, Od. 23, 134. 2) Esply in the Il.: *to lead, to command. a*) With dat. where the idea of going before prevails, 2, 864. 5, 211; ἐπὶ στίχας, 2, 687. (Others, for ἐφηγήσατό σφιν στίχας, who went before the ranks, Voss.) νήεσσιν ἐς Τροίην, 15, 169. *b*) With gen. like ἄρχειν, *to lead on, to command, to govern*, 2, 567. 620, 851.

ἡγερέθομαι, Ep. lengthened from ἀγείρομαι, only in the 3 plur. pres. and imperf. ἡγερέθονται and ἡγερέθοντο and infin. ἡγερέθεσθαι, 10, 127; which Spitz, after Aristarch. has adopted for ἡγερέεσθαι.

ἡγερέομαι, Ep. for ἀγείρομαι, only infin. pres. ἡγερέεσθαι, 10, 127; see ἡγερέθομαι.

ἤγερθεν, see ἀγείρω.

ἡγηλάζω (collateral Ep. form of ἡγέομαι), *to lead*, with accus. τινά, Od. 17, 217. κακὸν μόρον ἡγηλάζειν, to lead a wretched fate, i. e. to suffer, to endure it, *Od. 11, 618.

ἡγήτωρ, ορος, ὁ (ἡγέομαι), *a conductor, ὀνείρων*, epith. of Hermês, h. Merc. 14; *a leader, a commander*, in connexion with μέδοντες, 2, 79. Od. 7, 98.

ἡγοράασθε, see ἀγοράομαι.

ἡγορόωντο, see ἀγοράομαι.

ἠδέ, conj. poet. *and*; it connects, like καί, two words; sometimes τε precedes, 9, 99. σκῆπτρόν τ' ἠδὲ θέμιστες and τε—ἠδὲ καί, 5, 822; often ἠδὲ καί, and also, 1, 334. 2) Most commonly it follows ἠμέν, see ἤ.

ἤδεα, pluperf. of οἶδα, see ΕΙΔΩ.

ἤδη, adv. (δή). *already, now*, jam, 1) Of the immediate present: νῦν ἤδη, or ἤδη νῦν, *even now*, now, 15, 110. With a preterite it may be translated by *just, just now*; and with a fut. by *immediately, at once*, Od. 1, 303. 2) Of past events: *already*: 1, 250. 260. ἤδη ποτὲ πάρος, already before, 1, 453. 2, 205. 3) Of unexpected, or long since expected events: *now at length*, 1, 456.

ἤδομαι, depon. mid. aor. ἡσάμην, *to be pleased, to delight in*; ἥσατο πίνων, Od. 9, 353.†

ἦδος, εος, τό, *pleasure, joy, enjoyment, δαιτός*, the enjoyment of a feast, 1, 576. ἡμέων ἦδος, our joy, 11, 318. 2) *profit, advantage*, only Ep. τί μοι τῶν ἦδος;

what advantage have I from this? 18, 80. αὐτὰρ ἐμοὶ τί τόδ' ἦδος; [only by implication: *but thence what joy to me?* Cp.] Od. 24, 95.

ἡδυγελώς, ωτος, ὁ, ἡ (γέλως), *laughing sweetly, laughing amiably*, epith. of Pan, h. 18, 37.

ἡδυεπής, ές (ἔπος), *sweetly speaking, sweet-tongued*, epith. of Nestor, 1, 248;† *sweetly singing*, ἀοιδός, Μοῦσαι, h. 20, 4. 32, 2.

***ἥδυμος, ον**, poet. for ἡδύς, *sweet, agreeable*, epith. of sleep, h. Merc. 241. 419; see νήδυμος.

ἡδύποτος, ον (πίνω), *sweet to drink, pleasant*, οἶνος, *Od. 2, 340. 3, 391. h. 6, 36.

ἡδύς, εῖα, ύ (akin to ἅδω, ἀνδάνω), once an adj. of two endings: ἡδὺς αὐτμή, Od. 12, 369; superl. ἥδιστος, Od. 13, 80. 1) *agreeable, sweet, delightful*; spoken of objects of sense: of taste, οἶνος, Od. 2, 350. 3, 51; of smell, ὀδμή, Od. 9, 210; of hearing; ἀοιδή, Od. 8, 64; again: ὕπνος, κοῖτος, 4, 131. Od. 19, 510; and generally φίλον καὶ ἡδύ ἐστι, 4, 17. 7, 387. Od. 24, 435. 2) Metaph. of the mind, *agreeable, cheerful*. Often the neut. ἡδύ, as adv. esply ἡδὺ γελᾶν, to laugh pleasantly, heartily, 2, 270.

ἠέ, poet. for ἤ, *or*.

ἦε, see εἰμι.

ἠείδειν, ἠείδη, ἠείδης, Ep. pluperf. of οἶδα, see ΕΙΔΩ.

ἥλιος, ὁ, poet. for ἥλιος (ἕλη), always in the poet. form: *the sun*. Of its rising we find ἡλ ἀνιέναι, once ἀνορούειν, Od. 3, 1; and ἀνανεῖσθαι, Od. 10, 192; στείχειν πρὸς οὐρανόν, Od. 11, 17; of noon, μέσον οὐρανὸν ἀμφιβαίνει, 8, 68; of afternoon, μετενίσσετο βουλυτόνδε, 16, 779; or ἂψ ἐπὶ γαῖαν προτρέπεται, Od. 11, 18; of sunset, δύω, ἐπιδύω, καταδύω, and ἐμπίπτειν Ὠκεανῷ, 8, 485. φάος ἠελίοιο, the light of the sun : hence φάος ἠελίοιο ὁρᾶν = to live, 5, 120. Od. 10, 498. 2) To indicate the points of compass : *the east, the west*, Od. 13, 240. πρὸς Ἠῶ τ' Ἠέλιόν τε, in opposition to ζόφος, towards the dawn and the sun, always indicates the east, not the east and south, since the poet recognizes only two heavenly regions, the light side, and the obscure, or the east and the west, 12, 239. Od. 9, 26; cf. ζόφος, and Völcker's Hom. Geogr. § 15—19.

Ἠέλιος, ὁ, poet. for Ἥλιος (the last form, Od. 8, 271), *Helios*, god of the sun, son of Hyperion, Od. 12, 176; and Euryphaessa, h. 31; see Ὑπερίων. His wife was Persê, and his children Æêtês and Kirkê (Circê), Od. 10, 136, seq. He rises in the east from the ocean, and sinks into the same in the west. The nymph Neæra bore him Phaethūsa and Lampetia, who watched the herds of their father in Trinacria, Od. 12, 132. Oaths were sworn by him, because he hears and sees every thing, 3, 277. He betrayed to Hephæstus the amour of Aphroditê and

Ἥσ.   190   Ἥἰον.

Ἀρῆς, Od. 8, 271. With Zeus a boar is offered to him, 19, 197; and a white ram in opposition to a black one for the dark earth, 3, 104. Steeds and chariot are mentioned first in h. Merc. 69. It was only at a later period that Hēlios was confounded with Apollo and Phœbus.

ἦιν, see εἰμί.
ἠέπερ, adv. poet. for ἦπερ.
ἠέρα, see ἀήρ.
ἠερέθομαι, Ep. collat. form of ἀείρομαι, 3 plur. pres. ἠερέθονται, to hang, to hover, to flutter, spoken of tassels, 2, 448; of grasshoppers, 21, 12; metaph. ὁπλοτέρων φρένες ἠερέθονται, the minds of younger men are ever *unstable* [Cp.], *3, 108.

ἠέρι, see ἀήρ.
Ἠερίβοια, ἡ, Ep. for Ἐρίβοια, daughter of Eurymachus a son of Hermēs, the second wife of Alōeus; step-mother of the Aloīdæ, Otus and Ephialtes. From hatred to her step-sons she discovered to Hermēs the place where they held Arēs imprisoned, 5, 389. (Ἐρίβοια, one who brings many cattle.)

ἠέριος, η, ον, Ion. and Ep. for ἀέριος (ἀήρ), *in the darkness of the morning, dusk, in the morning, early,* 1, 497. 557. 3, 7; and Od. 9, 52. Voss derives it correctly from ἀήρ, since very early in the morning every thing is wrapt in vapour; he translates therefore: *in the misty dawn,* 1, 497; and *from the misty air,* 3, 7; with which Wolf, Vorles. 4, 189, agrees. Buttm., in Lex. p. 42, derives it from ἦρι, *early.*

ἠεροειδής, ές (εἶδος), gen. έος, Ep. for ἀεροειδής, that which is like to the distant dusky air (ἀήρ), *dusky, hazy, misty, cloudy, obscure,* epith. of the sea, from its blue misty colour, 23, 744. Od. 2, 263; of grottoes, Od. 12, 80. 13, 366; and of a distant rock, Od. 12, 233; and of the prospect of a man standing upon watch : ὅσσον ἠεροειδὲς ἀνὴρ ἴδεν ὀφθαλμοῖσιν, as far as a man with his eyes beholds the dark distance, i. e. as far as a man's vision extends over the blue expanse of the sea, 5, 770. (The word should be taken as a subst.; Köppen's explanation of ἠεροειδές as an adv. like ἠεροειδέως is incorrect; for it is not equivalent to ἐν ἀέρι.)

ἠερόεις, εσσα, εν, Ion. and Ep. for ἀερόεις (ἀήρ), *cloudy, dusky, gloomy, dark, murky,* epith. of Tartarus, 8, 13; and of ζόφος, as the under world and dark side of the earth, 12, 240. 15, 191; hence ἠερόεντα κέλευθα, the dark paths of death, Od. 20, 64.

ἠεροφοῖτις, ιος, ἡ (φοιτάω), *walking in darkness, veiled in darkness,* epith. of the Furies, since they threaten death and unforeseen calamity, *9, 571. 19, 87.

ἠερόφωνος, ον (φωνή), *crying through the air; clear, shrill-voiced,* epith. of heralds, 18, 505.†

Ἠετίων, ωνος, ὁ, 1) king of Hypo(?)placian Thebē in Cilicia, father of Andro-

mache, 1, 366. 6, 396. Achilles slew him together with seven sons, when he sacked Thebē, 6, 416. cf. 23, 827. 2) an Imbrian, a friend of Priam, who liberated Lycaon from slavery and sent him to Arisbe, 21, 42, seq. (According to Damm. from ἀετός.)

ἤην, see εἰμί.
ἤηρ, ὁ, from which Ep. the oblique cases ἠέρος, ἠέρι, ἠέρα of ἀήρ, are formed.

ἠθεῖος, είη, εῖον (ἦθος), *trusty, beloved, worthy, dear,* in the Il. mly in voc. as subst. ἠθεῖε, 6, 518. 10, 37. 22. 229; where the young brother always addresses the elder: ἠθείη κεφαλή, dear head, like our 'dear heart;' thus Achilles addresses the shade of Patroclus, 23, 94; and Eumæus calls Odysseus (Ulysses) ἠθεῖος, Od. 14, 147. (The deriv. from ἦθος, one with whom intercourse is wont to be held, is most prob.; improb. from θεῖος, uncle, or θεῖος, divine.)

ἦθος, εος, τό (Ion. for ἔθος), *an accustomed abode,* hence *a haunt, a dwelling,* spoken only of beasts; of horses: the *accustomed pasture,* Voss, Il. 6, 511. 15, 268; of swine, the *accustomed sty,* Od. 14, 411.

ἤϊα, τά (εἶμι), 1) the food which one takes with him on a journey, *provision for the road,* pros. ἐφόδια, Od. 2, 289. 410. 4, 363. 5, 266. 9, 212. 12, 329; and generally, *food, nourishment;* also λύκων ἤϊα, the food of wolves, 13, 103. 2) *chaff, husks, pods,* elsewhere ἄχυρα, as the Gramm. explain, ἠίων θημῶν καρφαλέων, Od. 5, 368; The Gramm. derive it from εἶμι, imperf. ἤϊον, and explain it τὰ φερόμενα, what is carried (food), and that which moves easily (chaff), see Thiersch, Gram. § 166, 2. (iota is commonly long in the arsis; twice short, Od. 4, 463. 12, 329; and at the close of the verse it is to be pronounced with synizesis, Od. 5, 266. 9, 212, where Wolf writes ἦια, perhaps also correctly, Od. 5, 368, ἤϊων.) [Fäsi, ἦα.]

ἤϊε, see εἰμί.
ἠίθεος, ὁ, Ep. for ἤθεος, *a youth who has arrived at manhood but who is yet unmarried, a young man,* παρθένος ἠίθεός τε, 18, 593. 22, 127. νύμφαι τ' ἠίθεοί τε, Od. 11, 38.

ἧικτο, see ἔοικα.
ἧιξε, see ἀίσσω.
ἠιόεις, εσσα, εν (ἠϊών), *having banks, deep-embanked* (Cp.), 5, 36;† epith. of the Scamander, to indicate its high banks (according to the common derivation of the Gramm. from ἠιών, ὄχθη, prop. ἠιονόεις, and by syncope, ἠιόεις, Etym. Mag. Buttm. Lex. p. 324, derives it from ἤϊον, akin to εἰαμένη, meadow, = 'meadowy,' 'skirted with meadowland'). [Död. makes it *muddy,* i. e. *full of earthy matter:* related to αἶα, εἴα, dry.]

ἤϊον, see εἶμι.

Ἠϊόνες. 191 Ἠλίβατος.

Ἠϊόνες, αἱ, *Eiones*, a village in Argolis, in the region of the promontory Scyllæum; later a port of the Mycenians, 2, 561. Strab.

ἠϊονεύς, ῆος, ὁ (an inhabitant of the shore), 1) a Greek, slain by Hector, 7, 11. 2) a Thracian, father of Rhesus, 10, 435.

ἤϊος, ὁ, an epith. of Phœbus, of uncertain derivation, 15, 365. 20, 152. h. Ap. 120; prob. the *far-shooter*, Voss; according to the Schol. for ἰηΐε from ἵημι, or, more correctly, from the original form ἄω, ἤϊος, Ep. ἤϊος, as ἤλιος and ἠέλιος. Aristarch., on the other hand, would write it ἤϊος. Others say, from ἰάομαι, *the healer* (but Phœbus never appears as the god of the healing art), or from the exclamation ἰή, ἰή, with which Apollo was addressed (of which traces are first found h. Ap. 500). Buttm., Lex. p. 246, regards it as a corruption of ἐΰς or ἠΰς.

ἤϊσαν, see εἶμι.
ἤϊχθη, see ἀΐσσω.
ἠϊών, όνος, ἡ, Ep. for ἠών, Batr. 13, *the sea-shore, the sea-coast, the coast, the strand*, 2, 92. ἠϊόνες προὔχουσαι, projecting shores, or sand-downs (dunes) running into the sea, Od. 6, 138.

ἦκα, adv. (ἀπή). 1) *softly, gently, low*. ἦκα ἀγορεύειν, 3, 155; spoken of a thrust or blow, *gently, softly*, 24, 508. Od. 18, 92; spoken of walking slowly, Od. 17, 254; spoken of shining: ἦκα στίλβοντες ἐλαίῳ, mildly shining with oil, 18, 596 (according to the old Gramm. to be taken as a comparison: and so Voss, 'bright as the soft lustre of oil'). 2) Generally *somewhat, a little*. ἦκ' ἐπ' ἀριστερά, 23, 336; and ἦκα παρακλίνειν κεφαλήν, to bend the head a little sidewise, Od. 20, 301. (Buttm., Lex. p. 327, correctly taking ἀκήν as the root, gives as the primary signif. *feebly*, and recognises it as the positive of ἧσσον, ἥκιστα; cf. Thiersch, § 198. 2.) [Död., asserting the relationship to ἀκήν, denies that to ἧσσον.]

ἧκα, see ἵημι.
ἤκαχε, see ἀκαχίζω.
ἠκέσατο, see ἀκέομαι.
ἤκεστος, η, ον, Ep. for ἄκεστος (κεστός), *ungoaded*, spoken of cattle that have not yet felt the goad of the driver, *unbroken, unused*, *6, 94. 275. 309.

ἥκιστος, η, ον (superl. from the adv. ἦκα), only in ἥκιστος δ' ἦν ἐλαυνέμεν ἄρμα, he was the *slowest* to drive the chariot, 23, 531, Wolf.† Others write ἥκιστος as superl. of ἧσσων, the *worst*. Buttm., Lex. p. 327, regards ἥκιστος as correct, only because it has the signif. *the weakest, worst*, although he finds in ἦκα the true positive of ἧσσων, ἥκιστα. [Död. the *quietest*, hence *slowest*: quite unconnected with ἥκιστα.]

ἥκω, to (*have*) *come, to arrive*, always with the idea of the action perfected; τηλόθεν, 5, 478; εἰς Ἰθάκην, Od. 13, 325.

ἠλάκατα, τά (plur. from the obsol. ἠλάκατον), *the wool on the distaff*, or the threads which are drawn from the distaff, Od. 6, 53; hence ἠλάκατα στρωφᾶν, to spin threads, Od. 6, 306. 7, 105; and στροφαλίζειν, †Od. 18, 315.

ἠλακάτη, ἡ, prop. *a reed*, then generally any thing made of or similar to a reed, *a spindle, a distaff*, 6, 491. Od. 1, 357. (Prob. from ἠλάσκω, to turn around.)

ἠλάκατον, τό, see ἠλάκατα.
ἤλασα, see ἐλαύνω.
ἠλασκάζω, poet. lengthened from ἠλάσκω, 1) Intrans. *to wander about*, 18, 281. 2) *to avoid, to flee*. ἐμὸν μένος ἠλασκάζει (mine anger), Od. 9, 457. It is not necessary, with Passow, to change it to ἠλυσκάζει; for ἠλασκάζει may have this different construction as well as φεύγειν, ἀτύζεσθαι, cf. Herm. ad Orph. Arg. 439.

ἠλάσκω (an Ep. form of ἀλάομαι)† a poet. lengthened form is ἠλασκάζω, 1) *to wander around, to rove up and down*; spoken of animals, καθ' ὕλην, 13, 104; of bees, to swarm about, 2, 470.

ἤλατο, see ἄλλομαι.
ἤλδανε, see ἀλδαίνω.
Ἠλεῖος, είη, εῖον, *Elean*, appertaining to Elis. οἱ Ἠλεῖοι, *the Eleans*, inhabitants of Elis, 11, 671.

Ἠλέκτρη, ἡ, 1) daughter of Oceanus and Tethys, wife of Thaumas, mother of Iris and the Harpies, h. in Cer. 418. 2) = Λαοδίκη, daughter of Agamemnon.

ἤλεκτρον, τό, and ἤλεκτρος, ὁ, ἡ, *electron*, either amber, or a metallic mixture of gold with perhaps a fifth of silver. Especially may the latter be understood in Od. 4, 73, where it is mentioned between gold and silver us an ornament of the walls; but in Od. 15, 460. 18, 296 (χρύσεον ὅρμον ἔχων μετὰ δ' ἠλέκτροισιν ἔερτο), we may understand a golden necklace with beads of amber, Ep. 15, 10. Eustath. ad Od. 4, 73, mentions both; he calls the first μίγμα χρυσοῦ καὶ ἀργύρου; Plin. IX, 65, calls it a mixture of three parts gold and one part silver. Voss ad Virg. Ec. 6, 62. Otfr. Müller (Archäol. p. 55), Buttm. Schrift. der Berl. Akadem. der Wissenschaft. histor. Classe 1818, p. 38, decide in favour of amber; on the other hand, Passow, Nitzsch (Anmerk. zu Od. 1, 238), Wiedasch consider it as a metallic mixture; cf. Dilthey de Electro et Eridano. 1824. (Without doubt it is derived from ἠλέκτωρ.)

ἠλέκτωρ, ορος, ὁ, *the shining sun*, as subst., 6, 513; and adj. ἠλέκτωρ Ὑπερίων, the beaming Hyperion, *19, 398. h. Ap. 369 (prob. from the same root with ἥλιος).

ἠλεός, ή, όν (ἠλός), *infatuated, foolish*, φρένας ἠλεέ, infatuated in mind; senseless, Od. 2, 243. 2) Act. *causing folly*, οἶνος, *Od. 14, 464; cf. ἠλός.

ἠλήλατο, see ἐλαύνω.
ἠλίβατος, ον, *ascending precipitously*;

Ἦλιθα.   192   **Ἠμών.**

and generally *very high*; mly as an epith. in H. of πέτρη, 15, 273. 16, 35. Od. 9, 243. 10, 88. 13, 196. h. Merc. 404; and of trees, h. Ven. 268. (Herm. has, however, included the verse in brackets as spurious.) The deriv. is uncertain; the most common deriv. is from ἥλιος and βαίνω (Apoll. ὑψηλή, ἐφ' ἦ ὁ ἥλιος πρῶτον βάλλει or ἧς ὁ ἥλιος μόνος ἐπιβαίνει), passed over only by the sun, upon which the sun rests all day; or, as others think, from ἧλος akin to ἀλιτεῖν, and hence = δύσβατος, *inaccessibl*, *precipitous*; or from ἀλιτεῖν and βαίνω for ἀλιτόβατος, upon which one easily makes a false step, cf. ἠλιτόμηνος. The last deriv. is adopted by Buttm. Lex. p. 329.

ἤλιθα, adv. (ἅλις), *sufficiently*, *abundantly*, always ἤλιθα πολλή, 11, 677. Od. 5, 483.

ἡλικίη, ἡ (ἧλιξ), generally *an age, the period of life*, æt a.s, *old age*. 22, 419; but chiefly, the *age of strength* and activity, from perhaps eighteen to fifty years; hence 2) Collect. *contemporaries, those of the same age*; esply *youthful companions*, *16, 808.

ἧλιξ, ικος, ὁ, ἡ, τό, *of ripe age*, *adult, full-grown, of equal age*, spoken of cattle, Ο.1. 18, 373.†

ἥλιος, prose form of ἠέλιος, q. v.

Ἴλιος, ὁ, Ep. Ἤλιος, q. v.

Ἦλις, ιδος, ἡ, *Elis*, a country on the western side of Peloponnesus, which was bounded by Achaia, Arcadia, Messenia, and the sea. H. knows nothing of the later division into Κοίλη, Πισᾶτις, and Τριφυλία, nor of any city of Elis. The Epeans were the ruling tribe, perhaps of Pelasgian origin; the southern part belongs to Nestor's dominions; and here dwelt the Achæans (or Achaians), 2, 615. 626. Od. 4, 635. 13, 275. H. has only the accus. Ἤλιδα in the passages quoted; Ἤλιν was used, at a later day, of the city.

ἤλιτε, see ἀλιταίνω.

ἠλιτόμηνος, ον (ἀλιταίνω, μήν), prop. missing the month, *untimely*, *born too soon*, 19, 118.†

ἤλησε, see ἐλκέω.

ἧλος, ὁ, *a nail, a stud*; only as an ornament of the sceptre, sword, and goblet. σκῆπτρον, χρυσείοις ἥλοισι πεπαρμένον, studded with golden nails, 1, 246. cf. 11, 29. 633.

ἠλός, ή, όν (ἀλή), *wandering, silly, foolish*. φρένας ἠλέ, senseless, 15, 128† (whence ἠλεός. q. v.).

ἤλυθον, see ἔρχομαι.

Ἠλύσιον πεδίον, τό, *the Elysian field*, *Elysium*, a beautiful plain, situated at the western extremity of the earth (this is indicated by the Zephyr), on the ocean, where, as in Olympus itself, no storm, rain, or snow approaches, but ever-during spring prevails. In this abode H. places heroes and favorites of the gods, e. g. Rhadamanthus son of Zeus, and Menelaus, and represents them as living there with the body without seeing death. Whether it is to be considered as an island, or as a plain situated on the margin of the ocean, is no where in H. clearly expressed; Hesiod. Op. 169, and later writers, speak of the 'islands of the blessed,' see Völcker, Hom. Geogr. § 78, p. 156. Nitzsch ad Od. 4, 563 (fr. ἤλυσις, = ἔλευσις, coming).

ἤλφον, see ἀλφαίνω.

ἥλω, see ἁλίσκομαι.

ἠλώμην, see ἀλάομαι.

Ἡλώνη, ἡ, a town of the Perrhæbians in Thessaly (Phthiōtis), on the Eurōtas; later Λειμώνη, according to Strab., 2, 739.

ἧμα, ατος, τό (ἵημι), *a cast, a throw*, the act of casting a missile. ἥμασιν ἄριστος, very excellent in casting the spear, 23, 891.†

Ἠμαθίη, ἡ, *Emathia*, a country between the rivers Erigon and Axius, north of Pieria, 14, 226. h. Ap. 217; later, a part of Macedonia (perhaps from ἤμαθος = ἄμαθος, sandy).

ἠμαθόεις, εσσα, εν (ἄμαθος), Ion. for ἀμαθόεις, *sandy*, epith. of the city Pylos, because it lay on the coast, 2, 77; and also in fourteen other passages, always Πύλος, ἀμαθόεις. The deriv. from a river Amathos, according to Strab. is improbable, since an adj. with the ending ὀεις from a river is unheard of.

ἧμαι (prob. perf. pass. from ἘΩ, ἕδω), imperf. ἥμην. Peculiar Ion. forms are the 3 plur. pres. ἕαται and Ep. εἵαται for ἧνται, and 3 plur. imperf. ἕατο, Ep. εἵατο for ἧντο, prop. *I am seated, laid, placed*. hence 1) *to sit, to lie, to remain*, with particp. ὀνειδίζων, 2, 255. Od. 4, 439. 8, 505. 2) *to sit still, quietly, idle*, with σιγῇ, 3, 134. Od. 11, 142.

ἧμαρ, ατος, τό, poet. for ἡμέρα, *a day*, χειμέριον, and ὀπωρινόν, a winter day, an autumn day, 11; again, αἴσιμον, μόρσιμον, the day of fate = the day of death, 8, 72. 15, 613. νηλεὲς ἧμαρ, 11, 484; ὀλέθριον, 19, 409; κακόν, 9, 251; ἐλεύθερον, the day of freedom, 6, 455; δούλιον, ἀναγκαῖον, the day of slavery, the day of force, often slavery itself, 6, 463. 16, 836; ὀρφανικόν, the day of orphanage, 22. 490; and νόστιμον, the day of return. Od. 1, 9; ἐν ἤματι, day by day, daily, Od. 12, 105. 14, 105; upon a day, 10, 48. Od. 2, 284; for a day, 19, 229.

ἠμάτιος, η, ον (ἧμαρ), *by day*, *during the day*, Od. 2, 104. 19, 149. 2) *οὐ ποτ' ἧμαρ, daily*, 9, 72.

ἤμβροτον, see ἁμαρτάνω.

ἡμεῖς, *we*, plur. of ἐγώ. Æol. and Ep ἄμμες, gen. ἡμέων, always dissyllabic, Ep. ἡμείων, dat. ἡμῖν, and according to the necessity of the metre ἧμιν or ἡμῖν, as enclitic, 11 415. Od. 11, 344; Æol. ἄμμι, ἄμμιν, accus. ἡμέας, ἡμας, Od. 16, 372; Æol. and Ep. ἄμμε, Rost. Dial. 44. Kühner, § 301.

ἠμέν—ἠδέ (ἧ), poet. for καί—καί, *both—and*, see ἧ.

'Ημέρη. 193 *Ηνις.

ήμέρη, ή (ήμαρ), *a day;* used seven times, 8, 541. Od. 11, 294. Hom. divides the day into three parts, ήώς, μέσον ήμαρ, δείλη, 21, 111. cf. Od. 7, 288.

ήμερίς, ίδος, ή, fem. of ήμερος, *tame,* esply used of trees; subst. *the cultivated vine* [*the garden-vine.* Cp.], Od. 5, 69. †

ήμερος, ον, *tame, tamed, domestic,* χήν, Od. 15, 162.

ήμέτερος, η, ον (ημείς), *our, belonging to us.* έφ' ήμέτερα, sc. δώματα, νέεσθαι, *to return to our homes.* 9, 619. Od. 15, 88. εις ήμέτερον, sc. δώμα, Od. 2, 55. 7, 301. ήμετερόνδε, Od. 8, 39.

ήμί, prop. Att. for φημί, only ή, 3 sing. imperf. *he spake,* always after a quoted speech; once with subject, 8, 390.

ήμι-, half, in composition.

ήμιδαής, ές (δαίω), *half-burnt,* νηΰς, 16, 294.

ήμίθεος, ό (θεός), *a demi-god;* as adj. *half-divine, heroic.* ήμιθέων γένος ανδρών, 12, 23.† h. 31, 19.

ήμιόνειος, η, ον (ήμίονος), *belonging to mules, drawn by mules.* άμαξα ήμιόνειος, *a carriage drawn by mules,* 24, 189. Od. 6, 72. ζυγόν ήμιόνειον, *a span of mules,* 24, 268.

ήμίονος, ή, rarely ό **(όνος),** *a mule.* 17, 742. They were difficult to tame, 23, 655; and were used particularly in mountainous regions (hence όρεύς, ούρεύς), for drawing waggons, &c., and for agriculture, 10, 352. Od. 8, 124. By the wild mules in Paphlagonia (2, 852), Köppen understands the Dschiggetai, *equus hemionus,* Linn. 2) As adj. βρέφος ήμίονον, *a mule-foal,* 23, 266.

ήμιπέλεκκον, τό (πέλεκυς), *a half-axe,* an axe with an edge on only one side, *23, 851. 858. 883 (κ doubled for metre's sake).

***ήμιπνοος, ον (πνέω),** *half-breathing, half-dead,* Batr. 255.

ήμισυς, σεια, συ (from μέσος), *half. the half or moiety;* sing. only in the neut. τιμής βασιληΐδος ήμισυ, *the half of the royal dignity,* 6, 193. 9, 579. 580; also in the plur. ήμίσεες λαοί, 21, 7. Od. 3, 155.

ήμιτάλαντον, τό (τάλαντον), *a half-talent,* χρυσού, *23, 571. 796.

ήμιτελής, ές (τελέω), *half-finished.* δόμος ήμιτελής, *a half-finished house,* half-built, 2, 701.† The most simple explanation is: the house which Protesilaus, just married, was building for himself and his wife, was not yet completed upon his sudden departure for Troy; for it was customary, at marriage, to build a new house. Thus Heyne (an unfinished mansion. Cp.). Another explanation is, according to Etym. M. and Poseidonius Strab. VII. p. 454, 'half-abandoned,' because now occupied only by the wife; thus Damm, Wolf, Passow; and a third: 'he left his house incomplete,' i. e. without children. Thus Schol. brev. and Runhken.

ήμος (prop. = ήμαρ), Ep. adv. for ότε, *at the time when, when, after,* spoken of past time, usually only of the time of day; the apodosis begins with τήμος. 11, 86 seq.; often with δή τότε, δή τότ' έπειτα, καί τότε, 1, 475. 8, 68. Od. 9, 58. It stands always with the indic., mly with the aor., rarely with the imperf. and pluperf., 1, 475. 8, 68; cf. Thiersch. § 316, 18.

ήμύω (μύω), aor. ήμυσα, *to nod, to incline or bend. to sink.* ήμυσε κάρη, the head sank (spoken of one dying), 8. 308; and of a horse: ήμυσε καρήατι, he drooped (with the head), 19, 405; of a harvest-field: έπί τ' ήμύει άσταχύεσσιν [the loaded ears *bow* before the gale. Cp.], 2, 148; έπί is adv. (Others incorrectly interpret it of the wind: έπημύει ασταχύεσσιν, it falls upon the ears, Hesych.): metaph. of cities: *to sink, to fall,* 2, 373. 4, 290. (ϋ in the pres.; ϋ in aor. 1.

ήμων, ονος. ό (ίημι), *one who hurls spears, a spearman, a lancer,* ήμονες άνδρες, 23, 886.†

ήν, conj. contract. from εάν, *if, when, whether.* On the construction see εί with άν. It stands with the subjunc. 9, 692. Od. 5, 120; with the optat. in the orat. obliq. Od. 13, 415.

ήναίνετο, see άναίνομαι.

ήνεικα, ήνείκαντο, see φέρω.

ήνεμόεις, εσσα, εν (άνεμος), *windy, gusty,* exposed to the wind, epith. of places situated in lofty positions (esply of Troy), of mountains and trees, 2, 606. b, 499, and Od. 3, 172. 19, 432.

ήνία, τά (ίημι), *the reins or lines* of chariot-horses, which were often adorned with gold or ivory, 5, 226. 583. Od. 6, 81. Only in the plur. (the sing. ήνίον is later, and means, *a curb*).

ήνίκα, adv. *when, at the time when,* with indic. pres. Od. 22, 198.† (Voss, ad Arat. Phænom. 561, would read ήν κεν άγωνης.)

Ήνιοπεύς, ήος, ό (rein-maker), son of Thebaus, charioteer of Hector, 8, 120.

ήνιοχεύς, ήος, ό, poet. for ήνίοχος, *5, 505. 8, 312.

ήνιοχεύω (ήνίοχος), *to hold the reins, to guide the horses, to drive,* absol., 11, 103. Od. 6, 319.

ήνίοχος, ό (έχω), prop. *the reins-holder,* then *the charioteer, the driver.* In the Hom. war-chariots (see άρμα) were always two warriors; prob. on the left the charioteer, and on the right the παραβάτης, i. e. the hero who fought from the chariot. The charioteer is also called ήνίοχος θεράπων, 5, 580. 8, 119. He was a warrior, as well as his companion, of noble family, as was Patroclus, the charioteer of Achilles, 16, 244. Also the bravest heroes are often called ήνίοχοι, as Hector, 8, 89. 15, 352; cf θεράπων.

ήνίπαπε, see ένίπτω.

ήνις, ις, ή (ένος), accus. plur. ήνις for ήνιας, 6, 94; *a year old, a yearling,* βούς, 10, 292. Od. 3, 382. (In the accus. sing. ήνιν, long ι is used.)

Ἠνοπίδης. 194 **Ἡρακλέης.**

Ἠνοπίδης, ου, ὁ, son of Enops = Satnius, 14, 444.

ἠνορέη, ἡ, Ep. dat. ἠνορέηφι (ἀνήρ), manhood, strength, manly courage, 4, 303. Od. 24, 509.

ἦνοψ, οπος, *, ἡ (poet. for ἄνοψ from ἀ and ὄψ), which cannot be looked upon for its lustre: dazzling, blinding, sparkling; always ἤνοπι χαλκῷ, 16, 408. Od. 10, 360. [Död. gives it the strange meaning of *bent. vast-, gnast-, gnampt-.*]

Ἥνοψ, οπος, ὁ. 1) a Mysian father of Satnius and Thestor, 14, 445. 16, 401. 2) father of Clytomēdēs, an Ætolian, 23, 634.

ἤνπερ, conj. *even if; although*, with subj. Od. 16, 276; see ἤν.

ἦντο, see ἧμαι.

ἠνώγεα, ἠνώγει, see ἀνώγα.

ᾖξε, see ἄγνυμι.

ἠοῖος, η, ον (ἠώς), 1) Of time: *early in the morning*, matutinus; hence: ἡ ἠοίη, sc. ὥρα, morning, Od. 4, 447. 2) Of a point of the compass: *east*, opposed to ἑσπέριος. ἠοῖοι ἄνθρωποι, eastern men, *Od. 8, 29.

ἧπαρ, ατος, τό, *the liver*, 11, 579; ὅτι φρένες ἧπαρ ἔχουσιν, Od. 9, 301. 2) Plur. ἥπατα, as a dish, Batr. 37.

ἤπαφε, see ἀπαφίσκω.

ἠπεδανός, ἡ, όν, *feeble, tottering, weak*, spoken of Hephæstus, Od. 8, 11. h. Ap. 316; and Il. 8, 104; of the servant of Nestor, because he did not drive rapidly. [The ancients explain it by ἀσθενής, and derive it from ἀ and πέδον. *not standing firmly*: according to Schneider it is an amplification of ἤπιος.)

ἤπειρος, ἡ, *the main land, the continent*. spoken of the main land in distinction from an island, and of an island in opposition to the sea, Od. 13, 114. 1) Acarnania, with Leucadia, 2, 635. Od. 24, 378; and according to some also ἤπειρος μέλαινα, Od 14, 97. 21, 109. (The ancients understood in part Samos or Ætolia.) 2) Hellas, or a part of it, h. Cer. 130; chiefly Attica, h. in Dion. 22; prob. also Od. 14, 97 seq. 3) The later Epirus, Od. 18, 84. 21, 109. (Derived from ἄπειρος, sc. γῆ.) Cf. Völcker, Hom. Geogr. p. 61.

ἤπερ, poet. ἤπερ, *than, than even, than indeed*, 1, 260. Od. 4, 819; see πέρ.

ἤπερ, see ὅσπερ.

ἠπεροπεύς, ῆος. ὁ, Od. 11, 364; † and **ἠπεροπευτής**, οῦ, ὁ (ἠπεροπεύω), *a deceiver, a seducer*,* 3, 39. 13, 769. h. Merc. 282.

ἠπεροπεύω, fut. σω, *to cheat, to deceive, to seduce*. to lead away by crafty discourse, with accus. esply γυναῖκας and φρένας γυναιξί, 5, 349. Od. 15, 421. h. Merc. 577; τινὰ ταῦτα, i. e. διὰ ταῦτα, 3, 399. (Prob. fr. εἰπεῖν, ἠπύω. Passow. [= ἀπροπευύν (ἀπρεπής), *to deal unhandsomely by.*]

*ἠπητής, οῦ, ὁ, *a cobbler, a botcher, a tailor*, Batr. 184.

ἠπιόδωρος, ον (δῶρον), *willingly giving, benevolent, bounteous*, μήτηρ, 6, 251.†

ἤπιος, ίη, ιον, 1) *gentle, mild, kind*, τινί, to any one, 8, 40. Od. 10, 337. ἤπια εἰδέναι τινί, to be kindly disposed towards any one, 16, 73. Od 13, 405. 2) Act. *calming, smoothing, alleviating*, φάρμακα, 4, 218. 11, 515. (Prob. from ἔπος.)

ἤπου, now ἦ που, or, and *thus perhaps*, see ἦ.

ἤπου, now, according to Wolf, ἦ που, *surely, indeed*, see ἦ.

ἠπύτα, ὁ, Ep. for ἠπύτης (ἠπύω), *the loud crier*, hence ἠπύτα κῆρυξ, the loud-crying (loud-voiced) herald, 7, 384.†

Ἠπυτίδης, ου, ὁ, son of Epytus = Periphas, a Trojan; 17, 324.

ἠπύω (akin to εἰπεῖν), 1) *to cry, to cry aloud, to call to*, τινά. Od. 9, 399. 10, 83. 2) Intrans. spoken of wind : *to roar, to whistle*, 14, 399; of the lyre: *to sound, to resound*, 17, 271. (ὕ in the pres., cf. Spitzner, Pros. § 52. 5.)

*ἦρ, poet. for ἔαρ, *spring*, in gen. ἦρος ἀεξομένοιο, h Cer. 455; see ἔαρ.

ἦρα, once in Hom. ἦρα φέρειν τινί, 14. 132; and thrice; ἦρα ἐπιφέρειν τινί, Od. 3, 164. 16, 375. 18, 56; *to do a kindness to, to gratify*. θυμῷ ἦρα φέροντες, gratifying their inclination, spoken of those who from love of life stood aloof from battle, 14, 162. [Cp. *attentive only to their own repose.*] The other explanation: *gratifying their anger*, with reference to Agamemnon, v. 49, is forced. (Buttm., Lexil. p. 335, properly supposes a tmesis of ἐπιφέρειν, and hence in 1, 572. 578, writes ἐπίηρα separately: cf. ἐπίηρα. With him agrees Nitzsch ad Od. 3, 164. Buttm. with Herodian considers ἦρα as an accus. sing from an obsol. word ἦρ = χάρις; Thiersch, G. § 199, 3, on the other hand with Aristarch. as an accus. plur. from an adj. ἦρος. (Root ἔραμαι, or more prob. ἄρω.)

Ἡρακλείδης, αο, ὁ, son of Heracles = Tlepolemus, 2, 653. 5, 628. [2] = *Thersalus*, 2, 679.]

Ἡρακλέης, Ion. and Ep. **Ἡρακλῆς**, gen. **Ἡρακλῆος, Heracles**, son of Zeus and Alcmēnē, 14, 324. 18, 118. His birth was retarded by Hērē, and that of Eurystheus accelerated, 19, 98—125. Of the twelve famous labours which Eurystheus imposed upon him, the command to bring the dog of Pluto is mentioned, 8. 362 seq. Od. 11, 623. When Laomedon would not give him the reward for delivering his daughter Hesionē, 20, 145 seq. he captured Troy and slew Laomedon and his sons, Priam excepted, 5, 642. On his return he was driven by Hērē to Cos, 14, 250 seq. In order to avenge himself on Neleus on account of the purification for the murder of Iphitus being denied, he captured Pylos and wounded there Pluto himself, 11, 689 seq. On his death, see 18, 117. In the under-world Odysseus (Ulysses) met his shade, Od. 11, 601 seq. although he, in connexion with Hebe, is blessed among the immortal gods, cf. v. 608. Of his wives there is mentioned Megara, Od. 11, 268; and of his

Ἡρακλήειος. 195 Ἤτοι.

sons Thessalus, 2, 679; and Tlepolemus, 2, 657. (Damm derives the name from ἤρα and κλέος, *love of glory*. Herm. *Popliciutus*.)

Ἡρακλήειος, είη, ειον, Ep. for Ἡράκλειος, *pertaining to Héraclēs, Herculean*, only in the fem. βίη Ἡρακληείη, 2, 658.

ἤραρε, see ἀραρίσκω.
ἤρατο, see αἴρω.
ἠρᾶτο, see ἀράομαι.

Ἥρη, ἡ, Ion. and Ep. for Ἥρα, *Hērē*, daughter of Kronus and Rhea, sister and wife of Zeus, 16, 432; the queen of heaven and the first of goddesses. She was nurtured in the house of Oceanus, when Zeus cast Kronus into Tartarus, 14, 202 seq. In character she is proud, ambitious of power, and deceitful; she often deceives her husband, cf. 14, 153; yet she often experiences on this account his anger, 15, 13–21. In the Hom. poems she appears as the enemy of the Trojans; she collects the Grecian army against Troy, 4, 26, seq. because she considered herself neglected by the Trojans. United with Poseidōn and Athēnē she aids the Greeks, 5, 768 seq. 20, 33; and then commands Hēphæstus to drive back the river-god Xanthus within his banks when pursuing Achilles, 21, 377 seq. From earlier traditions, it is mentioned that she accelerated the birth of Euristheus and retarded that of Hēraclēs, 19, 97; the latter on his return from Troy she drove to the coast of Cos by a storm, 14, 250; and was wounded by him in Pylos, 5, 392. To Zeus she bore Hebē, Ilithyia. Arēs, and Hephæstus. Argos, Mycenæ, and Sparta are her favorite cities, 4, 51, 52. (Prob. according to Herm. from ΑΡΩ, who translates the name *Populonia*, and understands by it the union of social life; Heffter, on the other hand, nuptial union.)

ἤρηρει, see ἀραρίσκω.
ἠρήρειστο, see ἐρείδω.
ἦρι, adv. *early in the morning*, μάλ' ἦρι or ἦρι μάλα, very early, 9, 360. Od. 19, 320. 20, 156. (Prob. dat. from ἦρ, contr. of ἔαρ, the spring-time, or from ἀήρ, ἠήρ.)

ἠριγένεια, ἡ (γίγνομαι), *early-born, rising early in the morning*, or with reference to ἀήρ, born of the morning mist, epith. of Ἠώς, Aurora (some explain it as act. *producing the morning*, which contravenes the etymol, cf. αἰθρηγενής), 1, 477. 2) As pr. n. the *goddess of the morning*, Od. 22, 197. 23, 347.

Ἠριδανός, ὁ, *Eridanus*, a fabulous stream of the ancient geogr. which rose in the north-west, coming from the Rhipæan mountains, and flowed into the ocean; first, Hesiod. Th. 338. Batr. 20. Most of the ancients referred it to the Padus, some to the Rhodanus or Rhenus.

ἤρικε, see ἐρείκω.
ἠρίον, τό (prob. from ἔρα), *a hill, a mound, a sepulchral mound*, 23, 126.†
ἤριπε, see ἐρείπω.

ἤρυγε, see ἐρεύγομαι.
ἠρώ, see ἀράομαι.
ἠρώησαν, see ἐρωέω.
ἥρως, ὁ, gen. ἥρωος, dat. ἥρωϊ, Ep. ἥρῳ, accus. ἥρωα, Ep. ἥρω. Instead of the gen. ἥρωος with the mid. syllable short, Od. 6, 303, some read ἥρως; instead of ἥρω as accus. we should write ἥρω without apostr. 6, 63. 13, 428. Od. 11, 520; with which, however, Spitzner does not agree. 1) *a hero, a noble*, esply are kings and princes, the commanders and their companions, so called in Hom.; but also all warriors, especially when addressed: ἥρωες Δαναοί, ἥρωες Ἀχαιοί, ἄνδρες ἥρωες, 2, 110. 15, 220. Od. 1, 101; and generally, all who distinguished themselves by their strength, courage, prudence, and skill as artists: also every freeman, an honorable man, 7, 44. Od. 8, 483. 2) *a demi-god*, a middle class between gods and men, who sprung from a god on the paternal or maternal side; of which we find the first trace 12, 25.

ἥσατο, see ἥδομαι.
ἥσειν, see ἵημι.
ἦσθα, see εἰμί.
ἤσκειν, see ἀσκέω.
ἧσο, see ἧμαι.

ἥσσων, ἥσσον, gen. ονος, *inferior, worse*, especially in strength, *weaker, feebler*, 16, 722. 23, 858. The neut. as adv. ἧσσον, *worse*, Od. 15, 365. (In the gram. an irreg. compar. to κακός; according to the root it belongs to ἧκα.)

ἧσται, see ἧμαι.
ἥστην, see εἰμί.

ἡσυχίη, ἡ, *rest, peace, tranquillity, enjoyment*, Od. 18, 22; † h. Merc. 356.
ἡσύχιος, ον, poet. for ἥσυχος, *quiet, still, gentle, unobserved*, 21, 598.† whence adv. ἡσυχίως, *quietly*, h. Merc. 438.

ᾐσχυμμένος, see αἰσχύνω.
ἧτε, by the τέ added the relation of equivalence is indicated; therefore it nearly = εἴτε; doubled, ἤτε, ἤτε, *either*, or, 17, 42; or single, 19, 148. cf. ἤ.
ἦτε, or according to Wolf, ἢ τε, see ἤ.
ἠτιάασθε, see αἰτιάομαι.
ἠτίωντο, see αἰτιάομαι.

ἤτοι, Ep. (prob. fr. ἤ and τοί), conj. *surely, certainly, verily*; it denotes 1) *an assurance*, and hence often stands with μέν and with the following correlative δέ, ἀλλά: *assuredly, verily, certainly, truly*, 7, 451. 17, 514; esply after a vocat. 7, 191. 21, 446. Od. 4, 78. 16, 309. 2) It introduces alone a sentence, like μέν, to an antithetic clause with δέ, when it may be sometimes translated *now*, 1, 68. Od. 15, 6. 24, 154; or it begins, like μήν, the antithesis to a preceding clause, *indeed, surely*, esply ἀλλ' ἤτοι, *but yet*, 1, 211. Od. 15, 488. 16, 278. 3) It stands also to convey the idea of assurance, after conj. which introduce adjunct clauses: ὡς ἤτοι, ὄφρ' ἤτοι, 23, 52. Od. 3, 419. 5, 24. 4) ἤτοι for ἤ, or, after a preceding ἤ, occurs once, Od. 19, 599.

K 2

ἦτορ. 196 Ἠώς.

Often in Pindar ἤ—ἤτοι stands for ἤ--ἤ. (As a strengthening particle we find also ἤ τοι (Bothe: ἤτοι). 11, 6, 56.)

ἦτορ, ορος, τό, *the heart*, as a part of the human body, 22, 452; on 15, 252, see ἀέω, and in a wider signif. = στῆθος, 2, 490. 2) Metaph. *a) the powers of life, life*, of which the beating of the heart is the index, 5, 250. 11. 115. *b) heart, spirit*, as the seat of feelings, propensities, wishes, etc. 3, 31. 5, 529. 8, 437; also *soul, spirit*, as the thinking principle, 1, 188. (Prob. from ἄημι, breathing, like *animus*.)

ηὐγένειος, ον, Ion. and Ep. for εὐγένειος.

ηὐγενής, ές, Ion. and Ep. for εὐγενής.

ηὔδα, see αὐδάω.

*ηὔζωνος, ον, Ep. for εὔζωνος, Fr. 54.

*ηὐθέμεθλος, ον, Ep. for εὐθέμεθλος.

ηὔκομος, ον, Ion. for εὔκομος.

ἠύς, ἠΰ, Ep. for ἐύς, q. v.

ηὗσε, see αὔω.

ηὖτε, Ep. partic. 1) *as, like*, with single words, 1, 359. 2, 87. *b)* Also after a comparative for ἤ, 4, 277; according to Spitzner ηὖτε stands in its ordinary sense and the comparison is elliptical: ' blacker than it really is.' So also Damm: *nubes magis atra veluti pix*. 2) In the signif. of ὡς ὅτε, *as when*, with indicat. 2, 87; with subj. 17, 547. (According to Buttm. Lexil. ηὖτε sprung from ᾗ εὖτε; once we find εὖτε for ηὖτε. 3, 10)

Ἥφαιστος, ὁ, *Hēphæstus*, son of Zeus and Hērē (1, 577. 578), god of fire and of the mechanic arts, which need the aid of fire, especially of working metals. He and his sister Athēnē are the teachers of all the arts mentioned in Hom. At his birth he was ugly in form, weak in the feet and lame, (ἠπεδανός, χωλός, ἀμφιγυήεις,) for which reason Hērē threw him into the sea. Two sea-goddesses, Thetis and Eurynōmē, received him, and he remained with them nine years, 18, 395. Zeus also once hurled him from Olympus, when he attempted to aid his mother, upon the island of Lemnos, where the kind Sintians received him, 1, 590. In 18, 382, Charis is assigned to him as a wife; in the Od. 8, 267, Aphroditē. At the request of Thetis he made new arms for Achilles, and here his workshop in Olympus and his working of metals are described to us, 18, 468 seq. Hom. mentions the infidelity of his wife Aphroditē, Od. 8, 267 seq. His common residence is Olympus, his favorite place on earth the island Lemnos, Od. 8, 283. The most noted of the productions of Hēphæstus are, 1) The arms of Achilles, and especially the shield, upon which the heavens and the earth and the most important scenes of life were depicted, 18, 478. 2) The net, in which he entangled Arēs and Aphroditē, Od. 8, 274. 3) The brazen dwellings of the gods, 1, 606. 4) The sceptre and the ægis of Zeus, 2, 101 15 309. Hom. often calls fire φλὸξ

Ἡφαίστοιο, 9, 468 [and also simply Ἡφαιστος, 2, 426]. II) As an appellat. for *fire*, 2, 426. (According to Herm. fr. ἅπτειν and αἴστος, *qui ignem ex occulto excitat*; according to Heffter more prob. fr. φαίω, φαίστος, with a prosthesis of η, *the light-producer*.)

ἤφι, Ep. for ᾗ, 22, 107.

*ἠχέω (ἠχή), aor. 1 ἤχησα, intrans. *to sound, to resound, to echo*, h. Cer. 38.

ἠχή, ἡ, *sound, echo, noise, roaring*, spoken of a multitude, 2, 209. 12, 252. Od. 3, 150; of battle; 8, 159. 15, 355; of wind, 16, 769.

ἠχήεις, εσσα, εν (ἠχή), *sounding, resounding, roaring*, spoken of the sea, 1, 157; δώματα, Od. 4, 72. h. 13, 5.

ἤχθετο, see ἔχθομαι.

ἦχι, Ep. for ᾗ, adv. *where*, 1, 607 (not ᾖχι as in the Od.).

*ἠχώ, όος, ἡ, *sound, noise*, but esply *echo, reverberation*, h. 18, 21.

ἠῶθεν, adv. (ἠώς), *from the morning, from the dawn*; *in the morning*, 7, 372, and often. 2) *at the dawn*, at day-break, 18, 136. Od. 1, 372. 15, 308.

ἠῶθι, adv. (ἠώς), *in the morning, at the dawn*; always ἠῶθι πρό, before day-light, 11, 50. Od. 6, 36.

*ἠῷος, η, ον (ἠώς), *in the morning, early*, h. Merc. 17.

ἠώς, gen. οῦς, dat. οῖ, accus. ἠῶ, 1) *the dawn of day, the early dawn*, 9, 618 seq. Od. 6, 48. 2) *the time of the morning dawn, morning*; accus. ἠῶ, during the morning, Od. 2, 434; the gen. ἠοῦς, on the morning (of the following day), 8, 470. 525. 3) *the rising day-light*, 8, 1 (according to Eustath., Voss, and others, *day-light* itself, and *the whole day*, 13, 794. Od. 19, 571); e. g. ὄτε δὴ τρίτον ἦμαρ ἐϋπλόκαμος τέλεσ᾽ Ἠώς, but when Aurora brought about (not brought to an end) the third day, Od. 5, 390. 9, 76. 10, 144; hence the days were counted by the mornings, 1, 493. Od. 19, 192. 571; cf. Völck. Hom Geog. p. 126. Nitzsch ad Od. 2, 434. 4) As a point of the compass: *morning, east*, in πρὸς ἠῶ τ᾽ ἠέλιόν τε, see ἠέλιος (from ἀέω. ἄημι, prop. the morning-air).

*Ἠώς, ἡ, as pr. n. *Aurora*, the goddess of the dawn or of the breaking day-light. She was according to h. 31, daughter of Hyperion and Euryphaessa; according to Hesiod. Th. 372, of Theia wife of Tithōnus, mother of Memnon, 11, 1. Od. 4, 188. h. Ven. 219. She bore away Orion and Clitus on account of their beauty, Od. 5, 121. 15, 250; and as a goddess had her residence in western Æa (according to Nitzsch, Od. 5, 1, prob. because an appearance similar to the dawn shows itself in the evening sky). She rises in the morning from the couch of her husband, to bring the light, 11, 1; or, according to 19, 1, 2. Od. 22, 197, from the waves of Oceanus; and the bright morning-star precedes her, 23, 226 She spreads her light over the whole earth, but the poets say nothing of her setting. According to

Od. 23, 246, she performs her journey with two horses. She is called χρυσόθρονος, εὔθρονος, ῥοδοπηχυς, ῥοδοδάκτυλος, ἠριγένεια, etc.

Θ.

Θ, the eighth letter in the Greek alphabet; and therefore the sign of the eighth book.

Θαάσσω, Ep. for θάσσω, to sit, 9, 194. 15, 124. Od. 3, 336. h. Merc. 172; only in the pres. and imperf. (According to Buttm. Lexil. p. 350, from the root θέ- or θά- (in the sense of sit), cf. τίθημι.)

Θαιρός, ὁ, the hinge of a door; the hinges were attached to the door, and not, as with us, to the door-post [the doors were so constructed as to have pivots above and below, which turned in sockets; the pivot is called στροφεύς, the sockets στρόφιγγες, cf. Bothe in loc.], 12, 459.†

Θαλάμη, ἡ, the lurking-place, lair, or den of a wild-beast, Od. 5, 432.†

Θαλαμηπόλος, ὁ (πολέομαι), attending in the sleeping-chamber or apartment of the women; the fem. the chamber-maid, lady's-maid, *Od. 7, 8. 23, 293.

Θάλαμος, ὁ, any apartment or chamber in the interior of a house, and 1) the sleeping-apartment of married persons, the nuptial chamber, 3, 423. 6, 243—250; the bridal-chamber, 18, 492. 2) the common apartment of the mistress of a family, 3, 127. Od. 4, 121; also any other room or chamber in the inner part of the house, 23, 317. 3) Also the store-room, in which clothes, arms, and provisions were kept, 4, 143. 6, 288; and according to Od. 2, 337, it would seem to be a vault below, cf. Nitzsch ad loc. cf. Od. 8, 439. 15, 99. (Prob. from θάλλω.)

Θάλασσα, ἡ (prob. from ἅλς), the sea, sea-water, the interior or Mediterranean sea, in distinction from the ocean, 1, 34. Od. 12, 1. 2.

Θαλάσσιος, or (θάλασσα), belonging to the sea; hence, nautical. θαλάσσια ἔργα (maritime affairs; mar. employs, Cp.), navigation, 2. 614: fishing, Od. 5, 67.

Θάλεα, τά (θάλυς), blooming fortune, happiness, a superfluity of all delights, res floridæ. θαλέων ἐμπλησάμενος ἦτορ, having filled his heart with contentment or joy [not, with delicacies, Cp.], 22, 504;† cf. θάλεια.

Θαλέθω, poet. form for θάλλω, to bloom, Od. 23, 191; metaph. spoken of men: to be in the bloom of life, Od. 6, 63. 2) to flourish, to abound in any thing, with ἀλοιφῇ, 9, 467. 23, 32.

Θάλεια, ἡ, as adj. used only in the fem. as an epith. of δαίς, 7, 475. Od. 3, 420. 8, 76. 99; a flourishing, i. e. rich, sumptuous feast. The old Gramm. derive it incorrectly from θάλεος; it is rather the fem. of an obsol. adj. θάλυς, an Ep. form of θῆλυς, to which also τὰ θάλεα belongs, Buttm.

Θάλεια, ἡ, Thalia, daughter of Nêreus and Dôris, 18, 39.

Θαλερός, ή, όν (θάλλω), blooming, flourishing; hence, fresh, vigorous, active; only in the metaph. signif. as αἰζηοί, πόσις; γάμος, blooming marriage, i. e. marriage in the bloom of youth, Od. 6, 66; μηρώ, strong, vigorous thighs, 15, 113; χαίτη, a full mane, 17, 439. 2) gushing, strong, rich, abundant; φωνή, the gushing, rich voice, 17, 696. Od. 4, 705: δάκρυ, abundant tears; the copious tear, 2, 266; γόος, unceasing lamentation, Od. 10, 457. (According to others, θαλερός signifies, in connexion with φωνή, loud, strong.)

Θαλίη, ἡ (θάλλω), prob. bloom; metaph. blooming fortune, abundance, joy. ἐν πολλῇ θαλίῃ, in full bliss, 9, 143; plur. Od. 11, 603.

Θαλλός, ὁ (θάλλω), a sprout, a sprig, a branch, Od. 17, 224.†

Θάλλω, only in h. Cer. 402; Ep. θηλέω, Od. 5, 73; aor. 2 ἔθαλον. Ep. θάλον. h. 18, 33; perf. 2 τέθηλα, partcp. τεθηλώς, fem. τεθαλυῖα (Ep. for τεθηλυῖα, for metre's sake), pluperf. τεθήλει, 1) to bloom, to flourish, to be verdant; spoken of the earth, ἄνθεσι, h. Cer. 402. 2) to have an abundance, to abound in, with dat. σταφυλῇσιν (spoken of a vine), Od. 5, 69; φυλλοῖσι. Od. 12, 103; metaph. ἀλοιφῇ, 9, 208. The partcp. mly absol. blooming, luxuriant, abundant, ἀλωή, εἰλαπίνη, ἀλοιφή. Od.

Θάλος, εος, τό, a sprout, a sprig, a sucker, metaph. spoken of men, 22, 87. λευσσόντων τοιόνδε θάλος χορόν εἰσοιχνεῦσαν, when they behold such a sprout (one so blooming in youthful beauty) entering the dance, Od. 6, 157. the partcp. agrees in gender with the object understood (κατὰ σύνεσιν), h. Ven. 279.

Θαλπιάω (θάλπω), to become warm, to be warm; only partcp. θαλπιόων for θαλπιῶν, Od. 19, 319.†

Θάλπιος, ὁ, son of Eurÿtus, grandson of Actor, commander of the Epêans before Troy, 2, 620 (from θάλπος, that warms).

Θάλπω, only pres. to make warm, to warm, with accus. στέατος, τροχόν, Od. 21, 179; τόξον, i. e. to make the bow flexible by rubbing it with fat over the fire, *Od. 21, 246.

Θαλπωρή, ἡ (θάλπω), prop. warming; always metaph. the act of refreshing, recreation, resting, 10, 223. Od. 1, 167; comfort, joy, opp. ἄχεα, 6, 412.

Θαλύσια, τά, subaud. ἱερά (θάλλω), the offerings of the first-fruits which were made to the gods, 9, 534. In this place it is represented as offered to all the gods; later, this offering was made only to Dêmêtêr, Theocrit. 7, 3.

K 3

Θαλυσιάδης, ου, ὁ, son of Thaly-ius = Echepoius, 4, 458

θαμά, adv. (ἅμα), always of time: *often, frequently, continually*, 16, 207. Od. 1, 143. θαμά θρώσκοντες οἰστοί, 15, 470; also of time; for the sense is, that the new bow-string might endure (not give way under) the arrows which should be shot in rapid succession.

*θαμβαίνω, poet. form θαμβέω, *to be amazed at, to regard with astonishment*, with accus. εἶδος, h. Ven. 84. h. Merc. 407.

θαμβέω (θάμβος), aor. ἐθάμβησα, Ep. θάμβησα, 1) *to be amazed, to be astonished*, absol. 1, 199. Od. 1, 323. 2) Trans. with accus. *to be astonished at, to behold with astonishment*, Od. 2, 155. 16, 178. 17, 367.

θάμβος, εος, τό (θάομαι), Ep. gen. θάμβευς, Od. 24, 394 : *astonishment, amazement, admiration, terrour*, 3, 342. Od. 3, 372.

θαμέες (θαμά), dat. θαμέσι, accus. έας, an Ep. adj. used only in the plur. masc. = θαμειός, *frequent, thick, in great numbers, in quick succession*. As a sing. θαμής or θαμύς are assumed, 10, 264. 11, 552. Od. 14, 12; see Thiersch, § 199. 5. Buttm. Ausf. Gram. § 64. Anm. 2.

θαμειός, ή, όν (θαμά), *frequent, close together, in great numbers*; only in the fem. plur. nom. and accus, *1, 52. 14, 422. 18, 68.

θαμίζω (θαμά), *to come* or *go frequently*, 18, 386. 425. Od. 5, 88. 8, 161. 2) *to be common* or *frequent*; with partep. οὔτι κομιζόμενός γε θάμιζεν, he was not often attended, Od. 8, 451.

θάμνος, ὁ (θαμινός), *a shrub, a bush, shrubbery, a thicket*, sing. Od. 23, 190. h. Cer. 100; plur. 11, 156. Od. 5, 471. 476.

Θάμυρις, ιος, ὁ, accus. Θάμυριν, ὁ Θρήιξ, a bard of the fabulous ages, of Thrace, son of Philammōn and Argiopē. He was conquered in a contest with the Muses, and deprived of his eyes and his art, 2, 595. Apd. 1, 3, 3.

θανατόνδε, *to death*, 16, 693.

θάνατος, ὁ (θανεῖν), *death*, both natural and violent, *slaughter*, 3, 309; in the plur. *kinds of death*, Od. 12, 311. Natural death is brought by the goddess of fate (μοίρα, μόρος), according to the universal law of nature; violent death, contrary to the common termination of life, by Κῆρ 'κῆρες θανάτοιο); sudden death in the bloom of life by Apollo and Artēmis, cf. μόρος and κήρ.

Θάνατος, ὁ, pr. n. *the god of death*, death personified; H. calls him the twin brother of Hypnos (Sleep), 14, 231. 16, 454. 672. His form is not further described by him. According to Hes Th. 759, he is the son of Νύξ (Night), and dwells in Tartarus.

θανέειν, contr. θανεῖν, see θνήσκω.

θάομαι, prop. Dor. for θηέομαι, q. v.; depon. mid. fut. θήσομαι, *to regard with astonishment, to admire, to wonder at*; only optat. aor. θησαίατ' for θήσαιντο, Od. 18, 191.†

θάπτω, aor. 1 θάψα, Ep. for ἔθαψα, plupf. pass. ἐτέθαπτο, to perform the last offices to a corpse, i. e. 1) *to burn* it, Od. 12, 12. 11, 21, 323. 2) *to bury, to inter* the collected bones, ὑπὸ χθονός, Od. 11, 52.

θαρσαλέος, έη, έον, Att. θαρραλέος (θάρσος), *bold, courageous, confident*, in a good sense. πολεμιστής. 5, 602 ; also in a bad, *rash, audacious*, Od. 17, 449. 19, 91; compar. θαρσαλεώτερος, 10, 223. Adv. θαρσαλέως, *boldly, audaciously*, Od. 1, 382

θαρσέω, Att. θαρρέω (θάρσος), aor. ἐθάρσησα. Ep θάρσησα, perf. τεθάρσηκα, *to be bold, courageous, of good courage, resolute*; mly absol., often imperat. θάρσει. τεθαρσήκασι λαοί, the people are full of courage, 9, 420 687. 2) Trans. with accus. θάρσει τόνγ' ἄεθλον, be of good courage in this contest, Od. 8, 197.

θάρσος, εος, τό, Att. θάρρος, 1) *resoluteness, good courage, confidence, boldness*. 2) In a bad sense: *rashness, imprudence*, 17, 570 21, 395.

θάρσυνος, ον (θάρσος), *courageous, confident, bold, πόλις*, 16, 70; *confiding* in, with dat. οἰωνῷ, 13, 823.

θαρσύνω, Att. θαρρύνω (θαρσύς), poet. for θρασύν), iterat. imperf. θαρσύνεσκε, *to make courageous, spirited, confident, to encourage, to inspirit*, τινά, 18, 325 ; ἥτόρ τινι ἐνὶ φρεσίν. 16, 242 ; and dat. instrum. ἐπέεσσι, μύθῳ, 4, 233. Od. 9, 377.

θάσσων, ον, *faster, swifter*, compar. of ταχύς, q. v.

θαῦμα, ατος, τό (θάομαι), 1) *an object of wonder, a miracle*, any thing which is beheld with admiration and astonishment; often with θαῦμα ἰδέσθαι and ἰδεῖν, a prodigy to behold, 5, 725. h. Ven. 206 : spoken of Polyphēmus : θαῦμα πελώριον, Od. 9, 190. 2) *astonishment, amazement*, Od. 10, 326.

θαυμάζω (θαῦμα), fut. θαυμάσομαι, Ep. σσ, aor. θαύμασα, 1) Intrans. *to wonder, to be astonished*, often with partep. 24, 692; with infin. οἷον δὴ θαυμάζομεν Ἕκτορα—αἰχμητήν τ' ἔμεναι καὶ θαρσαλέον πολεμιστήν! how wonder we so, that Hector is both a lancer and a brave warrior! 5, 601. 2) Trans. with accus. *to wonder at any thing, to regard with astonishment*. 10, 12. Od. 1, 382 ; connected with ἀγάασθαι, Od. 16, 203 ; οἷον ἐτύχθη, at what happened, 2, 320.

θαυμαίνω, Ep. form of θαυμάζω, fut. ανῶ, *to wonder at*, Od. 8, 108.†

Θαυμακίη, ἡ, a city in Magnesia (Thessaly), under the dominion of Philoctētēs; according to Eustath. the later Θαυμακοί 2, 716.

*θαυμάσιος, ίη, ιον (θαῦμα), *wonderful, astonishing*, h. Merc. 443.

*θαυμαστός, ή, όν. *wonderful, astonishing*, h. Cer. 10

*θαυματός, ή, όν. poet. for θαυμαστός h. Merc. 50. Bacch. 34.

ΘΑΦΩ, poet. obsol. root of the perf. τέθηπα, pluperf. Ep. ἐτεθήπεα for ἐτεθήπειν, and aor. 2 ἔταφον (in the perf. the second aspirate is changed into the tenuis, and in the aor. the first). The perf. has the signif. of the pres. *to wonder, to be astonished, to be amazed*, often in the partcp., 4, 243. 21, 29. 64. θυμός μοι ἐν στήθεσσι τέθηπεν, my mind in my breast is amazed (*my soul is stunn'd within me*, Cp.), Od. 23, 105; also ἐτεθήπεα θυμῷ. Od 6, 166. Of the aor. 2 only the partcp. ταφών, 9, 193. 11, 545 (see Buttm. Gram. p. 285).

ΘΑΩ, Ep. defect. of which only the infin. pres. mid θῆσθαι for θᾶσθαι, and 3 sing. aor. mid. θήσατο, partcp. θησάμενος, occur. 1) *to suck, to milk*. γυναικά τε θήσατο μαζόν, be sucked at a woman's breast, see γυνή, 24, 58. h. Cer. 236; spoken of sheep: αἰεὶ παρέχουσιν ἔπηετανὸν γάλα θῆσθαι, they always give milk the whole year (In., *milk to milk* [infin.]; *for* a man *to milk* it), Od. 4, 89. 2) *to suckle*. Ἀπόλλωνα θήσατο μήτηρ, the mother suckled Apollo, h. Ap. 123.

θεά, ἡ, fem. of θεός, *a goddess*; in connexion with another subst. θεὰ μήτηρ, 1 280, and θεαὶ Νύμφαι, 24, 615 (θεά retains the alpha through all the cases); hence θεᾶς, θεάν, the dat. plur. θεαῖς, but θεῆς, 3, 158; θῆσιν, 8, 305. Herm. ad h. Ven. 191, would always read θεαῖς; θεά must be pronounced as a monosyllable after πότνια, Od. 5, 215. 13, 391. 20. 61. Buttm., Ausf. Sprachl. I. p. 261, reads πότνα, and then θεά is disyllabic.

θεά, ἡ (θεάομαι), sight, view. αἰδέσσαί με θέας ὕπαρ, reverence me by thy countenance [*by thy sweet face*], h. Cer. 64; as an adjuration, a doubtful reading. Herm. would write θέης; Ilgen takes it as a pr. n. Θέη for Θεία, as Ῥέα, Ῥέη [see Bothe in loc.].

θέαινα, ἡ, poet. for θεά, *goddess*, 8, 5. Od. 8, 341.

Θεανώ, οῦς, ἡ, daughter of Cisseus, wife of Antēnôr, priestess of Athēnē in Troy, 5, 70. 6, 298. According to later poets, sister of Hecabē (Hecuba).

θέειον, τό, Ep. for θεῖον, q. v.
θεειόω, Ep. for θειόω.
θείω, see τίθημι.

θειλόπεδον, τό (εἴλη, πέδον), a place exposed to the sun for drying any thing, *a drying-place*. Od. 7, 123;† viz. a space in the vineyard exposed to the rays of the sun, where grapes were dried on the stocks, in order to prepare the *vinum passum*, cf. 18, 566. τῆς (subaud. ἀλωῆς) ἕτερον (sc. πέδον) θειλόπεδον λευρῷ ἐνὶ χώρῳ τέρσεται ἠελίῳ ἑτέρας δ' ἄρα τε τρυγόωσιν, ἄλλας δὲ τραπέουσι, in this, a drying-place, on the level ground, is warmed by the sun [*the arid level glows*, Cp.], and they are gathering some and treading out others. Voss translates, 'some grapes, spread out on the level place, are drying in the sun' (he understands, of course, a place in which the plucked grapes are dried), see Nitzsch ad loc.

θεῖμεν, see τίθημι.
θεῖναι, see τίθημι.

θείνω (akin to κτείνω and θάνω), aor. 1 ἔθεινα, partcp. θείνας, 20, 481; *to strike, to cut down, to goad*, with accus. 1, 588. 16, 339; and with dat. instrum. ἄορι, with the sword, βουπλῆγι, μάστιγι, 10, 484. 6, 135. On θεινομένου in Od. 9, 459, see ῥαίοιτο.

θείομεν, poet. for θῶμεν, see τίθημι.
θεῖον, τό, Ep. θέειον and once θήϊον, Od. 22, 493; *sulphur*, spoken of lightning, 8, 135. 14, 415. Od. 12, 417. It was used as a sacred means of purification, 16, 228. Od. 22, 493; see θειόω.

θεῖος, η, ον (θεός), *divine*, sprung from a deity, γένος, 6, 180; or sent by a deity, ὀμφή, 2, 41. 2) *consecrated to a deity, holy, sacred*, ἀγών, χορός, 7, 298. Od. 8, 264. 3) *divine, glorious*, spoken not only of men who are distinguished by peculiar powers and qualities, but also of every thing which is great, beautiful, sublime, or excellent in nature; ἅλς, 9, 214 [sacred salt, prob. because derived from the sea, ἐξ ἁλὸς δίας]; ποτόν, Od. 2, 341. 9, 205; cf. Nitzsch ad Od. 3, 265, p. 190.

θειόω, Ep. θεειόω (θεῖον), fut. ώσω, *to fumigate with sulphur, and purify*, δῶμα, Od. 22, 482. Mid. Od. 23, 50 (both times the Ep. form).

θείω, Ep. for θέω, θῶ, see τίθημι.

θέλγω, aor. ἔθελξα, ἐθέλχθην, *to stroke with the hand, to caress*, mulcere, and to overcome any one by such charms addressed to the sense, hence: 1) *to charm, to benumb*, spoken of bodies with the accus. of the wand of Hermēs: ἀνδρῶν ὄμματα θέλγει, with which he seals the eyes of men, Od. 5, 47. 24, 3. Il. 24, 343. θέλξας ὄσσε φαεινά, sealing the bright eyes, 13, 435. (It is not to be taken of the obscurity of death.) *b) to charm*, i. e. to transform by enchantment, τινά, Od. 10, 291. 318, 326. Others explain it in a metaph. sense, to restrain, to appease; but against the context, cf. v. 432; and Nitzsch ad loc. 2) *to charm, to infatuate*, metaph. of the mind: rely in a bad signif. to deprive a man utterly of his mental powers, *to overreach, to deceive, to blind, to seduce, to infatuate*, spoken of the Sirens, Od. 12, 40 : νόον, to deprive of reason, 12, 255. h. Cer. 36; θυμόν, to enfeeble the mind, 15, 594; and dat. instrum. λόγοισιν, ἐπέεσσιν, by words, Od. 1, 57. 3, 267; ψεύδεσσι. δόλῳ, 21, 276. 604; spoken of the suitors: ἔρῳ δὲ θυμὸν ἔθελχθεν, they were infatuated by love, Od. 18, 212. *b*) Rarely in a good signif.: *to charm, to chain* (by a narration), Od. 17, 521; pass. Od. 17, 514.

θελκτήρ, ῆρος, ὁ (θέλγω), a soother, an assuager, ὀδυνάων, h. 15, 4.

θελκτήριον, τό (θέλγω), any thing which has an enchanting power over the mind; *an instrument of enchantment, a charm, delight, rapture*, spoken of the girdle of

K 4

Θέλω.   Θεός.

Aphrodītē, 14, 215. Songs are called θελκτήρια βροτῶν, the delights of mortals, Od. 1, 337; and the Trojan horse: θεῶν θελκτήριον, the joy of the gods, Od. 8, 509. Others make θελκτήριον here an adj., and connect it with ἄγαλμα, a propitiatory offering.

θέλω, Ep. ἐθέλω, *to will, to wish*, whence θέλοι, h. Ap. 46; where however Herm. would read ἐθέλω.

θεμέθλον, τό (θέμα), *a foundation, a bottom*. ὀφθαλμοῖο θέμεθλα, the bottom, i. e. the cavities of the eye, 14, 493. στομάχοιο θέμεθλα, the bottom of the throat, *17. 47.

θεμείλιον, τό = θεμέθλιον, *the foundation*, τιθέναι, to lay the foundation; διατιθέναι, h. Ap. 254. Il. 12, 28; προβαλέσθαι, 23, 255; only in the plur.

θέμεν, and θέμεναι, see τίθημι.

θέμις, ιστος, Ep. for θέμιδος, ἡ (from θέω, τίθημι), in general, any thing which is introduced and sanctioned by use, *that which is proper, becoming*; hence 1) *order, custom, right*, 5, 761; often θέμις ἐστί, *it is right, reasonable*, with dat. of the pers and infin. Od. 14, 56. Il. 14, 386. ἦ or ᾗ θέμις ἐστί, as is the custom, as is fitting, 2, 73. 9, 33; cf. ᾖ, and with gen. ἣ θέμις ἀνθρώπων πέλει, 9, 134. 19, 177. ἥτε ξείνων θέμις ἐστίν, Od. 9, 168; in connexion with ἀγορή, the assembly of judges, 11, 807. 2) In the plur. οἱ θέμιστες, *ordinances, decrees*; of the gods: Διὸς θέμιστες, the oracles of Zeus, Od. 16, 403. *b*) Spoken of men: *laws, statutes, institutions*, 9, 112, 115; chiefly spoken of rulers and judges: οἵτε θέμιστας πρὸς Διὸς εἰρύαται, who guard the laws from Zeus [voluntate, auspiciis Jovis regnant, Heyn.], 1, 238. 2, 206; [cf. ἐρύω,] *judicial sentences, κρίνειν θέμιστας σκολιάς, to give unjust decisions (to pervert justice), 16, 387; and of subjects: λιπαρὰς τελεῖν θέμιστας, to pay rich tributes, customs, i. e. the customary gifts to the king, 9, 156. 298.

Θέμις, ιστος, ἡ, *Themis*, daughter of Uranus and Gæa, Tellus (Hes. Th. 135), occurs in H. only three times. She performs in Olympus the office of a herald, and calls the gods to an assembly, 20, 4; at a feast of the gods, she receives those who come, and preserves order in it, 15. 87; she arranges assemblies of the people and dismisses them, Od. 2, 68. In the Hymns she is called the friend of Zeus, h. 22, 2; and the companion of Nikē (Victory), h. 7, 4. Later, she appears as the protectress of legal order and the goddess of justice.

θέμιστα, θέμιστας, see θέμις.

θεμιστεύω (θέμις), *to give laws, to administer justice*, τινί, Od. 11, 569; spoken of the gods, βουλήν, to give an oracle, h. Ap. 253. 2) *to rule, to govern*, τινός, *Od. 9, 114.

*θεμιστοπόλος, ον (πολέω), *administering the laws, administering justice*, epith. of kings, h. Cer. 103. 473.

*θεμιτός, ή, όν, poet. for θεμιστός (θε-μίζω), *according to law, just, right*, h. Cer. 302.

θεμόω (τίθημι), *to set*, i. e. *to force*. τὴν θέμωσε χέρσον ἱκέσθαι, the wave forced the ship to come to the land, *Od. 9, 486. 542.

θέναρ, αρος, τό (θείνω), *the palm of the hand*, with which a man strikes, 5, 339.†

θεό, Ep. for θοῦ, see τίθημι.

θεοδμήτος, ον (δάμω), *built by a god, god-built*, πύργοι, 8, 519 †

θεοειδής, ές (εἶδος), *similar to a god, god-like*, epith. of distinguished heroes, still only in reference to physical superiority, 2, 623; also of the suitors, Od. 21, 186. 277; see θεουδής, cf. Buttm. Lex. p. 352.

θεοείκελος, ον (εἴκελος), *similar to a god*, like θεοειδής, 1, 131. Od. 3, 416.

θεόθεν, adv. (θεός), *from god*, Od. 16, 147.†

Θεοκλύμενος, ὁ, son of Polypheides, a descendant of Melampus and a famous prophet, Od. 15, 256.

θεοπροπέω (θεοπρόπος), *to prophesy, to communicate the will of the gods, to explain divine signs*, only partcp. 1, 109. Od. 2, 184.

θεοπροπίη, ἡ, prop. *the explanation of signs given by the deity, prophecy* = μαντεία, 1, 87; cf. Eustath. Od. 1, 415. 2) = θεοπρόπιον, *an oracle, a revelation*, 1, 385. 11, 794. 16, 36.

θεοπρόπιον, τό, any thing which is indicated by the gods, *a divine command, a divine response, an oracle, a revelation, a prophecy*, *1, 85. 6, 438.

θεοπρόπος, ὁ, *a prophet, a seer*, a general name of those who, from signs, interpret the will of the gods, 12, 228. Od. 1, 416. (Mly derived from θεός and προσπεῖν or τὰ θεοῖς πρέποντα λέγειν; accord. to Buttm., Lex. p 350, from πρέπω, in the signif. *to break forth, to sound out*, hence θεὸς πρέπει, a god sends a sign. (θεοπρόπιον is the sign, and the expounder is called θεοπρόπος.)

θεός, ὁ, ἡ, Ep. θεόφιν, gen. plur. 17, 101; dat. plur. 7, 366; nom. plur. θεοί as a monosyllable, 1, 18. 1) Masc. *god*; indefinite = δαίμων, *a god*, 17, 99. Od. 3, 131. σὺν θεῷ, with god, with god's help, 9, 49. ἐκ θεόφιν, through the gods, 17, 101. ὑπὲρ θεόν, against god. against god's will, 17, 327. 2) As fem. ἡ = θεά, often in H. θήλεια θεός, 8, 7. 3) As adj. in the compar. θεώτερος, *diviner*. Θύραι θεώτεραι, more used by the gods, Od. 13, 111. The Hom. gods have bodies with blood, and are formed like men, larger however and more handsome and far superior in their powers, 5. 859 seq. 15, 361. 24, 467. They are immortal and enjoy an eternal youth; sickness and other human infirmities they do not experience; still they are not secure from all misfortune, 5, 336. 883. 858 In intelligence and knowledge they far excel mankind, without however being omniscient, 5, 441. 2, 485. In a moral point of view they do not rise above

Θεουδής. 201 Θεσπιδαής.

men; they have desires and passions, failings and weaknesses. They govern the world, and especially the affairs of men; allot happiness and misfortune. Men, however, often draw evils upon themselves, by their own perverseness, and then it is the allotment of fate, see μοῖρα, Od. 1, 33, 34. They commonly appear to men in assumed forms or enveloped in a cloud, 5, 127. 14, 343. 20, 151. 150. Their dwelling is Olympus and heaven, see Ὄλυμπος.

Θεουδής, ές, *fearing god, reverencing the gods*; hence, *pious, upright*, νόος, θυμός, Od. 6, 121. 19, 364; βασιλεύς, *Od. 19, 109. (Buttm., Lex. p. 352, justly distinguishes this word from θεοειδής, the contraction of which rather would be θεώδης, and derives θεουδής from δαίδω and θεός Hesych. Θεοσεβής, Schol. Palat. θεοδεής or δεισιδαίμων. So Pass. and Nitzsch. Lobeck he-itates.)

θεόφιν, see θεός.

Θεράπευω (θεράπων), *to be a servant, to serve*, in opposition to ἄρχω, Od. 13, 265.† 2) Mid. = act. h. in Ap. 380.

*Θεράπνη, ἡ, poet. contr. fr. θεράπαινα, a *female servant*, h. Ap. 157.

Θεράπων, οντος, ὁ, *a servant, an attendant, a companion, a helper*. It is distinct from δοῦλος, and signif. a voluntary servant, not merely of free birth but often of noble descent, 15, 431, seq.; thus Patroclus is θεράπων, the comrade of Achilles, 16, 244; Meriones of Idomeneus, 23, 113; all heroes are called θεράποντες Ἄρηος, 2, 110. 7, 382; and especially those attendants of heroes who guide the horses, charioteers, ἡνίοχοι θεράποντες, 5, 580. So (a private) *herald* was often a θεράπ. in the *service* of an individual, Od. 18, 424. In the Od. the θεράποντες perform duties of various kinds in the house, Od. 1, 109; they are, however, always like the squires of knights, of noble descent, as Eteoneus, Od. 4, 22; (from θέρω, *fovere.* prop. devoted to a man's service.)

Θερέω, Ep. for θερῶ, see θέρομαι.

Θερμαίνω (θερμός), aor. 1 ἐθέρμηνα, *to warm, to make warm, to heat*, with accus. λοετρά, 14, 7. Pass. *to become warm, to be heated*, Od. 9, 376.

Θερμός, ή, όν (θέρω), *warm, hot*, in different degrees; warm, 14, 6. 11, 266; but also seething hot, Od. 19, 368; metaph. δάκρυα θερμά, hot tears, 7, 426. Od. 4, 523.

Θέρμω (θέρω), *to warm, to heat*, ὕδωρ, Od. 8, 426; pass. *to become warm or hot, to be warmed*, Od. 8, 437. πνοιῇ δ' Εὐμήλοιο μετάφρενον εὖρε τ' ὤμω θέρμετο, by the breath (of the steeds close behind him) were the back and broad shoulders of Eumelus warmed, 23, 381.

Θέρος, εος, τό (θέρω), gen. Æol. θέρευς, Od. 7, 118; dat. θέρει, 22, 151; prop. *warmth*; esply the warm season, *summer*, opposed to ὀπώρη, Od. 12, 76; opposed to χεῖμα, Od. 7, 118.

Θέρομαι, a defect. mid. fut. θέρσομαι,

aor. 2 pass. ἐθέρην, subj. θερέω, Ep. for θερῶ, *to become warm, to warm oneself, to become hot*, Od. 19, 64. 507; πυρός, by the fire, Od. 17, 23. 2) *to glow. to be burned*, πυρός, 6, 331. 11, 667. ₍The act. θέρω is rare.)

Θερσίλοχος, ὁ, a Pæonian, an ally of the Trojans, slain by Achilles, 17, 216. 21, 209.

Θερσίτης, ao, ὁ, the ugliest of the Greeks before Troy in body and mind. He was squint-eyed, lame of one foot, and hump-backed. His slanderous tongue found fault with every one, and in his impudent harangues he did not spare even the most dignified characters. Odysseus (Ulysses) compelled him to hold his tongue by a blow of his sceptre, 2, 211—271. (From θέρσος=θάρσος, the *hot, over-loud speaker.*) According to Apd. 1, 8, 1, son of Agrius.

θές, see τίθημι.

Θέσκελος, ον (θεός and ἔϊσκω, ἴσκω, origin.=θεοείκελος), *god-like*: *similar to the gods; divine, supernatural, wonderful*, spoken only of things, in a metaph. signif. (Θεοείκελος on the other hand in a proper signif.), ἔργα, 3, 130. Od. 11, 374. 610; as adv. ἔϊκτο θέσκελον αὐτῷ, he was wonderfully like him, 23, 107 (see Buttm. Lex. p. 357).

Θεσμός, ὁ (τίθημι), *an ordinance, law, decree, custom*. λέκτροιο παλαιοῦ θεσμὸν ἵκοντο, they went to the custom of their ancient couch [i. e. to the couch they habitually shared in years long past], Od. 23, 295.† θεσμοὶ εἰρήνης, the laws of peace, h. 7, 15.

Θεσπέσιος, ίη, ιον (θεός, εἰπεῖν), prop. *spoken or inspired by a god*; the signif. from εἰπεῖν is, however, obscure in ἀοιδή θεσπεσίη, 2, 600. θεσπέσιαι Σειρήνες, Od. 12, 158; generally. 1) *divine*, βηλός, 1, 591; ἄντρον, Od. 13, 363; and dat. θεσπεσίῃ, subaud. βουλῇ, as adv., by the counsel of the gods, by the divine decree, 2, 367. 2) Most commonly as an epith. of any thing great and glorious, whether proceeding from nature or men: *divine, grand, sublime, glorious, wonderful, powerful, violent*, χάρις, ὀδμή. χαλκός, φόβος, φύζα, powerful flight, 9, 2; so also νέφος, λαῖλαψ, 15, 669. Od. 9, 68. (As an epith. of φόβος, φύζα, etc. it has also been interpreted *supernatural, divinely sent*, but without necessity, see Buttm. Lex. p. 358 [a *great* and *general* flight. B.])

Θέσπια, ἡ, or Θέσπεια, Ep. for αἱ Θεσπιαί, *Thespiæ*, an ancient town, at the foot of Helicon in Bœotia, according to Strabo a colony of Thracians, or, according to a native tradition, named from Thespius, son of Erechtheus, famed for a temple of Erôs (Cupid) and the Muses, now *Rimocastri*, 2, 498. Wolf, after Herodian and Venet. has ῑ; Heyne, on the other hand, Θέσπεια, which Spitzner has adopted.

Θεσπιδαής, ές (δαίω), gen. έος, prop.

K 5

Θέσπις. **Θηέομαι.**

god-kindled; generally. *violent, terrible,* always an epith. of fire, 12, 441. Od. 4, 418 (see Butim. Lex. p. 358). In 12, 177, some take πῦρ in a metaph. signif., the heat of contest, cf. λάινον.

θέσπις, ιος, ὁ, ἡ (θεός, εἰπεῖν), *inspired by god, divinely inspired*, epith. of ἀοιδή and ἀοιδός, *Od. 1, 328. 8, 498. 17, 385. 2. divine, glorious, violent, ἆλλα,* h. Ven 209.

Θεσπρωτοί, οἱ, the *Thesprotians,* inhabitants of Thesprotia, a small region in the middle of Epirus. In the Od. they dwelt not only on the coast of the proper Epirus, but in the interior as far as Thessaly. They were of Pelasgic origin, and one of the main tribes of this region, Od. 14. 315. 327. 16, 65. 427.

Θεσσαλός, ὁ, Ion. for Θετταλός, son of Heraclês and Chalciope daughter of Eurypýlus king of Cos, father of Pheidippus and Antiphus, 2, 679. (As a national name the word does not occur.)

Θεστορίδης, ου, ὁ, son of Thestor = *Calchas,* 1, 69; = *Alcmæon,* 12, 394; [also a name found in Epigr. 5, 1.]

Θέστωρ, ορος, ὁ, 1) son of Idmon, a prophet and Argonaut, father of Calchas, of Alcmæon, of Leucippê and Theonoê, Hyg. f. 160. 2) son of Enops, a Trojan, slain by Patroclus. 16, 401.

θέσφατος, ον (θεός, φημί). 1) *spoken or communicated by God* (never in the *transferred* sense of *great, vast.* Buttm. Lex. p. 358], θέσφατόν ἐστι. It is appointed by God, 8, 477; τινί, Od. 4, 561. 10, 473. As subst. not *an oracle, a divine response,* as Buttm. explains it, but *the predetermination of the gods; divinely predestined fate;* hence with adj. παλαίφατα θέσφατα (= decrees of the gods declared of old=) *ancient oracles,* 5, 64. Od. 9, 507. 11, 151. 13, 172. See Nitzsch ad Od. 9, 507. 2) Generally, *procured or sent by god.* ἀήρ, Od. 7, 143.

Θέτις, ιος and ιδος, ἡ, gen. ιδος, 8, 370; dat. Θέτῑ for Θέτιι, 18, 407; daughter of Nereus and Doris, wife of Peleus and mother of Achilles, not from choice, but by an appointment of Zeus, 18. 431. 24, 62. She tenderly loves her son, and on his account supplicates Zeus to avenge the insult offered him, 1, 502, seq. Zeus is greatly moved, for once, when the gods had conspired to bind him, she had delivered him from this disgrace, 1, 397, seq. She has her dwelling in the depths of the sea, and she is therefore called ἁλοσύδνη, 20, 207. According to 24, 78. 753. cf. 1, 357. 18, 35, her dwelling is in the vicinity of the Trojan dominions.

θέω, and **θείω,** fut. θεύσομαι, 1) *to run, to fly, to hasten,* spoken of men and animals with the adjunct: πόδεσσι, ποσί, 23, 623. Od. 8, 247; μετά τινα, 10, 63; πόλεος πεδίοιο, through the wide plain, 4, 244; spoken of horses: περὶ τρίποδος θέειν, to run for a tripod (in a race), 11, 701; metaph. περὶ ψυχῆς Ἕκτορος θέειν, to run for Hector's life, 22, 161. (Both

Hector and Achilles ran thus rapidly, for the prize was the life of the first, which he sought to save and his adversary to destroy.) 2) Spoken of inanimate things, *to run, to fly,* spoken of a ship, 1, 483; often in Od. of a fragment of rock. 13, 141; of a potter's wheel, 18, 601; of a quoit, ἀπὸ χειρός, Od. 8, 193. 3) Of things without motion; φλὲψ ἀνὰ νῶτα θέουσα, a vein running along the back. 13, 547; ἄντυξ πυμάτη θέεν ἀσπίδος, 6, 118. 4) It is often connected as particp. with other verbs: as ἦλθε θέων, he came running, or he came quickly, hastily, 6, 54; and παρέστη, 15. 649; (the extended Ep. form θείω is found in the infin., partcp., and pres. subj.; see Thiersch, § 221. 82)

ΘΕΩ, obsol. root of τίθημι, q. v.

θεώτερος, α, ον, see θεός.

Θῆβαι, ῶν, αἱ, poet. Θήβη, ἡ, *Thebæ, Thebes.* 1) the oldest city in Bœotia, on the Ismênus, built by Cadmus, from whom the citadel was called Καδμεία, and enlarged by Amphion; now *Thivæ.* H. uses the sing. 4, 378. 406. Od. 11, 265; plur. 5, 804. 6, 223. It had epith. ἑπτάπυλος, seven-gated, Od. 11, 263; see Apd. 3, 6. 6; cf. Ὑποθῆβαι. 2) the ancient capital of upper Ægypt, *Thebais,* on the Nile, later called Διὸς πόλις, famed for its opulence; hence it is called ἑκατόμπυλος, only plur. 9, 381. Od. 4, 124. 126.

Θήβασδε, poet. for Θήβαζε *to Thebes.* 23, 279. [3) a city in Troas, 22, 479; see Θήβη.]

Θηβαῖος, αίη, αῖον. *Theban,* as subst. a Theban, an inhabitant of Thebes in Bœotia, Od. 10, 492.

Θηβαῖος, ὁ, a Trojan, father of Eniopeus, 8, 120.

Θήβη, ἡ, 1) Poet. for Θῆβαι, No. 1. 2) a city in Troas, on the borders of Mysia, which was inhabited by Cilicians. It was situated at the foot of mount Placus (hence Ὑποπλακίη), and was the residence of Eëtion, the father of Andromache. Achilles destroyed it; according to the Schol. the later *Adramyttium.* 1, 366. 6, 397; plur. Θήβησιν. 22, 479; once. Strab. XIII. p. 585. In later writers, only τὸ Θήβης πεδίον, a fruitful region, south of Ida, near Pergamus, is mentioned.

θήγω, fut. ξω, aor. 1 mid. ἐθηξάμην, 1) Act *to whet, to sharpen,* spoken of the wild boar, ὀδόντας, 11, 416. 13, 475. 2) Mid. *to sharpen any thing for oneself,* δόρυ. *2. 382.

Θηέομαι, Ion. for Θεάομαι, pres. optat. θηοῖο, contr. imperf. 3 plur. θηεῦντο, Ep. for ἐθηοῦντο, aor. 1 ἐθησάμην, optat. 3 plur. θησαίατο, fr. θάομαι, *to see, to behold, to look upon,* with the additional notion of wonder, hence *to regard with astonishment, to wonder, to wonder at,* with accus. 10, 524; πάντα θυμῷ, Od. 5, 76; absol. with θαμβεῖν. 23, 728. Βή; and often with the partcp. Od. 5, 75. 8, 17

Θήης.

Θήης, Ep. for θῆς, see τίθημι.
Θηητήρ, ῆρος, ὁ, Ion. for θεατής (θηέομαι), *a beholder, a judge or connoisseur, one acquainted with,* τόξων, Od. 21, 397.†
Θήίον, τό, Ep. for θεῖον. q. v.
Θήλεας, accus. plur. θῆλυς.
Θηλέω, Ep. (θηλή) = θάλλω, *to bloom, to be verdant,* with gen. Od. 5 73;† see θάλλω.
Θῆλυς, θήλεια, θῆλυ (Ep. also θῆλυς, gen. commun., 10, 97. 5, 269. 10, 216. Od. 5, 467). 1) *female, of the female sex,* opposed to ἄρρην), θήλεια θεός, a female deity, 8, 7; θήλειας ἵππους, 5, 269; αὐτή, female voice, Od. 6, 122. Since with the female sex the ideas of fruitfulness, softness, and tenderness are connected, it signif. 2) *fruitful, fructifying, fresh, tender.* ἐέρση θῆλυς, the fresh dew, Od. 5, 467. (Others, ' the fructifying dew,' incorrectly, on account of its connexion with the cutting morning frost.) The compar. θηλύτερος, η, ον, poet. positive; only, however, θηλύτεραι θεαι and γυναῖκες, 8, 520. Od. 8, 324, and that with the idea of the fruitful or tenderer sex, as Passow remarks (' the tender woman,' V.).
Θημών, ῶνος, ὁ (τίθημι), *a heap,* ἠίων, Od. 5, 368.†
Θήν, Ep. enclit. particle (primarily a dialect. form of δή); it expresses a subjective conviction; *surely, certainly,* 9, 394. Od. 3, 352; in H. always in an ironical signif., as δήπου (opinor), *assuredly, certainly,* 13, 620. 17, 29; and strengthened, ἦ θην, *certainly, indeed* ; often οὐ θην, *assuredly—not;* not—*I take it,* 2, 276 B, 448. οὐ μέν θήν γε, not—*I presume* (or *hope*). Od. 5, 211.
Θηοῖο, see θηέομαι.
ΘΗΠΩ, obsol. root of τέθηπα, see ΘΑΦΩ.
Θήρ, θηρός, ὁ, *a wild animal,* esply *a beast of prey, a wild beast,* 10, 184. h. 18, 13; see φήρ.
Θηρευτής, οῦ, ὁ (θηρεύω), only as an adj. κύνεσσι καὶ ἀνδράσι θηρευτῆσι, dogs and hunters, *12, 41. cf. 11, 325.
Θήρη, ἡ (θήρ), *the chase, the hunting of animals,* 5, 49. 10, 360; *prey,* Od. 9, 158.
Θηρεύω (θήρη), *to hunt,* Od. 19, 365; in the partcp.†
Θηρητήρ, ῆρος, ὁ, Ion. and poet. (θηράω), *a hunter,* Il., and ἄνδρες θηρητῆρες, 12, 170. αἰετὸς θηρητήρ, *21, 252.
Θηρήτωρ, ορος, ὁ, poet. for θηρητήρ, 9, 544.†
Θηρίον, τό (prop. dimin. of θήρ); *a wild animal; a (wild) beast,* without the diminutive force, spoken of a stag, μέγα θηρίον *Od. 10, 171. 180.
Θηροσκόπος, ον (σκοπέω), *lying in wait for wild animals,* h. 27, 11.
Θής, θητός, ὁ, *a hireling, a hired labourer,* Od. 4, 644,† where θῆτες are mentioned with δμῶες; they were free, but poor house-holders, who had. it is true, family establishments of their own, but

Θνήσκω.

derived their support from the wealthy land-holders, by performing menial offices, see θητεύω. The interpret. ' serfs is incapable of proof. (According to Buttm. Lex. p. 350. from ΘΕΩ, τίθημι θα- [θάακος, seat], like the Germ. *Sasse, Insasse.*)
Θησαίατο, see θηέομαι.
Θήσατο, see ΘΑΩ.
Θησεύς, ῆος and *έως,* accus. Θησέα, *Theseus,* son of Argeus and Æthra, or, by tradition, of Poseidôn, king of Athens. Among the many exploits ascribed to him, the most remarkable are: the slaughter of the Minotaur, in Crete, by the help of Ariadnê, Od. 11, 322; his contest with the Centaurs at the marriage of Peirithous, etc. He also, by uniting the inhabitants of Attica in one place, laid the foundation of the later city of Athens, l, 265. Od. 11, 631. This verse is, however, as borrowed from Hesiod, Sc. 182, marked as not genuine.
Θητεύω (θής), aor. ἐθήτευσα, *to labour for hire, to work as a hireling, as a daylabourer.* Cf. θής, 21, 444. Od. 18, 357; τινί, Od. 11, 389.
Θίς, θινός, ὁ, later θίν (from τίθημι), prop. any *heap.* πολὺς δ᾽ ἀμφ᾽ ὀστεοφιν θὶς ἀνδρῶν πυθομένων, around is a heap of bones of putrefying men, Od. 12, 45. 2) Chiefly *sand-heaps* on the sea-coast, *dunes;* and gener. *the coast, the strand,* θαλάσσης or ἁλός, in the dat. or accus. Od. 7, 290. 9, 46. The gender is to be recognized only in 23, 693; according to which it is masc. Later, it is masc. and fem. Incorrectly, the Gramm. distinguish ὁ θίς, a heap, and ἡ θίς, a shore.
Θίσβη, ἡ, poet. for Θίσβαι. αἰ, *Thisbe,* an ancient town in Bœotia at the foot of Helicon, between Creusa and Therpiæ, with a port. now *Gianiki;* accord. to Mannert = Σίφαι, sing. 2, 502; cf. Strab. p. 411.
Θλάω, aor. ἔθλασα, Ep. σσ, *to bruise in pieces, to dash in pieces, to grind to pieces, to crush,* with accus. κοτύλην, 5, 307; κυνέην, 12, 384; ὀστέα, Od. 18, 97.
Θλίβω, fut. θλίψω, *to press, to crush;* mid. θλίψεται ὤμους, he will chafe his shoulders, Od. 17, 221.†
Θνήσκω (for θανήσκω, from θάνω), fut. θανοῦμαι, infin. θανέεσθαι, aor. 2 ἔθανον, perf. τέθνηκα; also the syncop. forms: plur. τέθναμεν, τέθνασι, optat. τεθναίην, imp.rat. τέθναθι, infin. Ep. τεθνάμεν and τεθνάμεναι, particp. τεθνεώς; only dat. τεθνεῶτι, Od. 19, 331; Comm. Ep. τεθνηώς, ῶτος; sometimes in the gen. τεθνηότος, Od. 24, 56. Il. 13, 659; as fem. once τεθνηκυῖα, Od. 4, 734. (The reading τεθνειώς, Wolf, after Aristarchus, has banished from H. Spitzner agrees with Wolf, ad Il. 6, 70. Buttm. regards it as established, at least for the gen. τεθνειῶτος, see Rem. Ausf. Gram. § 110. 19, 6.) 1) *to die, to find a man's death,* spoken both of natural and violent death; ὑπὸ χερσίν τινος, by the hands of any one,

K 5

Θνητός. 204 Θρασύς.

15, 289, οἴκτιστῳ θανάτῳ θανεῖν, to die a most pitiable death, Od. 11, 412. 2) In the perf. *to be dead*, opposed to ζάω, Od. 2, 131; partcp. τεθνηκὼς *one dead, a corpse*, and even τεθνηὼς νεκρός, 6, 71; in like manner θανών, *a dead person*, 5, 176.

Θνητός, ή, όν (θνήσκω), *mortal*, an epith. of men; subst. οἱ θνητοί, *mortals*, in opposition to ἀθάνατοι, 12, 242. Od. 19, 593.

Θοινάομαι, in H. depon. pass. (θοίνη), *to feast*, aor. 1 infin. θοινηθῆναι, Od. 4, 36.†

*Θοίνη, ἡ, *a feast, a repast, food*, Batr. 40

Θοαί, αἱ νῆσοι, see θοός.

Θόας, αντος, ὁ, *Thoas*, 1) son of Andraemon and Gorgo, king of Pleuron and Calydon in Aetolia, 2, 638. 4, 275. Od. 14, 499. 2) son of Dionysus and Ariadne, king of Lemnos, father of Hypsipyle. He alone, in the slaughter of the men in Lemnos, was saved by his daughter, she sending him in a ship to Œnoē, 14, 230. 3) a Trojan, slain by Menelaus, 16, 311.

Θόη, ἡ (adj. θοή), *Thoē*, daughter of Nereus and Doris, 18, 40.

Θόλος, ἡ, *a dome*, particularly a circular building with a dome; in the Od. an adjoining building between the house and the court, in which were kept furniture and provisions, *kitchen-vault*, Voss, Od. 22, 442. 459. That it rested upon pillars is evident from the fact, that Odysseus (Ulysses) attached the cord to a column in hanging the maids, Od. 22, 466.

Θοός, ή, όν (prob. from θέω), *swift, rapid*. a) Spoken of warriors, *active, prompt, vigorous*, in battle; often in the Il. Ἄρης, 5, 430; also with infin. θοὸς ἔσκε μάχεσθαι, 5, 536. νῦν θοοὶ ἐστέ, 16, 422, now be active, i. e. alert in battle, as an exhortation to bravery, with which also the following passage agrees. Thus Heyne and Spitzner. Others, with Eustathius, think they find here a reproach for cowardice, and translate it in a sarcastic signification, 'now ye are swift!' ἄγγελος, h. 18. 29. b) Spoken of inanimate things which are moveable: βέλος, ἅρμα, μάστιξ. θοὴ δαίς, a hasty, quickly-prepared meal (take care that the meal be quickly prepared), Od. 8, 38; see αἶψα. θοαὶ νῆες, a constant epith. of ships, since they are swift and easily managed; the other interpretation, 'running to a point,' is less suitable, 1, 12. νὺξ θοή, swift night, either because it comes suddenly on, or, more correctly, because to men loving repose it seems to pass swiftly away (hence Voss, 'swift-flying night'). Buttm., Lex. p. 365, explains it, 'the swift night, as incessantly following the sun, and seizing on what he leaves;' with the implied notion of unfriendliness, 10, 394. 468. In Od. 12, 284, seq. Nitzsch, ' the sharp night-air,' c) Spoken of objects without motion : *running to a point*,

pointed; only θοαὶ νῆσοι, the pointed islands, Od. 15. 299; the little precipitous islands at the mouth of Achelous, which formed the extreme points of the Echinades, and form their cliffs or promontories projecting into the sea, were called θοαί or ὀξεῖαι, Strab. VIII. 350: now *Cursolari*. (The primary signif. is from θέω, running rapidly to an object; and therefore spoken of material objects running to a point, pointed; according to others. akin to θήγειν.)

Θοόω (θοός, c.), aor. 1 ἐθόωσα, *to point, to make pointed, to sharpen*, ὁμαλόν, Od. 9, 327.†

Θόρε, Ep. for ἔθορε, see θρώσκω.

*Θορικός, ὁ (Θόρικος, Thuc.), *Thoricus*, one of the twelve ancient cities in Attica, upon the east coast, founded by Cecrops; later, a place and borough (δῆμος) belonging to the Acamantian tribe; now, *Porto Mandri*; whence the adv. Θορικόνδε, h. in Cer. 126.

*Θορυβέω (θόρυβος), *to make a noise, to cry*, Batr 191.

ΘΟΡΩ, obsol. root of θρώσκω, q. v.

Θοῦρις, ιδος, ἡ, fem. of θοῦρος, q. v.

Θοῦρος, ὁ. fem. θοῦρις, ιδος, ἡ (θόρω), prop. springing upon, attacking, *impetuous, violent*, the masc. always an epith. of Ἄρης, 5, 30; the fem. spoken of arms with which one presses upon an enemy. ἀσπίς, 11, 32. 20, 162; αἰγίς, 15, 308; often θοῦρις ἀλκή, impetuous strength, in attacking and defence, often in the Il.; once in Od. 4, 527.

Θόωκος, ὁ. see θῶκος.

Θόων, ωνος, ὁ, 1) son of Phaenops, brother of Xanthus, a Trojan, slain by Diomēdēs, 5, 152. 2) a Trojan, slain by Odysseus (Ulysses), 11, 422. 3) a Trojan, who attacked the camp with Asius, 12, 140. 4) a Trojan, slain by Antilochus, 13, 545. 5) a noble Phaeacian, Od. 8, 113. 6) = Θόων.

Θοῶς, adv. from θοός, *swiftly, instantly*, 5, 533. Od. 5, 243. h. 7, 7.

Θόωσα, ἡ, a nymph, daughter of Phorcys, mother of Polyphēmus, Od. 1, 71. 72

Θοώτης, ου, ὁ, voc. Θοῶτα, the herald of Mnestheus, 12, 342, 343.

Θράσιος, ὁ, a Pӕonian, slain by Achilles, 21, 210.

Θράσος, τό. prop. only θάρσος with metath. *fearlessness, courage*, 14, 416.†

Θρασυκάρδιος, ον (καρδία,) *bold hearted, spirited, decided*, *10, 41. 13, 343.

Θρασυμέμνων, ον, gen. ονος (μένος), *boldly-enduring, ever-courageous*, epith. of Heraclēs, 5, 639. Od. 11, 267.

Θρασυμήδης, ους, ὁ. son of Nestor, who went with his father to Troy; leader of the watch, 9, 81, seq. He returned prosperously with his father, Od. 3, 39. 442.

Θρασύμηλος, ὁ. the charioteer of Sarpedon. slain by Patroclus, 16, 463 (otherwise Θρασυμήδης).

Θρασύς, εῖα, ύ (θράσος), *bold, brave, spirited*, epith. of heroes, 8, 89. 12, 60;

Θρέξασκον. 205 Θρόνος.

oftener χεῖρες, 11, 553; and πόλεμος, 6, 254. Od. 4, 146; later in a bad signif. (also Voss, *arrogant*.)
θρέξασκον, see τρέχω.
Θρεπτήριος, ον, *skilled in nourishing, in bringing up*. τὰ θρεπτήρια, wages for nursing or bringing up (see θρέπτρα), h. Cer. 168. 223.
θρέπτρα, τά (τρέφω), prop. the present, received by the person who nurses or brings up a child when the nursling is grown, *wages for nursing* or *bringing up;* then, *the gratitude* and *requital* which a child gives to his parents in age, for the care he has received. οὐδὲ τοκεῦσιν θρέπτρα φίλοις ἀπέδωκε, he requited not his dear parents' care [*liv'd not to requite their love*, Cp.] 4, 478. 17, 302.
θρέψα, Ep. for ἔθρεψα, see τρέφω.
Θρηΐκιος, ίη, ιον (Θρῄκη), *Thracian;* πόντος, the Thracian sea, the northern part of the Ægean sea. 23, 230; φάσγανον and ξίφος, see these words. Σάμος Θρηϊκίη Samothracia, see Σάμος, 13, 12.
Θρῇξ, ἴκος, ὁ, contr. Θρῄξ, Ion. for Θρᾴξ, *a Thracian*. The inhabitants of Thrace were auxiliaries of the Trojans, 2, 844. Sometimes in the full form, Θρήϊκα, Θρήϊκες, Θρηΐκας, 2, 595. 4, 533; sometimes contract. Θρῇκας, 24, 234; Θρῃκῶν, 4, 519 (Thiersch, Gram. § 170, 4, would write Θρηΐκων, as coming from Θρηΐκων); ι is short in H.
Θρῄκη, ἡ, Ion. for Θρᾴκη, *Thracia, Thrace*, a region north of Greece, by which it was bounded (through the Penēus and the sea) on the south, 23, 230. Towards the north, east, and west, Thrace in H. has no definite boundaries, and embraces all countries lying above Thessaly (8, 845). As a portion of them, he mentions Pieria, Emathia, Pæonia; as nations or tribes, the Pæonians and Ciconians; as mountains, Olympus, Athos, and the Thracian mountains (Θρηϊκων ὄρη, 14, 227; proh. accord. to Eustath. the Scomius and Hæmus); and the river Axius. It produces cattle, 11, 222; and wine, 9, 72; it is the habitation of the winds, v. 4; and, on account of the rudeness and savage valour of its inhabitants, the residence of Arēs, 13, 301. Od. 8, 360. From this comes the adv. **Θρῄκηθεν**, from Thrace, 9, 5; and **Θρῄκηνδε**, to Thrace, Od. 8, 361.
θρηνέω (θρῆνος), *to lament, to groan, to wail*, absol. Od. 24, 61; with accus. ἀοιδήν, to sing a dirge, 24, 722. (? See note.)
θρῆνος, ὁ (θρέω), *lamentation, wailing*, esply *the wailing for the dead*, which the singers commenced and women repeated, 24, 721; and gener. *any plaintive song*, spoken of the song of the birds, h. 18, 18.
θρῆνυς, υος ὁ (θρᾶνος), *a foot-stool*, which commonly stood by the θρόνος and κλισμός, 14, 240. Od. 1, 131. 2) *a bench for rowers*, the seat of the rowers, 15, 729; cf. ζυγόν.
Θρῇξ, ηκός, ὁ, Ion. for Θρᾷξ, see Θρῄξ.

*Θριαί, αἱ, the *Thriæ*, nymphs of Parnassus, who brought up Apollo, and invented the art of prophesying by little stones thrown into an urn, h. Merc. 552; cf. Herm. ad loc. and Apd. 3, 10. 2.
θριγκός, ὁ, the *projecting edge (coping, or cornice*) on the upper part of an (inner or outer) wall, the projecting part of a house-wall, which served to throw off the rain, *a battlement, a cornice*, Od. 17, 267. In the passage περὶ δὲ θριγκὸς κυάνοιο, Od. 7, 87, round about was a cornice of dark brass, it is commonly understood of the interior of the house, but Nitzsch ad loc. takes it as the coping of the exterior wall, for the description of the interior of the house commences v. 97.
θριγκόω (θριγκός), aor. ἐθρίγκωσα, *to furnish the upper part of a wall with a coping, to finish off*, and gener. *to enclose* or *fence*, ἀχερδῳ, Od. 14, 10.†
Θρινακίη, ἡ, νῆσος, Ep. for Θριναμρία (Θρίναξ), *Thrinacia*, i. e. the triangular island, or having three promontories, Od. 11, 107. The old and several modern critics understand by it the island of *Sicily*, and place in it the giants, Cyclōpes, Læstrygones, Siculi, and Sicani, see Strab. VI. p. 251. So Voss and Mannert. In H. it is a desolate island, and he gives it no occupants except the herds of Hēlios, Od. 11, 108. 109. G. F. Grotefend therefore justly remarks: "Italy was but obscurely known; it was confounded with several islands, Sicania, Od. 24, 306; and the land of the Siculi, Od. 20, 383; cf. 24, 366, if Sicania does not signify Sicily. The Sicani and Siculi are also later mentioned as inhabitants of lower Italy, Thuc. 6, 2. Also the giants, Cyclōpes, and Læstrygones seem not to dwell in Thrinacia, according to H. According to Völcker's Hom. Geog. p. 110, Thrinacia is not indeed the country of the giants, Cyclōpes, Læstrygones, etc., but a little island, distinct from Sicily, sacred to Hēlios.
θρίξ, τριχός, ἡ, dat. plur. θριξί, *the hair*, both of men and brutes, Od. 13, 399. 431. 11. 8, 83; ἀρνῶν, the wool of lambs, 3, 273; κάπρου, the bristles of the wild boar, 19, 254.
Θρόνιον, τό, *Thronium*, the chief town in Locris, on the Boagrius, later the capital of the Epicnemidian Locrians; now *Paleocastra* in Marmara, 2, 533.
θρόνον, τό, only in the plur. τὰ θρόνα, *flowers*, as ornaments in weaving and embroidery, 22, 442. In Theoc. II. 59, it is used of flowers and herbs.
θρόνος, ὁ, *a seat, a chair*, esply an elevated arm-chair, before which a foot-stool (θρῆνυς) was always placed. It was commonly wrought elaborately, and of costly materials, 14, 238. 8, 442. 18, 390. To make the seat soft, λῖτα, τάπητες, χλαῖναι, ῥήγεα were spread over it, Od. 1, 130. 10, 352. 20, 150 (from θρᾶνος).

θρόος.

θρόος, ὁ (θρέω), *a noise, a roar, a cry, a loud call*, 4, 337.†

*θρυλλίζω (θρύλλος), *to strike a discordant note on the lyre*, h. Merc. 488.

θρυλλίσσω (θρύλλος), fut. ξω, *to break in pieces, to crush*, θρυλλίχθην μέτωπον, 23, 396.†

*θρύλλος, ὁ, and **θρῦλος** (akin to θρόος), *noise, uproar, outcry*, Batr. 135. (Several ancient Gramm. prefer the reading with one λ.)

Θρυόεσσα, ἡ. poet. for Θρύον.

*θρύον, τό, *a rush*, juncus, a marsh-plant, 21, 351.†

Θρύον, τό, poet. Θρυόεσσα, ἡ, 11, 711, *Thryon*, a town in Elis, the boundary of the Pylians and Eleans, on the Alpheus, through which there was here a ford; it was situated upon a hill; according to Strab. the later *Epitalium*, 2, 592. It belonged to the dominion of Nestor; the passage 5, 545, where it is said of the Alpheus, that it flows through the land of the Pylians, does not conflict with 11, 711, where Thryon is named as a frontier town; for, although the river flowed by Thryon, it might still in other places flow through the interior of the realm, see Heyne ad loc.

θρώσκω. aor. 2 ἔθορον. Ep. θόρον, 1) *to spring, to leap, ἐκ δίφροιο*, 8, 320; χαμᾶζε, 10, 528. 1), 684; metaph. spoken of inanimate things; *to spring, to fly*, spoken of the arrow, 15, 314. 16, 774 : spoken of beans and vetches, 13, 589 2) *to leap upon, to make an attack*, ἐπί τινι, upon any one, 8, 252. Od. 24, 203; ἔν τινι, 5, 161.

θρωσμός, ὁ (θρώσκω), *a place springing up*, as it were, above another, *an elevation, a height*. θρωσμὸς πεδίοιο, the heights of the plain, 10, 160. 11, 56. Thus the more elevated part of the Trojan plain is called, which stretched from the high shore of the Scamandrus to the camp; Voss, not with exact propriety, calls it 'the hill of the plain;' still less is it the hill of Callicolôné, as Köppen, ad Il. 10, 160, has it.

θυγάτηρ, ἡ, gen. θυγατέρος and θυγατρός, dat. θυγατέρι and θυγατρί, accus. θύγατρα, 1, 13; nom. plur. θυγατέρες and θύγατρες, dat. θυγατέρεσσιν, 15, 197; H. uses both forms; *a daughter*. (υ is prop. short; but, in all cases which are more than trisyllabic, for metre's sake long.)

θυέεσσιν, dat. plur. from θυός.

θύελλα, ἡ (θύω), *a tempest, a whirlwind, a storm, a hurricane*, often ἀνέμοιο, ἀνέμων θύελλα, 6, 346. πυρός τ' ὀλοοῖο θύελλα (V. a consuming fire-tempest), Od. 12, 68: only spoken of a violent tempest, or of a storm-cloud rising with wind, 23, 366.

Θυέστης, ου, ὁ, Ep. and Æol. Θυέστα, 2, 107; (from θύω, *Furius*, Herm.) *Thyestes*, son of Pelops, grandson of Tantalus, brother of Atreus; he begot Ægisthus from his own daughter Pelopia. According to 2, 107, he succeeded Atreus in the government of Mycenæ. In Od. 4,

Θυμός.

517, the abode of Thestes is mentioned, prob. in Midia, on the Argolic gulf; for here Thyestes dwelt, according to Apd. 2, 4. 6 ; see Nitzsch ad Od. 1. c.

Θυεστιάδης, ου, ὁ, son of Thyestes = Ægisthus.

θυήεις, εσσα, εν (θύος), *smoking with offerings, exhaling incense, sending forth vapour*, epith. of βωμός, 8, 48. 23, 148. Od. 8, 363.

θυηλή, ἡ (θύω), *the portion of victim burnt in honour of the gods* (Schol. *ὲκ ἀπαρχαί*), *the offering of the first portion, [the consecrated morsel*, Cp.], 9, 220 ;† see ἄργμα.

*θυίω = θύω. *to rave, to be in a state of inspiration, of prophetic frenzy*, h. Merc. 560.

θυμαλγής, ές, gen. έος (ἄλγος), *heart-paining, distressing*, χόλος, λώβη, μῦθος, ἔπος, 4, 513. 9, 387. Od. 8, 272.

θυμάρης, ές, also θυμήρης (ἄρω), *pleasing the mind, agreeable, delightful*, pleasant, ἄλοχος, 9, 336. Od. 23, 232; σκῆπτρον, Od. 17, 199 (According to the Schol. ad Od. 23, 232, the accent of one form should be θυμαρής, of the other θυμῆρες.)

Θυμβραῖος, ὁ, a Trojan slain by Diomedes, 11, 322.

Θύμβρη, ἡ, *Thymbra*, a plain (τόπος) in Troas, on the river Thymbrius, from which the camp of the Trojan allies extended to the sea. Later, this place was called Θυμβραῖον πεδίον, and there was the temple of the Thymbrian Apollo, 10, 430.

θυμηγερέω (ἀγείρω), only partcp. pres. *gathering courage, recovering one's spirits*, Od. 7, 283.†

θυμηδής, ές (ἦδος), gen. έος, *delighting the heart, grateful*, Od. 16, 389.†

θυμήρες, neut from θυμήρης, as an adv. *agreeably*, see θυμαρής.

θυμοβόρος, ον (βορά), *heart-gnawing, soul-consuming*, ἔρις, *7, 210. 16, 476. 20, 253.

θυμοδακής, ές (δάκνω), *heart-biting, soul-stinging*, μῦθος, Od. 8, 185.†

Θυμοίτης, ου, ὁ, *Thymœtes*, a distinguished Trojan, 3, 146.

θυμολέων, οντος (λέων), *lion-hearted*, epith. of heroes, 5, 639. Od. 4, 724. 814.

θυμοραϊστής, οῦ, ὁ (ῥαίω), *life-destroying, deadly*, θάνατος, 13, 544. 16, 414; δήιοι, 16, 591.

θυμός, ὁ (θύω), prop. that which moves and animates in men, cf 7, 216; *the heart, the soul*, as the seat of feeling, will, and thought, but always regarded as in motion; chiefly the passions and desires; hence 1) *the soul, as life, the vital powers*, θυμὸν ἐξαίνυσθαι, ἀφελέσθαι, ὀλέσαι, Il. ἐξελέσθαι μελέων Θυμόν, Od. 11, 201 ; on the other hand, θυμὸν ἀγείρειν, to collect the vital powers, to recover, see ἀγείρειν; spoken also of the vital powers of beasts, 3, 294. 12, 150, etc. 2) *the soul*, as the seat of feeling, especially of the stronger passions, anger, courage, wrath, displeasure. ὀρίνειν θυμόν, to excite the soul, especially to pity, to fear, 4, 208. 5, 29; on the other hand, πᾶσιν κάππεσε θυμός the spirit of all fell, 15, 280; anger, displeasure, 2, 156. Od. 4, 694. b) Sometimes also spoken of the gentler emotions· ἐκ θυμοῦ φιλέειν, to love from the heart, 9, 486. ἀπὸ θυμοῦ μᾶλλον ἐμοὶ ἔσεαι, thou wilt be farther removed from my heart. 1, 561. 3) the soul, as the seat of willing or wishing. a) desire, inclination, eaply for food and drink, appetite, 1, 468. 4, 263. πλήσασθαι θυμόν, to satisfy the appetite. Od. 19, 198; again, θυμὸς ἀνώγει, ἐποτρύνει, κελεύει, κέλεται, with intin., my heart prompts, commands me. b) will, resolution, thought. ἐδαΐζετο θυμός, 9, 8. ἕτερος δέ με θυμὸς ἔρυκεν, another thought restrained me, Od. 9, 302. 3) Generally, mind, disposition, spirit. ἕνα or ἶσον θυμὸν ἔχειν, to have a like mind, 13, 487. 704. δόκησε δ᾽ ἄρα σφίσι θυμὸς ὣς ἔμεν, so seemed their heart to be (i. e. they seem to be affected, just as they would have been if, &c.), Od. 10, 415. 5) In many phrases we find the dat θυμῷ, 1, 24. Od. 19, 304; also κατὰ θυμόν, ἐν θυμῷ: and often κατὰ φρένα καὶ κατὰ θυμόν. a construction like mente animoque, in the inmost heart.

Θυμοφθόρος, ον (φθείρω). prop. soulwasting; hence, life-destroying, fatal; θυμοφθόρα πολλά, sc. σήματα, signs which commanded to put the bearer to death. 6, 169; φάρμακα, fatal poisons, or, with others, poisons destroying the understanding, infatuating, Od. 2. 329; ἄχος, κάματος, Od. 4, 716. 10, 363. 2) Generally, soul-harassing, Od. 19, 323.

*Θυμόω (θυμός), to make angry, to enrage, in the aor. pass Batr. 242.

Θύνω (θύω), intrans. to move oneself violently, to rush. to dash on, to run impetuously, ἂμ πεδίον, διὰ προμάχων, Il. κατὰ μέγαρον, Od., spoken eaply of warriors in battle; ἄμυδις, to rush on in crowds, 10, 524; with partcp. 2, 446. (Θύνω bears the same relation to θύω as δύνω to δύω.)

Θυόεις, εσσα, εν (θύος), odoriferous, fragrant, νέφος, 15, 153;† and epith. of Eleusis, h. Cer. 97.

Θύον, τό (θύω), a tree whose fragrant wood was used for incense. Plin. H. N. XIII. 16, understands by it citrus, the lemon-tree, or the pyramidal cypress. Theophrastus describes θύον as a shrub which Sprengel considers the thyia articulata. Büllerbeck (Flor. Classic. p. 234) thinks it the thyia cypressoides, Od. 5, 60.†

Θύος, εος, τό, incense, and generally oblation, sacrifice, 6, 27. 9, 499. Od 15, 261; only in the plur. (H. was not acquainted with incense see Nitzsch ad Od. 5, 60.)

Θυοσκόος, ὁ (from θύος and κέω, καίω). prop. the sacrifice-burner, the sacrificial priest, the inspector of the sacrifice, who from the the flame, and especially from the vapour of the victim prophesied, Od.

21, 145. According to 24, 221, distinguished from μάντις and ἱερεύς (Eustath. ad Od. 21, 145, would rather derive it from κοέω, Ion. for νοέω.)

Θυόω (θύος), fut. ώσω, to perfume by fumigation, to make fragrant; only partcp. of the perf. pass. τεθυωμένον ἔλαιον, fragrant, perfumed oil, 14, 172;† εἵματα, h. Ap. 184.

Θύραζε, adv. out of the door, out of doors, 18, 29. 2) Generally, out, without. ἔκβασις ἁλὸς θύραζε, an egress out of the sea, a landing-place Od. 5, 410.

Θυρεός, ὁ (θύρα), a door-stone, a stone placed before the entrance, *Od. 9, 240. 313. 340.

Θύρετρον, τό (θύρα), a door, a gate, used only in the plur., 2, 415. Od. 18, 385.

Θύρη, ἡ. Ion. for θύρα, a door, prop. an opening in the wall, whether of a single room or of the whole house; a gate, mly in the plur. folding-doors (i. q. σανίδες), θύραι δικλίδες, Od. 7, 267: ἐπὶ or παρὰ Πριάμοιο θύρῃσιν, at the doors of Priam, i e before the dwelling, 2, 788. 2) Generally, access, entrance, Od. 9, 243. 13, 109.

Θύρηθε, adv. poet. for θύραθεν, out of the door, out, out of [the water, Bothe], Od. 14, 352.†

Θύρηφι. Ep. dat. from θύρη, as adv. without, Od. 9, 238.

Θυσσανόεις, εσσα, εν, Ep. θυσσανόεις, fringed, furnished with tassels or fringes, epith. of the aegis, *5, 739. 15, 229: only in the Ep. form.

Θύσανος, ὁ (θύω), a tuft, a tassel, a fringe, as an ornament on the shield of Agamemnon, the aegis, and the girdle of Hērē, *2, 448. 14, 181.

Θύσθλα, τά (θύω), the sacred things used in the festivals of Bacchus, accord. to the Gramm. eaply the thyrsi, torches, etc., 6, 134 †

*Θυσίη, ἡ (θύω), the act of sacrifice; the victim itself, h. Cer. 313. 369.

Θύω, fut. θύσω, aor. ἔθυσα, I) Trans. to sacrifice, to slay or burn a victim, ἀργματα θεοῖς, Od. 14, 446; without accus 9, 219. Od. 15, 222. 260; ἄλφιτα, h. Ap. 491; absol. τινί, to sacrifice to a god, Od, 9, 231. II) Intrans. to move violently, to rush on, to roar. To θύω. a) Spoken of wind, Od. 12, 400. 408; of rivers and floods, 21, 324, 23, 230. δάπεδον αἵματι θύεν, the floor swam with blood, Od. 11, 420. 22, 309. b) Spoken of men, generally, to rage, to storm, to rush boisterously on, φρεσί, 1, 342; ἐγχεῖ, dat. instrum. 11, 180. 16, 669 (cf. θύω. In the second signif. θύω has always ῠ, and in the first likewise, except in the trisyllabi cases of the partcp. pres. θύων, see Spitzner, § 52. 4).

Θυώδης, ες (εἶδος), fragrant, perfumed, odoriferous, θάλαμος, Od. 4, 121; εἵματα, Od. 5, 264. 21, 52.

*Θυώνη, ἡ, an appellation of Semele, after she was received amongst the gods, h. 5, 21; (from θύω, accord. to Diod. 2·

62 : ἀπὸ τῶν θυομένων αὐτῇ θυσιῶν καὶ θυηλῶν.)

θωή, ἡ (τίθημι), as *imposed punishment, a fine*, Od. 2, 192 ; ἀργαλέην θωὴν ἀλέεινε Ἀχαιῶν (he avoided the ignominious punishment of the Greeks, Voss), 13, 669. According to the Gramm. it here means *blame, insult, reproach*, and Nitzsch, ad Od. 2, 92, approves this ; accord. to Od. 14, 239, χαλεπὴ δήμου φῆμις, the reproachful remarks of the people which compel one to go to war.

θῶκος, ὁ, Ep. for θόωκος, Od. 2, 26. 12, 318 (Att. θᾶκος), a *seat*. Od. 2, 14 ; θεῶν θῶκοι, 8, 439. 2) *a sitting* in council, an assembly, Od. 2, 26 ; θωκόνδε, to the council, at the council, Od. 5, 3.

Θών, ῶνος, ὁ, *Thón*, husband of Polydamna, a noble Egyptian, at the Canopic mouth of the Nile, who received Menelaus, Od. 4, 228. Strab. XVII. p. 801, mentions a tradition, that not far from Canópus there was a city Thonis, which received its name from the king Thon. This town is distinctly mentioned by Diodor. 1, 19. Heeren, however (Ideen II. 2. Absch. 3, p. 706), supposes that Diod. may have indicated the city Thonis, as the oldest port of Egypt, perhaps from the Thonis, which Herod. (II. 113) from the account of the Egyptian priests, calls a guard (φύλακος) of the Canopic mouth. Canopus itself, it is said, received its name from the pilot of Menelaus, who was buried there, Strab. (Θῶνος, according to Eustath. In the Od. stands for Θόωνος, or, rather by syncope, for Θώνιος.)

θωρηκτής, οῦ, ὁ (θωρήσσω), *one who is armed with a cuirass, a cuirass-bearer*; always in the plur. as adj. πύκα θωρηκταί, with closely fitted cuirasses, *12, 317; and often.

θώρηξ, ηκος, ὁ, Ion. for θώραξ, *the coat of mail, the cuirass*, a covering of metal for the upper part of the body from the neck to the abdomen, 3. 332 ; where the girdle (ζωστήρ) was attached to it. It was commonly of metal, for the most part of brass, and consisted of two curved plates (γύαλα), of which one covered the breast, and the other the back ; at the sides they were fastened together by hooks; it is hence called διπλόος, 4, 133. cf. 15, 530. It was not only carefully polished but ornamented; hence, ποικίλος, πολυδαίδαλος, παναίολος, cf. particularly the cuirass of Agamemnon, 11, 20—27. The edge was commonly encompassed with a border of tin. Besides metallic cuirasses there were also lighter ones, as the *chain-cuirass*, στρεπτὸς χιτών, q. v., and the linen corselet, 2, 529. 830. See Köpke, Kriegswes. der Griech., p. 95.

θωρήσσω (θώρηξ), aor. 1 ἐθώρηξα, Ep. θώρηξα, aor. 1 pass. ἐθωρήχθην, I) Act. *to put on a cuirass, to arm*, τινά, 2, 11; τινὰ σὺν τεύχεσιν, 16, 155. II) Mid. and aor. pass. *to put on one's cuirass, to arm oneself*, often absol. in the Il. : once χαλκῷ, Od. 23, 368 ; mly τεύχεσιν, also σὺν τεύχεσιν, Il. δὺς δέ μοι ὠμοῖιν τὰ σὰ τεύχεα θωρηχθῆναι, permit me to put thine armour about my shoulders, 16, 40; praegn. θωρήσσεσθαι Ἐφύρους μέτα, to march armed, 13, 301.

θώς, θωός, ὁ, a ravenous beast of prey, which, 11, 474, is named in connexion with the lion; in 13, 103, with panthers and wolves; in colour it is δαφοινός. Most critics understand by it the *jackal*, *canis aureus*, Linn., which in the shape of its body bears a great resemblance to the fox.

I.

I, *Iota*, the ninth letter of the Greek alphabet, and hence the index of the ninth rhapsody.

ἰα, ἰῆς, Ep. for μία, see ἰος.
ἰά, τά, heterog. plur. of ἰός.
ἰαίνω, aor. 1 ἴηνα, aor. 1 pass. ἰάνθην, 1) *to warm, to make warm, to heat*, ἀμφὶ πυρὶ χαλκόν, the kettle, Od. 8, 426; ὕδωρ, Od. 10, 359 ; hence, *to make soft* or *liquid*, ξηρόν. Od. 12, 175. 2) Metaph. *to warm, to enliven*, θυμόν τινι, Od. 15, 379. h. Cer. 435 ; often pres. θυμὸς εὐφροσύνησιν ἰαίνεται, the heart is warmed with joy, Od. 6, 156 ; and generally, *to rejoice, to gladden*, 23, 598. Od. 4, 549. 840 ; μέτωπον ἰάνθη, the brow is cleared up, 15, 103: also θυμὸν ἰαίνομαι, I am become cheerful in heart, φρένας, Od. 23, 47. 24, 382; τινί, *to delight in any one*, Od. 19, 537. *b*) *to soften, to mollify*, θυμόν, 24, 119. 147. (Prop. ῐ, on account of aug., and for metre's sake also ῑ.)

Ἴαιρα, ἡ (ῐ), daughter of Nereus, 18, 42. (From ἰαίνω, gladdening.)

ἰάλλω, aor. ἴηλα, infin. ἰῆλαι (ἴημι), 1) *to send, to send away, to shoot*, ὀϊστὸν ἀπὸ νευρήφιν, 8, 300. 309 ; χεῖρας ἐπ᾽ ὀνείατα, to extend the hands to the food, 9, 91 ; περὶ χερσὶ δεσμόν, to put chains on the hands, 15, 19 ; ἑτάροις ἐπὶ χεῖρας ἰάλλειν, to lay hands upon the companions, Od. 9, 288 ; uncommon is: ἰάλλειν τινὰ ἀτιμίησιν, to wound any one with insults, like βάλλειν τινά τινι, Od. 13, 142.

Ἰάλμενος, ὁ (ῐ, the attacker, from ἰάλλω), son of Ares and Astyoche, leader of the Boeotians from Orchomenus and Aspledon ; he is mentioned as an Argonaut, and as a suitor of Helen, Apd. 1, 9. 16, Il. 2, 512. 9, 83. According to Aristot. Epigr. Anth. he fell before Troy.

*Ἰάμβη, ἡ, (ῐ, fr. ἰάπτω, the female scoffer), an handmaid of Celeus and Metaneira, with whom Deméter tarried, when she was seeking her stolen daughter. Iambe forced the sad goddess

Ἰαμενός. 209 Ἰδαῖος.

to laugh by her jests, h. in Cer. 195. 203. [Apd. 1, 5. 1. According to the Schol. ad Orest. Eur. 662, daughter of Echo and Pan.
Ἰαμενός, ὁ (ῑ, partcp. ἰάμενος), a Trojan hero, slain by Leonteus, 12, 139. 193.
Ἰάνασσα, ἡ, (ῐ, the warmer, fr. ιαίνω), daughter of Nereus and Doris, 18, 47.
Ἰάνειρα (ῑ), *Ianeira*, 1) daughter of Nereus and Doris, 18, 47. 2) daughter of Oceanus and Tethys, h. in Cer. 421.
*Ἰάνθη, ἡ (ῐ = Ἰάνειρα), daughter of Oceanus and Tethys, h. in Cer. 418.
ἰάνθην, see ἰαίνω.
ἰάομαι, depon. mid. fut. ἰήσομαι, Ion. for ἰάσομαι, aor. 1 ἰησάμην, *to heal*, spoken only of external wounds, with accus. τινά, 5, 904 ; ὀφθαλμόν, Od. 9, 525 ; absol. 5, 899 (ῐ).
Ἰάονες, οἱ (ῑ), Ep. for Ἴωνες, *the Ionians*, in 13, 685.† h. Ap. 147 ; the inhabitants of Attica. In this appellation of the Athenians both ancient and modern critics have found difficulty, because the Ionians, almost 200 years before the Trojan war, emigrated from Attica to Ægialus, and not till eighty years after it in part returned. The name, however, with Heyne, Köppen, Bothe, may be very well defended, because the inhabitants of Attica still retained the name of Ionians, when Ion had taken possession of Ægialus, Hdt. 8, 44. The inhabitants of Ægialus, in distinction from the Attic Ionians, were called Αἰγιαλεῖς Ἴωνες, Paus. 7, 1. 2. Also the region of country from Sunium to the Isthmus was called Ionia, cf. Plut. Thes. 24.
Ἰαπετός (ῑ), a Titan, son of Uranus and Gæa (Tellus), husband of Clymene, father of Atlas, Prometheus, and Epimetheus, see Τιτῆνες, 8, 479. (According to Heffter, motion upon the earth personified, in oppos. to Ὑπερίων.)
ἰάπτω (akin to ἵημι), 1) *to send, to cast, to hurl*, cf. προϊάπτω. 2) *to touch, to hit, to wound, to injure*, τί (Schol. διαφθείρειν, βλάπτειν). prop. καταιάπτω, with tmesis ; only, ὡς ἂν μὴ κλαίουσα κατὰ χρόα καλὸν ἰάπτῃ, that she should not injure [impair, Cp.] her beautiful person by weeping, Od. 2, 376. 4, 749. (Some think it a separate verb, akin to ἵπτω, ἄπτω in the signif. *to injure*, Passow in Lex. supplies χεῖρας, and explains it, to lay hands upon, etc.)
Ἰάρδανος ὁ (ῑ), *Iardanus*, 1) A river in Elis near Pheia, 7, 135 ; according to Strab. VIII. p. 348, a tributary of the A-idon, which derived its name from the monument of the ancient hero Iardanus, near Chaa in Elis on the Arcadian borders; Paus. 5, 5, 5, says it is the Acidas or Acidon itself, but incorrectly, cf. Mannert, 8. p. 394. Otfr. Müll. Gesch. d. Hell. St. 1. p. 272. 2) a river in Crete, Od. 3, 292.
ἴασι, see εἶμι.
Ἰασίδης. ου, ὁ ("--"), son of Iasus, 1) =*Amphion*. Od. 11, 283. [2) = *Dmetor*, Od. 17, 443.]

Ἰασίων, ωνος, ὁ ("--"), son of Zeus and Electra, according to Apd. 3, 12. 1, brother of Dardanus, a beautiful youth. He was killed by lightning, Od. 5, 125. Accord. to Hesiod. Th. 962, where he is called Ἰάσιος, he was the father of Plutus by Demeter.
Ἴασον Ἄργος, τό, for Ἰάσιον, *the Iasian Argos*. The city Argos received its name from king Iasus, q. v. Od. 18, 246. Accord. to the Schol. Peloponnesus is here to be understood.
Ἴασος, ὁ (ῑ from εἶμι, *Egredus*, Herm.) 1) king of Orchomenus, father of Amphion, Od. 11, 283. 2) son of Argos I. and Evadne, father of Agenor, ruler of Peloponnesus. From him Argos derived the epith. Ἴασον, Apd. 2, 1. 2. 3) son of Sphelus, leader of the Athenians, slain by Æneas, 15, 332. 337. 4) Father of Dmetor in Cyprus, Od. 17, 443.
ἰαύω (αὔω), aor. 1 ἴαυσα, *to sleep*, and generally, *to lie, to rest*, νύκτας, 9, 325 ; and ἐν ἀγκοίνῃσίν τινος, 14, 213. Od. 10, 261 : also of beasts, Od. 9, 184.
*ἰαχέω=ἰάχω, aor. ἰάχησα, h. Cer. 20 ; in the pres. obsol.
ἰαχή, ἡ (ῑ), 1) *a cry*, both the shout of warriors in making an attack, and the cry of suppliants and of the shades, 4, 456. Od. 11, 43. 2) Spoken of inanimate things, *noise, uproar*, h. 13, 3.
*Ἰάχη, ἡ, a nymph, the playmate of Persephone, h. in Cer. 419.
ἰάχω (a word formed to imitate the sound, akin to ἄχω), aor. 1 ἰάχησα, h. Cer. 20 ; 1) *to cry aloud, to cry out*, spoken of the cry of applause, 2, 333. 394 ; partic. spoken of the battle-cry of warriors, 11, also of the lamentation of the wounded, 5, 343 ; and of mourners, 18, 29. 2) Spoken of inanimate things : *to make a loud noise, to sound, to roar*, spoken of waves and of flames, 11., *to twang*, spoken of the bow-string, 4, 125 ; *to clang*, spoken of the trumpet, 18, 219 : *to hiss*, spoken of glowing iron immersed in water, Od. 9, 392.
Ἰάων, ονος, ὁ, see Ἰάονες.
Ἰαωλκός, ἡ, Ep. for Ἰωλκός (ῐ), *Iolcus*, a town in Magnesia (Thessaly), on the Pelasgic gulf, not far from the port Aphetæ, the rendezvous of the Argonauts : later only a port of the new city Demetrias, now *Volo*, 2, 712. Od. 11, 255.
ἰγνύη, ἡ, *the ham*, poples, 13, 212.† (akin to γόνυ.)
*ἰγνύς, ύος, ἡ = ἰγνύη, h. Merc. 152 ; παρ' ἰγνύσι, but Herm. corrects παροιγνὺς λαῖφος.
Ἰδαῖος, αίη, αῖον (ῑ), *Idæan*, relating to Ida, in Phrygia. τὰ Ἰδαῖα ὄρεα, the Idæan mountains, on account of the different peaks = Ἴδη, 8, 170. 410. 12, 19. ὁ Ἰδαῖος, epith. of Zeus, because on the promontory Gargarus he had an altar and a grove, 16, 605. 24, 291.
Ἰδαῖος, ὁ (ῑ), 1) a herald of the Trojans, charioteer of Priam, 3, 248. 24, 325.

'Ιδέ. 210 'Ιερός.

2) son of Dares, the priest of Hephaestus, a Trojan, 5, 11; delivered from Diomedē, by Hephaestus, v 23.

ἰδέ, conj. Ep for ἠδέ, and. (The deriv. from ἰδέ. see, according to Thiersch. § 312. 12, cannot be proved.)

ἴδε, ἴδέειν, ἴδεσκον, see ΕΙΔΩ, Α.

ἰδέω, Ep. see ΕΙΔΩ, B.

Ἴδη, ἡ, Dor. Ἴδα, Ida, (ῑ), a lofty and steep mountain-range, beginning in Phrygia and extending through Mysia. Its slope formed the plain of Troy, and it terminated in the sea, in the promontories or Gargarus, Lectum, and Phalacra. On the highest point, Gargarus, stood an altar of Zeus, now Ida, or Kas Daghi, 2. 821. From this, an adv. Ἴδηθεν. down from Ida. 3, 276. (Ἴδη, fr. εἰδεῖν, according to Herm. Gnarius, from which one can see far.)

Ἴδηαι, see ΕΙΔΩ, A.

Ἴδης, εω, ὁ, Ep. and Ion. for Ἴδας, son of Aphareus, and brother of Lynceus from Messēnē, father of Cleopatra. He was an excellent archer, see Εὔηνος, 9, 558. (Ἴδης, according to Etym. M. the seer.)

ἴδιος, ίη, ιον, own, proper, peculiar, private, πρήξις ἰδίη, the private business of an individual, in opposition to δήμιος, *Od. 3, 82. 4, 314.

ἰδίω (ῑ long, from Ἴδος), Ep. for ἱδρόω, to sweat, to perspire, only imperat. ἴδιον, Od. 20, 204.†

ἴδμεν, ἴδμεναι, see ΕΙΔΩ, B.

ἰδνόω, fut. ώσω, only aor. 1 pass. ἰδνώθην, to bend, to curve; plur. to bend oneself, to cringe, 2, 266. 12, 205. Od. 8, 375.

ἰδοίατο, Ep. for ἴδοιντο, see ΕΙΔΩ, A.

Ἰδομενεύς, ῆος and έος, accus. ῆα, and έα (ῑ), son of Deucalion, grandson of Minos, king of Crete, 13, 449—454. Before Troy he distinguished himself by his bravery, 2, 645. 4, 252. seq. According to Od 3, 191, he returned prosperously home. A later tradition says that, having been banished from Crete, he sailed to Italy.

ἰδρείη, ἡ (ἴδρις), knowledge, experience. 7, 198. 16, 359.

ἴδρις, ι, gen. ιος (ἴδμεν), intelligent, skilful, wise, Od. 6, 233. 23, 160; with infin. Od. 7, 108.

ἰδρός, ὁ, Ep. for ἰδρώς, q. v.

ἱδρόω (ἱδρός), fut. ἱδρώσω, aor. ἴδρωσα. to sweat, to perspire, esply from effort. 18, 372; from fear, 11, 119; with accus. ἱδρῷ ἰδρώσαι, 4, 27. (On the forms ἱδρώοντα. ἱδρώουσα, see Thiersch, § 222, 8.5. 11. Rost, Dial. 71. 6.)

ἱδρύνω. an assumed form of ἱδρύω for the derivation of the aor. pass. ἱδρύνθην.

ἱδρύω, aor. 1 ἴδρυσα, aor. 1 pass. ἱδρύνθην. 1) Act. to cause to sit, to seat or bid to sit, with accus. λαούς, 2, 191; ἐν θρόνῳ, Od. 5, 86. Pass. to sit, to be seated, to seat oneself, 3, 78 [ἱδρύνθησαν. placed themselves, Buttm. Lex. p. 101]. 7, 56.

ἱδρώς, ῶτος, ὁ (Ἴδος), sweat, often is the 11. On the accus. ἰδρῶ for ἰδρῶτα, and dat. ἰδρῷ for ἰδρῶτι, 4, 27. 17, 385, see Thiersch, § 188, 13 1. Buttm. § 56, 5. 6. Rost, Dial 31. Rem. Kühner, § 266.

ἰδυῖα, ἡ. Ep. see ΕΙΔΩ, B.

ἴδω, ἴδωμι, see ΕΙΔΩ, A.

ἰέ, ἴεν, Ep., see εἶμι.

ἴει, see ἵημι.

ἰείη, Ep. for ἴοι, 3 sing. optat. of εἶμι. 19, 209. πρὶν δ' οὔπως ἂν ἐμοιγε φίλον κατὰ λαιμὸν ἰείη Οὐ πόσις, οὐδὲ βρῶσις, before there shall pass into my throat neither food nor drink. Thus Wolf correctly from MS. Townl. for ἰείη, see εἰμί.

ἵεμαι, pres. pass. and mid. from ἵημι. ἵεμαι, pres. and ἱέμην, imperf. mid., poet. form of εἶμι, q. v., to go, also with the idea of haste, 12, 274. Od. 22, 304. In other places now ἵεμαι.

ἱέμεναι, Ep. for ἱέναι, see ἵημι.

ἴεν, see ἵημι.

ἱέρεια, ἡ, fem. of ἱερεύς, a priestess, 6, 300.†

ἱερεῖον, τό, Ep. and Ion. ἱερήϊον. a victim, rare, spoken of sacrificing for the dead; elsewhere τόμιον or ἔντομον, Οd. 11, 23. 2) Generally, cattle for killing. as an adage. οὐχ ἱερήϊον, οὐδὲ βοείην ἀρνύσθην, they did not strive for a fat ox or a bull's hide (as was the case in combats), 22, 159. Od. 14, 250. H. always the Ιοη. form.

ἱερεύς, ῆος, ὁ, Ep. ἱρεύς, 5, 10 (ἱερός, a priest, one who sacrifices victims, the priest of a particular deity, who had the charge of the temple service in the presentation of victims, 1, 23. 370. Od. 9. 198. Besides, they explained the divine will from an examination of the entrails. 1, 62. 24, 221.

ἱερεύω (ἱερός), Ep. ἱρεύω, with ῑ, Οd. 19, 198. 20, 3; fut. σω, prop. to make holy, to consecrate and slay a victim, to sacrifice, βοῦς, ταύρους, αἶγας θεῷ, 11. 21 Generally, to slay, because, of every thing prepared to eat. some portion was presented to the gods, Od. ; ξείνῳ, in honour of a guest, Od. 14, 414.

ἱερήϊον, τό, Ιon. for ἱερεῖον.

ἱερόν, τό, Ep. ἱρόν (prop. neut. of ἱερός. but used entirely as a subst.). that which is consecrated ; hence, a votive offering. ὄφρ' ἱρὸν ἑτοιμασσαίατ' Ἀθήνῃ, 10, 571; esply a victim for sacrifice ; chiefly plur. τὰ ἱερά, 1, 147. Od. 1, 66; and ἱρά, 2, 420.

ἱερός, ή, όν, Ep. ἱρός, ή, όν, 1) consecrated to a deity, sacred, holy, divine, spoken of things which are above human power, and are the ordinances of higher beings, cf. Nitzsch ad Od. 3, 278; ἦμαρ, κνέφας. 8. 66. 11, 194; again, ῥόος Ἀλφειοῖο. 11. 726; ἄλφιτον, 11, 431; and also ἰχθύς. as a present from the gods, 16, 407 ; see no. 3. 2) holy, spoken of every thing which men consecrate to the gods ; βωμός, δόμος. Il., esply often ἐκατόμβη, ἄλσος, ἐλαίη, Od. 13, 372 ; ἀλωή, the

Ιζάνω.   211   Ἰθάκη.

sacred threshing-floor (upon which the fruits of Dêmêtêr were cleansed), 5, 499; again, countries, cities, islands, etc. were called sacred, as being under the protection of some tutelary deity, as Troy, Thebes, etc. 3) *glorious, excellent, admirable*, spoken of men, like *divine;* ἱς Τηλεμάχοιο, Od. 2, 409; τέλος φυλάκων, 10, 56; δίφρος, 17, 464. (ι is sometimes long in ἱερός; In ἱρός always.)

ἰζάνω (ἴζω), 1) intrans. *to seat oneself, to sit,* Od. 24, 209; metaph. *to sink,* spoken of sleep, 10, 92. 2) Trans. *to cause to be seated,* with accus. ἀγῶνα, 23, 258.

ἵζω, imperf. ἷζον, I) Act. 1) Intrans. *to seat oneself, to sit down, to sit, to rest;* ἐπὶ θρόνου, 18, 422; ἐς θρόνον, Od. 8, 469. ἐπ' ἀμφοτέρους πόδας ἵζει, he sits upon both feet, 13, 251; εἰν ἀγορῇ, 9, 13. βουλὴ ἷζε, 2, 53; spoken of warriors, to take their place, 2, 96. 2) Trans. *to cause to sit, to be seated.* once τινὰ ἐς θρόνον, 24, 553. II) Mid. like act. *to seat oneself, in place oneself in ambuscade,* 18, 522. Od. 22, 335 (only pres. and imperf.).

ἵηλα, infin. ἱῆλαι, see ἰάλλω.

Ἰηλυσός, ή, Ion. for Ἰαλυσός, a town on the island of Rhodes, in Strabo's time a village; now *Jaliso.* 2, 656; Strab. XIV. p. 653. (υ long in H.; hence in some editions Ἰηλυσσός, as Hdt. 1, 144; ϑ, Dion Per. 505.)

ἵημι (root ΕΩ), pres. 3 plur. ἱεῖσι, infin. ἱέναι, Ep. ἱέμεναι, 22, 206; partcp. ἱείς, imperat. ἵει, impf. ἵην (whence ἵεν, Æol. for ἵεσαν, 12, 331) and ἵουν (as if from ἱέω), often 3 sing. ἵει, fut. ἥσω, aor. 1 ἧκα, Ep. ἕηκα, except sing. only 3 plur. ἧκαν, Od 15, 458. Of the 2 aor. 3 sing. subj. ἥσιν, 15, 359. On ἴωμεν, see that word. Mid. only pres. and imperf. ἵεμαι, ἱέμην, and aor. 2 in tmesis, in ἐξ ἕρον ἕντο, see ἐξίημι. (ι is in H. mly short.) I) Act. 1) Trans. *to put in motion,* hence a) *to send, to send away, to let go,* τινὰ ἐξ ἀδύτοιο, 5, 513: ἄγγελόν τινι, (18, 182). ἐν δὲ παρηορίῃσιν Πήδασον ἵει (for ἐνίει), he attached Pēdasus with the side-rein, 16, 152; cf. παρηορίη; eaply spoken of what is sent by a god: δράκοντα φόωσδε, 2. 309; of inanimate things: σέλας, ἀστέρα; ἱεμενον οὐρόν τινι, to send to any one a favorable wind, 1. 479: and metaph. ὄπα, *to send out the voice, to utter,* 3, 152. 221; ἔπεα. 3, 222. b) *to cast, to throw, to hurl, to shoot, to let fly,* spoken of lying bodies, πέτρον, λᾶαν; eaply of missiles: βέλος, δόρυ, ὀϊστόν τινος, *to shoot an arrow at* one. 13, 650; sometimes without accus. 2. 774. 15, 359. Od. 9, 499. c) Spoken of water: *to pour out, to let flow,* ῥόον ἐς τεῖχος, 12, 25; of a river: ὕδωρ, 21, 158. d) *to let down, to let fall.* ἐκ δὲ ποδοῖιν ἄκμονας ἧκα δύω, from thy feet I made two anvils hang down (since Zeus. after attaching them, let them fall), 15, 19; ἐκ χειρὸς φάσγανον, Od. 22, 84; δάκρυον, Od. 16, 191. 23, 33; metaph. spoken of

hair: *to let fall or roll down,* ἐθείρας, 18, 383. 22, 316; κόμας, Od. 6, 231. 2) Intrans. a) *to flow along,* spoken of a river; ἐπὶ γαῖαν, Od. 11, 239; from the fountain: *to gush forth,* Od. 7, 130. b) *to cease from,* with gen. ἐπεὶ χ' ἵωμεν πολέμοιο, when we have retired from the war, 19, 402; see ἴωμεν. II) Mid. *to put oneself in motion, to move to,* often partcp. with gen. of the body only: ποταμοῖο ῥοάων, to turn oneself towards the current of the river, Od. 10, 529; absol. ἀκόντισσαν ἱέμενοι, striving, they hurled their javelins, Od. 22, 256 (cf. Nitzsch ad Od. 1, 58); mly spoken of the mere direction of the mind : *to aspire to, to strive for, to desire, to wish,* with infin. 2, 589. 5, 434, seq. The partcp. ἱέμενος, *striving for,* also with gen. πόλιος, 11, 168; νόστοιο, Od. 15, 69; elsewhere with adv. οἴκαδε, πόλεμόνδε. ἱεμένω κατὰ ὦλκα, struggling along the furrows, 13, 707 (another reading is ἱεμένω).

ἵηνα, see ἰαίνω.

*Ἰηπαιήων, ονος, ὁ, an appellation of Apollo, from the exclamation ἰὴ παιάν, h. Ap. 272. 2) a hymn.

ἰήσασθαι, see ἰάομαι.

ἴησι, Ep. for ἵη, see εἶμι.

Ἰησονίδης, ου, ὁ, son of Jason = Euneus, 7, 468, 469.

Ἰήσων, ονος, ὁ, Ep. and Ion. for Ἰάσων (the healer, from ἴασις), son of Æson and Polymēdē, leader of the Argonauts. He was sent by Pelias to Colchis, to bring the golden fleece. On the voyage thither he landed at Lemnos, and by Hypsipylē begat Euneus and Nebrophonus, 7, 468, 469. With the aid of Medēa, daughter of Aêtês, in Colchis, he obtained the golden fleece. He took her for his wife. Subsequently, however, he cast her off and married Creüsa, Od. 12, 69 seq.; see Πελίης.

ἰητήρ, ῆρος, ὁ (ῑ), poet. for ἰητρός, 2, 732 ; κακῶν, Od. 17, 384; νόσων, h. 15, 1.

ἰητρός, ὁ, Ion. for ἰατρός (ἰάομαι), a *physician, a surgeon ;* also with ἀνήρ, 11, 514, and Od.

ἰθαιγενής, ἐς, poet. for ἰθαγενής (ἰθύς, γένος), *straight-born.* i. e. legitimately born, born in lawful wedlock, Od. 14, 203.†

Ἰθαιμένης, εος, ὁ, a Lycian, 16, 586.

Ἰθάκη, ή (ῑ), *Ithaca,* a little island of the Ionian sea, between the coast of Epirus and the island Samos, the country of Odysseus (Ulysses); now *Theaki,* 2, 632. It extends from south-east to north-west, and is composed of two parts, which are connected by a small isthmus. It is called, Od. 9, 25, the most western island, and thus appears not to agree with the situation of the present Theaki, cf. Völcker, Hom. Geogr. § 32. (The poet may here be mistaken ; still, in an age destitute of all the means for chart-drawing, it cannot be a matter of reproach.) It was very mountainous ;

Ἴθακος. 212 Ἰκάριος.

H. mentions the Nēritus, Neïon, and the promontory Corax. It was therefore not adapted to horses, Od. 4, 605, seq.; but well suited for pasturing goats and cattle, Od. 13, 244; and fruitful in corn and wine. Besides the port Reithrum, he mentions only one town, Ithaca. 2) The town was situated at the foot of Neïon, Od. 2, 154. The citadel of Odysseus (Ulysses) was connected with the town. According to most critics, as Voss, Kruse, the town was in the middle of the island, on the west side, under the northern mountain, Neïon. By this mountain also was the port Reithrum formed, Od. 1, 185. At the town itself was also a port, Od. 16, 322. Völcker, Hom. Geogr. p. 70, strives to prove that the town must be placed on the eastern coast. From this, adv. Ἰθάκηνδε, to Ithaca, Od. 16, 322; and subst. Ἰθακήσιος, ὁ, an inhabitant of Ithaca.

Ἴθακος, ὁ (ῑ), an ancient hero, according to Eustath., son of Pterelaüs, from whom the island of Ithaca had its name, Od. 17, 207.

ἴθι, prop. imperat. from εἶμι, go! come! often used as a particle, like ἄγε, up! on! come on! 4, 362. 10, 53.

ἴθμα, ατος, τό (εἶμι), a step, gait; and generally motion, 5, 778.† h. Ap. 114.

ἰθύντατα, see ἰθύς.

ἰθύνω (ἰθύς, Ion. and Ep. for εὐθύνω), I) Act. 1) to make straight, to regulate: τι ἐπὶ σταθμήν, to regulate or measure any thing by the carpenter's line, Od. 5, 245. 17, 341. Hence pass. ἵππω δ᾽ ἰθυνθήτην, the steeds were made straight again, i. e. placed in a line by the pole, 16, 475. 2) to guide directly towards, to direct, to regulate, with accus. 4, 132; and with double arcus. 5, 290. Ζεὺς πάντ᾽ ἰθύνει, sc. βέλεα, 17, 632; in like manner, ἵππους, ἅρμα, νῆα, with the prep. ἐπί, παρά. II) Mid. to direct, with reference to the subject, with accus. Od. 22, 8. ἀλλήλων ἰθυνομένων δοῦρα, they directing the spears at each other, 6, 3; πηδαλίῳ νῆα, Od. 5, 270 (cf. ἰθύω).

ἰθυστίων, ωνος, ὁ, ἡ (ῑ), epith. of the spear, 21, 169.† μελίην ἰθυστίωνα ἐφῆκε. Most probably it is derived, according to Apoll., from ἰθύς and πέτομαι, as it were ἰθυπετίωνα, flying straight forward, straight to the mark, cf. 20, 99. Zenodotus read ἰθυκτίωνα, and derived it from κτείς, straight-grained, straight-fibred.

ἰθύς, ἰθεῖα, ἰθύ (ῑ). Ion. and Ep. for εὐθύς, 1) As adj. straight, direct; only the neut. τέτραπτο πρὸς ἰθύ οἱ, he was turned directly to him (others refer it to ἔγχος), 14, 403; with gen. ἰθύ τινος, directly to or at any one, 20, 99; metaph. straight, upright, just. ἰθεῖα ἔσται, sub. aud. δίκη or ὁδός, the sentence will be just, 23, 580. ἰθύντατα εἰπεῖν δίκην, 18, 508. 2) ἰθύ as an adv. like ἰθύ, directly towards, straight at, for the most part with the gen. Δαναῶν, 12, 106; προθύροιο, Od. 1, 119; with prep. ἰθὺς πρὸς

τεῖχος, straight to the wall, 12, 137. ἰθὺς μεμαώς, rushing straight upon, 11, 95. τῇ ῥ᾽ ἰθὺς φρονέειν, to think right onward, with direct purpose, 13, 135 [ἰθὺς φρονεῖν, like ἰθὺς μεμαώς, to stretch straight on, Passow]. τῇ ῥ᾽ ἰθὺς φρονέων ἵππους ἔχε, 12, 124. In this passage, Spitzner after the Schol. connects ἰθὺς with ἔχων, and translates φρονέων, of set purpose, with design, as 23, 343. ἰθὺς μάχεσθαι, to contend directly against, 17, 168. μόνος χειρῶν ἰθὺς φέρειν, to bring straight on the strength of hands [i. e. to come into direct conflict], 5, 506. 16, 602.

ἰθύς, ύος, ἡ (ἰθύω) (ῑ), a straight direction in motion, hence ἀν᾽ ἰθύν, directly up, 21, 303. Od. 8, 377; hence attack, an onset, an undertaking, a project, 6, 79. Od. 4, 434; and, in reference to the mind, a strong impulse, a desire, a longing, Od. 16, 304. h. Ap. 539.

ἰθύω (ἰθύς), aor. ἴθυσα, 1) to rush directly upon, to attack, to run impetuously upon, to rage; limited by an adv. or prep. ἐπὶ τεῖχος, διὰ προμάχων, 12, 443. 16, 582; with gen. νηός, to rush against the ship, 15, 693. 2) to stretch after, to strive, to desire ardently, with infin. 17, 353. Od. 11, 591. 22, 408 (υ is short, but before σ long).

Ἰθώμη, ἡ, a fortress in Thessaly (Hestiaeōtis), near the later Metropolis; subsequently also called Θούμαιον, 2, 729.

ἱκάνω, Ep. form of ἱκνέομαι (ἵκω, ῑ), to come, to reach, to arrive at, mly with accus., more rarely with ἐπί, ἐς, τί, 1, 431. 2, 17. 9, 354; prim., 1) Of living beings, 6, 370. Od. 13, 231. 2) Of inanimate things: φλὴψ ἡ αὐχέν᾽ ἱκάνει, a vein which reaches the neck, 13, 547. 3) Of all sorts of conditions and situations: to attain, to come upon, to befall, 10, 96; μόρος, 18, 465; eaply of human feelings: ἄχος, πένθος, ἱκάνει με, pain, grief came upon me; and with double accus., 2, 171. II) In like manner the Mid. ἱκάνομαι, 10, 118. 11, 610; and with accus., Od. 23, 7. 27.

Ἰκάριος, ὁ, Icarius, son of Perieres and of Gorgophonē, brother of Tyndareus, and father of Penelopē. He dwelt in Lacedaemonia; he fled with his brother to Acarnania, and remained there after the return of his brother, cf. Strab. X. p. 461. Od. 1, 276. 329. Accord. to others, he lived in Cephalēnia or Samos, Od. 2, 53; cf. Nitzsch ad loc. (The first ι long.)

Ἰκάριος, η, ον (ῐ), Icarian, belonging to Icarus or the island Icarus. ὁ πόντος Ἰκάριος, the Icarian sea, a part of the Aegean; accord. to tradition it received its name from Icarus, son of Daedalus, who was drowned in the sea. It was very stormy and dangerous, 2, 145. (The first ι long.)

Ἴκαρος, ἡ, or Ἰκαρίη (ῐ), an island of the Aegean sea, which at an early period was called Δολίχη, and received its name

Ἴκελος. 213 *Ἰλήϊος.*

from Icarus son of Dædalus; now Nicaria, h. Bacch. 26. 1.

ἴκελος, η, ον, (ἴ), poet. for εἴκελος, similar, like, with dat. 2, 478. Od. 4. 249.

Ἰκεταονίδης, ου, ὁ, son of Biketaon = Menalippus, 15, 547.

Ἰκετάων, ονος, ὁ (ῑ, ἱκέτης), son of Laomedon, and brother of Priam, father of Melanippus, 3, 147. 20, 238.

ἱκετεύω (ἱκέτης), aor. ἱκέτευσα, to come or go to any one as a supplicant, εἴς τινα, 16, 574; or τινά, Od. and generally, to beg suppliantly, to supplicate, to beseech, Od. 11, 530.

ἱκέτης, ου, ὁ, a suppliant, one who comes to another for protection against persecution, or to seek purification from blood-guiltiness; the persons of such suppliants were inviolable, when they had once seated themselves before the altar of Zeus (ἱκετήσιος) or at the hearth, 24, 158. 570. Od 9, 270. 19, 134. According to the Schol. on Od. 16, 422, it denotes also the receiver of the suppliant, the same relation existing as in ξένος. This signif. however ἱκέτης never has in H., and we may better understand here Penelopê and her son by ἱκέται.

ἱκετήσιος, ὁ (ἱκέτης), the protector of suppliants, epith. of Zeus, Od. 13, 213.†

ἴκηαι, Ep. for ἴκῃ, see ἱκνέομαι.

Ἰκμάλιος, ὁ, an artist in Ithaca, Od. 19, 57. (According to Damm from ἐξικμαίνειν = Meister Trockenholz, Mr. Drywood.)

ἰκμάς, άδος. ἡ. the moisture, which destroys all roughness, and yields smoothness and flexibility. ἄφαρ ἰκμὰς ἔβη. δύνει δὲ τ᾽ ἀλοιφή, quickly a softness comes and the oil enters (spoken of leather which is rendered soft by oil), 17, 392. Cp., like Voss, translates (ἔβη = ἀπέβη), *it sweats The moisture out and drinks the unction in.*' See Nitzsch ad Od. 2, 419.

ἴκμενος, ὁ, always in connexion with οὖρος, a favorable wind; prob. for ἱκμενος from ἱκέσθαι, the wind which comes upon the ship, secundus, Eustath. Schol. Venet. Others (Hesych. Etym. M.) a moist, gently blowing, or according to Nitzsch ad Od. 2, 419, a uniform breeze, (opp. one that drives the vessel about, &c.) from ἰκμάς, slipperiness, smoothness (cf. Od. 5, 478; ἄνεμοι ὑγρὸν ἀέντες), 1, 479. Od. 2, 420.

ἱκνέομαι, poet. depon. mid. (from ἴκω), fut. ἴξομαι, aor. ἱκόμην, to come, to go, to attain, to reach, with the accus. of the aim, or with εἴς τι; more rarely, with ἐπί, πρός, κατά, etc.; with dat. ἐπαιγομένοισι δ᾽ ἴκοντο, 12, 374. 1) Spoken of any thing living; ἐς χεῖράς τινος, to fall into any one's hands, 10, 448 ; ἐπὶ νῆας, 6, 69; esply to come to any one as a suppliant, 14, 260. 22, 123. 2) Spoken of any thing inanimate, conceived of as in motion; τινά, 11. 3) Of various states and conditions. Ἀχιλλῆος ποθὴ ἵξεται υἶας Ἀχαιῶν, regret for Achilles will at length come upon the sons of the Greeks, 1, 240. κάματός μιν γούναθ᾽ ἵκετο, fatigue attacked his knees, 13, 711; in like manner, σέβας, τένθος etc., with double accus. 1, 362. 11, 88. (ι is short, except when long by augm.)

ἴκρια, τά, always in the plur., Ep. gen. ἰκριόφιν (from ἴκριον, ἡ plank, a beam), the deck, which covered only the fore and hind part of the ship; the middle was open for the seats of the rowers, 15, 676. Od. 12. 229. 13, 74. In the difficult passage, Od. 5, 252, are commonly understood the ship's ribs, connected by cross-pieces, upon which the deck rested. Voss, more correctly, considers σταμῖνες the ribs; 'he placed around it planks, fastening them to the frequent ribs;' see ἐπηγκενίδες. Nitzsch ad loc. understands by ἴκρια the planks which formed the inner coating, as it were, of the ship's sides, cf. Od. 5, 163. In a large vessel this lining of boards was confined to the prow and stern, the centre-portion being left with naked timbers to form the hold.

ἴκω, Ep. imperf. ἴκον, aor. 2 ἷξον, ἷξες, the root of ἱκάνω and ἱκνέομαι. (Upon the aor. see Buttm. § 96, note 9. Root. Dial. 52, d); to go, to come, to reach, to arrive at, to attain, with accus. of the aim, 1, 317. 9, 525. ὅ τι χρειὼ τόσον ἴκει, what so great need is come, 10, 142 ; often with a partcp. ἐς Ῥόδον ἷξεν ἀλώμενος, he came to Rhodes in his wandering, 2, 667. (ι is regularly long.)

ἰλαδόν, adv. (ἴλη), in crowds, in troops, troop by troop, 2, 93.†

*ἴλαμαι, mid. poet. form for ἱλάσκομαι, see ἴληθι, h. 20, 5.

ἱλάομαι, Ep. for ἱλάσκομαι, to appease, to propitiate, ἱλάονταί μιν ταύροισι. 2, 550† (viz. Erechtheus, say the Gramm. and Voss ; others, as Heyne, refer it to Athenê).

ἵλαος (ἱ, ᾱ), propitiated, favorable, placatus, spoken of the gods: gracious, merciful, 1. 583; of men: gentle, kind, *9, 639. h. Cer. 204.

ἱλάσκομαι, depon. mid. (ἱλάω, ῑ), fut. ἱλάσομαι, Ep. σσ. aor. ἱλασάμην, Ep. σσ. spoken only of gods, to appease, to propitiate, to conciliate, to render gracious or favorable, with accus. θεόν, Ἀθήνην, 1, 100. 147. 386. Od. 3, 419 ; τινὰ μολπῇ, 1, 472. cf. h. 20, 5. (Kindred forms, ἴλαμαι, ἱλάομαι ; prop. ῐ, sometimes ῑ, 1, 100.)

ἴληθι, poet. (from root ἱλάω), only imperat ἴληθι. and perf. subj. ἱλήκῃσι, optat. ἱλήκοι, to be propitiated, gracious, favorable. ἴληθι, be gracious, in addresses to the gods, *Od. 3, 380. 16. 184. The perf. with signif. of pres. with dat. Od. 21, 365. h. in Ap. 165.

Ἰλιάς, άδος. ἡ, prop. adj. Trojan, of Troy; as subst. subaud. ποίησις, the Iliad.

Ἰλήϊος, ον, Ep. for Ἴλειον, Ilian, relating to Ilus. τὸ πεδίον Ἰλήϊον, the Ilian plain; the Schol. says it was so called from the monument of Ilus, cf. Ἴλος, 2. But, in the first place, this region was never so called; in the next, Agēnor would in that case have retired from Ida and gone back; more correctly. Lenz understands (Ebene von Troj. S. 226) the plain back of Troy towards Ida. Crates therefore has amended it to Ἰδή ἴον, and Voss translates, *the Idæan plain*, 21, 558; cf. Köpke Kriegswes. d. Griech. S. 193.

Ἰλιονεύς, ῆος, ὁ (ῐ), son of Phorbas, a Trojan, slain by Peneleus, 14, 489. (The first ι long.)

Ἰλιόθεν, adv. *from Ilium (Troy)*, 14, 251.

Ἰλιόθι, adv. *at Ilium (Troy)*, always Ἰλιόθι πρό, before Ilium (Troy), 8, 561. Od. 8, 581.

Ἴλιον, τό = Ἴλιος, q. v.

Ἴλιος, ἡ, (ῑ) (τὸ Ἴλιον, 15, 71†). *Ilios* or *Ilium*, the capital of the Trojan realm, afterwards called *Troja* (*Troy*). It received its name from its founder, Ilus. This city, with its citadel (Πέργαμος), in which was the sanctuary of Athēnē, and the temple of Zeus and Apollo (22, 191) called by the later Greeks τὸ παλαιὸν Ἴλιον, was situated upon an isolated hill in a great plain (20, 216), between the two rivers Simoeis and Scamandrus, where they approached each other. Their confluence was to the west of the city. It was thirty stadia beyond Novum Ilium, about six Roman miles from the sea. On the west side of the city, towards the Grecian camp, was the great gate, called the Σκαιαὶ πύλαι, also called Dardanian. Now the village *Bunar-Baschi* occupies its site. *New Ilium* lay near to the coast, only twenty stadia from the mouth of the Scamander; originally a village with a temple of Athēnē, which under the Romans grew into a city; now *Trojahi*, cf. Lenz, die Ebene vor Troja, 1797. Ἴλιος is also applied to the whole Trojan realm, 1, 71. 18, 58. 13, 717. (The first ι long; the second also long in 21, 104.)

Ἰλιόθιν, Ep. for Ἰλίου, 21, 295.

ἱλλάς, άδος, ἡ (ἴλλω, εἴλω), prop. that which is twisted (of thongs or any thing flexible), *a string, a rope*, plur. 13, 572.†

Ἶλος, ὁ, *Ilus*. 1) son of Dardanus and Bateia, king of Dardania, who died without children, Apd. 3, 12. 2 2) son of Tros and Calirrhoë, father of Laomedon, brother of Ganymede, founder of Ilium, 20, 232. His monument was situated beyond the Scamandrus, midway between the Scæan gate and the battle-ground, 10, 415. 11, 166. 371. 3) son of Mermerus, grandson of Pheres, in Ephyra, Od. 1, 259.

ἰλύς, ύος, ἡ, prob. from εἰλύω, *mud, mire*, 21, 318.†

ἱμάς, άντος, ὁ (ῐ, rarely ῑ, from ἵημι), a *leathern thong*, 21, 30. 22, 397; hence 1) *a thong* or *strap* for harnessing horses, 8, 544. 10, 475; also *a trace*, 23, 324. 2) the *straps* with which the chariot-body was fastened, 5, 727. 3) *the whip-thong, a whip*, 23, 363. 4) the *thong* for fastening the helmet under the chin, 3, 371; also the *thongs* with which the helmet was lined for protection, 10. 2, 265) *the magic-girdle, the cestus* of Aphroditē, which, by its magic power, inspired every one with love, 14, 214. 219. 6) *the thongs* of pugilists, cæstus, which were made of undressed leather and wound around the hollow of the hand, 23, 684. 7) In the Od., the *thong* fastened to the bolt of the door, and drawn through a hole. To shut the door, the bolt (κληΐς) was drawn forward, and fastened to the κορώνη; to open the door, the thong was first untied, and then the bolt pressed back with a hook, Od. 1, 4. 424, 802.

ἱμάσθλη, ἡ (ἱμάσσω), prop. *a whip-thong*, then *a whip*, 8, 43, and Od.

ἱμάσσω (ἱμάς), aor. 1 ἵμασα, Ep. σσ, to *whip, to lash, to strike*, ἵππους, ἡμιόνους, Il. and Od.; πληγαῖς τινα, 15, 17; metaph. γαῖαν, to strike (lash) the earth with lightning spoken of Zeus), 2, 782. h. Ap. 340.

Ἰμβρασίδης, ου, ὁ, son of Imbrasus=*Peirus*, 4, 520.

Ἴμβριος, ὁ, son of Mentor of Pedæon, husband of Medesicastē, son-in-law of Priam, slain by Teucer, 13, 171. 197. (ῑ) As adj. *of Imbrus, Imbrian*, 21, 43.]

Ἴμβρος, ἡ, 1) an island on the coast of Thrace, famed for the worship of the Caberi and of Hermēs; now *Imbro*, 13, 33. 24, 78. 2) a city on the above island, 14, 281. 21, 43.

ἱμείρω, poet. and Ion. ἱμέρω (ῑ). 1) *to long for, to desire ardently*, with gen. κακῶν, Od. 10, 431. 555. 2) Mid. as depon. aor. 1 ἱμειράμην; more frequently with gen. αἴης, Od. 1, 41; and with infin. Il. 14, 163. Od. 1, 59.

ἱμέν and ἵμεναι, see εἰμι.

ἱμερόεις, εσσα, εν (ἵμερος), *awakening desire* or *longing; enchanting, fascinating, lovely, agreeable,* χορός, 18, 603; ἀοιδή Od. 1, 421; γόος, the lamentation of longing desire, Od. 10, 398; chiefly *charming, exciting amorous passions*, στήθεα, 3, 397; ἔργα γάμοιο, 5, 429. Neut. as adv. ἱμερόεν κιθάριζε, 18, 570.

ἵμερος, ὁ (ῐ), *longing, ardent desire for* a person or thing, τινός, 11, 89. 23, 14, 108, and also connected with a gen. of the object: πατρὸς ἵμερος γόοιο, a strong desire to mourn his father [Cp.], Od. 4, 113; esply *amorous desire, love*, 3, 139. 14, 198.

ἱμερτός, ή, όν (ἱμείρω), *longed for, attractive, lovely*. epith. of a river, 2, 751;† of the harp, h. Merc. 310.

ἴμμεναι, see εἰμι, cf. Thiersch, §223, a.

ἵνα. 1) Adv. of place, *where*, in which place, 2, 558. Od. 6, 322; for ἐκεῖ, *there*, 10, 127. *b*) More rarely, *whither*, Od. 4, 821. 6, 55. In Od. 6, 27, it is explained

Ἰνδάλλομαι. 215 Ἰότης.

as au adv. of time, *when;* and Od. 8, 313, *how;* in both places, however, the *local* signif. is predominant; in the first, we may translate ἵνα, *whereat* (on which occasion); and in the second, *how* —*there*, cf. Nitzsch ad Od. 4, 621. II) Conjunct. *that, in order to,* denoting purpose. 1) With the subj. after a primary tense (pres., perf., fut.), 1, 203. 3, 252. 11, 290; and after an aor. with pres. signif. 1, 410. 19, 347. Apparently the indicat. is often found here, since the Ep. subj. shortens the long vowel, 1, 363. 2, 232. 2) With the optat. after an historical tense (imperf., pluperf., aor.), Od. 3, 2. 77. 5, 492. As exceptions, notice *a)* The subj. stands with a preceding historical teuse *a)* When the aor. has the signif. of the perf., Od 3, 15. 11, 93. β) In the objective representation of past events, 9, 495. *b)* The optat. follows a primary tense, when the declaration assumes the character of dependent discourse (in H. examples are wanting), cf. ὄφρα. Sometimes the subj. and optat. follow one after the other in two dependent clauses, 15, 596. 24, 584. Od. 3, 78. 3) ἵνα μή. that not, 7, 195. Od. 4, 70; construc. as in ἵνα, 1, 2; ἵνα μή, in Il. 7, 353, is explained by the Schol. by ἐὰν μή, if not; the verse is, however, suspected. 4) With other particles, ἵνα δή, ἵνα περ, 7, 26. 24, 382.

ἰνδάλλομαι (εἶδος, εἰδάλιμος), *to present ones-lf in view, to appear, to show oneself,* 23, 460. Od 3, 246. h. Ven. 179. The dat. τινί indicates him to whom any thing appears. ἰνδάλλετό σφισι πᾶσι τεύχεσι λαμπόμενος Πηλείωνος, he (viz. Patroclus) appeared to all, gleaming in the arms of Peleides, 17. 213 (As the sense appears to be 'he was like Achilles,' Heyne, Bothe, and Spitzner, after Aristarchus, have adopted Πηλείωνι. Commonly the nom. indicates the person who appears, or in whose character any one appears; the dat., however, is not unusual, cf. Od. 3, 246, where formerly stood ἀθανάτοις; h. Ven. 179, ὥς μοι ἰνδάλλεται ἦτορ, as he appears to me in my mind (= *recollection*), Od. 19, 224; for here Odysseus (Ulysses) is immediately described, as to his exterior. Damm takes it here as mid. = *concipere, conceives, imagines* [ἦτορ as nom.]; so also Voss, 'so far as my mind remembers.'

ἴνεσι, see ἴς.

ἰνίον, τό (ἴ, ἴς), the back bone of the head, *the neck, the nape of the neck,* *5, 73. 14, 495.

Ἰνώ, όος, ἡ, see Λευκοθέα.

*Ἴνωπος, ὁ (ῑ, Ἰνωπός, Strab.), a fountain and rivulet in Delos, h. Ap. 18.

ἴξαλος, ον, epith. of αἴξ ἄγριος, prob. *fast springing, climbing,* from ἀΐσσω or ἰκνεῖσθαι and ἄλλομαι, other say, *lascivious,* from ἰξύς, 4. 105.†

ἴξον, ες. ε, see ἴκω.

ἰξύς, ύος, ἡ, *the flank* or *side of the body,* the region above the hips, ἰξυῖ, Ep. contr. dat. for ἰξυΐ, *Od. 5, 231. 20, 544.

Ἰξίων, ίωνος, ὁ, *Ixion,* king of Thessaly aud husband of Dia, who bore Peirithous by Zeus; from this Ἰξιόνιος, ίη, ιον, *pertaining to Ixion;* ἄλοχος, 14, 317.

Ἰοβάτης, ου, ὁ, king of Lycia, father of Antia, and father-in-law of Prœtus, who sent Bellerophontes to him, that he might put him to death. H., 6, 173, mentions not his name, but Apd. 2, 2. 1; cf. Ἄντεια and Προῖτος.

ἰοδνεφής, ές (ῐ, from ἴον, νέφος), *violet-coloured, purple,* and generally, *dark-coloured,* εἶρος, *Od. 4, 135. 9, 426.

ἰοδόκος, ον (ῐ, from ἰός, δέχομαι), *containing arrows, arrow-holding,* φαρέτρη, Od. 21, 12. 60.†

ἰοειδής, ές (ῐ, from ἴον, εἶδος), *violet-coloured,* and generally, *dark-coloured,* cf. πορφύρεος, epith. of the sea, 11, 298. Od. 5, 56

ἰόεις, εσσα, εν (ῑ, from ἴον), *violet-coloured, dark-coloured* (as πολιός), σι δηρος, 23, 850.

Ἰοκάστη, ἡ, see Ἐπικάστη.

ἰόμωρος, ον (ῐ), a reproachful epith. of the Argives, *4, 242. 14, 479; according to most critics, *skilled with the arrow, fighting with arrows,* from ἰός and μῶρος [=μόρος. Schol. οἱ περὶ τοὺς ἰοὺς μεμορημένοι), cf. ἐγχεσίμωρος; sense: ye, who only fight at a distance with missiles, but will not attack the enemy in close conflict with sword and spear. It indicates, tnerefore, cowardice; and from many passages in H., it appears that archery was little reputable. Köppen, without probability, takes it as an honorary epithet. But as the ι here is short, and the ι in ἰός is always long, consequently several other explanations have been sought Schneider derives it from ἰά, voice, and translates, 'ready with the voice, boastful, braggarts.' Others, from ἰον, explaining it, 'destined to the fate of the violet,' i. e. a short-lived fate, or, to a violet-coloured, i. e. a dark fate, etc.

ἴον, τό (ῐ), *a violet,* Od. 5, 72.† h. Cer. 6. There were, according to Theophr. Hist. Plant. 6, 6, white, purple, and black.

ἰονθάς, άδος. ἡ, *shaggy, hairy,* epith. of wild goats, Od. 14, 50.† (From ἴονθος, akin to ἄνθος.)

ἰός, ὁ (ῑ, from ἵημι), plur. οἱ ἰοί and once τὰ ἰά, 20, 68;† prop. that which is cast, *an arrow.* cf. ὀϊστός.

ἴος, ἴη, ἴον, Ep. for εἷς, μία, ἕν, in gen. and dat. with altered accent, ἰῆς. ἰῷ, 6, 122; ἰῇ, one, 9, 319. τῇ δέ τ' ἰῇ ἀναφαίνεται ὄλεθρος, supply βοΐ, to one (cow) death appeared, 11, 174. Od. 14, 435.

*ἰοστέφανος, ον (στέφανος), *violet-crowned,* h. 5, 18.

ἰότης, ητος, ἡ (ῐ, prob. from ἵς), only in the dat. and accus. *will, resolution, counsel, bidding, advice,* 15, 41; often θεῶν ἰότητι, by the will of the gods, 19, 9. Od. 7, 214. ἀλλήλων ἰότητι, the counsel of each other. 5. 874.

Ίουλος. 216 Ίππυς.

ἴουλος, ὁ (οὖλος), *the first down, the earliest appearance of beard* only in the plur. Od. 11, 319.†

ἰοχέαιρα, ἡ (ἴ, from ἰός, χαίρω), *delighting in arrows, arrow-loving*, epith. of Artemis; as subst. *mistress of the bow*, huntress, 21, 480. Od. 11, 198.

ἱππάζομαι, depon. mid. (ἵππος), *to guide horses, to drive a chariot*, 23, 426.†

Ἱππασίδης, ου, ὁ, son of Hippasus = Charops, 11, 426: = Socus, 11, 431; = Hypsenor, 13, 411: = Apisãon, 17, 348.

Ἵππασος, ὁ, 1) father of Charops and Sôcus, a Trojan, according to Hyg. f. 90, son of Priam, 11, 425: 450. 2) father of Hyprênor, 13, 411. 3) father of Apisâon, 17, 348.

ἵππειος, η, ον (ἵππος), *of a horse, belonging to a horse*, ζυγόν, φάτνη, ὁπλή, Il., κάπη, Od. 4, 40. ἵππειος λόφος, a crest of horse-hair, Il. 15, 537.

ἱππεύς, ῆος, ὁ (ἵππος), plur. once ἱππεῖς, 11, 151; a knight; in H. *a charioteer, one who guides horses*, 11, 51; = ἡνίοχος, for the most part, opposed to πεζός, *one who fights from a chariot*, 2, 810. 11, 529; also a combatant for a prize in a chariot, 23, 262. cf. ἡνίοχος, παραιβάτης.

ἱππηλάσιος, η, ον (ἐλαύνω), *good for travelling with horses, passable for chariots*. ἱππηλάσιος ὁδός, a chariot-road, *7, 340. 439.

ἱππηλάτα, ὁ, Ep. for ἱππηλάτης, only nom. sing. (ἐλαύνω), *a charioteer, a horseman*, epith. of distinguished heroes, 4, 387. Od. 3, 436; always in the Ep. form.

ἱππήλατος, ον (ἐλαύνω), *suited to driving horses, convenient for travelling*, νῆσος (convenient for a race-ground, V.), *Od. 4, 607. 13, 242.

Ἱππημολγοί, οἱ, *the Hippomolgi*, prop. horse-milkers, from ἵππος and ἀμέλγω, Scythian nomades, who lived upon mare's milk; Strab., VII. p. 260. after Posidonius, places them in the north of Europe. H. calls them ἀγαυοί, from their simple mode of life, 13, 5.

ἱππιοχαίτης, ου, ὁ (χαίτη), *of horse-hair*, λόφος, 6, 469.

ἱππιοχάρμης, ου, ὁ (χάρμη), *that practises fighting from a chariot, a charioteer*, 24, 257. Od. 11, 259.

ἱππόβοτος, ον (βόσκω), *pastured by horses, horse-nourishing*, epith. of Argos, because the plain of this city, abounding in water, was suited to the pasturing of horses; also spoken of Tricca and Elis, 4, 202. Od. 21, 347.

Ἱπποδάμας, αντος, ὁ, a Trojan, slain by Achilles, 20, 401 (= ἱππόδαμος).

Ἱπποδάμεια, ἡ, *Hippodameia*. 1) daughter of Atrax, wife of Pirithous, mother of Polypœtes, 2, 742. 2) daughter of Anchises, wife of Alcathous, sister of Æneas, 13, 429. 3) prop. name of Briseis, according to Schol. ad Il. 1, 184; see Βρισηΐς. 4) a handmaid of Penelope, Od. 18 182.

ἱππόδαμος, ον (δαμάω), *horse-subduing, horse-taming*, epith. of heroes, and also of the Trojans and Phrygians, 2, 230. 10, 431. Od. 3, 17.

Ἱππόδαμος, ὁ, *Hippodamus*, son of Merops, from Percôtê, a Trojan, slain by Odysseus (Ulysses), 11. 335

ἱππόδασυς, εια, υ (δασύς), *thickly covered with horse-hair*, κόρυς, 3, 369; κυνέη, Od. 22. 111.

ἱππόδρομος, ὁ (δρόμος), *a race-course for chariots*, 23, 330.†

ἱππόθεν, adv. (ἵππος *from a horse*), *Od. 8, 515. 11, 531.

Ἱππόθοος, ὁ, 1) son of Lethus from Larissa, grandson of Teutamus, leader of the Pelasgians, 2, 840, seq.; he is slain, 17, 217—318. 2) son of Priam, 24 251.

ἱπποκέλευθος, ον (κέλευθος, *travelling by horses, fighting from a chariot*, epith. of Patroclus, in *16. 126. 584. 839; since being the charioteer of Achilles he fought not on foot. Thus the better Gramm. Eustath. Ven. Schol. The Interpret. ἵπποις κελεύεις, thou that commandest horses, is contrary to the *usus loquendi*. Bentley would write, ἱπποκελευστής.)

ἱππόκομος, ον (κόμη), *set with horse-hair, crested with horse-hair*, τρυφάλεια, κόρυς, *12. 339. 13, 132, seq.

ἱπποκορυστής, ον, ὁ (κορύσσω), *arming horses, or more correctly passive, furnished with horses for fighting*, epith. of heroes fighting from war-chariots, *2, 1. 16, 287. 21, 205.

Ἱπποκόων, ωντος, ὁ, a relative and comrade of the Thracian king, Rhesus, 10, 518. (From κοεῖν = νοεῖν, acquainted with horses.)

Ἱππόλοχος, ὁ, 1) son of Bellerophontes, father of Glaucus, 6, 119. 197; king of the Lycians, 17, 140. seq. 2) a Trojan, son of Antimachus, slain by Agamemnon, 11, 122.

Ἱππόμαχος, ὁ, son of Antimachus, a Trojan, slain by Polypœtes, 12, 189.

Ἱππόνοος, ὁ (acquainted with horses), 1) a Greek, slain by Hector, 11. 303. 2) prop. name of Bellerophontes, cf. Schol. ad Il. 6, 155.

ἱπποπόλος, ον (πολέω), *to go about with horses, horse-driving*, epith. of the Thracians, 13, 4. 14, 227.

ἵππος, ὁ, *a horse, a steed*; ἡ ἵππος, *a mare*; also θήλεες ἵπποι, 5, 269; and ἵπποι θήλειαι, 11, 681. H. uses both genders, but chiefly the fem., since mares were regarded as better suited for travelling and fighting, 2, 763. 5, 269. Od. 4, 635. The heroes of the Trojan war used horses only for drawing chariots: though 10, 513, is only understood of riding, but not with entire certainty. See κέλης and ἅρμα, Od 4, 590; hence, 2) In the plur., and rarely in the dual (5, 13. 237), *a pair of horses*, or *a team*, in connexion with ἅρμα, 12, 120; and often ἵπποισιν καὶ ὄχεσφιν. 12, 114. 119; hence also a) *the chariot itself*, 5,

Ἱπποσύνη. 217 Ἴσκω.

265. 5, 13, etc.; hence, ἁλὸς ἵπποι, the chariot of the sea, for a ship, Od. 4. 708. b) *warriors fighting from a chariot*, in opposition to πεζοί, Od. 14, 267. ἵπποι τε καὶ ἀνέρες, Il. 5, 554. 16, 1:7.

ἱπποσύνη, ἡ (ἵππος), *the art of managing horses* and *of fighting from a chariot*, 4, 403. 11, 503; also in the plur. 16, 776. Od. 24, 40.

ἱππότα, ὁ, Ep. for ἱππότης (ἵππος), a *charioteer, a warrior fighting from a chariot*, epith. of heroes, esply of Nestor, only Ep. form, often in the Il., and Od. 3, 68.

Ἱπποτάδης, ου, ὁ, a descendant of Hippotes = Æolus, Od. 10, 2. 36.

Ἱππότης, ου, ὁ, son of Poseidôn or of Zeus, father of Æolus, according to H. and Ap. Rh. 4, 778; others say grandfather of Æolus, through his daughter Arne, see Αἴολος.

Ἱπποτίων, ωνος, ὁ, a Mysian, father of Morys, 13, 392; slain by Meriones, 14, 514, or perhaps another.

ἱππουρις, ιδος, ἡ (οὐρά), as fem. adj. *furnished with a horse-tail*, κυνέη and κόρυς, 3, 337. 11, 42. Od. 22, 124.

ἵπτομαι, depon. mid. fut. ἵψομαι, aor. ἰψάμην, *to press, to squeeze*; but only in the metaph. sense, *to oppress, to afflict* (strike, V.) with accus. (spoken of Zeus and Apollo) λαόν, 1, 454. 16, 237; (of Agamemnon,) *to chastise, to punish*, 2, 193 (related to ἶπος, ἰπόω), †Il.

ἱραί, αἱ or ἶραι, different readings, 18, 531, for εἶραι, q. v.

ἱρεύς, Ep. and Ion. for ἱερεύς.

ἱρεύω, Ep. and Ion. for ἱερεύω.

Ἵρη, ἡ ed. Wolf, Ἴρη ed. Spitzner, a city in Messenia (different from Εἶρα,) one of the towns promised by Agamemnon to Achilles as a dowry, 9, 150. Paus. calls it the later Ἀβία; Strab. VIII. 360, incorrectly, Ἴρα. on the way from Andania to Megalopôlis. Spitzner has adopted Ἴρη, which was the common reading in Paus., and which the rule of accent requires. Aristarch., on the other hand, writes Ἴρη, cf. Spitzner.

ἴρηξ, ηκος, ὁ, Ion. and Ep. for ἱέραξ (ἱερός), *a hawk or falcon*, to which species also the κίρκος belonged, Od. 13, 86; prop. the sacred bird, because the soothsayers observed and divined from its flight, 13, 62. 16, 582 (only in the contr. form with ῖ).

Ἶρις, ιδος, ἡ, accus. Ἶριν, *Iris*, according to Hes. daughter of Thaumas and Electra; in the earlier rhapsodies of the *Iliad* only, she is the messenger of the gods, not only amongst each other, 8. 398. 15, 144; but also to men, 2, 786. She interposes of her own accord, 3, 122. 24, 74; and brings spontaneously the commands of Achilles to the winds, 23, 198. She commonly appears in a foreign form, e. g. as Polites, 2, 791; and Laodikê (Laodice), 3, 122. Her fleetness is compared to the fall of hail, or to wind, 15, 172; hence ἀελλόπος, ποδήνεμος. In the later poets she is goddess of the rainbow. (According to Herm. *Sertia*, from εἴρω, to join.)

Ἴρις, ιδος, ἡ, dat. plur. ἴρισσιν, 11, 27; *the rainbow*, which in ancient times passed with men as a message from heaven, 17, 547.

ἱρός, ή, όν (ῑ), Ep. for ἱερός.

Ἶρος, a beggar in Ithaca, who was prop. called *Arnæus*, but was denominated Ἶρος, *messenger* (from Ἶρις), because the suitors thus employed him. He was large in person, but weak, and insatiably greedy; he was beaten by Odysseus (Ulysses), whom he insulted, Od. 18, 1—7. 73. 239.

ἴς, ἰνός, ἡ, dat plur. ἴνεσι (ῑ), 1) *sinew, muscle, nerve*; in the plur. Od. 11, 219. Il. 23, 191; esply the neck-sinews, 17, 522. 2) *muscular power, bodily strength, vigour, strength*, prim. of men, 5, 245. 7, 269; also of inanimate things, ἀνέμου and ποταμοῦ, 15, 383. 21, 356. 3) Since strength is the prominent trait of every hero, the strength of the hero is spoken of by a circumlocution for the hero himself. κρατερή ἲς Ὀδυσῆος, the vigorous strength of Odysseus (Ulysses), for the powerfully strong Odysseus. 23. 720; Τηλεμάχοιο, Od. 2, 409; cf. βίη, σθένος.

ἰσάζω (ἴσος), fut. ἰσάσω, aor. 1 mid. Ep. iterat. form ἰσάσκετο, 24, 607; act. *to make equal*, spoken of a woman weighing wool in scales, 12, 435; see ἔχω. 2) Mid. *to make oneself equal, to esteem oneself equal*, τινί, 24, 607.

ἴσαν, 1) 3 plur. imperf. from εἶμι. 2) Ep. for ᾔδεσαν, see ΕΙΔΩ. Β.

Ἰσάνδρος, ὁ (man-like), son of Bellerophontes, slain by Ares in an engagement against the Solymi, 6, 197. 203.

ἴσασι, see ΕΙΔΩ. Β.

ἰσάσκετο, see ἰσάζω.

ἴσθι, imper. see ΕΙΔΩ. Β.

ἴσθμιον. τό (ἰσθμός), prop. what belongs to the neck, *a necklace, a neck-band*, Od. 18, 300.†

ἴσκω, Ep. (from root ΙΚ, εἴκω), poet. form of εἴσκω, only pres. and imperf. *to make equal, to make similar, to liken*, τί τινι. φωνὴν ἀλόχοις (for φωνῇ ἀλόχων) ἴσκουσα, making the voice like the voices of the wives [i. e. imitating their voices], Od. 4, 279. 2) In thought: *to deem like, to esteem equal or like*. ἐμὲ σοὶ ἴσκοντες. esteeming me like thee (i. e. taking me for thee, V.), 16, 41. cf. 11, 799. 3) In two places, Od. 19, 203, and 22, 31, some critics explain ἴσκε and ἴσκεν, 'he spake,' as it occurs also in Ap. Rhod. But Eustath., with the more exact critics, interprets it by εἴκαζε, ὡμοίου, Od. 19, 203. ἴσκε ψεύδεα πολλὰ λέγων ἐτύμοισιν ὁμοῖα, prop. uttering many falsehoods, he made them like the truth [uttered many 'specious fictions,' *Cp.*]; and Od. 22, 31, ἴσκεν ἕκαστος ἀνήρ, each one imagined, i. e. was deceived in thinking as the following words show, cf. Buttm. Lex. p. 279, who

L

Ἴσμαρος. 218 Ἱστίη.

conjectures that ἴσπε should be the reading in Od. 22. 31.
Ἴσμαρος, ἡ, a city in Thrace, in the realm of the Ciconians, near Maronia, famed for its strong wine, Od. 9, 40. 198.
ἰσόθεος, ον (ἴ, θεός), godlike, equal to a god, epith. of heroes, 2, 565, and Od.
ἰσόμορος, ον (ἴ, μόρος), having an equal share, an equal lot. 15, 209.†
ἰσόπεδον, τό (πέδον), an equal bottom, level ground, a plain, 13, 142.†
ἴσος, ἴση, ἴσον, Ep. for ἴσος, Ep. also in fem. εἴση, q. v. 1) equal in quality, number, value, strength; sometimes also similar; absol. ἴσον θυμὸν ἔχειν, 13, 704; with dat. δαίμονι, 5, 884; Ἄρηϊ, 11, 295; and even often with the dat. of the pers., although the comparison concerns only something belonging to the person. οὐ μὲν σοί ποτε ἴσον ἔχω γέρας for γέρας τῷ σῷ γέραϊ ἴσον, I never receive a reward equal to thine, 1, 163. cf. 17, 51. 2) equally shared. ἴση μοῖρα μένοντι καὶ εἰ μάλα τις πολεμίζοι, there is an equal portion to him who remains behind (at the ships), and to him who fights ever so vigorously, 9, 318; often ἴση alone, 11, 705. 12, 423. Od. 9, 42. 3) The neut. sing. as adv. ἴσον and ἴσα. ἴσον κηρί, like death, 3, 454. 15, 50; oftener the neut. plur. ἴσα τυκέεσσι, 5, 71. 15. 439; and with prep. κατὰ ἴσα μάχην τανύειν, to suspend the fight in equipoise, to excite it equally, 11, 336. ἐπ' ἴσα, 12, 436. The passage Od. 2, 203, is variously explained. χρήματα δ' αὖτε κακῶς βεβρώσεται, οὐδέ ποτ' ἴσα ἔσσεται, thy possessions are consumed, and never will the like be to thee, i. e. that which is consumed will never be replaced. Thus Nitzsch, and this appears most natural. Eustath. says, 'they will never remain equal,' i. e. will continually decrease. Others, as Voss, 'there will be no equity.' Both are contrary to the Hom. usus loquendi.
Ἶσος, ὁ, son of Priam, slain by Agamemnon, 11, 101.
ἰσοφαρίζω (ἴ, from ἴσος and φέρω), to put oneself on an equality with any man, to liken, to compare oneself to in any thing; τινὶ μένος, to any man in strength, 6, 101; ἔργα Ἀθήνῃ, 9, 390; and with the dat. alone, 21, 194.
ἰσοφόρος, ον (φέρω), bearing a like burden, of equal strength, βόες, Od. 18, 373 †
ἰσόω (ἴσος), only optat. ἰσωσαίμην, to make equal, mid. to become equal, with dat., Od. 7, 212.†
ἵστημι, imperf. ἵστην, 3 sing. Ep. iterat. form ἱστάσκε, ἵστασχ', Od. 19, 574; fut. στήσω, aor. 1 ἔστησα, also Ep. 3 plur. ἔστασαν for ἔστησαν, 12, 55. 2, 525 (ἵστασαν, Spitzner). Od. 3, 182. 18, 307 (cf. ἔκρεσε); aor. 2 ἔστην, Ep. iterat. form στάσκον, and 3 plur. Ep. ἔσταν and στάν, subj. στέω, 2 sing. στήῃς for στῇς, etc., 1 plur. Ep. στήωμεν and στείομεν for στῶμεν, infin. στήμεναι for στῆναι, perf.

ἕστηκα, and pluperf. ἑστήκειν; the dual and plur. only in the syncop. forms: dual ἔστατον, plur. ἔσταμεν, ἔστατε, and poet. ἔστητε, 4, 243. 246; 3 plur. ἑστᾶσι, subj. ἑστῶ, optat. ἑσταίην, infin. ἑστάμεναι, ἑστάμεν, partcp. only the obliq. case, ἑστεότος, etc., pluperf. dual ἑστάτον, 3 plur. ἕστασαν: mid. fut. στήσομαι, aor. ἐστησάμην, aor. pass. ἐστάθην, signif. I) Trans. in the pres. imperf. fut. and aor. 1, to place, to cause to stand, of animate and inanimate objects, hence 1) to put up, to set up, to place erect, with accus. 2, 525; ἔγχος, 15, 126; τρίποδα, 18, 344. 2) to cause to rise, to raise, νεφέλας, 5, 523. Od. 12, 405, κονίης ὀμίχλην, 13, 336; hence metaph. to excite, to stir up, φυλόπιδα, ἔριν, Od. 11, 314. 16, 292. 3) to cause to stand, to hinder, to bring to a stand, to check, to stop (in their course), ἵππους, 5, 368; νέας, to anchor the ships, Od. 2, 391. 3, 182; μύλην, to stop the mill, Od. 20, 111; hence, to cause to stand in the balance, i. e. to weigh, τάλαντα, 19, 247. 22, 350. 359. II) Intrans. and reflex. in the aor. 2 perf. and pluperf. act. 1) to place oneself, to stand, perf. ἕστηκα, I have placed myself, or I stand; ἑστήκειν, I stood, in which signif. the mid. is used to supply the pres. imperf. and fut. both of animate and inanimate things. 2) to stand, of warriors, 4, 334; νῆες, σκόλοπες, 9, 44. 12, 64. 3) to stand up, to arise, 1, 535; to stand forth, to lift oneself, χρημνοί, 12. 55. ὀρθαὶ τρίχες ἔσταν, the hair stood erect, 24, 359. ὀφθαλμοὶ ὡσεὶ κέρα ἔστασαν, the eyes stood out like horns, Od. 19. 211; hence metaph. ἕβδομος ἑστήκει μείς, the seventh month had begun, 19, 117; hence ἵσταται, begins, Od. 14, 162. 4) to stand still, to keep one's place, κρατερῶς, 11, 410. 13, 56. III) Mid. esply aor. 1. 1) to place for oneself, to put up, with accus. κρατῆρα θεοῖσι, 6, 528; ἱστόν, to put up the loom-beam, Od. 2, 94; ἱστόν, to raise the mast, 1, 480. Od. 9, 77. ἀγῶνα, to begin a combat, h. Ap. 150. 2) Oftener intrans. and reflex., to place oneself, in the passages cited under no. II. Il. 2, 473. πάντεσσιν ἐπὶ ξυροῦ ἵσταται ἀκμῆς [in balance hangs, poised on a razor's edge. Cp.], 10, 173; see ἀκμή. δοῦρα ἐν γαίῃ ἵσταντο, the spears remained sticking in the earth, 11, 574: metaph. νεῖκος ἵσταται, the contest begins, 13, 333. Cf. on ἕστασαν, Buttm. § 107. 6. Thiersch, § 223. Kühner, § 182.
Ἰστίαια, ἡ, Ep. and Ion. for Ἑστίαια, a town in Euboea, on the northern coast. later Ὠρεός, 2, 537.
ἱστίη, ἡ, Ion. and Ep. for ἑστία, the domestic hearth, which at the same time was a domestic altar of the household gods; it was the asylum of all suppliants, and an oath by it was peculiarly sacred, *Od. 14, 159. 17, 156. 19, 304 (The middle syllable is always long.)
Ἱστίη, ἡ (Ἱστίη, ed. Herm.), Ep. for Ἑστία, Vesta, daughter of Kronus (Saturn)

and Rhea, tutelary deity of the domestic hearth, of houses and cities, h. 23, 1. 28, 1.

ἱστίον, τό (dim. from ἱστός), prop. any thing woven, *cloth*; in H. a *sail*, ūly in the plur., 1, 480; sing., 15, 627. Od. 2, 427. The sails were commonly of linen (also called σπεῖρα). They were attached to the mast by yards. They were holsted (πετανύσθαι, ἀναπετανύναι) in a favorable wind, and furled (στέλλεσθαι) in an unfavorable, 1, 433. Od. 3, 11.

ἱστοδόκη, ἡ (δέχομαι), *the receptacle of the mast*, the place in which it was stowed when lowered [its *crutch*, Cp.], 1, 434.†

ἱστοπέδη, ἡ (πέδη), *the mast-stay*, a transverse piece of timber, in which the mast of a vessel was fixed, *Od. 12, 51. 162.

ἱστός, ὁ (ἵστημι), 1) *the mast*, which stood in the middle of the ship, and was attached by two ropes (πρότονοι) to the bows and stern of the ship. The mast was taken down, and lay in the ship when at anchor, 1, 434; at departure it was raised (ἀείρειν, στήσασθαι), Od. 2, 424. 9, 77. 2) *a loom-beam*, the beam upon which the warp was drawn up perpendicularly, so that the threads hung down, instead of lying horizontally upon the warp-beam as with us; hence ἱστὸν στήσασθαι, to put up the loom-beam, Od. 2, 94. ἱστὸν ἐποίχεσθαι, to go around the loom in order to weave; for the weaver sat not before it, as with us, but went around, 1, 31. Od. 5, 62. This kind of weaving is still in partial use in India. 3) *the warp* itself, and generally *the web*. ἱστὸν ὑφαίνειν, 3, 125. Od. 2, 104. 109.

ἴστω, imperat. see ΕΙΔΩ, B.

ἴστωρ, ορος, ὁ (εἰδέναι), one who is in-intelligent, one who knows: esply like cognitor, *an umpire*. ἐπ' ἴστορι, before the judge, or rather witness (μάρτυρι ἢ κριτῇ, Schol.), *18, 501. 23, 486. ἴστωρ stands in ed. Heyne, and in h. 32, 2, ed. Wolf. The derivation favours the spiritus lenis.

ἰσχαλέος, η, ον, poet. for ἰσχνός, *dry*, *dried*, Od. 19, 233.†

ἰσχανάω, Ep. form of ἴσχω; ἰσχανάᾳ, ἰσχανόωσιν, Ep. for ἰσχανᾷ, ἰσχανῶσιν, Ep. iterat. imperf. ἰσχανάασκον, 1) Act. *to hold*, *to hold back*, with accus., 5, 89. 15, 723. 2) *to attach oneself to*, *to strive after*, *to be eager for*, with gen. δρόμου, φιλότητος, 23, 300. Od. 8, 288; and with infin. 17, 572. II) Mid. *to check oneself*, *to delay*, *to tarry*, ἐπὶ νηυσίν, 12, 38. Od. 7, 161. (Only pres. and imperf.)

ἰσχάνω, poet. form from ἴσχω = ἰσχανάω, *to hold*, *to hold back*, *to hinder*, with accus., 14, 387. 17, 747. Od. 19, 42; see κατισχάνω, h. 6, 13.

ἴσχιον, τό, 1) Prop. *the hip-joint*, *the hip-pan*, i. e. the cavity in the hip-bone in which the head of the thigh-bone (μηρός) turns, 5, 305. 2) Mly *the hip*, *the loins*, esply the upper part, 11, 339. Od. 17, 234; plur. 8, 340. (Prob. from ἰσχύς, akin to ἰξύς.)

*Ἴσχυς, υος, ὁ, son of Elatus, the lover of Corônis, h Ap. 210.

*ἰσχύω (ἰσχύς), fut. ύσω, *to be strong*, *to be able*, Batr. 280.

ἴσχω, poet. form of ἔχω, only pres. and imperf. chiefly in the signif.: I) *to hold*, *to hold fast*, *to hold back*, τινά, 5, 812; ἵππους, 15, 546; metaph. θυμόν, *to restrain the spirit*, 9, 256; σθένος, 9, 352. II) Mid. *to hold oneself*, *to restrain oneself*, 2, 247; restrain yourself, i. e. be silent, Od. 11, 251. *b*) With gen. *to restrain oneself* from a thing, *to cease*, λώβης, πτολέμου, Od. 18, 347. 24, 531.

ἰτέη, ἡ, Ion. for ἰτέα, *willow*, 21, 350; *salix alba*, the common ozier, Od. 10, 510.

ἴτην, imperf. of εἶμι.

*Ἴτυλος, ὁ, son of Zethus and Aëdon, whom his mother killed in a fit of frenzy, Od. 19, 522; cf. Ἀηδών.

*Ἰτυμονεύς, ῆος, ὁ, son of Hyperôchus in Elis, who abstracted from Nestor a part of his herds, and was slain by him, 11, 671, seq.

ἴτυς, υος, ἡ, prop. any *circle*; in H. the *circumference* or *periphery* of a wheel, made of felloes of wood, 4, 486. 5, 724. (Prob. from ἰτέα.)

ἴτω, see εἶμι.

*Ἴτων, ωνος, ἡ (ῑ), a town in Larissa, in Phthiôtis (Thessaly), with a temple of Athênê, 2, 696. Ἴτωνος, ὁ, Strab.

ἰυγμός, ὁ (ἰύζω), *a cry*, *a cry of joy*, *a shout*, 18, 572.†

ἰύζω (ῑ), *to shout for joy*, *to cry aloud*; in H. to terrify an animal by loud crying and shrieking, 17. 66. Od. 15, 162.

Ἰφεύς, ῆος, ὁ (ῑ), see Ἶφις.

*Ἰφθίμη, ἡ, daughter of Icarius and sister of Penelope, wife of Eumêlus of Pheræ, Od. 4, 797.

ἴφθιμος, η, ον and ος, ον, 1) *highly honoured*, *greatly lauded*, and generally, *active*, *lively*, *noble*, 5, 415; spoken of women, ἄλοχος, 19, 116. Od. 10, 106. (Prob. from ἶφι and τιμή, greatly lauded. Schol.; so Wolf and Thiersch.) Hence, 2) *to be honored for one's strength*, *might*, &c., *strong*, *brave*, *mighty*, *powerful*, prim. as epith. of heroes possessing physical power, hence also spoken of head and shoulders, 3, 336. 11, 55.

ἶφι, adv. (prob. an old dat. from ἴς), *strongly*, *powerfully*, *with might*, *with power*, ἀνάσσειν, μάχεσθαι, 1, 38. 2, 720; δαμῆναι, Od. 18, 156.

*Ἰφιάνασσα, ἡ (ῑ, ruling with power), daughter of Agamemnon and Klytæmnestra (Clytæmnestra), called in the tragic writers Ἰφιγένεια, 9, 145.

*Ἰφιδάμας, αντος, ὁ (ῑ), son of Antênor and Theâno, who was educated in Thrace with his grandfather Cisseus, 11, 221.

*Ἰφικλήειος, η, ον, Ep. for Ἰφικλεῖος,

Ἴφικλος. 220 **Κάδμος.**

pertaining to Iphiclus. ἡ βίη Ἰφικληείη, Od. 11, 290.

Ἴφικλος, ὁ (ῑ in the beginning), son of Phylacus, from Phylacê in Thessaly, father of Protesilaus and Podarces, noted as a runner. His noble herds of cattle were demanded by Neleus of Bias as a price for his daughter of Pero, 2, 705. 23, 636. Od. 11, 289, seq. Cf. Βίας.

Ἰφιμέδεια, ἡ (ῑ in the beginning), daughter of Triops, wife of Alôeus, mother of Otus and Ephialtes by Poseidôn, Od. 11, 305 (from μέδομαι, the mighty ruler).

Ἰφίνοος, ὁ (the first ι long) son of Dexius, a Greek, slain by the Lycian, Glaucus, 7, 14.

Ἴφις, ιος. ὁ (not Ἰφεύς). accus. Ἴφεα, a Trojan, slain by Patroclus. 16, 417; see Buttm. Gr. Gram. § 51. Rem. 1. p. 192.

Ἴφις, ιος, ἡ, daughter of Eunyeus, a slave of Patroclus, 9, 667.

ἶφιος, η, ον (ἶφι), or Ἶφις, ἶφι, *strong,* reply *robust, fat, fatted,* only ἴφια μῆλα, 5, 556. Od. 11, 108 (the first ι long).

Ἰφιτίδης, ὁ, son of Iphitus = *Archeptolemus,* 8, 128.

Ἰφιτίων, ωνος, ὁ (ῑ in the beginning), son of Otrynteus of Hydê, slain by Achiles, 20, 382. (From τίω, avenging powerfully.)

Ἴφιτος, ὁ (ῑ in the beginning) 1) son of Eurytus, from Œchalia, brother of Iolê, an Argonaut. On the journey, when he was seeking the mares which had been concealed by Hêraclês, he gave his bow to Odysseus (Ulysses), in Messenia. When he found them with Hêraclês, he was slain by him, Od. 21, 14, seq. 2) son of Naubôlus, an Argonaut of Phocis, father of Schedius and Epistrôphus, 2, 518. 17, 306. 3) father of Archeptolemus, 8, 128.

ἰχθυάω (ἰχθύς), Ep. iterat. form, imperf. ἰχθυάασκον, Od. 4, 368; *to fish, to take fish,* *Od. 12, 95.

ἰχθυόεις, εσσα, εν (ἰχθύς), *fishy, abounding in fish,* epith. of the sea, and of Hyllus, 9, 4. 360. 20, 392; κέλευθα, Od. 3, 177.

ἰχθύς, ύος, ὁ, nom. and accus. plur. ἰχθύες, ἰχθύας, contr. ἰχθῦς. Od. 5, 53. 12, 331; *a fish;* taking fish in nets was already customary, Od. 22, 384, seq. (υ in nom. and accus. sing. long, 21, 127; elsewhere short.)

ἰχναῖος, αίη, αῖον (ἴχνος). *tracing, tracking,* epith. of Themis, who traces out the actions of men, h. in Ap. 94. According to the Gram. from the town *Ichnæ* in Thessaly, where she had a temple. The last derivation Herm. ad loc. prefers.

ἴχνιον, τό (prop. dimin. of ἴχνος), *a truce, a track, a footstep,* 18, 321. h. Merc. 220. μετ' ἰχνιά τινος βαίνειν, to follow a man's steps, Od. 2, 406; tracks, Od. 19, 436. 2) Generally, *gait, movement,* 13, 71.

ἴχνος, τό, *a track, a footstep, a trace,* Od. 17, 317.†

ἰχώρ, ῶρος, ὁ, accus. ἰχῶ, Ep. for ἰχῶρα (Kühner, § 266, 1. Buttm. § 56, note 6, ei; *ichor,* the blood of the gods,—a humour similar to blood, and which supplies its place in the gods, *5, 340. 416.

ἴψ, ἰπός, ὁ, nom. plur. ἶπες (ἰπτομαι), an insect which gnaws horn and vines, Od. 21, 395.†

ἴψαο, see ἴπτομαι.

ἰωγή, ἡ, *a shelter, a protection.* Βορέω ἀγκίνιστ the north wind, Od. 14, 533;† see ἐπιωγαί.

ἰωή, ἡ (ἰά, ῑ), *a call, a voice,* spoken of men, 10, 139; and generally. *clamour, noise,* of the lyre and the wind, Od. 17, 261. Il. 4, 276; of fire, 16, 127.

ἰῶκα, see ἰωκή.

ἰωκή, ἡ (from δίω and διώκω), metaplast. accus. ἰῶκα, as if from ἰώξ, 11, 601;† prop. pursuit in battle; and generally, *the tumult of battle, the noise of battle,* plur., 5, 521. 2) Ἰωκή, personified, like *Ἔρις, *5, 740.

ἰωχμός, ὁ (ἰωκή), *pursuit, the tumult of battle,* *8, 89. 158.

K.

K, the tenth letter of the Greek alphabet, and the sign of the tenth book.

κάββαλε, Ep. for κατέβαλε, see καταβάλλω.

Καβησσός, ἡ, a town in Thrace on the Hellespont, or in Lycia, from which is Καβησσόθεν, from K. (ἔνθον refers to Troy), 13, 363.

κάγ, Ep. for κατ' before γ; κὰγ γόνυ, for κατὰ γόνυ (accord. to Bothe, καγγόνυ). 20, 458.†

κέκαυνος, ον (καίω with a kind of redupl.), *that may be burned, dry,* ξύλα, 21, 364. Od. 18, 308. h. Merc. 136.

καγχαλάω (Ep. prs. καγχαλόωσι, καγχαλόων for καγχαλῶσι, καγχαλῶν), *to laugh aloud, to rejoice,* 6, 514. Od. 23, 1. 59; to laugh to scorn, 3, 43. (From ΧΑΟ, χαλάω, *cachinnor.*)

κἀγώ, contr. from καὶ ἐγώ, 21, 108;† yet rejected by Spitzner.

κάδ. Ep. for κατά before δ, e. g. κὰδ δέ· κὰδ δώματα, Od. 4, 72.

καδραθέτην, see καταδαρθάνω.

καδδῦσαι, see καταδύω.

Καδμεῖος, η, ον (Κάδμος), *derived from Cadmus, Cadmæan,* in Hom. plur. οἱ Καδμεῖοι, the inhabitants of the citadel Cadmeia, i. e. the Thebans, 4, 391. Od. 11, 276.

Καδμείων, ωνος, ὁ = Καδμεῖος, 4, 385. 5, 804.

Καδμηίς, ίδος, ἡ, peculiar fem. of Καδμεῖος, daughter of Cadmus = Σεμελή, h. 6, 57.

Κάδμος, ὁ (Herm. *lustrans*), *Cadmus,* son of the Phœnician king Agênor.

brother of Európa, husband of Harmonia. In his journeyings in quest of Europa, who had been seduced by Zeus, he came at last to Bœotia, and founded the fortress Cadmeia. H. mentions him only as the father of Ino, Od. 5, 334.

ΚΛΔ, see καίνυμαι.

Κάειρα, ή, fem. of Κάρ, a female Carian, prob. from the root Κάηρ, 4, 142.†

καήμεναι, see καίω.

καθαιρέω (αἱρέω), fut. ήσω, aor. καθεῖλον, subj. Ep 3 sing. καθέλησι, 1) to take (pull or let) down, τί; ἱστία, Od. 9. 149: ζυγόν, 24, 268 ; ὅσσι θανόντι, to close the eyes of a corpse, 11, 453 ; and in tmesis, Od. 11, 426. 2) Esply to take down with violence, to cast down, τινά, 21,327; hence, to overpower, to carry off, spoken of Fate, Od. 2, 100; metaph. of sleep, Od. 9, 372, 373.

καθαίρω (καθαρός), aor. 1 ἐκάθηρα and Ep. κάθηρα, to purify, to cleanse, to wash, with accus. κρητῆρας, θρόνους, τραπέζας ὕδατι, Od. 20, 152. 22, 439. 453 ; ῥυπόωντα, Od. 6, 87 ; trop. κάλλεϊ προσώπατα καθαίρειν, to adorn with beauty, see κάλλος. Od. 18, 192. 2) to bring away by cleansing, to wash away; ἀπὸ χροὸς λύματα, 14, 171 ; ῥύπα, Od. 6, 93; with double accus. εἰ δ' ἄγε—αἷμα κάθηρον Ἐλθὼν ἐκ βελέων Σαρπηδόνα, 16, 667. In this passage, which is variously explained, place with Spitzner a comma before and after ἐκ βελέων, so that it may signify extra jactum telorum. Thus Voss : 'Go, beloved Phœbus, to cleanse, beyond the reach of the enemy's spears, Sarpēdon from his blood.' Instead of Σαρπηδόνα, Aristarchus reads Σαρπηδόνι ; Eustath., however, defends the double accus. and compares 1, 236, 237. 18, 345. b) In a religious signif. θείῳ δέπας, to purify a goblet by fumigation with brimstone. 16, 228.

καθάλλομαι, depon. mid. (ἄλλομαι), to leap down ; metaph. to rush down, spoken of a tempest, 11, 298.†

καθάπαξ, adv. (ἄπαξ), once for all, entirely, Od. 21, 349.†

καθάπτομαι, depon. mid. (ἅπτω), to touch, to attack, always τινὰ ἐπέεσσιν, to approach any one with words, a) In a good sense : ἐπ. μαλακοῖσίν τινα, to address any one with kind words, 1, 582 ; or μειλιχίοις ἐπ., Od. 24, 393 ; absol. Od. 2, 39. 240, seq. b) In a bad signif. ἀντιβίοις ἐπ., to attack or assail with angry words, Od. 18, 415. 20, 323 ; absol. 15, 127. 16, 421. (The dat. depends upon κέλετο cf. Od. 2, 39.)

καθαρός, ή, όν, clean, unspotted, εἵματα, Od. 2) clean, clear. ἐν καθαρῷ, subaud. τόπῳ, in a clear place (a place free from dead bodies), 8, 491. 10, 199. 3) Metaph. pur., blameless. καθαρῷ θανάτῳ, by an honorable death, i. e. not by the halter, Od. 22, 462. Adv. καθαρῶς, purely, h. Ap. 121.

καθέζομαι, depon. mid. (ἔζομαι), only pres. and imperf. to sit down, to sit, ἐπὶ θρόνου, 1, 536; ἐπὶ λίθοισι, Od. 3, 406; to sit in council, to hold a session, Od. 1, 372. 2) to reside, to dwell, Od. 6, 295.

καθέηκα, see καθίημι.

καθείατο, see κάθημαι.

καθεῖσα (εἷσα), defect. aor. to seat, to cause any one to be seated, τινὰ ἐπὶ θρόνου, 18, 389. 2) to set down, to place, to cause to remain, 2, 549. 3, 382; τινὰ σκοπόν, to place a man as a spy, Od. 4, 524.

καθέξει, see κατέχω.

καθεύδω, imperf. Ep. καθεῦδον, only pres. and imperf. to sleep, to rest, 1, 611 ; ἐν φιλότητι, Od. 8, 313. According to Eustath. [ἀναπίπτειν ὡς ἐπὶ ὕπνῳ], it signifies in 11. 1, 611, 'to lie down to sleep.' [This, however, is not the necessary sense, since the usual signif. does not conflict with 2, 2, where οὐκ ἔχε νήδυμος ὕπνος forms an antithesis with εὗδον παννύχιοι, cf. Schol. ad 11. 2, 2. Am. Ed.]

καθεψιάομαι, depon. mid. (ἐψιάομαι), to deride, to mock, τινός, Od. 19, 372.†

κάθημαι (ἧμαι), imperf. ἐκαθήμην, 3 sing. καθῆστο and κάθητο, h. 6, 14 ; 3 plur. καθείατο, Ep. for κάθηντο, to sit down, παρά τινι, 7, 143 ; ἐν or ἐπί τινι, 11, 76. 14, 5 ; esply to sit at ease, to sit in state, to be throned, Od. 16, 264.

κάθηρα, see καθαίρω.

καθιδρύω (ἱδρύω), to seat, to cause to sit, τινά, Od. 20, 257.†

καθιζάνω (ἱζάνω), to seat oneself, θυκόνδε, Od. 5, 3.†

καθίζω (ἵζω), imperf. κάθιζον, once ἐκάθιζον. Od. 16. 408 (Buttm. Lex. p. 122, would read δὲ κάθιζον), aor. ἐκάθισα, part. Ep. καθίσσας, 1) Trans. to seat, to cause to sit, with accus. Il. ; ἀνδρῶν ἀγοράς, to constitute, to convoke assemblies of men, Od. 2, 69; proverbially, καθίζειν τινὰ ἐπ᾽ οὐδεῖ, to seat any one upon the ground, i. e. to plunder him of his property, h. Merc. 284: see οὔδας. 2) Intrans. to seat oneself, to sit, ἐπί, παρά τινι, 8, 436; and alone, 3, 426. Od. Od. 4, 649.

καθίημι (ἵημι), aor. 1 καθῆκα, inf. aor. 2 καθέμεν, Ep. for καθεῖναι, 1) to send down, to cast down, with accus. οἶνον λαυκανίης, to send or pour wine down the throat, 24, 642 ; ἵππους ἐν δίναις, to sink the horses in the waters, in order to propitiate the river-god. 21, 132; κεραυνὸν χαμᾶζε, 8, 134 (by tmesis). 2) to let down, to lower, ἱστία ἐς νῆας. Od. 11, 72. h. Ap. 503. 481. (On the dual aor. 2 κάθετον, see Buttm. Ausf. Gram. § 33, 3. Rem. 3.)

καθικνέομαι (ἱκνέομαι) only aor. καθικόμην, to go to, to reach, to arrive at, to touch, to hit ; only metaph. ; spoken only of disagreeable things. ἐμὲ καθίκετο πένθος, Od. 1, 342. μάλα πώς με καθίκεο θυμὸν ἐνιπῇ, thou hast exceedingly touched (= wounded) my heart by reproach, 14, 104.

καθίστημι (ἵστημι), imperf. pres. Ep. καθίστα, aor. 1 κατέστησα, aor. 1 mid. κατεστησάμην, 1) Only trans. to put

Καθοπλίζω. 222 **Καιροσέωϊ.**

down, to set down, to put away; with accus. κρητήρα, the mixer, 9. 202; νήα, to direct the ship down. i. e. to shore [appelle navem], Od. 12, 185; hence Πύλονδε καταστήσαί τινα, to convey any one to Pylos (connected with ἀφέσσαι, to put ashore [but Fäsi aft. Schol. *to take him on board*: a hysteron-proteron]), Od. 13, 274. II) Mid. = act. *to let down,* λαῖφος βοεῦσιν, h. Ap. 407.

*καθοπλίζω (ὁπλίζω), *to arm*; mid. *to arm oneself*, Batr. 122.

καθοράω (ὁράω), aor. κατεῖδον, part. κατιδών, *to look down*, ἐξ' Ἴδης. 11, 337; with accus. *to survey, to inspect* any thing, h. Ap. 136. Mid. as depon. ἐπ' αἶαν, 13, 4.

καθύπερθε, and before a vowel καθύπερθεν, adv. (ὕπερθε), 1) *from above, down from above*, 3, 337; with gen. Od. 8, 279. 2) *above, over*, 2, 754. λαοῖσιν καθύπερθε πεποιθότες, trusting to the men who were above [i. e. on the walls], 12, 153; of the situation of places, 24, 545; with gen. Χίοιο, above Chios, i. e. north of it, Od. 3, 170. 15, 404.

καί, conjunc. *and, even*, marking connexion or heightened force. I) As a copulative conjunc. καί connects 1) Ideas and sentences of every kind, whilst the enclit. τέ connects only related ideas. 2) τε—καί, *as well—as, both—and*, shows that the connected ideas stand in close and necessary union; in H. the two words stand together, 1, ,7. 17. Od. 3, 414. 3) καί τε, the Lat. *atque*, annexes something *homogeneous* and *equal* (in quantity, &c.); it often points to something special: *and indeed*, 1, 521. Od. 23, 13. In like manner we have ἠδὲ καί, Od. 1, 240; ἠμέν, ἠδὲ καί, 5, 128. 4) The ori ginal enhancing power shows itself, although feebly, in sentences which annex an action quickly following what precedes, ὡς ἄρ' ἔφη, καὶ ἀναΐξας—τίθει. 1, 584. 5) In an anacoluthon καί connects a partcp. and a finite verb, ὡς φαμένη, καὶ ἡγήσατο, 22, 247. In like manner in apodosis after temporal conjunctions, καὶ τότε, 1, 478. II) As an enhancing adverb: in the orig. signif. *even, also, still*, etiam, καί renders a single word or a sentence emphatic. According to the character of the antithesis, the augmenting force may be 1) Strengthening. *a*) With verbs, substantives, numerals: *even*. τάχα κεν καὶ ἀναίτιον αἰτιόωτο, he might easily blame even an innocent person, 12, 301. cf. 4, 161. *b*) Esply, καί with partcp. and adj. forms an antithesis to the main verb of the sentence; in which case it may be translated by *although, however*. Ἕκτορα, καὶ μεμαῶτα (however impetuous) μάχης σχήσεσθαι δίω, 9, 655. καὶ ἐσσύμενον, 13. 787. 16, 827. *c*) With compar. *still*. θεὸς καὶ ἀμείνονας ἵππους δωρήσαιτο, 10, 556. *d*) With adverbs: καὶ λίην, καὶ μάλα, 13, 237. 19, 408. Od. 1, 46. 2) Diminishing: ἰέμενος καὶ καπνὸν—νοῆσαι, *to see* if but the smoke, Od. 1, 58. III) καί in connexion with conjunctions: καὶ γάρ, since indeed, for indeed; καὶ γὰρ δή, for certainly, or really, καὶ — γε, and (indeed); καὶ δέ, and yet, but also; καὶ δή, and now, and certainly; καὶ εἰ, even if; καὶ μέν = καὶ μήν. and certainly, and surely, surely also, 23, 410; also (indeed), Od. 11, 582; καί τοι. and yet, although, etc. (To the above may be added καί as an expletive. κασίγνητος καὶ ὄπατρος, 12, 371; as also the use between numerals, sometimes = or. ἕνα καὶ δύο, 2, 346. cf. Od. 3, 115.]

Καινείδης, ὁ, son of Cæneus = Coronus, 2. 746.

Καινεύς, ῆος, ὁ, son of Elätus, king of the Lapithæ. father of the Argonaut Corônus, 1, 264. (From καίνυμαι, that overpowers.)

*καινός, ή, όν, *new, strange, unknown*, τέχνη, Batr. 116.

καίνυμαι, p et. depon. (root ΚΑΔ for καίδνυμαι), perf. κέκασμαι, pluperf. ἐκεκάσμην, 1) *to excel*, τινά, Od. 3, 282. More freq. the perf. and pluperf. in the signif. of the pres. and imperf. κεκάσθαι τινά τινι, *to excel a man in any thing*, 2, 530. 13, 431. Od 19, 395. Instead of the dat. the infin. stands in Od. 2, 159. 3. 283. 2) Alone with dat. without accus. of pers. *to be distinguished* in any thing, *to be remarkable* for any thing, *to be adorned with*, δόλοισι (for evil wiles renowned, 4, 339. c) With prep. accompanying the pers. and a dat. of the thing, παντοίῃ ἀρετῇσιν ἐν Δαναοῖσι, Od. 4, 725; μετὰ δμώησι, Od. 19, 82; ἐπ' ἀνθρώπους, 24, 535. (Others suppose a root ΚΑΖΩ.)

καίπερ, Ep. separated καί περ, except Od. 7, 224; *although, however, however much*; πέρ takes its place after the emphatic word. καὶ ἀχνύμενοί περ, however grieved they are, 2, 270. 24, 20. καὶ πρὸς δαίμονά περ. 17, 104.

καιρός, η, ον (καιρός), *happening at the right time, seasonable, hitting the right place*; in H. only in the neut. καίριον, the vital part of the body, where wounds are fatal. ὅθι μάλιστα καιρίον ἐστιν, where the blow is fatal, 8, 84 326. ἐν καιρίῳ, κατὰ καίριον, in a mortal part, 4, 185. 11, 439.

καιρόεις, εσσα, εν, *well-woven*, *close-woven*, from καῖρος, the threads which cross the chain or warp in weaving [the woof or filling], Lat. *licia*. καιροσέων ὀθονέων ἀπολείβεται ὑγρὸν ἔλαιον, Od. 7, 107,† from the close-woven linen flows off the liquid oil, i. e. the linen is wrought so thick that even the penetrating oil flows off; καιροσέων is the reading of Aristarchus, and is, according to the Schol., gen. plur. for καιροεσσῶν, καιροσῶν, Ion. καιροσέων. Voss translates differently, 'and as the woven linen gleams with the dripping oil,' see Nitzsch ad loc. [Bright as with oil the new-wrought texture shone, Cp]

καιροσέων, see καιρόεις.

καίω, Ep. for κάω, aor. 1 ἄκηα and κῆα, plur. subj. κήομεν for κήωμεν, 3 sing. and plur. optat. κήαι, κήαιεν, infin. κῆαι, in the Od. also κεῖαι, κείομεν, κείαντες, aor. 1 mid. ἐκηάμην, partcp κηάμενος (in the Od. κείαντο, κειάμενος, Od. 16, 2. 23, 51); aor. pass. ἐκάην, infin. Ep. κᾐμεναι, 1) *to kindle, to light up, to set in a blaze,* πῦρ, Il. 2) *to consume, to burn,* μηρία, νεκρούς, Il.; hence pass. *to burn,* πυραί καίοντο, 1, 52. *b*) *to be burnt,* Od. 12, 13. II) Mid. only aor. 1, *to enkindle for oneself, to kindle,* with accus. πῦρ, πυρά. 9, 88. Od. 16, 2. (On the exchange of η and ει, see Buttm. p. 287. Rost. p. 308; Kühner, § 151. A. The forms κήω and κείω are doubtful.)

κάκ, abbreviated κατά before κ; mly κὰκ κεφαλήν, κὰκ κόρυθα, 11, 351. Others, κακκεφαλήν, etc.

κακίζω (κακός), *to render bad.* 2) Mid. *to make oneself bad, to show oneself cowardly,* 24, 214.†

κακκείαι, see κατακαίω, Od. 11, 74.

κακκείοντες, see κατακείω.

κακκεφαλῆς, see κάκ.

κακκόρυθα, see κάκ.

***κακοδαίμων**, ον (δαίμων), *wretched, unhappy, miserable,* Ep. 14, 21.

κακοείμων, ον, gen. ονος (εἷμα), *wretchedly clothed, ill clad,* πτωχοί, Od. 18, 41.†

κακοεργίη, ἡ (κακοεργός), *a bad deed, a wicked act,* Od. 22, 374.†

κακοεργός, όν, poet. (ἔργον), *wicked;* γαστήρ, the abominable stomach [=hunger always counsellor of ill. *Cp.*], Od. 18, 54.†

Κἀκοίλιος, ἡ (Ἴλιος), *wretched Ilium,* *Od. 19, 260. 23, 19.

***κακομηθής**, ές (μῆδος), *crafty, deceitful,* h. Merc. 389.

κακομήχανος, ον (μηχανή), *contriving evil, destructive,* 6, 344. 9, 257. Od. 16, 418.

κακόξεινος, ον, Ion. and Ep. for κακόξενος (ξένος), *inhospitable, having bad guests.* Thus, Τηλέμαχ᾽ οὔτις σεῖο κακοξεινώτερος ἄλλος, no other one has worse guests, is more unfortunate in his guests than thou, Od. 20, 376.†

κακορραφίη, ἡ (ῥάπτω), *the machination of evil things, craftiness, treachery, trickery, malice,* 15, 16. Od. 12, 26; plur. Od. 2, 236.

κακός, ή, όν, *bad, evil,* hence 1) Spoken of external qualities of animate and inanimate things: of the external appearance of a person or thing, *ugly, homely.* κακὸς εἶδος, 10, 316. κακὰ εἵματα, esply of persons, *a*) In point of rank, *mean, vulgar, ignoble,* 14, 126. Od. 1, 411. 4, 64. *b*) *bad, worthless, miserable,* νομῆες, Od. 17, 246. 2) Of conditions and circumstances: *evil, bad, ruinous, injurious, wretched.* Κῆρες, δόλος, νύξ, θάνατος, etc. 3) Spoken of the character: *bad, mean, wicked;* in H. esply of warriors, *cowardly.* κακὸς καὶ ἄναλκις, 8, 153. 5, 643 Neut. κακόν and κακά as subst. *badness, vileness, misfortune, misery, wretchedness, evil;* spoken of Ares, τυκτὸν κακόν, an unnatural, monstrous evil, 5, 831, see τυκτός; as an exclamation, μέγα κακόν, a great evil (V. 'O shame!'), 11, 404. κακόν τι ποιεῖν, to do some harm, 13, 120. κακὸν or κακὰ ῥέζειν τινά, to do harm to any one, 2, 195. 4, 32; rarely τινί, Od. 14, 289. κακὰ φέρειν τινί, 11. 2, 304; also absol. κακὰ Πριάμῳ for εἰς κακά, to the ruin of Priam, 4, 28. 4) Adv. κακῶς, *badly, wickedly, basely, insultingly,* e. g. ἀφιέναι τινά, νοστεῖν, 1, 25. 2, 153. It often has a strengthening force. κακῶς ὑπερηνορέοντες, Od. 4, 766. 5) As a compar. in H. *a*) Regular: κακώτερος, η, ον, 19, 321. κακίων, ον, 9, 601; from which κακίους for κακίονας, Od. 2, 277. Superl. κάκιστος, η, ον, Il. and Od. *b*) Irregular: χερείων, together with the forms χέρηϊ, χέρηα, etc., χερειότερος, ἥσσων, q. v.

κακότεχνος, ον (τέχνη), *practising evil arts, deceitful, wily,* 15, 14.

κακότης, ητος, ἡ (κακός), *badness, worthlessness,* 1) *moral vileness, baseness, wickedness,* 3, 366. 13, 108. Od. 24, 455; spoken of warriors, *cowardice, timidity,* Il. 2, 368. 15, 721. 2) *evil, harm, misfortune,* 10, 71. Od. 3, 175; esply *the sufferings of war,* Il. 11, 382. 12, 332.

κακοφραδής, ές (φράζομαι), *evil-minded, irrational, foolish,* 23, 483.†

***κακοφραδίη**, ἡ, *evil intention, folly, indiscretion,* plur. h. Cer. 227.

κακόω (κακός), aor. ἐκάκωσα, perf. pass. κεκάκωμαι, *to do badly, to inflict evil upon, to make unhappy, to maltreat, to injure,* τινά, 11, 690. Od. 16, 212. κεκακωμένοι ἦμεν, we were in a bad case, 11, 689. κεκακωμένος ἅλμῃ, disfigured by sea-water, Od. 6, 137; metaph. μηδὲ γέροντα κάκου (imperat. for κάκοε) κεκακωμένον, do not afflict the afflicted old man, Od. 4, 754.

κάκτανε, see κατακτείνω.

κακώτερος, η, ον, see κακός.

καλάμη, ἡ, 1) *a stalk* or *straw* of corn, 19, 222. 2) *the stubble* (in harvesting only the ears were cut off); hence metaph. *the rest, the remnant.* ἀλλ᾽ ἔμπης καλάμην γέ σ᾽ ὀΐομαι εἰσορόωντα γιγνώσκειν, but still, I think, that on beholding, even the stubble, thou wilt recognize it, i. e. thou wilt recognize, in my still remaining strength, what I once was, Od. 14, 214. [But mark the stubble, and thou canst not much Misjudge the grain. *Cp.*]

***Καλαμίνθιος**, ὁ (καλαμίνθη), *the lover of calamint,* a frog's name, Batr. 227.

***κάλαμος**, ὁ, *a reed,* h. Merc. 47.

***καλαμοστεφής**, ές (στέφω), *crowned with reed, rush-covered;* βυρσαί, coria calamis obducta, Batr. 127.

καλαῦροψ, οπος, ἡ, *the herdsman's crook,* which the herdsmen bore, and threw at the cattle to drive them, 23, 845.

καλέω, infin. Ep. καλήμεναι, 10, 125; fut. καλέσω, Ep. σσ, and καλέω, Od. 4, 532; aor. 1 ἐκάλεσα, Ep. σσ. aor. 1 mid.

ἐκαλεσάμην, Ep. σσ, perf. pass. κέκλημαι, piuperf. 3 plur. κεκλήατο, fut. 3 κεκλήσομαι, Ion. iterative imperf. καλέσκον and καλεσκόμην, I) *to call*, i. e. (1 *to name, to call by name*; τινὰ ἐπώνυμον or ἐπίκλησιν, to call one by a surname, 9, 562. 18, 187; hence pass. *to be called, to be named*, often, 2, 260. 684. 4, 61. ἐμὴ ἄλοχος κεκλήσεαι. h. Ven. 489. 2) *to call, to call in*; spoken of several, *to call together*, with accus. τινὰ εἰς ἀγορήν, εἰς Ὄλυμπόν Od. 1. 90. Il. 1, 402; also ἀγορήνδε, θαλαμόνδε οἰκόνδε; with accus. alone, ὅσοι κεκλήατο βουλήν, whosoever had been called to the council, 10, 195; and with infin. *to call upon, to require, to challenge*, καταβῆναι, 3, 250. 10, 197; *to call, to invite to a repast*, Od. 4, 532. 11, 187. II) Mid. in the aor. *to call to oneself, to summon*, 5, 427. h. Ven. 126; τινὰ φωνῇ, 3, 161; λαὸν ἀγορήνδε, 1, 54.

καλήμεναι. see καλέω.

Καλήσιος, ὁ, a comrade and charioteer of Axylus, from Arisbê in Thrace; slain by Diomêdês, 6, 18.

Καλητορίδης, ου, ὁ, son of Calêtor = Aphareus, 13, 541.

καλήτωρ, ορος, ὁ (καλέω), *a crier*, 24, 577.†

Καλήτωρ, ορος, ὁ (καλέω), pr. n. 1) son of Clytius, a kinsman of Priam, 15, 419. 2) father of Aphareus.

καλλείπω, Ep. for καταλείπω.

Καλλιάνασσα, ἡ, daughter of Nereus and Doris, 18, 46.

Καλλιάνειρα, ἡ, daughter of Nereus, 18, 44.

Καλλίαρος, ἡ, a town in Locris, in Strabo's time destroyed, 2, 531.

καλλιγύναιξ. αικος (γυνή), *abounding in beautiful women or virgins*, epith. of Hellas [Achaia] and Sparta, only in accus., 2, 683 [3, 75]. Od. 13, 412.

*Καλλιδίκη, ἡ, daughter of Keleos (Celeus) in Eleusis. h. in Cer. 109.

καλλίζωνος, ον (ζώνη), *beautifully girdled* or [rather *having a beautiful girdle*, cf. Od. 5, 231], epith. of noble women, 7, 139. Od. 23, 147.

*Καλλιθόη, ἡ, daughter of Keleos (Celeus) in Eleusis, h. in Cer. 110.

καλλίθριξ, τριχος (θρίξ) *having beautiful hair*; epith. of horses: having beautiful manes, 5, 323; epith. of sheep: having beautiful wool, Od. 9, 936. 469.

Καλλικολώνη, ἡ (κολώνη), *Mount Beauty*, a beautiful hill in the Trojan plain, not far from Troy, on the right side of the Simoeis, 20, 53. 151. Not far from it was the valley Θύμβρη.

καλλίκομος, ον (κόμη), *having beautiful hair, having beautiful tresses*, epith. of handsome women, 9, 449. Od. 15, 58.

καλλικρήδεμνος, ον (κρήδεμνον), *having a beautiful head-band or fillet* (beautifully veiled, V.), ἄλοχοι, Od. 4, 623.†

κάλλιμος, ον, poet. for καλός, *beautiful*, *Od. 4, 130. 11, 529. 640.

κάλλιον, see καλός.

*Καλλιόπη, ἡ (from ὄψ), having a *beautiful voice*), the eldest of the nine Muses, later the goddess of Epic song, h. 31, 2.

καλλιπάρηος, ον (παρειά), *having fair cheeks*, epith. of beautiful women, I, 143. Od. 15, 123.

κάλλιπε, καλλιπέειν, see καταλείπω.

*καλλιπέδιλος, ον (πέδιλον,) *having beautiful sandals*, h. Merc. 57.

καλλιπλόκαμος, ον (πλόκαμος), *having beautiful locks, having lovely tresses*, epith. of fair women, Il. and Od.

καλλιρέεθρος, ον (ῥέεθρον). *beautifully flowing*, κρήνη, Od. 10, 107.† h. Ap. 240.

καλλίροος, ον, poet. for καλίρροος.

Καλλιρόη, ἡ, poet. for Καλιρρόη, daughter of Oceanus and Tethys, wife of Chrysâôr, h. in Cer. 419.

καλλίρροος, ον, Ep. καλλίροος, Od. 5, 441. 17, 206 (ῥόος), *beautifully flowing*, epith. of rivers and fountains, 2, 752. 22. 147.

*καλλιστέφανος, ον (στέφανος), *beautifully crowned*, epith. of Dêmêtêr, h. Cer. 252.

κάλλιστος, η, ον, see καλός.

καλλίσφυρος, ον (σφυρόν), prop. *having beautiful ankles or feet, slender-footed*, epith. of beautiful women, 9, 557. Od. 5, 333.

καλλίτριχες, see καλλίθριξ.

κάλλιφ' for κατέλιπε, see καταλείπω.

καλλίχορος, ον (χορός), *having beautiful dancing-places, or having beautiful plains*, Πανοπεύς, Od. 11, 581; Θήβαι, h. 14, 2; see εὐρύχορος.

[Καλλίχορος, ὁ, a sacred fountain near Eleusis, h. Cer. 273.]

κάλλος, τό (καλός), *beauty*, both of men and women, 3, 392. 6, 156. Od. 6, 18. 8, 457; spoken of Penelopê, κάλλεϊ μέν οἱ πρῶτα πρόσωπα καλὰ κάθηρεν ἀμβροσίῳ οἵῳ Ἀφροδίτη χρίεται, Athênê illumined her lovely countenance with ambrosial beauty, such as Aphroditê adorns herself with, Od. 18, 191. (Here critics take it, unnecessarily, for 'fragrant ointment.' Beauty, as Passow remarks, is in H. something corporeal, which the gods put on and take off from men like a garment, cf. Od. 23, 156. 162.)

*κάλον, τό, *wood*, esply dry wood for burning, h. in Merc. 112.

καλός, ή, όν, compar. καλλίων, superl. κάλλιστος, *beautiful*. 1) Spoken of the external form both of animals and inanimate objects: *beautiful, fascinating, lovely, agreeable*, spoken of men, καλός τε μέγας τε, Il.; often of women; of parts of the body, of clothes, arms, furniture, regions, etc.; λιμήν, a beautiful harbour. Od. 6, 263. 2) Of internal quality: *beautiful, noble, glorious, excellent*; in H. only neut. καλόν ἐστι, it is well, it is becoming, with infin., 9, 615. 17. 19. νῦν δὴ κάλλιον μεταλλῆσαι, now it is more fitting to ask, Od. 3, 69. οὐ μήν τόγε κάλλιον, this is by no means well. Il. 24, 52. Od. 7, 159. The neut. sing καλόν and plur. καλά are often used by κάλος. Η. as adv. *well, fitly, beautifully*, καλόν, Od. 1, 155. 8, 266; in the Il. καλά, 6, 326. 8, 400. The adv. καλώς, only Od. 2, 64, see διόλλυμι.

κάλος, ὁ, Att. κάλως, *a rope, a sailrope*, Od. 5, 260; † different from ὑπεραί and πόδες.

κάλπις, ιδος, ἡ, *a vessel for drawing or scooping up water, a pitcher, an urn*, Od. 7, 20.† h. Cer. 207.

*καλύβη, ἡ (καλύπτω), *a shelter, a hut, an harbour*, Batr. 30.

Καλύδναι, αἱ νῆσοι, *the Calydnæ islands*, according to Strab. X. p. 489, *the Sporades*, near the island of Cos, which received their name from the larger, afterwards called Καλύμνα, but in earlier times Καλύδνα. Others understood by the word, the two islands Leros and Calymna. According to Demetrius, the island was called Καλύδναι, like Θῆβαι, 2, 677.

Καλυδών, ῶνος, ἡ, *a very ancient town in Ætolia on the Evēnus, famed on account of the Calydonian boar*, 2, 640. 9, 340. 13, 217.

*καλυκῶπις, ιδος, ἡ (ὤψ), *with a florid countenance, having a blooming face*, h. Cer. 420. Ven. 285.

κάλυμμα, ατος, τό (καλύπτω), *an envelopment*; esply the head-covering of the women, *a veil*=καλύπτρη. It is called κυάνεον, dark-coloured, as used in mourning, 24, 93.† It would seem, however, to be more correct to distinguish κάλυμμα from καλύπτρη, and, with Voss, to translate it 'mourning robe,' since it is followed by τοῦ δ᾽ οὔτι μελάντερον ἔπλετο ἔσθος, cf. h. Cer. 42.

κάλυξ, υκος, ἡ, 1) Prop. *an envelope*; hence *a bud*, esply *a flower-bud, a flower-cup*, or *calyx*. 2) In H., 18, 401,† as a female ornament, perhaps *ear-pendants* in the form of a flower-cup. According to some Gramm. they are the σωληνίσκοι, σύριγγες (Voss, 'hair-pins'); al. small tubes to keep the hair in curl [*pipes*, Cp.], cf. h. Ven. 87. 164.

καλύπτρη, ἡ (καλύπτω), *a covering*, esply *a veil*, with which females cover the face upon going out, 22, 406. Od. 5, 232. 10, 543.

καλύπτω, fut. ψω, aor. 1 ἐκάλυψα, Ep. κάλυψα, aor. mid. ἐκαλυψάμην, perf. pass. κεκάλυμμαι, aor. pass. ἐκαλύφθην. 1) *to cover, to envelope, to wrap around*. πέτρον περὶ χεῖρ ἐκάλυψεν, the hand (just) covered the stone, i. e. it was as great as the hand could grasp, 16, 735. Mly constr. τί τινι, *to cover something with something*, 7, 462. 10, 29; more rarely, τί τινι, *to* (cover =) *spread something over any one*, 5, 315. 21, 321; ἀμφί τινι and πρόσθε τινός, e. g. σάκος, *to hold a shield before any one*, 17, 132. 22, 313. Pass. κεκάλυπτο φέρι, 10, 790. ἀσπίδι κεκαλυμμένος ὤμους, having the shoulders covered with a shield, 16, 360. 2) Metath. of death: τέλος θανάτοιο κάλυψεν αὐτόν, death enveloped him, 5, 553; with double accus. τὸν δὲ σκότος ὄσσε κάλυψε, 4, 461; and often spoken also of swooning, οἱ ὄσσε νὺξ ἐκάλυψε μέλαινα, 14, 439. Spoken of a mental state, 11, 249. II) Mid. *to envelope oneself* with any thing, *to cover*, τινί; ὀθόνῃσιν, κρηδέμνῳ, 3, 141. 14, 184: with accus. πρόσωπα, h. Ven. 184.

Καλυψώ, οῦς, ἡ (the concealer, *Occulina*. Herm.), daughter of Atlas; she dwelt in the island Ogygia, remote from all intercourse with gods or men, Od. 1, 50, 52. She received the shipwrecked Odysseus (Ulysses) into her abode, and wished ever to retain him with her, promising to make him immortal, Od. 7, 244, seq. He spent here seven years, till at last, in the eighth, the gods pitied him, and Hermês was sent by Zeus with the command to Calypso to permit him to return home, Od. 5, 28—81. Unwillingly she obeyed the command of the gods. Odysseus (Ulysses) built a ship under her direction; and, after he was furnished by Calypso with the necessary implements and provisions, he departed with a favorable wind, which the goddess sent after him, Od. 7, 265, seq. 5, 160, seq. According to h. Cer. 422; Hes. Th. 1010, she was a daughter of Oceanus.

Κάλχας, αντος, ὁ, voc. Κάλχαν, son of Thestor, a famous seer of the Greeks, who by his art guided the Grecian enterprises before Troy, since he knew the present, the past, and the future, 1, 69—72. 2, 300. 13, 45.

κάμ, Ep. abbrev. κατά before μ. κὰμ μέσσον, 11, 172. κὰμ μέν, Od. 20, 2.

κάμαξ, ακος, ἡ, *a stake, a pole; a vine-prop*, to which the vines were bound, 18, 563.†

*καματηρός, ἡ, όν (κάματος). *wearisome, burdensome*, γῆρας, h. Ven. 247.

κάματος, ὁ, 1) *labour, toil, hardship*, 15, 365. ἄτερ καμάτοιο, Od. 7, 325. 2) *fatigue, weariness, exhaustion*, 4, 230. 13, 711 (see ΔΔΕΩ), Od. 6, 2. 12, 281. πολυᾶϊξ κάματος, fiercely assailing weariness, or the fatigue of impetuous battle, 5, 811. 3) *labour*, i. e. *the gains of labour*, Od. 14, 417.

κάμε, Ep. for ἔκαμε, see κάμνω.

Κάμειρος, ἡ, *Cameirus*, a town on the western coast of the island of Rhodes, now *Jerachio*, 2, 656.

*καμῖνος, ὁ, *an oven* for baking; an oven for burning potters' ware, Ep. Hom. 14.

καμινώ, οῦς, ἡ, connected with γρῆυς, *an old oven-woman*, with the implied notion of loquacity, Od. 18, 27.†

καμμονίη, ἡ (Ep. for καταμονίη), prop. *endurance, perseverance in battle;* the victory thus obtained, *22, 257. 23, 661.

κάμμορος (Ep. for κακόμορος, according to Ap.), *ill-fated, miserable, unfortunate*, *Od. 2, 351. 5, 160.

*καμμύσαι, see καταμύω.

κάμνω, fut. καμοῦμαι, aor. ἔκαμον

Κάμπτω. 226 Κάρ.

3 sing. κάμε, Ep. subj. κεκάμω with redupl., aor. mid. έκαμόμην, perf. κέκμηκα, partcp. κεκμηώς, gen. ώτος, accus. plur. κεκμηότας, 1) Intrans. *to fatigue oneself with labour*. a) *to take pains, to toil, to suffer*, μάλα πολλά, 8, 22. 448 ; with part. ουδέ τόξον δήν έκαμον τανύων, I did not long weary myself in drawing the bow [Jν. δήν τανύων, Fäsi], Od. 21, 426 ; of works of art, κάμε τεύχων, Il. 2, 101. 7, 220. 8, 195. b) *to become fatigued, to become weary, to become relaxed*; with accus. χείρα, in the hand, 2. 389. 5, 797; γυία. Ώμον, often with a partcp. έπήν κεκάμω πολεμίζων, after I am fatigued in battle. 1, 168 ; so κάμνει θέων, έλαύνων, he is weary with running, rowing, 4, 244. 7, 5 κεκμηώς, a fatigued person, 6, 261. 11, 802 ; but οι καμόντες, the wearied ones; epith. of the dead who have escaped from their labours, 3, 278 (V. ' those who rest'). Od. 11, 476. According to Buttm , Lex. p. 371, ' the worn out, the *enfeebled*,' as a kind of euphemism for θανόντες, the word presenting, instead of the notion of non-existence, the lowest degree of life short of annihilation. 2) Trans. *to make with toil, to prepare*, with accus. esply works of art in brass, μίτρην. 4, 187. 18, 614; νήας, Od. 9, 126. Mid. *to work upon with pains-taking for oneself, to cultivate*, with accus. νήσον, Od. 9, 130. 2) *to earn by labour for oneself, to acquire*, δουρί τι, Il. 18, 341.

κάμπτω, fut. ψω, aor. έκαμψα, *to bend, to curve*, with accus. ίτυν, 4, 486; esply γόνυ, to bend the knee, in order to rest, 7, 118. 29, 72 ; γούνατα χείράς τε, Od. 5, 453.

καμπύλος, η, ον (κάμπτω). *curved, crooked, bent*, epith. of the bow, chariot and wheel, 5, 97. 231. 722. Od. 9, 156; άροτρον, h. Cer. 308.

*κάναστρον, τό (κάνη), a basket made of twisted osier; an earthen vessel, Ep. h. 14, 3.

καναχέω (καναχή), only aor. καναχησε, *to resound, to make a noise, to rattle, to ring*, spoken of brass, Od. 19, 469.

καναχή, ή (καναζω), *noise, sound, rattling, ringing*; spoken of brass, 16, 105 ; of the stamping of mules, Od. 6, 82 ; of the gnashing of teeth, 11. 19, 365 ; of the lyre, h. Ap. 185.

καναχίζω = καναχέω, only imperf. *to rattle, to ring, to resound*. καναχιζε δούρατα πύργων βαλλόμενα, the timbers of the towers being hit resounded, 12, 36. (The explanation 'δούρατα έπι τους πύργους άκοντιζόμενα' is contrary to the usus loquendi)

κάνειον, τό, Ep.=κάνεον, Od. 10, 355.†

κάνεον, τό, Ep. κάνειον (κάνη), prop. *a basket* make of twisted reeds ; *a reed basket*; generally *a basket, a vessel, a dish* for bread and for the sacred barley in a sacrifice; spoken of brass, 11, 630 ; and of gold, Od. 10, 355.

καννεύσας, see κατανεύω.

κανών, όνος, ό (κάνη), prop. *a reed rod*, any straight rule for measuring, etc.; in H. 1) κανόνες are two cross-bars (ράβδοι. Hesych.) on the inside of a shield. The left arm was put through one of these, whilst the left hand grasped the other, when an attack was made upon the enemy ; *a handle*. They were made of leather, and also of metal, 8, 193. 13, 407; later, όχανα. Others suppose these were two cross-bars to which the τελαμών was attached, cf. Köpke, Kriegsw. d. Gr. S. 110. 2) A straight piece of wood, or spool, upon which the yarn of the woof was wound, in order to throw it through the warp; Voss, *the shuttle* (it is incorrectly explained as ' the great beam of the loom') έπι δ' ώρνυτο δίος 'Οδυσσεύς "Αγχι μάλ' ώς ότε τις τε γυναικί ευζώνοιο Στήθεός έστι κανών. 23, 760. Here the gen. στήθεος depends upon άγχι, for the sense is, Odysseus (Ulysses) was as near Ajax, as the instrument with which the woof is inserted in the warp is to the breast of the woman. [Bothe supposes an hypallage : κανών τις γυναικί για κανών γυναικός τινος.] [*Cp.* " Near as some cinctured maid [industrious holds the distaff to her breast."]

κάπ, Ep. abbreviated for κατά before π and φ. κάπ πεδίον, κάπ φάλαρα, 11, 167. 16, 106.

Καπανεύς, ήος, ό, son of Hipponous and Laodice, father of Sthenelus, one of the seven princes before Thebes, was killed by lightning as he was mounting the walls, 2, 564.

Καπανηϊάδης, ου, ό, and Καπανήϊος υιός, son of Capaneus=Sthenelus, 5, 108, 109. 4, 367.

κάπετος, ή (σκάπτω), *a ditch, a fosse* = τάφρος, 15, 356; *a pit, a vault*, 24, 797; and generally *a trench*, *18, 564.

κάπη, ή (κάπτω), *a crib, a manger* with the food, 18, 433. Od. 4, 40.

καπνίζω (καπνός), aor. έκάπνισα, Ep. σσ, *to make a smoke, to kindle a fire*, 2, 399.†

καπνός, ό (ΚΑΠΩ), *smoke, fume*, distinct from κνίσση, 1, 317. Od. 1, 58; the vapour from waves, Od. 12, 219.

κάππεσον, see καταπίπτω.

κάπριος, ό, for κάπρος, 11, 414. 12, 42; and σύς κάπριος, 11, 293. 17, 282.

κάπρος, ό, *a boar, a wild swine*. The male swine was taken as an offering in forming a treaty, 19, 196.

καπύω (ΚΑΠΩ), aor. έκάπυσα, Ep. σσ, *to breathe, to breathe forth*. άπο δε ψυχήν έκάπυσσεν, 22, 467.†

Κάπυς, υος, ό, son of Assaracus, father of Anchises, 20, 239.

ΚΑΠΩ, see ΚΑΦΩ.

κάρ, Ep. abbrev. κατά before ρ. κάρ ρόον, 12, 33.

κάρ, according to the Schol. an ancient Ep. abbrev. form for κάρη: hence έπι κάρ, *upon the head*, *headlong*, 16, 392.† Later it was written έπίκαρ.

κάρ (δ'), a word of uncertain signif. prob. an ancient word for θρίξ, in the

Καρ.   ·   227   Κασίγνητος.

passage τίω δέ μιν ἐν καρὸς αἴσῃ, I value him equally with a hair, i. e. not at all, 9, 378.† According to Clarke and Heyne, probably of a common origin with ἀκαρής, Hesych., τὸ βραχύ, ὁ οὐδὲ κεῖραι οἶόν γε so that it has yielded a word κάρ (capillus rasus, from κείρω), like the Latin nec hilum or flocci facere. The ancients take it, some for κηρός, like death (cf. 3, 454); some for Καρός, like a' Carian, because the Carians were despised as soldiers. The quantity is at variance with both, and with the last also the state of things when H. lived. [Död. accepts the explanation of the Schol. Ven. = φθείρ, pediculus.]

Κάρ, Καρός, ὁ, a Carian, an inhabitant of Caria, the south-western country in Asia Minor, 2, 867. 10, 428.

Καρδαμύλη, ἡ, a town near Leuctra, in Messenia, which Agamemnon promised to give Achilles as a dowry; now Scardamoula, 9, 150.

καρδίη, ἡ, Ep. κραδίη, the last the common Ep. form; καρδίη only 2, 452. 1) the heart, as a part of the human body, the seat of the circulation of the blood and of life, 10, 94. 13, 282. 2) Metaph. the heart, as the seat of the feelings, desires, impulses, and passions, 1, 225. 395. Od. 4, 293; connected with θυμός, 2, 171. Od. 4, 548. 3) As the seat of the faculty of thought, the soul, the mind, the understanding, 10, 244. 21, 441.

*κάρδοπος, ὁ, a kneading-trough, a tray, Epigr. 15, 6.

κάρη, τό, Ion. and Ep. for κάρα, gen. κάρητος, καρήατος, dat. κάρητι, καρήατι, accus. κάρη, plur. nom. κάρα, h. Cer. 12 (from κάρατα, κάραα), καρήατα, 17, 437; accus. κράατα. Here belong the forms ΚΡΑΣ, gen. κρατός, κράατος, dat. κρατί, κράατι, accus. κρᾶτα, Od. 8, 92; plur. gen. κράτων (more correctly, κρατῶν), dat. κρασί; and from κάρηνον: καρήνου, κάρηνα, καρήνων, see Thiersch, § 197, 55. Rost, Dial. 39; the head, of men and of brutes, κάρη, only nom. and accus. Il. 2, 259. 6, 509; gen. κάρητος, Od. 6, 230; κάρητι, Il. 15, 75.

κάρηας, τό, a later nom., used of Antimachus, probably formed from the Ep. forms καρήατος, καρήατι, καρήατα, see κάρη.

καρηκομάω, only in the pres. partcp. καρηκομόωντες, Ep. for καρηκομῶντες (κομάω), long-haired, epith. of the Achæans, who wore the hair long; opposed to ὄπιθεν κομόωντες, 2, 542.

κάρηνον, τό, Ep. form of κάρη, q. v. 1) the head, καρήνου, h. 7, 12; often in periphr. ἀνδρῶν, ἵππων κάρηνα, 9, 407. 11, 500. νεκύων κάρηνα, Od. 10, 521. 2) Metaph. the top, the summit, of mountains, 1, 44. Od. 1, 102; citadels, the strong-holds of cities, Il. 2, 117. 9, 24.

Κάρησος, ὁ, a river in Mysia, which flowed into the Æsôpus; later Πίνυς, 12, 20.

καρκαίρω, to shake, to tremble, to quake, 20, 157.†

*καρκίνος, ὁ, a crab, Batr. 301.

Κάρπαθος, ἡ, Ep. Κράπαθος, an island between Crete and Rhodes, in the sea called from it the Carpathian; now Scarpanto, 2, 676. The first form is found in h. Ap. 43.

καρπάλιμος, ον (for ἁρπάλιμος from ἁρπάζω), fleet, rapid, hasty, πόδες, 16, 342. 809. Frequently the adv. καρπαλίμως, quickly, rapidly, hastily.

καρπός, ὁ. 1) fruit, both of trees and of the field, 6, 142. Od. 10, 242. 2) the wrist, the part of the hand near the wrist, 5, 458. 8, 328. Od. 18, 258.

καρρέζουσα, see καταρρέζω.

καρτερόθυμος, ον (θυμός), of strong spirit, steadfast, courageous, epith. of Heracles, Achilles, and the Mysians, 5, 277. 13, 350. Od. 21, 25.

καρτερός, ή, όν (κάρτος), Ep. for κρατερός, strong, mighty, powerful, powerful, for the most part spoken of men and human affairs; chiefly bold, brave, θυμός, 5, 806. καρτεραὶ φάλαγγες, the mighty or brave squadrons, 5, 592. b) Of things: ἔργα, mighty deeds, 5, 757; ὅρκος, 19, 105. Od. 4, 253. ἕλκος, 16, 517.

*καρτερόχειρ, ος, ὁ, strong-handed, powerful, epith. of Arês, h. 7, 3.

κάρτιστος, η, ον, Ep. for κράτιστος superl. from κραυύς or κράτος, the strongest, the mightiest, Il. and Od.

κάρτος, εος, τό, Ep. for κράτος, strength, might, power, 9, 254; and oftener connected with βίη and σθένος, see κράτος.

καρτύνω, Ep. for κρατύνω (κράτος), to make strong; only mid. to strengthen for oneself, always ἐκαρτύναντο φάλαγγας, *11, 215. 12, 415. 16, 563.

*κάρυον, τό, any kind of nut, esply walnut, Batr. 31.

Κάρυστος, ἡ, a city on the southern coast of Eubœa, famed for its marble; now Caristo, 2, 539.

καρφαλέος, η, ον (κάρφω). 1) dry, parched, ἧα, Od. 5, 369. 2) Metaph. spoken of a sound, dull, hollow, ἀσπὶς καρφαλέον ἄϋσεν, 13, 409.

κάρφω, fut. κάρψω, aor. κάρψα, to draw together, to wrinkle, to wither; only χρόα, to wrinkle the skin, *Od. 13, 398. 430.

καρχαλέος, η, ον (κάρχαρος), rough, sharp; metaph. δίψῃ, rough (in the throat) from thirst, 21, 541.† (καρφαλέοι is a gloss.)

καρχαρόδους, όδοντος, ὁ, ἡ (ὀδούς), having sharp teeth, κύνες, *10, 360. 13, 198.

κασιγνήτη, ἡ (fem. from κασίγνητος), an own sister, a sister, 4, 441, and often.

κασίγνητος, ὁ (κάσις, γεννάω), 1) a brother, a full, an own brother, ὅπατρος, 12, 371. 2) Generally a near kinsman, esply the child of a brother or sister, 15, 545. 16, 456. 3) As adj. for κασιγνητικός, πόλλ' ἀχέουσα κασιγνήτοιο φόνοιο, on account of the slaughter of her brothers; for Meleager slew several brothers of Althæa, Apd. 1, 8. 3. The poet, however, might mean Iphiclus, who con-

L 6

Κάσος.

tested with Meleager the honour of victory; hence Voss, 'on account of the slaughter of an own brother,' 9, 567.

Κάσος, ή, an island of the Ægean Sea near Cos. now *Casso*, 2, 676.

Κασσάνδρη, ή, daughter of Priam, had received from Apollo the gift of prophecy; but, because she did not return his love, he laid a curse upon her prophecies. She prophesied only misfortune, and no one believed her, 13, 366. After the sack of Troy she became the save of Agamemnon, and was slain by Klytæmnê-tra (Clytæmnestra) in Mycenæ, Od. 11, 420.

κασσίτερος, ὁ, *tin,* plumbum album, different from lead, plumbum nigrum. H. mentions it as an ornament of cuirasses and shields, 11, 25. 34. 18, 565. 575; and of chariots, 23, 503. Also greaves were made of tin, or for ornament coated with tin, 21, 592. 18, 613. According to 18. 474, it was melted and over other metal. χεῦμα κασσιτέροιο, tin-casting, 23, 561. Probably, however, it was also beaten into plates with the hammer, 20, 271, and hence called ἑανός. Beckmann, Geschich. der Erfind. c. 4, 3, considers it the *stannum* of the Romans, a mixture of silver and lead, because soft tin would have afforded no protection in war. (Schneider in his Lex. agrees with this view). *II.

Καστιάνειρα, ή. *Castianeira,* mother of Gorgythion, 8, 305.

Κάστωρ, ορος, ὁ, son of King Tyndareus and of Leda. or, by mythology, of Zeus, brother of Polydeukês (Pollux) and Helen, 3, 238, famed for his skill in managing horses. According to later mythology, he took part in the Calydonian hunt and in the Argonautic expedition. He was born mortal, and, when he was killed by Idas, Polydeukês (Pollux) shared immortality with him. Alternately they spent a day in the upper and a day in the under world. 3. 237. Od. 11, 299, seq. Mly, Kastôr (Castor) and Polydeukês (Pollux) together are called *Dioscūri*, i. e. sons of Zeus, see Διόσκουροι. 2) *Castor,* son of Hylacus, a fictitious personage, Od. 14. 204.

*καστορνύσα, see καταστορέννυμι.

κασχέθε, see κατέχω.

κατά, 1) Prep. with gen. and accus., prim. signif. *down from above* 1) With the gen. spoken only of place: *a)* To indicate a downward motion, *down from, down.* βῆ δὲ κατ' Οὐλύμποιο καρήνων, 1, 44. καθ' ἵππων ἆλτο; hence also with the implied notion of extension, *down from above.* κατ' ὀφθαλμῶν κέχυτο νύξ, down over the eyes the night was poured; again, κατ' ἄκρης, prop. from the summit down, i. e. entirely, 13, 772. cf. ἄκρος. *b)* To indicate direction to a place in a lower situation, *down upon, down to, under.* κατὰ χθονὸς ὄμματα πήξαι, to fasten the eyes upon the ground, 3, 217. νηχῇ κατὰ χθονὸς ᾤχετο, under the earth,

Καταβάλλω.

23, 100: and generally of direction to an object, Od 9, 330. 2) With accus. *a)* Spoken of place (here it forms an antithesis with ἀνά, in reference to the commencing-point, but agrees with it in expressing expansion over an object). *a)* To innicate direction to an object, mostly one in a lower situation, *ἐπί, ὑπό, εἰς.* βάλλειν κατὰ γαστέρα; in like manner, νύσσειν, οὐτᾶν κατά τι, κατ' ὄσσε ἰδών, looking into the eyes, 17, 167. β) To indicate extension from above downwards, *through, over, along upon.* κατὰ στρατόν, through the army, in the army. κατὰ λαόν, κατὰ γαῖαν. Thus often κατὰ θυμόν, in the heart. *b)* In reference to cause, manner, etc. *a)* To denote design, purpose : πλεῖν κατὰ πρῆξιν, o: business, Od, 3, 72. κατὰ χρέος ἐλθεῖν. Od. 11, 479. β) To denote suitableness, *according to,* secundum: κατὰ μοῖραν, according to propriety. κατὰ θυμίν, according to a man's power. γ) To denote the manner, etc. κατὰ λωτὸν ἐρύοιτο, after the manner of an onion-skin, Od. 19, 233. κατὰ μέρος, part by part, h. Merc. 53. κατ' ἔμ' αὐτόν, by myself, ll. 1, 271. κατὰ σφέας, by themselves, 2, 366. κατὰ φῦλα, by tribes, 2, 362. III) Adv. without case. κατά as an adv. has the signif. *down, downward, down from above,* 1, 40. 436; again, *fully, utterly, entirely.* κατὰ πάντα φαγεῖν, Od. 3, 315. III) In composition it has the same signif., and often strengthens the notion. IV) κατά may be placed after the subst. and then the accent is retracted: ὕμων κάτα. In the poets it is sometimes elided into κατ even before consonants. The accent is retracted and the τ assimilated to the following consonant: *καδ δύναμιν.* Other connect the prep. with the following word : καδδύναμιν

καταβαίνω (βαίνω), fut. καταβήσομαι, aor. 2 κατέβην, from this 1 plur. subj. καταβείομεν, Ep. for καταβῶμεν, aor. 1 mid. κατεβησάμην; also the Ep. forms κατεβήσετο and imper. καταβήσετο, 1) *to descend, to come down, to alight, εἰς τινος,* or with gen. alone, 5, 109; with the question whither, we have ἐς and ἐπί with the accus. 3, 252. 10, 541; or the accus. alone. κατεβήσατο θάλαμον, he descended to the chamber, Od. 2. 337. 2) With accus. *to descend* any thing. κλίμακα κατεβήσατο, he descended, went down, the stairs, Od. 1, 330. ξεστὸν ἐφόλκαιον καταβῆναι, to slide down by the smooth rudder (into the deep), Od. 14. 350; in a similar manner, ὑπερώϊα κατέβαινε, she descended the upper chamber, i. e. from the chamber, Od. 18, 206. 23, 85.

καταβάλλω (βάλλω), aor. 2 κατέβαλον, Ep. 3 sing. κάββαλε for κατέβαλε, 1) *to cast down, to tear down, to demolish,* with accus., 12, 206; to dash into, 15, 357; and κατὰ πρηνὲς βαλέειν μέλαθρον, i. e. καταβαλέειν, to demolish, 2, 414 ; to cast upon the land, Od. 6, 172. 2) *to lay down;* κρεῖον ἐν πυρὸς αὐγῇ, 9, 206. 3)

Καταβείομεν. 229 Καταθνητός.

to cause to fall, 5, 343. 8, 249; hence of a dog : οὔατα κάββαλεν, he dropt his ears (on recognizing his master), Od. 17, 302.

καταβείομεν, see καταβαίνω.

καταβήσετο, see καταβαίνω.

*καταβιβρώσκω (βιβρώσκω), aor. 2 κατέβρων, to devour, to consume, h. Ap. 127

*καταβλάπτω (βλάπτω), to hurt, to injure, with accus. h. Merc. 93.

καταβλώσκω (βλώσκω), only pres. to go or pass through, with accus. ἄστυ [to range the city-streets Cp.], Od. 16, 466. (καταβρόχω), only 3 sing. optat. aor. act. **καταβρόξειε**, to swallow, to swallow down, φάρμακον, Od. 4, 222 ; † see ἀναβρόχω.

καταγηράσκω and **καταγηράω** (γηράω), from which κατεγήρα, to grow old, *Od. 9, 510. 19, 360.

καταγίνέω, Ep. form of κατάγω, to bring down, to convey, to bring, with accus. ὕλην, Od. 10, 104.†

κατάγνυμι (ἄγνυμι), fut. κατάξω, aor. κατέαξα, to break, to dash in pieces, with accus. 8, 403. Od. 9, 283. τὸ κατεάξαμεν, ὃ πρὶν ἔχεσκον, we broke this (spear) which I was before accustomed to carry, 13, 257. That the plur. should be used is surprising, since the sing. follows ; still it may be very well accounted for: we (Idomeneus and Meriones), says the latter, broke, in our conflict, the spear which I used to bear, cf. Spitzner ad loc.

κατάγω (ἄγω), fut. κατάξω, Ep. infin. καταξέμεν, aor. act. κατήγαγον, aor. mid. κατηγαγόμην, 1) to conduct down, to bring down, with accus. τινὰ εἰς Ἀΐδαο, Od. 11, 164. 24, 100. 2) Generally, to lead away, to conduct, for the most part from a higher to a lower region, as ἵππους ἐπὶ νῆας, 5, 26. 6, 53. τινὰ Κρήτηνδε, to drive a man to Crete (of a wind), Od. 19, 186. Mid. to proceed from the high sea into port, to put into harbour, opposed to ἀνάγεσθαι, spoken of ships, Od. 3, 10 ; ἐς Γεραιστόν, Od. 3, 178 ; Ἰθάκηνδε, Od. 16, 322 ; spoken of seamen : νηΐ κατάγεσθαι, Od. 10, 140.

καταδαίομαι (δαίω), fut. δάσομαι, to tear in pieces, to devour. only in tmesis, κατὰ πάντα δάσονται, 22, 354.†

*καταδάκνω (δάκνω), to bite severely, Batr. 45.

*καταδάμναμαι, depon. mid. (δάμναμαι), poet. for καταδαμάω, to tame, to subdue, to overpower, h. Merc. 137.

καταδάπτω (δάπτω), aor. κατέδαψα, 1) to tear in pieces, to lacerate, with accus. spoken of dogs and birds of prey, 22, 339. Od. 3, 259. 2) Metaph. ἦτορ καταδάπτεται, my (tortured) soul is rent=wounded. distressed, Od. 16, 92.

καταδαρθάνω (δαρθάνω), aor. κατέδαρθον, poet. κατέδραθον, 3 dual. Ep. καθδραθέτην for κατεδραθέτην, Od. 15, 494 ; subj. καταδραθώ. which aor. sometimes passes into the pass. form ἐδάρθην, Od. 5,

471 ; only in the Ep. aor. to go to sleep, to sleep. οὕτω τοιόνδε κατέδραθον, subaud. ὕπνον, I never slept so soundly, *Od. 23, 18.

καταδέρκομαι, poet. (δέρκομαι), to look down, τινά, upon any one, Od. 11, 16.†

καταδεύω (δεύω), aor. κατέδευσα, to wet, to drench, χιτῶνα οἴνου. to deluge my vest with wine [Cp.], 9, 490.†

καταδέω (δέω), aor. κατέδησα, 1) to bind, to bind fast, ἵππους ἐπὶ κάπῃ 8, 434. Od. 4, 40 ; ἱστὸν προτόνοισιν, the mast with ropes, Od. 2, 425. 2) to bind together, to lock up, to obstruct, with accus. ἀνέμων κελεύθους, Od 5, 383. 10, 20.

καταδημοβορέω (δημοβόρος), prop. to consume the property of the people. 2) to consume in common, 18. 301.†

καταδραθώ, see καταδαρθάνω.

*καταδύνω. a form of καταδύω, h. Merc. 237.

καταδύω (δύω), aor. 2 κατέδυν, partcp. καταδύς, nom. plur. fem. καδδῦσαι for καταδῦσαι, 19, 25 ; fut. mid. καταδύσομαι. aor. 1 mid. κατεδυσάμην, with the Ep. form κατεδύσετο, only in an intrans. signif. 1) to descend into, to go into, to penetrate, εἰς Ἀΐδαο δόμους, Od. 10, 174 ; κατὰ ὠτειλάς, to enter into the wounds, Il. 19, 25 ; with accus. δόμον, to go into a house ; πόλιν, Od. 4, 246 ; often ὅμιλον, Il. 4, 86. 10, 517 ; in like manner μάχην, μῶλον Ἄρηος, 18, 134. 2) to put on, spoken of arms, τεύχεα. 7, 103. 3) Absol. to set, to go down, spoken of the sun, ἠέλιος κατέδυ, 1, 475. 592, and often.

καταειμένος, η. ον, see καταέννυμι.

καταείνυον, see καταέννυμι.

καταείσατο, see κάτειμι.

καταέννυμι, poet. for καθέννυμι (ἕννυμι), imperf καταείνυον, 23, 135 (as if from εἰνύω) ; perf. pass. κατεειμένος, to clothe, to cover. with accus. νέκυν, 23, 135 ; metaph. ὄρος κατααειμένον ὕλῃ, a mountain clothed with wood, Od. 13, 351. 19, 431.

καταζαίνω (ἀζαίνω), to wither up, to cause to dry, with accus. Ep. iterat. aor. καταζήνασκε, Od. 11, 587.†

καταθάπτω (θάπτω), aor. 1 infin. καταθάψαι, Ep. for καταθάψαι, 24, 611 ; to bury, to inter, τινά, *18, 228.

καταθείομαι, **καταθείομεν**, see κατατίθημι.

καταθέλγω (θέλγω), aor. 1 κατέθελξα, to charm, to transform, spoken of Circe [Kirkē], who metamorphosed the companions of Odysseus (Ulysses) into brutes, Od. 10, 213.† cf. θέλγω.

καταθνήσκω (θνήσκω), aor. κατέθανον, Ep. κάτθανε, perf. κατατέθνηκα, infin. κατατεθνάναι, Ep. κατατεθνάμεν, partcp. κατατεθνηώς. to die, to expire, to decease; chiefly the partcp. perf. dead, deceased, ἀνήρ, 7, 89 ; plur. νεκροί and νέκυες κατατεθνηῶτες the dead, the slain ; the corpses of the slain), 7, 409. Od. 22, 448.

καταθνητός, ή, όν (θνητός), mortal, ἀνήρ and ἄνθρωπος, 6, 123. Od. 3, 114.

Καταθρώσκω. Κατακτείνω.

καταθρώσκω (θρώσκω), only in tmesis, κἀδ δ' ἔθορε, to leap down, 4, 79. h. Cer. 28.

καταθύμιος, ον (θυμός), lying in the mind, in the heart. μηδέ τί τοι θάνατος καταθύμιος ἔστω, let not death come into thy mind, i. e. entertain no thought of it [Cp.], 10, 383. 17, 201. ἔπος, τό μοι καταθύμιόν ἐστιν, (such) order as is in my mind, as my mind suggests. Others (alt Eust., τὸ κατὰ νοῦν νόημα), transl. it according to my mind, as I wish, Od. 22, 392. [Cf. Jahr. Jahn und K. p. 269, where the last signif. is rejected.]

καταΐάπτω see ιάπτω.

καταιβατός, ή, όν. poet. καταβατός (βαίνω), descending, leading downwards, θύραι καταιβαταὶ ἀνθρώποισιν, doors, by which men descend. Od. 13, 110.†

καταικίζω (αἰκίζω), perf. pass. κατῄκισμαι, to abuse, to disfigure. τεύχεα κατῄκισται (by smoke and dirt), *Od. 16, 290. 19, 9.

καταισχύνω (αἰσχύνω), to shame, to insult, to disgrace, to dishonour, πατέρων γένος. Od. 24, 508. 512; δαῖτα, *Od. 16, 293.

καταΐσχω, poet. for κατίσχω=κατέχω: οὔτ' ἄρα ποίμνῃσιν καταΐσχεται, it (the island) was not inhabited by shepherds, *Od. 9, 122.†

καταῖτυξ, υγος, ἡ, a head-piece, a low, light helmet [or casque, Cp.], without a cone or crest, 10, 258. (Prob. from κατά and τεύχω.)†

κατακαίω (καίω), infin. pres. κατακαιέμεν (κατακηέμεν ed. Wolf), 7, 408; aor. 1 κατέκηα, su-j. 1 plur. Ep. κατακήομεν, infin. aor. κατακεῖαι, Od. 10, 533; Ep. κακκεῖαι, Od. 11, 74; aor. 2 pass. κατεκάην, to burn up, to consume, with accus. of victims and of the dead, Il. 1, 40. 6, 418. In the pass. intrans. κατὰ πῦρ ἐκάη, the fire burnt down (the flame declined. Cp.), 9, 212. The infin. pres. κατακηέμεν or κατακειέμεν is doubtful, for which reason Spitzner has adopted κατακαιέμεν, see Thiersch, § 213, 38. Buttm, p. 287. Cf. καίω.

κατακαλύπτω (καλύπτω), aor. κατεκάλυψα, only in tmesis, to envelope entirely, to cover, with the accus. μηροὺς κνίσσῃ, to wrap the thigh-bones with fat, 1, 460. 2, 423. Od 3, 104.

κατακείαι, see κατακαίω.

κατακείεμεν or κατακηέμεν, see κατακαίω.

κατάκειμαι, depon. mid. (κεῖμαι), to lie down, to lay oneself down, 17, 677; metaph. to rest: ἄλγεα ἐν θυμῷ κατακεῖσθαι ἐάσομεν, we will permit the pangs to rest in the mind, 24, 523. 2) to lie, to be in store. 24, 527. Od. 19, 439.

κατακείρω (κείρω), prop. to cut off; hence to consume, to plunder, βίοτον. οἶκον. *Od. 4, 686. 22, 36; μῆλα, *Od. 23, 356.

κατακείω (κείω), partcp. κακκείοντες, Ep. for κατακείοντες, desiderat., to desire to lie down, to go to rest, 1, 606. Od. 1, 424 (see κείω).

κατακήομεν, see κατακαίω.

κατακλάω (κλάω), aor. 1 pass. κατεκλάσθην, to break in pieces, to break, with accus. 13, 608. 20, 227; metaph. ἔμοιγε κατεκλάσθη ἦτορ, my heart was broken. i e. overcome, distressed, Od. 4, 481. 9, 256.

κατακλίνω (κλίνω), aor. κατέκλινα, to bend down, to lay down, δόρυ ἐπὶ γαίῃ, O.l. 10, 165.†

Κατακλῶθες, αἱ (κατακλώθω), according to Eustath. metaplast. plur. for Κατακλωθοί, from Κλωθώ, prop. the spinners, for the Parcæ, the Fates, Od. 7, 197.† πείσεται, ἄσσα οἱ Αἶσα Κατακλῶθές τε βαρεῖαι Γεινομένῳ νήσαντο, which Fate and the inexorable sisters spun for him. Plainly the Cataclôthês are here annexed to Aisa, as the special to the generic, although we cannot refer them to the three post-Homeric Moirae. The figurative expression to spin is current in H., see ἐπικλώθω. The other reading, καταλώθησι βαρεία, must be rejected, see Nitzsch ad loc.

κατακοιμάω (κοιμάω), only aor. pass. κατεκοιμήθην, to put to sleep. Pass. to go to sleep, to rest, παρά τινι, 1, 355. 9, 427; ἐν ἔτεσιν, *11, 730.

κατακοσμέω (κοσμέω), 1) to adjust, to put aright, with accus. ὀϊστὸν ἐπὶ νευρῇ, 4, 118. 2) Mid. to put in order, δόμον, Od. 22, 440.

κατακρεμάννυμι (κρεμάννυμι), aor. κατεκρέμασα, to hang up, to suspend, φόρμιγγα. Od. 8, 67; τόξα, h. 27, 16.

κατακρῆθεν, adv. according to Aristarch. κατὰ κρῆθεν, from above, down from the head, Od. 11. 588. h. Cer. 182, metaph. from the top to the bottom, entirely, thoroughly. Τρῶας κατάκρηθεν λάβε πένθος, grief took complete possession of the Trojans, 16, 548. (Prob. from κάρη, κάρηθεν, syncop. κρῆθεν, which is found as an Ep. gen. in Hes. sc. 7, on which account it is better written separately; others say from κατά and ἄκρηθεν, see Spitzner ad Il. 16, 548.)

*κατακρημνάω (κρημνάω), to hang down (trans.), only mid. to hang down (intrans.), κατεκρημνῶντο βότρυες, h. 6, 39.

*κατάκρημνος, ον (κρημνός), precipitous, steep, Batr. 154.

κατακρύπτω (κρύπτω), fut. ψω, to conceal, to hide, to dissemble, τί, 22, 120. οὔτι κατακρύπτουσιν, they (the gods) conceal nothing from him, Od. 7, 205; apparently intrans.: ἀλλὰ δ' αὐτὸν (for ἑαυτὸν) φωτὶ κατακρύπτων ἤϊσκεν, disguising he made himself like another man, (αὑτόν is to be referred to both verbs), Od. 4, 247.

κατακτάμεν and κατακτάμεναι, see κατακτείνω.

κατακτάς, see κατακτείνω.

κατακτείνω (κτείνω), fut. act. κατακτενῶ, 23, 412; κατακτανέω, Ep. for κτενῶ. 6, 409; aor. 1 κατέκτεινα, aor. 2 κατέκτανον, imperat. κάκτανε, Ep. for κατάκτανε, 6, 164; also the Ep. aor. κατέκταν, infin.

κατακτάμεν and κατακτάμεναι. partcp. κατακτάς, aor. 1 pass. κατεκτάθην, fut. mid. κατακτανέομαι, with pass. signif.—*to kill, to slay, to slaughter*, τινά; ὧδε κατακτανέεσθε καὶ ὔμμες, thus will you also be slain, 14, 481; κατέκταθεν, Ep. for κατεκτάθησαν, Il. and Od.

κατακύπτω (κύπτω), aor. κατέκυφα, *to stoop (bend* or *bow) the head forward*, *16, 611. 17, 527.

καταλαμβάνω (λαμβάνω), *to take possession of, to seize*, only in tmesis, see λαμβάνω.

καταλέγω, Ep. (λέγω), fut. καταλέξω, aor. 1 κατέλεξα, fut. mid. καταλέξομαι, aor. 1 κατελεξάμην and Ep. aor. syncop. 3 sing. κατέλεκτο, infin. καταλέχθαι, Od. 15, 304; partcp. καταλέγμενος, prim. *to lay down.* I) Act. *to lay down, to tell, to relate, to recount*, τί τινι, often with ἀτρεκέως and εὖ, 9, 115. 10, 413; καταλέξαι τινά, to relate of any one, Od. 4, 832. II) Mid. *to lay oneself down, to lie, to rest*, 9, 662. Od. 3, 353. (On the deriv. see λέγω.)

καταλείβω (λείβω), *to pour down.* Mid. *to drop down, to trickle down*, 18, 109.†

καταλείπω, and Ep. καλλείπω (λείπω), fut. καταλείψω, Ep. καλλείψω, aor. 2 κατέλιπον, Ep. 3 sing. κάλλιπε and κάλλιφ', ό, 223; infin. καλλιπέειν, Od. 16, 296; 1) *to leave*, with accus. Il. 6, 223; of battle, 12, 226. Od. 13, 208. 2) *to leave behind, to leave*, spoken esply of persons dying and departing on a journey, τινὰ χήρην, 24, 726; εὐχωλήν τινι, to leave an oject of desire to any one, 4, 173; τινὶ ὀδύνας, Od. 1, 243. 3) *to abandon, to give up*, τινά, with infin. ἄλωρ γενέσθαι. 17, 151. Od. 3, 271.

καταλέω (ἀλέω), aor. κατήλεσα, Ep. σσ, *to grind*, τί, in tmesis, Od. 20, 109.†

καταλήθομαι (λήθομαι, Ep. for λανθάνομαι), *to forget entirely*, 22, 389.†

κατάλοφάδια, adv. (λόφος), *on the neck*, φέρειν, Od. 10, 169.† (a and ι are Ep. used as long.)

καταλύω (λύω), fut. καταλύσω, aor. 1 κατέλυσα, *to dissolve;* hence, 1) *to destroy, to demolish*, πολέων κάρηνα, 2, 117. 9, 74. 2) *to loose, to unyoke*, ἵππους, Od. 4, 28.

καταλωφάω (λωφάω), *to rest (from)*, *to become free*, τινός; καδ δέ κ' ἐμὸν κῆρ λωφήσειε κακῶν [would lighter feel my wrong. Cp.], only in tmesis, Od. 9, 460.† cf. λωφάω.

καταμάρπτω (μάρπτω), aor. 1 κατέμαρψα, *to seize, to overtake, to lay hold of*, τινά, 5, 66. 16, 598; metaph. spoken of age, Od. 24, 390.

καταμάω (ἀμάω), only aor. 1 mid. καταμησάμην, *to amass, to heap up*, κόπρον, 24, 165.†

καταμίγνυμι and καταμίσγω (μίγνυμι), *to mingle;* καμμίξας, 24, 529; for which Wolf has adopted κ' ἀμμίξας. Mid. *to mingle themselves*, h. 18, 26.

καταμύσσω (ἀμύσσω), aor. 1 mid. καταμυξάμην Ep. for κατημ., *to lacerate, to scratch.* Mid. *to scratch oneself*, χεῖρα, to scratch one's hand, 5, 425.†

*καταμύω, Ep. καμμύω (μύω), aor. Ep. infin. καμμύσαι, *to close the eyes, to sleep*, Batr. 192.

κατανεύω (νεύω), fut. (once, 1, 524), κατανεύσομαι, aor. 1 κατένευσα, partcp. καννύσας, Ep. for κατανεύσας, *to nod, to beckon*, κεφαλῇ or κρατί, with the head, i. e. *to assent, to grant*, τινί τι, any thing to any one; νίκην, κῦδος, 8, 175; with the infin. 2, 112. 10, 393.

κατανύομαι, Ep. for κατανύομαι (ἄνω), only pass. πολλὰ κατάνεται, much is finished, i. e. much is destroyed, consumed, *Od. 2, 58. 17, 537.

κάταντα, adv. (κατάντης), *downwards*, 23, 116.†

κατάντηστιν, adv. (ἀντάω), *opposite*, Od. 20, 387.† ed. Wolf, where others read κατ' ἄντηστιν or ἄντησιν According to Eustath. from κατάνηστος with epenth. σ, as in προμνηστῖνοι.

καταντικρύ, adv. (ἀντικρύ), *directly down*, with gen. τέγεος, *Od. 10, 539. 11, 64.

καταπάλλω (πάλλω), Ep. aor. syn., mid. κατέπαλτο, *to hurl down.* Pass. *to hurl oneself down, to leap down, to descend*, οὐρανοῦ ἐκ, 19, 351.† (The Schol. explain it: καθήλατο, and write κατέπαλτο, as if from κατεφάλλεσθαι), cf. πάλλω.

καταπατέω (πατέω), aor. κατεπάτησα, *to tread down, to trample under foot*, i. e. *to despise*, with accus. ὅρκια, in tmesis, 4, 157.†

κατάπαυμα, τό (καταπαύω), *cessation, rest, alleviation, quiet*, γόου, 17, 38.†

καταπαύω (παύω), fut. σω, aor. κατέπαυσα, 1) *to cause to cease, to stop, to end*, with accus. πόλεμον, 7, 36; μηνιθμόν, 16, 62; to appease, χόλον θεῶν, Od. 4, 583. 2) Spoken of persons: τινά, *to stop any one, to check, to restrain*, 16, 618. Od. 2, 618. ἡμέας θηρῶν καταπαύσμεν (Ep. infin.), Od. 2, 244 (construct: ὁρ. [sc. 'Ιθακησίους] ἡμ. κατ. exhorting [the people] to restrain us; to put an end to our proceedings;) τινά τινος, to restrain a man from any thing; ἀγηνορίης, 22, 457; ἀφροσυνάων, Od. 24, 457.

καταπεδάω (πεδάω), aor. κατεπέδησα, prop. to bind with foot fetters; hence, *to fetter, to bind*, τινά, only in tmesis, 19, 94. Od. 11, 292; see πεδάω.

καταπέσσω (πέσσω), aor. κατέπεψα, *to boil down, to digest*, with accus. χόλον, to restrain anger (V. to check), 1, 81.†

καταπετάννυμι (πετάννυμι), *to spread over, to cover*, only in tmesis. κατὰ λῖτα πετάσσας, 8, 441.†

(καταπέφνω), defect obsol. pres. to the aor. κατέπεφνον, to which belongs the irregularly accented partcp. καταπέφνων, *to kill, to slay*, τινά, 17, 539. (cf. ΦΕΝΩ,) Il. and Od.

καταπήγνυμι (πήγνυμι), aor. 1 κατέπηξα, Ep. aor. syncop. mild. 3 sing. κατέπηκτο, 1) Act. *to strike into the earth, to infix*, ἔγχος ἐπὶ χθονί, 6, 213; σκόλοπας, 7, 441.

Καταπίπτω.   Κατατίθημι.

II) Mid. *to remain fixed, to stand firm*, Ep. aor. ἐν γαίῃ, *11, 378.
καταπίπτω (πίπτω), aor. κατέπεσον, Ep. κάππεσον, 1) *to fall down, ἀπὸ πύργου*, 12, 386; ἀπ' ἱκριόφιν, Od. 12, 414. 2) *to fall down, ἐν Δήμνῳ*, Il. 1, 593; *ἐν κονίῃσιν*, 4, 523; *to fall*, in battle, 15, 538; metaph. πᾶσιν παραὶ ποσὶ κάππεσε θυμός, the courage of all fell before their feet, i. e. sunk entirely, 15, 280.
καταπλέω (πλέω), *to sail down*, from the high sea to the coast, to make the land, Od. 9, 142.†
καταπλήσσω (πλήσσω), only aor. pass. κατεπλήγην, Ep. for κατεπλάγην, act. prop. *to strike down*; pass. metaph., *to be terrified, to be amazed* or *confounded*, 3, 31.†
*καταπνείω, poet. for καταπνέω (πνέω), *to breathe upon, to blow against*, h. Cer. 239
καταπρηνής, ές (πρηνής), *prone downwards*, epith. only of χείρ, the flat hand (the palm downwards), to represent the action of striking [or *pressing* forcibly down], 15, 114. Od. 13, 164. h. Ap. 333.
καταπτήσσω (πτήσσω), aor. 1 κατέπτηξα, Ep. aor. 2 sync. κατέπτην (from ΠΤΑΩ). *to stoop down from fear, to conceal oneself*, Od. 8, 190; ὑπὸ θάμνῳ, Il. 22, 191; metaph. *to be terrified, to be frightened*. ἵππω κατεπτήτην, the horses were terrified, 8, 136.
καταπτώσσω (πτώσσω) = καταπτήσσω, only pres. *to hide oneself fearfully, to cringe*, 4, 224. 340. 5, 254; metaph. *to be terrified, to be dismayed*, *5, 476.
καταπύθω (πύθω), aor. κατέπυσα, *to render putrid, to let putrefy*, with accus. h. Ap. 371. Mid. *to become putrid, to putrefy*, 23, 328.†
καταράομαι, depon. mid. (ἀράομαι), *to invoke any thing upon a man*, esply evil, *to imprecate*: ἀλγεά τινι, Od. 19, 330; absol. πολλὰ κατηρᾶτο, he cursed much, Il. 9, 454.
καταρέζω, poet. for καταρρέζω.
καταρίγηλός, ή, όν (ῥιγέω), *horrible, terrible, odious*, Od. 14, 226.†
καταρρέζω (ῥέζω), aor. 1 Ep. κατέρεξα, partcp. pass. καρρέζουσα, Ep. for καταρρέζουσα, 5, 424; to put down, to stroke down, and thus put down; metaph. *to caress, to soothe*, τινὰ χειρί, 1, 361. Od. 4, 610.
καταρρέω (ῥέω), *to flow down*, Od. 17, 209; ἐξ ὠτειλῆς, Il. 4, 149; and with gen. χειρός, 13, 539.
κατάρχομαι, mid. (ἄρχω), In a religious signif. *to begin a sacrifice*, spoken of the ceremony which precedes the proper act of sacrifice, rarely with accus. χέρνιβά τ' οὐλοχύτας, to begin the sacrifice with the lustral water and the sacred barley, Od. 3, 445.†
κατασβέννυμι (σβέννυμι), aor. 1 κατέσβεσα, *to extinguish, quench*, πῦρ, *21, 381; in tmesis, 16, 292.
κατασεύομαι, poet. (σεύω), only Ep.

aor. 2. mid. κατέσσυντο, *to rush down*; with accus. ῥέεθρα, to rush into the stream. 21, 382.†
κατασκιάω, poet. for κατασκιάζω (σκιάζω). *to shade, to cover*, with accus. Od. 12, 436.†
κατασμύχω (σμύχω), *to burn down*, only in tmesis, see σμύχω.
*κατασστείβω (στείβω), *to tread upon*, with accus. h. 18, 4.
*κατασστίλβω (στίλβω), *to beam down, to shine upon*; transit. πρηῢ σέλας, *to send down mild beams*, h. 7, 10.
καταστορέννυμι (στορέννυμι) and καταστόρνυμι, partcp. καστορνῦσα, Ep. for καταστορνῦσα, Od. 17, 32; aor. 1 κατεστόρεσα. 1) *to spread out, to spread upon, to lay down*, with accus. ῥῆγος. Od. 13, 73; κῶα, Od. 17, 32. 2) *to cover over*; κάπετον λάεσσιν, the pit with stones, Il. 24, 798.
καταστόρνυμι. see καταστορέννυμι.
*καταστρέφω (στρέφω), aor. 1 κατέστρεψα, *to turn about, to overturn*; τοσσί τι. pedibus evertere, h. Ap. 73.
καταστυγέω (στυγέω), aor. κατέστυγον. 1) *to be amazed. terrified, to start back terrified*, absol, 17, 694. 2) Transit. with accus. *to be terrified at*, Od. 10, 113.
*καταστύφελος, ον (στυφελός), *very hard, firm*. πέτρη, h. Merc. 124.
κατασχεθεῖν, poet. for κατασχεῖν, see κατέχω.
κατασχεῖν, see κατέχω.
*κατατανύω (τανύω), poet. for κατατείνω, aor. 1 κατάνυσα, Ep. for κατετάνυσα, *to pull down, to draw down*, ὅπλα, h. 6, 34.
κατατείνω (τείνω), aor. κατέτεινα, prop. *to pull down*, in tmesis, κατὰ δ' ἡνία τείνεν ὀπίσσω, he drew the reins back, 3, 261. 19, 311.†
κατατήκω (τήκω), aor. 1 act. κατέτηξα. 1) Act. trans. *to melt*, with accus. χιόνα, Od. 19, 206. 2) Mid. intrans. *to melt, to dissolve*; metaph. *to consume oneself, to pine away*; ἦτορ, at heart, *Od. 19, 136.
κατατίθημι (τίθημι), fut. καταθήσω, aor. 1 κατέθηκα, aor. 2 only plur. in the Ep. forms κάτθεμεν, κάτθετε, κάτθεσαν, for κατέθεμεν, κατέθετε, etc., subj. καταθείομεν, Ep. for καταθῶμεν, infin. κατθέμεν, Ep. for καταθεῖναι, aor. 2 mid. plur. κατέθεμεθα, κατθέσθην, Ep. for κατεθέμεθα, κατεθέσθην, and 3 plur. κάτθεντο, subj. καταθείομαι, Ep. for καταθῶμαι, 21, 111; *to set down, to put down, to lay down, to place in, to put away*, with accus. ἐπὶ χθονός and ἐπὶ χθονί, 3, 293. 6, 473; τινὰ ἐν λιχέεσσι, 18, 233; τόξα ἐς μυχόν, Od. 16, 285; τί τινι, to propose as a combat-prize, 23, 267. 851; ἄεθλον, to propose a contest, Od. 19, 572 (cf. 576]; τινὰ εἰς Ἰθάκην, to land any one in Ithaca, Od. 16, 230. Mid. *to lay down for oneself* (with reference to the subject); τεύχεα ἐπὶ γαίῃ, Il. 3, 114. 22, 111; ὅπλα νηός, h. Ap. 457; *of the dead, to lay out, to inter*, Od. 24, 190. 3) =

*Καταιρίζω. 233 Κατέρχομαι.

ing up, to keep, τὶ ἐπὶ δόρπῳ, Od. 18, 45.

*καταιρίζω (τρίζω), spoken of the piercing cry of birds, mice, etc., to squeak, to squeal; and generally, to wail, to lament, Batr. 88.

κατατρύχω (τρύχω), to wear out, to consume, to exhaust, λαοὺς δώροις, 17, 225. Od. 15, 309. 16, 84.

*καταιρώγω (τρώγω), aor. κατέτρωξα, to gnaw, to corrode, to consume, Batr. 126.

καταῦθι, adv. on the spot, there, 13, 253. Od. 10, 567; a false reading for κατ' αὖθι.

καταφαγεῖν, infin. aor. to κατεσθίω.

*καταφαίνω (φαίνω), to show; mid. to become visible, to show oneself, h. Ap. 431.

καταφέρω (φέρω), only fut. mid. κατοίσομαι, to bear down, to bring or conduct down. Mid. as depon. τινὰ Ἄϊδος εἴσω, any one to the realms of Hades, 22, 425.†

*καταφθινύθω, a form of καταφθίω, only pres. to destroy, to annihilate, τιμήν, h. Cer. 334.

καταφθίω (φθίω), fut. καταφθίσω, perf. pass. κατέφθιμαι, pluperf. κατεφθίμην, which is at the same time a syncop. aor. mid. infin. καταφθίσθαι, partcp. καταφθίμενος, 1) Act. trans. to destroy, to kill, to annihilate, τινά, Od. 5, 341. 2) Intrans. in the pass. and mid. to perish, to go to ruin, to vanish away. ἧα κατέφθιτο, the stores had vanished, Od. 4, 363; esply partcp. aor. destroyed, dead, Il. 22, 288; plur. subst. the dead, the shades, h. Cer. 347.

καταφλέγω (φλέγω), fut. ξω, to burn down, to consume, πάντα πυρί, 22, 512.†

καταφυλαδόν, adv. (φυλή), by tribes, divided into tribes, 2, 668.†

καταχέω (χέω), Ep. aor. 1 κατέχευα, Ep. aor. syncop. mid. κατέχυντο, 1) Prop. spoken of fluids: to pour over, to pour upon, to pour out. ἔλαιον χαιτάων τινί, to pour oil upon any one's hair, 23, 282; ὕδωρ.14, 435. 2) Of dry things: to pour down, to let fall, χιόνα, νιφάδας, Od. 19, 206. Il. 12, 158; πέπλον ἐπ' οὔδει, to let the robe fall on the floor, 1, 734; θύσθλα χαμαί, to let the staves, the thyrsi, fall to the ground, 6, 134; τεῖχος εἰς ἅλα, 7, 461. 3) Metaph. to pour out, to spread out, τί τινι; ὀμίχλην τινί, 3, 10; ἀχλὺν τινί, Od. 7, 42; χάριν τινί, Od. 2, 12. 8, 19; ἐλεγχείην, αἰσχός τινι, to pour reproach, insult upon any man, 23, 408. Od. 11, 433; πλοῦτόν τινι, Il. 2. 670. Mid. to flow down, to fall down, only Ep. sync. aor. εἰς ἄντλον, Od. 12, 411.

καταχθόνιος, ον (χθών), subterranean, Ζεύς = Hades (Pluto), 9, 457.†

κατέαξα, see κατάγνυμι.

κατέδω (ἔδω), Ep. for the prose κατεσθίω, fut. κατέδομαι, perf. act. κατέδηδα, in tmesis. 17, 542; to eat up, to devour, to consume, prim. spoken of brutes; with accus. Il. metaph. to consume, to waste,

οἶκον, κτήματα, Od. 2, 237. ὃν θυμὸν κατέδειν, to consume (devour, prey upon) one's own heart, to feed on grief [Cp.], Il. 6, 202.

*κατεέργω (εἴργω), aor. κατέερξα, to drive in, to shut up, βοῦς, h. Merc. 356.

κατείβω (εἴβω), poet. = καταλείβω, 1) Act. to let flow down, to shed, δάκρυ, Od. 21, 86. 2) Mid. to flow down, to trickle down, with gen. παρειῶν, Il. 24, 794; spoken of the water of the Styx, 15, 37; metaph. κατείβετο αἰών, life flowed away, Od. 5, 152.†

κατείδον (ΕΙΔΩ), partcp. κατιδών, 4, 508. Batr. 11; defect. aor. 2 of καθοράω, to look down.

κατειλύω (εἰλύω), fut. ύσω, to surround, to cover, τινὰ ψαμάθοις, any one with sand, 21, 318.† In tmesis.

κάτειμι (εἶμι), partcp. pres. κατιών, Ep. and aor. mid. κατασεισάμην for κατεισ-, 1) to descend, to go down; δόμον Ἄϊδος, into the abode of Hades 14, 457. 2) Metaph. spoken of a river, to flow down, 11, 492; of a ship, to proceed, ἐς λιμένα, Od. 16, 472; of missiles: δόρυ κατεσίσατο γαίης, the spear entered the earth, Il. 11, 358.

κατέπαθεν, see καταπτείνω.

κατεναίρω (ἐναίρω), only aor. mid. κατενηράμην, to slay, to kill, τινὰ χαλκῷ, Od. 11, 519.†

κατεναντίον, adv. (ἐναντίον), over against, opposite, τινί, 21, 567.†

*κατενήνοθε (ἐνήνοθα), an old perf. with the signif. of the pres. and imperf., to lie upon, to be upon. κόμαι κατενήνοθεν ὤμους, hairs covered the shoulders, h. Cer. 280; the connexion of the subst. fem. plur. with a verb in the sing. is called schema Pindaricum, cf. Rost Gram. § 100, p. 478. Kühner, § 370.

κατένωτα, adv. (ἐνωπή), directly before the face, opposite, with gen. Δαναῶν, 15, 320.† More correctly, κατ' ἐνῶπα, see ἐνώψ.

κατεπάλμενος, see κατεφάλλομαι.

κατέπαλτο, see κατασάλλω.

κατερείπω (ἐρείπω), prop. to snatch down; in the aor. and perf., aor. κατήριπον, perf. κατερήριπα, intrans. to fall down, to tumble down, spoken of a wall, 14, 55. Metaph. κατήριπεν ἔργα αἰζηῶν, the labours of the youths perished, Vors, Il. 5, 92.

κατερητύω (ἐρητύω), to restrain, to check, τινά, 9, 465. Od. 3, 31.

κατερικάνω, poet. for κατερύκω, 24, 218.†

κατερύκω (ἐρύκω), 1) to stop, to check, τινά, 6, 190. Od. 3, 345. 2) to retard, to detain, to hinder; in a bad sense, τινά, 23, 734. Od. 2, 242; hence pass. to linger, Od. 1, 197. 4, 498.

κατερύω (ἐρύω), aor. 1 κατέρυσα, perf. pass. κατείρυσμαι, to pull down, to draw down, always of ships, which are drawn down from the shore into the sea, with accus. Od. 5, 261. Pass. *Od. 8, 151.

κατέρχομαι, depon. (ἔρχομαι), fut. κατελεύσομαι, aor. κατῆλθον, poet. κατ-

Καυλός. **235** Κεΐσε.

were a remnant of the ancient Pelasgians, a part of whom migrated to Asia, Hdt. 1, 146. cf. Mannert. VIII. s. 352.

καυλός, ό, prop. *a stem, a handle;* in H. according to the Schol., the end of the shaft which was inserted into the socket of the spear's head, *the spear-shaft*, 13, 162. 16, 115; but 16, 338, *the hand-guard* of the sword. *II.

καῦμα, τό (καίω). *a fire, heat,* esply *the heat of the sun*, 5, 865.†

καυστειρός, ή, όν (καίω), *burning, hot,* μάχη, *4, 342. 12, 316.

Καΰστριος, ό, Ep. for Κάϋστρος, *Cayster*, a river in Ionia, which rises in Lydia, and flows into the sea near Ephesus, 2, 461 (ὡς διὰ κεκαυμένης ῥέων).

ΚΑΦΩ. Ep. obsol. pres. akin to κάπτω and καπνόω, *to gasp, to breathe forth,* from which only partcp. perf. in the accus. κακαφηότα θυμόν, the gasping soul, occurs 5, 698. Od. 5, 468.

κε, before a vowel κεν, an enclit. particle, Ep. and Ion. for ἄν, q. v.

Κεάδης, ου, ὁ, son of Κεας = *Trœzenius*, 2, 847.

κεάζω (κέω), aor. 1 ἐκέασα, Ep. σσ, perf. pass. κεκέασμαι, aor. pass. ἐκεάσθην, *to split, to cleave,* prop. spoken of splitting wood, Od.; *to split in pieces, to crash,* spoken of lightning, Od. 5, 132. Pass. κεφαλὴ ἄνδιχα κεάσθην, the head was split in two pieces, 16, 412. 578. 20, 387.

*κέαρ, αρος, τό, contr. κῆρ, *the heart*, Batr. 212.

κέαται, κέατο, Ep. and Ion. for κεῖνται, ἔκειντο, from κεῖμαι.

*Κεβρήνιος, ίη. ιον, *Cebrenian, belonging to the town Kebrēn (Cebren)* in Æolia; subst. the inhabitants of Kebrēn, Ep. 10.

Κεβριόνης, ου, ό, son of Priam, and charioteer of Hector, slain by Patroclus, 8, 318. 16, 738, seq.

κεδάννυμι, Ep. for σκεδάννυμι, aor. ἐκέδασα, Ep. σσ, aor. pass. ἐκεδάσθην, *to scatter, to disperse, to dissipate,* κύνας, φάλαγγας, 17, 283. 285. Od. 3, 131; pass. Il. 2, 398. κεδασθείσης ὑσμίνης, when the battle had scattered, i. e. when it was no longer fought in dense crowds, 15, 328. 16, 306. *b)* Of lifeless things, rare: *to tear away, to prostrate,* spoken of a torrent, γεφύρας, 5, 88. (H. has not the pres.)

κεδνός, ή. όν (κῆδος), superl. κεδνότατος, 9. 586. 1) Act. *careful, prudent, provident, trusty,* epith. of persons upon whom the conscientious attendance rests, Od.; hence neut. plur. as adv. κέδν' εἰδυῖα, of a careful, faithful disposition, Od. 1, 428. 2) Pass. *worthy of care, estimable, dear,* ἕταιροι, 9, 586; τοκῆες. 17, 28. Od. 10. 225.

κέδρινος, η, ον (κέδρος), *of cedar,* θάλαμος, 24, 192.†

κέδρος, ἡ, *the cedar-tree,* whose fragrant wood was used for fumigation, and of which a species is vet produced in Greece, Od. 5, 60; prob. *juniperus oxycedrus*, Linn.†

κειάμενος, κειάντες, see καίω.

κείαται, κείατο, see κεῖμαι.

κεῖθεν, adv. Ion. and Ep. for ἐκεῖθεν, *from there, thence,* Il. and Od. κεῖθεν φράσομαι ἔργον, then I will consider what is to be done, Il. 15, 234.

κεῖθι, adv. Ion. and Ep. for ἐκεῖθι, *there, in that place,* 3, 402. Od. 3, 110. κἀκεῖθι, another reading for καὶ κεῖθι, Il. 22, 390.

κεῖμαι (prop. perf. pass. from κέω), 2 sing. κεῖσαι. Ep. also κέιαι, h. Merc. 254; 3 plur. κεῖνται, Ep. κέαται, κείαται and κέονται, 22, 510; subj. κέωμαι, 3 sing. κῆται, 19, 32. Od. 2, 102; for the earlier reading κεῖται (which Buttm. Gram. ¶ 109, prefers), infin. κεῖσθαι, imperf. ἐκείμην, Ep. κείμην, 3 plur. ἔκειντο, Ep. κέατο and κείατο, 3 sing. iterat. κέσκετο, Od. 21, 41: fut. κείσομαι; primary signif. prop. to be laid; hence *to lie.* 1) Spoken of animate beings; of men: *to lie, to repose, to rest,* spoken of the sleeping, the inactive, the sick, the weak, the wounded, the miserable, and the dead; esply to lie unburied, 5, 685. 19, 32. 2) Spoken of inanimate things: *a)* Of regions, countries, islands: *to lie: to be situated,* Od. 7, 244. 9, 25. *b)* Of things: *to lie, to be,* esply of valuable objects, *to be treasured up, to be in store.* κτήματα, κειμήλια κεῖται ἐν δόμοις, 9, 382. 11, 132. κεῖται ἄεθλον, the prize is fixed, 23, 273: also spoken of chariots, ἅρματα κεῖτο, 2, 777 *c)* Metaph. spoken of conditions: πένθος ἐνὶ φρεσὶ κεῖται, sadness is in the soul, Od. 24, 423; and often ταῦτα θεῶν ἐν γούνασι κεῖται, see γόνυ.

κειμήλιον, τό (κεῖμαι), a valuable article which is laid aside and preserved, *a valuable, a jewel*, 6, 47. 9, 330; esply spoken of gifts of hospitality. Od. 1, 312. 4, 600. In the most general signif. it means property stored up, in opposition to herds and flocks. κειμήλιά τε πρόβασίς τε, stores and grazing animals, Voss, Od. 2, 75.

κεῖνος, κείνη, κεῖνο, *that one, he, she, it,* Ep. and Ion. for ἐκεῖνος, q. v.; κείνῃ, subaud. ὁδῷ, in that way, Od. 13, 111.

κεινός, κεινή, κεινόν, Ep. for κενός, *empty*, 3, 376. 4, 181. 11, 160. 15, 453.

κείρω, fut. κερῶ, infin. κερέειν, aor. 1 Ep. ἔκερσα, aor. 1 mid. ἐκειράμην, 1) *to cut off, to shear off.* κόμην τινί, 23, 146; δοῦρα, 24, 450. 2) *to consume, to devour, to graze,* spoken of brutes, λήϊον, 11, 560; δημόν, 21, 204; ἧπαρ, Od. 11, 578. 3) *to eat up, to waste, to destroy,* κτήματα, Od. 2, 312; in like manner βίοτον, Od. 1, 378. 2, 143: metaph. *to render void,* see ἐπικείρω. Mid. *to cut off a man's hair,* which the mourner consecrated to the dead. as an offering, κόμην, χαίτας, 23, 46. Od. 4, 198. 24, 46.

κεῖσε, adv. Ion. and Ep. for ἐκεῖσε,

which is not found in H., *thither*, 12, 356. Od. 4, 274.

κείω and κέω, Ep. fut. without the characteristic of the tense, from the obsolete root ΚΕΩ, *to wish to lie down, to desire to sleep or rest*, Od. 19, 340; often as partcp. βῆ δὲ κείων, Od. 14, 532. ἴομεν κείοντες, 14, 340 ὄρσο κέων Od. 7, 342; Infin. κειέμεν, Od. 8, 315.

κείω, ground form of κεάζω, *I split*, Od. 14, 425.†

κεκαδήσομαι, see κήδω.
κεκαδήσω, see χάζομαι.
κεκάδοντο, aor. of χάζομαι.
κεκαδών, see χάζομαι.
κεκάμω, see κάμνω.
κέκασμαι, see καίνυμαι.
κεκαφηώς, see ΚΑΦΩ.
κέκλετο, see κέλομαι.
κέκληγα, see κλάζω.
κεκλήατο, see καλέω.
κεκλόμενος, see κέλομαι.
κέκλυθι, κέκλυτε, see κλύω.
κέκμηκα, see κάμνω.
κεκοπώς, see κόπτω.
κεκόρημαι and κεκορηότε, see κορέννυμι.
κεκορυθμένος, see κορύσσω.
κεκοτηώς, see κοτέω.
κεκρδαντει, κεκρδαντο, see κραίνω.

κεκρύφαλος, ὁ (κρύπτω), a net, knit or twisted, with which women confined their hair, *a head-net, a net cap*, 22, 469.†

κεκύθωσι, see κεύθω, Od.

κελαδεινός, ή, όν (κέλαδος), *rushing, noisy*. Ζέφυρος, 23, 208. h. Merc. 95; chiefly an epith. of Artemis, as goddess of the chase, 16, 183; as prop. name, 21, 511.

κελαδέω, poet. (κέλαδος), aor. 1 κελάδησα, *to rush, to make a noise, to cry, to make a tumult*, spoken of men, 23, 869.† see ἐπικελαδέω.

κέλαδος, ὁ, *a rushing noise, a tumult, a cry*, esply of the chase, Il.; spoken of the suitors, Od. 18, 402.

κελάδω = κελαδέω, poet. only partcp. pres. κελάδων, *rushing, roaring*, spoken of water, 18, 576. 21, 16; of wind, Od. 2, 421.

Κελάδων, οντος, ὁ, prop. name, a little river, in Ells or Arcadia, which flows into the Alpheus, 7, 133. According to Strab. VIII. p. 348, some critics would here read 'Ακίδων, cf. Ottfr. Müller, Orchom. p. 372.

κελαινεφής, ές, poet. (νέφος), *cloudy*, generally *black, dark*, αἷμα, 4, 140. 16, 667. 2) Freq. an epith. of Zeus, *enveloped in black clouds*, as the god of rain and tempest, 2, 412; as prop. name, Od. 13, 147. (Some Gramm. and the Etym. M., p. 501, explain it actively, *cloud-darkener*. Modern critics have even derived it from κέλλω, cloud-compeller, like νεφεληγερέτης.)

κελαινός, ή, όν. Ep. for μέλας (Buttm. Gram. § 16, 2), *black, dark*, often αἷμα, also δέρμα, νύξ, κῦμα, λαῖλαψ. *5, 310. 6, 117. 11, 747. κελαινή χθών, 16, 384; for which Spitzner, far better, reads κελαινή. in reference to λαῖλαπι.

κελαρύζω, poet. *to rush, to roar, to gush, to flow*, spoken of blood, 11, 813; of water, 21, 261. Od. 5, 523.

*Κελεός, ὁ, *Celeus*, son of Eleusis, father of Triptolemus, king of Eleusis. h. Cer. 105.

κέλευθος, ἡ (κέλλω), plur. οἱ κέλευθα, and τὰ κέλευθα, in H., 1) *a way, a path, a course*, often ὑγρά and ἰχθυόεντα κέλευθα, the watery and fishy paths, spoken of the voyages of seamen, 1, 312. Od. 3, 71. 177; also ἀνέμων, Od. 5, 383. ἐγγὺς νυκτός τε καὶ ἤματός εἰσι κέλευθοι, the paths of night and day are near, Od. 10, 86. The ancient critics in part understood it of place (τοπικῶς) in the sense, that the pastures of the night, (for the kine,) and of the day, (for the sheep,) were situated near the city; and in part of time, as a figurative representation of the short nights and long days, the rising of Helios, as it were, coinciding with the night; hence a sleepless man might earn double wages. This last explanation, proposed by Crates, seems to be required by the context, as Nitzsch at loc. shows at large. The poet presupposes the well-known custom of driving out the kine very early, and folding the sheep very late. A man, therefore, who should renounce all sleep, might ear double wages, first with the kine, driving them out at day-break, and secondly, with the sheep, since it is scarcely dark before it becomes light again. The poet does not indeed here consider whether the herdsman is at home when the sheep must be driven out. It only occurred to him that the returning shepherd, if willing to forego sleep, might become the out-driving herdsman. 2) the act of going, the *course* which a man takes, a *journey*. χάζεσθαι κελεύθου, *to retire from one's course*, i. e. place, 11. 504. 12, 262. 14, 282. 3) Metaph. *walk, course of life*, θεῶν, 3, 406; see ἀποσκεδαίω.

κελευτιάω (frequentat. from κελεύω), only partcp. pres. κελευτιόων, Ep. for κε λευτιῶν, *to command now here and now there, to exhort frequently*, *12, 265. 13, 125.

κελεύω (κέλομαι), fut. κελεύσω, aor. 1 ἐκέλευσα, Ep. κέλευσα, prop *to urge on, to drive*, μάστιγι, 23, 642; hence, 1) *to call to, to exhort, to order, to command, to demand*. spoken not only of rulers, but also 2) Of equals: *to desire, to wish*, Il 781 Od. 10, 17. It is construed a) With the dat. τινί, very often : *to call to* any one, *to command*, 2, 151. 442; or with dat. of pers. and accus. of the thing, ἀμφιπόλοισι ἔργα, 6, 324; and instead of the accus. with the infin. 1, 50. Od. 2, 9. b) More frequently with accus. of the pers. and infin. 11. 2, 114. 5, 318. 10, 242. 17, 30, seq.; more rarely with accus. of the pers. alone : τινά, *to exhort any one, to demand*, 13, 784. Od.

Κέλης. 237 Κέρας.

4, 274. 8, 204. 9, 278; and c) With double accus., 7, 68. 349. 20, 87.
κέλης, ητος, ὁ (κέλλω), *a racer, racehorse, courser*, a riding-horse for running-races, ἵππος, Od. 5, 371.†
κελητίζω (κέλης), *to ride upon a race-horse*, and generally, *to ride*, ἵπποισι, 15, 679.†
κέλλω [~ *pello*; cf. κύαμος, πύαμος, &c., or κίω as obsol. *cillo* ~ *cio*. Lob. Techn. 117], poet. aor. 1 ἔκελσα, only in the aor. 1) Trans. *to drive, to urge on*; νῆα, *to propel the ship* to land, *appellere*, Od. 9, 549. 10, 511. 12, 5. 2) Intrans. *to strike the ground* [Cp.]. to run in to a low sandy shore. ἡ νηῦς ἔκελσα, *Od. 9, 144.
κέλομαι, poet. (κέλλω), fut. κελήσομαι, aor. 2 Ep. ἐκεκλόμην, κεκλόμην. partcp. κεκλόμενος, 1) = κελεύω, *to urge on, to exhort, to command. to bid. to advise*; an unusual meaning is: ἐπεὶ κέλετο μεγάλη ἴς (the wax melted), since a great force constrained it, Od. 12, 175; viz. the wax became soft through the strong pressure of the hands. since the following verse (176), which refers it to the sun, is probably not genuine. Construct. as with κελεύω, chiefly with accus. of pers. and with accus. and infin. 2) *to call to, to call*, chiefly in aor. with dat. of pers. 6, 66. 110. 8, 172; with accus. Ἥφαιστον, 18, 391.
κέλσαι, see κέλλω.
κεμάς, άδος, ἡ, poet. according to the Gramm. a kind of *deer* or *roe* [*hind*. Cp.]; according to Aristot. Hist. A. 9. 6, 2, a two-year old deer, 11. 10, 361.†
κέν, see κέ.
κενεαυχής, ές, poet. (αὐχή) *empty-boasting; vain-glorious* [Cp.], 8, 230 †
κενεός, ή, όν, Ep. and Ion. for κενός, *empty, void*, χείρ, Od. 10, 42. 2) κενεὸν νέεσθαι, *to return empty*, i. e. with un-accomplished object [*re infecta*], 2, 298. Od. 15, 214.
κενεών, ῶνος, ὁ (κενεός), prop. any void space, esply *the flank*, the sides of the abdomen between the hips and the ribs, 5, 284. 11, 381. Od. 22, 295.
κενός, ή, όν, *empty, vain*, metaph. *idle, groundless*. κενὰ εὔγματα, Od. 22, 249. Hom. uses elsewhere κενεός and κεινός, q. v.
κένσαι, see κεντέω.
Κένταυροι, οἱ, *the Centaurs*. 1) In H., an ancient savage tribe in Thessaly, between Pelion and Ossa, who were expelled by the neighbouring Lapithæ. According to H. 1, 268, they were rough mountaineers of great stature (φῆρες ὀρεσκῷοι), 11, 382. Od. 21, 295. 2) Later, prob. in Pindar's age, they were fabulously represented as possessing horses' feet, prob. because they were good riders, and gradually they were converted into monsters, half man, half horse, Batr. cf. Voss. Myth. Br. 11. 33; Κενταύρου for κεν ταύρου is the reading of Herm. h. Merc. 224. (Prob. from ταῦρος and κεντέω, ox-hunter.)

κεντέω, Ep. aor. infin. κένσαι, *to prick, to goad*, in order to urge on, ἵππον, 23, 337.†
κεντρηνεκής, ές (ἠνεκής), *urged with a goad, spurred*, *5, 752. 8, 396.
κέντρον, τό (κεντέω), *a goad* with which horses, oxen, and other draught-cattle are urged on, 23, 387. 430; the *horse goad*, or a whip ending in a goad (Voss).
κέντωρ, ορος, ὁ, poet. (κεντέω), *a goader, a driver*, ἵππων, an honorable epith. of the Cadmeans and Trojans, *4, 391. 5, 102.
κέομαι, Ep. and Ion. for κεῖμαι, from which κέονται.
κεραΐζω (akin to κείρω), *to destroy utterly, to lay waste, to raze*, with accus. πόλιν, σταθμούς, 5, 557. 24, 245. Od. 8, 516. 2) Of living beings: *to kill, to slay*, 2, 861.
κεραίνω, κεραίρω, another form of κεραίω, in 9, 203.
*κεραϊστής, οῦ, ὁ (κεραΐζω), *a destroyer, a plunderer*, h. Merc. 336.
κεραίω, Ep. for κεράννυμι, *to mingle, to mix*, only imperat. κέραιε, 9, 203.†
κεραμεύς, έως, ὁ (κέραμος), *a potter*, 18, 601.†
*κεραμήϊος, ίη, ιον (κέραμος), Ep. for κεράμειος, *of clay, earthen*, Ep. 14.
κέραμος, ὁ (ἔρα), 1) *potter's earth, potter's clay*, Ep. 14. 2) all kinds of ware burned of clay, *a bowl, a vessel, a pitcher*, 9, 469. 3) *a prison*, so called, according to the Schol., amongst the Cyprians, either from its form, or because any one was kept in it, as it were in a jug, χαλκέῳ ἐν κεράμῳ, 5, 387.
κεράννυμι, Ep. κεράω and κεραίω, also the poet. forms κιρνάω and κίρνημι, aor. 1 act. ἐκέρασα, Ep. σσ, aor. 1 mid. ἐκερασάμην, Ep. σσ; H. uses in the pres. act. κεράω, from which the partcp. κερώντας, Od. 24, 364; imper. κέραιε, 11. 9, 203, and κίρνημι, q. v., subj. pres. mid. κέρωνται, as if from κέραμαι, imperf. ἐκίρνα and κίρνη, imperf. mid. κερῶντο, Ep. for ἐκερῶντο from κηράω, Od. 8, 470; 1) *to mingle, to mix*, esply spoken of the mixing of wine and water, νέκταρ, οἶνον, Od. 5, 93. 24, 364; ἐνὶ κρητῆρσι, Il. 4, 260. 2) *to temper, to soften*, by mixing, spoken of bathing water, Od. 10, 362. Mid. *to mix for oneself*, often οἶνον ἐν κρητῆρσι,.to mingle wine for oneself in the mixers, Il. 4, 260 ; οἶνον alone Od. 3, 332. 8, 17; also κρητῆρα οἴνου, to mingle a mixer of wine, Od. 3, 393; and without gen. Od. 7, 179. 13, 50.
κεραοξόος, ον (ξέω), *smoothing* or *working horn*, τέκτων, 4, 110.†
κεραός, ή, όν, *horn-d*, ἔλαφος, 3, 24. 11, 475 ; ἄρνες, Od. 4, 85.
κέρας, τό, gen. Ep. κέραος, dat. κέρᾳ, plur. nom. κέρα, gen. κεράων, dat. κέρασι Ep. κεράεσσι. The α in κέρα is mly short. 1) *a horn*, chiefly of the bovine genus, as an image of fixedness, Od. 19, 211. 2) *horn*, as a material for artificial products, Od. 19, 563. 3) *every thing made of horn*, esply the *bow*, Od. 21,

Κῆαι. 239 **Κηρόθι.**

sleep, Od. 7, 342,† 2) as a form of καίω, it is doubtful, see Buttm. Gramm., § 114. p. 287.
κῆαι, κήαι (3 optat. aor.), κηάμενος, Ep. aor. forms from καίω
κήδειος, ον (κῆδος), Ep. also κήδεος, q. v. worth care, *dear, beloved*, 19, 224. (The other explanation : ' to be buried by us,' does not suit the connexion, 19, 294.) Superl. κήδιστος.
κηδεμών, όνος, ὁ (κηδέω), one who has the charge, *a guardian, a protector*, Il. •23, 163. 674, those who have charge of the interment of the dead.
κήδεος, ον, Ep. for κήδειος, οἷσι κήδεός ἐστι νέκυς, either generally, *dear*, or [less probably], according to Voss, ' upon whom devolves the care of the corpse,' 23, 160.† (Some Gramm. considered the word as gen. of κῆδος : ' to whom the dead is an object of care.')
κηδέω, absol. pres. of the fut. κηδήσω, see κήδω.
κήδιστος, η, ον (superl. formed from κῆδος, in signif. belonging to κήδειος), *dearest, most beloved*, 9, 642. Od. 10, 225. (In like manner, Od. 8, 583, without exactly indicating the nearest kindred.)
κῆδος, εος. τό, *care, sadness, trouble, grief*, τῶν ἄλλων οὐ κῆδος, about the others there is no care, i. e. there is no trouble with the others, Od. 22, 254. ὃσ' ἐμῷ ἐνὶ κήδεα θυμῷ. Il. 18, 53. κήδεα θυμοῦ, *heart-troubles*, Od. 14, 197 ; distinguished from ἄχος, Od. 4, 108 ; esply grief for the death of one dear to us, Il. 4, 270. 5, 156. 13, 464.-18, 8. 2) that which occasions care, *need, misery, wretchedness*; esply in the plur. 1; 445. 9, 592. Od. 1, 244 ; and often. (The signif. *relationship*, Voss, Il. 13, 464, 'if relationship touches thy soul,' is justly rejected by Passow.)
κήδω (ΚΑΔΩ), fut. κηδήσω, fut. mid. κεκαδήσομαι, iterat. imperf. κηδέσκετο, 1) Act. only Ep. *a) to render anxious, to sadden, to trouble, to distress*, τινά, 9, 615; θυμόν, 5, 400. 11, 458. *b) More frequently : to injure externally*, to violate, *to harass*, θεοὺς τόξοισιν, 5, 404 ; μῆλα, 17, 550 : οἶκον, Od. 23, 9. 2) Mid. *to be anxious, sad, to trouble oneself*, always partcp. 1, 196. Od. 3, 240. 3) *to be anxious about* any man, *to care for* any man, τινός, Il. 1, 56 ; Δαναῶν, 8, 353 ; βιότοιο, Od. 14, 4. (The aor. 2 κέκαδον and fut. κεκαδήσω, in the signif. *to deprive*, belongs to χάζομαι.)
κῆεν, see καίω.
κηκίω, *to gush forth, ro stream* (*from*), spoken of water, ἂν στόμα, out of the mouth, Od. 5, 455.† (from κίω, with reduplicat.)
κήλειος, ον, Ion. and Ep. for κήλεος, 15, 744.†
κήλεος, ον (κάω, καίω, like δαιδάλεος ·, *burning, flaming*, always πυρὶ κηλέῳ (the last dissyllabic), 8, 217. Od. 9, 328.
κηληθμός, ὁ (κηλέω), *enchantment, pleasure, transport*, *Od. 11, 334. 13, 2.

κῆλον, τό (καίω), prop. a dry stick of wood, esply *the shaft of an arrow : an arrow itself* in H. ; in the plur. κῆλα, *missiles, shafts:* used only of the gods, •1, 53. 12, 280. h. Ap. 444.
•Κηναῖον, τό, a promontory on the north-west coast of the island Eubœa, now *Cap Lithoda*, h. in Ap. 219.
κήξ, κός. ἡ = κηΰξ, a sea-bird, *the seahen*, or *sew-mew*, Od. 15. 479.†
κήομεν, Ep. for κήωμεν, see καίω.
κῆπος, ὁ, *a garden*, and generally a piece of land, inclosed and set with trees or other vegetation, 8, 305. Od. 4, 737. 7, 129.
Κήρ, κηρός. ἡ, *the goddess of death*, (distinct from Μοῖρα and Αἶσα), the personified power of death, which brings death in a particular form ; as death in battle, sickness, drowning in the sea, etc., hence, in sing. and plur. Κῆρες θανάτοιο, 2, 302. 11, 332; and Κήρ in connexion with φόνος, θάνατος. 2, 352. Od. 4, 273. 5, 387, 16, 169. He who was to die by a violent death had the Κήρ allotted him at birth, 23, 79. To Achilles were two Κῆρες allotted, 8, 411. Zeus laid the Κῆρες of Achilles and Hector in the scales, to determine which was to die first, 22, 210. The Κῆρες are μυρίαι, since one is allotted to each person who is destined to a violent death, 12, 326, 327. 2) As an appell. *fate, death*, in Wolf's ed. only once : τὸ δέ τοι κὴρ εἴδεται εἶναι, that seems to thee to be *death*, 1, 228. Bothe has it in many passages beside, 2, 352. 3, 32. 5, 22. e'c. which also Passow prefers. In 1, 97, Wolf, after a conjecture of Markland, has λοιμοῖο Κῆρας ἀφέξει instead of the reading of the Cdd. χεῖρας (κήρ prob. from κείρω, κείρω).
κῆρ, κῆρος. τό, contr. from κέαρ, Batr. *the heart*, esply 1) *the soul, the mind*, as the seat of the feelings and passions, 1, 44 ; chiefly the dative κῆρι as adv. *in the heart*, for the most part with περὶ preceding, (ed. Wolf) much at heart. 4, 46. 53. 13, 119. 430. Od. 5, 36, where πέρι is an adv. according to Passow. Spitzner rejects this and writes with the ancients περὶ κῆρι, in heart. That this is the true explanation is shown by the kindred phrases περὶ θυμῷ, περὶ φρεσίν, 22, 70. 16, 157. cf. περί. and Thiersch, § 264. p. 458. 2) As a periphrasis of the person, like βίη : Πυλαιμένεος λάσιον κῆρ, 2, 851. cf. Od. 4, 270.
κηρεσσιφόρητος, ον (φορέω), brought by *the Fates*, or *impelled by the Fates* [iniquo fato adrectus. Db.], [*these dogs*, κύνες, *whom Ilium's unpropitious fates Have wafted hither.* Cp.], i. e. the Greeks sent by the Κῆρες for the destruction of Troy 8, 527.
Κήρινθος, ἡ. a town in Eubœa, northeast of Chalcis, 2, 538.
•κηρίον, τό (κηρός), *a cake of honey, a honey-comb*, h. Merc. 559.
κηρόθι, adv. (κῆρ), *in the heart, heartily,*

Κηρόε.

strengthened by μᾶλλον, 9, 300. Od. 15, 369.

κηρός, ὁ, wax. *Od. 12, 48. 173. 175.

κῆρυξ, ῦκος, ὁ, *a herald*. The heralds were most respectable royal servants, and even of noble and often of royal blood, 1, 321. 3, 116. They receive as epithets, ἀγανοί, 3, 268; θεῖος, 4. 192. Their office was to convoke assemblies, and to preserve order in them. 2, 50. 280. In war they were employed to treat with the enemy, 7, 274, seq. Esply in time of peace all care of sacrifices and sacrificial feasts devolved upon them, Od. 1, 110. 3, 472. As an ensign of office they carried a sceptre, Il. 18, 505. Od. 2, 38. They were under the immediate protection of Zeus, Διὸς ἄγγελοι, Διΐ φίλοι, 1, 334. 8, 517. They placed the sceptre in the hand of one about to speak in the assembly, 24, 567, seq. Od. 2, 38; they waited at meals. Od. 1, 143. 146.

κηρύσσω (κήρυξ), 1) *to be a herald, to hold the office of herald*, 17, 325. 2) *to proclaim as a herald, to cry out*, 2, 438; with accus. λαὸν ἀγορήνδε, 2, 51. Od. 2, 7; πόλεμόνδε. Il. 2, 443.

κῆται, for κέηται, see κεῖμαι.

Κήτειοι, οἱ, the *Ceteans*, an unknown tribe In Mysia, so called from the river Κητώειε in the region of the later Elea or Pergamus, Od. 11, 521. (The old Gramm. were uncertain about them: Aristarchus explains ἑταῖροι κήτειοι by μεγάλοι from κῆτος; others read κήδειοι.)

κῆτος, εος, τό (according to Buttm., Lex. p. 378. from ΧΑΩ. χάσκω. prop. *a hollow, a chasm*, as appears in the deriv.), *any large sea-animal, a sea-monster*, 20, 147. Od. 5, 421; in Od. 4, 443. 446. 452 = φώκη.

κητώεις, εσσα, εν (κῆτος), only as an epith. of Lacedæmon, *having many chasms and hollows*; cf. Λακεδαίμων, 2, 581. Od. 4, 1: because it [the valley of the Eurotas] lies in a hollow, surrounded with mountains and narrow passes. Thus Buttm., Lex. p. 378, and Nitzsch; others, as Heyne, Voss, *spacious, vast, huge*, a definition less suited to fact.

Κηφισίς. ίδος, ἡ λίμνη, *the Cephisian lake*, 5, 709; elsewhere ἡ Κωπαῖς λίμνη, the *lake Copāis*, in Bœotia, which was nine geographical miles in circumference, and often occasioned a flood, now the lake of *Livadia* or *Topolia*. (It received its name from the river Κηφισός, q v.)

Κηφισός. ὁ, a river in Phocis; it rises near Lilæa, and flows into the lake Copais, now *Mauro-Nero*, 2, 522. (Κηφισσός, a later form, cf. Buttm. Gram. § 21.)

κηώδης, ες (κάω, καίω), *exhaling vapour, sweet-scented, fragrant*, κόλπος, 6, 467.† (according to Passow from an old subst. κῆος=θύος.)

κηώεις, εσσα, εν = κηώδης, *fragrant*, always epith. of θάλαμος, 3, 382. Od. 15, 99.

Κιμμέριοι.

κιθνάμαι (intrans.), Ep. mid. from ΐδ-νημι, poet. form of σκεδάννυμι, *to spread, to extend*, Ἠὼς ἐκίδνατο πᾶσαν ἐπ' αἶαν. *8, 1. 24, 695. ὑπεὶρ ἅλα, 23, 227.

κιθάρα, ἡ = κίθαρις, a later form, h Merc. 509. 515.

κιθαρίζω (κίθαρις), *to play upon the harp*, and generally, *to play upon a stringed instrument*, φόρμιγγι, 18, 570;† λύρῃ. h. Merc. 433.

κίθαρις, ιος, ἡ, accus. κίθαριν, *a harp, a lute*, a stringed instrument which differed in form from the lyre. According to Buretti in the Mémoir. des Inscript. de l'Acad. des Sciences à Paris IV. p 116, the *cithara* had two curved horns which at the top turned outwards and at the bottom inwards, and stood upon a hollow-sounding stand. Above and below were two cross-pieces for fastening the strings (ὑπολύριον and ζυγόν). The strings were strained above by pegs (κόλωπες). The *cithara* had a soft tone, and was closely related to the φόρμιγξ. 3, 54. Od. 1, 153. 2) *the act of playing upon the harp, the tone of stringed instruments*, Il. 13, 731. Od. 8, 248.

κιθαριστύς, ύος, ἡ, *the art of playing upon the cithara, harp playing*, 600.†

*κιθαριστής, οῦ, ὁ (κιθαρίζω), *a harp player, a harper*, h. 24, 3.

κικλήσκω, Ion. and Ep. form for καλέω in the pres. and imperf. 1) *to call*, τινά, 2, 404. 9, 11; *to call upon, to cry to*, Ἀΐδῃ, ν, 9, 569. 2) *to name*, with accus of the pers. and of the name, 2, 813. Od. 4, 355; and ἐπίκλησιν κικλήσκειν. *call by surname*, Il. 7, 139. Mid. Bat. 27.

Κίκονες, οἱ, sing. Κίκων, ονος, a people in Thrace, who dwelt along the southern coast of Ismarus to Lissus, 2, 846. Od. 39, seq.

κίκυς, ἡ, an ancient poet. word, *strength* Od. 11, 393.† h. Ven. 238. (According to Eustath. from κίω, *to go*; others write κηκίς, and explain it, *moisture, blood*.)

Κίλικες, οἱ, sing. Κίλιξ; the *Cilicians* had their seat in H.'s time in greater Phrygia. Here they were governed in two kingdoms, of which one had its capital at Thebe, at mount Placus, the other at Lyrnessus, 6, 397. 415. cf. 2, 692. At a later date they emigrated to the country called by their name.

Κίλλα, ἡ, a small town in Troas or in Æolis in Asia Minor, having a temple of Apollo, 1, 38. 452.

Κιμμέριοι, οἱ, *Cimmerii*, in H. a fabulous people, who dwelt in the western part of the earth, on Oceanus, north of the entrance to the under world; they are wrapped in clouds and storms, and live in perpetual night. Od. 11, 14, seq. The ancient critics place them either in Italy, in the region of Baiæ, or in Spain, cf. Strab. That the Cimmerian night indicates the extreme north

*Κίνδυνος.   241   Κλάζω.

cannot be denied; and we may certainly suppose that a dark rumour of a night lasting many months may have had a place in the poet's imagination, though he thought of no definite country. Völcker, Hom. Geogr. p. 154, derives the name from χειμέριος; Voss, on the other hand, from the Phoenician word *Kamar, Kimmer.*

κίνδυνος, ὁ, peril, danger, Batr. 9.

κινέω (κίω), poet. form, mid. κίνυμαι, fut. κινήσω, aor. 1 ἐκίνησα, aor. pass. ἐκινήθην, *to put in motion, to move, to excite, to urge on;* often κάρη, *to move the head,* 17, 200. Od. 5, 285; σφῆκας, *to excite the wasps,* Il. 16, 264; νεφέλην, 16, 297; κῦμα (spoken of wind), 2, 395; τινὰ λάξ, to thrust a man with one's foot (to awaken him), 10, 158; θύρην, Od. 22, 394. Mid. and pass. *to move oneself, to move.* κινήθη ἀγορή, ἐκινήθεν φάλαγγες, Il. 2, 144. 16, 280; *to move oneself forward,* i. e. *to go,* 1, 47.

κινητήρ, ῆρος, ὁ (κινέω), a mover, one who shakes; γαίης, *a shaker of the earth,* h. 21, 2.

κίνυμαι, mid. poet. form of κινέω, *to be moved.* κινύμενον ἐλαίων, 14, 173; often *to move oneself,* i. e. *to go, ἐς πόλεμον.* 4, 281. 332. 10, 280.

Κινύρης, αο, ὁ, Ion. for Κινύρας, ruler in Cyprus, 11, 20. Apd. 3, 14, 4; son of Sandacus, grandson of Phaëthon, at first king of Syria; he went afterwards to Cyprus and built Paphos, cf. Κινύρου πλουσιώτερος, Tyrt. III. 6.

κινυρός, ή, όν, *wailing, moaning, plaintive,* 17, 5.†

Κίρκη, ἡ, Kirkē (Circe), daughter of Helios and Persē, sister of Æētēs, a nymph, skilled in magic, who dwelt on the island Ææa. Od. 10, 136; see Αἶα. Odysseus (Ulysses), having escaped from the terrible Læstrygones, landed on her island. The enchantress metamorphosed his companions into swine; he compelled her to disenchant them, Od. 10, 230–364. He lived a year with Circe in perpetual feasting; and, in order to procure intelligence concerning his return, he visited, by her advice, the entrance of the infernal regions, Od. 10, 466, seq. 11, 1, seq. According to Hes. Th. 759, she bore two sons by Odysseus (Ulysses), Agrius and Latinus. (Herm. de Myth. Græc. Antiq. explains the name, *navigatio in orbem facta.*)

κίρκος, ὁ, *a hawk, a kind of falcon,* which describes circles in flying, 17, 757. 22, 139. Because his flight was regarded as ominous, he was called Ἀπόλλωνος ἄγγελος, Od. 15, 526; and also ἱρήξ κίρκος, *the circling hawk,* Od. 13, 87.

κιρνάω and κίρνημι, poet. form of κεράννυμι, *to mingle, to mix,* from which we have partcp. κιρνάς, Od. 6, 14; imperf. ἐκίρνα, Od. 7, 182. 10, 356; and from κίρνημι, imperf. κίρνη, *Od. 14, 78. 16, 52.

Κισσηΐς, ίδος, ἡ, daughter of Kisses

(Cisses)=*Thrāno*, 6, 299.

Κισσῆς, οῦ, ὁ, contr. from Κισσεύς, later Κισσεύς, έως, king of Thrace, father of Theāno, 11, 223. (Κισσεύς, from κισσός, crowned with ivy.)

κισσοκόμης, ου, ὁ (κομάω), having tresses of ivy, having the hair decorated with ivy, h. 25, 1.

κισσός. ὁ, ivy, a plant sacred to Dionysos, h. 6, 40.

κισσύβιον, τό, *a goblet, a cup,* prop. made of ivy wood, *Od. 9, 346. 14, 78. 16, 52.

κίστη, ἡ, *chest, a box,* Od. 6, 76.†

κιχάνω and* κιχάνομαι. Ep. imperf. ἐκίχανον, 2 sing. ἐκίχεις (cf. ἐτίθεις). dual ἐκιχήτην, 1 plur. ἐκίχημεν, fut. κιχήσομαι (as if from κιχέω), aor. 2 ἔκιχον, and aor. 1 mid. ἐκιχήσατο, partcp. pres. mid. κιχήμενος; also from an obsol. form κίχημι, pres. subj. κιχῶ, Ep. κιχείω, optat. κιχείην, inf. κιχῆναι, partcp. κιχείς, 1) *to reach, to attain, to overtake;* with accus. ποσσὶ τινά, *to overtake a man with the feet,* i. e. in running, 6, 228; δουρί, 10, 370; metaph. spoken of death and destruction, 9, 416. 11, 441. 451. κιχάνει δίψα τε καὶ λιμός, 19, 165. cf. κιχήμενον βέλος, *a hitting arrow,* with gen. of pers. 5, 187. 2) *to hit, to meet with, to find,* τινὰ παρὰ νηυσί, 1, 26. Od. 13, 228.

κίχλη, ἡ, *the thrush,* Od. 22, 468.†

κίχρημι (χράω), fut. χρήσω, to lend, mid. to borrow, only χρησαμένη, Batr. 187.

κίω, poet. form from εἶμι, ΊΩ, in pres. indicat. obsol., only optat. κίοιμι, partcp. κιών, imperf. ἔκιον, κίον, *to go, to go away,* like εἶμι, spoken of living beings; only, 2, 509. κίον νῆες.

κίων, ονος, ἡ, and masc. ὁ, Od. 8, 66. 473. 17, 29. 19, 38; *a pillar, a column,* only spoken of the pillars which supported the roof of the eating-room. Od. 1, 127. 6, 307. 19, 38, seq. 22, 466; metaph. spoken of Atlas, ἔχει κίονας μακράς, see Ἄτλας. *Od.

κλαγγή, ἡ (κλάζω), generally an inarticulate sound, produced by animate and inanimate objects; *a sound, a noise,* spoken of men; *a cry, a tumult,* spoken of warriors, 2, 100. 10, 523; of the dead, Od. 11, 604; of animals, reply of cranes, Il. 3, 2; of swine, Od. 14, 412; or the roar of lions, h. 13, 4; of the twang of the bow, Il. 1, 49.

κλαγγηδόν, adv. (κλαγγή), *with a cry, with a clamour,* 2, 463.†

κλάζω, aor. 1 ἔκλαγξα, Ep. perf. with pres. signif. κέκληγα, partcp. κεκληγώς, of this the plur. is κεκλήγοντες (as if from a pres. κεκλήγω), aor. 2 ἔκλαγον, spoken of any articulate sound, *to resound, to clang, to ring, to cry,* spoken of the cry of men, 2, 222. 12, 125; of the cry of the eagle, 12, 207. 16, 429; of herons and jackdaws, 10, 276. 17, 756; of the barking of dogs, Od. 14, 30; *to resound, to whiz* or *hum,* spoken of arrows, Il. 1,

Κλαίω. 242 **Κλῆρος.**

46; *to roar at him*, spoken of the wind, Od. 12, 408. ἔκλαγεν οἷος. in h. 18, 14, according to Herm. ad loc. *soius sub vesperam fistula canit* (Pan).
κλαίω, fut. κλαύσομαι, aor. 1 ἔκλαυσα, Ep. κλαῦσα, Ep. iterat. imperf. κλαίεσκον, 1) *to weep, to wail, to lament*, absol. κλαίοντά σε ἀφήσω, I will send thee forth weeping, i. e. I will punish thee, 2, 263; esply *to weep for the dead*, 7, 427. 19, 75. 2) With accus. *to weep for any man, to bewail*, 22, 87. 210. Od. 1, 363, and often.

*Κλάρος, ἡ, a small town near Colophon in Ionia, upon a point of land, with a temple and oracle of Apollo; now *Zille*, h. Ap. 40.
κλαυθμός, ὁ (κλαίω), *the act of weeping or wailing, lamentation*, 24, 717, and often Od.
κλάω, aor. 1 Ep. κλάσε, aor. pass. ἐκλάσθην, *to break, to break off*, with accus. πτόρθον, Od. 6, 128. Pass. intrans. *to break in pieces*, Il. 11, 584.
κληηδών, όνος, ἡ, once κληηδών, Od. 4, 317; Ion. and Ep. for κληδών (κλέος), 1) *report, rumour, fame*; πατρός, intelligence about one's father, Od. 4, 317. 2; Esply *a divine voice, an omen*, like ὄσσα, *Od. 18, 117. 20, 120.
Κλεισιδίκη, daughter of Keleos (Celeus), in Eleusis, h. in Cer. 109.
κλειτός, ή, όν (κλείω), *famous, glorious, excellent, illustrious*, spoken of persons, 3. 451. Od. 6, 54; of things: ἐκατόμβη, often Il.; Πανοπεύς, 17, 307.
Κλεῖτος, ὁ. *Clitus*, son of Pisênor, a Trojan, 15, 445, seq. 2) son of Mantius, grandson of Melampus, Od. 15, 249.
κλείω, poet. for κλέω (from κλέω; H. has only pres. pass. κλέομαι, imperf. ἔκλεο for ἐκλέεο, 24, 202; also fut. act. κλήσω. h. 31, 19); *to make known, to render famous; to praise*, with accus. ἔργα, Od. 1, 338. 17, 418. Pass. *to be made known, to be famous, ἐπ' ἀνθρώπους, Il. 21, 202; whereby κέρδεσιν, Od. 13, 299.
Κλεόβουλος, ὁ, a Trojan, slain by Ajax, son of Oïleus, 16, 330.
Κλεοπάτρη, ἡ, daughter of Idas and Marpessa, wife of Meleagros (Meleager), see Ἀλκυόνη, 9, 556.
κλέος, εος, τό (κλέω), 1) *report, rumour, fame*, 2. 486; with gen. κλέος Ἀχαιῶν, the report of the Greeks, 11, 227; πολέμοιο, 13, 364; πατρός, Od. 2, 308. 3, 83; σὸν κλέος, intelligence of thee, Od. 13, 415; ἐμόν, Od. 18, 255. 2) *a good report, fame, glory, honour*, in connexion with ἐσθλόν, μέγα, εὐρύ, and alone Il. 4, 197; and often in the plur. κλέα ἀνδρῶν, for κλέεα, famous deeds, *laudes*, 9, 189. 524. Od 8, 73.
κλέπτης, ου, ὁ (κλέπτω), *thief, robber*, 3, 11.†
κλεπτοσύνη, ἡ, *thievery, knavery, deception*, Od 19, 396.†
κλέπτω, aor. 1 ἔκλεψα, 1) *to steal, to procure by stealth*, 5, 269. 24, 24. 2)

Metaph. *to deceive, in cheat, to overreach*, νόον τινός, 14, 217; absol. μὴ κλέπτε νόῳ, cherish not deception in thy soul (Voss, 'meditate not deceit') I, 132.
κλέω, from which pass. κλέομαι, see κλείω.
Κλεωναί, αἱ, *Cleônæ*, a town in Argolis, south-west of Corinth, 2, 570.
*κλεψίφρων, ον (φρήν), *having deceitful purposes, cunning, crafty*, h. Merc. 413.
κληδήν, adv. (καλέω), *by name, namely*, 9, 11.†
κληηδών, όνος, Ep. form of κληδών, q. v.
κλήθρη, ἡ, Ion. for κλήθρα, *the alder*, alnus, *Od. 5, 64. 239.
κληίζω, as a form of κλείω. κλήϊω is incorrect, see Buttm. Ausführ. Gram. Th. 2, p. 169.
*κληΐθρον, τό, Ion. and Ep. for κλῆθρον, *a lock, a bolt*, h. Merc. 146.
κληΐς, ῖδος(ῑ), ἡ, Ion. and Ep. for κλείς, (only in the Ion. form), 1) Prop. that which locks, *a) the bolt or bar*, which locks the door inside, and which from without is pulled forward with a thong; to unlock, after untying the thong, the bolt is pressed back with a hook. ἐν κληῖδ'(ῑ) ἱμάντι, Od. 1, 442. II. 24, 455. This bolt is also called ἐπιβλής. 24, 453; and ὀχεύς, 12, 121. *b) the bolt*, which locked together two corresponding bars, 12, 456. 14, 168. *c*) Esply *a key*, of brass, with ivory handle, with which the door was locked and opened, Od. 21, 6. Il. 6, 89. It was a curved hook with which, in locking, the bolt was thrust forward; in opening, pushed back through a hole, into which the key was introduced, Od. 21, 6. 47. 241. *d*) the *hook* of a clasp, Od. 18, 294. 2) the *clavicle*, the bone between the neck and breast, Il. 5, 146. 8, 325. plur. 22, 324; (in the Od. it has not this signif. 3) κληΐδες(ῑ), only in the plur. the *rowers' seats* in the ship, i. e. the seats where the oars were worked in leather thongs in the manner of a key, Od. 2, 419. 4, 579. Il. 16, 170.† cf. Voss ad Arat. Phænom. 191.
κληϊστός, ή, όν (κληίω), Ion. for κλειστός, *locked, that may be locked*. Od. 2, 344.†
κληΐω, Ion. and Ep. for κλείω (κλῄζω), aor. 1 ἐκλήϊσα, *to shut up, to lock*, with accus. θύρας, Od. 19. 30. 24, 166. (κλήϊσσεν with σσ is incorrect, as ι is long), *Od.
*κληροπαλής, ές (πάλλω), *distributed by shaking lots*, by lot, h. Merc. 129.
κλῆρος, ὁ. 1) *a lot*, any thing used for casting lots; in the earliest times, stones, pieces of wood, etc., marked by those who were casting lots, 7, 175. In H. the lots are placed in a helmet, shaken, and he whose lot first leapt out of the helmet, was the individual destined by the lot, 3, 316. 325. Od. 10, 206. 2) that which is obtained by lot, esply

heritance, Il. 15, 198. Od. 14, 64. (From κλάω, because a fragment was used for a lot.)

κλητός, ή, όν (καλέω), 1) *called, called out*, hence *chosen*, 9, 165. 2) *summoned, invited*, Od. 17, 386.

κλήω = κλείω, *to celebrate, to render famous*, κλήω, h. 31, 16; κλήσαι, Ep. 4, 9.

κλῖμαξ, ακος, ἡ (κλίνω), *a ladder, a staircase*, *Od. 1, 330. 10, 558. 21, 5.

κλιντήρ, ήρος, ὁ (κλίνω), *an easy chair, a couch*, Od. 18, 190.†

κλίνω, aor. 1. ἔκλινα, perf. pass. κέκλιμαι, 3 plur. Ep. κεκλίαται, aor. pass, ἐκλίθην, Ep. ἐκλίνθην, ground signif., 1) Act. *to incline, to bend*. 1) *to incline, to lean*, τί τινι, any thing against another: σάκεα ὤμοισι, 11. 593. 13, 488; ἅρματα πρὸς ἐνώπια, 8, 435; τόξον πρὸς ἐνώπια, Od. 22, 121. 2) *to incline*, to change the direction, τάλαντα. *to bend* the balances, so that one scale rises and the other falls, 19, 223: ὄσσε πάλιν, *to turn back*, 3, 427. Esply 3) *to bend, to force to yield, to put to flight*, μάχην Τρώας, 14, 510. 5, 37. Od. 9, 59. II) Mid. with aor. pass. *to incline oneself to one side, to lie down*, Od. 19, 470. II. 10, 350; and perf. and pluperf. pass. *a) to be inclined, to support oneself*, τινί, on or against any thing. κεκλιμένος στήλῃ. inclined against a pillar, 11, 371. Od. 0, 307; ἀσπίσι, leaning upon the shields, Il. 3, 335. *b) to lie*, 10, 472. Od. 11, 194; spoken esply of places, *to lie, to be situated*, ἁλί, towards the sea, Od. 4, 608. 13, 235; also of persons, κεκλιμένος λίμνῃ, inclined to the lake, i. e. dwelling at, 11. 5, 709. 16, 68. 2) *to bend oneself, to sink*, esply in aor. pass. 3, 360. 7, 254. 13, 543.

κλισίη, ἡ (κλίνω), Ep. dat. κλισίηφι, 13, 168: prop. *a place where a man may lie down or recline*; hence 1) *a lodge, a hut, a tent*, made of posts, inwoven with ozier twigs and covered above with reeds. *a)* the *huts of herdsmen*, 18, 589. Od. 14, 45. 16, 1. *b)* Esply *the lodges of warriors*, which were in like manner built of wood, often in the plur. 1, 306. 2, 91, sq. The lodge of Achilles is described, 24, 450. Tents like those now used were probably of later invention, see Mitford's Greece, I. § iii. p. 147. 2) *an easy-chair, an arm-chair*, Od. 4, 123. 19, 55; mly κλισμός, q. v.

κλισίηθεν. *from the lodge, from the tent*, *1. 391 11, 603; and often.

κλισίηνδε, adv. (κλισίη), *to the lodge, to the tent*, 9. 712. Od. 14, 45. 48.

κλισίον, τό (κλισίη), *the domestics' house, a dwelling* for the servants of a family, Od. 24, 208.†

κλισμός, ὁ (κλίνω), *an easy-chair, an arm-chair*, distinct from θρόνος, Od. 3, 389; prob. somewhat lower, often elegantly wrought, and decked with shining ornaments, Od. 1, 132 11. 8, 436; also

κλιτύς, ύος, poet. accus. plur. κλιτύς, *inclination, declivity, a descent*, 16, 390. Od. 5, 470.

κλονέω, for the most part poet. only pres. and imperf. 1) Act. *to put in violent motion, to drive before a man, to chase*, with accus. φάλαγγας, 5, 96; spoken of lions : ἀγέλην, 15, 324; absol. *to make a tumult*, 11, 496. 526. 14, 14; metaph. of the wind: *to drive*, νέφεα, 23, 213; φλόγα, 20, 492. 2) Mid. and pass. *to put oneself in disorderly motion, to be in confusion, to be tumultuous*, 11, 148. 15, 448; ὁμίλῳ, 4, 302 : ὑπό τινι, *5, 93.

Κλονίος, ὁ, son of Alector, and leader of the Boeotians before Troy, 2, 495.

κλόνος, ὁ, poet. *any violent motion, a press, a tumult, a confusion*, esply of warriors, who are thrown into disorder, 16, 331. 713. 729; ἐγχειάων, *a press of spears*, *5, 167.

κλόπιος, η, ον (κλώψ), *thievish, stolen, stealthy, crafty*. Od. 13, 295.†

***κλόπος, ὁ κλώψ**), *a thief*, h. Merc. 276.

κλοποπεύω. 19, 149.† οὐ γὰρ χρὴ κλοπεύειν, from the connexion it seems to signify, 'it is not proper to employ fine words,' or 'to use plausible pretexts.' (The deriv. is uncertain, Hesych. and other Gramm. explain it by παραλογίζεσθαι, ἀπατᾶν, and derive it from κλέπτω, supposing it to be equivalent to κλοποπεύειν, to delay by plausible pretexts. One Schol. B. explains it καλλιλογεῖν καὶ κλυτοῖς ἔπεσιν ἐνδιατρίβειν, 'to employ fine words,' and derives it from κλυτός and ὄψ, proposing to write κλυτοπεύειν or κλυτ' ὀπεύειν.)

κλύδων, ωνος (κλύζω), *a wave, a dashing of the surge*, Od. 12, 421.†

κλύζω, κλύσω, fut. Ep. σσ, aor. pass. ἐκλύσθην. prob. a word formed to imitate the sound of agitated water. 1) *to dash upon, to plash, to beat*, spoken of waves, ἐπ' ἠϊόνος, 23, 61. *b)* τινά, h. Ap. 74. 2) Pass. *to roll in waves, to dash in waves*. ἐκλύσθη θάλασσα ποτὶ κλισίας, 14, 392. Od. 9, 484. Batr. 76.

κλῦθι, see κλύω.

Κλυμένη, ἡ, 1) a Nereid, 18, 47. 2) a handmaid of Helen, 3, 144. 3) daughter of Minyas or Iphis. wife of Phylacus, mother of Iphiclus, Od. 11, 326.

Κλύμενος, ὁ, son of Presben, king of the Minyæ in Orchomenos, father of Erginus and Eurydice, who was mortally wounded at Thebes, on a feast of Poseidon, Od. 3, 452. Apd. 2, 4. 11.
(κλύμει), an assumed root of κλύθι.

Κλυσώνυμος, ὁ, son of Amphidamas, slain by Patroclus, 23, 88.

Κλυταιμνήστρη, ἡ, daughter of Tyndareus and Leda, sister of Helen, wife of Agamemnon, q. v., 1, 113. Od. 3, 264. She lived in illicit intercourse with Ægisthus, who with her aid slew her husband upon his return from Troy. Orestes avenged his father's death, by the murder of his mother and her para-

Κλυτίδης.

Κλυτίδης, ov, ό. son of Clytius, 1) = Piraeus. of Elis. Od. 15, 539. 16, 327. 2) = Dolops, Il. 11, 302.

Κλυτίος, ό, 1) son of Laomedon, and brother of Priam, father of Caletor, one of the counsellors, 3, 147. 15. 419. 2) father of Piraeus of Ithaca, Od. 16. 327. 15, 539. 3) a Greek, father of Dolops, Il. 11, 302. The accentuation Κλύτιος is incorrect, cf. Göttling, Lehre vom Accent, § 23.

κλυτοεργός, όν, poet. (ἔργον), famed by works, illustrious by his products, an illustrious artist, epith. of Hephaestus, Od. 8, 345.†

Κλυτομήδης, εος, ό, son of Enops from Ætolia, whom Nestor conquered in a pugilistic combat, 23, 634

*κλυτόμητις, ι. poet. (μῆτις), famed for knowledge, intelligent, h. 19, 1.

Κλυτόνηος, ό, son of Alcinous, a fleet runner, Od. 8, 119. 122.

κλυτόπωλος, ov, poet. (πῶλος), famed for horses, or rather, having famous horses, cf. Schol. ad Il. 5, 754, and κλυτότοξος; in the Il. an epith. of Hades,*5, 654. 11, 445. 16, 625; of the country Dardania, Fr. 38.

κλυτός, ή, όν, rarely ός, όν. poet. 2, 742; and Od. 5, 422; (κλύω), prop heard, hence : of which one hears much. 1. e. famed, famous, glorious, often an epith. of gods and men; κλυτὰ φῦλα ἀνθρώπων in opposition to brutes, 14, 361; generally, spoken of animate and inanimate objects: famed, glorious, splendid, μῆλα, τεύχεα, δώματα, ἄλσος. (The signif. roaring, noisy, that makes itself heard, has been given to the word, in connexion with μῆλα, Λιμήν, Od. 9. 308. 10, 87; although the signf. glorious is suitable.)

κλυτοτέχνης, ου, ό, poet. (τέχνη), famous for art, an illustrious artist, 1, 571. Od. 8, 286.

κλυτότοξος, ov. poet. (τόξον), famed by the bow, or, rather, having a famous bow, cf. ἀργυρότοξος, ἀγκυλότοξος : an illustrious archer, epith. of Apollo, 4, 101. Od. 17, 494.

κλύω, poet. (akin to κλάω), imperf. ἔκλυον with signif. of aor., also imperat. aor. 2 κλῦθι, κλῦτε, and with redupl. ἐκλυθι, κέκλυτε, 1) to hear, to apprehend, mly with accus. δοῦπον, αὐδήν, 4, 455. 13, 757 ; more rarely with gen. of pers. and particp. ἔκλυον αὐδήσαντος, I heard him speaking, 10. 47 ; with gen. of pers. and thing, 16, 76; ἐκύρης ὀπός, 22, 451; κέκλυτέ μευ μύθων, Od. 10, 189. 311. 481. 12, 271. 340 ; ἐκ τινος, to hear of any man, Od. 19, 93; generally, to learn, to become acquainted with, Od. 6, 185. 2) to hear, to listen to, mly with gen. of pers. Il. 1, 43. 218; with dat. after κλῦθι and κλῦτε, 5, 115. Od. 2, 262, is rather dat. commod., yield to my desires ; in like manner. θεά οἱ ἔκλυεν ἀρῆς, the goddess listened to her prayer, Od. 4, 767. 3) to hear to any man, to obey, in

Κνωσός.

connexion with πείθομαι, Il. 7, 379. 8, 79. Od. 3, 477.

κλωμακόεις, εσσα, εν (κλῶμαξ), stony, rocky, poet. Ἰθώμη. ?, 729.†

κνάω, imperf. κνῆ, Ep. for ἔκνη, to scrape, to rub, τυρόν, 11, 639.† (κνῆ is not aor. cf. Buttm. Gram. § 105, note 5. Rost, p. 234.)

κνέφας, αος, τό (akin to νέφος), darkness, gloominess, esply the obscurity of evening twilight, 1, 475. Od. 5, 225; only nomin. and accus.

κνῆ, see κνάω.

κνήμη, ή, the leg between the knee and ankle, the shank, the tibia, 4, 147. 519. Od. 19, 469.

κνημίς, ίδος, ή (κνήμη), armour for the legs, greaves, a covering worn for protection in war. It consisted of two metallic plates, fastened together with buckles or clasps (ἐπισφύρια). 3, 3 6; prob. they were of tin or plated with tin. 18, 613. 21, 392. In Od 24, 228, leathern greaves or gaiters are mentioned, a kind of boots worn for a protection against thorns.

κνημός, ό, a mountain height, a mountain forest, the Lat. saltus, Pass.: plur. 2, 281. 11, 105. Od. 4, 337; sing. h. Ap. 283.

κνῆστις, ιος, ή (κνάω). a scraping knife, a scraper, a rasp, dat. κνῆστι for κνήστιι 11, 640.†

*Κνίδος, ή, Cnidus, a town on the promontory Triopion, upon an isthmus. with a temple of Aphrodite, h. in Apoll. 43.

κνίσση, ή, also κνίσα, ed. Spitzn. and Dindorf.) 1) vapour from the fat of burnt meat, the odour or vapour of fat, esply the sacrificial vapour, 1, 66. 317. 8. 549. 2) fat, esply the fat of the kidneys, mly called suet or tallow, in which the sacrifice was enveloped, 1, 460. Od. 3, 457 ; see Voss. mythol. Brief. 2. p. 316; according to Heyne the fat caul about the stomach and intestines, omentum, which is justly rejected by Voss.

κνισσήεις, εσσα, εν (κνίσση). full of the vapour of fat, full of sacrificial vapour, Od. 10, 10.†

*κνισσοδιώκτης. ό (διώκω), fat-smeller, that runs after roast meat, Batr. 231.

κνυζηθμός, ὁ (κνύζω), the whine, howl, or growl of a dog, Od. 16, 163.*

κνυζόω, fut. ώσω, aor. ἐκνύζωσα (akin to κνύω), to render obscure, to becloud, τινὶ ὄσσα. *Od. 13, 401. 433.

κνώδαλον, τό. 1) any living thing which is monstrous and dangerous of its kind, a monster, a reptile, a wild beast, Od. 17, 317.† 2) Adj. monstrous, horrible. γέρων. h. Merc. 188. according to Voss. and Passow. But this is not suitable, hence Herm. conjectures νωχαλόν, i. e. ῥᾴθυμον.

κνώσσω, poet. to sleep, to slumber, Od. 4, 809.†

Κνωσός, ή (also Κνωσσός), the chief town of the island of Crete, on the Ceratus, in H. the residence of Minos, at a later period famous for its Labyrinth, 2. 646. Od. 19, 178. From this Κνώσιος, ίη, ιον, Cnossian, from Cnossus.

κοίλος, η, ον (akin to κύω), 1) *hollow, excavated, deep,* often epith. of ships. κοίλος δόμος, the hollow structure, spoken of a wasp's nest, 12. 169; κοίλον δόρυ, the hollow wood; of the Trojan horse, Od. 8, 507; σπέος, a deep cave, Od. 2) Esply of places which lie in the valleys between mountains: κοίλη οδός, a hollow pass, a defile, Il. 23, 419. κοίλη Λακεδαίμων, the *hollow* Lacedæmon Il. e. lying in a deep situation), 2, 581: metaph. Αιμήν, a harbour encompassed by hills, Od. 10, 92.

κοιμάω (κείμαι), aor. έκοίμησα, aor. mid. έκοιμησάμην, partcp. aor. pass. κοιμηθείς, 1) Act. prop. *to lay down, to lay to rest, to put to bed,* τινά, Od. 3, 397: spoken of animals: e. g. of a hart laying her fawns to rest. Od. 4, 336. 17, 127. 2) *to close in sleep, to lull, ὄσσε,* Il. 14, 236; τινά ὕπνῳ, Od. 12, 372; metaph. *to calm, to still, to hush. ανέμους,* Il. 12, 281; κύματα, Od. 12, 169; *to assuage,* οδύνας, Il. 16, 524. II) Mid. and aor. pass., *to go to bed, to lie down to sleep, to go to sleep,* often in H. χάλκεον ὕπνον, to *sleep* the brazen sleep, i. e. the sleep of death, 11, 241: spoken of animals: to sleep, Od. 14, 411.

Κοίος, ό, Cœus, son of Uranus and Gæa (Tellus), husband of Phœbe, father of Latona, h. Ap. 62. (With ot shortened in Κοίοιο)

κοιρανέω, poet. (κοίρανος), 1) *to be ruler, to rule, to command,* spoken both of war: κατά πόλεμον, ανά μάχην, 2, 207. 5, 824; πολέας διά, 4, 230. πόλεμον κάτα κοιρανέουσιν, 5, 332; and of peace, 12, 318; 'Ιθάκην κάτα, Od. 1, 247. 2) *to domineer, to play the master,* spoken of the suitors, Od. 20, 234.

κοίρανος, ό (akin to κύρος), *ruler, commander,* λαών. 7, 234. 2) Generally, *lord, master,* Od. 18, 106.

Κοίρανος, ό, 1) a Lycian, slain by Odysseus (Ulysses), 5, 677. 2) a Cretan, from Lyctus, 17, 611.

κοίτη, ή (κείμαι), *a couch, a bed,* Od. 19, 341.

κοίτος, ό=κοίτη, 1) *a couch, a bed.* 2) *the going to sleep, sleep,* *Od. 19, 510. 5. 5. [κοίτοιο μέδεσθαι, to think about going to bed, 2, 358.]

κόακος, ό, the kernel of stone [granum] of fruits; of the pomegranate, h. Cer. 373. 412.

κολεόν, τό, Ep. κουλεόν, *a scabbard of a sword,* made of metal, or decorated with it, 11, 29, seq. H. has it only as neut. κολεόν. Od. 8, 404. μέγα κουλεόν, Il. 3, 372. 11, 30. The nom. κολεός does not occur in H.

κολλήεις, εσσα, εν, poet. κολλάω. *glued together, fastened together,* ξυστά, 15, 389.†

κ άλητός. ή, όν (κολλάω), *glued together,* and generally, *joined together,* δίφρος, άρματα, ξυστόν, 15, 678; σανίδες, Od. 21, 137. 164.

κόλλοψ, οπος. ό, *the key* or *peg of a lyre,* to which the strings were attached, Od. 21, 407 † (Prop. the thick skin on the neck of oxen.)

κολοιός, ό, *the jackdaw,* graculus, *16. 583. 17. 755 (akin to κολῳός).

*κολοκύντη, ή (also κολυκύνθη), *the round gourd, the pumpkin,* Batr. 53.

κόλος, ον (akin to κυλλός), *mangled, maimed;* δόρυ, a spear with its head lopped off [*his mutilated beam,* Cp.], 16, 117.†

κολοσυρτός, ό poet. (akin to κολῳός), *noise, tumult, uproar, hubbub,* of men and dogs, *12, 147. 13, 472.

κολούω (κόλος), *to maim, to cut short, to curtail;* only metaph. τό μεν τελέει (τό relates by synes. to μύθος), τό δέ καί μεσσηγύ κολούει, one he fulfils, another he cuts short in the midst, i. e. leaves half accomplished, 20, 370. ἑο δ' αυτού πάντα κολούει. Cp. ' he cripples his own interest,' Od. 8, 211; δώρα, to curtail your gifts [*scantily to impart,* Cp.], Od 11, 340.

κόλπος, ό, 1) *the bosom* of the human body. δέχεσθαι κόλπῳ, 6. 483. παίδ' επί κόλπῳ έχειν, as an expression of tender maternal love, 6, 400. 2) *the bosom, the swell* of the garment formed by the girdle, 22, 80. Od. 15, 469; plur. Il. 9. 570. 3) any thing formed like a bosom, *a gulf of the sea,* 2, 560; the bosom of the deep, 18, 140. Od. 5, 52. h. Ap. 431.

κολωάω (κολῳός), *to screech, to cry, to clamour, to wrangle* [in piercing accents *stridulous,* Cp.], spoken of Thersites, 2, 212.†

κολώνη, ή, *a hill, an elevation,* *2, 811. 11, 711.

*κολωνός, ό=κολώνη, h. Cer. 273.

κολῳός, ού, poet. *a screech, a cry, scolding strife* [prop. *a shrill chattering,* B.]. κολῳόν έλαύνειν, to make an uproar, to quarrel, 1, 575.† (according to Buttm. Lex. p. 391, akin to κολοιός, κέλω, κέλομαι: but, according to Döderlein, L. Hom. Sp. 1. p. 4, κολωάω is a collateral form of κέλλω).

κομάω (κόμη), fut. ήσω, *to let the hair grow long, to have long hair,* in Il. only partcp. 'Άβαντες όπιθεν κομόωντες, the Abantes, long-haired behind, 2, 542 (Strabo assigns as a reason, that no enemy might seize them by the hair); spoken of horses: furnished with manes. 8, 42. 13, 24. 2) Metaph, of fields and plants: *to be overgrown, to be verdant, to wave,* fut. άσταχύεσσι, h. Cer. 454. *II.

κομέω, poet. *to take care of, to tend, to provide for,* υιούς, γέροντα, Od. 11, 250. 24, 212; ίππους, Il. 8, 109. 113; κύνας, Od. 17, 310. 319.

κόμη, ή, *the hair, the hair of the head,* more rarely plur. κόμαι Χαρίτεσσιν όμοῖαι, 17, 51 (see όμοιος). Od. 6, 231. 2)

Κομιδή. 246 Κορίννυμι.

Metaph. κόμη ἐλαίης, the foliage of the olive-tree, Od. 23, 195.

κομιδή (κομίζω), care, attendance, the care of feeding, in the Il spoken of horses, 8, 186. 23, 411. in the Od spoken of men, and of the care of the garden, Od. 24, 245. 247. ἐπεὶ οὐ κομιδή κατὰ νῆα ἦεν ἐπηετανός, since I have not all along had (ample or) good accommodation in a ship: he had lost his ship and been obliged to swim, Od. 8, 232; see Damm and Nitzsch. Passow unnecessarily assumes here the signif. 'nourishment, provisions.' So also Cp.

κομίζω (κομέω), aor. ἐκόμισα, Ep. σσ, aor. mid. ἐκομισάμην, 1) *to take care of, to attend upon, to provide for*, like κομέω, spoken of things and persons: ἔργα, 6, 490. Od. 1, 356. 21, 350; κτήματα, to manage possessions, Od. 23, 355; τινά, to take care of any man, esply to entertain as a host, often in the Od. (in the Il. in this signif. only in the mid.). 2) *to take up* any thing, *to bear away, to carry away*, prim. to take care of, χλαῖναν, τρυφάλειαν, 2, 183. 13, 578; and generally, *to bear off, to carry off, to take away*, in a good and bad sense: νεκρόν, 13, 196; ἵππους, Il.; ἄκοντα κόμισε χροΐ, he bore off the spear in his body, i. e. he received it in the body, 11, 4.36 463. Mid. *to provide for in a man's house, to attend upon, to entertain,* τινά, 8, 284. Od. 6, 278. 14, 316. 2) *to take up for oneself, to receive.* Σίντιες ἐκομίσαντο αὐτόν, the Sintians took him up, 1, 594; τινα, to convey away (from the battle), 5, 359. ἔγχος ἐνὶ χροῒ κομίσασθαι, to receive a spear in the body, 22. 286. cf. Act. 2.

κομπέω (κόμπος), *to resound, to rattle, to clash* or *clang*, spoken of brass, 12, 151.†

κόμπος, ὁ, *a rattling, a noise, a clashing*, a sound arising from striking upon a body; spoken of the tread or stamping of dancers, Od. 8, 380; ὀδόντων, of the noise of the tusks of the wild boar, Il. 11, 417. 12, 149.

κοναβέω, kindr. from κοναβίζω, poet. (κόναβος), aor. 1 κονάβησα, *to resound, to rattle, to ring*, spoken of brass, 15, 648. 21, 593; *to resound, to re-echo.* νῆες δοῦμα, 2, 334. 16, 277. Od. 17, 542. (κοναβέω only in the aor.)

κοναβίζω =κοναβέω, only in the imperf. *2, 466. 13, 498. 21, 255.

κόναβος, ὁ, poet. *a sound, a clashing, a noise*, Od. 10, 122.† (Prob. from κόμπος)

κονίη, ἡ, poet. form κόνις, ἡ, 1) *dust*, esply the powdered dust of the earth. often in plur. ἐν κονίῃσι πίπτειν, Il. ἐν κονίῃσι βάλλειν τινά, to cast any one into the dust, i. e. to slay him, 8. 156. 2) *sand. river-sand*, 21, 271. 3) *ashes*, Od. 7, 153. 160 (s. in the arsis of the sixth foot is used by H. as long).

κόνις, ιος. ἡ=κονίη, *dust*, in connexion with ψάμαθος, to indicate infinity of number, 9, 385. (κόνι, Ep. dat. for κόνει. 24, 18. Od. 11, 191.) 2) *ashes*, κόνι αἰθαλόεσσα, Il. 18, 23.

κονίσαλος or κονίσσαλος, ὁ 1 (κόνις, *dust, a whirlwind of dust* *3, 13. 5, 503. 22, 401.

κονίω (κόνις), fut. κονίσω, aor. ἐκόνισα. perf. pass. κεκόνιμαι, 1) *to fill with dust, to cover with dust*, with accu. χαίτας 21, 407; pass. 21, 405; πεδίον, to fill the plain with dust, spoken of the flying Trojans, 14, 145; hence κεκονιμένοι, covered with dust, 21, 541. 2) Intrans. *to excite dust*, spoken of fleet horses and men; αἰψα· κονίοντες πεδίοιο, raising a dust through the plain, 13, 820. 23, 372. Od. 8, 122.

κοντός, ὁ, *a pole, a stick*, Od. 9, 487.†

*κοπόω (κόπος), *to weary, to fatigue*; pass. *to become weary*. Batr. 190.

Κοπρεύς, ῆος, ὁ, son of Pelops, from Elis, a herald of Eurystheus, 15, 639. seq.

κοπρίζω (κόπρος), fut. ἰσω, *to manure with dung*, Od. 17, 299.†

κόπρος, ὁ. 1) *manure, dung*. Od. 9, 329. 17, 297; and generally, *dirt, filth* Il. 22, 414. 24, 164. 2) *a stable, a yard for cattle*, 18, 575. Od. 10, 411.

κόπτω, aor. 1 ἔκοψα, perf. κέκοπα, aor. mid. ἐκοψάμην, 1) *to strike, to thrust,* τινά, spoken of persons fighting, Od. 18. 28. 335. κώληπα, Il. 23, 726; with double accus. τινά παρήϊον, 23, 690; and with dat. insrum. ἵππους τόξῳ, with the bow, σκηπανίῳ, 10, 514. 13, 60; spoken of a serpent: κόψε αἰετὸν κατὰ στῆθος, is struck or bit the eagle in the breast, 12, 204; also spoken of the blow with which oxen were stunned when they were to be slaughtered, 17, 521. Od. 14, 425. 2) *to strike off, to cut off*, κεφαλὴν ἀπὸ δειρῆς, Il. 13, 203. Od. 22, 477. 3) *to hammer, to forge,* δεσμούς, Il. 18, 379. Od. 8, 274. Mid. *to smite oneself,* κεφαλὴν χερσίν, to beat a man's head, Il. 22, 23.

Κόρακος πέτρη, ἡ, *the rock Κόραξ*. in Ithaca, near the fountain Arethusa, according to Gell, on the south east end of the island, still called Κοraka Petra: according to Voss, in the middle of the island upon the east side, on Neion; Völcker, Hom. Geogr., places it on the west side as a part of Neritus, Od. 13, 408. It received its name, according to the Schol., from Korax, son of Arethusa, who in a hunt fell from this rock.

κορέννυμι, fut. κορέσω, Ep. κορέω, 1. 379. 13, 831; aor. 1 ἐκόρεσα. Ep. σσ. aor. 1 mid. ἐκορεσάμην, perf. Ion. κεκόρημαι, also Ep pariep. perf. act. with pass signif. κεκορηώς, Od 18, 372; aor. pass. ἐκορέσθην, *to satiate, to satisfy,* τινά, any man. Il. 16, 747; with any thing, τινί: κύνας, ᾗδ᾽ οἰωνοὺς δημῷ καὶ σάρκεσσι, spoken of the corpses which lie unburied, Il. 8, 379. 13, 831. 17, 241 Mid. *to satiate oneself, to be sated or satisfied, have* (had; *one's fill*, also perf. pass. and

Κορέω. Κοσμέω.

aor. pass. 1) With gen. φορβῆς, 11, 562; σίτου, Od. 14, 46: also with θυμὸν δαιτός, Od. 8, 98; metaph. θυλόπιδος κορέσσασθαι, to be sated with battle, Il. 13, 635; also ἀέθλων, Od. 23, 350. 2) Often with partcp. κλαίουσα ἐκορέσσατο, she sated herself with weeping, Od. 20, 59. κλαίων ἐκορέσθην, Od. 4, 541. ἐκορέσσατο χεῖρας τάμνων, he was satiated in his hands with cutting, i. e. tired, Il. 11, 87. οὔπω κεκόρησθε ἐελμένοι; are ye not yet satisfied with being enclosed? 18, 287. (H. has not the pres. κορέννυμι.)
κορέω, fut. ήσω, to sweep, to take care of, to clean, δῶμα, Od. 20, 149.†
κόρη, ἡ, Ep. κούρη, q. v., h. Cer. 439.†
κορθύω (κόρθυς), to lift up, only mid. to lift oneself. κῦμα κορθύεται, the wave lifted itself up, 9 7.†
Κόρινθος, ἡ, Corinthus, mentioned 2, 570; afterwards, one of the most flourishing cities of the old world, situated on the isthmus According to Pausan. 2, 1. 1, built by Ephyra, daughter of Oceanus, of whom a descendant Corinthus changed the name; according to Apd 1, 9. 3, by Sisyphus, son of Æolus, cf. Ἐφύρη. In Hom. Κορ. is prob. fem., for ἀφνειός is common, as in Soph. and Herod. It is found masc. in an oracle, Herod. 5, 92. and in Strab. ὁ δὲ Κόρ. ἀφνειός, p. 580. From this the adv. Κορινθόθι, at Corinth, 13, 664.
κορμός, ὁ (κείρω), a piece cut off, a billet, a log, Od. 23, 196.†
κόρος, ὁ (κορέννυμι), satiety. the state of satiety, (one's) fill, φυλόπιδος, γοοῖο, 19, 221. Od. 4, 103. πάντων κόρος ἐστί, there is a satiety of all, Il. 13, 636.
κόρος, ὁ, Ep. and Ion. κοῦρος, q. v.
κόρση, ἡ, Ep. and Ion. for κόρρη, the temples, the temples of the head, *4, 502. 13. 574.
κορυθάιξ, ἰκος, ὁ (ἴ, ἀΐσσω). helmshaking, crest-waving, i. q. κορυθαίολος epith. of Ares, 22, 132.†
κορυθαίολος, ον (αἰόλος), helm-shaking, crest-waving, often an epith. of Hector, 2, 816; once of Ares, 20, 38. (Others explain it, ' with variegated helmet,' see αἰόλος.)
κόρυμβος, ὁ, plur. τὰ κόρυμβα (κορυφή), prop. the upper part of a thing, the point, the top, the peak, ἄκρα κόρυμβα νηῶν, the extreme points of the curved stern of the ships=ἄφλαστα (aplustria), which were commonly adorned with ornaments, 9. 241.† Thus Heyne after Hesych. Voss. on the other hand, ' the splendid beaks,' after Etym. M. ἄφλαστα μὲν λέγεται τὰ πρυμνήσια, κόρυμβα τὰ πρωρήσια; or the Schol. κάκροστόλια, ' the ships' beaks which were erected as trophies.' This was, however, a later custom. [our vessel-heads, Cp.]
κορύνη, ἡ, a club, a mace; σιδηρείη, iron or covered with iron, *7, 141. 143.
κορυνήτης, ου, ὁ, a mace-bearer, a warrior armed with a club, *7, 9, 138.
κόρυς, υθος, ἡ, accus. κόρυθα aud κόρυν,

13, 131. 16, 215; the helmet; it was coated with brass, χαλκήρης, χαλκείη, and differed in this respect from the leathern κυνέη, although this difference is not always regarded, 12, 184. The helmet had a crest, λόφος. made of horse-hair (ἱπποδάσεια, ἵππουρις); this was put into a conical elevation (φάλος), and many helmets had several φάλοι, hence ἀμφίφαλος, τετράφαλος, etc. The helmet itself was fastened with a strap (ὀχεύς) under the neck.
κορύσσω (κόρυς), aor. 1 mid. Ep. κορυσσάμενος, perf. pass. Ep. κεκορυθμένος, 1) Prop. to put on a helmet, hence generally, to equip, to arm, τινά, Batr. 123. 2) to raise, to excite, πόλεμον, 2, 273; κῦμα, 21, 306. Mid. often: 1) to equip oneself, to arm oneself for war, absol. 10, 37. Od. 12, 121; with dat. instrum. χαλκῷ, τεύχεσι, Il. 7, 206. 17, 199; in the partcp. κεκορυθμένος χαλκῷ, 4, 495. 5, 562. Od. 21, 434; metaph. spoken of arms: δοῦρα κεκορυθμένα χαλκῷ, spears armed with brass, Il. 3, 18. 11, 43. 16, 802. 2) to raise oneself, to rise, prop. for battle, metaph. spoken of strife, 4, 442. κῦμα κορύσσεται, the wave swells, 4, 424; in the Od. rarely.
κορυστής, οὗ, ὁ (κορύσσω), prop. one wearing a helmet; then generally, one armed, ἀνήρ, 4, 457, and often. *[i.
κορυφή, ἡ (κόρυς), prop. the extreme part of any thing, hence 1) the crown of the head, 8, 83. h. Ap. 309. 2) the top, of a mountain, the summit, often plur. with ὄρεος or ὀρέων, Il. and Od.
κορυφόω (κορυφή), to carry any thing to the highest point, hence mid. to reach the highest point, to tower aloft; only κῦμα κορυφοῦται, the wave towers aloft [curls its head on high. Cp.], 4, 426.†
Κορώνεια, ἡ, a town in Bœotia on the west side of the lake Copaïs, now Diminia, 2, 503.
κορώνη (κορωνός), prop. any thing curved, hence 1) the crow (from the curved beak), always the sea-crow or cormorant, εἰναλίη, Od 5. 66. 12, 418. 14, 308. 2) the ring on the house-door with which it is shut, Od. 1, 441. 7, 90. 21, 46. 3) the curved end of a bow, which was furnished with a knob or ring to which the string was fastened, Il. 4, 111. Od. 21, 138. 4) the curved stern of a ship, see κορωνίς. [Döll. thinks κορωνίζειν was=κρώζειν: cornix=cornix.]
κορωνίς, ίδος, ἡ (κορώνη), curved, beaked, epith. of ships, from the curved stern, Il. often, once Od. 19, 182.
*Κορωνίς, ίδος, ἡ, daughter of Phlegyas of Laceria in Magnesia, sister of Ixion, who bore Asklêpios (Æsculapius), to Apollo on the plain of Dotium, h. 15. cf. Apd. 3, 10, 3.
Κόρωνος, ὁ (appell. κορωνός), son of Cæneus, father of Leonteus. king of the Lapithæ, at Gyrton in Thessaly, 2, 746.
κοσμέω (κόσμος), aor. 1 Ep. κόσμησα,

M 4

Κοσμητός. 248 Κουρητρόφος.

aor. mid. ἐκοσμησάμην, aor. pass. ἐκοσμήθην. 1) *to put in order, to arrange, to draw up in line*, with accus. of warriors: ἵππους τε καὶ ἀνέρας, 2. 554. 704. 14, 379. πέντᾱχα κοσμηθέντες, arranged in five troops, 12, 87. διὰ τρίχα κοσμηθέντες, ἐϋ διακοσμέω. φθὰν μέγ᾽ ἱππήων ἐπὶ τάφρῳ κοσμηθέντες, they were drawn up at the trench before the charioteers, 11. 51. (The gen. ἱππήων depends upon φθάνω, since this contains a notion of comparison, and not upon κοσμέω, cf. Thiersch, Gram. § 254, *d*.) δόρπον, to prepare a repast, Od. 7, 13; ἀοιδήν, h. 6, 50. 2) *to adorn, to deck*, χρυσῷ, h. Ven. 65; σῶμα ἐν ἔντεσι, Batr. 121. Mid. *to put in order*, with reference to the subject, with accus. πολιήτας, 2, 806.

κοσμητός, ἡ, όν (κοσμέω), *set in order, arranged*. πρασιαί, Od. 7, 127.†

κοσμήτωρ, ορος, ὁ, poet. for κοσμητήρ, one who orders, *a commander*, always with λαῶν. l. 16. Od. 18, 152.

κόσμος, ὁ (prob. from κομέω), 1) *order, arrangement, suitableness, propriety*, κόσμῳ ἔρχεσθαι, to go in order, 12, 225; καθίζειν, Od. 13, 77; ἐσπλῃ κατὰ κόσμον, in order; and strengthened with εὖ, Il. 10, 472. 12, 85, according to propriety, as is befitting; often οὐ κατὰ κόσμον, not according to propriely, contrary to propriety; ἐρίζειν, εἰπεῖν; hence, ἵππον κόσμος, the arrangement, the construction of the (wooden) horse. Od. 8, 492. 2) *ornament, decoration*, of women, Il. 14, 187. h. Ven. 163; of horses, 4, 145.

κοτέω and κοτέομαι, poet. (κότος). Of the act. there occur: pres. indic. aor. 1 partcp. κοτέσας, h. Cer. 254; Ep partcp. perf. κεκοτηώς, always κεκοτηότι θυμῷ, inly mid. pres., fut. κοτέσομαι, Ep. σσ. aor. 1 ἐκοτεσσάμην, Ep σσ, *to be angry, enraged*, wit. dat. pers., 3, 345. 5, 177. 14, 143. τοίσιν τε κοτέσσεται for ἐκοτέσεται. 5. 747. 8, 391. On. 1, 101 (cf. Host, p. 629. Kühner, § 661. 4); with gen. of the thing. ἀπάτης. on account of deception, Il. 4, 168; and with accus. κοτεσσαμένη τόνδε θυμῷ, angry in mind at this, 14. 191.

κοτήεις, εσσα, εν, poet. (κοτέω), *wrathful, angry, enraged*. θεός}, 5. 191.†

κότος, ὁ, prop. a grudge; then, *anger, hatred*. κότον ἔχειν τινί, to have a grudge against any man, 13, 517. κότον ἐντίθεσθαί τινι, Od. 11, 102. 13, 342

κοτύλη, ἡ (akin to κοῖλος), prop. any cavity; hence 1) *a small vessel for fluids, a cup, a little goblet*, 22, 495. Od. 15, 312. 17, 12. 2) *the hip-pan*, the socket in which the head of the thighbone turns, Il. 5, 306, 307.

κοτυληδών, όνος, ὁ (κοτύλη), any cavity; esply, *a*) a little cavity in the arms of sea-polypi [like a small cuppling-glass, with which they attached themselves to the rocks, Passow], *b) the branching arms* themselves. πουλύποδος πρὸς κοτυληδονόφιν (Ep. for κοτυληδόσι) πυκιναὶ λάϊγγες ἔχονται, to the arms of the polypus many pebbles attach themselves, Od. 5, 433.† see πουλύπους.

κοτυλήρυτος, ον (ἀρύω), that may be drawn with a cup, *gushing, copious*, ἔρρεεν αἷμα [*followed by* goblets full], 23, 34.†

*κότυλος, ὁ=κοτύλη. *a cup*, Ep. 14.3.

κουλεόν, τό, Ep. and Ion. for κολεόν q. v.

κούρη, ἡ, Ion. for κόρη, *a maiden, a virgin*, 2, 872; *a daughter*, 1, 111; Διός, Il. 9, 536; mly with gen. of a prop. name, alone 6, 247. 2) *a bride*. Od. 16, 279; always the Ion. form, except h. Cer. 479.

*κουρήϊος, ίη, ιον, Ion. for κόρειος (κούρη), appertaining to virgins, *youthful*, h. Cer. 108.

κούρητες, οἱ (κοῦρος), *youths*, Παναχαιῶν, *19, 193. 248.

Κουρῆτες, οἱ, *the Curētes*, the most ancient inhabitants of the south-eastern parts of Ætolia, about Pleuron, probably belonging to the Lelèges; they were expelled by the Ætolians; for which reason they attacked them in their chief town Calydon, 9, 532. (Prob. from κουρά, tonsure, because they wore short hair, cf. Eustath. ad Il. 19, 193.)

κουρίδιος, ίη, ιον, Ion. and poet. (κούρος), *conjugal, legitimate*, connected with πόσις, ἀνήρ, ἄλοχος or γυνή, in opposition to illicit concubinage; as clearly appears from 19, 298, where Brisēis says that it is forbidden her to become the κουριδίη ἄλοχος, the lawful wife of Achilles; κουρίδιος πόσις, 5, 414. Od. 11, 430; also κουρίδιος φίλος, as subst beloved husband, Od. 15, 22; ἀνὴρ κουρ. Od. 19, 266; ἄλοχος, Il. 1, 114. Od. 14, 345; γυνή, Od. 13, 43; λέχος, the conjugal couch, Il. 15, 40; κοῦρε δῶμα, the house of the husband, Od. 19, 580. The common explanation *youthful*, after the Schol., a wife whom a man has married as κούρη is refuted by Buttm, Lex p. 593; although the derivation from κοῦρος, as denoting the bloom of life. or. of free, noble birth, is not rejected. According to Döderlein, κούριος is the Homeric form of the later κύριος.)

κουρίζω (κοῦρος), *to be young, juvenile*. only Od. 22, 185.†

κουρίξ, adv. (κουρά), *by the hair*, Od. 22, 118.†

κοῦρος, ὁ, Ion and Ep. for κόρος, 1) *a youth, a boy*. from the earliest age to the vigour of manhood; hence often the young warriors are called κοῦροι Ἀχαιῶν. 1, 473; spoken of one unborn, ὃ, 50; Καδμείων, 5. 807; also, *a son*, κοῦροι Ζηθοιο, Od. 19, 523. 2) the servants at sacrifices and entertainments, who were always free-born, and often of royal descent, Il. 1, 470. Od. 1, 148. 3, 339.

κουρότερος, η, ον, compar. of κοῦρος *younger*, and generally, *youthful*, ἀνήρ Od. 21, 310; subst. Il 4, 316.

κουροτρόφος, ον (τρέφω), *nourishing boys or youth*, epith. of Ithaca, Od. 9, 27.

κούφος, η, ον, light; [hence] *fleet:* σάνδαλα, h. Merc. 83. The neut. plur. as adv. κούφα προβιβάς, lightly striding along. 13, 158; and compar. κουφότερον μετεφώνεε, he addressed them more lightly, i. e. more cheerfully, Od. 8, 201.

*κοχλίας, ου, ὁ, *a snail* with convoluted shell, Batr. 165.

Κόων, ωνος, ὁ, son of Antēnor, a Trojan, slain by Agamemnon, 11, 248—260.

Κόως, ἡ, Ep. for Κώς q. v.

κράας, τά, obsol. nom. of the Ep. oblique cases, κράατος, κράατι, etc. see κάρη.

κραδαίνω, Ep. form of κραδάω, *to brandish, to hurl;* pass. αἰχμὴ κραδαινομένη, 13, 504. ἔγχος κραδαινόμενον, 17, 524.

κραδάω (κράδη), Ep. form κραδαίνω, only in pres. pass. partcp. *to brandish, to swing, to shake,* with accus. always κραδάων ἔγχος, δόρυ, 7, 213. Od. 19, 438. κραδίη, ἡ, Ep. for καρδίη.

κραιαίνω, Ep. length. form of κραίνω, q. v.

κραίνω, oftener the Ep. lengthened κραιαίνω (κάρη), imperf. ἐκραίαινον, fut. κρανέω, 9, 310, another reading for φρονέω, aor. 1 ἔκρηνα, Ep. ἐκρήηνα, imperat. κρήηνον, Il., κρῆνον, Od.; infin. κρηῆναι, Il., κρῆναι, Od.; perf. pass. κεκράανται, fut. mid. κρανέομαι, Il. 9, 626, with pass. signif.: 1) *to finish, to end, to accomplish, to complete, to fulfil, to perform,* with accus. ἐφετμάς, 5,508; ἐέλδωρ τινί, to fulfil a wish for any man, 1, 41. Od. 8.418; ἔπος, Od. 20, 115; absol. Od. 5, 170 (antith. νοῆσαι); hence pass. οὔ μοι δοκέει τῇδε ὀδῷ κρανέεσθαι, it seems to be that it [our object] will not be attained in this way, Il. 9, 626. χρυσῷ ἐπὶ χείλεα κεκράανται, the lips are finished off with gold, i. e. gilded (spoken of a cup), Od. 4, 616. 15, 116; κεκράαντο, Od. 4, 133. 2) *to be head, to rule, to reign,* Od. 8, 391 (κραίνω in the Od., κραιαίνω in the Il. except κρανέεσθαι). κραίνων ἀθανάτους τε θεοὺς καὶ γαῖαν, h. Merc. 427. Passow explains: he completed the gods and the earth, i. e. he represented them in his song as coming into being. as they really did come. Math. and Herm. think κραίνων corrupt; the latter conjectures κλείων. [Bothe after Hesych. renders κραίνων, *honorans, celebrans.*]

κραιπνός, ή, όν, compar. κραιπνότερος, Od. 5, 365. 2) *rapid, fleet, swift,* πόδες, πόμποι; metaph. κραιπνότερος νόος, a vehement spirit, Il. 23, 590. As adv. often neut. plur. κραιπνά, with κραιπνῶς, 13, 18. 5, 223. (Prob. from ΑΡΠΩ, ἁρπάζω.)

*κραιπνῶς, adv. (κραιπνός), *quickly, swiftly,* 10, 162. Od. 8, 247.

*κράμβη, ἡ, *cabbage,* Batr. 163.

*Κραμβοφάγος, ὁ (φαγεῖν), *Cabbageeater,* name of a frog, Batr. 221.

Κρανάη, ἡ (appellat. κραναή), *Crenaë,* an island to which Paris first brought Helen from Lacedæmon, 3, 445. According to the ancient critics, it is either the island Helena in Attica, Eur. Hel. 1690; or a small island in the Laconian gulf, now *Marathonisi,* Paus. 3, 22. 2. Ottfr. Müller, Orchom. p. 316, decides in favour of the latter. Others suppose it *Cythera.*

*κραναήπεδος, ον (πέδον), *having a hard, rocky soil,* h. Ap. 72.

κραναός, ή, όν, *hard, rough, stony, rocky,* epith. of Ithaca, 3, 201. Od. 1, 247.

κρανέεσθαι, see κραίνω.

κράνεια, ἡ, *the cornel-tree,* cornus, 16, 767. According to Od. 10, 242, swine were fed with the fruit [*cornel-fruit,* Cp.].

*κρανέϊνος, η, ον, *made of the cornel-tree,* ἀκόντιον, h. Merc. 460.

κρανίον, τό (κρᾶνον), *the skull,* 8, 84.†

Κράπαθος, ἡ. Ep. for Κάρπαθος, q. v.

κράς, ὁ, used only in the oblique cases, gen. κρᾱτός, dat. κρᾱτί, as a form of κάρη, q. v., *the head, the summit,* ὑπὸ κράτεσφι, under the head, 10. 156.

κραταιγύαλος, ον, poet. (γύαλον), *furnished with strong arched plates, strong-arched,* θώρηξ, 19, 361 †

κραταιΐς ἡ, Ep. (κράτος). τότ' ἀποστήψασκε κραταιΐς αὖτις, Od. 11, 597.† According to Schol. br. ἡ κραταιὰ δύναμις ὅ ἐστι τὸ βάρος, the overpowering force, the weight of the stone (for which also some of the ancients would write κραται-ις), rolled it back.' Aristarchus took it as an adv.: 'then rolled it violently back;' [cf. λικρῐφίς.] Nitzsch. (and so Fäsi) thinks κραταιΐς is (as in the next article) a personification; a sort of sprite, '*Mastery;*' or '*Force.*'

Κραταιΐς, ἡ, *the powerful,* the mother of Scylla. a nymph, Od. 12. 124.

κραταιός, ή, όν, poet (κράτος), *strong, powerful, mighty,* Μοῖρα, 5, 83; θήρ, 11, 119; φώς, h. Merc. 265.

κραταίπεδος, ον, poet. (πέδον). *having a firm, hard bottom* or *soil,* οὖδας, Od. 23, 46.†

*κραταίπους, οδος, ὁ, ἡ, poet. (πούς), *strong-footed,* Ep. 15, 9.

κρατερός, ή, όν (κράτος), Ep. κάρτερος, *strong, mighty, powerful,* a) Spoken of persons: Ἀρης, Ἔρις, esply of warriors; *brave, bold. courageous,* 11, 2) Of things: βέλος, ὑσμίνη, Il.; φύλοπις, Od. 16, 268; μῦθος, a violent, harsh word, Il. 1, 25. 326; [*a.pera vox,* Nägelsb.;] from this κρατερῶς, *strongly, mightily, powerfully,* μάχεσθαι, νεμεσσᾶν, Il. ἀγορεύειν, to speak powerfully, with emphasis, 8, 29.

κρατερόφρων, ον, gen. ονος, poet. (φρήν), of a firm, hard temper, *spirited, courageous, unterrified,* epith. of Heracles, 14, 524; of the Dioscuri, Od. 11, 298; of the lion, 10, 184.

κρατερῶνυξ, υχος, ὁ, ἡ poet. (ὄνυξ), *strong-hoofed,* ἵπποι. ἡμίονοι, 5, 329, 24, 277; *strong-clawed,* λύκοι [*talon'd wolves,* Cp.], λέοντες. Od. 10. 218.

κράτεσφι, see ΚΡΑΣ.

κρατευται, αἱ, Ep (κρατέω), *the forked*

M 5

Κ,ιατεω. 250 **Κρήτη.**

supports upon which the spit rested (Voss, *the supporting forks*), according to Aristarch., stones upon which the roasting spit was laid, 9, 214.†

κρατέω (κράτος), fut. ήσω, 1) *to have might, power: to exercise sway, to command*, absol. 5, 175. 16, 172. 2) *to rule, to command*, with gen., over any man, 1, 79. 288. rarely with dat. νεκύεσσιν, to have dominion amongst the dead, Od. 11, 485; ἀνδράσι, ἀθανάτοισι, Od. 16, 265. 3) With accus., to get any thing into one's power, *to hold, to grasp*, Batr. 63. 236.

κράτιστος, η, ον, Ep. κάρτιστος, q. v.

κράτος, εος, τό. Ep. κάρτος, *strength, might, power*, Od. 1, 70, 359; esply spoken of bodily strength, Il. 7, 142. 9, 39. 13, 486; of iron : *strength, hardness*, Od. 9, 393. 2) *mastery, superiority, victory*, Il. 1, 509. 6, 387; ἐγγυαλίζειν τινὶ κράτος, Il. 192. 753, φέρεσθαι, to bear away the victory, 13, 486

κράτός, gen. from ΚΡΑΣ, see κάρη.

κρατύς, ὁ, poet. (κράτος) = κρατερός, *powerful, mighty*, epith. of Hermes, 16, 184. Od. 5, 49.

*Κραυγασίδης, ου, ὁ (κραύγασος), *Vociferator*, a frog's name, Batr. 216.

κρέας, ατος, τό, nom. and accus. plur. κρέα. gen. κρεάων, h. 2, 130; κρειῶν, Od. 15, 98; Ep. κρειῶν, Il. 11, 551; dat. κρέασιν, 8, 162; *mrat, flesh*, in sing. only accus. Od. 8, 477; plur. *pieces of meat*. (The a in the last syllable in κρέα is short, and in the Od. is also elided, Od 3, 65. 470.) To be read with synizesis, Od. 9, 347; (see Buttm. Gram. § 54, note 3. Thiersch, § 188. Rost, Dial. 38.)

κρεῖον, τό (κρέας), a *meat-table, a dresser* [Cp.], upon which meat was cut up, 9, 206.†

κρείσσων, ον, gen. ονος, irreg. compar. of ἀγαθός, prop. from κρατύς or κράτος for κράσσων, *stronger, more powerful*, 1, 80; esply *superior, victorious*, in connexion with νικᾶν, 3, 71. 92. Od. 18, 46; sometimes with infin. Od. 21, 345.

Κρειοντιάδης, αο, ὁ, Ep. for Κρεοντιάδης, son of Creon, 19, 240.

κρείων, οντος, ὁ, fem. κρείουσα, ἡ, (prob. from κρᾶς, κραίνω), *ruler, commander*, spoken of kings and gods; also of Eteoneus, a servant of noble race, Od. 4, 22; κρείουσα, ἡ, only once, Il. 22, 48.

Κρείων, οντος, ὁ, Ep. for Κρέων, father of Megara, ruler in Thebes, Od. 11, 269. 2) father of Lycomedês, Il. 9, 84.

κρέμαμαι, depon. mid. *I hang*, see κρεμάννυμι.

κρεμάννυμι, fut. κρεμάσω, contr. κρεμῶ, and expanded κρεμόω, 7, 83; aor. 1 ἐκρέμασα, mid. κρέμαμαι, imperf. ἐκρεμάμην, 2 sing. ἐκρέμω and κρέμω, which has been falsely given as aor. 2 mid. 1) *to hang up, to suspend, to let hang*, τεύχεα προτὶ νηόν, 7, 83; σειρὴν ἐξ οὐρανόθεν, to let a chain hang down from heaven,

8, 19. Mid. *to hang, to be suspended*, ὅτι τ' ἐκρέμω ὑψόθεν, when thou u wert suspended on high, *15, 18. 21.

κρεμβαλιαστύς, ύος, ἡ (κρέμβαλον), a *rattling, a jingling*, h. Ap. 162.

κρέων, see κρέας, Od.

κρήγυος, ον, poet. *good, advantageous, profitable*, τὸ κρήγυον εἰπεῖν, 1, 106 † (According to Buttm., Lex. p. 305, from χρήσιμος, others think from κέαρ, γαῖω, that which rejoices the heart, see Thiersch, § 199. 7.)

κρήδεμνον, τό (κράς, δέω), prob. *a head-band, a veil*, a female head-covering, with which the whole face could be covered, and whose long ends were permitted to hang down over both cheeks, 14, 184 Od. 1, 334. Nitzsch, ad Od. 5, 346, thinks it perhaps differed from the καλύπτρη, in being attached to the head by a band, whereas the καλύπτρη was thrown over it. Odysseus (Ulysses) used the veil of the goddess Ino as a girdle in swimming, Od 5, 346. 2) Metaph. Τροίης ἱερὰ κρήδεμνα, the sacred battlements of Troy, which, like a band or fillet, encircled and protected the city, Il. 16, 100. Od. 13, 388. *b) the lid of a vessel*, since κάρη denotes the upper part of a thing, Od. 3, 392; perhaps *a cover tied over* the opening: cf. Od. 10, 23.

κρήηναι, Ep. for κρήναι, see κραίνω.

κρῆθεν, adv. (syncop. from κάρη, κάρηθεν), *from the head, from above*, 16, 548. Od. 11, 588; see κατακρῆθεν.

Κρηθεύς, ῆος, ὁ, son of Æolus and Enaretê or Laodicê, founder of Iolcus in Thessaly, husband of Tyro, brother of Salmoneus, father of Æson, Amythaon, and Pheres, Od. 11, 236, seq. 253—258.

Κρήθων, ωνος, ὁ, son of Diocles, brother of Orsilochus of Pheræ in Messenia, slain by Æneas, 5, 542, seq.

κρημνός, ὁ, *any overhanging edge: a precipice*, or *cliff*, of a mountain, &c.; or the *edge* of a deep trench, *12, 54. 21. 175. 234.

κρηναῖος, η, ον (κρήνη), *belonging to a fountain*. (Νύμφαι κρηναῖαι, fountain-nymphs, Od. 17, 240.†)

κρήνη, ἡ (akin to κάρη), *a fountain, a spring, a well*, 9, 14; κρήνηνδε, Od. 20, 154.

Κρής, ὁ, gen. Κρητός, plur. οἱ Κρῆτες, *the Cretans*, inhabitants of the island of Crete, 2, 645. Their reputation as liars, according to Damm, originated in the fiction of Odysseus (Ulysses), Od. 14, 200, seq.

Κρήτη, ἡ, and poet. αἱ Κρῆται, Od. 14. 199, a large island in the Mediterranean Sea, famed by the legislation of Minos and by the fable of Zeus and Europa: now *Candia*. Even in the time of Homer it was very populous, for he speaks of it as having a hundred cities, 2, 649; in round numbers, however, as in Od. 19, 174, he mentions only ninety. From this the adv. Κρήτηθεν, from Crete, Il. 3, 233. Κρήτηνδε, to Crete, Od. 19, 186

Κρητήρ. 251 Κροταλίζω.

κρητήρ, ήρος, ό (κεράννυμι), a mixing-vessel, a mixer, the vessel in which the wine was tempered with water, and from which it was poured into the goblets, 3, 247. Od. 1, 110. 7, 179. 9, 9. 13, 50. The mixing-vessel stood upon a tripod, Od. 21, 141. 145. 22, 341; was of silver, Il. 23, 741. Od. 9, 203; and prob. also furnished with a golden rim, Od. 4, 615. Il. 23, 219.

κρῖ, τό, Ep. abbreviated form for κριθή, in nom. and accus. barley. [Prob. the original form, see Buttm. § 57, note 3.] [" Every final consonant that the Greek language did not admit as a termination is either rejected or changed into a permissible consonant of the same organ, or assimilated to the nearest vowel. The earliest form of the language had some neuters without suffix: hence by the changes just enumerated we get δῶ (= δομ), κρῖ (= κριθ), βρῖ (= βριθ [βρίθος, βριθοσύνη]), γάλα (= γαλαν, γλάγος), κνῦ (κνυθός, Hes.), &c.," Düd., p. 231, note 163.]

κρίζω, aor. ἔκρικον (akin to κράζω), to crack, to snap, spoken of a breaking body, 16, 470.†

*κριθαίη, ἡ, prob. barley broth, Ep. 15, 7.

κριθή, ἡ, barley, only plur., 11, 69. Od. 9, 110. Sing. Ep. abbrev. κρῖ λευκόν, Il. 8, 564. Od. 4, 604. 12, 358. It is mentioned as food for horses. Prob. hordeum vulgare, Linn.

κρίκε, Ep. for ἔκρικε, see κρίζω.

κρίκος, Ep. for κίρκος, a ring, placed upon or over the pin on the pole, in attaching the horses to the chariot, 24, 272;† see ἕστωρ.

κρί νω, aor. 1 ἔκρινα. aor. 1 mid. ἐκρινάμην, perf. pass. κέκριμαι, aor. pass. ἐκρίθην, partcp. κριθείς and κρινθείς, 13, 129. Od. 8, 48: 1) to separate, to divide, to sunder, with accus. Il. 2, 362; καρπόν τε καὶ ἄχνας, 5, 502. 2) to choose out, to select, φῶτας ἐκ Λυκίης, 6, 188. Od. 4, 666. 10, 102; hence partcp. κεκριμένος and κρινθείς, selected, chosen, Il. 10, 417, Od. 13, 182; but οὖρος κεκριμένος, a decided wind, which blows steadfastly to one point of the compass, 11, 14, 19. 3) to deride, to judge, νείκεα, Od. 12, 440. σκολιὰς θέμιστας κρίνειν, to give tortuous sentences, i. e. to pervert the laws in judging. Il. 16, 387; spoken also of war: νεῖκος πολέμου, to decide the contest of battle, Od. 18, 264; hence pass. ὁπότε μνηστῆρσι καὶ ἡμῖν μένος κρίνηται Ἄρηος, when between the suitors and us the strength of Arês is decided, i. e. when it comes to open conflict, Od. 16, 269. Mid. 1) to separate oneself, to withdraw oneself, Od. 8, 36. 24, 507; esply from battle: κρίνεσθαι Ἀρηΐ, according to Wolf: ' to get clear, as it were, of each other by fighting,' and generally, to contend in open battle, to decide any thing by fighting, Il. 2, 385. 18, 209. 2) to select for oneself, to choose for oneself, ἑταίρους, Od. 4, 408. Il. 9, 521. 11, 697. 3) to decide, to judge, as depon. ὀνείρους, to explain dreams. 5, 150.

Κρῖσα, ἡ, later orthography Κρίσσα, h. Ap. 269, ed. Herm. and Ilgen; a very ancient city in Phocis, north of Cirrha, a colony of Cretans according to h. Ap. At a later day, it was destroyed by a decree of the Amphictyons, and its territory attached to Delphi; still it remained the port of Delphi; now Chriso, 2, 520. Whence ὁ Κρίσσης κόλπος, the Crisean Gulf, on the coast of Phocis, now Mare di Lipanto. Strabo distinguishes Κρίσα and Κίρρα, but Pausanias, 10, 37, 4, considers them as one place. With him accords Ottfr. Müller, Orchom. S. 495.

κριός, ὁ, a ram, *Od. 9, 447. 461.

κριτός, ή, όν (κρίνω), separated, chosen, selected, 7, 434. Od. 8, 258. 12, 439.

κροαίνω (κρούω), to strike, to stamp, spoken of a horse, *6, 507. 15, 264.

Κροῖσμος, ὁ, a Trojan, slain by Meges, 15, 523.

*κροκήϊος, η, ον, poet. (κρόκος), saffron-coloured, ἄνθος, h. Cer 178.

κροκόπεπλος, ον (πέπλος), having a saffron-coloured robe, epith. of [the saffron-mantled Morn. Cp.] Aurora, 8, 1, and elsewhere.

κρόκος, ὁ, saffron, a flower which grows in the mountains of southern Europe, crocus vernus, Linn., Il. 14, 348.†

Κροκύλεια, τά, a place in Acarnania according to Strabo, or in Ithaca according to Steph., Il. 2, 633.

κρόμυον, τό, an onion (allium cepa, Linn.); it is spoken of as food 11, 630. Od. 19, 233 (later orthography κρόμμυον).

Κρονίδης, ου, ὁ [also αω and εω, h. Cer. 414. h. 32. 2], son of Kronus=Zeus, often, standing alone, or connected with Ζεύς, 2, 375. Od. 1, 45.

Κρονίων, ίωνος and ίονος, son of Kronus=Zeus, also Ζεὺς Κρονίων (ῑ in nom. and gen. Κρονίονος, 14, 247. Od. 11, 620 ; elsewhere ῐ.)

Κρόνος, ὁ, Saturnus, son of Uranus and Gaia or Gæa (Tellus), husband of Rhea, father of Zeus, Poseidôn, Hadês, Hêrê, Dêmêtêr, and Hestin (Vesta). Before Zeus, he governed the world, till he was dethroned by his sons, and confined with the Titans in Tartarus, 8, 479. The sons divided the kingdom of their father, 15, 157. The golden age was during his dominion, Hes. Op. 111. (Κρόνος from κραίνω, the finisher, Perficus, as the last of the Titans, Herm.)

κρόσσαι, αἱ (akin to κόρση), τῶν πύργων, the battlements [?] of towers, Schol. ἄκραι, στεφάναι, *12, 258. 484. They are distinct from ἐπάλξεις. Hdt. 2, 125, compares them with ἀναβαθμοί, projecting stones by which the wall could be ascended ; hence κροσσάων ἐπέβαινον, 12, 444. Other critics incorrectly understand by it, scaling-ladders.

κροταλίζω (κρόταλον), to clatter, to

*Κρόταλον.   252   Κτήσιππος.

produce a rattling; with accus. ὄχεα, to hurry away the chariots with a rattling noise, 11, 160.†

κρόταλον, τό, a clapper, a bell, h. 13, 3.

κρόταφος, ὁ (κροτέω), *the temple* of the head, *the temples*, 4, 502: mly plur., 13, 188, and Od. 18, 378.

κροτέω (κρότος), *to cause to clatter or rattle*, ὄχεα, 15, 453.†

Κρουνοί, οἱ, *a fountain*, not far from Chalcis, of a little river in the southern part of Elis, with a village of the same name, cf. Strab. VIII. p. 351. Od. 15, 295. h. Ap. 425. (Barnes has introduced the verse from Strabo into the Od; Wolf, on the other hand, has enclosed it in brackets.)

κρουνός, ὁ 1) *a fountain, a spring*, 22, 208. 2) *the basin* in which the water is collected; *the bed* of a stream, 4, 454.

κρύβδα, adv. (κρύπτω), *secretly, privily*: with gen. Διός, without the knowledge of Zeus, 18, 168.†

κρύβδην, adv. i. q. κρύβδα, *Od. 11, 455. 16, 153.

κρυερός, ή, όν (κρύος), *cold, chilling*; metaph. *terrific, horrible*, φόβος (*icy fear*), γόος, 13, 48. 24, 524. Od. 4, 103.

κρυόεις, εσσα, εν (κρύος), *cold, chilling; icy, terrific*. φόβος, Ἰωκή, *5, 740. 9, 2.

κρυπτάδιος, η, ον (κρύπτω), *concealed, secret*, φιλότης, 6, 161. κρυπτάδια φρονεῖν, to devise secret plans, *1, 542.

κρυπτός, ή, όν (κρύπτω), *concealed, secret*, κληΐς, 14, 168.†

κρύπτω, Ep. iterat. imperf. κρύπτασκε, 8, 272, for κρύπτεσκε, h. Cer. 239; fut. κρύψω, aor. 1 ἔκρυψα, perf. pass. κέκρυμμαι, aor. pass. ἐκρύφθην, 1) *to conceal, to hide*, with accus. 18, 397. Od. 11, 244; for protection, τινὰ σάκεϊ, to cover any one with a shield. Il. 8, 272. κεφαλὰς κορύθεσσιν, 14, 373. 2) Metaph. *to conceal, to be silent*, τινὶ ἔπος, Od. 4, 350. τὸ δὲ καὶ κεκρυμμένον εἶναι (for the imperat.), let the other remain unspoken, Od. 11, 443. Mid. with aor. pass. *to conceal oneself, ὑπ' ἀσπίδι,* Il. 13, 405. κρύπτων Ἥρην, h. 26, 7, has been explained as reflexive, 'concealing oneself from Hêrê,' but unnecessarily; supply σέ from what precedes, and render, 'concealing thyself from Hêrê.'

κρύσταλλος, ὁ (κρύος), *any transparent, congealed, or frozen substance, ice*, 22, 152. 14, 477.

κρυφηδόν, adv. (κρύπτω), *secretly, in a concealed manner, clandestinely*, *Od. 14, 330. 19, 299.

Κρῶμνα, ἡ, a place in Paphlagonia; according to Strabo at a later day, with Sesamus and Cytôrus, it formed Amastris, 2, 885.

κτάμεναι, κτάμεναι, κτάμενος, see κτείνω.

κτάομαι, aor. 1 ἐκτησάμην, perf. ἔκτημαι, only infin. ἐκτῆσθαι, *to gain, to acquire, to earn, to procure, to purchase*, with accus. 9, 400; also τινί τι, to obtain any thing for any one, Od. 20,

265; perf. *to have acquired, to possess*, Il. 9, 402.

ΚΤΑΩ, assumed ground form of the Ep. aor. ἔκταν, ἐκτάμην, see κτείνω.

κτέαρ, ατος, τό, only dat. plur. ἐτεάτεσσι; poet. *that which is gained, property, possessions*, 5, 154. Od. 1, 218, and often.

κτεατίζω (κτέαρ), aor. 1 ἐκτεάτισα, Ep. σσ. perf. mid. ἐκτεάτισμαι, 1) *to acquire for oneself, to procure*, with accus. πολλά, Od. 2, 102; δουρί, in war, Il. 16.57. Mid, *to acquire for oneself*, h. Merc 522.

Κτέατος, ὁ, son of Actor and Moliond, or, according to fable, son of Poseidôn, twin brother of Eurytus; Heracles slew him, 2, 601. 13, 185; see Εὔρυτος.

κτείνω, fut. κτενῶ, κτενεῖ, Ep. κτενέω, έεις, und fut. partcp. κτανέοντα, 18, 309; aor. 1 ἔκτεινα, aor. 2 ἔκτανον, aor. 1 pass. 3 plur. ἔκταθεν for ἐκτάθησαν, Od. 4, 537; Ep. aor. act. ἔκταν, 3 plur. ἔκταν for ἔκτασαν, subj. κτέω, Ep. 1 plur. κτέωμεν, infin. κτάμεν, κτάμεναι for κτάναι, aor. 2 mid. ἐκτάμην, with pass. signif. infin. κτάσθαι, partcp. κτάμενος (akin to καίνω, θείνω), *to slay, to kill, to slaughter*, τινά, esply in battle, rarely spoken of the killing or slaughtering of a brute, 15, 587. Od. 12, 379. Pass. κτείνεσθαί τινι, to be slain by any one, Il. 5, 465; Ep. aor. 2 mid. with pass. signif. 3, 375. 5, 301. 15, 558.

κτέαρ, τό = κτέαρ, Ep. *possessions, property*, only sing. nom., *10, 216. 24, 235.

κτέρεα, τά (the nom. sing. κτέρος, i. q. κτέαρ, does not occur), prop. *possessions*; then, every thing bestowed upon a dead person as property, and burned with the funeral pile; generally, *funeral obsequies, the last offices to the dead*, extremi honores; mly κτέρεα κτερείζειν, Od. 1, 291. 3, 285. Il. 24, 38.

κτερείζω, fut. κτερείξω, a lengthened form of κτερίζω, 23, 646. 24, 657. Od. 1, 291. 2, 222.

κτερίζω (κτέρεα), fut. κτερίσω. Ep. κτεριῶ, aor. ἐκτέρισα, originally = κτερείζω, confined in use to the funeral rites of the dead. 1) With accus. *to inter a man with funeral honours*, 11, 455. 16, 334. 22, 236. κτερείζειν τινὰ ἀέθλοις, to solemnize the interment of any one with funeral games, 23, 646. 2) with the accus. κτέρεα, to perform the obsequies, *justa facere*, 24, 38. Od. 1, 291.

κτῆμα, ατος, τό, *that which is gained, possessions, property, estate*, sing. only Od. 15, 19. Plur. in the Il. mly *treasures, valuables*, 9, 382. Od. 4, 127; in the Od. rather, *property, estate*, Od. 1, 375. 404.

κτῆνος, εος, τό = κτῆμα, possessions, esply an ox, plur. oxen, *domestic animals*, h. 30, 10.

Κτήσιος, ὁ, son of Ormenus, father of Eumæus, of Syria, Od. 15, 414.

Κτήσιππος, ὁ (possessing horses), son of Polytherses of Samê, a suitor of Penelope, Od. 20, 288. 22, 279.

Κτῆσις.   Κύδιστος.

κτῆσις, ιος, ή, that which is gained, possessions, property, 5, 158. Od. 4, 687.
κτητός, ή. όν (κτάομαι), gained. 2) to be acquired, to be gained, 9, 407.† cf. ἐλετός.
κτίδεος, έη, εον (κτίς), for ἰκτίδιος, pertaining to a weasel, κυνέη κτιδέη, a headpiece of weasel-skin [of ferret's felt, Cp.], *10, 335. 458. (According to most critics, κτίς or ἰκτίς is mustela putorius, a polecat; some define it to be a ferret, viverra.)
κτίζω, fut. ίσω, aor. 1 ἔκτισα, Ep. σσ, to make a country habitable, to settle, to people; to found to build a city, with an ac. us 20, 216; Θήβης, ἕδος, Od. 11, 263. (Akin to κτάομαι.)
κτίλος, ὁ, prop adj tame; then subst. a ram, *3, 196. 13, 492.
Κτιμένη, ἡ, daughter of Laertes, sister of Odysseus (Ulysses); she was married and settled in Samê, Od. 15, 362, seq.
κτυπέω (κτύπος), aor. ἔκτυπον, to crack, to rattle, to resound, 13, 140. 23, 119; often Ζεὺς ἔκτυπε, Zeus thundered, 8, 75. Od. 21 413.
κτύπος, ὁ (τύπτω), a noise, crash, &c. produced by striking or stamping, noise, rattling, uproar, hubbub; ἵππων, the stamping of steeds, 10, 532. 535; ποδοῖιν (of men), Od. 16, 6. Il. 10, 363; of the tumult of battle, 12, 338; Διός, the thunder of Zeus, 15, 379. 20, 66.
κύαμος, ὁ, a bean, prob. the field-bean, 13, 589.† Batr. 125
κυάνεος, έη, εον (κύανος), dark-blue, black blue; and generally, dark-coloured, blackish ὀφρύες (of Zeus), 1, 528; of Herê, 15, 102; χαῖται, spoken of the hair of Hector and Odysseus (Ulysses), 22, 402. Od. 16, 176; δράκων, Il. 11, 26; κάλυμμα, 24, 94; νέφος, νεφέλη, 23, 188. 5, 345; trop. κυάνεον, Τρώων νέφος, 16, 66. κυάνεαι φάλαγγες, dark squadrons, which move on like dark clouds, 4, 282.
κυανόπεζα, ἡ (πέζα), having dark-blue feet, a table with dark-blue pedestal, V., 11. 629.
*κυανόπεπλος, ον (πέπλος), having a dark-c loured robe, dark-robed epith. of Dêmêtêr, h. in Cer. 320.
κυανοπρώρειος, ον and κυανόπρωρος, ον (πρώρα). having a dark-blue or black prow, black-beakrd [sable-prow'd, Cp.], νηῦς. 15, 693, and often. (κυανοπρώρειος only Od. 3, 299.)
κύανος, ὁ, a blue cast metal (according to Voss, blue cast steel); Beckmann, Geschich. der Erfind. 4 B. p. 356, with Voss, takes it for steel; and according to Köpkens Kriegswissensch. it cannot be denied that the ancients used steel, cf. 23, 850, and Od. 9, 391. As there is no other blue-black metal, whether produced by nature or art, H. very probably intends this by κύανος. Millin (Mineralogie d'Homère) considers it as tin or lead, and several ancients (Hesych.) thought it a dark colour. or a kind of mineral varnish or lacker. Thus Schneider in Lex. This metal was used for ornament, as upon the shield of Agamemnon ten strips. 11, 24; and in Od. 7, 87, in the hall of Alcinous, a cornice of κύανος is mentioned.
κυανοχαίτης, ου, ὁ (χαίτη), having dark hair, mly having dark locks, epith. of [the azure-haired, Cp.] Poseidôn (once ἵππος, black-maned, 20, 144); as subst. one having black locks, 20, 144 Od. 9, 536.
κυανῶπις, ιδος, ἡ (ὤψ), dark- or black-eyed, pith. of Amphitrîtê, Od. 12, 60.†
κυβερνάω, aor. infin. κυβερνῆσαι, to steer. to pilot. νῆα, Od. 3. 283.†
κυβερνητήρ. ἥρος, ὁ = κυβερνήτης, Od. 8, 557.†
κυβερνήτης, ου, ὁ (κυβερνάω), a pilot, gubernator, 19, 43. Od. 0. 78
κυβιστάω (κύβη), to place or throw oneself upon the head, esplv to plunge head foremost, to dive down, 16, 745. 749; spoken of fish, *21, 354.
κυβιστητήρ. ἥρος, ὁ (κυβιστάω), one who places himself upon his head, or who turns a somerset, a juggler, a tumbler, 18, 605. Od. 4, 18. 2) a diver, Il. 16, 750.
κυδαίνω (κῦδος). poet. κύδανω, fut. κυδανῶ, aor. 1 ἐκύδηνα. 1) Prop. to render famous; to honour, to distinguish, to glorify, τινά with τιμᾷν, 15, 612. 2) to place any one in an enviable condition, to honour, to distinguish. to glorify, spoken of the body (opposed to κακῶσαι); Αἰνείαν ἀκέοντό τε κύδαινόν τε, they healed Aeneas and restored his former beauty, 5, 448; [him—they healed and glorified, Cp.] cf. Od. 16, 212. The Schol. explain it: ἐδόξαζον, λόγῳ παρεμύθοντο: Damm; honore officiebant, notions which do not suit ἀκέοντο. b) Spoken of the mind, to rejoice, θυμὸν ἄνακτος, Od. 14, 438.
κυδάλιμος, ον, poet. (κῦδος), famous, renowned, lauded, epith. of individual heroes and of entire people, 6, 184. 204. 2) ambitious, noble, κῆρ, 10, 16. Od. 21, 147; spoken of lions, 12, 45.
κυδάνω, poet. for κυδαίνω, to honour, τινά ὁμῶς θεοῖσιν, 14, 73.† 2) Intrans. = κυδιάω, to vaunt oneself, to be proud, imperf. κύδανον, 20, 42.
κυδιάνειρα, ἡ (κυδαίνω), poet. man-honouring, man-ennobling, μάχη. Il. and once ἀγορή, *1, 490. It is derived not from κῦδος, but from κυδαίνω, hence Hesych. justly: ἡ τοὺς ἄνδρας δοξάζουσα.
κυδιάω (κῦδος), intrans. to boast, to be proud, to be puffed up, to stride proudly, spoken of warriors, 2, 579. 21, 519. of steeds, 6, 509. 15, 266; for the most part, the Ep. partcp. κυδιόων (glorying [in]); only εὐφροσύνῃ κυδιόωσιν, h. 30, 13.
*κύδιμος, ον (κῦδος) = κυδάλιμος, epith. of Hermês, only n. Merc. 46, and repeated nine times.
κύδιστος, η, ον (irreg superl. of κῦδος, as if formed from κῦδος), most famous,

Κυδοιμέω. 254 **Κυλίνδω.**

most honorable, most honoured, epith. of Zeus and Athênê, 4, 415; and of Agamemnon, 2, 434.

κυδοιμέω (κυδοιμός), fut. ήσω, 1) *to make a noise, to raise a disturbance, to make an uproar*, άν' ὅμιλον, 11, 324. 2) Trans. *to throw into confusion*, with accus. *15, 136.

κυδοιμός, ὁ, *noise, tumult, the tumult of battle*, Il., *confusion, panic*, 18, 218. 2) As a mythic being: *the deity of the tumult of battle*, as companion of Enyo (Heilona), 5, 593. 18, 535. (Bothe as appellat.) *11.

κῦδος, εος, τό. 1) *splendour, glory, honour, praise, dignity*, often connected with τιμή, 10, 84. 17, 251; in the address, κῦδος 'Αχαιῶν, glory or pride of the Greeks, 9, 673. Od. 3, 79 2) that which gives glory and fame, *prosperity, success, fortune*. κῦδος ὀπάζειν τινί. Od. 3, 57. 15, 320; in the Il. *success in war, the glory of victory*, 5, 225. 8, 141; *famous bodily strength, lofty courage*, κῦδος καὶ ἀγλαίη, Od. 15, 78. 11, 1, 405. 5, 906. Nitzsch ad Od. 3, 57.

κυδρός, ή, όν, poet. (κῦδος), *famous, famed, glorious*, always fem., epith. of Hêrê, Lêtô (Latona), Athênê, and of a mortal female, Od. 15, 26. The masc. h. Merc. 461.

Κύδων, ωνος, ὁ, plur. οἱ Κύδωνες, *the Cydônes*, a people who dwelt on the north-west side of the island of Crete. According to Strab. they were the aborigines of the island, and, according to Mannert, VIII. p. 679, prob. a division of the Etruscans. Their town Cydonia was prob. situated where stands the present Canea, Od. 3, 292. 19, 176.

κυέω. poet. old form for κύω, *to become pregnant, to be pregnant with; to conceive*, with accus. υἱόν, spoken of a woman, 19, 117; of a mare, 23, 266; mid. h. 26, 4.

κύθε, see κεύθω.

Κυθέρεια, ή, an appellation of Aphroditê, either from the island Cythêra, which was sacred to her, or from the town Cythera in Cyprus, Od. 8, 288. 18, 192. h. Ven. 6; with Κυπρογενής, h. 9, 8.

Κύθηρα, τά, an island on the Laconian coast, south-west (according to Strab. one mile) of the promontory of Malea, now *Cerigo*. According to later fable, Aphroditê landed upon it when she rose from the foam of the sea, 15. 432. Od. 8, 288. The chief town Cythêra, had a noted temple of Aphroditê. From this **Κυθηρόθεν**, from Cythera, Il. 15, 438; **Κυθήριος,** Born in Cythera, 10, 208.

κυκάω, partcp. pres. κυκόων, Ep. for κυκῶν, aor. 1 ἐκύκησα, aor. 1 pass. ἐκυκήθην, 1) *to touch, to mingle, to stir in*, 5, 903; with dat. instrum τυρόν οἴνῳ, Od. 10, 235. Il. 11, 637. 2) Metaph. *to confuse, to throw into confusion, to put into disorder*; only pass. *to be confused, to be thrown into disorder*, 11, 129. 18. 229; of horses: *to be terrified*, 20, 489; of rivers and waves: *to be in uproar, to be turbid*, 21, 235 Od. 12, 258. 241.

κυκείω and **κυκέω,** see κυκεών.

κυκεών, ῶνος. ὁ (κυκάω), Ep. accus. κυκειῶ and κυκεῶ, Ep. for κυκεῶνα, *a mixture, a potion, draught* (Cp.), or *jelly* which was prepared from barley-meal, goat's-milk cheese, and Pramn'an wine, 11, 624. 638. 640. In Od. 10, 234. 290, Circê casts in honey. That it was somewhat thick appears from the Od., where it is called σῖτος. In h. Cer. 208, it is prepared of barley-meal, water, and penny-royal. This jelly was taken to strengthen and recruit; and even in later times it was an article of food for the lower classes, Theoph. Char. 4, 1. (On the accus. see Thiersch, § 188, 15. Buttm. § 55, note.)

κυκλέω (κύκλος), fut. ήσω, *to carry away on wheels, to convey away*, νεκρούς βουσί, 7, 332.†

κύκλος, ὁ, plur. οἱ **κύκλοι** and τά **κύκλα.** spoken of a chariot, 1) *a circle, a ring, a circumference*, esp'ly the circular rim of a shield. κύκλοι, 11, 33. 12, 297; trop. *b) a circle*, spoken of men ἱερὸς κύκλος, of a popular assembly, 18, 504. c) δόλιος κύκλος, the deceitful circle, which hunters form around wild animals, Od. 4, 792; κύκλῳ, in the circle, Od 8, 278. 2) any thing circular; in form, *a wheel*, which is the signif. of τά κύκλα. Il. 5, 722. 18, 375. *b) the disc, the ball* of a planet, h. 7, 6.

κυκλόσε, adv. (κύκλος), *in a circle, round about*, *4, 212. 17, 392.

κυκλοτερής, ές (κύκλος), *round, circular*, ἄλσος, Od. 17, 209. κυκλοτερὲς τείνειν τόξον, to send the bow to a circle, Il. 4, 124.

Κύκλωπες, οἱ, sing. **Κύκλωψ, ὁ** (prop. *circular-eyed*), *the Cyclôpes*, in the Od. are a rude, gigantic race, who live in a scattered, nomadic manner, without laws or cities, Od. 9, 106. seq. Polyphêmus, the most powerful amongst them, sprung from Poseidôn, Od. 1. 63, seq. That they were only one-eyed, appears from the circumstance that Polyphemus, after losing his eye, saw no more, cf. Od 9, 397. 416. The ancients generally place them in Sicily, in the region of Ætna, Thuc 6, 2. Some regard the Leontines as springing from them. Amongst the moderns Voss places them on the south side of Sicily; Völcker, Hom. Geogr. § 58, with great probability, on the south-west coast, near the promontory Lilybaeum. Distinct from them are the Cyclopes mentioned by Hes.Th. 140, children of Uranus and Gaia (Tellus), who forge lightning and thunderbolts for Zeus.

κύκνος, ὁ, *a swan*, *2, 460. 15, 692.

κυλίνδω, only pres. and imperf. and aor. 1 pass. ἐκυλίσθην as if from κυλίω, *to roll, to move by rolling*, with accus. spoken of waves, ὀστέα, Od. 1, 162; of the wind, κῦμα, Od. 5, 296; metaph. πῆμά τινι, to bring a misfortune upon

Κυλλήνη. 255 . Κύπρις.

any one, Il. 17, 688. Mid. with aor. pass. *to roll oneself, to roll away*. spoken of a tempest and of waves, 5, 142. 11, 307; of a wounded horse: περὶ χαλκῷ, 8, 86; spoken of men, as an expression of vehement grief; κατὰ κόπρον, to roll (oneself) in the dirt, 22, 414. 24, 165 Od. 4, 541. Metaph. νῶϊν πῆμα κυλίνδεται, ruin is rolling upon us, Il. 11, 347. 17, 99. Od. 2, 163.

Κυλλήνη, ἡ. a mountain in northern Arcadia on the borders of Achaia, having a temple of Hermēs, 2, 603. h. Merc. 2, a town in Elis, now *Chiarenza*.

Κυλλήνιος, ὁ, the *Cyllenian*. 1) epith. of Hermēs, Od. 24, 1. 2) an inhabitant of the town of Cyllēnē in Elis, Il. 15, 518. according to Schol. Venet. and Eustath.

Κυλλοποδίων, ονος, ὁ (κυλλός, πούς), voc. Κυλλοπόδιον, *having crooked feet, lame*, epith. of Hēphæstus, *18, 371. 21, 331.

κῦμα, ατος, τό (κύω), *a wave, a swell* of rivers and the sea, often plur. κύματα παντοίων ἀνέμων, the waves excited by winds from every direction (gen. origin.), 2, 397.

κυμαίνω (κῦμα), *to swell into waves, to undulate*. only partcp. πόντος κυμαίνων, 14, 229. Od. 4, 425. and often.

κύμβαχος, ον (κύπτω, κύβη, κύμβη), adj. *head forwards, head foremost, headlong*. 2) Subst. *the upper arch* or *head of the helmet*, in which the crest was inserted, *15, 536.

*Κύμη, ἡ, a town in Æolis (Asia), a colony of Ætolians, Ep. 1, 2. 4, 16.

κύμινδις, ὁ, *a night-hawk*, Plin. H. N. *noeturnus accipiter*; according to 14, 291,† it was called in the earlier language χαλκίς, in the later κύμινδις.

Κυμοδόκη, ἡ (δέχομαι), a Nereid, prop. the wave-receiver, 18, 39.

Κυμοθόη, ἡ (θοός), a Nereid, prop. wave-swift, 18, 41.

κυνάμυια, ἡ (μυῖα), *a dog-fly*, i. e. according to Voss, an impudent fly, a term of reproach used in regard to women, who like dogs and flies are shameless and impudent. Arēs uses it to Athēnē and Hērē [*Wasp!* front of impudence! *Cp*.], 21, 394. 421. Others, as Bothe, read κυνόμυια, as common in prose.

κυνέη. ἡ (prop. fem. from κύνεος, subaud. δορά), *a dog's-skin*, from which head-coverings were made; generally, *a helmet, a head-piece*, without regard to the derivation; the κυνέη was made of ox-hide, ταυρείη, 10, 258; of weasel's (or *ferret's*)-skin, κτιδέη, 10, 335; and set with metal, χαλκήρης, χαλκοπάρῃος, also entirely of brass, πάγχαλκος, Od. 18, 378; κυνέη αἰγείη, a cap of goat's skin, is mentioned Od. 24, 231, which countrymen wore in labouring. The κυνέη Ἄϊδος rendered the wearer invisible (like the *Nebel-* or *Tarn-kappe* of the Niebelungenlied), 5, 845: it was made by the Cyclopes, Apd. 1, 2. 1.

κύνεος, έη, εον, *of a dog, canine, shameless, impudent*, 9, 373.†

κυνέω, aor. 1 ἔκυσα, Ep. σσ (from κύω), *to kiss*, with accus. υἱόν 6, 474. Od. 16, 190; γούνατα, χεῖρας, Il. 8, 371. 24, 478; and with double accus. κύσσε μιν κεφαλήν, Od. 16, 15. 17, 39; (κυνέω only in the pres. and imperf. Od. 4, 522. 17, 35.)

κυνηγέτης, ου, ὁ (ἡγέτης), that leads dogs to the chase, *an hunter*. Od. 9, 120.†

*Κύνθιος, η, ον, *Cynthian*, ὄχθος = Κύνθος, h. Ap. 27.

*Κύνθος, ὁ, a mountain on the island of Delos, the birth-place of Apollo and Diana, h. Ap. 141; and Κύνθου ὄρος, for Κύνθος, according to an emend. of Hollstein's ad Steph. cf. Herm. ad loc.

κυνοραιστής, ὁ (ῥαίω), *a dog-louse, a dog-tick*, acarus ricinus, Od. 17, 300.†

Κῦνος, ἡ, a city in Locris, on a peninsula of the same name, the port of Opus, now *Cyno*, 2, 531.

κύντερος. η, ον, compar. and κύντατος, η, ον, superl. formed from κύων: *more dog-like*, metaph. *more shameless, more impudent*, 8, 483. Od. 7, 216. Superl. κύντατον ἔρδειν, to act most impudently, Il 10, 503.

κυνώπης, ου, ὁ (fem. κυνῶπις, ιδος), *dog-eyed, dog-faced*, i. e. shameless, impudent; voc. κυνῶπα, spoken of Agamemnon, 1, 159.†

κυνῶπις, ιδος, ἡ, fem. of κυνώπης, dog-eyed, i. e. shameless, impudent, of Helen, 3, 180. Od. 4, 146; of Hērē, Il. 18, 396: of Aphroditē, Od. 8, 319.

Κυπαρισσήεις, εντος, ἡ, a town in Triphylia in Elis, on the borders of Messenia, according to Strab. in the ancient Macistia, and in his time an uninhabited place, called ἡ Κυπαρισσία, 2, 593.

κυπαρίσσινος, η, ον (κυπάρισσος), *made of cypress-wood*, Od. 17, 340.†

Κυπάρισσος. ἡ, *cypress*, cupressus semper virens, which in Greece was very abundant, Od. 5, 64.†

Κυπάρισσος, ἡ, a little town in Phocis on Parnassus, not far from Delphi, or a cypress-grove; according to Steph. at an early period *Eranos*, later *Apollonias*, 2, 519.

κύπειρον, τό. a meadow-plant, *the cyperus*, cyperus longus, Linn. Heyne, ad Il. 21, 351, understands by it *the fragrant cyperus*, cyperus rotundus, Linn. Voss, on the other hand, *the galangal*, pseudo-cyperus, Plin.; it was used as food for horses, Od. 4, 603.

*κύπειρος, ὁ, prob. = κύπειρον, h. Merc. 107.

κύπελλον, τό (κύπτω), *a goblet, a beaker, a drinking-cup*, often the same with δέπας, mly of metal, χρύσεια κύπελλα, 3, 248; and Od. 1, 142.

Κύπρις. ιδος, ἡ. accus. Κύπριδα, 5, 458; and Κύπριν (Κύπρος), 5, 330: *Cypris*, an appellation of Aphroditē, because she

*Κυπρογενής. was especially worshipt on the island Cypros, or was supposed to have been born there, *5, 422.

*Κυπρογενής, οῦς, ἡ, one born in Cyprus, epith. of Aphroditê, h. 8, 9.

Κύπρος, ἡ, an island of the Mediterranean sea, on the coast of Asia Minor, noted for the worship of Aphroditê, for its fruitfulness, and its rich mines of metals, now Cipro, 11, 21. Od. 4, 83. 8, 362. (υ prop. short, but Ep. also long.)

κύπτω, aor. 1 ἔκυψα, to bow oneself, to bend forwards, 4, 468. 17, 621. Od. 11, 585.

*κυρβαίη μάζα, ἡ, a kind of paste or broth, Ep. 16, 6; where Suid. has κυρκαίη; Herm. would read: πυρκαίη δ' αἰεὶ κατὰ καρδόπου ἄρπεο, μάζαν ἔμμεν, ignis mactram culefaciat, ut semper placenta suppetat.

κυρέω, Ion. and poet., rarely κύρω, imperf. κῦρε for ἔκυρε, 23, 821; aor. 1 ἔκυρσα (ἐκύρησα, Ep. 6, 6), pres. mid. κύρομαι=κυρέω, 1) with dat. to fall by chance upon any thing, to hit, to meet any thing, ἅρματι, 23, 428; κακῷ κύρεται, he is fallen into misfortune, 24, 530; ἐπὶ σώματι, spoken of a lion which meets with prey, 3, 23; αἰὲν ἐπ' αὐχένι κῦρε δουρὸς ἀκωκῇ, he aimed even at the neck with the spear's point, 23, 821. 2) With gen. to reach any point, to attain, to reach, Ep. 6, 6. (Pres. κυρέω is not found in H.)

κῦρμα, ατος, τό, any thing which one falls upon and finds, a windfall, spoil, booty, plunder, in connexion with ἕλωρ, 5, 488. 17, 151. 272. Od. 3, 271. 5, 473.

κύρσας, see κυρέω.

κυρτός, ή, όν, bent, curved, crooked, κῦμα, 4, 426. 13, 799. ὤμω, *2, 218.

κυρτόω (κυρτός), fut. ὤσω, to bend, to curve, to arch; κῦμα οὐρεῖ ἴσον κυρτωθέν, arched like a mountain, Od. 11, 244.†

κύστις, ιος, ἡ (κύω), a bladder, *5, 67. 13. 652.

Κύτωρος, ἡ, a town in Paphlagonia, later the port of Amastris, now Quitros, 2, 853; Strab. τὸ Κύτωρον.

κυφός, ή, όν (κύπτος), bent forwards, bowed down, γηραί, Od. 2, 16.†

Κύφος, ἡ, a town in Perrhæbia (Thessaly), upon a mountain of the same name, 2, 748; elsewhere ἡ Κύφος.

κύω, 1) a later form from κυέω, q. v. 2) the root of κυνέω.

κύων, gen. κυνός, ὁ, ἡ, dat. κυσί. Ep. κύνεσσι, 1) a dog, a bitch; κύνες θηρευταί, hunting dogs; hounds; τραπεζῆες, table-dogs. It was a heroic custom to take dogs into the assembly, Od. 2, 11. 17, 62. 2) As a term of reproach, to indicate shamelessness, impudence, as of Helen, Athênê, Hêrê, 6, 344. 356. 8, 423. 21, 481; used of a maid of Odysseus (Ulysses), Od. 18, 338, spoken of men it indicates rage, rashness; of Hector: κύων λυσσητήρ, a raging dog, 11. 8, 299; but also shameless cowardice, esply in the fem κακαὶ κύνες, ye dastardly dogs (spoken of Trojans), 13, 623. 3) κύω Ἀΐδαο, the dog of Hadês, is Cerberus, 8, 368. 4) κύων Ὠρίωνος, the dog of Orion (the dog-star, Σείριος, Hes.), which, with his master, was placed amongst the constellations. In hot regions it is the forerunner of fevers and epidemics, 22, 29. 5) a sea-dog, Od. 12, 96.

κῶας, τό, plur. κώεα, dat. κώεσιν, a soft, hairy skin; a sheep-skin, a fleece. Such skins were spread on the ground, or on chairs and beds, to sit or lie upon, 9, 661, once; Od. 3, 38. 16, 47, and often.

κώδεια, ἡ (κόττα), a head, esply, a poppy-head, 14, 499.† Cf. on the passage the word φή.

κωκυτός, ὁ (κωκύω), howling, lamentation, wailing, *22, 409. 447.

Κωκυτός, ὁ, Cocytus, a river in the under-world, which issued from the Styx, Od. 10, 514.

κωκύω, aor. 1 ἐκώκυσα, to howl, to lament, to wail, to groan, always spoken of women, 18, 37. 71. Od. 2, 361 (in the press. and imperf. ὕ, Od. 4, 259. 8. 527.

κώληψ, ηπος, ἡ (κῶλον), the ham, 23, 726.†

κῶμα, τό (κοιμάω), a deep, sound sleep, 14, 359. Od. 18, 201.

*κῶμος, ὁ, a feast, a festal entertainment, h. Merc. 481.

*κώνωψ, ωπος, ὁ, ἡ, a gnat, Batr. 203.

Κῶπαι, αἱ, Copæ, an old town on the north side of the lake Copaïs in Bœotia, now Topolia, 2, 502.

κώπη, ἡ (ΚΑΠΩ, κάπτω), a handle, hence 1) the hilt of a sword, the hilt of a dagger, 1, 219. Od. 8, 403. 11, 531. b) the handle of an oar, Od 9, 489. 12, 214; also the oar itself. [For the last signif. there is no sufficient proof, see Jahn Jahn und K. p. 271.] c) the handle of a key, Od. 21, 7.

κωπήεις, εσσα, εν (κώπη), furnished with a handle or hilt; hilted, ξίφος, *15, 713. 14, 332. 20, 475.

κώρυκος, ὁ, a leathern sack or wallet, In which provisions were carried, *Od. 5. 267. 9, 213.

*Κώρυκος, ὁ, a steep mountain in Ionia (Asia Minor), which forms a promontory, according to Steph. near Troy and Erythræ, h. Ap. 39.

Κῶς, Ep. Κόως, gen. Κῶ, accus. Κῶν, 2, 677; a little island of the Icarian sea, with a town of the same name; it was inhabited by the Meropes, 2, 677. h. Ap. 43. Adv. Κόωνδε, to Cos, 14, 255. 15. 28.

κωφός, ή, όν (κόπτω, cf. tusus, obtusus), blunt, obtuse, powerless, βέλος, 11, 390. esply 1) obtuse in the senses, deaf, h. Merc. 92. 2) mute, still. κῦμα κωφόν, the mute [or still, Cp.] wave, as a premonitory sign of a coming tempest, 14, 16; κωφὴ γαῖα, the mute or dead, i. e. the senseless earth, 24, 54.

257 Λαιστρυγόνες.

Λ.

Λ, the eleventh letter of the Greek alphabet ; hence the sign of the eleventh rhapsody.
λᾶας. contr. λᾶς, ὁ, gen. λᾶος, dat. λᾶϊ, accus. λᾶαν, dat. plur. λάεσσι, *a stone*, such as warriors hurl at one another in battle, 3, 12. 4, 521. 2) *a rock, a crag*, Od. 13, 163. [3) *a stone-seat*, Od. 6, 267.]
Λάας, contr. Λᾶς, ὁ, accus. Λάαν, an old town in Laconia, ten stadia from the sea; it was destroyed by the Dioscūri, who from this acquired the name Λαπέρσαι, 2, 385. (Λᾶς, nom. in Scyl. and Paus. According to Eustath, and Steph. ἡ Λᾶ and ὁ Λᾶς were used in the nom.)
λαβραγόρης, ου, ὁ (ἀγορεύω), *prating boldly, pertly; forward with the tongue*, 23, 479.†
λαβρεύομαι, depon. mid. (λάβρος), *to speak in a bold, rash*, or *pert manner*. *to prate inconsiderately*, *23, 474; μύθοις, 478.
λάβρος, ον superl. λαβρότατος, *vehement, impetuous, violent, rapid*, spoken of wind, 2, 148. Od. 15, 293; κῦμα, 11. 15, 625; ποταμός, 21, 271; and of rain, λαβρότατον χέει ὕδωρ Ζεύς, 16, 385. (The deriv. is obscure; the Gramm. derive it from λα and βορά, very voracious, greedy; that is, however, a post-Hom. notion; according to Passow from ΛΑΩ)
λαγχάνω. aor. 2 ἔλαχον, subjunc. λάχω. Ep. λελάχω, 7, 350; perf. λέλογχα, Ep. for εἴληχα; (3 plur. λελόγχασ'. Od. 11, 304, is a conject. of Eustath. instead of the vulgar λελόγχασι, with a short, Thiersch, § 211. 26. Rem.) 1) *to receive by lot, to receive* by fate or the will of the gods, because, to learn this, recourse was had to lots, and generally, *to receive, to obtain*. *a*) With accus. γέρας, 4, 49; οὐρανόν, 15, 192; αἶσαν, Od. 5, 40; πολλά, Od. 14, 233. h. Merc. 420; also κλήρῳ λαχεῖν, 11. 23, 862; with infin following, 23, 356, 357. cf. 15, 191; hence αὗνοί. ὅς τε λάχῃσιν, on whom the lot falls, 7, 171. 10, 430. cf. Od. 9, 334. In the perf *to be master of, to possess, to have*, τιμήν, Od. 11, 304. h. 18, 6. *b*) With gen. *to become partaker of a thing*, as it were, to obtain part of a thing, δαίρων, 11 24, 76; πτερέων, Od. 5, 311. 2) *to cause to partake of*, to make one a partaker of a thing, τινά τινος; however, the subj. nor. with redupl. has this signif. only in the Il θανόντα πυρός, *to yield the dead the honour of fire*, 7, 80. 15, 350. 23, 76. 3) Intrans. *to fall by lot, to be allotted to*. ἐς ἑκάστην ἐννέα λάγχανον αἶγες, nine goats fell to the lot of each ship. Od. 9, 160.
*λαγών, όνος, ἡ, or ὁ, prop. *a cavity*. 2) *the flank* (the space between the hips and the ribs), Batr. 225.
λαγωός. ὁ, Ion. and Ep. for λαγώς. *a hare*; its cry in mating-time is a hollow muttering; when distressed, it is like the crying of a child, 10, 361. Od. 17, 295.
Λάέρκης, ους, ὁ, 1) son of Αἰμῶν (Æmon), father of Alcimedon, a noble Myrmidon, 16, 197. 17, 467. 2) An artist in Pylos, Od. 3, 425. According to Eustath. ὁ λαοῖς ἐπαρωών, who aids the people.
Λαέρτης, αο, ὁ, son of Arcesius, father of Odysseus (Ulysses), king of Ithaca; in his youth he destroyed Nericus; he lived to an advanced age in the country, Od. 11, 186, seq. 24, 219, seq.: and fought with his son against the people of Ithaca, Od. 24, 498.
Λαερτιάδης, ου, ὁ, son of Laertes = Odysseus (Ulysses), 11. and Od.
λάζομαι. depon. only pres. and imperf. Ion. and Ep. for λαμβάνω, *to take, to seize, to grasp, to lay hold of*, with accus. ἡνία χερσί, 5, 365. Od. 3, 483: ἀγκὰς θυγατέρα, to take in the arms, to embrace, 11. 5, 371; γαῖαν ὀδάξ, to lay hold of the earth with the teeth, to bite the earth, to perish, 2, 418; metaph. μῦθον πάλιν, to take again the word, to answer, 4, 357. Od. 13, 255.
*λάζυμαι, a form of λάζομαι, h. Merc. 316.
λαθικηδής, ές (κῆδος), *that causes to forget troub e, soothing*, μαζός, 22, 83.†
λάθρη, Ion, and Ep. for λάθρα, adv. (λανθάνω), *secretly, unobserved*, 2, 515. Od. 4, 92; with gen. λάθρη τινός, without the knowledge of, 11. 5, 269. 24, 72. (λάθρα, h. Cer. 241.)
λᾶϊγξ, ιγγος, ἡ (dimin. of λᾶας), *a pebble, a stone*. *Od. 5, 433. 6, 95.
λαίλαψ, απος. ἡ, *a tempest* with a whirlwind, rain, and darkness, *a hurricane*, 4, 278. To it H. compares his heroes, 11, 747. 12, 375; esply *a sea-storm*, Od. b, 68. 12, 314.
λαιμός, ὁ (λάω), *the throat, the gorge, the gullet*, 13, 388. Od. 22, 15.
λάϊνεος, έη, έον (only 22, 154). and λάϊνος, ον (λᾶας), *stony, of stone*, οὐδος, 9, 404 λάϊνος χιτών. 3, 57 (cf. ἔννυμι). πάντη περὶ τείχος ὀρῴρει θεσπιδαὲς πῦρ λάϊνον, every where the dreadful fire arose around the wall of stone, 12, 177. Thus Damm explains this passage, constructing λάϊνον with τεῖχος by hyperbaton. Others (as Heyne and Voss) construct λάϊνον with πῦρ, and understand it in a trop. signif. 'around the wall arose the dreadful fire of rattling stones.' (Several Gramm. consider this verse as not genuine.)
λαισήϊον, τό (prob. from λάσιος), *the target, a kind of shield*, prob. of leather, and lighter than the ἀσπίς, hence πτερόεις, *5, 453. 12, 426. cf. Hdt. 7, 91.
Λαιστρυγόνες, οἱ, sing. Λαιστρυγών, όνος, *the Læstrygones*, an ancient rude race, who lived by grazing cattle. The

Λαιστρυγόνιος. 258 Λανθάνω.

ancients. Thuc. 6, 2, placed them on the east side of Sicily, where the city Leontini (afterwards called Lentini) was situated: Voss. and Völcker, with more probability, place them on the north-west coast. Some of the ancients supposed their place of abode was in Formiæ in lower Italy, Od. 10, 119, seq. cf. Cic. ad Atticum, II. 13.

Λαιστρυγόνιος, ίη, ιον, *Lœstrygonian*, Od. 10, 82; in Wolf's ed. Λαιστρυγονίη stands as prop. name. and τηλέπυλος as adj. Even the ancients were not agreed about the name of the city; it is best to take Τηλέπυλος as the prop, name, as Voss translates it, and even Wolf in Od. 23, 318. Cf. Λάμος. Nitzsch, however, ad loc., prefers Λαιστρυγονίην as prop. name.

λαῖτμα, ατος, τό (λαιμός), *the deep, an abyss*; always with ἁλός or θαλάσσης, the abyss of the sea, 19, 267. Od. 4, 504; and generally, *the depths of the sea; the Deep,* often Od.

λαῖφος, εος, τό, *a ragged garment, an old cloak* (pl. *tatters*), *Od. 13, 399. 20. 206. 2) *a sail,* h. Ap. 206. (Akin to λῶπος.)

λαιψηρός, ή, όν, *quick, rapid, fleet,* esply γούνατα, 20, 358. (= αἰψηρός, cf. αἶψα and λείβω, see Thiersch, Gram., § 158. 12.) *II.

λάκε, Ep. for ἔλακε, see λάσκω.

Λακεδαίμων, ονος, ἡ, *Lacedæmon,* 1) Prop. the name of the country, later *Laconia*, which in heroic times was settled only in country villages and residences. As it forms a wide basin between two mountains running down from Arcadia, it is called hollow, κοίλη: abounding in hollows, cavernous, κητώεσσα, 2, 581. 2) the chief town of Lacedæmon = Σπάρτη, Od. 4, 1; or, according to Buttm. Lex. p. 383, the country also, as a collection of villages.

λακτίζω (λάξ), *to strike with the heel,* and generally, *to thrust, to strike, ποσὶ γαῖαν,* Od 18, 99; *to struggle, to writhe,* *Od. 22, 88 Batr. 90.

*Λακωνίς, ίδος, ἡ, adj. *Laconian,* γαῖα, h. in Ap. 410.

λαμβάνω, aor. 2 ἔλαβον, Ep. ἔλλαβον and λάβον, aor. 2 mid. ἐλαβόμην, Ep. ἐλλαβόμην, infin. λελαβέσθαι, only in the aor. 1) *to take, in grasp, to lay hold of,* with accus. ἔγχος χειρί or χερσί, ἡνία ἐν χείρεσσι, 5, 853. 8, 116. The part taken hold of stands in the gen. τινὰ ποδῶν, by the feet, 4, 463; γούνων, by the knees, Od. 6, 142. The gen. often alone: ἑανοῦ, ποδῶν, γενείου; metaph. spoken of external and internal states: τρόμος ἔλλαβε γυῖα, Il. 8, 452; in like manner, χόλος, πένθος, with double accus. 4, 230 16, 335. 2) *to take, to receive, to take possession of, τὶ ἐκ πεδίοιο,* 17, 621; esply in a bad signif.: *to take any one prisoner,* 5, 159. 11, 126; *to make booty of, ἵππους,* 10, 545; κτήματα, Od. 9, 41; In a good signif.: *to acquire, κλέος,* Od. 1, 298. 3) *to receive, to receive into one's house,* Od.

7, 255. rarely. The partcp. λαβών apparently often stands superfluously. λαβών κύσε χείρα, he kissed his hand, prop. having taken it, Od. 24, 398. Mid. to *take any thing for oneself. In seize upon* any thing, with gen. σχεδίης, Od. 5, 325; with accus. Od. 4, 388.

Λάμος, ὁ (gorge), king of the Læstrygones, founder of the city Telepylos, according to Eustath. and the ancients generally, son of Poseidon, cf. Ovid. Metam. 14. 23. (Some take Lamus for the name of the city Λάμου πτολίεθρον, like 'Ιλίου πόλιν. 5, 642: cf. Τροίης στολ. Od. 1, 2.) Od. 10, 81.

λαμπετάω, poet. = λάμπω, *to shine, to blaze:* only partep pres. λαμπετόωσι πυρί, 1, 104. Od. 4, 662.

Λαμπετίδης, ου, ὁ, Ep. for Λαμπίδης, son of Lampus = Dolops, 15, 526.

Λαμπετίη, ἡ (the shining), daughter of Helius and Neæra, who with her sister pastured the herds of her father in Trinacria, Od. 12, 132 cf. 374.

Λάμπος, ὁ, 1) son of Laomedon in Troy, father of Dolops, a counsellor, 3, 147. 20, 237. 15, 825. 2) a horse of Aurora, Od. 23, 246.

λαμπρός, ή, όν, superl. λαμπρότατος, η, ον (λάμπω), *shining, gleaming, beaming,* spoken of the heavenly bodies, Il. and Od.; of brass, 13, 132. The neut. sing. as adv. 5. 6. 13, 265.

λαμπτήρ, ῆρος, ὁ (λάμπω), *a fire-vase, a lighter,* a vessel in which dry wood was burned for a light, *Od. 8, 307. 343. cf. Od. 19, 63.

λάμπω and λάμπομαι, fut. ψω, 1) *to give light, to shine, to glimmer, to beam, to flash,* prop spoken of fire, mly of brass, 10, 154. πᾶς χαλκῷ λάμφ' (= ἔλαμπε), of Hector, 11, 66: of the eyes: ὀφθαλμώ οἱ πυρὶ λαμπέτων, the eyes flashed with fire, 13, 474. Mid. in Il. and Od. only in the partcp. spoken of persons and things: λάμπετο δουρὸς αἰχμή, 6, 319: χαλκός, 20, 131; of Hector: λαμπόμενος πυρὶ τεύχεσι, 15, 623. 20, 46; but also λαμπομένη κόρυς, δαΐς, Od. 19, 48. λάμπετε φλόξ, h. Merc. 113.

λανθάνω, Ep. and Ion. oftener λήθω, Ep. iterat λήθεσκε. 24, 13; fut. λήσω, aor. 2 ἔλαθον. Ep. λάθον, subj. Ep. λελάθω, mid. λανθάνομαι, only imperf. oftener Ep. and Ion. λήθομαι, aor. 2 ἐλαθόμην, Ep. λελαθόμην, perf. mid. λέλασμαι; λανθάνω in the imperf. only three times, 13, 721. Od. 8, 93 532; and imperf. mid. once, Od. 12, 227. I) Act. 1) *to be concealed, to remain concealed or unobserved,* τινά, from any one: οὐ λήθε Διὸς υἱόν, 15, 461. Oftener there stands with it, *a*) A partcp. οὔ σε λήθω κινύμενος, I do not moving remain concealed from thee, i. e. I do not move without being observed by you, 10, 279. 13, 272. Od. 8, 93. 12, 17. *b*) With ὅτι: οὔ μη λήθεις, ὅττι θεῶν τίς σ' ἦγε, it was not concealed from me, that some one of the gods conducted thee, Il. 24, 563. *c*)

Λάξ. 259 **Λάχνη.**

The partcp. aor. often stands as adv. άλτο λαθών, he leapt down unobserved, 12, 390. 2) Trans. *to cause one to forget* a thing, only in the subj. aor, 2 with redupl. τινά τινος, 15, 60. cf. έκλανθάνω. 11) Mid. *to forget*, with gen. often άλκῆς, χάρμης, Il.; άθανάτων, Od. 14, 421. 2) *to neglect, to omit.* Il. 9, 537.

Λάξ, adv *(striking) with the heel,* or *(thrusting) with the foot,* also λὰξ ποδί, 10, 158. Od. 15, 45.

Λαόγονος, ὁ. 1) son of Onētor, a Trojan, slain by Meriones, 16, 604. 2) son of Bias, a Trojan, 20, 460.

Λαοδάμας, αντος, ὁ (subduer of the people), 1) son of Antēnor, a Trojan, slain by Ajax, 15, 516. 2) son of king Alcinous in Scheria, an excellent pugilist, Od. 8. 116. seq.

Λαοδάμεια, ἡ, daughter of Bellerophontes, who bore Sarpēdon by Zeus. Artemis, being angry, slew her, 6, 197, seq. 205.

Λαοδίκη, ἡ, 1) daughter of Priam in Troy, wife of Helicāon, 6, 252. 2) daughter of Agamemnon, 9. 145. 287 (on account of her beauty, in the tragic poets *Electra*).

Λαοδόκος or **Λαόδοκος,** ὁ (receiving the people), 1) son of Antēnor, a Trojan, 4, 87. 2) a Greek, a friend of Antilochus, 17, 699.

Λαοθόη, ἡ, daughter of Altes, king of the Leleges, mother of Lycaon, 21, 85. 22, 48. (Damm, ' *a concursu populi ad eam spectandam.*')

Λαομεδοντιάδης, ου, ὁ, son of Laomedon = *Priam* or *Lampus,* 3, 250. 15, 527.

Λαομέδων, οντος, ὁ, son of Ilus, father of Tithōnus, Priam, Lampus, etc., 5, 269. 20, 237. Poseidōn and Apollo served him, at the command of Zeus, for a year at wages. The former built the walls of Troy; the latter kept his herds. When they demanded their wages, he refused to pay them, and wished to sell them as slaves, 21, 441. cf. 7, 452. They left him in anger; Poseidōn sent a ravaging sea-monster, and Apollo a pestilence. According to the oracle, the anger of the gods could only be appeased by exposing his daughter Hesiōnē, as a victim, to the monster. This was done. Heracles delivered her, but Laomedon did not give him the promised reward: therefore Heracles sacked Troy and slew him, 5, 638, seq. 20, 145. cf. 'Ηρακλῆς.

Λαός, ὁ, *the people,* as a mass or collection of men 1) Esply plur. *troops, army,* sometimes *infantry.* in opposition to ἵπποι 7, 342. 9, 708. 18, 153; or the army in the ships, 9, 424. 2) In the Od. often λαοί, rarely λαός, people. λαοί άγροιῶται, country people, Il. 11, 676. λαοί ἕταροι, 13, 710.

Λαοσσόος, ον Ep (σεύω), *exciting the people, urging the people to battle, exciting the nations,* epith. of Arēs, of Eris, 17, 398 20, 48; of Athēnē, 13, 128. Od. 22, 210; of Apollo, 20, 79; of Amphiaraus, Od. 15, 244.

Λαοφόρος, ον, Ep. (φέρω), *bearing the people;* ὁδός, the public road, 15, 682.†

Λαπάρη, ἡ, *the flank* (between the ribs and hips), 6, 64, and often.

Λαπίθαι, οἱ, *the Lapithæ.* an ancient warlike race, about Olympus and Pelion in Thessaly, known by their contest with the Centaurs at the marriage of Pirithous, 1, 266. 12, 128. Od. 21, 295, seq.

Λάπτω, ψω, poet. *to lap, to lick up.* as cats and dogs drink; spoken of wolves: γλώσσησιν ὕδωρ, 16, 161.†

Λάρισσα, ἡ *(fortress.* a Pelasg. word), a town of the Pelasgians in Æolia, in Cymē, afterwards called *Phryconis,* 2, 841. 17, 301.

Λάρναξ, ακος, ἡ. *a chest, a box,* and generally, a repository for keeping any thing, 18, 413; *an urn* in which the bones of Hector were placed, *24, 795.

Λάρος, ὁ, a voracious sea-bird, *a seamew,* larus, Linn., Od. 5, 51.†

Λαρός, ἡ, όν. superl. irreg. λαρώτατος, Od. 2, 350; *agreeable, palatable, delicious, sweet,* spoken of taste, δεῖπνον, δόρπον, οἶνος. λαρόν οἱ αἷμ' ἀνθρώπων, sweet to it (the gnat or musquito) is the blood of man, Il. 17, 572 (λάω, *cupio,* hence *acceptus;* or from λάω, to wish.)

λασιαύχην, ενος, ὁ (αὐχήν), *having a hairy neck, shaggy-necked,* epith. of the bull, h. Merc. 224; of the bear, h. 6, 46.

λάσιος, ίη, ιον, *thick-haired, shaggy, hairy,* spoken of men: λάσια στήθεα, λάσιον κῆρ, the hairy breast, the hairy heart. as a mark of manhood and of distinguished bodily vigour, 1, 189. 2, 851; *woolly,* ὄἵς, 24, 125; γαστήρ, Od. 9, 433.

λάσκω. poet. aor. 2 ἔλακον, Ep. λάκον, perf. λέληκα partcp. λελήκώς, fem. λελακυῖα, aor. 2 mid. λελάκοντο, h. Merc. 145. 1) *to sound, to crack, to snap, to creak.* spoken of hard bodies which are struck; of brass, 14, 25. 20, 277. λάκε ὀστέα, the bones cracked, 13, 616. 2) *to cry, to bark,* spoken of the cry of the falcon, 21, 141; of the barking of Scylla, Od. 12, 85.

λαυκανίη, ἡ (λάω, λάβω), *the gorge, the gullet,* *22, 325. 24, 642.

λαύρη, ἡ, *a lane, street, a way* between houses, *Od. 22, 128. 137; (From λάω, λάβω, *a gorge-like opening.)

λαφύσσω (λάπτω), *to swallow greedily, to devour,* αἶμα καὶ ἔγκατα, spoken of lions, *11, 176. 17, 64. 18, 583.

Λάχε. Ep. for ἔλαχε, see λαγχάνω.

Λάχεια, ἡ, Od. 9, 116. 10, 509; as an epith. of νήσος, ἀκτή, Eustath. Apoll. Etym. M. explain it by εὔγεως ἡ εὔσκαφος, and derive it from λαχαίνω, having good arable land. More correct is the reading of Zenodotus: νῆσος ἕπειτ' ἐλάχεια and ἀκτή τ' ἐλάχεια, a little island, a little coast. Thus Voss, cf. Thiersch, Gram. § 201. 14. c.

Λάχνη, ἡ, *wool, woolly hair,* spoken of

Λαχνήεις. 260 **Λείπω.**

the human hair and beard, 2, 219. Od. 11, 320; of a mantle, Il. 10, 134.

λαχνήεις, εσσα, εν (λάχνη), woolly, hairy, shaggy, φῆρες, στήθεα, Il Λαχνῆεν δέρμα συός, the bristly skin, 9, 548; ὄροφος, the hairy reed, 24, 451.

λάχνος, ὁ = λάχνη. wool, Od. 9, 445 †

Λάω, an ancient Ep. word found only in three places; according to the best Gramm. it signifies, to see, to look at. κύων έχε έλλόν, άσπαίροντα λάων, (a dog held a fawn, looking at it palpitating,) Od. 19, 229: and v. 230 : ὁ μὲν λάε νεβρὸν ἀπάγχων, choking he looked at the fawn Clearer still is αἰετὸς ὀξὺ λάων, h Merc. 360. It is the root of γλαύσσω, and of ἀλαός, blind. Some explain it as meaning to s-ize, from the root ΔΑΩ = λαμβάνω, ἀπολαύω.

λέβης, ητος, τό (λείβω), prop. a vessel for pouring, a basin, a cauldron. 1) a vessel for boiling, made of brass, often connected with τρίπους, and prob. smaller than the tripod, 9, 123. 21, 362. 23, 267. 2) a basin or ewer, on which, before eating, water (χέρνιψ) was carried to strangers, in a golden laver. It was frequently made of silver, and ornamented with artificial work, Od. 1, 137. 3, 440; also for bathing the feet, Od. 19, 380.

λέγω, fut. λέξω, aor. 1 ἔλεξα, fut. mid. λέξομαι, aor. 1 mid. ἐλεξάμην, Ep. sync. aor. ἐλέγμην imperat. λέξο and λέξεο, aor. 1 pass. ἐλέχθην, I) Act. Ep. to lay any one down, to put to bed, τινά, only in the aor. 1 act. 24, 635; metaph. to quiet, to soothe, Διὸς νόον, 14, 252. 2) to lay single things together, to pick up, to gather, to collect, ὀστέα, 23, 239. 24, 72 ; αἱμασιάς, Od. 18, 359. 24, 224. 3) to place single things in a row, i. e. to count, to count out. ἐν δ' ἡμέας πρώτους λέγε κήτεσιν, he counted us first amongst the sea-calves, Od. 4, 452; hence pass. ἐλέχθην μετὰ τοῖσιν, I was counted with these, Il. 3, 188. 13, 276. 4) to recount, to relate, τί, often, esply Od. τί τινι, only ὀνείδεά τινι, to utter reproaches against any one, Il. 2, 222. II) Mid. 1) to lie down, to place oneself, to lie, aor. 1 mid. and the sync. aor 2 and imperat. λέξο, λέξεο. a) to lay oneself down to sleep, 14, 350. Od. 10, 320. λέξασθαι ὕπνῳ, Il. 4, 131; εἰς εὐνήν, Od. 17, 102. b) to place oneself, to lie down, (in ambush.) περὶ ἄστυ δὲ λόχον, Il. 9, 67. Od. 4. 413. 453. 2) to pick up for oneself, to gather, ξύλα, Π. 8. 507. 547; hence, to pick out for oneself, to select, Τρῶας, 2, 125. 21, 27; ἄνδρας, Od 24, 108. 3) to place oneself with, to count oneself amongst, to count for oneself. ἐγὼ πέμπτος μετὰ τοῖσιν ἐλέγμην, I reckoned myself as the fifth amongst them, Od. 9, 335; but λέκτο ἀριθμόν, he counted over their number (for himself), Od. 4, 451. 4) to recount any thing, to relate, to talk of, μηκέτι ταῦτα λεγώμεθα, let us speak no more about these things, Il 2, 435 13, 292. cf. 275. Od. 3, 240. The Schol. explain μηκ-

ταῦτ. λεγ. by καθήμεθα, κείμεθα : hence Wolf, 'let us not lay our hands in the lap,' but cf. Buttm., Lex. p. 398. (Buttm., Lex. p. 403, takes for the signif. to lay, the theme ΛΕΧΩ [Germ. legen], hence λέχος, λόχος, and for the other signi. the theme λέγω.)

Λειαίνω, Ep. for λεαίνω (λεῖος), fut λειανώ, aor. 1 ἐλείηνα, to make smooth. to smooth, to polish, κέρα, 4, 111 ; κέλευθον, to smooth the way, 15, 261 ; χορόν, Od. 6, 260.

λείβω (akin to εἴβω), aor. 1 ἔλειψα, to drop, to pour, to pour out, to shed, δάκρυα, esply to pour out wine as a libation to a deity, οἶνόν τινι, 10, 579. Od. 2, 432 ; and absol. Il. 24, 285.

λειμών, ῶνος, ὁ (λείβω), any moist place, a meadow, a field, a pasture, 2, 461. Od. 4, 605.

λειμωνόθεν, adv. from the meadow or pasture, 24, 451.†

λεῖος, η, ον, smooth, polished, spoken of the trunk of a poplar, 4, 484 ; level, plain, of places : πεδίον, ὁδός, and via gen. χῶρος λεῖος πετράων, a place free from rocks, Od. 5, 443. ποιεῖν λεῖα θεμείλια, to level the foundation (of the wall). Il. 12, 30.

λείουσι, see λέων.

λείπω, fut. λείψω, aor. 2 ἔλιπον, perf. λέλοιπα, aor. mid. ἐλιπόμην, perf. pass. λέλειμμαι, aor. 1 pass. ἐλείφθην, h. Merc. 195; aor. 2 pass. ἐλίπην, 16, 507 ; fut. pass. λελείψομαι, 24, 742. I) Act. = to leave, to quit, to forsake, to leave behind, with accus. of persons, things, and places, θάλαμον, Ἑλλάδα, Il. λείπειν φάος ἠελίοιο, to leave the light of the sun, i. e. to die, 18, 11 ; on the other hand, τὸν λίπε θυμός, ψυχή; ψυχὴ δὲ λοιπε, subaud. ὀστέα (' the soul left the bones,' Voss), Od. 14, 134 ; in like manner, v. 213 : in πάντα λέλοιπε, supply the accus. ἐμέ, all things have left me. (Some Gramm. take λέλοιπε as intrans.: this, however, is foreign to the Homeric usus loquendi.) Again, τί τινι, to bequeath, to leave behind, any thing to any one, Il. 2, 106. 722, seq. b) to abandon, to leave in the lurch, 16, 368. ἔλιπον ἰοὶ ἄνακτα, the arrows left the king, i. e. failed him, Od 22, 119. Il. Mid. and pass. 1) to be left behind, to be forsaken, spoken of persons and things, Il. 2, 700, 10, 256 ; hence, to remain, to survive, 5. 154. 12, 14. Od. 3. 196. 2) to remain back or behind (in the course), ἀπό τινος, far from any one, Il. 9, 437. 445 ; esply in foot and chariot races, 23, 407. 409. Od. 8, 125 : with gen. of the person, to remain behind any one, Il. 23, 523. 520. δουρὸς ἐρωήν (a spear's cast), hence, λελειμμένος οἰῶν, remaining behind the sheep (the ewes), Od. 9, 443; ἀπ' ἄλλων, h. Ven. 76. (In Il. 16, 507, ἐπὶ λίπεν ἅρματ' ἀνάκτων, λίπεν stands for ἐλίπησαν, aor. 2 pass. (Schol. Ven. ἐλείφθησαν). The Myrmidons held up the panting horses, which strove to fly, after

Λειριόεις. *Λεύκιππος.

the chariots were left by the kings. (The reading of Zenodot. which Voss follows, was λίινον, after they had left the chariots.)

Λειριόεις, εσσα, εν (λείριον), lily (as adj.), having the colour of a lily, only metaph. χρώς lily-white, i. e. tender, delicate skin, 13, 830; όψ. the tender (clearchirping, V) voice of the cicada [his slender ditty sweet, Cp.], 3, 152.

*λείριον, τό, a lily, eply the white, h. Cer. 427.

λείστός, ή, όν (λείζομαι), Ion. and poet. for ληϊστός, q. v.

*Δειχήνωρ, ορος, ὁ (άνήρ), Licker, name of a mouse, Batr. 205.

*Δειχομύλη, ή (μύλη), Lick-mill, one that licks up the flour in the mill, name of a mouse, Batr. 29.

*Δειχοπίναξ, ακος, ό (πίναξ), Platelicker, name of a mouse, Batr. 106.

Δειώδης, ου, ό, son of Ænops, a prophet and suitor of Penelope. He was opposed to the impiety of the suitors; still Odysseus (Ulysses) slew him, Od. 21, 144. 22, 310.

Δειώκριτος, ό, 1) son of Arisbas, a Greek, slain by Æneas, 17, 344. 2) son of Evenor, a suitor of Penelope, Od. 2, 242. 22, 294.

λείων, see λέων.

λέκτο, Ep. for έλεκτο, see λέγω.

Δεκτόν, τό (more correctly Λέκτον), a promontory on the Trojan coast, at the foot of Ida, opposite Lesbos, now Cap Baba, 14, 283 (h. Ap. 217, it stands incorrectly; hence Ilgen would read Δεύκης, Herm. Δύγκος).

λέκτρον, τό (λέγω), 1) a couch, a bed, mly in the plur. Il. and Od. λέκτρονδε, to bed, ιέναι, Od. 8, 292.

λελαβέσθαι, λελάβησι, see λαμβάνω.

λελάθῃ, λελάθοντο, see λανθάνω.

λελάκοντο, λελακυία, see λάσκω.

λέλασμαι, see λανθάνω.

λελάχητε, λελάχωσι, see λαγχάνω.

Δέλεγες, οἱ, the Leleges, an ancient race of the southern coast of Troas, about Pedasus and Lyrnessus, opposite Lesbos, 10, 429 20, 96. After the destruction of Troy, they migrated to Caria. According to Mannert, they together with the Curêtes were of Illyrian origin, and dwelt originally in Acarnania, Ætolia, etc. Prob. they were a Pelasgian race, having their earliest place of settlement in Greece.

λεληκώς, see λάσκω.

λελίημαι, an old perf. with pres. signif.: to strive, to hasten, only partcp. λελιημένος, used as an adj. eager [= sugerly], impetuous, 12, 106. 16, 552; with όφρα, 4, 465. 5, 690. (From λιλάομαι [simpler form of λιλαίομαι] for λελίημαι, see Thiersch, Gram. § 238. 85.) *il. [Buttm., Lex. p. 77.]

λέλογχα, see λαγχάνω.

λέξεο and λέξο, see λέγω.

Δεοντεύς, ῆος, ό, son of Corônus, one of the Lapithæ, a suitor of Helen; he went to Troy with twenty ships, 2, 745. 23, 841.

λέπαδνον, τό, the yoke-strap; mly in the plur., according to App. Lex. the leathern straps with which the yoke was fastened under the necks of the draughtanimals, and connected with the girth; but in H., the straps with which the yoke was made fast to the end of the pole. These straps served perhaps also to govern the horses, 5, 730. 19, 393; cf. Köpke, Kriegsw. d. G. S. 137.

λεπταλέος, έη, έον, poet. (λεπτός), slender, weak, delicate, φωνή, 18, 571.†

λεπτός, ή, όν (λέπω, prop. peeled), 1) thin, fine, delicate, mly spoken of the products of the loom, 18, 595. Od. 2, 95; of brass, Il. 20, 275: of barley, trodden fine, 20, 497; εἰσίθμη, a narrow entrance, Od. 6, 264. 2) little, slender, weak, μῆτις, Il. 10, 226.

*λεπτουργής, ές (έργον), wrought finely, h. 31, 14.

*λέπυρον, τό (λέπος). a rind, a husk, a shell, καρύοιο, Batr. 131.

λέπω, aor. έλεψα, to peel off, to strip off, with accus. φύλλα, 1, 236.†

Δέσβος, ή, an island of the Ægean sea, opposite the Adramyttian gulf, having a town of the same name, now Metteilino, 24, 544. Od. 3, 169; from which 1) Adv. Λεσβόθεν, from Lesbos, Il. 9, 660. 2) Λεσβίς, ίδος, ή, Lesbian; subst. a Lesbian female. 9, 129.

λέσχη, ή (λέγω), 1) talk. 2) a place frequented for talk and gossip [the public portico, Cp.]; a rendezvous for idlers and loungers, Od. 18, 329.†

λευγαλέος, έη, έον (from λυγρός as πευκάλιμος from πυκνός), wretched, sad, miserable, lamentable, bad, miser. 1) Of persons: πτωχός, Od. 16, 273. 17, 202. 20, 203. λευγαλέοι ἐσόμεσθα, we shall be miserable, i. e. weak (Ntz.), Od. 2, 61. 2) Of things: miserable, wretched, θάνατος, a miserable death, in distinction from a natural death, Il. 21, 281. Od. 5, 312; πόλεμος, 13, 97. λευγ. έπεα, harsh words, 20, 109. λευγ. φρένες, an evil mind, 9, 119. (According to the Schol. act. hurtful; but see Nitzsch ad Od. 2, 61.)

λευγαλέως, adv. sadly, lamentably, 13, 723.†

λευκαίνω (λευκός), to whiten, ύδωρ έλατῃσιν [to sweep the whit'ning flood, Cp.], Od. 12, 172 †

Δευκάς, άδος, ή, πέτρη, the Leucasrock, i. e. white-rock, is prop. a rock on the coast of Epirus, where the ancients placed the entrance into the under-world, also = Λευκαδία, now S. Maura. In H. Od. 24, 11, it is further west, near Oceanus, but still to be regarded as this side of it, on the light-side of the earth.

λεύκασπις, ιδος, ό, ή (ἀσπίς), having a while shield, epith. of Deiphobus [whiteshielded chief, Cp.], 22, 204.†

*Λευκίππη, ή, daughter of Oceanus and Tethys, n. Cer. 418.

*Λεύκιππος, ό, 1) son of Periêres,

Λευκοθέη. 262 **Λήϊτος.**

brother of Aphareus. 2) son of Œnomaus in Elis, who loved Daphne, h. Ap. 212.

Λευκοθέη, ή, i. e. white-goddess, a name of Ino, after she was reckoned amongst the sea-deities. She was the daughter of Cadmus, king of Thebes, and, being pursued by her raging husband Athamas, she precipitated herself with her son Melicertes, from the rock Moluris on the Corinthian isthmus, into the sea, Od. 5, 334. Cf. Apd. 3, 4. 2.

λευκός, ή, όν (λάω, λεύσσω), compar. **λευκότερος**, 1) *shining, gleaming, bright, clear.* 14, 185: αἴγλη, λέβης, hence also: λευκὸν ὕδωρ. clear water. 23, 282. Od. 5, 70; esply *white-shining;* πόλις, κάρηνα, ὀδόντες, Il. 2) Most nıly: *white, whitish*, in manifold degrees. λευκότεροι χιόνος, anoken of steeds. 10, 437; γάλα, 5, 902; ὀστέα. Od. 1, 161; ἄλφιτα, Il. 11, 640; χρώς, 11, 573; λευκοὶ κονισάλῳ, with white dust, 5, 503.

Λεῦκος, ὁ, 1) a companion of Odysseus (Ulysses). 4, 491 2) a river in Macedonia, h. Ap. 217; according to Ilgen for **Δέκτον.**

***λευκοχίτων, ωνος, ὁ, ἡ** (χιτών), *white-clad*, ἧπαρ, the liver wrapped in a white net, Batr. 37.

λευκώλενος, ον. Ep. (ὠλένη), *having white elbows, white-armed*, epith, of Hêrê, and of many women, Il. and Od.

λευρός ή, όν (λεῖος), Ion. *level, smooth,* χῶρος. Od. 7, 123.†

λεύσσω. poet. (λάω), prop. to emit light, then, *to see, to look;* ab-ol πρόσσω καὶ ὀπίσσω, forwards and backwards, i. e. to be prudent, wise, 3, 110; ἐπὶ πόντον, ἐς γαῖαν, 5, 771. Od. 9. 166. *h)* With accus. *to see, to behold,* Il. 1, 120. 16, 70. 127. Od. 6, 157. 23, 124.

λεχεποίης, ου, ὁ, fem. λεχεποίη, ή, Ep. only accus. λεχεποίην (ποία), overgrown with long grass, suitable for making beds, *abounding in grass, grassy*, as masc. epith. of the river Ἀσῶπος, 4, 383; as fem. of the towns Pteleus, Teumessus, and Onchestus, 2, 697. h. 224. It is incorrect to assume that λεχεποίην (with the names of cities) is an accus. fem. to λεχέποιος. Cf. Eustath. ad Il. 2, 679.

λέχος, εος, τό (λέγω, ΛΕΧ), 1) *a couch, a bed*, in the plur. *a bedstead*, 3, 391. Od. 1, 440, esply, *a)* *the nuptial bed*, Od. 8, 269. Il. 3, 411. 15, 39, hence. *the nuptial embrace*, in the construct. λέχος πορσύνειν, ἀντιᾶν, 1, 31. Od. 3, 403. *b) a death-bed*, for laying out a corpse, Il. 18, 233. 24. 589, and often.

λέχοσδε, adv. *to bed*, 3, 148.

λέων, οντος, ὁ, dat. plur. Ep. λείουσι, (Ep. form λῖς). *a lion*, often as a comparison for heroes, Il. once for Λάαινα: Ζεύς σε λέοντα γυναιξὶ θῆκε, Zeus made thee a lioness, i. e. a destroyer, for women, spoken by Hêrê, of Artemis, because the sudden death of women was ascribed to the arrows of Artemis, 21, 483.

λήγω, fut. λήξω, aor. ἔληξα, Ep. λήξα 1) Intrans. *to cease, to desist, to leave of obsol.* 21, 218; ἐν σοὶ μὲν λήξω, σέο δ' ἄρξομαι, in thee I will leave off and with thee begin, i. e I confine myself especially to thee. *a)* With gen. *to desist from, to rest from,* χόλοιο, ἔριδος, φόνοιο, χορείη, ἀπατάων. *b)* With partcp. λήγω ἀείδων, I cease singing, 9, 191. Od. 8, 87: ἐναρίζων, Il. 21, 224. h. Ap. 177. 2) Trausit. only poet. *to cause to cease, to quiet, to allay, τί*, any thing. μένος. 13, 424 21, 305. *b)* τί τινος ; λήγειν χεῖρας φόνοιο, to stay the hands from slaughter, Od. 22, 63 : (λήγω, akin to λέγω, to lay.)

Λήδη, ή, Ep. for Λήδα, daughter of Thestius, wife of Tyndareus; she bore to Zeus, who visited her in the form of a swan, Helen, Kastôr (Castor), and Polydeukês (Pollux), Od. 11, 298: (according to Damm. from Λῆδος, a thin robe.)

ληθάνω, poet. form in tmesis, see ἐκλαν-θάνω.

λήθη, ή (λήθος), *forgetfulness, oblivion.* 2, 33.†

Λῆθος, ὁ. son of Teutamus, king of the Pelasgians in Larissa, 2, 843. 17, 288.

λήθω, mid. λήθομαι, Ep. ancient form of λανθάνω. q. v

ληϊάς, άδος, ή, pecul. poet. fem. of **ληΐδιος** (ληΐς), *a female captive*, 20, 193†

ληΐβότειρα, ή, fem. from ληϊβοτήρ, poet. (βόσκω), *crop-devouring*, σῦς, Od. 18, 29.†

ληΐζομαι, depon. mid. (ληΐς), fut. ληΐσομαι, aor. 1 ἐληισάμην, Ep. 3 sing. ληΐσσατο. *to lead away as booty, to plunder*, to obtain in war, spoken of persons : τινά, 18, 28. Od. 1, 398; spoken of things : πολλά, Od. 23. 357.

ληϊον, τό, *a crop, a harvest*, standing in the field, 2, 147. Od. 9, 135.

ληΐς, ἴδος, ή, Ion. and Ep. for λεία. *plunder, booty in war*, spoken of men and cattle, 9, 138. 280. Od. 3, 106 ; (from λαός, as common property, divided amongst the warriors.)

ληϊστήρ, ῆρος, ὁ (ληΐζομαι), *a spoiler, a plunderer,* esply *a sea-rubber, a pirate.* *Od. 3, 73. 9, 254. Piracy and coast-robbery, according to Homeric notions, were not disgraceful, cf. Thuc. 1, 5.

***ληϊστής, οῦ, ὁ** =ληϊστήρ. h. 6, 7.

ληϊστός, ή, όν (ληΐζομαι), Ep. also λεϊστός, ή, όν. *plundered, robbed ; capable of being plundered*, ληϊστοὶ βόες, 9, 408: ἀνδρὸς δὲ ψυχὴ πάλιν ἐλθεῖν οὔτε λεϊστή. οὔτε, κτλ. the soul of man cannot be seized (and constrained) to return again [ἐλθεῖν=ὥστε ἐλθεῖν], 9, 408; cf. ἁπατός.

ληϊστωρ, ορος, ὁ = ληϊστήρ, Od. 13. 427.†

ληΐτις, ιδος. ή (ληΐς), *one who makes booty, the bestower of spoil*, epith. of Athênê, 10, 460.†

Λήϊτος, ὁ, son of Alectryon. leader of the Bœotians before Troy, 2, 494; wounded by Hector, 17, 601.

Λήκυθος. 263 Λικμητήρ.

λήκυθος, ή. an oil-flask, an oil-cruet, **Od 6, 79. 215.

*Δήλαντον πεδίον, τό, the Lelantian plain, a fruitful plain in the western part of the island of Euboea, near Er»tria, on the river Lelantus, having warm baths and iron mines, h. Ap. 220.

Δήμνος, ή, an island in the northern part of the Aegean sea, having in H.'s time perhaps a town of the same name, sacred to Hephaestus on account of the volcano Mosychlus, now Staltmene, 1, 594. 2, 722. Od. 8, 283.

*Ληνός, ή and ὁ, any tub-like vessel; esply a trough, for watering cattle, a watering-place, h. Merc. 104.

*Λησίμβροτος, ον, poet.(βροτός), stealing unawares upon men, deceiver, thief, h. Merc. 339.

λήσω, λήσομαι, see λανθάνω.

*Λητοΐδης, ου, ὁ, son of Lētō (Latona) = Apollo, h. Merc. 253.

Λητώ, οὓς, ή, voc. Λητοῖ, Lētō (Latona), daughter of the Titan Koios (Coeus), and Phœbe, mother of Apollo and Artemis by Zeus, 1, 9. Od. 6, 318: she cures the wounded Æneas, Il. 5, 447. On the way to Delphi she was violently attacked by Tityus, Od. 11, 580. (According to Herm. Supitia, akin to λήθειν.)

Λιάζομαι, depon. pass. aor. 1 ἐλιάσθην, Ep. λιάσθην, prop. to bend, mly, 1) to bend sidewise, to bend outwards, to retire, to retreat, for the most part spoken of men, ὕπαιθα, 15, 520. 21, 255. δεῦρο λιάσθης. retiredst hither, 22, 12; and so also νόσφι λιασθείς (going or turning aside), 1, 349. 11, 80. ἐκ ποταμοῖο, ἀπὸ πυρκαϊῆς, to escape from the river, to go away from the funeral pile, Od. 5, 462. Il. 23, 231; and with the gen. alone, 21, 255. ἀμφὶ δ' ἄρα σφι λιάζετο κῦμα, 24, 96; absol. to retire, Od. 4, 838. 2) to bend down, to sink, to fall, to slip, only Ep. ποτὶ γαίῃ, Il. 20, 418. πρηνὴς ἐλιάσθη, 15. 243. πτερὰ πυκνὰ λίασθεν for ἐλιάσθησαν, the thick wings sank, dropt, 23, 879 (see Buttm., Lex. p. 404).

Λιαρός, ή, όν (χλιαίνω, ἰαίνω), warm, tepid, αἷμα, ὕδωρ, 11, 477. 846. Od. 24, 25; οὖρος, a soft wind, Od. 5, 268. 2) Generally, mild, gentle, agreeable, ὕπνος, Il. 14. 164.

Λιβύη, ή, Libya, in H. the country west of Egypt as far as Oceanus; later entire North Africa, Od. 4, 85. 14, 295.

Λίγα. adv. from λιγύς for λιγέα, loudly, clear-sounding, mly with κωκύειν, 19, 284; with ἀείδειν, only Od. 10, 254.

Λιγαίνω (λιγύς), shrill-crying, to cry loudly, spoken of heralds, 11, 685.†

Λίγγω, aor. λίγξε, see λίζω.

Λιγδην. adv. poet. (λίζω). in the manner of grazing, scratching; βάλλειν χεῖρα, to wound the hand superficially [with a surface wound, Cp.], Od. 22, 278.†

Λιγέως, adv. from λιγύς, q. v.

*Λιγύμολπος, ον (μολπή), clear-singing, Νύμφαι. h. 18. 19.

Λιγυπνείων, οντος, ὁ, poet. (πνέω), clear or loud-blowing, roaring, ἀήτης, Od. 4, 567.†

*Λιγύπνοιος, ον (πνοιή)=λιγυπνείων, h. Ap. 28.

Λιγυρός, ή, όν (lengthened from λιγύς), clear-sounding, whistling, shrill, spoken of the wind, 5, 526. 13, 590; loud-cracking, spoken of a whip [shrill-sounding, Cp.], 11, 52; clear-sounding, of a bird, 14, 290; loud-singing, of the Sirens, Od. 12, 44. 183.

Λιγύς, εῖα, ύ, Ep. and Ion. in fem. λίγεια, poet. clear or loud-sounding, spoken of any fine, sharp, and piercing sound. 1) Of inanimate things: clear-whistling, roaring, of the wind, 13. 334. Od. 3, 176; clear-ringing, of the lyre, 11. 9, 186. Od. 8, 67. 2) Of living beings: of the muse, Od. 24, 62. h. 13, 2; esply of Nestor, clear-voiced, ἀγορητής, Il. 1, 248; adv. λιγέως: aloud, loudly, often with κλαίειν, 19, 5; of wind: φυσᾶν, to blow loudly, 23, 218. λιγέως ἀγορεύειν, to speak impressively, emphatically, 3, 214. (On the accentuation λίγεια, Ion. for λιγεῖα, see Thiersch, Gram. § 201. c.)

Λιγύφθογγος, ον, poet. (φθογγή), clear-sounding, clear-voiced, epith. of heralds, 2, 50, and once Od. 2, 6.

Λιγύφωνος, ον, poet. (φωνή), clear-voiced, loud-crying, spoken of the eagle, 9. 350.†

Λίζω, only aor. 1 λίγξε for ἔλιγξε, to twang, 4, 125.†

Λίην, Ion. and Ep. for λίαν, adv. 1) too much, exceedingly, very much, for the later ἄγαν, with verbs and adject. 1, 553. Od. 3, 227. 4, 371; more rarely, much, greatly, οὔτι λίην, Il. 13, 284. 14, 368. 2) Frequently καὶ λίην stands at the beginning of a sentence with emphasis, for καὶ μάλα, certainly, by all means, yes certainly. καὶ λίην οὗτός γε μένος θυμόν τ' ὀλέσειεν, certainly he would have lost his strength and his life, 8, 357. καὶ λίην κεῖνός γε ἐοικότι κεῖται ὀλέθρῳ, Od. 1, 46. 3, 203. 9, 477. (ι is prop. short, but in καὶ λίην always long.)

Λίθαξ, ακος, ὁ, ἡ (λίθος), stony, rocky, hard, πέτρη, Od. 5, 415.†

Λιθάς, άδος, ή = λίθος, a stone, a rock, *Od. 14, 36. 23, 193.

Λίθεος, η, ον (λίθος), of stone, 23, 202. Od. 13, 107.

*Λιθόρρινος. ον (ῥίνος), having a hard shell, stone-cased, χελώνη, h. Merc. 48.

Λίθος, ὁ, twice ή, 12, 287. Od. 19, 494; a stone, as an image of what is hard and unfeeling, Il. 4, 510. Od. 23, 103; esply a field-stone thrown by warriors at each other, Il., in the plur. λίθοι, οἱ, stone seats, 18, 504. Od. 3, 406. b) a rock, Od. 3, 296. 13, 156. (In later writers ἡ λίθος, a precious stone.)

Λικμάω (λικμός), to cleanse grain with the winnowing-fan, to winnow, καρπόν, 5, 500.†

Λικμητήρ, ἦρος, ὁ, poet. (λικμάω), a winnower, a grain-cleaner, 13, 590.†

*Λίκνον. 264 Λἶς.

λίκνον, τό, *a winnowing-fan*, probably of osier basket-work, h. Merc. 21, 63.

λικριφίς, adv. poet. *from the side, sideways, ἀἴσσειν*, 14, 463. Od. 19, 451.

Λικύμνιος, ὁ, son of Electryon and Midea, uncle of Heracles; he was slain by the son of that hero, Tlepolemus, by mistake, 2, 663. (According to Herm. *Subnlescentius*.)

Λίλαια, ἡ, a city of Phocis, at the source of the Cephīsus, now *Lellen*, 2, 523.

Λιλαίομαι, depon. Ep. (λι—λάω), only pres. and imperf. *to desire ardently, to strive for, to long for, to wish.* 1) With infin. poet. also spoken of inanimate things, of the spear, 21, 168; uncommonly is λιλαιομένη πόσιν εἶναι, i. e. τοῦ εἶναι αὐτόν οἱ πόσιν, desiring that he might be her husband, Od. 1. 15; cf. Thiersch, § 206. 2. *b.* 2) *to long for, to desire earnestly*, with gen. πολέμοιο, ὁδοῖο, Il. 3, 133 Od. 1, 315. 12, 326. (From this the Ep. perf. λελίημαι.)

λιμήν, ένος, ὁ (λείβω), *a haven, a bay*, or *harbour*, in general ὅρμος, the inner portion of it, 1, 432. Od. 2, 391.

λίμνη, ἡ (λείβω), properly, water which washes a neighbouring shore; hence 1) *a pool* or *lake*, 2, 711. 865. 5, 709; also, water overflowing from a river or the sea, *a marsh*, or *a sound* (fretum), between two neighbouring shores, generally, *the sea*, 24, 79. 13, 21. 32. περικαλλής λίμνη, in Od 3, 1, according to ancient critics, is a part of Oceanus; according to Voss, from a fragment of Æschylus in Strab. I. p. 33, a pool in which Helius bathes his horses, and from which he mounts the heavens; Nitzsch ad Od. p. 131, explains it generally, as the water of Oceanus standing near the shore.

*Διμνήσιος, ὁ, *an inhabitant of the marsh*, *Fenman* or "*Marsh*," a frog's name, Batr. 229.

λιμνοχαρής, ές, gen. έος (χαίρω), *delighting in a marsh*, epith. of the frog, Batr. 13.

*Λιμνόχαρις, ὁ, *Marshjoy*, a frog's name, Ba'r. 211.

Λιμνώρεια, ἡ, daughter of Nereus and Doris, 18, 41.

λιμός, ὁ (prob. from λείπω, λέλειμμαι), *hunger, famine*, 17, 166. Od. 4, 369; as fem., h. Cer. 12; according to the Gramm. Doric.

Λίνδος, ἡ, a town on the Island Rhodes, with a temple of Athēnē, now *Lindo*, 2, 656.

λινοθώρηξ. ηκος, Ep. (θώραξ), *wearing a linen cuirass* |*alnd in thick-woven mail*. Cp.], epith. of Ajax, son of Oïleus, and of Amphius, 2, 529. 830.

λίνον, τό, *fiax*. 1) any thing made of flax: *a) thread, yarn*; eply *an anglingline*, 16, 408; metaph. *the thread of life*, which the Fates spin for men, 20, 128. 24, 210. Od. 7, 198. 2) *a fisher's net*, Il. 5, 487. 3) *linen*, λίνοιο ἄωτον, 9, 661. Od. 13, 73; see ἄωτον, plur. h. Ap. 104.

Λίνος, ὁ, an ancient hero or a country youth, slain by Apollo because he engaged in a contest with him, Paus. 9. 29. 3. From this, as later, is distinguished the singer of Thebes, son of Apollo and a Muse (Calliope or Urania), teacher of Orpheus and Heracles, Hes. fr. l. apd. 1, 3. 2. From this,

Λίνος, ὁ, *the Linus song*, a song named after the hero of the famous mystic bard Linus (see Λίνος), which was originally serious and sad, but later of a joyful character, Hdt. 2, 79. Athen. XIV. p. 619. C; generally, *singing, a song, spoken of a song in vintage*, 18, 570.† Λίνον δ' ὑπό καλόν ἄειδε, he sang beautifully the Linus song. Thus Aristarch. and, amongst the moderns, Voss, Heinrichs, Spitzner. Others, as Köppen, Heyne, take λίνον as the accus. from τὸ λίνον, thread, the string of a lyre (since these strings were first made of thread), and construe, ὑπό λίνον καλόν ἄειδε, he sang beautifully to the string of the lyre. (This construct-on is not to be received, if only for the reason that thread does not make good lute strings.)

λίπα, Ep. λίπ' ἐλαίῳ ἀλείψαι, 18, 350; and ἀλείψασθαι, 10, 577. 14, 171; χρίσαι and χρίσασθαι, Od. 3, 466. 6, 96. 10, 364; *to anoint oneself with oil*. According to Herodian in Eustath. λίπα is origin. dat. from τὸ λίπα, *oil, fat*, gen. *dat*. λίπαΐ, λίπα; later, this dat. was by use shortened to λίπα (ἔλαιον is adj. from ἐλάα, olive; hence λίπ' ἐλαίῳ, with olive oil), see Buttm. Gram. § 56, p. 96. Kühner, § 270. Others consider λίπα an adv. *unctunusly* (as an abbrev. from λιπαρά), hence λίπα ἀλείφειν, to anoint with fat, see Thiersch, Gram. § 198. 2.

λιπαροκρήδεμνος, ον (κρήδεμνον), *having a shining head-band, splendidly veiled*, Χάρις, 18, 382.† h. Cer. 25.

λιπαροπλόκαμος, ον (πλόκαμος), *having annointed* or *glossy tresses*, 19, 126.†

λιπαρός, ή, όν (λίπας), superl. λιπαρώτατος, h. Ap. 33; originally 1) *fat, anointed*. Wealthy persons anointed themselves after bathing, and also on festival occasions, esply the head, face, and hair; hence λιπαροί κεφαλάς και καλά πρόσωπα, spoken of the suitors. (Od. 15, 332. 2) *shining, beaming, bright, beautiful*, nitidus, spoken of the external form, πόδες, nly of men, and of Hērē, Il. 14, 186; κρήδεμνα, the splendid veil, Od. 1, 334. 16, 416; but, the gleaming battlements, Od. 13, 388. Λιπαροί θέμιστες, rich, splendid tributes, Il. 9, 156. *b) agreeable, happy*, esply spoken of age, Od. 11, 136.. 19, 368; hence adv. λιπαρῶς, *happily*. γηράσκειν, Od. 4, 210.

Λιπάω (λιπάς), Ep. λιπόω, *to be fat*, is *shine*, an old reading for ῥυσόω, Od. 19, 72.†

λίς or **λῖς**, Ep. for ὁ λέων, *a lion*, a defect. subst., of which except the nomin. we have only the accus., λῖν, 11, 480. Spitzner, ad Il. 15, 275, prefers λίς.

λῖς, ἡ, abbrev. form for λισσή. smooth, λῖς πέτρη, *Od. 12, 64. 79. 2) λῖς, ὁ, see

Λίσσομαι. • 265 *Λοξοβάτης.

λίνς, occurring only in the dat. sing. λιτί and nccus. λίτα, an old Ep. defect. =λίνον, linen; in the phrase ἑανῷ λιτί κάλυψαν, they covered him with costly linen, Voss, Il. 18, 352. 23, 254 (spoken of the linen with which the dead was shrouded); and accus. sing. ὑπὸ λῖτα πετάσσας καλόν, Od. 1, 130. cf. Od. 10, 353. Il. 8, 441; spoken of linen cloth spread upon seats and over a chariot. Thus Apoll., Heyne, Butim., Gram. p. 91. Thiersch, Gram. § 197. 60. Wolf, on the contrary, in Anal. IV. p. 501, Passow, Rost, and Nitzsch ad Od. 1, 130, take λῖτα as accus. plur. from an old neut. λί, Ep. for λισσόν, λεῖον, smooth cloth without embroidered figures=λεῖα, Thuc. 2, 97. In favour of this are the epithets καλόν, δαιδαλέον, Od. 1, 130, which are generally used with θρόνος, but never with λῖτα, Il. 18, 390. Od. 10, 314. 366.

λίσσομαι, more rarely λίτομαι, poet. depon. mid. Ep. imperf. ἐλλισάμην, and iterat. λισσέσκετο, fut. λίσομαι, aor. 1 ἐλισάμην, Ep. ἐλλισάμην, Od. imperat. λίσαι, aor. 2 ἐλιτόμην, from the optat. λιτοίμην, Od. 14, 405; infin. λιτέσθαι, Il. 16, 47. 1) Absol. to supplicate, to entreat; ὑπέρ τινος, by any one, thus ὑπὲρ τοκέων, ὑπὲρ ψυχῆς καὶ γούνων, 15, 660. Od. 15, 261; and gen. alone, Od. 2, 68. 2) to beg, to implore, to adjure. a) With accus. of the person: τινά; the object of the entreaty stands a) In the infin. οὔ σε λίσσομαι μένειν, Il. 1, 174. 283. 4, 379; or in the accus. with the infin. 9, 511. Od. 8, 30; sometimes also ὅπως follows, Od. 3, 19. 327. β) In the accus. οἱ αὐτῷ θάνατον λιτέσθαι, to implore death for oneself. Il. 16, 47; and with double accus. ταῦτα οὐχ ὑμέας ἔτι λίσσομαι. these things I no longer entreat of you, Od. 2, 210. cf 4, 347. Λίσσεσθαί τινα γούνων, Il. 9, 451, supplicating to embrace the knees, for the usual λαβὼν γούνων, 6, 45. (λίτομαι stands only h. 15, 5. 18, 48.)

λισσός, ή, όν, poet. form of λεῖος, smooth, always λισσὴ πέτρη, *Od. 3, 293. 5, 412. cf. λίς.

λιστρεύω (λίστρον), to level, to dig, to dig about. φυτόν, Od. 24, 227.†

λίστρον, τό, a spade, a mattock, for digging the earth; a shovel for cleaning the ground, Od. 22, 455.† (From λισσός.)

λῖτα, see λίς.

Λιταί, αἱ (cf. λιτή), Prayers personified as mythic beings, daughters of Zeus, and sisters of Atë. They are penitent and timorous deprecations after the commission of a fault; hence the poet describes them as lame, wrinkled, squint-eyed maidens, since it is unwillingly that a man forces his spirit to deprecation after the commission of a crime, 9, 502 sqq. [they are also wrinkled from anxiety, and dare not look one in the face, Db.]

λιτανεύω (λιτή), fut. εύσω, 1) to beseech, to entreat, esply as a suppliant for protection, Od. 7, 145; γούνων, to entreat by one's knees, Od. 10, 481. cf. Il. 24, 357; with infin. following, 23, 196. 2) With accus. of the pers. to beseech or, supplicate any one, 9, 581. 22, 414. (The λ is doubled with an augm. ἐλλιτάνευε.)

λιτή, ἡ, the act of supplication, entreaty, prayer, Od. 11, 34.† Plur. αἱ Λιταί. q. v.

λιτί, see λίς.

*λίτομαι, a rare pres. for λίσσομαι, q. v.

λό for λόε, see λοέω.

λοβός, ὁ (prob. from λέπω), the lower part of the ear, the lobe of the ear, 14, 182.† h. 5, 8.

λόγος, ὁ (λέγω), a saying, a word; plur. words, discourse, only twice, 15, 393. Od 1, 57; but also in the Hymn. and Batr.

*λόγχη, ἡ, a lance, a spear, Batr. 129.

λόε, Ep. for ἔλοε, ser λούω.

λοέσσαι, λοεσσάμενος, see λούω.

λοετρόν, τό, ancient Ep. for λουτρόν (λοέω), a bath, the act of bathing, always plur.: nly θερμὰ λοετρά, warm bath, 14, 6; but λοετρὰ Ὠκεανοῖο, 18, 489. Od. 5, 275. The contr. form stands only in h. Cer. 50.

λοετροχόος, ον, old Ep. for λουτροχόος (χέω), prob. pouring out water for bathing, bath-filling; τρίπους, a bathing-kettle, i. e. a three-footed kettle, in which water for bathing was warmed, 18, 346. Od. 8, 435; subst. ἡ λοετροχόος, the maid who prepares a bath, Od. 20, 297.

λοέω, Ep. form of λούω, from which λοέσσαι, λοέσσασθαι, etc., see λούω.

λοιβή. ἡ (λείβω), dropping, pouring out; only in a religious sense, that which is poured out. a libation, mly with wine; connected with κνίσσα, 9, 500. Od. 9, 349.

λοίγιος, ον. poet. (λοιγός), bad. sad, ruinous, mischievous: ἔργα, pernicious things, 1, 518; οἴω λοίγι᾽ ἔσεσθαι, I think it will be ruinous, *21, 533.

λοιγός, ὁ (akin to λυγρός), destruction, mischief, ruin, death, *1, 67. 5, 603. 9, 495; spoken of the destruction of the ships, *16, 80.

λοιμός, ὁ (akin to λύμη), pestilence, a pestilential and deadly sickness, contagion, *1, 61. 97.

λοισθήιος, ον. Ep. for λοίσθιος (λοῖσθος), relating to the last, λοισθήιον ἄεθλον, a prize for the last, 23, 785; also subst. τὰ λοισθήια, *23, 751.

λοῖσθος, ον (λοιπός), the last, the extreme, 23, 536.†

Λοκροί. οἱ. the Locrians, inhabitants of the district of Locris in Hellas, who were divided into two races: the Epicnemidian or Opuntian at Mount Cnemis, and the Ozolae, on the Corinthian gulf. The first only are mentioned by H., 2, 527.

*Λοξοβάτης, ου, ὁ, going obliquely,

N

Λοπός. 266 Λυκηγενής.

slant-gaited, an epith. of the crab, Batr. 297.
λοπός, ὁ (λέπω), *a shell, a rind, a skin;* κρομύοιο, an onion-skin, Od. 19, 233.†
***λουέω**, Ep. form of λούω, from which ἐλούσον, h. Cer. 290.
***λουτρόν**, τό, contr. for λοετρόν.
λούω, Ep. resolved λοέω, λουέω, impert. ἐλούεον, aor. 1 ἔλουσα, Ep. λοῦσα, infin. λοέσσαι, partcp. λούσας, Ep. λοέσσας, fut. mid. λοέσσομαι, aor. 1 ἐλουσάμην, Ep. λουσάμην, with this the infin. λοέσσασθαι, partcp. λοεσσάμενος, perf. pass. λέλουμαι, 5, 6. In the pres. and imperf. are found the common and shortened forms λούεσθαι and λοῦσθαι, Od. 6, 216; imperf. ἐλόεον, Od. 4, 252; also an old aor. 2 ἔλοον, from the root ΛΟΩ, from which λόε, Od. 10, 361; λόον, h. Ap. 120; *to wash, to bathe*, always spoken of human beings, τινὰ ποταμοῖο ῥοῇσιν, Il. 16, 669; of horses only, 23, 282. Mid. *to wash* or *bathe oneself*, very often ἐν ποταμῷ, Od. 6, 210; and ποταμοῖο, in the river, Il. 6, 508. 15, 265; spoken of Sirius: λελουμένος Ὠκεανοῖο, having bathed in Oceanus, i. e. when he rises, 5, 6.

λοφάδια, see καταλοφάδια.
λοφιή, ἡ (λόφος), *the neck, with long, stiff hair*, spoken of the boar: *the bristles*, Od. 19, 446.†
λόφος, ὁ (λέπω). 1) *the neck*, prim. of draught-animals, which was rubbed by the yoke in drawing, 23, 508; then, of men, 10, 573. 2) *a crest*, mly made of the mane of horses, which was placed in a conical elevation (φάλος) upon the helmet, 6, 469; having coloured hair, v. 537. Od. 22, 124. 3) *a hill, an elevation*, Od. 11, 596. 16, 471. h. Ap. 520. In this signif. it is not found in the Il.
λοχάω (λόχος), aor. infin. λοχῆσαι, fut. mid. λοχήσομαι, partcp. aor. 1 λοχησάμενος, 1) *to lay an ambuscade*, 18, 520. Od. 4, 487. b) With accus. *to waylay* any one, *to lie in ambush* for any one, Od. 14, 181. 15, 28. Mid. as depon. *to place oneself in ambush*, Od. 4, 388. 463. 13, 268; with accus. τινά, to waylay any one, only Od. 4, 670.
***λοχεύω** (λόχος), fut. σω, *to bring into the world, to bear*, spoken of the mother, h. Merc. 230.
λόχμη, ἡ (λόχος), *a lair, a thicket*, Od. 19, 439.†
λόχονδε, adv. (λόχος), *to an ambuscade*, 1, 227. Od. 14, 217.
λόχος, ὁ (from λέγω or ΛΕΧΩ), 1) *concealment, ambush*, prim. spoken of place, 1, 227. 11, 379; of the Trojan horse: κοῖλος or πυκινὸς λόχος, Od. 4, 227. 8, 515. 11, 525. 2) *ambuscade*, as an action, *the act of waylaying*, 18, 513. 24, 779. Od. 4, 441; λόχος γερόντος, the way to seize the old man, Od. 4, 395. 3) *ambuscade*, spoken of the force composing it, Il. 4, 392. 6, 189. λόχον ἀνδρῶν ἐσίζεσθαι, to place oneself in the ambush of men, 13, 285. 8, 522; hence,

generally, 4) *a troop, a company* of warriors, Od. 20, 19.
***λύγξ, ὁ**, gen. λυγκός, *a lynx*, h. 14, 24.
λύγος, ὁ, *Abraham's balm*, vitex agnus castus, Linn., a kind of shrub, like willow; and generally, *a willow, a rod, an osier twig*, Od. 9, 427. 10, 167; δίδη μόσχοισι λύγοισι, he bound them with tender willows: thus Heyne. Il. 11, 105; for Apoll. explains μόσχοι by ἁπαλαῖς καὶ νεαῖς. Others consider λύγοισι as an adj., and μόσχοισι as subst., as Köppen and Voss: *with willow rods*, cf. μόσχος. [Db. with flexible rods, sc. osiers.]
λυγρός, ή, όν (λύζω), that which causes sighs: *sad, gloomy, lamentable, miserable, wretched*. 1) Spoken prim. of human conditions: ὄλεθρος, γῆρας, δαΐς, ἄλγος; τὰ λυγρά, sad things, 24, 531. Od. 14, 226; εἵματα, miserable garments, Od. 16, 457; apparently active, *pernicious, destructive*, φάρμακα, γαστήρ, Od. 4, 230. 17, 473. 2) Of men: *sad, miserable*, i. e. weak, cowardly, Il. 13, 119. Od. 18, 107: but = bad, destructive, Od. 9, 454. Adv. **λυγρῶς**, *miserably, wretchedly*, πλήσσων, Il. 5, 763.† Cf. λευγαλέος.
λύθεν, Ep. for ἐλύθησαν, see λύω.
λύθρον, τό or λύθρος, ὁ (λῦμα), prop *a stain of blood*; in H. the blood which flows from wounds, *the life-blood as shed*; according to the Gramm. blood mixed with dust, 11, 169; always dat. αἵματι καὶ λύθρῳ πεπαλαγμένος, defiled with blood and the dust of battle [or, battle-stains], 6, 268. Od. 22, 402, 23, 48.
λυκάβας, αντος, ὁ, *the year*, *Od. 14, 161. 19, 306 (probably from λύκη and βαίνω), the course of light, the progress of the sun; Eustath. strangely derives it from λύκος and βαίνω, because the days follow one another like wolves, which in passing over a river are said to seize one another by the tail.) [According to Ameis, *walker-in-light*, the composit. requiring an act. signif.]
Λύκαστος, ἡ, a town in the southern part of Crete, 2, 647.
Λυκάων, ονος, ὁ, 1) ruler of Lycia, father of Pandarus, Il. 2, 826. 4, 88. 2) son of Priam and Laothoë, Il. 3, 333. Achilles took him prisoner, and sold him to Lemnos; he escaped, and was finally slain by Achilles, 21, 35, seq.
λυκέη, ἡ, sc. δορά, prop. adj. from λύκος, *a wolf-skin*, 10, 459.†
Λυκηγενής, οῦς, ὁ (Λυκία, γένος), *born in Lycia* (V. Lycian). Apollo was a national deity of the Lycians, 4, 101. 119. Another deriv. is from λύκη, light, *the father of the light*, in allusion to the rising sun. This contravenes the usu. loq. because γενής in compos. is always passive. [According to K. O. Müller, Λυκηγενής = light-born, not one born in Lycia, cf. h. Apoll. 440, seq. Light played a great part both symbolically in

Λυκίη. 267 Λωβάομαι.

the cultus of Apollo, and in the poetic imagery connected with him.]
Λυκίη, ή. *Lycia*, 1) a district in Asia Minor, between Caria and Pamphylia, named by the Gramm. *Great Lycia*, 2, 877. 2) a district in the north of Asia Minor, at the foot of Ida, from the river Æsēpus to the city Zeleia. This the Gramm. call *Lesser Lycia*, 5, 173. Also adv. 1) Λυκίηθεν, from Lycia. 2) Λυκίηνδε, to Lycia.
Λύκιοι, οί, *the Lycians*, 1) the inhabitants of the district of Great Lycia, who were governed by Sarpēdon, 2, 876. 6, 194. 2) the inhabitants of the district of Little Lycia, led by Pandarus, 15, 486.
Λυκομήδης, ους, ὁ, son of Creon, a Bœotian, one of the seven heroes, who commanded the watch at the trench, 9, 84. 12, 366. 17, 345, 346.
Λυκόοργος, ό, Ep. for Λυκοῦργος, 1) son of Dryas, king of the Edōnes in Thrace, the insulter of Dionȳsos. He persecuted the god, so that he fled to Thetis in the sea. The gods for a punishment made him blind, and he lived but a short time, 6, 130, seq. 2) son of Aleus, king of Arcadia, grandfather of Agapēnor; he slew Areīthous, and presented his club to Ereuthalion, 7, 142, seq. (According to Damm, from λύκος and ὀργή, *wolf-spirited*; more correctly from ἔργω, *wolf-slaying*, cf. Hdt. 7, 76.)
λύκος, ὁ, *a wolf*, often used as a figure of ferocity and greediness, 4, 471. 16, 156. Od.
Λυκοφόντης, ου, ὁ, 1) a Trojan, slain by Teucer, 8, 275. 2) Another reading for Πολυφόντης, q. v.
Λυκόφρων, ονος, ὁ, son of Mastor, from Cythēra, a companion of the Telamonian Ajax, 15, 130, seq.
Λύκτος, ή, an ancient town in Crete, east of Cnossus, a colony of Lacedæmonians, 2, 647. 17, 611; in Polyb. Λύττος, (according to Herm *Crepusca*.)
Λύκων, ωνος, ὁ, a Trojan slain by Peneleus, 16, 335, seq.
λῦμα, ατος, τό (λύω, λούω), *uncleanness*, *dirt*, *filth*, *defilement*, 14, 171; the dirty water which is poured away after a purification, *1, 314.
λυπρός, ή, όν (λυπηρός), *sad*, *wretched*, *miserable*, epith. of Ithaca, Od. 13, 243.†
λύρη, ή. a lyre; a seven-stringed instrument, said to have been invented by Hermēs, h. Merc. 428. It had, like the cithara, two sides, which however were less curved. Its sounding-board was shaped like the turtle-shell, for which reason it did not stand upright, but was held between the knees. Its tone was stronger and sharper than that of the cithara, see Forkel's Gesch. der Mus. I. p. 250.
Λυρνησσός, ή (Λυρνησσός), a town in Mysia (Troas), in the kingdom of Thebes, the residence of king Mynes, 2, 690. 19, 60. 20, 92.

Λύσανδρος, ὁ, *Lysander*, a Trojan wounded by Ajax, 11, 491.
λυσιμελής, ἐς (μέλος), *relaxing the limbs*, *limb-relaxing*, ὕπνος, *Od. 20, 57. 23, 343.
λῦσις, ιος, ή (λύω), *the act of loosing, resolving;* hence, *setting free, liberating,* θανάτου, from death, Od. 9, 421; esply *ransoming* from slavery, Il. 24, 655.
λύσσα, ή, *frenzy*, *madness*, always spoken of warlike rage, *9, 239. 21, 542.
λυσσητήρ, ῆρος, ὁ, *one furious* or *frenzied, a rover*, κύων, 8, 299.†
λυσσώδης, ες (εἶδος), *like one raving* or *mad*, spoken of Hector, 18, 53.†
λύχνος, ὁ (ΛΥΚΗ), *a light*, *a lamp*, Od. 19, 34,† and Batr.
λύω, fut. λύσω, aor. 1 ἔλυσα, fut. mid. λύσομαι, aor. 1 ἐλυσάμην, perf. pass. λέλυμαι, 3 sing. optat. λελῦτο for λελῦιτο, Od. 18, 238; aor. pass. ἐλύθην, and Ep. pass. aor. without a connective vowel ἐλύμην, from this: λύτο and λύντο. I) Act. *to loose*, i. e. 1) *to unbind* or *loosen* any thing from an object, with accus. θώρηκα, ζωστῆρα, ζωνήν, Od. 11, 245. cf. ζώνη, frequently, ἱστία, πρυμνήσια, Od. (not in the Il.) ἀσκόν, Od. 10, 47. *b*) Spoken of horses: *to unyoke, to unharness,* ἵππους ἐξ or ὑπὲξ ὀχέων, ὑπὸ ζυγοῦ, ὑφ' ἅρμασιν, Il. 5, 369. 8, 504. 543. 18, 244. *c*) *to release, to free* from fetters, 15, 22; metaph. τινὰ κακότητος, to release any man from misery, Od. 5, 397; esply *to liberate, to release* any one from imprisonment, τινὰ ἀποίνων, for a ransom, Il. 11, 106; without ἀποίνων, 1, 20. 29. 2) *to dissolve, to dismiss, to loose*, ἀγορήν, Il. 1, 305. Od. 2, 257; pass. λύτο δ' ἀγών, Il. 24, 1; νείκεα, to dismiss contest, 14, 205. Od. 7, 74; metaph. λύειν γυῖα, γούνατα, to loose the limbs, i. e. to relax them, to deprive them of power, Il. 4, 469. 5, 176. 16, 425, seq.; frequently =*to kill*, also λύειν μένος, Od. 3, 450; but spoken also of one fatigued, sleeping, terrified, pass., Il. 7, 16. 8, 123; λύθεν δέ οἱ ἄψεα πάντα (of sleep), Od. 4, 794; λύτο γούνατα καὶ ἦτορ, knees and heart trembled, Od. 4, 703; again: λύθη ψυχή, μένος, Il. 5, 296. 8, 315, hence generally: *to dissolve, to destroy, to ruin;* λέλυνται σπάρτα, the ropes are ruined, 2, 135; λύειν κάρηνα, κρήδεμνα πόλιος, to destroy the citadels. the battlements, 2, 118. 16, 100. Od. 13, 388. 11) Mid. 1) *to unloose for oneself*, ἱμάντα, Il. 14, 214; ἵππους, to unyoke his horses: 23, 7. 11; τεύχεα ἀπ' ὤμων, to take off the arms for themselves, viz. from the dead, 17, 318. 2) *to ransom* any one *for oneself*, θυγατέρα, 1, 13. 10, 378. Od. 10, 284. (υ is short, long only before σ, twice υ in the pres. and imperf. Od. 7, 74. Il. 23, 513.)
λωβάομαι, depon. mid. (λώβη), aor. 1 ἐλωβησάμην, *to treat with insult* or *contempt, to dishonour; to insult*, 1, 232. 2,

Λωβεύω. 242; with accus. τινὰ λώβην, to offer an insult to any man, 13, 623.

λωβεύω (λώβη) = λωβάομαι, to insult, to deride, to revile, τινά, *Od. 23, 15. 26,·

λώβη, ἡ, insulting treatment, in word and deed, abuse, insult, injury, indignity. λώβην τίσαι, to expiate the injury, 11, 142 ; and ἀποδοῦναι, 9, 387 ; in connexion with αἶσχος, mockery and insult, 13, 622. Od. 18, 225; an occasion of insult, Il. 3, 42. 7, 97.

λωβητήρ, ῆρος, ὁ (λωβάομαι), 1) a reviler, 2, 275. 2) a vile man, a villain, *24, 239.

λωβητός, ή, όν (λωβάομαι), shamefully treated, insulted. λωβητόν τινα τιθέναι, to overwhelm one with insult, 24, 531.†

λωίτερος, η, ον, see λωίον.

λωίων, ον, gen. ονος (λάω), irreg. compar. of ἀγαθός, more desirable, more agreeable, better. only in the neut. 1, 229. 6, 339 ; from which a new compar. λωίτερος, η, ον, with ἄμεινον, Od. 1, 376.¹, 141.

λώπη, ἡ, poet. (λέπω), a covering, a woollen garment, a robe, Od. 13, 224.†

λωτεῦντα, see λωτόεις.

λωτόεις, εσσα, εν, poet. (λωτός), overgrown with lotus, πεδία λωτεῦντα, contr. for λωτοῦντα from λωτόεντα, plains full of lotus-trefoil, 12, 283.† Aristarch. here wrote λωτοῦντα ; others consider it as a partcp. of a verb not elsewhere found, λωτέω = λωτίζω.

λωτός, ὁ, 1) the lotus, lotus-trefoil, a species of trefoil used as food for horses, growing in the moist low-lands of Greece and Troy; according to Voss, ad Virg. Georg. 2, 84, trifolium melilotus, Linn., Il. 2, 776. 14, 384. Od. 4, 603. 2) the lotus-tree, later also called the Cyrenian lotus, a kind of tree with a sweet fruit, on the African coast, upon which some of the inhabitants chiefly lived. According to H. Od. 9, 84, it was the food of the Lotophagi. This species of tree is described by Hdt. 2, 96 ; he compares its fruit in size with the berry of the mastich-tree, and in taste with the date. According to Sprengel. Antiq. Botan. p. 51, it is the rhamnus lotus, Linn., or Zizyphus lotus. It is now known in Tunis and Tripoli under the name jujuba. From the words ἄνθινον εἶδαρ, Od. 9, 84, it has been incorrectly concluded that H. intended a plant; cf. Miguel, Hom. Flor. p. 18.

Λωτοφάγοι, οἱ, the Lotophagi, i. e. the lotus eaters (see λωτός), a peaceable, hospitable people, to whom Odysseus (Ulysses) came from Cythêra, after a ten days' voyage, Od. 9, 84. Without doubt, they must be sought on the Libyan coast, according to Völcker's Hom. Geogr. p. 100, at the Syrtis Minor. According to Hdt. 4, 177, they were upon a cape not far from the Gindānēs [an African tribe]; according to most of the old commentators, on the island Meninx, now Zerbi.

λωφάω (λόφος), fut. ήσω, prop. spoken of draught-cattle, which being unyoked, and having the neck at liberty, rest; generally, to rest, to recruit, 21, 292; κακῶν, to recruit oneself from miseries, Od. 9, 460; see καταλωφάω.

M.

M, the twelfth letter of the Greek alphabet; in H. the sign of the twelfth rhapsody.

μ', 1) With apostroph. for με. 2) Rarely and only Ep. for μοι, as 9, 673; cf. Thiersch, Gram. § 164. 2. Rem. 2.

μά, a particle of asseveration, connected with the accus. of the deity or thing by which one swore. It stands 1: Prim. in negative clauses : οὐ μὰ γὰρ Ἀπόλλωνα, no, by Apollo, 1, 86. 23, 43. Od. 20, 339. 2) Connected with ναί, it stands affirmatively: ναὶ μὰ τόδε σκῆπτρον, verily, by this sceptre, Π. 1, 234.

*μάγειρος. ὁ (μάσσω), a cook, Batr. 40.

Μάγνητες, οἱ, sing. Μάγνης, ητος, ὁ, the Magnētes, inhabitants of a district of Thessaly, Magnesia, a Pelasgian race, deriving its origin from Magnes, son of Æolus, 2, 756.

*μάζα, ἡ (μάσσω), kneaded dough and barley-bread prepared from it, κυρβαία μάζα, Ep. 15, 6.

μαζός, ὁ, a breast, a pap, distinct from στέρνον and στῆθος, 4. 528. 2) Chiefly of a woman, the (maternal-) breast, Il. 22, 80. 83. 24, 58. Od. 11, 448.

ΜΑΘΩ, obsol. root of μανθάνω.

μαῖα, ἡ, mother, a friendly mode of addressing aged women, *Od. 2, 349. 19, 16 (later, a wet-nurse). h. Cer. 147.

Μαῖα, ἡ, poet. also Μαιάς, άδος, ἡ, Od. 14, 435 ; Maja, Maia, daughter of Atlas and Pleïonē, mother of Hermês by Zeus, h. Merc. 3.

Μαίανδρος, ὁ, Meander, a river in Ionia and Phrygia, famed for its manifold sinuosities, which flows into the Icarian sea near the city Miletus, now Meinder, 2, 869.

Μαιάς, άδος, ἡ = Μαῖα, q. v.

Μαιμαλίδης, ου, ὁ, son of Maemalus = Pisandrus, 16, 194.

μαιμάω (μαίω), poet. aor. 1 Ep. μαίμησα, often in the Ep. form μαιμώωσι. μαιμώωσα for μαιμῶσι, μαιμῶσα, to desire earnestly, to rush impetuously, to rage, 15, 742; αἰχμὴ μαιμώωσα, the rushing spear; the impetuous spear, 5, 661. 15, 542. περὶ δούρατι χεῖρες μαιμῶσιν, 13, 78. cf. v. 75 ; metaph. μαίμησεν οἱ ἦτορ, violently was his heart agitated, 5, 670.

μαιμάω, μαιμώωσα, see μαιμάω.

μαινάς, άδος, ἡ (μαίνομαι), a frenzied, raging female, 22, 460.† h. Cer., 386.

μαίνομαι, depon. pass. (ΜΑΩ), only pres. and imperf. 1) *to become frenzied, to rave, to be furious, to rage.* a) Mly spoken of the gods and men, with reference to an attack in battle, 5, 185. 6, 101. Od. 11, 537; also of anger, Il. 8, 360 ; of Dionysus *to be under the influence of divine enthusiasm, of prophetic frenzy*, 6, 132 ; of the drunken, Od. 18, 406. 22, 298. b) Of inanimate things; of hands and of the spear, Il. 16, 75. 245. 8, 111; of fire, 15, 606.

μαίομαι, dep. mid. (ΜΑΩ), *to touch* [*to will; to strive.* Död.], esply *to seek, to explore*, Od. 14, 356. h. Cer. 44 ; with acc. κευθμώνας (to *explore* its secret nooks), Od. 13, 367 ; only pres. and imperf. (ἐπὶ χερσὶ μάσασθαι. Od. 11, 591, belongs to ἐπιμαίομαι.) *Od. [But cf. Död. p. 88.]

Μαῖρα, ἡ (the sparkling) 1) daughter of Nereus and Doris, 18, 48. 2) daughter of Prœtus and Anteia (Antēa), a companion of Artemis ; at a later period, when she became the mother of Locrus by Zeus, she was slain by the goddess, Od. 11, 326.

Μαίων, ονος, ὁ, son of Hæmon, a Theban, leader of the ambuscade with Polyphontes, 4, 394, seq.

*μάκαιρα, h. Ap. 14 ; see μάκαρ.

μάκαρ, αρος, ὁ, ἡ, pecul. poet. fem. μάκαιρα, superl. μακάρτατος, η, ον, 1) *happy, blessed*, prim. spoken of the gods. θεοὶ μάκαρες, 1, 339 ; but οἱ μάκαρες, the happy dead, *the blest*, Od. 10, 299. 2) Spoken of men : *happy*, i. e. *rich, opulent*, Il. 3, 182. 11, 68. Od. 1, 217. 6, 158. σεῖο δ', Ἀχιλλεῦ, οὔτις ἀνὴρ μακάρτατος, in comparison with thee was no one the most happy, or, no one was so entirely happy as thou, Od. 11, 483, where the compar. would naturally be expected; see Thiersch, Gram. § 282, 5.

Μάκαρ, αρος, ὁ, son of Æolus, king of Lesbos, 24, 544. h. Ap. 37.

μακαρίζω (μάκαρ), *to esteem happy*, τινά, any one, *Od. 15, 538. 17, 165.

μακεδνός, ή, όν, poet. *μακεδανός, tall, slender*, epith. of the poplar, Od. 7, 106.†

μάκελλα, ἡ (κέλλω), *a broad mattock, a shovel, a spade*, 21, 259.†

μακρός, ή, όν (μάκος=μῆκος), compar. μακρότερος, η, ον, poet. μάσσων, ον, Od. 8, 203 ; superl. μακρότατος, η, ον, Ep. μήκιστος ; *long*. 1) Spoken of space: *long*, i. e. *far-reaching, δόρυ, ἔγχος*, but also of perpendicular distance: *high*, Ὄλυμπος, οὔρεα, ἐρινεός ; μακρὰ φρείατα, deep wells, 21, 197 ; again : *far*, μακρὰ βιβάς. βιβῶν, *far-striding*, 3, 22. 7, 213 ; spoken of the voice: μακρὸν ἀΰτειν, to cry afar, i. e. aloud, 3, 81. 5, 101. 2) Spoken of time: *long-lasting, = long,* ἤματα, νύξ, Od.; ἔλδωρ, a long-cherished wish, Od. 23, 54.

μάκων, see μηκάομαι.

μάλα, adv., compar. μᾶλλον, superl. μάλιστα, *A*) μάλα, *very, exceedingly, entirely*. α) Strengthening a single word (adv., adj., and verb): μάλα πάντες, all (without exception): μάλα πάγχυ, altogether ; εὖ μάλα, *very well*; μάλ᾿ αἰεί, for ever and ever; with compar. μάλα πρότερος, much before or earlier, 10, 124. (b) With ἀλλά, having a compar. force=*sed potius,* but rather, Od. 6, 44.) c) Establishing and affirming an entire clause : *gladly, certainly, by all means*, μάλ᾿ ἐψόμαι, gladly will I follow, Il. 10, 108. cf. Od. 4, 733. Often ἢ μάλα, yes, certainly, and ἢ μάλα δή. ἀλλὰ μάλα, but rather, Od. 4, 472; εἰ μάλα, εἰ καὶ μάλα, although greatly ; though never so much, &c.; mly with optat., and μάλα πέρ, καὶ μάλα πέρ, with partcp. in the same signif. B) Compar. μᾶλλον, *more, more strongly, more vehemently*. It is often strengthened by πολύ, ἔτι, καί, also καὶ μᾶλλον, and rather, much more, Il. 8, 470. 13, 638. Od. 18, 154. b) *rather*, Il. 5, 231. Od. 1, 351. c) Also with compar. μᾶλλον ῥηίτεροι, still [much] more easy, Il. 24, 243. d) On the omission of μᾶλλον with βούλομαι, see this word. C) Superl. μάλιστα, *most, most strongly, for the most part, chiefly, especially, exceedingly*, with the positive as a periphrastic superl. 14, 460 ; it also stands for the purpose of strengthening it with a superl. ἔχθιστος μάλιστα, 2, 220. 24, 334.

μαλακός, ή, όν (μαλός), compar. μαλακώτερος, *soft, mild, gentle, tender*. 1) Spoken of corporeal things : εὐνή, κῶας. μαλακῇ νειῷ, a mellow fallow-field, 18, 541 ; λειμών, Od. 5, 72. 2) Metaph. *soft, mild, gentle*, θάνατος, ὕπνος, Il. 10, 2. Od. 18, 202 ; ἔπεα, 6, 337 ; of the slain Hector Achilles says : ἢ μάλα δὴ μαλακώτερος ἀμφαφάασθαι Ἕκτωρ, assuredly, Hector is now much more easy to be handled (is ' far more patient to the touch.' Cp.], Il. 22, 373. Adv. μαλακῶς, *gently, softly*, Od. 3, 350. 24, 255.

*μαλάχη, ἡ (μαλάσσω), *mallows*, Batr. 161.

Μάλεια, ἡ, Ep. for Μαλέα, Od. 9, 80; and Μαλειάων ὄρος, Od. 3, 287 ; Μαλειῶν, Od. 14, 137 ; *Malea*, a promontory in the south-eastern part of Laconia, dangerous to navigators, now *Cap Malio di St. Angelo*, Od. and h. Ap. 409.

μαλερός, ή, όν (μάλα), *fierce, violent, strong*, epith. of fire, *9, 242. 20, 316. 21, 375.

μαλθακός, ή, όν (poet. for μαλακός), *soft, tender, ἄνθος*, h. 30, 15 ; metaph. *cowardly*, αἰχμητής, 17, 588.†

· μάλιστα, μᾶλλον, superl. and compar. of μάλα.

μάν, Dor. and old Ep. for μήν, as a particle of asseveration : *truly, certainly, by all means, verily*. 1) Standing alone, 8, 373 ; ἄγρει μάν, up ! on ! 2) Strengthened : ἢ μάν, yes, verily ; *assuredly*, 2, 370. 3) With negat. οὐ μάν, surely not, certainly not, 12, 318; μὴ μάν, 8, 512. Od. 11, 344; see μήν.

μανθάνω (ΜΑΘΩ), aor. 2 ἔμαθον, Ep. μάθον and ἔμμαθον, only in the aor. is

*Μαντείη. 270 Μάστιξ.

learn, to have learnt, i. e. to understand, κακά έργα, Od. 17, 226; 18, 362; and with infin. Il. 6, 444.

*μαντείη, ή (μαντεύομαι), prophecy, the art of prophesying, h. Merc. 533; plur. 472.

μαντεΐον, τό, Ion. and Ep. μαντήϊον, prophesying, a response, an oracle, Od. 12, 272.†

μαντεύομαι, depon. mid. (μάντις), to communicate an oracle, to prophesy, 2, 300; with accus. κακά, 1, 107; τινί τι, 16, 859; without accus. 19, 420; and generally, to predict, Od. 2, 170.

Μαντινέη, ή, Ep. and Ion. for Μαντίνεια. Muntinēa, a town in Arcadia on the river Ophis, north of Tegea, 2, 607.

Μάντιος, ὁ, son of Melampus and brother of Antiphātes, Od. 15, 242, seq.

μάντις, ιος, ὁ (from μαίνομαι), prop. one entranced, one inspired by a deity, who unveils the future; a seer, a prophet, who penetrates the future, both with and without external omens. This name also often comprehends those who divine by birds, dreams, and sacrifices, 1, 62. Od. 1, 201.

μαντοσύνη, ή, the art of prophecy, the art of divination, Il. and Od.; also plur. Il. 2, 832.

(μάομαι), see μαίομαι.

Μαραθών, ώνος, ὁ and ή, a village and borough in Attica, on the eastern coast, later famed for the overthrow of the Persians, named from the fennel (μάραθον) growing there, Od. 7, 80.

μαραίνω, aor. 1 ἐμάρᾱνα, h. Merc. 140; aor. pass. ἐμαράνθην, ἀνθρακίην, h. Merc. 140. 2) Pass. to be extinguished, to burn out, to cease to burn, *9, 212. 23, 228.

μαργαίνω (μάργος), to rave, to be frantic, to be boisterous, ἐπί τινα, 5, 882.†

μάργος, η, ον, raving, raging, boisterous, Od. 16, 421; γαστήρ, Od. 18, 2; foolish, irrational, *Od. 23, 11.

Μάρις, ιος, ὁ, son of Amisodarus, a Lycian, wounded by Antilochus, 16, 319. 327.

μαρμαίρω (μαίρω), to glimmer, to twinkle, to shine, to sparkle, for the most part spoken of the splendour of metals, 12, 195. ὄμματα μαρμαίροντα, the sparkling eyes (of Aphroditē), *3, 397.

μαρμάρεος, ἐη, εον (μαρμαίρω), gleaming, shining, beaming, spoken of metals esply, αἰγίς, ἄντυξ, 17, 594. 18, 480. ἅλς, μαρ, the sparkling sea (in a calm), 14, 273.

μάρμαρος, ὁ (μαρμαίρω), in H. stone, a block of stone, with the notion of shining, 12, 380. Od. 9, 499; an adj., πέτρος, μάρμαρος, the gleaming stone, Il. 16, 735.

μαρμαρυγή, ή (μαρμαρύσσω), splendour, radiancy, twinkling, metaph. the quivering, rapid movements of the feet, spoken of dancers, Od. 8, 265.† h. Ap. 203.

μάρναμαι, depon. mid. Ion. and poet. Infin. μάρνασθαι, only pres. and imperf. like ἵσταμαι, pres. optat. μαρνοίμην, Od. 11, 513 (prob. from μάρπη), to fight, to do battle, to contend, a) Mly spoken of war; τινί, dat. of pers. with a man, mly, against a man, Il. 9, 327. Od. 22, 228; rarely ἐπί τινι, Il. 9, 317. 17, 148; and dat. instrum. χαλκῷ, ἔγχει; περί τινος. about or over a man, 16, 497; but περὶ ἔριδος, to contend from discord, 7, 301. b) to contend, to dispute, with words, 1, 257.

Μάρπησσα, ή, daughter of Evēnus, wife of Idas. She was carried away by Apollo, but Idas received her again, ή, 557; see Idas, Ἴδης, and Evenus. (From μάρπτω, one seized.)

μάρπτω, poet. fut. μάρψω, aor. 1 ἔμαρψα. 1) to lay hold of, to seize or grasp, to hold. with accus. Od. 9, 289; ἀγκάς τινα, to embrace any one with the arms, Il. 14, 346; χείρας σκαιῇ, 21, 489. 2) to touch, to overtake, τινὰ ποσσί, 21, 564; χθόνα ποδοΐιν, to touch the earth with the feet, 14, 228; spoken of the lightning of Zeus; μάρπτειν ἕλκεα, to inflict (Cp. imprese) wounds (= corripiendo infligere; of lightning], 8, 405. 519; metaph. ὕπνος ἔμαρπτε αὐτόν, sleep overtook him, 23, 62. Od. 20, 56; γῆρας, Od. 24, 390.

μαρτυρίη, ή (μάρτυρ), witness, testimony, Od. 11, 325.†

μάρτυρος, ὁ, Ep. for μάρτυς, a witness, in the sing. only Od. 16, 423, often in the plur. μάρτυροι ἔστων (plur. with dual), Il. 1, 338.

*μάρτυς, υρος, ὁ, a witness, h. Merc. 372.

Μάρων, ωνος, ὁ, son of Euanthēs, priest of Apollo at Ismarus in Thrace, who presented Odysseus (Ulysses) with wine, Od. 9, 197, seq.

Μάσης, ητος, ή, a town in Argolis, later the port of Hermiōnē, 2, 562.

μάσσων, ὁ, ή, neut. μάσσον or μᾶσσον, irreg. compar. of μακρός, longer, greater, Od. 8, 203.

μάσταξ, ακος, ή (μαστείω [which Död connects with ἁμάω]), 1) that with which one chews, the mouth [i. e. the interior mouth with its organs of mastication, Död.], Od. 4, 287. 23, 76. 2) food, esply that which a bird brings in its beak for its young ones. νεοσσοῖσι προσφέρει μάστακ' for μάστακα (τροφήν. Schol.), Il. 9, 324. Al. μάστακι, to the beak.

μαστίζω (μάστιξ), aor. Ep. μάστιξα, to wield the whip, to whip, to lash, ἵππους, 5, 768; often with infin. μάστιξεν δ' ἐλάαν, he whipt, in order to drive, 5 366. Od. 3, 484. (Another form is μαστίω.)

μάστιξ, ιγος, ή (μάσσω). Ep. also μάστις, from this dat. μάστι for μάστιγι. Il. 500; accus. μάστιν, Od. 15, 182; a whip, a scourge, for driving horses, 5, 226. 736. 2) Metaph. strife, punishment, Διός, 12, 37. 13, 812.

μάστις, ή, Ion. and Ep. for μάστιξ, q. v.

μαστίω, poet. for μαστίζω, to lash, 17, 622. Mid. spoken of lions: σύρῇ πλευράς μαστίεται, he lashes his sides with his tail, *20, 171.

Μαστορίδης, ου, ό, son of Mastor = Halitherses, Od. 2, 158; = Lycophron, Il. 15, 430. 438.

Μάστωρ, ορος, ό, 1) father of Lycophron from Cythēra, Il. 2) father of Halitherses, Od.

*μασχάλη, ή, the shoulder, and the armpit, h. Merc. 242.

ματάω (μάτην), aor. 1 ἐμάτησα, to be inactive, to delay, to loiter, 16, 474. 23, 510; spoken of horses: μὴ—ματήσετον for ματήσητον, *5, 233.

ματεύω (ΜΑΩ), poet. = μαστεύω, to seek, to look up, 14, 110.†

*μάτην, adv. in vain, to no purpose, h. Cer. 309.

ματίη, ή (μάτην), a vain undertaking, a fruitless attempt, levity, folly, Od. 10, 79.†

μάχαιρα, ή (akin to μάχη), a large knife, a dagger, a sabre, which hung beside the sword, and which was used particularly in slaughtering victims, a sacrificial knife, 3, 271. 18, 597; Machaon also used it for cutting out an arrow, *11, 844.

Μαχάων, ονος, ό, voc. Μαχᾶον, son of Asklepios (Æsculapius), ruler of Tricca and Ithomē in Thessaly, distinguished for his medical skill, 2, 732. Cheiron had given his father healing remedies, 4, 219.

μαχειόμενος, Ep. see μάχομαι.

μαχεούμενος, see μάχομαι.

μάχη, ή, (referred by Död. to ἀμᾶν, mactare, &c.), a battle, a combat, a contest, a fight, mly a battle between heroes. μάχεσθαι μάχην, to fight a battle, 15, 673. 18, 533; also of a duel, 7, 263. 11, 542. 2) contest, quarrel, dispute, with words, 1, 177. H. mentions four contests in particular: the first between the Simoïs and Scamandrus, 4, 446. 7, 305; the second between the city of Troy and the Grecian ships, 8, 53—488; the third on the Scamandrus, from 11—18, 242; the fourth embraces the deeds of Achilles, and ends with Hector's death, 20—22. Il. and Od.

μαχήμων, ον (μαχέομαι), eager for battle, warlike, κραδίη, 12, 247.†

μαχητής, οῦ, ό (μαχέομαι), a warrior, combatant, Il.; with ἀνήρ, Od. 18, 261.

μαχητός, ή, όν (μάχομαι), to be attacked, to be combated, that may be vanquished, κακόν, Od. 12, 119.†

μαχλοσύνη, ή (μάχλος), incontinence, luxury, voluptuousness, sensuality, 24, 30, spoken of Paris. Aristarchus wished to strike out the word, because it is elsewhere used only of women; but without reason; on the contrary, it suits Paris very well, cf. 3, 39.

μάχομαι, Ion. and Ep. (μαχέομαι,) depon. mid. fut. μαχέσομαι and μαχήσομαι (the Att. fut. μαχοῦμαι is not Homeric), aor. ἐμαχεσσάμην, ἐμαχησάμην, pres. μαχέομαι, μαχέονται, 2, 366; μαχεῖται, 20, 26. μαχέοιτο, μαχέοιντο, 2, 72. 344; in pres. partcp. for metre's sake, μαχειόμενος and μαχεούμενος. The fut. and aor. Wolf always writes with η; only in the infin. aor. 1, for metrical reasons, stands μαχέσασθαι, 3, 20. 433. 7, 40; and optat. μαχέσαιο, 6, 329. According to Buttm. Gram. p. 291, in the aor. ἐμαχεσσάμην, not ἐμαχησάμην, agrees with the MSS., a reading which Spitzner follows. 1) to contend, to fight, to war, to battle, a) Esply in a contest both between whole armies and between single warriors, 3, 91. 435. 19, 153; mly τινί, with or against any man, ἐπί τινι, 5, 124. 244; ἀντία τινός, 20, 80. 88; ἐναντίον τινός, 3, 433; πρός τινα, 17, 471; but σύν τινι, with any man, i. e. with any man's aid, Od. 13, 391. Of the thing for which a man fights we have mly περί τινος, also περί τινι, Il. 16, 568. Od. 2, 245; ἀμφί τινι, Il. 3, 70. 16, 565; and εἵνεκά τινος, 2, 377; sometimes a dat. instrum. is added: τόξοις, ἀξίνῃσι. 2) Generally, to contend, to fight, without reference to war: ἀνδράσι περί δαιτί, about a repast, Od. 2, 245; spoken of a contest with beasts, Il. 16, 429. 758. b) Spoken of a prize-combat: πύξ, to contend with the fist, 23, 621. c) Spoken of contest of words, with ἐπέεσι, 1, 304. 5, 875; and without ἐπ. 1, 8.

μάψ, adv. poet. = μάτην, 1) in vain, fruitlessly, to no purpose, 2, 120. μάψ ὁμόσαι, 15, 40. 2) without reason, foolishly, inconsiderately, often μάψ, ἀτάρ οὐ κατὰ κόσμον, foolishly and indecently, 2, 214. Od. 3, 138. (Prob. from μάρπω, μάπω.)

μαψιδίως, adv. poet. = μάψ, 5, 374. Od. 3, 72. 7, 310.

*μαψιλόγος, ον, poet. (λέγω), speaking in vain or without sense, h. Merc. 546.

ΜΑΩ, an obsolete root, of which some forms remain. Perf. μέμαα, with pres. signif. Sing. obsol. for which μέμονα, as, ε (cf. γέγονα with γέγαα) is used, dual μέματον, plur. 1 μέμαμεν, 3 plur. μεμάασι. Imperat. μεμάτω, partcp. μεμαώς, gen. μεμαῶτος and μεμαότος, 3 plur. pluperf. μέμασαν, to strive for, 1) to rush eagerly to any thing, to dash impetuously on, 8, 413; πρόσσω, 11, 615; ἐγχείῃσι, 2, 818; ἐπί τινι, 8, 327. 20, 326. Often the partcp. μεμαώς, as an adj. or connected with another verb: in haste, impetuously, zealously, earnestly. 2) to desire ardently, to long for. a) Mly with the infin. pres., 1, 590. 2, 543. b) With gen. of thing: ἔριδος, αὐτῆς, 5, 732. 13, 197. 20, 256; μάχονα, mly with infin., 5, 182. 7, 36. 3) It also gives tenses to μαίομαι, q. v.

Μεγάδης, ου, ό, son of Megas = Perimus, 16, 695.

μεγάθυμος, ον, poet. (θυμός), high-

Μεγαίρω. 272 Μέδων.

souled, noble-hearted; esp. *brave, courageous*, epith. of brave men and nations, 2, 541; of a bull, 16, 488; of Athênê, Od. 8, 520. 13, 121.

μεγαίρω (μέγας), aor. 1 ἐμέγηρα, prop. to regard any thing as too great, with the notion of vexation, envy; hence, 1) *to envy, to grudge, to deny* any thing to any man, as too great for him, τινί τι, 23, 865. Od. 3, 55. Δαναοῖσι μεγήρας (sc. βίον), 15, 173; and with infin. μηδὲ μεγήρῃς ἡμῖν τελευτῆσαι τάδε ἔργα, deem it not too great for us to accomplish this work, Voss, Od. 3, 55; with accus. and infin. Od. 2, 235; and generally, *to refuse, to deny*. κατακαιέμεν (*to refuse permission to burn the dead*), Il. 7, 408. οὔτι μεγαίρω, I hinder it not, Od. 8, 207. Il. 8, 54. Also with gen. τί τινος, any thing from any man; spoken of Poseidôn: αἰχμὴν βιότοιο μεγήρας, diverting the spear from the life (viz. of Antilochus: refusing it the life = refusing to permit it to take the life) of Antilochus: according to Buttm, Lex. p. 409, ll. 13, 563 (refusing the life. V.)

μεγακήτης, ες (κῆτος), prob. that which has a great hollow or belly, and generally, *vast, very great, prodigious*, νηῦς, 8, 222; πόντος, Od. 3, 158; δελφίν, Od. 21, 22.

μεγαλήτωρ, ορος, ὁ, ἡ (ἦτορ), *great-hearted, high-minded, magnanimous, courageous*, epith. of heroes and of whole nations, 13, 302. Od. 19, 176; *spirited, proud*, θυμός, Il. 9, 109. Od. 5, 298.

μεγαλίζομαι, mid. (μέγας), *to make oneself great, to elevate oneself, to be proud*, θυμῷ, 10, 69. Od. 23, 174.

*μεγαλοσθενής, ές (σθένος), *very strong*, Ep. 6.

μεγάλως, adv. (μέγας), *greatly, very*. μάλα μεγάλως, very greatly, 17, 723. Od. 16, 432.

μεγαλωστί, adv. (μέγας), *in a great space*, always μέγας μεγαλωστί, great and long, 16, 776. Od. 24, 40.

Μεγαμηδείδης, ου, ὁ, son of Megamêdês. So is the father of Pallas called, h. Merc. 100.

Μεγαπένθης, εος, ὁ (sorrowful), son of Menelaus by a female slave; he was married to the daughter of Elector, Od. 4, 10. 15, 100. He received his name from his father's feelings on account of the rape of Helen.

Μεγάρη, ἡ, *Megara*, daughter of King Creon, in Thebes, wife of Heracles, Od. 11, 268. 269.

μέγαρον, τό (μέγας), *a large room, a hall*, hence esply, 1) the assembling-room of the men, *the men's hall*. It was the main room, situated in the middle of the house, and in which the meals were taken. The roof was supported by pillars, and it was lighted by a front and side door, Od. 1, 270. 22, 127. cf. Od. 1, 127—130. 133. 2) Generally, *any large room*, as that of the mistress, of the maids, Il. 3, 125. Od. 18, 98. 19, 60. 3) in plur. *a house, a dwelling, a palace*, l, 396. 5, 805. Od. 2, 400.

μεγαρόνδε, adv. *to the house, to the dwelling*, *Od. 16, 413. 21, 58.

μέγας, μεγάλη, μέγα, compar. μείζων, ον, superl. μέγιστος, η, ον, 1) *great*, spoken of extension in various ways: *high, long, wide, broad*, of animate and inanimate things, thus Ὄλυμπος, οὐρανός, αἰγιαλός, πέλαγος, etc. 2) *great*, i. e. *strong, powerful, mighty*, spoken of the gods; also, ἄνεμος, κράτος, κλέος. μέγα ἔργον, a great, i. e. a difficult work. Od. 3, 261. 3) *too great, immoderate*. λίην μέγα εἰπεῖν, to say something too great, Od. 3, 227. The neut. sing. and plur. μέγα and μεγάλα as adv. *greatly, very, strongly, powerfully*; μέγα with verbs and adj. μέγα ἔξοχος, very conspicuous; also with compar. and superl. μέγ' ἀμείνων, far better, Il. 2, 239. 21, 315; and μέγ' ἄριστος, by far the best, 2, 82. 763; plur. μεγάλα with κτυπεῖν, εὔχεσθαι, etc.

Μέγας, ὁ, a noble Lycian, 16, 695.

μέγεθος, εος, τό (μέγας), *size, height*, always spoken of the size of the body, mly with εἶδος and κάλλος. 2, 58. Od. 6, 152. 18, 219.

Μέγης, ητος, ὁ, son of Phyleus, sister's son of Odysseus (Ulysses), commander of the Dulichians and of the inhabitants of the Echinâdes, 2, 625. 13, 692. 15, 302.

μέγιστος, η, ον, see μέγας.

μεδέων, οντος, ὁ, fem. μεδέουσα. ἡ. poet. for μέδων, *a ruler, a sovereign*. masc. spoken of Zeus: Ἴδηθεν, Δωδώνης *16, 234. Fem. *a female ruler*, Σαλαμῖνος, h. 9, 4.

Μεδεών, ῶνος, ὁ, a city in Boeotia, near mount Phoenicius, 2, 501.

μέδομαι, depon. (prop. mid. of μέδω), fut. μεδήσομαι, 9, 650.† 1) *to take care of, to have charge of, to think of, to consider about*, with gen. πολέμοιο, κοίτου, 2, 384. Od. 2. 358; δόρποιο, Il. 18, 245; νόστοιο, 9, 622. Od. 11, 110; often ἑλκ. to think of defence, Il. 2) *to prepare* any thing for any man, *to invent, to plot*, κακὰ τινί, 4, 21. 8, 458.

μέδων, οντος, ὁ, prop. partcp. pres. from μέδω, as subst. *one who cares for, ruler, sovereign*, sing. only ἁλὸς μέδων, Od. 1, 72; elsewhere always ἡγήτορες ἠδὲ μέδοντες.

Μέδων, οντος, ὁ, 1) son of Oïleus and Rhênê (2, 727), step-brother of Ajax, he dwelt in Phylace, whither he had fled, because he had slain his step-mother's brother. He was the leader of the warriors from Methônê when Philoctêtês remained behind in Lemnos. Æneas slew him, 2, 727. 13, 693, seq. 15, 332. 2) a Lycian, 17, 216. 3) a herald of Ithaca in the train of the suitors; he disclosed to Penelope the danger of her son Telemachus, and was on that account afterwards saved by him, Od. 4, 677. 22, 357.

Μεθαιρέω.

μεθαίρέω (αἰρέω), aor. μεθεῖλον, Ep. Iterat. form μεθέλεσκον, *to take, to catch*, spoken of a ball : ὁ δ' ἀπὸ χθονὸς ὑψόσ' ἀερθείς, ῥηϊδίως μεθέλεσκε, subaud. σφαῖραν, the other, springing high from the earth, caught it with ease, Od. 8, 374.† (Damm [*e contrario capto*] and Voss.)

μεθάλλομαι (ἅλλομαι), only partcp aor. sync. μεταλμενος, *to leap over, to spring upon* or *to*, absol. 5, 336. 11, 538 ; *to leap after*, *23, 345.

μεθείω, Ep. for μεθῶ, see μεθίημι.

μεθέλεσκε, see μεθαιρέω.

μεθέμεν, Ep. for μεθεῖναι, see μεθίημι.

μεθέπω (ἕπω), partcp. aor. 2 act. μετασπών and mid. μετασπόμενος, I) Act. intrans. *to be behind, to go after*, hence 1) *to pursue, to follow*, τινὰ ποσσί, 17, 190. Od. 14, 33.   b) *to seek, to seek for*, with accus. Il. 8, 126 ; spoken of regions : *to visit*, absol. *to arrive*, Od. 1, 175.   2) Trans. with double accus. *to cause to go after, to drive after*; ἵππους Τυδεΐδην, to drive the horses after Tydides [κατόπιν ἥλαυνε, Schol.], Il. 5, 329.   II) Mid. *to follow, to pursue*; τινά, only, 13, 567.

μέθημαι (ἧμαι), *to sit in the midst*; with dat. μνηστῆρσι, in the midst of the suitors, Od. 1, 118.†

μεθημοσύνη, ἡ (μεθήμων), *negligence*, *remissness*, *13, 108. 121.

μεθήμων, ον (μεθίημι), *negligent, remiss, lazy, supine*, 2, 241. Od. 6, 25.

μεθίημι (ἵημι), infin. pres. Ep. μεθιέμεναι and μεθιέμεν, fut. μεθήσω, aor. 1 μεθῆκα, μεθῆσα. Of the aor. 2 subj. μεθῶ, Ep. μεθείω : optat. μεθείην, infin. μεθέμεν for μεθεῖναι. Of the pres. indic. μεθείω, 2 and 3 sing. μεθεῖς, μεθεῖ : of the imperf. 2, 3 sing. μεθίεις, μεθίει ; but 3 plur. μεθίειν for μεθίεσαν, *to neglect*, 1) Trans. with accus. 1) *to let loose, to let go* (any thing bound or detained); τινά, to let a prisoner go, 10, 449. cf. 16, 762; spoken of missiles: ἰόν, 5, 48; τὶ ἐς ποταμόν, to let any thing fall into the river, Od. 5, 460; metaph. χόλον τινός, to give up anger about any man, Il. 15, 138; 'Ἀχιλλῆϊ, to remit his wrath against Achilles, 1, 283 ; κῆρ ἄχεος, to free the heart from care, 17, 539.   2) *to abandon*, τινά, 3, 414. Od. 15, 212. εἴ με μαθείη ῥίγος, Od. 5, 471.   3) *to give, to permit, to yield*, νίκην τινί, Il. 14, 364; and with infin. ἐρύσαι, to permit to draw, 17, 418.   II) Intrans. 1) Absol. *to be negligent, to relax, to become weary, to loiter, to linger*, often absol. 6, 523. 10, 121, also Od. 4, 372; βίῃ, in strength, Il. 21, 177.   2) *to neglect, to desist, to cease from*; with gen. πολέμοιο, from war, 4, 240. 13, 97; in like manner ἀλκῆς, μάχης, βίης, Od. 21, 126; χόλοιο Τηλεμάχῳ (against Telem.), Od. 21, 377.   b) With infin. and partcp. rarely in H. μάχεσθαι, *to cease* to fight, Il. 13, 334. 23, 434. ἀλαύσας μεθῆκε, he ceased weeping, 24, 48.   (On quantity, see ἵημι.)

μεθίστημι (ἵστημι), fut. μεταστήσω,

Μείρομαι.

1) Act. transit. *to transfer, to transpose, to change, to exchange*, τινί τι, Od. 4, 612. 2) Mid. intrans. *to transfer oneself*, i. e. to go elsewhere, with dat. ἑτάροισι, 5, 514.

μεθομιλέω (ὁμιλέω), *to have intercourse, to associate*; τινί, with any man, 1, 269.†

μεθορμάω (ὁρμάω), only partcp. aor. pass. μεθορμηθείς, *to drive after*.   2) Pass. *to follow, to pursue*, Od. 5, 325. Il. 20, 192.

μέθυ, υος, τό, *any strong, intoxicating drink*, esply *wine*, 7, 471. Od. 4, 796.

*μεθύστερος, η, ον (ὕστερος), *after, later*, the neut. as adv. h. Cer. 205.

μεθύω (μέθυ), only pres. and imperf *drink unmixed wine*, Od. 18, 240 ; Metaph. *to be thoroughly soaked or saturated* (with). βοείη μεθύουσα ἀλοιφῇ, an ox-hide soaked with fat [*drunken with slippery lard*, Cp.], Il. 17, 390.

μειδάω, only in aor. 1 ἐμείδησα, Ep. μείδασα ; and μειδιάω, from which only partcp. pres. μειδιόων, Ep. for μειδιῶν, *to smile*; on the other hand, γελᾶν, to laugh aloud, h. Cer. 204 ; βλοσυροῖσι προσώπασι, 7, 212; Σαρδάνιον, Od. 20, 803 ; see this word.

μειδιάω, see μειδάω.

μείζων, ον, irreg. compar. of μέγας.

μείλας, Ep. μέλας, 24, 79 ;† only μείλανι πόντῳ, see ὁ Μέλας πόντος.

. μεῖλα, τά (μέλι, μειλίσσω), any thing gladdening, rejoicing, esply *gratifying presents*, *9, 147. 289; spoken of the gifts which a father gives to his daughter as a portion ; *marriage presents* ; *dower*.

μείλιγμα, ατος, τό (μειλίσσω), *any thing which serves to soothe* or *please*. μειλίγματα θυμοῦ, dainties, which the master takes for his dogs, Od. 10, 216.†

μείλινος, η, ον, poet. for μέλινος, q. v. *11.

μειλίσσω, only pres. (akin to μέλι, prop. to make sweet), hence 1) Act. *to please, to rejoice*, esply *to soothe, to calm*; νεκρὸν πυρός, to appease the dead by fire (the funeral pile), 7, 408. The dead, according to the views of the ancients, were angry if their obsequies were not soon performed.   2) Mid. *to enjoy oneself, to rejoice*, h. Cer. 291.   b) *to be gentle, to use gentle words, to address kindly*, Od. 3, 96. 4, 326.

μειλιχίη, ἡ (μειλίχιος), *gentleness, mildness*; πολέμοιο, slackness in battle [i. e. the dealing gentle blows; or *making little exertion*], 15, 741.†

μειλίχιος, η, ον and μείλιχος, ον (μειλίσσω), prop. *sweet*; hence *mild, gentle, kind, affectionate*. a) Spoken of persons (of whom alone μείλιχος is used, except Od. 15, 374), Il. 17, 671. 21, 300.   b) μειλιχίοισι μύθοις, 10, 288; and μύθοισι, ἐπέεσσι μειλιχίοισι προσαυδᾶν, to address any man with friendly words, 6, 343. Od. 6, 143; and μειλιχίοισι alone, Il. 4, 256; αἰδώς, Od. 8, 172.

μείρομαι, from which ἔμμορε as 3 sing.

N 5

aor. 2, only 1. 278; elsewhere 3 sing. perf. pass. εἵμαρται, *to allot oneself, to receive as a share, to receive*, with accus. ἥμισυ μείρεο τιμῆς, the half of the honour, 9, 612. *b*) With gen. in the aor. and perf. act. *to participate in, to obtain*, τιμῆς, 1, 278. 15, 189. *c*) Perf. pass. εἵμαρται, together with the pluperf., *it is appointed by fate*, with accus. and infin., 21, 281. Od. 5, 312. 24. 34.

μείς, ὁ, gen. μηνός, Ion. for μήν: the nom. μείς is found, 19, 111. h. Merc. 11, *a month*. Neither the names nor the length of the months are definitely given; the only limiting expression is: τοῦ μὲν φθίνοντος μηνός, τοῦ δ' ἱσταμένοιο, when this month ends and that begins, Od. 14, 162. 19, 307.

μείων, neut. μεῖον, irreg. compar. of μικρός.

μελαγχροιής, ές, poet. = μελάγχροος (χρόα), *having a dark skin, swarthy*, Od. 16, 175.† See μελανόχροος.

μέλαθρον, τό (μέλας), *the ceiling of a room*, but esply the central projecting beam under the roof, through which the smoke passed (ἀπὸ τοῦ μελαίνεσθαι, according to Et. M.), Od. 8, 279. 22, 240. 2) *the roof-timber, roofing*, Od. 19, 544; hence, 3) Generally, *a roof*, *a covering*, and like tectum, for a *dwelling*, Il. 2, 414. 9, 204. Od. 18, 250. αἰδέσσαι μέλαθρον, reverence thy roof (with reference to hospitality, since every one who lived and ate under the same roof with one was inviolable), 9, 640.

μελαθρόφιν, Ion. and Ep. for μελάθρου, Od. 8, 279.†

μελαίνω (μέλας), *to blacken*, only mid. *to blacken oneself, to become black*, χρόα, as to the skin = the skin became livid (or purple: from blood), 5, 354; spoken of the newly-ploughed fallow field, *18, 548.

Μελάμπους, οδος, ὁ, son of Amynthaon and Idomenê, brother of Blas, a noted seer. He wished to fetch the famous cattle of Iphiclus from Phylacê in Thessaly, for his brother, but he was attacked and bound by the herdsmen. After a year he received his freedom, and the cattle as a present, because he had imparted to him good counsel, Od. 15, 225, seq. 11, 287, seq.

μελάνδετος, ον (δέω), poet. *bound with black*, φάσγανον (according to the Schol. having a black, i. e. iron handle; it is better to explain it of the sheath, as encompassed with iron), 15, 712.†

Μελανεύς, ῆος, ὁ, father of Amphimêdon in Ithaca, Od. 24, 103.

Μελανθεύς, ῆος, ὁ, in the nom. and voc., and Μελάνθιος, ὁ, in the remaining cases; son of Dolius, the scandalous goat-herd of Odysseus (Ulysses); he abused him when he came home in disguise, and was dreadfully punished, Od. 17, 212, seq. 22, 472, seq.

Μελάνθιος, ὁ, 1) = Μελανθεύς. 2) a Trojan, 6, 36.

Μελανθώ, οῦς, ἡ, daughter of Dolius, the dissolute maid of Penelope: she was devoted to the suitors, Od. 18, 320. 19. 60; her death is related, Od. 22 431, seq.

Μελάνιππος, ο, 1) a Trojan, slain by Teucer, 8, 276. 2) son of Hiketaon, slain by Antilochus, 15, 547, seq. 3) a Trojan, slain by Patroclus, 16, 695. 4) an Achaian, 19, 240.

μελανόχροος, ον, poet. for μελάγχροος (χρόα,) *of a black colour, swarthy*, Od. 19. 246.†

μελανόχρως, οος, ὁ, ἡ = μελανόχροος, κύαμοι, black beans, 13, 589.†

μελάνυδρος, ον, pnet. (ὕδωρ), *dark-watered*, κρήνη, 9, 14. Od. 20, 158.

μελάνω, poet. = μελαίνομαι, *to blacken oneself, to become dark*, spoken of the sea, μελάνει πόντος ὑπ' αὐτῆς (sc. φρικός), ed. Wolf. Il. 7, 64.† This explanation of Eustath. is rejected by Spitzner because verbs in αίνω and άνω have always in H. a trans. signif. He has therefore adopted the reading of Aristarch. μελάνει δέ τε πόντον, sc. Ζέφυρος.

μέλας, μέλαινα, μέλάν, gen. μέλανος, μελαίνης, μέλανος, poet. form μείλας, 24, 79; in dat. compar. μελάντερος, 1) *black, dark-coloured, dark*, spoken of what seems to the eye black, as αἷμα, οἶνος, ὕδωρ, νηῦς, γαῖα, 2, 699; ἔντερα, Od. 14, 97. 2) *black, dark, dusky*, ἕσπερος, Od. 1, 423; νύξ, Il. 8, 503. 3) Metaph. *black, dark, gloomy, horrible*, θάνατος. Il. 2, 634; Κήρ, 2, 859; ὀδύναι, 4, 117. Neut. as subst. τὸ μέλαν ἀρυός, poet. μελάνδρυον, the heart, the marrow of the oak, Od. 14, 12. [cf. Jahrb. Jahn und K p. 272.]

Μέλας, ανος, ὁ, son of Portheus, brother of Œneus, 14, 117.

Μέλας πόντος, ὁ, Ep. Μείλας π., 24. 79. The Schol. in part understand by this the *black bay* (also called ὁ Καρκινός πόντος), between the continent of Thrace and the Thracian Chersonesus. This explanation is followed by Heyne. Bothe. From the connexion it appears more correct with Wolf and Voss to take μείλας as an appell., since the poet seems to have no particular point in view.

μέλδω, *to melt* (trans.), *to dissolve*, mid. μέλδομαι, *to become melted, to melt* (intrans.) λέβης κνίσσην μελδόμενος, a kettle melting with fat, i. e. in which fat is melting. Heyne and Spitzner read with Aristarchus: κνίσσην μαλδόμενον (act. for μέλδων), melting the fat; so also Voss, 21, 363.†

Μελέαγρος, ὁ (from μέλει and ἄγρα, who cares for the chase), son of Œneus and Althæa, husband of Cleopatra; he collected heroes for slaying the Calydonian boar in Ætolia. Between the Curetes and Ætolians a strife arose touching the head and skin of the slain boar. As long as Meleager took part, the Ætolians were successful; when however he, in censed by the imprecations of his mother, withdrew, then the Curētes besieged Calydon itself. At, last, upon the prayer of his wife, he took part again in the contest, and repulsed the Curētes, 9, 541. see 'Αλθαία.

μελέδημα, ατος, τό, poet. (μελέδη), care, anxiety, always plur., 23, 62. μελεδήματα πατρός, anxieties about one's father, Od. 15, 8.

*μαλεδών, ῶνος, ἡ = μελεδώνη, h. Ap. 532.

μελεδώνη, ἡ, poet. care, trouble, Od. 18, 517.†

μέλει, see μέλω.

μελεῖστί, adv. (μέλος), limb by limb, 24, 409.† [Bothe and Nitzsch read διὰ μελεῖστί for διαμελεῖστί, Od. 9, 291.]

μέλεος, έη, εον, idle, vain, unprofitable, αἶνος, 23, 795. ὁρμή, Od. 5, 416; inactive, 10, 480. Neut. as adv. vainly, 16, 336. 21, 473.

*μελετάω (μέλω), aor. 1 ἐμελέτησα, 1) to care. 2) to take care of, to practise, with accus. h. Merc. 557.

*Μέλης, ητος, ὁ, a river in Ionia near Smyrna, where H. is said to have been born, h. 8, 3. Ep. 4, 7.

μέλι, ιτος, τό, honey, 1, 249; vessels of honey and fat were placed upon the funeral piles, 23, 170. Od. 24, 68.

Μελίβοια, ἡ, a town in Magnesia (Thessaly), at Mount Othrys, 2, 717.

μελίγηρυς, υ (γῆρυς), sweet-voiced, sweet-toned, ὀψ, Od. 12, 187.† ἀοιδή, h. Ap. 519.

μελίη, ἡ, the ash, fraxinus excelsior, 13, 178. 16, 767. 2) the ashen shaft of a spear, and often the spear itself, 2, 543. Od. 14, 281.

μελιηδής, ἐς (ἡδύς), sweet as honey, honey-sweet, οἶνος, πυρός, often metaph. sweet, lovely, θυμός, 10, 495; νόστος, ὕπνος, Od. 11, 100. 19, 551.

μελίκρητος, ον, Ion. for μελίκρατος (κεράννυμι), mixed with honey; τὸ μελίκρητον, a honey mixture, a drink of milk and honey, which was presented to the souls of the dead and to the infernal deities, *Od. 10, 519. 11, 27.

μέλινος, ίνη, ινον, Ep. μείλινος (μελίη), ashen, made of ash, μέλινος οὐδός, Od. 17, 339; in the Il. always μείλινος, as epith. of ἔγκος. δόρυ.

μέλισσα, ἡ (μέλι), a bee, 2, 87. Od. 13, 106.

Μελίτη, ἡ, daughter of Nereus and Doris, 18, 42. [2] a companion of Persephŏne, h. Cer. 419.]

*μελίτωμα, ατος, τό (μελιτόω), honey-cake, Batr. 39.

μελίφρων, ον (φρήν), by its sweetness delighting the soul, heart-refreshing, οἶνος, πυρός, σῖτος, Il. and Od., metaph. ὕπνος, Il. 2, 34.

μέλω, only pres. and imperf. prim. signif. to consider, in eo esse, ut, an auxiliary verb, which for the most part stands with the infin. fut., more rarely with pres and aor. It must be rendered, shall, will, should, would, must, may, according as it expresses the purpose of a man, or something dependent upon the will of another, or upon the condition of things; hence, 1) to will, to purpose, to design, to think, to be about to do, to indicate the human will. ἔμελλε διεξίμεναι πεδίονδε, he was about to go out, 6, 393; ἔμελλε στρέψεσθαι ἐκ χώρης, he designed, was on the point of, going away, 6, 515. cf. 6, 52. 10, 336. Od. 11, 553 rarely with infin. pres. Il. 10, 454. Od. 6, 110. 19, 94; and aor. Il. 23, 773. 2) to be destined, to be about, a) According to the will of a deity or of fate: οὐ τελέεσθαι ἔμελλε, it should not be, i. e. was not to be fulfilled, 2, 36. cf. Od. 2, 156. Il. 5, 686; with infin. pres. 17, 497; with infin. aor. ἔμελλε—λιτέσθαι, he was about to supplicate, 16, 46. b) According to human arrangement, 11, 700. c) According to the situation of things, 11, 22. Od. 5, 135; οὐκ ἄρ' ἔμελλες ἀνάλκιδος ἀνδρὸς ἑταίρους ἔδμεναι, it was to be [ἄρα = ut nunc apparet] no timid chief whose companions thou devouredst, &c. (ironical), Od. 9, 475. 3) to be obliged, must. a) According to right and duty: καὶ λίην σέγ' ἔμελλε κιχήσεσθαι κακὰ ἔργα, vengeance was sure to overtake thee (could not but overtake thee), Od. 9, 477. b) According to probable consequence, i. e. may, might, must, sometimes to seem, οὕτω που Διὶ μέλλει φίλον εἶναι, thus it seemed pleasing to Zeus, Il. 2, 116. μέλλω που ἀπέχθεσθαι Διΐ, 21, 83. τὰ δὲ μέλλετ' ἀκουέμεν, this you will have heard, 14, 125. μέλλεν ποτὲ οἶκος ἀφνειὸς ἔμμεναι, once the house may (or must) have been rich, Od. 1, 232. 4, 181; with infin. aor. 24, 46. Od. 14, 133. [So also πολλάκι που μέλλεις ἀρήμεναι, you must or will often have prayed (of a probable inference), Od. 22, 322.]

μέλος, εος, τό, a limb, always in the plur. Il. and Od. 2) an air, a melody, h. 18, 16.

μέλπηθρον, τό (μέλπω), diversion, play, sport. μέλπηθρα κυνῶν and κυσὶν γενέσθαι, to be a sport (refreshment, V.) of the dogs; spoken of the corpses of enemies, lying unburied, *13, 233. 17, 255. 18, 179.

μέλπω, 1) Prop. to sing, with dance and sports, to sing, to celebrate in song, Ἑκάεργον, 1, 474. 2) Mid. as depon. a) to sing, ἐμέλπετο θεῖος ἀοιδὸς φορμίζων, 18, 604. Od. 4, 17. 13, 27. b) to sing and dance, to lead a choir of dancers, Il. 16, 182; Ἄρηϊ, to dance in honour of Arēs, i. e. to fight bravely, 7, 241.

μέλω, rarely personal, mly impersonal, pres. μέλει, μέλουσι, fut. μελήσει, perf. Ep. μέμηλα, partcp. μεμηλώς, mid. Ep. fut. μελήσεται, perf. mid. μέμβλεται, and pluperf. μέμβλετο, Ep. for μεμήληται, μεμήλητο, 1) Active. a) Personal, only one sing. to be an object of care, to lie on the heart, ἀνθρώποισι μέλω, I am prized amongst men, V., Od. 9, 20, cf.

Μεμακυία.   276   Μενεσθεύς.

'Αργώ πασιμέλουσα, Od. 12, 70. 2) Impers. μέλει μοί τι, *it lies on my heart, it is an object of care to me, it is my concern.* The object stands in the nom., the pers. in the dat., Il. 6, 492. 10, 92; also plur. μέλουσί μοι, they are objects of concern to me, 20, 21; μή τοι ταῦτα μελόντων, let not these things trouble thee, 18, 463; μελήσουσί μοι ἵπποι, 5, 228; instead of the nom. we have also the infin. Od. 16, 465.. Poet. is esply *a*) Perf. and pluperf. with pres. signif. ἀνήρ, ᾧ τόσσα μέμηλε, upon whom lie so many cases, Il. 2, 25. ἔργα, 2, 614. Od. 1, 151. The partcp. perf. μεμηλώς has a person. signif., *caring for, addicted to, studious of,* with gen. πλούτοιο, πολέμοιο, Il. 5, 708. 13, 297; once also μέμηλας ταῦτα, these things hast thou devised, h. Merc. 437. II) Mid. rarely pres. μήτι τοι ἡγεμόνος γε ποθὴ μελέσθω, let not the desire for a guide trouble thee, Od. 10, 505. μελήσεταί μοι ταῦτα, Il. 1. 523; often perf. μέμβλεται for μέλει, 19, 343; and μέμβλετο for μεμήλει, 21, 516. Od. 22, 12.

μεμακυία, see μηκάομαι.
μεμαότες, μεμαώς, see ΜΑΩ.
μέμβλωκα, see βλώσκω.
μέμβλεται and μέμβλετο, see μέλω.
μεμηκώς, see μηκάομαι.
μέμηλα, see μέλω.
μεμνέῳτο, see μιμνήσκω.

Μέμνων, ονος, ὁ, son of Tithônus and Eôs (Aurora), king of the Æthiopians; he came to the aid of Priam, after Hector's death; he slew Antilochus, Od. 4, 187, 188. According to Pind. Nem. 111, 63, he fell by Achilles.

μέμονα, Ep. perf. with pres. signif. used only in the sing, *to desire ardently, to wish;* it is used in connexion with μέμαμεν, μέματε, etc., see ΜΑΩ.

μέμυκα, see μυκάομαι.

*μέμφομαι, depon. mid. *to blame, to chide,* Batr. 70.

μέν, a particle (originally=μήν, *truly,* i.e. in truth, indeed), used as conjunct. and adv. I) Conjunc. μέν in connexion with δέ unites different notions and clauses; μέν stands in the protasis, and indicates concession and admission, and points to the limitation expressed by δέ in the apodosia. The antithesis thus arising may be more or less strong. In the one case μέν — δέ may be translated by *indeed, but;* in the other, either not at all, or by *and* only. They are used. 1) In distributing according to place, time, number, order, and persons, Il. 1, 18. 54. 3, 114. ὁ μέν, ὁ δέ, *this, that;* cf. ὁ, ἡ, τό. τὰ μέν — πᾶν δέ, Il. 4, 110, 111; οἱ μέν — ἡμίσεες δέ, Od. 3, 153. 155. 2) In a repetition of the same word, in two different clauses, in order to render it emphatic (anaphora): περὶ μέν — περὶ δέ, Il. 1, 358. 3) The clauses related to each other by μέν and δέ are often widely separated by intervening clauses, 2, 494, and 511. 4) Also the protasis is doubled by μέν, μέν,

23, 311; mly however in H. μέν, μέν, introduces an apodosis with two members, 20, 41—47. 5) Instead of δέ may stand other adversative particles, ἀλλά, αἱ, αὖτε, αὐτάρ, 2, 704. 1, 51. Od. 22, 5, 6; or copulative conjunctions are also introduced, τέ, καί, ἠδέ, Od. 22, 475. 6) Frequently the antithetic clause with δέ is wanting, and must be supplied in thought, Il. 5, 893. Od. 7, 237. 7) μέν often stands in connexion with other particles: μὲν ἄρα, μὲν γάρ, μὲν δή; in μέν τε, the τε indicates a more intimate connexion of the two members (an equal validity), Il. 5, 139. 21, 260; and without apodosis=μέν τοι, *but yet; but,* 4, 341. μέν τοι=*certainly; indeed:* often like μήν, *assuredly,* 8, 294. Od. 1, 275. 4, 137. 11) Adv. Ep. and Ion. stands frequently in the original signif. instead of μήν, *truly, certainly, verily,* alone, Il. 7, 89. 15, 203; and often for emphasis with subst. and pron. 1, 440. 2, 145; frequently in connexion with other particles: ἦ μέν, οὐ μέν, καὶ μέν, ἀτὰρ μέν, etc., see μήν.

μενεαίνω (μένος), aor. 1 ἐμενέηνα, 1) *to desire ardently, to wish continually, to long for,* absol. and often with infin. pres. and aor.; with infin. fut. only, Il. 176. Od. 21, 125. 2) To having something in mind against any man (en vouloir) *to be angry, to be incensed,* τινί, Il. 15, 504. Od. 1, 20; often absol., and ἐπὶ μενεαίνειν, to become angry in a strife, Il. 19, 58. κτεινόμενος μενέαινε, he was wrathful even in falling, 16, 491. (Thus Damm and Passow; Voss after Eustath. contrary to the signif. of the word, 'he groaned out his spirit.')

μενεδήϊος, ον (δήϊος), resisting an enemy, holding him at a stand, *brave, courageous,* 12, 247. 13, 228.

Μενέλαος, ὁ, son of Atreus, king of Lacedæmon, 7, 470. 2, 408. 581, seq. He was brother of Agamemnon, and husband of Helen, whose rape caused the Trojan war. He was possessed of a strong, active body, but not of the same talent for command with his brother. In his disposition he exhibits benevolence and mildness; as a warrior, spirit and bravery, although he is not so impetuous and rash as Ajax and Diomedes, 17. 18, seq. After the Trojan war, he wandered about eight years before he reached home, Od. 4, 82, seq.

μενεπτόλεμος, ον, poet. (πόλεμος), enduring in battle, brave, warlike, epith. of heroes and of a nation, 2, 749.

Μενεπτόλεμος, ὁ, formerly incorrectly taken as a proper name in 13, 693.

μενεχάρμης, ου, ὁ, ἡ (χάρμη), enduring in battle, courageous, epith. of heroes and nations, *9, 529, and often.

μενέχαρμος=μενεχάρμης, 14, 376.†

Μενεσθεύς, ῆος, ὁ (μένος, σθένος), son of Peteüs, commander of the Athenians, an excellent charioteer, 2, 552. 12, 331. 15, 331.

Μενέσθης. 277 *Μέροπες.

Μενέσθης, ους, ὁ, a Greek, slain by Hector, 5, 609.

Μενέσθιος, ὁ, 1) son of Areïthous, sovereign of Arnæ in Bœotia, slain by Paris, 7, 9. 2) son of the Spercheius, or Borus and Polydōra, a leader of the Myrmidons, 16, 173—178.

μενοεικής, ές (εἴκω), prop. *gratifying the desire*; hence: *sufficient, plentiful, abundant,* spoken of food and drink, δαίς, ἐδωδή, οἶνος, τάφος, 23, 29; also θήρη, Ἀψίς, Od. and ὕλη, abundant wood, Il. 23, 139. 2) Generally: *agreeable, pleasing, wished for,* 9, 227. Od. 16, 429.

μενοινάω (μένος), Ep. μενοινώω, Ion. μενοινέω, aor. 1 ἐμενοίνησα, *to have in mind, to think, to consider, to wish, to will,* τί, or with infin. 10, 101. Od. 2, 36; and τινί τι, to purpose any thing against any man, κακά, Od. 11, 532. μενοίνεον (sc. κέ), εἰ τελέουσιν (fut.), they considered whether they should accomplish it, Il. 12, 59. [Bth. says: *deliberare et dubitare solent;* but Schol. προεθυμοῦντο (not supplying κε) and so Cowper and Voss.]

μενοινέω, Ep. for μενοινάω, q. v.

Μενοιτιάδης, ου [also εω, 16, 93], ὁ, son of Menœtius=*Patroclus,* Il.

Μενοίτιος, ὁ, son of Actor, father of Patroclus, an Argonaut, 11, 765. 16, 14. 23, 85, seq.

μένος, εος, τό (μένω), prop. perseverance in a thing, hence 1) any vehement manifestation of spirit, and particularly *a) impetuosity, fierceness, rage, anger,* l, 103. 9, 679; esply *warlike spirit, bravery.* μένος ἀνδρῶν, 2, 387; also plur. μένεα πνείοντες, the courage-breathing, 2, 536. 11, 508; connected with θυμός, ἀλκή, θάρσος, 5, 2. 470, 9, 706. *b) desire, longing, wish, purpose,* 13, 634; also plur. 8, 361. 2) *animation, life, vigour,* since this manifests itself in ardent desires, 3, 294; hence ψυχή τε μένος τε, life and strength, 5, 296. 8, 123. 3) *strength, force, power* of body, as a manifestation of a resolute will: to bear strength of hands against one another, 5, 506; thus also μένος καὶ χεῖρες, 6, 502. μένος καὶ γυῖα, 6, 27. *b)* Of animals, 17, 20. Od. 3, 450. *c)* Of inanimate things: of the spear, Il. 13, 444; of the wind, 5, 524; of fire, Od. 11, 220; of the sun, Il. 23, 190; of streams, 12, 18. 4) It is often used periphrastically, as βίη, ἴς, μένος Ἀτρείδαο, 11, 268. ἱερὸν μένος Ἀλκινόοιο, the blessed strength (Nitzsch), Od. 7, 167.

Μέντης, ου, ὁ, 1) leader of the Kikŏnes (Ciconians), 17, 73. 2) king of the Taphians, a friend of Odysseus (Ulysses) in Ithaca, under whose form Athēnē came to Telemachus, Od. 1, 105. 180.

μέντοι, Od. 4, 157, ed. Wolf; better separate, see μέν.

Μέντωρ, ορος, ὁ, 1) father of Imbrius, 13, 171. 2) son of Alcimus, an intimate friend of Odysseus (Ulysses) in Ithaca, to whom, on his departure, he entrusted his domestic affairs. Athēnē assumed his form when she accompanied Telemachus to Pylos, Od. 2, 225. 4, 654. 17, 68.

μένω, poet. μίμνω, fut. Ep. μενέω for μενῶ, aor. 1 ἔμεινα, 1) Intrans. *to remain, to abide;* esply *a*) In battle: *to maintain one's ground, to remain firm,* with τλῆναι. *b)* Generally, *to remain, to continue, to abide,* αὖθι, αὐτόθι, 3, 291. 14, 119; with prep. ἀπό τινος, παρά τινι, etc., spoken of inanimate things: *to remain standing,* 17, 434. *c) to wait,* with accus. and infin. 4, 247. μένον δ' ἐπὶ ἕσπερον ἐλθεῖν, they waited till the evening came on, Od. 1, 422; or εἰσόκε with subj., Il. 9, 45. 2) Transit. with accus. *to await, to wait for,* esply spoken of an attacking enemy: *to resist, to withstand, to stand against,* τινά, Il.; δόρυ, Il. 13, 830; spoken of beasts and lifeless things, 13, 472. 15, 620. *b*) Generally, *to wait for, to await,* Ἠῶ, 11, 723; τινά, 20, 480. Od. 4, 847. (The perf. 2 μέμονα belongs in signif. to μέμαα, see ΜΑΩ.)

Μένων, ωνος, ὁ, a Trojan, 12, 93.

Μεριδάρπαξ, αγος. ὁ (ἅρπαξ), Crumbsnatcher, name of a mouse in Batr. 265.

μερίζω (μέρος), perf. pass. μεμέρισμαι, *to divide,* Batr. 61.

μέριμνα, ἡ, care, solicitude, anxiety, h. Merc. 44. 160. (From μερίς, μερίζω.)

μέρμερος, ον, poet. (from μέρμηρα, Hes. poet. = μέριμνα), *exciting care, causing trouble,* spoken of actions: *wearisome, difficult, terrible, dreadful,* spoken only of warlike deeds, in the plur. μέρμερα ἔργα, 8, 453; and μέρμερα alone, *10, 48. 11, 502.

Μερμερίδης, αο, ὁ, son of Mermerus =Ilus, Od. 1, 259.

Μέρμερος, ὁ, 1) a Mysian, slain by Antilochus, 14, 513. 2) father of Ilus, Od.

μερμηρίζω (μέρμερος), aor. 1 Ep. μερμήριξα, 1) Intrans. *to be anxious, to be troubled, to revolve anxiously in the mind, to ponder;* esply δίχα and διάνδιχα, *to be irresolute, to be doubtful, to hesitate between two courses, to delay,* Od. 16, 73. Il. 1, 189. 8, 167. There follows it ὡς, 2, 3; ὅπως, 14, 159. Od. 20, 8; often ἠ—ἤ, whether—or, Il. 5, 672. 10, 503; also infin. ἐλθεῖν ἠδὲ πυθέσθαι. Od. 10, 152. 438. 24, 235; περί τινος, Il. 20, 17. 2) Trans. with accus. *to devise, to plot, to resolve upon,* δόλον, Od. 2, 93; πολλά, Od. 1, 427; φόνον τινί, Od. 2, 325. 19, 52.

μέρμις, ιθος, ἡ (prob. from εἴρω), *a bond, a cord, a rope,* Od. 20, 23.†

μέρος, εος, τό, *a part, a share.* κατὰ μέρος, each in his part, h. Merc. 53.

μέροψ, οπος, ὁ (μείρομαι, ὄψ), *endowed with* (*articulate*) *speech, discoursing, speaking,* epith. of men, who are distinguished from brutes by uttering articulate, instead of inarticulate sounds, 1, 250. 9, 340. Od. 20, 49. (Voss, 'the speaking tribes of men,' but in h. Cer. 'manytoned,' or speaking many tongues.)

*Μέροπες, οἱ, the ancient name of the

Μέροψ. 278 Μετά.

inhabitants of the island Cos, derived from a King Merops, h. Ap. 42.

Μέροψ, οπος, ὁ, a ruler and famous seer in the city Percote, on the Hellespont, father of Adrastus and Amphius, 2, 831. 11, 329.

μεσαιπόλιος, ον, poet. (πολιός), *half-gray, beginning to be grey*, epith. of Idomeneus [*with age half-grey*, Cp.], who was approaching old age, 13, 361.†

Μεσαύλιος, ὁ (having charge of the cattle-yard), a slave of Eumæus in Ithaca, Od. 14, 449. 455.

μέσσαυλος, ὁ, Ep. μέσσαυλος (or τὸ μέσαυλον) (αὐλή), *the court-yard*, between the out-buildings in the court; also a shepherd's or herdsman's dwelling, 24, 29; esply the yard for cattle, 11, 548. Od. 10, 435; always Ep. form.

μεσσηγύ, adv. Ep. μεσσηγύ before a vowel or to form a position μεσσηγύς. 1) *in the midst, between*, rarely without cases, 11, 573. 23, 521. *b*) With gen. *between*, 5, 41. Od. 4, 845. 2) Of time: *in the mean time*, Od. 7, 195. τὸ μεσσηγύ ἤματος, the half of the day, h. Ap. 108.

μεσήεις, εσσα, εν, poet. (μέσος), *in the midst, middle*, 12, 269.†

Μέσθλης, ου [not ους], ὁ, son of Pylæmenes and of the nymph Gygæa, leader of the Mæonians, 2, 864. 17, 216.

μεσόδμη, ἡ (for μεσοδόμη from δέμω), prop. the intermediate work, or juncture of two beams, hence 1) *the transverse beam* in a ship, or the hollow between the beams, in which the mast is fixed, Od. 2, 424. 15, 289. 2) *a depression* or *recess* in the wall between the pillars (*intercolumnia*), according to Aristarch. =μεσόστυλα, or the space between the beams in the ceiling, Voss, *Od. 19, 37. 20, 354.

*μεσόμφαλος, ον, in the middle of the navel; hence subst. τὸ μεσόμφαλον, the middle; according to the Schol. the lamp-cover, Batr. 129.

μέσον, τό, Ep. μέσσον, neut. of μέσος, q. v.

μεσσοπαγής, ές, see μεσσοπαλής.

μεσσοπαλής, ές, Ep. μεσσοπαλής (πάλλω), *hurled by the middle*. μεσσοπαλὲς ἔθηκε κατ' ὄχθης μείλινον ἔγχος, he fixed in the shore his ashen spear hurled by the middle, V. Il. 21, 172.† Eustath. [Död.] and others read μεσσοπαγές, infixed to the middle (*mid-length deep stood plunged the ashen beam*, Cp.). Aristarch. prefers μεσσοπαλές, because this word indicates greater force in the cast. [Db. *vibrating from the centre upwards.*]

μέσος, η, ον, Ep. μέσσος (according to the necessity of the metre), 1) *middle, in the midst*, spoken of space: βάλεν αὐχένα μέσσον, he smote the neck in the midst, 5, 657; μέσση ἁλί, in the midst of the sea, Od. 4, 844. *b*) Of time: μέσον ἦμαρ, mid-day, Il. 21, 111. 2) Freq. τὸ μέσον, *the middle*, as subst. often ἐκ μέσου, 4, 79. ἐν μέσσῳ, 3, 69, and μέσσῳ, 4, 444. κατὰ μέσον, into the midst, 5, 8; with gen. 9, 87. Od. 11, 187; metaph. ἐς μέσον ἀμφοτέροις δικάζων, to administer justice equally to both (impartially), Schol. ἐξ ἴσου, Il. 23, 574. Neut. μέσον, as adv. 12, 167.

μέσσατος, η, ον, Ep. for μέσατος· ἐν μεσσάτῳ, *in the midst*, *8, 223. 11, 6. (Perhaps an old superl., see Rost, Gram. p. 402.)

μέσσαυλος, ὁ, Ep. for μέσαυλος, q. v.

Μέσση, ἡ, a town and port in Laconia, near Tænarus, now *Massa*, 2, 582. Paus. 3, 25.

Μεσσηίς, ίδος, ἡ, a fountain in Hellas in Thessaly, cf. Strab. XIII. p. 431. II. 6. 457.

Μεσσήνη, ἡ, a small district about Pharæ in the later Messenia, where Odysseus (Ulysses) visited Orsilochus. Od. 21, 15. A town Messênê was not known to H.

Μεσσήνιος, η, ον. *Messenian*, subst. the Messenians, Od. 21, 18.

μεσσηγύ, poet. for μεσηγύ.
μεσσοπαλής, ές, Ep. for μεσσοπαλής.
μέσσος, Ep. for μέσος.
*μεστός, ή, όν, *full*, Ep. 15, 5.
μέσφα, poet. adv. =μέχρι, *till, until* ἠοῦς, 8, 508.†

μετά, 1) Prep. with gen. dat. and accus.; primary signif. *with*. 1) With gen. indicating concomitancy and community, when the discourse implies not a mere co-existence in space (as μετά and σύν with dat.), but an intimate and active union: *with, between, amongst*, 13, 790. 21, 458. Od. 10, 320. 16, 140. 2) With dat. only poet. *a*) To indicate a union in place, rely with plur., *with, amongst, between*. μετ' ἀθανάτοις, μετὰ Τρώεσσι: again, μετὰ χερσί, ποσσί, between the hands; μετὰ φρεσί, in the mind. *b*) To indicate concomitancy: μετὰ πνοιῇς ἀνέμοιο, like ἅμα, with the blasts of wind, i. e. fleet as the wind, Od. 2, 148. *c*) Rarely to indicate approach: ἀρχὸν μετ' ἀμφοτέροισιν ὄπασσα, I gave a leader to both, Od. 10, 204. cf. Od. 9, 335. 5, 224. 3) With accus. *a*) Spoken of space: *a*) To indicate direction or motion: *into the midst of, amongst*. ἱκέσθαι μετ' αὐτούς, Il. 3, 264. ἱκέσθαι μετὰ Τρώας καὶ Ἀχαιούς, 17, 458. βάλλειν τινὰ μετ' ἔριδας καὶ νείκεα, into the midst of contention. 2, 376; and generally, to indicate direction to a person or thing: *to, towards, after* [in this sense of a somewhat strengthened πρός it is poet.]. βῆναι μετὰ Νέστορα, 10, 73; but also in a hostile signif.: βῆναι μετά τινα, to pursue any man, 5, 152; in like manner, ὁρμᾶσθαι μετά τινα, 17, 605; and generally spoken of following: *behind, after*. μῆλα ἕσπετο μετὰ κτίλον, 13, 492; metaph. spoken of worth or rank: *according to, after, secundum*, 2, 674. *β*) Also to indicate co-existence, with verbs of rest, as with dat. μετὰ πληθύν, amongst the multitude, 2, 143. Od. 4, 652. *b*) Spoken of time, to indicate subsequence: *after*, Il. 8, 261. 18, 96. 23, 27. μετὰ κλέος, after the news, report, 11, 227. μετὰ ταῦτα, h. Merc. 126; often with partcp. μετὰ Πάτροκλον θανόντα, 24, 575. c) Spoken of cause, manner, etc. a) To indicate the object: *for, after*, 7, 418. ἰέναι μετὰ δόρυ, to go to bring a spear, 13, 247. βῆναι μετὰ πατρὸς ἀκουήν, to go in quest of intelligence from a father, Od. 2, 308. β) To indicate suitableness: *according to, after*. μετὰ σὸν κῆρ, Il. 15, 52. Od. 8, 583. II) Adv. without cases, 1) *together, moreover, besides*, 2, 446. 2) *behind, hereafter*, of space and of time, 23, 133. Od. 15, 400. Frequently it is separated from the verb by tmesis. III) In composition, it has, in addition to the definitions already given, this, that it indicates a change from one condition to another.

μέτα, with anastrophe for μετά, 1) When it follows the subst. 13, 308. 2) For μέτεστι, Od. 21, 93.

μεταβαίνω (βαίνω), μεταβήσομαι, aor. μετέβην, perf. μεταβέβηκα, *to go elsewhere, to go over*. 1) Spoken of the stars: μετὰ δ' ἄστρα βεβήκει, the stars had gone over, viz. *had traversed the mid sky* (Cp.), Od. 12, 312. 14, 483. 2) Spoken of singers: *to go over* from one subject to another, *to proceed*, *Od. 8, 492; with ἔς τι, h. 8, 9.

μεταβάλλω (βάλλω), aor. 2 μεταβαλών only in tmesis, *to cast around*, hence *to turn around*; νῶτα, to turn the backs (in flight), 8, 94.†

μεταβουλεύω (βουλεύω), *to change a resolution, to alter one's mind*, μετεβούλευσαν, Od. 5, 286.†

μετάγγελος, ὁ (ἄγγελος), one who bears intelligence from one to another, *a messenger* [internuncius], *15, 144. 23, 199. In 15, 144, Wolf reads μετ' ἄγγελος.

μεταδαίνυμαι, mid. (δαίνυμαι), fut. μεταδαίσομαι, *to eat with, to feast with*; ἱρῶν, to participate in the sacrificial feast, 23, 207; τινί, with any one, 22, 498. Od. 18, 48.

μεταδήμιος, η, ον (δῆμος), *existing amongst the people*. κακὸν μεταδήμιον, evil amongst the people, Od. 13, 46; spoken of an individual: *domestic, native*, at home, *Od. 8, 293.

μεταδόρπιος, ον (δόρπον), *in the midst of or during supper*, Od. 4, 194.†

μεταδρομάδην, adv. *running after, pursuing*, 5, 80.†

μεταίζω, poet. for μεθίζω (ἵζω), *to seat oneself with*, Od. 16, 362.†

μεταΐσσω (ἀΐσσω), partcp. aor. μεταΐξας, *to leap after, to pursue, to rush after*, only absol. in the partcp. aor. 15, 398. Od. 17, 236.

μετακιάθω, Ep. (κιάθω), only imperf. μετεκίαθον, 1) *to go after*, 11, 52; in a hostile signif. *to pursue*, τινά, 16, 685. 18, 581. 2) *to go to some other place, to visit*; τινά, any man, Od. 1, 22; πεδίον, to reach the plain, Il. 11, 714.

μετακλαίω, *to weep after, to deplore*, 11, 764.†

μετακλί̄νω (κλίνω), aor. pass. μετεκλίθην, *to bend to another quarter*. πολέμοιο μετακλινθέντος, when the battle has turned, i. e. is yielding, 11, 509.†

μεταλήγω (λήγω), Ep. aor. 1 optat. μεταλλήξειε. partcp. μεταλλήξας, *to cease, to desist from*; with gen. χόλοιο, from anger, *9, 157. 261. h. Cer. 340.

μεταλλάω (μετ' ἄλλα), aor. 1 μετάλλησα, prop. *to search after other things*, hence 1) *to search after, to seek after, to inform oneself about*, with accus. τινά or τί, 10, 125. Od. 3, 243. 2) *to inquire for, to ask after*; τινά, any man, and τινά τι, to ask a man about any thing, Il. 3, 177. Od. 1, 231; also ἀμφί τινι, Od. 17, 554. [Herm. Op. vii. 141, is dissatisfied with Buttmann's explanation, Lex. 412.]

μεταλλήγω Ep. for μεταλήγω.

μετάλμενος, partcp. aor. 2 from μεθάλλομαι.

μεταμάζιος, ον (μαζός), *between the breasts*; στῆθος, the middle of the breast, 5, 19.†

*μεταμέλπομαι, mid. (μέλπω), *to sing or dance amongst*, with dat. h. Ap. 197.

μεταμίγνυμι (μίγνυμι), Ep. μεταμίσγω, fut. μεταμίξω, *to mix with, to mingle amongst*, τί, Od. 18, 310; τινί τι, *Od. 22, 221.

μεταμώλιος, ον=μεταμώνιος.

μεταμώνιος, ον, poet. (ἄνεμος), prop. *with the wind*, i. e. *idle, vain, profitless*. νήματα, Od. 2, 98. πάντα μεταμώνια τιθέναι, to render all vain, Il. 4, 363; μεταμώνια βάζειν, to prate idly, Od. 18, 332. (Wolf has μεταμώλιον for μεταμώλιος, after the best MSS.)

μετανάστης, ου, ὁ (ναίω), one who goes from one place to another, *a stranger, a settler, a new-comer*, *9, 648. 16, 59.

Μετάνειρα, ἡ, wife of Celeus, mother of Demophon, h. Cer. 161. 206.

μετανίσσομαι, poet. (νίσσομαι), *to go over, to go to the other side*, spoken of Helios: μετενίσσετο βουλυτόνδε, Helios went to the unyoking of oxen, i. e. descended to his setting, 16, 779. Od. 9, 58.

*μετάνοια, ἡ (νοέω), *a change of mind, repentance*, Batr. 10.

μεταξύ, adv. (μετά), *in the midst*, 1, 156.†

μεταπαύομαι, mid. (παύω), *to cease in the midst, to take rest*, 17, 373.†

μεταπαυσωλή, ἡ (παύω), *intermediate rest, refreshment*, πολέμοιο, 19, 201. According to Heyne and Nägelsb. ad Il. 2, 386, to be written μετὰ παυσωλή.

μεταπρεπής, ές, poet. (πρέπω), *distinguished amongst*; with dat. ἀθανάτοισιν, amongst immortals, 18, 370.†

μεταπρέπω, poet. (πρέπω), *to distinguish oneself, to be eminent amongst*; with dat. of pers. ἡρώεσσιν, amongst the heroes, Il. and Od.; with dat. of the thing, γαστέρι, Od. 18, 2. b) With double dat.

*Μεταρίθμιος. 280 Μετοχλίζω.

έγχεϊ Τρώεσσι, with the spear amongst the Trojans, Il. 16, 835; πλούτῳ Μυρμιδόνεσσιν, 16, 596; and with infin. 16, 194.

*μεταρίθμιος, ον (ἀριθμός), belonging with the number, counted with, with dat. h 25, 6.

μετασεύομαι (σεύομαι), μετασσεύομαι, aor. sync. μετέσσυτο, 1) to hasten after, to follow swiftly, 6, 296. 2) to hasten, absol. and with accus. ποιμένα λαῶν, *23, 389.

μετασπόμενος, μετασπών. see μεθέπω.

μέτασσαι, αἱ, lambs which are born between early ones (πρόγονοι) and the late ones (ἕρσαι), later-born (or middle-aged) lambs, Od. 9, 221.† (From μετά, as περισσός from περί, see Thiersch, Gram. § 200, 11.)

μετασσεύομαι, Ep. for μετασεύομαι.

μεταστένω (στένω), to sigh over, to lament. ἄτην, Od. 4, 261.†

μεταστοιχί, adv. (στοῖχος), along in a row, *23, 358. 757.

μεταστρέφω (στρέφω), fut. ψω, aor. 1 μετέστρεψα, aor. pass. μετεστρέφθην, 1) Act. to turn about, to turn around, to turn, ἦτορ ἐκ χόλου, 10, 107. νόον μετὰ σὺν κῆρ, to turn the mind to thy desire, 15, 52. b) Intrans. to turn about, i. e. to retreat, 15, 203; to turn about, i. e. to requi·e, Od. 2, 67. 2) Pass. and mid. to turn oneself about, to turn, both to and from an enemy; only partcp. aor. pass. Il. 11, 595.

μετατίθημι (τίθημι), aor. 1 μετέθηκα, to put between or in the midst; κέλαδον, to excite a tumult, Od. 18, 402.†

μετατρέπομαι, mid. (τρέπω), aor. 2 mid. μετετραπόμην, to turn oneself around, absol. in tmesis, 1, 199. b) Metaph. to turn oneself to, to attend to, τινός, *1, 160. 9, 630. 12, 238.

μετατροπαλίζομαι, depon. mid. poet. =μετατρέπομαι, to turn oneself around, to turn (intrans.) esply for flight, 20, 190.†

μεταυδάω (αὐδάω), mly imperf. μετηύδα and μετηύδων, prop. to speak in the midst of several, then to speak to any one; always with dat. plur. ἕνεα Τρώεσσι, πᾶσιν, 8, 496. Od. 12, 153.

μετάφημι (φημί), aor. 2 μετέειπον, 1) to speak amongst or to several, to discourse, always with dat. plur. 2, 411. Od. 4, 660. [Once with accus., Il. 2, 795, where, however, the var. lec. προσέφη is, according to Ameis, to be preferred.]

μεταφράζομαι, mid. (φράζομαι), fut. μεταφράσομαι, to consider upon, to meditate, τί, 1, 140.†

μετάφρενον, τό (φρήν), the back, esply the part between the shoulders, which lies above the diaphragm, 5, 40. Od. 8, 528; also plur. Il. 12, 428.

μεταφωνέω (φωνέω), to speak amongst or to several; with dat. plur. τοῖσι, amongst them, 7, 384. Od. 8, 201.

μετέασι, Ep. for μέτεισι, see μέτειμι.

I. μέτειμι (εἰμί), pres. subj. Ep. μετείω and μετέω for μετῶ, infin. μετέιναι for μετεῖναι, fut. μετέσσομαι, to be amongst; with dat. ἀθανάτοισι, to be amongst the immortals. 3, 109. and Od. 15, 251; absol. to be in the midst, to intervene, spoken of time, Il. 2, 386.

II. μέτειμι (εἶμι), partcp. aor. 1 mid. Ep. μετεισάμενος, 1) to go after, to go behind, 6, 341. 2) to go to; πόλεμόνδε, to the battle, 13, 298. Mid. aor. to go into the midst, to penetrate, 13, 90. 17, 285.

μετεῖπον, Ep. μετέειπον (εἶπον), aor. of μετάφημι, to speak amongst or to several, with dat. 1, 73, and absol.

μετεισάμενος see μέτειμι.

μετείω, Ep. for μετῶ, subj. from μέτειμι, to be in the midst.

μετέμμεναι, see μέτειμι I.

μετέπειτα (ἔπειτα), afterwards, hereafter, 14, 310. Od. 10, 519.

μετέρχομαι, depon. mid. (ἔρχομαι), μετελεύσομαι, aor. 1 μετῆλθον, mly partcp. μετελθών, 1) to come or go into the midst, or to, absol., 4, 539. 5, 456. 13, 127. Od. 1, 239. a) With dat. to come amongst, ὑπερφιάλοισι. Od. 1, 134. κούρῃσιν, Od. 6, 222; esply in a hostile signif. to rush upon, Il. 16, 487. Od. 6, 132. 2) With accus. to go after any man, i. e. a) to go to any man in order to call him, Πάριν, Il. 6, 280; absol. to follow, 21, 422; or τί, any thing, in order to obtain it; πατρὸς κλέος, to go in quest of intelligence concerning one's father, Od. 3, 83; ἔργα, to visit the works (of servants), to inspect them, Od. 16, 314. Metaph. to go after a matter of business, i. e. to attend to it, ἔργα, Il. 5, 429. b) Spoken of a place: πόλινδε, to go to the city, 6, 86.

μετέσσυτο, see μετασσεύομαι.

μετέω, see μέτειμι.

μετέωρος, ον, poet. for μετήορος (ἀείρεται), suspended in the air, aloft, in the air, 8, 26; ἅρματα αἴξασκε μετήορα, the chariots sprang into the air, 23, 369. 2) Metaph. wavering, uncertain, h. Merc. 488.

μετοίχομαι, depon. mid. (οἴχομαι), to go into the midst, ἀνὰ ἄστυ, to go through the city, Od. 8, 7. 2) With accus. to go after any man, to overtake him, Il. 10, 111. Od. 8, 47; absol. to accompany, Od. 10, 24; in a hostile signif. to rush upon, to attack, τινά, Il. 5, 148.

μετοκλάζω (ὀκλάζω), to crouch down and keep shifting one's posture (of a cowardly soldier in ambush), 13, 281.†

μετόπισθε, before a vowel μετόπισθεν, adv. (ὄπισθεν), 1) Spoken of place: behind, behind the back, backwards, with gen. behind, 9, 504. Od. 9, 539. 2) Spoken of time: after, behind, παῖδες μετόπισθε λελειμμένοι, the children left behind, Il. 24, 687.

μετοχλίζω (ὀχλίζω), aor. 1 optat. 3 sing. μετοχλίσσειε, Ep. for μετοχλίσσαι, to remove by levers or by force, λέχος, Od. 23, 188; ὀχῆας, to thrust away the bars, Il. 24, 567.

Μετρέω. 281 Μήδομαι.

μετρέω (μέτρον), aor. 1 έμέτρησα, to measure; hence poet. πέλαγος, to measure the sea, i. e. to navigate, to sail over, Od. 3, 179.†
μέτρον, τό, a measure. 1) the instrument for measuring, a measure, 12, 422. 2) Esply a measuring vessel for liquids and dry goods, οίνου, 7, 471. 23, 268. ἀλφίτου, Od. 2, 355. (How much it held is not known.) 3) that which is measured. i. e. space, length, μέτρα κελεύθου, Od. 4, 389. 10, 539. ὅρμου μέτρον ἱκέσθαι, the space of the harbour, Od. 13, 101; metaph. μέτρον ἥβης, the full measure of youth, i. e. the bloom of life, Il. 11, 225. Od. 11, 317.
μετώπιον, τό = μέτωπον, the forehead, *11, 85. 16, 739; prop. neut. of the adj. μετώπιος.
μέτωπον, τό (ὤψ), the forehead, mly of men, plur., Od. 6, 107 : once of a horse, Il. 23, 454. 2) Metaph. the front, the fore-part, κόρυθος, 16, 70.
μεῦ, Ion. for μοῦ, see ἐγώ.
μέχρι, poet. before vowel μέχρις, prep. with gen. until, as far as. 1) Spoken of place: θαλάσσης, 13, 143. 2) Of time: τέο μέχρις; till when, how long? 24, 128.
μή, adv. and conj. not, that not. 1) Adv. μή, not; it never denies independently and directly (cf. οὐ), but always indirectly, and in reference to a preced. representation. It is found, therefore, only in a really dependent denial, or in one conceived of as dependent: and esply in such main and subordinate clauses as express a wish, will, command, a case or condition, a fear or anxiety. (The same holds true of the compounds: μηδέ, μηδείς, etc.) A) In main clauses : 1) In such as express a command, the act of forbidding or warning, where mly the imperat. pres. stands, 1, 32. 363: or instead of it the infin., 7, 413. 17, 501; or the subj. aor. μή δή με ἕλωρ ἐάσῃς κεῖσθαι, do not, do not let me lie as a prey [hoc tantum te rogo . . . ne], 5, 684; often with an implied threat, μή σε παρὰ νηυσὶ κιχείω, let me not meet thee at the ships, 1, 26. 21, 563. Rare and mly Ep. is the imperat. aor. 4, 410. Od. 16, 301; and the fut., 15, 115. 2) In sentences expressing a wish, either with the optat. or the indic. histor. tenses: μή τοῦτο φίλον Διὶ πατρὶ γένοιτο! may this not please father Zeus! Od. 7, 316. μή ὄφελες λίσσεσθαι, would that thou hadst not supplicated, Il. 9, 698. 22, 481; also with infin. μή πρὶν ἐπ' ἠέλιον δῦναι, 2, 413. 3) In sentences which contain an exhortation with the subj. μή ἴομεν for ἴωμεν, let us not go, Il. and Od. 4) In oaths, sometimes instead of the direct negative οὐ, (Il. 10, 330. B) In subordinate clauses : 1) In all clauses expressing design or a condition ; therefore with the conjunct. ἵνα, ὡς, ὅπως, ὄφρα, εἰ, ἤν, etc. On the construct. see these conjunct. (οὐ stands only when the negation is limited to a single word, 24, 296.) 2) With infin. only in dependent discourse in H.: ὄμνυθι, μή μὲν ἑκὼν τὸ ἐμὸν δόλῳ ἅρμα πεδῆσαι, swear to me, that thou didst not wittingly by craft obstruct my chariot, 23, 585. cf. 19, 261. II) Conjunct. that not : 1) After the primary tenses or an aor. with pres. signif. with subjunct., 1, 522. 17, 17 ; after a historical tense with optat., 10, 468. 2) After verbs to fear, to avoid, to beware, to prevent, etc., μή like the Lat. ne signifies that : δείδω μή τὸ χθιζὸν ἀποστήσωνται Ἀχαιοὶ χρέος, I fear that the Greeks will pay yesterday's debt, 13, 745. cf. 1, 553. 14, 261; after ἰδεῖν, to take heed, 10, 98. Such clauses with μή are often elliptical, so that δίδοικα or φοβοῦμαι must be supplied before them (cf. A 1), μήτι χολωσάμενος ῥέξῃ κακὸν υἷας Ἀχαιῶν, that in anger he may inflict some evil upon the sons of the Achaians, 2, 195. 5, 487. 17, 93. b) If οὐ is added, it is thereby shown that the apprehended event will not ensue, μή νύ τοι οὐ χραίσμῃ, lest haply it should avail thee nothing. 1, 28. μή οὔτις, 10, 39. μή with indicat., Od. 5, 300, is to be taken as an interrogative particle. III) An interrogative particle : μή as such stands, 1) In a direct question, when a negative answer is expected : ἦ μή πού τινα δυσμενέων φάσθ' ἔμμεναι ἀνδρῶν, you did not surely suppose it to be one of the enemy, Od. 6, 200. cf. Od. 9, 405. 2) In an indirect question : whether not, after ἰδεῖν, φράζεσθαι, mly with subjunct. and optat., Il. 10, 98. 101. 15, 164. Od. 24, 291; rarely with the indicat. when a man is convinced that the apprehended act will happen or is true : δείδω, μή δή πάντα θεὰ νημερτέα εἶπεν, I have my fears whether the goddess did not speak all things truly, Od. 5, 300.

μηδέ, adv. connects two clauses, prop. adversatively : but not, 4, 302. 10, 37. mly merely annexing : also not, and not, 2, 200. Od. 4, 752. 2) also not, not even, and repeated for the sake of emphasis, 6, 38. 10, 239. 2) Doubled μηδέ, μηδέ, neither, nor, 4, 303.

Μηδείδης, ου, ὁ, h. Bacch. 6, 43. ed. Wolf, after the conjec of Barnes for μή δείδειν, the name of a pilot. Herm. amends: νῆ' ἤδη, which Frank has adopted.

μηδείς, μηδεμία. μηδέν (μηδέ and εἷς), no one, none, in H. μηδέν, 18, 500.†

Μηδεσικάστη, ἡ (adorned with wisdom), daughter of Priam, wife of Imbrius, 13, 173.

μήδομαι, d-pon. mid. (μῆδος), fut. μήσομαι, aor. ἐμησάμην, to have in mind, like parare, not merely to devise, but also to execute: hence, 1) Absol. to devise, counsel, 2, 360. 2) to devise, to plot, to prepare, τί, Od. 5, 173. νόστον, Od. 3, 160. κακά, Od. 3, 166. τί τινι, Od. 5, 189. κακά τινι, Il. 6, 157. 7, 478. ὄλεθρόν τινι, Od. 3, 249. 9, 92; also with

Μῆδος. 282 Μηρίον.

double accus. κατὰ Ἀχαιούς, against the Greeks, Il. 10, 52. ἔργον Ἀχαιούς, Od. 24, 426.

μῆδος, εος, τό, 1) *resolution*, *counsel*, *purpose*, *plan*, always in the plur., 2, 340. Od. 2, 38. μάχης ἡμετέρης, our plans or efforts in this battle, Il. 15, 467; sometimes in the abstract signif. *prudence*, *cunning*, Od. 13, 89. 19, 353. 2) Plur. *the male pudenda*, Od. 6, 129. 18, 67. 87. 22, 476.

Μηθώνη, ἡ. Ep. for Μεθώνη, a town in Magnesia (Thessaly), near Melibœa, 2, 716.

μηκάομαι, depon. mid. Ep. aor. partcp. μακών, perf. μέμηκα, with pres. signif. partcp. μεμηκώς, fem. shortened μεμακυῖα, 4, 435; from the perf. as a new poet. imperat. ἐμέμηκον, Od. 9, 439. 1) A word imitating the cry of sheep, *to bleat*, 4, 435. Od.; spoken of deer and hares, *to cry*, Il. 10, 362. 2) The partcp. μακών is found only in the construction: κὰδ δ' ἔπεσ' ἐν κονίῃσι μακών, he sank screaming or crying in the dust, spoken of animals, 16, 469; and once of a man, Od. 18, 98.

μηκάς, άδος, ἡ (ΜΑΚΩ), *bleating*, epith. of goats, 11, 383. Od. 9, 124.

μηκέτι, adv. (ἔτι), *no more, no longer, no further*, 2, 259. Od. 3, 240.

Μηκιστεύς, ῆος, ὁ, 1) son of Talaus, brother of Adrastus, father of Euryalus; he took part in the Theban war, 2, 566. 2) son of Echius, a companion of Teucer, slain by Polydamas, 8, 333. 15, 339; accus. Μηκιστῆ.

Μηκιστιάδης, ου, ὁ, son of Mekisteus= Euryalus, 6, 28.

μήκιστος, η, ον (μῆκος), superl. of μακρός, *the longest*, neut. sing. and plur. as adv. μήκιστα, *at the furthest, finally, at last*, Od. 5, 299. 465. h. Cer. 259.

μῆκος, εος, τό, *length*, Od. 9, 324; *tallness*, *height (of stature)*, *Od. 11, 312. 20, 71.

μήκων, ωνος, ἡ (μῆκος), *a poppy, a poppy-head*, 8, 306.†

μηλέη, ἡ (μῆλον), *an apple-tree*, malus, Od. 7, 115. 11, 589 (to be pronounced as a disyllable); *Od. 24, 340.

Μηλόβοσις, ιος, ἡ (prop. sheep-pasturing), daughter of Oceanus, h. Cer. 420.

μηλοβοτήρ, ῆρος, ὁ (βόσκω), *a shepherd*, 18, 529.† h. Merc.

I) μῆλον, τό, a head of smaller cattle, sing. rare; *a sheep*, without distinction of sex, Od. 12, 301; also, *a goat*, Od. 14, 105; mly plur. τὰ μῆλα, *small cattle*, esply *sheep* and *goats*, often ἴφια μῆλα, μήτηρ μήλων, Il. 2, 696.

II) μῆλον, τό, *an apple*, and generally, *tree-fruit*, 9, 542. Od. 7, 120.

*μηλόσκοπος, ον, poet. (σκοπέω), from whence a man can oversee the sheep, *flock-inspecting*, κορυφή, h. 19, 11.

μήλωψ, οπος, ὁ, ἡ (ὤψ), that looks like an apple or a quince, *quince-coloured*, .ιυω, *golden*, καρπός, Od. 7, 104.†

μήν, Ep. μέν and μάν, adv. of confirmation and asseveration: *yes, verily*, *certainly, by all means*, vero; it stands more rarely alone than with other particles, and connects itself with the most important word in the sentence. It stands alone with the imperat. ἄγε μήν, come on now, 1, 302. Μὴν ἢ μήν (μέν, μάν), verily, truly, 9, 57; οὐ μήν (μάν), *truly, not*, 12, 318. 24, 52; μὴ μάν, I. 603. 10, 330; καὶ μήν (μέν), and truly, certainly also, 19, 45. 23, 410. 24, 463: and yet, but also, 9, 499.

μήν, μηνός, ὁ, *a month*, only in the oblique cases; see μείς.

μήνη, ἡ, *the moon*, 19, 374. 23, 455. 2 As prop. name, the *goddess of the moon*, h. 32.

μηνιθμός, ὁ (μηνίω), *anger, wrath*, *14, 62. 202.

μήνιμα, ατος, τό (μηνίω), *a cause of anger* or *wrath*. μή τοι θεῶν μήνιμα γένωμαι, that I may not awaken the wrath of the gods against thee, 22, 358. Od. 11, 73.

μῆνις, ιος, ἡ (μένω [al. μαίνομαι, or μηνα]), *lasting anger*, *wrath* (Ap. ἡ ἐπιμένουσα ὀργή), mly of the gods, 1, 7. Od. 3, 135; of men, 1, 1. 9, 517.

μηνίω (μῆνις), aor. 1 partcp. μηνίσας *to cherish a lasting anger, to persevere in wrath, to be wroth*, τινί, against any man, 1, 422. 18, 257; τινός, on account of any thing; ἱρῶν, 5, 178; and often also. (In the pres. and imperf. ι is short, only once in the arsis long. 2, 679.)

*μηνύτρον, τό (μηνύω), *a reward for discovery*, h. Merc. 284.

*μηνύω, fut. μηνύσω, *to indicate, to betray, to make known*, h. Merc. 373. in the pres. long and short.

Μῄονες, οἱ, Ion. for Μαίονες, *the Meonians*, the inhabitants of Mæonia, then =Λυδοί, 2, 864. 10, 431.

Μηονίη, ἡ, Ion. for Μαιωνία, prop. a district in Lydia, which lay east of Mount Tmolus, 3, 401.

Μῄονίς, ίδος, ἡ, Μæonian. 2) Subst. *a Mæonian woman*, 4, 142.

μήποτε (ποτέ), *that not even, lest perhaps*: on the construe. see μή with subj. 7, 343. Od. 19, 81. b) In asseverations *never*, with infin. following. Il. 9, 133.

μήπου or μή που, *lest perhaps*, Od. 4, 775.

μήπω (πώ), *not yet*, Il. 234. 2) by *means*, with imperat. 4, 234. 3) For μή που, Od. 9, 102.

μήπως (πώς), *that not perhaps, lest haply*, with subj. and optat., 3, 436. 1. 487; and after verbs of fearing, *that perhaps*. 2) Interrogatively, *whether perhaps*, 10, 101.

μῆρα, τά, rare plur. of μηρίον, q. v.

μήρινθος, ἡ, *a cord, a string*, *24, 854. 857. 866. 867. 869.

μηρίον, τό, only in the plur. μηρία rarely μῆρα, 1, 464. Od. 3, 179; *the thighbones*, *the thigh-pieces*, which were cut from the thighs (μηροί), of victims.

Μηριόνης. 283 Μίγνῦμι.

They were then covered with pieces of flesh from the other parts, enveloped with a doubled covering of caul, and thus burnt as a sacrifice to the gods, Il. 1, 460. Od. 3, 456; hence often πίονα μηρία, 1, 40; thus Nitzsch ad Od. 3, 456. Voss, Myth. Brief. I. 39, explains μηρία as the *hip-bones*, with the flesh belonging to them.

Μηριόνης, ους, ὁ, son of Molus of Crete, charioteer of Idomeneus, 2, 651. 7, 166.

μηρός, ὁ, the upper fleshy part of the hip, *the thigh*, spoken of men, 5, 305. 12, 162. ἄορ ἐρύσασθαι παρὰ μηροῦ, to draw the sword from the thigh, Il. 2) Spoken of beasts, only in the connexion, μηρούς ἐξέταμον, see μηρίον, 1, 460. Od. 12. 360.

μηρύομαι, depon. mid. aor. Ep. μηρῡσάμην, *to draw in, to take in, to furl*, ἱστία, Od. 12, 170.†

μήστωρ, ωρος, ὁ (μήδομαι), 1) an *adviser, a counsellor*, spoken of Zeus (governor of the world, V.), 8, 22; of heroes: μήστωρες μάχης, ἀϋτῆς, counsellors in battle (Voss: 'exciters of battle'), 4, 328. 17, 339. 2) which occasions any thing: φόβοιο, the occasion or cause of flight, 6, 97. 12, 39; but of horses, skilled in flying (impetuous steeds, V.), 5, 272. 8, 108.

Μήστωρ, ορος, ὁ, son of Priam, 24, 257.

μήτε (τε), *and not, and that not*. μήτε —μήτε, *neither—nor*, also with τε in the second member, 13, 230. On the construc. see μή.

μήτηρ, μητέρος, ἡ, contr. μητρός, a *mother*, spoken of animals, 2, 313. 17, 4. Od. 10, 414. 2) Metaph. spoken of regions in which any thing especially flourishes: μήτηρ μήλων, θηρῶν, mother of sheep; of wild beasts, i. e. abounding in sheep, etc., Il. 2, 696. 8, 47, and elsewhere.

μήτῑ, neut. of μῆτις, q. v.
μήτῑ, see μῆτις.

μητιάω (μῆτις), Ep. μητιόω, only pres. and imperf. 1) *to have in mind, to devise, to plan*, βουλάς, 20, 153; absol. 7, 45. 2) *to devise prudently, to plan, to plot*, τί, 10, 208; κακά, 15, 27. 18, 312; νόστον τινί, Od. 6, 14. Mid. *to conclude by oneself, to deliberate*, Il. 22, 174; with infin. 12, 17.

μητίετα, ὁ, Ep. for μητιέτης (μητίομαι), *counsellor, counselling* (ruling, V.), epith. of Zeus, 1, 175. Od. 14, 243, and often.

μητιόεις, εσσα, εν (μῆτις), 1) *rich in counsel, wise*, h Ap. 344. 2) *wisely prepared* or *devised*, φάρμακα, Od. 4, 227.†

μητίομαι, depon. mid. (μῆτις), fut. μητίσομαι, aor. 1 ἐμητῑσάμην; the pres. is not found in H.:=μητιάω, 1) *to have in mind, to deliberate upon*. Od. 9, 262. 2) *to invent, to devise, to plot*, ἔχθεα, Il. 3, 417; μέρμερα, to practise dreadful deeds, 10, 48; θάνατόν τινι, 15, 349; κακά τινα,

Od. 18, 27. (In the earlier edd. we find incorrectly μητίσσομαι.)
μητιόω, Ep. for μητιάω.

μῆτις, ιος, ἡ, dat. μήτῑ, Ep. for μήτιϊ, 1) *prudence, understanding, intelligence*, the ability to counsel, often Il. and Od. 2) *counsel, advice, plan, expedient*, esply μῆτιν ὑφαίνειν, Il. 7, 324. 10, 19. Od. 4, 678.

μῆτις or μή τις, neut. μήτι, gen. μήτινος (τις), *that none*, (that no) *that no one*, constr. of μή. 2) μήτι, frequently, as adv. *that not perhaps, indeed not perhaps*, 4, 42. 5, 567. Od. 2, 67.

μητροπάτωρ, ορος, ὁ, poet. (πατήρ), a *mother's father, a maternal grandfather*, 11, 224.†

μητρυιή, ἡ, a *step-mother*, *5, 389. 13, 697.

μητρώϊος, ίη, ίον, poet. for μητρῷος (μήτηρ), *maternal*, δῶμα, Od. 19, 410.†

μήτρως, ωος, ὁ (μήτηρ), a *mother's brother*, an uncle, *2, 662. 16, 717.

μηχανάομαι, depon. mid. (μηχανή), only pres. and imperf., 3 plur. imperf. μηχανόωντο, Ep. for ἐμηχανῶντο, 1) Prop. *to prepare with art, to build*, machinor, τείχεα, 8, 177. 2) *to invent, to devise, to purpose, to practise*, mly in a bad signif.: κακά, ἀτάσθαλα, to practise wickedness, 11, 695; τινί and ἐπί τινι, Od. 4, 822.

μηχανάω, Ep. μαχανόω = μηχανάομαι, from this the partcp. μηχανόωντας, Od. 18, 143.†

*μηχανιώτης, ου, ὁ, poet. for μηχανητής, machinator, one who practises cunning or prudence, *crafty*, h. Merc. 436.

μῆχος, εος, τό, poet. for μηχανή, *means, remedy, counsel*, 2, 342. οὐδέ τι μῆχός ἐστι, there is no remedy, i. e. it is impossible, 9, 249. cf. ἄκος, Od. 14, 238.

Μήων, ενος, ὁ (5, 43), see Μήονες.

μιαίνω, aor. 1 ἐμίηνα, aor. 1 pass. ἐμιάνθην, Ep. 3 plur. for ἐμιάνθησαν, 4, 146; according to Buttm. 3 dual aor. 2 sync. for ἐμιάνθην, 1) *to stain, to colour*, ἐλέφαντα φοίνικι, 4, 141. 2) *to stain, to defile, to foul*, αἵματι, κονίησι, *16, 797. 17, 439.

μιαιφόνος, ον (μιαίνεσθαι φόνος), *defiled with slaughter, stained with slaughter, reeking with gore* [gore-tainted, Cp.], epith. of Ares, *5, 31. 455. 844. Lobeck and Buttm. read μιαίφονος from μιαίνεσθαι and φόνος, and its connexion with βροτολοιγέ and τειχεσιπλῆτα requires an act. signif. *accustomed to stain oneself with blood* (Schol. μιαινόμενος (Mid.) φόνοις). Ameis.

μιαρός, ή, όν (μιαίνω), *stained, defiled, fouled*, 24, 420.†

μιγάζομαι, poet. for μίγνυμαι, mid. Od. 8, 271.†

μίγδα, adv. (μίγνυμι), *mixed, mingled together*, Od. 24, 77; with dat. θεοῖς, mixed among the gods, Il. 8, 437.

*μίγδην, adv. = μίγδα, h. Merc. 494.

μίγνῡμι, Ep. μίσγω, fut. μίξω, aor. 1 ἔμιξα, fut. mid. μίξομαι, Ep. aor. 2 sync.

Μίδεια, 284 Μίνυθα

3 sing. ἔμικτο, perf. pass. μέμιγμαι, aor. 1 pass. ἐμίχθην, and aor. 2 ἐμίγην, fut. pass. μιγήσομαι. (The pres. μίγνυμι is not in H.) I) Act. *to mix, to mingle,* prop. spoken of fluids, with accus. οἶνον, 3, 270. Od. 1, 110 ; φάρμακα, Od. 4, 230 ; pass. ἄλεσσι μεμιγμένον εἶδαρ, food seasoned with salt. According to others, food out of the sea, Od. 11, 123. *b)* Metaph. *to join, to bind, to unite,* to bring any thing to another in close contact, τί τινι: χεῖρας τε μένος τε, to mingle hands and spirit, i. e. to come into close fight, Il. 13, 510 ; ἄνδρας κακότητι καὶ ἄλγεσι, to bring men into wretchedness and suffering, Od. 20, 203. Pass. γλῶσσ' ἐμέμικτο, their speech was mingled, Il. 14, 435. Od. 19, 175. II) Mid. with aor. pass. 1) *to mingle themselves, to mingle,* spoken of sheep : νομῷ, in the pasture, Il. 2, 475 ; of tempests, Od. 5, 317. 2) Metaph. *to mix oneself, to touch* any thing, with dat. κάρη κονίῃσιν ἐμίχθη, the head plunged in the dust, Il. 10, 457 ; also spoken of men, 3, 55 ; of the spear : μιχθῆναι ἔγκασι φωτός, pierced into the entrails of the man, 11, 438. 8) Most frequently of men : *to mingle oneself with, to consort with, to have intercourse with, to have commerce or live with* ; with dat. προμάχοισι, amongst the front warriors, ἀθανάτοισιν, 24, 91 ; also ἐν προμάχοισι, Od. 18, 379 ; ἀλλοδαποῖσι, to have intercourse with strangers, Il. 3, 48 ; and ἔν τινι, 3, 209 ; and ἐς Ἀχαιούς, 18, 216 ; absol. Od. 4, 178 ; μίξεσθαι ξενίῃ, to mingle in hospitality, Od. 24, 314. *b)* In a hostile signif. : *to meet in battle,* i. e. to come into close fight, Τρώεσσιν, Il. 5, 143 ; ἐν δαΐ, 13, 286 ; ἐν παλάμῃσί τινος, to engage in a pugilistic contest with any one, 21, 469. *c)* Esply spoken of sensual love: ἐν φιλότητι τινος, 6, 161. 165 ; and τινί, 21, 143 ; also εὐνῇ, 4, 445 ; once with accus. εὐνήν, 15, 33 ; spoken of man and wife at once, and also of each person singly, when it may be translated, *to embrace in love, to have intercourse with any one.*

Μίδεια, ἡ, Ep. for Μίδεα, a town in Bœotia, on the lake Copaïs, which according to Strabo was swallowed up by this lake, 2, 507.

*Μίδης, εω, ὁ, Ep. for Μίδας, king of the Phrygians, Ep. 3.

μικρός, ή, όν, Ion. form σμικρός, *little, small, short,* accus. δέμας, 5, 801. Od. 3, 290 ; only twice. παρὰ μικρόν, almost, Batr. 241. Compar. μείων, q. v.

μίκτο, see μίγνυμι.

Μίλητος, ἡ, 1) a noted and opulent commercial city of the Ionians in Caria, with four ports, 2, 868. h. Ap. 42. 180. 2) a town on the island of Crete, mother city of the Ionian Miletus, 2, 647.

μιλτοπάρῃος, ον (παρειά), having red cheeks, i. e. sides, *red*, epith. of ships, whose sides were painted with vermilion, 2, 637. Od. 9, 125. (' Red-beaked,' V.)

Μίμας, αντος, ὁ, a promontory in Asia Minor, east of Chios, at the southern extremity of the Erithrean isthmus, Od. 3, 172.

*μιμέομαι, depon. mid. *to imitate,* with accus. h. Ap. 156. Batr. 7.

μιμνάζω, poet. form of μένω, *to remain.* 2, 392. 10, 549. 2) Trans. with accus. *to await, to wait for,* h. 8, 6.

μιμνήσκω (root ΜΝΑΩ), fut. μνήσω, aor. 1 ἔμνησα, fut. mid. μνήσομαι, aor. 1 ἐμνησάμην, iterat. μνησάσκετο, perf. mid. μέμνημαι, 2 sing. μέμνῃ for μέμνησαι, optat. μεμνήμην, 24, 745 ; and paenepto for μέμνηντο, 23, 361 ; fut. 3 paenehsomai, aor. 1 pass only infin. μνησθῆναι, Od. 4, 118. Also in the pres. μιμνήσκομαι and μνάομαι, contr. μνῶμαι, in the expanded forms, partcp. pres. μνωόμενος, imperf. ἐμνώοντο, *to remind. to put in mind,* τινά, Od. 12, 38 ; of any thing, τινά τινος, Il. 1, 407. Od. 3, 101. 14, 169. Mid. *to remember, to call to mind, to think of, to bethink oneself,* with gen. often ; ἀλκῆς, to bethink oneself of spirit, i. e. to show it, Il. 6, 112 ; χαρμῆς, 4, 222 ; πολέμοιο, νόστου, σίτου, βρώμης, κοίτου, etc. ; instead of the gen. once φύγαδε μνώοντο, they bethought themselves of flight, 16, 697. 2) *to mention, to bring to mind by speaking,* with gen. 2, 492. Od. 4, 118. 331 ; with accus. h. Ap. 159 ; and ἀμφί τινος, Od. 4, 151 ; ἀμφί τινα, h. 6, 1 ; and περί τινος, Od. 7, 192. 3) The perf. mid. has the pres. signif. like *memini*, I bethink myself, I remember ; fut. 3 μεμνήσομαι, I shall remain mindful. mly with gen. 5, 818 ; and with accus. Τυδέα, ἄργυρον, ἄλλα, 6, 222. 9, 527. Od. 14, 168. 24, 122 ; and with infin. Il. 17, 364 ; and the partcp. often absol. 5, 263. 19, 153.

μίμνω, poet. form for μένω, only pres. and imperf. 1) *to remain,* 2, 331. 7. With accus. *to wait for, to await,* 4, 342. Od. 11, 210.

μίν, accus. sing. of the pron. 3 pers. for αὐτόν, αὐτήν, αὐτό, always enclitic, often μίν αὐτόν, (the person) himself (not as a *reflexive*), 21, 245 ; but αὐτὸν μίν [only once], himself, as a reflexive (*se ipsum*), Od. 4, 244, for the plur. ; doubtful, cf. Thiersch, Gram. § 204. 5.

Μινύειος, η, ον, Ep. Μινυήϊος, Minyean, appellation of Orchomenus in Bœotia, named from the powerful tribe of the Minyæ, 2, 511 ; Ep. form Od. 11, 284.

Μινυήϊος, ὁ, Ep. for Μινύειος, 1) a river in Elis, according to Strab. VIII. 347. Paus. 5, 1. 7, the *Anigrus ;* according to others, the *Peneus.*

μινύθω (μινύς), poet. only pres. and imperf. iterat. imperf. μινύθεσκον, 1) Trans. *to diminish, to lessen, to impair. to weaken,* with accus., 15, 492. 493. 17. 242. Od. 14, 17. 2) Intrans. *to become smaller, to decrease, to be destroyed,* Il. 16, 392. 17, 738. Od. 12, 46 ; ἦτορ ἑταίρων, Od. 4, 374 ; πόθῳ, to pine away with desire, h. Cer. 202.

μίνυνθα, adv. (μινύς) *a little, a very*

Μινυνθάδιος.   Μοῖρα.

little, for a time, mly of time, 4, 466. Od. 15, 494.

μινυνθάδιος, ον (μίνυνθα), compar. **μινυνθαδιώτερος**, *lasting but a short time*, αἰών, 4, 178; *short-lived*, 1, 352. Od. 11, 307.

μινυρίζω (μινυρός), *to moan, to whimper, to lament, to wail*, prop. spoken of women, 5, 889. Od. 4, 719.

*Μινωίος, ον, Ep. for Μίνφος, Minoian, h. Ap. 393.

Μίνως, ος, ὁ, accus. Μίνωα and Μίνω ed. Wolf, Μίνων ed. Spitzner after Aristarch., Il. 14, 322; son of Zeus and Europa, king of Crete, famed as a wise ruler and lawgiver, 13, 450. 451. 14, 322. His wise laws he had received from Zeus himself, since he had for nine years intercourse with Zeus, Od. 19, 178. His daughter is Ariadne and his son Deucalion, Od. 11, 321. 19, 178. He also appears in the realm of shades as ruling king, Od. 11, 567. Later tradition alone makes him a judge in the under world.

μισγάγκεια, ἡ (ἄγκος), *a dell, glen, gulley, a defile, a ravine*, in which the mountain torrents meet, 4, 455.†

μίσγω, a form of μίγνυμι, q. v.

μισέω (μῖσος), aor. 1 ἐμίσησα, *to hate, to abominate, to detest*. μίσησέ μιν κυσὶ κύρμα γενέσθαι, it was an abhorrence to him to become a prey to the dogs, Voss, Il. 17, 272.

μισθός, ὁ, *a reward, wages. hire*, 10, 304. 21, 445. 450; plur., Od. 10, 84.

μιστύλλω (akin to μίνυλος), *to cut in small pieces, to cut up*, spoken of carving flesh, with accus., 1, 465. 2, 428. Od. 3, 462.

μίτος, ὁ, *the cord, the thread*, a single thread introduced into the warp (πηνίον), 23, 762.† (Others understand *the warp* by it. stamen. Cp. translates, 'she tends the flax, drawing it to a thread.')

μίτρη, ἡ, *a belt, a girdle*, a woollen belt worn by warriors about the abdomen, furnished with metallic plates as a defence against missiles, and distinct from ζωστήρ, *5, 857. 4, 137.

μιχθείς, see μίγνυμι.

μνάομαι, ground form of μιμνήσκομαι, *to remember*, contr. μνῶμαι, which occurs in the Ep. expanded forms of the pres. and imperf. see μιμνήσκω.

μνάομαι, contr. μνῶμαι, depon. mid. iterat. imperf μνάσκετο *to court, to woo, to seek in marriage*, with ἄκοιτιν, γυναῖκα, Od. 1, 39. 16, 431; and absol. *Od. 10, 77. 19, 529. (Only in the pres. and imperf. sometimes in the contract and sometimes in the expanded forms.)

ΜΝΑΩ, root of μιμνήσκω.

μνῆμα, ατος, τό (ΜΝΑΩ), *a memorial, a monument*, χειρῶν, Od. 15, 126. 21, 40; τάφον, a tomb, 23, 619.

μνημοσύνη, ἡ (μνήμων), *remembrance, memory*. μνημοσύνη τις ἔπειτα πυρὸς γενέσθω, then let there be some remembrance of the fire, 8, 181.†

*Μνημοσύνη, ἡ (Moneta, Herm.), daughter of Uranus, mother of the Muses by Zeus, h. Merc. 429.

μνήμων, ον, gen. ονος (μνήμη), *mindful, remembering*, Od. 21, 95; with gen. φόρτον, mindful of the lading [i. e. careful of the goods stowed in his ship], Od. 8, 163.

μνῆσαι, μνησάσκετο, see μιμνήσκω.

Μνῆσος, ὁ, a noble Pæonian, 21. 210.

μνηστεύω (μνηστός), fut. μνηστεύσω, *to woo, to solicit in marriage*, absol. Od. 4, 684; and with accus. γυναῖκα, a woman, Od. 18, 276.

μνηστήρ, ῆρος, ὁ (μνάομαι), *a suitor, a wooer*, often spoken of the suitors of Penelope; the number of them, *Od. 16, 245.

μνῆστις, ιος, ἡ, poet. for μνήμη, *remembrance, memory*, οὐδέ τις ἡμῖν δόρπου μ., = *we thought not of supper*, Od. 13, 280.†

μνηστός, ή, όν (μνάομαι), *wooed*, who is won by presents, and hence *a lawful wife*, always as fem. with ἄλοχος, κουριδίη, 6, 246. Od. I. 36.

μνηστύς, ύος, ἡ, Ion. for μνηστεία, *the act of wooing, soliciting in marriage*, *Od. 2, 199. 19, 13.

μνωόμενος, μνώοντο, Ep. for μνώμενος, ἐμνῶντο from μνάομαι, q. v.

μογέω (μόγος), aor. 1 ἐμόγησα, 1) Intrans. *to weary oneself, to fatigue oneself, to exert oneself, to suffer pain*, mly as part. with another verb, 11, 636. 12, 29. 2) Trans. with accus. *to endure, to bear, to suffer*, ἄλγεα, Od. 2, 343. πολλά, Il. 23, 607. ἄεθλους, Od. 4, 170. ἐπί τινι, about any thing, Il. 1, 162. Od. 16, 19.

μόγις, adv. (μόγος), *with difficulty, scarcely*. (22, 412. is long in the arsis,) 9, 355. Od. 3, 119.

μόγος, ὁ, *pains, labour, exertion*, 4, 27.†

μογοστόκος, ον (μόγις, τίκτω), *exciting pains (dolorum creatrix*, Ern.), that causes the woman to bear with pain. Thus according to Aristarchus. Others, 'aiding those that bring forth with difficulty,' but such paroxytones have an active signification (cf. θεοτόκος), epith. of Ilithyia (Εἰλείθυια), *11, 270. 16, 187. 19, 103.

μόθος, ὁ, poet. (akin to μόγος), *the tumult of battle, battle*, 7, 117. 18. 159; ἵππων, a tumult of horses, the battle-fray of cavalry, 7, 240.

μοῖρα (μείρομαι), 1) *a part*, in opposition to the whole, 10, 253. Od. 4, 97; *esply a share* in any thing, Od. 11, 534; in a repast, *a portion*, Od. 3, 40. 66 : and often metaph. οὐδ' αἰδοῦς μοῖραν ἔχειν, to have no particle of shame, Od. 20, 171; hence *fitness, propriety*: κατὰ μοῖραν, suitably, properly, often with εἰπεῖν, a'so ἐν μοίρῃ, Il. 19, 186; and παρὰ μοῖραν, contrary to propriety, Od. 15, 509. 2) Esply *the portion of life, the lot of life*, Od. 19, 192; in full, μοῖρα βιότοιο, the measure of life, Il. 4, 175; generally, *fate, destiny*, with infin. Od. 4, 475. Il 7, 52,

Μοίρα.

esply in a bad signif. *the lot of death*, 6, 488; connected with θάνατος, 3, 101. Also in a good signif. Od. 20, 76, *prosperity, good fortune*, opp. άμμορίη.

Μοίρα, ή, prop. name, *the goddess of fate*, the *Parca* of the Romans, who allotted to men the destiny of life. In H. mly sing. once plur. 24, 49. cf. Od. 7, 197. Fate appears in H. in general, without limitation, but still not in the sense of an absolute fatalism. Primarily, every thing is ascribed to fate, whose unconditional necessity is most striking, e.g. death, as a law of nature, Od. 17, 326; also every thing independent of the free will of man, e.g. birth, death, fortune, misfortune, etc. *Moira* is primarily the dispenser of fate, Od. 3, 236 —238; still Zeus is also mentioned as the ruler of fate, Od. 4, 208. 20, 76, he can accelerate or delay the destiny of *Moira*, or in doubtful cases decide it, Il. 12, 402. 16, 443; nor is all influence denied to the other gods, Od. 3, 269. 8, 167.

μοιρηγενής, ές (γένος), *favoured by fate at birth, born to happiness*, 3, 182.†

μοιχάγρια, τα (άγρα), *the penalty inflicted* upon one detected in adultery [*th' adulterer's forfeit*, Cp.], Od. 8, 332.†

μολείν, see βλώσκω.

μόλιβος, ὁ, poet. for μόλυβδος, *lead*, 11, 237.† Some prefer to read μόλυβος, see μολύβδαινα.

Μολίων, ίονος, ὁ, 1) son of Molione, wife of Actor; in the dual, τὼ Μολίονε, the two *Moliones*, Cteatus and Eurytus, 11, 709; see Ἀκτορίωνε and Εύρυτος. 2) A prop. name of a Trojan, charioteer of Thymbræus, 11, 322.

μολοβρός, ὁ, *a glutton, a parasite, a greedy beggar*, *Od. 17, 219. 18, 26; according to the deriv. of the Gramm. μολὼν εἰς βοράν, better according to Riemer akin to μῶλυς, μωλύνω, *a lazy, fat paunch*.

Μόλος, ὁ, son of Deucalion, father of Meriones of Crete, 13, 249. 10, 269.

μολπή, ή (μέλπω), *a song united with dancing*, 1, 472. Od. 4, 19; and generally, *play, pastime*, Od. 6, 101. 2) *song, playing on the lyre*, alone, Od. 1, 152. 4, 19; also *dancing* alone, Il. 18, 606.

μολύβδαινα, ή (μόλυβδος), *a leaden ball*, which was tied to the line above the bait, to sink it more deeply in the water, 24, 80.†

ΜΟΛΩ, root of the aor. ἔμολον, see βλώσκω.

*μονσήμερος, ον (ἡμέρα), Ep. for μονήμερος, *of one day, living only one day, ephemeral*, Batr. 305.

μόνος, η, ον, Ep. μοῦνος, in H. only Ep. alone, often μόνος, Batr. 257. 2) *alone, solitary*, 4, 388. Od. 3, 217.

μονόω (μόνος), Ep. μουνόω, Od., partcp. aor. pass. μονωθείς, *to make single, to leave alone*; with accus. γενεήν, to propagate the race singly (so that there is always only one), Od. 16, 117; hence

Μοῦσα.

pass. *to be left alone*, Il 11, 471. Od. 14. 380.

μόριμος, ον, poet. for μόρσιμος, q. v.

μορμύρω, poet. (μύρω), only pres. *to rush, to roar, to murmur*, spoken of a stream, ἀφρῷ, 5, 599. 21, 325; spoken of the ocean, *18, 403.

μορόεις, εσσα, εν, only μορόεντα ἔρματα. according to the best critics: *carefully or skilfully wrought ear-rings*, of rare art, 14, 183. Od. 18, 298. Voss, *brigh.* and according to Riemer to be derived from μαίρω, to shine.

μόρος, ὁ (μείρομαι), *the lot, fate, destiny*, assigned to a man, either by the deity or by fate, esply *a sad lot, death*, 19, 421; hence often, κακὸς μόρος, and connected with θάνατος, 6, 357. Od. 9, 61; *see* μόρον, see ὑπέρμορον.

μόρσιμος, ον (μόρος), Ep. μόριμος, 19, 302; † *appointed by fate, fated*, Od. 10, 392. 21, 162; once, *appointed to death*, 22, 13. μόρσιμον ἦμαρ, the day of fate, the day of death, 15, 613; and μόρσιμόν ἐστι, with infin., it is allotted by fate, 2, 674.

Μόρυς, υος, ὁ, son of Hippotion, a Mysian, 13, 792. 14, 514.

μορύσσω, fut. ξω, perf. pass. μεμόρυγμαι, *to defile, to discolour, to foul, to soil, εἵματα καπνῷ, Od. 13, 435.†

μορφή, ή, *form, figure, shape of body*. Od. 8, 170; metaph. μορφή ἐπέων, grace, ornament *of words*, *Od. 11, 367.

μόρφνος, ον, 24, 316; an adj. epith. of an eagle, of uncertain signif. prob. *dark-coloured, black*, for ὀρφνη, Hesych. other explanations, according to the Schol., are: 1) *beautifully formed*, from μορφή. 2) *rushing on, swooping, plundering*, for μάρπτω. 3) *death-bringing*, from μοροφόνος. 4) Arist. H. A. 9, 32, a kind of eagle, living in valleys and swamps, hence Voss: 'dwelling in valley and swamp.'

μόσχος, ὁ, *a sprout, twig, rod*; as adj. *young, tender*, 11, 105.† cf. λύγος.

Μούλιος, ὁ, 1) the husband of Agamede, 11, 739. 2) a Trojan, 16, 696. 3) a Trojan slain by Achilles, 20, 472. 4) a herald of Amphinomus, Od. 18, 422.

μουνάξ, poet. for μόναξ, adv. (μούνος), *singly, alone*, *Od. 8, 371. 11, 417.

μούνος, η, ον, see μόνος.

μουνόω, Ion. for μονόω, q. v.

Μοῦσα, ή (prob. = μῶσα from μάω, *perceiving, inventing*), *a Muse*, goddess of song, of the poetic art, etc.; even in H. plur., but the number *nine* is nowhere first, Od. 24, 60, without mentioning their names, which are found for the first time, Hes. Th. 76. They are, according to 2, 491. Od. 1. 10, daughters of Zeus; they inhabit Olympus, 2, 484; and entertain the gods by singing, 1, 604. They inspire the Epic poets, suggest to their minds the deeds they are to record, and accord to their style attraction and grace. [The derivation from μάω is rejected by Buttm., Mythol. 1. 289, seq. Am. Ed.]

μοχθέω (μόχθος), fut. ήσω, like μογέω, *to take pains, to trouble oneself, to be distressed*, κήδεσιν, 10, 106.†

μοχθίζω =μοχθέω, *to suffer, to be sick*, έλκεϊ, with a wound, 2, 723.†

μοχλέω (μοχλός), *to move with levers*; στήλας, to turn over the pillars, 12, 259.†

μοχλός, ό, 1) *a lever*, Od. 5, 261. 2) any *long, strong stake*, *Od. 9, 332.

Μυγδών, όνος, ό, king of Phrygia, in whose time the Amazons attacked Phrygia, 3, 186.

μυδαλέος, η, ον (μυδάω), *wet through, moist, damp*; αίματι, sprinkled with blood, 11, 54.†

Μύδων, ωνος, ό (appell. μυδών), 1) son of Atymnius, charioteer of Pylæmenes, a Trojan, slain by Antilochus, 5, 580. 2) a Trojan slain by Achilles, 21, 209.

μυελόεις, εσσα, εν (μυελός), *full of marrow, marrowy*, ὀστέα, Od. 9, 293.†

μυελός, ὁ, *marrow*, 20, 482; metaph. μυελός ἀνδρῶν, the marrow of men, spoken of nourishing food, Od. 2, 291. 20, 108.

μυθέομαι, depon. mid. (μύθος), fut. μυθήσομαι, aor. 1 ἐμυθησάμην, Ep. form 2 sing. μυθέαι and μυθεῖαι, Ep. iterat. imperf. μυθέσκοντο, 1) *to discourse, to speak, to tell*, absol. and with accus. and infin. 21, 462. 2) Trans. *to tell, to narrate, to call*, τινί τι, 11, 201. πάντα κατά θυμόν, to speak every thing according to one's mind [agreeably to me], 9, 645. ἀληθέα, νημερτέα, 6, 376. 382. ἐναίσιμα, Od. 2, 159. πόλιν πολύχρυσον, to call the city rich in gold, 11. 18, 289. ποτὶ ὂν θυμόν, to speak to a man's heart, i. e. to consider, 17, 200. Od. 5, 285; hence *to counsel*, Od. 13, 191. (3) *to explain, to indicate, to interpret*, Il. 1, 74.]

μυθολογεύω, fut. σω, *to relate, to tell*, τί τινι, *Od. 12, 450. 453.

μῦθος, ὁ, 1 *discourse, word*, as opposed to ἔργον 9, 443. Od. 4, 777; in special applications: *a*) *a public discourse*, Od. 1, 358. *b*) *narration, conversation*. μῦθος παιδός, the narration of the son, Od. 11, 492. 2, 314. 4, 324. *c*) *bidding, command, commission, counsel*, Il. 2, 252. 5, 493. 7, 358. 2) *a resolve, plan, project*, since it is presented in words, *undertaking*, 14, 127. Od. 3, 140. 22, 288. 3) Od 21, 70, 71 is explained as Æol. for μόθος, noise, confusion, but unnecessarily; it signifies *project, purpose*, as no. 2. οὐδέ τιν' ἄλλην μῦθον ποιήσασθαι ἐπισχεσίην ἐδύνασθο, you could not make any pretext for your undertaking, Voss.

μυῖα, ἡ, *a fly*, an image of unblushing impudence. *a*) *a house-fly*, 4, 131. *b*) *a musquito*, 2, 469. 17, 570. *c*) *a carrion-fly*, 19, 25.

Μυκάλη, ἡ, a mountain in Ionia (Asia Minor), opposite Samos, which formed a promontory; also called Trogilium, 2, 869.

Μυκαλησσός, ή (Μυκαλησσός, Herm. h. Ap. 224), a city in Bœotia, near Tanagra, 2, 498.

μυκάομαι, depon. (μῦ), aor. ἔμυκον, perf. μέμυκα, 1) *to bellow*, spoken of cattle, Od. 10, 413. Il. 18, 580. 2) *to crack, to rattle, to buzz, to roar*, spoken of doors and of a spear, 5, 749. 20, 260; of a river, 12, 460. 21, 237.

μυκηθμός, ὁ, *bellowing, roaring*, 18, 575. Od. 12, 265.

Μυκήνη, ἡ, 1) daughter of Inachus, wife of Arestor, who gave name to the city Mycēnē, Od. 2, 120. 2) Plur. Μυκῆναι, Mycēnæ, a town in Argolis, the residence of Agamemnon, at the time of the Trojan war famous esply for the treasury of Atreus, and by the Cyclopean walls; its ruins are near the village Krabata; plur. 2, 569; sing. 4, 52. From this 1) adv. Μυκήνηθεν, from Mycenæ. 2) Μυκηναῖος, η, ον, Mycenian, 15, 638.

μύκον, see μυκάομαι.

μύλαξ, ακος, ὁ (μύλη), prop. *a millstone*; and generally, *any large stone*, 12, 161.†

μῦλη, ἡ (μύλλω), *a mill*, *Od. 7, 104. 20, 106. The mills of the ancients were hand-mills, which were turned by maids; or rather mortars, in which the grain was broken.

μυλήφατος, ον (πέφαμαι), *broken or ground in a mill*, Od. 2, 355.†

μυλοειδής, ές (εἶδος), *similar to a millstone*, πέτρος. 7, 270.† Batr. 217.

μυνή, ἡ (akin to ἀμύνω), *a pretext, an excuse, a tarrying*, plur. Od. 21, 111.†

Μύνης, ητος, ὁ, son of Evenus, husband of Briseïs, ruler in Lyrnessus, 2, 692. 19, 296.

*μυοκτόνος, ον (κτείνω), *mouse-slaying*, μυοκτ. τρόπαιον, a trophy on account of the slaughter of the mice, Batr. 159.

μυρίκη, ἡ, *a tamarisk*, according to Miquels, Hom. Flora. p. 39, the French tamarisk, *tamarix Gallica*, a shrub common in southern marshy regions, *10, 466. h. Merc. 81. (ῑ in the arsis, 21, 350.)

μυρίκινος, η, ον, *of the tamarisk*; ὄζος, a tamarisk branch, 6, 39.†

Μυρίνη, ἡ, daughter of Teucer, wife of Dardanus, according to Strab. an Amazon, who lay buried here. The tradition of the Pelasgians called a mound the monument of Myrina, which the men of that day called thorn-hill, 2, 814; see Βατίεια.

μυρίος, η, ον, *very much, infinite, innumerable*. μυρίον χέραδος, immense rubbish, 21, 320; frequently in the plur. 1, 2, 12, 326. 2) *infinitely great, illimitable, a thousand-fold*, ἄχος, 20, 282; ὦνος, Od. 15, 452: often plur. ἄλγεα, κήδεα (μυρίοι, countless; but μύριοι, ten thousand, according to the Gramm.).

Μυρμιδόνες, οἱ, sing. Μυρμιδών, όνος, *the Myrmidons*, an Achaian race in Thessaly, Phthiōtis, under the dominion of Achilles, whose chief towns were Phthia and Hellas, 1, 180. Od. 4, 9. They had emigrated under Peleus from Ægina to Thessaly. On the fabulous explanation of the name by the metamorphosis of ants into men, see Ovid. Met. 7, 622.

μύρομαι, only mid. (act. μύρω, Hesiod.), *to dissolve in tears, to weep; ἀμφί τινα, about any one,* 19, 6; *to lament, to wail,* in connex. with κλαίω, γοάω, 22, 427. Od. 19, 119.

μυρσινοειδής, ές (εἶδος), similar to a myrtle, h. Merc. 81.

Μύρσινος, ἡ (=μύρρινος), a village in Elis near Dyme; later τὸ Μυρτούντιον, 2, 616.

μῦς, μυός, ὁ, a mouse, Batr.

Μῦσοί, οἱ, *the Mysians.* 1) the inhabitants of the district of Mysia in Asia Minor, which in the time of Homer extended from the Æsopus to Olympus. They had emigrated from Thrace, 2, 858. 10, 430. 14, 512. 2) a race in Europe, originally on the Danube, from which the Asiatic Mysians sprang, 13, 5. Strab. VII. p. 295.

μυχμός, ὁ (μύζω), *sighing, groaning,* Od. 24, 416.†

μυχοίτατος, η, ον, irreg. superl. of μύχιος. μυχοίτατος ἷζε, he sat in the innermost corner, i. e. farthest from the entrance, Od. 21, 146.†

μυχόνδε, adv. (μυχός), poet. *into the interior, to the innermost recess,* Od. 22, 270.

μυχός, ὁ (μύω). *the innermost place, the interior, the corner,* of a tent, house, fort; *an inlet,* 21, 23. μυχῷ Ἄργεος, in the interior of Argos, 6, 152. Od. 3, 263.

μύω, aor. ἔμυσα, perf. μέμυκα, intrans. *to shut up, to close,* spoken of the eye, 24, 637. ἕλκεα μέμυκεν, the wounds were closed, *24, 420. (υ is in the pres. doubletimed.)

μυών, ῶνος, ὁ (μῦς), a place in the body where several muscles unite; *a knot of muscles,* 16, 315 (V. 'the calf'). 324.

μῶλος, ὁ (akin to μόλος), *pains, labour;* esply μῶλος Ἄρηος, the labour or toil of Ares, i. e. *contest, battle,* 11.; also alone, *contest.* 17, 397; between Irus and Odysseus (Ulysses), Od. 18, 263.

μῶλυ, τό (only nomin. and accus.), a fabulous magical herb with black roots and white flowers. Theophr. Hist. Plant. 9, 15. 17, understands by it, *allium nigrum Gouan.*, a kind of garlic, Od. 10, 305.† (Later, *the garlic.*)

μωμάομαι, depon. mid. (μῶμος), fut. μωμήσομαι, *to blame, to reproach, to deride, to insult, τινά,* 3, 412.†

μωμεύω = μωμάομαι, Od. 6, 274;† only pres.

μῶμος, ὁ, *blame, mockery, derision.* μῶμον ἀνάψαι, to give an insult, Od. 2, 86.†

μῶνυξ, υχος, ὁ, ἡ (μόνος or μία and ὄνυξ), *with undivided hoof, having a solid hoof,* epith. of horses, 5, 236, and Od.

N.

N, the thirteenth letter of the Greek alphabet; hence the sign of the thirteenth rhapsody.

ναί, Att. νή, adv. of asseveration, always in affirmative clauses, *yea, truly, verily;* often in the constr. ναὶ δὴ ταῦτά γε πάντα κατὰ μοῖραν ἔειπες, 1, 286. 8, 146; and ναὶ μὰ τόδε σκῆπτρον, verily, by this sceptre, with accus. 1, 234.

ναιετάω, Ep. (ναίω), only pres. and imperf. iterat. form, imperf. ναιετάασκον. 1) Intrans. *to dwell, to abide,* with prep. ἐν ἐπί, and with the dat. merely, 3, 387. *b) to be inhabited, to lie,* spoken of countries, islands, etc. 4, 45. Od. 9, 23; often partcp. 2, 648. Od. 1, 404. 2) Trans. *to inhabit,* with accus. 2, 539. 17, 172. Od. 9, 21. (For the most part in the open forms, except ναιετάασκον, and irreg. ναιετάωσα.)

ναίω, imperf. iterat. ναίεσκε, poet. aor. 1 ἔνασσα, aor. 1 pass. ἐνάσθην, 1) Intrans. only pres. and imperf. *to dwell, to abide, to remain;* with prep. ἐν, also with κατά, περί, πρός, with accus. and παρά with dat. and accum., and with the mere dat. αἰθέρι ναίων, 2, 412; Φρυγίῃ, 16, 719. *b) to be inhabited, to lie,* spoken of places. 2, 626. *c) For ναίω, to be full,* Od. 9, 222, see ναίω. 2) Trans. *to inhabit,* with accus. 3, 74. 15, 13, 172. Od. 4, 811. *b)* In aor. 1 *to give to inhabit;* hence *to build, πόλιν,* Od. 5, 174. h. Ap. 298; hence aor. pass. *to settle, to remove to,* Ἀργεῖ νάσθη, 14, 119.

νάκη, ἡ, *a woolly skin, a fleece,* Od. 14, 530.†

*Νάξος, ἡ, at an earlier period Δία q. v., the largest of the Cyclades, an island having a town of the same name, on account of its productiveness in wine, sacred to Bacchus, h. Ap. 44.

νάπη, ἡ, Ep. for νάπος, *a valley, a forest, a ravine, a defile,* between mountains, *8, 558. 16, 300.

ναρκάω (νάρκη), aor. 1 poet. νάρκησα. *to become benumbed, stiff, lame,* 8, 328.†

*νάρκισσος, ὁ, *the narcissus,* h. Cer. 8, 428.

νάσθη, see ναίω.

νάσσα, Ep. for ἔνασσα. see ναίω.

νάσσω, fut. νάξω, *to press firmly, to stamp down closely,* γαῖαν, Od. 21, 122.*

Νάστης, ου, ὁ (the settler), son of Nomion, leader of the Carians before Troy, 2, 867.

Ναυβολίδης, ου, ὁ, 1) son of Naubolus = Iphiclus. 2) a Phæacian, Od. 8, 116.

Ναύβολος, ὁ, son of Oryntus, king of Phocis, father of Iphitus, 2, 518.

*ναυηγός, όν, Ion. for ναυαγός (ἄγνυμι), *shipwrecked,* Batr. 94.

Ναύλοχος. Νέκυς

ναύλοχος, ον (ΛΕΧΩ), affording a secure anchorage, a convenient station for ships; λιμήν (Cp. a commodious haven; Voss, 'a ship-protecting harbour'), *Od. 4, 846. 10, 141.

ναύμαχος, ον (μάχη), employed in naval battles, ξυστά [ναυσί poles ... for conflict maritime prepared, Cp.], *15, 389. 677.

Ναυσίθοος, ὁ (ship-swift), son of Poseidôn and Periboea, father of Alcinous and Rhexênor, sovereign of the Phaeaces in their new abode at Scheria, Od. 7, 56, seq. cf. 6, 7—11.

Ναυσικάα, ἡ, the beautiful daughter of the Phaeacian sovereign Alcinous in Scheria, who conducted the ship-wrecked Odysseus (Ulysses) to the house of her father, Od. 6, 17, seq.

ναυσικλειτός, ή, όν (κλειτός), poet. renowned in naval affairs, Od. 6, 22.† Εύβοια, h. Ap. 31. 219.

ναυσικλυτός, ή, όν (κλυτός). = ναυσικλειτός, epith. of Phaeaces, Od. 7, 39; of the Phœnicians, *Od. 15, 415.

Ναυτεύς, ηος, ὁ (= ναύτης), a noble Phaeacian, Od. 8, 112.

ναύτης, ου, ὁ (ναῦς), a sailor, a seaman, a mariner, 4, 76. Od. 1, 171.

ναυτιλίη, ἡ (ναυτίλος), navigation, Od. 8, 253.†

ναυτίλλομαι, depon. only pres. and imperf. to navigate, to go by ship, *Od, 4, 672. 14, 246.

ναῦφι, ναῦφιν, Ep. see νῆυς.

νάω and ναίω, Ep. only pres. and imperf. ναῖον, to flow, κρήνη νᾶει, Od. 6. 292. κρῆναι νάουσι, 11. 21, 197. ναῖον ὀρῷ ἄγγεα, the vessels flowed with whev, Od. 9, 222. (ᾱ, Od. 6, 292. ᾰ, Il. 21, 197.) 2) Root of ναίω.

Νέαιρα, ἡ (the younger), a nymph, who bore to Helios Lampetiê and Phaetusa, Od. 12, 133.

νεαρός. ή. ον (νέος), young, tender, παῖδες, 8, 289.†

νέατος, η. ον, Ep. νείατος (prob. old superl. of νέος), always in the Ep. form, except 9, 153. 295. 11, 712; the last, the extreme, the lowest, always spoken of place: πούς, ἀνθερεών, κενεών, Il. b) With gen. νείατος ἄλλων, the lowest of them all, Il. 6, 295. πόλις νεάτη Πύλου, the last city of Pylos, 11, 712; and plur νέαται Πύλου (not for νενέαται from ναίω), 9. 153.

νεβρός, ὁ (akin to νεαρός), the young of the stags, a fawn, also a deer, 4, 243. Od. 4, 336.

νέες, νέεσσι, see νῆυς.

νεῆνις. ιδος, ἡ, Ep. for νεᾶνις (νέος), adj. youthful, παρθενική, Od. 7, 20. 2) Subst. a virgin, a maiden, 18, 418.

*νεήφατος, ον (φημί), newly-said, new-resounding, h. Merc. 443.

νέιαι, Ep. for νέεαι, see νέομαι.

νείαιρος, only in the fem. νείαιρα, irreg. compar. of νέος, the latter, the outer, the lower, mly νειαίρη γαστήρ, the lower belly, the abdomen, *5, 539. 616, and elsewhere.

νείατος, η. ον, Ep. for νέατος, q. v.

νεικέω (νεῖκος), and according to the necessity of the metre νεικείω: as subj. νεικείησι, infin. νεικείειν, imperf. νείκειον and νεικείεσκον, fut. νεικέσω, aor. 1 ἐνείκεσα, Ep νείκεσα, and σσ. 1) Intrans. to quarrel, to dispute, to wrangle. τινί, with any one, Od. 17, 189. ἀλλήλησιν, Il. 20, 254. εἵνεκά τινος, 18, 498. νείκεα νεικεῖν, 20, 251. 2) to provoke, to irritate, to blame, to scold, to accuse, with accus. αἰσχροῖς ἐπέεσσιν. 3, 38; χολωτοῖσιν, 15, 210. Od. 22, 525; spoken of Paris: νείκεσσε θεάς — τὴν δ' ᾔνησε, to slight, in antith. to αἰνεῖν, since he gave Aphroditê the preference to Hêrê and Athênê, Il. 24, 29.

νεῖκος, τό, 1) quarrelling, contention, disputation, esply with words: the act of blaming, reproaching, abusing, 7, 95. 9, 448. Od. 8, 75; also in the assembly, Il 18, 497.. 2) Often also, contest in deed: fight, battle, Il. νεῖκος πολέμοιο, contest of war. 13, 271. Od. 18, 264; thus also φυλόπιδος, ἔριδος, Il. 17, 384. 20, 140.

νεῖμα, Ep. for ἔνειμα, see νέμω.

νειόθεν, Ion. for νέοθεν, adv. (νέος), from beneath. νειόθεν ἐκ καρδίης, deep from the heart. 10, 10.†

νειόθι, Ion. for νέοθι, adv. (νέος), in the lowest part; with gen. λίμνης, deep down in the lake, 21, 317.†

νειός, ἡ, subaud. γῆ (νέος), new land, fallow ground; also newly-ploughed land, which has lain for a season untilled, and is now fresh ploughed. νειὸς τρίπολος, thrice-plowed fallow, Od. 5, 127. Il. 18, 541.

νεῖται, contr. for νέεται, see νέομαι.

νεκάς, άδος, ἡ (νέκυς), a heap of corpses, 5, 886.†

νεκρός, ὁ, 1) Subst. a dead body, a corpse; also Ep. νεκροὶ τεθνηῶτες and κατατεθνηῶτες, the departed dead, 6, 71. b) the dead, the departed, as inhabitants of the under-world, 23, 51. Od. 10, 526. 2) Adj. perhaps, Od. 12, 11.

νέκταρ, αρος, τό, nectar, the drink

Νεμέθω.   290   Νεοπτόλεμος.

accus. plur. νέκυς for νέκυας, Od. 24, 417. 1) *a dead body, a corpse*, also νέκυς τεθνηώς, κατατεθνηώς, κατακτάμενος, Il. 7, 409. Od. 11, 37. 22, 401. 2) *the dead, the departed*, in the under-world, only in the plur. Od.

νεμέθω, poet. lengthened for νέμω, only imperf. mid. νεμέθοντο, 11, 635.†

νεμεσάω and often νεμεσσάω, poet. fut. νεμεσήσω, aor. 1 Ep. always νεμέσησα, fut. mid. νεμεσήσομαι, aor. 1 pass. Ep. always νεμέσηθεν for νεμεσσήθησαν. 1) Act. *to feel a just indignation against any one, to find fault with, to blame for, to take ill*, τινί τι, Od. 23, 213; and generally, *to be displeased, to be angry, to be offended*, with dat. of the pers. Il. 4, 413. 5, 17; and often absol. 11) Mid. and aor. pass. 1) *to be displeased with oneself, to regard as unbecoming, to deem unseemly*; often with infin. νεμεσσάται ἐνὶ θυμῷ ὑπεσβολίας ἀναφαίνειν, he deems it unbecoming to exhibit loquacity, Voss, Od. 4, 158. Hence also, *to be scrupulous, to be ashamed*, Od. 2, 64; with μή following, Il. 16, 544. 2) As act. *to take amiss, to be displeased, to be angry*, absol. and τινί, with any man, 10, 115. 129. 15, 103 ; with accus. and infin. Od. 4, 195. 18, 227. *b*) With accus. *to be offended with* (to resent, V.), κακὰ ἔργα, Od. 14, 284.

νεμεσητός, Ep. νεμεσσητός. ή, όν (νεμεσάω), 1) *worthy of displeasure, blameworthy, reprehensible*, mly neut. with infin. 3, 410. Od. 22, 59. 2) *whose displeasure is to be avoided, to be shunned*, Il. 11, 648. Thus Eustath. Others act. for ὁ νεμεσῶν, *disposed to displeasure*, Il. 11, 648.

νεμεσίζομαι, depon. mid. (νέμεσις)=νεμεσάω, only pres. and imperf. 1) *to be displeased, to be angry*, τινί, 8, 407. Od. 2, 239; τινί τι, *to take amiss* any thing at any one's hands, Il. 5, 757; also with accus. and infin. 2, 297. 2) *to deem unbecoming, to stand in awe*, with accus. and infin. 17, 254; θεούς, to stand in awe of the gods, Od. 1, 263.

νέμεσις, ιος, ή, Ep. dat. νεμέσσει for νεμέσει. 6, 335 (νέμω), 1) *just displeasure, blame, or anger about any thing unbecoming* (later, at undeserved prosperity). νέμεσις δέ μοι ἐξ ἀνθρώπων ἔσσεται, the blame of men will accrue to me, Od. 2, 136. 2) *that which excites displeasure or blame, blameworthy*. οὐ νέμεσις, with the infin., it is not to be blamed, it is no reproach, Il. 14, 680. Od. 1, 350; or accus. with infin. Il. 3, 156. 3) Subjective, according to Passow, *the fear of blame, dread*; with αἰδώς, according to Schol. *the blame of others*, like no. 1. Il. 13, 122.

νεμεσσάω, Ep. for νεμεσάω.
νεμεσσητός, Ep. for νεμεσητός.
νεμέσσει, Ep. dat. of νέμεσις.
νέμος, εος, τό, poet. (νέμω), *a meadow*, and generally, *a grove, a forest*, 11, 480.† [nemus.]

νέμω, aor. 1 ἔνειμα, Ep. νεῖμα; Ep. form νεμέθω. I) Act. *to divide, to distribute*, τι; κρέα, μέθυ, often τινί τι, any thing to any one, 3, 274. Od. 6, 188. *to allot as pasture, to pasture*, spoken of herds, Od. 9, 233. II) Mid. *to have* any thing which has been distributed, *to possess, to enjoy*, with accus. πατρίδα, Od. 20, 336; mly spoken of estates: *to cultivate*, τέμενος, ἔργα, Il.; and generally, *to inhabit*, ἄλσεα, Ἰθάκην. *b*) Spoken of brutes : *to pasture, to graze, to feed*, absol. 5, 777. Od. 13, 407 ; with accus. ἄνθεα ποίης, Od. 9, 449; metaph. spoken of fire : *to consume*, Il. 23, 177; and pass. πυρὶ χθὼν νέμεται, the land is consumed by fire, 2, 780.

νένιπται, see νίζω.
νεοαρδής, ές (ἄρδω), *newly-watered, fertilized*, ἀλωή, 21, 346.†

νεοιλός, ή, όν, *new-born*, γοννος, σκύλαξ, Od. 12, 86.† (According to Hesych. and Eustath. for νεογνός.)

*νεογνός, ον, contr. for νεόγονος, *new-born*, h. Cer. 141. Merc. 406.

νεόδαρτος, ον (δέρω), *just stripped of*, δέρμα, *Od. 4. 437. 22, 363.

*νεοδμής, ῆτος, ὁ, ἡ (δαμάω), *newly-broken, just tamed*, πῶλος, h. Ap. 231.

νεοθηλής, ές (θάλλω), *fresh-blooming, new-sprouting, just becoming tender*, ποιή. 14, 347;† metaph. fresh-flourishing, h. 30, 13.

νεοίη, ή, poet.=νεότης, *youth, youthful ardour*, 23, 604.†

*νεόλλουτος, ον, poet. for νεόλουτος (λούω), *newly-washed, fresh-bathed*, h. Merc. 241.

νέομαι, poet. depon. only pres. and imperf. Ep. contr. νεῦμαι, 18, 336; 2 and 3 sing. pres. νεῖαι, νεῖται, Od. 11, 114. 12, 188. 14, 152 ; infin. νεῖσθαι, Od. 15, 88 ; elsewhere uncontracted. subj. pres. 2 sing. νέηαι for νέῃ. *to go, to come*; esply *to go away, to go forth, to return*. οἴκαδε, οἰκόνδε, and with the prep. εἰς, πρός, ἐπί, with accus. and ἐπί with dat. Il. 22, 392; and with the accus. simply, πατρίδα, 7, 335; primar. spoken of gods and men ; metaph. of a stream : νέεσθαι κὰρ ῥόον, to return to its channel, 12, 32. The pres. like εἶμι, has for the most part the signif. of the fut. 18, 101. Od. 2, 238. 13, 61.

νέον, adv. see νέος.
νεοπενθής. ές (πένθος), *in new grief, newly-mourning*, Od. 11, 39.†

*νεόπηκτος, η, ον (πήγνυμι). *newly-coagulated, fresh-curded*, τυρός, Batr. 75.
νεόπλυτος, ον (πλύνω), *fresh-washed, newly-cleansed*, Od. 6, 64.†
νεόπριστος, ον (πρίω), *newly-sawed, newly-cut* (V. smoothed), Od. 3, 404.†

Νεοπτόλεμος, ὁ (young warrior), son of Achilles; he was brought up in Scyros, 19, 326, seq. ; from whence Odysseus (Ulysses) took him to Troy. Here he proved himself, both in the council and battle, worthy of his father. After the destruction of Troy, he conducted the

Myrmidons back to Phthia, and then married Hermionē, daughter of Menelaus, Od. 3, 188. 4, 9. 11, 506. According to other traditions, he emigrated to Epirus, and was slain in Delphi, Pind.

νέος, η, ον, compar. νεώτερος, superl. νεώτατος, new, i. e. 1) Spoken of things: *fresh, new, άλγος, άοιδή*. 2) Of persons: *young, juvenile, youthful*, παῖς (opposed to παλαιός), 14, 108; κοῦρος, γυνή. οἱ νέοι, the youth, in opposition to the γέροντες, 2, 789. 9, 36. Adv. νέον, *newly, fresh, lately, just now*. νέον γεγαώς, just born, Od. 4, 144.

νεός, see νηῦς.

νεόσμηκτος, ον (σμήχω), *newly-rubbed, newly-burnished*, θώρηξ, 13, 342.†

νεοσσός, ὁ (νέος), *a young one*, esply of animals, *2, 311. 9, 323.

νεόστροφος, ον (στρέφω), *newly-twisted*, 15, 469.†

*Νεοτειχεύς, έως, ὁ, an inhabitant of the Æolian town Neonteichus in Mysia, Epigr. 1.

νεότευκτος, ον (τεύχω), *newly made, newly-wrought*, κασσίτερος, 21, 592.†

νεοτευχής, ές = νεότευκτος, δίφρος, 5, 194.†

νεότης, ητος, ἡ (νέος), prop. *newness*; esply *youth, the age of youth*, 23, 445. ἐκ νεότητος, from youth up, *14, 86.

νεούτατος, ον (οὐτάω), *newly* or *just wounded*, *13, 539. 18, 536.

νέποδες, ων, οἱ, Od. 4, 404;† epith. of seals. The ancient Gramm. explain, 1) By ἄποδες, *footless* (from νή and πούς, in which case πη is shortened to νε; thus Apion). 2) By νηξίποδες, *having feet suited to swimming; web-fuoted* (from νέω πούς, according to Etym. Mag. Apoll. Lex.) 3) By ἀπόγονοι, *the young*, according to Ap. Lex. and Eustath. The last signif. was rejected by Apoll.; the second is most probable. Voss, ' web-footed.'

νέρθε, before a vowel νέρθεν, adv. poet. for ἔνερθε, *under, from beneath*. 2) Prep. *under, beneath*, with gen. γαίης νέρθεν, 14, 204. νέρθεν γῆς, Od. 11, 302.

Νεστόρεος, η, ον, *Nestorean*, appertaining to Nestor, νηΰς, 2, 54.

Νεστορίδης, ου, ὁ, son of Nestor, Od. 3, 482.

Νέστωρ, ορος, ὁ, son of Nēleus and Chlōris, king of Pylos (see Πύλος), engaged when an old man in the Trojan war, as he was reigning over the third generation, 1, 247 — 252; and distinguished himself by his wisdom and eloquence, 2, 370, seq. Of his former ex-

νεῦμαι, see νέομαι.

νευρή, ἡ, Ep. gen. νευρῆφι, νευρῆφιν, 8, 300; Ep. dat. νευρῆφι, Od. 11, 607; always *the bow-string;* in 11. 8, 328, ρῆξε δέ οἱ νευρήν,' he broke the string of the bow (not the cord of the hand: Teucer stood ready to shoot; the stone burst the string, and then grazed the hand).

νεῦρον, τό, 1) *a sinew, a tendon, the muscular cords*, only once, plur. 16, 316. 2) *a cord, a ligament, a thong;* the cord with which the point of the arrow was bound to the shaft, 4, 151; but νεῦρα βόεια, v. 122, seems to mean the bow-string, *II.

νευστάζω (νεύω), *to nod*, κεφαλῇ, Od. 18, 154; ὀφρύσι, to make signs with the eyes, Od. 12, 194; κόρυθι, to nod with the crest (as the consequence of a firm step), Il. 20, 162.

νεύω, fut. νεύσω, aor. always Ep. νεῦσα, 1) *to nod, to beckon, to give the wink*, τινί, 9, 223; and εἰς ἀλλήλους, h. 6, 9. b) *to nod to*, i. e. to promise, to assure, τί τινι, h. Cer. 445; mly with accus. and infin. c) *to nod, to incline*, i. e. to bend forwards, 13, 132; often spoken of the crest, 3, 337. 2) Trans. *to incline, to droop*, κεφαλάς, Od. 18, 237.

νεφέλη, ἡ (νέφος), *a cloud, mist, vapour*; often metaph. νεφ. κυανέη, spoken of the darkness of death, 20, 417; ἄχεος, cloud of grief, 17, 591. Od. 24, 315.

νεφεληγερέτα, αο, ὁ, Ep. for νεφεληγερέτης (ἀγείρω), *the cloud-collecter [cloud-assembler*, Cp.], who drives the clouds together, epith. of Zeus, 1, 511. Od. 1, 63.

νέφος, εος, τό, *cloud, mist*, often in the plur.; generally, *darkness*, νέφος θανάτοιο, 16, 350; ἀχλύος, 15, 668. b) Metaph. *a dense multitude, a troop*, that looks like a *cloud*, Τρώων, πεζῶν, ψαρῶν, 16, 66. 4. 274. 17, 755; πολέμοιο, the cloud of battle, i. e. the dense tumult of battle, 17, 243.

νέω, only pres. and imperf. ἔννεον, Ep. for ἔνεον, 21, 11; *to swim*, Od. 4, 344. 442.

νέω, later νήθω, *to spin*, only aor. 1 mid. νήσαντο, Od. 7, 198; τινί τι, to spin a man any thing.†

νή, Ep. inseparable particle, which in composition denies the notion contained in the word.

νῆα, see νηῦς.

νηγάτεος, έη, εον, poet. (for νεήγατος from νέος and γάω [γείνω, γέγαα' cf. τατός from τείνω. B.]), *newly-made, newly-wrought*, χιτών, κρήδεμνον, 2, 43.

ήδύς (cf. h. Merc. 241. 449); *sweet, gentle*, as Buttm., Lex. p. 414, after the Schol. Ven., has pretty satisfactorily proved. It had originally a digamma, hence Fηδύμος; when this was omitted, ν was attached to the preceding word, which was then connected with the word itself by Aristarch. Il. 2, 2. 10, 91. Od. 4, 793. 2) Aristarch. derives it from νή and δύω = άνέκδυτος, *from which a man cannot easily arouse himself*, consequently = νήγρετος, a deep sleep, which explanation is approved by Passow and Rost on Damm's Lex. ad Il. 16, 454.

νηδύς, ύος, ή, *the belly*, and every thing contained in it, 13, 290; *the stomach*, Od. 9, 296; *the womb*, Il. 24, 496.

νήες, νήεσσι, see νηϋς.

νηέω, Ion. for νέω, aor. 1 act. Ep. νήησα, aor. mid. ένηησάμην, 1) *to heap up, to collect together, to accumulate*, with accus. ύλην. ξύλα, 23, 139. 163. Od. 19, 64 : άποινα, Il. 24, 276. 2) *to load, to freight*, νήας, 9, 358. Mid. *to freight for oneself*; νήα χρυσού, to freight his ship with gold, 9, 137. 279.

Νήϊον, τό, a mountain in the northern part of the island Ithaca, on whose declivity was situated the town of Ithaca, Od. 1, 186. cf. Od. 3, 81. Thus Voss; Eustath. took it for a part of Neritus; Völcker in Hom. Geogr., § 38, places the mountain Neïon on the eastern coast of the island. cf. 'Ιθάκη.

Νηϊάς, άδος, ή = Νηΐς, *a Naiad*, *Od. 13, 104. 348.

νήϊος, η, ον (νηύς), *belonging to a ship*, δόρυ νήϊον, *timber for ship-building, shiptimber*, 3, 62. Od. 9, 384. 498; without δόρυ, Il. 13, 391. 16. 484.

Νηΐς, ΐδος, ή. Ion. for Naΐς (νάω), a *naiad, a fountain-nymph*, νύμφη νηϊς, *6, 22. 14, 444.

νήϊς, ΐδος, ὁ. ἡ (ί. from νή and είδέναι), *ignorant, inexperienced*, 7, 198. h. Cer. 256; with gen. Od. 8, 179.

νηκερδής, ές (νή, κέρδος), *without gain, profitless, unprofitable*, βουλή, έπος, 17, 469. Od. 14, 509.

νηκουστέω (άκούω), aor. 1 νηκούστησα, *not to hear, not to obey*, with gen. θεάς, 20, 14.†

νηλεής, ές, poet. (νή, έλεος), also νηλής, 9, 632; from this the dat. νηλεΐ, accus. νηλέα, *without pity, pitiless, ruthless, cruel*, spoken of persons, 9, 632. 16, 33; elsewhere often νηλεές ήμαρ, the cruel day, i. e day of death, 11, 484. Od. 8. 525; χαλκός, δεσμός, Il. 4, 348. 10, 443; ύπνος, the cruel sleep (during which one fell into misfortune), Od. 12, 372; θυμός, Il. 19, 229.

Νηλείδης, αο, ὁ = Νηλιάδης, 23, 652.

*νηλειής, ές, Ep. for νηλεής, h. Ven. 246.

Νηλεύς, ήος, ὁ, son of Poseidôn and Tyro, husband of Chloris, father of Pero and Nestor, Od. 11, 234—238; he was driven by his brother Pelias from Iolcos to Thessaly, and emigrated to Messenia, where he founded Pylos. His sons were slain in a war with Heracles; the twelfth alone, Nestor, remained alive, Il. 11. 691, seq. ; he also waged war against the Arcadians, 7, 133. Od. 3, 4. 309.

Νηληϊάδης, ου, ὁ, son of Neleus = *Nestor*, 8, 100. Od. 3, 79.

Νηλήϊος, ον, also η. ον, *Nelean*: ή Νηλήϊος Πύλος, Il. 682. Od. 4, 639; but also αἱ Νηλήϊαι ἵπποι, Il. 11, 597.

νηλής, ές, Ep.= νηλεής, q. v.

νηλίτης, ές (νή, άλείτης), *free from fault, guiltless, not to be blamed*, *Od. 16, 317. 19, 498. 22, 418.

νήμα, ατος, τό (νέω), *that which is spun, thread*, Od. 4, 134. Plur. *Od. 1. 98. 19, 143.

νημερτής, ές (νή, άμαρτάνω), *unerring, not deceptive, true*, epith. of Proteus, Od. 4, 349 ; βουλή, Od. 1, 86 ; έπος, Il. 1, 204 : νόος, Od. 21, 205 ; frequently neut. as adv. νημερτές and νημερτέα είπεΐν, to speak according to truth. Il. 6, 376; and adv. νημερτέως, Od. 5, 98. 19, 269.

Νημερτής, ούς, ή (more correctly. Νημέρτης), daughter of Nêreus and Doris. 18, 46.

νηνεμίη, ή (νήνεμος), *a calm, a quiet atmosphere*. νηνεμίης, in a calm, 5, 523. 1) As adj. γαλήνη, a calm at sea, Od. 5, 391. 12, 169.

νήνεμος, ον (νή, άνεμος), *calm, quiet, windless*, αἰθήρ, 8, 556.†

*νήξις, ιος, ή (νήχομαι), *the act of swimming*, Batr. 67, 149.

νηός, ὁ, Ion. for ναός (νάω), a *dwelling, a temple*, Il. and Od. άντρου νηόν, h. Merc. 148.

νηός, gen. of νηῦς.

νηπενθής, ές (νή, πένθος), *without suffering*; act. *grief-removing, grief-assuaging*, φάρμακον, an Egyptian charm, which, taken in wine, expelled trouble from the mind, Od. 4, 221.† Some of the ancients explained this magic potion allegorically, and understood by it the charm of discourse. Others, more correctly, understood by it a real plant (cf. Od. 4, 228, 229); Miquel, Hom. Flor. p. 48, and Sprengel think it opium.

νηπίας, see νηπίη.

νηπιαχεύω (νηπίαχος), *to be childish, to pursue childish sports*, 22, 502.†

νηπίαχος, ον (poet. lengthened from νήπιος), *under age, childish*, *2, 338. 16. 262.

νηπίη, ή (νήπιος), accus. plur. νηπίας, Ep. for νηπίας. 1) *minority, childhood*, 9, 491. 2) *childishness, childish sport*, Od. 1, 297; and generally, *foolishness*; in the plur. νηπιέησι, Il. 15, 363. Od. 24, 462.

νήπιος, ιη, ιον (νή, έπος), *childish, young, infans*, 9, 440; *early* νήπια τέκνα, also spoken of animals, 2, 311. Metaph. *childish, inexperienced, foolish, simple*, 2, 38. 5, 406. 7, 401. Od. 1, 8. b) *weak* (like a child), βίη, Il. 11, 561.

νήποινος, ον (ποινή), *without reason, without recompense; unpunished, unavenged*, spoken of persons, Od. 1, 338.

Νηπύτιος. 293 **Νίσσομαι.**

2, 145. Neut. as adv. νήπιον, Od. 1, 160. 377; and often. ⁴Od.

νηπύτιος, ίη, ιον (νή — ἀπύω), young, 20, 200; metaph. *childish, foolish, simple,* *13, 292. [According to Ameis, a lengthened form of νήπιος, found only in the three books, 13. 20. 21.]

Νηρεύς. ῆος, ὁ (from νή and ῥέω, *Nereus,* Herm.), *Nereus,* son of Pontus and Gæa (Tellus), husband of Doris, father of the Nereids; he ruled in the Ægean sea, under Poseidôn. The poet calls him ὁ γέρων, 18, 141. The name occurs first h. Ap. 319.

Νηρηίς, ίδος, ἡ, Ion. for Νηρείς, a *Nereid,* daughter of Nereus and Doris; in the Il. only plur. αἱ Νηρηΐδες, 18, 38, 52.

Νήρικος, ἡ, an ancient city on the island Leucas, according to Strab., where the isthmus formerly was connected with the main-land, Od. 24, 377. At a later day, the isthmus was pierced by the Corinthians, and the town Leucas founded, now *St. Maura.*

Νήριτον, neut. τό, Od. 13, 351; ὁ Νήριτος, Strab. a mountain in the southern part of Ithaca, according to Gell, now *Anoi,* Il. 2, 632. Od. 9, 22; see Ἰθάκη.

Νήριτος, ὁ, son of Ptereláus, brother of Ithacus, 17, 207.

Νησαίη, ἡ (belonging to an island), a Nereid, 18, 40.

νῆσος, ἡ (νάω), prop. floating land, *an island,* 2, 108. Od. 1, 50.

νῆστις, ιος, ὁ, ἡ (νή, ἐσθίω), *not eating, fasting, abstaining from food,* 19, 207. Od. 18, 370.

νητός, ή, όν (νέω), *heaped, accumulated,* Od. 2, 338.†

νηῦς, Ion. for ναῦς, gen. νηός and Ep. shortened νεός, dat. νηΐ, accus. νῆα, νέα, plur. νῆες, νέες, gen. νηῶν, νεῶν, ναῦφιν, dat. plur. νηυσί, νήεσσι, νέεσσιν, ναῦφιν, accus. νῆας, νέας, *a ship.* H. mentions two kinds: 1) *ships of burden,* φορτίδες Od. 9, 322. 2) *ships of war,* called by way of eminence, νῆες. According to the Catalogue of ships, they bore 50, and some even 150 men, and could not have been very small. As parts of the ships, are mentioned τρόπις, πρώρη, πρύμνη, ἰκρία, πηδάλιον, ἱστός, ζυγά; to the tackle belong ἱστία, ἐρετμά, πείσματα, πρυμνήσια; see these words. The station of the Greeks was between the two promontories Rhœteum and Sigeum; see 14, 30, seq. According to Strab. these promontories are sixty stadia apart. As the space could not contain the large number of ships (by the catalogue 1186), they probably lay in several rows, cf. 14, 31. Achilles held with his ships the right wing near Sigeum, Odysseus (Ulysses) the middle, and the Telamonian Ajax the left near Rhœteum. Between the rows of ships were the huts or lodges; towards Troy was the encampment surrounded by a ditch and wall. An exact description has been given by K. G. Lenz, in a work entitled: die *Ebene* von Troja, 1747, p. 189. Köpke in der Kriegsw. der Gr. 184, seq.

νήχω and νήχομαι, depon. mid. fut. νήξομαι, *to swim,* the act. Od. 5, 375. 7, 276; mid. *Od. 6, 364. 14, 352.

νίζω, takes the tenses of νίπτω (which in H. occurs only in the pres. ἀπονίπτεσθαι, Od. 18, 179.), fut. νίψω, aor. 1 Ep. νίψα, mid. aor. 1 ἐνιψάμην, perf. νένιμμαι, 1) *to bathe, to wash,* with accus. δέκα, τραπέζας, with double accus. νίψαι τινὰ πόδας, ' d. 19, 376. 2) *to wash off* or *away,* ἱδρῶ ἀπό τινος, Il. 10, 57; αἷμα, 11, 830. Mid. *to wash oneself,* with accus. χεῖρας (before a libation and generally before eating the Greeks were accustomed to wash the hands), 16, 230. Od. 12, 336; (as a religious service) χεῖρας ἁλός, from the sea, Od. 2, 261; with double accus. ἐκ ποταμοῦ χρόα ἄλμην, to wash the sea-water from the body, Od. 6, 224. *b*) With accus. *to wash oneself, to bathe,* Il. 24, 305. Od. 1, 138.

νικάω (νίκη), fut. νικήσω, aor. 1 ἐνίκησα and νίκησα, partcp. aor. 1 pass. νικηθείς, 1) Intrans. *to conquer, to vanquish, to have the mastery, to be superior,* 3, 71; hence νικήσας, the victor, 3, 178; metaph. cat. instrum. μύθοισιν, ἔγχει, 18, 252; δόλοισι, Od. 3, 121; absol. τὰ χερείονα νικᾷ, the worse prevails, Il. 1, 576. βουλὴ κακὴ νίκησεν, Od. 10, 46. *b*) In judicial language: to be acquitted, *to gain the cause,* Od. 11, 545. 2) Trans. *to conquer, to vanquish,* with accus. τινὰ μάχῃ, Il. 16, 79; πόδεσσι, 20, 410; metaph. *to excel, to surpass,* τινα ἀγορῇ, κάλλει, 2, 370. 9, 130; νόον νεοίη, 23, 604. *b*) *to gain, to bear off;* νίκην, to gain a victory, Od. 11, 545. πάντα ἐνίκα, he bore off all the prizes, subaud. ἆεθλα, Il. 4, 389.

νίκη, *victory,* nily in battle, 3, 457. 7, 26. *b*) *victory,* in a civil cause, Od. 11, 545. 2) Prop. name, *the goddess of victory,* daughter of Arês. h. 7, 4.

Νιόβη, ἡ, daughter of Tantalus and Dia, wife of King Amphίon of Thebes. Proud of her twelve children, and boasting over Lêtô (Latona), she was first deprived of her children, and then converted to a stone, 24, 602. 606.

νίπτω, see νίζω.

Νιρεύς, ῆος, ὁ, son of Charopus and Aglaia, from the island Symê, the handsomest Greek before Troy except Achilles, 2, 671, seq.

Νίσα, ἡ (otherwise Νύσσα), a town in Bœotia, 2, 508. According to Strab. there was no town of this name; hence, he understands Νύσα, a village near Helicon; cf. Ottf. Müller, Orchomen. p. 381.

Νῖσος, ὁ, son of Arêtus, a Dulichian, father of Amphinόmus, Od. 16, 395.

νίσσομαι, poet. (akin to νέομαι), fut. νίσομαι, 23, 76. 1) *to go,* πόλεμόνδε, 13, 186. 2) Esply *to go away, to return,* οἴκαδε, Od. 5, 19. ἐκ πεδίου, Il. 12, 119.

O 3

(The form νίσσομαι is now not found in Hom.)

Νίσυρος, ή, a little island, belonging to the Sporades near Cos, now Nizzaria, 2, 676. (ΰ in Anthol. III. 240.)

νιφάς, άδος, ή (νίφω), a snow-flake, mly plur. νιφάδες, a snow-storm, 12, 278; often as an image of multitude, *3, 222.

νιφετός, ό (νέφω), a snow-storm, Od. 4, 566; (in Il. 10, 7, it is incorrectly accented νίφετος.)

νιφόεις, εσσα, εν (νίφω), snowy, snow-clad, epith. of mountains, esply of Olympus, 18, 615. Od. 19, 338.

νίφω, infin. pres. νιφέμεν, to snow, 12, 280.†

νίψα. Ep. for ένιψα, see νίζω.

νοέω (νόος), fut. νοήσω, aor. ἐνόησα and νόησα. 1) to see, to observe, to perceive, τινά or τί, prim. with the eyes, ὀξύ νοήσαι, to see sharply or quickly, 3, 374. 5, 312; also ὀφθαλμοῖς, 15, 422. 24, 294; often in connexion with ἰδεῖν, 11, 599. Od. 13, 318; metaph. to perceive, to be aware, to see, θυμῷ, φρεσί, μετὰ φρεσί, ἐν φρεσί. 2) to think, to consider, to ponder, to deliberate, Il. 9, 537. Od. 11, 62. 20, 367. 3) to think upon, to devise, to plan, νόον, to devise a counsel or plan, Il. 9, 105; μῦθον, 12, 232; νόημα, Od. 2, 122; ἄλλο, Od. 2, 382; with infin. to purpose, to have in mind, Il. 5, 665. 22, 235. Mid. aor. 1, νοήσατο μάστιγα ἐλέσθαι, he thought, or was minded, to take the whip, 10, 501.†

νόημα. ατος, τό, 1) thought, a sentiment, often plur. as an image of velocity, Od. 7, 36. h. Ap. 187. 2) purpose, resolution, design, mly in the plur. Il. 10, 104. Od. 2, 121. 3) understanding, intelligence, wisdom, Od. 20, 346. Il. 19, 218.

νοήμων, ον, gen. ονος, thoughtful, considerate, intelligent, *Od. 2, 282. 3, 133. 13, 209.

Νοήμων, ονος, ὁ (cf. Cato), 1) a Lycian, Il. 5, 678. 2) a noble Pylian, 23, 612. 3) son of Phronius in Ithaca, who gave Telemachus a ship for his voyage, Od. 2, 386. 4, 630.

νόθος, η, ον, illegitimate, base-born, born out of wedlock; opposed to γνήσιος, 11, 102. κούρη νόθη, *13, 173.

νομεύς, ῆος, ὁ (νέμω), a herdsman, in the most general signif. ἄνδρες νομῆες, 17, 55.

νομεύω (νομεύς), fut. σω, to pasture, to tend, to guard, μῆλα, Od. 9, 336. 10, 85. 2) to graze, to feed down, βουσὶ νομούς, h. Merc. 492.

*νομή, ἡ (νέμω), a meadow, a pasture, Batr. 59.

*νόμιος, η, ον (νομή), relating to a pasture; νόμιος θεός, the pastoral deity Pan, h. 18, 5.

Νομίων, ἴονος, ὁ, father of Amphimachus in Caria, 2, 871.

νομόνδε, poet. adv. to pasture, 18, 575. Od. 9, 438.

νομός, ό (νέμω), a pasture. a) i. e. the place where cattle feed, pasture-ground,

ὕλης, a woodland pasture, Od. 10, 12. b) food, nourishment in the pasture, h. Merc. 198. c) Metaph. ἐπέων πολὺς νομὸς ἔνθα καὶ ἔνθα, on this side and that the pasture of words extends, i. e. the field from which one may draw topics of discourse is wide. [(man's tongue is nimble, &c.)... nor wants wide field and large, Cp. "There is a wide range in words." Lid. and Scott.] 20, 249.

*νόμος, ὁ (νέμω), that which is distributed; hence, custom, usage, law, not in the Il. and Od., only νόμοι φδῆς, the melodies of song, h. Ap. 20.

νόος, ὁ, contr. νοῦς, only Od. 10, 240. prop. thought, intelligence, i. e. the nobler part of the soul, which is wanting in brutes, sentiment, consciousness, 11, 813; hence, 1) understanding, reason, intelligence, 15, 643; νόῳ (with intelligence) καὶ βουλῇ, Od. 3, 128: connected with μῆτις, Il. 7, 448; νόῳ, with discretion, Od. 6, 326. 2) disposition, cast of mind, mode of thought, heart, soul, with θυμός, Il. 4, 369. Od. 1, 3. χαῖρε νόῳ, Od. 8, 78. ἔχειν νόον, Od. 2, 124. 281; ἔμπεδον, ἀκήλητος, ἀπηνής, ἀεικής. 3) thought, opinion, view, resolution, νόον νοεῖν, Il. 9, 104. νόον καταλέξαι, 2, 192. Od. 4, 256. 14, 490.

*νόσος, ἡ, see νοῦσος.

νοστέω (νόστος), fut. νοστήσω, aor. ἐνόστησα, 1) to turn back, to return, οἴκαδε, οἴκόνδε, ἐκ Τροίης, Il. δώματα, Ἰθάκηνδε, ἐς πατρίδα, Od. 2) Generally, to go, to come, Od. 4, 619 (or it must be assumed that Menelaus had been in Sidon twice).

νόστιμος, ον (νόστος), belonging to the return; hence, 1) νόστιμον ἦμαρ, the day of return: the return, the return home, Od. 1, 9. 354, and often. 2) returning home, that can or will return home, *Od. 4, 806. 19, 85.

νόστος, ὁ, a return, a journey home, 2, 155; both with the gen. of the person who returns, Ὀδυσῆος, Od. 1, 87. 2, 366; and of the place, to which one returns γαίης Φαιήκων, to the land of the Phæacians, Od. 5, 344; also ἐπί τι, Il. 10, 509. 2) Esply the return of the heroes from Troy, Od. 1, 325. 3, 132. The Cyclic poets have treated this subject circumstantially.

νόσφι, before a vowel νόσφιν, 1) Adv. poet. (from) (apart (from), away, aside with κἰειν, εἶναι, aside, in concealment, l. 408; also νόσφιν ἀπὸ φλοίσβοιο, 5, 322. 2) As prep. with gen. far from, away from, mly spoken of place, ἑτάρων, l. 349. πολέμοιο, 6, 443. b) alone, without, aside, Od. 1, 20. θεῶν, Il. 12, 466. c) Spoken of the mind: νόσφιν Ἀχαιῶν βουλεύειν, to think differently from the Greeks, i. e. otherwise than the Greeks, 2, 347.

νοσφίζομαι, mid. poet. (νόσφι), aor. 1 νοσφισάμην, Ep. aor. pass. νοσφίσθεις. 1) to remove oneself, to separate oneself, prim. spoken of place, with gen. πατρός, from one's father, Od. 23, 98; absol. aor. pass. Od. 11, 73. *b*) With accus. *to leave, to forsake* any thing, παίδα, δώμα, Od. 4, 264. 21, 104. ὄρεα. Od. 19, 339. 2) Metaph. spoken of the mind: *to separate oneself, to turn from* any one, from hatred or contempt, Il. 2, 81. 24, 222. N. B. νοσφισθεῖσα, in the signif. of the aor. mid. with accus. θεῶν ἀγορήν, h. Cer. 92.

νοτίη, ἡ, poet. (νότιος), subst. prop. *moisture*, then *rain*, plur. 8, 307.†

νότιος, ίη, ιον (νότος), *wet, moist*, ἱδρώς, 11, 811. ἐν νοτίῳ τήνγε ὥρμισαν, subaud. ναῦν, they anchored the ship high in the water (not the deep water, but the shore water), Od. 4, 785. 8, 55; see Nitzsch ad Od. 2, 414.

Νότος, ὁ, *the south wind*, or, more precisely, the *south-west wind*, 2, 145. It brings wet weather, 3, 10. 11, 306; and with the zephyr is the most stormy wind, Od. 12, 289.

νοῦσος, ἡ, Ion. for νόσος, h. 15, 1†; *sickness, disease*, and generally, *evil, wretchedness*, Od. 15, 408.

νύ, νύν, mly Ep. enclitic particle (shortened from νῦν), it marks, 1) The progress of the action or discourse (see νῦν 2), *now, then, thereupon* often at the same time moderately illative, 1, 382. Od. 4, 363; rarely Ep. in a temporal signif. Il. 10, 105. 2) It has a strengthening force, *a*) In exhortations, *now, then*, δεῦρά νυν, 23, 485. *b*) In other clauses: *then, therefore, now*, 10, 165. 17, 469; often with irony, *certainly*, οὔ νύ τι, not surely, Od. 1, 347. *c*) In interrogations, *now*, Il. 1, 414. 4, 31. Od. 2, 320. 4, 110.

νυκτερίς, ἴδος, ἡ (νύξ), *a night-bird*, esply *a bat*, *Od. 12, 433. 24, 6.

νύμφα, see νύμφη.

νύμφη, ἡ, vocat. poet. νύμφα, only 3, 130. Od. 4, 743 (perhaps from the obsol. νύβω, nubo, to envelope), *a bride* (who was conducted to the bridegroom, with the face veiled), Il. 18, 493; generally, *a*) *a young wife, a married woman*, 3, 130. Od. 4, 743. *b*) *a virgin, a maiden*, of nubile age, Il. 9, 560.

Νύμφη, ἡ, *a nymph*, a female deity of inferior rank. The nymphs inhabited islands, mountains, forests, fountains, etc. 20, 6, 9. H mentions Νύμφη Νηΐς, a fountain nymph, Il. Νύμφαι ὀρεστιάδες, mountain nymphs, 6, 420; ἀγρονόμοι, country nymphs, as companions of Artěmis, Od. 6, 105. They are daughters of Zeus, Il. 6, 420; springing from fountains, groves, and streams, Od. 10, 350; the handmaids of other goddesses, Od. 6, 105. 10, 348; and were worship in sacred grottoes with sacrifices, Od. 14, 435.

νύμφιος, ὁ (νύμφη) *a bridegroom, an affianced husband* (newly married, V.), 23, 223. Od. 7, 65.

νῦν, adv. 1) *now, immediately, at once, nunc*, prop. spoken of the immediate present, opposed to ὕστερον, 1, 27. Od. 4, 727. νῦν δέ, Il. 2, 82. καὶ νῦν, ἤτοι, and just now, Od. 4, 151. Sometimes like the English *now*, *a*) Spoken of the past, Il. 3, 439. Od. 1, 43. *b*) Of the future, Il. 5, 279. 2) Frequently metaph. for νῦν, *now, then, thereupon*, esply with the imperat. 10, 175. 15, 115. cf. νύ, νύν.

νύν, see νύ.

νύξ, νυκτός, ἡ, 1) *night*, both generally, and spoken of individual nights. H. divides the night into three parts, 10, 253. Od. 12, 312. νυκτός, by night, Od. 13, 278. νύκτα = διὰ νύκτα, through the night, Od. 3, 151. νυκτὶ πείθεσθαι, to obey the night, i. e. to cease, Il. 7, 282. 2) *the darkness of night*, and generally, *darkness, obscurity*, 5, 23. 13, 425; esply *a*) *the night of death, the darkness of death*, 5, 659. 13, 580. *b*) As an image of terrour, spoken of Apollo: νυκτὶ ἐοικώς, 1, 47. τάδε νυκτὶ ἔΐσκει, the things he esteemed as the night, Od. 20, 362.

Νύξ, κτός, ἡ, *the goddess of night*, 14, 78. 259; according to Hes. Th. 123, daughter of Chaos, who with Erebus begat Æther and Day. [In 14, 78, it should be appellat. νύξ, cf. Jahrb. Jahn und K., p. 275.]

νυός, ἡ, poet. *a daughter-in-law*, 22, 65. Od. 3, 451. 2) Generally, one related by marriage, *a sister-in-law*, Il. 3, 49. h. Ven. 136.

*Νῦσα, ἡ (akin to νύσσα), a name given to mountains and cities, whither Dionysus was said to have come, perhaps a mountain in Arabia, Τηλοῦ Φοινίκης, h. 26, 8. cf. 25, 5.

Νυσήϊον ὄρος, τό, the *Nysean mountain*, perhaps in Thrace, according to V. an Edonian mountain, 6, 133; others suppose it a mountain in Arabia or India.

*Νήσιον πεδίον, τό (Νῦσα), the *Nysean plain*, according to Creuzer in Asia, h. Cer. 17. cf. Apd. 3, 4. 3. Voss regards it as the Bœotian village *Nysa*, others still as *Phocis*.

νύσσα, ἡ (νύσσω), 1) a pillar on the race-ground, around which the runners were obliged to turn, the *goal*, meta, 23, 332. 358. 2) the point of starting, *the barriers*, 23, 758. Od. 8, 121.

νύσσω, aor. 1 Ep. νύξα, 1) *to prick, to thrust*; absol. with dat. instrum. ξίφεσιν καὶ ἔγχεσιν, 13, 147; with accus. τινά, to pierce, to wound any one, 5, 46. 12, 395; *to pierce, to thrust through*, σάκος 11, 564; τινὰ κατὰ χεῖρα, to wound any one in the hand, 11, 252; also with double accus. 11, 96. 2) Generally, *to thrust*, ἀγκῶνι νύσσειν τινά, to thrust any one with the elbow, Od. 14, 485.

νώ, see νῶϊ.

νωθής, ές, poet. (perhaps from νή, ὠθέω), *slow, lazy, dull*, epith. of the ass, 11, 559.†

νῶϊ, nom. dual, gen. dat. νῶϊν, accus. νῶϊ and νώ, the last only, 5, 219. Od. 15, 475. 16, 306; *both of us, we two*. (νῶϊν as nom. or accus. is to be rejected, and νώϊ

O 4

Ξεινοσύνη. 297 Ο.

ception and entertainment, Od. 1, 313. This bond descended by inheritance; hence ξεῖνος πατρώϊος, a paternal table-friend, a guest by inheritance, Il. 6, 215. Od. 1, 187. The ξεῖνος is both the guest who is entertained, Od. 8, 543, and the host who provides the entertainment, Il. 15, 532. 21, 42;=ξεινοδόκος.

ξεινοσύνη, Ion. for ξενοσύνη, *hospitality, rights of hospitality*, Od. 21, 35.†

ξενίη, ἡ (ξένος), *hospitality, hospitable reception and entertainment, guest-friendship*. *Od. 24, 286. 314.

ξείνιος, ίη, ιον, for the Ion. ξένιος, q. v.

ξερός, ή, όν, Ion. for ξηρός. *dry. ξερὸν ἠπείροιο*, the dry ground of the mainland, Od. 5, 402.†

ξέσσα, Ep. for ἔξεσε, see ξέω.

ξεστός, ή, όν (ξέω), *shaved, smoothed, polished*, spoken of wood, δίφρος, 24, 322; ἵππος, the artificial horse, Od. 4, 272; spoken of stones: ξεστοὶ λίθοι, hewn stones, for benches or seats before the door, Il. 18, 504. Od. 3, 406; in like manner αἴθουσα, portico, Il. 6, 243; spoken of horn, Od. 19, 566.

ξέω, aor. 1 ἔξεσα, always Ep. ξέσσα, *to shave, to scrape*; esply to work any thing carefully with fine tools, *to smooth, to polish, to plane*, *Od. 5, 245. 17, 341. 23, 199.

ξηραίνω (ξηρός), aor. pass. ἐξηράνθην, *to dry up, to make dry*, only ἐξηράνθη πεδίον, *21, 345. 348.

ξίφος, εος, τό (akin to ξύω), *a sword*; it seems to be not materially different from the φάσγανον, q. v.; and is spoken of as large and two-edged, 21, 118. It had a straight blade (ταννήκης), was carried in a sheath (κουλεόν), hung upon a belt (τελαμών). The handle (κώπη) was often decorated. ξίφος Θρηΐκιον, a Thracian sword; according to the Gramm. ad Il. 13, 576, it was large and broad.

*ξουθός, ή, όν, poet. *yellow, brownish*, h. 33, 3.

*ξύλινος, η, ον, *of wood, wooden*, δόλος, Batr. 116.

ξύλον, τό (ξύω), *wood* which is cut and split; only in the plur. *wood, fire-wood, logs*, sing. 23, 327.

ξύλοχος, ἡ (ἔχω), ground covered with wood; *a wood, a thicket*, as a lurking-place of wild animals, 11, 415. Od. 4, 335.

ξυμβλήμεναι, ξυμβλήτην, ξύμβλητο, ξύμβληντο, see συμβάλλω.

ξύμπας, ασα, αν, see σύμπας.

ξύν, Ep. and earlier form for σύν, which H. rarely uses, and then, for the most part, to support the metre. H. has the following compounds: ξυναγείρω, ξυνάγω, ξυνδέω, ξυνελαύνω, ξυνέχω, ξυνιέναι, which are to be found under συν.

ξυνάξε, see συνάγνυμι.
ξυνεείκοσι, Ep. for συνείκοσι, Od.
ξυνήκα, see συνίημι.
ξυνεοχμός, ὁ, see συνεοχμός.

ξύνεσις, ιος, ἡ, see σύνεσις.
ξυνήϊος, η, ον, Ep. and Ion. for ξυνός, *common, public*. ξυνήϊα, common property, belonging to the whole army, *1, 124, 23, 809.

ξυνίει, see συνίημι.
ξύνιον, Ep. for ξυνίεσαν, see συνίημι.
ξυνιόντος, ξύνισαν, see σύνειμι.

ξυνός, ή, όν, Ion. and poet. for κοινός, *common, in common, public; κακόν*, 16, 262. ξυνὸς Ἐνυάλιος, common is the god of war, i. e. he helps now this, now that party [*Mars his favour deals Impartial*, Cp.], 18, 309; with gen. γαῖα ξυνὴ πάντων, *15, 193.

ξυρόν, τό (ξύω), *a razor*; proverbial: ἐπὶ ξυροῦ ἵσταται ἀκμῆς, it stands upon the edge of the razor, i. e. this is the decisive instant, 10, 173.† (Cf ἴσταμαι.) The met., according to Köppen and Passow, is derived from the notion, that any thing resting upon a razor's edge must instantly incline to one of the two sides.

ξυνοχή, ἡ, see συνοχή.
ξυστόν, τό (ξύω), prop. a smoothed stake; *a spear-shaft, a spear*, 4, 269. 11, 260. ξυστὸν ναύμαχον, the pike or pole used in naval engagements, which, according to 15, 677, was twenty-two cubits long, and pointed with iron.

ξύω (akin to ξέω), aor. 1 ἔξυσα, *to shave, to rub, to smooth*; δάπεδον λιστροῖσιν, to clean the floor with shovels, Od. 22, 456. 2) Generally, *to do fine work*. ἑανὸν ἔξυσε ἀσκήσασα, she had woven the garment delicately with art. Voss, Il. 14, 179. Others: she had smoothed or polished it.

O.

O, the fifteenth letter of the Greek alphabet; and hence the sign of the fifteenth rhapsody.

ὁ, ἡ, τό, Ep. forms are: sing. gen. τοῖο, masc. and neut.; plur. nomin. τοί and ταί: gen. fem. τάων for τῶν; dat. τοῖσι, ταῖσι, τῃσι, and τῆς: ταῖς is not Homeric. (Some ancient Gramm. would write the unaccented cases ὁ, ἡ, οἱ, αἱ, with the acute; when standing alone, they are used as demonstrative, cf. Thiersch, § 284. 16, and Spitzner ad Il. 1, 9, who follows this in his ed. The opposite view is held by Buttm., Gr. Gram. § 75. Rem. 5. p. 305.) It has, like the German article *der, die, das*, in H. the signif. both of a demonstrative and of a relative pronoun.

I) ὁ, ἡ, τό, as a demonstrative pronoun, it points out an object, and indicates it as something known and already spoken of. Often, however, the demonstrative force is so weakened, that the transition to the Attic article clearly shows itself. 1) The pure demonstrative

O 5

Ὄαρ. force is seen esply. a) When the pronoun stands without a substantive, where it is translated by *this, that*, or, like αὐτός, by *he, she, it*, cf. 1, 9. 12, 29. 43, etc.; again, when it is separated from the substantive by the verb, and, as it were, prepares the way for the following substantive: ἡ δ' ἕσπετο Παλλὰς Ἀθήνη, she however followed, [viz.] Pallas Athēnē, Od. 1, 125. cf. Il. 1, 448. 5, 508. Od. 3, 69. *b)* When it stands as an adjective pronoun, and a relative clause follows it, it is commonly placed after the substantive. οὐδ' —ἐλήθετο συνθεσιάων τάων, ἃς ἐπέτελλε Διομήδης, he forgot not those commands which Diomēdes gave him, 5, 320. Od. 2, 119. sq. c) In connexion with *μέν, δέ, ὁ μέν, ὁ δέ, this here, that there, the one, the other, this, that.* τὸ μέν, τὸ δέ, the one thing, the other, Od. 4, 508; *partly, partly,* Od. 2, 46. So also in the plur. οἱ μέν, οἱ δέ, τὰ μέν, τὰ δέ. If a plur. is distributed into several sing., the former mly stands in the gen. 18, 595; often. however, in the same case with ὁ μέν, ὁ δέ, 5, 27. Od. 12, 73. Frequently ὁ δέ is found without a preceding μέν, Il. 22, 157. Frequently also ὁ μέν stands alone, and a substantive follows, as 23, 4. Od. 1, 115; or another word: τὰ μὲν —ἄλλα δέ, Il. 6, 147. 2) The demonstrative force of the pronoun is weaker, when it stands before the substantive, without any subsequent clause relating to it. Still it even then marks the object as known, and gives it emphatic prominence, of. 1, 11. 20, 33. 35. The pronoun in this case rarely succeeds the noun, see Od. 21, 41. Often almost like the later article, cf. τὰ θύραια, Od. 18, 385. 2) It approaches most nearly to the later article, *a)* When it converts adjectives and adverbs into substantives, ὁ γεραιός, Il. 24, 252; τὸ μέλαν ὀρυός, Od. 14, 12; τὸ πάρος, τὸ πρίν. *b)* When it connects prepositions and adverbs with substantives. ἄννγες αἱ περὶ δίφρον, Il. 11, 535. ἄνδρες οἱ τότε, 9, 559. 4) Some cases are used as absolute: *a)* τό, accus. neut. *therefore, on this account*, 3, 176. 7, 239. *b)* The dat. τῇ and τῷ, q. v. c) τοῖσι in τοῖσιν μετέφη, 1, 58, and the like constructions, Wolf ad Il. 1. c. would explain as neut. plur. *inter hæc.* It is better taken as a plur. masc. (cf. τῇσι, 24, 723), *among them,* and it stands thus even with only two, Od. 7, 27. 13, 374. *d)* With prepos. ἐκ τοῦ. *from that time, since*, Il. 15, 601.

II) ὅ, ἥ, τό, as a relative pronoun, in all the forms, *who, which, that.* The masc. ὅ stands, 16, 835; and κλῦθί μοι ὁ χθιζὸς θεὸς ἤλυθεν, hear me god, who camest yesterday, Od. 2, 262.

ὄαρ, ἀρος, ἡ, poet. (prob. from ἄρω), contr. ὤρ, from which dat. ὤρεσσιν, 5, 486; † *a female companion*, esply *a wife, a consort*, 9, 327.

ὀαρίζω, poet. (ὄαρ), iterat. imperf. ὀρίζεσκον, contr. for ὀαρίζ., h. Merc. 58; *to have intimate intercourse,* esply *to converse intimately, to be familiar.* τινί, with any one, 6, 516; ἀπὸ δρυὸς οὐδ' ἀπὸ πέτρης, down from the oak or the rock, i. e. securely and undisturbed to converse familiarly with any one, a proverbial expression, 22, 127; and generally, *to live,* μετά τινι, h. Merc. 170.

ὀαριστής, οῦ, ὁ, poet. (ὀαρίζω), *a companion, an associate,* Διός, Od. 19, 179.†

ὀαριστύς, ύος, ἡ, (ὀαρίζω), *intimate intercourse, familiar conversation, endearment* in the girdle of Aphroditē (Ven. toying), 14, 216. 2) Generally, *intercourse, society, commerce.* ἡ γὰρ πολέμου ὀαριστύς, this is the commerce of war (the way in which *it deals with* those who are engaged in it), 17, 228; προμάχων, *13, 291.

*ὄαρος ὁ, poet. (ὄαρ), *intimate intercourse, familiar converse*, h. 22, 3; esply *the converse of love*, h. Ven. 250.

ὀβελός, ὁ (βέλος), *a spit, a roasting spit*, only plur. 1, 465. Od. 3, 462.

ὀβριμοεργός, όν (ἔργον), *using violence,* always in a bad sense; *impious, wicked,* *5, 403. 22, 418. Batr.

ὀβριμοπάτρη, ἡ, poet. (πατήρ), *the daughter of a mighty* or *powerful father.* epith. of Athēnē, 5, 747. Od. 1, 101.

ὄβριμος, ον, poet. (from βρι, βριθύ,) 1) *strong, powerful, impetuous,* epith. of Ares, Hector, and Achilles, Il. 2) Spoken of inanimate things: *powerful, mighty*, i. e. great, heavy, epith. of the spear, of a stone, Od. 9, 241; of impetuous water, Il. 4, 453.

*ὀβριμόθυμος, ον (θυμόν), *stout-hearted, courageous,* epith. of Ares, h. 7, 2.

ὀγδόατος, η, ον, Ep. lengthened for ὄγδοος *the eighth,* 19, 246, and Od.

ὄγδοος, η. οον (ὀκτώ for ὀγδόFοσ), *the eighth.* (Od. 7, 261. 14, 287, it is to be pronounced as a dissyllable, see Thiersh. § 149. 3.)

ὀγδώκοντα, Ion. contr. for ὀγδοήκοντα, Indeclin. *eighty*, *2, 568. 652.

ὅγε, ἥγε, τόγε, the demonstr. pron. ὁ, ἡ, τό, strengthened by the particle γέ, *this here, that there*, and often to be translated by an emphatic *this* or *that*. 1) Sometimes it points out the near or remote place of an action, and can be translated only by an adv. κεῖνος, ὅτι, that one there, he there, 3, 351. 19, 344. 2) In the Epic language it stands often, in case of two consecutive clauses, in the second clause, to bring the subject again to mind, when it is translated ny an emphatic *he, she, it,* 2, 664. Od. 1, 4. As absol. there occur, 1) τῇγε, exactly here, Il. 6, 435. 2) τόγε, for that very reason, 5, 827.

ὄγκιον, τό (ὄγκος), *a coffer, a chest, a basket,* for keeping arrows and other iron instruments, Od. 21, 61.†

ὄγκος, ὁ (akin to ἀγκών), *a curvature: a bending;* hence *a hook,* especially *the barb* of an arrow, *4, 151. 214.

ὄγμος, ὁ (akin to ἄγω), prop. *a line, a*

Ογχηστός. 299 *Ὀδυσσεύς.*

ϝow, esply. 1) *the furrow* in ploughing, Il. 18, 546; or *the swath* which mowers or reapers cut and leave in rows, 11, 68. 18, 552; metaph. πίονες ὄγμοι, rich (*furrows*=) fields, h. Cer. 455. · 2) *the path* (of the heavenly bodies, h. 32, 11.

Ὀγχηστός, ὁ, a town in Bœotia, on the lake Copais, having a grove, sacred to Poseidôn; now the convent *Mazaraki*, 2, 506; from this the adv. Ὀγχηστόνδε, to O., h. Merc. 186.

ὄγχνη, ἡ. *a pear-tree*, Od. 11, 589. 2) *the pear itself*, *Od. 7, 120.

ὁδαῖος, η, ον (ὁδός), *belonging to the way*. τὰ ὁδαῖα, prop. that on account of which a journey is undertaken, according to the Schol. *merchandise* (V. *wares*), Od. 8, 163; and *provisions for a journey*, Od. 15, 445, Eustath. Better, according to Nitzsch, *the back freight*, or the wares received in exchange for those carried, hence ὦνος ὁδαίων, the gain in the back freight.

ὁδάξ, adv. (δάκνω, ὁδούς), *biting with the teeth*, λάζεσθαι γαῖαν, Il.; ἑλεῖν οὖδας, 11, 749. ὁδὰξ ἐν χείλεσσι φῦναι, to bite oneself in the lips, Od. 1, 381. 20, 268; see φύω.

ὅδε, ἥδε, τόδε, demonstr. pron. with the enclitic δέ, which strengthens its demonstrative force, in the dat. plur. Ep. τοῖςδεσσι and τοῖςδεσσιν, both parts being inflected; *this here, that there, this*. It indicates primar. the nearness of the subject. οὐκ ἔρανος τάδε γ' ἐστίν, Od. 1, 226; but is also often 1) To be referred to what immediately succeeds, Il. 1, 41. 504. 2) It also points emphatically to a near or remote place, esply in connexion with personal and other pronouns, and is then translated only by *here, there*. ὅδ᾽ ἐγώ, I here, Od. 16, 205. ἡμεῖς οἵδε, Od. 1, 76; δῶρα δ᾽ ἐγὼν ὅδε (εἰμί) πάντα παρασχεῖν, I am here, to present—to thee, Il. 19, 140. ἀνδρὶ ὅστις ὅδε κραίνει, who here governs, Il. 5, 175. νηῦς δέ μοι ἥδ᾽ ἕστηκεν ἐπ᾽ ἀγροῦ, there in the field, Od. 1, 185. Absol. use of single cases: 1) τῇδε, *here, there*, Il. 12, 345. Od. 6, 173. 2) τόδε, accus. *hither*, Il. 14, 298. Od. 1, 409. δεῦρο τόδε, Il. 1, 309. *b*) *therefore, for that reason*, Od. 20, 217. 23, 213.

ὁδεύω (ὁδός), *to go, to journey*, ἐπὶ νῆας, 11, 569.†

Ὀδίος, ὁ (Ion. for Ὀδίος = adj. ὅδιος), 1) leader of the Halizones, slain by Agamemnon, 2, 856. 5, 39. 2) a herald of the Greeks, 9, 170.

ὁδίτης, ου, ὁ (ὁδός), *a traveller, a wayfaring man*, also with ἄνθρωπος, 16, 263. Od. 13. 123.

ὀδμή, ἡ (ὄζω), Ion. and poet. *odour, fragrance*, Il., also *vapour, stench*, Od. 4, 406.

*ὁδοιπορίη, ἡ, *a journey, a way*, h. Merc. 85.

ὁδοιπόριος, ον (πόρος), *relating to a journey*. τὸ ὁδοιπόριον, recompense for a journey, passage-money for a voyage, Od. 15, 506.†

ὁδοιπόρος, ον (πόρος), *travelling*; subst. *a traveller, a travelling companion*, 24, 375.†

ὁδός, ἡ, Ion. οὐδός, Od. 17, 196;† *the way*. 1) Spoken of place: *a path, a street*, ὁδ. ἱππηλασίη, Il. 7, 340; ὁδ. λαοφόρος, 15, 682. πρὸ ὁδοῦ γενέσθαι, to go forwards, 4, 382. 2) Spoken of the act: *progress, travel, journeying*, 9, 626; also by sea, Od. ὁδὸν ἔρχεσθαι, generally, to go a journey, according to Voss, Il. 1, 151; (in distinction from ἶφι μάχεσθαι, Bothe: *embassy*.) It is not with the ancients to be explained by λόχος, but means any *journey* or *mission* (though by *implication*, it would usually have a warlike object).

ὀδούς, ὀδόντος, ὁ (ἔδω), *dens*; *a tooth*; in the boar, *a tusk*, 11, 416. Od. 19, 393; on ἕρκος ὀδόντων, see ἕρκος.

ὀδύνη, ἡ, *pain, pang*, *a*) Spoken of the body, always in the plur. 4, 117. 5, 397. 766, and often. *b*) Spoken of the soul: *grief, sadness*, Od. 2, 79; connected with γόοι, Od. 1, 242; sing. only ὀδύνη Ἡρακλῆος, pain about Heracles, Il. 15, 25.

ὀδυνήφατος, ον, poet. (φάω), *pain-destroying, pain-quieting, soothing, assuasive*, φάρμακα, *5, 401. 900. 11, 847.

ὀδύρομαι, depon. mid. partcp. aor. ὀδυράμενος, 24, 48. 1) Intrans. *to lament, to wail aloud, to complain, to grieve*, spoken of men; once of birds, 2, 315: often absol. and *a*) With gen. τινός, about any one, 22, 424. Od. 4, 104; ἀμφί τινα, Od. 10, 486. *b*) With dat. τινι, for any one, Od. 4, 740; ἀλλήλοισι, mutually to complain to each other, Il. 2, 290. 2) Trans. *to bewail, to lament for, to deplore*, with accus. of the person, 24, 740. Od. 1, 243; of the thing: νόστον, Od. 5, 153. 13, 219.

Ὀδυσσήϊος, ίη, ιον, Ep. for Ὀδύσσειος, relating to Odysseus (Ulysses), Od. 18, 353.

Ὀδυσσεύς, ὁ, Ep. Ὀδυσεύς, gen. Ὀδυσσῆος, Ὀδυσῆος, Ὀδυσσέος, and Æol. and Ep. Ὀδυσεύς, Od. 24, 398; dat. Ὀδυσῆϊ and Ὀδυσσεῖ, accus. Ὀδυσσῆα, Ὀδυσσέα and Ὀδυσῆ, Od. 19, 136; *Odysseus* (*Ulysses*, *Ulixes*), son of Laertes and Crimene, Od. 16, 117, seq., king of the Cephallenes, i. e. of the islands Ithaca, Same, Zacynthus, and of the neighbouring continent, husband of Penelope and father of Telemachus; he received this name from his grandfather Autolychus, because he came angry with many (ὀδυσσάμενος), Od. 19, 407. In him the poet presents to us a hero, who distinguished himself as much by spirit and bravery as by cunning, prudence, and steadfastness. He sailed to Troy with twelve ships, Il. 2, 631; and, after the destruction of this city, he made sail first with Menelaus to return to Ithaca, Od. 3, 162. He spent ten years in wanderings, so that he reached home in the twentieth year. His wanderings are described in the Odyssey. After he was landed in Ithaca by the Phæaces, Athênê communi-

O 6

(Ὀδύσσομαι.) 300 Οἰκεύς·

eated plans to him, by which he might punish the suitors, Od. 13, 287, seq. He goes clad as a beggar to Eumaeus, discovers himself to Telemachus, permits himself to be recognized by Penelope, and, in company with his son and the faithful herdsman, slays the suitors. He fights against the parents of the suitors who would revenge the death of their sons, until finally Athēnē established peace, Od. 24, 220, seq.

(ὀδύσσομαι), poet. depon. mid. pres. obsol. only in the aor. ὠδυσάμην, 3 plur. ὀδύσαντο, partcp. ὀδυσσάμενος, perf. ὀδώδυσμαι, with pres. signif. Od. 5, 423. 1) *to be angry, to be wroth, to hate*, τινί, Il. 6, 138. Od. 1, 62. 19, 275; ὀδυσσάμενος, Od. 19, 407, Passow would take in a pass. signif.: *hated, odious*, but it is act.: *angry, enraged*. 2) With accus. ὠδύσατο Ζῆνα, he excited the anger of Zeus, Ep. 6. 8. cf. Herm.

ὄδωδα, see ὄζω.

ὀδώδυσμαι, see ὀδύσσομαι.

ὄεσσι, see ὄἴς.

ὄζος, ὁ, *a knot* or *joint* in a tree, from which a branch springs; generally, 1) *a twig, a branch*. Il. Od. 2) Metaph. *a scion, descendant, a child, offspring*, Il. 2, 540. 12, 188.

ὄζω, perf. ὄδωδα, only 3 sing. pluperf. intrans. *to smell, to yield an odour*, ὀδμή ὀδώδει, the odour was diffused, from fumigation and from wine, *Od. 5, 60. 9, 210.

ὄθεν, adv. (ὅς), *whence, from which time, from which place*, also relating to a person instead of the relative, 2, 852. Od. 3, 319; also apparently, ὅπου, *from there, where*, Il. 2, 857.

ὄθι, adv. (poet. for οὗ), *where, in which place*, 13, 229; rarely with a gen. ὅθι αὐλῆς, where in the court, Od. 1, 425; also, *there, where*, and *b*) with the termination of a journey, *thither, where*, Od. 15, 101.

ὄθομαι, poet. depon. only pres. and imperf. *to trouble oneself about any thing, to be anxious about, to shun, to fear*, always with neg. absol. and(*a*) with gen. τινός, to trouble oneself about any one, 1, 181. 2) With infin. 15, 166; and with a partcp. οὐκ ὄθετ᾽ αἴσυλα ῥέζων, he shuns not to practise wickedness, *5, 403. Prob. only used in the pres., the imperf. use being doubtful, as e. g. 5, 403.

ὀθόνη, ἡ, *fine linen*, Od. 7, 107. *b*) *a veil* or *robe* made of it, Il. 3, 141. 18, 595.

ὄθριξ, ότριχος, ὁ, ἡ, poet. for ὁμόθριξ (θρίξ), *with similar hair (alike in their coat: of horses)*, 2, 765.†

Ὀθρυονεύς, ῆος, ὁ, a Trojan ally from Cabesus, 13, 363, seq.

οἱ, dat. sing. from οὗ.

οἴα, adv. sing. οἷος.

οἴγνυμι (οἴγω), aor. 1. Ep. ὦιξα and ᾦξα, 24, 457;† partcp. οἴξας, imperf. pass. ὠίγνυντο, *to open, to unlock*, with accus. θύρας, Il. or πύλας, τινί, to any one, 24, 457. οἶνον, to open the wine, Od. 3, 392.

οἶδα, οἶσθα, οἶδε, perf. *I know*, see ΕΙΔΩ.

οἰδάνω, Ep. for οἰδαίνω (οἶδος). 1) Act. *to swell*, i. e. to cause to swell, with accus. spoken of anger: νόον, to swell the heart, i. e. to excite, 9, 554. 2) Mid. *to swell*, οἰδάνεται κραδίη χόλῳ, *9, 646.

οἶδας, Ep. for οἶσθα, see ΕΙΔΩ.

οἰδέω, Ion. and Ep. for οἰδάω, imperf. 3 sing. ᾤδεε, intrans. *to swell, to puff up*, χρόα, in body, Od. 5, 455.†

Οἰδίπους, οδος, ὁ, Ep. gen. Οἰδιπόδαο, Il. 23, 679; (from οἰδεῖν and πούς, swollenfoot, because his feet were swollen when he was found, cf. Apd. 3, 5. 7), son of Laïus and Epicastē, father of Eteoclēs and Polynices. His father, on account of an oracle, caused him to be exposed at birth; a herdsman of the king of Corinth found him, and took him to his wife, who brought him up. Warned by the oracle at Delphi not to return to his native land, he proceeded to Thebes, slew unwittingly his father Laïus, solved the riddle of the Sphinx, and married his mother Epicaste. When the secret was discovered, Epicaste hung herself, but Œdipus reigned in Thebes and died there, Od. 11, 270. According to the tragic poets he put out his own eyes, and, being expelled from Thebes, fled to Attica. His funeral games are mentioned Il. 23, 679, seq.; see Ἐτεικάστη.

οἶδμα, ατος, τό, poet. *a swelling*, esply of the sea; *a roaring, a breaker*, 23, 230; θαλάσσης, h. Cer. 14; spoken of a river, *21, 234.

οἰέτης, ες, poet. (ἔτος), for ὁμοέτης, *of equal age*, βοῦς, 2, 765.†

οἰζυρός, ή, όν, poet. (οἰζύς), compar. οἰζυρώτερος, superl. οἰζυρώτατος, *lamentable, miserable, wretched, sad*, often as epith. of men, 1, 417. Od., and of inanimate objects: νύκτες, Od. 3, 95. 13, 337. πόλεμος, the miserable war, Il. 3, 112. (On the irreg. compar. and superl. see the Gram.)

οἰζύς, ύος, ἡ, poet. *misery, wretchedness, distress, suffering*, 6, 285. 14, 480; dat. contr. οἰζυῖ for οἰζύι, Od. 7, 270.

οἰζύω, poet. (οἰζύς), aor. 1 partcp. οἰζύσας, 1) *to lament, to utter lamentations, περί τινα*, about any one. 3, 408. 2) Trans. *to suffer, to endure*, κακά, Il. 14, 89; and absol. *to be wretched*, Od. 4, 152.

οἰήιον, τό, Ep. = οἴηξ, *a rudder*, Od. 9, 483: plur. 19, 43.

οἴηξ, ηκος, ὁ, Ep. for οἴαξ (οἴω), prop. *a handle*, esply of *a rudder, the rudder* or *helm* itself; in H. however οἴηκες, Il. 269,† *rings on the yoke*, through which the reins pass to the mouths of the animals.

οἴκαδε, adv. (from ad old root ΟΙΕ = οἶκος), *to the house, homewards, home*, Il. and Od.

οἰκεύς, ῆος, ὁ, Ion. (οἰκέω), *an inmate*

Οἰκέω. 301 **Οἶνος.**

of a family, 5, 413; as early as in the Od. *servant*, *slave*, 14, 4. 4, 245.
οἰκέω (οἶκος), fut. -ήσω, aor. 1 pass. 3 plur. ᾠκηθεν, Ep. for ᾠκήθησαν, 1) Intrans. *to dwell, to live*, mly with ἐν, 14, 116. Od. 9, 200. 2) Trans. *to inhabit*, with accus. ὑπωρείας, Il. 20. 218; hence pass. *a*) *to be inhabited*, οἰκέοιτο πόλις, 4. 18. *b*) *to be settled, to keep house*, as οἰκίζεσθαι: τριχθὰ ᾤκηθεν, they dwelt in three divisions, 2, 668.
οἰκίον, τό (dimin. only in form from οἶκος), *a house, an abode, a dwelling, a habitation*, always in the plur. mly spoken of men. *b*) Spoken of animals: *an abode, a nest*, of wasps, bees, 12, 168; of the eagle, 12, 221. *c*) Spoken of the underworld, 20, 64.
Ὀϊκλῆς, έος, ὁ, poet. Ὀϊκλείης, Od. 15, 244; accus. Ὀϊκλῆα, son of Amphiaraüs, father of Amphiaräus, Od. 15, 243. cf. Apd. 2, 6. 4.
οἴκοθεν, adv. (οἶκος), *from a house*, i. e. *a*) from a dwelling, 11, 632. *b*) from a man's own property, *7, 364. 391. 23, 556.
οἴκοθι, adv. (οἶκος), poet. = οἴκοι, *in the house, at home*, domi, 8, 513. Od. 3, 303.
οἴκοι, adv. (οἶκος), *to the house, to home*, 1, 113. Od. 1, 12, and often.
οἴκόνδε, adv. (οἶκος), poet. = οἴκαδε, *to one's house, home*. *a*) to the dwelling, 3, 390. *b*) to one's country, φεύγειν, 2, 158; ἄγειν), to conduct home, Od. 6, 159.
οἶκος, ὁ, 1) *a house*, i. e. *an abode, a dwelling* of any kind; the tent of Achilles, 24, 471; the cave of the Cyclops, Od. 9, 478. *b*) single parts of a house, *a chamber, a room*, Od. 1, 356, 362; also plur. οἶκοι, like aedes, spoken of a house, Od. 24, 417. 2) *house*, i. e. *household, family*, Od. 1, 232. 2, 64. 6, 181. Il. 15, 498.
οἰκτείρω (οἶκτος), aor. 1 ᾤκτειρα, *to pity, to commiserate, to grieve for*, τινά, 11, 814. πωλιόν τε κάρη, πολιόν τε γένειον, *24, 516. h. Cer. 137.
οἴκτιστος, η, ον, see οἰκτρός.
οἶκτος, ὁ (οἶ), *compassion; sorrow* (*for*), *commiseration, pity*, *Od. 2, 81. 24, 438.
οἰκτρός, ή, όν (οἶκτος), compar. οἰκτρότερος, superl. οἰκτρότατος, Od. 11, 421; oftener οἴκτιστος, *lamentable, deplorable, pitiable*, Il. and Od. neut. plur. οἴκτρα, as adv. ὀλοφύρεσθαι, to wail or complain piteously, Od. 4, 719; also superl. οἴκτιστα θανεῖν, Od. 22, 472.
οἰκωφελίη, ἡ (ὀφέλλω), *advantage for a house, domestic economy, domestic life*, Od. 14, 223.†
Ὀϊλεύς, ῆος, ὁ, king of Locris, husband of Eriopis, father of the Locrian Ajax, and of Medon, 2, 527. 727. 13, 694. 2) a Trojan charioteer, of Bianor, 11, 93.
Ὀϊλιάδης, ου, ὁ, son of Oïleus = Ajax, 12, 365.
οἶμα, ατος, τό, poet. (οἴω), *an assault*,

an attack, 16, 752; spoken of lions, and plur. of the eagle, *21, 252.
οἰμάω, poet. (οἶμα), aor. 1 οἴμησε, *to assault, to rush upon*, spoken of an attack, 22, 308. Od. 24, 538; of the hawk, μετὰ πέλειαν, to pounce upon a dove, Il. 22, 140.
οἴμη, ἡ = οἶμος, poet. prop. *a way, a path*, metaph. spoken of the course which a narration takes; hence, *a narrative, a lay, a song*, *Od. 8, 74. †81. 22, 347.
οἶμος, ὁ, poet. (οἴω = φέρω), *a way, a path*, metaph. *a*) *a strip*, οἶμοι κυάνοιο, strips of steel (upon the shield), 11, 24.† *b*) *the course of a song, an air, a melody*, h. Merc. 450.
οἰμωγή. ἡ (οἰμώζω), *lamentation, wailing, a cry of distress*, as of persons dying, 4, 450. Od. 20, 353.
οἰμώζω (οἴμοι), aor. 1 ᾤμωξα, partcp. οἰμώξας, prop. to cry οἴμοι (ah me); hence, *to lament, to wail, to howl*, often in the partcp. aor. with κάππεσεν, πέσεν, 5, 68. Od. 18, 398.
Οἰνείδης, ου, ὁ, son of Oeneus = Tydeus, 5, 813.
Οἰνεύς, ῆος, ὁ (the vintner, from οἶνος), son of Portheus, king of Calydon, husband of Althaea, father of Tydeus, Meleager, etc. 14, 117. Bellerophon was his table-friend, 6, 215. He once forgot Artemis in an offering of first-fruits; incensed thereat, she sent a wild boar upon him as a punishment, 9, 529, seq.
οἰνίζομαι, only mid. (οἶνος), imperf. without augm. *to procure wine for oneself, to purchase wine*, χαλκῷ, for brass, 7, 472; οἶνον, to fetch wine, *8, 506. 546. (The act. is not found in H.)
οἰνοβαρέω, Ep. οἰνοβαρείων, *to be heavy, or drunken with wine*, only partcp pres. in the Ep. form, *Od. 9, 374. 21, 304.
οἰνοβαρής, ές, poet. (βάρος), *heavy with wine, intoxicated, drunken with wine*, 1, 225.†
Οἰνόμαος, ὁ (*Vindemius*, Herm.), 1) an Aetolian, 5, 706. 2) a Trojan, slain by Idomeneus, 12. 140.
οἰνόπεδος, ον (πέδον), *having vineyards, producing wine, abounding in wine*, ἀλωή, Od. 1, 193. 11, 193; neut subst. τὸ οἰνόπεδον, *a vineyard*, Il. 9, 579.
Οἰνοπίδης, ου, ὁ, son of Oenopion = Helenus, 5, 707.
οἰνοπληθής, ές, poet. (πλῆθος), *full of wine, abounding in wine*, Συρίη, Od. 15, 406.†
οἰνοποτάζω, poet. for οἰνοποτέω (πότης), *to drink wine*, 20. 84. Od. 6, 309.
οἰνοποτήρ, ῆρος ὁ *wine-drinker, a winebibber*, Od. 8, 456.†
οἶνος, ὁ, *wine*; the Homeric heroes were wont to drink it mingled with water; the red wine seems to have been most common (μέλας, ἐρυθρός), Od. 12, 19. No other wine is mentioned in H. Andromache sprinkled with wine the wheat given as food to the ho.ses, Il. 8,

Οἰνοχοεύω. 302 Οἶος.

186; cf. Columella de Re Rust. VI. c. 30. Wine was preserved in jars (ἀμφιφορεῖς, πίθοι), Od. 2, 290. 340; or in skin bottles (ἀσκοί), Il. 3, 247.

οἰνοχοεύω, poet. οἰνοχοέω (οἰνοχόος), *to pour out wine*, only in the pres. 2, 127; elliptically, οἰνοχοεύει, sc. ὁ οἰνοχόος, Od. 21. 142.

οἰνοχοέω (οἰνοχόος), imperf. ᾠνοχόει and Ep. ἐῳνοχόει, 4, 3; aor. 1 infin. οἰνοχοῆσαι, *to pour out wine, to be cupbearer*, τινί, 1, 598. Od. 4, 233; with accus. νέκταρ, Il. 4, 3.

οἰνοχόος, ὁ (χέω), *a wine-pourer, a cup-bearer*, 2, 128. Od. 9, 10.

οἶνοψ, οπος, ὁ, ἡ, poet. (ὄψ), looking like wine, *wine-coloured*, i. e. dark-red, black, see οἶνος, mly an epith. of the agitated sea, like πορφύρεος, the dark, red-black sea, because in a violent agitation of the waves it assumes a dark-red appearance, see πορφύρω, 1, 350. 5, 771. 1, 183. *b*) an epith. of oxen: *dark-red, blackish* (Voss, dark), 13, 703.

Οἶνοψ, οπος, ὁ, ἡ, a noble of Ithaca, father of Leodes, Od. 21, 144.

οἰνόω (οἶνος), partcp. aor. pass. οἰνωθείς, *to intoxicate with wine*, pass. *to be intoxicated, drunken*, *Od. 16, 292. 19, 11.

οἴξασα, partcp. aor. 1 οἴγνυμι.

οἶο, Ep. for οὗ (see ὅς), *his*.

οἰόθεν, adv. poet. (οἶος), *from one side, alone*; always οἰόθεν οἶος, prop. alone from one side, i. e. *entirely alone*, *7, 39. 226.

οἴομαι, Ep. always in the pres. indic. ὀίομαι, depon. (ῑ), more frequently in the 1 sing. οἴω and ὀίω, 3 optat. pres. οἴοιτο, Od. 17, 580; imperf. ὠϊόμην, aor. 1 ὀϊσάμην, Ep. for ὠϊσ., aor. pass. ὠϊσθην only Od. 4, 453. 16, 475; partcp. ὀϊσθείς only Il. 9, 453; prim. signif. *to be of opinion, to believe, to think*. *a*) In reference to the future: *to suppose, to conjecture, to expect*, and according as it is good or bad, *to hope, to fear, to suspect*. *b*) *to intend, to purpose*, with infin. 13,-263; strengthened by θυμῷ, κατὰ θυμόν and θυμὸς ὀΐεταί μοι, Od. 9, 213. The construction is various: 1) Sometimes absolute, Il. 1, 561; mly with accus. and infin. according to the sense. *a*) The pres. with something present, 13. 263. Od. 1, 323; but mly with future things. Il. 5, 894. 12, 73. Od. 5, 290. *b*) The aor. with the past: σ᾽ ὀΐω, I believe that thou hast given the nod, Il. 1, 558. 10, 551. Od. 19, 569. *c*) Most frequently with infin. fut. In all these cases, the subject of the infin. is often omitted when it may be easily supplied. ὀΐσατο θεὸν εἶναι, he believed it was a god, Od. 1, 323. προΐσεσθαι ὀΐω, sc. αὐτούς, I think they will be wounded, Il. 12, 66 [cf. Od. 11, 101. 12, 212, and see Nitzsch]. 2) With the simple infin. where the main verb and the infin. have the same subject [κιχήσεσθαί σε ὀΐω, I think that I shall overtake thee], Il. 6, 341. Od. 8, 180. 3)

Trans. with accus. *to be of opinion, to believe*, τί, Od. 3, 255. 13, 427; κῆρας to expect the Fates, Il. 13, 283. 4) Often absol. introduced in the first pers. as a parenthesis, *I believe, I suppose*, to intimate a modest doubt. ἐν πρώτοισιν, ὀΐω, κείσεται, he will lie, I suppose, amongst the first, 8, 536. 13, 153. Od. 16, 309. 5) Once impersonal: ὀΐεταί μοι ἀνὰ θυμόν, it seems to me in my mind. Od. 19, 312. (ι is always long, only ὀΐω is sometimes short, see Spitzn. Pros. § 52. 2. *a*.)

οἶον, neut. sing. see οἷος.

οἰοπόλος, ον, poet. (πέλομαι), prop. being solitary; *lonely, solitary*, spoken of places, 13, 473. Od. 11, 574.

*οἰοπόλος, ον (πέλομαι), pasturing sheep, h. Merc. 314.

οἶος, οἴη, οἶον, poet. 1) *alone, forsaken*; strengthened, εἷς οἶος, one alone. δύ᾽ οἴω, two alone. οὐκ οἴη, 3, 143. *b*) With gen. τῶν οἶος, left by these, 11, 693; or with prep. ἀπό τινος, 9, 438. Od. 21, 364. 2) *single*, i. e. *excellent, chief*, 24. 499. οἶω, adv. *once*, according to Eustath. for οἴω μα, *me alone*. 9, 355.

οἷος, οἴη, οἶον (ὅς, ἥ, ὄν), *of what quality, what sort of, what a*, as, the relat. to the demonstrative τοῖος. οἷος ἀριστήν, what a man in bravery, 13, 275. Often it can only be translated by *how*. οἷος καλός τε μέγας τε, how beautiful and large, 21, 108. It stands, 1) In independent sentences, to express astonishment at any thing great and extraordinary (good or bad), and esply in exclamations. οἷον δὴ τὸν μῦθον ἐνέσπης ἀγορεῦσαι, what a word is this that thou hast brought thyself to utter! (Thiersch, Gram. § 317. 5); esply, often in the neut. οἷον, *how*, 5, 601. Od. 1, 32. 2) More frequently in dependent sentences, to indicate the same quality, with reference to a definite object: *a*) After a preceding τοῖος, Il. 18, 105. Od. 1, 371; and without it, Il. 4. 264. 16, 557. 22, 317. *b*) It often stands in reference to an entire sentence, as if for ὅτι τοῖος. οἷ᾽ ἀγορεύεις, οἷα μ᾽ ἔοργας, *pro iis qua dixisti, fecisti*. 18, 95. Od. 4, 611. οἷον (i. e. ὅτι τοῖον) ἔειπεν. Il. 17, 173. οἷος ἐκείνου θυμὸς ὑπέρβιος, οὐκ ἐθέλησει, etc. so insolent is his spirit, he will not wish, etc. (*quæ ejus est atrocitas*), 18, 262. Od. 15, 212. *c*) In connexion with other particles: οἷος δή, as indeed. οἷός περ, just as. οἷός τε, as perchance (τέ often only augments the connecting force of the relative). 3) οἷον with the infin. *to be of the kind*, i. e. *to be capable, to be able, to be in a condition to*. οἷος Ὀδυσσεὺς ἔσκεν, ἀρὴν ἀπὸ οἴκου ἀμῦναι, Odysseus (Ulysses) was able to repel the curse from his house, Od. 2. 59. cf. v. 272; and in like manner οἴκ τε, Od. 19, 160. 21, 117. 4) The neut. sing. and plur. οἷον and οἷα as adv. 1) *how*, with adj. Il, 24, 419; with verb sing. 13, 633. Od. 1, 32. 2) *just as, like*

Οἱός. 303 Ὀκτωκαιδέκατος.

ας, in comparisons, Od. 3, 73. 9, 128. 3) as indeed, because indeed, since indeed, cf. 2, b. Il. 17, 587. Od. 14, 392. (The first syllable is sometimes used as short, Il. 13, 275. Od. 7, 312.)

οἰός and οἶος, see ὄἴς.

οἰοχίτων, ωνος, ὁ, ἡ, poet. (χιτών), simply in the tunic (clad thus sparely, Cp.), Od. 16, 489.†

οἰόω (οἶος), only aor. pass. Ep. οἰώθη, to leave alone; pass. to be left alone, to remain alone, *6, 1. 11, 401.

ὄἴς, ὁ, ἡ, Ion. for οἶς, gen. ὄϊος, οἰός, accus. ὄϊν. plur. gen. ὄϊων, οἰῶν, dat. ὀΐεσσιν, οἴεσσιν, ὄεσσιν, accus. ὄϊς, contr. for ὄϊας, a sheep; ὁ ὄϊς, the ram, also ὄἴς ἄρσην, 12, 451.

ὀΐσατο, Ep. see ὀίομαι.

οἶσε, οἰσέμεν, οἰσέμεναι, see φέρω.

οἶσθα, 2 sing. of οἶδα, see ΕΙΔΩ.

ὀΐσθεις, see ὀίομαι.

ὀϊστεύω, poet. (ὀϊστός) aor. 1 ὀΐστευσα, to shoot with an arrow; τινός, at any one, 4, 100; often absol. with βάλλειν, 4, 196; τόξῳ, with the bow, Od. 12, 84.

ὀϊστός, ὁ, Ep. for οἰστός (οἴω), an arrow; it consisted of wood or reed; had a metallic point with barbs, 4, 139. cf. 151; sometimes three-pointed, 5, 393. Poisoned arrows are also mentioned, Od. 1, 261.

οἶστρος, ὁ, a gad-fly, œstrus, Od. 22, 300.†

οἰσύϊνος, η, ον (οἰσύα), willow, osier, made of willow, Od. 5, 256.†

οἴσω, see φέρω.

οἶτος, ὁ, Ep. (οἴω = φέρω, as fors from fero), lot, destiny, fate, mly in a bad signif.; misfortune, death, for the most part κακὸς οἶτος, 3, 417. 8, 554; without κακός, 9, 563. Od. 8, 489.

Οἴτυλος, ἡ, a town in Laconia, on the coast, now Vitylo, 2, 385; ὁ Οἴτ., Strab.

Οἰχαλίη, ἡ, a town in Thessaly on the Pēneius, the residence of Eurytus, according to 2, 730. 596. cf. Εὔρυτος. According to later tradition, Heracles destroyed it, because he refused him his daughter Iole, cf. O. Müller, Dorians, vol. 1. 2) a city in Messenia, called at a later day Carnesion, to which is also transferred the story of Eurytus. Thus it appears, Od. 8, 214. cf. Paus. 4, 2. 1. Strab. understood also this, Il. 2, 596. 3) At a still later day, the story of Eurytus was transferred also to Œchalia in Eubœa, from which Οἰχαλίηθεν, from Œch., 2, 596; from this the subst. Οἰχαλιεύς, ἦος, ὁ, the Œchalian, 2, 596.

οἰχνέω, poet. for οἴχομαι, Ion. iterat. imperf. οἴχνεσκον, 5, 790; to go, to come, 3 plur. pres. οἰχνεῦσιν, Od. 3, 322.

οἴχομαι, depon. mid. imperf. ᾠχόμην, only pres. and imperf. prop. to be away, rarely, to go away, to depart, and the latter mostly in the imperf., also simply to go, to come. 1) Spoken of animate beings: with prep. ἐς, ἐπί, κατά, μετά, with accus.; chiefly as an euphemism for to die. οἴχεται ἐς Ἀΐδαο [sc. δῶμα], he has departed to Hades, 22, 213. 2) Of inanimate things: of storms and missiles, to fly, to travel, 1, 53. 13, 505. Od. 20, 64. 3) Of other things: πῇ σοι μένος οἴχεται, where is thy courage gone, Il. 5, 472. ποῦ τοι ἀπειλαὶ οἴχονται, where are thy threats gone, 13, 220. cf. 24, 201. Often it is connected with a partcp., when it can be translated by away. οἴχεται φεύγων, he flew away, Od. 8, 356. οἴχεται προφέρουσα, the tempest bore away, Il. 6, 346; ἀνάγων, 13, 627. h. Cer. 74.

οἴω and οἰω, Ep. for ὀίομαι, q. v.

οἰωνιστής, οῦ, ὁ (οἰωνίζομαι), a diviner by birds, one who presages the future by the voice or the flight of birds, an augur, 13, 70; as adj. skilled in augury by birds, *2, 858.

οἰωνοπόλος, ον (πολέω), one who concerns himself about the ominous flight of birds; subst. an augur, *1, 69. 6, 76; see οἰωνός.

οἰωνός, ὁ (οἶος), 1) Prop. a bird which flies by itself, esply a bird of prey, as an eagle, a vulture, a hawk, 11, 453. Od. 16, 216. These were sacred birds, whose flight was especially observed, in order to predict the prosperous or disastrous issue of an undertaking. The flight to the right, i. e. to the east, indicated prosperity; to the left, i. e. to the west, on the other hand, adversity, Il. 12, 239. Other circumstances also, as the voice, were ominous, 12, 200; hence 2) Generally, an omen, an augury. εἷς οἰωνὸς ἄριστος, ἀμύνεσθαι, etc., one omen is the best, to fight for the country, 12, 243; see Nitzsch ad Od. 2, 146.

ὀκνέω, Ep. ὀκνείω, 5, 255: to delay, to loiter, to be slow, to hesitate, with infin. *20, 155.

ὄκνος, ὁ (from ἔχω), prop. delay, slowness, dilatoriness, spoken esply of bodily exhaustion; slothfulness, 5, 817. ὄκνῳ εἴκων, evercome by slothfulness, *10, 122.

ὀκριάω, poet. (ὄκρις), prop. to make sharp, metaph. to irritate; pass. to be irritated or made angry: 3 plur. imperf. Ep. ὀκριόωντο for ὀκριῶντο, Od. 18, 33.†

ὀκριόεις, εσσα, εν, poet. (ὄκρις=ἄκη), having several points, pointed, ragged, sharp-pointed; χερμάδιον, μάρμαρος, 4, 518. 12, 380. Od. 9, 499. (In other places now ὀκρυόεις.)

ὀκριόωντο, see ὀκριάω.

ὀκρυόεις, εσσα, εν, poet. (for κρυόεις with o prosthetic, from κρύος), cold, making cold; metaph. awful, horrible. dreadful, κύων, 6, 344; (Helen) and πόλεμος, *9, 64.

ὀκτάκνημος, ον (κνήμη), having eight spokes, κύκλα, 5, 723.†

*ὀκτάπους, ποδος (πούς), eight-footed, Batr. 290.

ὀκτώ, indeclin. eight, Il. and Od. often

ὀκτωκαιδέκατος, η, ον, the eighteenth.

Ὀλβ.οδαίμων. 304 **Ὀλοοίτροχος.**

only ὀκτωκαιδεκάτῃ, sc. ἡμέρῃ, *Od. 5, 297. 7, 268.

ὀλβιοδαίμων, ονος, ὁ, ἡ, poet. (δαίμων), having a happy destiny, *happy, fortunate, blessed*, 3, 182.

ὄλβιος, η. ον, poet. (ὄλβος), *happy, fortunate, blessed*, always spoken of external blessings; hence *rich, wealthy,* spoken of persons. δῶρα ὄλβια ποιεῖν, to make happy presents, i. e. to bless with prosperity, Od. 13, 42. Neut. plur. as subst. ὄλβια δοῦναι, to bestow blessings, Od. 8, 413. 7, 148. h. Ap. 466.

ὄλβος, ὁ (akin to ὄφελος), *prosperity, a happy condition, fortune, blessing,* spoken chiefly of external blessings, 16, 596. Od. 14, 206; and generally, *happiness, bliss,* Od. 3, 208. 4, 208.

ὀλέεσθαι, see ὄλλυμι.
ὀλέεσκε, see ὄλλυμι.

ὀλέθριος, ον (ὄλεθρος), *destructive, bringing destruction, ruinous.* ὀλ. ἦμαρ, the day of destruction, *19, 294. 499.

ὄλεθρος, ὁ (ὄλλυμι), *destruction, misfortune, ruin, death;* often ὀλέθρου πείρατα, the bounds of death, or according to Eustath. a periphrasis for τέλειος ὄλεθρος, complete destruction, Il. and Od. ὄλεθρος ψυχῆς, the destruction of life (Voss, the most perilous place), Il. 22, 325. λυγρὸν ὄλεθρον, annexed by way of apposition in the accus.: to sad destruction, 24, 735. Rost, Gram. p. 497. D. 4.

ὀλεῖται, see ὄλλυμι.

ὀλέκω, Ep. form of ὄλλυμι from the perf. ὀλώλεκα. only pres. and imperf. 1) Act. *to destroy, to kill, to slay,* τί, 5, 712. Od. 22, 305. 2) Mid. *to perish, to die,* Il. 1, 10. 10, 17.

ὀλέσαι, ὀλέσας, see ὄλλυμι.

ὀλέσσαι, ὀλέσσας, Ep. for ὀλέσαι, ὀλέσας, see ὄλλυμι.

*ὀλέτειρα, ἡ (ὀλετήρ), *a destroyer;* μυῶν, a mouse-trap, Batr. 117.

ὀλετήρ, ἦρος. ὁ, poet. (ὄλλυμι), *a destroyer, a murderer,* 18, 114.†

ὀλέω, obsol. root of several tenses of ὄλλυμι.

ὀλιγηπελέω (πέλομαι), *to be weak, to be powerless, feeble,* only partcp. pres. 15, 24. 246. Od. 5, 457.

ὀλιγηπελίη, ἡ, *weakness, feebleness,* Od. 5, 468.†

ὀλίγιστος, η, ον, see ὀλίγος.

ὀλιγοδρανέω (δραίνω, δράω), to be able to du little, *to be weak, feeble* = ὀλιγηπελέω, only partcp. pres. *15, 146. 16, 843. 22, 337.

ὀλίγος, η, ον, irreg. superl. ὀλίγιστος, η, ον, 1) *little,* prim. spoken of number, in opposition to πολύς; often of space: χῶρος, 10, 161; of time: *short,* 19, 157. 2) Spoken of size: *small,* 2, 529. Od. 9, 515. 10, 94. The neut. sing ὀλίγον as adv. *little, a little, very little,* Il. 5. 800. 11, 391. οὐδ᾽ ὀλίγον, not an instant, Batr. 192; the gen. ὀλίγου, nearly, almost (elsewhere ὀλίγου δεῖν), Od. 14, 37. The

superl. Il. 19, 223; always *the least.* As a compar. μείων used.

Ὀλιζών, ῶνος, ἡ (adj. ὀλίζων, small), a town in Magnesia (Thessaly), below Melibœa, 2, 717.

ὀλισθάνω, aor. 2 ὄλισθον, Ep. for ὤλισθον, *to slip, to slide, to fall,* 23, 774. ἐκ δέ οἱ ἦπαρ ὄλισθεν, the liver fell from him, 20, 470.

ὄλλυμι (root ΟΛΩ), fut. ὀλέσω, Ep. σσ, aor. ὤλεσα, Ep. ὄλεσα and σσ, mid. fut. ὀλοῦμαι, infin. Ep. ὀλέεσθαι, aor. 2 ὠλόμην, Ep. ὀλόμην. perf. 2 ὄλωλα, Ep. iterative imperf. ὀλέεσκεν from ὀλέω, 19, 135.† According to others, aor. 2 act. Buttm. prefers the reading ὀλέεσκεν, see Ausf. Gram. under ὄλλυμι. (The partcp. aor. 2 mid. ὀλόμενος, Ep. οὐλόμενος, is used as an adj.) I) Act. 1) *to destroy, to overthrow, to annihilate, to kill,* with accus. of animate and inanimate objects: νῆας, πόλιν, 8. 498: ὀδμήν, to dissipate the smell.Od. 4, 446 2) *to lose,* λαόν, Il. 2, 115; θυμόν, ἦτορ, μένος, often. II) Mid. *to perish, to die, to be undone;* ὑπό τινι, by any one or thing, Od. 3, 235; with accus. of the manner, κακὸν οἶτον ὀλέσθαι, to die a miserable death, Il. 3, 417; or with dat. ὀλέθρῳ ἀδευκεῖ, Od. 4, 489. νῦν ὤλετο πᾶσα κατ᾽ ἄκρης. Ἴλιος. now was all Ilium utterly ruined. Il. 13, 772. 2) *to be lost.* ὤλετο κλέος, νόστος. νόστιμον ἦμαρ, 2, 325. 9, 413. Od. l. 168. The perf. 2 ὄλωλα, I am lost. ruined, Il. 4, 164. Od. 3, 89. 4, 318.

ὄλμος, ὁ (ἔλω, εἴλω), origin. *a round stone, a boulder;* thus Hesych. Il. 11, 147; according to others, *a mortar* (from ὅλω). ὅλμον δ᾽ ὣς (sc. αὐτὸν) ἔσσευε κυλίδεσθαι (he made him (the dead body) roll round like a mortar, Voss), cf. Buttm. Lex.

*ὀλοιός, όν, Ep. for ὀλοός, *destructive,* h. Ven. 225.†

ὀλολυγή, ἡ (ὀλολύζω), prop. a loud cry. *a loud voice of women,* chiefly *the suppliant cry of women* imploring a divinity. 6, 301;† also a loud song, *a shout of joy,* h. Ven. 19.

ὀλολύζω (λύζω), aor. 1 ὠλόλυξα, always with augm. *to raise the voice aloud to the gods,* prop. used of women at a sacrifice: *to supplicate aloud [up-end their suppliant wailings to the skies,* Cp.], Od. 3, 450. According to Aineis, raised a loud cry when Thrasymêdes struck the heifer, 4, 767. b) Also spoken of a cry of joy: *to shout for joy,* Od. 22, 408. 411. h. Ap. 118. [According to Eustath. it was a sacred custom to cry ὀλολοῖ when the victim was slain, in order thereby to supplicate an omen, Hdt. 4. 189.) *Od.

ὀλόμην, Ep. for ὠλόμην, see ὄλλυμι.

ὀλοοίτροχος, Ep. for ὀλοίτρ. ed. Woll. or ὀλοοίτρ, ed. Spitzner, Il. 13, 137; *a rock or round stone,* such as, according to Hdt. 8, 52, were rolled upon the enemy. Prob. according to Buttm., Lex. p. 430, with App. Etym. M. from ὄλοος and τρέχω, ruin-roller (Voss, a crushing

Ὀλοός.

tone). The other form, with the spiritus asper, is supposed to be derived from ἴλος, whole, a completely round stone; a *rolling-stone*. This form is adopted by Spitzner after Cod. Ven., and Herod. 1, 92. 8. 52, sanctions it, cf. Nitzsch ad Od. 1, 52.

ὀλοός, ή, όν (ὀλῶ, ὄλλυμι), compar. ὀλοώτερος, ὀλοώτατος, Ep. form ὀλοιός, οὔλιος, *destructive, ruinous, mischievous, cruel*. spoken of persons: Κήρ, Μοῖρα, θεῶν ὀλοώτατος, of Apollo, 22, 15: of Zeus, ὀλοώτερος Od. 20, 201. *b*) Of things: ὄλεμος, λύσσα, πῦρ. Il. 3, 133. 9, 305. 13, 29. (We must remark ὀλοώτατος ὀδμή, Od. 4, 422, as fem., and ὀλοῇσιν, with εngthened ο, Il. 1, 342.) ὀλοὰ φρονέων, 6, 701.

Ὀλοοσσών, όνος, ἡ, a town in Perrhæbia (Thessaly), on the Eurotas, later Ἔλασσον, now *Alassona*, 2, 739.

ὀλοόφρων, ονος, ὁ, ἡ, Ep. (ὀλοός, φρήν), *plotting destruction, savage, deadly-minded* (*fall*, Cp.), epith. of the serpent, the lion, and the boar, 2, 723. 15, 630. 17, 21. *b*) Spoken of persons: *devising mischief* (*evil-minded, ill-disposed*), epith. of Atlas, Æëtês, Minos, Od. 1, 52. 10, 137. 1, 322. Thus Voss and Nitzsch translate; Wolf and Spitzner on the contrary take it with Eustath. and App. in the Od. for τῶν ὅλων φροντιστικός, *all-wise*, see Spitzner on Köppens Anm. ad Il. 5, 630. Passow, on the other hand, justly remarks, that in the earliest language any one might be denominated *evil-minded*, in so far as by superior power or intelligence he could become dangerous to others. [Herm. Opusc. VII. p. 250: Ut Æetes ut Minos ὀλοόφρονες, quod est *perniciosa meditati*, ab Homero appellantur, sic etiam Atlas, *fragilem truci committens pelago ratem*.]

ὀλοφυδνός, ή, όν, poet. (ὀλοφύρομαι), *railing, plaintive, complaining*, ἔπος, 5, 83. Od. 19, 362.

ὀλοφύρομαι, depon. mid. aor. Ep. ὀλοφυράμην, 1) Intrans. *to complain, to wail. to lament, to be troubled*, often absol. in partcp. 5, 871; with infin. πῶς ὀλοφύρεαι ἄλκιμος εἶναι, how lamentest thou to be brave, Od. 22, 232. *b*) With τινός, *to complain about any one, to compassionate* any one, Il. 8, 33. 202. 6, 17. 2) Trans. with accus. *to lament, to bewail, to deplore* any one, 8, 245. 7, 648; *to pity* any one, Od. 4, 364. 10, 57; (it is derived from ὀλοός.)

ὀλοφώϊος, ον, Ep. *destructive, mischievous, frightful*, only in the neut. plur. ὀλοφ. δήνεα, pernicious artifices, Od. 10, 289; and ὀλοφώϊα without a subst. *artifices*, according to the Schol. Od. 4, 410; ὀλοφώϊα εἰδώς, devising pernicious things, Od. 4, 460. 17, 248; (prob. from ὀλοός and ΦΑΩ = φαίνω, showing destruction; not from ὄλω and φώς, man-destroying.)

Ὀλυμπιάς, άδος, ἡ, pecul. fem. of

Ὁμαρτέω.

Ὀλύμπιος, *Olympian*, epith. of the Muses, 2, 491. h. Merc. 450.

Ὀλύμπιος, η, ον, *Olympian, dwelling in Olympus*, epith. of the gods, esply of Zeus, who is also called Ὀλύμπιος alone, 2, 309. Od. 1, 60. Ὀλύμπια δώματα, the dwellings of the gods in Olympus, Il. 1, 18.

Ὄλυμπος, ὁ, poet. and Ion. Οὔλυμπος, prop. a lofty mountain on the border of Thessaly and Macedonia, with several snow-capped peaks, now *Elimbo*, cf. 14, 225. Od. 11, 315. According to the popular belief, which the poet followed, Olympus was the abode of the gods, Il. 2, 30. 5, 360. In the Iliad, however, it is expressly distinguished from the broad heavens (οὐρανός), 5, 867. 868. 15, 192. Upon the highest point is the palace of Zeus, where the gods assemble in council, 1, 498. 8, 3. 44. Od. 1, 27. In the neighbourhood, upon the inferior peaks, the other gods have their palaces, Il. 11, 76. 18, 186. Od. 3, 377. The notion of the mountain is often confounded with the heavenly residence of the gods, since its heights lifted themselves into heaven, high above the clouds, cf. Il. 8, 18—26; the description of it, Od. 6, 42—46. Still Olympus as a mountain always remains the residence of the gods; from it the gods descend to earth, and to it they return, Il. 14, 225. Od. 1, 103. 6, 41. Voss supposes, without necessity, that the highest point pierces through an opening, into the brazen vault of heaven, cf. Mythol. Br. I. p. 170. Völcker, Hom. Geogr. p. 4, seq.

ὄλυρα, ἡ, only plur. a kind of grain, used as food for horses, and mentioned in connexion with barley, *5, 196. 8, 564; according to Schneider, perhaps *triticum monococcum*, Linn., *St. Peter's corn*; or, according to Sprengel, Geschich. Botan. *triticum spelta, spelt*, Od. 4, 41; ζειά is mentioned in its stead.

ὄλμλα, see ὄλλυμι.

ὁμαδέω. Ep. (ὅμαδος), aor. 1 ὁμάδησα, without augm. *to make a noise or tumult*, always spoken of the suitors, *Od. 1, 365. 4, 768. 17, 360.

ὅμαδος, ὁ, poet. (ὁμός), *noise, uproar, tumult, disturbance*, spoken of a tumultuous assemblage, 2, 96. 9, 573. 10, 13. Od. 10, 550 (where it is distinguished from δοῦπος). metaph. the *roaring* of a tempest, Il. 13, 797. 2) a *crowd itself, a throng*, 7, 3. 7. 15, 689.

ὁμαλός, ή, όν (ὁμός), *like*, even, smooth, Od. 9, 327.†

ὁμαρτέω, poet. (ὁμός, ἀρτάω), aor. optat. ὁμαρτήσειεν, partcp. aor. ὁμαρτήσας, imperf. ὁμαρτήτην, Ion. for ὁμαρτείτην, *to coincide* in a thing, *to do the same thing*, 12, 400. 13, 584. 2) Esply *to go together*, 24, 438; in the partcp. for the adv. ἁμαρτῇ, is common, together, Od. 21, 188; *to be equally swift*, spoken of the hawk, Od. 13. 87. [According to Ameis, this verb never governs the accus., and

"Ομβρος. 306 'Ομοκλάω.

the interpunction in Il. 12, 400, in Wolf and Spitzner after ὄμαρτ. is false, and should be a comma.]

ὄμβρος, ὁ, imber, rain, a shower of rain, esply a thunder-shower, a tempest of rain, 5, 91. Od. 4, 566. 2) of snow, Il. 12, 286.

ὀμεῖται, see ὄμνυμι.

ὀμηγερής, ἐς (ἀγείρω), collected together, assembled, mly ὀμηγερέες ἐγένοντο, 1, 57. Od. 8, 24.

ὀμηγυρίζομαι, depon. mid. (ὀμήγυρις), aor. infin. ὀμηγυρίσασθαι, to collect, τινὰ εἰς ἀγορήν, Od. 16, 376.†

ὀμήγυρις, ιος, ἡ (ἄγυρις), poet. assembly, 20, 142.† h. Ap. 167.

ὀμηλικίη, ἡ (ὀμῆλιξ), equal age, the same age, 20, 465; in H. for the most part the abstract for the concrete as collect. [cf. the English acquaintance], men of equal age: esply youthful friends, companions in years, coeval, 3, 175. 13, 431. 485. Od. 3, 364; also spoken of an individual: an equal in age, Od. 3, 49. 22, 290; and generally contemporaries, Od. 2, 158.

ὀμῆλιξ, ικος, ὁ, ἡ (ἧλιξ), of equal age, of the same age, coeval, often subst. πάντες ὀμήλικες, all of thy age [Cp.], 9, 54. Od. 15, 197. 16, 419.

ὀμηρέω (ὅμηρος), aor. ὠμήρησα, to meet, to go together, τινί, with any one, Od. 16, 468.

ὀμιλαδόν, adv. poet. (ὅμιλος), by troops, in crowds, μάχεσθαι, *12, 3. 17, 730.

ὁμιλέω (ὅμιλος), aor. 1 ὡμίλησα, 1) to be together or in company, to have intercourse, to hold converse with any one, τινί, 1, 261; in a good and bad signif. esply amongst a multitude: μετά, ἐνί, παρά, with dat. 5, 86. 834. 18, 194. Od. 18, 383; περί τινα, to collect about any one, Il. 16, 641. 2) Esply in a hostile signif. to meet in conflict, to come to close fight, to fight, τινί, 11, 523. Od. 1, 265; absol. Il. 19, 158.

ὅμιλος ὁ (ὁμου—ἴλη). prop. a dense troop, an assembly, a multitude, collected for feasting or for sport, Od. 1, 225. 18. 603. 23, 651. 2) Esply in the Il. a warlike troop; then the press, the throng, the tumult of battle, often with gen. ἀνδρῶν, Τρώων, and ἵππων, Il. 10, 338. 433. 499.

ὀμίχλη, ἡ, Ion. for ὁμίχλη, a cloud, a mist, thick air, 1, 359; also ὀμίχλην κονίης ἱστάναι, to raise a cloud of dust, *13, 336.

ὄμμα, ατος, τό ('ΟΠΤΩ), the eye, always in the plur. the countenance, 8, 349; sing. ἔκδικον ὄμμα, Batr. 97.

ὄμνυμι, fut. ὀμοῦμαι, εἶ, εἶται, infin. ὀμεῖσθαι, aor. 1 ὤμοσα, Ep. ὅμοσσα and σσ, imperat. pres. ὄμνυθι, 23, 585;† from the form ὀμνύω, imperf. ὤμνυε, 14, 278. 1) to swear, mly ὅρκον, also ἐπίορκον, 3, 279. 2) Absol. to swear to one, to promise on oath, mly τινί, also πρός τινα, Od. 14, 331. 19, 288; it is followed by ᾖ, μέν, with infin. fut. (that one will do something), Il. 1, 76. 10, 522; and often in a negative oath; μή

with infin. fut. Od. 5, 178; with aor. Od. 2, 373. 4, 254; with any thing past, infin. perf. Od. 14, 331; also μή with subj. Od. 12, 300. 18, 56; and once μή with fut. indic. Il. 10, 329. 3) With accus. to call any one by an oath to witness, to swear, Στυγὸς ὕδωρ, by the water of the Styx, 14, 271; h. Merc. 274.

ὀμνύω, see ὄμνυμι.

ὀμογάστριος, ον (γαστήρ), from the same womb; κασίγνητος, a uterine brother (a brother born from the same womb, Cp.). *24, 47. 21, 95.

ὁμόθεν, adv. from the same place. δίμνοι ἐξ ὁμόθεν πεφυῶτες, branches sprung from the same trunk, Od. 5, 477; metaph. of the same descent, h. Ven. 135.

ὁμοῖος, ὁμοίϊον, Ep. for ὁμοῖος, ον (i. prop. short, when however the last syllable is long, it is used as long; [gen. ὁμοίιου, ˘ ˘ ˘ ˉ, 9, 440]).

ὁμοῖος, η, ον, H. and Ion. for ὅμοιος. Ep. form ὁμοίιος, ἴον (ὁμός). 1) like, similar, with art. ὁ ὁμοίιος, one similar, Od. 17, 218. Il. 16, 53. α) Also = ὁ αὐτός, the same, 18, 329. b) Like in strength, equal, 23, 632. The object with which any thing is compared is in the dat. 9, 305, 306; but the thing in which the similarity consists stands: α) In the accus. πελειάσιν ἴθμαθ' ὁμοῖαι, similar in movement to doves, 5, 778. Od. 6, 16. β) With prep. ἐν πολέμῳ, Il. 12, 270. γ) With infin. ἵπποι θείειν ἀνέμοισιν ὁμοῖοι, equal to the winds in running, 10, 437. cf. 2, 553. δ) With οἷος following, h. Ven. 180. A peculiar abbrev. of expression is found in κόμαι Χαρίτεσσιν ὁμοῖαι, hair similar to the Graces, i. e. to the hair of the Graces, 17, 51. cf. Od. 2, 121; the thing or person standing for the real object of comparison, see Thiersch, § 261. 10. ?) common, general, appertaining to all, spoken of a thing whose power is experienced by all; in this signif. always the Ep. form in the masc. and neut. relax ὁμοίιον, the common contest, in which both parties take equal share, 4, 444; πόλεμος, 9, 440. 13, 358. Od. 18, 264; θάνατος, Od. 3, 336; γῆρας, Il. 4, 315; but ὁμοίη μοῖρα, 18, 120. (The ancient critics, without reason, explain the Ep. form perniciosus.)

ὁμοιόω (ὅμοιος), only aor. pass. infin. ὁμοιωθήμεναι, 1) Act. to make equal a similar. 2) Pass. to place oneself a equal, to compare, absol. 1, 187; μάτην, in craft, Od. 3, 120.

ὀμόκλα, see ὁμοκλάω.

ὁμοκλάω and ὁμοκλέω, poet. (ὁμοκλή) 3 sing. imperf. ὁμόκλα, 18, 156; aor. 1 ὁμόκλησα, and iterat. ὁμοκλήσασκον from ὁμοκλέω. 3 plur. imperf. ὁμόκλεον, Il. 658. Od. 21, 360), to call to, to cry to, τινί, in order to encourage, to threaten or to rebuke him; hence, to encourage, to urge on, to threaten, to reprimand; often absol. in partcp. aor. and with μύθῳ, ἐπέεσσιν, Il. 2, 199. 23, 363; and

Ὀμοκλή. 307 Ὄνειρος.

with infin. to exhort to do any thing, 16, 714.

ὀμοκλή, ἡ, poet. (καλέω), prop. the act of *calling together* several persons, *the threatening call* of enemies (V. a call of derision), 16, 147. 2) Mly, *calling to, encouraging, threatening* (a threatening cry, V.). 6, 137. 12, 413. Od. 17, 189.

ὀμοκλητήρ, ῆρος, ὁ, poet. (ὀμοκλάω), *one who calls to, encourages* or *threatens*, *12, 273. 23, 452.

*ὀμοργάζω, a form of ὀμόργνυμι, h. Merc. 361.

ὀμόργνυμι, poet. aor. mid. ὠμορξάμην, *to wipe off, to dry up*, only mid. *to wipe away*, in reference to the subject, *to dry up*, δάκρυα, Od. 8, 88 ; δάκρυα παρειάων, the tears from the cheeks, Il. 18, 124. Od. 11, 530.

ὁμός, ή, όν, poet. (akin to ἅμα), prop. 1) *equal, similar, the same*, γένος, often. 2) *common, in common*, spoken of space, νεῖκος, 13, 333 ; λέχος, 8, 291 ; ὀιζύς, Od. 17, 563.

ὀμόσαι, see ὄμνυμι.

ὁμόσε, adv. (ὁμός), *to one and the same place*, *12, 24. 13, 337.

ὁμόσσαι, Ep. see ὄμνυμι.

ὁμοστιχάω (στιχάω), *to go with, to go together*, with dat. βόεσσιν, *to walk among the cattle*, 15, 635.†

ὁμότιμος, ον (τιμή), *equally honoured*, equal in worth, 15, 186.†

*ὁμότροφος, ον (τρέφω), *brought up together, educated* or *grown up together*, h. Ap. 199.

ὁμοῦ, adv. (ὁμός), 1) *together, in the same place* (ἅμα, relating to time), ἔχειν, 11, 127 ; always spoken of space, so also 1, 61, where it seems to stand for ἅμα. 2) *together with, along with*, with dat. Od. 4, 723. 15, 364 ; and ὁμοῦ νεφέεσσιν, with the clouds, Il. 5, 867.

ὁμοφρονέω (ὁμόφρων), *to be like-minded, to have similar thoughts, to agree*. Od. 9, 456 ; also νοήμασιν, *Od. 6, 183.

ὁμοφροσύνη, ἡ (ὁμόφρων), *similarity in disposition, harmony, agreement*, Od. 6, 181 ; plur. *Od. 15, 198.

ὁμόφρων, ονος, ὁ, ἡ (φρήν), *like-minded, harmonious, united*, θυμός, 22, 263.†

ὁμόω, poet. (ὁμός), aor. pass. infin. ὁμωθῆναι, *to unite ;* pass. *to be united, to unite.* φιλότητι, 14, 209.†

ὀμφάλοεις, εσσα, εν, poet. (ὀμφαλός), *having a navel*, having a boss like a navel in the middle : ἀσπὶς ὀμφαλόεσσα [*his bossy shield.* Cp.], 4, 448. Od. 19, 32, and often ; ζυγόν, Il. 24, 269.

ὀμφαλός, ὁ (akin to ἄμβων), 1) *a navel*, 4, 525. 2) any navel-shaped elevation in the middle of a surface : *a) the boss of a shield*, 11, 34. cf. ἀσπίς. *b) a knob* on the yoke for fastening the reins, 24, 273. *c) Generally, the centre, the middle*, θαλάσσης, as the island of Calypso, Od. 1, 50.

ὄμφαξ, ακος, ἡ, *an unripe wine-grape*, Od. 7, 125.†

ὀμφή, ἡ, poet. (ἐπω, with epenthetic μ), *a voice*, in H. always *the voice of the gods, the voice of destiny*, which was thought to be recognized in dreams, in the flight of birds, and in other omens, 2, 41. 20, 129 ; θεοῦ, Od. 3, 215.

ὀμώνυμος, ον (ὄνομα), *having the same name*, 17, 720.†

ὁμῶς, adv. (ὁμός), 1) *together, at once, equally, in like manner*, frequently between two substantives, which are already connected by τὲ καί, 8, 214. 24, 73. 2) *alike, in the same way*, 1, 196. Od. 11, 565 ; with dat. ὁμῶς Πριάμοιο τέκεσσιν, like the sons of Priam, 5, 535. 9, 312.

ὅμως, conj. (ὁμός), *however, still, notwithstanding*, 12, 393.†

ὄναρ, τό, only nom. and accus. sing. *a dream, a dreaming vision*, in the nom. 1, 63. 10. 496 ; in opposition to ὕπαρ, Od. 19, 547. 2)=ὄνειαρ, in h. Cer. 269 ; according to a conjecture of Herm. (From ὄναρ are formed ὀνείρατα, ὄνειρος, see the latter.)

ὄνειαρ, ατος, τό, poet. (ὀνίνημι), 1) Prop. every thing profitable, *help, aid, profit, advantage*, 22, 433. 486 ; *refreshment*, Od. 4, 444. 15, 78. 2) In the plur. pleasing things ; hence, *valuables*, Il. 24, 367 ; elsewhere always *food, a refreshing repast*, 9, 91. Od. 1, 149. (In h. Cer. 270, εἰ in ὄνειαρ is shortened.)

*ὀνειδείη, ἡ, poet. for ὄνειδος, Ep. 4, 12.

ὀνείδειος, ον (ὄνειδος), *insulting, blaming, chiding, reproaching*, often with ἔπεα, also μύθος, *21, 393.

*ὀνειδείω, poet. for ὀνειδίζω, Fr. I. 18, ed. Wolf.

ὀνειδίζω (ὄνειδος), aor. 1 ὠνείδισα, partcp. ὀνειδίσας, 1) Absol. *to vituperate, to insult, to reproach*, ἔπεσιν, 1, 211. 2) *to cast reproach*, τινί, 2, 255 ; τινί τι, to allege any thing as a reproach against any one, to reproach him with —, Od. 18, 380. Il. 9, 34.

ὄνειδος, εος, τό, *insult, abuse*. *a) Esply* in words : *reproach, blame, vituperation*, often in the plur. ὀνείδεα μυθεῖσθαι, λέγειν, 1, 291. Od. 22, 463. *b)* that which brings reproach to others : σοὶ κατηφείη καὶ ὄνειδος ἔσσομαι, I shall be to thee a reproach and shame, Il. 16, 498. 17, 556. Od. 6, 285.

ὀνείρατα, τά, see ὄνειρον.

ὀνείρειος, η, ον (ὄνειρος), *of a dream, belonging to a dream*. ἐν ὀνειρείῃσι πύλῃσι, in the gates of dreams, Od. 4, 809.†

ὄνειρον, τό, see ὄνειρος.

ὀνειροπόλος, ον (πολέω), *conversant with dreams, i. e. expounding dreams*, γέρων, 5, 149. Subst. *an expounder of dreams*, *1, 63.

ὄνειρος, ὁ (from ὄναρ), a rare form is ὄνειρον, Od. 4, 841 ; irreg. nom. plur. ὀνείρατα [cf. ὄναρ], Od. 20, 87.† 1) *a dream, a vision*, mly sent by Zeus. According to Od. 19, 562 seq., dreams come from the under-world, cf. Od. 24, 12 ; δῆμος Ὀνείρων, through two gates : the true come through a gate of horn, and the false through one of ivory ; a

'Ονέω. 308 'Οπάζω.

pun with ἐλεφαίρω and κραίνω. q. v. 2) As a prop. name: *the god of dreams*, 3, 6. 16, 22. Od. 21, 12.

'ΟΝΕΩ, theme of ὀνίνημι.
ὀνήμενος, see ὀνίνημι.
ὄνησα, Ep. for ὤνησα, see ὀνίνημι.
*ὀνήσιμος, η, ον, poet. (ὄνησις), profitable, advantageous, h. Merc. 30.
ὄνησις, ιος, ἡ, poet. (ὀνίνημι), profit, help, advantage; and generally, *happiness, welfare*, Od. 21, 402.†
'Ονητορίδης, ου, ὁ, son of Onetor, Od. 3, 282.
'Ονήτωρ, ορος, ὁ (=ὀνήσιμος), a priest of Zeus on Ida near Troy, 16, 604, 605.
ὄνθος, ὁ, *dung, manure*, *23, 775. 777. 781.
ὀνίνημι, 24, 45; infin. ὀνινάναι, fut. ὀνήσω, aor. ὤνησα, Ep. ὄνησα, fut. mid. ὀνήσομαι, aor. 2 ὠνήμην, imperat. ὄνησο, partcp. ὀνήμενος, *to profit, to help, to rejoice, to promote*, absol. 8, 36; with accus. of person, 1, 503. 5, 205. 24, 45; apparently with double accus. σὺ δὲ τοῦτό γε γῆρας ὄνησαι, in this will age profit thee, Od. 23, 24; *in rejoice, to gladden*, καρδίην τινός, Il. 1, 395. Mid. *to have advantage or profit from any thing, to enjoy any thing, with gen.* δαιτός, Od. 19, 68; τινός, to have advantage from any one, Il. 10, 31. b) Often absol. *to be well, to enjoy uneself*, 6, 260. ἐσθλός μοι δοκεῖ εἶναι, ὀνήμενος, he seems to me to be good, a man favoured by the gods, Od. 2, 33. The partcp. stands as adj.; incorrectly the ancients [and so *Cp.*] supply εἴη, so that it may=ὄναιτο ταύτης, let him have the profit of it, see Nitzsch ad loc.
ὄνομα, τό, Ion. for οὔνομα, only three times, 3, 235. 17, 260. Od. 6, 194. 1) *a name*, the appellation of a person, Od. 19, 180. 409. 2) a *name, fame, reputation*, Od. 13, 248. 24, 93. (For τοὔνομα, Il. 3, 235, Herm. ad Vig. p. 708, reads καὶ τ' οὔνομα.)
ὀνομάζω (ὄνομα), aor. ὠνόμασα, *to name, to call by name*, τινά, Il. and Od. 2) *to mention, to enumerate, to recount*, δῶρα, Il. 9, 515.
ὄνομαι, Ep. and Ion. depon. 2 sing. ὄνοσαι, 3 plur. ὄνονται, imperat. ὄνοσο, fut. ὀνόσομαι, Ep. σσ. aor. ὠνοσάμην, optat. ὀνοσαίμην, also the Ep. form from the theme 'ΟΝ, pres. οὔνεσθε (24, 241.) for ὄνεσθε (for which Buttm. § 114, prefers οὔνοσθε) and aor. 1 mid. ὠνατο, 17, 25. 1) *to insult, to rebuke, to reproach, to blame*. a) Absol. Od. 17, 378. ἦ οὔνεσθε, ὅτι, blame you it, or are you still dissatisfied, that, Il. 24, 241. b) With μύθον, 9, 55; φάλαγγας, 13, 127. c) With gen. of the thing, κακότητος, to chide the misery, i. e. to esteem it too little, Od. 5, 379. 3) *to despise, to reject*, with accus. ἔργον, Il. 4, 539; also φρένας, 14, 95.
ὀνομαίνω, poet. form of ὀνομάζω (ὄνομα), pres. h. Ven. 291, in Il. and Od. only aor. 1 ὠνόμηνα, subj. ὀνομήνω. 1) *to name, to call by name*, τινά. 2) *to recount*, *to relate*, τι τινι, Il. 9, 121; with accus. and infin. Od. 24, 341. b) *to nominate, to appoint*, τινὰ θεράποντα, 23, 90.

ὀνομακλήδην, adv. (καλέω), *mentioning by name. namely*, Od. 4, 278.†
ὀνομάκλυτος, ον (κλυτός), *having an illustrious name, famous; uf. note*, 22, 51.† Heyne: ὄνομα κλυτόν.
ὀνομαστός, ή, όν (ὀνομάζω), *named, to be named*. οὐκ ὀνομαστός, not to be named, *nefandus*. Κακοΐλιος, *Od. 19, 260. 597. 23, 19. h. Ven. 255.
ὄνος, ὁ, *an ass*, 11, 558.†
ὀνοσσάμενος, ὀνόσσεσθαι, see ὄνομαι.
ὀνοστός, ή, όν, poet. (ὄνομαι), *reviled, abused, to be reviled, blameworthy, despicable*. δῶρα οὐκέτ' ὀνοστά, 9, 164.†
ὀνοτάζω, poet. form of ὄνομαι, *to revile*, h. Merc. 30.
'ΟΝΟΩ, an assumed theme, from which are derived the tenses of ὄνομαι.
ὄνυξ, υχος, ὁ, dat. plur. ὀνύχεσσι, prop. *a nail, a talon, a claw*, spoken only of the eagle, 8, 248. Od. 2, 153.
ὀξυβελής, ές, poet. (βέλος), gen. ές, having a sharp weapon, *sharp-pointed*, epith. of the arrow, 4, 126.† [βέλος however, never means 'point,' but always 'missile.' Hence ὀϊστὸς ὀξυβελής =ὀϊστὸς ὀξὺ βέλος ὤν. Ameis.]
ὀξύεις, εσσα, εν, poet. for ὀξύς, *sharp, pointed*, often epith. of ἔγχος and δόρυ, 14, 443. Thus Voss after Apion. (According to other Gram. incorrectly for ὀξυΐνος, *beechen*, from ὀξύα.)
ὀξύς, εῖα, ύ, superl. ὀξύτατος. *pointed, sharp*, μόχλος, Od. 9, 382; hence 1) *pointed, cutting*, spoken of weapons and other things, σκόλοπες, λᾶας. 2) Metaph. spoken of the senses: *sharp, cutting, piercing*. αὐγὴ Ἠελίοιο ὀξεῖα, the burning beam, 17, 372; ὀδύναι, ἄχος, 16, 518; αὐή, a piercing cry, 15, 313. d) Of the mind: *hot, violent, raging*, Ἄρης, 2, 440. The neut sing. and plur. ὀξύ and ὀξέα stand often as adv. 1) Spoken of sight: ὀξὺ νοεῖν, to observe closely. ὀξέα δέρκεσθαι, h. 18, 14. 2) Of the voice and the hearing: ὀξέα κεκληγώς, 2, 222; ἀκούειν, 17, 256. (On the elision of αι in ὀξεῖ' ὀδύναι, see Buttm.. Gr. Gram § 30, p. 126, who would read ὀξέαι.)
*ὀξύσχοινος, ὁ, *a kind of rush*, schœnus mucronatus, Batr. 169.
ὅον, Ep. for οὗ, see ὅς, ἥ, ὅ.
ὀπάζω, poet. (ὀπάων), fut. ὀπάσω, Ep. σσ, aor. 1 ὤπασα, Ep. ὄπασσε, imperat. ὄπασσον, mid. fut. ὀπάσομαι, Ep. σσ, aor. ὠπασάμην, 1) *to give as a companion, to cause to follow, to associate*, τινά τινι. spoken of persons: πομπόν, ἡγεμόνα τινί, 13, 416. Od. 15, 310; τινὰ πομπὸν τινι, to associate any one with another as a companion. Il. 24, 153; λαόν τινι, 8, 483. b) Spoken of things: *to add, to give, to bestow*, κῦδός τινι. 8, 141; in like manner αἰδοίην, κτήματα, with pleon. infin. 23, 151. 2) = διώκω, *to follow, to pursue, to press*, τινά, 8, 341; metaph. spoken of age, 8, 103; and absol. *to press*

Όπαῖος.   309   'Οπόθεν.

on, 5, 334. Pass. χειμάρρους ὀπαζόμενος Διὸς ὀμβρῳ, a torrent urged or driven on by the ra-n of Zeus, swollen, 11, 493. Mid. to cause to follow oneself, to associate to oneself, to take any man as a companion, τινά, 10, 238. 19, 238. Od. 10, 59.
ὀπαῖος, αίη, αίον (ὀπή), see ἀνοπαῖα.
ὄπατρος, ὁ, poet. for ὁμόπατρος, by the same father. κασίγνητος καὶ ὄπατρος, a brother, and sprung from the same father, *11, 257. 12, 371.
ὀπάων, ονος, ὁ (ὀπάζω), a companion, a comrade, an associate in war, esply an armour-bearer, 7, 165; also fem. a female companion, h. Cer. 440.
ὅπερ, Ep. for ὅσπερ.
ὅπη, Ep. ὅππη, adv. (πῇ), 1) Spoken of place: where, in which place, prop. dat. local, 22, 321. Od. 1, 347; for the most part with reference to direction, whither, Il. 12, 48. Od. 3, 106. 2) Spoken of manner, etc.: how, in what way, Il. 20, 25. Od. 1, 347. 8, 45.
ὀπηδέω, poet. (ὀπηδός), Ion. for ὀπαδέω, only pres. and imperf. ὀπηδεῖ and ὀπήδει, to follow, to attend or accompany, to go with, τινί, spoken of persons, also ἅμα τινί, Od. 7, 181; to help, h. Ap. 530. b) Spoken of things, Il. 5, 216. ἐκ Διὸς τιμὴ ὀπηδεῖ, honour and fame come from Zeus, 17, 251.
*ὀπηδός, ὁ, ἡ, following, accompanying, τινί, h. Merc. 450.
ὀπίζομαι, depon. poet. (ὄπις), only pres. and imperf. to dread, to fear, to regard, always from fear of guilt and punishment, with accus. μητρὸς ἐφετμήν, 18, 216; also τινά, to dread any one, 22, 332; in the Od. only in reference to the gods: Διὸς μῆνιν, θυμόν, Il. 14, 283. 13, 148.
ὄπιθε and ὄπιθεν, poet. for ὄπισθεν.
ὀπιπτεύω (ὀπτω), fut. σω, aor. ὀπιπτεύσας, to look about oneself at any thing, to observe with curiosity, to spy out, to look out for, with accus. πολέμοιο γεφύρας, 4, 371; γυναῖκας, to gaze at the women, Od. 19, 67; absol. λάθρῃ, to watch for secretly, Il. 7, 243.
ὄπις, ιδος, ἡ, poet. (ἕπω), accus. ὄπιδα, according to Apoll. prop. the consequence of human actions, in H. for the most part, of bad actions: θεῶν, punishment, vengeance of the gods, 16, 388. Od. 20, 215; without θεῶν, Od. 14, 82. 88. (According to others, from ὄψ, the monitory inspection of the gods; thus Nitzsch ad Od. 5, 146, and Köppen, contrary to the Gramm., cf. Spitzner ad Il. 16, 388.)
ὄπισθε, before a vowel ὄπισθεν, adv. Ep. also ὄπιθε, 16, 791; ὄπιθεν, 1) Spoken of place: behind, from behind, backwards. ὄπισθε μένειν, to remain behind, 9, 332. οἱ ὄπισθε, those behind, Od. 11, 66. τὰ ὄπισθεν, the hinder parts, he back, Il. 11, 613. b) As prep. with gen. behind. ὅπ. μάχης, Il. 13, 538. 2) Spoken of time: hereafter, henceforth, in future, 9, 519. Od. 2, 270. h. Merc. 8.

ὀπίσσω, Ep. for ὀπίσω, q. v.
ὀπίστατος, η, ον, superl. from ὄπισθε, the hindmost, the last, *8, 342. 11, 178.
ὀπίσω, Ep. ὀπίσσω, adv. (ὄπις), 1) Spoken of place: backwards, back; also strengthened, πάλιν ὀπίσσω, Od. 11, 149. ὀπίσσω χάζεσθαι, Il. 5, 443; νεκρῶν, 13, 193. 2) Spoken of time: henceforth, hereafter, in future, prop. that which is yet in the background, which cannot be seen, 3, 411. Od. 1, 222 ἅμα πρόσσω καὶ ὀπίσσω νοεῖν, λεύσσειν, ὁρᾶν, to see that which lies before and the following, i. e. the present and the future, Il. 1, 343. 3, 109. Od. 24, 452 (according to Heyne, Voss, and Nägelsbach, 'forwards and backwards,' i. e. into the future and the past, contrary to the usus loquendi).
'Οπίτης, ου, ὁ, a Greek, slain by Hector. Il. 11, 301.
ὁπλέω, poet. for ὁπλίζω, only imperf. ὥπλεον, to harness, to prepare, ἄμαξαν, Od. 6, 73.†
ὁπλή, ἡ (akin to ὅπλον), a hoof, of a horse, *11, 536. 20, 501; spoken of bovine cattle, h. Merc. 77.
ὁπλίζω (ὅπλον), aor. 1 ὥπλισα, Ep. σσ, aor. pass. ὡπλίσθην, without augm. ὁπλισάμεσθα and ὁπλίσθεν for ὡπλίσθησαν, to put right, to fit out, hence 1) to prepare, with accus. of food: κυκεῶ, 11, 641; ἧία, Od. 2, 289. 2) to harness, spoken of a chariot, Il. 24, 190. 3) Of ships: to fit out, Od. 17, 288. Mid. 1) to equip oneself, to adapt oneself to an employment, with infin. Il. 7, 417. ὁπλίσθεν γυναῖκες, the women prepared or adorned themselves (for the dance), Od. 23, 143; esply to arm oneself, Il. 8, 55; ἐπὶ πόλεμον, Batr. 140. 2) to prepare for oneself, (sibi), with accus. δεῖπνον, δόρπον; ἵππους, to harness one's horses, 23, 301.
ὁπλομαι, poet. for ὁπλίζομαι, mid. to prepare for oneself, δεῖπνον, *19, 172. 23, 159.
ὅπλον, τό, mostly in the plur., sing. only Od. Batr. equipment, instruments, furniture in general and in particular. 1) the tools of a forge, 18, 409. Od. 3, 433. 2) a ship's gear, tackle, every thing belonging to the equipment of a ship, a cable, a sail, in the last signif. twice in the sing. Od. 14, 346. 21, 390. 3) implements of war, esply arms, equipment, *Il. Sing. spoken of the lightning of Zeus, Batr. 282.
ὁπλότερος, η, ον and ὁπλότατος. η, ον, poet. compar. and superl. without positive, younger, later, the youngest, the latest; γενεῇ, younger in birth, 2, 707. Od. 19, 184. ὁπλότατος, γενεῆφιν, Il. 9, 58. ὁπλοτάτη, Od. 3, 465. (Originally from ὅπλον, capable of bearing arms, cf. Il. 3, 108. Ep. 4, 5.)
'Οπόεις, εντος, ὁ, Ep. for 'Οποῦς, the chief city of the Locrians, not far from the sea, founded by Opus, son of Locrus, and the native city of Patroclus, 2, 531. 18, 326.
ὁπόθεν, Ep. ὁππόθεν, adv. (πόθεν),

Ὁπόθι. *whence, from whence,* in a dependent question, *Od. 1, 406. 3, 80. 14, 47.

ὁπόθι, Ep. ὁππόθι, adv. poet. for ὅπου, *where, in which place,* 9, 577; ὁππόθ' ἄλωλεν, Od. 3, 89.

ὁποῖος, η, ον, Ep. ὁπποῖος, *of what kind, what sort of,* qualis, prop. in the dependent question: ὁπποῖ' ἄσσα for τινά, Od. 19, 218; and in the direct question, Od. 1, 171. 2) Also for οἷος in reference to τοῖος: ὁποῖόν κ' εἴπῃσθα ἔπος, τοῖόν κ' ἐπακούσαις, such a word as thou shalt have spoken thou mayest hear (*or* shalt hear) again, Il. 20. 250. Od. 17, 421.

ὀπός, ὁ, prop. *sap, the juice of plants;* esply the sap of the wild fig-tree, which was used for coagulating milk, 5, 902.† cf. Columell. de Re Rust. VII. 8.

ὀπός, see ὄψ.

ὁπόσε, Ep. ὁππόσε, adv. (πόσε), poet. for ὅποι, *whither,* Od. 14, 139.† h. Ap. 209.

ὁπόσος, η, ον, Ep. ὁππόσος and ὁπόσσος (πόσος), *how great, how many,* spoken of space and number, Il. 23, 238. Od. 14, 47.

ὁπόσσος, Ep. for ὁπόσος.

ὁπότ' ἄν, see ὁπότε.

ὁπότε, Ep. for ὁππότε, conj. (ποτέ), I) To indicate simultaneousness: *when, as.* 1) With indic. when the declaration is represented as something real, mly with things past, 1, 399. Od. 4, 731. In Il. 8, 229, ὁπότ' ἐν Λήμνῳ, supply ἦμεν. b) In comparisons, chiefly ὡς ὁπότε, as when, 11, 492; also however with subjunct. 2) With subjunct. a) Spoken of possible actions, present or future, in reference to a primary tense. The subjunct. aor. indicates a conceived action completed in the future, *if, in case, as soon as* (fut. exact.), 13, 271. Od. 1, 77. By an annexed ἄν, κέ: ὁπότ' ἄν, ὁπότε κεν, the designation of time is indicated as a condition, Il. 4, 40. Od. 8, 444; φθέγξομαι, Ep. for φθέγξωμαι, Il. 21, 340; in like manner Od. 1, 41. b) To mark an indefinite repetition: *as often as,* Il. 1, 163; with ἄν, Il. 4, 229. 9, 702. c) In comparisons, ὡς ὁπότε, only Ep., 11, 305. Od. 4, 335. 17, 126. 3) With subjunct. a) In reference to a historical tense of the main clause, Il. 7, 415. 19, 317. b) To mark an indefinite repetition, 3, 233. 4, 344. 13, 711. Also with ἄν or κέν annexed, 7, 415. II) In assigning a reason: *as, since, whereas* (quando); according to Thiersch, § 323, 8, here belongs Od. 20, 196; cf. Kühner, § 675, seq. Rost, § 121.

ὁπότερος, η, ον, Ep. ὁπποτέρος (πότερος), *which of the two,* uter, 3, 71. Od. 18, 46; spoken of single persons; in the plur. of two parties, Il. 3, 299; only in the Ep. form.

ὁποτέρωθεν, Ep. ὁπποτέρωθεν, adv. (ὁπότερος), *from which of two sides, from which of the two parts,* 14, 59.†

ὅπου, adv. (ποῦ), *where, wherever,* *Od. 8, 16. 16, 306.

ὁππόθεν, ὁππόθι, ὁπποῖος, ὁππύσι or **πόσος, ὁππότε,** Ep. for ὁπόθεν, ὁποῖ, ὁποῖος, etc.

ὅππως. Ep. for ὅπως.

ὀπτάλεος, η, ον (ὀπτάω), *roasted,* κρέα, 4, 345. Od. 12, 396.

ὀπτάω, aor. 1 ὤπτησα, *to roast,* spoken of flesh (never, to boil), κρέα, 1, 466. Od. 3, 33.

ὀπτήρ, ῆρος, ὁ ('ΟΠΤΩ), *a spy, a scout.* *Od. 14, 261. 17, 430.

ὀπτός, ή, ήν (ὀπτάω), *roasted,* *Od. 4, 66. 16, 443. +

'ΟΠΤΩ, an obsol. root which furnishes some tenses to ὁράω.

ὀπυίω, infin. pres. ὀπυιέμεν and ὀπυιέμεναι for ὀπύειν, only pres. and imperf. *to marry, to take as a wife,* spoken of the man, 13, 379. Od. 2, 336; absol. ὀπυίοντες, those married, in opposition to ἠίθεοι, Od. 6, 63. Pass. and mid. *to marry, to be married,* spoken of the woman, Il. 8. 304.

ὀπωπα, see ὁράω.

ὀπωπή, ἡ (ὄπωπα), poet. 1) *the act of seeing, a look,* Od. 3, 97. 4, 327. 2) *the sight, the visual power,* *Od. 9, 512.

***ὀπωπητήρ, ῆρος** = ὀπτήρ, poet. h. Merc. 15.

ὀπώρη, ἡ, the season of the year from the rising of Sirius to the rising of Arcturus, i. e. from July to the middle of September, consequently prop. *the warmest time of the year, dog-days,* or perhaps *late summer* or *early autumn* (H. recognizes four seasons: ἔαρ, θέρος, ὀπώρη, χειμών), 22, 27; in connexion with θέρος, Od. 12, 76. In this time there occurred not only great heat and drought, Il. 21, 346. Od. 5, 328; but also rain prevails, 16, 385; and because in it the fruits come to maturity, hence τεθαλυῖα ὀπώρη (the fruit-ripening season, Voss), Od. 11, 192.

ὀπωρινός, ή, όν (ὀπώρη), *in or of the time of dog-days, autumnal;* ἀστήρ, the autumnal star, i. e. the dog-star, see κύων, 5, 5; Βορέης, the autumnal Boreas, which brought heat and drought, Od. 5, 328. (ι in H. long; in itself, however, short.)

ὅπως, Ep. ὅππως (πῶς), I) Adverb. 1) Spoken of the way and manner: *how, in what way, as.* a) With indic. when the declaration is indicated as a real determination, 4, 37. 10, 545. The fut. frequently after verbs of considering, l. 136 4, 14. 17, 144. b) With subjunct. without ἄν or κέ, when the declaration is intended to be represented as an ideal or possible determination, Od. 1, 349; κέ is annexed when the sentence is at the same time to be taken as conditional, Il. 9, 681. Od. 1, 295. c) With optat. after a historical tense, Il. 18, 473. Od. 9, 554. 2) Spoken of time: *as soon as,* like ὡς, with indic. Il. 12, 208. Od. 5, 373. In Od. 4, 109, it is almost equivalent to ἐπεί, since. II) Conjunct. that, *in order that,* in sentences indicating

●*Ὅραμα. 311 Ὀρθαί.

esign or purpose. 1) With subjunct. without ἄν after a primary tense, 3, 110. Od. 1, 77. If ἄν or κέ is annexed, the expressed or implied condition is alluded to, Od. 4, 545. 2) With optat. after a historical tense, Il. 1, 344. Od. 3, 29. 3) With indic. fut. to indicate a certain expectation of the result, only Od. 1, 57; cf. Kühner, § 690. Thiersch, 341. 7. § 342. Rost, § 122.

*ὅραμα, ατος, τό (ὁράω), *a thing seen, a sight*, Batr. 83.

ὁράω, Ep. ὁρόω, imperf. without augment. ὁρῶν, fut. ὄψομαι, aor. εἶδον, perf. Ep. ὄπωπα. H. uses partly the contr. forms, as ὁρῶ, ὁρᾷς, etc. partly the Ep. expanded, as ὁρόω, ὁράᾳς, ὁράαν, ὁρόωσα; plur. optat. ὁρόῳτε for ὁρῷτε, etc. The mid. is depon.; rare forms are 2 sing. pres. ὅρηαι for ὁρᾷ, and 3 sing. imperf. ὁρῆτο, for which others write ὅρηαι, ὁρῆτο, as if from ὅρημαι. Also the aor. ἰδόμην, infin. ἰδέσθαι, *to gaze, to look*. 1) Absol. with the prep. εἴς τι or τινα, at any thing, or any one, 10, 238. Od. 5, 439; again, ἐπὶ πόντον, 1, 350; κατά τινα, 16, 646. b) Trans. with accus. *to see, to behold, to observe, to perceive*, 23, 323; with the adjunct ὀφθαλμοῖσιν, Od. 3, 94. ὁρᾶν φάος Ἠελίοιο, to behold the light of the sun, for to live, 5, 120; with ὅτι, 7, 448; with partcp. 9, 359. 2) Mid. a depon. *to see, to behold*, τινά, 1, 56. Od. 4, 226.

*ὀργή, ἡ (ἘΡΓΩ), prop. *impulse*, emotion, passion = θυμός, h. Cer. 205.†

*ὄργια, τά, *secret religious usages, mysteries, orgies*, spoken of the secret worship of Demeter, h. Cer. 274. 476; (from ὀργάω, ὀργή, because these usages were solemnized with enthusiastic movements;) the sing. does not occur.

*ὀργι ων, ί ονος, ὁ, *one initiated, a priest*, h. Ap. 369.

ὄργυια, ἡ (ὀρέγω), in H. ἁ (in the later language ὄργυια with ἁ), *a fathom*, the space between the hands when the arms are extended, 23, 327. Od. 9, 325.

ὀρέγνυμι, poet. form of ὀρέγω, from which partcp. ὀρεγνύς, *1, 351. 22, 37.

ὀρέγω, fut. ὀρέξω, aor. ὤρεξα, mid. aor. 1 ὠρεξάμην, Ep. ὀρεξάμην, perf. mid. ὀρώρεγμαι, 3 plur. ὠρωρέχαται, pluperf. 3 sing. ὀρωρέχατο, 1) *to stretch, to reach, to extend*, with accus. χεῖρα εἰς οὐρανόν (spoken of suppliants), 15, 371. Il. 1, 351; χεῖράς τινι, to stretch out the hands towards any one, Od. 12, 257. 2) *to reach, to present, to give*, often κῦδός τι ἐυχός τινι, κοτύλην καὶ πύρνον, Od. 15, 112. Mid. 1) *to stretch oneself, to extend oneself*, with dat. χερσί, with the hands, i. e. to reach to any thing, Il. 23, 99. ἵπποι ποσσὶ ὀρωρέχαται, the steeds stretched themselves with their feet, e. took long strides, *stept out*, 16, 834. εἰς ὀρέξατ᾽ ἰών, thrice he strode forth poken of Poseidon), 13, 20; ἐγχεῖ, ὀρρί, to stretch oneself with the spear, e. to thrust with the spear, 4, 307. 13,

190. 2) With gen. to stretch oneself towards any thing, *to reach after*, παιδός, 6, 466. 3) With accus. trans. *to reach* any thing, *to attain*, Od. 11, 392; *to hit*, σκέλος, Il. 16, 314. 322. 4)=act. ἀνδρὸς ποτὶ στόμα χεῖρ᾽ ὀρέγεσθαι, i. e. (according to the Schol. Vict.), χεῖρε ἀνδρὸς ποτὶ στόμα, to press the hands of the man (viz. of Achilles) to the mouth. This explanation is followed by Voss. It is confirmed also by v. 478, where Priam kisses Achilles' hand, 24, 506.

*ὀρείχαλκος, ὁ (ὄρος, χαλκός), orichalcum, *mountain brass*, a metal of uncertain composition; according to Beckmann, *copper-brass*, h. 5, 9.

ὀρεκτός, ή, όν (ὀρέγω), *stretched out, extended, μελίαι*, 2, 543.†

ὀρέομαι=ὄρνυμαι, only 3 plur. imperf. ὀρέοντο, they hastened, *2, 398. 20, 140. 23, 212.

Ὀρέσβιος, ὁ (living on mountains), a rich Bœotian of Hyle, 5, 707.

ὀρεσίτροφος, ον, poet. (τρέφω), *raised or nourished upon the mountains*, epith. of the lion, 12, 299. Od. 6, 130.

ὀρεσκῷος, ον, poet. (κέω), lying in the mountains, *dwelling in the mountains, wild*, 1, 268. Od. 9, 155.

ὀρέστερος, η, ον, poet. (ὄρος), for ὄρειος, *living upon mountains, in mountains*, epith. of the serpent, of wolves, 22, 93. Od. 19, 212.

Ὀρέστης, αο, ὁ (mountaineer, Herm. Excitus), son of Agamemnon and Klytæmnestra (Clytemnestra), 9, 142; he was brought by his sister to his uncle Strophius in Phocis, where he entered into the well-known bond of friendship with his son Pylades. H. does not mention this, unless Od. 11, 458—462 refers to it. According to Od. 3, 305, he returned in the eighth year of the reign of Ægisthus to Mycenæ, slew him and his mother Klytæmnestra (Clytemnestra), in order to avenge the death of his father, and then reigned in Mycenæ, Od. 11, 457, seq. Because all the traditions point to Phocis, Zenodot. wrote, Od. 3, 307: ἀπὸ Φωκήων for ἀπ᾽ Ἀθηνάων. 2) A Greek [slain by Hector], Il. 5, 705. 3) [A Trojan, 12, 139. 193.]

ὀρεστιάς, άδος, ἡ (ὄρος), *inhabiting mountains*. Νύμφαι, the mountain nymphs, 6, 420.

ὀρεσφι, see ὄρος.

ὀρεχθέω, poet. strengthened form of ὀρέγω, intrans. only βόες ὀρέχθεον ἀμφὶ σιδήρῳ σφαζόμενοι, 23, 30; the oxen stretched themselves about the iron, according to the Schol. ἀπετείνοντο ἀναιρούμενοι, 23, 30.† Others: *palpitated, struggled*, thus Suid. κινεῖν, and Bothe. Others, with Hesych.: *bellowed*, ἐμυκῶντο, ἐρρόχθουν. Thus Voss, cf. Spitzner, Excurs. XXXIV. [According to others it is akin to ὀργή, ὀργάω, and means *intumescere*, so Ameis, in Jahrb. Jahn und K., p. 276. Am. Ed.]

ὀρθαί, see ὄρνυμι.

Ὀρθαῖος, ὁ, a Phrygian of Ascania, 13, 791.

Ὀρθή, ἡ, a town in Thessaly (Perrhaebia), in the neighbourhood of Phalanna, 2, 739.

ὄρθιος, η, ον (ὀρθός), upright, straight. 2) Metaph. spoken of the voice: *high, loud, shrill*. The neut. plur. as adv. ὄρθια ἤυσε, Il, 11.† ἀβόησα ὄρθια φωνῇ, h. Cer. 432.

ὀρθόκραιρος, η, ον (κραῖρα), having straight horns, high-horned, epith. of cattle, 8, 231. Od. 12, 348. *b*) Spoken of ships: *high-beaked*; these amongst the ancients were so curved at both ends, as nearly to resemble the moon in the last quarter, Il. 18, 3. 19, 344.

ὀρθός, ή, όν (ὀρνυμι), upright, straight, erect, with στῆναι, 18, 246. 24, 359; with ἀναΐξας, Od. 21, 119. Batr.

ὀρθόω (ὀρθός), aor. ὤρθωσα, aor. 1 pass. ὀρθωθείς, *to erect, to set up, to lift up* (one fallen), τινά, 7, 272; often ὀρθωθεὶς ἐπ' ἀγκῶνος, *supported upon the elbow*, *2, 42.

ὄρθριος, η, ον (ὄρθρος), early, in the morning, h. Merc. 143.

ὄρθρος, ὁ (ὄρνυμι), the early dawn, the morning, h. Merc. 98. ὑπ' ὄρθρον, at daybreak, Batr. 103.

Ὀριγανίων, ὁ, the *Origanon-eater*, prop. patronym. from τὸ ὀρίγανον, a plant of a sharp, bitter taste, of which there are mentioned esply two kinds: *Origanum onites* and *Orig. heracleoticum* (winter marjoram or wild mint), Batr. 259.

ὀρίνω (poet. form of ὈΡΩ, ὄρνυμι), aor. ὤρῖνα, Ep. ὄρινα, aor. pass. ὠρίνθην, Ep. ὀρίνθην. 1) *to excite, to move*, with accus. πόντον, 9, 4; θάλασσαν. Od. 7, 273; and pass Il. 2, 294; metaph. often θυμόν τινι, *to move or excite any one's mind*, by pity, fear, anger, etc. 2, 142. 4, 208. Od. 4, 366; and passive: ὠρίνθη πᾶσιν θυμός, Il. 5, 29; in like manner, κῆρ and ἦτορ, Od. 17, 47; γόον, Il. 24, 760. 2) In pass. also spoken of suppliants: *to be driven away*, 9, 243. 14, 14.

ὅρκιον, τό (ὅρκος), the pledge or token of an oath, an oath, a covenant, 4, 158. 2) Mly plur. τὰ ὅρκια subaud. ἱερεῖα, *the victims* which were sacrificed in solemn covenants, 3, 245. 269. *b*) And generally, the victims and religious rites which were sacrificed and performed at the solemn conclusion of treaties; *a covenant-sacrifice*, hence, *a covenant by oath, the covenant or treaty itself*. ὅρκια πιστὰ ταμεῖν, to conclude a faithful *treaty*, like *fœdus ferire*, since victims were slaughtered on such occasions, 2, 124; ὅρκια μετ' ἀμφοτέροισιν τιθέναι, to make a covenant between both parties, Od. 24, 546. ὅρκια φυλάσσειν, τελεῖν, to keep, to fulfil a covenant, 3, 280. 7, 69. The opposite is δηλήσασθαι, καταπατεῖν, συγχεύαι. (ὅρκιον is not. as Buttm. would consider it, Lex. p. 433, a deriv. diminutive, but prob. a neut. of adj. ὅρκιος, belonging to an oath.)

ὅρκος, ὁ (from εἴργω, originally of like signif. with ἕρκος), prop. the check, what retains that which any one promised; therefore: *the object by which any one swears, the witness of an oath*, thus spoken of the Styx, by which the gods swore, 2, 755. 15, 38; men swore by Zeus, the Earth, and the Furies, 3, 276. seq. 19, 258, seq. Od. 14, 394; Achilles by his sceptre, Il. 1, 234. 2) *an oath*, Il. 239. 23, 42; cf. Buttm., Lex. p. 433.

ὁρμαθός, ὁ (ὅρμος), a series or string of things hanging together, a flock of bats, Od. 24, 8.†

ὁρμαίνω (poet. form of ὁρμάω), aor. ὥρμηνα, prop. *to move here and there*; in H. only metaph. *to move any thing here and there in mind*, animo volvere, *to ponder, to consider, to weigh*, often with the adjuncts κατὰ φρένα καὶ κατὰ θυμόν, 1, 193; κατὰ φρένα, alone. 10, 507; ἀνὰ θυμόν 21, 137. Od. 2, 156; ἐνὶ φρεσίν, Od. 4, 843; and φρεσί, Il. 10, 4; without these adjuncts, 10, 28. Od. 3, 169. Constr. *a*) With accus. *to consider any thing, to purpose, to meditate*, πόλεμον, Il. 10, 28; ὁδόν, Od. 4, 732; χαλεπὰ ἀλλήλοις, to devise evil against another, Od. 3, 151. *b*) Often absol with ὅπως, Il. 21, 137; εἰ, ἤ, whether Od. 4, 789; with ἤ—ἤ, whether—or whether, Il. 14, 20. 16, 455; and with infin. Epig. 4, 16.

ὁρμάω (ὁρμή), aor. ὥρμησα, aor. mid. ὡρμησάμην, aor. pass. ὡρμήθην. 1) Trans. *to put in motion, to urge on, to excite, to stimulate*, spoken of persons and things with accus. τινὰ ἐς πόλεμον, 6, 338; τὸ λεμον, Od. 18, 376. Pass. ὁ δ' ὁρμηθείς θεοῦ ἤρχετο, moved by a god, he began. Od. 8, 499. 2) Intrans. *to put oneself in motion, to raise oneself, to begin to address oneself to*. *a*) With infin. spoken of Achilles, Il. 21, 265; of the hawk: ὁρμᾷ διώκειν ὄρνεον, he rises to pursue a bird, 13, 64. *b*) *to rush upon, to attack*, τινός, any one, 4, 335. Mid. with aor. mid. and pass. like act. 2. 1) *to put oneself in motion, to begin*, (to be moved to do it), Od. 13, 82; with infin. Il. 8, 511. 10, 539; metaph. ἦτορ ὡρμᾶτο πολεμίζειν, the heart desired to fight, 21, 572. 2) *to rush upon, to attack, to assault, to press*, with gen. τινός, 14, 488; μετά τινα, 17, 605; ἐπί τινι, Od. 10, 214; also ὁρμᾶτ' ἐκ θαλάμοιο, she hastened from her bed-chamber. 3, 142. 9, 179; often absol. *to rush upon, to press*, 13, 388. 16, 402; ἔγχεῖ, ξιφέεσσι, σὺν τεύχεσι, Il.

Ὀρμενίδης, εω, ὁ, son of Ormenus-Amyntor, 9, 448.

Ὀρμένιον, τό, a town in Magnesia (Thessaly), in the time of Strabo, a village which was attached to the town Demetrias, 2, 734.

Ὄρμενος, ὁ, 1) son of Κερκαφος (Cercaphus), grandson of Αἰολος, father of Amyntor, according to later mythology,

Ὄρμενος. 313 **Ὄρος.**

founder of Ormenion, 9, 448. 2) a Trojan, 8, 274. 3) a Trojan, 12, 187. 4) father of Ctesius, Od. 15, 414.

ὄρμενος, see ὄρνυμι.

ὁρμή, ἡ (ὄρνυμι), a *vehement assault*, *an attack*, *a fierce onset*, *fury*, spoken of a warrior, 9, 355; of a beast, 11, 119. h. Cer. 382; often spoken of inanimate things : of the waves, Od 5, 320 : of fire (the *fierceness* of it), 11. 11. 157. *ἐς ὁρμὴν ἔγχεος ἐλθεῖν*, to come within the reach of a man's spear, 5, 118. 2) *the beginning* of an undertaking, 4, 466; the commencement of a journey, Od. 2, 403. 3) Generally, *impulse*, *inclination*, *effort*, Od 5, 416; ψυχῆς, h. 7, 13.

ὅρμημα, ατος, τό (ὁρμάω), of uncertain signif. occurring only twice. in the plur. *Il.* 2, 356. 590; in the verse: *τίσασθαι Ἑλένης ὁρμήματά τε στοναχάς τε*, Eustath. explains: ὅρμιμα (ἡ ἐξ ἀρχῆς ἑκουσία ἔλευσις), therefore: 'the undertaking of Helen and her groans,' i. e. her repentance *afterwards*; so also Bothe: *Helenæ ausa et gemitus*. Most ancient critics take ὁρμήματα for *troubles*, *cares*, hence Voss. translates : 'before he has avenged the troubles and groans of Helen,' and Buttm. [deriving it fm ὁρμαίνω] follows him, Lex. p. 439. More probable, according to Rost in Damm's Lex., is the first signif. *the undertaking*, and the gen. is explained as gen. object. : 'their toils and groans on Helen's account.'

ὁρμίζω (ὅρμος), prop. to bring into port; then, *to anchor*, νῆα, Od. 3, 11. 12, 317; and generally, *to make fast*, *to render secure*, ὑψι ἐπ' εὐνάων or ὑψοῦ νῆα ἐν νοτίῳ, a ship upon the sea, Il. 14, 77. Od. 8, 55; by means of a large stone, see εὐνή. Cf. Nitzsch ad Od. II. p. 118 (who thinks the ship was drawn partly up upon the moist, overflowed sand of the shore. *Am. Ed.*]; see νότιος.

ὅρμος, ὁ (εἴρω). 1) *a string*, *a chain*, esply *a necklace*, *a neck-chain*. as an ornament of women, 18, 401. Od. 15, 460. 2) *an anchorage*, *a harbour*, *a road*, *a haven*, Il. 1, 435. Od. 13, 101 Batr. 67. (For the second signif. ὅρνυμι is taken as the t'eme.)

Ὀρνειαί, αἱ, Ep. for Ὄρνεαι, a city in Argolis, with a temple of Priapus, 2, 571.

ὄρνεον, τό, poet. for ὄρνις, *a bird*. 13, 64.†

ὄρνις. ἴθος, ὁ and ἡ, plur. ὄρνιθες, dat. ὀρνίθεσσι (ὄρνυμι). 1) *a bird*, both wild and tame. 2) a bird from whose flight and voice omens were taken; hence generally, *omens*, 24, 219. (ι in the dissyllable cases is double-timed, 9, 323. 12, 218; in the triayllabic always long.)

ὄρνυμι, poet. Ep. form ὀρνύω (from this imperf. ὤρνυον), imperat. ὄρνυθι, infin. Ep. ὀρνύμεν, fut. ὄρσω, a.r. 1 ὦρσα. iterat. form ὄρσασκε. Ep. aor. 2 ὤροροι, mly trans. = ὦρσα. only for perf. intrans. 13, 78. Od. 8, 539. Mid. ὄρνυμαι, imperf. ὠρνύμην, fut. ὀροῦμαι, 3 sing. ὀρεῖται, aor. ὠρόμην, Ep. 3 sing.

ὦρτο, 3 plur. ὤροντο, Od. 3, 471; subj. ὄρηται, imperat. ὄρσο and ὄρσεο (contr ὄρσευ, Il. 4, 264), infin. Ep. ὄρθαι, 8, 474; partcp. ὄρμενος, η. ον, perf. act. intrans. only sing. ὄρωρε, subj. ὀρώρῃ, pluperf. ὀρώρει and ὠρώρει, 18, 498 (to be distinguished from aor. 2 ὦροροι). Of like signif is the perf. mid. ὀρώρεται, subj. ὀρώρηται, 13, 271 ; Ep. ὀρέοντο, see ὀρέομαι. 1) Trans. in the act. *to excite*, *to move*, *to arouse*, with accus. 1) Spoken of persons, and generally of animate beings : a) to put in motion bodily. *to urge on*, *to make to go*, τινὰ κατὰ μέσον, 5, 8; esply in a hostile signif. τινὰ ἐπί τινι, 5, 629 ; ἀντία τινός, 20, 79. β) *to cause to rise*, *to make to lift oneself*, Ἠριγένειαν ἀπ' Ὠκεανοῦ, Od. 23, 348 ; *to awaken*, Il. 10, 518; spoken of beasts. *to drive up*, *to rouse*, αἶγας, Od. 9, 154. b) Frequently in reference to the mind: *to excite*, *to impel*, *to encourage*, *to inflame*, τινά, spoken esply of excitement by the gods, Il. 5, 105. Od. 4, 712; with infin following, Il. 12, 142. 13, 794. 2) Spoken of things, *to excite*, *to move*, *to cause*, πόλεμον, μάχην, νοῦσον· spoken of states of mind, ἵμερον, γόον, φόβον : of natural objects, ἄνεμον, θύελλαν, κύματα. II) Intrans. in the mid. together with perf. 2 ὤρωρα, *to rouse oneself*, *to move oneself*, *to stir*. 1) Spoken of persons in reference to the body: *to move*, *to hasten*, 4, 421; with infin. Od. 2, 397; esply *to raise oneself*, *to arise*, ἐξ εὐνῆφιν, Od. 2, 2 ; ἐκ λεχέων, Il. 11, 2 ; ἀπ' Ὠκεανοῖο ῥοάων, 19, 2; ἀπὸ θρόνου, 11, 645; absol. esply in imperat. pres. and aor. ὄρσο and ὄρσεο, *stand up! rouse up!* hence in a hostile signif. *to leap upon*, *to rush upon*, *to run upon*, χαλκῷ, with the spear, 3, 349. 5, 17; ἐπί τινα, 5, 590; also with infin. *to raise oneself*, *to begin to do anything* : νιφέμεν, ἴμεν, 12, 279; and with partcp. ὄρσο κέων, up, to go to sleep, Od. 7, 342. 2) Spoken of things, *to rise*, *to be excited*. *to begin*, *to arise*, esply in perf. 2, *I have arisen* : spoken of bodily and mental states, εἰσόκε μοι φίλα γούνατ' ὀρώρῃ, as long as my limbs move (prop. have raised themselves), Il. 9, 610. 10, 90 : spoken of events in life, πόλεμος, μάχη, νεῖκος : of states of nature, νύξ, φλόξ, ἄνεμος. πῦρ ὄρμενον, the fire which has arisen, 17, 738. δοῦρα ὄρμενα πρόσσω, spears flying forwards, 11, 572; and with infin. πῦρ ὤρετο καίεμεν ὕλην, 14, 397. ὦρτο—οὖρος ἀήμεναι, the wind rose to blow, Od. 3, 176.

ὀρνύω, poet. form of ὄρνυμι, q. v.

ὀροθύνω, poet. lengthened form of ὄρνυμι, only act. *to excite*, *to arouse*, *to put in motion*, *to stimulate*, *to encourage*, only spoken of persons, τινά. b) Of things, ἐναύλους, to raise the mountain streams, 21, 312 ; ἄλλας, Od 5, 292.

ὄρομαι (akin to οὖρος, ὁράω), *to watch*, ὄρονται, Od. 14, 104.†

ὄρος εος, τό, Ion. οὖρος, dat. ὄρεσι, ὄρεσσι, Ep. gen. and dat. ὀρεσφιν, 4,

'Ορός.

452. 11, 474; a mountain, an elevation, a height, with gen. Κυλλήνης, Τηρείης, 2, 603. 829 (prop. that which is raised, from ὄρνυμι).

ὀρός, ὁ, whey, the watery part of coagulated milk, *Od. 9, 222. 17, 225. (Prob. from ῥέω, thin, fluid milk.)

ὀροὔω, poet. (ὄρνυμι), fut. ὀρούσω, h. Ap. 417; aor. ὄρουσα, to rise quickly or impetuously, to rush, spoken of animate and inanimate objects, ἐπί and ἔν τινι, upon any one, 14, 401. 15, 625; ἐς δίφρον, to leap upon the chariot, 11, 359; of serpents: πρὸς πλατάνιστον, *2, 310.

ὀροφή, ἡ (ἐρέφω), an arch, a roof, Od. 22, 298.†

ὄροφος, ὁ (ἐρέφω), a reed, for thatching houses, 24, 451.†

ὀρόω, Ep. for ὁρῶ, see ὁράω.

ὄρπηξ, ηκος, ὁ, Att. a sprout, a branch, a twig, 21, 38.†

ὄρσας, see ὄρνυμι.

ὄρσασκε, see ὄρνυμι.

ὄρσεο, contr. ὄρσευ and ὄρσο, see ὄρνυμι.

Ὀρσίλοχος, ὁ, 1) son of Alpheios (Alpheus), father of Diocles, sovereign of Pherae in Messenia, 5, 546. Od. 3, 488. 21, 16. 2) son of Diocles, brother of Crethon, Il. 5, 542. 549. 3) a fabulous son of Idomeneus, Od. 13, 260. 4) a Trojan, Il. 8, 274.

ὀρσοθύρη, ἡ (ὄρνυμι, θύρα), prob. a door to which there was an ascent by steps, a stair-door, Voss, *Od. 22, 126. 233. [not: a postern, Cp.]

*ὀρσολοπεύω, poet. to provoke, to attack, to assail, τινά, h. Merc. 308.

Ὀρτυγίη, ἡ, prop. Quail-land. 1) According to the ancient critics, an old name of the island Delos; for here Artemis slew Orion, Od. 5, 123. 15, 403. cf. Apd. 1, 43; or an island near Delos, Rhenia, h. Ap. 16. According to some modern critics, the little island Ortygia, off Syracuse, is to be understood by it, cf. Völcker, Hom. Geogr. § 17.

ὀρυκτός, ἡ, όν (ὀρύσσω), dug, excavated, τάφρος, *8, 179. 15, 344.

ὀρυμαγδός, ὁ, poet. (ὀρυγμός), tumult, hubbub, noise of many men, voices, Od. 1, 133; the uproar, the tumult of those in haste, Il. 2, 810; of hunters and dogs, 10, 185; of wood-cutters, 16, 633; spoken of the roaring of a stream, 21, 256; spoken of the crash of a fragment of rock, 21, 313; of a falling tree, Od. 9, 235.

ὀρύσσω, aor. ὄρυξα, in diq, to excavate, τάφρον, Ep. always without augm. (ὀρύξομεν, aor. subj.), 7, 341; to dig up, μῶλυ, Od. 10, 305.

ὀρφανικός, ἡ, όν, poet. for ὀρφανός, orphan, parentless, fatherless, παῖς, 6, 432. ὀρφ. ἦμαρ, the day of orphanage, i. e. the fate of an orphan, *22, 490.

ὀρφανός, ἡ, όν, destitute, orphan, Od. 20, 68.†

ὀρφναῖος, η, ον, poet. (ὄρφνη), dark, gloomy, epith. of night, 10, 83. 386. Od. 9, 143. h. Merc. 97

Ὅς.

ὄρχαμος, ὁ (akin to ἄρχομαι), the leader of a row, and generally, a leader, a commander, a sovereign, always with ἀνδρῶν and λαῶν, 2, 837. Od. 4, 316.

ὄρχατος, ὁ, poet. (from ὄρχος), a piece of ground planted in rows; a plot of garden-ground; φυτῶν, a vegetable-garden, a fruit-garden, 14, 123. Od. 7, 112. 24, 222.

ὀρχέομαι, depon. mid. imperf. ὀρχῶντο, aor. ὠρχησάμην, to spring, to leap, esply to dance, 18, 594. Od. 8, 371. 14, 465.

ὀρχηθμός, ὁ (ὀρχέομαι), Ion. the act of dancing, a dance, a choral dance, 13, 637. Od. 8, 263.

ὀρχηστήρ, ἦρος, ὁ (ὀρχέομαι), a dancer, 18, 494.†

ὀρχηστής, οὗ, ὁ = ὀρχηστήρ, 16, 617. 24, 261.

ὀρχηστύς, ύος, ἡ, Ion. for ὄρχησις, the act of dancing, a dance, 13, 731; dat. contr. ὀρχηστυῖ, Od. 8, 253. 17, 605.

Ὀρχομενός, ὁ, 1) ὁ Μινυήϊος, a very ancient town in Boeotia, at the mouth of the Kephīsos (Cephisus), on the lake Kōpāïs (Copais), chief city of the kingdom of the Minyæ, esply remarkable for the treasury of Minyas; the ruins are near the village Skripu, Il. 2, 541. Od. 11, 284. 2) a town in Arcadia, Il. 2, 605. (Passow makes both these towns fem. Thucyd. however, I. 113, makes the former fem., and V. 61, the latter masc. Am. Ed.]

ὄρχος, ὁ (prob. from ἔργω), a row of trees or vines, or a single trellis of espalier-plants, Od. 7, 127. 24, 341. cf. Nitzsch ad Od. 7, 127.

ὄρωρε, see ὄρνυμι.

ὀρώρεται, see ὄρνυμι.

ὀρωρέχαται and ὀρωρέχατο, see ὀρέγω.

ὅς, ἥ, ὅ, a relative pronoun, rarely demonstrative, Ep. forms: sing. gen. rarely ὅου, 2, 325; ἧς for ἧς, 16, 208.† Fem. dat. ἧς, ἧσι:

1) a relative pronoun, who, which, that, frequently in H. in connexion with ὁ, ἡ, τό. 1) Often the demonstrative, which should properly precede the relative, is omitted, and that not only as like, but also in unlike cases, Od. 1' 434. 2) Frequently the relative pronoun does not agree with the preceding substantive a) In gender: Διὸς τέκος, ἤν Il. 10, 278. b) In number: κῦτος, ἃ (such as)—βόσκει, Od 12, 97. τοὺς αἱ λόνς, ὅν κε κιχείω, Il 11, 367. 3) The relative clause is placed before the demonstrative (inversion), 9, 131. 17, 645 4) Often the relative suffers attraction 5, 265. 23, 649. 5) When two or more sentences connected by καί, τέ, δέ, succeed each other, which require different cases of the relative, Homer either entirely omits the relative in the second sentence, or there stands in its place a demonstrative or personal pronoun, l. 78. 3, 235. Od. 1, 161. 6) Construct is relative sentences, 1) With indicative without ἄν, where any thing is indicated

Ὅς.

with certainty, Ep. also with indicat. fut. and κέ, Il. 9, 155. b) With indicat. of the historical tenses and ἄν or κέ, Od. 5, 39. 14, 62; cf. ἄν. 2) With subjunct. with ἄν, κέ, and Ep. also without ἄν, after a primary tense, when the declaration is given as supposed or possible [hypothetical use], or can be resolved by ἐάν or τίς, Od. 1, 352. Il. 2, 231; hence also a) To indicate an oftenrecurring case, 2, 391. b) In comparisons, 13, 63. 17, 110. 3) With optat. without ἄν after a historical tense, 10, 20. 489; as with subjunct. again: b) As part of a wish, 14, 107. Also ἄν or κέ is added, 15, 738. 7) Absol. use of single cases, a) Gen. sing. οὗ, always ἐξ οὗ, since. b) Dat. sing. ᾗ, q. v. c) Accus. neut. ὅ very mly for ὅτι, that, 1, 120; for δι' ὅ, therent, that, Od. 1, 382; because. Il. 9, 493. 17, 207.

II) As a demonstrative pronoun, for οὗτος, this, and he, she, it, eaply with οὐδέ, μηδέ, γάρ, καί, 6, 59. 21, 198. Od. 1, 286. οἱ—οἱ, these—those, Il. 21,353. 354.

ὅς, ἥ, ὅν, a possessive pronoun of the third person for ἑός, ἑή, ἑόν, his, her, its; it has in the gen. sing. οἷο, 20, 235; without subst. ὅν, 15, 112. 2) Ep. it stands instead of the pronoun of the second and third person, Od. 1, 402. 13, 320. Doubtful is Od. 9, 28. Other places have been altered by Aristarch. Il. 19, 174. cf. Buttm. Lex. p. 251.

ὁσσάκι and ὁσάκις, Ep. ὁσσάκι, how many times, how often, as often as, always in the Ep. form, 21, 265. Od. 11, 585.

ὁσσάτιος, η, ον, Ep. ὁσσάτιος, poet. for ὅσος, λαός, 5, 587.†

ὁσίη, ἡ (prop. fem. of ὅσιος, holy), 1) divine or natural right, and every thing which in accordance with it is consecrated or permitted: hence οὐχ ὁσίη, with infin. it is not right, permitted, Od. 16, 423. 32, 412. 2) a sacred service, a holy usage, in sacrifices and the worship of the gods, h. Ap 237. ὁσίη κρεάων, the sacred use of the sacrificial flesh, h. Merc. 130. ὁσίης ἐπιβῆναι, to go to a sacred service, h. Cer. 211. Merc. 173.

*ὅσιος, η, ον. prop. consecrated by divine laws; spoken of persons: pious, devout, Ep. 6, 6.

ὅσος, ὅση, ὅσον, Ep. ὅσσος, 1) how great, how wide, how long, how much, how many, spoken of space, time, number, and degree; if the correlative demonstrative τόσος precedes, ὅσος is translated as [cf. 3, 12. 6, 450]; with the gen. it stands periphrastically: ὅσον πένθος for ὅσον πένθος. 11, 658. cf. 5, 267. c) In the plur. all who, as many as, with preceding τοσοίδε, 14, 94. οὔτις—ὁνόσσεται ὅσσοι Ἀχαιοί for οὕτις Ἀχαιῶν, 9, 55. ὅσσαι νύκτες καὶ ἡμέραι ἐκ Διός εἰσιν, all the days and nights, which come from Zeus, Od. 14, 93. 2) Frequently the neut. plur. and sing. as adv. as greatly, as much, as far, so greatly, so much, so far, with τόσον, 5, 786. Od. 4,

Ὥστε.

356; and without τόσον: ὅσσον, as far as, Il. 5, 860; absol. ἀλλ' ὅσον ἐς Σκαιὰς πύλας ἵκανεν, he came only, 9, 354. b) When with ὅσον τε the limitation of space stands in the accus. it signifies about ὅσον τε ὄργυιαν, Od. 9, 322 325. 10, 167; prop. an attraction, cf. Kühner, § 656, and Od. 10, 113. c) ὅσσον ἐπί and ὅσσον τ' ἐπί for ἐφ' ὅσον, as far as, Il. 2, 616. 3, 12. a) With compar and superl. by how much, how much. ὅσσον ἐγὼ—ἀτιμοτάτη εἰμί, how much I am the most dishonoured, 1, 516. On ὅσος τε and ὅσος περ, see τέ and πέρ.

ὅσπερ, Ep. also ὅπερ, ἥπερ, ὅπερ; the strengthening πέρ indicates, a) That the relative clause has equal compass with the main clause: entirely, the very same, the very—who. θεὸς ὅσπερ ἔφηνεν, the very god, who, 2, 318. cf. 4, 524. b) Or that the clauses oppose each other. ὑπόσχεσις, ἥντερ ὑπέσταν, i. e. ὑποστάντες, περ, which they nevertheless promised, although having promised, 2, 286. 6, 100. Od. 20, 46. Frequently, however, it can be translated only by the simple relative who, which, cf. πέρ.

ὅσσα, ἡ (akin to ὄψ, ἔπος), 1) Generally, a voice, sound, a tone, as of the cithara, h. Merc. 443. 2) fame, report, rumour, eaply that of which the author is not known; it is therefore, as every thing for which a reason cannot be given, derived from the deity, Od. 1, 282.

Ὅσσα, ἡ, as pr. n. Ossa, a messenger of Zeus, 2, 93. Od. 24, 413.

Ὅσσα, ἡ, a mountain in Thessaly, famed as the abode of the centaurs, now Kissavos, Od. 11, 315.

ὅσσα, Ep. for ὅσα.

ὁσσάκι, Ep. for ὁσάκι.

ὁσσάτιος, η, ον, Ep. for ὁσάτιος.

ὅσσε, τώ, only nom. and accus. dual neut. in Il. and Od.; later also plur. ὄσσοις, h. 31, 9; the two eyes, also (in two passages), with adj. neut. plur. φαεινά, αἱματόεντα, Il. 13, 435. 617.

ὅσσομαι (from ὄσσε), depon. mid. only pres-. and imperf. 1) Prop. to look with the eyes, to see, cf. Od. 7, 31; esply 2) to see with the mind, to foresee, to surmise, to think upon any thing, κακά or κακόν. Od. 10, 374. 18, 154; ἄλγεα θυμῷ, Il. 18, 224; πατέρα ἐνὶ φρεσίν, Od. 1, 115; and without θυμῷ, φρεσί, Od. 20, 81. 3) to indicate any thing by the countenance or aspect, to foretoken, to look, κακά (Voss, 'with threatening look'), Il. 1, 105; ὄλεθρον, to threaten destruction, Od. 2, 152; spoken of the sea, Il. 14, 17; and generally, τινί τι, to predict any thing to any one, 24, 172.

ὅσσος, η, ον. Ep. for ὅσος.

ὅστε, ἥτε, ὅ, τε, he who, she who, that which; τέ indicates the mutual internal relation of the main and adjunct clauses, 2, 365. Od. 3, 73. Plur. ἅτε [τά τ'] after a sing. like those which [=οἷά τε, qualia, with ref. to the collective notion. F.]. Od. 5, 438; hence also such as.

'Οστέον.

όστέον, τό, Ep. gen. plur. όστεόφιν, 7d. 12, 45; a bone, spoken of the living, Il. 12, 185. Plur. όστέα, the bones of the dead, 7, 334.

όστις, ήτις, ό, τι, gen. ούτινος, ήστινος, ούτινος, Ep. forms : sing. nominative, όστις, ό, ττι, gen. ότευ, όττευ, όττευ, dat. ότεω, accus. ότινα, ό, ττι, plur. nomin. neut. δτινα, 22, 450; gen. ότεων, dat. ότέοισι, accus. ότινας, neut. άσσα. whoever, whatever ; this pronoun expresses the notion of indefiniteness or universality ; hence frequently to be translated each who, any ne, 2, 188. 19, 260. On the construct. with the moods, see ός. 2) Sometimes it refers to a definite object of a particular kind, yet in such a way that the notion of indefiniteness lies at the bottom : such as, which, Od. 2, 124. 3) In the indirect question : who, what, Il. 3, 167. Od. 1, 401.

*όστοφυής, ές (φυή), of a bony nature. bony, Batr. 298.

*όστρακόδερμος, ον (δέρμα), having a testaceous covering, having a hard skin, Batr. 297.

*όστρακον, τό, the hard shell of the tortoise, h. Merc. 33.

όταν, in H. ότ' άν, see ότε.

ότε, conjunct. of time : I) To mark a point of time: as, when, after, mly spoken of the past, more rarely of the present and future. 1) With Indic. when the declaration respects a fact ; also in comparisons, 3, 33. 4, 275. In the fut. the Ep. κέ is sometimes added, 20, 235. 2) With subj. after a primary tense, when the declaration is expressed as ideal or possible : mostly with άν or κέ, ότ' άν, ότε κεν, whereby the designation of time also appears as conditional: when, in case, as soon as, 1, 519. 4, 53 ; without άν and κέ, 2, 395. 782. b) To mark a frequently returning case : as often as, with άν, 2, 397. Od. 9, 6. c) Esply frequently in comparisons with άν, Il. 2, 147. 3) With optat. a) Chiefly as with the subj. after a historical tense, Od. 14, 122; to mark an indefinite repetition, Il. 1, 610. 10, 11. 14. Od. 8, 70. h) After another optat. in assigning a doubtful condition, Od. 2, 31 ; and as the continuation of a wish, Il. 18, 465. II) Spoken of a reason : as, since, quando, rarely, 1, 244. Od. 5, 357. III) ότε μή for ει μή, except when, always with optat. Il. 13, 319. 14, 248. IV) ότε for ότι, that, after οίδα, μέμνημαι, ακούειν, etc. 14, 71. 15, 18. V) In connexion with other particles: ότε δή, ότε τε, ότε περ, πρίν γ' ότε, before when ; εις ότε κε, for the time when, Od. 2, 99; cf. Kühner, § 688, seq. Thiersch, § 322. Rost, § 121.

ότέ, adv. (orig. = ότε), sometimes, now and then, oftentimes, 17, 178; mly in double sentences : ότέ μέν—άλλοτε δέ, or άλλοτε μέν—ότέ δέ, now—now, one while—another, 18, 599. 11, 566.

ότέοισιν, Ep. for οίστισιν.

ότευ, Ep. for ούτινος, Od.
ότέω, Ep. for ώτινι.
ότι, Ep. όττι, conj. that, because. 1) In introducing (dependent) explanatory clauses after verbs of thinking and declaring : that, always with indicat. in Il. 4, 32. 6, 126; also ότι ρά, ότι δή. 2) In assigning a reason : since, because. always with indic. 1, 56. 16, 35. 3) With a superl. adj. to indicate the highest degree : ότι τάχιστα, as quick as possible [quam cilissime], 4, 193. Od. 5, 112.

ότινα, ότινας, see όστις.
ότις, Ep. for όστις.
ότραλέως, adv. (ότρύνω), quickly, busily, fleetly, with despatch, 19, 317. Od. 19, 100.

'Οτρεύς, ήος, ό, son of Dymas, brother of Mygdon, sovereign of Phrygia, 3, 186. h. Ven. 111.

ότηρρός, ή, όν (ότρύνω), busy, quick, fleet, hasty, epith. of θεράποντε and of ταμίη, 6, 381. Od. 1, 109.

ότηρπως, busily, quickly, Od. 4, 735.†
ότρίχες, see δθριξ.
'Οτρυντείδης, ου, ό, son of Otryntens = Iphition, 20, 383.
'Οτρυντεύς, ήος, ό, king of Hyde on the Tmolus, father of Iphition, 20, 384.

ότρυντύς, ύος, ή (ότρύνω), poet. for ότρυνσις, encouragement, instigation, command, V. *19, 234, 235.

ότρύνω, fut. ότρυνέω, Ep. for ότρυνώ, aor. ώτρυνα, to urge on, to excite, to encourage, τινά. 1) Mly spoken of persons : to awaken from sleep, 10, 158; εις τι, to drive or send any one to any place, 15, 59. Od. 1, 85 ; πόλινδε. Od. 15, 306 ; πόλεμόνδε, to drive to the war, Il. 2, 589. 17, 383. b) For the most part with infin. to arouse, to animate, to stimulate, πολεμίζειν, μάχεσθαι, ιέναι, 1. 204. 414. 2, 94. Od. 14, 374. 2) Rarely spoken of brutes : ίππους, κύνας, Il. 16. 167. 18, 584. c) spoken of things : to urge on. to accelerate, to further, πομπήν. Od. 8, 30 ; τινι οδόν. Od. 2, 253 ; μάχην. Il. 12, 277. II) Mid. to urge oneself, to move oneself, to make haste, 14, 369 ; κάλινδε ίέναι, Od. 17, 183 ; and thus once the act. ώτρυνον, Il. 7, 420; where Aristarchus however read : ότρύνοντο πάσαι αγέμεν.

όττι, Ep. for ότι.
ό, ττι, Ep. for ό, τι.

ού, adv. of negation ; before a vowel having the spiritus lenis, ούκ ; before a vowel having the spiritus asper, ούχ; to this add the Ep. forms ούκί and ούχί q. v. This particle denies independently and directly, not merely the notion (cf. μή), but the existence of the thing or fact itself being denied. It stands sometimes before single words to deny the notion contained in them : ού φημι, i. e. I deny, I refuse, 7, 393 ; ούκ έώ, 5, 256 ; sometimes in whole sentences. I) In main clauses, ού stands, 1) When any thing is denied positively, whether it is expressed as something certain by the indicat. or as something possible by the optat. In H. οὐ also stands in connexion with the subjunct. when it has the signif. of the future, 1, 262. Od. 6, 201. 2) In interrogative sentences, as non, nonne, when the speaker expects an affirmative answer, Il. 10, 165. 3) In sentences which imply a command, by the optat. with ἄν, with and without a question: οὐκ ἂν δὴ τόνδ᾽ ἄνδρα μάχης ἐρύσαιο, wilt thou not — save? 5, 456. Od. 7, 22. II) In subordinate clauses: 1) In such as are introduced by ὅτι, ὡς, that; because they have the character of independent principal clauses. 2) In subordinate clauses showing the time and reason, commencing with ἐπεί, ἐπειδή, ὅτε, etc. Il. 21, 95. 3) In relative clauses, when the thought contained in them is positively denied. III) The negation is repeated: 1) For emphasis' sake, Od. 3, 27; thus also οὐ—οὐδέ, Il. 17, 641. Od. 8, 280. 2) When a whole which is denied is distributed into parts: οὐ—οὔτε—οὔτε, Il. 6, 450. 3) Indefinite pronouns and adverbs in a negative sentence (as any one, any where, etc.) are expressed negatively, 1, 86. 88.

οὗ, gen. sing. of the defect. pronoun of the third pers. masc. and fem. Ep. ἕο, ἕθ, εἷο, ἕθεν, dat. οἷ, accus. ἕε (εὖ and ἕθεν are enclitics), prop. reflexive: of himself, of herself, of itself; but often a personal pron. his, her, to him, to her, she, it; the accus. ἕ as neut. 1, 236; and for the plur. h. Ven. 268.

οὖας, ατος, τό, Ep. and poet. for οὖς.

οὖδας, τό (akin to οὖδός), poet. gen. οὔδεος, dat. οὔδει and οὔδαι, 1) the floor or pavement in chambers or houses, Od. 23, 46. Il. 5, 734. 2) the ground, the earth, Od. 9, 135. 13, 395. οὖδας ὀδάξ ἑλεῖν, to seize the earth with the teeth, i. e. to fall, Il. 11, 749. ὕπτιος οὔδει ἐρείσθη, he sank backwards to the earth, 7, 145; οὐδάσδε, to the ground, 17, 457.

οὐδέ, conjunc. (δέ), but not, and not; nor (yet). οὐδέ unites 1) Entire sentences, and expresses prop. an antithesis: not however, but not, 24, 25. Od. 3, 143. Often οὐδέ stands, when the same notion is expressed first affirmatively and then negatively: μνήσομαι οὐδὲ λάθωμαι, h. Apoll. 1. Od. 9, 408. 2) Mly it serves to annex a new sentence: and not, also not, nor yet, Il. 9, 372; often οὐ, οὐδέ. 3) οὐδὲ —οὐδέ, when occurring in one sentence it is a strengthened οὐδέ: not at all, certainly not, 5, 22. Od. 8, 32. οὐδὲ—οὐδέ at the beginning of two clauses signifies: also not—and not (never: neither—nor), Il. 9, 372. Sometimes we have also οὐδέ —οὔτε, h. Cer. 22. 4) οὐδέ in the middle of a sentence also stands in an adverbial signif. and means: also not, not even (ne ... quidem); often οὐδ᾽ ἠβαιόν, οὐδὲ τυτθόν.

οὐδείς, οὐδεμία, οὐδέν, gen. οὐδενός, etc. (οὐδέ, εἷς), also not one, i. e. no one, nothing. The neut. οὐδέν often stands as an adv. not at all, not in the least, 1, 412. Od. 4, 195. [A still stronger form of speech is οὐχ εἷς, found only once, h. Merc. 284. Am. Ed.]

οὐδενόσωρος, ον, ὁ (οὐδείς, ὥρα) not to be esteemed, contemptible, worthless, τείχεα, 8, 178.†

οὐδέπῃ or οὐδέ πῃ, adv. in no wise, i. e. not at all; in H. separated, Od. 12, 433; οὐδέ πῃ ἔστιν, with infin., it is by no means possible, h. 6, 58.

οὐδέποτε or οὐδέ ποτε, adv., also not ever, i. e. never, spoken of the past and future. Wolf writes at one time οὐδέποτε, 5, 789; at another divided, οὐδέ ποτε, Od. 2, 203.

οὐδέπω or οὐδέ πω, adv. not yet, mly not at all, in no wise, in H. mly separated by a word or more, 1, 108.

οὐδετέρωσε, adv. (οὐδέτερος), on neither side, in neither direction, 14, 18.†

οὐδός, ὁ, Ion. and Ep. for ὀδός, the threshold of a house; then also used of any other entrance, 6, 375. Od. 1, 104; of the under-world, Il. 8, 15. b) Metaph. γήραος οὐδός, the threshold of old age, i. e. its commencement. Thus Voss and Heyne; according to the ancient Gramm. = ἔξοδος γήρως, extreme old age, 22, 60. 24, 487. Od. 15, 246.

οὐδός, ἡ, Ion. for ὀδός, a way, Od. 17, 196.†

οὖθαρ, ατος, τό, the udder, the breast, prop. of animals, Od. 9, 440. b) Metaph. fruitfulness, fertility. οὖθαρ ἀρούρης, the fruitfulness of the land, i. e. blessed land, a land of milk and honey, Il. 9, 141. 283.

οὐκ, before a vowel for οὐ.

Οὐκαλέγων, οντος, ὁ (οὐκ, ἀλέγω), Ucalegon, a Trojan counsellor, 3, 148.

οὐκέτι, adv. (ἔτι), no more, no longer, not again, strengthened by οὐδέ, 12, 73.

οὐκέτι πάγχυ, no more at all, 19, 343.

οὐκί, adv. Ep. and Ion. for οὐκ, not, mly at the close of a sentence, 15, 137, Od. 11, 493.

οὐλαί, αἱ [according to Eustath. ad Il. 1, 449; and Et. Mag. ol], Att. ὀλαί, coarsely ground barley-corn, (Voss: 'sacred barley,') which was strewn between the horns of the victim before the sacrifice, Od. 3, 441.† The Gramm. derive οὐλή from ὅλος, whole, and supply κρίθαι, whole barley-corns; more prob. according to Buttm., Lex. p. 455, ὀλή comes from ΕΛΩ, ἀλέω, as τομή from τέμω, and signifies prop. that which is ground; then plur. οὐλαί, bruised barley-corns, barley-grits, the simplest treatment of grain. This was retained in sacred rites as a memorial of the earliest kind of food. Perhaps it was first roasted and mixed with salt (mola salsa, amongst the Romans).

οὐλαμός, ὁ (εἴλω), a press, a tumult, a crowd, ἀνδρῶν, *4, 251. 20, 118.

οὔλε, see οὔλω.

P 3

Οὐλή. 318 Οὐρανός.

οὐλή, ἡ (οὔλω), *a cicultrized wound, a scar*, Od. 19, 391. 393. 464.

οὖλος, η, ον (= ὅλος), Ep. for ὅλος, *destructive, pernicious*, epith. of the dog-star, 11, 62.†

οὐλοκάρηνος, ον (κάρηνον), *having curled hair*, Od. 19, 246.† 2) οὐλοκάρηνα *for* ὅλα κάρηνα, whole heads, h. Merc. 137.

οὐλόμενος, η, ον, prop. poet. for ὀλόμενος, partcp. aor. 2 mid. from ὄλλυμι; as adj. always in act. signif. *destructive, mischievous, deadly, pernicious*, spoken both of persons and of things, 1, 2. 14, 84. Od. 10, 304. (The pass. signif. perditus, *ruined, wretched*, as Od. 4, 92. 11, 410, have been explained, is preferred by Heyne ad Il. 14, 84. cf. Nitzsch, Od. 4, 92.)

*οὐλόπους, ποδος (πούς), from this οὐλόποδ᾽ for ὅλους πόδας, *whole feet*, h. Merc. 137.

οὖλος, η, ον, 1) Ep. and Ion. for ὅλος, *whole, unconsumed, entire*: ἄρτος, a whole loaf of bread, Od. 17, 343; μήν, a whole month, Od. 24, 118. 2) *healthy, sound*; and generally, *powerful, vigourous, sound, stout*. a) Spoken of the voice: οὖλον κεκληγοντες, stoutly, loudly crying, Il. 17, 756. 759. b) Spoken of material substances: *thick, firm, woolly* (V. 'curled,'), epith. of woollen stuffs, 16, 224. Od. 19, 225. 4, 50. οὖλαι λάχνη, thick wool, Il. 10, 134. οὖλαι κόμαι, thick hair, Od. 6, 231. 3) Ep. adj. from ὀλείν for ὀλοός, *destructive* (V. 'noisy, raging'), epith. of Arēs and Achilles, Il. 5, 461. 21, 336; ὄνειρος, the pernicious dream, 2, 6; the dream is so denominated on account of its destination, cf. Nägelsb. ad loc. (Passow would explain it as a 'corporeal god of dreams,' according to 1, b.) Buttmann, Lex. arranges the signification of οὖλος in the following branches: 1) For ὅλος, *whole*. 2) Ep. for ὀλοός from ὀλείν, *destructive, evil, dreadful*; to this add: οὖλον κεκληγοντες, to cry dreadfully. 3) From εἰλείν, *οὐλαμός, rough, woolly, bushy, curled*, spoken of wool and hair; so also Voss and Arat. Phæn.

οὐλοχύται, αἱ (χέω)=οὐλαί, *the bruised barley-corns*, which before the sacrifice were strewn upon the victim: 'sacred barley.' V., 1, 449. Od. 3, 447. 2) *the strewing of the sacred barley*, Od. 3, 445.

Οὔλυμπος, ὁ, Ep. for Ὄλυμπος.

οὔλω (οὖλος), *to be healthy, well*, only imperat. οὖλε, as a greeting: *be well*. οὖλέ τε καὶ χαῖρε, 'health and joy be with thee,' V., Od. 24, 402.†

οὑμός, contr. for ὁ ἐμός, 8, 360.

οὖν, adv. *now, therefore*, is connected in H. with other particles, and points back to something preceding, ἐπεὶ οὖν, *since now*, 1, 57. Od. 16, 453; ὡς οὖν, Il. 3, 261; γὰρ οὖν, Od. 2, 123; and οὔτ᾽ οὖν, μήτ᾽ οὖν.

οὕνεκα, by crasis for οὗ ἕνεκα, *wherefore, on which account*, Od. 3, 61. 2)

illy therefore because, because, Il. 1, 11. Od. 4, 569; also with preceding, τοῦ ἕνεκα, Il. 1, 111; or a following τοὔνεκα, 3, 403. 3) In the Od. after some verbs: *therefore that, in as far, that*, like ὅτι, Od. 5, 216. 7, 300. 15, 42. h. Ap. 376. [4) In a single passage demonstrative= τοὔνεκα, Il. 9, 505.]

οὕνεσθε, Ep for ὄνεσθε, see ὄνομαι.

οὔνομα, Ion. and Ep. for ὄνομα, q. v.

οὔπερ and οὔ περ, adv. *by no means, not at all*, 14, 416.

οὔπῃ, adv. (πῇ), *no where, in no place*. 2) *in no way, in no manner*, 13, 191. Od. 5, 140.

οὔ ποθι (οὐ ποθί), *nowhere*, 13, 399. 23, 463; οὐδέ ποθι, also not in any way, *in no way*, Od.

οὔποτε, adv. (ποτέ), *never*, often separated by several words, 1, 163. 4, 48.

οὔπω (πώ), *not yet*, often separated by a word, 1, 224; esply οὐ γάρ πω, Od. 1, 196. 216.

οὔπως, adv. (πώς), not how, i. e. *in no wise, not at all*, often οὔπως ἐστίν, with infin. it is impossible, 12, 65. Od. 2, 130; so also οὔπως ἔτι εἶχεν, he was no longer able, Il. 7, 354; also separated, οὐ γάρ πως, 14, 63; οὐ μέν πως, 2, 203.

οὐρά, ἡ, see οὐρή.

οὐραι, τά, see οὖρον.

οὐραῖος, η, ον (οὐρά), *belonging to the tail*. τρίχες οὐρ., the hairs of the tail, 23. 520.

*Οὐρανίη, ἡ, name of a nymph. prop. *the heavenly (Urania)*, h. Cer. 423.

*οὐράνιος, η, ον (οὐρανός), *heavenly, in heaven*, h. Cer. 55. οὐράνια κτέρεα. Batr. 26.

[οὐρανίων, without a capital, defended by Freytag and Lange, see Οὐρανίων.]

Οὐρανίων, ωνος, ὁ (οὐρανός), 1) *heavenly, dwelling in heaven*, epith. of the gods, 1, 570; as subst. οἱ Οὐρανίωνες, the celestials, 5, 373. 2) Patronym. the sons of Uranus=the *Titans*, 5, 898.

*οὐρανόθεκτος, ον (δείκνυμι), *showing itself in heaven*, αἰγλη, h. 32, 3.

οὐρανόθεν, adv. (οὐρανός), *from heaven, down from heaven*, ἐξ οὐρανόθεν, 8, 19; and ἀπ᾽ οὐρανόθεν, 8, 365. Od. 11, 18.

οὐρανόθι, adv. (οὐρανός), *in heaven*, οὐρανόθι πρό, i. e. πρὸ οὐρανοῦ, in the lower air, 3, 3.†

οὐρανομήκης, ες (μῆκος), *heaven-high*, *extending into heaven*, ἐλάτη [cloud-piercing fir, Cp.], Od. 5, 239.†

οὐρανός, ὁ, *heaven*, i. e. 1) *the vault of heaven*, which rests upon the tops of the highest mountains, hence: οὐρανός, *a limit*, from ὁρεῖν, ὁρίζειν. It was conceived of as a hollow hemisphere, which was as far above the earth as Hades was beneath it, 8, 16. The arch is called *brazen* or *iron*, 17, 425. 5, 504. Od. 15, 329. In this vault the sun, moon, and stars daily accomplish their course, rising from Oceanus in the east, and sinking into it in the west, Od. 5, 275. Il. 18, 489.

Οὐρανός. 319 Οὖτις.

seq. The clouds cover the heavens, and hide from the inhabitants of the earth the view of it, of the æther and the constellations, Od. 5, 293. Il. 8, 555; hence 2) *the atmospheric space above the earth*, which was distinguished from the αἰθήρ, 2, 458. 8, 558, 15, 192. Since Olympus extends into the upper air, οὐρανός is called, 3) *the abode of the gods*, 6, 108. Od. 1, 67. (We nowhere, however, find in the poems of Hom. the observation of Voss confirmed, that the arch of heaven has an opening directly over Olympus.) 4) Metaph. *heaven*, to denote the highest region: οὐρανὸν ἱκάνειν, to reach, to pierce to heaven, Il. 2, 153. Od. 12, 73, and often; cf. Völcker's Hom. Geogr. p. 5—14.

Οὐρανός, ὁ, prop. name, son of Erebus and of Gæa (Tellus), husband of Gæa (Tellus), by whom he begat the Titans and Titanides, the Cyclôpes, the Hecatoncheires, Hes. Th. 125. Il. 15, 36. Od. 5, 184.

οὔρεα, τά, Ion. for ὄρεα, see ὄρος.

*οὔρειος, η, ον, Ion. and Ep. for ὄρειος (ὄρος), *mountainous*, h. Merc. 244.

οὐρεύς, ῆος, ὁ, Ion. for ὀρεύς (probably from ὄρος), *a mule*, 1, 50. 24, 716; see ἡμίονος.

οὐρεύς, ῆος, ὁ, Ion. for οὖρος, *a watch, a guard*, 10, 84;† in the gen. οὐρήων. This verse was rejected by the ancients because οὐρεύς was here made to signify *a watch*. Voss translates it *mule*, and Menelaus might be supposed looking for a mule that had strayed.

οὐρή, ἡ, Ion. for οὐρά, *the tail*, 20, 170. Od. 17, 302.

οὐρίαχος, ὁ (οὐρά), *the extreme end*; always with ἔγχεος, *13, 443. 16, 612.

οὖρον, τό, Ep. for ὅρος, *a boundary, extent, space*, plur. οὖρα. ὅσσον τ' ἐν νειῷ οὖρον πέλει ἡμιόνοιιν, as far in the fallow field as is the limit to the mules, i. e. as much as is required of a pair of mules in the same time in which Cytoneus ran; as oxen accomplish less, Od. 8, 124. ὅτε δὴ ῥ' ἀπέην ὅσσον τ' ἐπὶ οὖρα (thus Spitzner after the Schol. instead of the common ἐπίουρα), πέλονται ἡμιόνων, when he was so far removed as the space of mules extends, Il. 10, 350. The sense is: Dolon ran so far forward as a pair of mules could plough, viz. in the time that Odysseus (Ulysses) and Diomedes remain standing. The words αἱ γάρ τε βοῶν προφερέστεραί εἰσιν are added by Hom. to show that the distance between Dolon and the two heroes was considerable. Thus Heyne and Spitzner, Excurs. XX, correctly explain the passage. Less natural seems the explanation of Aristarchus followed by Voss. Aristarchus namely supposes two teams, and finds the point of comparison in the space by which a pair of mules in ploughing outstrips a yoke of oxen: (*for as mules surpass slow oxen furrowing the fallow field*, Cp.); ὅσα δίσκου οὖρα πέλονται, as far as

are the limits of the discus, i. e. as far as it flies, 23, 431.

οὖρος, ὁ, poet. *a favorable wind*, often ἵκμενος οὖρος (*secundus ventus*), 7, 5. Od. 2, 420; plur. Od. 4, 360. (From ὄρνυμι, or prob. akin to αὔρη.)

οὖρος, ὁ, Ion. for ὅρος. Ep. also οὖρον, τό, *a boundary, a limit*, dat. plur. 12, 421; accus. sing. *21, 405.

οὖρος, εος, τό, Ion. for ὅρος, q. v. *a mountain*.

οὖρος, ὁ, poet. (from ὁράω), *a watcher, a guard*, Od. 15, 89. Thus esply Nestor, οὖρος Ἀχαιῶν, guardian or protector of the Greeks, Il. 8, 80. Od. 3, 411. Damm derives it fm ὥρα, *cura*.

οὐρός, ὁ (ὈΡΩ, moveo), *the trench* or canal (ὄρυγμα), by which the ships were drawn into the sea. These canals must have been easily choked up, since they were cleaned out when the ships were to be run into the sea, 2, 153.†

οὖς, τό, gen. ὠτός, dat. plur. ὠσίν, Ep. and Ion. οὔας, ατος (dat. plur. οὔασι, 12, 442). (Of the comm. form only accus. sing. and dat. plur. 11, 109. 20, 473. Od. 12, 200.) 1) *the ear*. ἀπ' οὔατος, far from the ear, Il. 22, 454. 2) *an ear*, i. e. *a handle*, 11, 633. 18, 378.

οὐτάζω, fut. άσω; and οὐτάω, fut. ήσω. Of the first form H. has pres. and imperf. aor. οὔτασα, perf. pass. οὔτασμαι, 11, 661; and from οὐτάω only aor. 1 οὔτησα, aor. pass. οὐτηθείς. Besides the Ep. iterat. imperf. οὔτασκε and the aor. 1 οὐτήσασκε, we find the Ep. aor. 2 οὖτα, infin. οὐτάμεν and οὐτάμεναι, and partcp. aor. 2 mid. οὐτάμενος, *to wound, to hit, to strike*, with any kind of weapon, χαλκῷ, ἔγχει, δουρί, ξίφει: but spoken esply of weapons used with the hand, 11, 661. Od. 11, 536; with accus. of the pers. or the part wounded, and with double accus. τινὰ πλευρά, Il. 4, 469. 13, 438; also τινὰ κατὰ λαπάρην, κατ' ἀσπίδα, 6, 64. 11, 434; and spoken of things: οὐτάζειν σάκος, to injure the shield, 7, 258; also ἕλκος, to strike a wound, 5, 361; hence οὐταμένη ὠτειλή, 14, 518.

οὔτασκε, see οὐτάω.

οὐτάω, see οὐτάζω.

οὔτε, adv. *and not*, mly doubled: οὔτε, οὔτε, *neither, nor*, to connect negative members of a sentence. We also find the following constructions: οὐ—οὔτε, 6, 450. 22, 265; οὐδὲ—οὔτε, h. Cer. 22. A negative sentence is connected with a positive by οὔτε—τί, *not—and*, 24, 185.

οὐτήσασκε, see οὐτάζω.

οὔτι, neut. of οὔτις, q. v.

οὐτιδανός, ἡ, όν (οὔτις), *profitless, worthless, good for nothing, naught*, 1, 231. Od. 9, 460.

οὔτις, neut. οὔτι (τίς), *no one, no man*. The neut. οὔτι, stands after adv. *not at all, by no means*, Od. 4, 199; often separate, Od. 1, 202.

Οὖτις, ὁ, accus. Οὖτιν, a feigned name of Odysseus (Ulysses), which he assumed

Οὗτοι   320   Ὀφρύς

to Polyphêmus, in order to deceive him by the *double entendre*, Od. 9, 369.
οὗτοι, adv. (τοι), *certainly not, verily not, assuredly not*, 6, 335. Od. 1, 203.
οὗτος, αὕτη, τοῦτο (ὁ, τος), demonstrat. pron. *this, that*. H. rarely connects οὗτος by the article with the subst. τοῦτον τὸν ἄναλτον, Od. 18, 114. 1) Mly it refers to the nearest preceding object, not unfrequently however also to something following, as Il. 13, 377. Od 2, 306. 2) Frequently it is used to point out the near or remote place of an action, and can be translated only by an adverb: οὗτος τοι,—ἔρχεται ἀνήρ, there comes a man, 10, 341. τίς δ' οὗτος—ἔρχεαι, 10, 82. 3) Before a relative sentence with ὅς, it signifies: *he, the one*, Od. 2, 40. 6, 201. It is frequently however omitted before ὅς, Il. 10, 306. Od. 11, 433. seq.; also in exclamations, ἄλγιον, Od. 4, 292. 4) The neut. ταῦτα often signifies, *in this, therefore*, Od. 2, 180. Il. 3, 399.
οὕτω, and before a vowel οὕτως, adv. (οὗτος), *of this kind, in this way, i. e. thus, so*, under these circumstances, in this condition. *a)* Mly the οὕτως has for its correlative ὡς, *so—as*, 4, 178. *b)* Emphatically with the fut and imperf.: οὕτως ἔσται, so shall it be, Od. 11, 348; κεῖσ' οὕτω, lie there thus, Il. 21, 184. *c)* Like αὔτως: thus idly, μὰψ οὕτω, 2, 120. *d)* In wishes and asseverations, also after εἰ and αἴθε with ὡς following: εἰ γὰρ ἐγὼν οὕτω γε Διὸς παῖς εἴην, if I were indeed thus certainly (i. e. as truly as I wish it) the son of Zeus, 13, 825. *e)* It also stands connected: οὕτω δή, thus then; οὕτω νου, thus indeed: οὕτω πῃ, thus perchance (24, 373]. [*f*] So = *tam*, 13, 309; cf. II. δεύω.]
οὐχ, before an aspirate or a spiritus asper for οὐκ.
οὐχί, a strengthened form of οὐχ, *not, no*, *15, 716. 16, 762.
ὀφείλω, Ep. also ὀφέλλω, Od. 8. 332. 462. 3, 367; aor. 2 ὤφελον, Ep. ὄφελον, ὄφελλον and ὠφέλλον, 1) *to be indebted, to have to pay, to owe*, χρεῖός τινι, a debt to any man, Il. 11, 688; and pass. χρεῖος ὀφείλεταί μοι, a debt is owed to me, 11, 688. Od. 3, 367. 2) Generally, *to be under obligation, duty or necessity*, as expressed by ought, should, must, in H. only aor. 2 ὤφελον mly with infin. Il. 1, 353. 10, 117. 23, 546. Od. 4, 97. *b)* Esply this aor. with and without αἴθε, εἴθε, ὡς, expresses a wish which cannot be fulfilled; the infin pres. follows when the wish refers to the present; the infin. aor. when it refers to the past (cf. Rost's Gram. p. 577); αἴθ' ὄφελες παρὰ νηυσὶν ἀδάκρυτος ἦσθαι, O that thou mightest sit tearless at the ships, Il. 1. 415. ὡς, ὄφελες, αὐτόθ' ὀλέσθαι, would that thou hadst perished there, 3, 426. cf. 1, 173. 6, 346. Od. 1, 217; also with negat. μὴ ὄφελες, would thou hadst not —, Il. 9, 698. Od. 8, 312.

Ὀφελέστης, ου, ὁ, 1) a Trojan, 8, 274 2) a Paeonian, 21, 210.
ὀφέλλω, Ep. for ὀφείλω, q. v.
ὀφέλλω, besides pres. and imperf. only optat. aor. ὀφέλλειεν, Od. 2, 334; *to augment, to increase, to enlarge, to strengthen, to bless*, πόνον, στόνον, μένος, ἀρετήν: spoken of the wind: κύματα, to increase the waves, Il. 15, 383; οἶκος. to enrich the house, Od. 15, 21; pass. Od 14, 233; μῦθον, to amplify discourse, i. e. to make many words, Il. 16, 631; ὀφέλλειν τινὰ τιμῇ, to increase any man in honour, i. e. to show him greater honour, 1, 510.
ὄφελος, εος, τό (ὀφέλλω), *profit, advantage, furtherance*. αἴ κ' ὄφελός τι γενώμεθα, if perchance we may be of some use, 13. 236. ὅς τοι πόλλ' ὄφελος γένετο, who was of great use to thee, *17, 152. h. Merc. 34.
Ὀφέλτιος, a Trojan, 6, 20. 2) a Greek, 11, 302.
ὀφθαλμός, ὁ (ὀφθῆναι). 1) *the eye*. ὀφθαλμῶν βολαί, the looks of the eyes, Od. 4, 150. 2) Generally, *the sight, the countenance*, Il. 24, 204.
ὄφις, ιος, ὁ, *a serpent*, 12, 208.† (o is long through the arsis.)
ὄφρα, conjunc. Ep. and Ion. I) Conj. of time. 1) To indicate simultaneousness: *whilst, as long as*. *a)* With ind. c. when the declaration respects something real, 2, 769. 5, 788; in the apodosis mly τόφρα, 4. 220. 18, 257. *b)* With subj. when the declaration is represented as something ideal or possible, 4, 346. 5, 524; also ἄν, κέ are annexed, Il, 187; (ὄφρα κεν κεῖται, 24, 554: where Spitzner correctly reads κηται.) 2) To indicate something following *until, till, up to*. *a)* With indicat. mostly preterite, 5, 557. 10, 488; Isl. 5, 110. 16, 243. *b)* With subjunct. when an expected or designed end is expressed, mly in the aor. 1, 82. 6, 113. 17, 155; also ἄν and κέ are annexed, 6, 258. Od. 4, 588. *c)* With optat. Il. 10, 571; and with ἄν, Od. 17, 298. 3) Absol. as an adv. *for a time, a while, in the mean time*, Il. 15, 547. II) Conjunct. of purpose: in sentences indicating design, *that*. *a)* With subj. after a primary tense: also with ἄν, κε. 2, 440. Od. 12. 52; and after an aor. with pres. signif Od. 1, 311. Often with a short mood vowel, Od. 3, 419. Il. 1, 147. *b)* With optat. after an historical tense, or in dependent discourse, 4, 300. 5, 690. Od 1, 261; ὄφρα μή, that not, Kühner. § 468, seq. 644. seq. Thiersch, § 316. 338, 341. Rost, § 121, 122.
ὀφρυόεις, εσσα, εν (ὀφρύς), *having eminences, situated on lofty ground*. epith. of Troy, 22, 411.†
ὀφρύς, ύος, ἡ, accus. plur. ὀφρῦς, contr. for ὀφρύας, 16, 740. 1) *the eye-brow*, mly plur. 13, 88. Od. 4, 153. 2) *an elevation, an eminence, the brow of a hill*, Il. 20, 151.

ὄχα, adv. Ep. (ἔχω, ὄχος), prop. *prominently;* then, *by far, far,* always in connexion with the superl. ὀχ' ἄριστος. 1, 69. Od. 3, 129.

ὄχεσφι, poet. dat., see ὄχος.

ὀχετηγός, όν, poet. (ἄγω), *cutting a trench* or *canal; cutting channels* or *water-courses for irrigation.* ἀνήρ [a peasant conducting a rill (through his garden), Cp.], 21, 257.†

ὀχεύς, ῆος, ὁ, poet. (ὀχέω), *a holder,* an instrument for carrying or fastening; hence, 1) the strap or thong with which the helmet was bound under the chin, 3, 372; the clasps of the girdle. 4, 132. 2) Frequently the *bolts* or *bars* which fastened the gate, 12, 121. 291. Od. 21, 47.

ὀχέω (ὄχος), iterative imperf. ὀχέεσκον, fut. mid. ὀχήσομαι, 24, 731; aor. ὀχησάμην. 1) *to carry, to convey, to conduct,* hence metaph. νηπιάας, to practise puerilities, Od. 1, 297. 2) *to endure, to bear,* ὀϊζύν, μόρον, Od. 7, 211. 11, 619. Mid. *to be borne, to suffer oneself to be borne,* κύμασιν, Od. 5, 54; chiefly by ships, chariots, and beasts; *to travel, to ride,* νηυσίν, Il. 24, 731; ἵπποισιν, h. Ven. 218; ἵπποι ἀλεγεινοὶ ὀχέεσθαι, horses difficult to manage, 10, 403. 17, 77.

Ὀχήσιος, ὁ, an Ætolian, 5, 843.

ὀχθέω, Ep. (akin to ἄχθεσθαι), *to be heavy at heart,* from pain, anger, despondency; hence *to be displeased, sad, dispirited, troubled;* often μέγ' ὀχθήσας ἔφη or εἶπε, 4, 30. Od. 4, 332.

ὄχθη, ἡ (ἔχω), prop. prominence; an *elevation of earth, a wall of earth;* esply *a shore, a coast,* 4, 475. Od. 6, 97; spoken of a trench, Il. 15, 356.

ὄχθος, ὁ=ὄχθη, a mound of earth, a hill, h. Ap. 17.

ὀχλέω, Ion. for ὀχλεύω (ὀχλεύς), prop. to move forward with a lever, *to roll on,* only pass. ὑπὸ ψηφῖδες ἅπασαι ὀχλεῦνται, 21, 261.

ὀχλίζω (ὀχλεύς), = ὀχλέω, only optat. aor. 1 ὀχλίσσειαν, prop. to remove with a lever, *to convey away, to roll away,* τὶ ἀπ' οὔδεος ἐπ' ἄμαξαν, something from the ground to the carriage, 12, 448. Od. 9, 242.

ὄχος, εος, τό (ἔχω), always in the plur. τὰ ὄχεα, Ep. dat. ὀχέεσσιν and ὄχεσφιν, *a chariot,* often παρ' ἵπποισι καὶ ὄχεσφιν, 5, 794. 12, 114; also ὑπ' ὄχεσφι τιτύσκεσθαι, 13, 23.

ὄχος, ὁ (ἔχω), *a holder, a bearer;* νηῶν ὄχοι, a holder or protector of ships, spoken of a port, Od. 5, 404.† 2) *a carriage, a chariot*=τὸ ὄχος, h. Cer. 19.

ὄψ, ὀπός, ἡ (ἔπος), accus. ὄπα, *the voice* of men and of animals, 2, 182; spoken of the shriek of Cassandra, Od. 11, 421; of the weeping of Penelope, Od. 20, 92; of the voice of the cicāda, Il. 3, 152; of the bleating of lambs, 4, 135. 2) *utterance, discourse,* 7, 53; ὀπ' for ὀψ', h. 27, 18.

ὀψέ, adv. (akin to ὄπις), *late, long after,* esply *late in the day, at evening,* 21, 232. Od. 5, 272.

ὀψείω (ὄψομαι), desiderat. *to wish to see,* with gen. αὐτῆς καὶ πολέμοιο, 14, 37.†

ὀψίγονος, ον (γόνος), *late-born, born after,* h. Cer. 141; ἄνθρωποι, posterity, 3, 353. Od. 1, 302.

ὄψιμος, ον, poet. (ὀψέ), *late, late-fulfilled,* τέρας, 2, 325.†

ὄψις, ιος, ἡ (ὄψομαι), dat. ὄψει, *the sight,* i. e. *the aspect, the appearance, the countenance,* 6, 468. Od. 23, 94. h. 18, 29.

ὀψιτέλεστος, ον (τελέω), *late-fulfilled,* or *to be fulfilled,* τέρας, 2, 325.† [Like ὄψιμος, Passow. The emphasis lies not merely in the synonym, but also in the asyndeton: see Nägelsbach ad Il. 1, 99.]

ὄψομαι, fut. of ὁράω.

ὄψον, τό (from ἕψω, prop. any thing cooked), esply any thing eaten with bread, particularly *meat,* Od. 3, 480; generally, *viands,* Il. 11, 630; the onion is called ὄψον ποτῷ, a luncheon with drink. Later, fish were so called, but these in the Homeric age were eaten only in case of necessity.

Π.

Π, the sixteenth letter of the Greek alphabet; hence in Hom. the sign of the sixteenth rhapsody.

πάγεν, Ep. for ἐπάγησαν, see πήγνυμι.

πάγη, Ep. for ἐπάγη, see πήγνυμι.

παγίς, ίδος, ἡ (πήγνυμι), a trap, a snare, Batr. 50.

παγκράτιον, τὸ (κρατέω), the pancratium, a kind of combat including at once wrestling and boxing, prop. *the all-combat,* Batr. 95.

πάγος, ὁ (πήγνυμι), *a point of rock, a cliff of rock, a rocky summit,* *Od. 5, 405 [*a craggy mass,* Cp.]. 411.

παγχάλκεος, ον (χαλκός), *all of brass, entirely brazen,* 20, 102; ἄορ, Od. 8, 403; ῥόπαλον, Od. 11, 575.

πάγχαλκος, ον = παγχάλκεος, *Od. 18, 378. 22, 102.

παγχρύσεος, ον (χρυσός), *all of gold, entirely golden,* 2, 448.† h. 8, 4.

πάγχυ, adv. (πᾶς), poet. for *πάνυ, altogether, entirely,* with augment μάλα πάγχυ, 14, 143. Od. 17, 217; once πάγχυ λίην, Od. 4, 825.

πάθε, Ep. for ἔπαθε, see πάσχω.

παθέειν, Ep. for παθεῖν, see πάσχω.

παιδνός, ή, όν (shortened from παιδικός), *childish, childlike,* in H. as subst. for παῖς, a boy, *Od. 21, 21. 24, 338.

παιδοφόνος, ον (φονεύω), *slaying children* or *boys,* 24, 506.†

παίζω (παῖς), fut. σω, mly in pres. and imperf., imperat. aor. only Od. 8, 251, παίσατε, prop. to behave like a child, hence 1) *to play, to trifle, to sport,* to amuse oneself, Od. 6, 106. 7, 291. h. Cer. 5, 425. 2) Esply *to dance,* Od. 8, 251.

P 5

Παιήων.   322   Πάλιν.

23, 147 *b*) *to play*, σφαίρῃ, with a ball, *Od. 6, 100. *c*) Spoken of a musical instrument, h. Ap. 206.

Παιήων, ονος, ὁ, Ion. for Παιάν, Παιών, Pæon, prop. *the healer, the deliverer*, from παω = παύω, according to Etym. Mag. In Hom. the physician of the gods, who cured the wounded Hades and Arēs, 5, 401. 899. He is distinct from Apollo, who is not yet mentioned as a physician, 5, 445. Eustath. ad Od. 4, 232: later an appellation of Apollo and Asklēpios (Æsculapius), as even h. in Ap. 272.

παιών, ονος, ὁ, as appell. *the pæan*, a solemn hymn to Apollo for deliverance from pestilence, 1, 473; and generally, *a hymn of praise, a song of rejoicing*, *22, 391.

Παίονες, οἱ, sing. Παίων, *the Pæōnes*, or Pæonians; inhabitants of Pæonia, who were famed as archers, 2, 848. 10, 428.

Παιονίδης, ου, ὁ, son of Pæon=*Agastrŏphus*, 11, 339.

Παιονίη, ἡ (Παίων), a region in the north of Thrace, on the Orbelus, between the Axius and Strymon, 17, 350.

παιπαλόεις, εσσα, εν, of uncertain signif., prop. according to Herm. ad h. Ap. 39, and Lucas, from πάλλειν with the reduplication παι, much twisted or wound, hence *rough, rocky, jagged*, epith. of mountains, 13, 17. Od. 10, 97; spoken of steep (rugged) ways, Il. 12, 168. Od. 17, 204; and of rocky islands, Chios, Samos, Imbros, Od. 3, 170. 4, 671. 11. 13, 33. [Död. identifies the root παλ- with Germ. *Fels, rock;* the '*fell*' of Cumberland, &c.]

παῖς, παιδός, ὁ and ἡ, often in the Ep. language. nom. πάϊς, voc. πάϊ. Buttm. and Herm. ad Orph. Præf. p. 15, would place the diæresis everywhere when the verse does not require the monosyllabic form. Otherwise Spitzner see Rost, p. 381; *a child*. *a*) In respect to age: *a boy, a girl, a lad, a virgin;* as adj. παῖς συφορβός, a young swineherd, 21, 282. *b*) In respect to descent: *a son, a daughter*, 1, 20. Od. 4, 263. παῖς παιδός, a child's child, a grandchild, Od. 19, 404; plur. Il. 20. 308.

Παισός, ἡ=Ἀπαισός, q. v.

παιφάσσω (φάω), poet. *to look, around wildly, restlessly*, only partcp. παιφάσσουσα (V. far-shining), Il. 2, 450.† (Wolf in his Comment. on Il. explains it, with the Schol and Eustath. *to rush wildly on*.)

Παίων, ονος, ὁ, see Παίονες.

πάλαι, adv. *anciently, from ancient times, formerly*, in opposition to νῦν, 9, 527. 2) *long ago, even earlier*, 23, 871. Opposed to νῦν, 9, 105. Od. 17, 366.

παλαιγενής, ές (γένος), *born long since, old, aged*, epith. of γεραιός. ἄνθρωπος, 3, 386. Od. 22, 395. h. Cer. 113.

παλαιός, ή, όν (πάλαι), compar. παλαίτερος, η, ον, 1) *old*, from former times, Ἶλος, ξεῖνος; spoken of things: οἶνος, neut. plur. παλαιά, Od. 2, 188. 2) *old,*

aged, full of years, in oppos. to νέος, Il. 14, 108. 136; γέρων, Od. 13, 432.

παλαισμοσύνη, ἡ, poet. (παλαίω), *wrestling, the art of wrestling*, 23, 701. Od. l. 103.

παλαιστής, οῦ, ὁ (παλαίω), *a wrestler,* Od. 8, 246.†

παλαίφατος, ον (φημί), *spoken a long time since, very old, ancient*, θέσφατα. Od. 9, 507. 13, 172. *b*) *of which the* is an old fable, *fabulous*. οὐ γὰρ ἀπὸ δρυός ἐσσι παλαιφάτου, not from the oak in the fable art thou sprung, V., Od. 14, 163. cf. δρῦς.

παλαίω (πάλη), ἐπάλαισα, *to wrestle, engage in a wrestling-match*, 23, 621; τινί, with any man, *Od. 4, 343. 17, 134.

παλάμη, ἡ (πάλλω), Ep. gen. and dat. παλάμηφι, 1) *the palm of the hand*, generally, *the hand* itself. 2) As a symbol of strength: *the hand* or *fist*, 3, 128. 5, 558.

παλάσσω (πάλλω), fut. παλάξω, perf. pass. πεπάλαγμαι, 1) *to sprinkle, to stain, to defile;* τί τινι, any thing with any thing, αἵματί τ᾽ ἐγκεφάλῳ τε σύδε. Od. 13, 395; often pass. Il. 5, 100; Ιόθρῳ πεπαλαγμένος, 6, 268. ἐγκεφαλος πεπάλακτο, the brain was defiled (viz. with blood) (V., mingled with blood). 11. 98. 12, 186. *b*) Mid. *to sprinkle ourself;* χεῖρας λύθρῳ, to defile one's hands with blood, 11, 169. cf. h. Merc. 554. 2) Like πάλλω only in the perf. pass. κλήρῳ πεπαλάχθαι, *to be taken by lot, to decide by lot, to cast lots*, 7, 171. Od. 9, 331. (According to Eustath. παλάσσω signifies not merely to sprinkle, but also to strike generally, cf. βάλλειν.)

πάλη, ἡ (πάλλω), *wrestling, a combat of wrestling* (luctus), 23, 635. Od. 8, 206.

παλίλλογος, ον (λέγω), *collected again*. παλίλλογα ἐπαγείρειν, to bring together things again collected; to collect together again, 1, 126.†

παλιμπετής, ές (πίπτω), prop. *falling back*, only the neut. παλιμπετές as adv. *back;* ἔρχειν, to drive backwards, 16, 395. ἀπονέεσθαι, Od. 5, 27. The Gramm. take it incorrectly as a syncope for the plur. παλιμπετέες, see Buttm., Lex. p. 296.

παλιμπλάζομαι (πλάζομαι), only partcp aor. pass. παλιμπλαγχθείς, poet. *to wander back, to wander round again*. παλιμπλαγχθέντες (Bothe: *iterum errantibus acti*), 1, 59. Od. 13, 5. [Nägelsbach ad Il. explains it by πλάζειν τινά, *to come a man to wander from his road;* hence from his object; οἱ μὲ μέγα πλάζουσι (Il. 2, 132). sc. τῆς ὁρμῆς. Hence he agrees with Eustath.: ἀντὶ τοῦ ὀπίσω μάτην (Schol. ἀπράκτους, infecta re) ἀνονοστήσαντες.]

πάλιν, adv. 1) *back, backwards*, always spoken of place in H. πάλιν δοῦναι. οἴχεσθαι, τρέπειν, to give, go, turn back, 1, 116; 380. 13, 2; sometimes with gen. πάλιν τρέπειν ἔγχος τινός, to turn back the spear from any man, 20, 439. πάλιν αὖ

Παλινάγρετος.   525   Πάναιθος.

Θυγατέρος, 21, 504; sometimes strengthened. πάλιν αὖτις, back again, 5, 257. ἄψ πάλιν and πάλιν ὀπίσσω, 18, 280. Od. 11, 149. 2) *back*, with the notion of opposition: πάλιν ἐρέειν, to contradict, Il. 9, 56. πάλιν λάζεσθαι μῦθον, to take back the word, i. e. *to speak otherwise than before*, 4, 357. Od. 13, 254. 3) Later: *again, anew*, Batr. 115.

παλινάγρετος, ον, poet. (ἀγρέω), prop. taken back; then *to be taken back, to be re-called*. τέκμωρ οὐ παλινάγρετον, an irrevocable pledge, 1, 526.†

παλινόρμενος, ον, poet. (ὄρνυμι), *turning back, hastening back*, 11, 326.†

παλίνορσος, ον, poet. (ὄρνυμι), *turning back, hastening back*, 3, 33.†

παλίντιτος, ον, poet. (τίνω), *paid back, requited*, hence *punished, avenged*. παλίντιτα ἔργα γίγνονται, the deeds were avenged, *Od. 1, 379. 2, 144.

παλίντονος, ον (τείνω), *stretched back*, epith. of the bow, which can be drawn back, hence a general epith. in reference to its elasticity; *flexible, elastic*, 8, 266. Od. 21, 11. Thus Köppen and Spitzner ad Il. 15, 443. Some critics take it in a double sense: *a) stretched back*, spoken of the bow, whose string is drawn back when an arrow is to be shot, 8, 266. 15, 443. *b) loosed, unbent*, spoken of the bow in a state of rest, 10, 459. Others, with Eustath. ad Il. 8, 266, understand by παλίντονον τόξον, a bow which has a repeated curvature, as the Scythian bow, or which was bent upwards at both ends.

παλιρρόθιος, ον (ῥόθος), *rushing back, flowing back*, κῦμα, *Od. 5, 430. 9, 485.

*παλίσκιος, ον, poet. (σκιά), *deeply-shaded, dark*, ἄντρον, h. 17, 6.

παλίωξις, ιος, ἡ, poet. (ἰωκή), *the act of turning and driving back*, when the flying party turns and repels the pursuer, and in turn becomes the pursuer, *12, 71. 15, 69.

παλλακίς, ίδος, ἡ, *a concubine*, 9, 449. 452. Od. 14, 203.

Παλλάς, άδος, ἡ, epith. of *Athênê*, from πάλλω, as brandishing the spear, or on account of the expertness of her hands in certain arts, mly Παλλὰς Ἀθήνη or Ἀθηναίη, Il.

Πάλλας, αντος, ὁ, father of Selene, h. Merc. 100.

πάλλω, aor. 1 ἔπηλα, Ep. sync. aor. masc. 3 sing. πάλτο, 15, 645. 1) *to brandish, to hurl, to cast*; with accus. τινὰ χερσίν, to toss (a child) in one's hands, 6, 474. Esply *a)* Spoken of weapons: δοῦρα, ἔγχος, λίθον. *b)* Spoken of lots: κλήρους, to shake the lots, viz. in the helmet till one should fly out whose owner was destined, 3, 316; and without κλήρους: *to cast lots*, 3, 324. 7, 181. Mid. *to leap, to spring*. ἐν ἀσπίδος ἄντυγι πάλτο, he sprang upon the rim of the shield, 15, 645 (cf. Spitzner, Excurs. XVI.); metaph. *to tremble, to palpitate*, with fear or joy. πάλλεται ἦτορ ἀνὰ στόμα, my heart leaps up to my mouth, 22, 451; δείματι, h. Cer. 294. 2) *to cast lots*, μετά τινος, with any man, 24, 400. παλλομένων, subaud. ἡμῶν, 15, 191; spoken of those casting lots, not pass. as explained by Heyne, κλήρων being understood.

Πάλμυς, υος, ὁ (the brandisher), an ally of the Trojans from Ascania, 13, 792.

πάλτο, Ep. for ἔπαλτο, see πάλλω.

παλύνω (akin to πάλλω), *to strew, to strew upon*, ἄλφιτα, 18, 560. Od. 4, 77. *b) to bestrew, to cover*; with accus. τὶ ἀλφίτου ἀκτῇ, any thing with barley flour, Od. 14, 429; spoken of snow: ἀρούρας, Il. 10, 7.

*παμβώτωρ, ορος, ὁ (βώτωρ), *all-nourishing*, Fr. 25.

παμμέλας, αινα, αν (μέλας), *entirely black*, ταῦροι, *Od. 3, 6. 10, 525.

*παμμήτειρα, ἡ (μήτηρ), *mother of all, all-mother, universal mother*, epith. of the earth, h. 30, 1.

Πάμμων, ονος, ὁ (the wealthy, from πᾶμα), son of Priam and Hecabê (Hecuba), 24, 250.

πάμπαν, adv. (πᾶς), *entirely, altogether*, 12, 406. Od. 2, 49.

παμποίκιλος, ον (ποικίλος), *exceedingly variegated, beautifully wrought*, πέπλοι, 6, 289. Od. 15, 105.

πάμπρωτος, ον (πρῶτος), *the very first*, Il. 7, 324. The neut. sing. and plur. as adv. *first of all*, Il. and Od.

παμφαίνω, poet. (from φαίνω, formed by reduplic.), only pres. and imperf., whence παμφαίνησι, 3 sing. pres. indic. as if from παμφαίνημι (where, however, with Spitzner, the subj. παμφαίνῃσι should stand), 5, 6; *to shine brightly, to beam, to gleam brightly*, spoken of stars, l. c. 11, 63; and of brass, with pres. partcp.; sometimes with dat. χαλκῷ, 14, 11. οτήθεσσι παμφαίνοντας, v. 100; Ep. παμφανόων.

παμφανόων, gen. ωντος, fem. παμφανόωσα, Ep. partcp. from παμφαίνω, as if from παμφανάω, resolved from παμφανών, always as adj. *brightly shining, gleaming, beaming, flashing*, epith. of arms and of brass; ἐνώπια, beaming walls, because they were on the sunny side, 8, 435. Od. 4, 42.

Πάν, gen. Πανός, ὁ, *Pan*, son of Hermês, by the daughter of Dryops, according to h. 18, 28; or son of Zeus and Thymbris, Apd.; a field, forest, and pastoral divinity of the Greeks, esply of the Arcadians. Particularly sacred to him was the mountain Lycaon, in Arcadia. He was represented as having a rough, hairy form, goat's ears, short goat's horns, and goat's feet. He mly bears a pipe, cf. h. Pan. 2, seq. According to h. 18, 47, his name is derived from πᾶς, ὅτι φρένα πᾶσιν ἔτερψεν.

πάναγρος, ον (ἄγρα), *all catching, all embracing*, λίνον, 5, 487.†

πάναιθος, η, ον, poet. (αἴθω), *all burning, all radiant*, κόρυς, 14, 372.†

Παναίολος. 324 Παπταίνω.

παναίολος, ον, poet. (αἰόλος), very easily mored, very flexible (Lexil. p. 66); less probably, very bright, exceedingly variegated: epith. of the girdle, shield, and cuirass, *4, 186. 13, 552 [cf. αἰόλος].
πανάπαλος, ον, poet. (ἀπαλός), very tender, very young, Od. 13, 223 † (here the fir-t α is long).
πανάποτμος, ον, poet. (ἄποτμος), very unfortunate, *24, 493. 255.
πανάργυρος, ον (ἄργυρος), all of silver, very silvery, *Od. 9, 203. 24, 275.
παναφῆλιξ. Gen. ἰκος, ὁ, ἡ (ἀφῆλιξ), without youthful companions, παῖδα παναφήλικα τιθέναι, to rob the child of all playmates, 22. 490.†
*πανάφυλλος, ον (φύλλον), all-leafless, h. Cer. 452.
Παναχαιοί, οἱ, the collective Achæans, by which name in Hom. the wide-spread tribe of the Achæans was designated, 2, 404. Od. 1. 239. 14, 369. cf. 'Αχαιοί.
πανάωριος, ον, poet. (ἀώριος), very untimely; παῖς, a child dying prematurely, 24, 540.†
πανδαμάτωρ, ορος, ὁ, poet. (δαμάω), that subdues all, all conquering (V. 'all-powerful'), epith. of sleep. 24, 5. Od. 9, 373.
Πανδάρεος, ὁ, son of Merops from Miletus in Crete, and friend of Tantalus; his eldest daughter Aëdon, according to Ionic tradition, was the wife of King Zethus in Thebes, Od. 19. 518, seq. Other daughters of Pandareus are mentioned, Od. 20, 66, whom later writers called Merōpe and Cleothēra, Paus. 10, 30. 1.
Πάνδαρος, ὁ, son of Lycaon, leader of the Lycians and an excellent archer, who by wounding Menelaus prevented the conclusion of peace, 2, 827. 4, 93. He was slain by Diomēdes, 5, 290.
πανδήμιος, ον, poet. (δῆμος), amongst or of the whole people, πτωχός, a common beggar, who begs of all, Od. 18, 1.†
*Πανδίη, ἡ, daughter of Zeus and Selēne, h. 32, 15.
Πανδίων, ονος, ὁ, a Greek, a companion of Teucer, 12, 372.
Πάνδοκος, ὁ, a Trojan slain by Ajax, 11, 490.
*πάνδωρος, ον (δῶρον), giving every thing, all-yielding, epith. of the earth, Ep h. 7.
Πανέλληνες, οἱ, the collective Greeks, a comprehensive name of the Grecian tribes in connexion with 'Αχαιοί, 2, 530; see 'Έλληνες. [The Greeks in the time of Hom. had no common name, and the poet employs the two names above to embrace the whole nation, see Mitford I. p. 192.]
πανῆμαρ, adv. (ἦμαρ), the whole day long, Od. 13, 31 †
πανημέριος. η, ον (ἡμέρα), lasting or doing something the whole day, adj. for a Iv. 1, 572. Od. 3, 486. 4, 356. The neut. as adv. Il. 11, 279.

Πανθοίδης, ου, ὁ, son of Panthoos = Polydamas, Euphorbus, 13, 756 16. 808
Πάνθοος, ὁ, contr. gen. Πάνθου. 15, 9: Πάνθῳ, v. 10; son of Othryades, father of Euphorbus and Polydamas, a priest of Apollo at Delphi, whence Antenor took him on account of his beauty. Priam made him priest of Apollo in Troy. He is mentioned amongst the old men of the council, 3, 146.
πανθυμαδόν, adv. (θυμός), in high anger in vehement wrath, Od. 18, 33. †
παννύχιος, η, ον (νύξ), lasting the whole night, or doing any thing the whole night. adj. for adv. 2, 2. 24. Od. 2, 434.
πάννυχος, ον=παννύχιος, 10, 150.
*πανόλβιος, ον (ὄλβιος), very happy, h 6, 54.
πανομφαῖος, ὁ, poet. (ὀμφή), the author of all omens ('all-disclosing,' V.), appellation of Zeus, as the giver of all oracles and signs, 8, 250.†
Πανοπεύς, ῆος, ὁ, a town in Phocis on the Cephisus on the borders of Bœotia. now Blasies, 2, 520. 17, 307. Od. 11, 58. (2) Prop. name of a man, the father of Epeus, 23, 665.
Πανόπη, ἡ, daughter of Nereus and Doris, 18, 45.
πάνορμος, ον (ὅρμος), very convenient for landing, λιμήν ('sheltering,' V.), 11. 195.†
πανόψιος, ον, poet. (ὄψις), visible to all. clear-shining, ἔγχος, 21, 397.†
πανσυδίη, adv. (σεύω), with all haste, with all dispatch, 2, 12. 29. 11, 709.
πάντη or πάντῃ, adv. (πᾶς), everywhere, at all events, in every direction, 1, 384. 11, 156. Od. 2, 383
*παντοδαπός, ή, όν (πᾶς), every kind, manifold, h. Cer. 402.
πάντοθεν, adv. poet. (πᾶς), from all sides or places, 13, 28. Od. 14, 270.
παντοῖος, η, ον (πᾶς), of every kind, manifold ('from all sides,' V.), both sing. and plur. παντοῖοι ἄνεμοι, winds from all sides, i. e. a confusion of gusts, 2, 397. Od. 5, 293.
πάντοσε, adv. (πᾶς), in every direction, to all sides, 5, 300. Od. 11, 606.
πάντως, adv. (πᾶς), entirely, altogether, exceedingly, always with οὔ, 8, 450. Od. 19, 91.
πανυπέρτατη. η ον, poet. exceedingly elevated, the highest of all, Od. 9, 25.†
πανύστατος, η, ον, poet. (ὕστατος), the very last, the last of all, 23, 532. Od. 1, 452.
πάομαι, furnishes tenses to πατέομαι, q. v.
παππάζω (πάππας), to say papa, πατέρα to call any one father, 5. 408.†
πάππας, ον, ὁ, vocat. πάππα, papa, father, a tender mode of address, formed from the language of children, Od. 6. 57.†
παπταίνω, aor. 1 ἐπάπτηνα, always without augm.; prop. to be timorous, α to look around uneasily, and generally. absol., ἀμφί ἕ, 4, 497; ἀνά, κατά τι, 11,

333. 18, 84; πάντη, Od. 12, 233. 2) With accus. *to look around for* any one who is missed, Il. 4, 200. 17, 115.

πάρ, poet. shortened: 1) for παρά. 2) for πάρεστι, 9, 43.

παρά, Ep. παραί, and shortened πάρ, I) Prep. with gen., dat., and accus., primar. signif. *by, near, at* [*apud*]. *A*) With gen. 1) spoken of space: *a*) to indicate withdrawment from the vicinity of a place or person, prop. from the side, *nly from*: φάσγανον παρὰ μηροῦ ἐρύσσασθαι, to draw the sword from his side [lit. *thigh*], 1, 190; ἐλθεῖν παρὰ Διός, to come from Zeus, like *de chez qln*, 21, 444; φέρειν τεύχεα παρὰ Ἡφαίστοιο, to bring arms from Hephæstus, 18, 137; φθέγξασθαι παρὰ νηός, 11, 585; ἀπονοστεῖν παρὰ νηῶν, 12, 114. 15, 69; ἔρχεσθαι παρὰ ναῦφιν, 12, 225; more rarely spoken of a state of rest: *al, by,* παρ᾽ ἀσπίδος, 4, 468. 19, 253. 2) To indicate a causal relation in naming the *author*, still closely bordering on the signif. of place: δέχεσθαι τεύχεα παρά τινος, to receive from any man, 19, 10. 24, 429; τυχεῖν παρά τινος, Od. 6, 290; φράζειν τι παρὰ Ζηνός, 11, 795. *B*) With dat. 1) spoken of space: *a*) In marking continuance with an object or person: *by, near, at, before*: ἧσθαι παρὰ κλισίῃ, to sit by the tent, 1, 329; μένειν παρ᾽ ἀλλήλοισιν, to remain near one another, 5, 577; ἀείδειν παρὰ μνηστῆρσιν, to sing by or before the suitors, Od. 1, 154. 2) In a causal signif. perhaps. also φιλέεσθε παρ᾽ αὐτῇ, Il. 13, 627, where however it may be taken in the *local* sense: to be hospitably entertained with or by any one, cf. Od. 1, 123. *C*) With accus. 1) spoken of space: *a*) In indicating an aim. *a*) Spoken of motion or direction to the vicinity of a person or thing, *to, towards*: παρὰ νῆας ἰέναι, to go to the ships, 1, 347; ἔρχεσθαι παρὰ Μενέλαον, Od. 1, 185. *β*) Of motion or direction by a place: *by, along*: βῆναι παρὰ θῖνα, to go along the shore, Il. 1, 34; οἱ δὲ – παρ᾽ ἐρινεὸν ἐσσεύοντο, they hastened along by the fig-tree hill, 11, 167. *b*) To indicate an extension in the vicinity of an object without special reference to the motion of it: *along, around*. οἱ δὲ κοιμήσαντο παρὰ πρυμνήσια νηός, Od. 12, 32; cf. Il. 1, 463. 16, 312. 2) Metaph. spoken of immaterial states, prop. *along by*, i. e. without touching; hence, *against, contrary to*, πὰρ δύναμιν, beyond a man's power, 13, 787; often παρὰ μοῖραν, against fate, Od. 14, 509; opposed to κατὰ μοῖραν. Note: παρά in all three cases can be placed after the nouns, but is then in anastrophe [i. e. cum accentu retracto], Il. 4, 97. II) As adv. only Ep. *thereby, by the side, thereupon*, 1, 611. 2, 279. III) In composition it has all the significations cited, and, in addition to this, it denotes a transformation or change, as the German *um, ver* [*irans*].

πάρα, in anastrophe stands 1) for παρά. when it is placed after the case governed, 6, 177. 2) for πάρεστι, 5, 603. Od. 3, 324. πάρα σοί, it rests with thee, Il. 19, 148.

παραβαίνω (βαίνω), partcp. perf. παραβεβαώς, Ep. for παραβεβαώς, *to mount beside*, hence in the perf. *to stand in the chariot beside* any one, with τινί, 11, 522. 13, 708; see παραβάτης.

παραβάλλω (βάλλω), aor. παρέβαλον, prop. *to cast beside*; *to cast before*, τινί τι, any thing to any one, spoken of food, 5, 369. Od. 4, 41: always in tmesis. Mid. prop. *to throw*, or *put down by one*-*self*, as the sum one stakes; hence, *to hazard* or *stake upon, to venture*, ψυχήν, 9. 322.

παραβάσκω (βάσκω), Ep. form of παραβαίνω, only imperf. 3 sing. παρέβασκε, he stood by him, 11, 104.†

παραβάτης, ου, ὁ, Ep. παραιβάτης (παραβαίνω), *one who stands beside the warrior*, i. e. the hero who stands beside the charioteer in the chariot, 23, 132.† in Ep. form.

παραβλήδην, adv. (παραβάλλω), properly, in the manner of being thrown beside; hence metaph. in an ironical signif. παραβ. ἀγορεύειν. *to speak covertly, allusively*, 4, 6.† According to Schol. 'to speak deceitfully or in reply;' or, according to Wolf, 'falling into the discourse,' interrupting; = ὑποβλήδην.

παραβλώσκω (βλώσκω), perf. Ep. παρμέμβλωκα, *to go to the side, to help*, τινί, any one. *4, 11. 24, 73.

παραβλώψ, ῶπος, ὁ, ἡ, Ep. (παραβλέπω), *looking sidewise, looking askance* [*slanieyed*, Cp. It is of the Λιταί], 9, 503.†

*παράβολος, ον, poet. παραίβολος; only παραίβολα κερτομεῖν like παραβλήδην, *to rebuke in a sly. covert manner*, to tease by oblique insinuations, to make sidethrusts at, h. Merc. 56.

παραγίγνομαι (γίγνομαι), *to be beside* or *at*, with dat. δαιτί, Od. 17, 173.†

παραδαρθάνω (δαρθάνω), aor. παρέδαρθον, Ep. παρέδραθον, infin. παραδραθέειν, *to sleep beside* or *with* any one, τινί, Od. 20, 88; τινὶ φιλότητι, Il. 14, 163.

παραδέχομαι, depon. mid. (δέχομαι), aor. παρεδεξάμην, *to take, to receive*, τί τινος, any thing from any one, 6, 178.†

παραδραθέειν, see παραδαρθάνω.

παραδραμέτην, see παρατρέχω.

παραδράω (δράω), 3 plur. pres. παραδρώωσι, Ep. resolved for παραδρῶσι, *to serve, to render service*, τινί, to any one, Od. 15, 324.†

παραδύω (δύω), infin. aor. 2 παραδῦμεναι, poet. for παραδῦναι. only intrans. *to glide along, to creep by*, 23, 416.†

παραείδω (ἀείδω), *to sing by* or *before*; τινί, to sing before any one, Od. 22, 348.†

παραείρω (ἀείρω), aor. pass. παρηέρθην, *to raise beside*, pass. *to hang beside*, 16, 341.†

παραί, poet. for παρά.

παραιβάτης, ου, ὁ, Ep. for παραβάτης, q. v.

Παραίβολος. 326 Παρατίθημι.

*παραίβολος, ον, poet. for παράβολος.
παραιπεπίθησιν, see παραπείθω.
παραίσιος, ον, poet. (αίσιος), of unfavorable omen, inauspicious, σήματα, 4, 381.†
παραΐσσω (άίσσω), aor. παρήϊξα, to spring away from, to rush or run by, 5, 690. 20, 414; τινά, any one, *11, 615.
παραιφάμενος, see παράφημι.
παραίφασις, ιος, Ep. for παράφασις.
παρακάββαλε, see παρακαταβάλλω.
παρακαταβάλλω (βάλλω), only aor. 2 παρακάββαλον, Ep. for παρακατέβαλον, prop. to cast down beside, to lay down, ύλην, 23, 127; ζωμά τινι, to put a girdle about any one, *23, 683. cf. 685. (Voss, on the other hand, 'he laid the girdle by him.')
παρακαταλέγομαι, mid. (λέγομαι), only sync. Ep. aor. 3 sing. παρκατέλεκτο, to lie down beside any one, τινί, *9, 565. 664.
παράκειμαι (κείμαι), iterat. imperf. παρεκέσκετο, Od. 14, 521; to lie beside, to stand or be placed beside, Il. 24, 476; with dat. τραπέζη, by the table, Od. 21, 416. 2) Metaph. to lie before, to be free to, ύμιν παράκειται, Od. 22. 65.
παρακίω (κίω), to go by, τινά, in tmesis, 16, 263.†
παρακλιδόν, adv. (κλίνω), in the manner of averting, turning aside. τρέπειν όσσε, to avert the eyes, h. Ven. 183; άλλα παρέξ ειπείν παρακλιδόν, turning aside to speak other things, i. e. to deviate from the truth, Od. 4, 348. 17, 139.
παρακλίνω (κλίνω), aor. 1 παρέκλινα, to incline or bend sidewise, κεφαλήν, Od. 20, 301. 2) Intrans. to turn aside, 23, 424.
παρακοίτης, ου, ό (κοίτη), a bed-fellow, a husband, *6, 430.
παράκοιτις, ιος, ή, Ep. dat. παρακοίτῑ, Od. 3, 381; a female bed-fellow, a wife, Il. 3, 53.
παρακρεμάννυμι (κρεμάννυμι), aor. partcp. παρακρεμάσας, to hang beside, to let hang, with accus. χείρα, 13, 597.†
παραλέγομαι, mid. (λέγω), only aor. 3 sing. παρελέξατο and subj. 1 sing. παραλέξομαι, Ep. for παραλέξωμαι, 14, 237; syncop. 2 aor. 3 sing. παρέλεκτο, h. Ven. 168; to lay oneself beside; τινί, to sleep with any one, 2, 515. Od. 4, 305; έν φιλότητι, to have amourous commerce with any one, Il. 14, 237.
παραμείβομαι, mid. (άμείβω), only aor. παρεμειψάμην, to go by, to ride by, τινά, any one, *Od. 6, 310. h. Ap. 409.
παραμένω, Ep. παρμένω and παραμίμνω (μένω), aor. 1 παρέμεινα, to remain by or beside, to persist, to hold out, 13, 151; τινί, to remain with any one, *11, 402.
παραμίμνω, poet. for παραμένω, *Od. 2, 297. 3, 115.
παραμυθέομαι, depon. mid. (μύθος), aor. 1 παρεμυθησάμην, to address, in order to comfort or animate, τινί, any one, 9, 417. 684; with infin. *15, 45.
παρανηνέω, poet. for παρανέω (νέω), to heap up by, to store up, σίτον έν κανέοισιν, *Od. 1, 147. 16, 51.

παρανήχομαι, depon. mid. (νήχομαι), fut. παρανήξομαι, to swim beside or by, Od. 5, 417.†
*παρανίσσομαι, depon. mid. (νίσσομαι), to go by, with accus. h. Ap. 430.
πάραντα, adv. (άντα), sidewise, obliquely, 23, 116.†
παραπαφίσκω (άπαφίσκω), aor. παρήπαφον, to mislead, to seduce, to infatuate, with infin. 14, 360.†
παραπείθω, poet. παραιπείθω (πείθω), aor. παρέπεισα, Ep. aor. 2 with Ep. reduplic. παραιπεπίθον, whence the subj. παραιπεπίθησι, Od. 22, 213; partcp. παραιπεπιθών, ούσα, and παρπεπιθών, prop. by crafty discourse to convert from one opinion to another, generally, to persuade, to wheedle, to win over, with accus. τινά, Od. 24, 119; φρένας τινός, Il. 7, 120. 13, 788; τινά έπέεσσιν, 14, 286; with infin. Od. 22, 213.
παρπεπιθών, see παραπείθω.
παραπέμπω (πέμπω), aor. παρέπεμψα, to send by, to convey by, Od. 12, 72.†
παραπλάζω (πλάζω), aor. 1 παρέπλαγξα, aor. pass. παρεπλάγχθην, 1) to lead from the right way, to conduct astray, to cause to err, τινά, with gen. of the place, Od. 9, 181. 19, 187; hence pass. to turn aside, to wander, spoken of the arrow, Il. 15, 464. 2) Metaph. to cause to err, to confuse, νόημα, Od. 20, 346.
παραπλήξ, ήγος, ό, ή (πλήσσω), prop. beaten sidewise. παραπλήγες ήιόνες, shores on which the waves beat only sidewise, i. e. low (V. sloping) shores, Od. 5, 418. 440.
παραπλώω (πλώω), Ep. for παραπλέω, 3 sing. Ep. aor. παρέπλω, to sail by, Od. 12, 69.†
παραπνέω (πνέω), aor. subj. παραπνεύσῃ, to breathe through a side opening, to blow by, to breathe by, spoken of the bottle of Æolus, Od. 10, 24.
παραρρητός, ή, όν (ρητός), addressed, a) that can be addressed, appeased; έπέεσσιν, by words, 9, 526. b) τά παραρρητά, addresses, admonitions (monita), cf. άμήχανος, *13, 726.
*παρασκέπτω (σκέπτω), to deride aside, to deride covertly, h. Cer. 203.
παρασταδόν, adv. (παρίστημι), standing near, 15, 22. Od. 10, 173.
*παραστείχω (στείχω), aor. παρέστιχον, to go by, with accus. h. Ap. 217.
παρασφάλλω (σφάλλω), aor. 1 παρέσφηλα, to thrust aside, to drive away, οϊστόν, 8, 311.†
παρασχέμεν, see παρέχω.
παρατανύω (τανύω), to place beside, τράπεζαν, Od. 1, 138. 7, 174; in tmesis.
παρατεκταίνομαι, mid. (τεκταίνω), aor. 1 παρετεκτηνάμην, to ruin in constructing, to construct falsely, metaph. to transform, to metamorphose, τί, 14, 54; έπος, to falsify a word, i. e. to devise a lie (to invent a tale, V.), Od 14, 131.
παρατίθημι (τίθημι), pres. 3 sing. παρατιθεΐ, fut. παραθήσω, aor. παρέθηκα, 1 aor. 3 plur. πάρθεσαν for παρέθεσαν,

Παρατρέπω. 327 Παρέκ.

subj. παραθείω, Ep. for παραθώ, optat. 3 plur. παραθείεν, imperat. παραθές, mid. aor. 2 optat. 3 sing. παραθεῖτο, partcp. παρθέμενος for παραθ., 1) *to sit by or near, to place beside,* τινί τι; τράπεζαν, δίφρον, Od. 5, 92. 20, 259; spoken esply of food: *to place before,* δαῖτα, Il. 9, 90; βρῶσίν τε, πόσιν τε, Od. 1, 192. *b*) Generally, *to present, to give, to bestow,* ξεινιά τινι, Il. 11, 779. 18, 408; δύναμίν τινι, Od. 3, 205. Mid. *to set or put before oneself,* δαῖδας, Od. 2, 105. 19, 150. 2) *to place upon* (prop. spoken of a stake), *to venture upon, to peril,* κεφαλάς, Od. 2, 237; ψυχάς, Od. 3, 74.

παρατρέπω (τρέπω), aor. 1 παρέτρεψα, *to turn sidewise, to turn aside, to guide away.* παρατρέψας εἶχεν ἵππους, turned (a little) out of his course and guided his horses by, *23, 398; ἐκτὸς ὁδοῦ, 423; other forms, παρατροπέω, τρωπάω.

παρατρέχω (τρέχω), only aor. 2 παρέδραμον, Ep. παραδραμέτην. *to run by,* 10, 350. 2) *to outrun, to outstrip any one,* τινὰ πόδεσσιν, 23, 636. h. 18, 16.

παρατρέω (τρέω), aor. 1 παρέτρεσα, Ep. σσ, *to tremble at the side, to start timorously aside,* 5, 295.†

παρατροπέω (τροπέω), poet. for παρατρέπω, only partcp. metaph. τί με ταῦτα παρατροπέων ἀγορεύεις, wherefore sayest thou these things to me turning aside, i. e. dissembling (Prôteus well knew the design of Menelaus, but dissembled, pretending not to know), Od. 4, 465.†

παρατρωπάω, poet. = παρατρέπω, only pres. *to turn about;* θεοὺς θυέσσι, to prevail on the gods by the vapour of sacrifice, 9, 500.†

παρατυγχάνω (τυγχάνω), *to be close by, to come to,* τινί, 11, 74.†

παραυδάω (αὐδάω), partcp. aor. παραυδήσας, 1) *to address, to comfort.* Od. 15, 53; θάνατόν τινι, to comfort any one concerning death, Od. 11, 488. 2) *to say or tell,* Od. 18, 178.

παράφασις, ἡ, Ep. παραίφασις and πάρφασις, 1) the act of *addressing, persuading, encouraging,* 11, 793. 15, 404. *b*) *allurement,* 14, 217; in the girdle of Aphroditê; according to the Schol. to be taken as adj. with ὁαριστύς; ὁμιλία παραινετική, intimate intercourse.

παραφεύγω (φεύγω), aor. 2 Ep. infin. παραφυγέειν, *to flee by,* with dat. Od. 12, 99.†

παράφημι (φημί), to which aor. παρείπον, mid. παράφαμαι, partcp. παρφάμενος for παραφάμ., infin. παρφάσθαι for παραφ., 1) *to persuade, to counsel,* τινί, 1, 577; mly mid. with accus. τινὰ ἐπέεσσιν, to persuade any one by words, to wheedle, with the notion of craft, 12, 249. Od. 2, 189.

παραφθάνω (φθάνω), only aor. optat. παραφθαίησι, partcp. παραφθάς, and aor. 2 mid. παραφθάμενος, *to outstrip, to surpass,* τινὰ πόδεσσι, 10, 346. Mid. = act. τινὰ τάχει. 23, 515.

παρβεβαώς, see παραβαίνω.

παρδαλέη, ἡ, poet. for παρδαλῇ, subaud.

δορά, *a leopard-skin* [cf. πάρδαλις], 3, 17. 10, 29; prop. fem. of παρδάλεος, έη, εον (πάρδαλις), *belonging to a leopard.*

*πάρδαλις, ιος, ἡ, *a leopard* or *panther* [animals then undistinguished], 13, 103. 21, 573, where Spitzner has adopted this form as approved by Aristarch. for πορδαλίων, πόρδαλις, cf. πόρδαλις, h. Ven. 71.

παρέζομαι, depon. mid. (ἕζομαι), *to sit by, to seat oneself;* absol, τινί, by any man, 1, 557; esply to converse with him, Od. 4, 738.

παρειά, ἡ, *a cheek,* prop. spoken of human beings; rarely of the eagle, Od. 2, 153. 2) the cheek-pieces of the helmet, h. 31, 11.

παρείθη, see παρίημι.

πάρειμι (εἰμί), pres. 3 plur. πάρεασι, imperf. 3 plur. πάρεσαν, infin. παρέμμεναι, poet. for παρεῖναι, fut. παρέσομαι, Ep. σσ, 1) *to be beside, present, near,* absol. 2, 485. 14, 299; with dat. τινί, *to be near any one;* often for support or assistance; hence *to aid,* 11, 75. 18, 472; also spoken of things: μάχῃ, to be present in the battle, Od. 4, 497; and ἐν δαίτῃσι, Il. 10, 217. 2) Generally, *to be there, to be ready, to be in store;* hence τὰ παρεόντα, property, stores, Od. 1, 140. εἴ μοι δύναμίς γε παρείη, if I had the power, Od. 2, 62. ὅσῃ δύναμίς γε πάρεστι, as much as is in my power, Il. 8, 294. 13, 786.

πάρειμι (εἶμι), partcp. παριών, *to go near* or *by, to pass by,* *Od. 4, 527. 17, 233. Ep. 3, 6.

παρεῖπον (εἶπον), defect. aor. 2 to παράφημι, 1) *to persuade, to address, to wheedle,* τινά, 1, 555. 2) With accus. of the thing: *to advise, to counsel,* αἴσιμα, 6, 62. 7, 121; absol. 11, 793.

παρέκ, before a vowel παρέξ, also before consonants, 11, 486. Od. 12, 216. 14, 168 (in later writers πάρεξ). I) Prep. 1) With gen. *without, out of.* (as with the notion of παρά), παρὲξ ὁδοῦ, Il. 10, 349. h. in Merc. 188; παρὲκ λιμένος, not far from the harbour, Od. 9, 116. 2) With accus. *near by, without, out of, beyond, aside from.* (παρά with the notion of ἐκ). παρὲξ ἅλα, Il. 9, 7. παρὲκ μίτον, 23, 762 Od. 12, 443. 16, 165. 343; *along by.* παρὲξ τὴν νῆσον ἐλαύνειν νῆα, Od. 12, 276. 15, 199. h. Ap. 410. In Il. 24, 349, the prep. stands after the accus. when, according to Spitzner, παρέξ would better be connected with the verb and the accus. depend upon it, cf. Od. 12, 53. *b*) Metaph. παρὲκ νόον, *beyond reason,* i. e. *without reason, foolishly,* Il. 10, 391. 20, 133. h. Merc. 547. β) *without, except.* παρὲξ Ἀχιλῆα, without Achilles's knowledge, 24, 434. II) Adv. 1) *near, near by, close by,* ῦπό στῆναι, 11, 486; νηχεῖν, Od. 5, 439; ωθεῖν, Od. 9, 488. νῆα παρὲξ ἐλάαν, Od. 12, 109. cf. v. 53. 2) Metaph. *aside,* i. e. contrary to right and truth. hence *a*) ἀλλὰ παρὲξ εἰπεῖν, παρακλιδόν, turning aside from

Παρεκέσκετο. 328 Παρίστημι.

the truth, Od. 4, 348. 17, 139. **παρὲξ ἀρεῖν**, Od. 23, 16. παρὲξ ἀγορεύειν, contrary to propriety, i. e. unskilfully, foolishly, Il. 12, 213. b) *besides, yet*, Od. 14, 168.

παρεκέσκετο, see παράκειμαι.

παρεκπροφεύγω (φεύγω), aor. subj. παρεκπροφύγω, *to flee away from*, metaph. *to escape*, τινά, 23, 314.†

παρελαύνω (ἐλαύνω), fut. ἐλάσω, aor. παρήλασα, poet. παρέλασα (σσ), *to drive by*, hence a) Intrans. *to ride by, to travel by* (subaud ἵππους or ἅρμα), 23, 342; τινα ἵπποισιν, *beyond any one, to conquer one* in a chariot-race, 23, 638. b) *to sail by*, νηΐ, Od. 12, 186; τινά, *beyond any one*, Od. 12, 197.

παρέλκω (ἕλκω), *to draw beside, to prolong, to delay any thing*; absol. *to loiter, to linger*, μύησαι, by pretexts, Od. 21, 111. Mid. *to draw to oneself, to procure for oneself*, by cunning and deceit, δῶρα, *Od. 18, 282.

παρέμμεναι, see πάρειμι.

παρενήνεον, see παρανηνέω.

παρέξ, see παρέκ.

*παρέξειμι (εἶμι), *to go out by*, metaph. *to overstep, to exceed, to transgress*, h. Cer. 478.

παρεξελαύνω (ἐλαύνω), aor. subj. παρεξελάσησθα, ed. Spitzner (παρὲξ ἐλάσησθα, ed. Wolf), *to drive out by*; only intrans. *to ride out by*, 23, 344.†

παρεξέρχομαι, depon. mid. (ἔρχομαι), aor. 2 infin. παρεξελθεῖν, 1) *to go out by, to go over, to go by*, Od. 10, 573: πεδίοιο, Il. 10, 344. 2) Metaph. *to overstep, to transgress, to violate*, Διὸς νόον, etc. Od. 5, 104; ἄλλον θεόν, Od. 5, 138.

παρέπλω, see παραπλώω.

παρέρχομαι, depon. mid. (ἔρχομαι), fut. παρελεύσομαι, aor. 2 παρήλυθον and παρῆλθον, infin. Ep. παρελθέμεν, 1) *to go by, to pass over*, Od. 12, 62; τί, before a thing, Il. 8, 239; hence absol. *to pass away*, κῦμα, Od. 5, 429. With accus. *to come before any one, to surpass him, to outstrip*, τινά, Il. 23, 345. 3, 239: ποσίν, in running, Od. 8, 230; ἐν δόλοισιν, Od. 13, 291; hence generally *to overreach, to deceive*, Il. 1, 132.

πάρεσαν, see πάρειμι.

παρευνάζομαι, pass. (εὐνάζω), *to lie or sleep by*, τινί, any one, Od. 22, 37.†

παρέχω (ἔχω), fut. παρέξω, aor. 2 παρέσχον, Ep. παρέσχεθον, subj. παρασχώ, infin. Ep. παρασχέμεν, 1) *to hold near, to present*, τί, any thing: δράγματα, 18, 556. cf. 23, 50; φάος, Od. 18, 317. 2) Generally, *to reach to, to present, to give, to accord, to bestow*, ἱερηΐα, δῶρα, σῖτον, ἰχθῦς, φιλότητα, *to accord friendship, hospitality*, Il. 3, 354; ἀρετήν, Od. 18, 133; γέλω τε καὶ εὐφροσύνην, Od. 20, 8; with infin. παρέχουσι γάλα θῆσθαι, they always give milk for milking, Od. 4, 89. Mid. παρεχέσκετο, var. lec. for παρεκέσκετο, Od. 14, 521.

παρηέρθη, see παραείρω.

παρήϊον, τό, ion. for the unusual παρεῖον, 1) *the cheek*, spoken of animals, 16, 159. Od. 22, 404. 2) *a cheek-ornament* upon the horse's curb, the part of the bit lying upon the cheek, Il. 4, 142.

παρήλασε, see παρελαύνω.

πάρημαι, depon. mid. (ἧμαι), *to sit by or near*: absol. and with dat. τινί, any one, Od. 1, 339; νηυσί, Il. 1, 421. b) Generally, *to remain by, to dwell, to reside at or in*, 9, 311. Od. 11, 573.

παρηορίη, ἡ, poet. (παρήορος), *the rein of the παρήορος* (vid.), the thong with which he is attached, *8, 87. 16, 152.

παρήορος, ον, poet. (παραείρω), 1) *hanging at the side*, subaud. ἵππος, an extra horse not attached to the yoke with the regular pair, but going beside, an *outrigger*, 16, 471. 474: elsewhere παράσειρος. 2) *lying beside, extended near*, 4, 156; metaph. *beside oneself, crazy, infatuated*, *23, 603.

παρήπαφε, see παραπαφίσκω.

παρθέμενος, see παρατίθημι.

παρθενική, poet. for παρθένος, *a virgin*, 18, 567. Od. 11, 39; prop. fem. of παρθενικός = παρθένιος; hence παρθενικὴ νεῆνις. Od. 7, 20.

παρθένιος, η, ον (παρθένος), *maidenly, pertaining to virgins*, ζώνη, Od. 11, 245; subst ὁ παρθένιος, kc. παῖς, *a virgin's son*, Il. 16, 180. 2) *innocent, pure, clear*, h. Cer. 99.

Παρθένιος, ἡ, *a river in Paphlagonia* which separates it from Bithynia, and flows into the Pontus; now *Bartin*, 2, 854.

παρθενοπῖπης, ου, ὁ (ὀπιπτεύω), *one who eyes maidens, a maid-gazer*, Il. 385.†

παρθένος, ἡ, *a virgin, a maiden*, Il. and Od. 2) *a young wife*, 2, 514.

πάρθεσαν, see παρατίθημι.

παριαύω (ἰαύω), *to sleep by or with*, τινί, any one, 9, 336.†

παρίζω (ἵζω), *to seat oneself by*, τινί, any one, Od. 4, 311.†

παρίημι (ἵημι), aor. 1 pass. παρείθη, *to let down beside*; pass. *to hang down*, 23, 868.†

Πάρις, ιος, ὁ, also called Ἀλέξανδρος, son of Priam; he seduced Helen, under the protection of Aphroditē, and was the cause of the Trojan war, 3, 45, seq. The poet mentions the occasion of this seduction, 24, 25, seq.; of his voyage, he only mentions that he returned with Helen by way of Phœnicia, 6, 290. seq He was a friend of the female sex and of music, 3, 59, seq.; and also not unacquainted with war, though often dilatory and cowardly, 6, 350.

παρίστημι (ἵστημι), aor. 2 παρίστην, subj. Ep. παραστήετον for παραστήητον, optat. παρσταίην, partcp. παραστάς and παραστάς, perf. παρίστηκα, infin. παρεστάμεναι, 3 plur. pluperf. παρέστασαν, fut. mid. παραστήσομαι, Od. 24, 28. 1) Trans. *to place near*, in H. not used. II) Intrans. mid. also aor. 2 perf. and pluperf. a) *to place oneself near*, to

Παρίσχω.   Πατέομαι.

come to, to approach, τινί, any one, esply in the pres. and imperf. mid. in a good sense, hence to help, to aid, to stand by, Il. 5, 809. 10, 290. Od. 13, 301; and in a bad sense, Il. 3, 405. 20, 472; often the partcp. aor. 2 παραστάς. 2) to stand by, to be near, esply in the perf. and pluperf. τινί, any one, 15, 255. 17, 563; also spoken of things: νῆες παρέστασαν, the ships were there, 7, 167. b) Metaph. to be near, to be before. ἀλλά τοι ἤδη ἄγχι παρέστηκεν θάνατος, but now death stands immediately before thee, is at hand, 16, 853. αἶσα παρέστη ἡμῖν, Od. 9, 52.

παρίσχω (ἴσχω), poet. form from παρέχω, infin. Ep. παρισχέμεν, 1) to hold near, ἵππους, 4, 229. 2) to reach to, to present. τί τινι. 9, 638.

παρκατέλεκτο, see παρακαταλέγομαι.
παρμέμβλωκε, see παραβλώσκω.
παρμένω, Ep. for παραμένω.

Παρνησός, ὁ Ion. for Παρνασσός, a large mountain in Phocis on the borders of Locris, at the foot of which lay Delphi; now Japura, Od. 19, 431; with σσ, h. Ap. 269. Adv. Παρνησόνδε, to Parnassus, Od. 19, 394. On the orthography, see Buttm. Ausf. Gram. § 21, p. 86.

*παροίγνυμι (οἴγνυμι), to open at the side, to open a little, h. Merc. 152, according to Herm. conject.

πάροιθε, before a vowel πάροιθεν, adv. (πάρος), a) Spoken of place: before, in front [20, 473, of a javelin; = at the point], 8, 494. οἱ πάροιθεν (ἵπποι), the first, or foremost (in the race), opp. οἱ δεύτεροι, 23, 498. b) Of time: before, previously, formerly, 15, 227. τὸ πάροιθεν. Od. 1, 322. οἱ πάροιθεν, those before, Il. 23, 498. 2) Prep. with gen. before, in view, opposite, τινός, 1, 360. 14, 428.

παροίτερος, η, ον, compar. of πάροιθε, the former, the earlier, *23, 459. 480.

παροίχομαι (οἴχομαι), perf. παρῴχηκα, to go by, to pass beyond, 4, 272; spoken of time: to pass away, *10, 252.

πάρος, adv. of time: a) before, formerly; in like manner: τὸ πάρος, with the pres. at other times. πάρος οὔτι θαμίζεις, t' ou dost not at other times come often; thou hast hitherto not been a frequent visitor, 18, 386. Od. 5, 88. cf. Il. 12, 346; with πρίν γε following: before, 5, 218. Od. 2, 127. b) As relat. partcp. with infin. before, ere. πάρος τάδε ἔργα γενέσθαι, ere these deeds occurred, 6, 348. Od. 1, 21. c) rather, Il. 8, 166; according to Damm: πάρος τοι δαίμονα δώσω, where it likewise signifies 'before.' 2) As prep. before, for πρό only 8, 254 †

*Πάρος, ἡ, one of the Cyclades, an island in the Ægean sea, fam-d for its white marble, h. Ap. 44; now Paro.

παρπεπιθών, see παραπείθω.

Παρρασίη, ἡ, a town in Arcadia according to 2, 608; later, a district in the south-western part of Arcadia.

παρστaίην. παρστάς. see παρίστημι.
παρστήετον, see παρίστημι.
παρτιθεί, see παρατίθημι.

πάρφαμαι, see παράφημι.
πάρφασις, ἡ, see παράφασις.
παρῴχηκα, see παροίχομαι.

πᾶς, πᾶσα, πᾶν, gen. παντός, πάσης, παντός, dat. plur. Ep. πάντεσσι for πᾶσι, and gen. plur. fem. πασέων for πασῶν, 1) every one, in sing. 16, 265. Od. 13, 313. Plur. all; when the notion of union or exclusion is expressed: ἐννέα πάντες, nine all of them = nine together or all nine [al. nine in all], Il. 7, 161. Od. 8, 258. 2) (the) whole, including all the parts. πᾶσα ἀληθείη, Il. 24, 407. Od. 11, 507; οἶκος, Od. 2, 48. 3) Pecul. uses = παντοῖος, of every kind. δαίδαλα πάντα. οἰωνοῖσι πᾶσι, Il. 1, 5. γίγνεσθαι πάντα, to become all things, i. e. to assume every form, Od. 4, 417. 4) The neut. plur. as adv. entirely, altogether, Il. and Od.

Πασιθέη, ἡ, one of the Graces, whom Hērē promised to the god of sleep for a bride, 14, 269. 276.

πασιμέλουσα, ἡ (μέλω), an appellation of the ship Argo, prop. which is a care to all, known to all, Od. 12, 70. †

πάσσαλος, ὁ (πήγνυμι), Ep. dat. πασσαλόφι, a wooden pin, a peg, to hang anything upon, Il. ἀπὸ πασσαλόφι αἱρεῖν, to take down from the pin, 24, 268.

πάσσασθαι, see πατέομαι.

πάσσω, only pres. and imperf. to strew, lay, or sprinkle upon, spoken of dry and of liquid things, prop. with accus. φάρμακα. also with gen. ἁλός, to strew some salt upon, *9, 214; see ἐμπάσσω.

πάσσων, ον, compar. of παχύς.

πάσχω, fut. πείσομαι. aor. 2 ἔπαθον, perf. πέπονθα, also πέπoσθε for πέπονθτε, πεπόνθατε, see Buttm., Gram. § 110, note 5 (according to Thiersch, perf. pass. § 212, 36); also Ep. partcp. perf. fem. πεπαθυῖα, Od. 17, 555 (prop. to receive an impression, both good and bad); in H. always in a bad sense: 1) to suffer, to endure, to bear, to sustain, spoken both of the body and the soul, with accus. κακόν, κακά, ἄλγεα, πήματα. often ἀλγέα θυμῷ, κατὰ θυμόν, Il. 9, 321. Od. 1, 4; ἔκ τινος, Od. 2, 134. b) Often absol. μήτι — πάθῃ, = lest any thing should happen to him, i. e. lest he should die, Il. 5, 567. 10, 538. Od. 17, 596. 2) In the interrogation τί πάθω; what am I to do? as an expression of the greatest embarrassment, Il. 11, 404. Od. 5, 465; and in like manner in the partcp. aor. τί παθόντε λελάσμεθα ἀλκῆς; what has happened to us, that we have forgotten our strength? Il. 11, 313. cf. Od. 24, 106.

πάταγος, ὁ, any loud noise arising from the collision of bodies, cracking of breaking trees, 16, 769; the chattering of the teeth. 13, 282; the dashing of the waves, *21, 9.

πατάσσω (akin to πάταγος), to strike, to beat, to knock, to palpitate, spoken of the heart, *7, 216. 13, 282.

πατέομαι, Ep. depon. mid. aor. ἐπασάμην, Ep. πασσάμην, pluperf. πεπάσμην,

Πατέω. 330 Πεδάω.

24, 642; *to taste, to eat, to consume,* with accus. σπλάγχνα, Δαμήτερος ἀκτήν, 1, 464. 21, 76; elsewhere with gen. σίτοιο, οἴνοιο, δείπνου, 19, 160. 24, 642. Od. 1, 124. (The pres. is not found in H.) πατέω, see καταπατέω.

πατήρ, ὁ, gen. πατρός, poet. πατέρος, dat. πατέρι, plur. gen. πατρῶν, 1) *father,* πατρὸς πατήρ, *grandfather,* 14, 118. Zeus is called, by way of eminence, πατὴρ ἀνδρῶν τε θεῶν τε. 2) As an honorary mode of address, ξεῖνα πάτερ, Od. 7, 48. 3) Plur. οἱ πατέρες, *the fathers,* i. e. the forefathers, 4, 405.

πάτος, ὁ, 1) *the act of stepping, a step,* Od. 9, 119. 2) *a trodden way, a path,* 20, 137. 6, 202.

πάτρη, ἡ (πατήρ), *country, father-land,* 1, 30. Od. 2, 365. (2) = πατριά, *family, stock, descent,* 13, 354.

πατρίς, ίδος, ἡ (πατήρ), prop. poet. fem. *belonging to country, native,* γαῖα, 2, 140; often subst. *country,* 5, 213. Od. 9, 34.

πατρόθεν, adv. (πατήρ), *from the father.* πατρόθεν ἐκ γενεῆς ὀνομάζειν, to name after the father, 10, 68.

πατροκασίγνητος, ὁ (κασίγνητος), *a father's brother, an uncle,* 21, 469. Od. 6, 330.

Πάτροκλος, ὁ, and after the 3 dec. gen. Πατροκλῆος, accus. κλῆα, voc. Πατρόκλεις, 17, 670. 11, 602. 1, 337; son of Menœtius and Sthenelê, a friend and companion of Achilles, from Opus, 18, 326; he fled when a youth, on account of the slaughter of the son of Amphidamas, to Peleus, 11, 765, seq. 23, 84, seq.; he accompanied Achilles to Troy, and withdrew from battle till the Trojans cast fire into the ships. Then first he went to battle in the arms of Achilles, and was slain by Hector, 16, 38, seq. His funeral solemnities see Il. 23.

πατροφονεύς, ῆος, ὁ (φονεύω), *a parricide,* Od. 1, 299. 3, 307.

πατροφόνος, ὁ = πατροφονεύς, 9, 461.†

πατρώιος, ίη, ιον, poet. for πατρῷος (πατήρ), *belonging to a father, paternal,* μένος, 5, 125; γαῖα, father-land, Od. 13, 188. πατρώια ἔργα, the deeds of the father, Od. 2, 22. *b) descending or inherited from a father,* Od. 1, 387; σκῆπτρον, Il. 2, 46; ξεῖνος, a paternal guest-friend, 6, 215.

παῦρος, η, ον, compar. παυρότερος, η, ον, *little, feeble, small;* λᾶος, a small people, 2, 675; mly in the plur. 9, 333. Od. 2, 276. Often in the compar. 1, 407.

παυσωλή, ἡ (παύω), *ceasing, resting, rest,* 2, 386.†

παύω, Ep. infin. pres. παυέμεν, iterat. imperf. παύεσκον, fut. παύσω, aor. ἔπαυσα, Ep. παῦσα, aor. mid. ἐπαυσάμην, Ep. παυσάμην, perf. mid. πέπαυμαι. I) Act. *to cause to cease, to bring to a stand, to restrain, to check, to cause to rest,* 1) With accus. *a)* Of persons, τινά, 11, 506. *b)* Of things: *to terminate, to restrain, to allay, to sooth,* χόλον, μένος,

μάχην, πόλεμον, 1, 192. 207. 7, 29. 11, 459. 2) τινά τινος, *to cause any one to cease, to restrain,* χαρμῆς, ἀλκῆς, μάχης τινὰ ἀοιδῆς, *to deprive any one of* a song, 2, 595; ἄλης καὶ ὀϊζύος, to deliver any one from wandering and wretchedness, Od. 15, 342. Instead of the gen. stands the infin. Il. 11, 442. *c)* Also with the partcp. as among the Attics, 11, 506. II) Mid. with perf. pass. *to cease, to rest, to leave off, to retire from. a)* Absol. spoken of persons and things, 3, 134. 11, 267. 14, 260. *b)* With gen. of the thing: πόνου, *to cease from the labour,* 1, 467; πολέμοιο, μάχης, with partcp. instead of the gen. ἐπαύσατο νηπιαχεύων, he ceased playing, 22, 502. N. B. The act. stands intrans. Od. 4, 659. καὶ παῦσαν ἀέθλων, and they rested from the combats; but cf. Buttm., Ausf. Sprachl. II. p. 264, seq. where the reading μνηστῆρας is defended.

Παφλαγών, όνος, ὁ, plur. οἱ Παφλαγόνες, *the Paphlagonians,* inhabitants of a country of Asia Minor upon the Pontus, between the river Halys, the Parthenius and Phrygia, 2, 851. 5, 577.

παφλάζω (φλάζω with redupl.), *to boil up, to bubble, to roar,* spoken of the sea, 13, 798.†

Πάφος, ἡ, a town on the west side of the island Cyprus, with a famous temple of Aphroditê, Od. 8, 363; later Παλαίπαφος, to distinguish it from Νεάπαφος, a port situated not far from the ancient Paphos on the coast, now *Baffo,* h. Ven. 58.

πάχετος, τό (παχύς), according to the Schol. poet. for πάχος. *thickness,* Od. 21, 191. 2) Ep. for παχύτερος, *thicker,* Od. 8, 187. According to Nitzsch ad loc. it may very well in both be adj., either of the positive form, *very thick,* or comparative, θάμνος — πάχετος δ' ἦν ἠΰτε κίων, it was thick as a pillar, Od. 23, 191, λάβε δίσκον μείζονα καὶ πάχετον, a large and very thick discus, Od. 8, 187.

πάχιστος, η, ον, superl. of παχύς. πάχνη, ἡ (πήγνυμι), *rime, hoar frost.* Od. 14, 476.†

παχνόω (πάχνη), prop. *to rime, to congeal into frost;* pass. *to be congealed by frost;* metaph. *to be chilled.* τοῦ ἦτο παχνοῦται, his heart shuddered, 17, 112.

πάχος, εος, τό (παχύς), *thickness,* Od. 2, 324.†

παχύς, εῖα, ὑ (πήγνυμι), compar. Ion. πάσσων, ον, Od. 6, 230; superl. πάχιστος, η, ον, Il. 16, 314; *thick, clotted,* spoken of blood, 23, 697. 2) *thick, fat, fleshy, solid, muscular,* spoken of human limbs, αὐχήν, μηρός, χείρ. 3) Generally *thick, heavy,* λᾶας, 12, 446; αὐλὸς αἵματος, a thick stream of "spouted blood" (Cp.), Od. 22, 18.

πεδάᾳ, see πεδάω.

πεδάω (πέδη), 3 sing. pres. πεδάᾳ, Ep. for πεδᾷ, aor. 1 ἐπέδησα, Ep. πέδησα, πεδάασκον, iterat. imperf. Od. 23, 353; prop. *to put on foot-fetters;* and generally, *to bind, to fetter, to restrain,* to

Πέδη.   331   Πείπαρ.

·inder, *to hold, to stop*, with accus. ἄρμα, -ῆα, Il. 23, 585. Od. 13, 168; with double accus. τινὰ βλέφαρα, *to blind any one's eyes*, Od. 23, 17. 2) Spoken esply of the supposed influence of a deity, who obstructs men in the accomplishment of their purposes: *to restrain, to entangle, to ensnare*, spoken of Atē, Moira, Διόρεα Μοῖρ' ἐπέδησαν, Il. 4, 517; ἀπὸ πατρίδος γαίης, *to hold back from one's country*, Od. 23, 353; and simply gen. κελεύθου, *from the way*, Od. 4, 380; with infin. Ἔκτορα μεῖναι Μοῖρα ἐπέδησε, Fate compelled Hector to remain, Il. 22, 5. Μοῖρά μιν ἐπέδησε δαμῆναι, Fate entangled him to be slain, Od. 3, 269. (Nitzsch and Bothe correctly refer μίν to the inger; the following ἀοιδόν is not superfluous, but opposed to ἐθέλουσαν. Eustath., and amongst the moderns Passow and Voss refer it to (Clytemnestra) Klytæmnestra; Voss translates, after the fate of the gods had ensnared her for destruction;' and Passow, 'that he was overcome,' i. e. that she yielded to his will. But H. uses this phrase always of one who is about to die, Il. 16, 434. 17, 421; cf. δαμάω. Others so the most recent editor, *Fäsi*] refer it, with equal incorrectness, to Ægisthus.

πέδη, ἡ (πέδον), *a foot-fetter* for horses, the tether with which horses pasturing in the field were bound; in the plur. 13, 16.†

πέδιλον, τό, *a sandal*; these were bound upon the feet in going out, Od. 15, 550. They were made of ox-hide, Od. 14, 23; and sometimes ornamented. With the gods they are ambrosial and golden, and have a motive power of their own, Il. 24, 340; see Voss, Myth. Br. I. p. 126.

πεδίον, τό (πέδον), *plain, field, level surface*, Il. and Od.; plur. πεδία with ᾱ, Il. 12, 283.

πεδίονδε, adv. *to the plain*, 6, 693. Od. I, 421.

πεδόθεν, adv. (πέδον), *from the ground*; metaph. *fundamentally, thoroughly*, φίλος, Od. 13, 295.†

*πέδον, τό, *the ground, the floor*, the earth, h. Cer. 455.

πέδονδε, adv. *down to the ground, to the earth*, 13, 796. Od. 11, 598.

πέζα, ἡ (akin to πούς), *the foot*, mly *the end, the extremity*, of the pole, 24, 272.†

πεζός, ὁ (πέζα), *going on foot, one who walks*, in opposition to one who rides, 4, 231. 5, 13. 2) *by land*, in distinction from those who go by ship, 9, 329. Od. 1, 73. 11, 58.

πείθω, fut. πείσω, aor. 1 ἔπεισα, only optat. πείσειε, Od. 14, 123; aor. 2 Ep. πέπιθον, subj. πεπίθω, optat. πεπίθοιμι, infin. πεπιθεῖν, partcp. πεπιθών, imperat. πέπιθε, h. Ap. 275; fut. mid. πείσομαι, aor. 2 ἐπιθόμην with redupl., optat. πεπίθοιτο, only Il. 10, 204; perf. 2 πέποιθα, *trust*, pluperf. πεποίθεα, Od. 4, 434; also the syncop. form ἐπέπιθμεν, Il. 2,

341. Also an Ep. form from aor. 2, fut. πιθήσω, ἐπίθησα, see ΠΙΘΕΩ, and fut. πεπιθήσω, trans. 22, 223. I) Act. *to move by representations and friendly means;* hence a) By words or prayers, *to persuade, to induce, to convince, to influence by entreaty*, with accus. τινά, 1, 132. Od. 14, 363; often with φρένας τινί, Il. 4, 104; θυμόν τινος, 9, 587; and with infin. 22, 223; primar. in a good sense, but also *to persuade, to wheedle*, through craft, 1, 132. Od, 2, 106. *b*) By presents: *to persuade, to appease, to conciliate*, Il. 1, 100. 9, 181. *c*) *to induce to obedience*, τινά, 9, 345; poet. θυέλλας, *to excite storms*, 15, 26. II) Mid. *to move oneself, to let oneself be persuaded, won over*, hence 1) *to be convinced, to believe, to trust*, often absol. 8, 154. 2) *to obey, to follow, to yield to*, τινί, any one, with double dat. τινὶ ἔπεσι, 1, 150; γέραί, *to obey or give up to age*, i. e. to accommodate oneself to the disabilities of age, 23, 645; νυκτί, *to obey the night*, i. e. to take rest, 7, 182; πάντα, *to obey in every thing*, Od. 17, 21. ἅ τιν' οὐ πείσεσθαι ὀΐω, in which I do not think any one will obey him, Il. 1, 289. cf 20, 466. Od. 3, 146. 3) The perf. πέποιθα, *to trust in, to confide in, to rely, to be confident*, esply often in the partcp. with dat. ποδωκείῃσι, ἱπποσύνῃ, ἀλκί, Il. 2, 792; absol. 1, 524; and with infin. following, 13, 96. Od. 16, 71.

πείκω, see πέκω.

πεινάω (πεῖνα), contr. πεινῶ, hence infin. πεινήμεναι, Od. 20, 137. elsewhere uncontr. *to be hungry, to hunger*, Il. 3, 25; τινός, *to hunger for a thing*, Od. 20, 137.

πείνη, ἡ, Ep. for πεῖνα, *hunger, famine*, Od. 15, 407.†

πειράζω = πειράω, *to tempt, to put to the proof*, absol. Od. 9, 281; τινός, *Od. 16, 319.

Πειραΐδης, ου, ὁ, son of Piræus=Ptolemaus, 4, 228.

Πείραιος, ὁ, son of Clytius, Od. 15, 539, 540.

πειραίνω, poet. for περαίνω, aor. 1 ἐπείρηνα, perf. pass. πεπείραμαι. 1) *to bring to an end, to accomplish*. πάντα πεπείρανται, Od. 12, 37. 2) *to pierce through, to transfix*. πειρήνας διὰ νῶτα χελώνης, sc. δόνακας, h. Merc. 48. 3) *to bind to, to attach*, prop. opposite ends (πείρατα), to fasten with a knot; σειρὴν ἐκ τινος, *Od. 22, 175.

πεῖραρ or πείρας, ατος, τό, Ep. for πέρας, 1) *an end, a limit, a boundary*, γαίης, πόντου, 14, 200. 8, 478. 2) *termination, completion, issue*. πεῖραρ ἑλέσθαι, to receive the issue (viz. of the contest), to bring the contest to an end, 18, 501. πείρατα νίκης ἔχονται ἐν θεοῖσιν, the end, i. e. the attainment of victory depends upon the gods, 7, 102. πείρατα ὀλέθρου ἱκνεῖσθαι, to reach the limit of destruction, 6, 143; in like manner πειρ. ὀλ. ἐφῆπται, the end of destruction depends over the Trojans, 7, 402. 12, 79

Πειράω. 332 Πέλαγος.

Od. 22, 33, where this is rather a poetical periphrasis for complete, utter destruction (τέλειος ὄλεθρος, Eustath.); hence 3) *the extremity, that which is most important* in a thing, as in a race, Il. 23, 350. πείρατα τέχνης, the tools or implements of art; i. e. the *finishers, executors,* or ministers of art. Od. 3, 433. 4) *a rope, a cord, a cable,* Od. 21, 51. 162; metaph. πολέμοιο πείραρ, Il. 13, 359, see ἐπαλλάσσω; according to Passow ad no. 1, prop. the ends of the cable.

πειράω (πεῖρα), Ep. πειρήσω, aor. 1 ἐπείρησα. mid. fut. πειρήσομαι, aor. 1 ἐπειρησάμην, perf. mid. πεπείρημαι, aor. 1 pass. ἐπειρήθην, 1) *to try, to strive, to take pains,* absol. and with infin. 8, 8. 19, 30; and with ὡς or ὅπως, 4, 66. Od. 2. 316. 4, 545. 2) *to try* any one, *to put* any one *to the proof,* with gen. of the object proved, τινός, Il. 24, 390. cf. 9, 345; esply in a hostile signif.; *to venture an attack,* μήλων, 12, 301. Od. 6, 134. Mid. embracing aor. mid. and pass. with reference to the subject, 1) *to attempt, to take pains, to undertake,* absol. and with infin. Il. 4, 5. 12, 341. It is not in H. combined with a partcp., for πάντα γιγνόμενος πειρήσεται, Od. 4, 418, means: he will, assuming every form, attempt, subaud. ἁλύξαι, (Voss incorrectly translates, 'he will attempt to become everything'), cf. Od. 21, 184. 2) *to try, to prove,* most frequently with gen. of the object which is tried. *b)* Spoken of persons: *to try, to prove* any one, *with words: to examine, to interrogate* any one, Il. 10, 444. Od. 13, 336; mly in a hostile signif. Il. 19, 70. 20, 352; once ἀντιβίην τινί, 21, 225. *c)* Of things: σθένεος, to try his strength, 15, 359; χειρῶν καὶ σθένεος, Od. 21, 282; esply *to try oneself* in any thing, ἔργου, ἀέθλου, Od. 18, 369. Il. 23. 707; τόξου, Od. 21, 159; once περί τινος, Il. 23, 553. 3) With dat. of the instrum. and means: ἔπεσι, to practise oneself with words, 2, 75; ἐγχείῃ, 5, 279; also ἐν ἔντεσι, ὅπλα, τεύχεσι, 5, 220 11, 386. πεπείρημαι μύθοισι, I have exercised myself in words, i. e. I am experienced, Od. 3, 23. 4) Rarely with accus. *to try, to prove* any thing, τροχόν, Il. 18, 601; τί, to spy out any thing, Od. 4, 119. 24, 238.

*Πειρεσίαι, αἱ, a town in Magnesia, h. Ap. 32. ed. Herm. for Εἰρεσίαι.

πειρητίζω, Ep. form of πειράω, only pres. and imperf. *to try, to prove,* absol. and with infin. 12, 257. 1) With gen. of pers. and thing, 7, 235. Od. 21, 124. 22, 237; to prove, to examine, Od. 14, 459. 2) With accus. στίχας ἀνδρῶν, to try the ranks of the men (in battle), Il. 12, 47.

Πειρίθοος, ὁ (with ι in attacking, from πείρω and θόος), *Peirithous,* son of Ixion or Zeus and Dia, of Larissa in Thessaly, king of the Lapithae, and friend of Theseus. He was present at the Calydonian chase, and was the husband of Hippodameia, at whose nuptials the celebrated quarrel of the Centaurs and the Lapithae arose, Il. 1, 263. 14, 318. Od. 21, 296.

πείρινς, ινθος, ἡ, *a carriage-basket,* for persons and things, 24, 190. 267. Od. 15. 131.

πείρω (πέρας), aor. ἔπειρα, Ep. νύξ. perf. pass. πέπαρμαι, to pierce through from end to end, hence 1) Intrans. to *go through, to sail through;* κέλευθον, to sail through the way, i. e. to accomplish the voyage, Od. 2, 434. ἀνδρῶν πτολέμους, ἀλεγεινά τε κύματα (by a zeugma. Il. 24, 8. Od. 8, 183. 13, 91. 2) Trans *to pierce, to transfix;* with accus. spec ὀβελοῖσιν, to pierce the flesh with the spits, Il. 7, 317. Od. 19, 422. ἰχθῦς δ̓ ὡς πείροντες ἀτερπέα δαῖτα φέροντο (i. e. ἰχθύας ὡς διαπείροντες τριαίναις), akin spearing fishes they bore them, etc. Od. 10, 124. This is the correct explanation. [Thus Cp. 'whom speared like fishes their home they bore,' etc.] The other explanation, according to which ἰχθῦς nom. and πείροντες = περῶντες τοῦ λιμένα, is incongruous; ἀμφ' ὀβελοῖσιν. i. 465. 2, 428; τινὰ αἰχμῇ διὰ χειρός. to pierce any one through the hand with the spear, 20, 479; without accus. 16. 405. ἥλοισι πεπαρμένος. studded with nails, embossed with studs, spoken of a sceptre and a goblet, 1, 246. Il. 433 περὶ δουρί, 21, 577; metaph. ἄλγεσι pierced with pangs, 5, 399.

Πείροος, ὁ, gen. Πείροω, 70, 484, son of Imbrasus of Aenus, leader of the Thracians, 2, 844.

πεῖσα, ἡ (πείθω), poet. for πειθώ, τῷ ἰ ἐν πείσῃ κραδίη μένε, his heart remained at rest (V. in composure), Od. 20, 23 (According to the Schol. for ἐν πείσματι.)

Πείσανδρος, ὁ, *Peisander* (*Pisander*). 1) son of Antimachus, a Trojan, slain by Agamemnon, 11, 122. 2) son of Menelaus, a leader of the Myrmidons, 16, 193. 3) a Trojan, 13, 601, seq. 4) son of Polyctor, a suitor of Penelope. Od. 18, 299. 22, 243.

Πεισηνορίδης, ου, ὁ, son of Pisenor = Ops, Od. 1, 429. 2, 347.

Πεισήνωρ, ορος, ὁ, 1) father of Clitus, 15, 445. 2) a herald in Ithaca, Od. 2. 38.

Πεισίστρατος, ὁ, the youngest son of Nestor; he travelled with Telemachus to Sparta and Pherae, Od. 3, 486. 15, 125.

πεῖσμα, ατος, τό (πείθω), *a cable, a rope, a hawser,* esply the rope with which the stern of the ship was made fast to the land, *Od. 6, 269. 13, 77 [more prob. the *anchor-cable,* or *stern-cable,* cf. Od. 9, 136, 137].

πείσομαι, fut. of πάσχω and πείθω.

πέκω, Ep. πείκω, aor. 1 mid. ἐπεξάμην. 1) Act. *to shear, to pick,* to comb; also to card wool, Od. 18, 316, in the Ep. form. 2) Mid. *to comb oneself,* χαίτας Il. 14, 176.

πελάαν, see πελάζω.

πέλαγος, εος, τό, *the sea,* esply *the open*

Πελάγων. 338 Πέλω.

igh sea, in the plur. ἁλὸς ἐν πελάγεσσιν *in the gulfs of ocean*, Cp.), Od. 5, 335. h, Λp. 73.

Πελάγων, οντος, ὁ, a leader of the Pylains, Od. 4, 295. 2) a Lycian, a companion of Sarpêdon, Il. 5, 695.

πελάζω (πέλας), aor. 1 ἐπέλασα, Ep. ἐλασα (σσ), mid. aor. 1 ἐπελασάμην, or. pass. ἐπελάσθην, Ep. syncop. aor. nid. ἐπλήμην, from which πλῆτο, plur. -λῆντο, perf. pass. πεπλημένος, Od. 12, 08; also Ep. form πελάω, infin. πελάαν, ι. 6, 44. 1) Act. 1) Trans. *to bring near, to cause to approach*, spoken of hings animate and inanimate: τινά, or ἰ τινι, Il. 2, 744. Od. 3, 300; νευρὴν μαζῷ, o bring (draw) the string to the breast, l. 4, 123; τινὰ χθονί or οὔδει, to stretch a man upon the earth, 8, 277; ἱστὸν ἱστοδόκῃ, to let down the mast into its receptacle, 1, 434; metaph. τινὰ ὀδύνῃσι, o put any one in pangs, 5, 766; sometimes absol. without dat. and accus. 15, 18. 21, 93. *b*) Instead of the dat. in Od. εἰς τι, ἔν τινι, Od. 7, 254. 10. 404: τινὰ οὐδάσδε, Od. 10, 440; τινὰ δεῦρο, Od. 5, 111. 2) Intrans. *to near, to approach*, Od. 12, 41; with dat. νήεσσι, Il. 2, 112. II) Mid. 1) Intrans. esply in the aor. 1 pass. and Ep. aor. mid. *to approach, to come near, to go to*, absol. 12, 420; with dat. 5, 282. πλῆτο χθονί, he sank to the earth, 14, 438; οὔδει, v. 467. ἀσπίδες ἔπληντ' ἀλλήλῃσι, the shields pressed upon one another, 4, 449. 2) Trans. *to bring near, to cause to approach*, only in the aor. τινὰ νηυσίν, to convey any one to the ships, 17, 341.

πέλας, adv. *near, close by*, Od. 10, 516, with gen. Τηλεμάχου πέλας, *Od. 15, 257.

Πελασγικός, ή, όν, Pelasgian. τὸ Πελασγικὸν Ἄργος, the Pelasgian Argos in Thessaly, 2, 681 (see Ἄργος). 2) ὁ Πελασγικός, an appell. of Zeus in Dôdôna, 6, 233.

Πελασγοί, οἱ, *the Pelasgi*, one of the oldest and greatest of the tribes of Greece. They dwelt originally in the Peloponnesus, in Thessaly and Epirus, 2, 681. 6, 234. Thence they spread themselves to Asia Minor, esply about Larissa, 2, 440: to Crete, Od. 19, 177. According to Hdt. 1, 56, 57, they were the aboriginal inhabitants of the country. They were probably a different race from the Hellênes, and migrated from Asia into Greece. The name is derived from πελάζειν; it signifies, therefore, *one approaching, a stranger*, and according to Strab. V. p. 221, it is equivalent to Πελαργοί.

*πελάω, poet. form of πελάζω, q. v.

πέλεθρον, τό, poet. for πλέθρον, *an acre, a piece of land*, prob. as much as one can plough in a day with a team, 21, 407. Od. 11, 577.

πέλεια, ἡ (πελός, πέλιος), *the wild dove*, of a bluish colour, 21, 494. Od. 15, 527.

πελειάς, άδος, ἡ = πέλεια, only in the plur. 11, 634. 5, 775.

πελεκάω (πέλεκυς), aor. 1 ἐπελέκησα Ep. πελέκκησα, *to cut with an axe, to hew*, χαλκῷ δοῦρα, Od. 5, 244;† in the Ep. form.

πελέκκησα, see πελεκάω.

πέλεκκον, τό. Ep. πέλεκκον (πέλεκυς), *the helve* or *handle of an axe*, 13, 612.†

πέλεκυς, εος, ὁ, dat. plur. πελέκεσσι, *a hatchet, an axe*, for carpenter's work and for the slaughter of victims, 13, 391. Od. 3, 499; *a battle-axe*, only Il. 15, 711.

πελεμίζω, Ep. aor. 1 πελέμιξα, aor. pass. Ep. πελεμίχθην, 1) *to put in violent motion, to wave, to cause to tremble, to shake*, with accus. οὐρίαχον, 13, 443; σάκος, 16, 108; ὕλην, 16, 766; τόξον, to shake a bow, spoken of one who begins or attempts to draw it, Od. 21, 125. Pass. *to put oneself in violent motion, to tremble, to shake*, spoken of Olympus, Il. 8, 413; often aor. *to be violently repulsed*, πελεμίχθη χασσάμενος, 4, 535. 5, 626.

πελίσκεο, see πέλομαι.

πέλευ, see πέλομαι.

Πελίης, ου, ὁ, Ion. for Πελίας, son of Crêtheus, or, according to fable, of Poseidôn and Tyro, sovereign of Iolcos. He wrested from his brother Æson the dominion of Iolcos, and also banished his other brother, Nêleus. Jason, the son of Æson, he compelled to undertake the expedition to Colchis, Od. 11, 254, seq

πέλλα, ἡ, *a milk-pail*, a vessel for milking, 16, 642 †

Πελλήνη, ἡ, a city in Achaia, between Sicyon and Æveira, in the time of Strabo a village; now, the ruins near Trikala, 2, 574.

*Πελοπόννησος, ἡ, *the Peloponnesus*, Pelops's island. It received this name from the Phrygian Pelops; earlier it was called Ἀπία, Πελασγία, Ἄργος, h. Ap. 250. 290.

Πέλοψ, οπος, ὁ, son of Tantalus, husband of Hippodameia, father of Atreus, Thyestês, etc. Expelled from Phrygia, he went with a colony to Elis, to king Œnomäus; whose daughter Hippodameia he won in a race, together with the kingdom of Elis. He extended his dominion over the greater part of the Peloponnêsus, so that this peninsula received a name from him, 2, 104, seq.

πέλω, mly πέλομαι, depon. mid. poet. only pres. and imperf. Of the act. 3 sing. pres. πέλει, imperf. 3 sing. πέλεν and ἔπλε. More frequently the mid. in the imperf. also syncop. forms: 2 sing. ἔπλεο, contr. πέλευ, 3 sing. ἔπλετο, Ep. iterat. πελέσκεο, 22, 433; Ep. imperat. πέλευ for πέλου. 1) Prop. *to be in motion, to stir oneself, to move oneself*, rarely: πέλει κλαγγὴ οὐρανόθι πρό, the cry rose to heaven, 3, 3. cf. Od. 13, 60. Il. 11, 392. 2) Mly *to be*, like *versari*, with the implied notion of motion. *a*) With subst. οἴμωγὴ καὶ εὐχωλὴ πέλεν, 4, 450. ἔπλετ' ἔργον ἄπαστιν, now was a work for all, 12, 271. *b*) With adj τοῦτο δὴ οἴκτιστον πέλεται βροτοῖσι, this is most pitiable to

Πέλωρ. 334 Πέπυσμα.

mortals, 22, 76. σέο δ' έκ πάντα πέλονται. from thee comes every thing, 13, 632. c) With adv. κακῶς πέλει αὐτῇ, it goes ill with it (the bird), 9, 324. 3)=εἶναι: τοῦ δ' ἐξ ἀργύρεος ῥυμὸς πέλεν, and attached to it was a silver pole [or, from it proceeded a silver pole], 5, 729. (On the imperf. which seems to stand as a pres. see Kühner, Gram. § 332. 4. Rost, § 116, p. 574)

πέλωρ, only nom. and accus. *a monster, a prodigy*, spoken of the Cyclôpes, Od. 9, 428; of Scylla, Od. 12, 87; of the serpent Python, h. Ap. 374; of Hêphæstus, Il. 18, 410.

πελώριος, η, ον (πέλωρ), *monstrous, huge, gigantic, prodigious*, spoken of every thing remarkable for its size; of persons and things, ἔγχος, 5, 594; λᾶας, Od. 11, 594. θαῦμα πελώριον, a prodigious spectacle, Od. 9, 190.

πέλωραν, τό = πέλωρ, *a monster, a prodigy*, Gorgô, 5, 741; a large stag, Od. 10, 168. δεινὰ πέλωρα, frightful prodigies of the gods, Il. 2, 321; spoken of the men changed into brutes by Calypsô, Od. 10, 219.

πέλωρος, η, ον = πελώριος, *monstrous*, epith. of a serpent, 12, 202; of a goose, Od. 15, 161. Neut. πέλωρα as adv. h. Merc. 225. Subst. *a monster*, spoken of the Cyclops, Od. 9, 257. (In H. πέλωρος is common gend., see Od. 19, 161; in Hesiod we find also πελώρη.)

πεμπάζομαι, mid. (πέμπε, πέντε), only aor. mid. subj. πεμπάσσεται, with shortened mood-vowel, *to count on the five fingers*, and generally, *to count*, τί, Od. 4, 412.†

πεμπταῖος, η, ον (πέμπτος), *on the fifth day*, adj. for adv. Od. 14, 257.†

πέμπτος, η, ον (πέντε), *the fifth*, Il. πέμπτος μετὰ τοῖσιν, Od. 9, 335. h. Ven.

πέμπω, fut. πέμψω, aor. 2 ἔπεμψα, Ep. πέμψα, also mid. *to send*, i. e. 1) *to send away, to dismiss, to send to*, spoken of persons and things: τινά or τί τινι; κακόν τινι, 15, 109; also a) With prep. ἐς πόλεμον, 18, 237; ἐς Χρύσην, 1, 390; ἐπί τινα, against or upon any one, 10, 464; ἐπί τινι, to any one, 2, 6. b) With adv. ἐνθάδε, οἴκαδε, πόλεμόνδε. c) With infin. φέρειν, in order to bring, 16, 454; ἔπεσθαι, 16, 575. cf. 7, 227. 18, 240. 2) *to send away from oneself, to let go, to dismiss, to send home*, Od. 4, 29. 13, 39. 3) *to escort, to accompany*, Il. 1, 390. 6, 255. 11, 626; also *to send with*, εἵματα, Od. 16, 83.

πεμπώβολον. τό (πέντε, ὀβελός), *a fork with five prongs or tines*, used esply in sacrifices, 1, 463. Od. 3, 460.

πενθείετον, see πενθέω.

πενθερός ὁ (πενθέω), *the wife's father, a father-in-law*, 6, 170. Od. 8, 582.

πενθέω, Ep. πενθείω, 23, 283 (πένθος), infin. pres. πενθήμεναι, Ep. for πενθεῖν, Od. 18, 174; aor. infin. πενθῆσαι, 1) Intrans. *to mourn, to grieve*, Od. 19, 120. 2) Trans. *to bewail, to lament*, τινά, Il.

23, 285; νέκυν γαστέρι, a dead pers: with the stomach, i. e. *to mourn for b* fasting, 19, 225.

πένθος, εος, τό, *sorrow, grief, lamentation*. πένθος τινός, grief for any one, Il. 249. Od. 21, 423.

πενίη, ἡ (πένομαι), *poverty, penury*, Od. 14, 157 †

πενιχρός, ή, όν, poet. for πενής. *poor, needy*. Od. 3, 348.†

πένομαι, depon. only pres. and imperf. *to earn one's support by labour*; hence generally, 1) *to labour, to be employed*, 1, 318. Od. 10, 347; περί τι, about any thing, Od. 4, 624. 2) Trans. *to prepare, to make ready*, with accus. esply δεῖπνον, Il. 18, 558. Od. 4, 428.

πενταέτηρος, ον, poet. (ἔτος), *five years old, of five years*, βοῦς, ὅς, 2, 403. Od. it. 419.

πενταετής, ἐς (ἔτος), *five years old, five* which adv. *πεντάετες, five years long*, Od. 3, 115.†

πένταχα, adv. (πέντε), *five fold, in five folds or parts*, κοσμηθέντες, 12, 87.†

πέντε, indeclin. *five*, Il. and Od.

πεντήκοντα, indeclin. *fifty*, Il. and Od.

πεντηκοντόγυος, ον, poet. (γύα), *having fifty acres*, τέμενος, 9, 579.†

πεντηκόσιοι, αι, α, Ep. for πεντακόσιοι, *five hundred*, Od. 3, 7.† (Nitzsch conjectures the reading should be πεντηκοστύς.)

πεπαθυῖα, see πάσχω.

*πεπαίνω (πέπων), *to make ripe, to become ripe*, from which aor. 1 p. optat. 3 plur. πεπανθεῖεν, Ep. 14, 3.

πεπαλάγμαι, see παλάσσω

*Πεπάρηθος, ἡ, one of the Cyclades, famed for its wine, now Scopilo, h. 4; 32.

πεπαρμένος, see πείρω.

πεπάσμην, see πατέομαι.

πεπερημένος, see περάω.

πέπηγε, see πήγνυμι.

πεπιθεῖν, see πείθω.

πεπιθμεν, see πείθω.

πεπιθήσω, see πείθω and ΠΙΘΕΩ

πέπληγον, see πλήσσω.

πεπληγώς, see πλήσσω.

πεπλημένος, see πελάω.

πέπλος, ὁ, 1) *the upper garment of women, an ample robe of fine texture* which was thrown over the other clothing, and covered the whole body, 5, 734. Od. 6, 38. 18, 292; fastened at the breast with a brooch or clasp, Il. 5, 425. Il. 180; 2) Generally, *a covering, a covering* for covering a chariot, 5, 194. 24, also *to spread over a chair*, Od. 7, 96.

πέπνυμαι, see πνέω.

πέποιθα, see πείθω.

πέπονθα, see πάσχω.

πέποσθε, see πάσχω.

πεποτήαται, see ποτάομαι.

πεπρωμένος, πέπρωτο, see πόρω.

πέπταμαι, see πετάννυμι.

πεπτεῶτα, see πίπτω.

πεπτηώς, see πτήσσω.

πεπύθοιτο, see πυνθάνομαι.

πέπυσμαι, see πυνθάνομαι.

Πέπων. **Περί.**

πέπων, ονος, ὁ, ἡ (πέσσω), prop. cooked by the sun; hence, *ripe, mellow, tender*; spoken of fruits, in H. always metaph. in an address: 1) In a good sense, *ὦ πέπον, friend, companion, beloved*, 5, 109. 5, 437; and κρὶ πέπον, Od. 9, 447. 2) [in a bad sense: *dastard, coward*, Il. 2, 235; (according to Voss, also Il. 13, 120.)

πέρ, an enclitic particle, shortened from περί, signifies prop. *through and through, throughout;* it strengthens the word to which it is annexed, in respect to the *compass* of the notion. It signifies hence: 1) *very, entirely* [*valde*], when it stands by itself, without reference to another thought; a rare and only Ep. use is with adj. and adv.: ἀγαθός περ ἐών, very good, 1, 131; cf. Od. 1, 315. φράδμων περ, Il. 16. 638. ἐπεί μ' ἔτεκές γε μινυνθάδιόν περ ἐόντα, being very short-lived, 1, 352. μίνυνθά περ, for a very short time, 1, 416. ὀλίγον περ, 11, 391. 2) More frequently in the Ep. language it is used in reference to another thought; *a)* If the two corresponding notions, of which one is to be supplied, be concordant, πέρ has an enhancing force: *entirely, indeed, by all means.* καὶ αὐτοί περ πονεώμεθα, let us work ourselves' (not merely others), 10, 70; οἴκαδέ περ νεώμεθα, let us by all means return home', 2, 236. *b)* If the two notions are antithetical, περ signifies *by all means yet, at least.* ἐπεί μ' ἔτεκές γε μινυνθάδιόν περ ἐόντα, τιμήν πέρ μοι ὄφελλον Ὀλύμπιος ἐγγυαλίξαι, Zeus should yet have by all means accorded honour to me, 1, 353. cf. 9, 301. *c)* Esply it then stands with partcp. and signifies, *how much soever, although, though*: ἱέμενός περ, however much thou desirest; ἀχνύμενός περ, although grieved; οὐτάμενός περ. 3) Very often πέρ stands after conjunct. or relatives: 1) If the two members of a sentence, or the sentences relating to each other are concordant, πέρ signifies, *entirely, in like manner, throughout; ὅσπερ, the very same, who*, in like manner οἷός περ; ὅπου περ, wheresoever; ὅθεν περ, whencesoever, etc. 2) In antithetic members πέρ signifies *still, also; ὅσπερ*, who yet; εἴ περ, although, q. v.; cf. Kühner, § 595. Rost, § 133.

περάαν, see περάω.

Περαιβοί, οἱ, poet. for Περραιβοί, the *Perrhæbi*, inhabitants of Perrhæbia in Thessaly. They dwelt first on the Peneus, as far as the sea; subsequently being driven back by the Lapithæ, further in the interior, 2, 749. The comm. form h. Apoll. 218.

περαιόω (περαῖος), aor. pass. περαιωθέντες, 1) *to convey over, to bring over*; pass. *to pass over, to travel over*, Od. 24, 437.†

περάτη, ἡ, fem. from πέρατος, subaud. γῆ or χώρα, *the region beyond, the country opposite*, esply the opposite quarter of the heavens, ἐν περάτῃ, as opposed to Ἠώς, in the western sky (V. 'at the end of the path'), Od. 23, 243.†

περάω (πέρα), pres. infin. περάαν, Ep. for περᾶν, iterat. imperf. περάασκε, fut. περήσω, 1) Intrans. *to pierce through, to go through, to pass through*, spoken of missiles, absol. 21, 594; διὰ κροτάφοιο, 4, 563; of the rain, Od. 5, 480; with accus. of the place, ὀδόντας, Il. 5, 291 ὀστέον εἴσω, 4, 460. 6, 10; hence generally, *to go through, to pass through, to steer through*, spoken of persons: πόντον, Od. 24, 118; τάφρον, to pass over the ditch, Il. 12, 63; πύλας Ἀΐδαο, to pass through the gates of Hades, 5, 646; also absol. with prep: διὰ Ὠκεανοῖο, through Oceanus, Od. 10, 508; ἐπὶ πόντον, to sail over the sea, Il. 2. 613. 2) Trans. only poet. *to convey through, to conduct through*, τὶ κατὰ δειρῆς, h. Merc. 133; perhaps also Il. 5, 291.

περάω (πέρα), aor. ἐπέρασα, Ep. σσ, perf. pass. πεπέρημαι, 21, 58; =the later τιπράσκω, prop. *to bring over for sale*; hence, *to sell*, with accus. 21, 102. h. Cer. 132; τινὰ Λῆμνον, to sell any one to Lemnos, 21, 40; or ἐς Λῆμνον, v. 58, and πρὸς δώματα, Od. 15, 387. The pres. περάω does not occur; for which we have the poet. form πέρνημι.

Πέργαμος, ἡ (among later writers τὸ Πέργαμον and τὰ Πέργαμα), the citadel of Ilium, see Ἴλιος, 4, 508. 5, 146. 460.

Περγασίδης, ου, ὁ, son of Pergasus = *Deïkuon*, 5, 535.

πέρην, Ep. and Ion. for πέραν, prep. with gen. 1) *beyond*, on the other side, 24, 752. 2) *opposite to*; Εὐβοίης, *Il. 2, 535.

περησέμεναι, see περάω.

πέρθαι, κεε περθω.

πέρθω. fut. πέρσω. aor. 1 ἔπερσα, aor. 2 ἔπραθον, mid. fut. with pass. signif. πέρσομαι, infin. of the syncop. aor. 2 πέρθαι, 1) *to lay waste, to destroy, to desolate*, spoken only of cities and countries, with accus. πόλιν, 2, 660. Od. 1, 2. οὐ νύ τοι αἶσα, πόλιν πέρθαι Τρώων, it is not appointed to thee by fate to destroy the city of the Trojans, 16, 708. Pass. 2, 374. 4, 291. πόλις πέρσεται, 24, 729. 2) *to pillage, to plunder*, τὶ ἐκ πολίων, 1, 125.

περί, I) Prep. with gen. dat. and accus. primar. signif. *round about*, spoken both of the full circumference of an object, as also of only that part embraced by one view. *Α*) With gen. 1) Spoken of place: a) To indicate existence about an object, poet. and rare: *around*. τετάνυστο περὶ σπείους ἡμερίς, around the cave, Od. 5, 68. περὶ τρόπιος βεβαώς, riding upon the keel, Od. 5, 130. 2) In a causal relation, in manifold applications: *a*) In presenting an object, about which as a centre the action moves, almost like ἀμφί, *around, about, concerning, for, over, before*. *a*) Almost local, still with verbs signif. to fight, to contend in order to plunder, to defend,

Περιδρύπτω. 837 Περιπέλομαι.

δρύπω open, κολώνη, 2, 812; αὐλή, Od. 14, 7.

περιδρύπτω (δρύπτω), Ep. aor. pass. περιδρύφθην, to tear round about; pass. to ὁ· torn or lacerated; ἀγκῶνας περιδρύφθη, his elbows were lacerated, 23, 395.†

περιδύω (δύω), aor. 1 Ep. περιδύσα, to draw off round about, to pull or strip off (elsewhere ἀπέδυσε), with accus χιτῶνας, 11, 100.†

περιδώμεθον, see περιδίδωμι.

περιειδον (ΕΙΔΩ), defect. aor. 2 in. H. only perf. περίοιδα, infin. περιίδμεναι, Ep. for περιειδέναι, pluperf. περιῄδειν, 3 sing. περιῄδη, with pres. signif. to know or understand better [than others, or than most], with infin. [= to know well how to—], 10, 247; with accus. of the thing and gen. of the pers. τινός, than another, Od. 3, 214. b) to be more intelligent in any thing, to be wiser in any thing, τινί, Od. 17, 317. βουλῇ περιίδμεναι ἄλλων, to excel others in counsel, Il. 13, 728.

περίειμι (εἰμί), 1) to be above, i. e. to be more excellent than any one, to excel, to be superior, with gen. of the pers. and accus. of the thing: φρένας, νόον, in intelligence, wisdom, Od. 18, 248, 19, 326. Il. 1, 258; in tmesis.

περιέπω, only in tmesis, see ἔπω, 15, 555.

περιέχω (ἔχω), only aor. 2 Ep. mid. περισχόμην, imperat. περίσχεο, to encompass, to embrace. Mid. to hold oneself around anything, i. e. to embrace any one protectingly, to protect, to shelter any one, with gen. of pers. 1, 393; with accus. Od. 9, 199.

Περιήρης, ους, ὁ, father of Borus, 16, 177.

*περιζαμενῶς, poet. adv. (ζαμενής), very powerfully, very vehemently, h. Merc. 495.

περιηχέω (ἠχέω), aor. περιήχησα, to resound round about, to ring, to rattle, 7, 267.†

περιίδμεναι, see περιείδον.

περιίστημι (ἵστημι), aor. 2 περίστην, Ep. for περιίστην, subj. περιστήωσι for περιστῶσι, optat. περισταίεν, aor. 1 mid. περιστησάμην, aor. pass. περιστάθην. H. only intrans. aor. 2 act. mid. and aor. pass. : 1) to place oneself about, to stand about, 4, 532; also aor. pass. Od. 11, 243. 2) to place oneself about any one or any thing, to surround him, to encircle, with accus. βοῦν περιστήσαντο, they placed themselves around the ox, Il. 2, 410; τινά, 17, 95. Od. 20, 50.

περικαλλής, ές (κάλος), very beautiful, exceedingly beautiful, fascinating, mly epith. of things; more rarely spoken of persons, 5, 389. Od. 11, 281. h. Merc. 323.

περικαλύπτω, only in tmesis, see καλύπτω.

περίκειμαι, depon. mid. (κεῖμαι), to lie around any thing, to surround, to embrace, with dat. τόξῳ, Od. 21, 54; τινί, to hold any one encompassed, Il. 19, 4; metaph. οὐδὲ περίκειταί μοί τι, nor have I any advantage or benefit [any thing peculiar in store, or reserved, for me], 9, 321.

περικήδομαι, mid. (κήδω), to be very anxious, to be troubled, τινός, about any one. Od. 3, 219; τινὶ βιότου, to be anxious for any one concerning property, *Od. 14, 527.

περίκηλος, ον, poet. (κῆλον), parched, very dry, *Od. 5, 240. 18, 309.

Περικλύμενος, ὁ, son of Neleus and Pero; he had received from Poseidon the gift of metamorphosing himself into many forms, Od. 11, 286.

*περίκλυστος, η, ον (κλύζω), washed on all sides by the waves, sea-girt, Δῆλος, h. Ap. 181.

περικλυτός, όν (κλυτός), heard on all sides, hence: speaking loud, singing loud: It is thus explained as an epith. of ἀοιδός, Od. 1, 325. (V. on the other hand 'far celebrated'), mly, 2) heard of round about, i. e. celebrated, famous, glorious, epith. of persons and things, Il. 1, 607. 7, 299.

περικτείνω. only in tmesis, see κτείνω.

περικτίονες. οἱ (κτίζω), only plur. those dwelling round about, neighbours, 19, 104; also as adj. with ἄνθρωποι, Od. 2, 65; ἐπίκουροι, Il. 17, 220.

περικτίται, ων, οἱ, Ep. = περικτίονες, Od. 11, 288.†

περιλείπω, only in tmesis, see λείπω.

περιμαιμάω, Ep. (μαιμάω), only pres. partcp. Ep. περιμαιμώωσα for περιμαιμάουσα, to seek eagerly round about, to be in eager quest of, with accus. σκόπελον, Od. 12, 95.†

περίμετρος, ον (μέτρον), immensely great, ἱστόν, *Od. 2, 95. 19, 140.

Περιμήδης, εος, ὁ (very wise, see μῆδος), 1) a companion of Odysseus (Ulysses), Od. 11, 23. 2) father of Schedius, Il. 15, 515.

περιμήκετος, ον, poet. = περιμήκης; ἐλάτη, 14, 287; Τηΰγετον, Od. 6, 103.

περιμήκης, ες (μῆκος), very long, very high, spoken of mountains, 13, 65. Od. 13, 183; of the wand of Kirkē (Circe), Od. 10, 293; of the neck of Scylla, Od. 12, 90.

περιμηχανάομαι, depon. mid. (μηχανάω), 3 plur. pres. περιμηχανόωνται, Ep. resolved: to prepare craftily on all sides; generally, to resolve upon craftily, to devise or contrive, τί, Od. 7, 200; δούλιον ἦμάρ τινι, *Od. 14, 340.

. Πέρίμος, ὁ, son of Meges, a Trojan, slain by Patroclus, 16, 695.

περιναιετάω, poet. (ναιετάω), to dwell round about, *Od. 2, 66. 8, 551. 2) Intrans. to be inhabited, to lie, spoken of cities, Od 4, 177.

περιναιέτης, ου, ὁ, poet. (ναίω), one of those dwelling round about, a neighbour, 24, 488.†

περιξεστός, ή, όν (ξεστός), hewed round about, smoothed, smooth, πέτρῃ, Od. 12, 79.†

περίοιδα, see περιείδον.

περιπέλομαι, depon. mid. poet. (πέλο-

Q

Περιπευκής. 338 Περιτροπέω.

ται), only syncop. partcp. περιπλόμενος, 1) *to turn oneself around, to roll around, to revolve in a circle,* spoken of time: περιπλομένων ἐνιαυτῶν, in the course of the seasons (lit. the years), Od. 1, 16. 11. 23, 833. h. Cer. 266. 2) Spoken of place, with accus. *to go about* any thing, *to encompass,* 18, 220.

περιπευκής, ές, poet. (πεύκη), *very bitter, very unpleasant, very painful,* βέλος, 11, 845.†

περιπλέκω (πλέκω), only aor. pass. Ep. περιπλέχθην, without augm. *to twist around, to wind about;* pass. *to wind oneself about* any thing, *to coil or twine about,* with dat. ἱστῷ, Od. 14, 313; *to embrace,* γρηΐ, *Od. 23, 33.

περιπληθής, ές (πλῆθος), *very full, very populous,* Ὀρτυγίη, Od. 15, 404.†

περιπλόμενος, see περιπέλομαι.

περιπρό, adv. (πρό), *very much, exceedingly, particularly,* 11, 180. 16, 699; ed. Spitzner; in Wolf separated: περὶ πρό.

περιπροχέω (χέω), only partcp. aor. pass. περιπροχυθείς. *to pour round about;* pass. *to pour oneself about,* metaph. ἔρος θυμὸν περιπροχυθεὶς ἐδάμασσε, love has overpowered my heart, poured about it [a full tide of love is poured into my breast, *Cp.*], 14, 316.†

περιρρέω (ῥέω), imperf. περίρρεε, *to flow round about,* with accus. Od. 9, 388.†

περιρρηδής, ές (περιρρέω), *falling about* any thing. περιρρηδὴς τραπέζῃ κάππεσε δινηθείς, staggering he fell prostrate upon the table, Od. 22, 84.†

περίρρυτος, ον (ῥέω), *flooded all around, sea-girt,* epith. of Crete, Od. 19, 173.†

περισαίνω (σαίνω), Ep. περισσαίνω, only pres. *to wag with the tail around, to flatter, fawn upon,* τινά, Od. 16, 4. 10; οὐρῇσιν. *Od. 10, 215.

περισείω (σείω), Ep. περισσείω, only Ep. form, *to shake round about;* only pass. *to shake oneself round about, to wave,* spoken of the crest, *19, 382. 22, 315. h 6, 4.

περισθενέω. poet. (σθένος), only partcp. pres. περισθενέων, *to be superior, to be very strong,* Od. 22, 368.†

περίσκεπτος, ον (σκέπτομαι), *to be seen round about;* hence, *lying open, elevated,* (V. 'wide looking,') *Od. 1, 426. 10, 211. 14, 6.

περισσαίνω, poet. for περισαίνω.
περισσείω, poet. for περισείω.

περισταδόν, adv. (περιΐστημι), *standing around,* 13, 514.†

περιστάθη, see περιΐστημι.

περιστείχω (στείχω), aor. 1 partcp. περιστείξας for περιστείξας, *to go round about, to walk around,* Od. 4, 277.†

περιστέλλω (στέλλω), aor. 1 partcp. περιστείλας, *to dress, to clothe,* eυply to *less or lay out a corpse,* with accus. Od. 14, 293.†

περιστεναχίζω, poet. (στεναχίζω). only in the mid. pres. and imperf. *to resound round about, to echo,* with dat. ποσσίν, from the feet, Od. 23, 147; and in tmesis, Od. 10, 454. δῶμα περιστεναχίζεται αὐλῇ, the house resounded round a out in the court-yard. Od. 10, 10. Thus Wolf; on the contrary, Voss and Bothe after Cdd.: αὐλῷ, i. e. αὐλήσει, with the sound of flutes.

περιστένω (στένω), 1) = στεναχίζω, *to groan around, to echo around,* with accus. h. Ap. 18, 21. 2) = στείνω, only mid περιστένεται γαστήρ, the stomach is too small, is filled up, 16, 163.†

περιστήωσι, see περιΐστημι.

περιστέφω (στέφω), *to crown round about, to surround,* τί τινι, any thing with another, Od. 5, 303.†

περιστοναχίζω, an old reading for περιστέν. Od. 10, 454. 23, 146.

περιστρέφω (στρέφω), partcp. aor. περιστρέψας, *to turn round about, to whirl around,* with accus. δίσκον, Od. 8, 183; τινὰ χειρί, Il. 19, 131. h. 2, 409. Πασι μάλα ὦκα περιστρέφεται κυκώοντι, καὶ γάλα, very quickly is it stirred by the mixer, 5, 903; the reading περιστρέφεται is better, according to Eustath., *to curdle, to coagulate.*

περίσχεο, see περιέχω.

περιτάμνω, Ep. and Ion. for περιτέμνω (τέμνω), *to cut off round about,* hence mid. *to cut off any thing for oneself,* and *bear away as booty: to plunder, to pillage,* βοῦς, *Od. 11, 402. 24, 112; cf. τέμνω.

περιτέλλομαι, depon. mid. (τέλλω), poet. only pres. *to accomplish its course, to roll around, to revolve.* ἄψ περιτελλομένων ἔτεος, the year rolling round again, Od. 11, 295. 14, 294. περιτελλομένων ἐνιαυτῶν, in the course or revolution of the years, i. e. as often as the day of the feast returned. Il. 2, 551; cf. 8, 404. 418; see περιπέλομαι.

περιτίθημι, only in tmesis, see τίθημι.
*περιτιμήεις, εσσα, εν (τιμήεις), *greatly honoured, highly valued,* h. Ap 65.

περιτρέπω (τρέπω), only intrans. *to turn oneself about, to return,* in tmesis, Od. 10, 469;† see τρέπω.

περιτρέφω (τρέφω), *to cause to curdle or congeal round about;* pass. *to curdle or congeal round about,* τινί, any thing. σακέεσσι περιτρέφετο κρύσταλλος, the ice formed about the shields. Od. 14. 477;† and Il. 5, 903; see περιστρέφω.

περιτρέχω (τρέχω), *to run round about,* in tmesis, περὶ δ' ἔδραμε, 14, 413.†

περιτρέω, poet. (τρέω), aor. Ep. περίτρεσα, *to tremble round about, to scatter in every direction in terrour,* 11, 676.†

περιτρομέομαι, depon. mid. (τρομέω = τρέμω), *to tremble round about.* σώρεντι περιτρομέοντο μέλεσσιν, upon the limbs, Od. 18, 77.†

περιτροπέω, Ep. and Ion. for περιτρέπω, only partcp. pres. 1) *to turn oneself around, to accomplish a course, to revolve,* spoken of time, 2, 295. 2) Spoken of persons: *to turn in every direction.* μῆλα περιτροπέοντες ἐλαύνομεν, we drove the sheep away, i. e. very circuitously, Od.

435; with accus. φῦλα ἀνθρώπων, to ive commerce or intercourse with the ibes of men, h. Merc. 542.

περίτροχος, ον (τρέχω), running around a circle, hence circular, 23, 455.†

περιφαίνομαι, pass. (φαίνω), to appear and about, to be visible round about, ily partcp. περιφαινόμενον: ὄρος, a far-en mountain, 13, 179. h. Ven. 100. ἐν ριφαινομένῳ, in a conspicuous place, d. 5, 476.

Περίφας, αντος, ὁ, 1) son of Ocheslus, Ætolian, who was slain by Arês, 5, 2, seq. 2) son of Epytus, a herald of e Trojans, 17, 323.

Περιφήτης, ου, ὁ, son of Copreus of ycēnæ, slain by Hector, 15, 639. 2) a ysian, 14, 515.

περιφραδής, ές (περιφράζομαι), very siderate, prudent, wise, h. Merc. 464; ten adv. περιφραδέως, thoughtfully, considerately, 2, 406. Od. 14, 431.

περιφράζομαι, mid. (φράζω), to consider all sides, carefully to ponder, νόστον, d. 1, 76.†

περίφρων, ον (φρήν) very considerate, evident, intelligent, epith. of women, 412. Od. 1, 329; and often.

περιφύω (φύω), only aor. 2 infin. περιῦναι and partcp. περιφύς, intrans. to ow round about; hence περιφῦναί τινι, intwine oneself about any one, to embrace, Od. 19, 416; mly with accus. Od. 1, 236. 320; without case, *Od. 16, 21.

περιχέω (χέω), aor. 1 περιχεῦα. Ep. for ριέχευα, aor. 1 mid. subj. περιχεύεται ith shortened vowel, Od. 6, 232. cf. d. 3, 426; to pour around, to pour ιον, τί Il. 21, 319; esply spoken of orkers in metal: χρυσὸν κέρασι, to put old about the horns, spoken of a victim lorned for sacrifice by putting gold ates about the horns, or gilding them, d. 3, 426. Il. 10, 294; metaph. χάριν νί, to pour grace over any one, Od. 23, 32. Mid. 1) to pour about ourself; υσὸν ἀργύρῳ, to put gold about silver, e. to gild it, Od. 6, 232. 23, 159. 2) to read or extend over any thing, metaph. tmesis, Il. 2, 19.

περιχώομαι (χώομαι), aor. Ep. περιχωσάμην without augm. to be violently ηγιη, τινί τινος, at any one on account some one, *9, 449. 14, 266.

περιωπή, ἡ (ὤψ), a place from which e can take a wide observation, an elettion, a height, 14, 8. Od. 10, 146.

περιώσιος, ον, poet. for περιούσιος, excessive, very great; neut. as adv. excessely, too much, 4, 359. Od. 16, 203. lur. h. 18, 41; with gen. περιώσιον λων, far beyond the others, h. Cer. 33.

περκνός, ή, όν, poet. blackish, dark, inky, sable (V. black-winged), epith. of the gle. 24, 316.† Schol. μέλας, cf. μόρφνος.

Περκώσιος, ὁ, of Percōte, 2, 831. 6, 30.

Περκώτη, ἡ, a city in Asia Minor on he Hellespont, between Abydos and ampsacus, 2, 835. 11, 229; in the time of Straho, a village near Parion: Παλαιπερκώτη. (Περκώπη is a false reading.)

πέρνασχ᾽ for πέρνασκε, see πέρνημι.

πέρνημι, Ep. form of περάω, partcp. περνάς, iterat. imperf. 3 sing. πέρνασχ᾽ for πέρνασκε, to lead out and sell, τινά, any one, 22, 45. 24, 752. κτήματα περνάμενα, goods (brought) for sale, *18, 292.

περονάω (περόνη), aor. Ep. περόνησα, aor. mid. περονησάμην always without augment. 1) to pierce with a clasp or buckle, generally, to pierce through, τινὰ δουρί, 7, 145. Mid. to fasten any thing (for oneself) with a clasp or buckle, with accus. χλαῖναν, 10, 133; τί ἐνετῆσι, with buckles, *14, 180.

περόνη, ἡ (πείρω), prop. the tongue of a buckle; generally, a buckle, a brooch, for fastening a cloak, 5, 425. Od. 18, 293. 19, 226.

περόωσι, see περάω.

Πέρραιβοί, see Περαιβοί, h. Ap. 218.

*Περσαῖος, ὁ (Πέρσης, Hes. Th. 377), son of the Titan Krios (Crius) and Eurybia, father of Hecate, h. Cer. 24.

πέρσα, Ep. for ἔπερσα, see πέρθω.

Περσεύς, έως, Ion. and Ep. ῆος (Herm. Pertrius), 1) son of Zeus and Danaë, daughter of king Acrisius in Argos. His grandfather caused him with his mother to be cast in a chest into the sea; he was, however, rescued by king Polydectes in Seriphus. When he had grown up, Polydectes, in order to remove him, commissioned him to bring the head of Medūsa. He accomplished the task prosperously, and upon his return liberated Andromēda, daughter of Cepheus, who was bound to a rock and destined to be the prey of a sea-monster. Andromeda became his wife and bore to him Alcæus and Electryon, 14, 320. 2) son of Nestor and Anaxibia, Od. 3, 414. 445.

Περσεφόνεια, ἡ, Ep. for Περσεφόνη, daughter of Zeus and Dēmētēr, 14, 326; wife of Hades, who bore her off from her mother. She rules with her husband the shades, and generally the underworld, Od. 10, 491. 11, 47. Il. 9, 457. Her sacred groves are on the western margin of the earth, on the borders of the realms of shades, Od. 10, 509. (According to Eustath. ad Od. 10, 491, from φέρειν and φόνος, who brings death, prop. Φερσεφόνη. Ion. Περσεφόνη.)

Πέρση, ἡ, daughter of Oceanus, wife of Helios, mother of Æetes and Kirkê (Circe), Od. 10, 139. Περσηίς, ίδος, ἡ, Hes. Th. 356.

Περσηϊάδης, ου, ὁ, poet. for Περσείδης, son or descendant of Perseus=Sthenelus, 19, 116.

πεσέειν and πεσέεσθαι, see πίπτω.

πεσσός, ὁ, Att. πεττός, a stone used in playing draughts, Od. 1, 107.† πεσσοῖσι θυμὸν τέρπειν. Eustath. ad loc. and Etym. M. mention the following games: 1) Two persons play, each with five stones. For this purpose a surface of

Πέσσω.   Πεφυλαγμενος.

clay is used, with lines, the middle of which is called ἱερά. The stones of the two parties, of different colours, are placed, and each seeks to shut up the other to the middle line. 2) A second kind is said to have been invented in Egypt, and is connected with astronomy and astrology. 3) A third kind is mentioned by Athenæus, I. p. 61, seq., which Apion heard about from a certain Cteson of Ithaca, and which, according to tradition, the suitors themselves invented. "The suitors," says he, "one hundred and eight in number, placed a like number of stones, in equal parts, opposite each other, so that fifty-four stood on each side. In the middle remained a small empty space, in which a stone was placed called Penelŏpē. At this, the suitor to whom the lot fell cast, by means of the stones. If he hit the Penelŏpē, and jerked her from her place, he placed his stone in the place of Penelŏpē. Then he put up Penelŏpē upon the place to which she had been jerked, and struck his own stone from the middle at her. If he hit, without touching another, he won, and this passed for a good omen. Eurymachus won most frequently." These explanations appear, however, to be only inventions of the Gramm., and deserving of little credit, cf. Wiedemann's Humanist. Magazin 1787, St. 3. p.237; and Nitzsch ad Od. l. c.

πέσσω, Ep. infin. pres. πεσσέμεν, to soften by heat, hence 1) Spoken of the sun, *to soften, to ripen, to mature*, τί, Od. 7, 119. 2) Metaph. *to digest*, hence χόλον, to digest (or *swallow one's*) anger, i. e. to restrain, Il. 4, 513. 9, 565; κήδεα, to keep troubles to oneself, 4, 513. 9, 565; γέρα, to digest presents, i. e. quietly to enjoy them, 2, 237. *b) to nurse, to heal*, βέλος, 8, 513.

πεσών, see πίπτω.

πέταλον, τό (πετάννυμι), *a leaf*, mly plur. 2, 312. Od. 19, 520.

πετάννυμι, aor. ἐπέτασα, Ep. πέτασα (σσ), perf. pass. πέπταμαι, aor. pass. ἐπετάσθην, also πιτνάω, 1) *to spread out, to unfold*, with accus. λῖτα, ἱστία, Od. 5, 269. 6, 94; χεῖρέ τινι, to spread out the arms to any one, Il. 4, 523. 13, 549. Od. 5, 374; spoken of doors: pass. πύλαι πεπταμέναι, folding-doors thrown open. 21, 531. 2) Metaph θυμόν, to expand the heart of any one, i. e. to swell, Od. 18, 160; and in the pass. αἴθρη πέπταται ἀνέφαλος. the cloudless serenity extended, Od. 6, 45; αὐγὴ Ἡελίοιο, Il. 17, 371.

πετηνός, ή, όν (πέτομαι), poet. for πτηνός, *flying, winged, feathered*, epith. of birds; plur. subst. τὰ πετηνά, *fowls, birds*, 15, 238. 2) Spoken of young birds; *fledglings*, callow birds, Od. 16, 218.

Πετεών, ῶνος, ἡ, a village of the Theban dominion in Bœotia, near Haliartus, 2, 500.

Πετεώς, ώ. poet. ῶο, ὁ (according Eustath. Att. for Πετεός, from whi gen. Πετεοῖο and Πετεῶο [Buttm. § note 3]), son of Orneus, fat er of Menestheus, who was expelled by Thes from Attica, 2, 552.

πέτομαι, depon. mid. aor. ἐπτόμην subj. 3 sing. πτῆται, 15, 170; and act. form ἔπτην, Batr. 207 (Ep. form τέομαι, πωτάομαι), 1) *to fly*. prim spoken of birds and insects, 2, 89. 16 265 2) Spoken of the rapid movemen gods, men, and brutes: *to fly, to hasen*. *to run*, 15, 150. Od. 5, 49; spoken men, Il. 13, 755. Od. 8, 122; oftes horses: οὐκ ἄκοντε πετέσθην. *b*) Spok of inanimate things: of arrows, sore and hail; of a river: *to flow away*, l. 13, 140. 592. 15. 170.

πετραῖος, η, ον, *rocky, stony, dwelling in rocks*, Σκύλλη, Od. 12, 231; spoyes h. Ap. 385.

πέτρη, ἡ, Ion. for πέτρα, *a rock, cliff*, often. 2) *a stone, a fragment of rock*; as an image of firmness, Od. 463; and of insensibility, Il. 16. proverbial: οὐκ ἀπὸ δρυὸς οὐδ᾽ ἀπὸ πέτρης, see δρῦς.

πετρήεις, εσσα, εν, poet. (πέτρη) rock stony, Πυθώ, 9, 405; νῆσος, Od. 4, h. 16, 7.

πέτρος, ὁ, poet. *a rock, a stone*, 270. 20, 288. Batr. 218.

πεύθομαι, poet. for πυνθάνομαι, q.v.

πευκάλιμος, η. ον, H. epith. always φρεσὶ πευκαλίμῃσι, Il. 8, 366. 14. 14 15, 81; *prudent, intelligent*. (Prob. according to Buttm., Lex. p. 321, a form πυκινός, like λυγαλέος from λυγρός, according to the Gramm. from πτυα point; *sharp, piercing*.) *ll.

πευκεδανός, ή, όν, poet. (πεύκη) explained, *bitter, sour*, as an epith. war, 10, 8.† (According to Buttm. L p. 320, from πεύκη, prop. the *pointed the pricking-tree*, a point, pointed; *sharp, painful*, cf. ἐχεπευκής.)

πεύκη, ἡ, *a fir tree, a pine tree*, 494.

πεύσομαι, see πυνθάνομαι.

πέφανται, see φαίνω.

πέφανται, see ΦΕΝΩ.

πεφάσθαι, see ΦΕΝΩ.

πεφασμένος, 14, 127, partcp. perf. pass. from φαίνω.

πεφήσομαι, Ep. 1) Fut. pass. φαίνω, 17, 155. Od. 22, 217. 2) Fut. pass. from ΦΕΝΩ, Il. 13, 829. 11, 14 q. v.

πεφιδέσθαι, see φείδομαι.

πεφιδήσομαι, see φείδομαι.

πέφνον, Ep. for ἔπεφνον. see ΦΕΝΩ.

πέφραδον, πεφραδέειν, see φράζω.

πέφρικα, see φρίσσω.

πεφύασι, see φύω.

πεφυγμένος, see φεύγω.

πεφυζότες, Ep. for πεφευγότες, partcp. perf. nom. plur. *flying*, from ΦΙΖΩ, φεύγω, 21, 6 528.

πεφυλαγμένος, see φυλάσσω.

Πεφυυία. 341 Πημαίνω.

πεφυυία, Ep. see φύω.
πέφυρμαι, see φύρω.
πῆ or πῇ (ed. Spitzner), adv. interrog. 1) *how, in what way, wherefore, why*, 10, 385. Od. 2, 364. 2) Spoken of place: *whither*, Il. 5, 472. 6, 377. Od. 17, 219; *where*, 13, 307.
πή or πῄ (ed. Spitz.), enclit. adv. 1) *in any way, in some way, perchance*. οὕτω πη, thus perhaps [*tali quodam modo*], 24, 373. 2) *to any place*. οὔτε τη ἄλλῃ, Od. 2, 127; *any where*, Od. 22, 25.
πηγεσίμαλλος, ον (μαλλός), *thick-woolled, having a thick fleece*, ἀρνειός, 3, 197.†
πηγή, ἡ, *a fountain, a spring*, 2, 523.
πήγνυμι, fut. πήξω, aor. ἔπηξα, Ep. πῆξα, perf. II. πέπηγα, pluperf. 3 sing. ἐπεπήγει, pass. aor. 2 ἐπάγην, Ep. πάγην, aor. 1 pass. only πήχθεν, Ep. for ἐπήχθησαν, 8, 298. I) Act. prop. *to make firm*, hence 1) *to stick in firmly, to stick in, to thrust in, to drive in*, τί, any thing; the place is accompanied by a prep. ἔγχος, δόρυ ἐν μετώπῳ, γαστέρι, 4, 460. 13, 372; ἐρετμὸν ἐπὶ τύμβῳ, to fix an oar upon the grave, Od. 11, 77: and dat. alone, Od. 11. 129; κεφαλὴν ἀνὰ σκολόπεσσι, *to fix his head upon stakes* [*to impale it*], 18, 177; metaph. ὄμματα κατὰ χθονός, *to fasten one's eyes upon the ground*, 3, 217. 2) *to join together, to construct, to build*, νῆας, 2, 664. II) Mid. and aor. 1 and 2 pass. and perf. 2. 1) Intrans. *to become firm*, hence *a*) *to remain infixed, to stick fast*, 4, 185. 5, 616. δόρυ δ' ἐν κραδίῃ ἐπεπήγει, the spear remained infixed in the heart, 13, 442. cf. 16, 772. 2) *to become firm, hard*. γοῦνα πήγνυται, the limbs become stiff, 22, 453. 3) Trans. in aor. 1, *to join together, to construct, to build*, ἴκρια ἐπ' αὐτῆς (sc. νηός), Od. 5. 163.
πηγός, ή, όν, poet. (πήγνυμι)=εὐπηγής, *thick, firm, compressed*; hence ἵπποι, well-fed, powerful horses, Schol. εὐτραφεῖς. 9, 124. 266. κῦμα πηγόν, *a dense*, i. e. huge, mighty wave, Od. 5, 388. 23, 235 (On the critics, who explain it now ' white,' and now ' black,' see Nitzsch ad Od. 5, 388.)
πηγυλίς, ίδος, ἡ, poet. (πήγνυμι), *frosty, cold, freezing*, νύξ, Od. 14, 476.†
Πήδαιον, τό, according to Eustath. an unknown place in Troy, or a river of the island Cyprus, in Ptolem. *Pediaeus*, cf. Mannert VI. 1. ν. 412. Il. 13, 172.
Πηδαῖος, ὁ, son of Antênor, who was slain by Meges, 5, 69.
πηδάλιον, τό (πηδόν), *the rudder, the helm*, in the stern of a ship, *Od. 3, 281. h. Ap. 418.
Πήδασος, ἡ, 1) a city of the Leleges in Troas, on the Satnioeis, the residence of king Altes, which Achilles destroyed, 6, 35. 21, 85 ; according to Pliny=*Adramyttium*. 2) a town in Messene, according to Strab. VIII. p. 369, the later *Methône*, 9, 152. 294.
Πήδασος, ὁ, 1) son of Bucolion, brother

of Æsêpus of Troy, 6, 21, seq. 2) a steed of Achilles, 16, 152.
πηδάω, imperf. 3 sing. ἐπήδα, aor. 1 ἐπήδησα, *to spring, to leap*, ποσσίν, 21, 269; spoken of missiles: *to go, to fly*, *14, 455.
πηδόν, τό (πέζα), prop. the lower part of an oar, *an oar-blade*, generally, *a rudder*, *Od. 7, 328. 13, 78.
πηκτός, ή, όν (πήγνυμι), *joined together, bound fast, firm*, ἄροτρον, 10, 353. 13, 703. Od. 13, 32. h. Cer. 196.
πήλαι, πῆλε, see πάλλω.
Πηληγών, όνος, ὁ, son of the river-god Axius and the nymph Peribœa, 21, 141, seq.
Πηλείδης, ao and εω, ὁ, Ep. Πηληϊάδης, ao, son of Peleus=*Achilles*, 1, 146. (Gen. Πηληϊάδεω, 1, 1, is pentesyllabic with synizesis.)
Πηλείων, ωνος, ὁ = Πηλείδης, 1) 1, 188. Od. 5, 310. 2) *Mud-dweller*, the name of a frog, Batr. 209.
Πηλείωνάδε, adv. *to Pelides*, 24, 338.†
Πηλεύς, ῆος and έος, ὁ (Herm. *Pulsantius*), son of Æacus, sovereign of the Myrmidons at Phthia in Thessaly, 2, 188, 189. He fled, on account of the slaughter of his brother Phocus, to Phthia, to Eurytion, whose daughter Antigône he married. She bore him Polydôra, 16, 175. He then took part in the Argonautic expedition and in the Calydonian hunt. After the death of Antigône, he married the Nereïd Thetis, who bore him Achilles, 16, 33. 20, 206. In the marriage festival the gods took part and made him presents, 24, 59, seq. 16, 143. 2) *the mud-dweller*, the name of a frog (from πηλός), Batr. 29.
Πηληϊάδης, Ep. for Πηλείδης, q. v.
Πηλήϊος, η, ον, Ep. for Πηλείος Πηλεύς), *Peleian*, δόμος, 18, 60. 441.
πήληξ, ηκος, ἡ (πάλλω), *a helmet*, so called from the waving crest, *8, 308. 15, 608. Od. 1, 256.
Πηλιάς, άδος, ἡ, *Pelian*, from the mountain Pelion; ἡ μελίη, the Pelian spear, which was presented to Peleus by Chiron, *16, 143. 19, 390.
Πήλιον, τό, a high, woody mountain in Thessaly, lying over against Ossa, which terminated in the promontory Sepias; now *Zagora*, 2, 744. 16. 114.
*Πηλοβάτης, ου, ὁ (βαίνω), *the mud-walker*, a frog's name, Batr. 210.
πηλός, ὁ, mud, mire, clay, Batr. 240.
πῆμα, ατος, τό (πέπηθα, πάσχω), *evil, wretchedness, misfortune, injury, ruin*, often plur. πήματα πάσχειν. πῆμα κακοῖο (V. the punishment of wickedness), Od. 3, 152. δύης πῆμα, Od. 14, 348. Often spoken of persons instead of *evil-bringing*: ἔτραφε πῆμα Τρωσί, Zeus nourished him as a great pest to the Trojans. Il. 6, 282. cf. 3, 50. 10, 453. 11, 347. Od. 12, 125. 17, 446. h. Ap. 304.
πημαίνω (πῆμα), fut. πημανῶ, Ep. -ανέω, aor. 1 ἐπήμηνα, aor. pass. Ep. πημάνθην, 1) Intrans. *to devise mischief*,

Πηνειός. 342 Πικρός.

to do injury, to do wrong; ὑπὲρ ὅρκια, contrary to the treaty, 3, 299. 24. 781. 2) Trans. with accus. *to injure, to harm, to destroy,* 15, 42. Pass. Od. 8, 563. 14, 255.

Πηνειός, ὁ, *Peneus,* a river in Thessaly, which rises in Pindus, flows through the vale of Tempe, and falls into the Thermaic gulf; now *Salambria,* 2, 752.

Πηνέλεως, ω, Att. for Πηνέλαος, Ep. ω (that cares for the people, from πένομαι and λαός), from the form Πηνέλεος, gen. Πηνελέοιο, 14, 489 (according to Thiersch, § 184. 17, the reading Πηνελάῳ is to be preferred, which Bothe has adopted); son of Hippalcmus, leader of the Bœotians before Troy. He was wounded in the fight about the corpse of Patroclus, by Polydamas, 2, 494. 17, 597.

Πηνελόπεια, ἡ, Ep. for Πηνελόπη (unravelling the web, from πήνη and λέπω), daughter of Icarius and Periboea, Od. 1, 329; the wife of Odysseus (Ulysses); her conjugal fidelity and love is celebrated in the Odyssey. During the absence of Odysseus (Ulysses), there were many youths who aspired to her hand. She put off the suitors a long time by an artifice, professing that she would choose one of them for a husband when she had finished weaving a shroud for Laertes which she had begun. But it was never finished; for she unravelled by night what she had woven by day, Od. 2, 88, seq. 19. 139, seq. A female slave at last betrayed her artifice; when Odysseus (Ulysses) returned, after twenty years, and slew the suitors, Od. 21, 22.

πηνίον, τό (πῆνος), dimin. *the thread of the woof wound upon a spool* or *bobbin* (the yarn for the woof, V.), 23, 762.† Close after Ajax, hastened Odysseus (Ulysses) on, and was as near to him, as the shuttle with which the woof (πηνίον) is drawn through the warp is to the breast of the woman weaving. According to others, the *spool* upon which the weft was wound. Damm incorrectly makes πηνίον an adject. to be connected with μίτον, the thread spun upon the spindle, see μίτος.

πηός, ὁ, poet. *a relative,* esply a relative by marriage, 3, 163. Od. 8, 581. 10, 441. (Prob. from πέπαμαι, to acquire.)

Πήρεια, according to Eustath. a place in Thessaly, prob. the region about Pheræ, 2, 766. ed. Wolf, e Cod. Ven. Steph. and Vous. in transl. Bothe has adopted the reading of the old editions, Πιερίῃ; since here Apollo pastured the herds of Admetus, h. Merc. 69. Others read: Φηρείῃ, the region about Pheræ.

πήρη, ἡ, Ion. for πήρα, *a travelling sack, a wallet,* *Od. 13, 432. 17, 197.

πηρός, ἡ, όν, *disabled, maimed,* esply *blind,* 2, 599.† [Related to πῆ-μα! *Rost.*]

Πηρώ, οῦς, ἡ, daughter of Neleus and Chloris, famed for her beauty. Her father demanded as a bridal present for his daughter the cattle of Iphiclus. She loved her, and his brother Melampus procured for him the wished-for cattle, Od. 11, 287. cf. 15, 225, seq.; see Bias.

πῆχυς, εος, ὁ (prob. akin to παχύς), 1) *the elbow;* the arm from the wrist to the elbow, the arm itself, 5, 314. in E. only dual. 2) *the central curve* which connected the two ends (τόξα) of the bow together, and upon which the arrow was laid in shooting, 11, 375. 13, 583. Od. 21, 419. 3) In the plur. *the curved ends* or *handle* of the lyre, h. Merc. 50.

πίαρ, τό (πίων), poet. only nom. and accus. *fat, tallow, grease.* βοῶν ἐκ ταλέϊσθαι, to take away the fat of the oxen; spoken of the lion, either in the literal sense (thus Buttm. Lex. p. 473. and Heyne), or it is equivalent to 'the fattest of the cattle,' 11, 550. 17, 659. πίαρ ἑλοῦσα. h. Ven. 30. metaph. *fertility.* 2) It is explained as adj. Od. 9, 135. h. Ap. 60. ἐπεὶ μάλα πίαρ ὑπ' οὖδας [so uncteous is the glebe, Cp.]. According to Buttm. l. c. πίαρ is a subst. and ὑπό is prep., for there is great fatness (richness, fertility) under the surface.

πίδαξ, ακος, ἡ, *a fountain, a spring,* 16, 825.†

πιδήεις, εσσα, εν, poet. (πίδαξ), *springy, abounding in fountains,* epith. of Ida, 11, 183.†

Πιδύτης, ον, ὁ, a Trojan from Percote whom Odysseus (Ulysses) slew, 6, 30.

πίε, πιέειν, see πίνω.

πιέζω, Ion. and Ep. πιεζέω, from which imperf. πιέζευν for ἐπίεζουν, Od. 12, 174. aor. pass. ἐπιέσθην, *to press, to squeeze,* and generally, *to press down, to hold fast,* 71, 11. 16, 510. 4, 419; τινὰ ἐν δεσμοῖς, *to hold any one fast in bonds,* Od. 12, 164. Pass. Od. 8, 336.

πίειρα, ἡ, a pecul. fem. of πίων, q. v.

Πιερίη, ἡ (prob. from πίαρ), a region of Macedonia, on the borders of Thessaly, in the vicinity of mount Olympus, h. 226. Od. 5, 50. Adv. from it, Πιερίηθε h. Merc. 85.

πιθέσθαι, see πείθω.

ΠΙΘΕΩ, from which are derived the Ep. forms of πείθω (prop. from the ar. 2, ἐπίθον), fut. πιθήσω, aor. ἐπίθησα. : the signif. *to obey, to follow, to trust* τινί, esply partcp. aor. 4, 398. 6, 161. Od. 21, 315.

πίθος, ὁ, *a vessel,* mly an *earthen one,* prop. a large earthen jar, for keeping wine, 24, 527. Od. 2, 340. 23, 305.

ΠΙΘΩ, obsol. root of πείθω.

πικρόγαμος, ον (γάμος), *whose marriages is unfortunate, unhappily wedded,* *Od. 1, 266. 4, 346. 17, 137.

πικρός, ἡ, όν (from πευκή), also of two endings, Od. 4, 406. 1) Prop. pungent *sharp, piercing, βέλος, διστός,* 11. 4, 118. 217. 2) *sharp* in respect of sense, because a) Of taste: *bitter, sour,* ῥίζα, 11, 846 δάκρυον, Od. b) Spoken of smell: *offensive,* Od. 4, 406. c) Spoken of feeling *bitter, virulent,* ὠδίνες, 11. 11, 271; and

Πίλναμαι. 343 Πίτυς.

generally, *disagreeable, odious*, Od. 17, 448. cf. Buttm., Lex. p. 319.

πίλναμαι, Ep. form of πελάζω, *quickly to approach a thing, to touch, to rush upon* or *to*, with dat. χθονί, 23, 368. h. Cer. 115; also ἐπ' οὐδεῖ, 19, 93; absol. ἀμφὶ δὲ χαῖται πίλναντο, round about the hair fluttered, 22, 402.

πῖλος, ὁ, *felted wool, felt*; a kind of helmet was made of it, 10. 265.†

πιμπλάνω, Ep. form of πίμπλημι; 3 pres-. mid. πιμπλάνεται, 9, 679.

πίμπλημι, pres. 3 plur. πιμπλᾶσι, fut. πλήσω, aor. ἔπλησα. Ep. πλῆσα, mid. πίμπλαμαι, aor. mid. ἐπλησάμην, aor. pass. ἐπλήσθην, 3 plur. πλῆσθεν for ἐπλήσθησαν, also Ep. aor. II. ἐπλήμην, only 3 sing. and plur. πλῆτο and πλῆντο, 1) *to fill, to make full, to fill up*, τί, 14, 35; τινός, with any thing; ἐναύλους νεκύων, τινὰ μένεος, 16, 72. 13, 60; τινί, 16, 374. Mid. with aor. 1, 1) *to fill for oneself, to satiate oneself, to satisfy*, with accus. δέπας οἴνοιο, 9, 224; θυμὸν ἐδητύος καὶ ποτῆτος, to satisfy the desire with food and drink, Od. 17, 603. 19, 198. 2) Intrans. in aor. pass. and Ep. aor. 2, *to fill oneself, to be full*, μένεος, of rage, 11. 1, 104; ἀλκῆς. 17, 211. h. Cer. 281. τῶν δὲ πλῆτο σπέος, the cave was full, 18, 50. cf. Od. 8, 57; Ep. form πιμπλάνω and πλήθω.

πίμπρημι, not found in Hom., see πρήθω.

πίναξ, ακος, ὁ, *a board*, Od. 12, 67; generally, a wooden table, e<ply 1) *a writing-table*, prob. made of two small boards, which were laid together, and fastened with a seal. b) *a plate, a vessel*, small boards upon which meat was laid, Od. 1, 141.

πινύσσω (from πνέω, πέπνυμαι), *to make wise, to instruct, to inform*, τινά, 14, 249.†

πινυτή, ἡ (πινύσσω), poet. *understanding, wisdom*, 7, 239. Od. 20, 71.

πινυτός, ή, όν (πινύσσω, πινύω), *intelligent, prudent, wise*, *Od. 1, 229. 4, 211; and often.

πίνω, pres. infin. πινέμεναι, imperf. iterat. πίνεσκε, fut. πίεσκε, aor. 2 ἔπιον, imperat. πίε, Od. 9, 347; infin. πιεῖν, Ep. πιέειν, πιέμεν, perf. pass. *to drink*, spoken of men and animals, mly with a cus. οἶνον, Il. 5, 341; also κρητῆρας οἴνοιο, to drink jars of wine, 8, 232; σύπελλα, 4, 346. b) Rarely with gen. Od. 11. 96. 15, 373. (Iota is in the fut. long; in the aor. short; long by the arsis in the infin. πιέμεν, Od. 18, 3.)

πίομαι, see πίνω.

πιότατος, η, ον, superl. of πίων.

πίπτω (for πιπέτω from root πέτω), fut. πεσέομαι, aor. 2 ἔπεσον, Ep. πέσον, perf. partcp. πεπτεώς, with synizesis of εω; accus. plur. πεπτεῶτας, Od. 22, 384; *to fall*, i. e. *to fall down, to plunge, to fall from a higher to a lower place*, spoken of persons with prep. showing whence, ἐξ ἵππων, ὀχέων, Il. 7, 16. 16, 379; of things: of missiles, of snow, fire, 17, 633. 12, 156; whither by prep. ἐν, ἐπί, παρά, with dat. or dat. alone πεδίῳ, 5, 82; or by adv. ἔραζε, χαμαί. Esply 1) *to fall out, to drop*, spoken of reins: ἐκ χειρῶν, 5, 583. μετὰ ποσσὶ γυναικός, to fall from the lap of the mother, i. e. to be born, 19, 110. ἐκ θυμοῦ τινι, to fall from any one's heart, i. e. to lose his favour, 23, 595. 2) *to fall down, to fall around*, often spoken of trees, harvests, etc. 11, 69. 18, 552. 3) In the *constructio prægnans*: *to fall dying, to fall, to perish*, spoken of men who are slain in battle, ὑπό τινος and τινι, 6, 453. 17, 428; in full: θνήσκοντες πίπτουσι, 1, 243. 4) *to fall*, i. e. *to rush upon, to cast oneself upon*; ἐν νηυσί, upon the ships, 9, 235. 11, 311. 823. 12, 107. 126. 15, 63. 17, 639; cf. ἔχω. (Voss. incorrectly translates, 11, 823, ἐν νηυσὶ πεσέονται, they were stretched about the ships); of wind, Od. 14, 475; metaph. spoken of discord. Il. 21. 385. 5) *to fall, to sink*, i. e. to become weak and faint, spoken of courage, 14, 418; of the wind, Od. 19, 202.

πῖσος, εος, τό, poet. (πίνω), *a moist place, a meadow, a meadow-pasture, marshy land*, 20, 9. Od. 6, 124. h. Ven. 99; (less correct is πεῖσος.)

πίσσα, ἡ (πίνυς), *pitch*, 4, 277.†

πιστός, ή, όν (πείθω), superl. πιστότατος, *who is believed or trusted: credible, faithful, trusty, trustworthy*, ἑταῖρος, 16, 147; ὅρκια, 2, 124; οὐκέτι πιστὰ γυναιξίν, no confidence can be placed in the women, Od. 11, 456.

πιστόω (πιστός), aor. mid. ἐπιστωσάμην, aor. pass. ἐπιστώθην, *to make trusty, true*; hence, pass. *to be assured, to believe, to trust*, Od. 21, 218. Mid. *to give mutual security, to become security, to promise fidelity*, Il. 6, 233; ἐπέεσσιν, by words, 21, 286; also in the aor. pass. ὅρκῳ πιστωθῆναί τινι, to give security to any one upon oath, Od. 15, 436.

πίσυνος, η, ον, poet. (πείθω), *trusting to, confiding in* any thing, with dat. τόξοισι, Διΐ, 5, 205. Od. 18, 140.

πίσυρες, οἱ, αἱ, πίσυρα, τά, Æol. and Ep. for τέσσαρες, *four*, 15, 680. Od. 5, 70.

Πιτθεύς, ῆος, ὁ, the well-known Pittheus was son of Pelops, king of Trœzêne, father of Æthra; but from 2, 105, seq. it would appear that the son of Pelops and the father of the Æthra mentioned in 3, 144, were probably distinct persons; hence Damm, s. v. *Alius erat filius Pelopis*.

πιτνάω and πίτνημι, poet. form of πετάννυμι, *to spread out, to stretch out*, ἠέρα πίτνα for ἐπίτνα, 21, 7; πιτνὰς εἰς ἐμὲ χεῖρας, Od. 11, 392.

Πιτύεια, ἡ, Ep. for Πιτύα, a town in Asia Minor, between Parion and Priapus, 2, 829 (prop. the *fir-town*).

πίτυς, υος, ἡ, *a fir, a pitch-pine*, pinus abies, 13, 390; dat. plur. πίτυσσιν, Od. 9, 186.

Q 4

Πιφαύσκω. 344 Πλευρών.

πιφαύσκω, and mid. πιφαύσκομαι, Ep. form by lengthening and prefixing redupl. from ΦΑΩ, i. e. φαίνω, only pres. and imperf. 1) Act. to cause to appear, to lay open, hence: *to indicate, to point out*, τινί, 10, 502; esply by speaking: *to give to understand, to tell, to report*, τινί τι, 10, 478. Od. 11, 442; also ἔπεα ἀλλήλοισι, to speak words with one another, Il. 10, 202; cf. Od. 22, 131. II) Mid. πιφαύσκομαι, like the act. 1) τί τινι, e. g. of Zeus: τὰ κῆλά τινι, to show his bolts to any one, i. e. to send, Il. 12, 280; φλόγα, Il. 21, 333. 2) To indicate by words, *to tell, to report, to communicate*, τί, 15, 97. Od. 2, 32; τί τινι, Il. 16, 12. 18, 500. Od. 2, 162; Od. 15, 518.

πίων, ον, gen. πίονος, to this an Ep. fem. πίειρα (as if from πίηρ), compar. πιότερος, η, ον, superl. πιότατος, η, ον, 9, 577. 1) Fut. in a literal sense, μηρία, δημός, Il. 2) Metaph. spoken of the soil: *fat, fertile, fruitful*, πεδίον, ἔργα, πίειρα ἄρουρα, 18, 541. Od. 2, 328. *b) rich, opulent, wealthy*, νηός, οἶκος. Il. 2, 549. Od. 9, 35; πίειρας πόλεις, Il. 18, 342.

Πλαγκταί, αἱ, πέτραι (from πλάζω), *the wandering rocks*; two rocks, which, upon the approach of a ship, struck together like the Symplēgădes; according to the ancient critics, they lay before the western opening of the Sicilian straits. Modern critics understand by them the volcanic islands *Lipari*, Od. 12, 61.

πλαγκτός, ή, όν (πλάζω), *wandering, restless*. 2) Metaph. *wandering, out of one's senses, simple*, Od. 21, 363.†

πλαγκτοσύνη, ἡ, poet. (πλαγκτός), *the act or state of wandering, roaming*, Od. 15, 313.†

πλάγχθη, see πλάζω.

πλάζω, syncop. form of πελάζω; ἐπλαζε δὲ καὶ ὤμους καθύπερθεν, i. e. according to Eustath. εἰς τοὺς ὤμους ἐπέλαζεν, 'the water washed his shoulders from above' (Voss). Others refer the form to πλάζω, i. e. ἐπλάνα καὶ διεσάλευεν ὤμους, the water shook his shoulders (so that he could not go straight on). Thus Damm, and perhaps the Gramm. in better keeping with the context, 21, 269.†

πλάζω, aor. ἔπλαγξα, fut. mid. πλάγξομαι, Od. 15, 312; aor. pass. ἐπλάχθην, Ep. πλάγχθην. I) Act. *to drive around, to cause to wander*, esply to turn from the right way, to drive from, τινὰ ἀπὸ πατρίδος, Od. 1, 75. 24, 307. Il. 17, 751. *b*) Metaph. *to confuse, to lead astray*, Od. 2, 396; *to mislead, to hinder*, τινά, Il. 2, 132. II) Pass. with fut. mid. *to wander, to roam about*, ἐπὶ πόντον, Od. 3, 106; κατὰ πτόλιν, Od. 15, 312; often absol. Il. 10, 91. Od. 1, 2. 3, 95. *b*) *to be turned aside, to wander*; spoken of a missile, *to rebound*, Il. 11, 351.

Πλάκος, ἡ, a mountain in Mysia, at which lay the city Thebe, 6, 396; see Ὑποπλάκιος.

*πλακοῦς, οῦντος, ὁ, contr. from πλακόεις, *a cake*, Batr. 36.

πλανάω (πλάνη), prose, = πλάζω, fr. ἥσω, *to lead astray*, Batr. 96. Mid. *to go astray, to wander about*, 23, 321.†

*πλανοδίη, ἡ, (ὁδός), *a wrong way*, μαζε (only h. Merc. 75: πλανοδίας ἤλαυνε διὰ ψαμαθώδεα χῶρον; it is more correct to consider it as accus. plur. fem. of an adj. πλανόδιος, ον, *astray*, and to refer it to βοῦς, v. 74).

Πλάταια, ἡ, poet. mly αἱ Πλαταιαί, town in Bœotia, in a plain on the Asopus, between Helicon and Cithaeron, now *Palæo-Castro*, 2, 504.

*πλαταμών, ῶνος, ὁ (πλατύς), a level surface, esply *a broad stone*, h. Merc. 128.

πλατάνιστος, ἡ, poet. for πλάτανος, *the plane-tree, platanus orientalis*, Linn., Il. 2, 307. 310.

*πλάτος, εος, τό, *breadth, width*, Pt. 4, 2.

*πλατύνωτος, ον (νῶτος), *broad backed*, Batr. 298.

πλατύς, εῖα, ύ, *broad, wide, flat*, τελαμών, 5, 796. *b*) *broad, spacious*, of great compass, Ἑλλήσποντος, 7, 86. αἰπόλια πλατέα, great, wide-wandering herds, 2. 474. Od. 14, 101. 103.

ΠΛΑΩ or ΠΛΗΜΙ, syncopated form of πελάζω, from which are derived the Ep. forms πλῆτο, πλῆντο.

πλέες, accus. πλέας, Ep. for πλείους and πλέονας, Il. 395. 2. 129; see πλείων.

πλεῖος, η, ον, Ion. and Ep. for πλέως. compar. πλειότερος, Od. 11, 359; *full, filled*, with gen. οἴνου, full of wine, Il. 9, 74. Od. 4, 319. (Always the Ion. form except πλέον, Od. 20, 355.)

πλεῖστος, η, ον, Irreg. superl. of πολύς, *the most, very much*. πλεῖστον κακόν, the greatest evil, Od. 4, 697; πλεῖστον as adv.

πλείω, Ep. for πλέω, *to sail*.

πλείων, πλεῖον, and πλέων, πλέον, compar. of πολύς. (H. uses both forms, also plur. nom. πλείους for πλείονες, dat. πλείοσιν and πλεόνεσσιν; also the Ep. plur. πλέες and πλέας, *more, greater*: πλέων νύξ, the greater part of the night, 10, 252; τὸ πλεῖον πολέμοιο, the greater part of the war, 1, 165. Od. 8, 475; οἱ πλέονες, the greater part.

πλεκτός, ή, όν (πλέκω), *twisted, twined*, τάλαροι, ἀναδέσμη, 18. 568. 22, 469. Od. 9, 247; σειρή, Od. 22, 175.

πλέκω, aor. 1 act. ἔπλεξα, aor. mid. ἐπλεξάμην, 1) *to twist, to twine, to curl*, with accus. πλοκάμους, the locks, 14. 176. Mid. *to twist for oneself*, χαίτας 14, 176; πεῖσμα, to twist a cord for oneself, Od. 10, 168.

πλέον, neut. of πλέος, see πλεῖος.

πλευρή, ἡ, *the side of the* human or of an animal body, *a rib*; mly in the plur. 11, 437. Od. 17, 232.

πλευρόν, τό, poet. form of πλευρή, 4, 468.†

Πλευρών, ῶνος, ὁ, an ancient city in

Πλέω. Πλοχμός.

Ætolia, on the river Evēnus, the abode of the Curētes, with a temple of Athēnē, 2, 639. 13, 217; from which Πλευρώνιος, η, ον, Pleuronian; subst. a Pleuronian.

πλέω, Ep. form πλείω; from which πλείειν, πλείοντες, fut. πλεύσομαι, Od. 12, 25. (Ep. form πλώω,) to sail, to travel by sea; to voyage, ἐπὶ πόντω, Il. 7, 88; ἐνὶ πόντῳ, Od. 16, 367; with accus. of place: ὑγρὰ κέλευθα, to navigate the watery paths, Od. 3, 71. 9, 252. (πλέων, Od. 1, 183, monosyllabic.)

ΠΛΕΩ, falsely assumed root for some of the tenses of πίμπλημι.

πλέων, πλέον, see πλείων.

πληγή, ἡ (πλήσσω), a stroke, a blow, a lash, Od. 4, 244; esply the cut of a whip, Il. 11, 532. 2) Διὸς πληγή, ἡ, a blow of Zeus=lightning, 14, 414.

πλῆθος, εος, τό (πλήθω), dat. πληθεῖ, prop. fulness; mly multitude, crowd; *17, 330. 23, 639.

πληθύς, ύος, ἡ. Ion. for πλῆθος, dat. πληθυῖ, 22, 458. Od. 16, 105; prop. fulness, multitude; mly a crowd of men, with verb plur. Il. 2, 278. 15, 305. Od. 11, 514; esply spoken of great multitudes, the people, in distinction from the leader, Il. 2, 143.

πλήθω, only pres. and imperf. to be full, to fill oneself, to become full, with gen. Ἵππων καὶ ἀνδρῶν, 8, 214; σίτου, Od. 9, 8; spoken of rivers: to rise, to swell, Il. 5, 87. 11, 492. πάντες ποταμοὶ πλήθουσι ῥέοντες, the flowing rivers rise, 16, 389; metaph. spoken of the moon: πλήθουσα Σελήνη, the full moon, 18, 484. cf. h. 32, 11.

Πληϊάδες, αἱ, Ion. for Πλειάδες, the Pleiades, the seven daughters of Atlas and Pleïone; they were placed by Zeus amongst the stars and formed the constellation of the seven stars in Taurus. Their rising brought summer, their setting winter, and so the beginning and end of navigation, 18, 486. Od. 5, 272. h. 7, 7. (The name is derived by some from πλέω, as the stars of navigation; by others, as Voss ad Arat. from πέλομαι, versari; according to others still = πελειάδες, a flight of wild doves, cf. Nitzsch ad Od. 5, 272.)

πληκτίζομαι, depon. mid. (πλήκτης), to strike, to fight, to contend, τινί, 21, 499.†

*πλῆκτρον, τό, prop. an instrument for striking: the plectrum, for playing upon the lyre, h. Ap 185.

πλημμυρίς, ίδος, ἡ, the flow or flux of the sea, in opposition to the ebb, Od. 9, 486.† In Hom. ῡ, in Eurip. ῠ, in like manner, πλήμυρα. (According to Buttm., Gr. Gram. § 7, 17, note, from πλήν and μύρω, according to others, from πλῆμα.)

πλήμνη, ἡ (πλήθω), prop. the filling; then, the nave of the wheel, in which the axle runs, and into which the spokes are inserted, *5, 726. 23, 339.

πλήν, as prep. besides, except, with gen. Od. 8, 207.†

πλῆντο, 1) Ep. 3 plur. aor. sync. pass. of πίμπλημι, Od. 8, 57. 2) 3 plur. aor. sync of πελάζω, Il. 14, 468.

πλῆξα, see πλήσσω.

πλήξιππος, ον (ἵππος), horse-spurring, horse-taming, *2, 104.

πλησίος, η, ον (πέλας), near, neighbouring, mly with gen. 6, 249. Od. 5, 71; with dat. Il. 23, 732. Od. 2, 149; as subst. a neighbour, the nearest person, πλησίος ἄλλος, Il. 2, 271. Neut. as adv. near, in the vicinity, with gen. 3, 115; rarely with dat. 23, 732.

πλησίστιος, ον (ἱστίον), filling or swelling the sails, οὖρος, *Od. 11, 7. 12, 149.

πλήσσω, aor. 1 ἔπληξα, always Ep. πλῆξα, Ep. aor. 2 πέπληγον and ἐπέπληγον, perf. πέπληγα, always in act signif. Mid. aor. 1 ἐπληξάμην, Ep. aor. 2 πεπληγόμην, aor. pass. ἐπλήγην, 1) to strike, to smite, to thrust, τινά, any one: πληγῇσιν, to punish any one with blows, 2, 264: σκήπτρῳ μετάφρενον, 2, 266. ποδὶ πλῆξαι, to strike with the foot, Od. 22, 20; χορὸν ποσίν, Od. 8, 264; ἵππους ἐς πόλεμον, to drive the steeds to the battle, Il. 16, 728; hence, b) Esply spoken of arms, for the most part of the sword: to smite, to wound, to hit; often with double accus. τινὰ κληῖδα, to strike any one upon the clavicle, 5, 147; τινὰ αὐχένα, 11, 240. Pass. in aor. 1, to be struck, 23, 694; esply to be struck by lightning, κεραυνῷ, 8, 455 (here stands πληγέντε masc. instead of πληγείσα), Od. 12. 416. b) Metaph. to be violently attacked, Il. 13, 394. 16, 203; see ἐκπλήττω. Mid. to strike oneself, with accus. στήθεα, upon the breast, 18, 51; μηρώ, 12, 162. 16, 125. h. Cer. 218.

πλῆτο, Ep. aor. sync. from πίμπλημι. 2 3 sing. Ep. aor. sync. from πελάζω, 14, 438.

πλίσσομαι (from πλίξ. Dor. = βῆμα), mid. (elsewhere also πλίσσω), to stride, prop. according to the Gramm. to weave the legs, by putting one foot before the other; or, generally, to stride with extended legs, spoken of running mules: εὖ πλίσσοντο πόδεσσιν, well strode they forward with the legs, Od. 6, 318.†

πλόκαμος, ὁ (πλέκω), curled hair, a curl, a lock, in the plur. 14, 176.†

πλοκμός, η, ον (πλέκω), curled, entangled, for πλόκιμος, Od. 13, 295.†

πλόος, ὁ (πλέω), the act of sailing, navigation, Od. 3, 169.† h. 33, 16.

*πλούσιος, η, ον (πλοῦτος), rich, h. Merc. 171.

πλοῦτος, ὁ (πλέος, not from πολύ, ἔτος), abundance, wealth, property, connected with ἄφενος, 1, 171; ὄλβος, Il., and Od. 14, 206.

†Πλοῦτος, ὁ, son of Jasion and Dēmētēr, god of wealth, h. Cer. 489

*Πλουτώ, οῦς, ἡ, daughter of Oceanus and Tethys, companion of Proserpina, h Cer. 422.

πλοχμός, ὁ, poet. (πλέκω) = πλόκαμος, twisted hair, a curl, 17, 52.†

Πλυνός. 346 Ποιέω.

πλυνός, ὁ (πλύνω) a washing-tank, or a cistern of stone, in which foul clothes were laid and cleansed, 22, 153. Od. 6, 40. 86. cf. Nitzsch ad Od. 6, 85.

πλύνω, fut. πλυνώ, Ep. πλυνέω, aor. Ep. πλῦνα, to wash, to rinse, to cleanse, πλύνεσκον, 22, 155. Od. 6, 93.

πλωτός, ή, όν (πλώω), sailing, esply swimming, floating, νῆσος, Od. 10, 3†; epith. of Æolia (see Αἰολίη); according to others, circumnavigable.

πλώω, Ep. form of πλέω, only in the signif. to swim, to float; imperf. τεύχεα πλῶον, 21, 302. Od. 5, 240. h. 21, 7.

πνείω, poet for πνέω.

πνεύμων, ονος, ὁ (πνέω), the lungs, 4, 528.

πνέω, poet. πνείω, perf. mid. πέπνυμαι; H. has the pres. and imperf. act. m:y in the poet. form (πνείω only Od. 5, 469), 1) to blow, to breathe, spoken of the wind and the air, Od. 4, 361. 5, 469; to exhale, Od. 4, 446. 2) Spoken of animate beings: to breathe, to respire,=to live, Il. 17, 447. Od. 18, 131; of horses: to pant, to puff, Il. 13, 385; metaph. spoken of men: μένεα πνείοντες, breathing courage, animated with courage, epith. of warriors, 2, 536. Od. 22, 203. 3) The perf. mid. πέπνυμαι, infin. πεπνῦσθαι. prop. to be animated; hence, to have recollection, to have intelligence, spoken of Tiresias, who alone possesses recollection in the under-world, Od. 10, 495; esply to be intelligent, prudent, Il. 24, 377. Od. 23, 210; most frequently the partcp. πεπνυμένος, as adj. intelligent, prudent, thoughtful, considerate, spoken of persons and things: as μήδεα, Il. 7, 278. πεπνυμένα βάζειν, to speak intelligently, 9, 58; ἀγορεύειν, Od. 19, 352.

πνίγω, fut. ξω, to strangle, to drown, τινά, Batr. 158.

πνοιή, ή, Ep. and Ion. for πνοή (πνέω), 1) blast, breath, air, with the adjunct. ἀνέμοιο, Βορέαο, also plur. 5, 526: then ἅμα πνοιῇς ἀνέμοιο πέτεσθαι, to fly with the blasts of wind, i. e. fleet as the wind, spoken of a bird, 12, 207; of horses, 16, 149. 2) the breath, of men and of animals: breath, respiration, 23, 380. πνοιῇ Ἡφαίστοιο, the breath of Hêphæstus, i. e. the flame of fire, 21, 355.

ΠΝΥΜΙ, ΠΝΥΩ, assumed root of πέπνυμαι. see πνέω.

ποδαλείριος, ὁ, Podaleirius, son of Asklêpius (Æsculapius), brother of Machaon, from Tricca in Thessaly; a famous physician, 2, 732. 11, 832.

ποδάνιπτρον (νίπτω), water for washing the feet, mly plur. Od. 19, 343. 504.

Ποδάργη, ή, (the swift-footed), one of the harpies, from whom Zephyrus begat the two horses of Achilles, Xanthus and Balius, 16, 150.

Πόδαργος, ὁ (swift-foot, from ἀργός), 1) a steed of Hector, 8, 185. 2) a steed of Menelaus, 23, 295.

ποδάρκης, ές (ἀρκέω), prop. enduring with the feet; hence, strong-footed, swift-footed, often epith. of Achilles, *1, 121.

Ποδάρκης, ους, ὁ, son of Iphiclus, brother of Protesilaus, who, after the death of his brother, led the warriors of Phylacê and Pyrasus, 2, 704. 13, 693.

ποδηνεκής, ές ('ΕΝΕΚΩ), reaching to the feet, spoken of a lion's skin, *10, 24. 178; of a shield, 15, 646.

ποδήνεμος, ον (ἄνεμος), wind-footed, swift-jooted, epith. of Iris, *2, 786; and often.

Ποδῆς, οῦς, ὁ, for Ποδέης, son of Eëtion, a wealthy and brave Trojan, friend of Hector, slain by Menelaus, 17, 575 seq.

ποδώκεια, ή (ποδώκης), swiftness of foot in plur. 2, 792.†

ποδώκης, ες (ὠκύς), swift-footed, often an epith. of Achilles, 2, 860. Od. 11, 471 also of Dolon, Il. 10, 316; of horses, 2, 764. 17, 614.

ποδέεσκε, see ποθέω.

πόθεν, adv. interrog. (πός), whence? from whence? spoken of place and race. Od. 17, 368. 373; often with gen. πόθεν ἀνδρῶν, who and whence, Il. 21, 150. Od. 1, 170. h. Cer. 113.

ποθέν, enclit. adv. from somewhere, from any place, mly εἴ ποθεν, 9, 380; μή πῶς and εἰ καί ποθεν ἄλλοθεν, Od. 7, 52.

ποθέω (ποθή), pres. infin. Ep. ποθήμεναι for ποθεῖν, Od. 12, 110; aor. Ep. ἐπόθησα and πόθεσα, to wish, to desire, to long for, τί or τινά, esply to long for something absent or lost; hence for the most part, to miss, τινά, 2, 793. 726. 5, 414. 11, 161. Od. 1, 343.

ποθή, ή, poet.=πόθησις, wish, desire, longing, esply for something absent τινός, 1, 240; ποθή ἐμεῖο, for me, 6, 36; βιότοιο, Od. 2, 126. κείνου δ᾽ οὔτι λυγρή ποθή ἔσσεται, there will be no great longing for him, i. e. we shall not greatly miss him, Il. 14, 368; also once, σῇ ποθῇ, in desire of thee, 19, 321.

πόθι, adv. interrog. poet. for πού, where?*Od. 1, 170. 10, 325.

ποθί, enclitic adv. poet. for πού, 1 anywhere, 10, 8. 2) Of time: at any time. αἴ κέ ποθι, 1, 128. 3) Mly somehow, perhaps, perchance, 19, 273. Od. l. 348.

πόθος, ὁ, wish, desire, longing, rare for any one, 17, 439.† In Od. 4, 596. 11. 202. 14, 144. h. 18, 33.

Ποιάντιος, ον, sprung from Poeas, υἱός, Od. 3, 190.

ποιέω, fut. ήσω, aor. ἐποίησα, D ποίησα, perf. pass. πεποίημαι, fut. m·d -ήσομαι, aor. ἐποιησάμην, Ep. ποιησάμην, ground signif. to make. 1) to make, i. e. to produce, to bring into being, to prepare, with accus. a) Prim. spoken of things which are produced by external action; it is to receive a translation suited to the subst. with which it is connected: δῶμά τινι, to build a man a house, 1, 608; in like manner πρός θάλαμον, κλισίην, etc. πύλας δ᾽ ὑψηλάς

Ποίη 347 Πολεμόνδε.

7, 339: σάκος ταύρων (gen. mater.), a shield of ox-hide, 7, 222; τύμβον to cast up a sepulchral mound, 7, 435. είδωλον, Od. 4, 796. b) Spoken of states and of things, to which esply mental action belongs: τελευτήν, to make an end, Od. 1, 250; φόβον, to excite fear, Il. 12, 432; νύημά τινι έν φρεσίν, to put a thought into any one's mind, Od. 14, 274; άθύρματα, to pursue pastimes, Il. 15, 363; κακόν μείζον, to prepare a greater evil, 13, 120; γαλήνην, Od. 5, 452; pass. ή σοι άριστα πεποίηται κατά οίκον πρός Τρώων (ironical), truly, excellent things have been done to thee in thy house by the Trojans, Il. 6, 57. 2) *to make*, i. e. to place a man in a condition; *a*) With double accus. *to convert, to render*: with subst. τινά βασιλέα, to make a man a king, Od. 1, 387; κείνον ταμίην άνέμων, Od. 10, 21; λαούς λίθους, the people to stones, Il. 24, 611; θεάν άκοιτιν θνητώ, to make a goddess bride to a mortal, 24, 537; with adj. τινά άφρονα, to render a man senseless, Od. 23, 12; άϊστον, Od. 5, 235; θεμείλια λεία, to make the ground smooth, i. e. level, Il. 12, 30; cf. δίπτυχα. Mid. 1) *to make any thing for oneself*, like the act. *a*) With a more or less distinct reference to the subj.: οίκία, to build houses or dwellings for oneself, 12, 168; τείχος, νηόν, 12, 5. h. Ap. 286; σχεδίην, Od. 5, 251. *b*) άγορήν, to make an assembly, Il. 8, 2; κλέος αύτή ποιείται, she acquired glory for herself, ρήτρην ποιείσθαι, Od. 14, 393. 2) With double accus. τινά άλοχον, to make any one a wife, Il. 3, 409; τινά άκοίτην, Od. 5, 120; τινά υίόν, to take any one as a son, Il. 9, 495.

ποίη, ή, Ion. for πόα, *grass, herbage, pasturage*, 14, 347.† Od. 9, 499; and often.

ποιήεις, εσσα, εν (ποίη), *grassy, verdant, green*, epith. of towns and islands, 2, 503; πίσεα, 20, 9; άγκεα, Od. 4, 337.

ποιητός, ή, όν (ποιέω), *made, prepared*; in H. *well-wrought* or *built*, spoken of dwellings, 5, 198. Od. 1, 333; of arms and vessels, Il. 10, 262.

ποικίλλω (ποικίλος), *to variegate*, spoken of embroidering and painting; especially *to adorn with various colours, to work or form with skill*, χορόν, 18, 590.†

ποίκιλμα, ατος, τό (ποικίλλω), *variegated work*, esply *painting, embroidery*, ποικίλμασι κάλλιστος, spoken of a robe, 6, 294. Od. 15, 107.

ποικιλομήτης, ου, ό (μήτις), *full of manifold devices*, *abounding in expedients*, *cunning*, epith. of Odysseus (Ulysses), 11, 482. Od. 3, 163; of Zeus and Hermes, h. Ap. 322. Merc. 155.

ποίκιλος, η, ον, 1) *variegated, having divers colours*, παρδαλέη, 10, 30. 2) *adorned, painted, embroidered*, spoken of garments, 5, 735. Od. 18, 293; and gen. *wrought with art, beautifully formed*, epith. of arms, chariots, etc. ποικίλα χαλκώ άρματα, chariots adorned with

brass, Il. 4, 226; in like manner τεύχεα, 3, 327; δεσμός, Od. 8, 448.

ποιμαίνω (ποιμήν), *to pasture, to drive to pasture*, spoken of shepherds; μήλα, Od. 9, 188; also absol. έπ' οίεσσι, to be a shepherd with sheep, Il. 6, 25. Mid. *pasture, to graze*, spoken of flocks, 11, 244.

ποιμήν, ένος, ό (πάομαι), *a herdsman*, esply *a shepherd*, 5, 137; then metaph. ποιμήν λαών, a shepherd of the people, frequently an epith. of princes, Il. and Od.

ποίμνη, ή (ποιμαίνω), *a flock or herd of cattle* pasturing, Od. 9, 122.†

ποιμνήιος, η, ον (ποίμνη), Ion. for ποιμνείον, *belonging to the flock or herd*, σταθμός, the fold of the flock or herd, 2, 470.†

ποινή, ή (akin to ΦΕΝΩ), prop. *compensation for a committed homicide*, the money with which a man redeems himself from blood-guiltiness; hence, 1) *penalty, vengeance* (which I take or which is taken of me), with gen. for or on account of any one, παιδός, 13, 659; κασιγνήτοιο, 14, 483; cf. 16, 398. 9, 633; and generally, *recompense, requital*, 5, 266. Od. 23, 312; τών ποιμνήν, ό, as appos. Il. 17, 207; cf. 21, 28.

ποίος, η, ον (πός), *what sort of, of what kind* (qualis). ποίον τόν μύθον έειπες! what a word hast thou spoken, and next ποίον έρεξας! 23, 570. With infin. ποιοί κ' είη 'Οδυσήι άμυνέμεν, how would you be able to defend Odysseus (Ulysses), Od. 21, 195.

ποιπνύω, partcp. aor. ποιπνύσας (prob. from πνέω, πέπνυμαι, with redupl.), prop. to be out of breath from haste; hence, 1) *to be hasty, active, to move hastily*, άνά μαχήν, 14, 155. 8. 219; in a sacrifice, Od. 3, 430. Esply 2) *to serve with assiduity, to wait upon assiduously*, Il. 1, 600. 18. 421. Od. 20, 149 (υ is in the pres. and impref. short, with a following short syllable, long with a following long, Il. 1, 601. 24, 475).

πόκος (πέκω), *wool shorn off, a fleece*, 12, 451.†

πολέες, Ep. for πολλοί. see πολύς.

πολεμήιος, ον, Ion. for the unusual πολεμείος, *warlike*; έργα, 2, 338. Od. 12, 116; τεύχεα, Il. 7, 193.

πολεμίζω. Ep. πτολεμίζω (πόλεμος), fut. πολεμίξω, 1) *to war, to fight, to contend*, τινί, with any one: άντα τινός, against any one, 8, 428; τινός έναντίβιον, 20, 85; μετ' Άχαιοίσιν, 9, 352; also πόλεμον, to wage a war, 2, 121. 2) *to make war upon, to invade*. ρήίτεροι πολεμίζειν, more easy to assail, 18, 258.

πολεμιστά, ό, Ep. for πολεμιστής.

πολεμιστής, ού, ό. Ep. πτολεμιστής (πόλεμος), *a warrior, a combatant*, 5, 289; and often; Od. 24. 499.

*πολεμόκλονος, ον (κλόνος), *making a warlike noise or tumult*, Batr. 4, 276.

πολεμόνδε. adv. Ep. πτόλεμόνδε, *to the war*, 8, 313, and often.

Q 6

πόλεμος, ὁ, Ep. also πτόλεμος (πέλω), *the tumult of war, the tumult of battle*, and generally, *war;* particularly in H. *contest, battle*, πόλεμος Ἀχαιῶν, war with the Achaians, 3, 165; ἀνδρῶν πτόλεμοι, 24, 8. Od. 8, 183.

πολεύω, poet. (πόλος), only intrans. *to go about, to remain, to abide*, κατὰ ἄστυ, Od. 22, 223.†

πολέων, Ep. for πολλῶν, see πολύς.

πόληας, πόληες, see πόλις.

πολίζω (πόλις), aor. ἐπόλισα, Ep. πόλισσα, perf. pass. πεπόλισμαι, prop. to found a city, general.y, *to found, to build*, τεῖχος, *7, 453. 20, 217.

πολιήτης, ου, ὁ, poet. for πολίτης, 2, 806.†

πόλινδε, adv. *to the city, into the city*, Il. and Od.

πολιοκρόταφος, ον (κρόταφος), *having gray hairs upon the temples* ('becoming gray,' V.), 8, 518.†

πολιός, ή, όν, also ός, όν, 20, 229; (πελός), *whitish, gray*, canus, spoken of the hair, 22, 74. 77; κεφαλή, Od 24, 317; of a wolf, Il. 10, 334; of iron, 9, 365; often of the sea on account of the white foam. 1, 350. Od. 4, 580.

πόλις, ιος, ἡ, Ep. also πτόλις (πέλω). H. has the gen. πόλιος dissyllabic, 2, 811; πτόλιος, πόλεος and πόληος, dat. πτόλεί, πόλει, πόληΐ, nom. plur. πόλιες, πόληες, gen. πολίων (πόλεων, false reading, 5, 744), dat. πολίεσσι, accus. πόλιας (trisyllabic and dissyllabic), πόλεις, πόληας, prop. a place of commerce, *a city*. ἄκρη πόλις, the highest part of the city, *a citadel*, 6, 88, 257. 2) *the region round about a city*, Od. 6, 177. πόλις καὶ ἄστυ, Il. 17, 144; cf. ἄστυ. On the declen. see Thiersch, Gram. § 190. 24; Kühner, § 268. 3.

*πολισσόος, ον (σώζω), *town-protecting*, h. 7, 2.

πολίτης, ου, ὁ. Ep. πολιήτης, 2, 806; *a citizen, an inhabitant of a city*, 15, 558. Od. 7, 131.

Πολίτης, ου, ὁ, 1) son of Priam, in whose form Iris appeared to his father, 2 791. 13, 339, seq. 2) a faithful companion of Odysseus (Ulysses), who was metamorphosed by Kirkê (Circe), Od. 10, 224.

πολλάκι or πολλάκις (with ε only, 8, 362. Od. 4, 101), adv. (πολλός), *many times, i. e. often, frequently*, Il. 3, 232; πολλάκι, h. Pan, 12, 13.

πολλός, πολλόν, Ep. and Ion. for πολύς, πολύ.

Πολυαιμονίδης, ου, ὁ, son of Polyæmon. 8, 276.

πολύαινος, ον (αἰνέω), *much praised, greatly lauded, praiseworthy;* epith. of Odysseus (Ulysses), 9, 673. 10, 544. 11, 43.). Od. 12, 184. According to Buttm., Lex. p. 60, *distinguished by shrewd and crafty discourse*: αἶνος, *a speech full of meaning, &c*.]

πολυάϊξ, ϊκος, ὁ, ἡ (ϊ), poet. (ἀΐσσω), prop. spoken of violent motion; hence,

impetuous, tumultuous, fatiguing, πόλεμος, 1, 105. Od. 11, 314; κάματος, Il. 5, 811.

πολυανθής, ές, (ἄνθος), *very blooming*, ὕλη, Od. 14, 353 ;† ἔαρ, h. 18, 17.

πολυάρητος, ον, Ion. (ἀράομαι), *greatly wished, much prayed for*, τινί, *Od. 6, 280. 19, 404. h. Cer. 220.

πολύαρνι, metaplast. dat. of πολύαρνος, ον, *rich in sheep, abounding in flocks*, 2, 106.†

πολυβενθής, ές, poet. (βένθος), *very deep*, epith. of the sea, 1, 432. Od. 4. 406.

Πόλυβος, ὁ (rich in oxen), 1) son of Antênor in Troy, 11, 59. 2) a suitor of Penelope, whom Eumæus slew, Od. 22. 243. 284. 3) a rich Egyptian in Thebes, husband of Alcandra, with whom Menelaus lodged, Od. 4, 126. 4) a Phæacian, Od. 8, 373. 5) an inhabitant of Ithaca, father of the suitor Eurymachus, Od. 16, 519. 16. 345.

πολυβότειρα, ἡ, Ep. πουλυβότειρα, poet. (βόσκω), prop. fem. of πολυβοτήρ, *much nourishing, fruitful productive*, epith. of the earth and of Achaia, 3, 89. 11, 770. Od. 8, 378; only in Ep. form.

πολύβουλος, ον, poet. (βουλή), *of great wisdom, intelligent, well-advised, counselling well*, epith. of Athênê, 5, 260. Od. 16, 282.

πολυβούτης, ου, ὁ, poet. (βοῦς), *rich in horned cattle, rich in oxen*, *9, 154. 296.

πολυγηθής, ές, poet. (γηθέω), *much delighting, greatly rejoicing*, epith. of the Hours, 21. 450.†

πολυδαίδαλος, ον, poet. (δαίδαλος), *rich in art, i. e. 1) wrought with great art, beautifully wrought*, spoken of metals. 2, 358. Od. 13. 11. 2) *skilled in art, ingenious*, Σιδόνες, Il. 23, 743.

πολυδάκρυος, ον = πολύδακρυς, whence μάχης πολυδακρύου, according to the Cod. Venet. ed. Bothe and Spitzner, Il. 17, 192. for πουλυδακρύτου, because υ in this word is always long.

πολύδακρυς, υ, poet. (δάκρυ), *tearful, much lamented, lamentable*, epith. of Arês, of battle, and of war, *3, 132. 17, 544.

πολυδάκρυτος, ον, poet. (δακρύω), *much lamented, much deplored*, epith. of battle, 24, 620; γόος, Od. 21, 57. 19, 213.

Πολυδάμας, αντος, ὁ, Ep. Πουλυδάμας (much conquering), voc. Πουλυδάμα, 12, 231; son of Panthôus and Phronis, a wise and brave Trojan, 11, 57. 18, 249.

Πολυδάμνα, ἡ, wife of the Egyptian Thon, who presented many magic herbs to Helen, Od. 4, 228.

*Πολυδέγμων, ονος, ὁ (δέχομαι), *the much embracing*, as subst. for Hades, who receives all mortals into his dominions, h. Cer. 17, 31.

πολυδειράς, άδος, ὁ, ἡ (δείρη). prop. *having many necks;* hence, *many peaked, having many summits*, epith. of Olympus *1, 499. 5, 754.

*Πολυδέκτης, ου, ὁ (δέχομαι), the much

Πολυδένδρεος. 349 Πολύλλιστος.

embracing, epith. of Hades, =Πολυδέγμων h. Cer. 9.
πολυδένδρεος, ον (δένδρον), abounding in trees, woody, *Od. 4, 737. 23, 139. h. Ap. 475.
πολυδέσμος, ον, poet. (δεσμός), well-bound, well-joined, σχεδίη, *Od. 5, 33. 7, 264.
Πολυδεύκης. ους, ό, accus. Πολυδεύκεα, Polydeukés (Pollux), son of Zeus and Leda, brother of Kastôr (Castor), one of the Dioscûri, famous as a pugilist; he alone as the son of Zeus was immortal, see Κάστωρ, 3, 237. Od. 11, 299, seq.
πολυδίψιος, ον (δίψα), very thirsty, destitute of water, epith. of Άργος, 4, 171. It refers to the tradition that the realm of Argos was once destitute of water, cf. Apd. 2, 1. 4. According to others, long looked for, Fr. 2, 1.
Πολυδώρη, ή, daughter of Peleus and Antigone, wife of Borus and mother of Menesthius, 16, 175.
πολύδωρος, ον (δῶρον), richly gifted, i. e. πολυέδνος, epith. of ἄλοχος, who on account of her beauty had received many presents, 6, 394. 22, 88. Od. 24, 293 In the last passage it has been translated well-portioned. [Cf. Lenz Gesch. d. Weiber, S. 170. Am. Ed.]
Πολύδωρος, ό, son of Priam and Laothoë. Because he was the youngest and most beloved of his sons, Priam would not permit him to take part in the battle. Disobedient to the command, he exposed himself in the fight and was slain by Achilles, 20, 407, seq. 21, 85, seq. (2) One of the Epigoni, conquered by Nestor, 23, 637.
Πολύειδος, ό, see Πολυΐδος.
*πολυεύχετος, ον (εὔχομαι), much wished, much prayed for, h. Cer. 165.
πολύζυγος, ον, poet. '(ζυγόν), having many banks of rowers, well-oared, νηῦς, 2, 293.†
πολυήρατος, ον (ἐράω), much beloved, greatly wished for, dear, Ἥβη, γάμος, *Od. 11, 275. 15, 126. 306. h. Ven. 226.
πολυηχής, ἐς (ἠχή), loud sounding, i. e. 1) loud singing, full-voiced, spoken of the nightingale, Od. 19, 521. 2) loud echoing, loud resounding, spoken of a shore. 4, 422.
πολυθαρσής, ἐς (θάρσος), very bold, very courageous, spirited, 17, 156. Od. 13, 387.
Πολυθερσείδης, ου, ό, son of Polytherses, = Ctesippus, Od. 22, 287.
Πολυΐδος, ό (ΐ), (who knows much, from πολύς and ἰδεῖν, according to Wolf. Heyne, on the other hand, writes Πολύειδος, according to Etym. M. and also Eustath. mentions this orthography, so also Paus. Plat.) son of Coeranus, a prophet of Corinth, of the family of Melampus, father of Euchênor, 13, 663. 2) son of Eurydamas, a Trojan, 5, 148.
πολυΐδρείη, ή, poet. (πολυΐδρις), much knowledge; hence, wisdom, intelligence, plur. *Od. 2, 346. 23, 77.

πολυΐδρις, ιος, ό, ή, poet. (ἴδρις), much knowing; hence, wise, intelligent, crafty, *Od. 15, 459. 23, 82.
πολύιππος, ον (ἵππος), having many horses, abounding in horses, 13, 171.†
*πολυίχθυος. ον (ἰχθύς), abounding in fish, h. Ap. 417.
πολυκαγκής, ές, poet. (κάγκανος), very parching; δίψα, burning thirst, 11. 642†.
πολύκαρπος, ον (καρπός), abounding in fruits, ἀλωή, *Od. 7, 122. 24, 221.
Πολυκάστη, ή (the much adorned), daughter of Nestor and Anaxibia, Od. 3, 401. According to Eustath, wife of Telemachus.
πολυκέρδεια, ή (πολυκερδής). great craftiness, cunning, in the plur. Od. 24, 167.*
πολυκερδής, ές (κέρδος), very crafty, cunning, νόος, Od. 13, 255.†
πολύκεστος, ον (κεστός), much embroidered, richly embroidered, ἱμάς, 3, 371.†
πολυκηδής, ές, poet. (κῆδος), full of care, causing trouble (νόστος), *Od. 9, 37. 23, 351.
*πολύκλαυτος, ον, poet. for πολύκλαυστος (κλαίω), much wept, greatly lamented, Ep. 3, 5.
πολυκλήϊς, ἴδος, ή, poet. (κλίς), furnished with many benches of oars, well-oared, epith. of ships, 2, 74. 20, 382. Od. (Iota long in all the cases.)
πολύκληρος, ον (κλῆρος), prop. of a great lot; having a great inheritance, very rich, wealthy, Od 14, 211.†
πολύκλητος, ον (καλέω), called from many places, called from far, epith. of allies, *4, 438. 10, 420.
πολύκλυστος, ον, poet. (κλύζω), prop. much washed; heaving, rolling great waves, πόντος, *Od. 4, 354. 6, 204.
πολύκμητος, ον (κάμνω), wrought with much toil and effort, prepared with toil, prop. spoken of iron which was hard for the ancients to work (V. beautifully wrought), 6, 48. 10, 379; and often; θάλαμος only Od. 4, 718.
πολύκνημος, ον, poet. (κνημός), having many wooded hills, abounding in woods, 2, 497.†
πολυκοιρανίη, ή (κοίρανος), a multiplicity of rulers, 2, 204.†
*πολύκροτος, ον (κρότος), very noisy, loud-resounding, h. 18, 37.
πολυκτήμων, ον (κτῆμαι), having great possessions, wealthy, 5, 613.†
Πολυκτορίδης, ου, ό, son of Polyctor = Pisander, Od. 18, 299.
Πολύκτωρ. ορος. ό wealthy, (from κτέαρ), 1) son of Pterelaus, one of the oldest heroes of Ithaca, Od. 17, 207. 2) father of Pisander, Od. 22, 243. (3) a fictitious Myrmidon, feigned by Hermès as his father, Il. 24, 397.)
πολυλήϊος, ον (λήϊον), rich in harvests, rich in fields, 5, 613.† h. Merc. 171.
πολύλλιστος, ον, Ep. for πολύλιστος, poet. (λίσσομαι), much prayed for, Od. 5, 445;† νηός, a temple in which the deity

Πολυμήλη. 350 Πολύς.

is often supplicated: *much frequented*, h. Ap. 347. h. Cer. 28.

Πολυμήλη, ή, daughter of Phylas, the beloved of Hermes and mother of Eudorus, afterwards wife of Echeclus, 16, 181.

πολύμηλος, ον (μήλον), rich in small cattle, *abounding in sheep*, *rich in flocks*. epith. of men and of regions, *2, 705; and h. 18, 2.

Πολύμηλος, ὁ, son of Argeas, a Lycian, 16, 417.

πολύμητις, ιος, ὁ, ή, poet. (μῆτις), *very prudent*, *very wise* (rich in invention, V.), epith. of Odysseus (Ulysses), 1, 311. Od. 21, 274; and Hephaestus, Il. 21, 355; of Hermes, h. Merc. 319.

πολυμηχανίη, ή, fertility in expedients, *invention, contrivance, prudence*, Od. 23, 321; † from

πολυμήχανος, ον (μηχανή), *rich in expedients, inventive, ingenious, very wise*, epith. of Odysseus (Ulysses), 2, 173. Od. 1, 205; and of Apollo, h. Merc. 319.

πολυμνήστη, ή, poet. (μνάομαι), *much wooed, much courted*, βασίλεια, *Od. 4, 770. 14, 64. The masc. is obsol.

πολύμυθος, ον (μῦθος), of many words; *loquacious, talkative*, 3, 214. Od. 2, 200.

Πολυνείκης, ους, ὁ, *Polynices*, son of Œdipus and brother of Eteocles. When according to his engagement the latter would not yield him the throne of Thebes, Polynices fled to Adrastus at Argos, and raised the expedition of the seven heroes against Thebes, in order to obtain the kingdom. The two brothers finally slew each other in a single combat, 4, 377.

Πολύνηος, ὁ (having many ships), son of Tecton, a noble Phæacian, Od. 8, 114.

Πολύξεινος, ὁ, Ion. and Ep. for Πολύξενος (very hospitable), 1) a prince of Eleusis in Attica, h. in Cer. 154. 2) son of Agasthenes and grandson of Augias, leader of the Epeans, 2, 623.

*πολυοινέω (οἶνος), fut. ήσω, *to be rich in wine*, h. Merc. 91.

πολυπαίπαλος, ον, poet. (παίπαλος) [rather from πάλλω], prop. very tortuous; only trop. *very crafty, very cunning*. Od. 15, 419; † see παιπαλόεις.

πολυπάμων, ον, gen. ονος (πᾶμα), *possessing much, wealthy, rich*, 4, 433.†

*πολυπείρων, ον, poet. (πείρας), having many borders, *from many regions, multifarious*, λαός, h. Cer. 297.

πολυπενθής, ές (πένθος), *very sad, mournful, grievous*, 9, 563. Od. 14, 386. 23, 15

Πολυπημονίδης, ου, ὁ, son of Polypæmon. Thus Odysseus (Ulysses) calls his grandfather, in allusion to his sufferings, Od. 24, 305.

*πολυπήμων, ον, gen. ονος, poet. (πῆμα) *very injurious*, h. Merc. 37. Cer. 230.

*πολυπίδακος, ον = πολυπίδαξ, h. Ven. 54.

πολυπίδαξ, ακος, ὁ, ή, poet. (πίδαξ),

abounding in fountains, epith. of Ida, 4, 47. 14, 157; but Ἀρκαδίη, h. 18, 20.

πολύπικρος, ον (πικρός), *very bitter, very painful*, Od. 16, 255.†

πολύπλαγκτος, ον, poet. (πλάζω), *far-wandering, restless*, ἄνθρωπος, Ἀνεμο... Od. 17, 511. 20, 195; as epith. of the wind, *raging around*, Il. 11, 308. Others explain it actively: *wide-scattering*.

Πολυποίτης, ου, ὁ (taking vengeance on many, as it were Πολυποινίτης from ποινή), son of Pirithous and Hippodameia, who went with forty ships from Argissa, Gyrton, etc. to the siege of Troy, 2, 740. 23, 836.

*πολυπότνια, ή, poet. (πότνια), *the highly venerable*, h. Cer. 211.

πολύπους, οδος, ὁ, Ερ. πουλύπους (πούς), that has many feet; then, the *sea-polypus*, in the Ep. form, Od. 5, 432.† h. Ap. 77. The ancients understood by it, the eight-armed polypus, *sepia octopodia*, Linn., which belongs to the molluscas, and is found in almost all seas. It is about eight feet long, and its arms are furnished upon the under-side with an apparatus with which it attaches itself firmly to the objects around. It is very ferocious, and attacks any animal which it can conquer.

πολύπτυχος, ον (πτύξ), prop. having many folds; metonym. *abounding in ravines, abounding in mountain glens*, epith. of Olympus and Ida, *8, 411. 21, 449.

*πολύπυργος, ον (πύργος), having many towers, *well-fortified*, h. Ap. 242; a false reading.

πολύπυρος, ον (πυρός). *abounding in wheat*, spoken of countries and islands, 11, 756. Od. 14, 335. h. Ap. 232.

πολύρρην, ηνος, ὁ, ή (ἈΡΗΝ), *abounding in sheep, rich in flocks*, ἄνδρες, *, 154. 296.

πολύρρηνος, ον = πολύρρην, Od. 11, 257;† see Thiersch, § 200. 10.

πολύς, πολλή, πολύ. besides the comm. forms, we have the following Ep.: nom. πουλύς, gen. πολέος, acc'us. πουλύν, plur. nom. πολέες and πολεῖς, gen. πολλάων. πολέων, πολλέων, dat. πολέσι, πολέσσι and πολέεσσι. accus. πολέας and πολεῖς; πολύς is used by H. as comm. gend. 14. 27. Od. 4, 709. H. has also nom. sin. πολλός, neut. πολλόν, compar. πλείων, ον, superl. πλεῖστος, η, ον, 1) Prop. spoken of a multitude: *many, numerous*, but also of power, size, strength: *great, strong, vehement, violent*. πολὺς ρεύστη. πολλῇ λαίλαψ, a great snow-storm, a violent tempest. π. ὕπνος, a deep sleep. Od. 15, 394. πολέος ἄξιος, worth much. Il. 23, 562. Od. 8, 405. 2) Spoken of place: *great, wide, broad, long, extended*. π. πεδίον, a wide plain. πολλὴ γαῖα, the wide earth. πολλός τις ἔκειτο παρησάμενος he lay extended wide. Il. 11, 156. 3) Spoken of time: *long*. πολὺν χρόνον, for a long time, 2, 343. πολλὸν ἔτι χρόνον, Od. 12, 407. As peculiarities of

*Πολυσημάντωρ. 351 Πολυωπός.

expression, observe 1) It stands often with the gen. to express the notion of a part. πολλοὶ Τρώων, many of the Trojans, Il. 18, 271. Also the neut. sing. πολλὸν σαρκός, βίης, Od. 19, 450. 21, 185. 2) Mly πολύς is treated as a complete predicate, and hence is connected with another adj. by καί, Ep. τὲ καί. πολλοὶ καὶ ἄλλοι, many others. πολλὰ καὶ ἐσθλά, many valuables, Od. 4, 96. πολέες τε καὶ ἐσθλοί, Il. 6, 152. 21, 586; or τέ, τέ, in which case πολύς takes the second place. παλαιά τε πολλά τε, Od. 2, 188. 2) Often it stands alone as subst. in H., very rarely with article. τὰ πολλά, the many, i. e. the most, Od. 2, 58. 17, 537; so also πολλά, Il. 9, 333; πολλοί also stands sometimes for οἱ πολλοί, the most, the multitude, 2, 483. 21, 524. 3) The neut. sing. and plur. as adv. much, greatly. very, strongly, long, often, πολλόν, θ, 506. 20, 173; πολλά, often μάλα πολλά, Il. 1, 35. Od. 2, 151. b) It enhances also the compar. and superl. πολὺ μᾶλλον, much more. πολλὸν ἀμείνων, much better. πολλὸν ἄριστος, by much the bravest.

*πολυσημάντωρ, ορος, ὁ, poet. who rules many, epith. of Hades, h. Cer. 31. 84. 377.

πολύσκαρθμος, ον, poet. (σκαίρω), leaping strongly, springing actively, epith. of the Amazon Myrina, 2, 814,† in reference to dancing; or, according to some, hastening away with steeds.

πολυσπερής, ές, poet (σπείρω), widesowed, widely-scattered, ἄνθρωποι, 2, 804. Od. 11, 365.

πολυστάφυλος, ον (σταφυλή), abounding in grapes, abounding in wine, *2, 507.† h. 25, 11.

πολύστονος, ον (στένω), much-groaning, unfortunate, Od. 19, 118. b) Act. causing many groans, epith. of Strife, of the arrow, Il. 1, 445. 11, 73.

πολύτλας, αντος, ὁ, poet. (τλῆναι), that has endured much, much-enduring, muchsuffering, epith. of Odysseus (Ulysses), only nom. 8, 97. Od. 5, 171; and often.

πολυτλήμων, ονος, ὁ, ἡ (τλήμων), muchenduring, much-sustaining, epith. of Odysseus (Ulysses), Od. 18, 319; θυμός, the much-enduring spirit, Il. 7, 152.

πολύτλητος, ον, poet. (τλῆναι), that has suffered much, much-enduring, γέροντες, Od. 11, 38.†

πολυτρήρων, ωνος, ὁ, ἡ (τρήρων), abounding in doves, epith. of regions, *2, 502. 582.

πολύτρητος, ον (τρητός), much-pierced, much-perforated, σπόγγος, *Od. 1, 111. 22, 439.

πολύτροπος, ον (τρέπω), that has endured much, far-travelled, epith. of Odysseus (Ulysses), Od. 1, 1. 10, 230. Thus Voss, Myth. Br. p. 102, and Nitzsch ad .oc., as also the epexegesis shows; on the contrary, Damm and Wolf: very versatile, crafty, and so also h. Merc. 13, 439.

*πολύυμνος, ον, poet. (ὑμνέω), muchsung, highly celebrated, h. 25, 7.

πολυφάρμακος, ον (φάρμακον), acquainted with many remedies or magic drugs, ἰητροί, 16, 28; Κίρκη, Od. 10, 276.

Πολυφείδης, ους, ὁ, son of Mantius, grandson of Melampus, Od. 15, 249.

πολύφημος, ον (φήμη), many-toned, much-speaking; ἀοιδός, abounding in songs, Od. 22, 376; βάτραχος, the muchcroaking frog, Batr. 12; ἀγορή, the many-voiced, noisy market-place, Od. 2, 150.

Πολύφημος, ὁ, 1) son of Poseidōn and of the nymph Thoōsa, one of the Cyclōpes in Trinacria, Od. 1, 70. After he had devoured six of the companions of Odysseus (Ulysses), the latter avenged himself by making him drunk and then putting out his eye with a glowing stake, Od. 9, 371, seq. cf. Κύκλωψ. 2) son of Elatus, brother of Cæneus, a Lapithe of Larissa, who took part in the Argonautic expedition. Having been left in Mysia, he founded the city Cios, Il. 1, 264.

πολύφλοισβος, ον, poet. (φλοῖσβος), much-roaring, loud-resounding, epith. of the sea, 1, 34; and Od. 13, 85.

Πολυφήτης, ου, ὁ, a Mysian of Ascania, 13, 791; it should prob. be read Περιφήτης, according to Strab. XIV. p. 511.

Πολυφόντης, ου, ὁ, son of Autophŏnus, who was slain by Tydeus before Thebes in an ambush, 4, 395.

πολύφορβος, ον, poet. (φορβή), muchnourishing, abounding in nourishment, epith. of the earth, 14, 200. 301; also πολυφόρβη, *9, 365.

πολύφρων, ονος, ὁ, ἡ, poet. (φρήν), very intelligent, very wise, very crafty, epith. of Odysseus (Ulysses), Od. 14, 424; and of Hēphæstus, Il. 21, 367. Od. 8, 297.

*πολύφωνος, ον (φωνή), many-voiced, loud-croaking, Batr. 216.

πολύχαλκος, ον, poet. (χαλκός), abounding in brass or copper, spoken of persons and places, having many copper utensils, 10, 315. 18, 289. Od. 15, 424. 2) made of much brass, adorned with much brass, brazen, epith. of heaven, 5, 504. Od. 3, 2. According to Voss, Myth. Br. 1, 27, in the literal sense; on the other hand, Völcker, Hom. Geogr. p. 5, metaph. imperishable, enduring.

*πολυχρόνιος, ον (χρόνος), long-enduring, lasting, h. Merc 123.

πολύχρυσος, ον (χρυσός), abounding in gold, rich in gold, epith. of persons and places, 7, 180. 10, 315. Od. 3. 305; adorned with gold, epith. of Aphroditē, h. Merc. 1.

*πολυώνυμος, ον (ὄνομα), 1) having many names, epith. of Hades. h. Cer. 18, 32. 2) having a great name, much-renowned, h. Ap. 82.

πολυωπός, όν (ὀπή), having many holes, having meshes, δίκτυον, Od. 22, 386.†

Πομπεύς. 352 Πόρος.

πομπεύς, ήος, ὁ (πέμπω), a companion, a conductor upon a journey, Od. 3, 325. 376: metaph. spoken of a ship: πομπῆες νηῶν, the companions of ships, *Od. 4, 362.

πομπεύω (πομπεύς), to accompany, to conduct, Od. 13. 422.†

πομπή, ἡ (πέμπω), 1) the act of accompanying, escorting, with the notion of protection, spoken of men and gods, 6, 171. Od. 5, 32. 2) dismissing, sending home, Od. 7, 151. 191. 8, 30. πομπήσιν ὑπ' Εὐρυσθῆος, sent by Eurystheus, Il. 14, 5.

πομπός, ὁ, a companion, a conductor, 13, 416. 16, 671; also ἡ πομπός, Od. 4, 826.

πονέομαι (πόνος), fut. πονήσομαι, aor. Ep. πονησάμην, pluperf. πεπόνητο (the act. πονέω not found in H.) 1) Intrans. to have labour and pains, to work, to weary oneself, to be busy, to exert oneself, often absol. 2, 409; esply spoken of battle, 4, 374. 13, 288; περί τι, about any thing, 24, 444; κατά τι, in any thing, 15. 447; κατά δῶμα, Od. 22, 377; often κατά ὑσμίνην, to exert oneself in the battle, Il. 5. 84; with dat. instrum. τοῖς ἐπονεῖτο, 13, 413; with which he worked, referring to the tools; in like manner Od. 16, 13. b) With partcp. ὄφελεν πονέεσθαι λισσόμενος, to weary oneself with praying, Il. 10, 117. 2) Trans. with accus. to produce by labour and pains, carefully to prepare any thing, to pursue diligently. πολλά, 9, 348. 18, 380; ἔργα. Od. 9, 250. 11, 9.

πόνος, ὁ (πένομαι), work, esply (like labour), hard work, pains, exertion. πόνος ἐμεῖο κυνός, the labour about my shameless self, 6, 355: esply the labour of war, battle, 5, 607. 6, 77; and often connected with νεῖκος, 12, 348; δῆρις, 17, 158; in the plur. πόνοι, in oppos. to ἀγοραί, Od. 4, 818; hence 2) fatigue, pain, distress, suffering, Il. 2. 421; connected with οἰζύς, 13, 2: with κήδεα, 21, 525; ἀνίη, Od. 7. 192; ἦ μὴν καί πόνος ἐστίν ἀνιηθέντα νέεσθαι, Il. 2, 291, Indeed, it is also hard (a pitiable case) to be obliged to endure suffering so long, and then to go home. viz. re infecta. Thus correctly Wolf. Aliter: nimirum laboribus fungimur, ut molesie ferentis redire velimus. thus Lehrs de Aristarch. S'nd. [p. 88; cf. also ἀνιάω]. (It does not signify pain either in Il. 13, 227, or 21, 525; but prob. in Batr. 46.)

Ποντεύς, έως, ὁ, a Phæacian, Od. 8, 113.

*πόντιος, ον (πόντος), from or in the sea, epith. of Poseidōn, the ruler of the sea, I- 21, 3.

ποντόθεν, adv. (πόντος), from the sea, 14, 395.†

ποντόνδε, adv. (πόντος), into the sea, *Od. 9, 495.

Ποντόνοος, ὁ (acquainted with the sea), a herald of the Phæaces, Od. 8, 65.

ποντοπορεύω and ποντοπορέω (ποντοπόρος, to navigate the sea, to sail upon the sea, to travel by sea, Od 5, 277. 278. 7, 267. The form ποντοπορέω only partcp. pres. *Od. 11, 11.

ποντοπόρος, ον (πείρω), sailing over the sea, sea-traversing, sea-navigating, epith. of ships, 1, 439. 3, 46. Od. 12, 269; ναύται, Ep. 8, 1.

πόντος, ὁ, Ep. gen. ποντόφιν, Od. 24, 83; the sea; esply the open sea. θάλασσα πόντου, the waters of the sea, Il. 2, 145. πόντος ἁλός, the sea of brine, the briny deep, 21, 59.

ποντόφιν, see πόντος.

*ποντοτίνακτος, ον (τινάσσω), shaken by the sea, Ep. 4, 6, for the false reading ποτινιάνακτος, according to Pierson.

πόποι, interj. akin to πάπαι, an exclamation of astonishment, displeasure, and grief, always at something unexpected, and mly unpleasant, except. 2, 272, where it is an expression of joyful surprise; always also ὦ πόποι. strange. impossible, awful, horrible; ἢ δή, ἢ μάλα, ἢ ῥα often follow, 2, 337. Od. l. 3, 4, 169. h. Merc. 309. According to Ap. Lex. and the Schol. it means O gods! as the Dryopes called their gods πόποι; hence we find ὦ πόποι, h. Merc. 309, it being taken as a vocat., cf. Müll. Geschich. Hell. St. II. p. 41. Spitzner ad Il. 15, 184.

πόρδαλις, ιος, ὁ, ἡ, Ep. for πάρδαλις, the panther, 13, 103. 21, 573. Od. 4, 457. ed. Wolf, where now Spitzner reads πάρδαλις, cf. πάρδαλις. According to the Gramm. πάρδαλις is fem. but falsely; for Il. 21, 573, πόρδαλις is also fem. The Greeks understood by this name panthers, leopards, etc. Cf. Bothe ad Il. 13, 103.

πορεύω (πόρος), to bring; mid. to go, to procced, Batr. 174.

Πορθεύς, ῆος, ὁ (the destroyer) (Παρθάων, Apd. 1, 7. 7), son of Agenor and Epicaste, king of Calydon, father of Œneus, Agrius, etc. 14, 115.

πορθέω (πέρθω), fut. ήσω. to destroy, to desolate, to pillage, πόλιας, τείχεα, h 30. Od. 14, 264; to rob, to plunder, τρίποδας, h. Merc. 180.

πορθμεύς, ῆος, ὁ (πορθμεύω), one who conveys travellers over water, a ferryman, Od. 20, 187.†

πορθμός, ὁ (πόρος), a place of passage, a ferry; esply a strait, a sound, *Od. 4, 671. 15, 29.

*πορίζω (πόρος), prop. to bring into the passage; hence, to bring to pass, to procure, τινί τι, Ep. 14, 10.

πόρις, ιος, ἡ, poet. for πόρτις, Od. 14, 410;† see πόρτις.

πόρπης, ου, ὁ, the ring about the shaft of the spear, for holding fast the head. *6, 320. 8, 495.

πόρος, ὁ (πείρω), prop. a passage, esply through shallow water; the ford of a river, Ἀλφειοῖο, 2, 592. 14, 433. b) Spoken of the sea in distinction from

Πόρπη. 953 Ποτάομαι.

ὁδός : πόροι ἁλός, the paths of the sea, Od. 12, 259.

πόρπη, ἡ (πείρω), the ring of a buckle, upon which the tongue (περόνη) lies, hence a buckle, a brooch, a clasp, 18, 401.† h. Ven. 154.

*πορσαίνω =πορσύνω, fut. πορσανέουσα. Ep. for πορσανοῦσα, ed. Spitzner, according to Cod. Ven. Il. 3, 411. h. Cer. 156.

πορσύνω (ΠΟΡΩ), poet. fut. πορσυνέω, to bring in pass. to further, to prepare, only λέχος, εὐνήν τινι, to prepare a bed, a couch for any one, always spoken of the wife who herself shares the couch with the husband, 3, 411 (cf. Nitzsch ad Od 1. c.), Od. 3, 403.

πόρταξ, ακος, ἡ =πόρτις, a calf, a heifer, 17, 4.†

πόρτις, ιος, ἡ, another form πόρις, Od. 10, 410; a calf, a heifer, Il. 5, 162.† h. Cer. 174.

*πορτιτρόφος, ον, nourishing calves or young cattle, h. Ap. 21.

πορφύρεος, η, ον (πορφύρα), purple, purple-coloured, a) coloured with purple, dark red in different degrees; spoken of garments and carpets, φᾶρος, 8, 221. Od. 4, 115; αἷμα, Il. 17, 361. 2) Metaph. spoken of the sea: πόρφ. κῦμα, the purple wave, spoken of the sea disturbed by the wind or the stroke of the oar, 1, 482. Od. 2, 428. πόρφ. ἅλς, Il. 16, 391 ; νεφέλη, a dark cloud, 17, 351. πόρφ. θάνατος, dark death, like μέλας, 5, 85. 16, 334 (according to Passow also blood-red, bloody).

πορφύρω, poet. (πορφύρα), only pres. to become purple, to be purpied or darkened [Cp.]. spoken of the disturbed sea, which assumes a dark colour, 14, 16. b) Metaph. spoken of the heart: to swell, to be restless. πολλά οἱ κραδίη πόρφυρε, his heart was greatly agitated, spoken of the unquiet spirit of one who cannot come to a resolution, 21, 551. Od. 4, 427.

ΠΟΡΩ (πόρος), obsol. pres. poet. from which aor. ἔπορον, Ep. πόρον, partcp. πορών. perf. pass. πέπρωται, partcp. πεπρωμένος, prop. to bring to pass. hence to procure, to give, to grant, to bestow, τινί τι, for the most part spoken of things and states: δῶρα, φάρμακα, πένθος: of persons: τινὶ υἱόν, 16, 185. ἀνδρὶ παράκοιτιν, to give a wife to a man, 24, 60. b) For the accus. constr. with infin. πόρε καὶ σὺ Διὸς κούρησιν ἕπεσθαι τιμήν, grant also thou, that to the daughter of Zeus honour be yielded, 9. 513. 2) The perf. pass. is impers. ; prop. it is divided or distributed to ; then it is fated, allotted by destiny, τινί, to any one, with accus. and infin. 18. 329. The partcp. πεπρωμένος, fated, destined, and with dat. of the thing, ὀμῇ αἴσῃ, to the same fate, 15, 209. 16, 441.

πόσε, adv. (πός), whither? 16, 422. Od. 6, 199.

Ποσειδάων, ωνος, ὁ, voc. Ποσείδαον, Ep. for Ποσειδῶν (according to Herm.

from πόσις and εἴδεσθαι, quod potabilis videtur), Poseidōn, son of Kronus (Saturn) and Rhea, brother of Zeus, of Hades, etc., husband of Amphitrite, 15, 187. He is ruler of the sea, esply of the Mediterranean sea, which fell to him by lot, 14, 156. 15, 189. Although he reigns independently in his vast dominion, yet he recognizes the precedence of Zeus as the elder, 8, 210. 13, 355; and even unharnesses his steeds, 8, 440. He has his dwelling in the depths of the sea near Ægæ (see Αἰγαί), 13, 21. Od. 5, 381. Here stand his steeds ; but he also comes to the assemblies of the gods in Olympus, Il. 8, 440. 15, 161. As sovereign of the sea he sends storms, Od. 5, 291 ; he gives also favorable winds and a prosperous voyage, Il. 9, 362. Od. 4, 500. He shakes the earth (ἐνοσίχθων, ἐννοσίγαιος), but he also holds it firm by his element (γαιήοχος). As the creator of the horse, he is the inventor and overseer of horses-races, Il. 23, 307. 584 ; and as such he is the god of the house and country of the horseman Nestor, see Nitzsch ad Od. 3, 7. In the Iliad he appears as the enemy of the Trojans, Æneas excepted, Il. 21, 442, seq., since Laomedon refused him the promised reward, when he and Apollo built the walls of Troy (see Λαομέδων). In the Od. he persecutes Odysseus (Ulysses) because he had blinded his son Polyphēmus, Od. 1, 20. 5, 286, seq. The symbol of his power is the trident; with this he excites and subdues the sea, Il. 12, 27. Od. 4, 506. He was worshipt at Onchēstus, Helicæ (see Ἑλικώνιος). Black bulls were sacrificed to him, Od. 3, 6. Il. 20, 404; also boars and rams, Od. 11, 130. Of his numerous progeny Homer mentions Eurytus and Cteatus, Nausithòus, Polyphēmus. Peleus, and Neleus.

Ποσιδήϊον, τό, a temple of Poseidōn, Od. 6, 266 †

Ποσιδήϊος. η, ον, Ion. for Ποσείδειος, sacred to Poseidōn, ἄλσος, 2, 506.†

πόσις, ιος, ὁ, poet. dat. πόσει and πόσει, 5, 71 ; a husband, Il. and Od.

πόσις, ιος, ἡ (πίνω), drink, often connected with ἐδητύς, 1, 469 ; and βρῶσις, 19, 210. Od. 1, 191.

ποσσήμαρ, adv. Ep. for ποσήμαρ (ἦμαρ), in how many days? 24, 657.†

πόστος, η, ον (πόσος), how much? Od. 24, 288.†

ποταμόνδε, adv. into the river, 21, 13. Od. 10, 150.

ποταμός, ὁ, a river, a stream, spoken also of Oceanus, 14, 245. 2) a river-god, 5, 544. 20, 7. 73. To the river deities were sacrificed bulls and horses, 21, 131. (From πίνω, πόω, prop. potable water.)

ποτάομαι, Ep. form of πέτομαι, to fly, pres. ποτῶνται, 2, 462. h. Merc. 558; perf. πεπότηαται, Ion. for πεπότηνται, 2 29 ; sing. πεπότηται, Od 11, 221.

πότε, adv. interrog. *when? at what time?* 19, 227. Od. 4, 642.

ποτέ, enclit. adv. *once, on a certain time,* often in connexion with other words, spoken both of past and future: ἤδη ποτέ, already; *ere now,* 1, 260; ἤ ποτε, 1, 240; [ὥς ποτέ,] 4, 182.

ποτέομαι, Ion. for ποτάομαι, *to fly,* Od. 24, 7.†

πότερος, η, ον, *which of the two?* 5, 85.†

ποτή, ἡ (πέτομαι), *the act of flying, flight.* Od. 5, 337.†

ποτής, ῆτος, ἡ (πότος), *the act of drinking, drink,* in connexion with ἐδητύς, βρωτύς, 11, 780. Od. 18, 408.

ποτητός, ή, όν (ποτάομαι), Ep. *flying, winged;* τὰ ποτητά, fowls, Od. 12, 62.†

ποτί, Ep. and Dor. for πρός, often alone and in composition.

ποτιβάλλω, Dor. for προσβάλλω.
ποτιδέγμενος, see προσδέχομαι.
ποτιδέρκομαι, Ep. for προσδέρκομαι.
ποτιδόρπιος, ον, Ep. for προσδόρπιος.
ποτικέκλιται, see προσκλίνω.
ποτινίσσομαι, Ep. for προσνίσσομαι.
ποτιπεπτηυῖα, see προσπίπτω.
ποτιπτύσσομαι, for προσπτύσσομαι.
ποτιτέρπω, Ep. for προστέρπω.
ποτιφωνήεις, εσσα, εν, Ep. for προσφωνήεις.

πότμος, ὁ, poet. (πίπτω), prop. *that which falls to any one, lot, destiny,* in H. always in a bad sense: *fate, misery, death,* ἀεικέα πότμον ἐφιέναι τινί, 4, 396. πότμον ἀναπλῆσαι, 11, 263. πότμον ἐπισπεῖν, to overtake one's fate, i. e. to die, 6, 412; hence often in connexion with θάνατος, 2. 359; and θανεῖν καὶ πότμον ἐπισπεῖν, Od. 4, 196.

πότνια, ἡ, and πότνα, h. Cer. 118; only nom. voc. and accus. πότνιαν, h. Cer. 203; poet. a female title of honour, 1) Adj. *honoured, venerable,* spoken of goddesses and of mortal women, πότνια Ἥρῃ, 1, 551; μήτηρ, 6, 264. 2) As subst. *sovereign, mistress,* θηρῶν, 21, 470. (Nitzsch would prefer πότνα ad Od. 5, 215; cf. on the word, Buttm., Ausf. Gram. I. p. 161.)

[ποτνιάνακτος, a false reading for ποτνιοτίνακτος, Ep. 4, 6; *regali nomine clara,* Barnes.]

ποτόν, τό (πίνω), *the act of drinking, drink,* 1, 470. 11, 630. Od. 9, 354.

ποῦ, adv. interrog. (πός), 1) *where?* 5, 171. Od. 1, 407. 2) *whither?* ποῦ δέ σοι ἀπειλαὶ οἴχονται; where are thy threats? what is become of thy threats? 11, 13, 219.

του, enclitic. adv. 1) *any where, some where,* 16, 514. Od. 1, 297. 2) *any how, perhaps, perchance,* very often in connexion with other particles, οὕτω που, 11. 2, 116; ἤ που. μέν που, νύ που, etc.

πουλυβότειρα, ἡ, Ep. for πολυβότειρα, which see.
Πουλυδάμας, Ep. for Πολυδάμας.
πουλύπους, Ep. for πολύπους.
πουλύς, πουλύ, Ep. for πολύς, πολύ,
q v.

πούς, ποδός, ὁ, r at. plur. ποσί, Ep. ποσσί and πόδεσσι, dual. ποδοῖν for τοῖν, 1) *a foot,* spoken of men and brutes, also of birds: the claws, the talons, Od. 15, 526. a) *a step,* conn. running, race, Il. 9, 523 (cf. ἐλέγχω ποσὶν ἐρίζειν, with feet, i. e. to contest in the race, 13, 328; ποσὶ νικᾶν, 20, 410. Od. 13, 201. b) Proverb. phrases: οἱ πόδας ἐκ κεφαλῆς, from the head to the feet, Il. 18, 353; πρόσθεν or προσφερῆς ποδῶν, before the feet, spoken of any thing lying near, 20, 324. 21, 601; vad ποσί. Od. 8, 376; cf. Il. 15, 280. 2) Metaph. *a foot;* a) the lower part of a mountain, 2, 824. 20, 59. b) *the extremity of a sail,* or *the rope* at the lower extremity of a sail, with which the sails were set, cf. Köpke, Kriegsw. d. Gr. p. 171. Od. 5, 260. 10, 32.

Πράκτιος, ὁ, a river in Troas, which falls into the Hellespont between Abydos and Lampsacus, now *Bargas,* 2, 835.

Πράμνειος οἶνος, ὁ, *Pramnian wine,* 11, 639. Od. 10, 235. According to Eustath. named from the mountain *Pramne* on the island Icaria (now *Nikaria*); according to other critics it grew near Smyrna or Ephesus, Plin. Hist. N. 14, 5, 6. It was used in the preparation of a strengthening drink, and probably the ancients understood by it, all strong and sour wines without reference to the origin. Some would therefore derive the word from παραμένειν (wine which keeps good), Ælian, V. h. 12, 31.

πραπίδες, αἱ, poet. 1) Prop. = φρένες the diaphragm, 11, 579. 17, 349. 2) Metaph. *the understanding, thought, mind,* because the diaphragm was regarded as the seat of thought, mly ἰδυίῃσι πραπίδεσσιν, 1, 608. Od. 7, 92.

πρασία, ἡ, *a garden-bed,* only plur. Od. 7, 127. 24, 247.

*Πρασσαῖος, ὁ, Ep. Πρασαῖος (πράσσω). *Garlic-green,* name of a frog, Batr 225.

*πράσον, τό, *garlic,* a sea-plant similar to garlic, Batr. 56.

*Πρασσοφάγος, ὁ, Ep. for Πρασοφάγος (φαγεῖν), *Garlic-eater,* name of a frog, Batr. 235.

*πράσσω, Att. for πρήσσω, Batr. 186 *

*πρέμνον, τό (akin to πρυμνός), *a trunk, a block,* h. Merc. 238.

πρέπω (akin to πείρω) prop. to shine, to gleam out; mly *to be prominent, to distinguished,* διὰ πάντων, 12, 104; tmesis, μετὰ πρέπει ἀγρομένοισιν, Od. 8, 172; τινί, in any thing, Od. 18, 2. h. Cer. 214.

*πρέσβειρα, ἡ, poet. = πρέσβα, h. 2. 32.

πρέσβα, ἡ, Ep. fem. of πρέσβυς, *an aged woman, a venerable female, veneranda,* an epith. of honour in 5, 721. 8, 383; in the Od. also of mortals, Od. 3, 452.

πρεσβήϊον, τό (πρέσβυς), *a present which the eldest received, a gift of honour,* 8, 289.†

*πρεσβηίς, ίδος, ή, poet. fem.=πρέσβα; τιμή, worthy honour, h. 29, 3.
*πρέσβις, ή, poet.=πρεσβεία, age, h. Merc. 4 1.
πρέσβιστος, η, ον. see πρέσβυς.
πρεσβυγενής, ές (γένος), elder in years, fr. si-born, 11, 249.†
πρέσβυς, ό, poet. for πρεσβύτης, not occurring in Hom., but the fem. Ep. πρέσβα, πρέσβειρα, πρεσβηίς, compar. πρεσβύτερος, η, ον, 11, 787; superl. πρεσβύτατος, η, ον and πρέσβιστος, h. 30, 2; old, venerable, πρεσβύτατος γενεῇ, eldest in birth, 6, 24. Od. 13, 142.
πρήθω, poet. form of πίμπρημι, which is not found in Hom.; aor. 1 ἔπρησα, Ep. πρῆσα, 1) to burn, to inflame, τί, with gen. mater. (cf. Kühner, § 455. Rem.); θύρετρα πυρός, with fire. 2, 415; cf. ἐνιπρήθω. 2) to blow upon, to swell, spoken of wind, τί; μέσον ἱστίον, Od. 2, 427. b) to cast out, to breathe out, to blow out, αἷμα ἀνὰ στόμα, Il. 16, 350. (According to Buttm., Lex. in voc., akin to πρίω and πέρθω; it is uncertain whether its prop. signif. is to kindle, to inflame, or to spout out, to emit; according to Rost it is to rattle, to crack.)
πρηκτήρ, ῆρος, ὁ (πρήσσω), Ion. for πρακτήρ, 1) a performer, a doer, an author, ἔργων, 9, 443. 2) Esply a tradesman, Od. 8, 162.
πρηνής, ές, Ion. for πρανής (akin to πρό), bent forwards, headlong, κατά (adv.) πρηνὲς βάλλειν τι, to cast any thing down, 2, 414; πρηνὴς ἤριπε, he fell forwards. 5, 58. ἔπεσε, ἐλιάσθη, also πρηνὴς ἐν κονίῃσι, 2, 418.
πρῆξις, ιος, ἡ (πράσσω), 1) doing, an action, business, undertaking, κατὰ πρῆξιν, on business, in opposition to μαψιδίως, Od. 3, 72. esply traffic, h. Ap. 398. 2) the produce of it, gain, advantage, οὔτις πρῆξις πέλεται γόοιο, there is no advantage from lamentation (V. 'we effect nothing'), Il. 24, 524; or οὔτις πρ. ἐγίγνετο μυρομένοισιν, there was no help to them complaining, Od. 10, 202.
πρήσσω, Ion. for πράσσω, fut. πρήξω, aor. ἔπρηξα, prop. to do, to act; hence, 1) to effect, to accomplish, to attain, with accus. Od. 16, 88; ἔργον, Od. 19, 324; absol. Il. 18, 357; esply partcp. πρήξας, Od. 3, 60; often with οὔτι, Il. 1, 562. 11, 552. Od. 2, 191. 2) Esply spoken of a way: to finish, to pass over, with accus. κέλευθον, Il. 14, 282. Od. 13, 83; ἅλα, to sail over the sea, Od. 9, 491; with gen. ὁδοῖο, Il. 24, 264. Od. 3, 476. 3) to collect, to gather, τινὰ τόκους, usury from any one, Batr. 186.
*πρηΰνω, Ion. for πραΰνω (πραΰς), to render mild, to calm, to appease, with accus. h. Merc. 417.
πρηΰς, ύ, Ion. for πραΰς, mild, gentle, h. 7, 10. cf. Gramm.
πρίασθαι, mid. defect. verb, of which only aor. 2 is in use, 3 sing. πρίατο, to buy, τί, any thing, κτεάτεσσιν, for treasures, *Od. 1, 430. 14, 115. 452.

Πριαμίδης, ου, ὁ, son of Priam (the first ι long by the arsis).
Πρίαμος, ὁ, son of Laomedon, king of Troy, husband of Hecuba (Hekabê). According to H. he had fifty sons, nineteen of them by Hecuba. Hector was the dearest of them all, 24, 493, seq. Of the time before the Trojan war, it is mentioned that he aided the Phrygians against the Amazons, 3, 184, seq. At the beginning of the siege of Troy he was already at an advanced age, and took no part in the contest, 24, 487. He appears only once on the battle field, to conclude the treaty concerning the duel of Paris and Menelaus, 3, 261. After Hector's death, he went, under the conduct of Hermês, into the tent of Achilles, and redeemed the corpse of his son, 24, 470, seq. According to later tradition he was slain by Neoptolemus, son of Achilles. (On the name Πρίαμος, cf. Apd. 2, 6, 4.)
πρίν, adv. and conjunct. I) Adv. of time: in independent sentences, before, ere, first, sooner, and, generally, earlier, at an earlier time; mly opposed to νῦν, 2, 112. 344; πολὺ πρίν, long before, Od. 2, 167. 2) Often with the article, τοπρίν or τὸ πρίν, ed. Spitzner, Il. 6, 125. 16, 373; but Od. τὸ πρίν, Od. 3, 265. 4, 32; formerly (olim). 3) As adv. it stands also with indicat. πρίν μιν καὶ γῆρας ἔπεισιν, first (i. e. sooner) shall old age come upon her, Il. 1, 29; cf. Thiersch, § 292. 2. Il. 18, 283; with optat. πρίν κεν ἀνιηθεὶς σὴν πατρίδα γαῖαν ἵκοιο, thou wouldst be wearied out and return to thy native land before [the tale was ended], Od. 3, 117. II) Conjunct. in relative clauses of time: before, ere; in this signif. πρίν—πρίν, πρίν—πρίν γε, πάρος—πρίν γε, etc., often stand in Hom. 1) With indicat. in the H. poems alone only in h. Ap. 357; but πρίν γ' ὅτε, as long as, until, Il. 9, 588. 12, 437. Od. 4, 180. 13, 322. h. Ap. 47. 2) With the future only in concuived actions, when the main clause is always denied. a) With subjunct. after a primary tense in the main clause, Il. 24, 551. Od. 10, 175; with πρίν γε, Il. 18, 135. Od. 13, 336; with πρίν γ' ὅτ' ἄν, Od. 2, 374. b) With optat. after an historical tense in the main clause, Il. 21. 580; after πρίν γ' ὅτε, 9, 488. 3) Most frequently with infin. aor. when the action of the subordinate clause appears as a temporal consequence of the main clause: οὐδ' ὅγε πρίν—Κῆρας ἀφέξει, πρίν γ' ἀπὸ πατρὶ δομέναι — κουρήν, 1, 98. 9, 387; and often. The infin. with accus. occurs when the dependent clause has a new subject, 6, 82. 22, 156. Od. 23, 138. Also πρίν γ' ἤ (cf. priusquam), Il. 5, 288. 22, 266. 4) In H. passages also occur where the infin. is exchanged with the optat, 17, 504, seq. 5) πρίν stands elliptically, Od 15, 394; πρίν ὥρη, subaud. ᾖ, before it is time, (ι is short, but is used as long Ep.)

Πριστός. 336 Προεῖπον.

πριστός, ή, όν (πρίω), prop. *sawn, cut*; ἐλέφας, polished ivory, *Od. 18, 196. 13, 564.

πρό, I) Prep. with gen.; ground signif. *before*. 1) Spoken of place: *before*, pro; in oppos to μετά and ἐν, πρὸ ἄστεος, before t e city; πρὸ πυλάων, also with the notion of withdrawing: πρὸ ὁδοῦ ἐγένοντο, they were forward upon the way, further on. 4, 382. 2) Spoken of time: *before*, πρὸ γάμοιο, Od. 15, 524; and separated from the case: καί τε πρὸ ὃ τοῦ ἐνόησεν, i. e. ὁ ἕτερος πρὸ τοῦ ἑτέρου, one perceived it before the other, Il. 10, 224. Thus Voss, correctly with the Schol. shorter and Heyne. (Köppen, 'the one thinks for the other.') 3) In causative relations: *a)* To indicate protection, primarily, still bordering on the notion of place: *for, in defence of* (pro). μάχεσθαι πρό τινος, to fight for any one, 4, 156. 8, 57. ἀεθλεύειν πρὸ ἄνακτος, 24, 734; ὁλέσθαι πρὸ πόληος, *pro patria mori*, 22, 110. *b)* In assigning the cause: *for*; πρὸ φόβοιο, for fear, 17, 667. But since φόβος in Hom. is said always to signify flight, others explain it *before flight*. Cf. Lehrs de Aristarch. p. 89. Sometimes πρό is separated from its case by other words, 23, 115. II) Adv. 1) Of place: *before, forwards, in front*, 1, 195. 13, 799. 17, 355; in connexion with adv. πρὸ Ἰλιόθι, before Troy, 8, 561; *forth, forward*; πρὸ φόωσδε, forth to the light, 16, 188. h. 9, 119. *b)* Spoken of time: *before, formerly*, 1, 70. Od. 1, 37; ἠῶθι πρό, before morning, Od. 5, 469. *c)* Often with other prep.: ἀπὸπρό, διαπρό, περιπρό, etc. III) In composition it has the significations of place: *before, forwards, onward, forth*; of time: *before, formerly*; and of preference: *sooner, rather*.

προαλής, ές (ἅλλομαι), leaping forward, i. e. *descending, prone, steep*, χῶρος, 21, 262.†

προβαίνω (βαίνω), only perf. προβέβηκα, pluperf. προβεβήκει, also Ep. partcp. pres προβιβάς and προβιβῶν. 1) Intrans. *to stride furward, to go forward, to step along*, ποσί, 13, 18; προβέβηκε ἄστρα, the stars have already gone far forward, i. e. are near to setting, 10, 252. 2) *to go before*, τινός τιν, any one in any thing, i. e. to excel, 6, 25. 16, 54.

προβάλλω (βάλλω), only aor. 2 without augm. πρόβαλον, iterat. προβάλεσκε. Od. 5, 331; aor. 2 mid. προβαλοίμην, *to cast before*, τινί τι or τινα; Νότος Βορέῃ προβάλεσκε φέρεσθαι, sc. αὐτόν, Notus cast him (Ulysses) to Boreas to drive him, Od. 5, 331; metaph ἔριδα, to begin a strife, Il. 11, 529. Mid. *to cast before oneself, to sprinkle* or *strew*, with accus. σύλοχύτας, 1, 458. Od. 3, 447; θεμέλια, to lay the foundation, Il. 23, 255. *b)* to cast oneself beyond any one, i. e. *to excel* any one, τινός νοήματι, 19, 218.

πρόβασις, ιος, ἡ, Ep. prop. the act of stepping forwards; hence, *moveable possessions*, in distinction from κειμήλια, esply *herds*, Od. 2, 75.†

πρόβατον, τό (προβαίνω), that which goes forward, mly in the ulur, *cattle, herds of cattle*, *14, 124. 23, 500 (later. *a sheep*).

προβέβουλα, defect. perf. from an obsol. verb, προβούλομαι (βούλομαι), Ep. *to choose rather, to prefer*, τινά τινος, one to another, 1, 113.†

προβιβάς, Ep. as partcp. pres. *striding forward*, of προβαίνω, from a form προβίβημι, 13, 18. Od. 17, 27.

προβιβῶν, ῶντος, Ep. partcp. pres. of προβαίνω, from a form προβιβάω, 13, 807. 16, 609. Od. 15, 555.

προβλής, ῆτος, ὁ, ἡ (προβάλλω). prop. *cast forth; mly prominent, springing upwards*. σκόπελος, πέτρη, 11. στῆλαι, projecting pillars upon the walls, *buttress*, prop. 12, 259; ἀκταί, Od. 5, 405. 13, 97.

προβλώσκω (βλώσκω), aor. προέμολον. Ep. without augm. *to go* or *come forth, to go out*, 18, 382. 21, 37; Θύραζε, Od. 19, 25. 21, 239. 385.

προβοάω (βοάω), *to cry out before* others, i. e. *to cry aloud*, 12, 277†.

πρόβολος, ον (προβάλλω), *prominent, projecting*, subst. ὁ, *a projecting rock*, Od. 12. 251.†

προβούλομαι, see προβέβουλα.

προγενέστερος, η, ον, compar. earlier born; *older, more aged*, and superl. προγενέστατος, η, ον, from an obsol. positive, προγενής, *the eldest*, compar. with γενεῇ, 9, 161†; superl. h. Cer. 110.

προγίγνομαι (γίγνομαι), only aor. 2 προγενόμην, without augm. prop. to happen before. 2) *to be before, to go before*, 18, 525.† ἐπί τι. h. 7, 7.

*προγιγνώσκω (γιγνώσκω), only inf. aor. 2 προγνῶναι, *to know before, to learn before*, τί, h. Cer. 258.

πρόγονος, ὁ (γίγνομαι), one born first *the elder*; πρόγονοι, the older sheep, Od. 9, 221.†

προδαῆναι (ΔΑΩ), Ep. partcp. aor. 2 pass. προδαείς, *to learn* or *know before*, Od. 3. 396†; see ΔΑΩ.

προδοκή, ἡ (προδέχομαι), a place where one lies in wait, *an ambush; a lurking place*, ἐν προδοκῇσιν [in ambush placed, Cp.], 4, 107.†

πρόδομος, ὁ (δόμος), *a vestibule*, sometimes the place before the door of the house, sometimes the passage from the house to the court, *a front entry, a porch*, 24, 673. Od. 4, 302. 14, 5.

προέργω, Ep. for προείργω (εἴργω), *to avert before, to repel*, τινά, and infin. 1, 569.†

προέηκα, see προίημι.

προεῖδον (εἶδον), partcp. προϊδών, mid. 3 plur. subj. προΐδωνται, Od. 13, 155; aor. 2 of προοράω, *to look forwards, to see at a distance, to espy at a distance*, τί, spoken only of place, Il. 17, 756. Od. 5, 393. Mid. = act.

[προεῖπον, in tmesis, Od. 1, 37; ὅ πρό may be adv.]

προέμεν, see προίημι.
προερέσσω (έρέσσω), aor. 1 προέρεσα, Ep. σσ, to row forwards, onwards, ές λιμένα, Od. 13, 279; trans. τὴν (νῆα) δ' εἰς ὅρμον προέρεσσαν ἐρετμοῖς, Il. 1, 435; a reading adopted by Spitzner for προρύσσαν, because προερύειν signifies 'to draw forward,' and hence cannot be spoken of oars. Also in Od. 9, 73; αὐτὰς —προερέσσαμεν ἠπειρόνδε.
προερύω, poet. (έρύω), aor. 1 προέρυσα, Ep. σσ, to draw forwards, onwards; spoken always of ships, a) From the shore into the sea, ἅλαδε, 1, 308. b) From the open sea to propel by rowing to the land, ἠπειρόνδε, Od. 9, 73. Il. 1, 435; but cf. προερέσσω.
πρόες, see προίημι.
προέχω, contr. προὔχω (ἔχω), always in the contr. form, except imperf. 3 sing. πρόεχε, Od. 12, 11. 2) Intrans. to be before, to come before, spoken of persons: προὔχων, the prominent man, Il. 23, 325. 453; δήμου, to be eminent among the people, h. Cer. 151; spoken of things: to project, to be prominent, Od. 12, 11. Mid. to have or hold before oneself, ταύροντ, Od. 3, 8 (where others read, προὔθεντο).
προήκης, ες (ἀκή), pointed before, Od. 12, 205.†
*προθαλής, ές, poet. (θάλλω), growing well, h. Cer. 241.
προθέλυμνος, ον, poet. (θέλυμνον), by the roots, utterly, entirely (Schol. πρόρριζος), προθελύμνους ἔλκετο χαίτας, he tore his hair out by the roots, 10, 15. προθέλυμνα χαμαὶ βάλε δένδρεα [" trees he cast on earth Uprooting them," Cp.], 9, 541; φράσσειν σάκος σάκεῖ, shield pressed on shield compactly, densely, in close array, 13, 130. They locked the shields so closely together that no space remained between. (Others take it in reference to τετραθέλυμνος, with close layers. The derivation from θέλυμνον = θεμέλιον, from the foundation, is most probable; the signif. close, one upon another (Schol. ἐπ' ἀλλήλοις), seems borrowed from the last passage; still Voss follows it, and Köppen ad Il. 13. 130.)
προθέουσι, 1, 291; see προτίθημι.
προθέω (θέω), Ion. iterat. imperf. προθέεσκε, to run before, 10, 362. 22, 459. Od. 11, 515.
Προθοήνωρ, ορος, ὁ, son of Areïlycus, leader of the Bœotians, 2, 495.
Πρόθοος, ὁ, son of Tenthrêdon, leader of the Magnetæ, 2, 756.
προθορών, see προθρώσκω.
Προθόων, ωνος, ὁ, a Trojan, slain by Teucer, 14, 515.
προθρώσκω (θρώσκω), partcp. aor. προθορών, to leap before, to spring before, *14, 363. 17, 522.
προθυμίη, ἡ (θυμός), readiness, good will, good courage, plur. 2, 588.† (Poet. with ι.)
*προθύραιος, ον (θύρα), before the door, τὰ προθύραια = πρόθυρα, h. Merc. 384.

πρόθυρον, τό (θύρα), mly plur. the doorway to the court, Il. and Od. 2) the place before the door, a porch, Od. 20, 355. 21, 299. 22, 474.
προϊάλλω (ιάλλω), poet. only imperf. to send forth, to send away, τινὰ ἀπ' οὐρανόθεν, 8, 365; ἐπὶ νῆας, 11, 3; ἀγρόνδε, Od. 5, 369.
προϊάπτω (ιάπτω), fut. προϊάψω, aor. προΐαψα (ῑ), prop. to thrust forth; then, to send away, to send, τινὰ Ἄϊδι, any one to Hades, 1, 3. 6, 487; 'Αϊδωνῆϊ, *5, 190.
προϊεῖν, see προίημι.
προΐημι (ἵημι), imperf. Ion. and Att. προίειν, aor. 1 προῆκα or προέηκα, 2 aor. 3 plur. πρόεσαν, imperat. πρόες, προέτω, infin. προέμεν, Ep. for προεῖναι, prop. to send forwards; hence, 1) Spoken of persons: to send forth, to send away, to let go, τινά, 1, 326; with infin. following, καλήμεναι, in order to call, 10, 125. cf. v. 388. 563. b) Of things: νῆας, 7, 468; of missiles: to let fly, to cast, to hurl, ὀϊστούς, βέλος, ἔγχος, 8, 297. 17, 516; of a river: ὕδωρ ἐς Πηνειόν, it sends out, i. e. pours its water into the Peneus, 2, 752. 2) to let go, to let fall, προβάλλον ἐκ χειρῶν, Od. 5, 316; ἔπος, to let a word drop, Od. 14, 466. πόδα προέηκε φέρεσθαι, Od. 19, 468; φήμην, Od. 20, 105. 3) to send to, τινά or τί τινι, Il. 1, 127; ἀγγελίας, to send an embassy, Od. 2, 92; and generally, to give, to bestow, like διδόναι: κῦδός τινι, Il. 16, 241. ἐμοὶ πνοιὴν Ζεφύρου προέηκεν ἀῆναι, he let the breath of the Zephyr blow upon me, Od. 10, 25; οὖρον, Od. 3, 183. [But πρό cannot signify to; it rather means forth, and these citations may better be referred to no. 2.]
προΐκτης, ου, ὁ (προίξ). a beggar, a mendicant, Od. 17, 449. ἀνὴρ προΐκτης, *Od. 17, 347. 352.
προΐξ, contr. προίξ, gen. προικός, a gift, a present. γενέσθαι προικός, to enjoy his present [to taste his menditcated mess, Cp.], Od. 17, 413; then προικός, as adv. gratuitously, i. e. without a (present in) return, χαρίζεσθαι, Od. 13, 15 (cf. Thiersch, § 198. 6). Another Schol. connects προικός as a subst. with χαρίζεσθαι; hence Voss and Passow: 'to bestow generous gifts.' Cf. Od. 1, 140.
προΐστημι (ἵστημι), aor. 1 partcp. προστήσας, trans. to place before, to put before; τινὰ μάχεσθαι, any one to fight, 4, 156.†
Προῖτος, ὁ, son of Abas, king of Tiryns, husband of Antia. Being expelled by his brother Acrisius, he fled to king Iobâtes in Lycia. He gave him his daughter Antia, and restored him to his kingdom, 6, 157, seq.
προκαθίζω (ἵζω), to sit down before, to settle, spoken of cranes, 2, 463.†
προκαλέω (καλέω), only mid. aor. 1, Ep. προκαλεσσάμην, subj. προκαλέσσεται with shortened vowel, 7, 39, 1) to call forth to oneself, to challenge, τινά, absol. Od. 8, 142; and χάρμῃ, to battle,

Προκαλίζομαι. 358 Πρός.

Il. 7, 218. 285; or μαχέσασθαι, 4, 432. 2) Metaph. *to solicit, to court,* ὕπνον, h. Merc. 241.

προκαλίζομαι, Ep. form, only mid. pres. and imperf. *to challenge, to call forth* to battle, τινά, 5, 807; and with infin. 3, 19. Od. 8. 228; χερσί, to a pugilistic combat, Od. 18, 20.

*προκάς, άδος, ή=πρόξ, h. Ven. 71.

*προκατέχω (ἔχω), only mid. *to hold down before oneself,* τί, h. Cer. 197.

πρόκειμαι, depon. mid. (κεῖμαι), *to lie or be placed before, to be ready,* only προκείμενα ὀνείατα, 9, 91. Od. 1, 149.

πρόκλυτος, ον, poet. (κλύω), *heard before.* πρόκλυτα ἔπεα, words formerly heard, i. e. old traditions, 20. 204.†

Πρόκρις, ιδος, ἡ, daughter of Erechtheus, king of Athens, wife of Cephalus (Kephalos), known for her want of fidelity to her husband. She is said to have been unintentionally slain by Cephalus, who took her for a wild animal, Od. 11, 321.

πρόκροσσος, η, ον (κρόσσα), according to the Schol. *step-wise.* προκρόσσας ἔρυσαν νῆας, they drew the ships up in the form of steps, 14, 35; † i. e. in several rows one behind another as in a theatre, because the shore could not contain them all side by side. Schneider and Passow, on the other hand: *prominent like the battlements of a wall,* so placed, that their high sterns formed a kind of wall with projecting battlements, see Hdt. 7, 188.

προκυλίνδω (κυλίνδω), *to roll forward;* only mid. *to roll oneself forward, to roll on,* spoken of the sea, 14, 18.†

προλέγω (λέγω), *to select, to choose,* partcp. perf. pass. προλελεγμένοι, the most select, 13. 689.†

προλείπω (λείπω), aor. partcp. προλιπών, infin. προλιπεῖν, perf. προλέλοιπα; prop. *to leave before,* generally, *to abandon. to leave behind,* νεκρούς, 17, 275; with accus. metaph. μῆτις σε προλέλοιπε, prudence forsook thee, Od. 2, 279.

προμαχίζω, poet. (πρόμαχος), *to be a champion, to fight in the front ranks;* Τρωσί, amongst the Trojans. 3, 16. 2) *to fight as a champion* with any one, τινί, 20, 376.

προμάχομαι (μάχομαι), *to fight before, to fight in the front ranks,* τινός, before any one, *11, 217. 17, 358.

πρόμαχος, ὁ (μάχη), *a champion,* one who fights in the front ranks, often in the plur. 4, 505. Od. 18, 379.

Πρόμαχος, ὁ, son of Algenor, a leader of the Bœotians, 14, 476. 482.

προμίγνυμι (μίγνυμι), aor. pass. infin. προμιγῆναι, *to mingle before;* pass. *to unite oneself* with any one *before,* τινί, 9, 432.†

προμνηστῖνοι, αι, α, only plur. *singly, one after another,* Od. 11, 233. 21, 230. (According to Eustath. and the Gramm. from μένω, fut. μενέσω for προμενετῖνοι.)

προμολών. see προβλώσκω.

πρόμος, ὁ (πρό). prop. *the front man;* always *a champion,* ἀνήρ, 5, 333. Od. 11, 493; τινί, against any one, Il. 7, 75.

προνοέω (νοέω), aor. 1 Ep. προνόησα 1) *to see before, to perceive before,* with accus. δόλον, 18, 526. 2) *to consider beforehand, to devise beforehand,* ἀμείνω τι, Od. 5, 365.

Πρόνοος, ὁ, a Trojan, slain by Patroclus, 16, 399.

πρόξ, προκός, ἡ, prob. *a deer,* Od. 17, 295.† (The Schol. explain it by δορκάς and ἔλαφος.)

προπάροιθε, and before a vowel προπάροιθεν, poet. (πάροιθε), 1) Adv. *of place. before, in front,* κιών, 15, 260; ἰέναι, Od. 17, 277. b) Spoken of time: *before, previously,* Il. 10, 478. 11, 734. 15, 356; in oppos. to ὀπίσσω, Od. 11, 483. 2) Prep. with gen. spoken of place: *before,* πύλος, Il. 2, 811. 6, 307. b) *along before, along.* ἠϊόνος, 2, 92. Also it stands after the gen. 14, 297. 15, 66.

πρόπας, ᾶσα, ᾶν, poet. (πᾶς), *whole,* ἦμαρ, 1, 601. Od. 9, 161. h. Merc. 206.

προπέμπω (πέμπω), aor. 1 προὔπεμψα, 1) *to stand before,* τινά, Od. 17, 54. 117: mly *to send forth, to send;* εἰς Ἀΐδαο, sc. δόμον, to send any one to the abode of Hades, Il. 8, 367.

προπέφανται, see προφαίνω.

προπίπτω (πίπτω), partcp. aor. προπεσών, *to fall forwards,* Batr. 255. 2) *to bend forwards, to lean forwards.* προπεσόντες ἔρεσσον, bending forward they rowed (*incumbentes*), *Od. 9, 490. 12, 194.

προποδίζω (ποδίζω), *to put forward the foot, to step forward,* *13. 158. 806.

*πρόπολος, ὁ, ἡ (πολέω), *a servant,* a handmaid. h. Cer. 440.

προπρηνής, ές, poet. (πρηνής), *bending forwards, prone,* oppos. to ὀπίσω. 3, 218. τύπτειν τινὰ προπρηνεῖ, sc. φασγάνῳ, to strike any one with the sweep of his sword; with his sword swung round, Od. 22, 98 (in distinction from thrusting with the point, Eustath. supplies χειρί= "*pur une main poussée en avant,*" i. e. by the point). ἐκτανύειν προπρηνέα τινά, to stretch out prone, Il. 24, 18.

προπροκυλίνδομαι, poet. strengthened κυλίνδω. 1) *to roll oneself forward:* τινός, to roll hither and thither before any man's feet, to supplicate him, 22, 221; metaph. *to wander continually around* Od. 17, 523.

προρέω (ῥέω), poet. for προρρ., *to flow forwards, to flow on,* ἅλαδε, 5. 593. 12, 19; εἰς ἅλαδε, Od. 10. 351. 2) *to cause to flow,* ὕδωρ, h. Ap. 380. cf. Herm. ad loc.

πρόρριζος, ον (ῥίζα), *with the root, from the foundation, radical,* *14, 415. 11, 157.

πρός, Dor. and Ep. προτί and ποτί, I) Prep. with gen., dat., and accus.; it is derived from πρό, and has likewise the signif. *before,* but by construction with the three cases, in manifold relations. προτί and ποτί occur mly with the accus., rarely with the dat., and each form

Προσάγω. 359 Προσεῖπον.

mly once with gen. 11, 831. 22, 198. **1)** With gen. 1) Spoken of place: *a)* Prop. to indicate motion from an object: *rum*. ἵκετο—ἠὲ πρὸς ἠοίων ἢ ἑσπερίων ἀνθρώπων, from eastern or western men, Od. 8, 29; mly πρός indicates only motion, hence to a point, *to, towards*. πρὸς ἁλός, to the sea, Il. 10, 428. 430. πρὸς νηῶν, 15, 670. πρὸς Βορέαο, to the north, Od. 13, 110. 21, 347, cf. 3) With accus. *b)* In indicating near approach to an object: *close upon, near by, before* [c oram]. ποτὶ πτόλιος πέτετ' ἀεί, he flew always close by the city, Il. 22, 198. τοῦτό σοι πρὸς Τρώων κλέος ἔσται, this shall redound to thy glory before the Trojans, 22, 514. cf. 16, 85. 2) In causative relations, as indicating any thing which proceeds from or is effected by a person or thing: *from, through, by means of, by virtue of*. *a)* Spoken of the author: ἔχειν τιμὴν πρὸς Ζηνός, Od. 11, 302. ἀκούειν τι πρός τινος, from any man, i. e. from his mouth, Il. 6, 525. οἴτε θέμιστας πρὸς Διὸς εἰρύαται, from Zeus (*auctore Jove*), 1, 339; and with the pass. διδάσκεσθαι πρός τινος, to be taught by any one, 11, 831. cf. 6, 57. *b)* Spoken of the possessor: πρὸς Διός εἰσι ξεῖνοι, strangers belong to Zeus, Od. 6, 207. 14, 57. *c)* In oaths and asseverations: πρὸς θεῶν, by the gods (for the sake of the gods), 1, 339. 19, 188. Od. 11, 67. 13, 324. *B)* With dat. spoken only of place in indicating continuance with an object: *before, by, near, beside, upon, at*. πρὸς ἀλλήλῃσι ἔχονται, by one another, Od. 5, 329. Often with the implied notion of motion: λιάζεσθαι ποτὶ γαίῃ, βάλλεσθαι προτὶ γαίῃ, Il. 20, 420. 22, 64. 2) In indicating approach: *to, towards*, Od. 10, 68. *c)* With accus. 1) Spoken of place: *a)* In indicating motion or direction to an object: *to, towards, against*. ἰέναι πρὸς Ὄλυμπον, φέρειν τι προτὶ ἄστυ; also εἰπεῖν, μυθήσασθαι πρός τινα, to speak to any one; spoken also of the situation of places: πρὸς 'Ἠῶ τ' 'Ηέλιόν τε, Il. 12, 239. Od. 9, 26. cf. Il. 8, 364. *b)* In a hostile signif.: μάχεσθαι πρὸς Τρῶας, to fight against the Trojans, 17, 471; metaph. πρὸς δαίμονα, against the deity, i. e. against the will of the deity, 17, 98. 104. 2) Spoken of time: *towards*, ποτὶ ἕσπερα, Od. 17, 191. 3) In causative relations; only of exchange: ἀμείβειν τι πρός τινα, to exchange any thing with any one, Il. 6, 235. 11) Adv. without cases: mly πρὸς δέ, *besides, moreover, in addition*, 1, 245. 5, 307. III) In composition, πρός has the signif. already given: *to, towards*, etc.

προσάγω (ἄγω), aor. 2 προσήγαγον, *to lead to, to bring to. to procure for*, τί τινι, Od. 17, 446 †: δῶρά τινι, to present gifts to any one, h. Ap. 272.

*προσαΐσσω (ἀΐσσω), partcp. aor. προσαΐξας, *to rush upon, to leap or spring* k, *Od. 22, 337. 342. 365.

προσαλείφω (ἀλείφω), *to rub on, to anoint; φάρμακόν τινι*, to anoint one with a drug, Od. 10, 392.†

προσαμύνω (ἀμύνω), infin. aor. προσαμῦναι, 1) *to repel, to avert*, τινά, 5, 139. 2) With dat. τινί, *to come to protect*, Od. 2, 238. 16, 509.

*προσαναγκάζω (ἀναγκάζω), aor. προσηνάγκασε, poet. σσ, *to constrain still further, to compel*, with infin. h. Cer. 413.

προσάπτω, Dor. and Ep. προτιάπτω (ἅπτω), *to attach*; metaph. *to dispense, to grant*, κῦδός τινι, 24. 110.†

προσαραρίσκω ('ΑΡΩ), only partcp. perf. προσαρηρώς, intrans. *to fit to, to suit; ἐπίσσωτρα προσαρηρότα, close fitting tires, 5, 725.†

προσαρηρότα, see προσαραρίσκω.

προσαυδάω (αὐδάω), poet. 3 sing. imperf. προσηύδα, 3 dual προσαυδήτην, *to speak to, to address*, often absol. and with accus. τινά, ἐπέεσσιν, 11, 136. Od. 15, 440; and μειλιχίοισιν, sc. ἐπέεσσιν, to address with friendly words, 11. 4, 256; κερτομίοισιν, 1, 539. *b)* Most frequently with double accus. τινὰ ἔπεα, to speak words to any one.

προσβαίνω (βαίνω), partcp. aor. 2 προσβάς, aor. mid. Ep. προσεβήσατο, 1) *to go to, to step to; λὰξ προσβάς, treading upon any thing with the heel, 5, 620. 2) With accus. 'Ὄλυμπον, to mount Olympus, 2, 48; κλίμακα, Od. 21, 5; πρὸς δειράδα, h. Ap. 281.

προσβάλλω (βάλλω), Ep. and Dor. προτιβάλλω, aor. 2 προσέβαλον, mid. προτιβάλλεαι, Ep. for προσβάλλῃ, 1) Prop. to cast to; generally, *to cast*, τί γαίῃ, only in tmesis, 1, 245. *b)* With accus. to cast upon any thing, *to hit* or *touch* any one, or any thing, thus 'Ἤλιος προσέβαλλεν ἀρούρας, Helios touched the fields, i. e. illumuiated them, 7, 421. Od. 19, 433. Mid. *to cast oneself upon* any one, *to attack* any one, τινὰ ἔπει, ἔργῳ, any one with words, in act, Il. 5, 879.

προσδέρκομαι, Dor. and Ep. ποτιδέρκομαι, poet. (δέρκομαι), *to look upon, to behold*, τινά, Od. 20, 385; ποτιδ., Il. 16, 10. Od. 17, 518.

προσδέχομαι, depon. mid. Dor. and Ep. ποτιδέχ. (δέχομαι), only partcp. aor. sync. ποτιδέγμενος, prop. to receive, to take up; only metaph. *to expect, to await*, τινά or τί, 10, 123. 19, 234 Od. 2, 403; absol. *to wait, to stay*, with ὁππότ' ἄν or εἰ, Il. 7, 415. Od. 23, 91.

προσδόρπιος, ον, Ep. ποτιδόρπ. (δόρπον), *pertaining to eating, or serving for eating; for supper*, *Od. 9, 234. 249.

προσειλέω, Ep. προτιειλέω (εἰλέω). infin. προτιειλεῖν, *to press on, to drive*, τινὰ προτὶ νῆας, 10, 347.†

πρόσειμι (εἶμι), only partcp. pres. προσιών, *to go to, to come to, to rush upon*, 5, 515. 7, 308. Od. 16, 5.

προσεῖπον (εἶπον), aor. of πρόσφημι, always Ep. προσέειπον optat. Dor. and Ep. ποτιείπω. 22, 329 prop. to speak

Προσερεύγομαι. 360 **Πρόσωπα.**

to; hence, *to address*, τινά έπέεσσιν, 1, 224 ; also with double accus. μύθόν τινα, 7, 16. 8, 280. Od. 6, 21.

προσερεύγομαι. mid. (έρεύγομαι), prop. to vomit or belch forth with a noise; metaph. spoken of the waves of the sea: *to dash roaring upon, to beat upon*, with accus. πέτρην, *a rock*, 15, 621.† (Others read ἀκτήν for αὐτήν).

πρόσθε, I) Adv. 1) Of place: *before, forwards*, in oppos. to όπιθεν, 6, 181; όπλαι αί πρόσθεν, the fore hoofs, h. Merc. 77; έχειν, to hold before, 4, 113; ίππους πρόσθε βάλλειν, to drive the horses forwards, 23, 572; but *to drive away*, p r æ v e r t e r e, 23, 639. 2) Spoken of time: *before, formerly*, 5, 851. οί πρόσθεν. men of former times, 9, 524; also τὸ πρόσθεν, 12, 40. II) Prep. with gen. 1) Spoken of place: *before*, πρόσθεν έθεν, 5, 56. 107. πρόσθε ποδών, before the feet, Od. 22, 4; then, with the implied notion of protection: ίστασθαι πρόσθε τινός, to place oneself before any one, Il. 4, 54. τάων πρόσθε, before these for defence, 16, 833. cf. 21, 587. Sometimes the dative appears to be connected with it, which would better be referred to the verb, 5, 300. 315. Od. 5, 452. 2) Of time: *before*. Il. 2, 359.

πρόσκειμαι (κείμαι), *to lie* or *to be upon*, spoken of a tripod, οὔατα προσέκειτο, there were handles (ears) upon it, 18, 379.†

προσκηδής, ές (κήδος), *careful, interested* (V. 'intimate'), Od. 21, 35 ;† according to others, *related*.

προσκλι΄νω, Ep. ποτικλι΄νω (κλίνω), perf. pass. ποτικέκλιμαι, *to lean upon, to lay upon*, τί τινι ; βέλος κορώνη, Od. 21, 138. θρόνος ποτικέκλιται αὐγῆ, others (αὐτῆ), a seat stood in the light, *Od. 6, 308.

προσλέγομαι, mid. (λέγω), aor. sync. προσέλεκτο, *to lay oneself beside*, or *near*, Od. 12, 34.†

προσμυθέομαι, depon. mid. Dor. and Ep. προτιμυθ (μυθέομαι), infin. aor. 1 προτιμυθήσασθαι, *to speak to, to address*, τινί, Od. 11, 143.†

προσνίσσομαι, Dor. ποτινίσ., poet. (νίσσομαι), *to go to* or *come to*, with εἰς τι, 9, 381 ;† in the Dor. form.

προσόσσομαι, see προτιόσσομαι.

προσπελάζω, poet. syncop. προσπλάζω (πελάζω), Od. 11, 583. 1) Trans. *to bring near, to cause to approach* ; νήα άκρη, to urge the ship to the promontory, Od. 9, 285. 2) Intrans. *to approach, to come near*, spoken of the waves of the sea: to come rolling on, Il. 12, 285. Od. 11, 583; in the syncop. form.

προσπίλναμαι. mid. (πίλναμαι), only imperf. *to approach, to draw near*, τινί, to any thing, Od. 13, 95.†

προσπίπτω (πίπτω), partcp. perf. Ep. προσπιπτούσαι, *to fall upon* ; metaph. *to happen upon* or *to* ; in the perf. *to lie upon* or *near*. ἀκταί λιμένος ποτιπεπτηυίαι, the shores lying near, towards the harbour (V. ' falling into, or forming a bay'), Od. 13, 98.†

προσπλάζω, Ep. for προσπελάζω. q. v.

προσπτύσσομαι, mid. Dor. and Ep. ποτιπτύσ., Od. 2, 77 ; (πτύσσω) ; fr. προσπτύξομαι, aor. subj. προσπτύξομαι Od. 8, 478 ; prop. to lie closely in fold. Mly metaph. *a) to embrace, to encompass, to enfold*, τινά. Od. 11, 451; *b*) to address, to petition with words: Od. 2, 77 ; to show oneself friendly, έν έργω, h. Cer. 109 ; *b*) generally, *to address in a friendly manner, to greet*, Od. 3, 22. 4, 647. 17, 509.

πρόσσοθεν, adv. poet. for πρόσωθεν, *forwards*, 23, 533.†

πρόσσω, Ep. for πρόσω.

προστείχω, poet. (στείχω), aor. 2 προέστιχε, *to stride to, to go to*, Όλυμπον. Od. 20, 73.

προστέρπω, Dor. and Ep. ποτιτέρπω (τέρπω), *to delight at, to animate, to entertain*, τινά, 15, 401 ;† Dor. form.

προστίθημι (τίθημι), aor. 1 προσέθηκα *to place at* or *upon*, λίθον, Od. 9, 305. 2) *to attach to*, τί τινι, h. Merc. 129.

*προστρέπω (τρέπω), aor. mid. προεστραπόμην, *to turn to*. Mid. *to turn self to*, τινά, any one, Ep. 15.

προσφάσθαι, see πρόσφημι.

πρόσφατος, ον (ΦΑΩ. ΦΕΝΩ). *just before, newly slaughtered* or *slain*, 24, 757.*

πρόσφημι (φημί), mly imperf. προσέφην, as aor. προσέειπον, is used; in mid. προσφάσθαι, Od. 23, 106 ; *to address*, τινά, Il. 1, 84; absol. *to speak*. Il. 369 [also 21. 212; although in both passages an αὐτόν is implied, and hence they are not prop. absol.]

προσφυής, ές (φύω), prop. to grow to; generally, *clinging* or *attached to*, ά τινος, Od. 19, 58.†

προσφύω (φύω), only aor. 2 partcp προσφύς, ύσα, ύ: 1) Trans. *to let grow to cause to grow*; metaph. *to cling to, to hold fast to*, with dat. τῷ προσφύς ἐθμήν, I held fast clinging to it, Od. 12. 433; absol. προσφῦσα, Il. 24. 213.

προσφωνέω (φωνέω), prop. *to sound to, to call to* ; generally, *to address*, τινά, 2, 22 ; and often absol. ; with dat. instr. τοῖσιν, sc. έπεσσιν, with these words, O. 22, 69.

προσφωνήεις, εσσα, εν, Dor. and Ep ποτιφων., poet. (προσφωνέω), *capable of addressing* (V. ' if thou understandest language'), Od. 9, 456.†

πρόσω, poet. πρόσσω, adv. (πρό). II Spoken of place, *forth, forwards*, Il. 572. 12, 274. 16, 265. 2) Of time; *forwards, in future*, only in connexion with όπίσσω, 1, 343. 3, 109. 18, 250. (In the two forms, 17, 598. Od. 9, 542.)

προσώπατα, τά, old Ep. plur. of πρόσωπον.

πρόσωπον, τό (ὤψ), Ep. plur. προσώπατα. Od. 18, 192 (elsewhere πρόσωπα); dat. προσώπασι. Il. 7, 212; *face, countenance, aspect*, for the most part plur. (see Thiersch, § 185, 22.)

Προτέμνω. Προφέρω.

προτέμνω (τέμνω), aor. 2 προταμών, optat. aor. mid. προταμοίμην, 1) *to cut off before, to curve (for)*, 9, 489. 2) *to cut off in front, at the end*, with accus. κορμόν, ἐκ ῥίζης, to cut off the trunk at the root, Od. 23, 196. Mid. *to cut off for oneself*; metaph. ὦλκα διηνεκέα, to cut a straight furrow, Od. 18, 375.

πρότερος, η, ον (πρό), compar. without posit. *the former, the earlier*, prior, 1) Spoken of time: *former, earlier, elder*, γενεῇ, 15, 166. πρότεροι ἄνθρωποι, men of former times, *ancestors, forefathers*, 5, 637; also πρότεροι alone: πρ. παῖδες, children of a former marriage, Od. 15, 22. τῇ προτέρῃ sc. ἡμέρᾳ, on the former day, Od. 16, 50; with gen. ἐμέο πρότερος, earlier than I, 11. 10, 124. 2) Of place: *before, fore-, that is before*, 16, 569. πόδες πρότεροι, the fore-feet, Od. 19, 228.

προτέρω, adv. (πρότερος), *further, further forwards*. πρ. ἵεσο, step nearer, Od. 5, 91; ἄγειν, Il. 3, 400. Od. 5, 91; metaph. *forward, more violent*. ἔρις προτέρω γένετο, the contest went forward, waxed more violent, 23, 490.

*προτέρωσε, adv. (πρότερος), *forwards*, h. 32, 10.

προτεύχω (τεύχω), perf. pass. προτέτυγμαι, *to make or to prepare before*. τὰ μὲν προτετύχθαι ἐάσομεν, these things we will allow to have happened, i. e. what is past we will let alone, 16, 60. 18, 112. 19, 65.

προτί, Dor. for πρός.
προτιάπτω, see προσάπτω.
Προτιάων, ονος, ὁ, a Trojan, father of Astynoüs, 15, 455.
προτιβάλλειν, see προσβάλλω.
προτιειλεῖν, see προσειλέω.
προτιείποι, see προσεῖπον.

προτίθημι (τίθημι), 3 plur. pres. προθέουσι for προτιθέασι, 1, 291; as if from the theme ΘΕΩ, cf. Thiersch, § 224. Kühner I. § 202. 2. aor. 1 προύθηκα, 1) *to place before, to put before, to lay before*, τὶ κυσίν, to devour, 24, 409. 2) *to put out, to expose publicly* for sale, for use; hence metaph. *to allow, to permit*, τινί, with infin. 1, 291. Mid. *to place before oneself*, τραπέζας, Od. 1, 112.

προτιμυθήσασθαι, see προσμυθέομαι.
προτιόσσομαι, Dor. for προσόσσομαι (ὄσσομαι), 1) *to look upon, to behold*, τινά, Od. 7, 31. 23, 365. ἦ σ' εὖ γιγνώσκων προτιόσσομαι οὐδ' ἄρ' ἔμελλον πείσειν, indeed knowing thee well, I behold thee, i. e. indeed, I see thee now as I have ever known thee (and I was not about to persuade thee), Il. 22, 356. Thus Passow and Bothe. Krause takes it as a pres. perf.: 'I anticipated it and anticipate it still.' 2) *to foresee, to anticipate*, ὄλεθρον, θάνατον, Od. 5, 389. 14, 219.

πρότμησις, ιος, ἡ (τέμνω), 1) *the part cut off*. 2) Metaph. spoken of the human figure: *the region about the loins and navel, the waist*, 11, 424.†

πρότονος, ὁ (τείνω), in the plur.; a rope, primar. the two great ropes that extend from the top of the mast, the one to the bow and the other to the stern of a ship, to support the mast and also to lower it, 1, 434. Od. 12, 409. h. Ap. 504.

προτρέπω (τρέπω), only mid. aor. 2 Ep. προτραπόμην, 1) *to turn forwards*. 2) Mid. *to turn oneself forward, to betake oneself, to turn in flight*, ἐπὶ νηῶν, 5, 700; spoken of Helios: ἐπὶ γαῖαν, to turn to the earth, Od. 11, 18. 2) Metaph. *to turn oneself to, to yield to*; ἄχεϊ, to grief, Il. 6, 336.

προτροπάδην, adv. (προτρέπω), prop. *turned forwards*; φοβέοντο, they fled ever forward. i. e. on and on, without stopping, 16, 304.†

προτύπτω (τύπτω), aor. προὔτυψα, prop. trans. *to strike forwards*; in Hom. only intrans. *to press forwards, to push forward*, 13, 136. 15, 306. 17, 262. ἀνὰ ῥῖνάς οἱ δριμὺ μένος προὔτυψε, fierce wrath pressed into his nose, Od. 24, 319.

προὔθηκε, see προτίθημι.
προὔπεμψε, see προπέμπω.
προὔφαινε, see προφαίνω.
προὔχω, for προέχω.

προφαίνω (φαίνω), imperf. προὔφαινον, perf. pass. 3 plur. προπέφανται, aor. 2 pass. partcp. προφανείς, 1) Act. trans. *to exhibit, to cause to appear*, with accus. τέραα, Od. 12, 394. b) Intrans. like mid. *to appear, to shine forth*, spoken of the moon, Od. 9, 145. II) Mid. with aor. pass. *to shine forth, to show oneself, to become visible*, Od. 13, 169. οὐδὲ προὐφαίνετο ἰδέσθαι, nothing appeared so that one could behold it, or to the sight, Od. 9, 143. προπέφανται ἅπαντα, every thing is visible at a distance, is exposed to view (Cp.), Il. 14, 332. b) Esply of persons: *to appear, to step forth*, Od. 24, 160; ἀνὰ γεφύρας πολέμοιο, Il. 8, 378; ἐς πόλεμον for ἐν πολέμῳ Il. 17, 487; ἐς πεδίον, 24, 332.

πρόφασις, ιος, ἡ (πρόφημι), *a pretext, a pretence, appearance*; absol. πρόφασιν, in appearance, in pretence, *19, 262. 302.

προφερής, ές (προφέρω), compar. προφερέστερος, η, ον; superl. προφερέστατος, η, ον, Od.; prop. borne before, placed before; then generally, *eminent, distinguished, excellent*, with dat. of the thing, ἄλματι, βίῃ, Od. 8, 128. 221. 21, 134; with infin., Il. 10, 352.

προφέρω (φέρω), only pres. and imperf. *to bring forward*; hence 1) *to bear onward, to carry forward, to bear away*, spoken of a storm, τινὰ εἰς ὄρος, 6, 346. Od. 20, 64. 2) *to bear to, to convey to*, τινί τι, 11. 9, 323. 17, 121; metaph. in a bad sense (nearly=our *to bring up against* any body; or *cast in his teeth*), ὀνείδεά τινι, to cast reproaches upon any one, δῶρά τινι, 3, 64, to reproach with. 3) *to bring forward*, i. e. *to bring to light, to present, to show*. μένος, 10, 479; ἔριδα, to exhibit emulation, Od. 6, 92. II) Mid. with reference to the subject: ἐριδά

Προφεύγω. 362 Πρωτεσίλαος.

τινι, to present a contest to any one, i. e. to challenge him to it, Il. 3, 7; άέθλων, Od. 8, 210.
προφεύγω (φεύγω), aor. 2 optat. 2 sing. προφύγοισθα, partcp. προφυγών, 1) to fly forward or forth, 11, 340. 2) Trans. to escape, with accus. χείρας, μένος, 7, 309. 14, 81; θάνατον, Od. 22, 318.
πρόφρασσα, ή (φράζω), an Ep. fem. of πρόφρων, willing, kind, compliant, well-disposed, or provident, considerate, decided, cf. Thiersch, § 201. Rem., 11. 10, 290. Od. 5, 161. 10, 386.
προφρονέως, Ep. προφρόνως, adv. from πρόφρων, readily, willingly, μάχεσθαι, 5, 810; with confidence, 7, 160; h. Merc. 558.
πρόφρων, ονος, ὁ, ἡ (φρονέω), 1) having a well-inclined disposition, kind, compliant, willing. θυμός, 8, 40. 9, 480. 2) having a decided mind, intentional, serious, earnest, 1, 77. 8, 23. 14, 317. Od. 2, 230 ; Ironically: πρόφρων κεν δη έπειτα Δία λιτοίμην, then could I pray to Zeus, with my whole heart [with great boldness, Cp.], i. e. I could not, Od. 14, 406.
*προφυλάσσω (φυλάσσω), Ep. imperat. προφύλαχθε for προφυλάσσετε, to watch or guard a place, νηόν, h. Ap. 538.
προχέω (χέω), to pour out, to pour forth, spoken of a river, 21, 219. h. Ap. 2, 41. Pass. to pour forth, to stream forth, spoken of masses of men, *2, 465. 15, 360. 21, 5.
πρόχνυ, adv. (γόνυ), upon the knees, upon the knee; καθέζεσθαι, to sit upon one's knees, i. e. to sink upon one's knees, 9, 570. b) Metaph. spoken of vanquished enemies: πρόχνυ ἀπολέσθαι κακώς, to perish miserably, sinking on their knees, "to be brought low and perish" (Lidd. and Scott), 21, 460; ὀλέσθαι, Od. 14, 69.
προχοή, ή (προχέω), an outlet, the mouth of a river, 17, 263 ; of a fountain, h. Ap. 383. 2) In the plur. a place which is washed by flowing water, a wave-washed shore, Od 5, 453. 11, 242. 20, 65.
πρόχοος, ή (προχέω), a vessel for pouring out water, a pitcher, an ewer, 24, 304. Od. 1, 136; a wine-can, Od. 18, 397.
πρυλέες, ων, οἱ, Ep. dat. πρυλέεσσι and πρύλεσσι, Ep. heavy-armed foot-soldiers, in oppos. to cavalry, *11, 49. 5, 744. [According to Herm., Opusc. IV. p. 288, seq., "praesules sive praesultores, qui ante caeteros progressi saltationem cum armis praeeunt." Ameis.]
Πρυμνεύς, έως, ὁ (the pilot), a Phæacian, Od. 8, 112.
πρύμνη, ή, Ion. and Ep. for πρύμνα, prop. fem. of the adj. πρύμνος, sc. νηῦς, the stern, the poop of a ship. It was rounder and higher than the prow, and the seat of the pilot; often in full, πρύμνη νηῦς, 7, 383. Od. 2, 417.
πρυμνηθεν, adv. poet. from the stern ; λαμβάνειν, to lay hold of the stern, 15, 716.†

πρυμνήσιος, η, ον (πρύμνη), belonging to the stern or poop; mly τὰ πρυμνήσια (retinacula), a hawser, the rope with which a ship was made fast when she lay at the shore; also πείσματα (the two words are, however, distinguished Od. 9, 136, 137. cf. πείσμα), the stern-cable. Upon departure they were loosed; hence πρ. λύειν, Od. 2, 418. The opposite καταδήσαι, ἀνάψαι, Il. 1, 436. Od. 9, 137.
πρυμνός, ή, όν, superl. πρυμνότατος, η, ον, Od. the extreme, the last, the hindmost, the lowest ; βραχίων, the end of the arm (at the shoulder), Il. 13, 532; ὦμος, the lower leg, 16, 314 ; γλῶσσα, the root of the tongue, 5, 292. πρ. κέρας, 13. 705 ; spoken of a stone : πρυμνὸς παχὺς thick beneath, 12, 446 ; hence also πρυμνὴν ἐκτάμνειν, to cut up the tree by the root, 12, 149. Neut. as subst. πρυμνὸν θέναρος, the end of the hand, 5. 339.
πρυμνώρεια, ή (ὄρος), the lowest part, the foot of a mountain, 14, 307.†
*πρυτανεύω (πρύτανις), fut. σω, to rule, to govern, with dat. h. Ap. 68.
Πρύτανις, ιος, ὁ (a ruler, akin to πρῶτος), a Lycian, slain by Odysseus (Ulysses), 5, 678.
πρωΐν, adv. in H. lately, very recently, formerly, spoken of time past, *5, 832. 24, 500 ; (contr. for πρωϊήν, subaud. ὥραν.)
πρωθήβης, ου, ὁ, Ep. for πρωθήβος, 8. 518. Od. 8, 263. h. Ap. 450.
πρωθήβος, ον, Ep. also πρωθήβη, Od. 1. 431.† (πρώτος, ἥβη), just entering the age of puberty, manly, marriageable. ἀνήρ, h. 7, 2.
πρωΐ, adv. (πρό), early, in the morning, on the next morning, *8, 530. 18, 27. 303.
πρωΐζα, adv. (πρωΐζος), early ; generally formerly. χθιζά τε καὶ πρωΐζα, yesterday and day before, 2, 303.†
πρώϊος, η, ον (πρωΐ), early, early in the day. The neut. πρώϊον as adv. early the morning, or, more correctly, early yesterday, 15, 470.† cf. Spitzner ad loc.
πρών, πρῶνος, ὁ, Ep. expanded from ονος (πρό), prop. any thing. projecting, hence a summit, an elevation, esply a point of land projecting into the sea, a cape, a promontory, 8, 557. 12, 282; always in the full form, except nom. sing. πρών, *17, 747.
Πρωρεύς, έως, ὁ (πρωράτης, the pilot's mate), a Phæacian, Od. 8, 113.
πρώρη, ή, Ep. and Ion. for πρώρα (πρό), the prow of a ship ; it runs to a point that the ship may more easily cut the waves. Hom. νηὸς πρώρη, Od. 12, 230.† (Prop. adj. from the obsol. πρώρος.)
πρώτα, adv. see πρῶτος.
Πρωτεσίλαος, ὁ, son of Iphiclus of Phylacê in Thessaly, leader of the Thessalians of Phylace. He was properly denominated Iolâus, and received this name because he leaped upon land first amongst the Greeks (πρῶτος τοῦ λαοῦ)

Πρωτεύς 363 Πτύγμα.

He was, according to the Cypr. Carm., soon after slain by Hector. After his death, he was worshipt as a hero in the Chersonêsus, 2, 698, seq. 13, 681.

Πρωτεύς, έος, ὁ, a fabulous sea-god; according to Od. 4, 385. He was father of Εἰδοθέη (Idothea), servant of Poseidôn, and attended his sea-calves in the Ægyptian sea. He had the gift of prophecy, and of changing himself into every possible form, Od. 4, 456, seq. Upon the advice of Idothea, Menelaus bound him, and forced him to inform him how he could return home. The later tradition made him king of Egypt, Hdt. 2, 112, seq.; or represented him as coming from Thrace to Egypt, Ap. 2, 5, 9.

πρώτιστος, η, ον, poet. superl. from πρώτος, *the first of all;* also of two endings, κατὰ πρώτιστον ὀπωπήν, upon the very first look, h. Cer. 157. The neut. sing. and plur. πρώτιστον and πρώτιστα, as adv. *first of all*, 1, 105. Od. 8, 57. τὰ πρώτιστα, h. Ap. 407.

πρωτόγονος, ον (γόνος), *first-born*, *4, 102. 23, 864.

πρωτοπαγής, ές (πήγνυμι), *now first constructed, just* or *newly made, new*, ἅρμα, *Il. 5, 194. 24, 267.

πρωτόπλοος, ον (πλόος), *sailing for the first time, newly made*, νηῦς, Od. 8, 35.†

πρῶτος, η, ον (πρό), superl. contr. from πρόατος, *the first, the foremost*, often with ὕστατος, 2, 281. 11, 299; then *the most distinguished, the noblest*, hence a) οἱ πρῶτοι = πρόμαχοι, the first, the front warriors, 5, 536. 12, 306. 321: also pleonast. πρῶτοι πρόμαχοι, Od. 18, 379. b) τὰ πρῶτα, sc. ἆθλα, the first prizes, 11. 23, 275. The neut. sing. and plur. as adv. πρῶτον, πρῶτα, in like manner with the article, τοπρῶτον, ταπρῶτα, Il. (also separate, τὸ πρῶτον, τὰ πρῶτα, ed. Spitz. and in Od.) 1) *first, at first, for the first time*, Il. 9, 32; often πρῶτον καὶ ὕστατον. 2) *too early.* ἤ τ' ἄρα καὶ σοὶ πρῶτα παραστήσεσθαι ἔμελλε Μοῖρα, truly fate was destined to approach thee too early, Od. 24, 28. 3) After an adv. of time: *once*, ἐπεὶ and ἐπειδὴ πρῶτον or πρῶτα, *quum primum*, when once, as soon as, 6, 489. Od. 3, 183. ἐξ οὗ δὴ πρῶτα, Il. 1, 6. Also aft. a relat. cf. Il. 1, 319.

πρωτοτόκος, ον (τίκτω), *bearing for the first time*, μήτηρ, 17, 5.†

Πρωτώ, οῦς, ἡ, daughter of Nereus and Doris, 18, 43.

πρώονος, ονι, etc. see πρών.

πταίρω, aor. 2 ἔπταρον, *to sneeze*, as a sign of good omen, Od. 17, 541.†

πτάμενος, πτάτο, see πέτομαι.

πτελέη, ἡ, an *elm*, ulmus campestris, *Il. 6, 419. 21, 242.

Πτελεός, ἡ [rather ὁ or τό, see Λεχεποίης] (πτελέη, an elm), 1) a place in Elis, a colony from the Thessalian Pteleos; in Strabo's time ruinous, 2, 594. τὸ Πτελεόν, Strabo. 2) an Achæan town in Thessaly, between Antrum and Pyrasus, with a port, 2, 697.

πτέρνα or πτέρνη, ἡ, *the heel*, 22, 397.† 2) Poet. for πέρνα, *the ham*, Batr. 37.

*Πτερνογλύφος, ὁ (γλύφω), *Ham-hollower*, name of a mouse, Batr. 227.

*Πτερνοτρώκτης, ου, ὁ (τρώγω), *Ham-gnawer*, name of a mouse, Batr. 29.

*Πτερνοφάγος, ὁ (φαγεῖν), *Ham-eater*, name of a mouse, Batr. 230

πτερόεις, εσσα, εν, poet. (πτέρον), prop. *feathered, winged*, epith. of an arrow. since it was furnished with feathers at the upper end, 4, 117. 5, 171. 2) Metaph. πτερόεντα λαισήια, easily-brandished shields (as if leather-light), 5, 453; often πτερόεντα ἔπεα, winged words, which escape quickly from the lips, Il. and Od.

πτέρον, τό (πέτομαι), a *feather*, a *wing*, a *pinion*, mly in plur. πτέρα βάλλειν, to strike the wings, 11, 454; as an image of swiftness, Od. 7, 36. 2) Metaph. *an oar* or *tail of a ship*, Od. 11, 125. 23, 272.

πτέρυξ, υγος, ἡ (πτέρον), a *wing*, a *pinion*, 2, 316. 462. Od. 2, 149. ὑπὸ πτερύγων, under the stroke of the wings, h. 20, 1.

πτήσσω (πίπτω, πέτω), aor. 1 ἔπτηξα, Ep. perf. πεπτηώς, ῶτος, intrans. to creep away for fear, *to crouch*, *to cringe, to shrink.* κείμην πεπτηώς, I lay crouched together, Od. 14, 354. 22, 362. ὑπὸ τεύχεσι πεπτηῶτες, Od. 14, 474; generally, *to be in fear*, hence 2) Trans. in the aor. 1, *to put in fright, to terrify.* στῆξε θυμὸν Ἀχαιῶν, he terrified the hearts of the Achæans, Il. 14, 40; πτήσσω as trans. is uncommon, hence some read στῆξε from στήννυμι; others consider the verse not genuine, as Bothe. (Spitzner ad loc. defends πτῆξε.)

πτοέω, Ep. πτοιέω, poet. (akin to στήσσω), aor. pass. Ep. 3 plur. ἐπτοίηθεν, *to put in terrour, to terrify.* Pass. *to be terrified, to fear*, Od. 22, 298.†

Πτολεμαῖος, ὁ (a warrior), son of Piræus, father of Eurymedon, 4, 228.

πτολεμίζω, Ep. for πολεμίζω.

πτολεμιστής, οῦ, ὁ, Ep. for πολεμιστής.

πτολεμόνδε, adv. for πόλεμόνδε.

πτόλεμος, ὁ, Ep for πόλεμος.

πτολίεθρον, τό. Ep. for πόλ. (πόλις), a *city*; always with the name in the gen. Ἰλίου πτολίεθρον, 2, 133. Od. 1, 2. (The form πολίεθρον is not used.) [It cannot, with Passow, be regarded as a dimin. of πόλις, for H. knows nothing of diminutives.]

πτολιπόρθιος, ὁ = πτολίπορθος, *Od. 9, 504. 530.

πτολίπορθος, ὁ, ἡ, Ep. for πολίπορθος (πέρθω), city-destroying, *the destroyer of cities*, epith. of Arês, Odysseus (Ulysses), Achilles, and of heroes, 2, 278. 8, 372; as fem. epith. of Enyo (Bellona), 5, 333. (The form πολίπορθος is not used.)

πτόλις, ιος, ἡ, Ep. for πόλις.

πτόρθος, ὁ (πείρω), a *sprout*, a *twig*, a *branch*, Od. 6, 128.†

πτύγμα, ατος, τό (πτύσσω), a *fold*, a

R 2

Πτυκτός. 364 Πύθώ.

plait; πέπλοιο, the folds of a robe, 5, 315.†

πτυκτός, ή, όν (πτύσσω), folded, doubled together. πτ. πίναξ, 6, 169;† see πίναξ.

πτύξ, πτυχός, ή (πτύσσω), that which is several times doubled; hence a fold, a layer, a plait, spoken of a garment, h. Cer. 176. πτύχες σάκεος, the layers of a shield, of brass or leather, placed one above another, for a protection, 7, 247. 18, 481. 2) Metaph. spoken of mountains: a curve, a hollow, a ravine, a valley, 11, 77. Od. 19, 432. Sing. rare, Il. 20, 22. h. Ap. 269. h. Merc. 555.

πτύον, τό (πτύω), Ep. gen. πτυόφιν, a winnowing-shovel, made of wood or iron, and having the form of the palm of the hand; the wooden ones were used for sifting earth, the other, as here, for cleaning grain, 13, 588.†

πτυόφιν, see πτύον.

πτύσσω (akin to πετάννυμι), aor. 1 έπτυξα, to lay in folds, to fold, to plait, with accus. χιτώνα, είματα, Od. 1, 439. 6, 111. 252. Mid. to fold themselves together. έγχεα έπτύσσοντο, the spears were entangled, since the combatants, standing in thick ranks, threw many at once (Mel in the air, and so deviated from their destined course. Db.), Etym. M. είς τό αύτό συνήγετο, Il. 13, 134. (V. 'they shook;' Passow, 'they bent;' both contrary to the usus loq.) ["Close-pressed upon one another were the spears hurled from brave hands," Lucas: ap. Ameis.]

πτύω, to vomit forth, to cast out, αίμα, 23, 697.†

*πτωκάς, άδος, ή (πτώξ), timid, fearful, Ep. 8, 2.

πτώξ, πτωκός, ό, ή (πτώσσω), timid, trembling, fearful, epith. of the hare, 22, 310. 2) Subst. poet. a hare, *17, 676.

πτωσκάζω, poet. (πτώσσω), to shrink, to be fearful, to be timorous, 4, 372.†

πτώσσω (akin to πτήσσω). 1) Intrans. to conceal oneself for fear, to crouch, to shrink away, ύπό τινι, before any one, 7, 126; καθ' ύδωρ, to flee into the water; ύπό κρεμνούς, 21, 14. 26. b) Generally, to be in fear, to be timorous, to be fearful, 4, 371. 6, 634. c) Spoken of a beggar: to crouch, Od. 17, 227; then = πτωχεύω, to beg, Od. 18, 363. 2) Trans. to fly in fear from any one. άλλήλους, Il. 20, 427; όρνιθες έν πεδίω νέφεα πτώσσουσαι· ίενται, the birds flying from the clouds, flutter in the plain, Od. 22, 304. (V. 'these fly terrified from the clouds into the plain.') (The explanation by the Schol. of νέφεα, as a net, is unnatural; the birds pursued by vultures, leave the clouds and seek protection on the earth, in perfect accordance with nature.)

πτωχεύω (πτωχός), fut. σω. 1) Intrans. to be poor as a beggar, to beg, Od. 15, 309. 19, 73. 2) Trans. to beg, to procure by begging, δαίτα, *Od. 17, 11. 18, 2.

πτωχός, ή, όν (πτώσσω), properly, that crouches, begging; as subst. ό πτωχός, a beggar, Od. 14, 400; also πτ. άνήρ, *Od. 21, 327.

Πυγμαίοι, οί (from πυγμή), the Pygmies, a fabulous nation of dwarfs, located in the southern part of the earth towards Ethiopia or India, 3, 6.

πυγμαχίη, ή (μάχομαι), a pugilistic combat, *23, 653. 665.

πυγμάχος, ό (μάχομαι), a pugilistic combatant, Od. 8, 246.†

πυγμή, ή (πύξ), a fist, a pugilistic combat, 23, 669.†

πυγούσιος, η, ον, poet. (πυγών), a cubit long, *Od. 10, 517. 11, 25.

πύελος, ή, a trough, a tub, esply for feeding animals, Od. 19, 553.†

πυθέσθαι, see πυνθάνομαι.

*Πύθιος, η, ον, Pythian; (see Πυθώ), ό Πύθιος, epith. of Apollo, either because he had an oracle in Pytho, or because he slew the dragon Python, h. Ap. 373.

πυθμήν, ένος, ό, the lower end, the foundation; hence, 1) Esply the trunk, the root, έλαίης, Od. 13, 122. 372. 23, 204. 2) the bottom, the basis, the foot, of goblets and tripods. The passage: δώ δ' ύπό πυθμένες ήσαν, Il. 11, 635, has given critics great trouble. The discourse relates to the mixer of Nestor: the easiest explanation seems to be, to take πυθμήν, as a foot; hence, 'there were two feet under it,' and if these were broad, as in the case of tables, this was possible. Such a cup, with two silver feet, according to Athen. Deipn. XI. 12, was shown at Capua as the goblet of Nestor. This signif. is also warranted by another passage, 18, 375, where the discourse relates to the artificial tripods of Hephaestus: χρύσεα δ' σφ' ύπό κύκλα έκάστω πυθμένι θήκεν, he placed golden wheels under each foot, for the wheels must plainly have been under the feet of the tripods, and not under the bottom. In the first passage Voss translates according to the ancient critics, who explain it as a bottom: there were two (i. e. double) bottoms under, and so, also, 18, 375. Others, as Köppen, Cammann, after Athen. XI. 488, understand it of the cavities or bellies, which were one over another.

πύθω, fut. πύσω. 1) to cause to decay, to putrefy, to consume, with όστέα, 4, 174. h. Ap. 369. Mid. to moulder, to decay, to putrefy, 11, 395. Od. 1, 161. 12, 46.

Πυθώ, ούς, ή, dat. Πυθοί, accus. Πυθώ, h. Ap. 372; dat., 9, 405; also Πυθών, ώνος, ή, an earlier form, 2, 519; accus. Πυθώνα, h. Merc. 178; Pytho, the oldest name of the region, on Parnassus, in Phocis, where was the temple and oracle of the Pythian Apollo; later also a name of the city of Delphi, which was well known to Hom.; Herod. I. 54. understands Πυθώ of the seat of the oracle, and Δελφοί of the town and the inhabitants. According to h. Ap. 372, the name comes from πύθεσθαι, to putrefy,

Πῦθώδε.

because the dragon slain by Apollo decayed there; according to others, from πυθέσθαι, to enquire of the oracle, but the short first syllable is unfavorable to this notion.)
Πῦθώδε, adv. *to Pytho*, Od. 11, 581.
πύκα, adv. poet. 1) *thickly, firmly*, βάλλειν, 9, 588; ποιητός. 18, 608. Od. 1, 333. 2) Metaph. *carefully, intelligently*, τρέφειν, Il. 5, 70: φρονεῖν. 9, 554.
πυκάζω (πύκα), aor. ἐπύκασα, Ep. πύκασσα, partcp. perf. pass. πεπυκασμένος, η, ον, 1) *to make close, firm, to press closely together* ἐντὸς σφέας αὐτούς, Od. 12, 225. 2) *to cover closely, to veil, to conceal*, τινὰ νεφέλη, Il. 17, 551; νέκυν, 24, 581; spoken of a helmet: πύκασε κάρη, 10, 271; in the pass. 2, 777: dat. instrum. ὄζοισιν, χρυσῷ. 14, 289. 23, 503. 3) Metaph. *to envelope, to overshadow, to encompass*; spoken of pain, τινὰ φρένας, 8, 124. 17, 83.
πυκιμήδης or πυκιμηδής, ές (μῆδος), of a considerate mind, *careful, prudent, wise*, Od. 1, 438;† h. Cer. 153.
πυκινά, adv. prop. neut. plur. from πυκινός=πυκνός.
πυκινός, ή, όν, Ep. for πυκνός, q. v.
*πυκινόφρων, ον (φρήν), *intelligent, wise*, h. Merc. 538.
πυκνός, ή, όν, poet. πυκινός, ή, όν (πύκα), 1) *thick, firm*. a) In respect of the mass: *firm, strong*, θώρηξ, ἀσπίς, χλαῖνα. b) In respect of single parts: *close, pressed together*, λέχος, 9, 621 (because several coverings were laid one upon another); νέφος, 5, 751; φάλαγγες, στίχες, dense phalanxes, columns, 4, 281. 7, 61; πτέρα, thickly feathered wings, 11, 454; βέλεα, λᾶες, thick arrows or stones, which were thrown in great numbers, Il.; c) also spoken of time: *frequent*, 10, 9. d) Spoken of something done: *thick, strong*, δόμος, 10, 267. Od. 6, 134; closelocked, θύρα, Il. 14, 167. 2) Generally, *great, strong*, ἄχος, ἄτη. 16, 599. 24, 480; πυκινὸν ἀχεύων, Od. 11, 88. b) Spoken of the mind: *considerate, prudent, wise, intelligent*, φρένες, νόος, μῆδεα, βουλή, ἔπος: also ἐρετμή, μῦθος. The neut. πυκνόν and πυκνά, πυκινόν and πυκινά, as adv., so also πυκινῶς. 1) *thickly, firmly*, θύραι πυκινῶς ἀραρυῖαι, closely fitted doors, Od. 2, 344. 2) Metaph. *strongly, greatly, exceedingly*, πυκινῶς ἀκάχημαι, Il. 19, 312; *considerate, intelligent*, Od. 1, 279. πυκινὰ φρονεῖν, to be wise of heart, Od. 9, 445.
Πυλαιμένης, ους, ὁ, king of the Paphlagonians, who came to the aid of Priam. Menelaus slew him, 2, 831. 5, 576. In 13, 643, seq., Pylæmēnes, prince of the Paphlygonians, appears accompanying the corpse of his son Harpalion. The ancient critics attempted to remove the contradiction, by supposing two persons of this name. Modern critics imagine themselves to have found in the circumstance a proof that the Iliad was put together at a later period.

Πύλος.

Πύλαιος, ὁ (adj. πυλαῖος), son of Lethus, leader of the Pelasgians, 2, 842.
πυλάρτης, αο, ὁ (ἄρω), *who locks fast the gates of the under world, the doorkeeper*, epith. of Hades, 8, 367. Od. 11, 276.
Πυλάρτης, αο, ὁ, prop. name of a Trojan, slain by Patroclus, 11, 491. 16, 696.
πυλαωρός, ὁ (ὥρα), Ep. for πυλωρός, *door-keeper, door-watch*, 21, 530. 24, 681; spoken of dogs, *22, 69.
πύλη, ἡ, *a door, a gate*, of a chamber, a house, or a town, mly in the plur. Ἀΐδαο πύλαι, the gates of Hades, as a periphrasis for death, 5. 646. 9, 312; poet. also πύλαι οὐρανοῦ, Ὀλύμπου, 5. 749. 8, 411; ὀνείρων, Od. 19, 562. In Hom. always in the plural; with reference to the two wings or leaves (valvæ); hence, a folding-door.
Πυληγενής, ές, see Πυλοιγενής.
*πυληδόκος, ὁ (δέχομαι), one who receives at the door, *a door-keeper*, h. Merc. 15.
Πυλήνη, ἡ, a town in Ætolia, later Proschium, 2, 639. Strab.
Πύλιος, η, ον (Πύλος), *of Pylos*, Pylian, ὁ Πύλιος γέρων = Nestor. Subst. the Pylian, 1, 248. Od. 3, 59.
Πυλόθεν, adv. *from Pylos*, Od. 16, 323.†
Πυλοιγενής, ές (γίγνομαι), *born in Pylos*, epith. of Nestor, 2, 54. 23, 303. The form Πυληγενής, h. Ap. 398. 424.
Πυλόνδε, adv. *to Pylos*, Od. 13, 274.
πύλος, ἡ = πύλη, *a door, a gate*; however only ἐν πύλῳ, which reading Wolf has adopted after Aristarch. 5, 397.† Ἀΐδου (Voss. 'at the gate Hades') is supplied, and it is referred to the fable, that Heracles, when he wished to bring up Cerberus, fought with Hades; cf. 8, 367. But as πύλος for πύλη does not occur elsewhere; and as we do not know who the νέκυες are, the reading ἐν Πύλῳ is adopted by Heyne. He refers it to the contest of Heracles with Neleus, in which he wounded Hades himself, cf. Apd. 2, 7. 3. Paus. 2, 7. 3, who quotes vs. 395—397; and Pind. Ol. 9, 31. cf. Ottf. Müller, Orchomen. I. p. 364.
Πύλος, ἡ (ὁ Strab.). According to Strabo and the well-known verse: Ἔστι Πύλος πρὸ Πύλοιο, Πύλος γε μέν ἐστι καὶ ἄλλη, Arist. Eq. 1059, there were in the Peloponnesus three cities of this name: 1) a town in the north of Elis on the Peneus, ὁ Ἠλειακός in Strab. 2) a town in Triphyllis (Elis), south of the Alphēus, near Lepreon and Samicon: ὁ Τριφυλιακός, Δεπρεατικός in Strab. 3) a town in Messenia, on the coast (hence called sandy) on the Pamisus, upon an elevation on the promontory Coryphasium, a city founded by Neleus, cf. Apd. 1, 9. 9. Strabo calls it ὁ Μεσσηνιακός, now the port *Old Navarino*. Even in anti-

Πύλων.

quity it was debated which of the last two towns was the city of Nestor. It is probable, at least in the Od., that it was the Messenide, as is maintained by Paus. 2, 3, and 4, 36; and amongst the moderns, by Mannert, Sickler, and Nitzsch, Rem. ad Od. I. p. 132. Strab. VIII. p. 342. regards the Triphylian Pylos as the residence of Nestor, and the river Alpheus seems to favour this opinion, Il. 11, 671—760; otherwise the Pylians would not have been able to convey to Pylos in the night the herds plundered from the Epeans, cf. Müller, Orchomen. I. p. 364. However, Πύλος in Hom., like Ἄργος, indicates not merely the city, but also the whole dominion of Nestor, which lay on both sides of the Alpheus, and extended to Messenia, cf. Strab. VIII. p. 337. If Pylos is taken in this sense, the passage may be very well reconciled with the supposition of Paus. Il. 1, 252. Od. 1. 93.

Πύλων, ωνος, a Trojan, slain by Polypoites, 12, 187.

πύματος, η, ον, Ep. (from πυθμήν), *the extreme, the last, the hindmost*, 4, 254. 10, 475. The neut. πύματον and πύματα, as adv. *at last, finally*. πύματόν τε καὶ ὕστατον, for the very last time, V.: 'yet once and finally,' also ὕστατα καὶ πύματα, Od. 4, 685. 20, 13.

πυνθάνομαι, poet. πεύθομαι, depon. mid. fut. πεύσομαι, aor. ἐπυθόμην, Ep. optat. πεπύθοιτο, perf. πέπυσμαι, pluperf. ἐπεπύσμην. (The form πυνθάνομαι only Od. 2, 315. 13, 256.) 1) *to seek, to ask for, to enquire after*, mostly with accus. νόστον πατρός, to seek for the return of his father, Od. 2, 360; with gen. πατρὸς οἰχομένοιο, Od. 1, 281. 2) Mly *to learn, to perceive, to hear*, often with accus. Il. 5, 702; also with gen. ἀγγελίης, to hear of news, 17, 641; μάχης, 15, 224; τί τινος, to hear any thing from or through any one, 17, 408; also ἐκ τινος, 20, 129; with partcp πυθόμην ὁρμαίνοντα ὁδόν, I had perceived him proceeding on his way, Od. 4, 732. πέπυστο υἱὸς πεσόντος, he perceived his son had fallen, 13, 522; with ὅτι, 13, 674. The pres. has the signification of the perf. Od. 3, 187. ἵπποι—πυθέσθην, plur. with dual, since horses were thought of in pairs, 17, 427.

πύξ, adv. (akin to πύκα), *with the fist, in pugilistic combat*. πὺξ ἀγαθός, excellent in boxing, 3, 237; μάχεσθαι, 23, 621; νικᾶν, Od. 8, 130.

πύξινος, η, ον (πύξος), *of box-wood*, 21, 269.†

πῦρ, πυρός, τό, plur. τὰ πυρά, the watch-fires (after the 2d decl.), *fire*, esply a sacrificial fire, also a funeral pile, 7, 410. 15, 350; often as an image of violence, danger, and destruction; hence proverb. ἐν πυρὶ γενέσθαι, to go into the fire, i. e. be destroyed, 2, 340. ἐκ πυρὸς αἰθομένοιο νοστῆσαι, to return from flaming fire, i. e. from great danger, 10,

Πυροφόρος.

246. The plur. τὰ πυρά, *watch-fires*, 8, 509. 9, 77. 10, 12.

πυρά, see πῦρ.

πυράγρη, ἡ (ἀγρέω), *a pair of tongs*, 18, 477. Od. 3, 434.

Πυραίχμης, ου, ὁ, Πυραίχμα (fire-fighter, αἰχμή), leader of the Paeonians, an ally of the Trojans, slain by Patroclus, 2, 848. 16, 287.

πυρακτέω (ἄγω), *to turn about in the fire, to harden*, τί, Od. 9, 328.†

Πέρασος, ὁ, 1) a Trojan, slain by Ajax, 17, 491. 2) ἡ, a town in the Thessalian Phthiōtis, having a grove sacred to Dēmētēr, 2, 695. (From πυρός the wheat-town.)

*πυραίθουσα, ἡ, Ep. 14, 11; perhaps a part of a potter's oven, ed. Herm. and Frank., but Wolf πῦρ' αἰθουσαν.

*πυραυγής, ές (αὐγή), *bright as fire, shining, brilliant*, Ep. 7, 6.

πυργηδόν, adv. (πύργος), prop. *turretwise*, metaph. *in troops* (in well-arranged squadrons, V.), espl in a square, *12. 43. 13, 152. 15, 618; see πύργος.

πύργος, ὁ, 1) *a tower*, espl upon a city wall, prob. only a kind of framework of wood, upon which armed men stood, 3, 153. 9, 574; hence also a wall with towers, 7, 338. Od. 6, 262. b) Metaph. *a bulwark, a bastion, a protection*, spoken of Ajax, Od. 11, 556; of a shield, Il. 7, 219. 11, 485. 2) *a body of troops arranged in a square*, generally, *a close squadron, a troop*, 4, 334. 347. 12, 332.

πυργόω (πύργος), aor. Ep. πύργωσα, *to furnish with towers, to fortify*, τί, Od. 11, 263.† Ep. 4, 3.

πυρετός, ὁ (πῦρ), *burning heat, glow or fever*, 22, 31.†

πυρή, ἡ (πῦρ), prop. a fire-place, espl *a funeral pile*, 1, 51. 4, 99. Od. 16, 521.

*πυρήϊον, τό, Ion. for πυρεῖον (πῦρ), is the plur. pieces of wood, with which fire was kindled by rubbing, *fire-implements*, h. Merc. 111.

πυρηφόρος, ον = πυροφόρος.

πυρίπηπς, ες (ἀκή), *pointed in the fire*, Od. 9, 387.†

πυρίκαυστος, ον (καίω), *burned with fire* ('hardened in the flame,' V.), σκῆλος, 13, 564.†

Πῦρις, a Trojan, slain by Patroclus, 16, 416.

Πυριφλεγέθων, οντος, ὁ (poet. for πυριφλέγων. flaming with fire), a river in the under world. Od. 10, 513.

πυρκαϊή, ἡ, Ion. for πυρκϊά (καίω), prop. *a blazing fire-place*; espl *a funeral pile*, *7, 428. 23, 158.

πύρνον, τό (sync. from πύρινον, adj. from πυρός, sc. σιτίον), *wheaten bread*, Od. 15, 312; plur. *Od. 17, 362.

πυρός, ὁ, *wheat*, in the plur., 11, 69. Od. 4, 604; as food for horses, 8, 188. 18, 569.

πυροφόρος, ον (φέρω), poet. also πυρηφόρος, ον, Od. 3, 495; *wheat-bearing*

*Πυρπαλαμάω.

(" sowed with wheat,' V.), ἄρουρα, πεδίον, *Il. 12, 314. 14, 123. 21, 602.
*πυρπαλαμάω (παλάμη), elsewhere depon. prop. to work with fire; according to Eustath. = κακοτεχνέω, to practise crafty devices. διὰ πυρπαλάμησεν ὀδοῦ, h. Merc. 157. ed. Wolf and Herm. But others διαπυρπαλάμησαν, cf. Frank.
πυρπολέω (πυρπόλος), to kindle a fire, to keep a watch-fire, Od. 10, 30.†
πυρσός, ὁ (πῦρ), a fire-brand, a torch, 18, 211.†
πώ, enclitic particle, somehow, in some way, yet; always in connexion with a negative, often compounded οὔπω, μήπω, not yet, or separately: οὔτε τί πω, 1, 108. Od 3, 23; οὐ γάρ πω, Il. 1, 262; μή δή πω, 15, 426.
πωλέομαι, depon. mid. (Ep. frequentat. of πέλομαι,) pres. 2 sing. πωλέ', i. e. πωλέεαι, partcp. Ion. πωλεύμενος, iterat. imperf. πωλέσκετο, fut. πωλήσομαι (veraor), to be frequently in a place, to frequent, to have intercourse, to come or go anywhere frequently, εἰς ἀγορήν, πόλεμον, 1, 490. 5, 788; εἰς ἡμέτερον, sc. δῶμα, Od. 2, 55; ἐς εὐνήν, h. Ap. 170; μετ' ἄλλους, Od. 9, 189.
πωλέσκετο, see πωλέομαι.
*πωλέω, ήσω, to sell, Ep. 14, 5.
πῶλος, ὁ, a young horse, a foal, a colt, 11, 681. Od. 23, 246. h. in Ap. 231.
πῶμα, τό, the cover of a quiver, of a chest and a cup, 4, 116. Od. 2, 353.
πώποτε, adv. (ποτέ), at some time, at any time, mly after a negat.: οὐ πώποτε, not at any time, never yet, 1, 106. 3, 442.
πῶς, adv. interrog. how? in what way? and often connected with other particles: πῶς γάρ; for how! πῶς δή; how indeed! πῶς γὰρ δή; πῶς ἄρα; πῶς νῦν; how now? i. e. what thinkest thou? Od. 18, 223. It stands a) With indicat. Il. 1, 123. 10, 61. b) With subj. 18, 188. Od. 3, 22. c) With optat., Il. 11, 838. d) πῶς ἄν and πῶς κε, with optat. 9, 437. Od. 1, 65.
πώς, enclitic particle (πός), in some way, somehow, in any way, after another particle: αἴ κέν πως, if by any means, 1, 66; οὐ μέν πως, in no way, 4, 158; οὐκ ἄν πως, Od. 20, 392.
πωτάομαι, poet. form of πέτομαι, to fly. λίθοι πωτῶντο, 12, 287.† h. Ap. 442. 30, 4.
πῶϋ, εος, τό, dat. plur. poet. πώεσι, a flock, always spoken of sheep: hence, οἴων πῶϋ and πώεα μήλων, 3, 198. 11, 678. Od. 4, 413.

P.

P, the seventeenth letter of the Greek alphabet; hence the sign of the seventeenth rhapsody.

Ῥάπτω.

ῥα, an enclitic particle, Ep. for ἄρα, often before a vowel, ῥ', see ἄρα.
ῥάβδος, ἡ (ῥάπις), = rod, a staff, a wand; in the plur. rods for fastening the leather to the shield, 12, 297; esply, 1) the wand of Hermes, the magic-rod, to compose to sleep and to awaken men, 24, 343. Od. 5, 47. 24, 2. h. Merc. 210. 526. 2) the magic wand of Kirkê (Circe), Od. 10, 238. 319; of Athênê, Od. 13, 429. 3) an angling rod, Od. 12, 251.
ῥαδαλός, ἡ, όν, a reading of Zenodot. for ῥοδανός, 18, 576; which is explained as a form of κραδαλός, easily moved.
ῥαδανός, a false reading in 18, 576; see ῥοδανός.
'Ραδάμανθυς, υος, ὁ, son of Zeus and Europa, brother of Minos, 14, 321, 322. According to Od. 4, 565, he was translated, as being the son of Zeus, to Elysium. The Phæaces conveyed him at one time to Eubœa, Od. 7, 322. According to a later tradition, he was expelled by his brother from Crete, and fled to Bœotia. On account of his justice he was made judge in the under world, Apd. 3, 1. 2.
ῥαδινός, ἡ, όν, poet. slender, flexible; ἱμάσθλη, 23, 585; † hence, agile, active, fleet, πόδες, h. Cer. 183. [From this was derived the false reading ῥοδανός, in 18, 576.]
ῥαθάμιγξ, ιγγος, ἡ, poet. (ῥαθαμίζω), a drop. plur. 11, 536; metaph. κονίης ῥαθάμιγγες, drops, i. e. particles of dust, 23, 502.
ῥαίνω, from theme 'ΡΑΖΩ, Ep. aor. Imperat. ῥάσσατε, Od. 20, 150; perf. pass. 3 plur. Ion. ἐῤῥάδαται, pluperf. ἐῤῥάδατο, see Buttm. § 103. IV. 3. Rost, Dial. § 52. c, to sprinkle, to besprinkle, to bestrew, τί τινι, any thing with another, esply with dust, αἵματι δ' ἐῤῥάδαται τοῖχοι, the walls are drenched with blood, Od. 20, 354; ἐῤῥάδατο, Il. 12, 431.
ῥαιστήρ, ῆρος, ἡ, poet. (ῥαίω), a hammer, 18, 477;† elsewhere masc.
ῥαίω, poet. fut. Ep. infin. ῥαισέμεναι for ῥαίσειν, aor. 1 ἔῤῥαισα, aor. pass. ἐῤῥαίσθην, to break in pieces, to strike in pieces, to destroy, to dash in pieces, νῆα, Od. 13, 151; τινά, to dash about any one, esply spoken of shipwrecked persons, Od. 5, 221. 6, 326. Pass. to burst asunder, to fly in pieces, Il. 16, 339. τῷ κέ οἱ ἐγκέφαλος διὰ σπέος θεινομένου ῥαίοιτο πρὸς οὔδει, then should the brain of him dashed in pieces, fly through the cave over the ground, Od. 9, 459. The gen. of the partcp. comes from the circumstance that Hom uses the dat. of the pron. instead of the gen. Kühner II. § 587.
ῥάκος, εος. τό (ῥήγνυμι), prop. a piece torn off, a rag, a shred, a fragment of cloth; an old garment, a frock, Od. 14. 342.
ῥαπτός, ἡ, όν (ῥάπτω), sewed together, patched, *Od. 24, 228, 229.
ῥάπτω, aor. 1 Ep. ῥάψα, 1) to sew

Ράριος.

together, to join together, to stitch. τί, any thing. βοείας θαμειὰς χρυσείης ῥάβδοισι διηνεκέσιν, to fasten the numerous hides with golden rods running quite around (that the leather might not warp), 12, 296. 2) Metaph. to plot, to machinate, to derive craftily, κακά τινι, 18, 367. Od. 3, 718; φόνον, Od. 16, 379. 422.

Ράριος, ιη, ιον, Rharian; τὸ Ῥάριον, the Rharian plain, in Eleusis, which was sacred to Dêmêtêr, and upon which the first grain is said to have been sown, h. Cer. 350. Ῥάριος is to be written without the spiritus asper, cf. Herm. ad l. c.

ῥάσσατε, see ῥαίνω.
*ῥαφάνη, ἡ, radish, Batr. 53.
ῥαφή, ἡ (ῥάπτω), a seam, Od. 22, 186.†
ῥάχις, ιος, ἡ (ῥάσσω), a back-bone, a back-piece, 9, 208.†
ῥαψῳδία, ἡ (ῥάπτω, ᾠδή), prop. a poem chanted by a rhapsodist; esply a single book of the Hom. poems, a rhapsody.

Ῥέα, ἡ, mly Ep. and Ion. Ῥείη, h. Ap. 93; gen. Ῥείης, 14, 203. Ῥέα, monosyllabic, 15, 187.† Ῥέη, h. Cer. 459; daughter of Uranus and Gaea, wife and sister of Kronus (Saturn), mother of Zeus, Poseidôn, Hades, Hestia (Vesta), Dêmêtêr, and Hêrê, 14, 203. 15, 187. h. Cer. 60, 442. (According to Plat. Cratyl. p. 402, from ῥεῖν, to flow, Herm. Fluonia, quod ex ea omnia effluxerint; according to others, ἔρα, the earth by metathesis.)

ῥέα and ῥεῖα, adv. poet. of ῥᾴδιος, easily, without trouble, θεοὶ ῥεῖα ζώοντες, the gods who live without labour or trouble, 6, 138. Od. 4, 805. (ῥέα is used by Hom. as monosyllabic, Il. 5, 304. 12, 381; and often.)

ῥέεθρον, τό, Ion. and poet. for ῥεῖθρον (ῥέω), a current, a stream; always plur. ῥέεθρα, the floods, the waves, 2, 461. Od. 6, 317; once ῥείθρα. h. 18, 9.

ῥέζω, poet. fut. ῥέξω, aor. 1 ἔρρεξα, and ἔρεξα, pass. only aor. pass. infin. ῥεχθῆναι, partcp. ῥεχθείς, cf. ἔρδω, from which it is formed by metathesis. 1) to do, to make, to effect, with adv. or with accus. αἴσυλα, to practise impiety, 5, 403; with double accus. τινά τι, to do any thing to any one: κακόν or κακά τινα, 2, 195. 4, 32; rarely τί τινι, Od. 20, 314; εὖ ῥέζειν τινά, to benefit any one, Il. 5, 650; on the other, κακῶς τινα, to abuse any one, Od. 23, 56; pass. ῥεχθὲν κακόν, 9, 250. ῥεχθὲν δέ τε νήπιος ἔγνω, even a simpleton knows what has happened, Il. 17, 32. 2) Esply to sacrifice; prop. ἱερά, to offer sacrifices, θεῷ, to a god, 8, 250; ἑκατόμβην, to offer a hecatomb, θαλύσια, to present the first fruits, 9, 535; βοῦν θεῷ, 10, 292.

ῥέθος, εος, τό, poet. a limb, only plur. *16, 856. 22, 68, 362.
ῥεῖα, adv. = ῥέα, q. v.
Ῥείη, ἡ, see Ῥέα.
ῥεῖθρον, τό, poet. for ῥέεθρον, q. v.

Ῥηιδιος.

Ῥεῖθρον, τό, a port in Ithaca, north of the city, Od. 1, 186; see Ἰθάκη.

ῥέπω (akin to ῥέω), to bend down, to sink; esply spoken of a balance, to sink and thereby give the preponderance or decision. ῥέπε αἴσιμον ἦμαρ Ἀχαιῶν, the fated day of the Greeks preponderated. i. e. the misfortune of the Greeks was decided, 8, 72; spoken of Hector, 22, 212.

ῥερυπωμένος, see ῥυπόω.
ῥεχθείς, see ῥέζω.
ῥέω, imperf. ἔρρεον, Ep. ῥέον, an. ἐρρύην, Ep. ῥύη, Od. 3, 455. 1) to flow, to run, spoken of water, blood, and sweat: also of brains, Il. 3, 300; with dat. πηγῇ ῥέει ὕδατι, the fountain runs with water. 22, 149; ῥέεν αἵματι. γαῖα, the ground flows with blood, 4, 451. 2) metaph. to flow, to stream forth spoken of discourse: ἀπὸ γλώσσης μέλι αὐδή, 1, 249; of missiles: ἐκ χειρῶν, issue from the hands, 12, 159; τῶν δὲ μελέων τρίχες ἔρρεον, the hairs fell from their limbs, Od. 10, 393.

ῬΕΩ, from this the aor. pass. partc. ῥηθείς; ἐπὶ ῥηθέντι δικαίῳ (a just sentence, V.). Od. 18, 114. 20, 322; see εἴπω and φημί.

ῥηγμίν, ῖνος, ὁ (ῥήγνυμι), in the nom. not used: 1) a high shore, upon which the waves break, a breaker, 1, 437. Od. 1, 430. 2) breaking waves themselves, the dashing waves, Il. 20, 229. Od. 12, 214. Voss maintains that it never means shore (as the Scholiasts assert), but always the waves breaking upon the shore.

ῥήγνυμι, another form ῥήσσω, item. imperf. ῥήγνυσκε, fut. ῥήξω, aor. ἔρρηξα, Ep. ῥῆξα, mid. aor. 1 ἐρρηξάμην, Ep. ῥηξάμην, 1) to tear, to tear in pieces, to break in pieces, to dash in pieces, with accus. χαλκόν, ἱμάντα, νευρήν; πύλας, to break through gates, 13, 124. b) Esply in war: to break through the ranks. φάλαγγας, ὁμίλον, στίχας, 6, 6. 11, 53. 15, 615. 2) Absol. to stamp, to strike. prop. πέδον ποσί, to stamp the ground with the feet, in the form ῥήσσω, 18, 571. h. Ap. 516. Mid. 1) to break, spoken of the sea, ῥήγνυτο κῦμα, 18, 67. 4, 425. 2) to break through any thing for oneself, to dash through, with accus. τεῖχος, φάλαγγας, 12, 90. 440. 11, 92. 3) to let break out, with accus. ἔριδα, 20, 55.

ῥῆγος, εος, τό (ῥήγνυμι), prop. a piece torn off, a rug, a covering, a carpet, prob. of wool, in oppos. to λίνον, Od. 13, 73; often in the plur. coverings, coverlets which were spread over beds, Il. 9, 661. 24, 644. Od. 3, 349; or over chairs, Od. 10, 352.

ῥηίδιος, η, ον, Ion. and Ep for ῥᾴδιος, compar ῥηίτερος, η, ον, superl. ῥηίτατος and ῥήιστος, η, ον (from ῬΗΞ) compar without pains, with infin. τάφρον εὑρεῖαν ῥηιδίῃ, a ditch easy to pass, with dat. of the pers. and infin. 20, 265. Od. 16, 211 [ῥηῖδ. ἔπος, an easy response, one easily complied with, Od. 11, 146]; ῥηιτέρα πολεμίζειν ἦσαν Ἀχαιοί for ῥηίτερον ἦν πόλεμ. τοῖς Ἀχαιοῖς, the Greeks were more easy to war against, Il. 18, 258. cf. 4, 243.

ῥηιδίως, adv. *easily, without trouble,* t, 390. Od. 8, 376.

ῥήιστος, η, ον, superl. of ῥηίδιος.

ῥηίτατος, η, ον, superl. of ῥηίδιος.

ῥηίτερος, η, ον, compar. of ῥηίδιος.

ῥηκτός, ή, όν (ῥήγνυμι), *torn, that may be torn,* poet. spoken of a man: χαλκῷ ῥηκτός, *that may be injured by the brass weapon), (vulnerable by it,* V. *"Whose flesh the spear can penetrate,"* Cp.), 13, 323.†

*'Ρήναια. ἡ, Ep. (more correctly 'Ρήναια), for 'Ρήνεια ('Ρηνέη, Hdt. 'Ρηνία, Plut.), an island, one of the Cyclades separated from Delos only by a strait, where all the dead of Delos were buried, now *Great Delos,* h. Ap. 44.

'Ρήνη, ἡ, concubine of Oileus, mother of Medon, 2, 728.

ῥηξηνορίη, ἡ (ῥηξήνωρ), *the valour that breaks through troops or ranks of men* (*"phalanx-breaking might,"* Cp.), Od. 14, 217.†

ῥηξήνωρ, ορος, ὁ (ἀνήρ), *dashing men in pieces;* breaker of the ranks of war (Cp.), epith. of Achilles, 7, 228. Od. 4, 5.

'Ρηξήνωρ, ορος, ὁ, son of Nausithöus, brother of Alcinöus, Od. 7, 63.

ῥῆσις, ιος, ἡ ('ΡΕΩ), *the act of telling, speaking; discourse, speech,* Od. 21, 291.†

'Ρῆσος, ὁ, 1) son of Eioneus, king of the Thracians, 10, 435, seq.; or, according to Apd. l. 3. 3, son of Strymon and a Muse; Diomēdes and Odysseus (Ulysses) slew him and seized his famous horses, Il. l. c. 2) a river in Troas which flowed into the Granīcus, 12, 20.

ῥήσσω, a form of ῥήγνυμι, q. v.

ῥητήρ, ῆρος, ὁ, poet. ('ΡΕΩ), *an orator, a speaker,* μύθων, 9, 443.†

ῥητός, ή, όν ('ΡΕΩ), *said, spoken; esply expressly mentioned, definite,* μισθός, 21, 445.†

ῥήτρη, ἡ ('ΡΕΩ), *a speech, a sentence;* hence, *an agreement, a convention,* Od. 14, 393.†

ῥιγεδανός, ή, όν (ῥιγέω), *shivering, that inspires shuddering, horrible, odious,* epith. of Helen, 19, 326.†

ῥιγέω, poet. (ῥῖγος), fut. ῥιγήσω, aor. ἐρρίγησα, perf. ἔρριγα, prop. *to shiver with cold, to be cold,* in H. always metaph. 1) Intrans. *to shudder, to be terrified, to be struck with fear,* mly absol. 3, 259; with partcp. 4, 279. 12, 331; or with a particle of time, 12, 108. 2) Trans. *to shudder before, to shrink trembling before,* τί; *to fear,* πόλεμον, 5, 351. 17, 175. Instead of the accus. the infin. 3, 353; or with μή following, Od. 23, 216. The perf. has a pres. signif. Il. 7, 114.

ῥίγιον, poet. compar. of ῥῖγος, used only in the neut.; also superl. ῥίγιστος,

ῥ, ων, 1) *more chilly, more cold,* Od. 17, 191. 2) Metaph. *more terrible, more fearful, more horrible.* τὸ δὲ ῥίγιον, Il. 1, 325. Od. 20, 220. τὰ ῥίγιστα, *the most terrible things, most horrible,* Il. 5, 873.†

'Ρίγμος, ὁ, son of Peirous, from Thrace, an ally of the Trojans, 20, 485, seq.

ῥῖγος, εος, τό, *cold, chilliness,* Od. 5, 472.†

ῥιγόω (ῥῖγος), fut. infin. Ep. ῥιγωσέμεν, *to be cold, to feel chilly,* Od. 14, 481.†

ῥίζα, ἡ, *a root* of plants; also as a remedy, 11, 846; metaph. spoken of the eye, Od. 9, 390.

ῥιζόω (ῥίζα), aor. ἐρρίζωσα, perf. pass. ἐρρίζωμαι, *to cause to take root, to plant,* ἀλωήν, Od. 7, 122. 2) *to root, to fasten,* spoken of a ship which Poseidōn changes to stone, *Od. 13, 163.

*ῥικνός, ή, όν (ῥῖγος), *stiff,* contracted with cold; generally, *bent, crooked,* πόδας, h. Ap. 317.

ῥίμφα, adv. (ῥίπτω), prop. *hurled,* hence *quickly, fleetly, swiftly,* 6, 511. Od. 8, 193.

ῥίν, better ῥίς, q. v.

ῥινόν, τό = ῥινός, *a shield.* εἴσατο δ' ὡς ὅτε ῥινὸν ἐν-πόντῳ, it appeared to him as a shield in the sea (spoken of Phæacia). The neut. is the later form, Od. 5, 281.†

ῥινός, ἡ, 1) *the skin* of the human body, 5, 308; also plur. Od. 5, 426. 14, 134. 2) *the skin* of an animal drawn off, *the hide,* Il. 7, 474. ῥινὸς λύκοιο, a wolf's skin, 10, 334; esply of horned cattle, 10, 155; hence 3) *a shield* which was made of ox-hide, with βοῶν, 12, 263; and often alone, 4, 447. ῥινοῦ τε, βοῶν τ' εὐποιητάων seems, according to Aristarch., a case of hendiadys, like πόλεμόν τε μάχην (V. *leather* and *well-prepared ox-hide),* 16, 636.

ῥινοτόρος, ὁ (τορέω), *piercing the skin* or the shield, *shield-breaking,* epith. of Arēs, 21, 392.†

ῥίον, τό, *the projecting point of a mountain;* hence 1) *a peak, a mountain-summit,* 8, 25; a rock, h. Ap. 383. 2) Esply *a promontory,* Od. 3, 295.

ῥιπή, ἡ (ῥίπτω), *a cast, a thrust, a throw, violence, force* with which any thing is thrown, 8, 355. h. Ap. 447. b) the force which any thing thrown has. ῥ. λᾶος, a stone's cast, 12, 462. Od. 8, 192; αἰγανέης, the cast of a spear, Il. 16, 589; and generally, *force, violence* of the wind and of fire, 15, 171. 21, 12.

'Ρίπη, ἡ, a town in Arcadia near Stratus, 2, 606.

*ῥιπίζω (ῥιπίς), partcp. aor. ῥιπίσσας, *to put in motion, to excite,* ἔριν, Fr. Hom. 26.

*ῥιπτάζω (frequent. from ῥίπτω), *to fling hither and thither, to hurl about,* as abuse, θεοὺς κατὰ δῶμα, 14, 257.+ 2) Intrans. *to move convulsively, to twitch,* ῥιπτάζεσκεν ὀφρῦσι, h. Merc. 279.

ῥίπτασκον, see ῥίπτω.

ῥίπτω, Ep. iterat. imperf. ῥίπτασκον,

ῥίπτω, aor. ἔρριψα, Ep. ῥίψα, to cast, to sling, to hurl, τινὰ ἀπὸ βηλοῦ, 1, 591; ἐς Τάρταρον, 8, 13. Bair. 97; τὶ μετά τινα, to cast any thing at any one, 3, 378. Od. 6, 115; ἔριψεν (Matthiæ ἔραψεν), h. Merc. 79.

ῥίς, ῥινός, ἡ, later ῥίν, *the nose*, plur. ῥῖνες the nostrils, 14, 467. 19, 39. Od. 5, 456.

ῥίψ, ῥιπός, ἡ, dat plur. ῥίπεσσι, *a reed, a rush*; plur. *osier-work, a hurdle, a mat*, Od. 5, 256.†

*ῥοδάνη, ἡ, *the thread* of the woof, the woof, Batr. 186.

ῥοδανός, ἡ, όν, *pliant, flexible* [= εὐκίνητος]. 18, 576. παρὰ ῥοδανὸν δονακῆα, by a waving thicket of reeds. This is the reading of Wolf after Aristarch., which Damm after Eustath. strangely derives from ῥοή, whence ῥοανός, ῥοδανός; it is akin to κραδάω. Other readings are: ῥαδαλός, ῥαδανός, ῥαδινός, the last according to Apoll. from ῥᾳδίως δονεῖσθαι.

*Ῥόδεια, ἡ (the rosy), daughter of Oceanus and Tethys, companion of Persephōnē, h. Cer. 419.

Ῥόδιος, η, ον, see Ῥόδος.

Ῥόδιος, ὁ, or Ῥοδιός (with accent changed), a river in Troas, north of cape Dardanis, 12, 20.

ῥοδοδάκτυλος, ον, poet. (δάκτυλος), *rosy-fingered*, epith. of (Eos) Aurora. since she was conceived of as youthful, or according to Eustath. from the colour of the dawning east, 6, 175. Od. 2, 5.

ῥοδόεις, εσσα, εν. poet. (ῥόδον), *of roses, rosy*; ἔλαιον, oil of roses, which in the opinion of the ancients prevented putrefaction, 23, 186.†

*ῥόδον, τό, *a rose*, h. Cer. 6.

*Ῥοδόπη, ἡ (having a rosy countenance), daughter of Oceanus and Tethys, h. Cer. 422.

*ῥοδόπηχυς, ὁ, ἡ, poet. (πῆχυς), *rosy-armed*, h. Cer. 31. 6.

Ῥόδος, ἡ, Rhodus, *Rhodes*, a famous island in the Carpathian sea, on the coast of Asia, with three cities, Lindus, Ialysus, and Cameirus; now *Rhodis*, 2, 655. The chief city, Rhodus, was built at a later date, whose harbour is famed on account of the Colossus, Strabo; from this Ῥόδιος, η, ον, *Rhodian*; subst. a *Rhodian*, 2, 654.

ῥοή, ἡ (ῥέω), *a flowing, a current*, always in the pur. *the floods, the waves*, spoken of Oceanus and of rivers, 2, 869. Od 6. 216.

ῥόθιος, η, ον (ῥόθος), *roaring, resounding*, esply spoken of water, κῦμα, Od. 5, 412.†

ῥοιά, ἡ, *the pomegranate*, both fruit and tree, Od. 7, 15. 11, 589. h. Cer. 373. 412.

ῥοιβδέω (ῥοῖβδος), aor. optat. ῥοιβδήσειεν, prop. *to sup or gulp up, to swallow with noise*, spoken of Charybdis, Od. 12, 106.†

ῥοιζέω (ῥοῖζος), aor. 1 Ep. ῥοίζησε, to *whizz, to hiss*, and generally spoken of any sharp sound, *to whistle*, 10, 502.†

ῥοῖζος, ὁ, Ion. and Ep. ἡ, *whistling, whizzing, hissing*, spoken of arrows and spears in rapid motion, 16, 361; of the whistling of the Cyclops, Od. 9, 315. (Akin to ῥέω.)

ῥόος, ὁ (ῥέω), *flowing; a river, a stream, a current*; only sing often with gen. Ἀλφειοῖο, Ὠκεανοῖο. 11, 726. 16, 151. κὰρ (Ep. for κατά) ῥόον, down the stream, 12, 33. κατὰ ῥόον, Od. 14, 254. ἀνὰ ῥόον up stream, Il. 12, 33.

ῥόπαλον, τό (ῥέπω), a *staff* that is thicker towards the top, *a cudgel, a club*, 11, 559. 561; of the Cyclops, Od. 9, 319. παγχάλκεον, the brazen club of Orion, Od. 11, 575.

ῥοχθέω, poet. (ῥόχθος), *to roar, to resound*, spoken of the waves which dash upon the shore, *Od. 5, 402. 12, 60.

ῥύατο, see ῥύομαι.

ῥυδόν, adv. (ῥέω, ῥυῆναι), *in a stream, abundantly, immoderately*, ἀφνειός, Od. 15, 426.†

ῥύη, Ep. for ἐρρύη, see ῥέω.

ῥυμός, ὁ (ἐρύω), *the pole by which draught-animals draw the chariot*, *Il. 729. 10, 505. cf. ἅρμα.

ῥύομαι, depon. mid. (prop. mid. of ῥύω, but only in the signif. *to deliver*, aor. 1 ἐρρυσάμην, Ep. ῥυσάμην, syncop. form of the pass. infin. ῥῦσθαι, 15, 141. imperf. 3 plur. ῥύατ' for ἐρρύοντα, 15, 515; iterat. imperf. 2 sing. ῥύσκευ, 1 *to deliver, to rescue, to liberate*, τινὰ ἐκ κακοῦ, any one from evil, Od. 12, 107. ὑπ' ἠέρος, Il. 17, 645. cf. Od. 1, 6. 2) Generally, *to deliver, to protect, to shelter, to preserve, to defend*, with acc. a) Spoken of gods and men, Il. 15, 257. ὑπό τινος, from any one, 17, 224. b) Spoken of things, esply of weapons, Il. 239. 12, 8: μήδεα φωτός, to protect, i e. to cover the man's shame, Od. 6, 619. 3) *to have under guard, to detain, to restrain*, Ἡδ, Od. 23, 246. (υ has a variable quantity in the pres. and imperf.; on the other hand, it is long in the derived tenses before σ, cf. Spitzner, Pros. § 2. 6. According to Buttm., Lex. in voc. ν is short in the fut. and aor. cf. Rost Gram. p. 302.)

ῥύπα, τά, see ῥύπος.

ῥυπάω, Ep. ῥυπόω, *to be dirty, foul*, Od. 19, 72. 23, 115. Partcp. ῥυπόωντα *Od. 13, 435. 6, 87. 24, 227. *Od.

ῥύπος, ὁ, metaplast. plur. τὰ ῥύπα *filth, foulness*, Od. 6, 93.† (Sing. τὸ ῥύπον or ῥύπος is doubtful.)

ῥυπόω, partcp. perf. Ep. ῥερυπωμένα for ἐρρυπ., *to defile, to soil*, Od. 6, 59.† 2) Ep. for ῥυπάω, q. v.

ῥῦσθαι, see ῥύομαι.

ῥύσιον, τό (ἐρύω), PYΩ), prop. *that which is dragged away, booty, plunder*, esply τὰ ῥύσια, that which is taken away from one who injures us, in order to compel satisfaction, *a pledge, a hostage*,

*Ρύσκεν. ρύσια ἐλαύνεσθαι, to drive off booty as a reprisal, 11, 674.†

ρύσκεν, Ep. for ρύσκον, see ρύομαι.

ρῡσός, ή, όν (ἐρύω), prop. drawn together, hence shrivelled, wrinkled, epith. of the Litae, 9, 503.†

ρυστάζω (frequent. from 'ΡΥΩ, ἐρύω), Ep. literat. imperf. ρυστάζεσκεν, poet. to draw hither and thither, to drag, to trail, with accus. of the corpse of Hector, 24, 755. 2) Generally, to pull about, to abuse, γυναίκας, Od. 16, 109. 20, 319.

ρυστακτύς, ύος, ή, poet. (ρυστάζω), the act of dragging around, pulling about, generally, abusing, Od. 18, 224.†

ρῡτήρ, ἠρος, ὁ ('ΡΥΩ, ἐρύω), prop. one drawing; hence 1) a drawer of the bow, Od. 21, 173; ὀϊστῶν, the shooter of arrows, Od. 18, 262. 21, 173. 2) the strap on the bit of horses in which they draw, or a rein. ἐν δὲ ῥυτῆρσι τάνυσθεν, they ran in the reins, see τανύω, Il. 16, 475. 3) (ῥύομαι), a protector, a watch, σταθμῶν, Od. 17, 187. 223.

'Ρύτιον, τό, a town in Crete, later prob. 'Ριθυμνία, now Retimo, 2, 648.

ρῡτός, ή, όν, poet. ('ΡΥΩ, ἐρύω), drawn on, drawn to, dragged on, spoken of large stones, *Od. 6, 267. 14, 10.

ρωγαλέος, η, ον (ρώξ), torn asunder, split, cut apart, 2, 417. Od. 13, 435. 17, 198.

ρώξ, ρωγός, ὁ and ἡ, poet. (ἔρρωγα, perf. from ῥήγνυμι), a rent, a fissure. ρῶγες μεγάροιο are according to Eustath. δίοδοι, passages; Apoll. θυρίδες, sidedoors of the hall; Etym. Mag. ἀναβάσεις; and Voss translates: ἀνὰ ῥῶγ. μεγ., up the stairs of the house; Wiedasch [and Cp.] correctly. the galleries of the house, Od. 22, 143.†

ῥώομαι, depon. mid. only 3 plur. imperf. ἐρρώοντο and ῥώοντο, and aor. ἐρρώσαντο, 1) to move oneself violently and rapidly. γούνατα δ' ἐρρώσαντο, Od. 23, 3. cf. Il. 18, 411. χαῖται ἐρρώοντο, the manes fluttered, 23, 367. 2) Esply to go rapidly, to hasten, to run, to rush, 11, 60; ἀμφί τινα, 16, 166. 24, 616; πυρὴν πέρι, Od. 24, 69. ὑπὸ δ' ἀμφίπολοι ῥώοντο ἄνακτι, the handmaids hastened with the king, Köppen; or, they exerted themselves for the king (supported the king, V.), Il. 18, 417. 3) Trans. with accus. χορόν, to speed the dance i. e. to dance, h. Ven. 262.

ῥωπήϊον, τό, Ion. for ῥωπεῖον (ῥώψ), a place grown up with bushes, a thicket, a coppice, mly plur. πυκνὰ ῥωπήϊα, 13, 199. 21, 559. Od. 14, 473. h. 18, 8.

ῥωχμός, ὁ (ῥώξ), a rent, a fissure, a cleft, 23, 420.†

ῥώψ, ῥωπός, ή, poet. (akin to ῥίψ), a low bush, bushes, shrubbery, brambles, plur. *Od. 10, 166. 14, 19. 16, 47.

Σ.

Σ, the eighteenth letter of the Greek alphabet; the sign, therefore, of the eighteenth book.

σ', apostroph. for σά. 2) More rarely for σοί [perhaps in 1, 170, but cf. φύσω, Am. Ed.]. 3) For σά, Od. 1, 356.

*Σαβάκτης, pr. n. a domestic goblin, Ep. 14, 9.

Σαγγάριος, ὁ, the largest river in Bithynia, rising near the village Sangia at the mountain Didymus, flowing through Phrygia and falling into the Pontus, now Sakarja, 3, 187. 16, 719.

*Σαιδήνη, ή, a lofty mountain in Asia Minor, near Cymê, Ep. 1, 3.

σαίνω (akin to σεύω), aor. ἔσηνα, to wag, to move, prop. spoken of dogs, Od. 10, 217. 219. 16, 6; οὐρῇ, with the tail, *Od. 17, 302; of wolves, h. Ven. 70.

σακέσπαλος, ὁ (πάλλω), shield-shaking, (shield-brandishing), epith. of Tydeus, 15, 126.†

σάκος, εος, τό, a shield; prop. distinct from ἀσπίς, prob. larger than that. It was made of several ox-hides stretched one over another; the largest shield mentioned by Homer consisted of seven layers of ox-hide, above which was a plate of beaten brass, 7, 219, seq. It was besides variously adorned, see 11, 32, seq., and esply the description of the shield of Achilles received from Hêphaestus, 18, 478, seq.

Σαλαμίς, ῖνος, ή, later Σαλαμίν, 1) an island off the coast of Attica, which at an earlier period constituted a state, but afterwards came under the dominion of Athens, now Κoluri; from it Αἴας (Ajax) conducted twelve ships to Troy, 2, 557. 2) a town in Cyprus, founded by the Salaminian Teucros (Teucer), now Porto Constanza, h. 9, 4.

Σαλμωνεύς, ῆος, ὁ, son of Æolus and Enaretê, father of Tyrô; he reigned first in Thessaly, migrated to Elis, and built the city Salmônê. In his pride he wished to be equal to Zeus, and imitated thunder and lightning by riding in a brazen chariot upon a copper floor and hurling down blazing torches. Zeus struck him with lightning, Od. 11, 236.

σάλπιγξ, γγος, ή, a trumpet with which the signal of attack was given, 18, 219.† This is the only passage in which this instrument is mentioned; perhaps it was used as a signal in sieges.

σαλπίζω, fut. σαλπίγξω, to sound a trumpet, Batr. 203; metaph. to resound like a trumpet. ἀμφὶ δὲ σάλπιγξεν οὐρανός (the heaven round about resounded like a trumpet, V.), spoken of thunder, 21, 388.† 2) Trans. with accus. to peal forth, to trumpet, Batr. 202.

Σάμη, ή, or Σάμος, 2, 634. Od. 4, 671;

B 6

Σάμος.   372   **Σαφέως.**

an island near Ithaca, which belonged to the kingdom of Odysseus (Ulysses), later *Cephallenia*, now *Cephallonia*. It is separated from Ithaca by a narrow strait, Od. 1, 246. 9, 24. h. Ap. 429.

Σάμος, ή 1) = Σάμη, q v. 2) Σάμος Θρηϊκίη, later Σαμοθράκη, *Samothrace*, an island of the Ægean sea, on the coast of Thrace, opposite the mouth of the river Hebrus, later famed by the mysteries of the Cabeiri, having a town of the same name, now *Samothraki*, 13, 12; also simply Σάμος, 24, 78. 753. 3) an island in the Ægean sea, on the coast of Ionia, having a town of the same name, famed for its splendid temple of Hêrê, h. Ap. 41.

*σάνδαλον, τό, *a sole of wood*, which was bound to the feet by thongs, *a sandal*, h. Merc. 79. 83.

σανίς, ίδος, ή. 1) *a board, a plank*. 2) *any thing made of boards*; hence *a) doors*, always plur. σανίδες, *folding doors* [valvæ]. 9, 583. Od. 2, 344. *b) a scaffold of boards, a stage*, sing. Od. 21, 51.

ΣΑΟΣ, obsol. ground form of σώς, σόος, from which the compar. σαώτερος, η, ον. σαώτερος ώς κε νέηαι, that thou mayest return the more safely home, 1, 32;† prop. compar. with only a slight degree of augmentation (cf. Thiersch, § 202. 10). On the other hand, Buttm., Gr. Gram. § 49. N. 8, considers it as a simple positive.

σαοφροσύνη, ή, Ep. for σωφροσύνη (φρήν), prop. *a sound understanding, discretion, prudence*, *Od. 23, 13. 30.

σαόφρων, ονος, ό, ή, Ep. for σώφρων (φρήν), *discreet, intelligent, prudent*, 21, 462. Od. 4, 158 (later, *temperate, abstinent*).

σαόω, contr. σώ. from which poet. σόω and σόω, Ep. form of σώζω (which occurs only once, Od. 5, 490, in the partcp. pres., but where prob. the reading should be σώων). Hom. has 1) From σαόω, fut. σαώσω, aor. έσάωσα, fut. mid. σαώσομαι, Od. 21, 309; aor. pass. έσαώθην, also imp. pres. act. σάω for σάοε, contr. σώ, and extended by α, σάω, cf. ναιετάωσα, Od. 13, 230. 17, 595; 3 sing. imperf. σάον for έσάοε, contr. σώ, and extended σάω, Il. 16, 363. 2) The contracted form σώ does not occur; but the extended forms, *a)* σόω (from which σώζω), whence partcp. σώοντες and imperf. σώεσκον. *b)* σόω, from this subj. pres. σόη, σόης, σόωσι. 1) *to sustain in life, to save, to keep unconsumed, to preserve, to deliver*, τινά, also ζωούς. 21, 238; hence pass. *to be saved, to remain alive*, 15, 503: in oppos. to ἀπολέσθαι, 17, 228. *b)* Spoken of things: νῆας, πόλιν; also σπέρμα πυρός [semina flamma, Virg.], to preserve the seeds of fire, Od. 5, 490. 2) *to rescue, to deliver, to bring safely*, with accus. from what? έκ φλοίσβοιο, πολέμου, Il. 5, 469. 11, 752; υπό τινος, 8, 363. *b)* to what? ές προχοάς, Od. 5, 452; επί νῆα, Il. 17, 692;

πόλινδε, 5. 224; μεθ' ὁμίλον, 17, 149. On this, cf. Thiersch, § 222.

σαπήη, Ep. for σαπῆ, see σήπω.

Σαρδάνιος, η, ον, rd. Wolf, from which μείδησε δὲ θυμῷ Σαρδάνιον μάλα τοίοισιν οι άκροισι χείλεσι), hence also σαρδίζω. and signifies prop. *showing the teeth, grinning.* Others write σαρδόνιον, and derive it from σαρδόνιον, a poisonous plant, which distorted the countenance to an involuntary laugh. It was said to grow chiefly in Sardinia (Σαρδώ); Eustath. quotes still other explanations [*Sardonic*, Cowper. whose explanation from the Schol., see ad Od. 20, 359. *Ja. Ed.*]

σάρξ, σαρκός, ή, dat. plur. σάρκεσσι. *flesh*, the sing. only Od. 19, 450; elsewhere plur. of men and beasts, Il. 8, 380. Od. 9, 293.

Σαρπηδών, όνος, ό, Ep. form Σαρπηδόντος, 12, 379; Σαρπήδοντι, 12, 373: voc. Σαρπῆδον, 5, 633; from the obsol. Σαρπήδων, son of Zeus and Laodamia, l. 198, seq. (According to a later tradition, son of Evander and Didamia, grandson of an elder Sarpedon, Apd.), sovereign of the Lycians, an ally of the Trojans, l. 876; he was slain by Patroclus, 16, 480 seq. Upon the command of Zeus, Apollo cleansed the dead body from blood and dust, and anointed it with ambrosia, 16, 667.

*σατίνη, ή, *a chariot, a war-chariot*, h. Ven. 13.

Σατνιόεις, εντος, ό, a large torrent in Mysia, 6, 34. 14, 445; Σαφνιόεις, Strab. Σάτνιος, ό, son of Enops and a river nymph, slain by Ajax, 14, 443.

*σαύλος, η, ον (akin to σάλος), *vain, mincing, affected*. σαύλα βαίνειν, h. Merc. 28.

σαυρωτήρ, ῆρος, ὁ, *the lower end of a spear*; elsewhere ούρίαχος. *the point or spike of the shaft*, which was furnished with iron, that it might be set upright in the ground, 10, 153 † (prob. from σαύρα, a kind of snake or perhaps a point).

σάφα, adv. (from σαφής for σαφά), *clearly, certainly, definitely*; connected with είδέναι, έπίστασθαι, 2, 192. Od. 4, 730. σάφα είπεῖν, *to speak distinctly, to speak truly*, Il. 4, 404.

*σαφέως, adv. = σαφῶς from σαφής, h. Cer. 149.

*σαφής, ές, clear, certain, sure, h. Merc. 208.
σάω, for σάου, see σαόω.
σαώσαι, σάωσε, etc., see σαόω.
σαώτερος, η, ον, Ep. compar. from ΣΑΟΣ.
σβέννυμι, only aor. 1 ἔσβεσα. Ep. infin. σβέσσαι, aor. 2 ἔσβην. 1) Trans. in the aor. 1, to extinguish, to quench, to put out, with accus. πυρκαϊήν, 23, 237. 24, 791. b) Metaph. to moderate, to check, to restrain, χόλον, 9, 678; μένος, 16, 621. 2) Intrans. in the aor. 2, to go out, spoken of fire, 9, 471. b) Metaph. to become calm, spoken of wind, Od. 3, 182.
σεβάζομαι, depon. mid. (σέβας), aor. 1 only Ep. 3 sing. σεβάσσατο, to stand in awe, to be afraid of, τι θυμῷ. *h, 167. 417.
σέβας, τό (σέβομαι), only used in nom. and accus. 1) reverential fear, awe, that respect for the opinion of gods and men which restrains a person from doing any thing; fear, shame, with infin. 18, 178. h. Cer. 10. 2) astonishment, wonder, admiration, at uncommon occurrences; σέβας μ' ἔχει, Od. 3, 123, 4, 75.
σέβομαι, depon. (akin to σεύω), to stand in awe, to be ashamed, absol. 4, 240.†
σέθεν, Ep. for σοῦ, see σύ.
σεῖ', abbreviated for σεῖο, see σύ.
*Σειληνός, ὁ (later orthography Σιληνός). Silenus, foster-father and companion of Dionȳsus (Bacchus), who followed him always drunk and riding upon an ass. In the plur. οἱ Σειληνοί, generally, the ancient Satyrs, companions of Dionȳsus. h. Ven. 263.
σεῖο, Ep. for σοῦ, see σύ.
σειρή, ἡ (εἴρω), a rope, a cord, a string, 23, 115. Od. 22, 175; σ. χρυσείη, a golden chain, Il. 8, 19.
Σειρήν, ῆνος, ἡ, mly plur. αἱ Σειρῆνες (from σειρή, the entangling, the enticing), the Sirens, mythic virgins, who, according to Homer, dwelt between Ææa and the rock of Scylla, and by their sweet voices allured passengers and put them to death, Od. 12, 39. 52. Hom. knows but two, for v. 56, we have the dual Σειρήνοιϊν. At a later day there were supposed to be three or four, cf. Eustath. ad loc. They were in antiquity, for the most part, placed in the Sicilian sea, on the south-west coast of Italy, hence also the three small dangerous rocks not far from the island of Caprea, were called Σειρηνοῦσαι. Strab. They are the daughters of the river god Acheloüs and a muse, Ap Rh. 4, 895. Apd. 1, 34. At a still later period they were represented as birds with the faces of virgins.
σείω (akin to σεύω), aor. 1 Ep. σεῖσα, aor mid. Ep. σεσάμην always without augm., to shake, to brandish, with accus. ἔγχεϊσι, 3, 345; and pass. 13, 135; θύρας, to shake the doors, i. e. to knock at the doors, 9, 583; ζυγόν, to shake the yoke, spoken of running horses, Od. 3, 486. Mid. to move oneself, to shake, to

quake, Il. 14, 285. 20, 59; σείσατο εἰνὶ θρόνῳ, she was violently agitated, 8, 199.
σέλα for σέλαΐ, see σέλας.
Σέλαγος, ὁ, father of Amphius from Pæsus, 5, 612.
σέλας, αος, τό (akin to εἵλη), dat. σέλαΐ and σέλᾳ, light, splendour, brightness, a beam, spoken of fire, 8, 509. Od. 21, 246; of constellations and meteors, Il. 8, 76. h. Ap. 442. b) a torch, h. Cer. 52.
σελήνη, ἡ (σέλας), the moon, 8, 555; πλήθουσα, the full moon, 18, 484; an image of splendour, Od. 4, 45.
Σελήνη, ἡ, prop. name, Luna, the goddess of the moon; in the Il. and Od. we find nothing of her origin or of her rising and setting. In h. 31, 6, seq., she is called the daughter of Hyperion and Euryphaëssa (of Theia, Hes. Th. 375); in h. Merc. 94, daughter of Pallas, cf. h. 32.
Σεληπιάδης, ου, ὁ, son of Selēpius = Evēnus, 2, 693.
σέλινον, τό, parsley, a plant which belongs to the family of celery, and grows chiefly in depressed situations, 2, 776. Od 5, 72. Batr. 54. According to Billerbeck, Flor. Class. p. 70, hipposelinum s. Smyrnium olus atrum, Linn.; according to Heyne, apium graveolens, Linn.; also ἐλειοσέλινον; it is mentioned as a food of horses.
Σελλήεις, εντος, ὁ. 1) a river in Elis between the Penēus and the Alphēus, now Pachinta, 2, 659. 15, 531. 2) A river in Troas near Arisbe, 2, 839. 12, 97.
Σελλοί, οἱ ('Ελλοί, in a Frag. Pind. in Strab. VII. c. 7), the Selli, priests of Zeus in Dodōna, who communicated or explained oracles, 16, 234. They appear, perhaps in accordance with a priestly vow, to have led a very austere life, hence they were called ἀνιπτόποδες. According to Strab. VII., the original inhabitants of Dodōna.
*σέλμα, ατος, τό (akin to σελίς), a rower's bench, generally the upper deck (transtrum), h. 6, 47. cf. ζυγόν.
Σεμέλη, ἡ (according to Diod. Sic. 3, 61, from σεμνός), daughter of Cadmus, mother of Dionȳsus by Zeus. She implored Zeus that he would show himself to her in the full glory of his divinity. He fulfilled her request, but she was destroyed by his lightning, 14, 323; h. in Bacch. 6, 57. (According to Heffter from σέω, Bœot. = θέω, the frantic, Herm. soiseequa from σέβειν and ἔλη = ciliis.)
*σεμνός, ή, όν (σέβομαι), venerable, honoured, holy, prop. spoken of the gods, h. 12, 1. Cer. 486.
σέο, Ep. for σοῦ, see σύ.
σεῦ and σευ, see σύ.
σεύα, Ep. for ἔσσευα, see σεύω.
*Σευτλαῖος, ὁ (σεῦτλον), Beet-eater, a frog's name, Batr. 212.
*σεῦτλον, τό, a beet, a soft culinary

Σεύω. 374 Σιγαλόεις.

vegetable, *beta vulgaris*, Linn. Batr. 162.

σεύω, poet. (akin to θέω), aor. Ep. ἔσσευα and σεῦα, aor. mid. ἐσσευάμην, perf. pass. ἔσσυμαι, pluperf. ἐσσύμην. The perf. pass. often has a pres. signif. hence partcp. ἐσσύμενος, η, ον, with retracted accent. The pluperf. is at the same time Ep. aor. 2 ἐσσύμην, ἔσσυο, ἔσσυτο, Ep. σύτο, 21, 167. The pres. act. not found in Hom., the augment tenses have double Sigma. I) Act. trans. prop. *to put in violent motion, to drive;* hence, according to the prepos. *a) to drive, to urge, to chase*, τινὰ κατὰ Νυσσήϊον, 6, 133; τινὰ ἐπί τινι, any one against any one, 11, 293, 294; ἵππους, 15, 681. *b) to drive away, to chase away*, κύνας, Od. 14, 35; κατὰ ὀρέων, to drive down from the mountains, Il. 20, 189. *c)* Spoken of inanimate things: *to cast, to hurl*, κεφαλήν, 11, 147. 14, 413; αἷμα, to drive out the blood, i. e. to cause to flow, to draw, 5, 208. II) Mid. with Ep. aor. 2 and perf. pass. 1) Intrans. *to move oneself violently, to run, to hasten, to rush*, ἀνὰ ἄστυ, 6, 505; ἐπί τι, 14, 227. ψυχὴ κατ' ὠτειλὴν ἔσσυτο, the soul rushed to the wound, i. e. escaped through the wound, 14, 519; with infin. σεύατο διώκειν, he hastened to pursue, 17, 463. *b)* Metaph. spoken of the mind: *to desire ardently, to long for*, θυμός μοι ἔσσυται, Od. 10, 484; esply partcp. ἐσσύμενος, *ardently desiring, longing for, desirous*, with gen. ὁδοῖο, of the journey, Od. 4, 733; and with infin. πολεμίζειν, Il. 11, 717. Od. 4, 416. 2) With accus. trans. *a) to drive, to chase*, *c) to hunt*. esply wild beasts, with accus. κάπριον, λέοντα, 11, 415. *b) to chase away, to drive*, 3, 26; τινὰ πεδίονδε, 20, 148; metaph. κακότητα, h. 7, 13.

σηκάζω (σηκός), aor. pass. 3 plur. σηκάσθεν for ἐσηκάσθησαν, prop. to drive into the fold, *to fold*, spoken of sheep; generally, *to shut up, to enclose*, 8, 131.†

σηκοκόρος, ὁ (κορέω), one that cleans the stall, *a stable-cleanser, a stall-boy*, Od. 17, 224† [*a sweeper of my stalls*, Cp.].

σηκός, ὁ, an inclosed place: *a fold, a stall*, 18, 589. Od. 9, 219.

σῆμα. ατος, τό, *a sign*, to point out any thing; *a token*, of a lot, 7, 188; of theft, h. Merc. 136; esply 1) *a sign sent by the deity, an atmospheric sign, an aerial token*, such as thunder and lightning, which were regarded as omens and indications of the will of the gods, 2, 253. 351. 4, 381. 13, 244. · 2) *a monumental sign, a mound*; hence σῆμα χεῦαι, 2, 814. 7, 86. Od. 1, 291; generally, *a monument*. 3) *a written sign*. σήματα λυγρά, characters of fatal import [but not alphabetical], Il. 6, 168. Od. 1, 291; see γράφω. 4) *a mark*, 23, 843. Od. 8, 192.

σημαίνω (σῆμα), fut. σημανέω, aor. Ep. σήμηνα, aor. mid. ἐσημηνάμην. 1) *to give a sign* to do any thing; hence, *to command, to order*, τινί, 1, 289. 10, 58: rarely with gen. τινός, Il. 14, 85; and ἐπί τινι, about any one, Od. 22, 427. 2) Trans. with accus. *to mark, to indicate*. τέρματα, Il. 23, 358. 757. Od. 12, 26. Mid. *to mark* any thing *for oneself*, κλῆρον, one's lot, Il. 7, 175.

σημάντωρ, ορος, ὁ, poet. (σημαίνω), prop. one who gives a signal, *a leader, commander, sovereign*, 4, 431; esply *a driver of horses*, 8, 127; βοῶν, a keeper of cattle, a herdsman, 15, 315.

σήμερον, adv. (from τήμερα), *to-day*, 7, 30. Od. 17, 186.

σήπω, perf. σέσηπα, aor. 2 ἐσάπην from which Ep. 3 sing. subj. σαπήῃ for σαπῇ, 19, 27. Act. *to cause to decay, to rot*. Pass. and perf. intrans. *to become putrid, to rot, to moulder away*. χρὼς σήπεται, 14, 27. 24, 414. δοῦρα σέσηπε the timbers are decayed, *2, 135.

*σησαμόεις, εσσα, εν (σήσαμον), *full of sesame*, Ep. 15, 8.

Σήσαμος, ἡ, a town in Paphlagonia, later the citadel of Amastris, 2, 853.

*σησαμοτυρός, ὁ (τυρός), *sesame-cheese*, i. e. a kind of food made of sesame and cheese, Batr. 36.

Σηστός, ἡ, a little town on the Hellespont, in the Thracian Chersonesus, opposite the city of Abydos in Asia, later rendered famous by the love of Leander and Hero, now *Ialowa*, 2, 836.

σθεναρός, ή, όν, poet. (σθένος), *strong*, *powerful, mighty*, epith. of Atέ, 9, 505.†

Σθενέλαος, ὁ, son of Ithæmenes, slain by Patroclus, 16, 586.

Σθένελος, ὁ (abbrev. from Σθενέλαος), 1) son of Capaneus and Evadne, one of the Epigoni and a leader before Troy, 2, 564. 23, 511; a companion of Diomedes, 9, 48. 2) son of Perseus and Andromeda, husband of Nicippe, father of Eurystheus, king of Argos and Mycenæ, 19, 116.

σθένος, εος, τό, poet. *strength, power, might*, primar. spoken of the bodies of men and beasts. 5, 139. Od. 18, 373. more rarely of inanimate things, Il. 17, 751. 18, 607; esply of strength of heart, courage in war: μέγα σθένος ἐμβάλλει καρδίῃ, 2, 451. 14, 151. 2) Generally, *power, might*, 16, 542; *forces*, 18, 274: esply in periphrasis with gen. of the person (like βίη): σθένος Ἕκτορος, the might of Hector, i. e. the mighty Hector, 9, 351; Ἰδομενῆος, 13, 248.

σίαλος, ὁ, prop. *fat, fattened*. σῦς σίαλος, a fat swine, 9, 208. Od. 14, 41. 2) Subst. *a fat hog*, Il. 21, 363. Od. 2, 380.

σιγαλόεις, εσσα, εν, poet. (akin to σίαλος), (nitidus,) *shining, white, gleaming, bright, splendid* ('magnificent, costly,' V.), 1) Spoken of costly variegated or embroidered clothing, χιτών, εἵματα, ῥήγη, δέσματα, Il. and Od. 2) Of reins for horses, polished and perhaps adorned with metal, Il. 5, 226. Od. 6, 81. 3) Spoken of household furniture and of the dwelling, Od. 5, 86. 16, 449. (Other

Σιγάω. significations, as *tender, soft, covered with foam,* are not proved.)

σιγάω (σιγή), *to be silent, to be still,* only the imperat. σίγα, 14, 90. Od. 14, 493; σιγᾶν, h. Merc. 93.

σιγή, ἡ (σίζω), *silence,* only σιγῇ, dat. as adv. *in silence, still, quietly.* σιγῇ ἐφ' ὑμείων, still before you, 7, 195. σιγῇ νῦν, Od. 15, 391 (false reading σιγῇ νῦν).

σιδήρειος, η, ον, poet. for σιδήρεος, 7, 141. 8, 15, etc.

σιδήρεος, η, ον (σίδηρος), 1) *of iron,* iron, κορύνη, δέσματα; ὀρυμαγδός, the iron tumult, i. e. of iron arms, 17, 424; οὐρανός, the iron heaven, like χάλκεος, because the ancients conceived of it as made of iron. Od 15, 329. 17, 565; or, more correctly, in a metaph. sense. 2) Trop. *hard as iron, firm, strong;* θυμός, an iron mind, i. e. inexorable, Il. 22, 357; thus ἦτορ, κραδίη. σοίγε σιδήρεα, πάντα τέτυκται, to thee every thing is iron, Od. 12, 280. σιδ. πυρὸς μένος, the iron, i. e. the unwasting strength of fire, Il. 23, 177. (The forms with ει or ε change with the necessity of the metre.)

σίδηρος, ὁ, 1) *iron;* this metal is often mentioned in Homer; he calls it πολιός, αἴθων, ἴοεις; this last epithet, 'violet-coloured,' seems to indicate iron hardened to steel and become blue; also the method of hardening iron by immersing it in water was known to Hom., Od. 9, 391; as an image of hardness, Il. 4, 510. Od. 19, 211. 2) Metonym. *every thing made of iron, arms, furniture,* hence πολύμητος, Il. 6, 48; and often.

Σιδονίηθεν, adv. *from Sidon,* 6, 291.†

Σιδόνιος, η, ον (Σιδών), Ep. for Σιδώνιος, *Sidonian,* of *Sidon,* 6, 289; from which, 1) ἡ Σιδονίη, the district of Sidonia in Phœnicia, or the entire coast of the Phœnicians, with the chief town, Sidon, Od. 13, 285. 2) ὁ Σιδόνιος, a Sidonian, Od. 4, 84. 618.

Σιδών, ῶνος, ἡ, the famous capital of the Phœnicians, situated on the sea, with a double port, now *Seida,* Od. 15, 425.

Σιδών, όνος, a *Sidonian,* an inhabitant of the city of Sidon, 23, 743.

σίζω, a word formed to imitate the sound; *to hiss,* primar. the sound of red-hot bodies immersed in water, hence also spoken of the eye of the Cyclops in which Odysseus (Ulysses) twisted the burning stake; only imperf. Od. 9, 394.†

Σικανίη, ἡ, the original name of the island of *Sicelia,* which it received from the Sicani, according to Thucyd. 6, 2. Diodor. 5, 6. When, at a later period, the Sicani were pressed by the Siceli immigrating from Italy, and confined to the region about Agragas, the latter was called Sicania, and the whole island Sicelia, Od. 24, 307.

Σικελός, ή, όν, *Sicelian* or *Sicilian,* elsewhere Θρινακίη. γυνὴ Σικελή, Od. 24, 211. 366. 389. Subst. οἱ Σικελοί, *the Siceli,* according to Thuc. 6, 2, an Italian people, who, being pressed by the Pelasgi, emigrated to Italy, and first settled near Catana. Hence they dwelt on the eastern coast of the island, Od. 20, 383.

Σικυών, ῶνος, ὁ and ἡ, a town in the country Sicyonia, in the Peloponnesus, at an earlier day Αἰγιαλοί and Μηκώνη, famed for its traffic, and later the chief seat of Grecian art; now *Vasilika,* 2, 572.

Σιμόεις, εντος, ὁ, *Simois,* a small river in Troas, which rises in Ida, and flows north from the city of Troy and unites in the Trojan plain with the Scamander; now *Simas.* 4, 475. 5, 774. cf. Τρωϊκός. 2) the river-god of the Simois, 20, 53.

Σιμοείσιος, ὁ, son of the Trojan Anthemion, slain by Ajax, 4, 474, seq.

σίνομαι, depon. mid. only pres. and imperf. iterat. form σινέσκοντο, Od. 6, 6. 1) Prop. *to carry off, to plunder,* with accus. ἑταίρους τινί, Od. 12, 114. *b) to attack in order to plunder, to rob,* τινά, Od. 6, 6; spoken of herds, Od. 11, 112. 2) Generally, *to hurt, to injure, to harm.* αἰδὼς ἄνδρας σίνεται, shame injures men, Il. 24, 45.

σίντης, ὁ, poet. (σίνομαι), *a robber, a murderer,* as adj. *plundering, ravaging,* λίς, λύκος, *11, 481. 16, 353. 20, 165.

Σίντιες, οἱ (=σίνται, robbers), *the Sinties,* the earliest inhabitants of the island of Lemnos, who received Hephæstus when hurled down by Zeus, 1, 594. Od. 8, 294.

Σίπυλος, ὁ (Dor. for Θεόπυλος), a branch of mount Tmōlus, on the borders of Lydia and Phrygia, now *Minus,* 24, 615.

Σίσυφος, ὁ (Æol. for σόφος), son of Æolus and Enarētē, husband of Merope, father of Glaucus, founder of Ephyra or Corinth, noted for his cunning and propensity to robbery, 6, 153. He was doomed to roll a stone up a mountain in the under world, which always rolled back, because he betrayed to Asōpus that Zeus had seized his daughter, or because he had betrayed the secrets of the gods in general to men, Od. 11, 593. Apd. 1, 9. 3.

σιτέω (σῖτος), imperf. mid. σιτέσκοντο; act. *to give to eat, to feed.* Mid. *to give oneself food, to eat, to feed upon,* Od. 24, 209.†

σῖτος, ὁ, only sing. *wheat,* generally, *grain,* and esply 1) *flour, bread,* prepared from it; in opposition to flesh. σῖτος καὶ κρέα, Od. 9, 9. 12, 19. 2) Generally, *food, victuals, nourishment,* hence often σῖτος καὶ οἶνος, Il. 9, 706. Od. 3, 479. σῖτος ἠδὲ ποτής, Il. 19, 306. Od. 9, 87. (It never appears as neut. in Hom.; but clearly as masc., Od. 13, 244. 16, 83. 17, 533.)

σιτοφάγος, ον (φαγεῖν), *eating grain* or *bread,* Od. 9, 191.† Batr. 244.

σιφλόω (σιφλός [πόδα σιφλός = πηρός, Ap. Rhod. 1, 204]), aor. optat. σιφλώσειεν, prop. *to deform,* hence generally

Σιωπάω.

to bring into disgrace, to destroy, to ruin, τινά, 14, 142 † [al., less well, *to bring to shame.*]

σιωπάω (σιωπή), aor. optat. σιωπήσειαν, infin. σιωπῆσαι, *to be silent, to be still,* 2, 280. 23, 560. Od. 17, 513.

σιωπή, ἡ, *silence, stillness,* Hom. only dat. as adv. σιωπῇ, *in silence, still,* 6, 404. Od. 1, 325. ἀκὴν ἐγένοντο σιωπῇ they were entirely still, Il. 3, 95. Od. 7, 154. σιω. ἐπινεύειν, to give the nod in silence, Il. 9, 616; and often.

σκάζω (akin to σκαίρω), *to limp, to hobble,* 19, 47; ἐκ πολέμου, 11, 811. Batr. 251.

Σκαιαί, αἱ. πύλαι, *the Scaean gate,* also called *the Dardanian* (Δαρδάνιαι); it was upon the west side of the city of Troy, hence the name *west gate* (σκαιός); it was the main gate, and led to the Grecian camp. From its turret were to be seen the oak, the watch-station, the fig-tree, and the monument of Ilus, 3, 145. 6, 237. 11, 170. cf. Τρωικὸν πεδίον.

σκαιός, ή, όν, *left.* ἡ σκαιή, sc. χείρ, *the left hand*; hence σκαιῇ, with the left, 1, 501. 16, 734. 2) *western,* perhaps σκαιὸν ῥίον, Od. 3, 295.

σκαίρω (akin to σκάζω), *to leap, to spring,* Od. 10, 412; ποσί, to dance, Il. 18, 572. h. 31, 18.

*σκαλμός, ὁ, *the pin,* a block upon the ship, upon which the oar rests, h. 6, 42.

Σκαμάνδριος, η, ον, *Scamandrian,* on the Scamander. τὸ Σκαμάνδριον πεδίον, the Scamandrian plain, = τὸ Τρωικὸν πεδίον, q. v., 2, 465; also λειμὼν Σκαμάνδριος, 2, 467. 2) Subst. name of Astyanax, which his father gave him, 6, 402; see Ἀστυάναξ. b) son of Strophius, a Trojan, 5, 49, seq.

Σκάμανδρος, ὁ (σκ never forms posit., cf. Thiersch, § 146. 9), *Scamander,* a river in Troas, called by the gods *Xanthus*; it rises, according to 22, 147, seq., near the city of Troy, from two fountains, of which the one had cold, the other warm water; it then flows south-west from the city through the plain, unites with the Simoeis, 5, 774, and falls into the Hellespont somewhat north of Sigeum, 21, 125. Il. 12, 21 seems to clash with the origin of the Scamander in 22, 147, according to which passage it rises upon Ida, as says also Strabo XIII. p. 602. [Lechevalier, and others maintain that both sources still exist, but that the steam of the warm one is only visible in winter.] Now the river is called *Menderé-Su.* 2) the river-god *Xanthus.* His contest with Achilles is found 20, 74. 21, 136, seq.

Σκάνδεια, ἡ, a harbour on the southern coast of the island Cythêra, now *Cerigo,* 10, 268.

*σκάπτω, fut. ψω, *to dig,* φυτά, h. Merc. 90, 207.

*σκαπτήρ, ῆρος, ὁ (σκάπτω), *a digger,* Fr. 2.

Σκάρφη, ἡ (Σκάρφεια, Strab.), a small town in Locris, not far from Thermopylae, 2, 532. (According to Strab. L. 60 already, 400 years before Christ, destroyed by a earthquake.)

σκαφίς, ίδος, ἡ (σκάπτω), a small vessel for preserving any thing, *a bowl,* a tub. Od. 9. 123.†

σκεδάννυμι, aor. 1 ἐσκέδασα, Ep. σκέδασα, only aor. as pres. the poet. form *to scatter, to drive apart* or *let go,* with accus. λαόν, 19, 171. 23, 162; ἠέρα, 17, 649. Od. 13, 352. ἀχλὺν ἀπ᾽ ὀφθαλμῶν, *to scatter the darkness from any one's eyes,* Il. 20, 341; metaph. αἷμα, to shed blood, 7, 330.

σκέδασις, ιος, ἡ (σκεδάννυμι), *the act of scattering, dispersion,* *Od. 1, 116. 20, 225.

σκέλλω (or σκελέω), Ep. aor. 1 optat.: sing. σκήλειε, *to dry, to parch, to wither,* χρόα, 23, 191.†

σκέλος, εος, τό, in the broader sense, the entire leg from the hip to the foot. In the narrower, *the shank* (tibia) with the calf; hence πρυμνὸν σκέλος, the calf (Schol. γαστροκνημίαν), 16, 314.†

σκέπαρνον, τό (prob. from σκάπτω), a double-edged axe, for hewing wood, a carpenter's axe [used also for smoothing], *Od. 5, 237. 9, 391.

σκέπας, αος, τό (σκεπάω), *a cover, a covering, a shelter*; ἀνέμοιο, a shelter from the wind, *Od. 5, 443. 6, 210.

σκεπάω, poet. (σκέπας), 3 plur. pres. σκεπόωσι, Ep. for σκεπῶσι, *to cover, to protect*; spoken of the coast, σκεπάω κῦμα ἀνέμων, *the wave or the sea from the winds,* Od. 13, 99.†

σκέπτομαι, depon. mid. aor. Ep. σκεψάμην, *to look at a distance with the hand held over the eyes, to look sharply, to look around,* ἔς τι; μετά τινι, Od. 12, 247; with αἰ κεν, Il. 17, 652; ἐκ θαλάμοιο, h. Cer. 245. 2) Trans. *to examine, to contemplate,* with accus. ὀϊστῶν, ῥοῖζον. 16, 361. h. Merc. 360.

*σκευάζω (σκεῦος), *to prepare, to make ready*; absol. *to arrange domestic affairs;* κατ᾽ οἶκον, in the house, h. Merc. 285.

σκηπάνιον, τό (σκῆπτω), = σκῆπτρον, *a staff, a sceptre,* the ensign of imperial dignity; of Poseidôn, 13, 59; of Priam, *24, 247.

σκηπτοῦχος (σκῆπτρον, ἔχω), *sceptre-bearing,* holding the sceptre, epith. of kings, 2, 86. Od. 5, 9.

σκῆπτρον, τό (σκῆπτω), 1) *a staff, a cane* to support oneself upon, Od. 11. 437. 14, 31. 17, 199. 2) Esply *a sovereign's sceptre,* the sceptre, a spear without a metallic point, and, according to Il. 1, 246, adorned with golden studs. It was an ensign of imperial dignity in peace. Kings esply bore it, 1, 234. Od. 2, 411; also priests and prophets, Il. 1, 15. Od. 11, 91; heralds, Il. 7, 277; also judges, 18, 505. It was generally an ensign of public action; whoever spoke in an assembly was obliged to hold the sceptre in his hand, and received it from the herald, 23, 568. Od. 2, 37; in taking an oath the sceptre was raised, Il. 7, 412.

Σκήπτω. 377 Σκύμνος.

0, 327. 3) Metaph. *the royal power, the imperial dignity*, 6, 259. σκῆπτρον καὶ ἔμιστες, marks the union of the imperial and judicial power, 2, 206. 9, 99.

σκήπτω, act., a false reading, 17, 437, from ἐνισκίμπτειν; now only mid. *to support oneself, to lean* upon a staff, spoken of old men and beggars, Od. 17, 03. 338; with dat. καί μιν ὄϊω αὐτῷ Ἔκοντι) σκηπτόμενον· κατίμεν δόμον Ἄϊ- ος εἴσω, and I think that he will descend to the abode of Hades, supporting himself on the spear [will 'lean on it in his descent to Hell,' Cp.], sarcastic for 'he will die pierced through by my spear,' Il. 14, 457.

σκηρίπτω (σκήπτω), only mid. *to support oneself, to lean upon*, Od. 17, 196; spoken of Sisyphus rolling the stone, χερσίν τε ποσίν τε, to resist or push against it with hands and feet [to *shove* it, Cp.], Od. 11, 595.

σκιάζω, poet. form σκιάω, aor. subj. σκιάσῃ, *to shade* or *overshadow, to envelope with shade, to veil*, with accus. of the light, ἄρουραν, 21, 232.†

σκιάω, poet. σκιάζω, only mid. *to become shady, to be darkened*. σκιόωντο, Ep. for ἐσκιόωντο πᾶσαι ἀγυιαί, all the streets were dark, *Od. 2, 388. 3, 487.

σκίδναμαι, mid. poet. a form of σκεδάν- νυμι, in the pres. and imperf. *to scatter, to separate*, spoken of men: κατὰ κλι- σίας, 1, 487; ἐπὶ ἔργα, Od. 2, 252; πρὸς δώματα, Od. 2, 258; ἐπὶ νῆα, Il. 19, 277; with infin. 24, 2; spoken of the foam of the sea: ὑψόσε, to dash on high, 11, 308; of dust: ὑπὸ νεφέων, to whirl upward, 16, 375; of a fountain: ἡ ἀνὰ κῆπον σκίδναται, is distributed through the garden, Od. 7, 130.

σκιερός, ή, όν, poet: (σκιή), *shadowy, shady, dark*, νέμος, 11, 480; ἄλσος, Od. 20, 278.

σκιή, ή, Ion. for σκιά, *a shadow, a shade*, spoken of the souls in Hades, *Od. 10, 495. 11, 207. h. Cer. 100.

σκιόεις, εσσα, εν, poet. (σκιά), *shady, shaded*, i. e. by trees, ὄρεα, 1, 157; *dark, gloomy*, μέγαρα, Od. 1, 365. 4, 768. 'There were no windows in the hall, and it received light through the door; or, according to Eustath., because it protected from the heat.) νέφεα, Il. 5, 525. Od. 8, 374.

σκιρτάω, optat. pres. σκιρτῷεν, aor. 1 infin. σκιρτῆσαι, Batr. 60; *to leap, to spring*, ἐπὶ ἀρούραν, upon the earth. *20, 226; and v. 228, ἐπὶ νῶτα θαλάσσης.

σκολιός, ή, όν, *crooked, curved, tortuous, oblique*: metaph. σκολιὰς κρίνειν θέμιστας, to give perverse judgements, 16, 387.†

σκόλοψ, οπος, ὁ (from κόλος), a body having a sharp point, *a spit*, 18, 177. 2) Esply *a stake, a pale* for fortifying the walls of towns and encampments, 8, 343. 15, 1. Od. 7, 45.

σκόπελος, ὁ (σκοπός, prop. = σκοπιή), *a mountain peak, a rock, a cliff*, 2, 396; often Od., 12, 73. 95, 101.

σκοπιάζω (σκοπιά), prop. *to look abroad from a lofty place*; generally, *to spy, to watch, to observe*, 14, 58. Od. 10, 260. 2) Trans. *to spy out, to explore*, τινά, Il. 10, 40.

σκοπιή, ή, Ion. for σκοπιά (σκοπός), any elevated place from which observations can be taken, *a watch-station*, in Hom. always *a hill-top* [' a rocky point,' Cp.], 4, 275. Od. 4, 524; esply a place near Troy, Il. 22, 145. 2) *the act of spying*, observation, Od. 8, 302. h. Merc. 99.

σκοπός, ὁ (σκέπτομαι), 1) *a looker-out*, who from an elevated position surveys the region, *a watch*, Od. 4, 524; spoken of Helios, h. Cer. 63; also, *a scout*, = ἐπί- σκοπος, Il. 10, 324. 526. 561; generally, *an overseer*. 23, 359; also *a female superintendent*, δμωάων, Od. 22, 396; in a bad sense, *a lier in wait*, Od. 22, 156. 2) In the Od. *the point* to which one looks, Od. 22, 6; metaph. *aim, purpose*. ἀπὸ σκοποῦ, contrary to the design, Od. 11, 344.

σκότιος, η, ον (σκότος), *dark, gloomy;* metaph. *secret, clandestine*, 6, 23.†

σκοτομήνιος, ον (μήνη), *in which the moon is obscured, dark, moonless*, νύξ, Od. 14, 457.†

σκότος, ὁ (akin to σκιά), *darkness, obscurity*, Od. 19, 389; esply metaph. *the darkness of death*, often spoken of the dying, τὸν δὲ σκότος ὄσσε κάλυψεν, Il. 4, 461. h. Ap. 370. In the Il. always in the metaph. signif.; in the Od. only once in the literal.

σκυδμαίνω, poet. form of σκύζομαι, Ep. infin. σκυδμαινέμεν, *to be angry at*, τινί, 24, 592.†

σκύζομαι, depon. only pres. and imperf. poet. (from κύων, to snarl like a dog), *to mutter, to be angry, to be displeased*, absol. 8, 483; τινί, at any one, 4, 23. 8, 460. Od. 23, 209.

σκύλαξ, ακος, ὁ, ἡ (κεύω, κύων), a young animal, esply *a young dog, whelp, puppy*, *Od. 9, 289. 12, 86. 20, 14; in Hom. always fem.

Σκύλλα, ἡ. mly in Hom. Σκύλλη (the nom. Σκύλλα, only Od. 12, 235; *that tears in pieces*, from σκύλλω), a sea-monster of the Italian coast in the Sicilian straits, opposite Charybdis, dwelling in a cavern, Od. 12, 85, seq. She is called the daughter of Cratais, Od. 12, 124 (according to Ap. Rh. 4, 828, daughter of Phorcys and Hecate). She had six dragon throats and twelve sharp claws, and her body was surrounded with half-projecting dogs and other horrible objects. She tore in pieces every living thing which approached her. She robbed Odysseus (Ulysses) of six of his companions. According to mythology, she was afterwards changed into a rock. This rock, named Scyllaeum, lies opposite the promontory of Pelorum, on whose east side there lies at this day a small town Scilla or Seiglio.

σκύμνος, ὁ (κύω), like σκύλαξ, *a young*

Σκῦρος. 378 Σπάρτη.

animal; esply the young of the lion, (lion's) whelp, 18, 319.†

Σκῦρος, ἡ, an island of the Ægean sea, north-west of Chios, with a town of the same name, birth-place of Neoptolemus, now *Skyro*, 9, 668. Od. 11, 509; from which Σκυρόθεν, from Scyros, Il. 19, 332.

σκῦτος, εος, τό (ο υ τ i s), *the skin*; esply dressed skin, *leather*, Od. 14, 34.†

σκυτοτόμος, ὁ (σκῦτος, τέμνω), prop. cutting leather; hence, *a worker in leather* [often = armourer, fm the use made of leather in the ancient shields, &c.], 7, 221.†

σκύφος, ὁ, (akin to κυφός), *a goblet, a cup*, Od. 14, 112.† (Aristoph. Byz. read σκύφος as neut.)

σκώληξ, ηκος, ὁ, *an earth-worm*, lumbricus, 15, 654.†

σκῶλος, ὁ = σκόλοψ, *a pointed stake*, or, according to Etym. Mag., a kind of thorn, 13, 564.†

Σκῶλος, ἡ, a village of the Theban dominions in Bœotia, 2, 497.

σκώψ, σκωπός, ὁ, *an owl*, the wood-owl, *strix aluco*, Linn. According to Schneider ad Arist. H. A. 9, 19. 11, the *small horned-owl, strix scops*, Linn., Od. 5, 66.† (Either from σκέπτομαι, on account of its staring eyes, or from σκώπτω, from its droll form.)

σμαραγέω (akin to μαράσσω), aor. subj. σμαραγήσῃ, *to resound, to roar*, spoken of the sea and of thunder, 2, 210. 21, 199; spoken of the meadow, which resounded with the cry of the cranes, *2, 463.

*Σμάραγος, ὁ, *the blusterer*, a divinity, Ep. 14, 9.

σμερδαλέος, έη, έον, lengthened from σμερδνός, ή, όν, poet. *frightful, fearful, terrific, odious, horrible*, spoken esply of the appearance, δράκων, 2, 309. Od. 6, 137; κεφαλή. Od. 12, 91; hence spoken of brass and of weapons: χαλκός, αἰγίς, σάκος, Il. 12, 464. 20, 260. 21, 401. Od. 11, 609; the neut. sing. and plur. σμερδαλέον, σμερδαλέα, as adv. once of the look, δέδορκεν, 22, 95; elsewhere spoken with verbs of sound, βοᾶν, κοναβίζειν, κτυπεῖν, τινάσσεσθαι, 15, 609.

σμερδνός, ή, όν=σμερδαλέος, and much more rarely used; Γοργείη κεφαλῆς, 5, 742; the neut. σμερδνόν, as adv. 15, 687. h. 31, 9.

σμήχω, Ep. Ion. for σμάω, *to wipe off, to rub off*, χνόον ἐκ κεφαλῆς, Od. 6, 226.†

σμίκρός, ή, όν, Att. for μικρός, *small*; in H. on account of the metre, 17, 757. h. Ven. 115.

Σμινθεύς, ῆος, ὁ, epith. of Apollo, according to Aristarch. from Σμίνθη, a town in Troas, because he had a temple there, or from the Æolic σμίνθος, *a mouse*, because these as well as other animals living under the earth, were a symbol of prophecy, 1, 39. According to other critics, as Apion, Eustath., it signifies, mouse-killer, because he once freed one of the priests from a plague of mice in Chrysa, or because he indicated to the Teucri, on the march to Troy, the place of their settlement by mice, Strab. XIII. p. 604.

*Σμύρνη, ἡ, Ion. and Ep. for Σμύρνα, a noted town in Ionia, on the river Meles with an excellent harbour, now Ismir, Ep. 4, 6.

σμύχω, poet. aor. ἔσμυξα, *to consume any thing by a smothered fire, to burn down*. κατά τε σμῦξαι πυρὶ νῆας, 9, 653. Pass. *to be consumed by fire*, πυρί, *22, 411.

σμώδιγξ and σμῶδιξ, ιγγος. ἡ, *a weal or weal, a tumour, a stripe*, livid with blood, nom. σμῶδιξ, 2, 267; and plur. σμώδιγγες, *23, 716.

σόη, see σαόω.

σοίο, see σύς

σόλος, ὁ (σίλλω), *a mass of iron formed for throwing*; according to the Schol and Apoll. *a spherical quoit* (V. 'a ball.' Cp. *an iron clod*). According to Apion and Tryphon, the same with the discus, except that this was always made of stone, the σόλος of iron; cf. Valken. ad Ammon. de differ. voc. p. 60. *Il. 23, 826. 839.

Σόλυμοι, οἱ, the Solymi, a warlike nation, in the country of Lycia in Asia Minor, 6, 184. According to Od. 5, 283. they were neighbours of the eastern Æthiopians. According to Herod. 1, 173. they were the original inhabitants of Lycia, and according to Strab. they inhabited the points of the Taurus in Lycia or Pisidia.

σόος, η, ον, Ep. shortened from σῶς, which is expanded from σῶς, a contr. form of ΣΑΟΣ. 1) *healthy, sound*, αἰεὶ 7, 310; spoken of the moon, 7, 367. 2) *alive, preserved, delivered*, antith. w. ὀλέσθαι, 1, 117. 5, 331; ὑπάλυξε, safe, Il. 382. Od. 13, 364.

σορός, ὁ (akin with σωρός), *a vessel for preserving the bones of the dead*, as urn 23, 91.†

σός, ή, όν (σύ), Ep. gen. σοῖο for σοῦ. Od. 15, 511; *thy, thine*, mly without the article: with an art. τὸ σὸν γέρας, Il. 1, 185. 18, 457; the neut. as subst. ἐν σοῖσι, with thy friends, Od. 2, 369. (Ep. form, τεός, ή, όν.)

Σούνιον, τό, the southern cape of Attica, with a temple of Athenê, now Capo Colonni, Od. 3, 278.

σοφίη, ἡ (σοφός), *dexterity, skill, intelligence, wisdom*, spoken of a ship architect, 15, 412;† of music, h. Merc. 483. 511.

*σοφός, ή, όν, *expert, experienced, intelligent*, Fr. 1, 3.

σόω, Ep. form from σαόω, from this, σόῃς, σόῃ, and σόωσι, see σαόω.

*σπαργανιώτης, ου, ὁ, *a child in swaddling-clothes*, h. Merc. 301.

*σπάργανον, τό (σπάργω), *swaddling-clothes*, h. Merc. 151. 237.

*σπάργω, fut. ξω, *to wrap, to envelope*, τί ἐν φάρει, h. Ap. 121.

Σπάρτη, ἡ, *the chief town of Lacedaemon*, the residence of Menelaus, on the

Σπάρτον.   379   Σπονδή.

Εurōtas, in a valley almost entirely surounded by mountains, the ruins now ear Magula, see Λακεδαίμων, 2, 582. Od. 1, 93; from which adv. Σπάρτηθεν, from Sparta, Od. 2, 327.

σπάρτον, τό, a rope made of spartum a kind of broom); generally, a rope, a able. σπάρτα λέλυνται, Ep. (see Rost, § 00. 4. a. Kühner, § 369.), Il. 2. 135.† ὁ, σπάρτος is a shrub with tough branches, partium scoparium, Linn.: genista in Pliny. (The reference is prob. not to the Spanish Spartos; and Varro ad Gell. 17, doubts whether in Hom. the shrub have the name.)

σπάω, aor. 1 ἔσπασα, aor. 1 mid. ἐσπασάμην, Ep. σπασάμην and with σσ, mperat. σπάσσασθε, partcp. σπασσάμενος, aor. 1 pass. ἐσπάσθην, to draw, to draw out, τί. h. Merc. 85; in tmesis, 5, 59; hence pass. σπασθέντος, sc. ἔγχεος, when the spear was drawn out, 11, 458. 2) Mid. to draw out for oneself, to snatch, ὦπας, Od. 10, 166; χεῖρα ἐκ χειρός τινος, Od. 2, 321. ἄορ παρὰ μηροῦ, to draw the word from the thigh, Il. 16, 473; φάσγανον, Od. 22, 74; ἐκ σύριγγος ἔγχος, Il. 9, 387.

σπείω, see ἔπομαι.

σπεῖος, τό, Ep. for σπέος, q. v.

σπεῖρον, τό (σπεῖρα), prop. cloth for a covering; a cover, a cloth; a robe, a garment, Od. 4, 245. 6, 179; esply linen cloth for shrouding the dead, Od. 2, 102. 9, 147. 2) Generally cloth, a sail = σπεῖρα, *Od. 6, 269. 5, 318.

σπεῖσαι, σπείσασκε, see σπένδω.

Σπειώ, οῦς, ἡ (from σπέος, a dweller in a cave), daughter of Nēreus and Dōris, 18, 43.

σπένδω, fut. σπείσω, aor. ἔσπεισα, Ep. σπεῖσα, 2 sing. subj. pres. σπένδῃσθα, Od. 4, 591; iterat. imperf. σπένδεσκε, Il. 16, 227; aor. σπείσασκε, to sprinkle, to pour out; prop. a word used of sacred rites, since a portion of the wine was poured out in honour of the gods upon the earth, the table or the altar, Lat. libare; mly absol. (make a libation) or with a dat. of the deity to whom the offering is made: Διί, to present a drinkoffering to Zeus. 6, 259; θεοῖς, Od. 3, 34. 7, 137. b) Sometimes with an accus. of that which is offered: οἶνον, Il. 1, 775. Od. 14, 417; or with dat. ὕδατι, to sprinkle with water, Od. 12, 363. c) With dat. of the vessel: δέπαϊ, to pour out of a cup, Il. 23, 196. Od. 7, 137.

σπέος, τό, Ep. σπεῖος, gen. σπείους, dat. σπῆϊ, 24, 83; accus. σπεῖος, Od. 194; plur. gen. σπείων, h. Ven. 264; dat. σπέσσι, Od. 1, 15; σπήεσσι, 9, 00; a cave, a grotto, a cavern. σπέος appears to be more comprehensive than ἄντρον, cf. h. Merc. 228; and Nitzsch ad Od. 5, 57. (According to Ameis, σπέος is used when speaking of the exterior, and ἄντρον of the interior of a hollow place, cf. Od 9, 182. 216. Am. Ed.]

σπέρμα, ατος, τό (σπείρω), seed, seedcorn, prop. spoken of plants, h. Cer. 208. 2) Metaph. σπέρμα πυρός, the seed of fire, Od. 5, 490.†

Σπερχειός, ὁ (that hastens, from σπέρχω), Spercheius, a river in Thessaly, which flows from Mount Tymphrēstus into the Malean gulf, now Agramela, Il. 23, 142. 2) a river-god, father of Menesthius, 16, 174.

σπέρχω, poet. only pres. and imperf. Act. prop. trans. to drive on, to press, once intrans. like the mid. ὅθ' ὑπ' ἀνέμων σπέρχωσιν ἄελλαι, when the storms hasten on before the winds, 13, 334. h. 33, 7. Mid. to move oneself violently, i. e. to hasten, to run, to rush, spoken of men, with infin., 19, 317; absol. often in the partcp. hastening, fleet, 11, 110. Od. 9, 101; ἐρετμοῖς, to hasten with oars, i. e. to row swiftly, Od. 13, 22; spoken of a ship, to hasten, Od, 13, 115; of storms. Od. 3, 283.

σπέσθαι, see ἔπομαι.

σπεύδω, aor. ἔσπευσα, from this subj. σπεύσομεν for σπεύσωμεν, 17, 121; fut. mid. σπεύσομαι, 18, 402; mly in partcp. pres. 1) Intrans. to hasten, to speed, to make haste, often absol. ἐς μάχην, 4, 225; ὑπέρ τινος, before any one, 11, 119; εἴς τινα. 15, 402; with partcp., Od. 9, 250. b) to take pains, to strive, περὶ Πατρόκλοιο θανόντος, about the fallen Patroclus, i. e. to fight about him, Il. 17, 121. 2) Trans. with accus. to hasten any thing, to accelerate, to urge zealously, τί, 13, 237; γάμον, Od. 19, 137. (Of the mid. only the fut.)

σπῆϊ, σπήεσσι, see σπέος.

σπιδής, ές (σπίζω), extended, wide. διὰ σπιδέος πεδίοιο, through the wide plain, 11, 754;† the reading of Zenodotus; others read incorrectly δι' ἀσπιδέος π., assuming an adj. ἀσπιδής, similar to a shield. According to Apoll. Etym. Mag. σπιδής is from στίζω = ἐκτείνω, and accord. to the Gramm. Aeschylus and Antimachus used σπίδιος and σπιδόθεν for μακρός, μακρόθεν.

σπιλάς, άδος, ἡ, a rocky cliff, a rock in the sea, *Od. 3, 298. 5, 401.

*σπινθαρίς, ίδος, ἡ = σπινθήρ, h. Ap. 442

σπινθήρ, ἦρος, ὁ, a spark, 4, 77.†

σπλάγχνον, τό, only in the plur., τὰ σπλάγχνα, entrails, esply the more important, the heart, liver, and lungs. These were immediately cut out after the victim was slain, roasted and eaten, whilst the offering was burning. Afterwards followed the sacrificial feast, 1, 464. Od. 3, 9. 40, 461.

σπόγγος, ὁ, Att. σφόγγος, a spunge (fungus), for cleaning the hands, 18, 414; the table and chairs, Od. 1, 111.

σποδιή, ἡ, Ion. for σποδιά, a heap of ashes, generally = σποδός, ashes, Od. 5, 488.†

σποδός, ἡ, ashes, Od. 9, 375.† h. Merc. 258. (Akin to σβέννυμι.)

σπονδή, ἡ (σπένδω), a libation, a drink-

*Σπουδαίος. 380 Στέλλω.

offering (libatio), of unmixed wine, which was poured out in honour of the gods at feasts and esply in making treaties; hence in the plur. σπονδαί, a solemn *league, a covenant*, 2, 341. 4, 159.

σπουδαίος, η, ον (σπουδή), hasty, zealous, important. χρῆμα, h. Merc. 332.

σπουδή, ἡ (σπεύδω), 1) *haste, real, care, diligence,* ἄτερ σπουδῆς, without care, Od. 21, 409. 2) *earnestness.* ἀπὸ σπουδῆς, in earnest. Il. 7, 359. 12, 235. 3) Eśply often in the dat. σπουδῇ, as adv. in *haste,* Od. 13, 279. 15, 209. b) With zeal, with pains; hence, *scarcely,* with great difficulty, Il. 2, 99. 11, 562. Od. 3, 297. 24, 119.

σταδίη, ἡ, see στάδιος.

στάδιος, η, ον (ἴστημι), *standing, firm.* ἡ σταδίη ὑσμίνη, a standing-fight, *a close battle,* i. e. a pitched-battle, in which man and man fought with spears or swords, or hand to hand, in distinction from a skirmish, cf. αὐτοσταδίη, 13, 314. 713; also ἐν σταδίῃ alone: in close conflict, *7, 241. 13, 514.

στάζω, aor. Ep. στάξα, *to drop, to trickle;* τινί τι κατὰ ῥινῶν, ἐν στήθεσσι, *19, 39. 348. 354. Batr. 232.

στάθμη, ἡ (ἴστημι), *a marking-cord, a carpenter's cord,* for making a straight line, or a *level* or *line,* for making an even surface, 15, 410; δόρυ ἐπὶ στάθμην ἰθύνειν, to hew the wood straight by the line, Od. 5, 245. 17, 341. 23, 197 [squaring it by line, Cp.].

σταθμόνδε, adv. *into the pen,* into the stall, Od. 9, 451.†

σταθμός, ὁ (ἴστημι), 1) a place of stopping for men and beasts; *a station, a stall, a stable, a pen, an enclosure,* 2, 470. 5, 140. Od. 16, 45. 2) *a post, a pillar,* often in the Od., 1, 333. 6, 19. 3) *a weight* in the scales, Il. 12, 434.

στάμεν, στάμεναι, Ep. for στῆναι.

σταμίν, ἴνος, ἡ (ἴστημι), that stands upright, *the ribs* or *side-timbers* of a ship, which rise from the keel; ἴκρια ἀραρὼν θαμέσι σταμίνεσσι, 'fitting the *deck* or *deck-planks* (ἴκρια, vid.) to the numerous ribs,' V., Od. 5, 252.† Others, as Eustath., understand by it the *cross-pieces,* the *side-boards,* by which the upright timbers were connected, see Nitzsch ad loc. (a short from Ep. licence.)

στάν, see ἴστημι.

στάξ, Ep. for ἔσταξε, see στάζω.

στάς, see ἴστημι.

στάσις, ιος, ἡ (ἴστημι), sedition, strife, contention, Batr. 135.

στατός, ή, όν (verbal adj. from ἴστημι), *placed, standing;* ἵππος, a horse standing in the stall, *6, 506. 15, 263.

σταυρός, ὁ (ἴστημι), *a stake, a pale,* 24, 453. Od. 14, 11.

σταφυλή, ἡ, *the wine-grape, the vine, a shoot of a vine,* 18, 561. Od. 7, 120. 9, 358. (In Od. 7, 120. 121. Franke ad Callim. p. 167, as also Bothe, rejects the words: μῆλον δ' ἐπὶ—σταφυλή.)

σταφύλη, ἡ, *the plummet,* in the carpenter's *level;* then, *a plumb-line, a level* ἴσωσι σταφύλῃ ἐπὶ νῶτον ἐΐσας (ς), horses equal on the back by the level (i. e. exactly matched in height), 2, 765.†

στάχυς, υος, ἡ, Ep. also ἄσταχυς, *an ear* of grain, 23, 598.†

ΣΤΑΩ, ground form of ἴστημι.

στέαρ, ατος, τό (ἴστημι), *congealed fat, tallow,* *Od. 21, 178. 183. (στέατος is to be read as a dissyllable.)

στείβω, only pres. and imperf. *to tread, to trample, to tread in pieces,* with accus. spoken of horses, νέκυας, 11, 534. 21, 409; εἵματα ἐν βόθροισι, to tread clothes in a cistern in order to cleanse them, Od. 6, 92.

στεῖλα, Ep. for ἔστειλα, see στέλλω.

στειλειή, ἡ (στέλλω), *the hole* or *ear* of an axe for inserting the helve, Od. 21. 422.†

στειλειόν, τό (στέλλω), *the handle* of an axe, Od. 5, 236.†

στεῖνος, εος, τό, poet. (στείνω), 1) *narrowness, a narrow space,* 8, 476. 12, 66. 15, 426. Od. 22, 460. στεῖνος ὁδοῦ a narrow way, a narrow pass, Il. 23, 419. 2) Metaph. *pressure, distress, trouble,* h. Ap. 533.

στείνω, Ep. for στείνω (στενός), *to make narrow, to contract;* in H. only pass. στείνομαι, *to become narrow, contracted,* θυρετρὰ φεύγοντι στείνεται, the gate is too narrow to one flying, Od. 14 386; λαοὶ στείνοντο, the people were contracted, i. e. pressed together, Il. 14, 34; hence, a) *to be oppressed, burdened* τινί, by any thing, νεκύεσσιν, 21, 220; λαχνῇ, Od. 9, 445. b) *to be full, to fill oneself,* ἀρνῶν, Od. 9, 219.

στεινωπός, όν, Ion. for στενωπός (στενός, ὤψ), *narrow, contracted;* στειν. ὁδός, a narrow way, a narrow *pass, a gorge,* 7, 143. 23, 416; and without ὁδός, Od. 12, 234.

στείομεν, Ep. for στῶμεν, see ἴστημι.

στείρη, ἡ, Ion. for στεῖρα (στείρος), the main timber in the bottom of a ship, the *keel,* 1, 482. Od. 2, 228.

στείρος, ον, Ion. form of στερρός prop. *stiff, hard;* hence metaph. *unfruitful,* unsuitable for cultivation (*sterilis*). βοῦς στεῖρη, *Od. 10, 522. 11, 3 20, 186.

στείχω, poet. aor. 2 ἔστιχον, prop. *to enter in ranks, to march in,* 9, 86. 16, 258; generally, *to go, to proceed, to travel;* ἐς πόλεμον, to go to the war, 2, 833; ἐπ' ἄστυ, Od. 7, 72; spoken of the sun, Od. 11, 17.

στέλλω, fut. στελέω, Ep. for στελῶ, aor. ἔστειλα, Ep. στεῖλα, mid. *deriv.* λάμψην, 1) *to place;* esply *to bring into* a becoming condition, with accus. *to arm, to arrange the companions,* 4, 294; hence *to prepare, to fit out,* νῆα, Od. 2, 287. 14, 248. 2) *to send,* τινὰ ἐς μάχην, Il. 12, 325; ἀγγελίην ἐπί, to send upon an errand, *Batr.* 4, 381. 3) *to take in, to draw in,* ἱστία, Od. 3, 11. 16, 353. It signifies either to take down or *to furl* the sails;

ιere the latter, because ἀείραντες follows; the sails were drawn up to the sail-yard and tied fast to it. They were often let down with the yard. Mid. *to place oneself*, i. e. to prepare oneself, to fit oneself, Il. 23, 285. 2) *to draw in*, ἱστία (with reference to the subject [vela contrahere, Db.]), 1, 433.

στέμμα, ατος, τό (στέφω), prop. *a garland*; and plur. στέμμα 'Απόλλωνος, the garland or wreath (laurel-wreath) of Apollo. According to Eustath. and the best critics, a garland, sacred to Apollo, wound with woollen cords; this the priest bears, as a suppliant, upon his staff, 1, 14. 28. Heyne incorrectly rejects this explanation, and understands by it, 'the holy priestly fillet' (*infula*), h. in Ap. 179.

στενάχεσχ' for στενάχεσκε, see στενάχω.
στεναχίζω, poet. form = στενάζω, *to sigh, to groan*, 19, 304. Od. 1, 243. Mid. with like signif., Il. 7, 95; metaph. spoken of the earth; ὑπὸ ποσσὶ στεναχίζετο γαῖα, the earth resounded, groaned under their feet, 2, 84. (Only pres. and imperf. The form στοναχίζω is rejected by Wolf, after the Cod. Ven., cf. Buttm. Lex. s. v., who defends it.)

στενάχω, poet. form of στενάζω; iterat. imperf. στενάχεσκε, only pres. and imperf. 1) *to sigh, to groan*, spoken of men, 8, 334. 13, 423; of beasts, *to pant*, 16, 393. 489. *b*) Metaph. spoken of the sea and of rivers; *to resound, to roar*, 16, 391. Od. 4, 516; *to bemorn, to bewail*, τινά, 11, 19, 392. Mid. = act. intrans. 19, 301; and trans., Od. 9, 467.

Στέντωρ, ορος, ὁ, a herald of the Greeks before Troy, who could cry as loud as fifty others; according to the Schol. an Arcadian, who contended with Herês in shouting and lost his life, 5, 785.

στένω, Ion. στείνω, only pres. and imperf. for the most part poet. to make narrow, to contract; then, *to sigh, to groan*. in which signif. H. uses the form στείνω, 10, 16. 13, 33; metaph. spoken of the sea: *to roar, to resound*, 23, 230. Cf. στείνω.

στερεός, ή, όν (ἵστημι), compar. στερεώτερος. 1) *stiff, rigid, hard*, λίθος, σίδηρος, Od. 19, 494; βοέη, Il. 17, 493. 2) Metaph. *hard, severe*, ἔπεα, 12, 267; κραδίη, Od. 23, 103. The adv. στερεῶς, *just, firmly*, Il. 10, 263. Od. 14, 346; metaph *firmly, severely*, ἀποειπεῖν, Il. 9, 510. h. Ven. 25.

στερέω, aor. 1 infin. στερέσαι, Ep. for στερῆσαι, *to plunder*, τινά τινος, Od. 13, 262.

στέρνον, τό (στερεός), *the breast*, prop. the upper long part of it, 2, 479. 7, 224. Od. 5, 346; also spoken of beasts, Il. 4, 106. 23, 365. Od. 9, 443.

στεροπή, ἡ, poet. = ἀστεροπή (ἀστράπτω), 1) *lightning*, 11, 66. 184. 2) splendour similar to lightning, *a flash, a gleam, a beam, brightness*, spoken of metals, 19, 363. Od. 4, 72.

στεροπηγερέτα, αο, ὁ, Ep. for στεροπηγερέτης, epith. of Zeus, who collects the lightning (ἀγείρω), or according to Apoll. who excites (ἐγείρω) the lightning, *the lightning-sender*, 16, 298.†

(στεῦμαι), poet. akin to ἵσταμαι, only 3 sing. pres. στεῦται, and 3 sing. imperf. στεῦτο, prop. *to stand* in order to begin any thing; hence, 1) to assume the air of being about to do something, to place oneself, *to strive*. στεῦτο διψάων, thirsting he strove [*to drink*; πιέειν, to be borrowed fm the following clause, Fäsi], Od. 11, 584; according to Eustath. ἵστατο, thirsting he stood. 2) *to promise, to assure, to boast, to threaten*, with infin. fut., Il. 2, 597 3, 83. 9, 241; and infin. aor., Od. 17, 525. According to Eustath. it arose from a contraction of the form στέομαι into στεῦμαι, the resulting diphthong passing into the other persons also, Kühner, § 242. Anm. Thiersch § 223, *f*.

στεφάνη, ἡ (στέφω), prop. any thing encompassing the upper part of a body; hence *a*) *a garland, a crown*, as a female head-ornament, 18. 597. *b*) *a rim, a brim, a border*, of the helmet, 7, 12. 11, 96; also the helmet itself, 10, 30. *c*) *the brow* of a mountain. *13, 138.

στέφανος, ὁ (στέφω), *a garland, a crown*, h. 6, 42. 2) Generally any thing which encompasses; hence metaph. [spoken of a company or circle of warriors. κύκλος πολεμούντων, Schol.] πάντη στέφανος πολέμοιο δέδηε περί σε, the crown of battle burns every where around thee [War, like a fiery circle, all around Environs thee, *Cp.*], *13, 736.†

στεφανόω (στέφανος), perf. pass. ἐστεφάνωμαι, in H. only mid. to encompass a thing as a border, *to wind oneself*. ἦν περὶ πάντη φόβος ἐστεφάνωται, round about which fear wound itself (which fear encompassed), 5, 739. 11, 36. ἀμφὶ δέ μιν νέφος ἐστεφάνωτο. a cloud wound itself about him, enveloped him; 15, 153. περὶ νῆσον πόντος ἐστεφάνωτο, Od. 10, 195. h. Ven. 120. 2) With accus. *to surround, to encompass* any thing. τά τ' (πείρεα) οὐρανὸς ἐστεφάνωται, Il. 18. 485; or pass. with which the heaven is crowned. accus. of object with the pass. Cf. Kühner, § 485. Anm. 2. (The act. is not found at all in H.)

στέφω, 1) *to surround, to encompass, to encircle*; τὶ ἀμφί τινι, to put any thing around any man, 18, 205; 2) Metaph. *to adorn, to ornament*; μορφὴν ἔπεσσι, his form with the gift of words [better, *formam addit sermoni*: crowns his discourse with beauty], Od. 8, 170.

στεῶμεν, Ep. for στῶμεν, see ἵστημι.
στῆ, Ep. for ἔστη; στῆ, Ep. for στῆ. see ἵστημι.

στῆθος, εος, τό (στῆναι), prop. that which projects), Ep. gen. and dat. στήθεσφι, *the breast*, both male and female, in the sing. and plur. 2, 218. 544. 23, 761; also spoken of beasts, 11, 282. 2) Metaph. *the breast* as the seat of the feel-

Στήλη. 382 Στρεπτός.

ings, passions, and thoughts, 3, 63. 6, 51. Od. 2. 304.

στήλη, ή (ἴστημι), *a column*, 13, 437; esply *a*) *a pillar, a buttress* for the support of walls, 12. 259. *b*) *a monumental pillar, a grave-stone*, 11, 371. 16, 457. Od. 12, 14; and often.

στήμεναι, see ἴστημι.

στήμων, ονος, ὁ, the warp in the loom, Batr. 83.

στηρίζω (ἴστημι), aor. 1 ἐστήριξα, and Ep. στήριξα, aor. mid. infin. στηρίξασθαι, 3 sing. pluperf. mid. ἐστήρικτο, 1) Trans. *to support, to place firmly, to sustain*, with accus. ἰρίδας ἐν νέφεϊ, 11, 28; κάρη οὐρανῷ, to sustain the head in the clouds, i. e. to extend, 4, 443. 2) *to support oneself, to stand firmly*, ποσίν, Od. 12, 434; in like manner mid. intrans. πόδεσσιν. to stand firmly with the feet, 1. 21, 242. *b*) With dat. κακὸν κακῷ ἐστήρικτο, evil pressed upon evil, 16, 111. δεκατὸς μεὶς οὐρανῷ ἐστήρικτο, the tenth month ascended the heavens, h. Merc. 11.

στιβαρός, ή, όν (στείβω), compar. στιβαρώτερος, η, ον, prop. firmly trodden; hence *pressed, thick, firm, stout, strong*, spoken of human limbs and of arms, 3, 335. 5, 400. 746. Od. 8, 187.

στιβαρῶς, adv. *thick, firmly*, 12, 454.†

στίβη, ή (στείβω), prop. condensed vapour), rime, hoar-frost, esply *morning frost*, *Od. 5, 467. 17, 25.

*στίβος, ὁ (στείβω), *a trodden path, a way, a foot-path*, h. Merc. 353.

στίλβω, *to gleam, to shine, to beam*, ἐλαίῳ, with evil, 18, 596; metaph. spoken of the shining of the skin, κάλλεϊ, χάρισιν, 3, 392. Od. 6, 237; ἀπό τινος, h. 31, 11.

στιλπνός, ή, όν, poet. (στίλβω), *shining, gleaming, beaming, ἔερσαι*, 14, 351.†

ΣΤΙΞ, Ep. in the nom. absol. for the prose στίχος, from which gen. sing. στιχός, and nom. and accus. plur. στίχες and στίχας, *a row, a rank*, esply *a rank in battle*, sing. 20, 362; my plur. στίχες ἀνδρῶν, the ranks of men Il. and Od. κατὰ στίχας, in close ranks, by ranks, also ἐπὶ στίχας, 18, 602.

στιχάομαι, mid. poet. (στίχος), only 3 plur. imperf. ἐστιχόωντο for ἐστιχῶντο, *to proceed in a line*, generally, *to march, to advance*, spoken of warriors, εἰς ἀγορήν, 2, 92; ἐς μέσσον, 3, 266; of ships, *2, 516. 602.

Στιχίος, ὁ, leader of the Athenians before Troy, slain by Hector, 13, 195. 15, 329, seq.

*στοιχεῖον, τό (prop. dimin. from στοῖχος), prop. a small pole, a pin. 2) *a letter*; and as these are the simplest component parts of speech, hence in the plur. 3) στοιχεῖα, the simplest component parts of things. *the elements*, Batr. 61.

στόμα, ατος. τό, 1) *the mouth* of animals, *the jaws*, hence metaph. στόμα πολέμοιο, ὑσμίνης, the jaws of war, of the battle, poet. for the desolating

war, 10, 8. 19, 313. 20, 359. (The explanation of Heyne, 'the first line, the van,' belongs to a later period;) proverbial, ἀνὰ στόμα ἔχειν. διὰ στόμα ἄγεσθαι, to carry in the mouth. i. e. to utter, 14, 91. ἀπὸ στόματος εἰπεῖν, to speak out freely, Batr. 77. 2) *the mouth, the opening* of rivers, 12. 24. Od. 5, 441 στ. ἠϊόνος (V. an inlet of the shore, 14, 36. (It was a coast stretching far into the sea [rather, into the land bounded on both sides by promontoria λαύρης, the termination of the street. Od. 22, 137. 3) Generally, *the most conspicuous part*; hence *the face*, Il. 6, 43. 16, 410. *b*) Spoken of a spear: στόμα. at the point, 15, 389. *c*) *the pincers* of a crab, Batr. 300.

στόμαχος, ὁ (στόμα). a mouth, hence in Hom. *the gorge, the throat*, *3, 27. 17, 47. 19, 266.

στονᾰχέω, poet. (στοναχή), only inf. aor. στοναχῆσαι, *to sigh, to lament*, Il. 124.† cf. Butm., Lex. p.

στοναχή, ή, poet. (στένω), *the act of sighing, groaning, a sigh*, often in the plur. 2, 356. Od. 5, 83.

στοναχίζω. see στεναχίζω.

στονόεις, εσσα, εν, poet. (στόνος), *full of sighs*, i. e. *causing many sighs*, hence *lamentable, mournful, κήδεα, βέλεα*: also Od. 17, 102; ἀοιδή, a dirge, Il. 24. 721.

στόνος, ὁ, poet. (στένω), *the act of sighing, groaning*, the rattling in the throat of the dying, 4, 445. 10, 483. Od. 23, 40.

στορέννυμι, aor. 1 ἐστόρεσα, Ep. στόρεσα from στρώννυμι, perf. pass. ἔστρωμαι, 3 sing. pluperf. pass. ἔστρωτο (the pres. does not occur), 1) *to spread, to lay down* any thing (sternere); λέχος, to prepare a couch, 9, 621. Pass. h. Ven. 158: also δέμνια, τάπητας, Od. 4, 301 13, 73; ἀνθρακιήν, to spread the coals Il. 9, 213. 2) *to make level, to render passable*, prop. spoken of a road, then πόντον, Od. 3, 158.

Στρατίη, ή (appell. στρατιή, an army) a town in Arcadia, in Strabo's time destroyed, 2, 608.

Στρατίος, ὁ (appell. στρατιός, an army), son of Nestor and Anaxibia, Od. 3, 413.

στρατός, ὁ (στράω = στορέννυμι,) Ep. gen. στρατόφιν, 10, 347; *a camp, an encamped army*, and generally, *an army*, 1, 10. Od. 2, 30.

στρατόομαι, mid. (στρατός), 3 plur. imperf. ἐστρατόωντο, Ep. for ἐστρατῶντο, *to be encamped*, 3, 187; πρὸς τείχεα, *4, 377. cf. Buttm., Gr. Gram. I. p. 492.

*στρεβλός, ή, όν (στρέφω), 1) *turned, twisted, crooked*. 2) Spoken of the eyes *squint*, Batr. 297.

στρεπτός, ή, όν (στρέφω), verb. adj. *twisted, wound*. στρ. χιτών, a chain coat of mail, which was formed of metallic rings, according to Aristarch.; or perhaps we are to understand the rings with which the two plates of the cuirass were united, 5, 113. (Passow, with

Στρεύγομαι.   389   Συγκλονέω.

Schol. Ven.: a tunic of twisted work.) 2) that may be easily turned, *pliable, volυble, γλώσσα*, 20, 248; hence *tractable, manageable, φρένες*, 15, 203; θεοί, 9, 497.

στρεύγομαι, depon. pass. poet. (akin to στράγγω), prop. to be expressed drop by drop, hence *to become gradually enfeebled, exhausted, to become weary, έν αίνῇ δηϊοτῆτι*, 15, 512; *έν νήσῳ*, Od. 12, 351.

στρεφεδινέω, poet. (στρέφω, δινέω), *to whirl around in a circle*; pass. *to turn oneself round in a circle*. στρεφεδίνηθεν (Ep. for έστρεφεδινήθησαν) δέ οί όσσε, his eyes ['*swam dizzy* at the stroke,' *Cp.*], 11. 16, 792.† [According to Meiring, from στρέφεσθαι δίνῃ. *Am. Ed.*]

στρέφω, fut. στρέψω, aor. Ep. στρέψα, iterat. στρέψασκον, fut. mid. στρέψομαι, perf. pass. έστραμμαι, aor. 1 pass. έστρέφθην, 1) Act. intrans. *to turn, to turn about, to bend*, with accus. *ούρον*, Od. 4, 520; esply *ίππους*, to turn the horses, 11. 8. 168. Od. 15, 205; pass. στρεφθείς, firmly twisted, Od. 9, 435. 2) Intrans. *to turn oneself, to turn about*, Il. 18, 544; *άνά όγμους*, v. 546. *εις "Ερεβος στρέψας*, Od. 10, 528. Mid. with aor. pass. 1) *to turn oneself, to turn*, Il. 18, 488. *ένθα καί ένθα στρέφεται*, to turn oneself hither and thither, 24, 5; hence 1) *to turn oneself to*, 12, 42. *έστραμμέναι άλλήλῃσιν*, h. Merc. 411; or *to turn oneself from; έκ χώρης*, to go from the region, 5, 516. 15, 645. 2) Like *versari, to turn oneself about, to have intercourse with*, with accus. b. Ap. 175.

στρέψασκον, see στρέφω.

στρόμβος, ό (στρέφω), prop. a twisted body, hence *a whirlwind*, 14, 413.†

στρουθός, ή, *a sparrow*, *2, 311. 317 (elsewhere also ό στρ.)

στροφάλιγξ, ιγγος, ή (στροφαλίζω), *a whirlwind*, esply *κονίης*, of dust, 16, 775. 21, 503. Od. 24, 39.

στροφαλίζω, poet. (στρέφω), a strengthened form, *to turn, ήλάκατα*, Od. 18, 315.†

Στρόφιος, ό (dexterous, from στροφή), father of Scamandrius, 5, 49.

στρόφος, ό (στρέφω), *a twisted cord, a string, a rope, a girdle*, the band of a wallet, *Od. 13, 438. 17, 198. 2) *a swathing-band*, h. Ap. 123.

στρώννυμι, see στορέννυμι.

στρωφάω, poet. form of στρέφω, *to turn, ήλάκατα*, Od. 6, 53. 17, 97. Mid. *to turn oneself, κατά τινα*, to any one, 11. 13. 557. *b*) to turn *oneself* hither and thither, i. e. *to abide, to remain, κατά μέγαρα*, 9, 463; *έκάς*, 20, 422. h. Cer. 48.

στυγερός, ή, όν, adv. στυγερώς (στυγέω), prop. *hated, abhorred*; generally, *hateful, abominable, horrible*. *a*) Spoken of persons: 'Αΐδης, 8. 368; στυγερός δέ οί έπλετο θυμῷ, he was odious to her in the soul, 14, 158. *b*) Of things: *πόλεμος, σκότος, γάμος, πένθος*, 4, 240. Od.
1, 249. 16, 126. Adv. στυγερώς, *terribly, horribly*, Il. 16, 123. Od. 21, 374. 23, 23.

στυγέω, aor. 2 έστυγον, aor. 1 έστυξα, causat. 1) Pres. with aor. 2 *to hate, to abhor, to fear, τινά*, 7, 112. Od. 13, 400. *b*) *to stand in awe of, to fear*, with infin., Il. 1, 186. 8, 515. 2) In the aor. 1 *to render odious, frightful, τῷ κέ τεῳ στύξαιμι μένος*, Od. 11, 502.

Στύμφηλος, ή, Ion. for Στύμφαλος, a town in Arcadia on the Stymphalian lake, 2, 608; famous in mythology on account of the Stymphalian birds.

Στύξ, Στυγός, ή (the horrible). 1) A river in the under world, by which the gods swore the most dreadful and sacred oath, 2, 755. Od. 8, 369. The Cocytus is a branch of it, Od. 10, 514. 2) As a nymph, daughter of Oceanus and Tethys, Hes. Th. 361. h. Cer. 424. She dwelt, according to Hes. Th. 778, at the entrance of the under world; her stream is a branch of Oceanus, and, as a part of it, flows from the world above to the world below, Il. 15, 37. Zeus granted to her, Hes. Thes. 383, the honour to be the most sacred oath of the gods, 14, 271. Od. 5, 183. According to Hes. Th. 783, seq., any one of the immortals, who had sworn a false oath, was obliged to lie down a full year breathless in sickness. Perhaps the fable was derived from the Arcadian fountain near Nonakris, whose water was said to be deadly, Hdt. 6, 74.

Στύρα, τά, a town on the island of Euboea, 2, 539.

στυφελίζω (στυφελός), fut. στυφελίξω, aor. έστυφέλιξα, Ep. στυφέλιξα, 1) *to strike, to thrust, to shake*, with accus. *άσπίδα*, 5, 437; *τινά*, 7, 261; *νέφεα*, to scatter the clouds, 11, 305. *b*) *to thrust away, to chase away, τινά έξ έδέων, έκ δαιτύος, έκτός άταρπιτοῦ*, 1, 581. Od. 17, 234. 2) Generally, *to push hither and thither, to abuse, to insult, τινά*, Il. 21, 380. 512; pass., Od. 16, 108. 20, 318.

σύ, person. pron. of the second person, nom. Ep. τύνη. gen. Ep. σέο, σεῦ, σεῖο, τεοῖο, 8, 37; σέθεν, dat. σοί, τοί, accus. σέ (σε). The common gen. σοῦ is not found in Hom., σοί is always orthotone, τοί always enclitic: *thou*, gen. *thine*. σύγε, σύπερ, and connected with αύτός, in which case it always retains the accent, 3, 51. 19, 416; hence we should write σοί αύτῷ for σοί αύτῷ, Od. 4, 601. 5, 187. 6, 39; cf. Thiersch, § 204, 205. Rost, Dial 44. Kühner, § 301.

συβόσιον, τό (βόσις), *a herd of swine*, with συών, 11, 679. Od. 14, 101 (with ε lengthened).

συβώτης, αο, ό (βόσκω), *a swine-herd*; often, *Od. 4, 640.

σύγε, see σύ.

συγκαλέω (καλέω), partcp. aor. συγκαλέσας, *to call together, to collect*, with accus. *2, 55. 10, 302.

συγκλονέω, poet. (κλονέω), *to confound, to put in confusion*, with accus. 13, 722.†

Συγκυρέω. 384 *Σύμφωνος.

συγκυρέω, poet. (κυρέω), aor. 1 optat. συγκύρσειαν, *to strike together, to meet, to jostle* (of chariots), 23, 435.†

συγχέω (χέω), aor. 1 συνέχευα, infin. συγχεύαι, partcp. συγχέας, Ep. syncop. aor. 2 mid. σύγχυτο, 1) *to pour together*, esply with the ruling notion of disorder. *to confound, to confuse, to blend, to cast together*, ψάμαθον, 15, 364; and pass. 16, 471. 2) Metaph. a) Spoken of things: *to render null, to make void*, ὅρκια, 4, 269; κάματον, ἰούς, 15, 366, 473. b) In a mental respect, *to confuse, to sadden, to disquiet*, θυμόν, νόον, 9, 612. 13, 808; ἄνδρα, Od. 8, 139. (V. 'to destroy.')

συκέη, ἡ, contr. συκῆ, *a fig-tree*, Od. 7, 116. 11. 590; only once the longer form, which is to be pronounced as a monosyllable, *Od. 24, 341.

σῦκον, τό, *a fig*, Od. 7, 121. †Batr. 31.

συλάω, fut. σω, aor. optat. συλήσειε, subj. συλήσω, partcp. συλήσας, also often 3 sing. imperf. ἐσύλα, and dual συλήτην, 13, 202. 1) *to take away, to take down*, with accus. πῶμα φαρέτρης, 4, 116; τόξον, *to take out* (of the case), 4, 105. 2) Esply spoken of despoiling slain enemies, *to take away, to plunder, to strip*, τεύχεα ἀπ᾿ ὤμων, 6, 28; and τεύχεα, alone, 4, 466. b) With accus. of the pers. *to rob, to plunder, to despoil*, νεκρούς, 10, 343; and τινὰ τεύχεα, to despoil any one of arms, 6, 71. 15, 428. 16, 499; poet. form συλεύω, *11.

συλεύω, poet. form of συλάω, *5, 48. 24, 436.

συλλέγω, Ep. and Att. ξυλλέγω (λέγω), partcp. aor. συλλέξας, aor. 1 mid. συνελεξάμην, Ep. συλλεξάμην, fut. mid. συνλέξομαι. 1) *to put together, to bring together, to collect*, τί, 18, 301. Mid. *to lay together for oneself*, ὅπλα ἐς Λάρνακα (his implements), 18, 413. b) Spoken of persons, *to assemble*, with accus., Od. 2, 292. (Bothe in his ed. has always ξυλλ.)

συμβάλλω or ξυμβάλλω (βάλλω), aor. 2 συνέβαλον, Ep. σύμβαλον, aor. mid. συνεβαλόμην; of the Ep. syncop. aor. act. ξυμβλήτην (as if from βλῆμι), Od. 21, 15; infin. ξυμβλήμεναι, Il. 31, 578; Ep. syncop. aor. mid. ξύμβλητο, 14, 39; ξύμβληντο, 14, 27; subj. ξύμβληται, Od. 7, 204; partcp. ξυμβλήμενος, Od. 11, 127; from which Ep. fut. συμβλήσομαι, Il. 20, 335. 1) Trans. *to cast together, to bring together*, with accus. spoken of rivers. ὕδωρ, *to unite the water*, 4, 453; ῥόας, 5, 774; esply in war, ῥινούς, ἔγχεα, *to clash spears and shields together*, 4, 447. 8, 61; metaph. πόλεμον, *to begin a battle*, 12. 181. b) Spoken of persons: *to bring together, to put together, to set together*, in battle, ἀμφοτέρους, 20, 55; with infin. μάχεσθαι, 3, 70. 2) Intrans. like the mid. *to fall in with, to meet*, τινί, Od. 21, 15; esply, *to meet* in battle, *to fall upon* another, with infin., Il. 16, 565; Ep. aor. 21, 578. Mid. *to fall in with, to meet*, with any one, τινί, often in the Ep. aor. 2. Il. 14. 27. 231. Od. 6. H esply *to meet*, in battle, *to come to close conflict*, Il. 16, 565.

Σύμη, ἡ, an island between Rhodes and Cnidus, on the coast of Caria, now Symi; from which Σύμηθεν, from Syme 2, 671.

συμμάρπτω, poet. (μάρπτω), partcp. aor. συμμάρψας, *to grasp together, to break off*, τί, 10, 467.†

συμμητιάομαι, depon. mid. (μητιάομαι). Infin. pres. συμμητιάασθαι, Ep. for συμμητιᾶσθαι, *in consult together, to deliberate*, 10, 197.†

συμμίγνυμι, Hom. συμμείγνυω (μίγνυμι). aor. συνέμιξα, aor. pass. συνεμίχθην. 1) *to mingle together, to unite*, τί, h. Merc. 81; esply spoken of love, θεοὺς γυναιξί, h. Ven. 80. Mid. *to mingle, to unite* (with reference to the subject), spoken of rivers, with dat. Πηνειῷ, 2, 753; of a pugilistic combat, in tmesis, 23, 687; as μίγνυμι.

συμμίσγω, Hom. for συμμίγνυμι.
συμμύω, in tmesis. see μύω.

σύμπας, ᾱσα, ᾱν, Ep. and Att. ξύμπας (πᾶς strengthened by σύν), only in the plur. *all together*, 1, 241. (The Att. form πάντα stands, Od. 7, 214. 14, 198, without metrical necessity; cf. Thiersch. § 175, 4)

συμπήγνυμι (πήγνυμι), aor. 1 συνέπηξα. *to join together, to cause to coagulate, to curdle* or *concrete*, γάλα, 5, 903.†

συμπίπτω (πίπτω), *to fall together, to meet* in battle, only aor. 2 in tmesis, 7 256. 21, 687; spoken of the wind, Od. 5, 295; cf. πίπτω.

συμπλαταγέω (πλαταγέω), aor. συμπλατάγησα, Ep. for συνεπλατ., *to strike together*, χερσί, *to clap the hands*, 21 192.†

συμφερτός, ή, όν (συμφέρω), *brought together*; hence, *united, connected*, συμφερτὴ δ᾿ ἀρετὴ πέλει ἀνδρῶν, καὶ μάλα λυγρῶν, *the united force, even of very weak men, avails somewhat*, 13, 137 (Thus Köppen, Spitzner, aft. Eustath. πέλει must then be rendered by, *sensi. effects* [Arist. καὶ σφόδρα κακῶν ἀνθρώπων εἰς ταὐτὸν συνελθόντων γίνεταί τι ἀρετή]. The other explanation, συμφερτὴ for συμφέρουσα, i. e. ὠφέλιμος does not suit the context.)

συμφέρω (φέρω), fut. mid. συνοίσομαι. prop. *to bring together*, only mid. *I meet with*, like congredi, *to meet in conflict, to engage in combat*, πτόλεμόνδε, 8, 400; μάχῃ, *11, 736.

συμφράδμων, ονος, ὁ, ἡ, poet. (φράδμων), *deliberating with, aiding with counsel*, 2, 372.†

συμφράζομαι, mid. (φράζομαι), aor. συνεφρασάμην, Ep. συμφρασσάμην. 1) *to consult*, τινί, with any one, Od. 15, 202; βουλάς τινι, *to give counsel to any one*, Il. 1, 537. 9, 374. 2) *to deliberate by oneself, to ponder*, θυμῷ, Od. 4, 442.

σύμφωνος, ον (φωνή), consonant, harmonious, h. Merc. 51.

σύν, Ep. and old Att. ξύν, the latter rarely used, and only for some metrical reason. I) Prep. with dat. primary signif. *with* (cum). 1) Spoken of place, in indicating coexistence of persons: *with, together with, in company with*; σὺν ταίροις. often with the implied notion of assistance, σὺν θεῷ, with the help of the deity, 3, 439. 9, 49; σὺν Ἀθήνη, 10, 90. Od. 8, 493. b) Spoken of things: ὺν νηυσί, σκήπτρῳ, Il. 1, 179. 2, 187; ὺν τεύχεσι, ἔντεσι, ἄνεμος σὺν λαίλαπι. 7, 57. 2) Spoken of causal relations:) In indicating the means, by which any thing is produced: *with, by means f*, σὺν νεφέεσσιν, Od. 5, 293. b) In asigning the measure by which the action s limited, σύν τε μεγάλῳ ἀπέτισαν, Il. 4, 61. II) As adv. *at once, at the same time, together*, 1, 579. 4, 269. 23, 879; ὺν δύο. *two together*, 10, 224. III) In omposition it has the signif. of the adv., *with, at once, together*, and also that of ccomplishing.

συναγείρω, Ep. and Att. ξυναγείρω ἀγείρω), aor. 1 Ep. ξυνάγειρα, aor. 1 mid. Ep. ξυναγείρατο, Od. 14, 323 ; Ep. aor. 2 mid. συναγρόμενος, *to bring together, to collect*, spoken of persons and things, Il. 0, 21; βίοτον, Od. 4, 90. Mid. *to collect or bring together for oneself*, with accus. :τήματα, Od. 14, 323 ; ἵππους, Il. 15, 80 (συναγείρεται, shortened subj. aor. 1 mid. where Spitzner has adopted συναείερται, after the Schol. A.). b) Intrans. *to assemble*, in partcp. aor. 2 mid. 11, 87. 24, 802.

συνάγνυμι, Ep. and Att. ξυνάγνυμι ἄγνυμι), aor. 1 Ep. ξυνέαξα, *to break in pieces, to shiver, to shatter*, with accus. γχος, 13, 166; νῆας, Od. 14, 383 ; τέκνα *breaks in pieces*, Cp. (of a lion)], Il. 11, 14. (Hom. employs the form with ξ ven without metrical necessity.)

συνάγω, Ep. and Att. ξυνάγω (ἄγω), ut. ξω. aor. 2 συνήγαγον, *to lead together, to bring or gather together*, with ccus. γεραιὰς νηόν, 4, 446. 8, CO; to collect the marons into the temple, 6, 87 ; ὅρκια θεῶν, . 269; φόρτον τινί, Od. 14, 291. b) Metaph. as συμβάλλειν Ἄρηα, *to join or ιgin a battle*, Il. 2, 381; also ἔριδα Ἄρηος, 6, 361; ὑσμίνην, 16, 764; πόλεμον. h. Cer. 267.

συναείρω, poet. (ἀείρω), aor. συνήειρα, rop. 1) *to lift up together*, in tmesis, 4, 590. 2) *to take together*, σὺν δ' ἤειρεν μάσι, viz. ἵππους ('he bound them together with straps,' V.), 10, 499. Mid. ίσυρας συναείρεται ἵππους. ed. Spitzner, *to harness together*, cf. συναγείρω, *15, 80. (Eustath. explains it in the two ast passages, by συμπλέκειν, συζευγνύειν ; ἀείρειν is compounded of ἀ (ἅμα) nd εἴρω, and thus equivalent to ὁμοῦ ἵρειν; but cf. παρήορος and συνήορος).

συναίνυμαι, poet. (αἴνυμαι), *to take together, to collect*, with accus. 21, 502.†

συναίρω (αἴρω), aor. 2 συνεῖλον, *to take together, to gather together* (with violence and haste), with accus. χλαῖναν Od. 20, 25. 2) *to take away, to tear away, to crush* (Schol. συνέτριψε), ὀφρῦς [dashed both his brows *In pieces*, Cp.], Il. 16, 740

συναντάω, poet. ἀντέω (ἀντάω), imperf. dual. συναντήτην, aor. 1 mid. συνηντησάμην, *to meet with any one*, Od. 16, 333. Mid.=act. *to come against, to meet*, τινί, Il. 17, 134.

συνάντομαι, poet. form of ἀντάω, in the pres. and imperf. 7, 22. 21, 34. Od. 4, 367. 15, 538.

συναράσσω (ἀράσσω), fut. ξω, aor. Ep. συνάραξα, *to strike together, to dash in pieces*, with accus. 12, 384. Od. 12, 412 ; only in tmesis.

*συναραρίσκω ('ΑΡΩ), only in the perf. συνάρηρα, intrans. *to be joined together, to be united*, h. Ap. 164.

*συναρωγός, ὁ (ἀρωγός), *an assistant, an aid*, h. 7, 4.

συνδέω, Ep. and Att. ξυνδέω (δέω), aor. 1 Ep. συνδῆσα and ξυνέδ., infin. ξυνδῆσαι. 1) *to bind together, to bind fast, to fetter*, τινά, 1, 399; πόδας, Od. 10, 168. h. Merc. 82. 2) *to bind up*, spoken of a wound, Il. 13, 599. (In the Il. always the Att. form.)

*σύνδύο, as dual (δύο), *two and two, two together*, h. Ven. 74 (in Il. separate).

συνέδραμον, see συντρέχω.

συνεεργάθω, Ep. form for συνέργω (εἴργω), *to enclose, to shut up*, 14, 36.†

συνείργω, Ep. for συνείρω, prop. *to enclose together*: then, *to bind together*, τί λύγοισιν. Od. 9, 427. 12, 424; χιτῶνα ζωστῆρι, *to bind together the tunic with the girdle*. *Od. 14, 72.

συνείκοσι, Ep. and Att. ξυνείκοσι, *twenty together*, Od. 14, 98.†

σύνειμι (εἰμί), fut. infin. Ep. and Att. ξυνέεσθαι, *to be together, to live with*, ἀζηί πολλῇ. Od. 7, 270.†

σύνειμι (εἶμι), Ep. and Att. imperf. 3 plur. ξύνισαν, partcp. ξυνιόντες ; on the other hand, συνίτην, 6, 120. 16, 476 (Bothe with ξ), *to go or come together*, ἐς χῶρον ἕνα, 4, 446. 8, CO; ἐς μέσον, 6, 120; esply in a hostile signif *to meet together*, *to fall upon one another*, 14, 393; with μάχεσθαι, 20, 159; or ἔριδι, 20, 66; absol. *to fight*: περὶ ἔριδος, from a spirit of strife (prae ira), *16, 476.

συνελαύνω, Ep. and Att. ξυνελαύνω (ἐλαύνω), aor. 1 συνήλασα, Ep. συν ἔλασσα, infin. ξυνελάσσαι. *to drive together*, with accus. ληΐδα ἐκ πεδίων, 11, 677 ; βοῦς. h. Merc. 106; *to draw together*, κάρη χεῖράς τε, h. Merc. 240; ὀδόντας, *to chatter with the teeth*, in tmesis, Od. 18, 98: esply *to bring together in battle, to urge to engage in contest*, θεοὺς ἔριδι, Il. 20, 134. Od. 18, 39. 2) Intrans. *to meet, to engage* in battle. Il. 22, 129.

σύνελον, Ep. for συνεῖλον, see συναιρέω.

συνεοχμός, ὁ (Att. ξυνεοχμός, Bih.), poet. for συνοχμός (συνέχω), *a joining*, κεφαλῆς τε καὶ αὐχένος [where neck and spine unite, Cp.], 14, 465.†

Συνερείδω. 386 Σφάζω.

συνερείδω (έρείδω), *to press together*, in tmesis, στόμα, Od. 11, 426.†

συνέρίθος, ό, ή (ἔριθος), *a coadjutor*, Od. 6, 32.†

συνέσευε. see συσσεύω.

σύνεσις, ή, Ep. and Att. ξύνεσις (συνίημι), prop. *the act of meeting, uniting*, confluence, ποταμών, Od. 10, 515.†

συνεχής, ἐς (συνέχω), *holding together*. 2) spoken of time: *perpetual, unceasing*. The neut. sing συνεχές as adv., *perpetually, unceasingly* (continenter), 12, 26; also συνεχές αἰεί, Od. 9, 74.

συνέχω, Ep. and Att. ξυνέχω (ἔχω), Ep. perf. συνόχωκα, prop. *to hold together*, i. e. intrans. *to strike together, to unite*, 4, 133. 20, 415. 478. τὼ δὲ ὤμω ἐπὶ στῆθος συνοχωκότε, his shoulders were curved together towards the breast [were o'er his breast contracted, Cp.], 2, 218. (Perf. simple ὄχα, ὦχα, and with Att. redupl. ὄκωχα, see Thiersch, § 232, 61. Buttm., p. 283. Kühner, § 168.

*συνήθεια, ή (ἦθος), 1) *dwelling together*. 2) *custom, a customary manner*. συνήθειαι μαλακαί, consuetudines molles, = consuetudo leniter tangendi fides. Franke, h. Merc. 485.

συνημοσύνη, ή (συνήμων), *connexion, union*, hence *a promise, an agreement*, 22, 261.†

συνήορος, ον (συνείρω), *associated, united*. φόρμιγξ δαιτὶ συνήορος (' *the seasonable companion of a banquet* '), Od. 8, 99.†

συνθεσίη, ή, poet. (συντίθημι), *an agreement, contract, covenant*, 2, 339; in the plur. *a commission*, *5, 319.

συνθέω (θέω), fut. συνθεύσομαι, *to run together*; metaph. *to run happily, to go well*, Od. 20, 245.†

συνίημι. Ep. and Att. ξυνίημι (ἵημι), pres. imperat. ξυνίει. Od. 1, 271; imperf. 3 plur. ξύνιον for ξυνίεσαν (but Spitzner, with Aristarch., ξύνιεν), Il. 1, 273; aor. 1 ξυνέηκα, Ep. for ξυνήκα, aor. 2 imperat. ξύνες, aor. 2 mid. ξύνετο. subj. 1 plur. συνώμεθα. I) Act. 1) Prop. *to send together, to bring together*, spoken of battle: *to cause to engage*, with accus. ἔριδι μάχεσθαι, *to contend in strife* [rather ἔριδι ξυνέηκεν (commisit) (ὥστε) μάχεσθαι (ἔριδι), N.], 1, 8. 7, 210. 2) *to understand, to observe, to hear* (cf. conjicere); mly with accus. of the thing and gen. of the pers. ὄπα θεᾶς, ἔπος τινός, 2, 182. Od. 6, 289. *b*) With gen. pers. Il. 2, 26; ῥεῖ, 1, 273. II) Mid. 1) *to unite, to come together, to agree*, ἀμφί τινι, 13, 282. 2) Like act. *to perceive, to observe*, τοῦ ξύνετο, Od. 4, 76.

συνίστημι (ἵστημι), only intrans in the perf. partcp. *to stand together*. *b*) *to arise, to begin*, πολέμοιο συνεστᾰότος, 14, 96.†

συνοισόμεθα. see συμφέρω.

συνορῑ́νω, poet. (ὀρίνω), *to move with or together*, act. only in tmesis, 24, 467. Mid. *to move oneself, to put oneself in motion*, spoken of warlike forces, 4, 332.†

συνοχή, ή, Ep. and Att. ξυνοχή (συνέχω), the act of *holding together*, meton. ἐν ξυνοχῇσιν ὁδοῦ (V., with the Schol. in the narrow part of the way), 23, 330.

συνοχωκότε, see συνέχω.

συνταράσσω (ταράσσω), *to throw into confusion*, only in tmesis, 1, 579 [Sam. ' *with confusion mar the feast*,' Cp.]; see ταράσσω.

συντίθημι (τίθημι), only aor. 2 mid. 1 sing. σύνθετο, imperat. often σύνθες. act. *to put together*. Mid., which also Hom. uses. prop. *to put any thing together for oneself*; hence with and without θυμῷ (animo componere), *to observe, to notice, to perceive, to understand*, with accus. βουλήν, ἀοιδήν, 7, 44. Od. 1, 328. 16, 259. *b*) Absol. *to be attentive, to attend*, II. 1, 76. Od. 15, 27.

σύντρεις, neut. σύντρια, *three together*. Od. 9, 429.†

συντρέχω (τρέχω), aor. 2 συνέδραμον, *to run together*, in a hostile sense. *i rush upon each other*, *16, 335. 337. (On the constr. of the dual with the plur. see Rost, § 100. 4. *e*. Kühner, § 371.)

*Σύντριψ, ιβος, ὁ, ή (τρίβω), Crusher, prop. name of a domestic goblin that breaks vessels, Ep. 14.

συνώμεθα, see συνίημι.

Σύρίη, ή, Ep. for Σύρος, an island in the Ægean sea, between Delos and Paros, now Sira, according to Strab. X. p. 487; see Ottfr. Müller's Orchomen. p. 326, and τροφή, Od. 15, 403. The moderns seek it on the eastern coast of Sicily, see Ὀρτυγίη; cf. Voss alte Weikund. II. p. 295. Völcker, Hom. Geog. p. 24.

σῦριγξ, γος, ή, prop. *any reed, hence* 1) *a pipe*, esply *a shepherd's pipe or pipe of Pan*, 10, 13. 18, 526. h. Merc. 512. : *a spear's case, a spear-sheath* (prop. of the spear's head), *19, 387.

*σῡρίζω (σύριγξ), *to whistle*, spoken of a spear, Fr. 72.

συρρήγνυμι (ῥήγνυμι), fut. ξω, *to strike together, to strike in pieces, to break in pieces*. metaph. κακοῖσιν συνέρρηκται (he is *battered* with troubles, Cp. Od. 8, 137.†

*σύρω, *to draw, to pull, to drag*, with accus. Batr. 87.

σῦς, συός, ὁ and ή dat. συΐ, plur. nom. σύες, always uncontr. dat. συσί. Ep: σύεσσι, accus. σύας and σῦς, *a swine*. *boar*, *a sow*, mly masc. σῦς κάπρος and κάπριος, 5, 783. 7, 257; also ἄγριος, 8, 338. cf. ὗς.

*σύσσευω (σεύω), aor. συνέσσευα, *to drive together*. βοῦς, h. Merc. 94.

σύτο, Ep. for ἔσσυτο, see σεύω.

συφειός and συφεός, ὁ (σῦς), *a sty*, *hog-pen*, Od. 10, 234. 14, 13; συφεοῖσι to the sty, *Od. 10, 320.

συφορβός, ὁ (φέρβω), *a swineherd*, often Od. παῖς συφ., *the young swineherd*, II. 21, 282. cf. ὑφορβός.

σφάζω, aor. 1 ἔσφαξα and Ep. σφάξα perf. pass. ἔσφαγμαι, *to slay*, with accus. βοῦν, 9, 466; frequently spoken of sacri-

Σφαῖρα. 387 Σχέδον.

ἄγεα: to cut off the neck after they were slain, to slaughter, 1, 459. Od. 3, 454. Pass. Il. 23, 31. Od. 10, 532.

σφαῖρα, ἡ, a sphere; and generally, any round body, a ball. σφαίρῃ παίζειν, to play at ball, *Od. 6, 100. 115. 8, 372.

σφαιρηδόν, adv. in the form of a sphere, 13, 204.†

σφάλλω, aor. 1 Ep. σφῆλα, infin. σφῆλαι, to cause to fall, esply by striking out a leg (supplantare); generally, to throw a man, τινά, 23, 719. Od. 17, 469.

σφαραγέομαι, mid. poet. = σμαραγέω, to rattle, to roar, to hiss, Od. 9, 390. 2) to be filled, to be full. οὔθατα σφαραγεῦντο, Od. 9, 440.

σφάς, enclit. for σφέας, see σφεῖς.

σφέ, enclit. accus. plur. of σφεῖς.

σφεδανός, ή, όν, poet. violent, impetuous, terrible, only neut. adv. κελεύειν, *11, 165. 16, 372. (It is mly derived from σπεύδειν, as if σπεδανός; others from σφαδάν, akin to σφοδρός.)

σφεῖς, plur. of the pron. of the third person, gen. σφῶν, Ep. σφέων (always monosyllabic), σφείων, dat. σφίσι (ν), Ep. and Ion. σφί (ν), accus. σφέας (monosyllabic and dissyllabic), Ep. σφάς and rarely σφέ, 19, 265. The nom. and the neut. are not found in Hom. at all; all the forms except σφείων are enclitic; σφάς and σφέ always; σφέ, according to Buttm., in Lexil., is shortened from σφωέ, and prop. dual. 1) they, their, in Hom. always personal, cf. Od. 10, 355; strengthened, σφέας αὐτούς, Od. 12, 225. 2) Rare and poet. is the use of this pronoun for ὑμεῖς, Il. 10, 398; cf. Thiersch, § 204, 205. Rost, Dialect. 44. p. 204. Kühner, § 301.

σφείων, see σφεῖς.

σφέλας, αος, τό, plur. Ep. σφέλα, Od. 17, 231; a footstool, Od. 18, 394. cf. Buttm., Gram. § 54. Rem. 3.

σφενδόνη, ἡ. a sling, esply the string of the sling, spun of wool, which later was made of leather, 13, 600.† It was an unusual weapon with the Greeks; only the Locrians are mentioned as slingers, 13, 712—721.

σφέτερος, η, ον (σφεῖς), pron. of the third pers. plur. their, as it now stands, with Aristarch., everywhere in Hom. 4, 409; strengthened by αὐτός, Od. 1, 7. ἐπὶ σφέτερα, substantively (ad sua), Od. 1, 274. 14, 9.

σφηκόω, poet. (σφήξ), perf. pass. ἐσφήκωμαι, to draw closely together, into the form of wasps; generally, to bind fast, πλοχμοὶ χρυσῷ τε καὶ ἀργύρῳ ἐσφήκωντο, the locks were wound about With twine of gold and silver [Cp.], 17, 52.†

Σφῆλος, ὁ (adj. σφηλός, easy to shake), son of Bucolus of Athens, 15, 338.

σφῆλεν, Ep. for ἔσφηλε, see σφάλλω.

σφήξ, σφηκός, ὁ, a wasp, *12, 167. 16, 259. According to Bothe we are not here to understand common wasps (vespæ vulgares), but hornets (vespæ crabrones). Linn.

σφί and σφίν, see σφεῖς.

*σφίγγω, to contract, to draw together πόδας κατὰ γαστέρος, to draw the legs to the body, Batr. 71, 88.

σφοδρῶς, adv. (from σφοδρός), vehemently, violently, impetuously, Od. 12, 124.†

σφονδύλιος, ὁ, Ep. for σφόνδυλος, a vertebra of the back-bone; plur. the vertebræ, 20, 483.†

σφός, σφή, σφόν (σφεῖς), sing. his, her, it (suus), plur. their, like σφέτερος, 1, 534. Od. 2, 237. σὺν σφοῖσιν τεκέεσσι. h. Ap. 148. Herm. reads: αὐτοῖς σὺν τεκέεσσι.

σφῦρα, ἡ, a hammer, a mallet, Od. 3, 434; where in ed. Wolf, σφύραν stands incorrectly, see Buttm., Ausf. Gram. § 33, 4. p. 142.

σφυρόν, τό, the ankle, 4, 518; plur. *6, 117.

σφώ, 1) Abbrev. for σφῶϊ. 2) For σφωέ, Ep.

σφωέ, see σφωΐν.

σφώ, Ep. σφῶϊν and σφῶϊ, gen. and dat. σφωΐν, contr. σφῶν, Od. 4, 62; cf. Thiersch, Gram. § 204, 6; accus. σφωέ and σφώ, dual of the second personal pronoun, ye two; often ἀμφοτέρω σφῶϊ, Il. 7, 280; see Thiersch, § 204. Rost, Dial. 44. p. 412. Kühner, § 301.

σφωΐν, dat. dual of the third personal pronoun, accus. σφώ, Ep. σφωέ; the nom. is not in use; all the forms are enclitic: of them both, to them both; strengthened: σφωΐν ἀμφοτέροιϊν, Od. 20, 327. σφω' for σφωέ stands Il. 17, 531; σφώ, on the other hand, is found in Bothe, cf. Thiersch, Gram. § 204, 6. Rem.

σφωΐτερος, η, ον (σφῶϊ), your two, belonging to you two, Il. 1, 216.†

σχεδίη, ἡ, prop. fem. of σχέδιος, subaud. νηῦς, a vessel built in haste, by Odysseus (Ulysses) for a shift: a raft, *Od. 5, 33. 163. According to Nitzsch ad loc. a hand-boat, which one man can manage alone. [According to Ameis. it is derived from σχεῖν, akin to σχεδόν; cf. the German Gebünde, contignatio. Am.]

σχεδίην, Ep. adv. (prop. fem. of σχέδιος), near, in the vicinity, 5, 830.†

Σχέδιος, ὁ (adj. σχέδιος), 1) son of Iphitus and Hippolytê, leader of the Phocians, slain by Hector, 2, 517. 2) son of Perimides, another leader of the Phocians, 15, 515.

σχεδόθεν, adv. poet. from the vicinity, 16, 807. 17, 359. 2) in the vicinity, near, with gen. Od. 19, 447; and dat. Od. 2, 267.

σχεδόν, adv. poet. (σχεῖν, ἔχω). in the vicinity, near, absol. οὐτάζειν, ἐλαύνειν, εἶναι, 5, 458. 11, 488. b) As prep. with gen. ἐλθεῖν τινος, to come near any one, 5, 607. Od. 4, 439; with dat. Od. 2, 284. οὐ σχεδὸν ἦν ὑπερθορέειν, it was not near to leap over, i. e. the other side of the ditch was not so near that the horses

Σχεθεῖν.

could reach it, Il. 12, 53. 2) *near*, spoken of time: σοὶ δ᾽ αὐτῷ φημι σχεδὸν ἔμμεναι, 13, 817.

σχεθεῖν, Ep. σχεθέειν, infin. of a poet. lengthened aor. ἔσχεθον for ἔσχον, in the signif. *to hold, to restrain*; see ἔχω.

σχεῖν, σχέμεν, see ἔχω.

σχέο, see ἔχω.

Σχερίη, ἡ (prob. from σχερός, the land), *Scheria*, the blessed land of the Phæaces, Od. 5, 34. 280. According to the local indications furnished Od. 6, 204. 279, it may be considered as the island furthest north of Ithaca, near the land of the Thesprotians; according to the ordinary explanation of the ancients, the later Κέρκυρα, now *Corfu*, cf. Thuc. I, 25. Strab. These are followed amongst the moderns by Voss and Völcker: others place it towards Thesprotia or Campania (cf. Nitzsch ad Od. 7, 129). Others still regard it as a fabulous land in the vicinity of Elysium, as F. G. Welker in the treatise: *die homerischen Phäaken u. die Inseln der Seligen*, in the Rhein. Museum, St. 2, 1833, attempts to prove at large. Not inappropriately has the German *Schlaraffenland* (Pays de Cocagne), been compared with it.

σχέτλιος, η, ον (σχεῖν, ἔχω), the fem. only 3, 414. Od. 23, 150; that sustains or abides any thing; hence, 1) *strong, powerful, impetuous, bold, rash;* mly spoken in a bad sense, of those who from impetuous courage, or from a bad use of their strength, are terrible, as Heracles, Achilles, Hector, Il. 5, 403. 9, 630. 16, 203. 17, 150. Od. 9, 351. 478. The fem. σχετλίη, Il. 3, 414; plur. Od. 4, 729. It stands in a more favorable sense in Il. 10, 164, where Nestor, on account of his restless activity, is called σχέτλιος by Diomedes. Here and in 18, 13. Od. 12, 279, expositors endeavour to apply the meaning, *miserable, wretched;* it is, however, an expression like the Latin *improbus*, to be translated *wicked or prodigious, astonishing.* b) Often spoken of gods, and esply of Zeus, *harsh, severe, cruel*, 2, 111. 9, 19. Od. 3, 161; spoken of the gods generally, Il. 24, 133. Od. 5, 118. 2) Spoken of things, *violent, cruel, impious*, always with ἔργα, Od. 9, 295. 14, 83. 22, 413.

σχέτο, Ep. for ἔσχετο, see ἔχω.

ΣΧΕΩ, obsol., another form of ἔχω, q. v.

σχίζη, ἡ (σχίζω), *split wood, a billet of wood*, 1, 462. Od. 14, 425.

σχίζω, aor. 1 ἔσχισα, *to split, to cleave*, with accus. in tmesis, Od. 4, 507; generally, *to separate, to divide*, h. Merc. 128.

σχοίατο, Ion. for σχοῖντο, see ἔχω.

σχοῖνος, ὁ, *a rush, a bulrush*, also a place overgrown with rushes, Od. 5, 463.† Batr. 213.

Σχοῖνος, ἡ, a town in Bœotia, on the river Schœnus, not far from Thebes, 2, 497 Strabo calls it χώρα; the region received the name from the rushes growing thereabouts.

σχόμενος, η, ον, see ἔχω.

σώεσκον, see σαόω.

σώζω, the comm. form instead of the Ep. σαόω, only σώζων, Od. 5, 490; † see σαόω.

σῶκος, η, ον, Ep. (σωκέω), *strong, powerful* (V. 'that blesses'), epith. x Hermês, 20, 72. (The derivation from σάοικος, that preserves the house, according to Apion, is fanciful.)

Σῶκος, ὁ, a Trojan, son of Hippasus slain by Odysseus (Ulysses), 11, 427.

σῶμα, ατος, τό, *a body*, spoken both of men and beasts; in Hom. *a dead body, a corpse*, 7, 79. 23, 169. Od. 11. 53. [According to Aristot., sanctioned by Passow and Ameis, it is always spoken of a dead body in Hom., which brev. ad Il. 3, 23, it is there spoken of a living animal, cf. Eustath. ad l. c.]

σῶς, contr from σάος, occurs in Hom. only in the nom. sing. *safe, unhurt*, 332. Od. 15, 42. 2) *sure, certain*, according to the Schol. *complete*. σῶς ὄλεθρος, Il. 13, 773. Od. 5, 305; cf. σάος.

*σωτήρ, ῆρος, ὁ (σώζω), *a deliverer, preserver*, h. 21, 5. 33, 6.

Σώχ᾽, poet. shortened from Σῶκε, voc. from Σῶκος.

σώω, see σαόω.

T.

T, the nineteenth letter of the Greek alphabet, hence in Hom. the sign of the nineteenth rhapsody.

τ᾽, with an apostrophe 1) for τέ. More rarely in Hom. doubtful for τε in μέντ᾽ according to Bothe, Il 4, 54; Wolf μέν τ᾽, and in τάρ, see this word.

ταγός, ὁ (τάσσω), *an arranger, a leader*, a commander, 23, 160.† (Mly ά, hence Bothe and Spitzner have adopted τ᾽ ἐγώ which is the ancient reading.)

ΤΑΓΩ, obsol. theme of the defect. partcp. aor. 2 with Ep. redupl. τεταγών, *to seize, to grasp, to lay hold of*, ποδὸς τεταγών, seizing by the foot, *1, 591. 15, 23. According to the Schol. = λαβών and akin to ΤΑΩ, τείνω, cf. Buttm., Lex. p.

ταθείς, τάθη, see τείνω.

*Ταίναρον, τό (also ὁ Ταίναρος, Orph. Scylax; ἡ Ταίναρος, Pind.). *Tænarus*, a promontory in Laconia, the middle of the southern capes of the Peloponnesus, now *Cap Matapan*. Upon it there was a famous temple of Poseidôn, above a cave, where was the entrance to Hades, h. Ap. 412.

Ταλαεργός, 389 Τάμνω.

ταλαεργός, όν, poet. (ἔργον). enduring in labour, toil-enduring, burden-bearing [strong to toil, Cp.], epith. of the mule, 23. 654. 662. Od. 4, 636. 21, 23.
Ταλαιμένης, ονς, ὁ, poet. for Ταλαμένης, a leader of the Maeonians, 2. 865.
Ταλαϊονίδης, αο, ὁ, Ep. for Ταλαονίδης, son of Talaus = Adrastus, 2, 566. 23, 678.
τάλαντον, τό (ΤΑΛΑΩ, prop. that bears), prop. a scale, in the plur. the balance, scales, 12, 433. b) Metaph. the scales for the decision of Zeus (since Zeus weighs the fates of men in a golden balance), 8. 69. 16, 658. 19, 223; δίκης, h. Merc. 324. 2) that which is weighed, a specific weight, whose value cannot be determined, the talent, always with χρυσοῦ, sing. Od. 8, 393. Plur. Il. 9, 122. 18, 507. Od. 4, 129.
ταλαπείριος, ον (πεῖρα), that has sustained many trials, = τλήμων, miserable, wretched, ξεῖνος and ἱκέτης, *Od. 7, 24. 14, 511. h. Ap. 168.
ταλαπενθής, ές (πένθος), enduring-sufferings, patient, θυμός, Od. 5, 222.†
τάλαρος, ὁ (prob. from ΤΑΛΩ), a basket, a spinning-basket, so called because the wool which was daily weighed out to the slaves, was put in it, Od. 4, 132; also a fruit and cheese-basket, Il. 18, 568. Od. 9, 247. Mly of wicker-work; but also made of metallic rods, Od. 4, 132.
τάλας, τάλαινα, τάλαν (ΤΑΛΩ), voc. τάλαν, h. Merc. 160; enduring, suffering, miserable, wretched, Od. 18, 327; sometimes impudent, Od. 19, 68.
ταλασίφρων, ονος, ὁ, ἡ. poet. (φρήν), having an enduring soul, spoken of one who has sustained many battles, generally, courageous, spirited, brave, unterrified, Il. 4, 421; often spoken of Odysseus (Ulysses), Od. 3, 84. 4, 241.
ταλαύρινος, ὁ (ΤΑΛΑΩ, ῥινός). epith. of Arês, who makes resistance with a leathern shield, or who fights against shields, generally, steadfast, unwearied, invincible. 5, 289. 20, 78. The n-ut. as adv. τό μοί ἐστι ταλαύρινον πολεμίζειν; according to the Schol. τό stands for δι' ὅ, therefore can I steadfastly combat: or τό is metaleptic for ᾗ, referring to βῶν, *7, 239. cf. Thiersch, § 267. Damm, on the other hand, explains τό by ὅ. and refers it to the whole clause: which enables me, etc.
ταλάφρων, ονος, ὁ, ἡ, poet. shortened for ταλασίφρων. 13, 300.†
ΤΑΛΑΩ, an assumed theme for the defect. aor. 1 ἐτάλασα. Ep. σσ, subj. ταλάσσω, to venture, to dare, to undertake, with infin. following, *13, 829. 15, 164. 17, 166.
Ταλθύβιος, ὁ, a herald of king Agamemnon before Troy. In Sparta, at a later period, he was worshipt as a hero, 1, 320.
τάλλα, contr. for τὰ ἄλλα.
τάμε, ταμέειν, see τάμνω.
ταμεσίχρως, οος, ὁ, ἡ (χρώς), cutting or wounding the skin, lacerating the body (V. body-piercing), chiefly epith. of spears, *4, 511. 13, 340.
ταμίη, ἡ (τάμνω), a stewardess, a house-keeper, also γυνή, ἀμφίπολος ταμίη, 6, 381. Od. 1, 139; ἧε ταμίης.
ταμίης, ου, ὁ (τάμνω), prop. a distributor, that divides to each one his portion, a steward, a provider, a ruler, 19, 44; hence spoken of Zeus: ταμίης πολέμοιο (arbiter of war, V.), 4. 84. 19, 224; of Æolus: ἀνέμων, Od. 10, 21.
τάμνω, Ep. and Ion. for τέμνω, fut. τεμῶ, aor. 2 ἔταμον, Ep. τάμον, always without augment, infin. ταμεῖν, Ep. ταμέειν, aor. 2 mid. ἐταμόμην, infin. ταμέσθαι, perf. pass. τέτμημαι. (From τέμνω, only pres. infin. τέμνειν, Od. 3, 175; imperf. τέμνον, h. Cer. 382; and fut. τεμεῖ, Il. 13, 707; but where Buttm. and Spitzner would read τέμει as pres.), Ep. for τμήγω, 1) to cut, to hew, to split, and, according to the relation indicated by the prep., to cut in pieces, to hew in pieces, to split in pieces, to cut through, to hew through, to cut off, to cut out, spoken of things animate and inanimate, ἀρνῶν ἐκ κεφαλέων τρίχας, 3, 273, βέλος ἐκ μηροῦ, 11, 844; κεφαλὴν ἀπ' ὤμοιϊν, 17, 20; esply a) Spoken of persons: χρόα χαλκῷ, 13, 501; τινὰ διαμελεϊστί, to hew a man limb by limb [Cp.], Od. 18, 339. b) Spoken of beasts: prop. to carv-, generally, to slay, 11. 19, 197 (as a sacrifice); esply ὅρκια τάμνειν, to conclude a treaty, like fœdus ferire, from the slaughtering of the victim on such occasions, 2, 124; and often, see ὅρκια; also φιλότητα καὶ ὅρκια πιστά, 3, 73. 94. 256. cf. 4, 155. b) Spoken of trees and wood; to cut down, to fell, also to hew, δένδρεα, 11, 83; δούρατα, Od. 5, 243; pass. μελίη χαλκῷ ταμνομένη, Il. 13, 180. cf. Od. 17, 597. c) Spoken of motion through space, like secare, of a ship: πέλαγος, κύματα, Od. 3, 175. 13. 88; ἤέρα, h. Cer. 382; of the plough: τεμεῖ δέ τε τέλσον ἀρούρης, Il. 13, 707; supply, with Heinrichs, from the preceding ἄροτρον, and take the sentence as a parenthesis: it cuts through the end or boundary of the field. Instead of τεμεῖ as fut., Spitzner, after the Cod. Ven., has adopted τέμει, because the fut. can hardly be defended, cf. Buttm., Gr. Gram. p. 388. The early critics improperly refer τεμεῖ to ζυγόν; Voss follows the conjecture of Barnes, and translates: they cut diligently the furrow down to the end of the field. 2) to cut out, i. e. to separate, to cut off, to measure off, hence τέμενός τινι, 6, 194. 20, 184. Mid. 1) to cut off for oneself, to cut in pieces, with accus. κρέα, Od. 24, 304; to fell for oneself, δοῦρα, Od. 5, 243. τάμνοντ' ἀμφὶ βοῶν ἀγέλας, they cut off for themselves the herds, i. e. they drove them away, Il. 18, 528. cf. περιτέμνω. 2) to cut out for oneself, to separate, ταμίεσθαι ἄροσιν, 9, 580. It is better, with Spitzner, to take ταμέ

Ταναηκής.

σθαι as dpt on ἄροσιν πεδίοιο ταμέσθαι, sc. ἀράτρῳ, arable land, to plough. *(And half of land commodious for the plough,* Cp.]
ταναηκής, ές, gen. έος, poet. (ἀκή), with a long point or blade, *long-pointed, long-headed, long-bladed,* epith. of the spear and the sword, 7, 77. 24, 754. Od. 4, 257.
ταναός, όν, poet. (τείνω), *stretched, extended, long, lofty,* αἰγανέη, Il. 16, 589 ;† ἀσταχύες, h. Cer. 454. (Later also three endings.)
ταναύπους, ποδος, ὁ, ἡ, Ep. for ταναόπους (πούς), *stretching the feet, long-legged,* or *swift-running,* μῆλα, Od. 9, 464.† h. Ap. 304.
τανηλεγής, ές (ταναός, λέγω), *that stretches out long, that extends at length,* epith. of death, because the dead body appears longer ('for a long time' seems unsuitable, since death stretches out for ever', 8, 70. Od. 2, 100 ; and often.
Τάνταλος, ὁ, son of Zeus and Hades, or of Tmôlus, king of Sipylus in Phrygia, grandfather of Atreus and Thyestes. Blessed by the gods with riches, and even entertained at their table, he betrayed their secrets, and also he once served up his son Pelops at a feast of the gods in order to prove their omniscience. As a punishment, he was made to stand in Hades up to the neck in water, and yet obliged to suffer eternal thirs', Od. 11, 583. According to another fable, a rock was suspended over him and threatened to fall upon him; hence his name from ταντολεία, akin to τάλαντον. Plato, Cratyl. p. 395, derives it from τάλας, wretched.
τανύγλωσσος, ον, poet. (γλῶσσα), *having a long tongue, long-tongued,* κορώνας, Od. 5, 66.†
τανυγλώχιν, ινος, ὁ, ἡ (γλωχίν), *having a long point, long-pointed,* epith. of an arrow, 8, 297.†
τανυήκης, ες, poet. (ἀκή), *having a long point, long-pointed, long extended.* ἄορ, 14, 366. Od. 10, 439 ; once ὄξοι, Il. 16, 768.
τάνυμαι, poet. for τανύομαι, after the conjug. in μι; from this τάνυνται, 17, 393 ;† see τανύω.
τανύπεπλος, ον, poet. (πέπλος), *having a long upper garment* or *robe,* as the noble women wore it (whereas slaves tucked it up), as Helen, 3, 228. Od. 12, 375. ταν. πλακούς, jocularly : a cake surrounded by sugar and spices, Batr. 36.
*τανύπτερος, ον, poet. shortened from τανυσίπτερος, h. Cer. 89.
τανυπτέρυξ, υγος, ὁ, ἡ, poet. (πτέρυξ). with outspread wings, *long-winged, broad-winged,* i. e. swift-flying, οἰωνοί, ἄρπῃ, *12, 237. 19, 350.
τανυσίπτερος, ον (πτέρον), = τανυπτέρυξ, *Od. 5, 65. 22, 468.
τανυστύς, ύος, ἡ, poet. (τανύω), *the act of stretching* or *drawing,* τόξου, Od. 21, 111.†
*τανύσφυρος, ον, poet. (σφυρόν), prop.

390

Ταρβέω

having stretched ankles, *slender-footed,* h. Cer. 2, 77.
τανύφλοιος, ον, poet. (φλοιός), prp. *having a long bark,* prob. *of a late growth, lofty,* perhaps because in peeling it tears into long pieces, κράνεια. Κ 767.†
τανύφυλλος, ον. poet. (φύλλον), *having long leaves* or *thick leaved,* ἐλαία, *Od. 13, 102. 23, 190.
τανύω, poet. lengthened from ταν. fut. ύσω, Ep. σσ, and τανύω, Od. 2, 174; aor. 1 Ep. ἐτάνυσσα. τάνυσα, 2, τάνυσσα ; aor. 1 mid. Ep. ἐτανυσσάμην and τανυσσάμην, perf. pass. τετάνυσμαι aor. 1 pass. Ep. τανύσθην (τάνυται, Ep. shortened for τανύεται, 11. 17, 393, after the conjug. in μι), I) *to stretch, i. e. to extend, to expand, to spread out,* with accus. ἴριν, 17, 547. b) *to stretch,* i. e. *to draw to bend,* to *strain,* τόξον, βίον, χορδῇν ιτ. κόλλοπι, Od. 21, 407 ; hence pass. *to be stretched, to be tense* or *strained,* γνάμψα τάνυσθεν, Od. 16, 176 ; ἵππους, to guide. Il. 23, 334 ; κανόνα, *to fly* or *pass the shuttle,* 23, 761; metaph. *to move violently, to excite,* ἔριδα πτολέμοιο, 14, 389 ; μάχην. 11, 336 (ἔριδος πεῖραρ ἐπ' ἀμφοτέροισι τάνυσσαν, 13, 359 ; see ἐναλλάσσω :: πόνον, 17, 401; hence pass. *to exert oneself, to hasten, to run, to leap,* 16, 375 : ἐν ῥυτῆρσι τάνυσθεν, 16, 475. 2) *to stretch out, to prostrate, to place, to set,* ὀβελοῖσιν, 9, 213 : τράπεζαν often, τινα ἐν κονίῃς, 23, 25. Od. 18, 92 ; hence pass. *to lie extended,* Il. 9, 468. 10, 116. 13, 392 ; νήσος τετάνυσται, Od. 9, 116. cf. Od. 4, 135. Mid. 1) *to bend a stretch for oneself,* with accus. τόξον, Il. 4, 112 ; χορδάς, h. Merc. 51. 2) *to extend oneself, to stretch oneself out,* Od. 9. 298.
τάπης, ητος, ὁ, *a carpet, a cover,* which was spread over seats and beds, 9, 204. Od. 4, 124.
τάρ, according to some Gramm. contr. from τοὶ ἄρ ; hence Buthe : τάρ, 1, 8. !, 268 ; according to others doubtful, hence Wolf : τ' ἄρ for τὲ ἄρ, cf. Buttm., G: Gram. § 29. 4. Note 22 ; and Spitzner.
ταράσσω, aor. 1 ἐτάραξα, Ep. intrans perf. τέτρηχα, from the Att. form θράττω Ion. θρήττω, 1) *to stir, to stir up, speak of storms:* πόντον, *to stir up the sea,* Od. 5, 291; metaph. *to perplex, to disquiet, to disturb,* φρένας, Batr. 14 δαῖτα, Il. 1, 579 ; see συνταράσσω. The perf. 2 τέτρηχα has an intrans. signif. *to be unquiet, stormy,* spoken of an assembly of the people, 2, 95. 7, 346. (The form θράττω arose by metathesis from τραάσσω, where τ passes in θ on account of ρ. and the vowel is lengthened (partcp. θράττον); from this the perf. τέτρηχα, see Buttm., in Lexil., and Gram., p. 302. Rost, p. 330. Kühner. § 155)
*ταρβαλέος, η, ον, poet. (τάρβος), *horrible, terrified,* h. Merc. 165.
ταρβέω, poet. (τάρβος), aor. 1 Ep. τάρ-

βήσα, iterat. imperf. τάρβεσκον, 1) Intrans. *to be terrified, to be fearful*, Il.; with the adjunct θυμῷ, 7, 51. 2) Trans. *to fear, to be afraid of*, with accus. 6, 469. 11, 405.

τάρβος, εος, τό, *terrour, fear, fright, alarm,* *24, 152. 181.

ταρβοσύνη, ή, poet. = τάρβος, Od. 18, 342.†

Τάρνη, ή, a town in Lydia, at mount Tmōlus, later *Sardes*, 5, 44.

ταρπήμεναι, ταρπήναι, see τέρπω.

ταρσός, ὁ (τέρσω), 1) *a crate* or *frame* of wicker-work for drying any thing upon [*a strainer*, Cp.], Od. 9, 219. 2) any level surface, eχply ταρσὸς ποδός, *a foot-sole, a sole*, Il. 11, 377. 388.

Τάρταρος, ὁ, a deep abyss under the earth, which lies as deep below Hades as the earth is below the heavens. It has iron gates and brazen thresholds, 8, 13, seq. cf. Ἀΐδης. Here are the Titans, Κronus (Saturn), Iapetus, etc., 8, 481. b. Ap. 336. h. Merc. 256. 374.

ταρφέες, οἱ, ταρφέα, τά (τάρφος, τρέφω), defect. adj. used only in the plur., to which as fem. ταρφειαί belongs; *thick, frequent, dense*, epith. of arrows, ἰοί, 11, 387. 15, 472. Od. 22, 246. Neut. plur as adv. *thickly, frequently, densely, often*, Il. 12, 47. 13, 718. (The derivation from ταρφής is incorrect; on the other hand, at a later date, in Æschylus ταρφύς actually occurs: see Buttm., Gr. Sprachl. § 64. Rem. 2.)

ταρφειός, ὁ, only in the fem. plur. ταρφειαί, *thick, crowded, frequent*, νιφάδες, κόρυθες, 12, 158. 19, 357. (According to Buttm., Gr. Sprachl. § 64. Rem. 2, to be accented prop. ταρφεῖαι.)

Τάρφη, ή, a town in Locris, west of Œta, according to Strabo the later *Pharygæ*, 2. 533.

ταρφής, see ταρφέες.

τάρφθη, Ep. for ἐτάρφθη, see τέρπω.

τάρφος, εος, τό (from τρέφω by a transposition of the letters), *thickness, a thicket*, only in the dat. plur. ἐν τάρφεσιν ὕλης [*in the deep recess of a wood*, Cp.], *5, 555. 15, 606.

ταρχύω (poet. for ταριχεύω), fut. ταρχύσω, aor. subj. ταρχύσωσι, prop. to embalm, and generally, *to inter, to bury*, aor. ψίκυν, 7, 85; τύμβῳ τε στήλῃ τε, *16, 456.

ταύρειος, η, ον (ταῦρος), prop. of a bull; then *of bull's hide, of ox-hide*, epith. of a shield and of a helmet, *10, 258. 13, 161. 16, 360.

ταῦρος, ὁ. *a bull, an ox*, ταῦρος βοῦς, 17, 389. Bulls were eχply offered in sacrifice to the superior gods, also to river-gods, 11, 728. 21, 131.

ταφήϊος, η, ον, Ep. and Ion. ταφεῖος (τάφος), *belonging to burial*. ταφ. φάρος, a shroud, *Od. 2, 99. 19, 144.

Τάφιοι, οἱ, a tribe of the Leleges, who prop. dwelt partly on the western coast of Acarnania, partly upon the small islands between Acarnania and Leuca-dia. From the largest of these, Taphos, they received their name. The Taphians were engaged in navigation, and also in piracy, Od. 1, 105. 181. 14, 452. 15, 427. They were also called *Teleboæ*, Apd. 2, 4. 5. cf. Mannert VIII. s. 96.

Τάφος, ή, the largest of the islands inhabited by the Taphians; according to Dodwell, now *Meganisi*, Od. 1, 417. Voss places it, Alt. Weltkunde, p. 6, at the Acheloüs.

τάφος, ὁ (θάπτω), 1) *interment*, and the customary solemnities connected with it, *a funeral solemnity*, Πατρόκλοιο τάφ., 23, 619. 680. 2) Esply *a funeral feast*, δαινύναι τάφον, to give a funeral feast, 23, 29. Od. 3, 309.

τάφος, εος, τό, poet. (ΘΑΦΩ), *astonishment, amazement, wonder*, *Od. 21, 122. 23, 93. 24, 441. h. 6, 37.

τάφρος, ή (akin to τάφος). *a trench*. 7, 341. 450. Od. 21, 120; esply about walls, Il. 8, 179. 9, 349.

ταφών, partcp. aor. 2 of ΘΑΦΩ, q. v.

τάχα, adv. (from ταχέα), *quickly, swiftly, immediately, soon*, only of time, τάχα δή, quickly indeed, Od. 1, 251; and ἦ τάχα, Od. 18, 73. 19, 69; τάχα ποτέ, quickly sometime, Il. 1, 205: in Hom. never: *perhaps, probably*, cf. Nitzsch. ad Od. 8, 202.

ταχέως, adv. (ταχύς), *quickly, soon*, 23, 365.†

τάχιστος, η, ον, see ταχύς.

τάχος, εος, τό (ταχύς), *swiftness, rapidity*, *23, 406. 515.

ταχύπωλος, ον (πῶλος), *having swift horses*, an epith. of the Greeks, *4, 232; and often.

ταχύς, εῖα, ύ, compar. θάσσων, neut. θᾶσσον, superl. τάχιστος, η ον, *swift, quick, active, hasty*. ταχὺς πόδας, swiftfooted. 13, 249; and with infin. θέειν, 16, 186. Od. 3, 112. The neut. of the comp. θᾶσσον stands as adv., Il. 2, 440. Od. 2, 307. Of the superl. Hom. has only the neut. plur. as adv. τάχιστα, most quickly, very fleetly. ὅ,ττι τάχιστα, as quickly as possible, Il. 4, 193. Od. 5, 112.

ταχυτής, ῆτος, ή (ταχύς), *fleetness*, 28, 740. Od. 17, 315.

ΤΑΩ, an assumed theme, 1) for the derivation of the imperf. τῆ, q. v. 2) Incorrectly for ·the formation of the tenses of τείνω.

τέ, an enclitic particle: *and* (q u e), the most universal copula, unites related and co-ordinate notions and clauses. It stands 1) Single, chiefly in connecting notions which receive a casual adjunct clause, or which rise as a natural consequence from what precedes, 1, 5. cf. 57, 159. 2) When doubled, τέ ... τέ, it marks the correspondence of connected clauses, *as—so, both—and*, πατὴρ ἀνδρῶν τε θεῶν τε, 1, 544; also often in a series, 1, 177. 2, 58. Od. 3, 413. 3) It is often connected with other particles, τέ περ, Od. 21, 142, τὲ καί and καί τε, see καί: Ep. also τ' ἠδέ, Il. 2, 206. 9, 159; and

Τεγέη, 392 Τείνω.

more rarely τ' ἰδέ, ed. Spitz., 8, 162. 4) By τέ H. also connects different modes and tenses, 8, 347. 10, 224. cf. Thiersch, Gram. § 312. 11. 5) By a use peculiar to the Epic poets τέ very frequently stands after relative pronouns and conjunctions, as an exterior indication of the internal connexion of the sentences; a) With relatives, ὅστε, he who, namely he, ὅστις τε, οἷός τε, ὅσος τε, ἅτε. b) After relative particles, ἔνθα τε, ὅτε τε, ὥς τε, ὡσεί τε, ἵνα τε. c) Ον γάρ τε, μέν τε, δέ τε, see these conjunctions.

Τεγέη, ἡ, an old town in Arcadia, having a famous temple of Athênê, now in ruins. *Paleo Episcopi* near *Tripulitza*, 2, 607.

τέγος, ον (τέγος), *under the roof*, τέγεοι θάλαμοι, apartments under the roof for the daughters of Priam, 6, 248.† The Schol. explain it by ὑπερῷοι, apartments in the highest part of the house, occupied by the females of the family, but these apartments were opposite to those of the men, and situated on the interior of the court; hence, more correctly with Heyne and Köppen, under the roof of the house, not under the porch.

τέγος, εος, τό. *a roof, a cover*, Od. 10, 559. 11, 64. 2) Any covered part of the house, *a room, a chamber, a hall*, *Od. 1, 333. 8, 458.

τεθαλυῖα, τέθηλα, see θάλλω.

τέθηπα, see ΘΑΦΩ.

τίθναθι, τεθναίην, and τεθνάμεναι, τεθνᾶσι, see θνήσκω.

τεθνεώς, τεθνηώς, and τεθνειώς, see θνήσκω.

τείν, Dor. for σοί, see σύ.

τείνω, aor. 1 ἔτεινα, perf. pass. τέταμαι, 3 sing. τέταται, pluperf. 3 sin·. τέτατο, 3 dual τετάσθην, aor. 1 pass. ἐτάθην, Ep. τάθην. 1) *to stretch*, a) *to extend, to stretch out, to spread out*, ἡνία ἐξ ἄντυγος, to bind the reins fast to the chariot seat, 5, 262. 322; and pass. ὀχεὺς τέτατο ὑπ' ἀνθερεῶνος, the fastening extended under the chin, 3, 372; τελαμῶνε τετάσθην, 14, 404; τέταθ' ἱστία, Od. 11, 11. Metaph. λαίλαπα τείνειν, to spread a storm, Il. 16, 365; νύκτα, Od. 11, 19. b) *to stretch, to bend, to draw, to make tense*, τόξον, Il. 4, 124; ἶσον πολέμου τέλος, to draw equally the end of the war, i. e. to accord to both parties a similar issue. 20, 101; pass. 12, 436; metaph. ἐπὶ Πατρόκλῳ τέτατο κρατερή ὑσμίνη, a fierce battle arose about Patroclus, 17, 453; ἵπποισι τάθη δρόμος, the race was strained by the horses, i. e. the horses stretched to the race, 23, 375; ἀπὸ νύσσης, their race was stretched from the barriers, 23, 758. Od. 8, 121. 2) *to stretch along, to lay down*. φάσγανον τέτατο, the sword hung down, Il. 22, 307; esply *to stretch upon the ground*, τινὰ ἐπὶ γαίῃ, 13, 655; ἐν κονίῃσιν, 4, 536. 544.

Τειρεσίης, ao. Ep. for Τειρεσίας, *Tiresias*, son of Eueres and the nymph Chariclo, a noted prophet of Thebes. He was changed to a woman, and did not become a man again till the expiration of seven years. Angry at a decision which displeased her, Hêrê made him blind; Zeus, on the contrary, gave him the gift of prophecy, and a life of nine ages, Od. 10, 492. 11. 32. 267. 23. 251.

τείρος, εος, τό, Ep. for τέρας, cf. Thiersch, Gram. § 188, 13; used only in the plur. τὰ τείρεα, *the heavenly ones*, the constellations by which seamen and travellers by land direct their course, Il. 485.† h. 7, 7.

τείρω, only pres. and imperf. prop. *to rub, to rub off*, metaph. *to rub out, to exhaust, to enfeeble, to oppress, to weaken*, spoken of the body, by age, wounds, hunger, with accus. 4, 315. 5, 153. 13, 251. Of the soul, by care and anxiety: *to torment, to distress*, τινὰ κατὰ φρένας, 15, 61; κῆρ, Od. 1, 342; often pass., τείρεσθαι, to be pressed, exhausted in battle, Il. 6, 387. 9, 248; χαλκῷ, 17, 376; τεύθει, Od. 2, 71.

τειχεσιπλήτης, ου, ὁ (πελάζω, ἐπλήμην), approaching the walls, *the assaulter of walls, the assailer of fortresses*, epith. of Arês, *5, 31. 455.

τειχίζω, aor. 1 mid. Ep. ἐτειχίσσαντο, to build a wall; mid. *to build a wall for oneself*; τεῖχος, 7, 449.†

τειχιόεις, εσσα, εν (τεῖχος), surrounded with walls, *walled*, epith. of fortified towns, *2, 559. 646.

τειχίον, τό = τεῖχος, of which it is a dimin., but only in form, *a wall*, esply of a court, *Od. 16, 165. 348.

τεῖχος, εος, τό, *a wall*, e-ply a *city wall*, which served as a fortification; in Hom. any kind of a wall or entrenchment made of cast up earth, before Troy, ἀμφίχυτον τεῖχος, 20, 145. The margin was prob. covered with stone. So also at the Grecian camp, 9, 349. 12, 399. 438.

τείως, adv. Ep. for τέως.

τέκε, τεκέειν, see τίκτω.

τεκμαίρομαι, depon. mid. (τέκμαρ), aor. 1 Ep. τεκμήραμην, prop. to place a mark, hence 1) *to establish, to appoint, to determine*, spoken esply of the deity and of fate, κακά τινι, 6, 349. 7, 70; also of Alcinous, πομπήν τινι, Od. 7, 317; generally, *to indicate, to communicate, to predict*, ὄλεθρόν τινι, Od. 11, 112. 2) Later, *to decide with oneself, to conclude*, h. Ap. 285. (The act. is later.)

τέκμωρ, τό, indecl. poet. 1) *a mark, a border, an end*, 13, 10; εὐρεῖν τέκμωρ to find an end or an issue, Od. 4, 373. 466; εὑρέσθαι τέκμωρ, Il. 16, 472; τέκμωρ Ἰλίου, the end of Troy, i. e. the destruction. 7, 30. 9, 48. 2) Generally. *a sign, a token, a pledge*, by which any thing is assured. μέγιστον τέκμωρ ἐξ ἐμέθεν the greatest token from me (V. 'the most sacred pledge of my promises'), 1, 526; *a divine omen*. h. 31, 13.

τέκνον, τό (τίκτω), *that which is born*,

Τέκον. 393 Τέλος.

a child; often as a friendly address, with adj. masc. φίλε τέκνον, 22, 84. b) *a young one*, of animals, 2, 311. 11, 113. Od. 16, 217.

τέκον, Ep. for ἔτεκον, see τίκτω.

τέκος, εος, τό, poet. = τέκνον (τίκτω), dat. plur. τέκεσσι and τεκέεσσι, *a child*, Διὸς τέκος, 2, 157 Od. 2, 177. 2) *a young one*, of beasts, 11. 8, 248. 12, 222.

τεκταίνομαι, depon. mid. (τέκτων), aor. 1 Ep. τεκτηνάμην, *to construct, to build, to prepare*, with accus. νῆας, 5, 63; χέλυν, h. Merc. 25. Metaph. *to devise, to plot*, μῆτιν, *10, 19.

Τεκτονίδης, ἀο, ὁ, son of Tecton, Od. 8, 114.

τεκτοσύνη, ἡ (τέκτων), *building, construction, architecture*, plur. ('works of architecture,' V.), Od. 5, 250.†

τέκτων, ονος, ὁ (akin to τεκεῖν, τεύχω), one who prepares or makes any thing, *a workman, an artist*; κεραοξόος, one who works in horn, 4, 110; esply *a carpenter, a builder* or *architect*, 5, 59. Od. 17, 384; also τέκτονες ἄνδρες, 6. 315. (In Il. 5, 59, many, as Damm, regard it as a pr. n. *Am. Ed.*|

ΤΕΚΩ, absol. theme of τίκτω.

τελαμών, ῶνος, ὁ (τλῆναι), prop. *a bearer, a holder*, esply 1) *a belt*, a leathern strap on which the sword was carried, 2, 388. 5, 796. 798; and also the shield, 7, 304; sometimes also the short sword, 18, 598; hence two are mentioned in 14, 404; often of costly fabric, 11, 38. Od. 11, 610. 2) *a band*, for binding up wounds, Il. 17, 290.

Τελαμών, ῶνος, ὁ, son of Aeacus, brother of Peleus, king of Salamis, father of Aias (Ajax) and Teucer, 17, 293. Od. 11, 553.

Τελαμωνιάδης, ου, ὁ, son of Telamon = Ajax and Teucer, 9, 623. 13, 709.

Τελαμώνιος, η, ον, *Telamonian*, of Telamon, by way of distinction from Ajax, son of Oïleus, 2, 528. 13, 67. 76. 170.

τελέθω (poet. lengthened from τέλλω), pres. and iterat. imperf. τελέθεσκε, h. Cer. 241, *to arise, to become, to be*, with the implied notion of coming into being, νὺξ ἤδη τελέθει, it is already night, 7, 282. 293. cf. 9, 441. Od. 4, 85. 17, 486.

τέλειος, ον (τέλος), superl. τελειότατος, η, ον, *finished*, hence, *perfect, complete*, spoken of sacrificial animals, which were required to be spotless and perfect, 1, 66. 24, 34 (or, as others say, because they must be full-grown); the eagle is called τελειότατος πετεηνῶν, the most perfect among birds of omen, because his omen, as coming from Zeus, was most certain, *8, 247. 24. 315.

τελείω, Ep. lengthened for τελέω.

*τέλεος, η, ον=τέλειος, h. Merc. 129.

τελεσφόρος, ον (φέρω), prop. act. *bringing the end. bringing to perfection* or *maturity*; Ζεύς, who brings the end of all things, h. 22, 2; and often τελεσφόρον εἰς ἐνιαυτόν, to the *full-perfecting year* (because, according to the Schol.,

in this every thing comes to maturity). According to others, reflex. to the *self-perfecting* or *complete* year, 9, 32. Od. 4, 86. Thus Nitzsch ad Od 4, 86.

*τελετή, ἡ (τελέω), *accomplishment, end*, Batr. 305.

τελευτάω (τελευτή), σω, aor. 1 Ep. τελεύτησα, fut. mid. τελευτήσομαι, with pass. signif. 13, 100; aor. 1 pass. ἐτελευτήθην, 1) *to finish, to accomplish, to bring into operation*, with accus. ἔργα, 8, 9; γάμον to consummate, Od. 24, 126; ὅρκον. to finish an oath, i. e. to give in the best form, complete, Il. 14, 280. Od. 2, 378; κακὸν ἡμάρ τινι, to bring to any one the day of evil, Od. 15, 524. 2) *to cause to be fulfilled, to fulfil*, spoken of promises and wishes; τί, Il. 13, 375; ἐέλδωρ, Od. 21, 200. cf. 3, 62; hence pass. with fut. mid. *to be accomplished, to be fulfilled*, to come to pass, Il. 15, 74. Od. 2, 171.

τελευτή, ἡ (τελέω), 1) *accomplishment, completion*, τελευτὴν ποιῆσαι. to bring to pass, Od. 1, 249. 16, 126. 2) *a termination, an end*; βιότοιο, Il. 7, 104. h. 6, 29; metaph. *an end, an aim, an object*, μύθοιο, 9, 625.

τελέω, Ep. τελείω, according to the necessity of the metre (τέλος), fut. τελέσω, Ep. τελέω, aor. 1 ἐτέλεσα, Ep. σσ, and τέλεσα, perf. pass. τετέλεσμαι, aor. pass. ἐτελέσθην. 1) *to bring to an end, to finish, to end*, τί, δρόμον, 23, 373. 768; ὁδόν, Od. 10, 490; with particp. οὐδ' ἐτέλεσσε φέρων, he did not quite bring it, Il. 12, 222; hence pass. *to be finished, accomplished, fulfilled*, often τὸ καὶ τετελεσμένον ἔσται, which will also be accomplished, 1, 212; τετελεσμένος also signifies, *that may be fulfilled, that may be accomplished*, 1, 388. 2) *to accomplish, to execute*; κότον or χόλον. to satisfy one's anger, 1, 82. 4, 178; spoken of wishes and promises: *to bring to pass, to fulfil*, ὑπόσχεσιν, ὅρκια, Od. 10, 483. Il. 7, 69; μῦθον, Od. 4, 776; ἔπος τινί, Il. 1, 108. 3) *to accord, to grant, to present*, τινί τι. Il. 9, 157; ἀγαθόν, Od. 2, 34; γῆρας, Od. 23, 286; δῶρα, h. Cer. 369; esply *to pay*, spoken of established tributes, θέμιστας, Il. 9, 156. 298.

τελήεις, εσσα, εν (τελέω), *complete, perfect*, like τέλειος, spoken of victims: τελήεσσαι ἑκατόμβαι, perfect hecatombs (either full in number, or in which the animals were without blemish), 1, 315. Od. 4, 582. τελήεντες οἰωνοί, perfect birds of omen, which give sure omens, h. Merc. 544.

τέλλω, aor. 1 ἔτειλα, perf. pass. τέταλμαι, in H. only in tmesis, ἐπιτέλλω, q. v.

τέλος, εος, τό, 1) *end, boundary, aim*, very often spoken of things and actions: *accomplishment, completion, issue*. τέλος ἔχειν, to have an end. to be finished, 18, 378. τέλος μύθων ἱκέσθαι, to reach the end of the discourse, i. e. to have said every thing, 9, 56; hence τέλος μύθων, the whole of the discourse, 16, 83; πολλά·

Τέλοσδε. 394 Τέρπω.

μοιο, the end of the war, 3, 291 : hence also, *the issue, the decision, ἐν γὰρ χερσὶ τέλος πολέμου, ἐπέων δ' ἐνὶ βουλῇ* ['tongues in debate, but hands in war decide,' Cp.], 16, 630; often periphrastically, τέλος θανάτου, the end of death, the end brought on by death, 3, 309. Od. 5, 326. *b) accomplishment, completion,* γάμοιο, Od. 20, 74. τέλος ἐπιτιθέναι μύθῳ, to give accomplishment to the word. i. e. to execute, Il. 19, 107. 20, 369. τέλος ἐπιγίγνεται, the accomplishment is come, Od. 17, 496. *c)* The point of time in which any thing must happen, *the appointed time, μισθοῖο,* the time of reward, Il. 21, 450. 2) *the aim, the object, the design,* Od. 9, 5. *b) the extremity,* εἰς τέλος, to the extreme, h. Merc. 462. 3) *a troop, a squadron of warriors,* 7, 380. 10, 470. 11, 730.

τέλοσδε, Ep. for εἰς τέλος, adv. *to the end, to the limit,* θανάτοιο τέλοσδε, *9, 411. 13, 602.

τέλσον, τό, poet. for τέλος, *the end, the limit, the boundary,* ἀρούρης, the boundary of the field, i. e. the bounded field, *13, 707. 18, 544.

*Τελφοῦσα, Ep. and Ion. for Τιλφοῦσα (Τιλφοῦσσα, Apd., Τιλφώσσα, Pind.), 1) a fountain in Bœotia, sacred to Apollo, not far from Haliartus, near the town Tilphussion. 2) the nymph of this fountain, h. Ap. 246. (The correct orthography is Τιλφοῦσσα, contr. from Τιλφόεσσα. from τίλφη, Att. for σίλφη, a beetle, cf. Ilgen & h. Ap. l. c.)

*Τελφούσσιος, ὁ, epith. of Apollo, h. Ap. 387.

τέμενος, εος, τό (τέμνω), 1) a piece of land separated from the public possessions for a ruler, *a royal demesne; a lot* assigned to aby, 6, 194. Od. 6, 293; generally, *a field, cultivated land,* Il. 18, 550. 2) Esply a portion of land dedicated to a deity, often *a grove,* with a temple, 2, 696. 8, 48. Od. 8, 363.

Τεμέση, ἡ, a town famous for its copper mine, Od. 1, 184. Most of the old critics, and amongst the moderns Grotefend, Spohn, Nitzsch, understand by it Temese or Tamasus in Cyprus, which was famed for that metal, cf. Köpke, Kriegsw. d. Gr. p. 44. Others, cf. Strab. VI. p. 255, suppose that the town Tempsa or Temsa in lower Italy is meant. See Ovid. Fast. V. 441.

τέμνω = τάμνω, q. v.
τέμω, theme of τέμνω.

ΤΕΜΩ, from which the defect. aor. 2 ἔτεμον and τέτμον (prop. for ἐτέτεμον with syncop.), subj. τέτμης, τέτμῃ, *to reach, to attain, to overtake,* with accus. 4, 293. Od. 3, 256. h. Cer. 179; cf. Thiersch, Gr. § 232. 144.

Τένεδος, ἡ, an island of the Ægean Sea, on the coast of Troas, with a town of the same name, now *Tenedo,* 1, 452. Od. 3, 159.

Τενθρηδών, όνος, ὁ, a leader of the Magnētes from Thessaly, 2, 756.

τένων, οντος, ὁ (τείνω), prop. *the drawer; a tendon, a sinew,* esply *a muscle of the neck,* 4, 521; and often : Od. 3, 449 : only dual or plur. in Hom.

τέξω and τέξομαι, see τίκτω.
τέο, Ep. and Ion. for τινός and τίνος.
τεοῖο, Ep. for σοῦ, see σύ.
τεός, ἡ, όν, Ep. and Dor. for σός, *thy, thine,* often, 1, 138, and Od. 1, 295.

τέρας, ατος, Ep. αος, τό, nom. plur. Ep. τέραα, Od. 12, 394 ; Ep. τείρεα, gen. τεράων, dat. τεράεσσι, *a sign, a token, an omen, a miracle, a prodigy* (prodigium, portentum), esply spoken of natural phenomena, as thunder, lightning, rainbows, etc., by which the gods presaged the future. τέρας Διός, a sign sent by Zeus, 12, 209. Od. 16, 320 ; but τέρας ἀνθρώπων, a sign for men, Il. 11, 28. *b)* Spoken of any uncommon appearances, in which were seen the displeasure of the deity, 12, 209. 2, 324. h. Ap. 302; hence, *a terrific sign, a signal,* πολέμοιο, 11, 4. 17, 548 ; spoken of Gorgo, τέρας Διός, 5, 742.

*τερατωπός, όν (ὤψ), of wonderful appearance, *wonderful to behold,* h. 19, 36.

τέρετρον, τό (τερέω), *a gimlet,* *Od. 5, 246. 23, 198.

τέρην, εινα, εν (τείρω), gen. ενος, prop. rubbed off; hence *tender, soft, delicate.* esply ἄνθεα, φύλλα ; masc. only, τέρην χρόα, 4, 237; fem. τέρεινα γλήχων, h. Cer. 209.

τέρμα, ατος, τό (akin to τέρας), *end, limit, goal,* esply in the race-course, around which the chariots turned, otherwise νύσσα, 23, 309. 323. *b) the mark* at which the discus was hurled, Od. 8, 193.

τερμιόεις, εσσα, εν, poet. (τέρμα), *extending to the earth;* ἀσπίς, χιτών, a shield [that swept his ancle, Cp.], a tunic reaching to the ground, 16, 803. Od. 19, 242.

Τερπιάδης, ου, ὁ, son of Terpis = *Phēmius,* Od. 22, 330.

τερπικέραυνος, ὁ (κέραυνος), delighting in lightning, *the thunderer,* epith. of Zeus, 1, 419. Od. 14, 268 ; and often.

τερπνός, ή, όν (τέρπω), *rejoicing, charming,* only as a *varia lectio,* Od. 8, 45 ; see τέρπειν.

τέρπω, aor. 1 ἔτερψα, h. Pan. 47; fut. mid. τέρψομαι, aor. 1 mid. optat. τερψαίτο, h. Ap. 153 ; τερψάμενος, Od. 12, 188.† Hom. has also the aor. 2 mid. with a change of the vowel. ἐταρπόμην (only ταρπώμεθα, Il. 23, 10. 24, 636. Od. 4, 295); and often with redupl. τεταρπόμην (τετάρπετο, τεταρπώμεσθα, τεταρπόμενος); also the aor. pass. in a triple form: 1) The aor. 1 pass. ἐτέρφθην, Od. 5, 74. 8, 131. 17, 174. h. 18, 45; and with a change of the vowel. ἐταρφθην, Od. 19, 213 ; 2 plur. τάρφθεν, Od. 6, 99. 2) The aor. 2 pass. ἐτάρπην, 3 plur. τάρπησαν, subj. 1 plur. τραπείομεν, Ep. for ταρπῶμεν, Il. 3, 441. 14, 314. Od. 8, 292 ; infin. ταρπῆναι, Ep. ταρπήμεναι, *to satisfy, to refresh, to recreate, a*

Τερπωλή. 395 Τέτριγα.

rejoice, io charm, τινά, and dat. instrum. λόγοις, by words, Il. 15, 393; θυμὸν φόρμιγγι, 9, 189; θυμὸν πεσσοῖσι, Od. 1, 107; *to cheer,* ἀκαχήμενον, Il. 19, 312; with paricp. ἀείδων, Od. 17, 385. Mid. with aor. mid. and pass. 1) *to satisfy oneself, to refresh oneself, to recruit oneself,* with gen. ἐδητύος ἠδὲ ποτῆτος, Il. 11, 780. Od. 3, 70; ὕπνου, εὐνῆς, Il. 24, 3. Od. 23, 346; ἥβης, to enjoy youth, Od. 23, 212; metaph. γόοιο, to sate oneself with lamentation, Il. 23, 10; and often. 2) Generally, *to rejoice oneself, to delight oneself;* with dat. of the thing. φόρμιγγι, with the harp, 9, 186; αὐδῇ, δαιτί, etc. b) With partcp. 4, 10. Od. 1, 369; and often. c) With the adjunct: θυμῷ, φρεσίν, Il. 19, 313. Od. 8, 368; also with accus. θυμόν, φρένα, ἦτορ, κῆρ, to rejoice one's heart, Il. 1, 474. 9, 705. Od. 1, 310. λέκτρονδε τραπείομεν εὐνηθέντε, Od. 8, 292, constr. εὐνηθέντε λέκτρονδε; τραπείομεν is not derived from τρέπω, but from τέρπω, cf. Buttm., Gr. Gram. § 114, under τέρπω, Note.

τερπωλή, poet. for τέρψις, *satisfaction, delight, merriment,* Od. 18, 37.†

τερσαίνω (τέρσομαι), aor. 1 ἐτέρσηνα, Ep. τέρσ-, trans. *to dry, to dry up, to wipe off,* αἷμα, 16, 529.†

τερσήμεναι, see τέρσομαι.

τέρσομαι, Ep. aor. 2 ἐτέρσην; from this, infin. τερσῆναι and τερσήμεναι, 16, 519. Od. 6, 98; *to dry, to become* or *to be dry,* ἕλκος ἐτέρσετο, Il. 11, 267; ἠελίῳ, Od. 7, 124; with gen. ὅσσε δακρυόφιν τέρσοντο, the eyes were dried from tears, Od. 5, 152.

τερψίμβροτος, ον (βροτός). *man-rejoicing* or *cheering,* epith. of Helios, *Od. 12, 269. 274. h. Ap. 411.

τεσσαράβοιος, ον (βοῦς), *worth four oxen* or *cattle,* Il. 23, 705.†

τεσσαράκοντα, indecl. *forty,* Il. often, and Od. 24, 341.†

τέσσαρες, οἱ, αἱ, τέσσαρα, τά, *four* (with which Hom. has also the ÆoI. πίσυρες), 2, 618. Od. 10, 349.

τεταγών, see ΤΑΓΩ.

τέταλμαι, perf. pass. from τέλλω, see ἐπιτέλλω.

τέταμαι, see τείνω.

τετάρπετο, τεταρπώμεσθα, τεταρπόμενος, see τέρπω.

τέταρτος, η, ον, Ep. τέτρατος, by transposition, 21, 177 (τέσσαρες); *the fourth.* The neut. τέταρτον and τὸ τέταρτον, as adv. *for the fourth time,* 5, 438. 13, 20. Od. 21, 128.

τετάσθην, see τείνω.

τετεύξομαι, see τεύχω.

τετεύχαται, see τεύχω.

τετεύχετον, see τεύχω.

τετευχῆσθαι, infin. perf. pass. derived from τεύχεα, *to be armed, equipped,* Od. 22, 104;† see Thiersch, Gram. § 232. 146.

τετίημαι (from the obsol. theme ΤΙΕΩ, akin to τίω), a perf. pass. with pres. signif.; from this 2 dual τετίησθον, 8, 447; partcp. τετιημένος, also partcp. perf. act. τετιηώς, *to be troubled, dejected, sad.* τετιημένος ἦτορ, troubled in heart, 8, 457. The perf. act. has the same signif. τετιηότες, 1, 13; and τετιηότι θυμῷ, 11, 555.

τετιηότες, see τετίημαι.

τέτλαθι, τετλαίην, τετλάμεν, τετλάμεναι, see τλῆναι.

τετληώς, ότος, see τλῆναι.

τετμημένος, η, ον, see τάμνω.

τέτμον, ες, ε, see ΤΕΜΩ.

τετράγυος, ον (γύα), *four acres in size,* ὄρχατος, Od. 7, 113. Subst τὸ τετράγυον, a field four acres in size [Cp.], *Od. 18, 374.

τετραθέλυμνος, ον, poet. (θέλυμνον), *having four layers;* σάκος [a four-fold buckler, Cp.], a shield having four coats of ox-hide, 15, 479. Od. 22, 122.

τετραίνω (a form of τιτράω), only aor. Ep. τέτρηνα, *to bore, to pierce through,* τί, 22, 396; τερέτρῳ, Od. 5, 247. 23, 298.

τετράκις, adv. *four times,* Od. 3, 306.†

τετράκυκλος, ον (κύκλος), *having four wheels, four-wheeled,* ἀπήνη, ἅμαξα, 24, 324. Od. 9, 242; in the last passage ἅ.

τετράορος, ον (ἄρω), *drawn by four horses, harnessed four together,* ἵπποι, Od. 13, 81.

τετραπλῆ, adv. in a *four-fold manner, four-fold,* 1, 128.†

τέτραπτο, poet. for τέτραπτο, see τρέπω.

τετράς, άδος, ἡ, the number *four.* 2) *a period of four days' time.* τετράδι τῇ προτέρῃ, on the fourth day of the month, h. Merc. 19.

τέτρατος, η, ον, poet. for τέταρτος, 13, 20. Od. 2, 107.

τετραφάληρος, ον (φαληρός), according to the Schol. and App. = τετράφαλος, *having four knobs* or *bosses.* Thus Heyne and Köppen; or, *with four-fold rings* or *chains;* since φάλαρα are rings on the back of the helmet (κρίκοι τινὲς ἐν τοῖς παραγναθίοιν). These explanations are rejected by Buttm., Lex. sub voc. φάλος, since in both passages, *5, 743. 11, 41, the poet has ἀμφίφαλος κυνέη τετραφάληρος together. He compares φαληρός with φαληριάω and takes it as a *crest,* or an epith. of the crest, hence : ' having a quadruple crest.'

τετράφαλος, ον (φάλος), an epith. of the helmet; the common definition is: a helmet *having four studs* or *bosses;* according to Buttm., Lex. in voc. φάλος, and Köpke, Kriesgw. de Griechen. p. 94, better, a helmet *with four cones for the crest,* *12, 384. 22, 315; see φάλος.

τετραφάτω, see τρέπω.

τετραχθά, adv. poet. for τέτραχα, *four-fold,* in four parts. 3, 363. Od. 9, 71.

τετράχυτρος, ον (χύτρος), *containing four pots,* as wide as four pots, Batr. 258.

τέτρηνα, see τετραίνω.

τέτρηχα, τετρήχει, see ταράσσω.

τέτριγα, τετριγῶτας, see τρίζω.

S 6

Τέτροφα, see τρέφω.

τέττα, a friendly mode of address used by a younger person to an older, *father*, 4, 412.†

τέττιξ, ιγος, ὁ, dat. plur. τεττίγεσιν, a cicada or locust (*cicada ornis*, Linn.), *s. cicada plebeia*, a winged insect which dwells in trees, and by a movement of the under wings against the breast, produces a clear, shrill sound, regarded by the ancients as agreeable. The poets used it as a comparison for the clearness of the human voice, 3, 151.†

τέτυγμαι, see τεύχω.

τετυκεῖν, τετυκέσθαι, τετυκοίμην, see τεύχω.

τετύξαι, τετύχθαι, see τεύχω.

τετύχηκα, see τυγχάνω.

τεῦ, contr. from τεο, see τίς.

Τευθρανίδης, ου, ὁ, son of Teuthras = *Axylus*. 6, 13.

Τεύθρας, αντος, ὁ, 1) a Greek from Magnesia, slain by Hector, 5, 705. 2) the father of Axylus, q. v.

Τεῦκρος, ὁ. son of Telamon (Τελαμώνιος) and of Hesione of Salamis, and step-brother of Ajax, the best archer in the Grecian army before Troy, 6, 31. 8, 281, seq. 13, 170. According to a later tradition, he was banished by his father, because he returned without his brother. He found a new country in the island of Cyprus, and built there the city Salamis, Pind.

*Τευμησσός, ὁ, or Τευμησσός, Strab., a village in Boeotia, not far from Thebes, where Zeus concealed Europa, h. Ap. 224.

Τευταμίδης, ου, ὁ, son of Teutamias = *Lethus*, 2, 843.

*τεῦτλον, τό, Att. for σεῦτλον, *a beet* (*beta*), Batr.

τευχέω, from this τετευχῆσθαι, q. v.

τεῦχος, εος, τό (τεύχω, prop. what is made), *a tool, an implement, an instrument*; exply a) *a warlike implement, equipment, weapon,* always in plur.; also ἀρηΐα and πολεμήϊα τεύχεα, 6, 340. 7, 193; so also Od. 4, 784. 11, 74. 12, 13. b) *ships' furniture, ships' tackle*, according to Eustath., Od. 15, 218. 16, 326. 360. According to Nitzsch ad Od. 4, 784, *luggage*, or better, *equipments of arms*, and not = ὅπλα.

τεύχω, poet. fut. ξω, aor. ἔτευξα, Ep. τεῦξα, perf. only partcp. τετευχώς, intrans. Od. 12, 423 :† fut. mid. τεύξομαι, aor. (ἐτευξάμην), infin. τεύξασθαι, h. Ap. 16, 221; perf. pass. τέτυγμαι, Ep. and Ion. 3 plur. τετεύχαται, Infin. τετύχθαι, pluperf. pass.· ἐτετύγμην, Ep. 3 plur. ἐτετεύχατο, aor. 1 pass. ἐτύχθην, fut. 3 τετεύξομαι, Il. 12, 345. 358. Also the purely Ep. aor. with redupl. and a change of the aspirate : aor. act. only infin. τετυκεῖν, aor. 2 mid. τετύκοντο, infin. τετυκέσθαι. with middle signif. (N.B. τετεύξεται ἄλγεα, 13, 346. ed. Wolf, which, according to the Schol. and the context, is 3 plur. imperf., is in form inadmissible;

the correct reading is ἐτεύχετον, cf Buttm., Gr. Gram. § 114, under τεύχω; Rost, p. 410; the old reading τετεύχατον as perf. with act. signif. according to Passow and Thiersch, § 232. 146, is likewise to be rejected. 1) *to prepare, to make ready, to make, to build*, prim. spoken of human labours of the hands and mind, with accus. δώματα, σκῆπτρον, σάκος, εἴδωλον; again spoken of repasts : δαῖτα, δόρπον, κυκεῶ, Il. 624; ὄμβρον (of Zeus), 10, 6. Μetaph. *to prepare, to occasion, to cause,* ἄλγεα τινι, κήδεα, 1, 110. Od. 1, 244 ; φύλοπιν, πόλεμον, Od. 24, 476 ; καλλιξιν, 11. 15, 70 ; θάνατόν τινι, Od. 11, 409, δόλον, Od. 8, 276 ; γάμον, Od. 1, 277. b) With double accus. αὐτοὺς ἑλώρια τεῦχε κύνεσσιν, he made themselves (i. e. the bodies), a prey to the dogs, Il. 1, 4; hence, 2) Pass. *to be prepared,* ἔκ τινος: fut. mid. with pass. signif. 5, 653 ; often in the perf., pluperf., and aor. a) *to be prepared, made, formed*, with gen. of the material, χρυσοῦ, of gold, 18, 574 ; κασσιτέροιο, Od. 19, 226 ; in like signif τετευχώς, Od. 12, 423; with dat. ἄριστα, Od. 19, 563. The perf. partcp. pass. τετυγμένος is often used as an adj. and signifies : *well wrought, well made, beautifully wrought;* also metaph. νόος ἐν στήθεσσιν τετυγμένος οὐδὲν ἀεικής, the mind in my breast is by no means perplexed or despicable, Od. 20, 366. b) Esply in the 3 sing. perf., pluperf., aor. pass., and fut. 3, *to become, to arise, to be*, Il. 4, 84. 5, 78. 402 ; οἷον ἐτύχθη, 2, 155. 17, 690. 18, 120. Od. 21, 303. Mid. *to prepare for oneself, to build for oneself*, in the imperf. δαῖτα, Od. 10, 182 ; fut mid. δόρπον, Il. 19, 208 ; aor. 1 mid. νηόν, h. Ap. 248 ; and often in the aor. 2. δαῖτα, 1, 467. Od. 8, 61.

τέφρη, ἡ, Ep. and Ion. for τέφρα (θρύπτω), *ashes*, with which the head and clothes were sprinkled as a token of grief, *18, 25. 23, 251.

τεχνάω, act. only infin. aor. τεχνῆσαι, Od. 7, 110 ; mly τεχνάομαι, mid. fut. τεχνήσομαι, aor. ἐτεχνησάμην, *to form with art, to make, to make beautifully*, with accus. Od. 5, 259. 11, 613. Metaph. *to devise cunningly, to prepare artfully,* τί, Il. 23, 415 ; generally, to use craft, h. Ap. 326.

τέχνη, ἡ (τεκεῖν), 1) *art, trade,* 3, 61. Od. 3, 433. 11, 614. 2) *dexterity in art,* Od. 6, 234 ; esply in a bad sense : *artifice, cunning*, Od. 4, 455. 529 ; in the plur., Od. 8, 327. h. Merc. 317.

τεχνήεις, εσσα, εν, poet. (τέχνη), *artificial, ingenious, artful,* Od. 8, 297.† Adv. τεχνηέντως, *artificially*, Od. 5, 270.†

τέῳ, τέων, see τίς.

τέως, Ep. and Ion. τείως, adv. 1) *usual then, as long as, in the mean time,* always spoken of time, prop. answering to the relative ἕως, 20, 42. Od. 4, 91 ; or to ὄφρα. Il. 19, 189. b) Often abs.

Τῆ. 397 **Τηλύγετος.**

meanwhile, in the meantime, 24, 658. Od. 10, 348. 15, 231. 16, 130. 2) Poet. for ἕως, to avoid the hiatus, h. Ven. 226. Cer. 66. 138. (τέως is also to be read as monosyllabic, Od. 15, 231. 16, 370; but Il. 20, 42, τέως at the beginning of the verse is trochaic, unless τεῖος stood there, cf. Thiersch, Gram. § 168. 10. Rem.— ταίως, only in the Od.)

τῆ, old Ep. imperat. derived from the ground theme ΤΑΩ, *take,* and always in connexion with an imperat. 14, 219. 24, 287. Od. 9, 347, except Il. 23, 618. It never takes an accus.; the only apparent exception is Od. 10, 287, but the acc. there belongs to ἔχων.

τῇ, adv. (prop. dat. fem of ὁ), 1) *in this place, here, there,* 5, 858; and often metaph. *in this manner, thus,* Od. 8, 510. 2) Relat. Ion. and poet. for ᾗ, *in which place, where,* Il. 12, 118. 21, 554. 3) Rarely, *thither,* 5, 752.

τῇδε, adv. = τῇ, cf. ὅδε.

τῆθος, εος, τό, *an oyster,* plur. τήθεα, 16, 747.†

Τηθύς, ύος, ἡ, daughter of Uranus and Gæa, wife of Oceanus, mother of the river-gods and the Oceanides (prob. from τήθη, grandmother), 14, 201. 302.

τηκεδών, όνος, ἡ (τήκω), the act of liquefying or dissolving, hence, *a wasting away, a consumption,* Od. 11, 201.†

τήκω, perf. 2 τέτηκα, with pres. signif. 1) Trans. in the act. *to melt, to dissolve,* with accus. metaph. θυμόν, *to consume the heart* (by grief), Od. 19, 264. 2) Mid. with perf. II. intrans. *to melt, to flow down, to dissolve,* spoken of snow, Od. 19, 207; generally, *to vanish, to disappear, to pine away,* from grief or desire, Od. 5, 396. 19, 204; τέτηκα κλαίουσα, I pine away with weeping, Il. 3, 176.

*τηλαυγής, ές (αὐγή), *far-shining, beaming, illuminating,* h. 31, 13.

τῆλε, adv. like τηλοῦ, *in the distance, far, abroad,* Od. 2, 183. 2) With gen. *fur from,* φίλων, Il. 11, 817. Od. 2, 333; also ἀπό τινος, Od. 3, 313; ἐκ τινος, Il. 2, 863.

τηλεδαπός, ή, όν (τῆλε), *from a distant land, foreign, strange,* ξεῖνοι, Od. 6, 219. 19, 351. 2) *situated at a distance,* νῆσοι, Il. 21, 254. (According to the Gramm. contr. from τῆλε and ΔΑΠΟΣ = δάπεδον; according to Buttm. τῆλε and ἀπό, see ἀλλοδαπός.)

τηλεθάω, poet. lengthened from θάλλω, θηλέω, θαλέθω, only in the partcp. pres.: τηλεθάων, fem. τηλεθώσα, by Epic extension for τηλεθοῦσα, τηλεθάον, *to become verdant, to be in bloom, to flourish,* 6, 148. 17, 55. h. 6, 41; metaph. παῖδες, 22, 423; χαίτη, blooming, i. e. abundant hair, 23, 142. (On the change of θ into τ when a syllable is inserted, see Buttm., Gr. Gram. § 18. p. 79.)

τηλεκλειτός, όν, poet. (κλείω), *far-famed,* epith. of illustrious men, 14, 321. Od. 11, 308. 19, 546.

τηλέκλητος, ον poet. (καλέω), *far-called, called from a distance,* epith. of allies, *5, 491. 6, 111. 11, 564. 12, 108; which Wolf has adopted for τηλεκλειτός; against this Buttm. contends, Lex. sub voc., because allies are often called κλειτοί, Il. 3, 451. cf. 12, 101; and this word does not elsewhere occur. Spitzner and Bothe have therefore adopted τηλεκλειτός.

τηλεκλυτός, όν (κλυτός) = τηλεκλειτός, 19, 400. Od. 1, 30.

Τηλέμαχος, ὁ (adj. τηλεμάχος, fighting at a distance), son of Odysseus (Ulysses) and Penelope, Od. 1, 216; he received, according to Eustath., the name, because he was born when his father was about to depart to the siege of Troy. When he had grown up, he went to seek his father, and Athênê accompanied him under the form of Mentor, Od. 1—4. On his return, he found his father already in Ithaca, and aided him in slaying the suitors, Od. 15—24.

Τήλεμος, ὁ, son of Eurymus, a famous prophet, who communicated to Polyphêmus the misfortunes that were to befall him, Od. 9, 507, seq.

τηλέπυλος, ον, poet. (πύλη), *wide-gated,* Od. 10, 82; It stands as an adj. in Wolf's ed. cf. Λαιστρυγόνιος.

Τηλέπυλος, ἡ, a town of the Læstrygônes, as prop. name, Od. 10, 82. ed. Bothe, 23, 318; in Wolf's ed., after the ancients, *Formiæ,* now *Mola di Gaëta,* Cic. Ep. ad Att. 2, 13.

τηλεφανής, ές, poet. (φαίνομαι), *that appears at a distance, visible at a distance,* Od. 24, 82.†

Τηλεφίδης, ου, ὁ, son of Telephus = Euryphylus, Od. 11, 519. Telephus, son of Heracles and Auge; he emigrated from Arcadia to Mysia, cf. Apd. 2, 7, 4.

τηλίκος, η, ον (correlat. of ἡλίκος), *of the size, of such an age, as old, as large,* spoken of younger and older persons, 24, 487. Od. 1, 297. h. Cer. 116.

τηλόθεν, adv. poet. (τῆλε), *from a distance, from afar,* ἥκειν, 5, 478. 2) *far,* 23, 359. Od. 6, 312. h. Ap. 330.

τηλόθι, adv. poet. (τῆλε), 1) *far, at a distance,* εἶναι, 8, 285. Od. 1, 22. 2) *far away, far hence,* Il. 1, 30. Od. 2, 365.

τηλόσε, adv. (τηλοῦ), *at a distance, far, far away,* *4, 455. 22, 407. h. Merc. 414.

τηλοτάτω, adv. superl. of τηλοῦ, *furthest, at the greatest distance,* Od. 7, 322.†

τηλοῦ, adv. *far,* 5, 479. 2) *far from,* with gen., Od. 13, 249. 23, 68.

τηλύγετος, η, ον, a Hom. epith. of children according to the explanation of the old Gramm. (from τῆλε or τηλοῦ and ΓΕΝΩ, γέγαα), prop. *late-born,* i. e. born in the old age of the parents, 5, 153. Od. 4, 11; hence 2) *very dear tenderly beloved,* for the most part spoken of sons, Il. 9, 143. 285. 492. Od. 16, 19. h. Cer. 164: of a daughter, Il. 3, 175; and 3) In a bad sense: *tender, weakly, puny, because*

Τῆμος. 398 Τίθημι.

such late-born children are commonly spoilt by tenderness (cf. 9, 143). τηλύγετος ὤς, as a nurseling, 13, 470. Buttm., Lex. sub voc., would derive it from τελευτή, so that τελεύγετος arose by a standard composition, and τηλύγετος, by an inversion of quantity, and translates, *born last, tenderly beloved*. Another derivation is attempted by Döderlein in Comm. de Voc., τηλύγετος; and Bothe ad Il. 3, 175, from θῆλυς (θάλλω), and γάω, so that it signifies prop. *being of a blooming age*. (The derivation of the ancients deserves the preference; espy since Apoll. Dysc. (de pron. 329) tells us that τηλυ was a collat. form of τῆλε.)

τῆμος, adv. of time, Ep. (= τῆμαρ), *then, at that time*; it refers prop. to a foregoing ἦμος, Il. 23, 228; often τῆμος ἄρα, 7, 434. Od. 4, 401; τῆμος δή, Od. 12, 441. 2) Absol. without protasis, h. Merc. 101. ἐς τῆμος, to that time, Od. 7, 318. cf. Buttm., Lex.

τῆπερ or τῇ περ, Ep. for ᾗπερ, *where*, 24. 603. Od. 6, 510.

Τήρεια, ἡ, a high mountain in Mysia near Zelia, τὸ Τηρείης ὄρος, 2. 829 (according to Eustath. from τηρεῖν τὰ κύκλῳ).

*τηρέω, fut. ήσω, *to keep, to watch, to guard*, with accus. δώματα, h. Cer. 142.

Τηύγετον, τό, Ion. for Ταΰγετον, *Taygĕtus*, a mountain of Laconia, which terminated in the south with the promontory Tænarum, now *Monte de Maina*, Od. 6, 103.

τηύσιος, η, ον, poet. *empty, vacant, unprofitable, vain, fruitless*, ὁδός, *Od. 3, 316. 15, 13; ἔπος, h. Ap. 540. (Of uncertain derivation; according to some, Ion. for ταύσιος = αὔσιος from αὔτως.)

τίεσκον, see τίω.

ΤΙΕΩ, obsol. theme of τετίημαι and τετιηώς, q. v.

τίη, poet. strengthened for τί, *why, wherefore, why then*, also τίη δέ, 15, 244; τίη δή, 21, 436. Od. 15, 326. (τιή from τί, like ἐπειή from ἐπεί, cf. Buttm., Lex. sub voc. δείλη, 9.)

τιθαιβώσσω, *to build, to construct*, spoken of bees, Od. 13, 106.† (Akin to τιθάς, τιθασσός.)

τιθέω, poet. form of τίθημι, of which Hom. uses only 3 sing. pres. τιθεῖ, and imperf. ἐτίθει and τίθει, see τίθημι.

τιθήμεναι and τιθήμενος, see τίθημι.

τίθημι, pres. 2 sing. Ep. τίθησθα, 3 plur. τιθεῖσι, infin. τιθήμεναι, Ep. for τιθέναι, 23, 83; imperf. only 3 plur. τίθεσαν: also from the form τιθέω, 3 sing. imperf. ἐτίθει and τίθει, fut. θήσω. Ep. infin. θησέμεναι, aor. 1 ἔθηκα and θῆκα, only sing. and 3 plur. ἔθηκαν, 6. 300; aor. 2 from this, 3 plur. without augment. θέσαν, subj. θῶ, Ep. θείω, 2 and 3 sing. θείῃς, θείῃ. Od. 10, 301. 341; better θήῃς, θήῃ, (as in the Il. ed. Wolf, to distinguish it from the optat.), 1 plur. θείωμεν, Od. 24. 485; and θείομεν for θῶμεν, Il. 23, 244; optat. θείην, 3 plur.

θείεν, imperat. θές, infin. θεῖναι, Ep. θέμεναι, θέμεν, mid. pres. particp. Ep. τιθήμενος for τιθέμενος, fut. θήσομαι. aor. 1 only 3 sing. θήκατο, 10. 31. 14, 187; aor. 2 ἐθέμην, often 3 sing. θέτο, optat. sing. θεῖτο, imperat. θέο for θοῦ. infin. θέσθαι, particp. θέμενος, η, ον, cf. Thiersch. § 224. 89. Ground signif. to *place, put*, or *lay*, any one or any thing any where; hence 1) Prop. spoken of space: *to put, to place, to lay*, and according to the different constructions, to *put away, to lay aside, to place upon, to lay before*, etc., mostly in τὶ ἔν τινι, like *ponere in aliqua re*, also with dat. without prep., Od. 13, 364; more rarely to τὶ, ἐπί with dat., and gen. μετά with dat., ἀμφί with dat., ἀνά with dat. and accus., ὑπό with dat. and accus. τὶ ἐν πυρί, to put any thing in the fire. Il. 5. 215; τὶ ἐν χείρεσσι, 10, 529; ἐν λάρνακι. 24. 795. 797; κυνέην ἐπὶ κρατί, to put the helmet on the head, 15. 480; ἐπ᾿ ἀπήνης, to lay any thing upon a vehicle, Od. 6, 252; τὶ ἀμ βωμοῖσι. Il. 8, 441; ἀνὰ μυρίκην, 10, 466; τὶ ὑπ᾿ αἰθούσῃ, 24, 644; ὑπὸ ῥίνα, Od. 4, 445. b) Metaph. spoken of mental states: μένος τινὶ ἐν θυμῷ, to put courage into one's heart. Od. 1, 321; θυμόν τινι, Il. 24, 49; νόον, βουλὴν ἐν στήθεσσιν, 13, 732. 17, 470; ἔπος τινὶ ἐν φρεσί, to put a word into any one's mind, i. e. to give to consider, Od. 11, 146; τέλος μύθον, Il. 16, 83. Esply a) *to place, to put up*, spoken of prizes: ἄεθλα, 23, 263; δέπας, 23, 656. 758. Od. 11, 546. b) *to establish, to appoint, to order*, τέρματα, Il. 23, 333; τιμήν τινι, 24, 57; hence spoken of the gods: *to allot, to ordain*, Od. 8, 465. c) *to put up, to arrange*, ἀγάλματα, Od. 12, 347. cf. Il. 6, 92. 2) *to present* any thing, *to place before*, and generally, like *ποιέω*, *to make* any thing, *to prepare, to produce*; primar. spoken of an artisan, 18. 541. 550. 561; metaph. ἄλγεά τινι, to occasion woes to any one, 1, 2; φόως ἑτάροισιν, to afford light or safety to the companions, 6, 6; ἔργα, to occasion works (troubles), μετ᾿ ἀμφοτέροισιν, 3, 321; σκέδασιν, to cause a dispersion, Od. 1, 116. 3) *to make*, i. e. to bring into any state, with double accus. with subst. τιθ. τινὰ ἱέριαν, to make any one priestess, Il. 6. 300; again, τινὰ ἄλοχον, 19, 298. Od. 13 163; adj. τινὰ πηρόν, to make any one blind, Il. 2, 599. cf. 5, 122. 9, 483; and often. Mid. like the act. only with reference to the subject, *to put, place, lay, for oneself*, e. g. κολεῷ ἄορ, to put the sword in the sheath, Od. 10, 333; ἀμφὶ ὤμοισιν ἔντεα, to put arms upon the shoulders, Il. 10, 34. 149; ξίφος, Od. 8, 416; metaph. τὶ ἐν φρεσί, to put any thing in one's heart, or to consider it by oneself, Od. 4, 729; κότον τινί, to cherish anger against any one, Il. 8, 449; αἰδῶ ἐν στήθεσσι, 13, 122. 2) *to make, prepare, cause, for oneself*, δαῖτα, 7. 475. d) τίθεσθαι ἀσπίδα, to prepare well one's

✲Τιθηνέομαι. 399 Τίνω

a**h**ield, 2, 382; οἰκία, δῶμα, to build a house, 2, 750. Od. 15, 241; μάχην, to begin the ba**t**tle, Il. 24, 402. cf. 17, 158. 3) *to make*, with d**o**u**b**le accus. θυμὸν ἄγριον, to make one's spirit fierce, 9, 629; τινὰ θέσθαι γυναῖκα, Od. 21, 72.

*τιθηνέομαι, depon. mid. (τιθήνη) (rarely act.), *to wait upon, to nurse, to bring up*, prop. spoken of the nurse, παῖδα, h. Cer. 142.

τιθήνη, ἡ (τιθή), a *nurse, a female attendant*, 6, 384. Διωνύσοιο τιθῆναι, the n**u**rs**e**s of Dionÿsus. are the Hyades, nymphs of Nysa, who brought him up, cf. Apd. 3, 4, 4.

τίθησθα, Dor. and Ep. for τίθης, see τίθημι.

Τιθωνός, ὁ, son of Laomedon, 20, 337; whom E**o**s (Aurora) bore away on account of his beauty, and took as a husband, see 'Ηώς. He received, at the desire of the goddess, immortality, but not immortal youth, h. Ven. 219—239.

τίκτω, fut. τέξω, mly τέξομαι, Ep. also τεκοῦμαι, from this τεκεῖσθαι, h. Ven. 207; aor. 2 ἔτεκον, Ep. τέκον, infin. τεκεῖν, Ep. τεκέειν, Ep. ἐτεκόμην and τεκόμην, *to bring into the world, to bear*, prop. spoken of the mother, with accus. παῖδα, υἱόν, mly τινί, 6, 22; also ὑπό τινι, 2, 714. 728. *b*) *to beget, to generate*, spoken of the father; often in the aor. m**i**ld. 5, 154. 546; but not solely, cf. 2, 742. 22, 48; of both parents, 22, 234. Od. 4, 64. *c*) Spoken of beasts and birds: *to produce young, to hatch*, Il. 16, 150. 2, 313.

τίλλω, 1) *to pluck, to pick, to pull, to tear out*, with accus. κόμην, the hair, 22, 406. cf. v. 78. Batr. 70; πέλειαν, Od. 15, 527. Mid. *to pluck out*, with reference to the subject, χαίτην, Od. 10, 567 (as a mark of grief); hence, τίλλεσθαί τινα, to bewail any one (by plucking out the hair), Il. 24, 711.

*τίμάοχος, ον, poet. (ἔχω), having honour, *honoured*, h. Cer. 258.

τιμάω (τιμή), fut. τιμήσω, aor. ἐτίμησα, fut. mid. τιμήσομαι, with pass. signif. h. Ap. 485; aor. 1 mid. ἐτιμησάμην, 22, 235; perf. pass. τετίμημαι, *to value*. 1) Spoken of persons: *to honour, to esteem, to venerate*, to hold in honour, τινά; also τινὰ δωτίνῃσι, to honour any one with presents, 9, 155; hence pass. τετιμῆσθαι σκήπτρῳ, 9, 38; ἔδρῃ, κρέασιν, 12, 310; once with gen. τετιμῆσθαι τιμῆς, to be esteemed worthy of honour, 23, 649. cf. Kühner, § 469. *c*. 2) Of things: *to value, to esteem*, ἀοιδήν, h. 24, 6. Mid.= act. with reference to the subject, τινά, 22, 235; πάρι κῆρι, Od. 19, 280. 20, 129.

τιμή, ἡ (τίω), *value*, hence 1) *estimation, honour, esteem*, esply *a place of honour, office, the dignity of gods and of kings*, Od. 5, 335; βασιληίς. Il. 6, 193; also alone, *the royal dignity, dominion*, 2, 197. Od. 1, 117. 2) *the valuation of a thing*, esply a determination of value as a recompense for any thing plundered;

hence *requital, punishment, compensation, restitution, satisfaction*. ἀρνυσθαί τινι τιμήν, to seek requital or procure satisfaction for any one, Il. 1, 159. 5, 552. ἀποτίνειν, τίνειν τιμήν τινι, 3, 286. 288. 459; ἄγειν, Od. 22, 57.

τιμήεις, εσσα, εν (τιμή), contr. τιμῆς, accus. τιμῆντα, 9, 605. 18, 475. Comp. τιμηέστερος, Od. 1, 398. Superl. τιμηέστατος, Od. 4, 614. 1) Spoken of persons: *valued, honoured, esteemed*, Il. 9, 605. Od. 13, 129. 2) Spoken of things: *valuable, precious, costly*, Od. 1, 312. Il. 18, 475. The posit. with contr. τιμῆς for τιμήεις (as Wolf has substituted for the gen. τιμῆς). 9, 601; and accus. τιμῆντα, Cf. Buttm., Gr. Gram. § 41. 9. 15.

τιμῆντα, τιμῆς, see τιμήεις.

τίμιος, η, ον, *valued, honoured*, spoken of persons, Od. 10, 38.† h. Ap. 483. 2) Of things, h. Ven. 143.

τινάσσω, aor. 1 ἐτίναξα, aor. mid. ἐτιναξάμην. aor. pass. ἐτινάχθην, *to shake, to move, to brandish*, δοῦρα, ἔγχος, hence also ἀστεροπήν, αἰγίδα, 13, 243. 17, 595; τινά, to shake any one in order to arrest his attention, 3, 385; θρόνον, to overturn the seat, Od. 22, 88; spoken of the wind: *to strow*, Od. 5, 368. Pass. *to be shaken*, Il. 15, 609. Od. 6, 43. cf. ἐκτινάσσω. Mid. τιναξάσθην πτερά, they shook their wings, or struck with their wings, 2, 151.

τίνυμαι, poet. form of τίνομαι, mid, *to cause to atone, to punish*, τινά, 3, 279. 19, 260. Od. 13, 214; τί, Od. 24, 326. (τίνυμαι is preferred by Buttm., Gr. Gram. II. § 112. Rem. 19.)

τίνω (τίω), fut. τίσω, aor. ἔτισα, infin. τίσαι, fut. mid. τίσομαι, aor. 1 ἐτισάμην (without perf.), 1) *to atone, to pay, to discharge*. τιμήν τινι, to pay a compensation (make satisfaction or amends) to any one, as a punishment, 3, 289; θωήν, Od. 2, 193. *b*) *to expiate, to atone for*, with accus. of the thing for which one makes expiation, δάκρυα, Il. 1, 42; ὕβριν, φόνον, Od. 24, 352. Il. 21, 134; more rarely with accus. of the pers. τίσεις γνωτόν, thou shalt make atonement for the brother, 17, 34; with dat. κράατι, Od. 22, 218. 2) Generally, *to pay, to discharge*, with accus. ζωάγρια, Il. 18, 407; εὐαγγέλιον, to reward the tidings, Od. 12, 382. Mid. 1) *to cause to atone, to cause to pay to oneself*, Od. 13, 15; hence 2) Mly *to punish, to chastise, to revenge, a*) With accus. of the person who is made to make atonement, Il. 2, 743. 3, 28. Od. 3, 197. *b*) With accus. of the deed which is avenged: φόνον τινός, Il. 15, 116; βίην, λώβην, Od. 23, 31. Il. 9, 218. *c*) Mly accus. of the pers. and gen. of the thing: τινὰ κακότητος, to punish any one for wickedness, 3, 366; ὑπερβασίης, Od. 3, 206; absol. Od. 3, 266. *d*) Rarely with two accus. ἐτίσατο ἔργον ἀεικὲς Νηλῆα, he caused Neleus to expiate the impious deed, Od 15 236. (ι is long in the Ep. writers.)

τίπτε, Ep. syncop. for τίποτε, before an aspirate τίφθ', 4, 243: *what then? why then?* 1, 202. Od. 1, 225.

Τίρυνς, θος, ἡ, *Tiryntha*, a town in Argolis, fortified by the Cyclôpes with great walls (τειχιόεσσα), the residence of Perseus, 2, 559.

τίς, τί, an indefin. pron. (enclit.) Ep. and Ion. declen. gen. τέο, τεῦ, 2, 388. Od. 3, 348; dat. τέω, τῷ, accus. τινά, τί, dual τινέ, plur. nom. τινές, accus. τινάς. 1) Any one, *a certain one, some one*; with subst. it is translated by *a, an*, τις ποταμός, τις νῆσος, neut. τί, *any thing, something*. εἴ τις, if any one, εἴ τι, if any thing; mly with special emphasis: *who but, what but*. 2) An indefinite single person from a large number: *many a one* (aliquis), Il. 6, 459. 479. Od. 2, 324; also collectively: *each one, every one*, for πᾶς; εὖ μέν τις δόρυ θηξάσθω, Il. 2, 382. 16, 209. 17, 254. Od. 1, 302. So also sometimes τί after a negation, h. Merc. 143. 3) In connexion with adj. and pron. it gives prominence to the notion, which according to the connexion may consist in strengthening or weakening, *somewhat, tolerably, very*, ζάκοτός τις, 3, 220 ; τίς θαρσαλέος, Od. 17, 449. cf. Od. 18, 382 ; 20, 140. The neut. τί stands as an adv. in connexion with adverbs, in the signif. *somewhat, a little, in some degree*, in a certain respect, Il. 21, 101. 22, 382; and often with negat. 1, 115.

τίς, τί, gen. τίνος, interrog. pron. (always orthotone), Ep. and Ion. declen. gen. always τέο and τεῦ, plur. gen. τεών, Il. 24, 387. 1) *who? what one? τί, what? what sort of?* ἐς τί, how long? 5, 465. τί μοι ἔριδος, καὶ ἀρωγῆς, supply πρᾶγμα, what have I to do with contention and aid? 21, 360. 2) Rarely as dependent interrogative, 18, 192. Od. 15, 423. 17, 368. 3) τί often stands absol., *how? why? wherefore?* Il. 1, 362. Od. 1, 346 ; see τίπτε for τί ποτε. 4) τί with a partcp. and a verb forms in Greek one sentence, which we may express in two, Il. 11, 313; see πάσχω.

τίσις, ιος, ἡ (τίω), *value*; hence, 1) *recompense, requital, satisfaction*, Od. 2, 76. 2) Esply *atonement, expiation, punishment, vengeance*, Il. 22, 19; τινός, for any thing, h. Cer. 368. ἐκ γὰρ Ὀρέσταο τίσις ἔσσεται Ἀτρείδαο, vengeance will come from Orestes for the son of Atreus, Od. 1, 40.

τιταίνω, poet. (a form from τείνω with redupl.), aor. ἐτίτηνα, to *bend*, τόξα, 8, 266. 1) to stretch, *to draw out*; hence also, *to draw*, ἅρμα, ἄροτρον, 2, 390. 13, 704. 2) *to extend, to spread out, to stretch out*, χεῖρε, 13, 354; τάλαντα, to hold up the balance, 8, 69; τράπεζαν, Od. 10, 334 ; generally, 3) Intrans. *to stretch oneself, to hasten, to speed*, Il. 23, 403; like the mid. Mid. *to stretch* or *draw for oneself* (sibi), τόξα. 5, 97. 11, 370. Od. 21, 259; ἐπί τινι. b) *to stretch oneself, to exert oneself*, spoken of birds,

Od. 2, 149. Esply spoken of horses: *to exert themselves in running, to stretch in the race*, Il. 22, 23. 23, 518.

Τιτανοκτόνος, ὁ (κτείνω), *Titan-slayer*, Batr. 282.

Τίτανος, ὁ, a mountain in Thessaly, named from τίτανος = γύψος, 2, 735.

Τιταρήσιος, ὁ, a river in Thessaly, not far from Olympus, afterwards called Eurôtas, which flowed into the Pêneios, 2, 751.

Τιτήν, ῆνος, ὁ, Ep. and Ion. for Τιτάν. plur. οἱ Τιτῆνες, the Titans, son of Uranus and Gæa 5, 898 ; an earlier race of gods, to which belonged Oceanus, Cœus, Creius, Hyperion, Iapetus, Kronus (Saturn). In an insurrection under Kronus (Saturn), they hurled their father from the throne, and in company with their brother ruled heaven. But soon after Kronus (Saturn) hurled them to Tartarus ; enraged at which, Gæa (Terra) instigated Zeus, the son of Kronus (Saturn), to rebellion, who dethroned his father, and banished him to Tartarus They are first mentioned 5, 898, where they are called Οὐρανίωνες. The name Τιτῆνες stands in 14, 279 h. Ap. 33. Batr. 283. According to Hes. Th. 207, the name signifies *those striving*, from τιταίνω, according to Etym. Mag., as it were, οἱ τιταίνοντες τὰς χεῖρας, *Tesdones*, Herm.

τιτρώσκω, see τρώω.

Τιτυός, ὁ, son of Gæa (Terra), a monstrous giant, who in Hades, lay extended over nine acres of land. He attempted to offer violence to Lêto (Latona), and was slain by her children ; in Hades, a vulture constantly preyed upon his liver, as a punishment, Od. 7, 324. 11, 576, seq. According to Hom. he dwelt in Eubœa ; later writers say in Panopeus. The latter call him the son of Zeus and Elara, Apd. 1, 3. 12.

τιτύσκομαι, Ep. (from the Ep. τιτυσκέθαι), only in the pres. and imperf., and having a like signif. with τεύχειν and τυχεῖν. 1) With accus. *to prepare, to arrange*; πῦρ, to kindle a fire, 21, 342; spoken of horses, ἵππους ὑπ᾽ ὀχεσφι, to harness the horses in the chariot, 8, 41. 13, 23. 2) More frequently = τυχεῖν, *to aim at*, ἄντα, Od. 21, 48 ; esply with missiles, absol., Il. 3, 80. Od. 21. 421. 22, 117 ; with a gen. of the object aimed at, Il. 11, 350. 13, 159. 498; with dat. of the weapon : δουρί, ἰοῖσι, 13, 159. 21, 582. b] Metaph. φρεσί, *to aim in mind*, i. e. *to have in view, to have in mind*. 13, 558 : spoken of ships, ὄφρα σε τῇ πέμπωσι τιτυσκόμεναι φρεσὶ νῆες, that the ships aiming in mind may bring thee thither (where the poet represents the ships as animated), Od. 8, 556.

τίφθ' for τίπτ', see τίπτε.

τίω, poet. imperf. iterat. τίεσκον and τίεσκετο, fut. τίσω, aor. 1 ἔτισα and τίσα, perf. pass. τετιμένος = τιμάω. 1)

Τλῆμι. 401 **Τοκόs.**

ει, value, to esteem worth. to prize at, with accus. τρίποδα δυωδεκάβοιον, to **value a tripod at twelve oxen**, 23, 703; cf. v. 705; τίειν τινὰ ἐν καρὸς αἴση, 9, 378. (see κάρ.) 2) Metaph. *to value, to esteem, to honour, to distinguish*, τινά, often ἶσον or ἶσά τινι, 5, 467. 13, 176; ὁμῶς τινι, 5, 535; περί τινος, before any one, 18, 81. Pass. *to be honoured*, τινί, **by** any one, 5, 78. 11, 58; partcp. τετιμένοs, 20, 426. Od. 13, 28. h. Ap. 479 (the signification *to alone*, from τίσω, ἔτισα, belongs to τίνω).

ΤΛΗΜΙ, an assumed pres. for τλῆναι.
τλημοσύνη, ἡ (τλήμων), *endurance, patience, suffering, distress*, h. Ap. 191.
τλήμων, ονος, ὁ, ἡ (τλῆναι), 1) *suffering, enduring, patient.* 2) That ventures much, *venturing, adventurous, bold*, as epith. of Odysseus (Ulysses), 10, 231. τλήμων θυμόs, *5, 670. 21, 430; impudent. h. Merc. 296.

τλῆναι (verb defect. from the obsol. theme ΤΛΑΩ, of which there occur, aor. 2 ἔτλην, often 3 sing. Ep. τλῆ, Ep. ἔτλαν for ἔτλησαν, optat. τλαίην, imperat. τλῆθι (also Ep. aor. ἐτάλασα), perf. with pres. signif. τέτληκα, ας, ε, only in the sing. imperat. τέτλαθι, ἄτω, optat. τετλαίην, infin. τετλάμεναι and τετλάμεν, poet. for τετλάναι, partcp. τετληώς, ότος. 1) *to bear, to endure, to suffer.* absol. and with accus. ῥίγιστα, 5, 873; πολλὰ ἔκ τινος, 5, 384; τετληότι θυμῷ, Od. 4, 447. 11, 181; also κραδίη τετληυῖα, Od. 20, 23. 2) *to take upon oneself, to venture, to undertake, to be bold, to dare*, with θυμῷ and infin. following, Il. 1, 228. 4, 94; τάδε μὲν καὶ τετλάμεν εἰσορόωντες, we must bear these things, when we see them, Od. 20, 311. There is here an infin. as an expression of necessity, and χρή is to be supplied, as in h. Cer. 148. cf. Herm. ad loc. Buttm., however, in the Schol. ad Od. prefers the old reading τέτλαμεν, i.e. τετλήκαμεν. So also Voss (Bothe, Fäsi).

Τληπόλεμος, ὁ, son of Heracles and Astyoche (Astydamela, Pind.), he slew his uncle Licymnius by mistake, and fled to Rhodes; here he became king, and led the Rhodians in nine ships to Ilium, 2, 653, seq. 2) Son of Damastor, a Trojan, whom Patroclus slew, 16, 416.

τλητόs, ή, όν (τλῆναι), prop. *suffered, endured;* act. *enduring, patient, stedfast,* θυμόs, 24, 49.†

τμάγεν, Ep. for ἐτμάγησαν, see τμήγω.
τμήγω, Ep. form of τέμνω, *to cut;* from this aor. 1 ἔτμηξα, aor. 2 ἔτμαγον, aor. 2 pass. ἐτμάγην, of which there occurs only, τμήξας, 11, 146; in tmesis and 3 plur. aor. pass. τμάγεν.

τμηθῆν, adv. (τέμνω), *so as to cut; so as to make a gash*, or *draw blood;* of a spear, ἐπῆλθε, 7, 262.†

Τμῶλος, ὁ, a mountain in Lydia, near Sardis, abounding in wine and saffron, now Bosdag, 2, 866. 20, 385.
τόθι, adv. poet. *there*, Od. 15, 239;† h App. 214. cf. Herm. ad h. Ven. 258.

τοί, enclit. partic. according to Buttm. and Passow prop. an old dat. for τῷ; origin. *therefore, accordingly, consequently,* but even in Hom. simply, *truly, certainly, indeed.* It serves 1) To limit and give prominence to a thought: τοῦτο δέ τοι ἐρέουσα ἔπος, 1, 419; μήτε τοι, 23, 315. 2) Esply it is used when what is said has a proverbial character: οὐκ ἀρετᾷ κακὰ ἔργα· κιχάνει τοι βραδὺς ὠκύν (the slow overtakes the swift), Od. 8, 329. 2, 276. Often with other particles: δέ τοι, γάρ τοι, ἦ τοι, etc. (According to Damm, it is prop. dat. of the personal pron. (for σοί); he is followed by Nägelsbach ad Il. p. 175 [and it is a probable opinion].)

τοί, 1) Dor. and Ep. for σοί, q. v. 2) for οἱ, see ὁ, ἡ, τό.

τοιγάρ, partic. (from τοί and γάρ), it stands mly at the beginning of a sentence, and signifies: *therefore, then, accordingly, hence,* τοιγὰρ, ἐγὼν ἐρέω, 1, 76. Od. 1, 179 (τοιγάρ τοι, Il. 10, 413. Od. 1, 214, the second τοί stands for σοί.)

τοῖος, η, ον (τός), demonstr. pron. *such, such like, thus constituted (talis),* answers prop. to the relative οἷος; but often stands for οἷος, also ὁποῖος, 20, 250. Od. 17, 421; ὅς, 11, 7, 231. 24, 153. Od. 2, 286; rarely ὅπως, Od. 16, 208; for the most part absolute, also with dat. τεύχεσι τοῖοι, 11. 5, 450. 2) With infin. it signifies: *to be capable, to be able,* ἡμεῖς δ' οὔ νύ τι τοῖοι ἀμύνεμεν, able to ward off, Od. 2, 60. 3) With an adj. of the same gender and case, it signifies: *exceedingly, entirely, perfectly,* τύμβος ἐπιεικὴς τοῖος, prop. τοῖος οἷος ἐπιεικής, Il. 23, 246. cf. Od. 3, 321; also with μάλα, Od. 11, 135. 4) The neut. τοῖον, as adv. *very, exceedingly,* Il. 22, 241. θάμα τοῖον, Od. 1, 209. σιγῇ τοῖον, in perfect silence, Od. 4, 776.

τοιόσδε, ήδε, όνδε = τοῖος strengthened by the enclitic δέ, it refers in the main to what follows, yet also to what precedes, 5, 372. 21, 509. Od. 1, 371; with accus. τοιόσδε δέμας καὶ ἔργα, such in form and deeds, Od. 17, 313. b) With infin. Il. 6, 463; cf. τοῖος.

τοιοῦτος, αὕτη, οὖτο, Ep. and Att. in the neut. τοιοῦτον (τοῖος, οὗτος), Od. 7, 309. 13, 330; a strengthened τοῖος, *such, so constituted,* refers prop. like οὗτος to what precedes, still also to what follows, Il. 16, 847. Od. 4, 269.

τοῖσδεσι and τοίσδεσσι, see ὅδε.

τοῖχος, ὁ, *a wall;* esply a wall of a house, and of a court, 9, 219. 16, 212. Od. 7, 86. 2) *the side of a ship,* Il. 15, 382. Od. 12, 120.

τοκάς, άδος, ἡ (τίκτω), *bearing, having borne,* σῦς, Od. 14, 16.†

τοκεύς, έως, and ῆος, ὁ, poet. (τίκτω), one who begets or bears, in Hom. always in the plur. *parents,* 3, 140. h. Cer. 138; and dual, Od. 8, 312.

τόκος, ὁ (τίκτω), 1) *the act of bearing, birth,* 17, 5. 19, 119. h. Cer. 101. 2)

Τολμάω. 402 Τοῦ.

that which is born, a *child, posterity,* γενεή τε τόκος τε, 15, 141. Od. 15, 175. 3) Metaph. *usury, interest, reward,* Batr. 186.
τολμάω (τόλμα), fut. τολμήσω, aor. Ep. τόλμησα, like τλῆναι, 1) *to take upon oneself, to venture, to undertake, to dare,* to have boldness and spirit, with infin. 8, 424. Od. 9, 332; with partcp. Od. 24, 162; absol. θυμός μοι ἐτόλμα, Il. 10, 232. 17, 68. 2) Rarely with accus. *to undertake,* πόλεμον, Od. 8, 519.
τολμήεις, εσσα, εν (τόλμα), *full of spirit, bold, daring, rash,* θυμός, 10, 205; steadfast, Od. 17, 284.
τολυπεύω (τολύπη), prop. to wind the cleansed wool into a ball, hence, metaph. *to bring about any thing with painstaking, to prepare, to finish,* δόλους, *to devise a stratagem,* Od. 19, 137; πόλεμον, to finish the war, Il. 14, 86. 1, 235. Od. 1, 238. 4, 490; τί, Il. 24, 7.
τομή, ἡ (τέμνω), *a cut*, i. e. the act of cutting. 2) the part cut off, *the stump of a tree*, 1, 235.†
*τόμος, ὁ (τέμνω) = τομή; τόμος ἐκ πτέρνης, a slice of ham, Batr. 37.
Τομοῦραι, αἱ = αἱ μαντεῖαι, the oracle of Zeus in Dodôna; thus read some critics for θέμιστες, Od. 16, 403. cf. Strab. VII. p. 474.
τοξάζομαι, depon. mid. poet. (τόξον), pres. optat. τοξαζοίατο, fut. σομαι, Od. 22, 72; *to shoot with the bow*, absol. and τινός, at any one, *Od. 8, 218. 22, 27.
τοξευτής, ὁ (τοξεύω), *an archer*, 23, 850.†
τοξεύω (τόξον) = τοξάζομαι, with gen. 23, 855.†
τόξον, τό, 1) *a bow* (for shooting), poet. often in the plur. τὰ τόξα, because it consisted of two parts [or according to Herm. Suph. Phil. 652: "τόξα, de arcu et sagittis et quidquid ad arcum pertinet." *Am.Ed.*]. The bow, more rarely a weapon in battle, served for occasions of treachery and ambush. The bow of Pandarus, according to 4, 109, seq., was of horn, and consisted of two parts, each of which was 16 palms long. The two were so joined by the πῆχυς, that they received the form of a bow. Upon each of the extremities was a knob (κορώνη), to which the bow-string (νευρά) was attached. When it was to be used, it was drawn, by placing it against the earth, and drawing firmly the string (τιταίνειν τόξον). In shooting, the bow was grasped by the middle (πῆχυς), the arrow laid upon the string, and this drawn to the breast to impel the arrow (τόξον ἕλκειν, ἀνέλκειν), cf. 4, 105, seq. 11, 375. 582. Od. 19, 572. 2) Poet. *the act of shooting, archery*, Il. 2, 718. 12, 350.
τοξοσύνη, ἡ (τόξον), the act of shooting with the bow, *archery*, 13, 314.†
τοξότης, ου, ὁ, Ep. τόξοτα (τόξον), *an archer*, 11, 385.†
τοξοφόρος, ον (φέρω), *bearing a bow; archer*, epith. of Artĕmis, 24, 483.† of Apollo, h. Ap. 13, 126.
τοπρίν, adv. see πρίν.

τοπρόσθεν, adv. see πρόσθεν.
τορεῖν, Ep. defect. aor. 2 ἔτορον, and partcp. aor, 1 τορήσας, h. Merc. 119, *pierce through, to thrust through*, τί, any thing, 11, 236.†
τορνόω (τόρνος), Hom. only in the mid. aor. 1 Ep. 3 plur. τορνώσαντο. subj. τορνώσεται, Ep. for τορνώσωνται, Od. l. c. *to make round, to round off*, with accus. σῆμα, Il. 23, 255; ἔδαφος νηός, to form the bottom of a ship with its due curve. Od. 5, 249.
ΤΟΣ, ΤΗ, ΤΟ, obsol. ground form of the article.
τοσάκι, Ep. τοσσάκι, adv. *so many times, as often*, with reference to ὁσσάκι, 21, 268. 22, 197. Od. 11, 586.
τόσος, η, ον, also τόσσος. η. ον, *as great, as much, as far, as long, as strong*, used of time, number, etc.; it corresponds prop. to ὅσος; very often it stands absol.; spoken of a known number or size, 4, 430; Od. 2, 28. τρὶς τόσσοι, thrice as much, Il. 1, 213. 21, 80. 2) The neut. τόσον and τόσσον, often used as adv. = *much, so very, so far*, with verbs and adj. and with ὅσον correlating, 3, 12. 5, 450; more rarely with ὡς, 4, 130. 22, 424; ἄλλο τόσον, the rest entirely. τοῦ δὲ καὶ τόσον, κ. τ. λ., whose body the armour elsewhere entirely covered (according to Spitz.), 22, 322. cf. 23, 554.
τοσόσδε, τοσήδε, τοσόνδε, Ep. also τοσσόσδε, τοσσήδε, τοσσόνδε; = τόσος strengthened by the enclitic δέ, with a correlating ὅσος, 14, 94; and connected with τοιόσδε, 2, 120. τοσόνδε, and τοσσόνδε, as an adv. 22, 41. Od. 21, 253.
τοσοῦτος, τοσαύτη, τοσοῦτο, Ep. also τοσσοῦτος, τοσσαύτη, τοσσοῦτο or τοσσοῦτον, Od. (τόσος and οὗτος), a strengthened τόσος, 1) *so great, so much*, καί σε τοσοῦτον ἔθηκα, I reared thee thus great, Il. 9, 485. 2) τοσοῦτο or τοσσοῦτο, Od. 8, 203, *so very, so much*, Od. 21, 402; with a superl., Il. 23, 476.
τοσσάκι, Ep. for τοσάκι.
τόσσος, η, ον, Ep. for τόσος.
τοσσοῦτος, αύτη, οὗτο, Ep. for τοσοῦτος.
τότε, adv. of time: *then, at last, at that time*, 1, 100. Od. 4, 182; spoken of a time sufficiently definite from what precedes, or which is known; often τότε καί, τότε γε, καὶ τότε δή, καὶ τότ' ἔπειτα. 3) With an article, οἱ τότε, those at that time, or the then living, Il. 9, 559. 3) It often forms the apodosis, esp'y in sentences of time, 21, 451; esp'y Ep. δὴ τότε, 1, 476. Od. 9, 59; also καὶ τότε δή, Il. 8, 69; καὶ τότ' ἔπειτα, 1, 478; rarely after conditional clauses. 4, 36. Od. 11, 112.
τοτέ, adv. *once, sometimes*, τοτὲ μέν—τοτὲ δέ, now—now, Od. 24, 447, 448. It also stands alone, Il. 11, 63, ed. Spitzner (where Wolf reads τότε.)
τοτρίτον, adv. *for the third time*, τρίτος.
τοῦ, gen. of ὁ, and of τίς; but not enclit. for τινός.

Τοὔνεκα. 403 Τρέχω.

τοὔνεκα, contr. for τοῦ ἕνεκα, therefore, on that account, 1, 96. Od. 13, 194.
τοὔνομα, contr. for τὸ ὄνομα, q. v.
τόφρα, adv. of time, 1) so long, in the mean time, the while, prop. it answers to ὄφρα, which generally follows it, but often precedes, 4, 221. 9, 550; it also relates to ἕως, 10, 507. Od. 2, 76; ὅτε δή, Od. 10, 571; πρίν, Il. 21, 100. 2) so long as, until, until the time, here also follows ὄφρα, 1, 509. h. Cer. 37. 3) Absol. meantime, in the meantime, 10, 498. 13, 83. 17, 79. Od. 3, 303. 464; and often.
τράγος, ὁ, a he-goat, Od. 9, 239.†
τράπεζα, ἡ (prop. for τετράπεζα, having four feet), a table; ξενίη, the guest-table, as a symbol of hospitality, Od. 14, 158. 17, 155. Mly each guest had his own table, Od. 15, 466. 17, 333; and esply Od. 22, 74, where the suitors use the table as shields. Still this was not always the case, since Od. 4, 54, two guests used a table, and often all the guests had but one table, see Il. 9, 216. 11, 628. Od. 1, 138; see Nitzsch ad Od. 1, 109.
τραπεζεύς, ῆος, ὁ (τράπεζα), at the table, belonging to the table, only as adj. κύνες τραπεζῆες, table or house-dogs, 23, 173. Od. 17, 309; and πυλαωροί, Il. 22, 69.
τραπείομεν, Ep. for ταρπῶμεν, see τέρπω.
τραπέω, Ep. to tread grapes, Od. 7, 125.†
τραφέμεν, see τρέφω.
τράφεν, see τρέφω.
τραφερός, ἡ, όν (τρέφω), congealed, solid, compact, firm; hence ἡ τραφερή, the solid land, the continent, ἐπὶ τραφερήν τε καὶ ὑγρήν, 14, 308. Od. 20, 9. h. Cer. 43.
*τράχηλος, ὁ, the neck, Batr. 82.
τρεῖς, οἱ, αἱ, τρία, τά, three, 9, 144. οἱ τρεῖς, Od. 14, 26. On the number three, see τρίς.
τρέμω (τρέω), only pres. and imperf. to tremble, to shake, to quake, 13, 19; spoken of a robe, 21, 507. 2) Esply for fear, 10, 390. Od. 11, 527. (Another form is τρομέω.)
τρέπω, fut. τρέψω, aor. 1 ἔτρεψα, Ep. τρέψα, aor. 2 ἔτραπον, sometimes intrans. 16, 657. Mid. aor. 1 ἐτρεψάμην, h. Cer. 203. Od. 1, 422. 18, 305; very often aor. 2 ἐτραπόμην, Ep. τραπόμην, perf. pass. τέτραμμαι, esply τετραμμένος, imperat. τετράφθω, Il. 12, 273; pluperf. 3 sing. τέτραπτο, and 3 plur. τετράφαθ', Ep. for τετράφατο, aor. 1 pass. ἐτρέφθην, Ep. 14, 7, mly ἐτράφθην, from which τραφθῆναι, Od. 15, 80 (τραπείομεν, Od. 8, 292, belongs to τέρπω). 1) Act. to turn, to direct, to guide, to govern, with accus. according to the relation indicated by the connected adv. and prepos. a) to turn away, to direct, to a place, ἔς τι, Il. 13, 7; πρός τι, 5, 605; παρά τι, 21, 603; ἀνά τι, 19, 212; ἐπί τινι, 13, 542; ἐπί τι, 13, 4; τέτραπτο πρὸς ἰθύ οἱ, he was turned directly towards him, 14, 403; τινὰ εἰς εὐνήν, to bring any one to bed, Od. 4, 294; μῆλα πρὸς ὄρος, to drive the sheep to the mountain, Od. 9, 315; θυμὸν κατὰ πληθύν, to turn one's mind to, Il. 5, 676; ἵππους φύγαδε, the horses to flight, 8, 157. 257; and without ἵππους, 16, 657; spoken of battle: to turn to flight, to repulse, τινά, 15, 261. b) to turn around, to turn about, πάλιν τρ. ἵππους, to turn back the horses, 8, 137; πάλιν ὄσσε, 13, 3. c) to turn from, to avert, to repel ἀπό τινος, 16, 645. 22, 16. d) Metaph. to turn, to change, φρένας τινός, 6, 61. 2) Intrans. to turn oneself, like the mid. aor. 2 act., φύγαδε, 16, 657. II) Mid. and Pass. 1) to turn oneself, to betake oneself, to apply oneself, ἐπὶ ἔργα, 3, 432; εἰς ὀρχηστύν, Od. 1, 422; aor. 1 mid. absol. αἰχμὴ ἐτράπετο, the point bent. Il. 11, 237. Esply a) like versari, to have intercourse, to travel, τραφθῆναι ἀν' Ἑλλάδα, Od. 15, 80. b) πάλιν τραπέσθαι τινός, to turn from any one, 18, 138; ἑκάς τινος, Od. 17, 73. c) Metaph. to change, to turn, τρέπεται χρώς, his colour changes (spoken of one in fear), Il. 13, 279. 17, 733. Od. 21, 412; τράπεται νόος, φρήν, the mind changes, Il. 17, 546. 10, 45; ἤδη μοι κραδίη τέτραπτο νέεσθαι, already was my heart disposed to return, Od. 4, 260 (poet. from τροπάω).
τρέφω, fut. θρέψω, h. Ven. aor. 1 ἔθρεψα, Ep. θρέψα, aor. 2 ἔτραφον (trans. in 23, 90, where now stands ἔτρεφε, see at the end); perf. τέτροφα, intrans. aor. 1 mid. ἐθρεψάμην, only optat. θρέψαιο, aor. 2 pass. ἐτράφην, 3 plur. τράφεν for ἐτράφησαν. 1) Act. 1) to make compact or thick, to cause to congulate or curdle, with accus. γάλα, Od. 9, 246. 2) Mly to feed, to nourish, to rear, to bring up, to nurse, spoken of children, τινά, Il. 1, 414. 2, 548; τινὰ πῆμά τινι, to rear any one as a pest, 6, 282; of beasts: ἵππους, κύνας, to keep horses, dogs, 2, 766. 22, 69; of plants: to raise, 11, 741. b) Metaph. ὕλη τρέφει ἄγρια, the forest nourishes wild beasts, 5, 52; to cause to grow, ὕεσσιν ἀλοιφήν, Od. 13, 410; χαίτην, Il. 23, 142. II) Mid. 1) Trans. to rear for oneself, rear, Od. 19, 368.† 2) Intrans. mid. with perf. 2 and aor. pass. 1) to congeal, to attach itself firmly, περὶ χροῒ τέτροφεν ἄλμη, Od. 23, 237. 2) to be nourished, to grow, to grow up, Il. 1, 251. 4, 723. The forms ἐτραφέτην ὑπὸ μητρί, 5, 555: τραφέμεν for τραφέειν, 7, 199. 18, 436. Od. 3, 28; ἔτραφ' for ἔτραφε, Il. 21, 279, are explained as forms of the aor. 2 act. with intrans. signif., cf. Buttm., Ausf. Gram. under τρέφω, Kühner, § 244. Thiersch, on the contrary, § 215. 45, supposes an Ep. shortening for ἐτραφήτην, τραφῆναι, etc., accented ἐτράφ' with Herodian, as aor. 2 pass.
τρέχω, aor. 1 ἔθρεξα, only Ep. iterat.

Τρέω. Τρίσμακαρ.

from θρέξασκον, 18, 599. 602; aor. 2 ἔδραμον, to run, to haste, to hasten, πόδεσσι, 18, 599 ; metaph. spoken of inanimate things, of an auger, Od. 9, 38ʜ.
τρέω, 3 sing. τρεῖ, aor. 1 ἔτρεσα, Ep. τρέσσα, to tremble, to quake ; in Hom. according to Aristarch. always: to fly from fear, 5, 256 11, 546.. Od. 6, 138; ὑπὸ τεῖχος, to fly under the wall, II. 22, 143 (the aignif, to quake, prob. 17, 332. 21, 288). 2) Trans. to fear, to tremble at. τί, 11, 554. 17, 663. N.B. φωνὴ τρεῖ, the voice trembles, Herm. conject. h. Ven. 238, for ῥέει.
τρήρων, ωνος, ὁ, ἡ (τρέω), trembling, timorous, fearful, epith. of doves, 5, 778. 22, 140 Od. 12, 63.
τρητός, ή, όν, verb. adj. from τιτράω, pierced, perforated, λίθος, Od. 13, 77; often τρητὰ λέχεα, spoken of royal beds, prob. beautifully perforated, of perforated work, II. 3, 448. Od. 1, 440. Others think they were so called because they were thus pierced to admit girths or cords, Od. 23, 198.
Τρηχίς, ῖνος, ἡ, Ep. and Ion. for Τραχίς, an old town in Thessaly on the Malean gulf, so called from the mountainous region in its vicinity; after its destruction, it was rebuilt at a distance of six stadia, and called Ἡράκλεια, 2, 682.
Τρῆχος, ὁ, an Ætolian, slain by Hector, 5, 706.
τρηχύς, εῖα, ύ, Ion. for τραχύς, rough, uneven, rugged, steep, stony, λίθος, 5, 308 ; ἀκτή. Od. 5, 425; also epith. of towns and islands, II. 2, 717. Od. 9, 27.
(τρήχω), an erroneously assumed pres. for the Hom. perf. τέτρηχα, see ταράσσω.
τρίαινα, ἡ (τρεῖς), a tridrnt, the comm. weapon of Poseidôn, 12, 27. Od. 4, 506.
Τρίβος. ὁ (τρίβω), prop. rubbing, exercise, practice, expertness, h. Merc. 447.
τρίβω, infin. pres. Ep. τριβέμεναι, aor. 1 ἔτριψα, infin. τρίψαι. 1) Prop. to rub ; hence spoken of grain: to thresh, κρῖ, 23, 496 (which was done by oxen); μοχλὸν ἐν ὀφθαλμῷ, to turn the stake in the eye, Od. 9, 333. 2) Metaph. to exhaust, to enfeeble, τρίβεσθαι κακοῖσι, to exhaust oneself by sufferings, II. 23, 735.
τρίγληνος, ον (γλήνη), having three eyes, ἅρματα τρίγληνα, either with three eyes or openings, or having three stars ['triple-gemmed,' Cp.], 14, 183. Od. 18, 298.
τριγλωχίν, ῖνος, ὁ, ἡ. poet. (γλωχίν), three-pointed, triple-barbed, epith. of an arrow, *5, 393. 11, 507.
τριετής, ἐς (ἔτος), of three years, three years old, only adv. τρίετες (with retracted accent), three years long, *Od. 2, 106. 13. 377.
τρίζω, perf. τέτριγα, with pres. signif., partcp. Ep. τετριγῶτας for τετριγότας, a word formed to imitate the sound, to twitter, spoken of young birds, 2, 314; to squeak, to gibber, to utter a sharp sound, spoken of bats and of the noise of departing souls, Od. 24, 5 9. 11.

23, 101 [cf. Shaksp. 'the ghosts.—Did squeak and gibber in the Roman street. Am Ed.]; to crack, to creak [Cp.]. spoken of the backs of wrestlers, II. 23 714.
τριήκοντα, indecl. Ep. and Ion. for τριάκ., thirty, *2, 516. 680. 733.
τριηκόσιοι, αι, α, Ep. and Ion. for τριακ.. three hundred, 11, 697. Od. 13, 380.
Τρίκη, ἡ, prose Τρίκκη, Strab., a town in Thessaly on the Peneius, with a temple of Asklêpios (Æsculapius), the residence of the Asclepiades, 2, 729. 4, 202.
τρίλλιστος, ον, poet. for τρίλιστος (λίσομαι), thrice prayed for, i. e. often & earnestly supplicated, νύξ, 8, 488.† cf. τρίς.
*Τριόπης, ου, ὁ, Ion. for Τριόπας (triple-eyed, from ὤψ), father of Phorbas, h. Ap. 211.
*τριπέτηλος, ον (πέτηλον), triple-leaved, h. Merc.
τρίπλαξ, ακος, ὁ, ἡ (πλέκω), threefold, triple, ἄντυξ, 18, 480.†
τριπλῆ, adv. (τρίπλοος), threefold, 1. 128.†
τρίπολος, ον, poet. (πολέω). thrice turned around or ploughed, νειός, 18. 542. Od. 5, 127.
τρίπος, ου, ὁ, poet. for τρίπους, 22, 164.†
τρίπους, οδος, ὁ, ἡ, prop. adj. three-footed, mly ὁ τρίπους, a tripod : as a three-footed kettle for boiling, 18, 344. 346. Od. 8, 434 ; hence ἐμπυριβήτης. II. 23, 702. b) Or, a beautifully wrought three-footed stand for kettles, dishes, basins, ἄπυρος, 9, 122. 264. They are often mentioned as prizes and presents, 8, 290. 9, 122. 11, 700. Od. 13. 13.
*Τριπτόλεμος, ὁ, the rural deity dwelling upon the thrice-ploughed land (τριπόλῳ), according to Hom. h. Cer. 153, a prince of the Eleusinians ; according to the fable of the Athenians, son of Celeus and Metaneira, to whom Dêmêter presented a chariot yoked to a dragon, to travel through the earth and teach agriculture to mankind.
τρίπτυχος, ον (πτύσσω), triple, three-fold ; τρυφάλεια, a helmet which is formed of three plates laid one upon another, 11, 353.†
τρίς, adv. (τρεῖς), thrice, often, τρὶς τόσσον, τόσσα, 1, 213. 5, 136. The number three appears even in Hom. to have been a sacred number, and generally to indicate that which occurs several times, 5, 436. 6, 435. 22, 165 ; see Spitzner ad II. 16. 702.
τρισκαίδεκα, indecl. poet. for τριακαίδεκα, thirte·n, 5, 387. Od. 24, 340.
τρισκαιδέκατος, η, ον, the thirteenth, 18. 495 ; τῇ τρισκαιδεκάτῃ, sc. ἡμέρα, Od. 19, 202.
*τρισκοπάνιστος, ον (κοπανίζω), thrice-pounded, τρ. ἄρτος, bread made of very fine flour, Batr. 35.
τρίσμακαρ, αρος, ὁ, ἡ, thrice-blessed i. e. happy in the highest degree, Od. 4

Τρισσός. 405 **Τρόφις.**

154. τρισμάκαρες καὶ τετράκις, *Od. 5, 306.

*τρισσός, ή, όν (τρίς), three-fold, three and three. h. Ven. 7.
τριστοιχί, adv. (στοίχος), in three rows [ἐν triple order. Cp.], 10, 473.† ed. Wolf; otherwise τριστοιχεί.
τρίστοιχος, ον (στοίχος), in three rows, divided into three parts, Od. 12, 91.†
τρισχίλιοι, αι, α (χίλιοι), three thousand, 20, 221.†
τρίτατος, η, ον, poet. lengthened for τρίτος, the third, 1, 252. Od. 4, 97; and often.
Τριτογένεια, ἡ (γένος), the Triton-born, epith. of Athēnē, prob. named from Triton, a stream at Alalcomenæ, in Bœotia, where was the most ancient seat of her worship, 4, 515. 8, 39. Paus. 9, 33. According to the old Gramm. it means head-born, from τριτώ, in Cretan = κεφαλή; but the fable that Athēnē was born from the head of Zeus is first found h. 28, 4. A later fable derives the name from the lake Triōtnis in Lybia, where she was said to have been born, Ap. 1, 3. 0.
*Τριτογενής, έος, ἡ, a rare form of Τριτογένεια, h. 28, 4
τρίτος, η, ον (τρεῖς), the third. τοῖσι ἐπὶ τρίτος ἦλθε, Od. 20, 185. Neut. τὸ τρίτον, or, with Wolf, τοτρίτον, thirdly, for the third time, 3, 225.
τρίχα, adv. (τρίς), three-fold, in three parts, Od. 8, 506. διὰ τρίχα κοσμηθέντες, i. e. διακοσμ. τρ., Il. 2, 655; with gen. τρίχα νυκτὸς ἔην, it was in the third part or watch of the night, Od. 12, 312. 14, 483.
τριχάϊκες (ᾰ, ῐ), οἱ Δωριεῖς, Od. 19, 177;† according to Eustath. the triply-divided (ἀΐσσω), because they dwelt in Eubœa, in the Peloponnesus, and in Crete, or named from the triple race of the Dorians, the Hylleis, Dymanes, and Pamphyli, hence V., of treble race. According to others (Damm), with triple waving crest, like κορυθάϊξ; or from θρίξ, with waving hair, cf. Strab. X. p. 475.
τρίχες. αἱ, nom. plur. from θρίξ.
τρίχθα, poet. for τρίχα, three-fold, 2, 668. 15, 189. Od. 9, 71.
Τροιζήν, ῆνος, ἡ, Trœzene, a town in Argolis, not far from the coast on the Saronic gulf, with a port, Pogon, 2, 561.
Τροιζηνος, ον, son of Ceas, father of Euphēmus, 2, 847.
Τροίη, ἡ. Ep. and Ion. for Τροία, Troja, 1) the Trojan country in Asia Minor, with its capital, Ilium, extending along the coast from the river Æsēpus to Caïcus, or, according to Strabo, from the promontory of Lectum to the Hellespont. Often in Hom. 2, 162; in prose mly Τρωάς. 2) the chief town in Troja, otherwise Ilium, 1, 129. 2, 141. Od. 1, 2; from this Τροίηθεν and Τροίηθε, adv. from Troy, Od. 3, 257 [ἀπὸ Τροίηθε μολόντα, Il. 24, 492, is rejected by Spitzner in his Programm. de adverb. quæ in θεν de-

sinunt, usu Homerico, p. 6, who prefers the old reading, Τροίηθεν ἰόντα). Τροίηνδε, adv. to Troy, 22, 116. Od. 3, 268.
τρομέω, a form of τρέμω, only pres. and imperf. mid. 3 plur. optat. τρομεοίατο for τρομέοιντο. 1) to tremble, to quake. τρομέει ὑπὸ γυῖα, 10, 95. τρομέουσι φρένα, they tremble in heart, 15, 627. 2) With accus. to tremble at, to fear, any one, 17, 203. Od. 18, 79. Mid =τρομέω. τρομέοιντό οἱ φρένες, Il. 14, 10; θυμῷ. 10, 492; with accus. θάνατον, Od. 16, 446.
τρόμος, ὁ (τρέμω), the act of trembling, quaking, 3, 34. 8. 452. Od. 18, 88; hence anxiety, terrour, Il. 6, 137; and often.
*τρόπαιον, τό (τροπή), a trophy, Batr. 159.
τροπέω, poet. form of τρέπω; ὄχεα, to turn the chariot round, 28, 224.†
τροπή, ἡ, the act of turning, return τροπαὶ ἠελίοιο, the turning of the sun, the solstice, Od. 15. 404.† The passage Νῆσός τις Συρίη—Ὀρτυγίης καθύπερθεν, ὅθι τροπαὶ ἠελίοιο, is variously explained; Voss: beyond Ortygia, where is the solsticial point. According to most ancient critics, cf. Strabo X. p. 487, and Eustath. ad loc., by Syria is to be understood Syros, one of the Cyclades, and by Ortygia the island of Delos. The τροπαὶ ἠελίοιο Eustath. explains as a poetical description of the west, and compares with it Od. 11, 18. Also, according to Voss and Nitzsch ad Od. 1, 22, it is the quarter of the heaven where the sun declines to his setting. With him agrees G. F. Grotefend in Geogr. Ephem. B. 48. St. 3. p. 281. "Ortygia or Delos is the centre of the earth's surface in Homer, over which the sun reaches the highest point of its path. A line from north to south divides the earth into two parts." Others consider the words as meaning the real solstice, rejecting the above explanation because Syros is not west, but rather east from Delos. This Eustath. intimates, in saying that the solstitial point had been pointed out in a cave in this island; or it was referred to the gnomon of Pherecydes, cf. Diog. Laert. Pherecyd. According to Oilfr. Müller, cf. Orchomenos, p. 326, the words are the addition of a rhapsodist, and obviously refer to the gnomon of Pherecydes of Syros. Voss, Alte Weltkunde, p. 294, understands by Ortygia, the small island of Ortygia lying off Syracuse; and here also, he thinks, is Syria to be sought, see Συρίη.
τρόπις, ιος, ἡ (τρέπω), the keel of a ship, a ship's bottom; it was made small, in order easily to cut the waves; from it arose the two sides of the vessel, *Od. 7, 252. 19, 278.
τροπός, ὁ (τρέπω), a leathern thong with which the oar was made fast, and in which it turned, Od. 4, 782. 8, 53.
τρόφις, τρόφι, gen. ιος, Ep. short form =τροφόεις. τρόφι κῦμα, a huge, mighty wave, 11, 307.†

τροφόεις. εσσα, εν, poet. (τρέφω), well-nourished; hence thick, strong, huge, κύματα, huge billows 15, 621. Od. 3, 290. Aristarch reads τροφέοντα, incorrectly.

τροφός, ὁ and ἡ (τρέφω), one who nourishes, one who brings up: only as fem. a nurse, a female attendant, *Od. 2, 361. 4, 742.

*Τροφώνιος, ὁ, son of Erginus, a king of Orchomenos, brother of Agamēdes, h. Ap. 296.

τροχός, ὁ (τρέχω), any thing which runs, mly any thing circular, hence 1) the wheel of a chariot, 6, 42. cf. ἅρμα. 2) a potter's wheel. 18, 600. 3) a round mass of wax, tallow, Od. 12, 173. 21, 178.

τρυγάω (τρύγη), 3 plur. pres. τρυγόωσι, Ep. for τρυγῶσι, to gather the fruits of the trees and the field, to reap, to gather, Od. 7, 124; to strip off fruits, ἀλωήν, Il. 18, 556.

*τρύγη, ἡ, autumnal fruits, whether of field or tree, esply wine. 2) the autumnal harvest, h. Ap. 55.

*τρυγηφόρος, ον (φέρω), bearing wine, h. Ap. 529.

τρυγόω, see τρυγάω.

τρύζω, a word formed to imitate the sound, to coo, to utter a murmuring sound, esply spoken of the turtle dove; of men: to mutter, to murmur from displeasure; τινί, to complain of any thing to any one, 9, 311.†

τρύπανον, τό (τρυπάω). an augur, a carpenter's tool, Od. 9, 385.†

τρυπάω (τρύπη), pres. optat. 3 sing. τρυπῷ, to bore, to pierce, δόρυ, Od. 9, 384.†

τρυφάλεια, ἡ, poet. a helmet, 3, 372. Od. 18, 378. According to the common explanation, for τρυφάλεια, a helmet with three cones; according to Wolf and Buttm., Lex. in voc. φάλος, it was the current name of a helmet, and prob. derived from τρύω, to pierce, because the cone or knob was perforated for the reception of the crest, in distinction from καταίτυξ, Heyne ad Il. 3, 372.

*τρυφερός, ή, όν (τρυφή), soft, delicate, tender, Batr. 66.

τρύφος, εος, τό (θρύπτω), that, which is broken off, a piece, a fragment, Od. 4, 508.†

τρύχω, poet. = τείρω, fut. τρύξω, to wear away, to consume, to destroy, οἶκον, the property, Od. 1, 248. 16, 125; metaph. to drain, to vex, to torment, to distress. πτωχὸν οὐκ ἄν τις καλέοι, τρύξοντά ἑ αὐτόν, no one would call to him (invite) a beggar, to torment himself, Od. 17, 387. Pass. Od. 1, 288. τρύχεσθαι λιμῷ, *Od. 10, 177.

Τρωαί, αἱ, only plur. the Trojan women, 3, 384. 411, see Τρωός.

Τρωάς, άδος, ἡ, a pecul. fem. to Τρωός, Trojan, ἡ τροφός, h. Ven. 114; esply with and without γυνή, a Trojan woman, always in the plur. 6, 442.

*τρώγλη. ἡ (τρώγω), a hole, a cave, Batr. 52. 113.

*Τρωγλοδύτης. ου, ὁ, that lives in a hole, the name of a mouse, Batr. 205.

*τρωγλοδύω (δύω), to creep into a hole or cave. to dwell in a hole, only partcp. Batr. 35.

τρώγω, to gnaw, to crop, to chew, to nibble, spoken of mules, ἄγρωστιν, Od 6, 60; † of mice, Batr. 34.

Τρωϊάς, άδος, ἡ. poet. pecul. fem. of Τρώϊος, Trojan, ληΐς, Od. 13, 263: mly in the plur. with γυναῖκες, Il. 9, 139. 16, 831. Subst. the Trojan women, 13. 122.

Τρωϊκός, ή, όν, Trojan; τὸ Τρωϊκὸν πεδίον, 10, 11. 23, 464. the Trojan plain, between the rivers Scamander and Simois, the scene of the Trojan war; also Τρώων πεδίον, 11, 836. 15, 739: for the most part called simply πεδίον. This plain extended from the camp of the Greeks to the city of Ilium, and was broken by both these rivers and by several hills. In proceeding directly from the camp to the city, it was necessary to cross a ford of the Scamander. The following points in it are mentioned by Hom.: 1) The sacred oak of Zeus. at the Scaean gate, see φηγός. 2) The fig-hill, see Ἐρινεός. 3) The watchstand, not far from the fig-hill, see σκοπιή. 4) The sepulchral mound of Batieia, see Βατίεια. 5) The mound of Ilus, see Ἶλος. 6) The sepulchral mound of Aesyetes, from which the Grecian camp could be seen, 2, 793. 7) The height of the plain, near the Hellespont, see θρωσμός. 8) The entrenchment of Heracles (τεῖχος), in the neighbourhood of the sea, constructed by Athēnē and the Trojans for the protection of Heracles, 20, 145, seq. 9) The Hill of Beauty, see Καλλικολώνη, cf. Spohn de agro Trojan. p. 17, seq.

Τρώϊλος, ὁ, son of Priam and Hecuba, 24, 257.

Τρώϊος, ίη, ϊον. Ep. and Ion. for Τρωός, Trojan. 1) belonging to Tros. Τρώϊοι ἵπποι, 5, 222. 23, 378. 2) peculiar to the nation, δούρατα, Τρώϊα, 14, 262.

τρώκτης. ου, ὁ (τρώγω), a gnawer, a glutton; as epith. of Phoenician merchants: a cheat, a knave, a sharper *Od. 14, 289. 15, 406.

*Τρωξάρτης, ου, ὁ (ἄρτος), bread-eater name of a mouse, Batr. 20.

Τρωός, ή, όν, Trojan. 1) belonging to Tros, ἵπποι, 23, 291. 2) belonging to the nation, Τρωαὶ ἵπποι, 16, 393. Τρ. κύνες, 17, 255. 273; but Τρωαί, as subst., Trojan women, without iota subscript, q. v.

τρωπάω, poet. form of τρέπω, Ep. iterat. imperf. τρωπάσκετο, 11, 568; to turn, to change, to utter, φωνήν. Od. 19, 151. Mid. to turn oneself; πάλιν τρωπᾶσθαι, to turn back, to go back. Il. 16, 95; πρὸς πόλιν, Od. 24, 536; φόβονδε, to betake oneself to flight, Il 15, 666.

Τρώς, Τρωός, ὁ 1) son of Erichthonius

Τρωτός. 407 Τϋρός.

d Astyŏchê, grandson of Dardanus, husband of Callirhoê, who bore him us, Assaracus, and Ganymêdes. The art of Phrygia in which he reigned received from him the name of Troja, 20, 30, seq. 2) son of Alastor, 20, 462. 3) ιur. οἱ Τρῶες, gen. Τρώων (on the irregular accent, see Buttm. § 43. note 4. Lost, § 37. B. 1. Kühner, § 264), the Trojans, the inhabitants of the kingdom of Troy, of whom the Dardanians were a more ancient stock. They were prob. Pelasgian race; of their emigration to Crete Hom. knows nothing, 1, 152. cf. Idt. 7, 122.

τρωτός, ή, όν (τρώω), wounded, vulnerable, 21, 568.†

τρωχάω, Ep. form of τρέχω, to run, 22, 163. Od. 6, 318.

τρώω, poet. only in the pres. (theme of τιτρώσκω), aor. 1 ἔτρωσα, fut. τρώσομαι, aor. pass. ἐτρώθην, Batr. 193, to wound, esply to injure, to harm. ἀλλήλους, Od. 16, 293; ἵππους, Il. 23, 341; ὄφι τρώσεσθαι (sc. ἱππεῖς) ὀίω, where, I think, they will be wounded, 12, 66; metaph. to infatuate, to stupefy, οἶνός σε τρώει, Od. 21, 293.

τυγχάνω, imperf. Od. 14, 231.† fut. τεύξομαι, aor. 2 ἔτυχον. Ep. τύχον, subj. 1 sing. τύχωμι, also Ep. aor. ἐτύχησα, perf. τετύχηκα, only intrans. 1) Trans. with gen. to hit, to hit a mark. a) Prim. with missiles, τινός, Il. 16, 609. 23, 857; with accus. only in connexion with βάλλειν, οὐτάν, νύσσειν. ὄν ῥα—ὑπὸ στέρνοιο τυχήσας—βεβλήκει, 4, 106. cf. 5, 582. 12, 394. 13, 371; absol. 5, 287. 7, 243; and with prepos.: κατὰ ὦμον, 5, 98. 579. 12, 189. b) Generally, to hit, to attain, to find, to meet with, to reach, τινός, Od. 14, 334. 19, 291; absol. Od. 21, 13. c) Spoken of things: τύχε ἀμάθοιο βαθείης, he struck in the deep sand, Il. 5, 587; πομπῆς, Od. 6, 290; φιλότητος, Od. 15, 158. d) Absol. ὅς κε τύχῃ, whoever happened, Il. 3, 430; to attain an end, to be fortunate, 23, 466. 2) Intrans, to chance, to happen, to come to pass, 11, 116. πρὶν πεδίοιο διαπρύσιον τετυχηκώς, extending entirely through the plain, 17, 748. Od. 10, 88. b) Spoken of things: to fall to one's lot, to happen to, τινί, Il. 11, 684. Od. 14, 231. c) to be casual, with partcp. τύχησεν ἐρχομένη νηῦς, a ship chanced to be going, Od. 14, 334. 19, 291.

Τυδείδης, ου, ὁ, son of Tydeus=Diomêdes, 14, 380.

Τυδεύς, Ep. ῆος and έος, ὁ, son of king Œneus, of Calydon, in Ætolia, father of Diomedes. Because he slew his uncle Alcathous, he fled to Argos to Adrastus, who received him kindly and gave him his daughter Deiphyle as a wife. He marched with Polyneices to Thebes, and was slain there by Menelippus, 2, 406; esply 4, 372, seq. 5, 801, seq.

τυκτός, ή, όν, verb. adj. from τεύχω, prop. prepared, made. Ἄρης, τυκτὸν κακόν, an evil which men prepare for themselves, in opposition to a natural evil; an unnatural, a great evil (according to Köppen, formed of sheer evil), 5, 831. τ. κρήνη, an artificial fountain, Od. 17, 206. 2)=εὔτυκτος, artificially wrought, well-wrought, 11. 12, 105; δάπεδον, Od. 4, 627. 17, 169.

ΤΥΚΩ, obsol. theme of τεύχω.

τύμβος, ὁ (τύφω), prop. a place where a corpse is burned, esply a sepulchral mound, a hill of earth, which was heaped up above the ashes, 7, 336. 435. Od. 4, 584.

τυμβοχοή, ἡ (χέω), the act of heaping up a mound, sepulture, interment, 21, 323.† οὐδέ τί μιν χρέω ἔσται τυμβοχοῆς, ed. Wolf, with Crates. Aristarch., whom Eustath., and, among the moderns, Heyne, follow, reads τυμβοχοῆσ', shortened for τυμβοχοῆσαι; the latter, according to Buttm., Gr. Gram. § 305. A. 5, incorrect; cf. Thiersch, Gr. § 164. 2. A. 1.

Τυνδάρεος, ὁ, Att. Τυνδάρεως, Tyndareus, son of Œbalus and the nymph Batia; he was expelled from Sparta by his brothers, fled to Thestius to Ætolia, who gave him his daughter Leda as a wife. He was subsequently restored to Sparta by Heracles. His wife bore him Klytæmnêstra (Clytemnestra), Helen, Kastor (Castor), and Polydeukês (Pollux), Od. 11, 298.

*Τυνδαρίδης, ου, ὁ, son of Tyndareus, esply in the plur. οἱ Τυνδαρίδαι, the Tyndaridæ=Kastor (Castor) and Polydeukês (Pollux), h. 16, 2. 32, 2.

τύνη, Ep. and Ion. for σύ [5, 485].

*τύπανον, τό (τύπτω), a stroke, a thrust, a cut, in the plur. 5, 886.†

τύπτω, aor. 1 ἔτυψα, poet. τύψα, perf. pass. partcp. τετυμμένος, aor. 2 pass. ἐτύπην, to strike. 1) Prop. with a staff, τινά, 11, 561; spoken esply of weapons used in close conflict (opposed to βάλλειν, 11, 191. 13, 288. 15, 495); to cut, to hit, to thrust, to wound, τινὰ φασγάνῳ, ἄορι, δουρί, ξίφει, 4, 531. 13, 288. 782; with double accus. τινὰ λαιμόν, 13. 542; metaph. τὸν ἄχος κατὰ φρένα τύψε, pain smote him in the soul, 19, 125. 2) Improp. or poet. ἅλα ἐρετμοῖς, to strike the sea with the oars, Od. 9, 104; χθόνα μετώπῳ, Od. 22, 86; χνία πόδεσσι [' to press his footsteps, ere the dust filled them again, Cp.], Il. 23, 704; spoken of Zephyr, βαθείῃ λαίλαπι τύπτων, sc. νέφεα, smiting them with the full tempest, 11, 306. Pass. to be struck, ἐγχείῃσιν, 13, 782; but also with accus. ἕλκεα ὅσσ' ἐτύπη, 24. 421; cf. Rost, Gr. § 112. 6 Kühner, § 558.

*τύραννος, ὁ, prop. lord, commander, mly sovereign, prim. spoken of Ares, with dat. ἀντιβίοισι, h. 7, 5.

*Τυρογλύφος, ὁ (γλύφω), cheese excavator, the name of a mouse, Batr. 137.

τυρός, ή, cheese; αἴγειος, goats milk cheese, 11, 639. Od. 4, 88.

*Τυροφάγος, ὁ (φαγεῖν), cheese-eater, the name of a mouse, Batr. 226.

*Τυρσηνός, ὁ, Ion. for Τυῤῥηνός, a Tyrrhenian, an inhabitant of the country Tyrrhenia (Etruria), in Italy, h. 6, 8.

Τυρώ, οῦς, ἡ, daughter of Salmōneus and Alcidice, wife of Cretheus. She loved the river-god Enīpeus; Poseidōn appeared to her in the form of the river-god, and she bore to him Pelias and Neleus, Od. 2, 120. 11, 235, seq.

τυτθός, όν (later also of three endings), small, young, spoken of human beings, 6, 222 τυτθὸς ἐοῦσα, 22, 480. The neut. sing. τυτθόν as adv. little, a little, esply spoken of space, τυτθὸν ὀπίσσω, 5, 443; ἀποπρὸ νεῶν, 7, 334; τυτθὸν ὑπ' ἐκ θανάτοιο φέρονται, they sail a little removed from death, i. e. scarcely, 15, 628; in other connexions, τυτθὸν ἔτι ζώειν, to live a little longer, 19, 335; φθέγγεσθαι, to speak low, 24, 170. The neut. plur. only τυτθὰ διατμῆξαι or κεάσσαι, to cut small, to split small, Od. 12, 174 388.

Τυφάων, ονος, ὁ, poet. pecul. Ep. for Τυφών, see Τυφωεύς.

τυφλός, ή, όν, blind, 6, 139.† h. Ap. 172.

Τυφωεύς, έος, ὁ, Ep. contr Τυφώς, in Hom. gen. Τυφωέος, dat. Τυφωέϊ, 2, 782, 783; also Τυφάων, only in the accus. Τυφάονα, h. Ap. 306. 352; in prose Τυφῶν, ῶνος, prop. that smokes, from τύφω, the symbol of volcanoes and storms. According to 2, 780, a giant who lay in the land of the Arīmi in Cilicia, under the earth. In Hes. Th. 820, seq. he is described as a monster having a hundred dragon heads vomiting flames, whom Gæa (Terra) bore to Tartarus and sent against Zeus when he hurled the Titans into Tartarus. After a long contest, Zeus dashed him down to Tartarus. A later fable calls Cilicia his birth-place; after he was conquered by Zeus in a battle here, he fled into Sicily, where that deity hurled Ætna upon him, Pind. Pyth. 1, 32; cf. Ἄριμα.

ΤΥΧΕΩ, an assumed theme to some tenses of τυγχάνω.

*Τύχη, ἡ, fate, chance, destiny, esply good fortune, first found h. 10, 5.

*Τύχη, ἡ, daughter of Oceanus, h. Cer. 420

Τυχίος, ὁ (the maker, from τεύχω), a famous artist of Hylæ in Bœotia, 7, 220.

τῷ, prop. dat. sing. from τό, often used absol. 1) in this way, frequently in the apodosis, then, 2, 373. 4, 290. Od. 1, 239. 3, 258. cf. Nitzsch ad loc. 2) therefore, Il. 2, 250. Od. 2, 254. 7, 25.

τώς, adv. poet. = ὡς, οὕτως, thus, 2, 330. 3, 415. 14, 48. Od. 18. 271 19, 234. According to Apollon. de Adverb. p. 582. 17, τώς is correct only when it correlates to ὡς, as in Il. 3, 415. In other places he read ὅ' ὥς, and so reads Spitzner after good MSS., Il. 2, 330. 14, 48.

Υ.

Υ, the twentieth letter of the Greek alphabet, and the sign of the twentieth book.

Ὑάδες, ων, αἱ, the Hyades, according to the Schol. from ὕω, the raining ones, Pluviæ, or from their similarity to the letter Υ, a constellation, consisting of four stars of the third and some of the fourth magnitude, in the head of Taurus, the rising of which brought rain, 18, 486. The name has also been derived from ἱ. Suculæ, the constellation being conceived of as a herd of wild boars, cf. Gell. XIII. 9; and Nitzsch ad Od. 5, 272.

ὑακίνθινος, η, ον (ὑάκινθος), of the colour of hyacinth, hyacinthine, ἔσθς Od. 6, 231. 23. 158; see ὑάκινθος.

ὑάκινθος, ὁ (in Hom. in gender not indicated), the hyacinth, prob. the blue sword-lily (iris germanica, Linn.), or the larkspur (delphinium ajacis, Linn.), 14. 348.† h. Cer. 7, 426. h. 17, 25. Theocritus X. 28, calls it black; hence the poet compares to it the dark hair of Odysseus (Ulysses), Od. 6, 231. cf. Voss. ad Virg. Ecl. 3, 106. The flower had nothing in common with our hyacinth.

Ὑάμπολις, ιος, ἡ, a town in Phocis on the Cephīsus, between Opus and Orchomenus. Its name is compounded of Ὑάντων πόλις, having been built by the Hyantes, the original inhabitants of Bœotia, who were driven by Cadmus to Phocis, 2, 521.

ὑββάλλειν, Ep. for ὑποβάλλειν.

ὑβρίζω (ὕβρις), only partcp., pres. to be insolent or arrogant (in word or deed), spoken esply of men, to satisfy one's unbridled desires, to be wicked, to behave in a contumelious, insolent, or violent manner, Od. 1, 227. 3, 207. 17, 588. 2) Trans τινά, to do one wrong, to abuse any one to insult him, Il. 11, 695. Od. 20, 170.

ὕβρις, ιος, ἡ (akin to ὑπέρ), arrogance insolence, wickedness, any violence arising from the consciousness of power or from the preponderance of sensual desire, Od. 14, 262; spoken esply of the suitors Od. 1, 368. 4, 321; with βίη, Od. 14, 329. 17, 565. 2) wickedness towards others, violence, abuse, Il. 3, 203. 214.

ὑβριστής, οῦ, ὁ (ὑβρίζω), an arrogant person, an insolent, wicked, or violent man, ἀνήρ, 13, 633. In opposition to δίκαιος, φιλόξεινος, Od. 6, 120. 9, 175 h. Ap. 279.

ὑγιής, ές, gen. έος, healthy, sound vigourous, well, metaph. μῦθος, a healthful word (an useful, salutary thought) 8, 524.†

ὑγρή, ἡ, see ὑγρός.

ὑγρός, ή, όν (ὕω), 1) wet, moist, fluid ὑγρὰ κέλευθα, the watery paths, poet. for

*Ὑδατοτρεφής. 409 Ὑπαΐσσω.

the sea, Od. 3, 71; hence subst. ἡ ὑγρή, *the waters*, poet. for the sea, Il. 10, 27; connected with τραφερή, 14, 308. Od. 20, 18; ἄνεμοι ὑγρὸν ἀέντες, moist-blowing winds, Od. 5, 478. 2) Metaph. *languishing*, πόθος, h. 18, 33.

ὑδατοτρεφής, ές, gen. έος (τρέπω), *water-nourished* [Cp.], *loving the water*, epith. of the poplar (alder), Od. 17, 208.†

Ὕδη, ἡ, a town on the Tmōlus in Lydia, according to the Schol. the later Sardis, 20, 385.

ὑδραίνω (ὕδωρ), only aor. 1 mid. partcp. ὑδρηνάμενος, *to water*, mid. *to wash oneself*, *to bathe oneself*, *Od. 4, 750, 759, 17, 48. 58.

ὑδρεύω (ὕδωρ), only pres. and imperf. *to dip* or *fetch water*, Od. 10, 105. Mid. *to dip* or *fetch water for oneself*, *Od. 7, 131. 17, 206.

ὑδρηλός, ή, όν (ὕδωρ), *watery, moist, wet*, Od. 9, 133.† h. Ap. 41.

*Ὑδρομέδουσα, ἡ (μέδουσα), *the water-queen*, name of a frog, Batr. 19.

ὕδρος, ὁ (ὕδωρ), *the water-snake*, 2, 723.† Batr 81.

*Ὑδρόχαρις, ὁ (χαίρω), *a friend of the water*, *Water-joy*, a frog's name, Batr. 224.

ὕδωρ, ὕδατος, τό (ὕω), *water*; originally prob. rain-water, as 16, 385; plur. ὕδατα, *waters*, only once, Od. 13, 109; proverb ὕδωρ καὶ γαῖαν γενέσθαι, see γαῖα. (ν prop. short, but also long in the thesis, cf. Herm. ad h. Cer. 382.)

ὑετός, ὁ (ὗ, ὕω), *rain, a shower*, 12, 133.† ὑία, υἱάσι, see υἱός.

ΥΙΕΥΣ, a form of υἱός, obsol. in the nom. from which oblique cases are formed.

υἱός, ὁ (from this form there occur in Homer besides the nom. sing., the gen. and accus. sing, and the gen. and dat. plur. The accus. plur. υἱούς, as a varia lectio, 5, 159). Besides this, the Ep. language declined the obl. cases after two themes: ΥΙΣ and ΥΙΕΥΣ. gen. υἷος and υἱέος, dat. υἷι and υἱεῖ, υἱῖ, accus. υἷα and υἱέα, 13, 350; nom. pl.: υἷες, υἱεῖς, and υἱέες, in the dat. plur. only υἱάσι. 5, 463. Od. 3, 387; *a son*, often υἷες Ἀχαιῶν = Ἀχαιοί: once υἷες Δαπιθάων = Δαπίθαι, 11. 12, 128. (The diphthong υι is sometimes used as short, 6, 130. 17, 575), see Thiersch, Gram., § 185. 25. Buttm., § 58. p. 101.

υἱωνός, ὁ (υἱός), *a child's child, a grandson*, 2, 666. Od. 24, 515.

ὑλαγμός, ὁ (ὑλακτέω), *the act of barking, a howl*, 21, 575.†

Ὑλακίδης, ου, ὁ, son of Hylacus, whom Odysseus (Ulysses) pretends to be, Od. 14. 204.

ὑλακόμωρος, ον (ὗ), poet. *always* or *frequently barking; barking, howling*, κύνες, *Od. 14, 29. 16, 4. On the doubtful derivation of the termination μωρος, see under ἐγχεσίμωρος.

ὑλακτέω, poet. ὑλάω (ὗ), *to bark*, spoken of dogs, 18, 586; metaph. of wrath of heart, κραδίη οἱ ἔνδον ὑλάκτει

['so growled Ulysses' heart,' Cp.], Od. 20, 13, 16.

ὑλάω and ὑλάομαι, depon. mid. poet. form of ὑλακτέω, *to bark*, act. Od. 16, 9. Mid. Od. 16, 162. 2) Trans. *to bark at*, τινά, *Od. 16, 5. 20, 15.

ὕλη, ἡ (ὗ), 1) *a forest, a wood*, 5, 52. Od. 5, 63. 2) *felled wood, building timber, fire-wood*, Il. 23, 50. 111 Od. 9, 234. 3) *the ballast* of a ship, prob. properly wood, brush-wood, then rubbish, Od. 5, 257.

Ὕλη, ἡ, pros. αἱ Ὕλαι, a little town in Bœotia on the lake Copaïs, in the time of Strabo destroyed, 2, 500. 5, 708. 7, 221. (ῦ is short in 5, 708. 7, 221; hence some critics would write Ὕδη.)

ὑλήεις, εσσα, εν (ὗ, ὕλη), *woody, abounding in wood, well-wooded*, χῶρος. 10, 362; νῆσος, Od. 10, 308. h. 13, 5; as adj of two endings, Od. 1, 246.

Ὕλλος, ὁ, a river in Ionia, which rises in Lydia, and flows into the Hermus, 20, 392.

ὑλοτόμος, ον (ὗ, τέμνω), *wood-felling, wood-cutting*, πέλεκυς, 23, 114; spoken of men, *23, 123.

ὑμεῖς (ὗ), plur. of the personal pron. of the second person. Of the common form Hom. uses only, in addition, the dat. ὑμῖν. Nom. Æol. and Ep. ὕμμες, gen. Ion. ὑμέων, dat. Æol. and Ep. ὕμμι(ν) and ὕμμ', 10, 551; accus. Ion. ὑμέας, Æol. and Ep. ὕμμε. (The gen. ὑμέων, and accus. ὑμέας, are often disyllabic); *you, your*, with a collective sing. Od. 12, 81, 82; cf. Thiersch, § 204. 9. Rost, Dial. 44. Kühner, § 301.

ὑμέναιος, ὁ (ὑμνος), *a bridal song, the hymeneal song*, which the companions of the bride sung in conducting the bride to the house of the bridegroom, 18, 493.†

ὑμέτερος, η, ον (ὗ, ὑμεῖς), *your*, ὑμέτερόνδε, to your house. Ep., 23, 86.

ὕμμε, ὕμμες, ὕμμι, see ὑμεῖς.

ὑμνέω (ὕμνος), *to celebrate-, to praise, to extol*, with accus. h. Ap. 19, 190. h. 8. 1.

ὕμνος, ὁ, 1) *a song, a melody*, ὕμνος ἀοιδῆς = οἷμος ἀοιδῆς, the melody of the song, Od. 8, 429.† 2) *a song, a hymn*, h. Ap. 161. 8, 19.

ὑμός, ή, όν (ὗ), Dor. and Ep. for ὑμέτερος, *your*, 5, 489. Od. 1, 375.

ὑπάγω (ἄγω), only imperf. 1) *to lead under*, ἵππους ζυγόν, to put the horses under the yoke [to lead them to the yoke, Cp.], 16, 148. 23, 291; ἡμιόνους, to harness, Od. 6, 73. 2) *to lead away from under*, *to convey away*, τινὰ ἐκ βελέων, 11, 163.

ὑπαείδω, Ep. for ὑπᾴδω, *to sing in addition*, in tmesis, 18, 570; see ἀείδω.

ὑπαί, Ep. for ὑπό.

*ὑπαιδείδοικα, see ὑποδείδω.

ὑπαιθά, adv. (ὑπό), 1) *away from under, sidewise*, 15, 520. 21, 271. 2) As prep. with gen. *along by, sidewise from* any one, 18, 421.

ὑπαΐσσω, poet. (ἀίσσω). fut. ὑπαΐξω, partcp. aor. ὑπαΐξας, *to leap* or *to rush*

Ὑπακούω. 410 Ὑπεξαναδύω.

from under, with gen. βωμοῦ, forth from under the altar, 2, 310. 2) With accus. spoken of the fish, φρίχ' (i. e. φρίκα) ὑπαίξει, ed. Wolf, will rush up to the agitated wave ['rippled surface,' Cp.], (to devour the fat of Lycaon), 21, 126; cf. φρίξ. Heyne and Bothe: ὑπαλύξει φρίκ', he will escape from the rippling flood (viz. into the deep), when he has satiated himself, cf. Bothe. This explanation is contrary to the sense. The main thought is : the fishes will devour thee ; In order to do this, the fish must come up from beneath to the floating corpse ; this is expressed by ὑπαίξει, but not by ὑπαλύξει, cf. Spitz. ad loc.

ὑπακούω (ἀκούω), aor. Ep. ὑπάκουσα, infin. ὑπακοῦσαι, *to hear to*, 8, 4; in tmesis. 2) to give ear to, or *to answer*, *Od. 4, 283. 10, 83.

ὑπαλεύομαι, depon. mid. poet. (ἀλεύω), aor. partcp. ὑπαλευάμενος, *to avoid, to scape*, with accus. θάνατον, Od. 15, 275.†

ὑπάλυξις, ιος, ἡ (ὑπαλύσκω). the *act of avoiding, escaping, fleeing*, 22, 270. Od. 23, 287.

ὑπαλύσκω (ἀλύσκω), fut. λύξω, Batr. 97; aor. Ep. ὑπάλυξα for ὑπήλ., partcp. ὑπαλύξας, *to avoid, to escape, to fly*, with accus. τέλος θανάτοιο. Κῆρας, 11, 451. Od. 4, 512; ἀέλλας, Od. 19, 189 ; χρείος, to escape a debt, i. e. not to pay, Od. 8, 355.

ὑπαντιάω (ἀντιάω), aor. 1 partcp. ὑπαντιάσας, *to come against* or *meet unexpectedly*, absol. 16, 17.†

ὕπαρ, τό, only nom. accus., *a real appearance* in a state of wakefulness, οὐκ ὄναρ, ἀλλ' ὕπαρ, not a dream, but a reality [*no fleeting dream, but a truth*, Cp.], *Od. 19, 547. 20, 90.

ὑπάρχω (ἄρχω), aor. subj. ὑπάρξῃ, *to begin, to do first*, Od. 24, 286 †

ὑπασπίδιος, ον (ἀσπίς). *under the shield, covered by the shield*, from this neut. plur. ὑπασπίδια as adv., with προποδίζειν and προβιβᾶν, *13, 158. 807. 16, 609.

ὕπατος, η, ον (from ὕπερ for ὑπέρτατος), *the highest, most exalted, supreme*, often epith. of Zeus, 5, 756 ; and Od. *ἐν πυρῇ ὑπάτῃ*, upon the highest part of the funeral pile, Il. 23, 165. 24, 787.

ὑπέασι, see ὕπειμι.

ὑπέδδεισαν, see ὑποδείδω.

ὑπέδεκτο. see ὑποδέχομαι.

ὑπεθερμάνθη, see ὑποθερμαίνω.

ὑπείκω, Ep. also ὑποείκω (εἴκω), fut. ὑποείξω, aor. ὑπόειξα, fut. mid. ὑπείξομαι and ὑποείξομαι, 23, 602. 1) *to yield, to retire from*, τινὶ ἕδρης, to retire from a seat for any one, Od. 16, 42 ; with gen. alone, νεῶν, to go away from the ships, Il. 16, 305. *b*) With accus. χεῖράς τινος, to escape a man's hands, 15, 227. 2) Metaph. *to yield, to submit to, to comply with*, to obey, τινί, 15, 211. 23, 602. Od. 12, 117; τινί τι, to yield to any one in any respect, Il. 1, 294. 4, 62. (The fut. mid. is, in use, equivalent to the fut. act.)

ὕπειμι (εἰμί), pres. 3 plur. Ion. ὑπέασι. *to be under*, μελάθρῳ, to be under a roof, 9, 204 ; πολλῇσι (ἵπποις), under many were colts, 11, 681 ; in tmesis, Od. 1, 131.

ὑπείρ, poet. for ὑπέρ.

ὑπειρέχω, poet. for ὑπερέχω.

ὑπείροχος, ον, poet. for ὑπέροχος.

Ὑπειροχίδης, ου, ὁ, son of Hyperochus = Itymoneus, 11, 673.

Ὑπείροχος, ὁ, poet. for Ὑπέροχος, a Trojan, slain by Odysseus (Ulysses), 11, 335.

Ὑπείρων, ονος, ὁ, a Trojan, slain by Diomedes, 5, 144.

ὑπέκ, before a vowel ὑπέξ (ὑπό, ἐκ), in the Il. ed. Wolf ὑπ' ἐκ. 1) Prepos. with gen. *from under, out from under, forth from beneath*, 5, 854. 13, 89. 15, 628 ; ex τυτθόν. 2) Adv. Od. 3, 175.

ὑπεκπροθέω, poet. (θέω), only pres. *to run forth from beneath*, 21, 604. Od. 1, 125. *b*) With accus. *to run before, to outstrip*, Il. 9, 506.

ὑπεκπρολύω, Hom. (λύω), aor. 1 ὑπεκπροέλυσα, *to loose from under*, ἡμιόνοις ἀπήνης, to unharness the asses from the carriage, Od. 6, 88.†

ὑπεκπρορέω (ῥέω), *to flow out from under*, Od. 6, 88.†

ὑπεκπροφεύγω (φεύγω), aor. 2 ὑπεκπροφύγοιμι, and partcp. ὑπεκπροφυγών, *to escape from under, to escape secretly*, absol. 20, 147. 21, 44. Od. 20, 43 ; with accus. Χάρυβδιν, Od. 12, 113.

ὑπεκσαόω, Ep. (σαόω), aor. 1 ὑπεξεσάωσα, to save or *deliver from unperceived*, τινά, 23, 292.†

ὑπεκφέρω (φέρω), imperf. poet. ὑπέκφερον, aor. ὑπήνεικα. 8, 883. 1) *to bear away from under* or *secretly*, τινὰ πολέμοιο, to withdraw any one from the war, 5, 318. 377. 885; generally, *to bear away*, spoken of horses, Od. 3, 496. 2) *to convey any thing away*, σάκος, Il. 8, 268.

ὑπεκφεύγω (φεύγω), aor. 2 ὑπεξέφυγον, and Ep. ὑπέκφυγον, infin. poet. ὑπεκφυγέειν, *to flee secretly from*, generally, *to escape, to flee*, 8, 243. 20, 191 ; with accus. Κῆρα, ὄλεθρον, ῥέεθρα, 5, 22. 6, 57. 16, 687. Od. 9, 286 (in Od. 3, 175, ὑπέκ υ adv.)

ὑπεμνήμυκε, see ὑπημύω.

ὑπένερθε and ὑπένερθεν, adv. (ἔνερθε). 1) *beneath, below*, 13, 30 ; esply in the under world, 3, 278. Od. 10, 353. 2) With gen. *under*, ποδῶν ὑπένερθε, Il. 2, 150 ; ὑπέν. Χίοιο, Od. 3, 172.

ὑπέξ, see ὑπέκ.

ὑπεξάγω (ἄγω), only aor. optat. ὑπεξαγάγοι, *to lead out under* or *secretly*, esply out of danger, τινὰ οἴκαδε, Od. 14, 147.†

ὑπεξαλέομαι (ἀλέομαι), only aor. infin. ὑπεξαλέασθαι, *to escape secretly, to avoid*, with accus. χεῖρας, 15, 180.†

ὑπεξαναδύω (δύω), aor. 2 ὑπεξανέδυν, intrans. *to emerge from beneath*, or *unobserved*, with gen. ἁλός, *from the sea*, 13, 352.†

Ὑπέρ. 411 Ὑπερηνορέω.

ὑπέρ, Ep. also ὑπείρ (the latter when the last syllable must be long before a vowel, ὑπείρ ἅλα), 1) Prepos. with gen. and dat., ground signif. *over* (**super**). *A*) With gen. 1) Of place: *a*) in indicating motion over a place or object, *away, over, above*, ὑπὲρ τοίχων καταβῆναι, 15, 382; cf. 20, 279; ὑπὲρ οὐδοῦ βῆναι, Od. 17, 575. *b*) In indicating continuance over a place: *above, upon*, on *the upper side*, ὑψοῦ ὑπὲρ γαίης ἔχειν, to hold high above the earth, Il. 13, 200; ὑπὲρ μαζοῖο, 4, 528. Od. 1, 137; hence also: ὑπὲρ κεφαλῆς στῆναί τινι, to stand above any one's head, i. e. to stand behind the head, Il. 2, 20. Od. 4, 803. β) *over, beyond*, ὑπὲρ τάφρου, Il. 18, 228. 23, 73. Od. 13, 257. 2) In causative relations, almost always like περί: *a*) in assigning the cause, as if still local: *for, for any one's good*; in expressions of protection and defence, τεῖχος τειχίσσασθαι νεῶν ὑπέρ, for the ships, Il. 7, 449; ῥέξειν τι ὑπὲρ Δαναῶν, 1, 444. *b*) With verbs of praying, *by* any one, *for one's sake*, λίσσεσθαι ὑπὲρ τοκέων, ὑπὲρ ψυχῆς καὶ γούνων σῶν, 15, 660. 665. 22, 338. Od. 15, 261. *c*) Generally, in indicating a reference of any kind: *of, about*, ὑπὲρ σέθεν αἴσχε' ἀκούω, Il. 6, 521. *B*) With accus. 1) Spoken of place, in indicating motion over an object: *away*, with the notion of accomplishment, *away over, over*; ὑπὲρ ὤμων, 5, 16; ὑπεὶρ ἅλα, 22, 227. Od. 3, 73. *b*) Spoken of measure: *beyond, against*, only metaph. ὑπὲρ αἶσαν, against propriety, Il. 3, 59; ὑπὲρ μοῖραν, against fate, 20, 336; ὑπὲρ θεόν, 17, 327. II) In composition, it expresses the signif. of the prepos. and also the notion of excess, of exaggeration.

ὑπεραής, ές, poet. (ἄημι), *blowing from above*, ἀέλλα, 11, 297.†

ὑπεράλλομαι, depon. mid. (ἄλλομαι), partcp. Ep. sync. aor. ὑπεράλτο, partcp. ὑπεραλμένος, *to leap over*, αὐλῆς, 5, 138. 2) *to leap over*, with accus. στίχας, to leap over the ranks, *20, 327.

ὑπερβαίνω (βαίνω), aor. 2 ὑπερέβην, 3 sing. Ep. ὑπέρβη, 3 plur. Ep. ὑπέρβασαν, Ep. for ὑπέρβησαν, 3 sing. subjunct. ὑπερβήῃ, Ep. for ὑπερβῇ, 1) *to stride over, to mount over, to go over*, with accus. τεῖχος, 12, 468; οὐδόν, Od. 8, 80. 16, 41. h. Merc. 20. 2) Metaph. *to overstep*, absol. *to transgress, to commit a fault*, Il. 9, 501.

ὑπερβάλλω, Ep. also ὑπειρβ. (βάλλω), aor. 2 ὑπειρέβαλον, 23, 637, and ὑπέρβαλον, without augm. 1) *to cast over*, with accus. σήματα πάντων, to cast beyond all the marks, 23, 843; spoken of the stone of Sisyphus: ἄκρον ὑπερβάλλειν, to cast it upon the summit, Od. 11, 597; rarely with gen. τόσσον παντὸς ἀγῶνος ὑπέρβαλε, he cast (the ball) so far beyond the whole circle, Il. 23, 847. 2) *to cast beyond* any one, τινὰ δουρί, i. e. to excel any one in casting the spear, 23, 637.

ὑπέρβασαν, see ὑπερβαίνω.

ὑπερβασίη, ἡ (ὑπερβαίνω), prop. *overstepping*, always metaph. *transgression, wickedness, impiety, insolence*, 3, 102. Od. 3, 206; plur., Il. 23, 589; and often.

ὑπερβήῃ, see ὑπερβαίνω.

ὑπέρβιος, ον (βία), *haughty*, mly in a bad sense, *insolent, violent, overbearing*, θυμός, 18, 262; ὕβρις, Od. 1, 368. Neut. ὑπέρβιον, as adv. *haughtily, overbearingly*, Il. 17, 19.

*Ὑπερβόρεοι, οἱ, pros. Ὑπερβόρειοι, *the Hyperboreans*, a fabulous people said to dwell beyond the north wind, and whose country was conceived of as a paradise, h. 6, 26. Pindar, Pyth. 10, 49, places it upon the Ister; Hdt. 4, 13. beyond Scythia.

ὑπερδεής, ές, gen. έος (δέος), ὑπερδέα, Ep. for ὑπερδεέα, see Thiersch, Gram. § 293; *raised above fear, incapable of fear*, δήμιος, 17, 330.† Thus Eustath. (ἀπτόητος); and Voss. [Cp. *disdaining fear*]. Still other Gramm., as Apoll., derive it from δέω, and explain it, *far less* (ὑπερδέοντα).

Ὑπέρεια, ἡ, 1) a fountain in the town of Pheræ in Thessaly, 2, 734. G, 451. 2) the ancient abode of the Phæaces, before they emigrated to Scheria, Od. 6, 4. According to this passage, it is in the vicinity of the Cyclopes; hence the ancient critics, for the most part, take it to be a town of Sicily, and particularly for the later *Camarina*.

ὑπερείπω (ὑπό, ἐρείπω), aor. 2 ὑπήριπον, prop. to demolish by mining; only in the aor. 2, *to undermine, to overthrow*, 23, 691.†

ὑπερέπτω (ὑπό, ἐρέπτω), imperf. ὑπέρεπτε, without augm., *to eat away beneath*, then generally, *to take away from beneath*, spoken of a river: κονίην ποδοῖιν, to wash away the sand beneath the feet, 21, 271.†

ὑπερέσχεθον, see ὑπερέχω.

ὑπερέχω, poet. ὑπειρέχω, always im perf. 2, 426 (ἔχω), aor. 2 ὑπερέσχον, poet. lengthened ὑπερέσχεθον, 11, 735. 1) Trans. *to hold above*; τί τινος, any thing above another, σπλάγχνα, Ἡφαίστοιο, 2, 426; eaply for protection, χεῖρα or χεῖράς τινι, to hold the hand over any man, to shelter him, 4, 249. 5, 433. Od. 14, 184; and instead of dat. with gen. Il. 9, 420. 687. 2) Intrans. *to project, to be prominent*, with gen. 3, 210. *b*) *to rise above*, spoken of the sun, γαίης, 11, 735; of a star, 23, 13, 93.

ὑπέρη, ἡ, *a sail yard rope*, in the plur. the ropes fastened to both ends of the yard and to the mast, which served to turn the sail, Od. 5, 260.†

ὑπερηνορέω (ὑπερήνωρ), only partcp. pres. *to have a haughty spirit, to be insolent*, in a bad sense, 4, 173. 13, 258; eaply in the Od. spoken of the suitors, and also strengthened by κακῶς ['the proud, injurious suitors,' Cp.], Od. 2, 266. 4, 766.

'Υπερήνωρ.

'Υπερήνωρ, ορος, ὁ (exceedingly manly), son of Panthöus, slain by Menelaus, 14, 616. 17, 24.

'Υπερησίη, ἡ, a town in Achaia, according to Paus. the later Ægeira, 2, 573. Od. 15, 254.

ὑπερῃφάνεω (φαίνω), only partcp. to exalt oneself above others, to be insolent, to be proud, 11, 694.†

ὕπερθε, before a vowel ὕπερθεν, 1) Adv. (ὑπέρ), from above, esply from heaven, 7, 101. Od. 24, 344. h. Cer. 101; generally, above, in the upper part, II. 2, 218. 5, 122. Od. 16, 47.

ὑπερθορδειν, see ὑπερθρώσκω.

ὑπερθρώσκω (θρώσκω), only fut. ὑπερθορέομαι, Ep. and Ion. for ὑπερθοροῦμαι, and aor. 2 Ep. ὑπέρθορον, infin. Ep. ὑπερθορέειν, to leap over, to spring over, with accus. τάφρον, 8, 179; ἑρκίον, *9, 475; absol. 12, 53.

ὑπέρθυμος, ον (θυμός), exceedingly spirited, noble-hearted, magnanimous, epith. of heroes and of an entire people, always in a good sense, 2, 746. Od. 16, 326. Voss takes it often in a bad sense, and translates haughty, proud, 4, 365. 5, 881; insolent, Od. 11, 269.

ὑπερθύριον, τό (θύρα), the lintel of a door-frame, opposed to οὐδός, Od. 7, 90.†

ὑπερίημι (ἵημι), fut. ὑπερήσω, to cast beyond, to excel, viz. δίσκον, Od. 8, 198.+

ὑπερικταίνομαι, to move oneself quickly, from which πόδες ὑπερικταίνοντο, Od. 23. 3† ['with nimbleness of youth she stepp'd,' Cp.]. According to Aristarch. in Apoll. ἄγαν πάλλοντο from ὑπό and ἐρικταίνοντο, or, according to Eustath., also=ὑπερεξετείνοντο, i. e. ἄγαν ἱκνοῦντο from ἵκταρ. The readings ὑποαικταίνοντο and ὑπεραικταίνοντο are to be rejected.

'Υπεριονίδης, ου, ὁ, son of Hyperion = Helios, Od. 12, 176.

'Υπερίων, ἴονος, ὁ, 1) son of Uranus and Gæa, one of the Titans, who from Thea begat Helios, Selene, and Aurora, Hes. Theog. 371 h. Cer. 26. cf. h. 31, 3. 2) It stands as a patronymic epith. 8, 480. Od. 1, 8. 'Υπερίων Ἥλιος (like Ζεὺς Κρονίων), son of Hyperion, according to Eustath. for euphony's sake shortened from 'Υπεριονίων, cf. Μαλίων. This explanation is confirmed by Od. 12, 133. 176. Others would explain it according to the derivation from ὑπὲρ ἰών, that goes over us, cf. Nitzsch ad Od. 1, 8.

ὑπερκαταβαίνω (βαίνω), aor. 2 ὑπερκατέβην, to descend over, to go over; with accus. τεῖχος, over the wall, *13, 50. 87.

ὑπερκύδαντας, poet. defect. accus. plur. from a nomin. ὑπερκύδας, αντος, ὁ, exceedingly famed, very glorious, *4, 66. 71. (According to Schol. a partcp. aor. 1 from an old word κύδω, κυδαίνω, whence κύδας, like γήμας; some take it as an adj. ὑπερκυδᾶς, Dor. for ὑπερκυδής, contr. from ὑπερκυδήεις, hence prop. to be accented ὑπερκυδᾶντας, cf. Spitzner ad loc.)

412

'Υπερφίαλος.

ὑπερκύπτω (κύπτω), fut. ψω, to bend oneself over, Ep. 14, 22.

ὑπερμενέτης, ὁ, poet. for ὑπερμενής. h. 7, 1; in the accus. ὑπερμενέτα.

ὑπερμενέω, poet. to be superior in vigour or strength, only prꝭs. partcp. ὑπερμενέοντες, Od. 19, 62.† from

ὑπερμενής, ές, gen. ἔος (μένος), superior in strength, powerful, almighty, epith. of Zeus and of kings, 2, 116. 8, 236. Od. 13, 205.

ὑπέρμορον, poet. adv. (μόρος), beyond fate, contrary to fate, i. e. more than fate allots or from the beginning appoints to man, 20, 30. 21, 517. Od. 1, 34; once ὑπέρμορα, as if formed from an adj. ὑπέρμορος, Il. 2, 155. cf. Μοῖρα. (Prob. ὑπὲρ μόρον should be written separately, as ὑπὲρ μοῖραν, αἶσαν, but they were joined for euphony, see Nitzsch ad Od. 1, 34.)

ὑπεροπλίη, ἡ, poet. (ὑπέροπλος), only in the plur. arrogance, esply in reference to prowess in arms, generally, pride, haughtiness, 1, 205.† (ἱ long.)

ὑπεροπλίζομαι, poet. depon. mid. (ὑπέροπλος), to behave oneself haughtily, to act insolently, hence with accus. to disdain, to despise, οὐκ ἄν τίς μιν ἀνὴρ ὑπεροπλίσσαιτο, no man could despise it (the dwelling), Od. 17, 268.† (Schol. Vulg. and Eustath. ὑπερηφανήσειαν.) This explanation Buttm., in Lexil., [and Fäsi] approves. According to Aristarch. on the contrary (cf. Apoll.), = νικήσειεν, to subdue or take by force of arms [No man should e'er achieve by force his entrance here, Cp.].

ὑπέροπλος, ον, poet. (ὅπλον), haughty, insolent, only neut. sing. as adv. ὑπέροπλον εἰπεῖν, *15, 185. 17, 170.

ὑπέροχος, ον (ἔχω), Ep. ὑπείροχος, projecting, prominent, distinguished, with gen. ἄλλων, above others, *6, 208. 11, 784; absol. h. 11, 2.

ὑπερπέτομαι, depon. mid. (πέτομαι), aor. 2 Ep. 3 sing. ὑπέρπτατο, to fly over, to fly beyond, 13, 408. 22, 275; with accus. σήματα, to fly beyond the marks, Od. 8, 192.

ὑπερράγη, see ὑπορρήγνυμι.

ὑπερσχεθεῖν, a lengthened aor. of ὑπερέχω, q. v.

ὑπέρτατος, η, ον, poet. (prop. superl. of ὑπέρ), uppermost, highest. κεῖτο ὑπέρτατος, it (the stone) lay uppermost, *12, 381; ἧστο — ὑπέρτατος ἐν πωρυσσῇ, 23, 457.

ὑπερτερίη, ἡ (ὑπέρτερος), the highest part (body or frame-work) of a carriage, on which the load was carried, Od. 6, 70.†

ὑπέρτερος, η, ον (prop. compar. from ὑπέρ), upper, that is above. κρέ' ὑπέρτερα, the upper flesh, in opposition to σπλάγχνα, Od. 3, 65. 470. 2) higher, superior, more excellent, more exalted, εὖχος, Il. 11, 290. 12, 437; γενεῇ, in race, 11, 786.

ὑπερφίαλος, η, ον, only in a metaph. signif. haughty, proud, insolent, often as

Ὑπερφιάλως. 413 Ὑπό.

epith. of the suitors, Od. 1, 134. 2, 310; of the Cyclōpes, Od. 9, 10; of the Trojans, Il. 3, 106. 13, 621; θυμός, a haughty spirit, 15, 94. 23, 611; ἔπος, Od. 4, 503. Antinous uses it, Od. 21, 289, of himself and the suitors, to the supposed beggar, where it signifies *proud, high-spirited* [in a good sense]. [Art thou not contented to partake of the feast unmolested with us high-souled (nobles)?] Adv. ὑπερφιάλως, *haughtily, insolently*, Od. 1, 227. 4, 663; generally, *excessively, exceedingly*, Il. 13, 293. Od. 17, 481. (The deriv. is doubtful: the ancients [Schol. Vulg. ad Od. 1, 134, Etym. Mag.], derived it from φιάλη, a dish, hence that which runs over the brim of the dish, *excessive*: Buttm., Lexil. (in voc.), derives it with Damm from φυή, hence prop. ὑπερφύαλος, *supernatural*, setting oneself above all others; Nitzsch ad Od. 4, 663, prop. = ὑπερφυής, *overgrown*, that overgrows oneself and others; according to Passow, poet. for ὑπερβίαλος = ὑπέρβιος.)

ὑπερφιάλως, adv. see ὑπερφίαλος.

ὑπέρχομαι, depon. mid. (ὑπό, ἔρχομαι), aor. 2 ὑπήλυθον, 1) *to go under, to go into, to enter (subire)*, with accus. θάλαμους, δῶμα, Od. 5, 476. 12, 21. 2) Metaph. of mental states, *to enter unobserved, to steal upon*. Τρῶας τρόμος ὑπήλυθε γυῖα, trembling seized the Trojans in their limbs (trembling seized upon the limbs of the Trojans), 7, 215. 20, 44. h. 28, 3.

ὑπερωέω (ἐρωέω), aor. Ep. ὑπερώησα, *to go back, to retire*, *8, 122. 15, 452.

ὑπερῴη, ἡ (prop. fem. from ὑπερῷος), *the palate*. elsewhere οὐρανίσκος, 22, 495.†

ὑπερωϊόθεν, adv. (ὑπερῷον), *from the upper story, from an upper apartment*, Od. 1, 328.†

ὑπερώϊον, τό, or ὑπερῷον (ὑπέρ), the upper part of the house, *the upper story*, an apartment in the upper story, *an upper chamber*, the apartment of the women, sing. 2, 514. Od. 6, 362; plur. in both forms, 16, 184. Od. 16, 449; because the apartments of the women were in the upper story, hence often, εἰς ὑπερῷ' ἀναβαίνειν, Od. 2, 358. 4, 751. (Prop. neut. of the adj. ὑπερῷος, subaud. οἴκημα.)

ὑπέστην, see ὑφίστημι.

ὑπέσχεθον, see ὑπέχω.

ὑπέχω (ἔχω), aor. ὑπέσχον, poet. ὑπέσχεθον, 7, 188; partcp. ὑποσχών, *to hold under, to hold before*, χεῖρα, 7, 188; θήλεας ἵππους, to cause the mares to couple, 5, 269.

ὑπεμνύω (ἠμύω), perf. ὑπεμνήμυκε, *to incline, to bow*, to make the head sink. πάντα δ' ὑπεμνήμυκε (ever casts down his eyes; dooms him to sad looks), 22, 491.† Thiersch, Gram. § 232. 94 (as intrans.); is entirely bowed down, i. e. hangs down his head. [Död. (denying that ὑπό- = 'down') explains it: *must knock under to every body* (lit. *bows the head under*), = παντὶ ὑπόχειρ ἐστί, or

πάντα (quemlibet) ὑπάρχεται ἐμνημυκώς.] This perf. arose thus: ἤμυκε, redupl. ἐμήμυκε, then strengthened *metri gr.*, ἐμνήμυκε. cf. νώνυμνος. (Bothe has adopted ὑπεμμήμυκε, after Toup.)

ὑπήνεικα, see ὑποφέρω.

ὑπηνήτης, ου, ὁ (ὑπήνη), *that gets a beard*. πρῶτον ὑπηνήτης (whose beard is just beginning to grow), 24, 348. Od. 10, 279.

ὑπηοῖος, η, ον (ἠώς), *towards the morning, early*, Il. 8, 530. Od. 4, 656. στίβη ὑπ', morning frost, Od. 17, 25.

ὑπισχνέομαι, depon. mid. Ion. ὑπίσχομαι, (Od. 2, 91. h. Merc. 275; aor. 2 ὑπεσχόμην, imperat. ὑπόσχεο, infin. ὑποσχέσθαι prop. a strengthened form of ὑπέχομαι), to hold oneself under, i. e. to *undertake*, hence *to promise, to engage*. τί τινι, Il. 9, 263. 12, 236; ἐσπλ θυγατέρα, to betroth a daughter to a man, 13, 376. *a*) *to vow any thing to the gods*, ἱερά, ἑκατόμβας, 6, 93. 115. 23, 209. *b*) With infin. fut. 6, 93. 13, 366. 368. Od. 4, 6; and with accus. and infin. Od. 8, 347. Instead of the fut. of the infin. the pres. ἀπονέεσθαι occurs, Il. 2, 112. 19, 19, with signif. of the fut.

ὑπίσχομαι, Ion. and Ep.=ὑπισχνέομαι.

ὕπνος, ὁ, *sleep*, very often (γλυκύς, ἡδύς, λυσιμελής, νήδυμος, πανδαμάτωρ). χάλκεος ὕπνος, poet. for the sleep of death (*ferreus* somnus, Virg.], 11, 241.

Ὕπνος, ὁ, *the god of sleep*, twin brother of death, 14, 231. 24, 5; ruler both of gods and men (14, 233). According to Hes. Th. 758, he has his dwelling in the under world; in Hom. Here seeks him in Lemnos, 14, 233.

ὑπνόω, contr. ὑπνῶ, hence expanded ὑπνώω, only partcp. ὑπνώοντες, intrans. *to sleep, to slumber*, 24, 344. Od. 5, 48 24, 4.

ὑπό, also Ep. ὑπαί. 1) Prepos. with gen., dat., and accus.; ground signif. *under*. A) with gen. 1) Spoken of place: *a*) In indicating motion *forth from under* an object, *under, from under, from beneath*, only poet. (elsewhere ὑπέκ), ἀνίστασθαι ὑπὸ ζόφου, to come forth from the darkness, 21, 56. ἐρύειν νεκρὸν ὑπ' Αἴαντος, *away from* (under) Ajax, 17, 235. cf. 9, 248. 13, 198. ἄγειν ἀνδροκτασίης ὑπό, *to lead away from (the consequences of— or, after) my killing a man*, 23, 86. λύειν ἵππους ὑπὸ ζυγοῦ, 8, 543. Od. 4, 39. *b*) In indicating continuance under an object, Il. 1, 501. 2, 268. 8, 14. 2) In causative relations: *a*) In assigning the author, with passive and intransitive verbs: *under*, more frequently, *by, through, before*, δαμῆναι ὑπό τινος, to be vanquished by any one, 3, 436. 4, 479. cf. 6, 134. 16, 434. θνῄσκειν ὑπό τινος, to perish by any one, 1, 242. φεύγειν ὑπό τινος, to flee before any one [i. e. *under* the influence of terrour inspired by him], 18, 149. φοβεῖσθαι ὑπό τινος, 10, 303. *b*) In assigning the efficient cause: ὑπ' ἀνάγκης, by force, Od. 2, 110. 19, 156. *c*) Often in assigning operating or accompanying circumstances: *under, by*, αὐσάντων ὑπ' Ἀχαιῶν,

ὑποβάλλω. 414 Ὑποθῆβαι.

under the shout of the Greeks, Il. 2, 334. δηίων ὑπὸ θυμοραϊστέων, 16, 591. 18, 492. Od. 19. 48. 23, 290. *d*) In indicating subordination, Od. 19, 114. *B*) With dat. almost like the gen. 1) Spoken of place, very often: *under*, esply in defining localities, ὑπὸ Τμώλῳ, Il. 2, 866. cf. 22, 479. 2) In causative relations, a) Spoken of the author, as with gen., rather poet., *under*, *by*, δαμῆναι ὑπό τινι, 5. 646. Od. 4, 790. ὑπὸ χερσί τινος, Il. 2, 860. *b*) Spoken of intermediate causes: ὑπὸ πομπῇ, under the conduct, 6, 171. φέβεσθαι ὑπό τινι, 11, 121. cf. Il. 5, 699. *c*) Of subordination, *under*, *by*, Od. 3, 304: also ὕπνῳ ὕπο, *somno obsecutus*, Il. 24. 636. Od. 4, 295. *C*) With accus. 1) Spoken of place, *a*) in indicating motion to a lower place, ἰέναι ὑπὸ γαῖαν, under the earth, Il. 18, 333; also spoken of motion to elevated places (*sub*), *to*, *towards*, ἔρχεσθαι ὑπὸ Ἴλιον, 2, 216. ὑπὸ τεῖχος, 4, 407. *b*) Of a quiet continuance, εἶναι ὑπ' ἠῶ τ' ἠέλιόν τε, 5, 267. cf. Od. 11, 498. 619. 2) Spoken of time: *against*, *about* (*sub*), νύχθ' ὕπο, Il. 2, 102: *during*, 16, 202. II) As adv. *amongst*, *under*, often ὑπὸ δέ, Od. 4, 636. 21, 23. 2) *secretly*, *unobserved*, Il. 23, 153. 24, 507. We may often also suppose a tmesis, 17, 349. 18. 347. III) In composition it has the signif. of the adv. sometimes it means also *somewhat*, *a little*.

ὑποβάλλω (βάλλω), infin. Ep. ὑββάλλειν for ὑποβάλλειν, 19, 80. 1) *to cast under*, *to lay under*, with accus., λῖτα, Od. 10, 353. 2) Metaph. to interpose a word, *to fall into the discourse*, *to interrupt*, 19, 80 [cf. Herm., Opusc. V. 302, seq. VII. 66, sq. esply 72].

ὑποβλήδην, adv. (ὑποβάλλω), prop. to cast between, hence, *interposing*, *interrupting* in the discourse [Herm. says, *admonendo occurrens*: see ὑποβάλλω]. ἀμείβεσθαι, 1, 292.† 2) *with sidelong glances* [*limis oculis*], ἐσκέψατο, h. Merc. 415. [So in 1, 292, according to Död.]

ὑπόβρυχα, adv. *under water*, τὸν ὑπόβ. θῆκε, it held him, Odysseus (Uysses), long submerged (according to Voss, the subject is: the raft, σχεδίη: according to Nitzsch, the surge itself), Od. 5, 319.† Mly it is taken as an adv. According to Buttm., in Lexil., a metaplast. accus. sing. of the adj. ὑπόβρυχος, or later ὑποβρύχιος.

*ὑποβρύχιος, ον (βρύχιος), *under water*, *in the depth*, of three endings, h. 33, 12.

*ὑπογνάμπτω (γνάπτω), *to bend under*, *to bend around*; *to repel*, *to withstand*, ὁρμήν, h. 7, 13.

ὑποδαίω, only in tmesis, see δαίω.

*ὑποδαμάω (δαμάω), *to subdue*, *to subject*, only pass. λάθρῃ ὑποδμηθεῖσα Κρονίωνι, secretly forced by Zeus, h. 6, 4.

*ὑποδάμναμαι, mid. from the form ὑποδάμνημι = ὑποδημνάω, only pres. 2 sing. ὑποδάμνησαι, *to subject oneself*, *to humble oneself*, *Od. 3, 214. 16, 95.

ὑποδέγμενος, see ὑποδέχομαι.

ὑποδίδρομε, see ὑποτρέχω.

ὑποδείδω (δείδω), aor. 1 Ep. ὑπέδδεισα, ὑποδδείσας. but imper. ὑποδείσατε, Ep. perf. 2 ὑποδείδια, 3 plur. pluperf. ὑποδείδισαν, Ep. perf. 1 ὑπαιδείδοικα, h. Merc. 165; *to be a little afraid of*, *to fear* any one or any thing, τινά or τί, 1, 406. 5, 32. 12, 413. Od. 2, 66.

ὑποδεξίη, ἡ (ὑποδέχομαι), *reception* esply hospitable reception, *hospitable entertainment*, 9, 73.† (ι long.)

ὑποδέχομαι, depon. mid. (δέχομαι), fut. ὑποδέξομαι, aor. 1 ὑπεδεξάμην, and Ep. aor. sync. 2 sing. ὑπέδεξο, 3 sing. ὑπέδεκτο, partcp. ὑποδέγμενος, infin. ὑποδέχθαι, 7, 93. 1) *to receive*, *to take*. a) Esply a guest, 9, 480. Od. 14, 52; metaph. spoken of misfortune, and of a place of repose, Od. 14, 275. 22, 470. 2) *to take upon oneself*, i. e. *to bear*, *to endure*, *to suffer*, βίας ἀνδρῶν, Od. 13, 310. 16, 189. *b*) Metaph. *to promise*, τί, Il. 7, 93. Od. 2, 387.

ὑποδέω, only in tmesis, see δέω.

ὑπόδημα, ατος, τό (δέω), prop. that is bound beneath: *a sole*, *a sandal*, *Od. 15, 369. 18, 361.

ὑποδμηθεῖσα, see ὑποδαμάω.

ὑποδμώς, ῶος, ὁ (δμώς), subjected, hence, *a slave*, *a servant*, τινός, Od. 4, 386.†

ὑπόδρα, adv. poet. looking up from beneath, i. e. *darkly*, *fiercely*, *angrily*, always, ὑπόδρα ἰδών, 2, 245. Od. 8, 165 (without doubt from ὑπέδρακον, cf. Thiersch, § 192. 2).

ὑποδράω (δράω) Ep. ὑποδρώωσιν, 3 plur. pres. for ὑποδρῶσι, *to serve*, *to wait upon*, τινί, Od. 15, 333.†

ὑποδρηστήρ, ῆρος, ὁ, Ep. (ὑποδράω), *a servant*, *a waiter*, *an attendant*, Od. 15, 330.†

ὑποδύω (δύω), aor. 2 ὑπέδυν, fut. mid. ὑποδύσομαι, Ep. aor. 2 ὑποδύσετο; only intrans. mid. together with aor. 2 act. 1) *to go under*, *to go into*, *to sink into*, with accus. θαλάσσης κόλπον, Od. 4, 435; absolute: *to step under*, *to stoop*, in order to take any one upon the shoulders, Il. 8, 332. 13, 421; metaph. with dat. πᾶσιν ἱμερόεις ὑπέδυ γόος, a joyful sorrowing came over them all [tears followed, but of joy,' Cp.], Od. 10, 398. 2) *to emerge amongst*, *to come forth*, with gen. θάμνων, Od. 6, 127. κακῶν ὑποδύσεαι, thou wilt escape from evils, Od. 20, 53.

ὑποείκω, poet. for ὑπείκω.

ὑποζεύγνυμι (ζεύγνυμι), fut. ὑποζεύξω, *to yoke*, *to bring under the yoke*, *to harness*, ἵππους, Od. 15, 81.† cf. Od. 6, 73.

ὑποθερμαίνω (θερμαίνω), aor. pass. 3 sing. ὑπεθερμάνθη, *to warm*, pass. *to become warm*, αἵματι, with blood, 20, 746.†

Ὑποθῆβαι, αἱ, a place in Boeotia, 5, 505. In regard to this place, even the ancients were at variance. According to Strab. IX. p. 412. some understood by it the later Ποτνιαί, others, with greater probability, the lower town of Thebes; and they would consequently read ὑπὸ Θήβας: for Cadmēa, the citadel, and the upper town of Thebes were destroyed by the Epigŏni, and at that time not yet rebuilt, cf. Maunert VIII. p. 226.

ὑποθημοσύνη, ἡ (ὑποτίθημι), *instruction, counsel, exhortation,* only plur. 15, 412. 16, 233.

ὑποθωρήσσω (θωρήσσω), *to arm privately,* only mid. *to arm oneself privately,* λόχῳ, for ambush, 18, 513.†

ὑποκάμπτω, *to bend under* or *about,* 24, 274.† See κάμπτω.

ὑπόκειμαι, only in tmesis, 21, 364. See κεῖμαι.

ὑποκινέω (κινέω), aor. 1 ὑποκινήσας, *to move beneath, to move gently,* spoken of Zephyr, 4, 423.†

ὑποκλίνω (κλίνω), aor. pass. ὑπεκλίνθην, *to bend.* Pass. with dat. σχοίνῳ, to lay oneself among the rushes, Od. 5, 463.†

ὑποκλονέω, poet. (κλονέω), only mid. ὑποκλονέεσθαί τινι, to fly in confusion ['in tumultuous flight,' Cp.] before any one, 21, 556.†

ὑποκλοπέω = ὑποκλέπτω, *to conceal under.* Mid. *to conceal* or *hide oneself under,* Od. 22, 382.†

ὑποκρίνομαι, depon. mid. (κρίνω), aor. 1 ὑπεκρινάμην, prop. *to give a decision to a question,* esply spoken of a prophet: *to give a decision, to reply, to return answer,* 12, 228; generally, τινί, to answer any one, 7, 407. Od. 2, 111. 15, 170. 2) *to explain, to interpret,* ὄνειρον, Od. 19, 535. 555. cf. Il. 5, 150.

ὑποκρύπτω (κρύπτω), aor. pass. ὑπεκρύφθην, *to conceal* or *hide under.* Pass. ἡ νηῦς ἄχνῃ ὑπεκρύφθη, was entirely concealed in the foam, 15, 626.†

ὑπόκυκλος, ον (κύκλος), *round beneath, rounded below* (Eustath. κυκλοτερής); τάλαρος, Od. 4, 131.† 2) Others explain it, without probability, *furnished with small wheels,* Apoll. and Schol. Vulg.

ὑποκύομαι, Ep. mid. (κύω), only aor. 1 partcp. ὑποκυσαμένη, *to become pregnant,* 6, 26. Od. 11, 254; spoken of beasts: to be big with young, Il. 20, 225 (still ὑποκυσαμένη is more correct., and it is adopted by Spitzuer; cf. Buttm., Gr. under κύω).

ὑπολαμβάνω, only in aor. 2 by tmesis, 3, 34. Od. 18, 88; see λαμβάνω.

ὑπολάμπω, 18, 492. Od. 19, 48, now written separately; see λάμπω.

ὑπολείπω (λείπω), fut. mid. ὑπολείψομαι, Od. 17, 276; *to leave behind,* τί, Od. 16, 50. Mid. *to remain behind, to be left,* Il. 23, 615. Od. 7, 230. 17, 282.

ὑπολευκαίνω (λευκαίνω), *to make white beneath,* only pass. *to grow white beneath,* ὑπολευκαίνονται ἀχυρμιαί, 5, 502.†

ὑπολίζων, ον, gen. ονος, poet. (ὀλίζων), *somewhat smaller* or *less,* λαοί, 18, 519.†

ὑπολύω (λύω), aor. 1 ὑπέλυσα, aor. 1 mid. ὑπελυσάμην, Ep. aor. 2 mid. 3 plur. ὑπέλυντο, 16, 341: *to loose beneath, to relax, to loose,* metaph. γυῖά τινος, to loose one's limbs beneath him, i. e. to deprive the limbs of their power, to render the feet lame or tottering; often spoken of the severely wounded, 15, 581; of the slain, 11, 579. 13, 412. Pass. 16, 341; and by tmesis, 15, 581; spoken of a wrestler who falls, 23, 726 (cf. λύω), μένος καὶ γυῖα τινος, 6, 27. Mid. *to loose from under, to deliver,* τινὰ δεσμῶν, to set free any one secretly from his bonds, 1, 401.

ὑπομένω (μένω), aor. ὑπέμεινα. 1) Intrans. *to remain behind* (to remain in one's place), Od. 10, 232. 258; esply spoken of a warrior, who makes opposition to the enemy, *to maintain one's post, to wait, to hold out,* Il. 5, 498; with infin. οὐδ᾽ ὑπέμεινεν γνώμεναι, he waited not till he was known [lit. *for us to know him*], Od. 1, 410. 2) Trans. *to await, to abide, to sustain,* τινά, Il. 16, 814. 17, 25; or ἐρωὴν τινος, 14,'489.

ὑπομιμνήσκω (μιμνήσκω), fut. ὑπομνήσω, aor. ὑπέμνησα, *to remind,* τινά τινος, any one of any thing, *Od. 1, 321. 15, 3.

ὑπομνάομαι (μνάομαι), 2 plur. imperf. ὑπεμνάασθε, Ep. for ὑπεμνᾶσθε, *to woo a woman illicitly,* γυναῖκα, Od. 22, 38.†

(ὑπομνημύω), see ὑπημύω.

Ὑπονήιος, ον, *lying at the foot of Mount Nēion,* epith. of Ithaca, Od. 3, 81: see Ἰθάκη.

ὑποπεπτηῶτες, see ὑποπτήσσω.

ὑποπερκάζω (περκάζω), *to become gradually of a dark colour* ['*to gather fast their blackness,*' Cp.]; of ripening grapes, Od. 7, 126.†

Ὑποπλάκιος, η, ον, *Hypoplacian, lying at the foot of Mount Placus,* epith. of Thebes in Troas, 6, 397; see Πλάκος. [According to others from πλάξ, situated in a low plain.]

ὑποπτάννυμι, only by tmesis, 1, 130; see πετάννυμι.

ὑποπτήσσω (πτήσσω), only partcp. perf. plur. ὑποπεπτηῶτες, Ep. for ὑποπεπτηκότες, *to crouch from fear, to cower,* spoken of birds: πετάλοις, to cower timidly under the leaves, 2, 312.†

ὑπόρνῡμι (ὄρνυμι), only aor. 2 ὑπώροροον, *to excite beneath* or *near, to awaken,* τοῖον ὑπώρορε Μοῦσα, thus moved the muse, Od. 24, 62.† Od. 4, 113; see ὄρνυμι.

ὑπορρήγνυμι (ῥήγνυμι), aor. 2 pass. ὑπερράγην, *to tear in pieces beneath.* Pass. οὐρανόθεν ὑπερράγη, in heaven the æther divided *or* opened itself beneath [cf. αἰθήρ], *8. 558. 16, 300.

ὑπόρρηνος, ον, poet. (ῥήν, ἀρήν), *having a lamb under it;* (each) *with its lamb,* 10, 216.†

ὑποσείω, Ep. ὑποσσείω (σείω), *to shake beneath,* or *gently, to turn beneath,* τρύπανον, Od. 9, 385.†

ὑποσταίην, see ὑφίστημι.

ὑποσταχύομαι (στάχυς), *to grow gradually,* prop. spoken of ears of corn, metaph. of herds, *to increase,* Od. 20, 212.*

ὑποστενᾰχίζω (στεναχίζω), *to groan beneath,* spoken of the earth, γαῖα δ᾽ ὑπεστενάχιζε, 2, 781.†

ὑποστορέννῦμι (στορέννυμι), aor. infin. ὑποστορέσαι, *to spread beneath, to lay under*, δέμνιά τινι, Od. 20, 139.

ὑποστρέφω (στρέφω), fut. ὑποστρέψω, aor. 1 ὑπέστρεψα, fut. mid infin. ὑποστρέψεσθαι, aor. pass. ὑπεστρέφθην, Od. 18, 23. 1) Trans. *to turn about, to turn around, to turn back*, with accus. ἵππους, Il. 5, 581. 2) Intrans. *to turn about, to turn back*, 5, 505. 12, 71; φύγαδε, *to turn oneself to flight*, 11, 446. Ὄλυμπον, *to return* to Olympus, 3, 407. Mid. and aor. pass. *to turn back*, ἐς μέγαρον, Od. 18, 23. Il. 11, 567.

ὑποσχεθεῖν, a lengthened Ep. aor., see ὑπέχω.

ὑποσχέσθαι, see ὑπισχνέομαι.

ὑποσχεσίη, ἡ, Ep. = ὑπόσχεσις, *a promise*, 13, 369.†

ὑπόσχεσις, ιος, ἡ (ὑπισχνέομαι), *a promise*, 2, 286. 349. Od. 10, 483.

ὑποταμνόν, τό (τέμνω), an herb cut off, for magic purposes, h. Cer. 228.

ὑποτανύω, poet. = ὑποτείνω, only by tmesis, see τανύω.

ὑποταρβέω (ταρβέω), *to be somewhat afraid of*; τινά, only partcp. aor. ὑποταρβήσαντες, 17, 533.†

ὑποταρτάριος, ον (Τάρταρος), *dwelling eneath* in Tartarus, Τιτῆνες, 14, 279.†

ὑποτίθημι (τίθημι), only mid. fut. ὑποθήσομαι, aor. 2 ὑπεθέμην, imperf. ὑπόθευ, .nfin. ὑποθέσθαι, *to put under, to lay under*, act. only in tmesis, 18, 375. Mid. *to put* any thing *under* any one, always metaph. *to give* any thing to any one, *to grant, to counsel* (with reference to the subject), βουλήν τινι, *to give counsel to* any one, 8, 36; ἔπος ἠδ ἔργον τινί, *to suggest* a word to any one, Od. 4, 163. *b*) Without accus. τινί, *to advise* any one, *to remind, to exhort*, Od. 2, 194. Il. 21, 293.

ὑποτρέμω, only in tmesis, 10, 390; see τρέμω.

ὑποτρέχω (τρέχω), aor. ὑπέδραμον, perf. 2 ὑποδέδρομα, 1) *to run under*, metaph. ὑποδέδρομε βῆσσα, a valley extended beneath, h. Ap. 284. 2) *to run to under*, ὁ δ' ὑπέδραμε καὶ λάβε γούνων κύψας, he ran up to him beneath his arm and spear, and clasped his knees, 21, 68. Od. 10, 323. (Others explain, *to run to*.)

ὑποτρέω (τρέω), aor. 1 ὑπέτρεσα, *to retire trembling, to retreat, to fly*, 7, 217. 15, 636. 2) Trans. with accus. *to flee trembling from, to run away from*, *17, 587.

ὑποτρομέω (τρομέω), Ep. iterat. imperf. ὑποτρομέεσκον, *to tremble thereupon, to quake*, 22, 241. 2) Trans. with accus. *to flee* from any one, *22, 241.

ὑπότροπος, ον (ὑποτρέπω). *turning back, returning home*, always adverbial, with ἱκνεῖσθαι, 6, 367. 501. Od. 21, 211 ; and εἶναι, h. Ap. 476.

ὑπουράνιος, ον (οὐρανός), *under the heaven*, πετεηνά, 17, 675; metaph. extending to heaven, i. e. very great, κλέος, 10, 212. Od. 9, 264.

ὑποφαίνω (φαίνω), aor. ὑπέφηνα, *to make visible* or *to show* any thing *under*, τί, θρῆνυν τραπέζης, to show the footstool under the table, Od. 17, 409.†

ὑποφέρω (φέρω), aor. 1 ὑπήνεικα, for. *to bear away from under*, *esply to deliver* from danger, τινά, 5, 885.†

ὑποφεύγω (φεύγω), *to flee from under*, *to flee from, to escape*, τινά, 22, 200.†

ὑποφήτης. ao, ὁ (ὑπόφημι), prop. that speaks under any one, or as the servant of any one; hence, *a diviner, an interpreter* of the divine will, epith. of the Selli, 16, 235.†

ὑποφθάνω (φθάνω), only in the partcp. aor. 2 ὑποφθάς, and partep. aor. mid. ὑποφθάμενος, *to be beforehand, to do before, to anticipate*, ὑποφθὰς ὠρόνησεν, 7, 144. Od. 4, 547 ; and with accus., to anticipate one, Od. 15, 171 (in the aor. ό).

ὑποχάζομαι, always in tmesis, see χάζομαι.

ὑποχείριος, ον (χείρ), *under the hand, in the hand*, χρυσός, Od. 15, 448.†

ὑποχέω (χέω), aor. 1 Ep. ὑπέχευα, *to pour under, to strew under*, spoken of dry things, μῶσς, Od. 14, 49 ; to spread out, βοείας, Il. 11, 843.

ὑποχωρέω (χωρέω), imperf. and aor. ὑπεχώρησα, *to retire, to retreat, to go back*, *6, 107. 13, 476 ; also in tmesis, 4, 505.

ὑπόψιος, ον, Ep. ὕποπτος, looked upon from beneath, i. e. with angry, contemptuous look : hence, *despised, odious*. ὑπόψιος ἄλλων, 3, 42 ;† ed. Wolf. (Others read ἐπόψιος, V. 'a spectacle to all.' This word which elsewhere occurs in a good sense, is opposed to the context.)

ὕπτιος, η, ον (ὑπό), *bent backwards, supine, backwards*, opposed to πρηνής, 11, 179 ; often with πίσε, 15, 434. Od. 9, 371 ; ἐρείσθη, Il. 12, 192.

ὑπώπιον, τό (ὤψ), the part of the face below the eyes ; generally, *countenance, aspect* (since anger and displeasure are expressed in the region of the eyes), 12, 463.†

ὑπώρεια, ἡ (ὄρος), the region at the foot of a mountain, *the foot* or *declivity* of a mountain, 20, 218 † (prop. fem. from adj. ὑπώρειος).

ὑπώροφος, see ὑπόρωμι.

ὑπωρόφιος, ον (ὀροφή), *under the roof, in the house*, ὑπωρόφιοι δέ τοί εἰμεν, we are under the roof with thee, i. e. tablefriends, 9, 640.†

Ὑρίη. ἡ, a little town in Bœotia on the Euripus, in the time of Strabo destroyed, 2, 837.

Ὑρμίνη, ἡ, a town in Elis, prob. near the cape Hyrmina or Hormina, 2, 616.

Ὑρτακίδης, ου, ὁ, son of Hyrtacus = Asius, 2, 837.

Ὕρτακος, ὁ, a Trojan, husband of Arisbe, Apd. 3, 12, 5.

Ὕρτιος, ὁ, son of Gyrtius, a Mysian. 14, 511.

ὕs, ὑός, ὁ and ἡ (ῦ in the obliq. cases), accus. ὗν, dat. plur. Ep. only ὕεσσι for ὕεσι, a swine, a hog, both the boar and the sow; mly the tame hog. Hom. uses ὅς and σῦς according to the necessity of the metre, 10, 264. 23, 32. Od. 15, 556; see Thiersch, Gram. § 158. 12; and 197. 59.

ὑσμῖ´νη, ἡ, Ep. also metaplast. dat. ὑσμῖνι, a contest, a fight, a battle, ὑσμίνηνδε ἰέναι, to go into the battle, 2, 477; the Ep. dat. ὑσμῖνι μάχεσθαι, 2, 863. 8, 56.

ὑσμίνη, see ὑσμίνη.

ὑστάτιος, η, ον, poet. = ὕστατος, 15, 634; the neut. as adv. ὑστάτιον, at last, 8, 353. Od. 9, 14.

ὕστατος, η, ον, superl. of ὕστερος (ὑπό), the last, the extreme, spoken of space, ὕστατος ὁμίλου, 13, 459; of time, 5, 703. 11, 299; connected with πύματος, 22, 203; neut. sing. as adv. at last; also πύματον καὶ ὕστατον, Od. 20, 116; ὕστατα καὶ πύματα, at the very last, Od. 4, 685.

ὕστερος, η, ον, compar. (prob. from ὑπό), that follows, next behind, 5, 17; mly spoken of time: later, next, posterior, with gen. σεῦ ὕστερος, 18, 333; γένει ὕστερος, 3, 215. The neut. sing. as adv. ὕστερον, afterwards, in future, also plur. ὕστερα, Od. 16, 319.

ὑφαίνω, aor. ὕφηνα, iterat. imperf. ὑφαίνεσκεν, and also from an Ep. from ὑφάω, the 3 plur. pres. ὑφόωσιν, Od. 7, 105; to weave, with accus. ἱστόν, Il. 3, 125; and often φάρεα, Od. 13, 108. 2) Metaph. spoken of crafty plots or discourse: to weave, to plot, to devise, to plan, μῆτιν, Il. 7, 324. Od. 4, 678; δόλον, Il. 6, 187; often with ἐνὶ φρεσί: δόλους καὶ μῆτιν, Od. 9, 422; μύθους καὶ μήδεα πᾶσιν, to present words and counsels before all, Il. 3, 212.

ὑφαιρέω, to take away from under, only in tmesis, 2, 154; see αἱρέω.

ὑφαντός, ή, όν, verb adj. (from ὑφαίνω), woven, ἐσθής, εἷμα, *Od. 13, 136. 218. 16, 231.

ὕφασμα, ατος, τό (ὑφαίνω), a web, that which is woven, Od. 3, 247.†

ὑφάω, poet. shortened for ὑφαίνω, from which ὑφόωσι, Ep. expanded for ὑφῶσι, Od. 7, 105.†

ὑφέλκω (ἕλκω), to draw from under, τινὰ ποδοῖιν, to drag away any one by the feet, 14, 477.†

ὑφηνίοχος, ὁ (ἡνίοχος), prop. the servant of the warrior in the chariot, generally, a charioteer, 6, 19; cf. θεράπων.†

ὑφίημι (ἵημι), aor. 2 partcp. ὑφέντες, 1, 434; elsewhere in tmesis. 1) to take down, to let down, ἱστόν, 1, 434. h. Ap. 504. 2) to bring or lay under, τί τινι, in tmesis, 14, 140. Od. 9, 309.

ὑφικάνω, only in tmesis, 11, 117;† see ἱκάνω.

ὑφίστημι (ἵστημι), aor. 2 ὑπέστην, 3 plur. Ep. ὑπέσταν, partcp. ὑποστάς, only in the aor. 2 in intrans. signif. 1) to place oneself under, to take upon oneself, to undertake, to attempt (Schol. τλῆναι), with infin. σαῶσαι, 21, 273; hence: 2) to promise, to covenant, to vow, with accus. 9, 519; τινί τι, 5, 715. 13, 375; with κατανεῦσαι, 4, 267; with infin. fut. 9, 445. 19, 195; ὑπόσχεσιν, to make a promise, 2, 286. Od. 10, 483. 3) to put oneself under one, to yield to one, τινί, Il. 9, 160.

ὑφορβός, ὁ (ὗς, φέρβω), according to the necessity of the metre, for συφορβός, a swineherd, esply δῖος ὑφορβός, Od. 14, 3; often ἀνέρες ὑφορβοί, *Od. 14, 410.

ὑφόωσι, see ὑφάω.

ὑψαγόρης, ου, ὁ (ἀγορεύω), voc. speaking loftily, speaking proudly, boasting, *Od. 1, 385. 2, 85. 303.

ὑψερεφής, ές (ἐρέφω), Ep. also ὑψηρεφής, ές, from which only gen. ὑψηρεφέος, 9, 582. h. Merc. 23; having a high roof, ὑψερεφὲς δῶμα, 5, 213. Od. 4, 15; δώματα ὑψερεφέα, Od. 4, 757; and often (ea with synizesis).

ὑψηλός, ή, όν (ὕψος), high, lofty, spoken of trees, mountains, buildings, etc., 3, 384. 5, 560. 12, 282. Od. 1, 426.

Ὑψήνωρ, ορος, ὁ (from ἀνήρ, courageous), 1) son of Dolopion, a Trojan, 5, 76. 2) son of Hippasus, a Greek slain by Deïphobus, 13, 411.

ὑψηρεφής, ές, see ὑψερεφής.

ὑψηχής, ές (ἦχος), gen. έος, high or loud sounding, epith. of horses, loud neighing, or loud stamping, *5, 772. 23, 27.

ὕψι, adv. high, on high, ἤμενος, 20, 155. Od. 16, 264. 2) high, up, on high, ἀναθρώσκειν, Il. 13, 140; βιβάς, high striding, i. e. with great steps, 13, 371. h. Ap. 202.

Ὑψιβόας, ου, ὁ, poet. (βοάω), high or loud crier, name of a frog, Batr. 205.

ὑψιβρεμέτης, ου, ὁ, poet. (βρέμω), high roaring, high or loud-thundering, epith. of Zeus, 5, 54. 12, 68. Od. 5, 4.

ὑψίζυγος, ον, poet. (ζυγόν), prop. that sits high upon the rower's seat or at the helm; metaph. high-sitting, high-ruling, epith. of Zeus, *4, 166. 7, 69. = ὑψιμέδων.

ὑψικάρηνος, ον, poet. (κάρηνον), having a lofty head or summit, having a lofty top, δρύες, tall oaks, 12, 132.† h. Ven. 265.

ὑψίκερως, ων, poet. (κέρας), high-horned, with lofty antlers, ἔλαφος, Od. 10, 158.†

ὑψίκομος, ον (κόμη), prop. high-haired, high-leaved, leafy, δρῦς, 14, 398. Od. 12, 357.

*ὑψικρήμνος, ον, poet. (κρημνός), with high precipices, high-projecting, Ep. 6, 5.

*ὑψιμέδων, οντος, ὁ (μέδω), high-ruling, Ep. 7, 3.

*ὑψιμέλαθρος, ον, poet. (μέλαθρον), high-built, αὔλιον, h. Merc. 103. 134.

*ὑψιπετήεις, εσσα, εν, poet. = ὑψιπέτης, αἰετός, 22, 308. Od. 24, 538.

ὑψιπέτηλος, ον, Ep. for ὑψιπέταλος (πέταλον), high-leaved, δένδρεον, 13, 437. Od. 4, 458.

ὑψιπέτης, ου, ὁ, poet. (πέτομαι) h'ynh flying, high-soaring, αἰετός, 12, 201. 209 Od. 20, 243.

T 5

Ὑψιπύλη. 418 Φαίνω.

Ὑψιπύλη, ἡ, Ep. Ὑψιπύλεια, daughter of Thoas, king of Lemnos, wife of Jason, see Ἰήσων, 7, 469.
ὑψίπυλος, ον, poet. (πύλη) having high gates, high-gated, Θήβη, 6, 416. Τροίη, *16, 698.
ὑψόθεν, adv. (ὕψος), from on high, from above, 11, 53. 12, 383. Od. 2, 147.
ὑψόθι, adv. poet. (ὕψος) high, on high, εἶναι, *10, 16. ὑψόθ' ὄρεσφι, 10, 376.
ὑψόροφος, ον. poet. (ὀροφή)=ὑψερεφής, having a lofty roof, high-roofed, θάλαμος, 3, 423. Od. 2, 337.
ὑψόσε, adv. poet. (ὕψος), on high, up, upward, 10, 461. Od. 8, 375, and often.
ὑψοῦ, adv. poet. (ὕψος). high, above, up, on high, 1, 486. 6, 509. Od. 4, 785.
*ὑψόω (ὕψος), partcp. aor. ὑψώσας, to elevate, to lift up, δέμας, Batr. 80.
ὔω (ῠ), only imperf. and partcp. pres. pass., prop. to make wet, esp'y to cause to rain, Ζεὺς ὕε, Zeus sends rain, 12, 25. Od. 14, 457. Hence pass. λέων ὑόμενος καὶ ἀήμενος, a lion that goes through rain and wind [lit. rained and blown upon], Od. 6, 131.

Φ.

Φ, the twenty-first letter of the Greek alphabet; hence the sign of the twenty-first rhapsody.
φάανθεν, see φαίνω.
φαάντατος, η, ον, Ep. irreg. superl. from φαεινός, or from φαεννός, the brightest, ἀστήρ, Od. 13, 93.†
φαγεῖν, Ep. φαγέμεν, infin. of the defect. aor. ἔφαγον, poet. φάγον, subj. Ep. 3 sing. φάγῃσι, for φάγῃ; to eat, to consume; belonging to ἐσθίω or ἔδω, with accus. 24, 411. Od. 9, 94; with gen. Od. 9, 102.
φάε, 3 sing. imperf., see φάω.
Φαέθουσα, ἡ (the shining), the daughter of Hēlios and Neaira, Od. 12, 132.
φαέθων, οντος, ὁ (poet. lengthened from φάων), luminous, shining, beaming, bright, epith. of Helios, 11, 735. Od. 11, 16.
Φαέθων, οντος, ὁ, proper name, a horse of Eōs (Aurora), Od. 23, 246.
φαεινός, ή, όν, Ep. comp. φαεινότερος, 18, 610. h. Ven. 86; superl. φαάντατος, Ep. resolved from the contr. φαεννότατος, luminous, shining, beaming, gleaming, often spoken of metal; again, of fire, 5, 215; of the moon, 8, 554; of the eyes, 13, 3; of Eōs (Aurora), Od. 4, 188; φοίνικι, with purple, Il. 6, 219; of splendid clothes, 5, 315.
φαείνω, poet. = φαίνω, only pres.; prop. trans., to make light, to feed the light, Od. 18, 243. Mly intrans. signif. to shine, to beam. to gleam, spoken of Hēlios, Od. 12, 383. 385; of fire vessels, *Od. 18, 308.

φαεσίμβροτος, ον. poet. (φάω, βροτός) enlightening or bringing light to mortals, epith. of Eōs (Aurora), 24, 785; of Hēlios, Od. 10, 138. 191.
Φαίαξ, ακος. ὁ, see Φαίηκες.
φαιδιμόεις, ὁ, poet, a rare form of φαίδιμος, ον (φαίνω), prop. shining, hence, still never spoken of the external brightness of arms, but always metaph. noble glorious, beautiful; spoken of the limbs of the body, γυῖα, ὦμος, 6, 27. Od. 11, 128 b) glorious, illustrious, famous, spoken of heroes, Il. 4, 505. Od. 2, 386, and often.
Φαίδιμος, ὁ, a king of the Sidonians, who hospitably entertained Menelāus, Od. 4, 617. 15, 117.
Φαίδρη, ἡ, Ep. for Φαίδρα, daughter of king Minōs in Crete, wife of Theseus. She loved her step-son. Hippolytus, and being alighted by him, was the cause of his death, Od. 11, 321 Apd. 3, 1. 4.
φαινέσκετο, see φαίνω.
φαινολίς, ἡ (φαίνω), light-bringing, epith. of Eōs (Aurora), h. Ap. 51.
Φαίηκες, οἱ, the Phaeacians, the fabulous blessed inhabitants of Scheria; see Σχερίη At an earlier period they dwelt in Hyperia, near the Cyclōpes, and emigrated under Nausithōus to Scheria, Od. 6, 7, 8. Twelve princes ruled over them, whose chief was Alcinōus, Od. 8, 390, seq. They were occupied with navigation, and engaged also in piracy, although not otherwise warlike, Od. 7, 20. Their fleet vessels are described by Hom., Od. 7, 34, seq. He further describes them as a people at peace, fortunate, industrious, and happy; they love the pleasures of the table, the song, and the dance, Od. 8. 244, seq. cf. Nitzsch ad Od. 6, 3 5, 248. Voss, Mythol. Briefe III. p. 173. Uckert, and Mannert, believe that they originated in an obscure rumour in regard to the Tyrrhenians. Welcker in the Abhandl. im Rhein. Mus., die Homerischen Phäaken, etc. II. 1833, p. 1, regards them as the ferrymen of death, borrowed from a foreign religion. The name he derives from φαίος, dusky, dark : the dark men.
φαινομένηφι (ν), Ep. for φαινομένῃ.
Φαίνοψ, οπος, ὁ, son of Asius, from Abȳdus, father of Xanthus and Thoōn, 5, 152, 17, 312. 583.
φαίνω (for φάω), Ep. infin. φαινέμεν, aor. ἔφηνα, infin. φῆναι, fut. mid. φανοῦμαι, infin. Od. 12, 230; aor. 2 pass. ἐφάνην, poet. φάνην, 3 plur. φάνεν fu ἐφάνησαν, subj. 3 sing. Ep. φανήῃ for φανῇ, infin. Ep. φανήμεναι Ep. aor. 1 ἐφαάνθην expanded from φάνθην, 3 plur. φάανθεν for ἐφαάνθησαν, Il. 1, 200; perf pass. πέφασμαι, 3 sing. πέφανται, 2, 122; fut. 3 πεφήσομαι, 17, 155 (not to be confounded with the similar form from ΦΕΝΩ); φάνεσκεν, 11, 64, is according to Buttm. Gr. p. 504, and Thiersch, Gr. § 210. c. more prob. to be derived from ἐφάνην. Prim. signif. 1) Transit. &

*Φαινώ, bring to light, to cause to appear, to make visible, to show, with accus. ἐπιγουνίδα, μηρούς, Od. 18, 67. 74; αὐτὸν Ἄρην, Batr. 265; ὁδόν τινι. Od. 12, 334; spoken of the gods, τέρας τινί, to cause a sign to appear, Il. 2, 324. Od. 3, 173; σήματα, Il. 2, 353; γόνον τινί, to give offspring to any one, Od. 4, 12. *b)* Generally, to show, to disclose, to express, νοήματα, Il. 18, 295; ἀοιδήν, to begin a song, Od. 8, 499; ἀεικείας, Od. 20, 309. 2) Intrans. to shine, to be clear, τινί, Od. 7, 102. 19, 26. Mid. with aor. pass. 1) to come to the light, to appear, to shine, to become visible, to show oneself, τινί, Il. 1, 198. 7, 7. Od. 7, 201; also τί, where: φαίνετο (sc. Ἕκτωρ or ὁ χρώς), he was visible at the neck, i. e. his neck was unshielded, Il. 22, 325; hence partcp. φαινόμενοι, those present, 10, 236, and often: where also belongs the Ep. aor. ἐφάνεσκε, 11, 64. Od. 11, 587. 12, 241, 242. With infin. Od. 11, 336. 14, 355; and with partcp. Il. 5, 867. 2) Esply spoken of the appearance of the heavenly bodies, 1, 477. 8, 556; often, ἅμα ἠοῖ φαινομένηφι, as soon as Eôs (Aurora) appeared, 9, 618. Od. 4, 407. *b)* to shine, to be bright, spoken of fire, Il. 8, 562; δεινώ οἱ ὄσσε φάανθεν, terribly beamed his eyes [her eyes, Felton and Heyne], 1, 200. [According to Ameis, φαίνεσθαι never means to shine, but always to appear; hence οἱ is referred to Achilles, and ὄσσε to Athênê, 'terrible to him appeared her eyes.' *Am. Ed.*]

*Φαινώ, οὖς, ἡ, a nymph, a playmate of Persephônê, h. Cer. 418.

Φαίνωψ, οπος, ὁ = Φαίνοψ.

Φαῖστος, ὁ (adj. φαιστός, clear), son of Borus of Tarne in Mæonia, an ally of the Trojans, slain by Idomeneus, 5, 43.

Φαιστός, ἡ, a town in the island of Crete, near Gortyna, founded by Minos, 2, 648. Od. 3, 296.

φαλαγγηδόν, adv. (φάλαγξ), by troops, in squadrons, 15, 360.†

φάλαγξ, αγγος, ὁ, a line of battle, a troop, a phalanx, a band, 6, 6, elsewhere in the plur. φάλαγγες Τρώων, 3, 77; ἀνδρῶν, 19, 158; φάλαγγες ἐλπόμενοι, construct κατὰ σύνεσιν, 16, 281; cf. Kühner, § 365. *a.* *Il.

φάλαρα, τά, 16, 106.† βάλλετο (πήληξ) δ' αἰεὶ κὰκ φάλαρ' εὐποιήθ'—ed. Wolf; on the other hand, Spitzner after Aristarch., καὶ φάλαρα εὐπ., which must be connected with δεινὴν—καναχὴν ἔχε, v. 104; φάλαρα, Ep. shortened for φαληρά; according to the comm. explanation = φάλοι, shining studs or plates in front of the helmet as an ornament (Schol. A. τὰ κατὰ τὸ μέσον τῆς περικεφαλαίας μικρὰ ἀσπιδίσκια). More probably they were, according to Buttm., in Lex., with a Schol. ad Il. 5, 743 (οἱ ἐν ταῖς παραγναθίσι κρίκοι, annuli s. fibulæ), to be distinguished from φάλοι, and considered as the squamous, or metal-covered bands of the helmet, which held it fast.

φαληριάω (φαληρός), only partcp. φαληριόων, Ep. for φαληριῶν, prop. to be white, spoken of waves, to foam, 13, 799.†

Φάλκης, ου, ὁ (the plank of a vessel), a Trojan, slain by Antilŏchus, 14, 513.

φάλος, ὁ (adj. φαλός, clear), according to the old Gramm. metal studs or knobs on the helmet (Schol. ἧλοι, ἀσπιδίσκοι), for protection and ornament. According to Buttm., in Lexil., more correctly, a metallic ring, or conical elevation (later κῶνος), running over the helmet from the forehead to the neck, and in which the crest was inserted. It terminated, both before and behind, in a small kind of brim. Voss translates, the cone of the helmet, cf. Köpke, Kriegswesen der Griechen, p. 93. Mly the helmet had one φάλος, 3, 362. 4, 459. 6, 9, etc. That the φάλος was closely connected with the crest, is shown by 10, 258, and 13, 614; cf. ἄφαλος, ἀμφίφαλος, τετράφαλος. *Il.

φάν, see φημί.

φάνεν, φάνεσκε, see φαίνω.

φανήῃ, φανήμεναι, see φαίνω.

φάος, εος, τό (φάω), and older poet. form for φῶς, Ep. φόως, dat. sing. φάει, Od. 21, 429; accus. φάος, φόως, φόωσδε, plur. φάεα, Od. 16, 15. 17, 39, (cf. Thiersch, § 189. 19, 3.) 1) light, e. g. of candles, Od. 19, 24. 34. 18, 317; light, in distinction from ἀχλύς, Il. 15, 669; esply day-light, day, day-break, 1, 605. 2, 49. 3, 465; often ὁρᾶν, or ὄψεσθαι, φάος ἠελίοιο for ζῆν, 5, 120; and λείπειν φάος ἠελίοιο for θνήσκειν, 18, 11. ἰέναι φόωσδε, to send to the light, 2, 309. ἐν φάει, in the light, in the day, 17, 647. Od. 21, 429. 2) Poet. *a)* the light of the eyes, only nom. plur. φάεα, Od. 16, 15. 17, 39. *b)* Metaph. light, as the image of joy, aid, happiness, victory: welfare, happiness, victory, Il. 6, 6. 8, 282. 11, 797. 15, 741. 16, 39; in the address γλυκερὸν φάος (sweet life, V.), Od. 16, 23. 17, 41.

φαρέτρη, ἡ (φέρω), a quiver, 1, 45. ἰοδόκος, Od. 21, 11; and often.

Φᾶρις, ιος, ἡ, an old town in Laconia, on the river Phellias, south of Amyclæ, 2, 582.

φάρμακον, τό (akin to φύρω, prop. a mixture), any artificial means of effecting physical changes; both in a good and a bad sense. 1) a remedy, both external and internal; esply medicinal herbs for wounds, 4, 191. 218. 5, 401. 900. 11, 515. 831. 2) poison, esply poisonous herbs, a poisoned draught, κακά, ἀνδροφόνα, θυμοφθόρα, 22, 94. Od. 1, 261. 2, 329; for poisoning arrows, Od. 1, 261. 3) a charm, a magic drug, a magic drink, Il. 11, 741. Od. 4, 220; and esply spoken of the charms of Kirkê (Circê), Od. 10 236. 292. 392. 394; and of Hermês, Od. 10, 287. 302.

φαρμάσσω (φάρμακον), to apply an artificial means, spoken of working in
T 6

metals: *to harden,* πέλεκυν ἐν ὕδατι, Od. 9, 393.†

φᾶρος, εος, τό, generally, any large piece of cloth, *cloth, linen,* for covering any thing; esply φᾶρ. ταφήϊον, a shroud, Od. 2, 97. 24, 132; also φᾶρος alone. Il. 18, 353; *sail-cloth,* Od. 5, 258. 2) *a mantle, a cloak,* which was worn over the other clothing, Il. 2, 43. 8, 221. Od. 3, 467. It was worn also by women, Od. 5, 230. 10, 543; h. 6, 5.

Φάρος, ἡ, a little island, before the coast of Egypt, where at a later day Alexander the Great founded Alexandria. It was subsequently connected with the main land by a dike, and had a famous light-house, Od. 4, 355.

φάρυγξ, υγγος. ὁ, poet. gen. φάρυγος, *the gullet,* Od. 9, 373; hence generally, *the throat, the neck,* *Od. 19, 480.

φάσγανον, τό (σφάζω, for σφάγανον), prop. an edged tool, *a death-steel,* a *sword,* the weapon which the ancient Greeks always wore; it is called ἀμφηκες, two-edged, perhaps rather a dagger, and probably distinguished by its shorter length from ξίφος, 10, 256. 15, 713. Od. 22, 74; Θρηίκιον, either distinguished by its size, or the present of a Thracian, Il. 23, 808.

φάσθαι, see φημί.

φάσκω (φημί). only imperf. ἔφασκον, ες, ε, etc., in the signif. *to declare, to affirm, to allege,* with infin. fut. 13, 100. Od. 5, 135; and often.

φασσοφόνος, ον (πέφνον. ΦΕΝΩ), *slaying wild doves* (φάσσα), ἰρηξ ['*the dove-destroyer falcon,*' Cp.], 15, 238† (*falco palumbarius,* Linn.).

φάτις, ιος. ἡ (φημί) = φήμη, *discourse, report, fame,* that circulates amongst the multitude, Od. 21, 323; μν,στήρων, Od. 23, 362. 2) *rumour, report,* in a bad sense, δήμου, Il. 9, 460; in a good sense, ἐσθλή, Od. 6, 29.

φάτνη, ἡ (from πατέομαι), *a manger, a crib,* ἱππείη, 10. 568. Od. 4, 535.

Φαυσιάδης, ου, ὁ, *son of Phausius,* 11, 578.

φάω, a theme, 1) of φαίνω, of which occurs the 3 sing. imperf. with the signif. of the aor. φάε 'Ηώς, Εὼς (Aurora) appeared, Od. 14, 502;† and fut. 3 πεφήσομαι, see φαίνω, cf. Buttm., Gr. Gram. § 114. Thiersch, § 232. 150. 2) From φημί, *to say.*

ΦΑΩ, theme of πεφήσομαι, πέφαται, see ΦΕΝΩ.

Φεαί, αἱ, see Φειά.

φέβομαι, depon. poet. = φοβέυμαι, only pres. and imperf. with and without augment, in Hom. *to become terrified, to flee, to retreat hastily,* opposed to διώκειν, 5, 223. Od. 22, 299; ὑπό τινι, before any one, Il. 11, 121. 2) Trans. with accus. τινά, *to flee from any one,* 5, 232. (φέβομαι, the theme of φόβος, φοβέω.)

*φέγγος, εος, τό (φάος), *light, splendour, brightness,* h. Cer. 279.

Φειά, ἡ, 7, 135; and Φεαί, αἱ, Od. 15, 297; a town in Elis on the river Iardanus, on the borders of Elis Pisatis. According to Strab. VIII. p. 342, there was also, at a later day, a small town named Pheia on the promontory Pheia, now *Castell Torneso.* He remarks, however, VIII. p. 348, that the monument of the hero is near the town of Chaa; hence some ancient critics read Χαᾶς παρ' τεί-χεσσιν.

Φείδας, αντος, ὁ (from φείδομαι, one who spares), a leader of the Athenians, 13, 691.

Φείδιππος, ὁ, *Phidippus,* son of Thessalus, grandson of Heracles, a leader of the Greeks from the Sporades, 2, 678.

φείδομαι, depon. mid. aor. 1 Ep. φεισάμην; also Ep. aor. with redupl. πεφιδόμην, optat. πεφιδοίμην, infin. πεφιδέσθαι, and from this the Ep. fut. πεφιδήσομαι, 15, 215. 24, 158; *to spare, to save,* with gen. 5, 202. 15, 215. Od. 9, 277; δέπαος, Il. 24, 236.

φειδώ, όος, contr. οῦς, ἡ (φείδομαι), *the act of sparing, covetousness, penuriousness, parsimony.* οὐ γάρ τις φειδὼ νεκύων —γίγνεται πυρὸς μειλισσέμεν ὦκα, for sparing in respect to the dead does not exist, i. e. it may not be omitted to pacify them quickly by fire, 7, 409. Od. 14, 92. 16, 315.

φειδωλή, ἡ = φειδώ. δούρων, 22, 244.†

Φείδων, ωνος, ὁ (sparing), king of the Thesprotians, Od. 14. 316. 19, 287.

Φένεος, ἡ, mly Φενεός, a town in Arcadia, upon a lake of the same name, now *Phonea,* 2, 605.

ΦΕΝΩ, obsol. theme of the Ep. syncop. aor. 2, with redupl., ἔπεφνον and πέφνον, paricp. πέφνων, with the accent of the pres. 16, 827. Also from the theme ΦΑΩ, the perf. pass. πέφαμαι, 5, 531. Od. 22, 54; infin. πεφάσθαι, and fut. 3 πεφήσομαι, 15, 140; *to slay, to kill,* with accus., 4, 397. 6, 12. On Il. 13, 447, see εἴσκω.

Φεραί, ῶν, αἱ, dat. Φερῇς, 1) the chief town in Thessaly Pelasgiôtis, the residence of Admêtus, with a port, Pagasae, 2, 713. Od. 4, 798. 2) Perhaps = Φαραί, h. Ap. 427, if the reading, as in Od. 15, 247, should not be Φεαί. (According to Eustath. ad Od. 3, 488, Φεραί is a town in Thessaly, Φηραί a town in Messenia.)

*φέρασπις, ιδος, ὁ, ἡ (ἀσπίς), *shield-bearing,* h. 7, 2.

*φέρβω, poet. pluperf. 3 sing. ἐπεφόρβει, h. Merc. 105; *to pasture, to feed, to nourish,* with accus. h. 30, 2; τινός, with any thing, h. Merc. 105. Pass. τάδε φέρβεται ἐκ σέθεν ὄλβου, that derive happiness from thee, h. 30, 4.

*φερέσβιος, ον (βίος), *bringing life, giving nourishment,* γαῖα, h. Ap. 341; ἄρουρα, h. 30, 9.

Φέρεκλος, ὁ, son of Harmonides, the builder of the ship in which Paris bore off Helen, 5, 59.

φέρετρον, τό (φέρω). Ep. contr. φέρτρον, τό, *a bier,* only Ep. ἐν φέρτρῳ, 18, 236.†

Φέριστος. 421 Φή.

φέριστος, η, ον, Ep. = φέρτατος, 9, 110. Od. [1, 405.]

Φέρης, ητος, ὁ, son of Crêtheus and Tyro, father of Admetus, founder of Pheræ in Thessaly, Od. 11, 259.

Φέρουσα, ἡ, daughter of Nereus and Doris, 18, 43.

φέρτατος, η, ον, superl. to φέρτερος.

φέρτερος, η, ον, compar. Ep. (φέρω), superl. φέρτατος and φέριστος. η, ον, better; espy spoken of external qualities: more powerful, stronger, 2. 201; with dat. βίη φέρτερος, 3, 431. Od. 18, 134. ἔγχει φέρτατος, Il. 7, 289; also with infin., Od. 5, 170. πολὺ φέρτερόν ἐστι, it is far better, Il. 4, 307. κακῶν δέ κε φέρτατον εἴη, of evils that would be the best [i. e. the least], 17, 105; φέριστε, most noble, as an address, 6, 123. Od. 1, 269.

φέρτε, Ep. for φέρετε, see φέρω.

φέρτρον, τό, see φέρετρον.

φέρω, from this Ep. pres. indic. 3 sing. φέρησι (as if from φέρημι), Od. 19, 111 for which others read φέρησι for φέρῃ); imperat. Ep. φέρτε for φέρετε, Il. 9, 171; imperf. iterat. φέρεσκον, ες. ε, fut. οἴσω th. 'ΟΙΩ), aor. 1 Ep. and Ion. ἤνεικα, and ἔνεικα, infin. ἐνεῖκαι and forms of the aor. 2 optat. 3 sing. ἐνείκοι, 18, 147; infin. ἐνεικέμεν, 19, 194; also Ep. aor. 2 only imperat. οἶσε, Il. 3, 103. Od. 22, 106; infin. οἰσέμεν and οἰσέμεναι, Il. 3, 20. Od. 3, 420; mid. fut. οἴσομαι, aor. 1 νεικάμην; primar. signif. to bear (ferre),) to bear, to take or to have any thing pon oneself. σάκος, λᾶαν, 7, 219. 12, 45; τὶ ἐν ἀγκαλίδεσσι, to have any thing in one's arms, 18, 555; δράκοντα νύχεσσι, 12. 202: metaph. to bear, to endure, to suffer, λυγρά, Od. 18, 135. 2) bear, with the implied notion of motion, poet. spoken of the feet and knees, l. 6, 511. 15, 405; again : to convey, draw, to carry, to drive, spoken of horses and other draught animals, τινά, 838. 11, 283; ἅρμα, to draw a chariot, 232; of ships, 9, 306. 15, 705; of 'inda, κνίσσην οὐρανὸν εἴσω, 8, 549. 'ass. φέρεσθαι θυέλλῃ, to be driven by a storm, Od. 10. 54. 14, 314. Esply according to the relations indicated by the prep. and the context: a) to bear away, convey away, to bring, to present, to fer, often δῶρά τινι, τευχεά τινι. Il. 18, 17 ; τὶ προτὶ Ἴλιον, 7. 82; τινὰ ἐπὶ ἧας, 13, 423; τινὰ ἐς Τροίην, 15, 705; ὔθον or ἀγγελίην τινί, to bring word or message to any one, 10, 288. Od. 1, 08; metaph. χάριν τινί, to confer a favour upon any one, to gratify one, Il. 211. Od. 5, 307; ἦρα and ἐπίηρα φέρειν, see these words; φόως τινί, Il. 11, ; μένος χειρῶν ἰθὺς [= ἐναντίον, Sch.) ἰρειν, to bring forward strength of hands, i. e. to lift up their powerful hands, 5, 506; φόνον καὶ Κῆρά τινι, to bring death and destruction upon any one, 2, 352. Od. 4, 273 ; κακόν or κακά τι, Il. 2, 304 ; κακότητα, 12, 332 ; δηϊοτῆτά τινι, Od. 6, 203. b) to bear off, to bear away, to take away, τὶ παρά τινος, Il. 18, 137. 191; τινὰ ἐκ πολέμοιο, πόνου, 13, 515. 14, 429; ἀπάνευθε μάχης, 11, 283; proverbial: ἔπος φέροιεν ἀναρπάξασαι ἄελλαι, may the storms snatch up the word and bear it away, Od. 8, 409 ; esply in war : to bear away as spoil, to plunder, often, Il. 2, 302. Od. 12, 99; to bear away and lead away, Il. 5, 484, see ἄγω ; generally, to bear off, to acquire, to obtain by effort, κράτος, 18, 308. c) to bear around, 7, 183. 3) to bear, to produce, spoken of the earth and of plants, Od. 4, 229. 9, 110; τρύγην, h. Ap. 55; of a mother: τινὰ γαστέρι φέρ., to bear any one in the womb, Il. 6, 58. 4) The partcp. stands often with verbs: ἔδωκε φέρων, he brought and gave, 7, 302; ἔστησε φέρων, Od. 1, 127. Mid. 1) to bear oneself forth, to move forth ; for the most part spoken of a violent movement occasioned by external force ; to fall, to plunge, to run, to fly, to shoot away, Il. 1, 592. ἧκε ποταμόνδε φέρεσθαι, he hurled him, so that he flew into the river, 21, 121. ἧκα πόδας καὶ χεῖρε φέρεσθαι, I let feet and hands fall [I dash'd into the flood, Cp.], Od. 12, 442. ἰθὺς φέρεσθαι, to rush on, Il. 20, 172 ; ἐπὶ νηυσίν, 15, 743. 2) to bear away for oneself, also to bear or bring by or with oneself, δῶρα παρά τινος, 4, 97. Od. 2, 410 ; δόρυ, to bring for oneself, Il. 13, 168; often, to acquire for oneself, to obtain by effort, ἔναρα, 22, 245; ἄεθλα, 9, 127 ; τὰ πρῶτα, to bear off the first prize, 23, 275. 538 ; οἰχόνδε, 23, 856 ; κράτος, κῦδος, 13, 486. 22, 17.

φεύγω, pres. infin. Ep. φευγέμεν, iterat. imperf. φεύγεσκεν, fut. φεύξομαι, aor. 2 ἔφυγον, Ep. φύγον. Ep. iterat. φύγεσκε, Od. 17, 316 ; infin. φυγέειν. Ep. for φυγεῖν, perf. πέφευγα, in the optat., Il. 21, 609 ; partcp. πεφευγότες, Od. 1, 12 ; also the Ep. form πεφυζότες, Il. 21, 6 ; and Ep. perf. mid. πεφυγμένος, η, ον, escaped. 1) Intrans. to fly, to escape, to run away, often absol. ὑπό τινος, to fly before any one, 18, 150 ; ἐκ πολέμοιο, 7, 118 ; or ὑπὲκ κακοῦ, 13, 89 ; ἐς πατρίδα, 2, 140 : and often πρὸς ἄστυ, 14, 146. 2) Trans. with accus. to flee from, to shun, to avoid, to escape from any one, τινά, 11, 327 ; often θάνατον, πόλεμον, κακόν, 1, 60. 12, 322. 14, 80 ; Κῆρα, 18, 117. b) Metaph. Νέστορα ἐκ χειρῶν φύγον ἡνία, the reins fell (or escaped) from the hands of Nestor, 8, 137. 23, 465; with double accus. ποῖόν σε ἔπος φύγεν ἕρκος ὀδόντων, 4, 330; and often. The partcp. perf. πεφυγμένος, having escaped, has mly the accus. μοῖραν, ὄλεθρον, 6, 488. Od. 9, 455 ; only Od. 1, 18 ; with gen. δίδλων, in the signif. released from labours, where the gen. indicates the notion of deliverance, see Nitzsch ad Od. 1, 18.

φῆ, Ion. and Ep. for ἔφη, see φημί.

φή or φῆ, according to the Schol. an old Ep. particle, said to signify as, as if. Thus

Φηγεύς.   422   Φθά νω

wrote Zenodot. φή κύματα for ως κύμ., 2, 144; and δ δὲ φὴ κώδειαν, κ.τ.λ. 14, 499; and Herm. has adopted it h. Merc 241. Buttm. (in Lexil.), Thiersch, § 158. 14, and Voss defend it. The passage φή κώδειαν ἀνασχών, πέφραδέ τε Τρώεσσι, 14, 499, Voss [and so *Cp.*] translates: then he lifted it (the head) up, like a poppy's head, and showed it to the Trojans. Buttm. would derive it from ἥ, *ᾗ, as;* Voss, in the Rem. on Il. p. 39, compares it with the German syllabic ending *sam* or the Lat. *ceu,* and considers it an original subst. from φάω, 'the appearance' (cf. *instar*). Aristarch. takes it in Il. 14, 499, as a verb φῆ, *he spoke,* and strikes out the following verse. The reading of Zenod. is shown to be inadmissible by Spitzn. Exc. 25.

Φηγεύς, ἦος, ὁ, son of Dares, priest of Hephæstus in Troy, slain by Diomēdēs, 5, 11.

φήγινος, η, ον (φηγός), *of beech-wood, beechen* or *oaken.* ἄξων, 5, 838.†

φηγός, ἡ (φαγεῖν), a tree which bore an edible fruit similar to the acorn, prob. *Quercus esculus,* Linn., *an oak* (red beech is wrong). Esply the poet makes mention of a lofty, beautiful oak at the Scæan gate, *5, 623. 6, 237. 9, 354. [See Mitford I. p. 8, 9, for proof that the φηγός, Lat. *fagus,* was not the beech. *Am. Ed.*]

*φηλητεύω (φηλητής), fut. σω, *to deceive, to rob,* h. Merc. 159.

*φηλητής, οῦ, ὁ, *a deceiver,* h. Merc. 67, 146, φηλήτης, Hesiod.

φήμη, ἡ (φημί), pron. *speech, rumour, discourse,* esply a human voice, a word or sound in which there is casually contained a good omen (*omen*), like κληδών, *a favorable word, an omen,* *Od. 2, 35. 20, 100. 105.

φημί, pres. Ep. 2 sing φῆσθα, 21, 186 Od. 14, 149; subj. 2 sing. φήῃ, Ep. for φῇ, Od. 11, 128; 1 plur. optat. φαῖμεν for φαίημεν, Il. 2, 81; imperf. ἔφην, with aor. signif., Ep. φῆν, 2 sing. φῆς, 5, 473; and ἔφησθα, φῆσθα, 1, 397; 3 plur. ἔφαν, φάν for ἔφασαν, also infin. φάναι, fut. φήσω. 8, 148. Mid. pres. φάμαι, imperat. φάο, infin. φάσθαι, imperf. ἐφάμην, often 3 sing. φάτο, plur. φάντο, perf. pass. partcp. πεφασμένος, 14, 127; also the iterat. imperf. Ep. ἐφάσκον, ες, ε, plur. Od. 22, 35. The imperf. ἔφην has an aor. signif.; in like manner φάναι. Here belongs as fut. ἐρέω (see εἴρω); as aor. εἶπον. On the pres. as enclitic, except the 2 sing. φῄς, see the grammars. Prim. signif. from the theme ΦΑΩ (from which also φαίνω), to disclose any thing by language; hence 1) *to tell, to say, to speak, to relate,* both absol. and with accus., often ἔπος; esply μῦθον, ἀγγελίην, 18, 17; ψεῦδος, 2, 81; τινὰ κακόν, to call any one cowardly, 8, 153; also in a more decided sense, *to affirm, to allege, to maintain.* 2) Prop. to speak in the mind, i. e. *to mean, to think, to believe,*

to imagine, 1, 521. 2, 37. 3, 220. 8, 23. and often. In both significations follows *a)* The simple infin. when it is the same subject with the main clause, 4, 351. 8, 229. *b)* With accus. and infin. when the subject of the infin. is different from that of the main clause, οὐδέ κ φαίη ἀνδρὶ μαχησάμενον τόγ' ἐλθεῖν ἀλλὰ χοροῦδε ἔρχεσθαι, thou wouldst not suppose he was just come from the battle, but that he was going to a dance, I. 392. cf. 2, 129. 350. 5, 103. Of the pass. only the perf. partcp. occurs.—The mid. has the same signif. with the act. ἴσον ἐμοὶ φάσθαι, to think himself equal τ me, 1. 287. 15, 167.

Φήμιος, ὁ (φήμη), son of Terpis, a famous singer of Ithaca, who, by compulsion, was obliged to entertain the suitors by his songs, in the house of Odysseus (Ulysses), Od. 1, 154. 22, 330.

φῆμις, ιος, ἡ, poet. = φήμη, *speech, rumour, discourse,* 10, 207. 2) *talk, conference, report, fame,* Od. 6, 273. δημω φῆμις, the talk, i. e. the judgement of the people, Od. 14, 230. cf. 16, 75. οἱ μέν ῥ' ᾤχοντο πρόμολον, δημοιό τε φῆμιν θέντ went to the assembly and the conference of the people, Od. 15, 468. (According to the Schol. φῆμις is = ἐκκλησία, συνέδριον, hence Voss: for deliberation in the assembly of the people.)

φήν, Ion. and Ep. for ἔφην, see φημί. φήναι, φήνειε, see φαίνω.

φήνη, ἡ, a kind of eagle, according to Billerbeck Dissertat. de Avibus ab Aristot. Pliniæque Commemor., *a sea-eagle, an osprey (ossifraga),* Od. 3, 372; plur. *Od. 16, 217.

φήρ, gen φηρός, ὁ, Æol. for θήρ (because the Lat. *fera*), *a beast, a wild animal,* then generally, *a monster, a prodigy,* esply were the Centaurs so called, *1. 268. 2, 733. [Mitford, I. p. 58, 59, denies that these passages refer to the Centaurs. Hesiod and Homer, he affirms, never speak of them as a savage race, and know nothing of their equine form. In Od. 21, 295, the Centaur Eurytion receives as an epith. ἀγακλυτός. *Am. Ed.*]

Φηραί, al. Ion. for Φαραί, Ep. also τ Φηρή, 5, 543: a town in Messenia, on the river Nedon, in the vicinity of the present Kalamata. In the time of Home it belonged to the Laconian dominions, 9, 151. 293. Od. 3, 488. cf. Φεραί.

Φηρητιάδης, ου, ὁ, Ep. for Φερητιάδης son of Pheres or grandson = Εὐμήλος, 2. 763. 23, 376.

φῂς, φῆς, φῆσθα, see φημί. φθάν. see φθάνω.

φθάνω, fut. φθήσομαι, 23, 444; αοr.! ἔφθην, Ep. φθῆν, 3 plur. φθάν, Ep. για ἔφθασαν, subj. φθῶ, Ep. 3 sing. φθῇ and φθῇσιν for φθῇ, 16, 861. 23, 805;1 plur. φθείωμεν for φθῶμεν, 3 plur. φθίως for φθῶσι, Od. 24, 437; optat. φθαίην, infin. φθῆναι, partcp. φθάς, also the Epartcp. aor. mid. φθάμενος, η, ον. 1) *to anticipate, to do before, to come before,*

Φθέγγομαι.

to be before, aosol. spoken of Atē, φθάνει πᾶσαν ἐπ᾽ αἶαν, βλάπτουσ᾽ ἀνθρώπους, she goes first over the whole earth, injuring men, Il. 9, 506; thus Wolf and Voss. It is better with Heyne and Bothe to erase the comma, and connect φθάνει βλάπτουσα, i. e. πρὶν βλάπτει, which also Köppen and Spitzner prefer; τινά, to anticipate one, 21, 262. 2) Mly with partcp. of the action in which one is first. In English, the verb φθάνω may be best translated by the adv. *first, sooner, before,* etc., φθῆ σε τέλος θανάτοιο κιχήμενον, the end of death first overtook, 11, 451. ἀλλ᾽ ἄρα μιν φθῆ Τηλέμαχος βαλών, but Telemachus hit him first (μίν depends upon βάλλω), Od. 22, 91, cf. Il. 9, 506. 10, 368. 16, 314. 23, 805. Od. 16, 383; with πρίν following, Il. 16, 322. On account of the implied comparat. ἤ sometimes follows, 23, 444. Od. 11, 58; and also the gen. φθὰν δὲ μέγ᾽ ἱππήων ἐπὶ τάφρῳ κοσμηθέντες, they were arranged at the trench far before the horsemen, Il. 11, 51. Thus Voss, cf. κοσμέω; more rarely with the partcp. pass. ἦ κε πολὺ φθαίη πόλις ἁλοῦσα, surely, the city would have been captured before, 13, 815. εἰ κε—φθήῃ ἐμῷ ὑπὸ δουρὶ τυπεὶς ἀπὸ θυμὸν ὀλέσσαι, whether he may not, smitten by my spear, first lose his life, 16, 861 (the infin. is here to be explained as the consequence of τυπείς, for ὥστε ὀλέσσαι θυμόν); cf. Od. 24, 437. 3) The partcp. mid. φθάμενος is on the other hand used as a supplement of the main verb, ὅς μ᾽ ἔβαλε φθάμενος, he hit me first, Il. 5, 119. 13, 387. 21, 576. Od. 19, 449 (Herm. ad Viger. p. 761, takes as a ground signif. *crasso, desino,* and explains these passages accordingly).

φθέγγομαι, depon. mid. (φέγγος), fut. φθέγξομαι, aor. ἐφθεγξάμην, Ep. 3 sing. φθέγξατο. subj. φθέγξομαι, with a shortened vowel, 21, 341; to utter a sound of a tone; hence, 1) *to speak, to call, to cry,* in Hom. spoken only of men, 10, 67. 139. Od. 10, 228; also ὀλίγῃ ὀπί, Od. 14, 492. 2) *to sing,* h. Ap. 164; spoken of the lyre, *to sound,* h. Merc. 486; φωνήν, Batr. 272.

Φθειρῶν ὄρος, τό (the pine *mountain,* from φθείρ, the fruit of a species of pine), a mountain of Caria, according to Strab. the mountain *Latmus* or *Grion,* 2, 868.

φθείρω (φθέω, φθίω), only pres. *to corrupt, to spoil, to destroy,* with accus. μῆλα, Od. 17, 246. Mid. *to perish, to be unfortunate,* Il. 21, 128.

φθέωμεν, φθέωσιν, see φθάνω.

φθῇ, φθήῃ, φθήῃσι, see φθάνω.

Φθίη, ἡ. Ion. for Φθία, Ep. dat. Φθίηφι. 1) Prop. a very ancient town in Thessaly on the river Sperchius, chief city of the Myrmidons, residence of Peleus, 2, 683. 2) the district about the town Phthia, hence often in connexion with Hellas for the kingdom of Achilles, 1, 155. 9, 395. Od. 11, 496; Φθίηνδε, Il. 1, 169.

Φθῖος, ὁ, *a Phthian,* an inhabitant of the town and district of Phthia, 13, 686.

φθίμενος, see φθίνω.

φθινύθω, poet. form of φθίνω, only pres. and imperf.; iterat. imperf. φθινύθεσκε, 1, 491; both intrans. and trans. 1) Intrans. *to pine away, to waste away, to vanish away,* 6, 327. 17, 364. 21, 466. Od. 8, 530; φθινύθει δ᾽ ἀμφ᾽ ὀστεόφιν χρώς, Od. 16, 145; τούσδε δ᾽ ἔα φθινύθειν, let these perish, Il. 2, 346. 2) *to cause to vanish, to destroy,* with accus. οἶκον, οἶνον, Od. 1, 250. 14, 95; κῆρ (with grief), Il. 1, 491. 10, 485; αἰῶνα, to consume the life. Od. 18, 204.

φθίνω, Ep. form φθίω. only 18, 446. Od. 2, 368; fut. φθίσω. aor. ἔφθισα, Ep. φθῖσα, infin. φθῖσαι, mid. intrans. fut. φθίσομαι, perf. ἔφθιμαι, Od. 20, 340; pluperf. ἐφθίμην, 3 plur. ἐφθίαθ᾽, Ep. for ἔφθιντο, Il. 1, 251; of the same form is the aor. 2 syncop. ἐφθίμην. subj. φθίωμαι, Ep. shortened φθίομαι. φθίεται, for φθίωμαι, φθίηται, 20, 173; φθιόμεσθα for φθιώμεσθα, 14, 87; optat. φθῖμην, Od. 10, 51; 3 sing. φθῖτ᾽ for φθῖτο, Od. 11, 330 (elsewhere φθεῖτο); imperat. φθίσθω, infin. φθίσθαι, partcp. φθίμενος. (The ι is long Ep. both in φθίνω and φθίω, but in the perf. and aor. 2 always short.) The trans. and intrans. signif. is divided amongst these forms as follows: 1) Intrans.: in Hom. the pres. φθίνω always, φθίω sometimes, Od. 2, 368; and the middle forms, *to vanish away, to waste away, to dwindle, to consume oneself.* a) Spoken of men, εὔχεται, θυμὸν ἀπὸ μελέων φθίσθαι, that the spirit departs from the limbs, Od. 15, 354; generally, *to perish, to die.* Il. 1, 251. 9, 246. 11, 821. 19, 329; hence, φθίμενος, one dead, 16, 581. Od. 11, 558: δόλῳ φθίειν, Od. 2, 368; ὑπὸ νούσῳ φθίσθαι, Il. 13, 667; φθίσεσθαι κακὸν οἶτον, to perish a wretched death, Od. 13, 384. b) Spoken of time: esply the pres. φθίνω: νύκτες καὶ ἤματα φθίνουσι, Od. 11, 185. 13, 338; also νὺξ φθίει, Od. 11, 330; μηνῶν φθινόντων, the months wasting, Od. 10, 470; τοῦ φθίνοντος μηνός, this month expiring, see μείς, Od. 14, 162. 19, 307. 2) Transit.: in the pres. φθίω, Il. 18, 446;† fut. and aor. act. *to cause to vanish, to destroy, to annihilate, to kill,* τινά, 6, 407. 16, 471. 22, 61. Od. 4, 741. 16, 369. 428. h. Cer. 352; metaph. φθίειν φρένας, to consume one's heart, Il. 18, 446.

φθισήνωρ, ορος. ὁ, ἡ (ἀνήρ), *man-destroying* or *slaying,* πόλεμος, *2, 833. 9, 604; and elsewhere.

φθισίμβροτος, ον (φθίω, βροτός), *man-destroying, man-slaying,* μάχη, 13, 339. Od. 22, 297.

φθογγή, ἡ (φθέγγομαι) = φθόγγος, 2, 791. 13, 216. 16, 508; of beasts, Od. 9, 167.

φθόγγος, ὁ (φθέγγομαι), *a voice, a sound, a call,* esply of men, 5, 234; of the Cyclopes, Od. 9, 257; of the Sirens, Od. 12, 41. 159; *noise,* Od. 18, 199.

φθονέω, only pres. (φθόνος). 1) *to be*

envious, *to envy, to deny,* absol. 4, 55, 56. 2) With dat. of the pers. and gen. of the thing, *to envy* one any thing, *to grudge, to refuse, to deny,* τινὶ ἡμιόνων, Od. 6, 68. 17, 100. 3) With infin. *to envy, to deny, to be unwilling,* Od. 11, 381; with accus. and infin., Od. 1, 346. 18, 16. 19, 348.

φι and φιν, a syllabic ending common in the Ep. language, in forming the gen. and dat. both in the sing. and plur.: e. g. εὐνῆφι for εὐνῆς; ἀγέληφι for ἀγέλη; δακρυόφιν for δακρύων; θεόφιν for θεοῖς. We find an example of the accus. in ἐπὶ δεξιόφιν ... ἢ ἐπ᾽ ἀριστερόφιν, 13, 308. cf. Thiersch, § 177. 16. Buttm., § 56. not. 9. Rost, Dial. 23. p. 396. Kühner, § 236.

φιάλη, ἡ, a vessel with a flat bottom, a *bowl* [=patera], esply for drinking, 23, 270. 616; for preserving the ashes of the dead, *an urn,* *23, 243. 253.

φίλαι, φίλατο, see φιλέω.

φιλέω (φίλος); fut. ήσω, infin. Ep. φιλήσεμεν, aor. ἐφίλησα, Ep. φίλησα, fut. mid. φιλήσομαι, Od. 1, 123; aor. pass. ἐφιλήθην, 3 plur. Ep. ἐφίληθεν; pecul. Ep. infin. pres. φιλήμεναι, Il. 22, 265 (cf. Thiersch., Gram. § 217); Ep. aor. mid. ἐφιλάμην (as if from φίλω), 3 sing. ἐφίλατο, φίλατο, 5, 61. 20, 304; imperat. φίλαι (Wolf φίλαι), 5, 117; subj. φίλωνται, h. Cer. 117; iterat. imperf. φιλέεσκε. 1) *to love, to hold dear,* to exhibit love and good will towards, τινά, often with περὶ κῆρι, ἐκ θυμοῦ, 9, 486. 13, 430; also spoken of things; σχέτλια ἔργα, Od. 14, 83; with double accus.: τινὰ παντοίην φιλότητα, to show every regard to any one, Od. 15, 245; hence pass. ἔκ τινος, *to be beloved* by any one, Il. 2, 668. 2) Esply a) *to treat any one in a kind and friendly manner, to receive kindly, to entertain hospitably and courteously,* spoken of hosts, 3, 207. 6, 15. Od. 4, 29. 171. 5, 135, and often; hence pass. φιλεῖσθαι παρά τινι, to be hospitably entertained by any one, Il. 13, 627; and παρ᾽ ἄμμι φιλήσεαι (fut. mid. intrans.), thou wilt be welcomed by us, Od. 1, 123. 15, 281. b) spoken of sensual love, 9, 450. Od. 18, 325. Mid. only in the Ep. aor. *to love* any one, like the act. τινά, Il. 5, 61. 117. 10, 280 (spoken only of the gods); περὶ πάντων, 20, 304. h. Cer. 117.

φιλήρετμος, ον (ἐρετμός), *oar-loving,* epith. of the Taphians and Phaeaces, *Od. 1, 181. 8, 96.

Φιλητορίδης, ου, ὁ, son of Philêtôr = Dêmûchus, 20, 457.

Φιλοίτιος, ὁ (lengthened from φίλος), a faithful herdsman of Odysseus (Ulysses), Od. 20, 185. 21, 189, seq.

φιλοκέρτομος, ον (κέρτομος), *delighting in jeers* or *mockery,* Od. 22, 287.†

*φιλόκροτος, ον (κροτέω), *noise-loving,* epith. of Pan, h. 18, 2.

φιλοκτέανος, ον, poet. (κτέανον), superl. φιλοκτεανώτατος, *loving possessions* or *gain,* hence, *covetous, avaricious,* 1, 122.†

Φιλοκτήτης, ου, ὁ, son of Poas, of Melibœa in Thessaly, an excellent archer, who possessed the bow and the arrows of Heracles, without which Troy could not be taken. On the island of Lemnos he was dangerously wounded by a poisonous snake, so that the Greeks left him there, 2, 716, seq. Od. 3, 190. 8, 219. According to a later tradition, he was brought to Troy by Odysseus (Ulysses), after having been cured by Machâon, Pind.

*φιλοκυδής, ές (κῦδος), *loving fame, loving joy, joyful,* ἥβη, κῶμος, h. Merc. 375. 481.

*φιλοληΐος, ον (ληΐη, λεία), *loving booty, desirous of plunder,* h. Merc. 335.

Φιλομέδουσα, ἡ, ed. Wolf; Φυλομέδουσα, ed. Spitzn., wife of the mace-bearer Areithous, of Arnê in Bœotia, 7, 10.

φιλομειδής, ές (μειδάω), mly poet. φιλομμειδής, *laughter-loving, sweetly smiling,* epith. of Aphroditê, 3, 424. 5, 375. Od. 8, 362, and often.

Φιλομηλείδης, ου, ὁ, according to Eustath. a king of Lesbos, who challenged passers by to wrestling combats, and so also the Greeks landing there, Od. 4, 343. 17, 134. Another explanation takes the word improb. to mean the son of Philomela = *Patroclus.* [According to Ameis, the last explanation is prob., since no other proper names in -ίδης and -άδης occur in Hom.]

φιλόξεινος, ον, Ion. and poet. for φιλόξενος (ξένος) *loving guests* or *strangers, hospitable.* *Od. 6, 121. 8, 576.

φιλοπαίγμων, ον, gen. ονος (παίζω) *loving play* or *sport, sportive,* ὀρχηθμός, Od. 23, 134.†

φιλοπτόλεμος, ον, poet. for φιλοπόλεμος (πόλεμος), *loving war, warlike,* *16, 65. 90. 17, 224.

φίλος, η, ον, compar. φίλτερος, η, ον, Ep. φιλίων, ον, Od. 19, 351; superl. φίλτατος, η, ον. 1) *dear, valued; beloved, grateful, agreeable,* spoken of persons and things, τινί. Il. 1, 381. 3, 102; esply in a case of address, φίλε ἑκυρέ, Il. 3, 172; also τέκνον, Od. 2, 363. 2) As subst. *a friend, a female friend,* often in the address, φίλε and φίλος, as vocat., Il. 4, 189. Od. 1, 301: esply a) In the neut. sing., φίλον ἐστί τινι, it is dear to any one, it is agreeable, it is pleasing. μή τοῦτο φίλον Διὶ πατρὶ γένοιτο, Od. 7, 316; cf. Il. 7, 387, and φ. ἔπλετο θυμῷ, Od. 13, 145. 335; sometimes with the infin. Od. 1, 82; and in the neut. plur. ἔνθα φίλ᾽ ὀπταλέα κρέα ἔδμεναι, there it is pleasant to you to eat roasted meat, Il. 4, 345. b) Often poet. as a periphrasis of the possessive pronoun, because that is dear to any one which belongs to him; prim. spoken of the nearest relatives, 1, 345. 9, 555. 22, 408. Od. 2, 17; then of parts of the human body, Il. 7, 271. Od. 8, 233; also φίλα εἵματα, Il. 2, 261. c) The neut. plur. φίλα, as adv. φίλα φρονεῖν τινι, to cherish friendly feelings towards one, to be kind to him, 4, 219. 5

*Φιλοστέφανος. Φοινί‾κη

116; in like manner φίλα εἰδέναι, Od. 3, 477. 2) Act. loving, kind, Od. 1, 313. φίλοι ξένοι, has been so explained, but without necessity, it means simply: dear guests; in like manner, φίλα μήδεα εἰδέναι, to cherish friendly sentiments, Il. 17, 325. (ι is short, but in φίλε, at the commencement of a verse, also long, 4, 155. 5, 359.)

*φιλοστέφανος, ον (στέφανος), garland-loving, epith. of Aphroditê, h. Cer. 102.

φιλότης, ητος, ἡ (φίλος), 1) love, friendship, also between nations, φιλότητα τάμνειν, 3, 73; βάλλειν, 4, 16; esply 2) hospitality, hospitable reception, 3, 354. Od. 15, 55. 197. b) (sexual) love, sexual intercourse, connected with εὐνή, Il. 3, 445. 14, 209. Od. 8, 267.

φιλοτήσιος, ίη, ιον (φιλότης), belonging to love, φιλοτήσια ἔργα, works of love, Od. 11, 246.†

φιλοφρονέω, an old reading, Od. 16, 17; now φίλα φρονέων, Wolf.

φιλοφροσύνη, ἡ (φιλόφρων), a friendly, kind disposition, kindness, affection, 9, 256.†

φιλοψευδής, ές, gen. έος (ψεῦδος), loving lies, false, a friend of deception, 12, 164.†

φίλτατος, φίλτερος, see φίλος.

*Φίλτραῖος, ὁ (φίλτρον), that tastes or licks up love-potions, a name of a mouse, Batr. 229.

φίλως, adv. with love, gladly, ὁρᾶν, 4, 347.†

φιτρός, ὁ, a log, a billet of wood, 12, 29. 21, 314. Od. 12, 11 (according to Damm, syncopat. from φίτυρος, fm φύω, φιτύω).

φλεγέθω. poet. form of φλέγω, only in the pres. 1) Transit. to burn, to consume, with accus. πόλιν, 17, 738. 2) Intrans. to burn, to be in flames, 18, 211; in like manner mid. *23. 197.

φλέγμα, ατος, τό (φλέγω), a conflagration, a flame, a fire, 21, 237.†

Φλεγύαι and Φλέγυες, οἱ (from which Φλεγύων, h. Ap. 278), the Phlegyans, a warlike and predatory people, who dwelt, according to Strab., Steph., and the Schol. Ven., near Gyrton in Thessaly; from hence they subsequently emigrated to Bœotia, 13, 302.

*Φλεγύας, ου, ὁ, son of Arês, king of the Lapithæ, father of Corônis, 15, 8.

φλέγω, poet. φλεγέθω. 1) Trans. to burn, to singe, to scorch, πῦρ φλέγει, sc. ἀκρίδας, 21, 13. 2) Pass. πυρὶ φλέγεσθαι, to burn in the fire, *21, 365; aor. pass. optat. φλεχθείη, Ep. 14, 13.

φλέψ, βος, ἡ (φλάω), a vein, a blood-vessel, 13, 546.†

φλιά, ἡ, Ep. a door-pillar, a door-post, elsewhere σταθμός, Od. 17, 221.†

φλόγεος, η, ον (φλόξ), flaming, sparkling, shining, according to Eustath. = ὀξέα, rapid, ὄχεα, *5, 745. 8, 389.

φλοιός, ὁ (φλάω), bark, the bark of a tree, 1, 237.† h. V. n. 272.

φλοῖσβος, ὁ (φλέω, φλοίω), roaring, noise, esply the tumult of battle (the storm of battle, V., the boisterous war, Cp.), *5, 322. 469. 10, 416. 20, 377.

φλόξ, φλογός, ἡ (φλέγω), a flame, a fire, Ἡφαίστοιο, the flame of Hêphæstus, i. e. a great fire, in oppos. to the flame of Hestia (Vesta), 17, 88. 23, 33; and often as an image of swiftness, 13, 39. 20, 423; in Od. 24, 71; often in the Il., only once in the Od.

φλύω, to overflow, in tmesis, see ἀνα-φλύω.

φοβέω (φόβος), aor. ἐφόβησα, poet. φόβησα, fut. mid. φοβήσομαι, aor. pass. ἐφοβήθην, 3 plur. ἐφόβηθεν, perf. pass. πεφόβημαι, 3 plur. pluperf. Ep. and Ion. πεφόβηατο. 1) Act. to scare away, to put to flight (fugare), (so always in Hom. according to Aristarch.), τινά, 11, 173. 406. 13, 300. 16, 689; δουρί, 20, 187; and often. b) to terrify, to frighten, 15, 91; αἰγίδι, v. 230. cf. 17, 547. 2) Mid. with aor. pass. to be scared, to flee in terrour, 5, 140; ὑπό τινος, 8, 149 (to fly before a man: lit. by his agency); and ὑπό τινι, 15, 637; also τινά, to flee any one, 22, 250. In the Od. it occurs only once, 16, 163. (The signif. to fear, is unknown to Hom., hence μή never follows it, cf. Lehrs. Aristarch. p. 90.)

φόβονδε, adv. for εἰς φόβον, see φόβος.

φόβος, ὁ (φέβομαι), terrour, fright, 9, 2 [see the close], esply flight from terrour, oft. Il., in Od. only 24, 57. μνήστωρ φόβοιο, 11, 5, 272. 8, 108. φόβον Ἄρηος φορέειν, to excite the flight of Arês, 2. 767. φόβον ποιεῖν Ἀχαιῶν, 12, 438. φόβονδε ἔχειν ἵππους, to direct to flight, 8, 139; τρωπᾶσθαι, 15, 666. φόβονδε ἀγορεύειν, to advise to flight, to speak of flight, 5, 252. [According to Amels, φόβος always means flight. So in 11, 9, 2, where φύζα means terrour. Am. Ed.]

Φόβος, ὁ, personified: son and companion of Arês, brother of Terrour [Δεῖμος], 4, 440. 13, 299; mentioned as his charioteer, 15, 119.

Φοῖβος, ὁ, epith. of Apollo, mly Φοῖβος Ἀπόλλων, sometimes Ἀπόλλων Φοῖβος, 20, 68. According to the Schol. pure, beaming (καθαρός), akin to φάος, on account of his bright youthful beauty; according to others, the enlightened, in regard to prophetic gifts. The more correct deriv. is prob. from φέβω, Februus, i. e. removens noxia, Hermann de Myth. Græc. Op. II, p. 376. cf. Κοῖος.

φοινήεις, εσσα, εν (φοινός), blood-red, blood-coloured = δαφοινός, epith. of a serpent, *12, 202. 220.

Φοίνικες, οἱ, sing. Φοίνιξ, ῖκος, ὁ, the Phœnicians, inhabitants of the country of Phœnicia in Asia, 23. 744. Hom. even knows them as a trafficking people, distinguished by navigation, art, and piracy, Od. 4, 84. 13, 272, seq 14, 288.

Φοινίκη, ἡ (φοίνιξ, prop. Date-land), Phœnicia, a maritime country in Asia, between the river Eleutherus and Mount Carmel, with Sidon for its capital, Od. 4, 83. 14, 291.

Φοινικόεις. 426 Φορύ να.

φοινικόεις, εσσα, εν=φοινίκεος (φοίνιξ), purple, shining with purple, χλαῖνα, 10, 133. Od. 14, 500; σμώδιγγες αἱματι φοινικόεσσαι, Il. 23, 717.

φοινικοπάρηος, ον (παρειά), having purple cheeks, with red sides, νηῦς, *Od. 11, 124. 23, 271; cf. μιλτοπάρηος (V. redbeaked; crimson-prow'd, Cp.).

Φοῖνιξ, ἶκος, ὁ, a Phœnician, see Φοίνικες. 2) son of Agēnōr, brother of Cadmus and Εurōpa; according to Hom. 14, 321, the father of Europa, if it is not rather to be taken as the name of a people. 3) son of Amyntor, the fosterfather and faithful companion of Achilles before Troy. Being cursed by his father on account of a forbidden passion, he fled to Peleus in Phthia, who named him as ruler of the Dolopians, 9, 448, seq. 16, 196. 17, 555, seq. 19, 311.

φοῖνιξ, ἶκος, ὁ, as appell. 1) purple, the colour of purple, because the discovery of this was ascribed to the Phœnicians, 4, 141. 6, 219. 7, 305. Od. 23, 201. 2) the palm, the date-palm, Od. 6, 163 h. Ap. 117. 3) As adj. purple-red, generally, dark-red, brownish-red, spoken of a horse, Il. 23. 454.

φοίνιος, η, ον, poet. (φοινός), blood-red, dark-red, αἷμα, Od. 18, 97.†

Φοίνισσα, ἡ, a Phœnician woman, Od. 15, 416. 425.

φοινός, ή, όν (φόνος), bloody, dark-red, αἷμα, 16, 159.† b) murderous, h. Ap. 362.

φοιτάω (φοῖτος), aor. 1 ἐφοίτησα, Ep. 3 dual imperf. φοιτήτην for ἐφοιτάτην, 12, 266; to go here and there, to stride, to stalk, always with the implied notion of a frequent, restless, or rapid movement, 2, 779. 12, 266. 13, 760. Od. 10, 119; διὰ νηός, to walk through the ship, Od. 12, 420; also spoken of birds: to move about, ὑπ' αὐγὰς Ἡελίοιο, Od. 2, 181.

*φοιτίζω, poet. = φοιτάω, h. 25, 8.

φολκός, ὁ, 2, 217:† epith. of Thersites, according to the old Gramm. squinting, in deriv. from φάεα and ἕλκειν; hence φάολκος, φολκός. More correct, if we may judge from the connexion, is the signif. given by Buttm., Lex. p. 541; bandy-legged (valgus), since the poet. commences the description with the feet. He derives it from ἕλκω, prop. ὁλκός and with the digamma φολκός, as φοῖτος and οἶτος.

φονεύς, ἦος, ὁ (φονεύω), a slayer, a murderer, κασιγνήτοιο φονῆος; Wolf elsewhere φόνοιο, cf. κασίγνητος, 9, 632. 18, 335. Od. 24, 434.

φονή, ἡ (ΦΕΝΩ), slaughter, homicide, murder, only plur. dat. φονῇσι, *10, 521. 15, 633 (the Gramm., see Ven. Schol., explain it in part: a place of slaughter; this is contradicted by Heyne, it being only a form of φόνος)

φόνος, ὁ (ΦΕΝΩ), 1) slaughter, homicide, in connexion with Κήρ, 2, 352. Od. 4, 273; hence, bloodshed, massacre, promiscuous slaughter, in connexion with πάντες, Il. 10, 298; plur. 11, 612. Od. 22,

376. 2) Poet. it stands, a) for the instrument of slaughter, spoken of the spear, 16, 144. 19, 391; and for the cause, Od. 21, 24. b) For blood shed in slaughter, gore, κεῖσθαι ἐν φόνῳ, Il. 24, 610; like φόνος αἵματος, bloody slaughter 16, 162.

φοξός, ή, όν, 2, 219.† φοξὸς ἔην κεφαλήν, having a conical head, according to the Gramm., l. q. ὀξυκέφαλος. The last deriv. is from ὀξύς with the digamma; according to Buttm., Lex. p. 536, with Etym. Mag. from φώγειν, to dry, prop. φωξός, that which is warped by the fire.

Φόρβας, αντος, ὁ, 1) king of the island Lesbos, father of Diomede, 9, 665. 2) The father of Ilioneus, a Trojan, 14, 490. 3) Son of Triopas, father of Pellen, h. Ap. 211. Paus. 7, 26.

φορβή, ἡ (φέρβω), pasturage, food, nourishment, *5, 202. 11, 562.

φορεύς, ἦος, ὁ (φέρω), a carrier in the harvest, 18, 566.†

φορέω, a form of φέρω, aor. 1 ἐφόρησα, Ep. φόρησα, pres. subj. Ep. 3 sing. φορῇσι for φορῇ, infin. optat. 3 sing. φοροίη, Od. 9, 320; pres. infin. φορῆναι, φορήμεναι for φορεῖν, prop. to bear continually or commonly; then generally, to bear, to bring, with accus., often spoken of clothes, arms, etc., Il. 4, 137. 144. 5, 149. Od. 9, 10. a) Improp. of horses, of wind, and of ships, Il. 5, 499. 8, 89. Od. 2, 390. b) Metaph. ἀγλαΐας φορέειν, to cherish ostentation or pride, Od. 17, 245.

φορήμεναι, φορῆναι, see φορέω.

Φόρκυνος λιμήν, ὁ, Phorcys-port in Ithaca, according to most critics, it lay on the eastern coast of the island, in the middle of it, Od. 13, 96. 17, 35; see Ἰθάκη.

Φόρκυς, υνος and νος, 1) son of Pontus and Gæa (Terra); by his sister Cēto he begat the Græœ and Gorgons, father of Thoosa, Od. 1, 72. 2) Son of Phænops, a Phrygian, Il. 2, 862. 17, 312, seq.

φόρμιγξ, ιγγος, ἡ, a lute, a lyre, a harp, a stringed instrument, differing from the cithara perhaps only in size, see κίθαρις. Hom. mentions, 9, 187, the cross-bar (ζυγόν), by which the two arms were connected, and Od. 21, 406, 407. the pegs by which it was tuned (κόλλοπες). He calls it γλαφυρή, Od. 23, 144. It is pre-eminently the instrument of Apollo, Il. 1, 603. 24, 63. h. Ap. 183. 505; Achilles uses it, 9, 186; and the minstrel, Od. 8, 67, seq. (According to Hesych. from φορέω: κιθάρα τοῖς ὤμοις φερομένη, the portable lute.)

φορμίζω (φόρμιγξ), to play upon the lyre or cithara, 18, 605; spoken of the κίθαρις, Od. 1, 155. 4, 18.

φορτίς, ίδος, ἡ (φόρτος), sc. νηῦς, a transport ship, a freight ship, *Od. 5, 250. 9, 323.

φόρτος, ὁ (φέρω), a load, a burden, esply a freight, cargo, *Od. 8, 163. 14, 296.

φορύνω (φύρω), prop. to stir or knead together, mly to stain, to defile, pass. Od. 22, 21.†

Φορύσσω.   427   Φρίξ.

φορύσσω = a form of φορύνω, aor. 1 φορύξας αἵματι, having stained him with blood, Od. 18. 336.†

φάως, τό, Ep. expanded from φῶς = φάος, q. v.

φάωσδε, adv. *to the light*, see φάος.

φραδής, ές, gen. έος, poet. (φράζω), *intelligent, wise, discreet*, νόος, 24, 354.†

*φραδμοσύνη, ἡ (φράδμων), *understanding, prudence, intelligence*, h. Ap. 99.

φράδμων, ον, gen. ονος, poet. (φράζω), *intelligent, sagacious, wise, skilful*. Thus Voss, according to the Schol. Ven. ὁ ἔμπειρος ; according to Eustath. ἐπιστήμων, γνωστός, *an acquaintance*, 16, 638.†

φράζω, mly poet aor. 1 ἔφρασα, Od. 11, 22.† h. Ven. 122. h. Merc. 442; Ep. aor. 2 πέφραδον and ἐπέφραδον (the last according to Thiersch, Gram. § 232. p. 406, from ἐπιφράζω), often 3 sing. πέφραδε and ἐπέφραδε, opt. πεφράδοι infin. πεφραδέειν and πεφραδέμεν, Od. 7, 49. (Of the act. Hom. never uses the pres.), mid. fut. φράσομαι, aor. 1 ἐφρασάμην (σσ), and φρασάμην (σσ), aor. pass. ἐφράσθην. Od. 19, 485. 23, 260; Ep. iterat. imperf. φραζέσκετο, h. Ap. 346. I) Act. according to Aristarch. in Apoll. Lex. always, *to indicate, to show, to cause to observe, to point out* (never prop. *to say*, although it sometimes inclines to that sense, as Od. 1, 273. cf. Lehrs de Aristarch. p. 93. Thiersch, Gram. § 232. p. 406), τί τινι, Il. 14, 335; to show any thing to any one, 14, 500; ὁδόν, Od. 1, 444. 11, 22; μῦθον πᾶσι, to lay the word before all, Od. 1, 273 : ἀοιδήν, h. Merc. 442. *b*) *to indicate*, δόμον, Od. 7, 49; σήματα, Od. 19, 250. 23, 206; *to signify, to bid*, with infin., Il. 10, 127. Od. 8, 68. II) Mid. prop. *to show any thing to oneself*, hence : 1) *to consider, to contemplate, to deliberate upon*, often with the adjuncts, θυμῷ, ἐνὶ φρεσίν, κατὰ φρένα, κατὰ θυμόν; with accus. and with a following εἰ, whether, Il. 1, 84 ; ἦ, ἤ, 9, 619 ; for the most part with ὅπως, 4, 14. 9, 680 ; with ὡς, Od. 1, 205 : φράζεσθαι, with μή following, like the Lat. *videre ne*, Il. 5, 411. 15, 163. 16, 446 ; ἀμφὶς φράζεσθαι, to be of different opinions, to be at variance, 2, 14. 2) *to devise, to project, to plan, to resolve, to machinate*, with accus. ἐσθλά, 12, 212 ; βουλήν, μῆτιν, 18, 313. 17, 634 ; or, κακά τινι, Od. 2, 367 ; ὄλεθρον, Od. 13, 373. 16, 371 ; θάνατον, Od. 3, 242 ; τινι ἠρίον, to think to prepare a monument for any one, Il. 23, 75. 3) Generally, *to observe, to perceive, to regard, to understand*, with accus. 10, 339. 15, 671. 23, 450. Od. 4, 71. 17, 161 ; also ὀφθαλμοῖσιν, Od. 24, 217; in connexion with ἰδεῖν, ἰδέσθαι and εἰσέσθαι, Od. 19, 501. 21, 222. h. Ap. 415; λαυρήν, to keep the street in the eye, Od. 22, 129. With infin. οὐ γὰρ ἔτ' ἄλλον φράζετο τοῦδέ τί μοι χαλεπώτερον εἶναι ἄεθλον, for he perceived, there is no contest more difficult than this, Od. 11, 624.

φράσσω, aor. 1 Ep. φράξα, partcp.

φράξας, aor. mid. ἐφραξάμην, Ep. φραξάμην, aor. pass. ἐφράχθην (Hom. has only the aor.), *to encompass, to enclose, to shut in*, eaply for protection, *to shelter*, σχεδίην ῥίπεσσι, a raft with osier-work, Od. 3, 256 ; ἐπάλξεις ῥινοῖσι βοῶν, to encompass the battlements with shields, so that they formed, as it were, shelter (Ernesti strangely imagines that they were, according to a later custom, real ox-hides stretched out), Il. 12, 263 ; hence pass. φραχθέντες σάκεσιν, encompassed with shields, 17, 268 ; φράσσειν δόρυ δουρί, to crowd spear upon spear, 13, 130. Mid. with reference to the subject, νῆας ἕρκεῖ, to enclose the ships with a wall, 15, 566.

φρέαρ, ατος, τό, Ep. φρεῖαρ, *a well*, φρείατα, 21, 197 ;† the prose form, h. Cer. 99.

φρεῖαρ, see φρέαρ.

φρήν, gen. φρενός, plur. φρένες, 1) in Hom. and the earliest writers, the *diaphragm, the midriff* (præcordia), which separated the heart and lungs from the remaining entrails, mly plur. 10, 10. 16, 481. 504. Od. 9, 301 ; because the most ancient Greeks regarded this as the seat of the collected spiritual life; it signifies, 2) *soul, spirit*, often like our *heart*, still closely bordering on the first signif. : θυμός, ἦτορ, κραδίη ἐνὶ φρεσίν, Il. 8, 202. 413. 16, 242. 435. *a*) Spoken of the faculty of thought, often : φρεσὶ νοεῖν, φράζεσθαι, κατὰ φρένα εἰδέναι, μετὰ φρεσὶ βάλλεσθαι, μερμηρίζειν, ἐνὶ φρεσὶ γνῶναι, θεῖναί τινί τι ἐν φρεσὶ and ἐπὶ φρεσί, to put any thing into any one's mind, 8, 2, 18. 16, 83. Od. 1, 89. φρένες ἐσθλαί, wise thoughts, an intelligent mind, Il. 17, 470 ; wise invention, spoken of female works, Od. 2, 117. 7, 111. φρένας βλάπτειν τινί, to injure a man's understanding, to infatuate him, Il. 15, 724 ; also ἐλεῖν. 16, 805 ; ἐξελέσθαι, 6, 234. *b*) Spoken of the will : *mind, resolution, will*, φρένας τρέπειν and πείθειν. Διὸς ἐτράπετο φρήν, the mind of Zeus changed, 10, 45. αεχρήσθαι φρεσὶν ἀγαθῇσιν, Od. 3, 266 ; *c*) Spoken of the feelings : *the heart, feelings*, φρεσὶ χαίρειν, κατὰ φρένα δεδοικέναι, ἄχος μιν φρένας ἀμφιβέβηκε, Od. 8, 541. 3) Generally, the principle of life, *the vital power*, vis vitalis (Voss, recollection), which the shades lacked, Il. 23, 104. Od. 10, 493; also the brutes have φρένες. Il. 4, 245. 16, 157.

φρήτρη, ἡ, Ion. for φράτρα, Ep. dat. φρήτρηφιν, a division of a people by the relationship of families, *a family, a clan, a race*, a subdivision of the φῦλον, *2, 362. 363. (According to the ancient critics, κατὰ φρήτρας, according to their localities.) Later, it was a mere political subdivision of the φύλη.

Φρίκων, ωνος, ὁ, the founder of Cyme in Æolia (Asia), Ep. 4.

φρίξ, φρικός, ἡ, prop. the roughening of a smooth surface : always in Hom.,

Φρίσσω. 428 Φυλακή.

of the sea, or of water, *the curling*, or *ruffling of the waves*, Βορέη, 23, 692. μέλαινα φρίξ, 21, 126. Od. 4, 102. οἴη Ζεφύροιο χεύατο πόντον ἔπι φρίξ, as under the breath of Zephyrus the ruffling-wave spreads itself over the sea, Il. 7, 63. [Cf. Catull. *placidum mare* .. Horrificans *Zephyrus*, 52, 286.]

φρίσσω (akin to ῥίγος), aor. 1 ἔφριξα, perf. πέφρικα, 1) *to be rough* and *uneven, to be stiff, to bristle* (*hurrere*), τινί, with any thing, or τί, in any thing; generally, spoken of the motion of the surface of an agitated body, thus of a corn-field, φρίσσουσιν ἄσταυρα, the cornfields bristle up [*the spiry grain erect Bristles the field*, Cp.], 23, 599; spoken of warlike troops: μάχη ἔφριξεν ἐγχείῃσιν, 13, 339; ἔγχεσι καὶ σάκεσι, 4, 282. 7, 62. *b*) With accus. as if trans. in the pres. and aor. 1, spoken of a raging boar; νῶτον, to bristle on the back [*to arch his bristly spine*, Cp.], 13, 473; λοφίην, Od. 19, 446. 2) Metaph. *to shiver* from cold; *to shudder, to tremble at, to fear*, τινά, Il. 11, 383. 24, 775.

φρονέω (φρήν), only in the pres. and imperf.; it indicates the various operations of the mind, esply of the faculties of thought and desire; hence 1) *to think*, i. e. to have understanding, intelligence, *to be wise, intelligent, discreet*, in Hom. rarely; opposed to μάχεσθαι. 6, 79; absol. φρονέων, intelligent, 23, 343, and v. 305 (according to Wolf, εἰς ἀγαθὰ φρονέων, considerate in regard to good things); poet. = ζῆν. ἐμὲ ἔτι φρονέοντ' ἐλέησον, while I yet have sense, 22, 59. *b*) With accus. *to comprehend, to understand*, Od. 16, 136. 17, 193. 281. 2) *to think*, i. e. to have an opinion or sentiment, *to mean, to have an opinion. to think, to will*, often with ἀνὰ θυμόν, ἐνὶ θυμῷ, ἐνὶ φρεσί. *a*) With infin., Il. 9, 608. 17, 286; *to be of opinion, to hope*, with accus. and infin. 3, 98. *b*) τί τινι, to have any thing in mind in regard to any one; ἀγαθά τινι, to be well disposed toward any one, also to have a noble soul, 6, 162; φίλα, to cherish friendly sentiments, 4, 219. 15, 116. Od. 6, 313; κακά τινι, to cherish evil thoughts against any one, Il. 10, 486. 22, 264; ἁλοά, 16, 701; ἀταλά, to have a child-like, joyous disposition, 18, 567; πυκά, to be intelligent, wise, 14, 217. Od. 9, 445; ἴσον τινι, to be like minded, to have the same mind with any one, Il. 15, 50. τὰ φρ., to think that, often, 4, 361. τὰ ἃ φρονέων, sua cogitans, following his own opinion, 8, 430; μέγα, to be proud, 8, 553. *c*) With adv. εὖ φρονεῖν τινι, to be well disposed to any one, in opposition to κακῶς, Od. 18, 168; ἀμφίς, to think differently, Il. 13, 345; ἄλλῃ, h. Ap. 469; ἰθύς, to think straight on, 12, 124. 13, 135. (According to Voss, ἰθύς is to be construed with ἔχε, cf. ἰθύς.) *d*) Poet. spoken of animals: μέγα φρονεῖν, to be spirited, proud, 11, 325. 16, 758. 22, 264.

*Φρόνιος, ὁ (the observer), father of Noëmôn, Od. 2, 386. 4, 630.

φρόνις, ιος, ἡ=φρόνησιν, 1) *prudence, intelligence*, Od. 3, 244. 2) *knowledge, information*, κατὰ δὲ φρόνιν ἤγαγε πολλήν, he brought back much information (viz. from Troy, into which he had gone by stealth), *Od. 4, 258.

Φρόντις, ιδος, ἡ, wife of Panthous, 17, 40.
Φρόντις, ιος, ὁ (appell. φροντίς), son of Onêtôr, pilot of Menelaus, Od. 3, 279, seq
Φρύγες, ων, οἱ, sing. Φρύξ, νγός, ὁ. *Phrygian;* they resided, in the time of Homer, on the river Sangarius in Asia Minor, 2, 862. 3, 185. According to Hdt. 7, 73, they had emigrated from Thrace.

Φρυγίη, ἡ, *Phrygia*, a country in Asia Minor; it embraced in part a district on the Hellespont (Φρυγίη καθύπερθε, 24, 545), and in part a portion of the later Bithynia, on the river Sangarius, and of the greater Phrygia, 3, 184. 16, 719. 16. 291. It was subsequently divided into Great Phrygia, a country in the interior of Asia Minor, and Lesser Phrygia, a district on the Hellespont.

*φρύγω, fut. ξω, aor. 1 pass. ἐφρύχθην, *to dry, to bake*, spoken of potters' vessels: *to burn*, Ep. 14, 4.

φῦ, Ep. for ἔφυ, see φύω.

φύγαδε, adv. (φυγή), *into flight, in flight*, as if from ΦΥΗ, like οἴκαδε, 8, 157. 11, 446. 16, 697.

φυγή, ἡ (φεύγω), *flight*, *Od. 10, 117. 22, 306; in the Il. φύζα, except φυγάδε.

φυγοπτόλεμος, ον, Ep. for φυγοπόλεμος (πόλεμος), *flying war, cowardly*, Od. 14, 213.†

φύζα, ἡ. poet. for φυγή (Wolf, less correctly, φύζα), *flight*, 9, 2 [see close]. φύζαν ἐνορνύναι, 15, 62; ἐμβάλλειν, Od. 14, 269. (According to Aristarch. in Apoll Lex., φύζα and φόβος are distinguished by the circumstance that the former has the implied notion of cowardice.) [According to Ameis, afi. Aristarch., φύζα in Il. 9, 2, means *terrour, panic* [ἐκπληξις]: see φόβος.]

φυζανικός, ή, όν, poet. (φύζα), *fugitive, timorous*, ἔλαφος, 15, 102.†

ΦΥΖΑΩ or ΦΥΖΩ, from which πεφυζότες, q. v.

φυή, ἡ (φύω), *the growth, the shape, the form of the body, the appearance*, connected with δέμας, 1, 115. Od. 5, 212; μέγεθος, Il. 2, 58; εἶδος, 22, 370. Od. 6, 16.

φυκιόεις, εσσα, εν (φύκιον), *abounding in sea-grass* or *sea-weed*, θίς, 23, 693.†

φῦκος, εος, τό, *sea-weed, sea-grass* (*fucus*), 9, 7.†

φυκτός, ή, όν, verb adj. (φεύγω), prop. *fled*; then, *that may be fled*. οὐκέτι φυκτὰ πέλονται, it is no longer to be escaped, 16, 128. Od. 8, 299. 14, 489.

[φυλαδόν, see καταφυλαδόν, by some separated.]

φυλακή, ἡ (φυλάσσω), *a watch, a guard*. 1) As an action, φυλακὰς ἔχειν, 9, 1; esply the night watch, 7, 371. 16, 299.

429 Φύω.

0, 416. δ) Spoken town in Thessaly hrys, belonging to Ίλαus, 2, 695. Od.

n of Phylacus = of φύλαξ, accus. ding to Aristarch.

Ion and Diomêdê, inder of the town , 705. Od. 15, 231. l, 35.
φύλαξ, *9, 66. 80. ur. φυλακτῆρες. άσσω), dat. plur. 3ich, a guard, in 1e watchers or sen- κες ἄνδρες. *9, 477. ther of Polymêlê Ephyra in Thes-

pres. φυλασσόμε- t. φύλαξα, subj. 1 shortened vowel, α, 23, 343; aor. 1 ι, h. Ap. 544. 1) keep watch, to be 20, 53; περὶ μή- ρα φυλάσσειν, to ight, Od. 5, 466; agers, Il. 10, 312. ətch, to guard, to h accus. στράτον, τινά, 5, 809. Od. rve the wine, Od. observe, to watch νόστον, to watch 251; metaph. to ων, 16, 30; ὅρκια, Mid. to watch for 10, 188: φρεσί, h. ne's guard, to take ναι, to be careful,

f Phyleus=Meges,

δος, ὁ, 10, 110, son of Meges of Elis. I not give to Hera- aning the stables, rbiter, decided in 'or this reason, he ther from Elis and 128. 23, 637.
olive-tree, Apoll. to others lentiscus e, Linn., Od. 5,

leaf, always in the 146. 21, 464. Od.

λομέδουσα.
a stock, a race, a sense, φύλον θεῶν, plur. spoken of a to the same race, γυναικῶν, 9, 130.

14, 361. 15, 54. Od. 3, 282; spoken of Insects: φῦλα, μυίας, Il. 19, 30. 2) In a stricter sense, a nation, a people, Πε- λασγῶν, 2, 480; Γιγάντων, Od.7, 206. 3) In the strictest sense, a tribe, a clan, a family, κατὰ φῦλα, Il. 2, 362; φῦλον Ἑλένης, Od. 14, 68.

φύλοπις, ιδος, ἡ, Ep. accus. φυλόπιδα, Od. 11, 364,† and φύλοπιν, 1) the battle- cry, the tumult of battle, a battle, also φύλοπις πολέμοιο, 13, 635. Od. 11, 314; elsewhere πόλεμός τε καὶ φύλοπις, Il. 4, 379. 2) an army equipped for battle, 4, 65. (According to the Gramm. from φῦλον and ὄψ, cry.)

Φυλώ, οῦς, ἡ, a handmaid of Helen, Od. 4, 125. 133.

φύξηλις, ιος, ὁ, ἡ, poet. (φύξις), fugitive, fearful, cowardly, 17, 143.†

φύξιμος, ον, poet. (φύξις), to which one may fly, τὸ φύξιμον, an asylum, a place of refuge, Od. 5, 359.†

φύξις, ιος, ἡ, poet. form for φυγή, flight, *10, 311. 398. 447.

φύρω, fut. φύρσω, perf. pass. πέφυρμαι, to mingle together, to stir; easly to mingle with a fluid, hence to moisten, to defile, τί τινι, any thing with any thing, δάκρυ- σιν αἵματα, 24, 162; also τί τινος; στή- θος αἵματος, Od. 18, 21; and pass. πεφυρ- μένος αἵματι, Od. 9, 397; δάκρυσι, Od. 17, 103. 18, 173.

φῦσα, ἡ (φύω), prop. wind, breath; hence a bellows, *18, 372. 409. 412. 468. 470.

φυσάω (φῦσα), only in the pres. and imperf. to blow, spoken of the bellows, 18, 470; of the wind, *23, 218.

φυσιάω (φυσάω), to blow vehemently, to pant, to puff, spoken of steeds, only partcp. φυσιόωντες, Ep. for φυσιῶντες, *4, 227. 16, 506.

*Φυσίγναθος, ου (γνάθος), Cheek-blower, Puff-cheek, a frog's name, Batr. 17.

φυσίζοος, ον, poet.(ζωή), life-producing, life-giving or supporting, γαῖα, 3, 243. Od. 11, 301.

φύσις, ιος, ἡ, prop. production, mly nature, i. e. the natural quality of a thing, φάρμακον, Od. 10, 303.† Batr. 32.

φυταλιή, ἡ (φυτόν), a plantation, a place where trees and grapes are planted, in distinction from arable land, *6, 195. 12, 314. 20, 185.

φυτεύω (φυτόν), aor. 1 ἐφύτευσα, to plant, prop. spoken of plants, πτελέας, δένδρεα, 6, 419. Od. 9, 108. 18, 359. 2) Metaph. to produce, to procure, to pre- pare, κακόν, πῆμά τινι, Il. 15, 134. Od. 4, 668; φόνον καὶ Κῆρά τινι, Od. 2, 165 κακά τινι, Od. 5, 340.

φυτόν, τό (φύω), a plant, a tree, 14, 123. Od. 9, 106; and elsewhere.

φύω, fut. φύσω, aor. 1 ἔφυσα, aor. 2 ἔφυν, 3 sing. φῦ for ἔφυ, and 3 plur. ἔφυν, perf. πέφυκα, 3 plur. πεφύασι, Od. 7, 128; partcp. fem. πεφυυῖα, Il. 14, 288; πε- φυῶτας for πεφυκότας, Od. 5, 477; plu- perf. πεφύκειν. 1) Trans.: pres. (once intrans., Il. 6, 149), fut. and aor. 1. to

*Φώκαια. 430 Χαίρω.

beget to produce, to let grow, to put forth, with accus. φύλλα, ποιήν, 1, 235. 6, 148. 14, 347. Od. 7, 119; τρίχας, to make the hair (or bristles) grow, Od. 10, 393; hence also, ό φύσας, the begetter, Batr. 23; φύσαί τινα δόλον, h. Cer. 8. 2) Intrans.: mid. together with aor. 2 and perf. to be produced, to grow, to spring, primar. spoken of plants, Od. 9, 109; once pres. act. intrans. ἀνδρῶν γενεή ἡ μέν φύει (nascitur), 11. 6, 149; esply perf. and pluperf. 4, 483. 484. 14, 288. cf. Od. 5. 63 7, 114. 128; also κέρα πεφύκει. Il. 4, 109; the aor. 2 only Od. 5, 481. 23, 190; metaph. often in the phrases, ἐν δ' ἄρα οἱ φῦ χειρί, and ἐν χείρεσσι φύοντο; ὀδάξ ἐν χείλεσσι φύντες, see ἐμφύω.

*Φώκαια, ἡ, a town in Ionia (Asia), on the river Hermus, famed for traffic and navigation, now in ruins, Fokia, h. Ap. 35.

Φωκεῖς, οἱ, sing. Φωκεύς, ῆος, ὁ, the Phocians, inhabitants of the country Phocis in Hellas, 2, 517. 15, 516.

φώκη, ἡ, a seal, a sea-calf, *Od. 4, 436. 448. h. Ap. 77.

φωνέω (φωνή), aor. 1 ἐφώνησα, Ep. φώνησα, to utter or sound a tone, spoken esply of men; to speak, to discourse, only [according to Ameis, always] intrans. 1, 333; and often connected with other similar words, ἔπος φάτο φώνησέν τε, Od. 4, 370; or ἀμείβετο, Od. 7, 298; καί μιν φωνήσας ἔπεα προσηύδα, Il. 1, 201; and προσέφη, 14, 41. (The accus. belong to the other verb.) 2) to cause to sound, to raise, ὄπα, 2, 182. 10, 512. Od. 24, 535.

φωνή, ἡ (φάω), a sound, a tone, mly spoken of men, a voice, speech, discourse, esply a loud voice, a cry, 14, 400. 15, 686. b) Of animals, Od. 10, 239. 12, 86, 396; the song of the nightingale, Od. 19, 521.

*φωρή, ἡ (φώρ), theft, h. Merc. 136.

*φώρης, ου, ὁ, poet. for φώρ, a thief, h. Merc. 385.

φωριαμός, ὁ (φέρω), a chest, a coffer, a box, for keeping clothes, 24, 228. Od. 15, 104.

φώς, gen. φωτός, ὁ, poet. for ἀνήρ, plur. φῶτες, a man, 2, 164; παλαιός, 14, 136; δέκτης, Od. 4, 247; κακός, Od. 6, 186; also in opposit. to the gods, Il. 17, 98. b) Often, a brave man, a hero, 4, 194. 5, 572. Od. 21, 26. (Prob. from ΦΑΩ, φημί, one who speaks.)

X.

X, the twenty-second letter of the Greek alphabet, hence the sign of the twenty-second rhapsody.

Χάα, see Φειά.

χάδε, χαδέειν, see χανδάνω.

χάζομαι, depon. mid. fut. χάσομαι, Ep. σσ, aor. ἐχασάμην. Ep. χασσάμην. Ep. aor. 2 with redupiic. κεκάδοντο for κεχά-δοντο. also from the act. form χάζω, Ep. aor. 2 κέκαδον. and fut. κεκαδήσω, 1 = retreat, to retire, to yield, to go back. w withdraw (never in the Od.), with ἀπ ὀπίσω, 3, 32. 5, 702; with gen. of the thing, κελεύθου, πυλάων, 11, 504. 12, 17; νεκροῦ, 17, 357; also with prep. ἐκ βελέων without, beyond, the cast of weapons, 16. 122; ὑπ' ἔγχεος, to retire from the spear. 13, 153; often ἑτάρων εἰς ἔθνος, 3, 32: οὐδὲ δὴν χάζετο φωτός, and not long did the stone remain removed from the man, i. e. it smote him quickly, 16, 736. (V., nor slowly flew it to the man.) In this passage, according to Köppen, Voss and Spitzner, the stone is the subject; according to Heyne, but by a forced construction, Patroclus. 2) Generally, to cease. to remove, to rest, with gen. μάχης, 15, 426. μίνυνθα χάζετο δουρός, he rested little from the spear, i. e. he fought continually, 11, 539; only Il. 3) The Ep. aor. 2 κέκαδον and the fut. κεκαδήσω have a trans. signif, prop. to cause one to retreat from a thing, to deprive one of a thing, τινὰ θυμοῦ καὶ ψυχῆς, 11, 334 Od. 21, 153. 170 (Passow refers it to κήδω); cf. Buttm., p. 307.

χάζω, see χάζομαι.

χαίνω or χάσκω (ΧΑΩ), in Hom. only aor. 2 ἔχανον, h. Cer. 16; optat. χάνοι and partcp. χανών, of the perf. only the partcp. accus. κεχηνότα, 1) to yawn, to gape, to open. h. Cer. 16. τότε μοι χάνοι χθών, then may the earth yawn for me, i. e. engulf me, 4, 182. 6, 281. 8, 150. 2) Esply to open the mouth wide, to gasp, spoken of men and animals, 16, 350. 18. 20, 168; hence πρὸς κῦμα. to gape at the wave, i. e. to drink it, Od. 12, 350.

χαίρω, fut. χαιρήσω, 20, 363; aor. ἐχάρην, Ep. χάρην, optat. χαρείη, 6, 481; partcp. χαρέντες, 10, 451; perf. κεχάρηκα, only in the Ep. partcp. κεχαρηώς, i. 312; perf. mid. κεχάρημαι, h. 7, 10. also the Ep. forms fut. κεχαρήσω, infin. κεχαρησέμεν and κεχαρήσομαι, aor. I mid. χήρατο, 14, 270; aor. 2 with replicat. κεχάροντο, optat. κεχάροιτο and κεχαροίατο, and iterat. imperf. χαίρεσκε. 1) to rejoice, to be cheerful, gay, often with θυμῷ, ἐν θυμῷ, φρεσίν and φρένα. also χαίρει μοι ἦτορ, 23, 347; but νῷ χαίρειν, to rejoice at heart, Od. 8, 78 2) With dat. to rejoice at any thing, to delight oneself in, to be pleased at, νίκῃ. ὄρνιθι, φήμῃ, Il. 7, 312. 10, 277. Od. 2, 35; with accus. χαίρει δέ μιν (ἀλωῇ) ὅστις ἐθείρῃ, he rejoice· in it who cultivates it, according to Wolf and Passow (V. joyfully the cultivator beholds it), Il. 21, 347. (Heyne refers μιν to ἀνέρι, but, cf. 9, 77, and γηθέω.) 3) With partcp. instead of infin. χαίρω ἀκούων, I rejoice to hear, 19, 185.—18, 259. Od. 14, 377. Dat. and partcp. for accus. and infin., Il. 7, 54. Od. 19, 463. The partcp. with its prop. signif., Il. 11, 73. Od. 3, 76. 12, 380. A peculiar use is - a) The fut. with the negat. οὐ χαιρήσεις, thou

Χαίτη. **Χαλκοβαρής.**

wilt not rejoice, i. e. thou wilt rue it, Il. 20, 363. Od. 2, 249. *b*) The imperat. χαίρε is a common formula of greeting: *hail to thee, health to thee, joy to thee,* at meeting, Il. 9, 107. Od. 1, 123; at departure, *farewell,* Od. 5, 205. 13, 59; to the gods, χαίρε ἀοιδῇ, praise be to thee in the song, h. 8, 7.

χαίτη, ἡ (χάω), *the dishevelled hair, the streaming hair, the hair,* spoken of gods and men, 10, 15. 14, 175. Od. 4, 150; spoken of horses, *the mane,* Il. 6, 509.

χάλαζα, ἡ (χαλάω), *hail, hail-stones,* •10, 6. 15, 170.

χαλάω (χάω), aor. ἐχάλασα, Ep. σσ, *to unbend, to relax,* βιόν, τόξα, h. Ap. 6. h. 27, 12.

χαλεπαίνω (χαλεπός), aor. ἐχαλέπηνα, infin. χαλεπῆναι, in Hom. only intrans., prop. *to be severe, ingravescere, to roar* [*to rave,* Cp.], spoken of storms, 14, 344. Od. 5, 485; for the most part of gods and men, *to be angry, to be displeased, to rage, to chide,* esply *to treat in a severe* or *hostile manner* ; absol., Il. 14, 256. Od. 16, 72; ὅτε ἄνδρεσσι κοτεσσάμενος χαλεπήνῃ, when he rages, angry with men, Il. 16, 386. Od. 5, 147. 19, 83. οὔτε τί μοι πᾶς δῆμος ἀπεχθόμενος χαλεπαίνει (μοί belongs to ἀπεχθόμενος), the whole people is not angry, being odious to me, i. e. because I hate them, Od. 16, 114. cf. 10, 75. According to the critics ἀπεχθέσθαι is here transitive (V. prefers ἀπεχθομένῳ. and translates: nor has the whole people risen against me hated); ἐπί τινι, any thing, Od. 18, 415. 20, 323. [Fäsi says: ἀπεχθόμενος, having become an enemy, then itself hating, ἐχθαίρων, cf. v. 96.]

χαλεπός, ή, όν, comp. χαλεπώτερος, *hard, difficult,* i. e. 1) connected with pains and danger in the execution, *troublesome, dangerous,* τινί, to any one, 1, 546. Often in the neut. with infin. χαλεπόν τοι, παισίν ἐριζέμεναι, 21, 184. Od. 4, 651; with accus. and infin., Il. 16. 620. Od. 20, 313; χαλεπὸν γάρ, ἐπιστάμενόν περ ἐόντα, supply from the preceding, ὑββάλλειν τινά, it is always vexatious, although one very experienced does it, Il. 19, 80. 2) making trouble and danger, *burdensome, oppressive, hard, cruel. grievous, κεραυνός, θύελλα, γῆρας, δεσμός, ἄλγος, ἔπος,* hard, threatening speech or discourse, 2, 245. χαλεπή φῆμις, an injurious report, Od. 14, 239. *b*) Spoken of persons: *severe, violent, angry, displeased,* Od. 1, 198; τινί, with any one, Od. 17, 388. χαλεποὶ θεοὶ ἐναργεῖς φαίνεσθαι, it is dangerous, when the gods appear visibly, Il. 20, 131. h. Cer. 111.

χαλέπτω, poet.=χαλεπαίνω, *to oppress, to press, to persecute,* τινά, Od. 4. 433.†

χαλεπῶς, adv. *in a severe, harsh,* or *difficult manner,* •7, 424. 20, 186.

χαλινός, ὁ (χαλάω), *a bridle, a check, a rein,* mly plur. 19, 393 †

χαλιφρονέω (χαλίφρων), *to be frivolous,* *simple, foolish,* in opposition to σαόφρων, Od 23, 13.†

χαλιφροσύνη, ή. *frivolity, simplicity, folly,* plur. Od. 16, 310.†

χαλίφρων, ον (χαλάω, φρήν), prop. *to be of a slack, negligent mind,* hence *light-minded, frivolous, simple, foolish,* connected with νήπιος, •Od. 4, 371. 19, 530.

χάλκειος, η, ον, poet. for χάλκεος, 3, 380 4, 461, and often.

χαλκεοθώρηξ, ηκος, ὁ, ἡ, poet. (θώρηξ), *having a brazen cuirass,* *1, 448. 8, 62.

χάλκεος, η, ον, poet. (χαλκός). χάλκειος, η, ον, and the Ion. form χαλκήϊος, only Od. 3, 433. 18, 328 (ὀψ χάλκεος, of two endings, Il. 18, 222 †), 1) *of copper* or rather *of bronze*: usually rendered *brazen* [see χαλκός], often spoken of arms: θώρηξ, χιτών, ἔγχος, ἔντεα; also οὐδός, ἄξων, κύκλοι, ὅπλα, Od. 3, 433; also, covered with brass, σάκος, or coming from brass, χαλκείη αὐγή, *the splendour of brass,* Il. 13, 341. 2) Metaph. *as if of brass,* i. e. *hard, firm, immoveable, strong,* ἦτορ, 2, 490. χάλκεος Ἄρης, *imperishable Ares,* 5, 704; or having a brazen cuirass: ὄψ, a strong voice, 18, 222; ὕπνος, the sleep of death, 11. 241. Also some explain, οὐρανὸς χάλκεος, metaph.; others, however, with Voss, take it literally, 17, 425. cf. Völcker, Hom. Geog., p. 5.

χαλκεόφωνος, ον (φωνή), *having a brazen voice, brass-throated,* epith. of Stentor, 5, 785.†

χαλκεύς, ῆος, ὁ (χαλκός), prop. *an artist in brass, a copper-smith,* connected with ἀνήρ. 4, 167. 216. 15, 309; generally, *a worker in metal,* i. q. χρυσοχόος, Od. 3, 432 ; *an iron-smith,* Od. 9, 391.

χαλκεύω (χαλκεύς), *to work in brass* or *metal,* τί, 18, 400.†

χαλκεών, ῶνος, ὁ, Ep. for χαλκεῖον, *a smith's furge, a smith's shop,* Od. 8, 273.†

χαλκήϊος, η, ον, Ion. for χάλκειος, δόμος = χαλκεών, *a smith's dwelling,* Od. 18, 328; ὅπλα, Od. 3, 433; see χάλκεος. *Od.

χαλκήρης, ες. gen. εος (ἄρω), *joined* or *furnished with brass, brass-covered, brazen,* epith. of various weapons, 3, 316. 13, 714. Od. 1, 262.

χαλκίς, ίδος, ἡ, an unknown bird of prey. According to 14, 291,† it is called χαλκίς, in the language of the gods, and amongst men κύμινδις, q. v.

Χαλκίς. ἴδος, ἡ. 1) the chief town of the island Eubœa, subsequently connected with the mainland by a bridge; an important commercial town, now *Egripo,* 2, 537. 2) a town in Ætolia, at the mouth of the Evēnus, at the foot of Mount Chalcis, now *Galata,* 2, 640; in Strab. also Ὑποχαλκίς. 3) a place in Elis, not far from the fountain Krunol h. Ap. 425; cf. Strab. VIII. p. 350. 4 a small river in southern Elis, near th village of the same name, Od. 15, 295.

χαλκοβαρής, ές, gen. έος, poet. (βαρύς)

χαλκοβαρύς.

heavy with brass, brazen, ίός, 15, 465. Od. 21, 423.

χαλκοβάρυς, εια, ν = χαλκοβαρής, of this Hom. uses the fem. χαλκοβάρεια, στεφάνη, 11, 96; μελίη, 22, 328. Od. 22, 259. 276.

χαλκοβατής, ές, gen. έος, poet. (βαίνω), going upon brass; hence, founded or standing upon brass, brazen, mly an epith. of the dwelling of Zeus, 1, 426. Od. 8, 321; and of Alcinous, Od. 13, 4. It has also been explained, having a brazen floor, cf. Od. 7, 83.

χαλκογλώχιν, ινος, ό, ή (γλωχίν), brasspointed, Cp. (brazen-armed, V.), μελίη, 22, 255.†

χαλκοκνημίς, ίδος, ό, ή (κνημίς), having brazen greaves; brass-greaved (brassbooted, V.), epith. of the Greeks, 7, 41.†

χαλκοκορυστής. οῦ, ὁ (κορύσσω), voc. **χαλκοκορυστά**, having brazen armour, armed with brass (brazen-mailed, V.; brazen-armed, Cp.), epith. of heroes, *5, 699; and of Ares, h. 7, 4.

χαλκοπάρῃος, ον, Ep. for χαλκοπάρειος (παρειά), having brazen cheeks (brazencheeked, V.), epith. of the helmet, 12, 183. Od. 24, 523.

χαλκόπους, ό, ή, neut. πουν, gen. ποδος (πούς), brazen-footed, having brazen hoofs (brazen-hoofed, V.), epith. of horses, *8, 11. 13. 23.

χαλκός, ὁ. Ep. gen. χαλκόφιν. 1) brass, metal, esply copper. Copper, compounded with zinc, tin, and lead, is called brass [not our brass, but rather bronze], which was probably the earliest metal used. As edged instruments of copper are often mentioned by the poet, it has been supposed that the word stands poetically for iron. But Hom. carefully distinguishes iron and brass, cf. 4, 510. 5, 723. 11, 133; hence, with more probability, it may be said that the ancients possessed an art of hardening brass unknown to us, cf Köpke, Kriegsw. der Gr. p. 55. seq. It is called χαλκός έρυθρός, 9, 365; it is mentioned with iron, 6, 48; as a purchase-price, 7, 473. 2) all furniture, weapons, equipments, made of brass [or bronze], 1, 236. 5, 75.

χαλκότυπος, ον (τύπτω), smitten with a brazen weapon, ώτειλαί, 19, 25.†

χαλκοχίτων, ωνος, ὁ (χιτών), having a brazen cuirass, epith. of heroes, 1, 371. 2, 47. Od. 1, 286.

Χαλκωδοντιάδης, ου, son of Chalcōdōn = Elephēnōr, 2, 541.

Χαλκώδων, οντος, ὁ (having brazen teeth, ὀδούς), king of the Abantes, in Euboea, father of Elephēnōr, who was slain in a battle with Amphitryon, 2, 541. 4, 464.

Χάλκων, ωνος, ό, a Myrmidon, father of Bathycles, 16, 595. seq.

χαμάδις, adv. (χαμαί), poet. for χαμάζε, upon the earth, to the ground, 3, 300. 6, 147. Od. 4, 114.

χαμάζε, adv. (χαμαί), upon the earth,

to the earth, άλλεσθαι, 3, 29. 4, 419. Od. 16, 191.

χαμαί, adv. 1) upon the earth, on the ground, έρχεσθαι, 5, 442. Od. 7, 160. 2) to the earth, πίπτειν, 11. 4, 482. Od. 1, 490; and often (from an obsol. word χαμός, χαμή).

χαμαιγενής, ές (γένος), produced upon or from the earth, earth-born, h. Ven. 106. Cer. 353.

χαμαιευνάς, άδος, ή. fem. of χαμαιεύνης; χαμ. σύες, *Od. 10, 243. 14, 15. (In both places αι is used as short.)

χαμαιεύνης, ου, ό (εὐνή), lying upon the ground, sleeping upon the earth, epith. of the Selli, 16, 235.†

χανδάνω, poet. (χάω), fut. χείσομαι, aor. έχαδον, Ep. infin. aor. χαδέειν for χαδείν, perf. κέχανδα, with pres. signif., partcp. κεχανδώς, 3 pluperf. κεχάνδει, to embrace, to encompass, to hold, to contain, with accus. spoken of vessels, ἐξ μέτρα, 23, 742; λέβης τέσσαρα μέτρα κεχανδώς, 23, 268; ὡς αἱ χείρες ἐχάνδανον. Od. 17, 344; of the coast, νῆες, Π. 14, 34; of the threshold, Od. 18, 17; improp. ἤύσεν, ὅσον κεφαλή χάδε φωτός. be cried as much as the head of the man held, i. e. as loud as he could, Il. 11, 462. Ἥρη οὐκ ἔχαδε στῆθος χόλον, the breast of Hērē did not contain her anger, i. e. she could not restrain it, 4, 24 (old reading: Ἥρῃ); also οὐκέτι μοι στόμα χείσεται, my mouth will not be able, h. Ven. 253.

χανδόν, adv. (χαίνω), yawning, opening the mouth, metaph. greedy, ἐλαῖν οἶνον. Od. 21, 294.†

χάνος, see χαίνω.

χαράδρη, ή (χαράσσω), a cleft, a chasm or gorge in the earth, esply formed by rushing water, κοιλή, 4, 459; hence also the stream itself, a torrent, a rapid stream, *16, 390.

χαρείη, χάρη, see χαίρω.

χαριδώτης, ου, ό, poet. (δίδωμι), the giver of joy, epith. of Hermēs, h. 17, 2.

χαρίεις, εσσα, εν (χάρις), superl. χαριέστατος, η, ον, charming, sweet, beautiful, pleasing, spoken of parts of the human body, 16, 798. 18, 24. 22, 403; of clothes, 5, 905. Od. 5, 211; generally, agreeable, lovely, joyous, dear; of things. δώρα, έργα, άοιδή, άμοιβή, grateful requital [see άμοιβή], Od. 3, 58; χαριεστάτη ήβη, most lovely youth, Od.10, 279. The neut. plur. as adv. χαρίεντα, gratefully, 1, 39; and as subst., Od. 8, 167.

χαρίζομαι, depon. mid. (χάρις), aor. 1 έχαρισάμην, perf. pass. κεχάρισμαι, often partcp. 1) to show something agreeable to any one, to show a favour, to be agreeable, to gratify, τινί, often in the partcp. 5, 71. 11, 23. Od. 8, 538; esply to gratify a deity by sacrifice, Od. 1, 61; with double dat. τινι ψεύδεσι, to please one with lies, Od. 14, 387. 2) With accus. of the thing, to give freely, to distribute, to bestow, δώρα, Od. 24, 283; άπουρά τω, Il. 6, 49. 11, 139; and with gen. of the

Χάρις. 433 Χεῖμα.

thing, *to impart freely, to give a share of*, ἀλλοτρίων, Od. 17, 452; esply, often, παρεόντων, Od. 1, 140. 4, 56; absol., Od. 13, 15 ; cf. προικός. 3) In the perf. and pluperf. pass. *to be agreeable, lovely, pleasing, grateful*, with dat θυμῷ, Od. 6, 23; often partcp., Il. 5, 243; κεχαρισμένος ἦλθεν, he came desired, or welcome, Od. 2, 54 ; κεχαρισμένα θεῖναί τινι, to show kindness to any one ; to gratify him much (Cp.), 24, 661 ; or εἰδέναι, Od. 8, 584.

χάρις, ιτος, ἡ (χαίρω), acc. χάριν, 1) *grace, fascination, loveliness, agreeableness, beauty*, esply spoken of persons, χάριν κατέχευαί τινι, Od. 2, 12. 6, 235. 8, 19 ; also χάριτες, charms, Od. 6, 237. b) Spoken sometimes of things, of an earring, Il. 14, 183. Od. 18, 298 ; of words, Od. 18, 175 ; ἔργοισιν χάριν καὶ κῦδος ὀπάζειν, Od. 15, 320. 2) *favour, kindness*. a) In sentiment: *benevolence, good-will, affection*, esply *thanks, gratitude*, obligation for favour received, χάριν ἀρέσθαι τινί, to receive thanks from any one, Il. 4, 95; χάρις τινός, thanks for any thing, Od. 4, 695. 22, 319; also with infin. οὔ τις χάρις ἦεν μάρνασθαι, one had (or I had) no thanks for fighting, Il. 9, 316. 17, 147; δοῦναι χάριν ἀντί τινος, to give thanks for any thing, to make requital for any thing, 23, 650; χάριν εἰδέναι τινί, to feel gratitude, 14, 235. b) Of actions : *kindness, beneficence, favour ;* often χάριν φέρειν τινί, to show favour to any one, 9, 613. 5, 211. 874. Od. 5, 307 ; esply also, *the pleasures of love*, Il. 11, 243 ; cf. ΕΙΛΩ A. 3) Phrases : accus. χάριν, with gen. *for one's sake, for one's pleasure*, 15, 744. Batr. 184.

Χάρις, ιτος, ἡ, prop. n., more frequently plur., αἱ Χάριτες, dat. Ep. Χαρίτεσσιν. 1) Hom. mentions a *Charis*, 18, 382, as wife of Hêphæstus; in Hes. Theog. Aglaia is named as such. In the Od. 8, 267, Aphroditê is his wife; in both fictions the same notion lies at the bottom, that a goddess of grace is wedded to a god skilled in art. 2) More frequently in the plur. *the Graces*, the goddesses of grace, and esply of grateful companionship, Il. 17, 51. Od. 6, 18. Homer mentions no definite number of them, and names but one, Pasithéa. Il. 14, 269. In v. 267, younger graces are mentioned; he recognizes, consequently, several classes ; or this epith. may, according to Heyne, be a mere indication of perpetual youth. Hesiod (Th. 997), mentions three as daughters of Zeus, *Aglaïa, Euphrosýnê, and Thalïa* (Theog. 909). They are prim. companions and hand-maids of Aphroditê, Od. 8, 364. 18, 194. h. Ven. 98 ; still Hêrê has them in her train, Il. 5, 338. [The last citation not in point.]

χάρμα, ατος, τό (χαίρω), *joy, rapture, enjoyment*. a) The cause of joy, χάρμα τινί, 14, 325. 17, 636. h. 15, 4 ; plur., Od. 6, 185 ; esply a *scandalous joy, a scoff*, χάρ-

μα γίγνεσθαί τινι, Il. 3, 51. 6, 82. 10, 193. 2) Generally, *joy, pleasure*, Od. 19, 471. h. Cer. 372.

χάρμη, ἡ, Ep. (χαίρω), prop. *joy*, esply *the lore of battle, battle*, often μνήσασθαι χάρμης [to be mindful of the fight, Cp.], 4, 222. 8, 252. Od. 22, 73 ; λήθεσθαι χάρμης, Il. 12, 203 ; χάρμην ἐμβάλλειν τινί, 13, 82. 2) Generally, *contest, battle*, 14, 101. 17, 161.

*χαρμόφρων, ονος, ὁ, ἡ (φρήν), *glad at heart, joyful*, h. Merc. 227.

χαροπός, ή, όν, prob. (χαρά, ὦψ), prop. *glad-looking*, spoken of the bright look of a joyful mind ; hence, *bright-looking, clear-eyed*, spoken of the brightness of the eyes, λέοντες. Od. 11. 611. h. Merc. 569; κύνες, h Merc. 194 ; afterwards it was borrowed to indicate the common colour of the eyes, *light-brown*. (Schol. φοβεροί ; according to Eustath. spoken of the colour of the eyes.)

Χάροπος, ὁ, with accent changed, prop. name, king of the island Symê, father of Nireus. 2, 672.

Χάροψ, οπος, ὁ, son of Hippasus, a Trojan, slain by Odysseus (Ulysses), 11, 426.

Χάρυβδις, ιος, ἡ, a dangerous whirlpool in the Sicilian straits, and on the coast of Sicily, opposite Scylla, which swallowed up every thing that approached it, Od. 12, 104, seq. 441. 23, 327. Later also a whirlpool was so called near the present *Capo di Furo*. Now it is called *Charilla, Remo*, or *Carofalo*. According to a later tradition, *Charybdis* was the daughter of Poseidôn and the Earth, Serv. ad Virg. A. 111. 420. Modern travellers find no whirlpool in the above vicinity, but merely a great agitation of the waves setting from the north towards the west, which is not dangerous.

χατέω, poet. (ΧΑΩ), only pres., prop. *to snap at any thing*: hence: *1) to desire, to covet, to wish*, absol. 9. 518. Od. 2, 249 ; with infin. Od. 13, 280. 15, 376. 2) *to want, to have need*, with gen. πάντες θεῶν χατέουσ' ἄνθρωποι, all men stand in need of the gods (according to Melanchton, the most beautiful verse in Hom.). Od. 3, 48.

χατίζω, Ep. = χατέω, 1) *to desire, to long for*, with gen. 2, 225. Od. 8, 156. 11, 350. 2) *to need*, τινός, Il. 17, 221. 18, 392.

ΧΑΩ, obsol. theme of χαίνω, χανδάνω.

χείη, ἡ (χάω), *a hole, a cavity*, a cleft, esply of snakes, *22, 93. 95.

χεῖλος, εος, τό (prob. from ΧΑΩ), *a lip*, χείλεσι γελᾶν, 15, 102 ; see γελάω ; proverb. spoken of a miser, χείλεα μέν τ' ἐδίην', ὑπερῴην δ' οὐκ ἐδίηνεν, he moistens his lips, but not his palate, 22, 485. 2) Metaph. *the rim, the margin* of a thing, Od. 4, 132. 616. Il. 12, 52.

χεῖμα, ατος, τό (χέω), prop. what is poured out, *a tempest, a rain-storm*, and because in the southern countries winter

Χειμάρροος. 434 Χεῦμα.

consists in this, *winter, winter-cold,* Od. 11, 190. 14, 437; as a season of the year in oppos. to θέρος, Od. 7, 118.

χειμάρροος, ον (ῥέω), contr. χειμάρρους, Il. 493; and Ep. shortened, χείμαρρος. 4. 452. 5, 88; *flowing* or *swollen with wintry waters*, i. e. with rain and melted snow, *a torrent*, epith. of rapid rivers, ποταμός, *13, 138.

χείμαρρος, Ep. shortened for χειμάρροος.

χειμέριος, η, ον (χεῖμα), pertaining to winter, *wintry*, ἄελλα, a winter storm, Il. 2. 294; νιφάδες, winter snow-flakes, 3. 222; ἧμαρ, a winter day, 12, 279; ὕδωρ, 23, 420; ὥρη, Od. 5, 485.

χειμών, ῶνος, ὁ (χεῖμα), stormy, rainy weather, *a storm, rain, winter-weather,* Od. 4, 566; mly, *winter,* Il. 3, 4. 21, 283.

χείρ. ἡ, gen. χειρός. Besides the regular forms, there occur the Ion. forms: dat. χερί, thrice; χέρα, h. 18, 40, and dat. plur. χείρεσι and χείρεσσι (see Thiersch, § 187. 11). 1) *the hand,* the *fist,* often χεῖρες καὶ πόδες, 5, 422. 15, 364; the forefoot, poet. spoken of animals, Batr. 88; also as in English for *side, ἐπ' ἀριστερὰ χειρός,* to the left hand, Od. 5, 277; often plonastic, χειρὶ λαβεῖν, χερσὶν ἑλέσθαι. On the phrases: χεῖρας ἀνασχεῖν θεοῖς, χεῖρας ἀείρειν, ὀρέξαι and πετάσαι τινί, see these verbs. 2) Esply in the plur. *activity, strength, power, force,* often connected with μένος, βίη. Il. 6, 502. 12, 135. *a*) In a good sense. ἔπεσιν καὶ χερσὶν ἀρήγειν, to help with word and deed, 1, 77; χεῖρα ὑπερέχειν τινί, to hold one's hand over anybody for protection, 4, 249; χεῖρες ἀμύνειν εἰσὶ καὶ ἡμῖν, we also have hands for protection, 13, 814. *b*) In a hostile signif. χεῖρα ἐπιφέρειν τινί, to lay one's hand (hands) on any one, 1, 89; χεῖρας ἐφιέναι τινί, Od. 1, 254; εἰς χεῖρας ἐλθεῖν or ἱκέσθαι τινί, to fall into any one's hands, Il. 10, 448; poet. also χεῖρας ἱκέσθαι, Od. 12, 331.

χειρίς, ίδος, ἡ (χείρ), a covering for the hand, *a glove,* Od. 24, 230.†

*χειροτένων, οντος, ὁ, ἡ (τείνω), stretching out the hand, *long-armed,* Batr. 299.

χειρότερος, η, ον, poet. for χείρων, *15, 513. 20, 436.

χείρων, ον, gen. ονος, prop. compar. of χέρης, mly irreg. comp of κακός (Ep. form χειρότερος, and χερειότερος, χερείων), *meaner, smaller, worse, inferior,* in worth, 15, 641. 14, 377; opposd to μείζων, in rank and race, Od. 21, 325.

Χείρων, ωνος, ὁ, *Chiron (Cheirôn),* son of Kronus (Saturn) and Philyra; a centaur, famed for his skill in medicine and prophecy, celebrated as the teacher of Asklêpios (Æsculapius), Heracles, and Achilles, Il. 4, 219. 11, 831.

χείσομαι, see χανδάνω.

χελιδών, όνος, ἡ, *a swallow,* *Od. 21, 411. 22, 240. Ep. 15, 11.

*χέλυς, υος, ἡ, *a turtle, a tortoise,* from the shell of which Hermês constructed the first lyre, by drawing strings over it, h. Merc. 33. 2) *the lyre* itself, v. 24. 153.

*χελώνη, ἡ=χέλυς, *a tortoise,* h. Merc. 42. 48.

χέραδος, εος, τό, poet. for the com. χεράς, άδος, ἡ, *dirty sand, gravel.* pebbles that swollen rivers bring down, χέραδος μυρίον [sands *Infinite,* Cp.], 21, 319. (Some Gramm. accented it as gen. and connected it with ἅλις, cf. Apoll. Lex.)

χερειότερος, η, ον, Ep. compar. *a χείρων, *2, 248. 12, 270.

χερείων, ον. gen. ονος, Ep. for χείρων, *inferior, worse,* oppond to ἀρείων, Il. 237; with accus. δέμας, φυήν, 1, 114. Od. 5. 411. Neut. plur. τὰ χερείονα, Il. 1. 576. In the neut. with infin., in which case the notion of comparison does not appear, οὔ τι χέρειον ἐν ὥρῃ δεῖπνον ἑλέσθαι, it is not at all bad to take food at the proper time, Od. 17, 176.

ΧΕΡΗΣ, an Ep. defect. adj. only used in the sing. gen. χέρηος, adv. χέρηϊ, accus. χέρηα, nom. plur. χέρηες, accus. nem. χέρηα, in the Od. χέρεια, 18, 229. 20. 510. This word, which is positive only in form, is the theme of the Ep. compar. χερείων, χερειότερος, in prose χείρων, but always has the signif. of the compar. *inferior, worse, weaker,* esply εἴο χέρηα μάχῃ, worse in the battle than he, Il. 4. 400; χέρηϊ opposed to κρείσσων, 1, 80. Od. 15, 324; in like manner, χέρηα χέρονι, Il. 14, 382. (According to Passow. it is to be derived from χείρ, and its signif. = χείριος, *under any one's power.* The form χέρεια, in the Od. seems incorrect, see Thiersch, § 202. 23, and Buttm. Gram. § 68)

χερμάδιον (χείρ), *a stone,* prop. as large as can be grasped in the hand, 4, 518. 5. 302. Od. 10, 121.

χερνῆτις, ιδος, ἡ, fem. of χερνήτης (χείρ), prop. living by the labour of the hands, γυνή, *a female who spins for wages,* 12, 433 †

χέρνιβον, τό (νίπτω), *a washing-basin, a hand-basin,* for washing the hands before sacrifice, 24, 304.†

χερνίπτομαι, depon. mid. (νίπτω), sec. Ep. *to wash one's hands,* esply before a sacrifice, 1, 449.†

χέρνιψ, ιβος, ἡ (νίπτω), *washing-water,* sacred or *holy water,* with which the hands were washed before eating, and before religious ceremonies, always accus. χέρνιβα, *Od. 1, 136. 3, 445, and often.

Χερσιδάμας, αντος, ὁ, son of Priam, slain by Odysseus (Ulysses), 11, 423.

χέρσονδε, adv. (χέρσος), on or to the mainland, 21, 238.† h. Ap. 29.

χέρσος, ἡ (akin to σκηρός, ξηρός), the shore, *the firm land,* in oppos. to water, 4, 425. Od. 10, 459; ποτὶ χέρσον, to the shore, Od. 9, 147. Il. 14, 394. (Od. 4, 95. Nitzsch reads as adj. ποτὶχέρσος θάλασσα.)

χεῦαι, χεῦαν, χεῦε, see χέω.

χεῦμα, ατος, τό (χέω), *that which is*

Χέω. **Χίμαιρα.**

poured out, a *casting, κασσιτέροιο*, a casting of tin, 23, 561.†

χέω, fut. χεύσω, χεύω, Od. 2, 222; aor. 1 Att. έχεα, only έχεαν, Il. 24, 799;† elsewhere Ep. έχευα and χεύα, infin. χεύαι, subj. χεύομεν, for χεύωμεν, 7, 336; aor. 1 mid. έχευάμην, always 3 sing. χεύατο, perf. pass. κέχυμαι, aor. pass. έχύθην, only opt. χυθείη. Also the Ep. syncop. aor. 2 mid. έχύμην, from which χύτο, έχυντο, Od. 10, 415; χύμενος, Od. 8, 527. The pres. and imperf. always uncontr. except infin. χείσθαι, Od. 10, 518. Prim. signif. *to pour;* 1) Prop. spoken of fluids: *to pour, to pour out, to shed,* with accus. ύδωρ, δακρυ; spoken of Zeus, χέει ύδωρ, pours out water, i. e. causes it to rain, Il. 16, 385; absol. χέει, sc. χιόνα, 12, 281. 2) Spoken of things dry: *to pour out, to shed, to scatter,* κρέας είν έλεοίσιν, 9, 215; spoken of wind, φύλλα, φύκος, καρπός, 6, 147. 9, 7. Od. 11, 588; esply σήμα, to heap up a mound, Il. 7, 86. Od. 1, 291; and τύμβον, Il. 7, 336. Od. 4, 584; poet. καλάμην χθονί, to stretch the stalks upon the ground, 19, 222; ηνία έρασε, to let the reins fall to the earth, 17, 619; δέσματα άπό κρατός, 22, 468. 3) *to pour out, to emit,* metaph. φωνήν, to let the voice resound, Od. 19, 521; αύτμένα κατά τινος [*pouring his breath upon his neck behind,* Cp.], 23, 765; poet. often = *to spread,* άχλύν κατ' όφθαλμών, to pour darkness over the eyes, 20, 321; ύπνον έπί βλεφάροισιν, 14, 165. Od. 2, 395; κάλλος κάκ κεφαλής, Od. 23, 156. Mid. 1) with aor. 1, *to pour out for oneself,* with accus. χοήν χείσθαι νεκύεσσιν, to pour out a grief-offering to the dead, Od. 10. 518. 11, 26; κόνιν κάκ κεφαλής, to scatter dust upon the head, Il. 18, 24. Od. 24, 317; βέλεα, to pour out his missiles, i. e. to shoot in a multitude, Il. 8, 159; άμφί υίόν έχεύατο πήχεε, she threw her arms about her son, 5, 314. 2) Mid. with perf. pass. and the syncop. aor. *a) to pour itself out, to stream,* prop. spoken of tears, Od. 4, 523. Il. 21, 385; of things dry, *to be poured out in abundance,* χιών, Il. 12, 285; κόπρος, Od. 17, 298; *to lie extended,* Od. 19, 539; άγχιστίναι κέχυνται, Il. 5, 141 (cf. άγχιστίναι); metaph. spoken of living beings, *to pour out, to stream forth, to issue,* έκ νεών, 16, 267. 19, 356. Od. 10, 415; in the sense, *to spread, to extend, to spread itself,* κατ' όφθαλμών κέχυτ' άχλύς, Il 5, 696; spoken of death, Il. 344; of sleep, Od. 19, 590; and άμφ' αύτω χυμένη, poured about him, i. e. embracing him, Il. 19, 284. Od. 8, 527.

χηλός, ή (ΧΑΩ), *a chest, a box,* for the preservation of clothes, 16, 221. Od. 2, 339. 8, 424.

χήν, χηνός, ό, ή (ΧΑΩ), *a goose,* 2, 460; masc. Od. 19, 552; fem. Od. 15, 161. 174.

χηραμός, ό, poet. (ΧΑΩ), *a cleft, a cavity,* 21, 495.†

χήρατο, see χαίρω.

χηρεύω (χήρος), intrans. *to be emptied, bereft, deprived of,* with gen. άνδρών, Od. 9, 124.†

χήρη, ή, *a widow,* prop. fem. of χήρος, as adj. widowed, μήτηρ, 20, 499; γυναίκες, 2, 289; as subst. χήρη σευ έσομαι, *6, 408. 432. 22, 484.

χήρος, η, ον (ΧΑΩ), *bereft,* see χήρη.

χηρόω (χήρος), aor. 1 Ep. χήρωσα, trans. *to make empty, desolate, bare,* άγυιάς, 5, 642; esply *to deprive of a husband,* to reduce to widowhood, γυναίκα, 17, 36.

χηρωστής, ού, ό, *collateral relatives,* who succeed to the property of one who dies childless, only plur. 5, 158.†

χήτος, εος, τό (χατέω), *want, need,* only in the dat. χήτει or χήτεί, from want, from desire, with gen. 6, 463. 19, 324. Od. 16, 35. h. Ap. 78.

χθαμαλός, ή, όν, compar. χθαμαλώτερος, superl. χθαμαλώτατος, 13, 683; lying on the earth; generally, *low, flat,* τείχος, 13, 683; νήσος, Od. 9, 25. 10, 196 (from χαμαι with epenthetic θ); εύνή, Od. 11, 194.

***χθές,** adv. *yesterday,* h. Merc. 273.

χθιζά, neut. plur. from χθιζός.

χθιζός, ή, όν (χθές), *appertaining to yesterday,* yesterday, χθιζόν χρόος, 13, 745; often instead of the adv. χθιζός έβη, he went yesterday, 1, 424. The neut. sing. and plur. as adv. χθιζόν, *yesterday,* 19, 195. Od. 4, 656; χθιζά τε καί πρώίζα, yesterday and the day before, i. e. *formerly,* Il. 2, 303; an indefinite expression of the old language for any past time, like *nuper* in Lat., cf. Cic. de Divin. 1, 39. 86. Thus Herod. uses χθές καί πρωίην (Il. 53), for a time long past; and so often in the Bible, cf. Exod. 2, 10. If we construct these words, according to Wolf, with ότ' ές— ήγερέθοντο, the sense is: Formerly, when the ships of the Greeks assembled, and the aporiosis v. 307, ένθ' έφάνη. Others deny this *usus loqu.* to Hom., and connect these words with Κήρες—φέρουσαι, v. 304, i. e. ye are all witnesses, who have not recently perished. Nägelsb. explains the passage by supplying ήν: it was since yesterday or the day before, i. e. it was at the time of the sacrifice now some days, that the ships were gradually gathering; but τέ καί can never be translated by *or.* [Lohrs: *vix cum Aulida advecti eramus, tum* (v. 308) *portentum accidit.*]

χθών, χθονός, ή, poet. *earth, ground,* έπί χθονί δέρκεσθαι = ζην, 1, 88; σίτον έδοντες, Od. 8, 222. χθόνα δύναι, to go under the earth, i. e. to die, Il. 6, 411.

χίλιοι, αι, α, *a thousand,* χίλι' ύπέστη αίγας, *11, 244; neut. with fem.

Χίμαιρα, ή, *Chimaera,* a frightful monster, of divine origin, in Lycia (according to Hes. Th. 321, daughter of Typhon and Echidna), which above had the form of a lion, in the middle of a goat, and below of a dragon. From its mouth issued fire; it was slain by Belerophontes. 6, 179, seq. 16, 328. h. Ap. 368. According to Scylax, a volcano in Lycia, not far from Phaselis, or, according to Strabo, a volcanic rocky valley in the Cragus, gave rise to the fable of the Chimaera.

Χίος, ή, an island of the Aegaean sea, on the coast of Ionia, famed for its excellent wine, now Scio or Saki Andassi (mastic-i-land), Od. 3, 170.

χιτών, ώνος, ό, *a tunic,* the under garment of the ancients; it was a woollen garment, without sleeves, similar to our shirts, which was worn next to the body, both by men and women, and confined by a girdle, 10, 21. Od. 15, 60. 14, 72; above the cloak was worn, Il. 2, 42. 2) Generally, a garment, esply *the coat of mail, the cuirass,* 2, 416. 5, 736; χάλκεος, 13, 439; στρεπτός, 5, 113 (cf. that word); proverbial: λάϊνον χιτώνα έννυσθαι, see λάϊνος.

χιών, όνος, ή (χέω), *snow,* 10, 7. Od. 6, 44. νιφάδες χιόνος, snow-flakes, Il. 12, 278.

χλαίνα, ή, *the upper garment, the mantle* of the men; according to Hase, Gr. Alterthumskunde, p. 66, a piece of cloth, cut square or round, which was commonly passed from the left arm backwards under the right arm, and the end thrown over the left shoulder, where it was fastened with a buckle, 2, 183. 10, 133. This garment was worn chiefly as a protection against cold and stormy weather, hence άνεμοσκεπής and άλεξάνεμος, 16, 224. Od. 14, 529. It was of wool, and thick, ούλή, πυκινή, Od. 4, 50. 14, 520; often purple. Od. 14, 500; double or single, διπλή, απλούς. 2) Generally, *a robe, a covering, a carpet,* to wrap around one-self in sleep, Od. 3, 349. 351. 4, 299. Il. 24. 646

*χλεύνη, ή, *jesting, jeer, mockery,* in the plur. h. Cer. 202.

*χλοερός, ή, όν, poet. for χλωρός, *green,* Batr. 161.

χλούνης, ου, ό, Ep. epith. of the boar, σύς άγριος, 9, 539; † a word whose deriv. and signif. was not known even by the ancients. Most prob. according to Eustath., Apoll., and Hesych., from χλόη and εύνή, prop. χλοεύνης, ό έν χλόη ευναζόμενος, lying in the grass, hence = εύτραφής, *well fed;* according to Aristarch. = μονιός, solitary; according to the Ven. Schol. = άφριστής, the foaming; according to Aristot. = τομίας, castrated, whence ή χλοϋνις, castration.

χλωρηίς, ίδος, ή, pecul. poet. fem. of χλωρός, *pale-green, yellowish,* as an epith. of the nightingale, Od. 19, 518; † according to the Schol. Vulg. prob. from its pale colour, or ' which lives in the green fields.'

Χλώρις, ιδος, ή, daughter of Amphion, the son of Iasius, king of Orchomenus, wife of Neleus, who bore him Nestor, Chromius, Periclymenus, and Pero, Od.

11, 281. (According to Apd. 3, 5. 6, Χλωρίς, daughter of the Theban Amphion.)

χλωρός, ή, όν, poet. χλοερός (χλόη), 1) *greenish, a yellowish green, yellowish,* of the colour of young shrubbery, ράπιτ. Od. 16, 47; of honey, Il. 11, 631. Od. 10, 234; generally, *pale, white,* χλωρόν ύπαί δείους, Il. 10, 376. 15. 4; esply δέος. Il. 10, 479. 8, 77. Od. 11, 43. 450. h. Cer. 190. 2) Metaph. *green,* i. e. fresh, in opposition to dry, μοχλός, ρόπαλον, Od. 9, 320. 379.

χνόος, ό, contr. χνούς (κνάω), that is upon the surface and may be scraped off, e. g. the down upon fruits; poet. άλός χνόος, the foam of the sea, Od. 6, 226.†

χόανος, ό (χέω), *the cavity* (before the bellows' pipe) in which the metal to be melted was put (the smelting-oven, V.), 18, 470.† Hesych. κοίλωμα; Köpke, Kriegswes. d. Gr. p. 51, understands by it a kind of *crucible,* of fire-proof clay, in which was put the metallic ore.

χοή, ή (χέω), that which is poured out, esply *a libation, a drink-offering,* in sacrifices for the dead, *Od. 10, 528. 11, 26.

χοΐνιξ, ικος, ή, *a corn-measure,* containing four κοτύλαι, or as much as a man uses in a day; hence *food, bread.* άντεσθαι χοίνικός τινος, to touch any one's corn-measure, i. e. to eat of any one's bread, Od. 19, 28.†

χοίρεος, έη, εον, poet. for χοίρειος (χοίρος), *belonging to young swine.* χοίρεα, sc. κρέατα, swine's flesh, pork, Od. 14, 81.†

χοίρος, ό, prop. *a porker, a pig,* Od. 14, 73.†

χολάς, άδος, ή, mly plur. αί χολάδες, *the entrails, the bowels,* *4, 526. 21, 181. h. Merc. 123.

χόλος, ό, poet. for χολή (χέω, prop. that pours itself out), *the gall,* 16, 203. 2) Metaph. *anger, hatred, wrath,* connected with μήνις, 15, 122. χόλος τινός, enmity which any one cherishes, *Hym. 18, 119. Od. 1, 433. 4, 583; but τινί, against any one, h. Cer. 351. 410; also spoken of animals: *rage,* Il. 22, 94.

χολόω (χόλος), fut. χολώσω, infin. Ep. χολωσέμεν, aor. έχόλωσα, fut. mid. χολώσομαι, more frequently κεχολώσομαι, aor. 1 έχολωσάμην, perf. pass. κεχόλωμαι, aor. pass. έχολώθην, to provoke one's gall, i. e. *to make angry, to enrage, to irritate, to incense,* τινά, 1, 78. 18, 111. Od. 8, 205. Mid. and pass. *to become angry, to be enraged, to be irritated,* to be incensed, often with the adjuncts θυμώ, ένι φρεσίν, κηρόθι, also with accus. θυμόν, ήτορ. a) With dat. of the pers. τινί, at any one, Il. 1, 9. 2, 629. Od. 8, 276. b) With gen. τινός, on account of a person or thing, Il. 4, 494. 501. Il. 703, 21, 146. Od. 1, 69; and with prep. είνεκα νίκης. Od. 11, 554; άμφί τινι. Il. 23, 88; έξ άρέων μητρός, Il. 9, 562; έπί τινι, Batr. 109.

Χολωτός.   Χρεώ.

χολωτός, ή, όν, adj. from χολόω, enraged, angry, passionate, έπεα, 4, 241. Od. 22, 26. 225

χορδή, ή, a gut, Batr. 225; a string of a musical instrument, Od. 21, 407.†

Μerc. 51.

***χοροήθης**, ες, gen. εος (ήθος), accustomed to the choir or the dance, h. 18, 3.

χοροιτυπίη, ή (τύπτω), the stamping of the ground in dancing, a choral dance, a dance, plur. 24, 261.†

***χοροίτυπος**, struck or played for a dance, λύρα, h. Merc. 31.

χορόνδε, adv. (χορός), to a dance, 3, 393.†

χορός, ὁ, 1) a choral dance, a circular dance, a dance, espiy a festal dance connected with singing, χορόνδε έρχεσθαι or εἰς χορόν, 3, 393. 15, 508. Od. 8, 65. χορῷ καλῇ, beautiful in the dance, 11. 16, 180; ἐν χορῷ μέλπεσθαι, 16, 182. On χορὸν ποικίλλειν and ἀσκεῖν, to represent a dance, see these words. b) a choir, a troop of dancers, h. Ven. 118. h. 5, 13. 2) a dancing-place, Od. 8, 260. 264. 12, 4. 318.

χόρτος, ὁ (akin to χορός), prop. an inclosed place, an inclosure, an interior space (Schol. περίφραγμα, τείχος), αὐλῆς ἐν χόρτῳ, 11, 774. Plur. 11. 24, 640. *11. (Köppen: grass, is a later signif.)

ΧΡΑΙΣΜΕΩ, Ep., an obsol. pres.; from which aor. 2 ἐχραισμε and χραίσμε, subj. χραίσμῃ, χραίσμωσι, Infin. χραισμεῖν, fut. χραισμήσω (χραισμήσει, and infin. χραισμησέμεν), aor. 1 only χραίσμησε, and infin. χραισμῆσαι, 1) Prop. to repel or ward off any thing from any one; espiy όλεθρόν τινι, 7, 144. 11, 120. 20, 296. 2) to help, to assist, to aid, to be of use, with the notion of protection, with dat. of the person, 1, 28. 3, 54; and often. In the passage 1, 566, μή νύ τοι οὐ χραίσμωσιν–ἀσσον ἰόνθ', the Schol. and Eustath. with Zenodot. explain ἰόντε, and as dual for plur., all the gods, coming (pressing) towards me, could not aid thee, cf. 11. 5, 487. So Buttm., Lex. p. 543, and Nägelsbach. Eustath. explains the dual by supposing that gods and goddesses may be meant. If we compare 15, 104. 18. 62, we shall find this explanation as nom. confirmed. Others make it accus. ἰόντα and supply ἐμέ, although it is the only passage where a person is the object to he repelled. Thus Voss: should I approach; Küppen. Spitzner, Wolf [and Dübner]. ne a te non depelluni me aggredientem.

χράομαι, depon. mid. Ion. χρέομαι, partcp. χρεώμενος, perf. κέχρημαι, only partcp. κεχρημένος, 3 sing. plupr rf. κέχρητο, Od. 3, 266. (Homer has only the partcp. pres., the partcp. perf., and the 3 sing. pluperf.) 1) to employ, only 11. 23, 834, absol. 2) to have in use, espiy in the perf. with pres. signif. to use continually, to have, only φρεσί κέχρητ' ἀγαθῇσιν, she had good feelings, Od. 3, 266. 14, 422. 16, 398. b) In

Hom. the perf. partcp. has the signif. to want, to long for, to desire, with gen. εὐῆς, Il. 19, 262; νόστου καὶ γυναικός, Od. 1, 13. 14, 124. Absol. as adj. needy, destitute, Od. 14, 155. 17, 347.

χραύω, prop. χραFω, Æol. for χράω, prop. to touch lightly, to scratch, to graze, to wound slightly, τινά, only subj. aor. χραύσῃ, 5. 138.†

χράω, a theme with the prim. signif. to approach, to draw near, in a good and bad sense, to which, besides χράομαι, belong the following forms of flexion:

1. **χράω**, Ep. defect. only imperf. 3 sing. ἔχραε, 2 plur. χράετε, Od. 21, 69; prop. to touch, to seize, esply in a hostile signif.: to attack any one, to rush upon any one, to set upon any one, with dat. στυγερός οἱ ἔχραε δαίμων, Od. 5, 396. 10, 64. b) absol. with infin. to strive, to endeavour, to exert oneself, 11. 21, 369; where the infin. κήδειν must be construed with ῥόον (see Thiersch, Gr. § 232. 162); in like manner Od. 21, 69, δώμα with ἐσθιέμεν, and not with χράω.

2. **χράω**, Ion. χρέω, Ep. χρείω, from which only partcp. pres. χρείων, Od. 8, 79. h. Ap. 396; χρέων, h. Ap. 253; fut. χρήσω, h. Ap. 132; fút. mid. χρήσομαι, only partcp.; prop. to present that which is desired, esply spoken of an oracle: to give an answer, to communicate an oracle or divine response, Od. 8, 79. h. Ap. 396; βουλήν τινι, h. Ap. 132. Mid. to cause an oracle to be given to oneself; hence, to consult an oracle or a deity, to ask counsel, absol., Od. 8, 81. h. Ap. 252. 292; with dat. τινί, to inquire of a god, or ask a god: ψυχῇ τινος, *Od. 10, 492. 505. 11, 165.

3. As a theme of κίχρημι, q. v. **χρεῖος**, εος, τό, Ep. for χρέος. q. v. **χρείω**, Ep. for χράω, see χράω. **χρειώ**, οῦς, ἡ, Ep. for χρεώ. **χρεμετίζω** (ΧΡΕΜΩ), to neigh, spoken of a horse, 13, 51.†

χρέος, τό, Ep. χρεῖος, only in the nom. and accus. sing., and χρέος only in Od. 1) want, need, necessity; generally, affair, business, ἐμὸν αὐτοῦ χρεῖος, my own affair, Od. 2, 45. κατὰ χρέος τινὸς ἐλθεῖν, to come for any one's sake, prop. after any one's need, Od. 11, 479. 2) what one must fulfil, a debt, what one has borrowed or lent, χρεῖος ὀφείλειν τινί, to owe a debt to any one, Il. 11, 688. Od. 21, 17. Pass. χρεῖος ὀφείλεται μοι, a debt is due to me, 11. 11, 686. Od. 3, 367. χρεῖος ἀποστήσασθαι, see ἀφίστημι, Il. 13, 746. 3) Metaph. obligation, propriety, κατὰ χρέος, h. Merc. 138.

χρεώ, ἡ, Ep. χρειώ (χρῆ), gen. χρεοῦς, dat. χρειοῖ, 8, 57; need, want, necessity, distress, 10, 172. 9, 197. Od. 4, 312. 11, 164; χρεὼ ἀναγκαίη, 11. 8, 57. 1) With gen. χρειὼ ἐμέιο γίγνεται, there is need of me, 1, 341. χρεὼ πείσματος ἐστιν, Od. 9, 136; with infin., 11. 23, 308. 2) χρειώ ἱκάνεται, ἵκει, ἱκάνει, necessity comes, there is need, 10, 118. 142. 11, 610. Od.

Χρεώμενος. 438 Χρύσεος.

6, 136; and with accus. of the pers. ἐμὲ χρεὼ τόσσον ἵκει, necessity presses me so exceedingly, Od. 5, 189; cf. 2, 28. This accus. stands even with γίγνεσθαι and εἶναι: ἐμὲ δὲ χρεὼ νηός I need a ship, Od. 4, 634; οὐδέ τί μιν χρεὼ ἔσται τυμβοχοῆς, Il. 21, 322; from this is explained, 3) The elliptical use of χρεώ with accus. of the pers., which is employed entirely like χρή: τίπτε δέ σε χρεώ, sc. γίγνεται or ἱκάνει (according to Herm. ad Viger. ἔχει), wherefore needest thou this? Od. 1, 225. Il. 10, 85. a) With gen. of the thing: οὔτε με ταύτης χρεὼ τιμῆς. I need not this honour, 9, 608; βουλῆς, 9, 75. 10, 43. 11, 606. b) With infin. τὸν μάλα χρεὼ ἑστάμεναι κρατερῶς, there is great need that he should stand firmly, 11, 409. 18, 406. Od. 4, 707. (Hom. uses χρεώ only in the elliptical phrase, and every where as a monosyllable.)

χρεώμενος, Ion. for χρώμενος, see χράομαι.

χρή, only 3 sing. pres. indic. (χράω), impers. *it is necessary, there is need, must, should.* 1) With infin. 1, 216. Od. 3, 209. 2) With accus. of the pers. and infin. χρή σε πόλεμον παῦσαι, thou must cause the battle to cease, Il. 7, 331. 9, 100. Od. 1, 296. Sometimes the infin. is wanting, and must be supplied from the foregoing: οὐδέ τί σε χρή, for thou must not, underst. ἀποπαύεσθαι, Π. 16, 721. 19, 420. Od. 19, 500. 2) With accus. of the pers. and gen. of the thing: χρή μέ τινος, I need a thing, I want any thing. ὅττεό σε χρή, Od. 1, 124. οὐδέ τί σε χρὴ ἀφροσύνης, thou needest not folly, i. e. fully becomes thee not, Il. 7, 109. cf. Od. 3, 14. 21, 110.

χρηΐζω, Ep. for χρῄζω (χράω), *to need, to want, to stand in need of,* with gen. 11, 835. Od. 17, 121; absol. partcp. *needy,* Od. 11, 340.

χρῆμα, ατος, τό (χράομαι), 1) prop. *a thing which is used or wanted,* hence in the plur. χρήματα, *property, possessions, goods,* Od. 2, 78. 203. 13, 203, and often, *Od. 2) Generally, a thing, any affair, an occurrence,* h. Merc. 332.

*χρησαμένη, see κίχρημι, Batr. 187.

*χρηστήριον, τό (χράω), an oracle, prim. the place where an oracle is communicated, h. Ap. 81 214.

*χρηστός, ή, όν (χράομαι), useful, profitable, agreeable, good, μελίτωμα, Batr. 39.

χρίμπτω, poet. strengthened from χρίω, aor. 1 mid. ἐχριμψάμην, h. Ap. and partcp. aor. pass. χριμφθείς; prop. *to glance upon the upper surface of a body;* mid. with aor. pass. *to approach very near a thing, to press upon,* absol. χριμφθεὶς πέλας, Od. 10, 516; † with dat. spoken of a ship, ἀμάθοισιν, h. Ap. 439.

χρίω, aor. ἔχρισα and χρῖσα, imperat. χρῖσον, fut. mid. χρίσομαι, aor. 1 ἐχρισάμην, prop. to rub upon the surface of a body; hence, mly 1) *to anoint,* often with λούω, because it was done after bathing, τινὰ ἐλαίῳ, Od. 3, 466. 4, 212. 10, 364. h. Ven. 61; also spoken of the dead, Il. 23, 186. 24, 587; ἀμβροσίῃ, 16, 670. Mid. *to anoint oneself,* ἐλαίῳ, Od. 6, 96. 220; κάλλει, Od. 18, 194 (cf. ειλ- λος); b) Generally, *to rub over, to besmear,* with accus. ἰούς (φαρμάκῳ), *to poison one's arrows,* Od. 1, 262; conic. *to smear,* μέτωπον, Batr. 241.

χροιή, ἡ, Ion. for χροιά (χρώς), the surface of a body; esply *the skin* of the human body; hence, *the body,* 14, 164.†

χρόμαδος, ὁ (ΧΡΕΜΩ), a creaking noise, *a gnashing or grinding of the teeth,* γενύων, 23, 688.†

Χρομίος, ὁ, 1) son of Priam, slain by Diomedes, 5, 160, seq. 2) son of Neleus and Chloris, Od. 11, 286. 3) a Lycian. Il. 5, 677. 4) a Trojan, 8, 275. 5) a Trojan, 17, 218. 494. [6) an Epean, a companion of Nestor, 4, 295.]

Χρόμις, ιος, ὁ, son of Midon, leader of the Mysians before Troy, 2, 858.

χρόνιος, ίη, ιον (χρόνος), *in time,* i. e. *after a long time,* χρόνιος ἐλθών, having (come) returned after a long absence, Od. 17, 112.†

χρόνος, ὁ, *time, duration* (whether a longer or a shorter time); peculiar phrases: πολὺν χρόνον, *a long time,* 3, 157; ὀλίγον χρόνον, 23, 418; χρόνον, *a while,* Od. 4, 599. 6, 296. 9, 138; ἐπὶ χρόνον, *for a time,* Il. 2, 299. Od. 14, 193; ἕνα χρόνον, *at one time, once,* Il. 15, 511.

χροός, χροί, χρόα, Ion. and Ep. cases of χρώς; q. v.

χρυσάμπυξ, υκος, ὁ, ἡ, poet. (ἄμπυξ), *with a golden head-band* or *frontlet,* ἵπποι, *5, 358. 720; *Ὧραι, h. 5, 5. 12.

χρυσάορος, ὁ, ἡ (and χρυσάωρ, ορος, ὁ, h. Ap. 123), from ἄορ, *having a golden sword,* mly an epith. of Apollo, *5, 509. 15, 256. h. Ap. 123; but of Demeter, h. Cer. 4. Thus Etym. Mag. χρυσοῦν ἄορ ἔχων, ὅ ἐστι φάσγανον. According to some Gramm. we should understand by ἄορ generally, *equipment, armour,* so that in the case of Apollo, it refers to his bow and arrows, and even to his cithera (Suid. χρυσοκίθαρις), cf. Schol. B. ad Il. 15, 256; in the case of Demeter, it refers to the sickle. Still this signif. is not usual in Hom.; on the other hand, the gods of the ancients are often armed, Hdt. 8, 77; cf. Mitscherl. in h. Cer. 4; Heyne ad Apd. p. 698; and Kämmerer ad h. in Cer. 4. Herm. on the contrary considers the word χρυσάορον as an interpolation for χρυσοθρόνον.

χρύσειος, είη, ειον, Ep. for χρύσεος.

*χρυσεοπήληξ, ηκος, ὁ, ἡ, poet. (πήληξ), *having a golden helmet,* h. 7, 1.

χρύσεος, έη, εον, Ep. χρύσειος. 1) *golden, of gold,* made of gold, or adorned with gold; espec. spoken of every thing which belongs to the gods, cf. 4, 2. 3, 724. 8, 44, seq. χρυσέη Ἀφροδίτη, decorated with gold, 3, 64. Od. 8, 337. 2)

Χρύση.

of the colour of gold, a golden yellow, **golden**, ἔθειραι, Il. 8. 12. 13, 24; νέθεα, 13, 523. 14. 351. (Hom. uses both forms according to the necessity of the metre; υ is always long; hence χρυσέη, χρυσέην, χρυσέω, and similar forms must be read with synizesis.)

Χρύση, ἡ, a town on the coast of Troas, near Thebes, with a temple of Apollo Smintheus, and a port, 1, 37, 390.

Χρυσηίς, ίδος, ἡ, 1) daughter of Chryses = *Astynome*, see Ἀστυνόμη, 1, 111. 2) a Nereïd, h. Cer. 421.

χρυσηλάκατος, ον, poet. (ἠλακάτη) *having a golden distaff*, inly an epith. of Artemis, Il. 16, 183. 20, 70. Od. 4, 122. h. Ven. 16, 116. Most ancient Gram. (Eustath., Ven. Schol., Apoll.), explain it: χρυσῷ βέλει χρωμένη, *carrying golden arrows*. It has been, however, justly suggested that in Hom. ἠλακάτη never signif. *arrow*, cf. 6, 191; cf. Spitzner ad Köppen, Il. 16, 183.

Χρύσης, ου, ὁ, voc. Χρύση, a priest of Apollo in Chrysé, father of Astynōmē, who came into the camp of the Greeks to redeem his daughter. Agamemnon, to whom she had been allotted, dismissed him with harsh language. Then Apollo avenged the priest by sending a pestilence. Agamemnon restored her, 1, 11, seq. 430, seq.

χρυσήνιος, ον, poet. (ἠνία), *having golden reins*, epith. of Ares, Od. 8, 285; of Artemis, Il. 6, 205.

*χρυσόζυγος, ον, poet. (ζυγόν), *having a golden yoke*, h. 31, 15.

Χρυσόθεμις, ιδος, ἡ, daughter of Agamemnon and Klytaemnēstra (Clytemnestra), 9, 145. 287.

χρυσόθρονος, ον, poet. (θρόνος), *upon a golden throne*, *golden-throned*, epith. of Hērē, 14, 153; of Artemis, θ, 533; of Ēōs (Aurora), Od. 10, 541. 12, 102.

χρυσοπέδιλος, ον, poet. (πέδιλον), *having golden soles* or *sandals*, *golden-sandalled* (Cp.), epith. of Hērē, Od. 11, 604.†

*χρυσοπλόκαμος, ον (πλόκαμος), with golden locks, *having golden tresses*, h. Ap. 205.

χρυσόπτερος, ον (πτερόν), *having golden pinions*, *golden-winged*, epith. of Iris, *8, 398. 11, 185. h. Cer.

χρυσόρραπις, ιος, ὁ (ῥαπίς), *having a golden rod* or *staff*, *with a golden wand*, *Od. 5, 87. 10, 331. h. Merc. 539.

χρυσός, ὁ, *gold*, often in Homer, not only wrought, but also unwrought, being weighed in exchange and traffic, χρυσοῖο τάλαντα, 9, 122. 264. 19, 247. Od. 4, 129. 2) that which is made of gold. Il. 6, 48. 8, 43; esply are the utensils of gods and heroes made of gold, as goblets, drinking-cups, girdles, neck-chains; also particular arms, as sword-belts, girdles, cuirasses, etc., are adorned with golden nails and studs, 1, 246. 2, 268, seq.

*χρυσοστέφανος, ον (στέφανος), *having a golden crown*, h. 5, 1.

χρυσοχόος, ὁ (χέω), *a gold-smelter, a goldsmith*, Od. 3, 425.† The reference is not here to proper casting, but it is an artist who covers the horns of the victim with gold plate.

χρώς, ὁ, gen. χρωτός, 10, 575; accus. χρῶτα, Od. 18, 172. 179: mly Ep. and Ion. gen. χροός, dat. χροΐ, accus. χρόα, Il. 4, 137. 5, 354. 7, 207. 1) Prop. the surface of a body, esply of the human body; *the skin*, 4, 210. Od. 16, 145. 19, 204; hence 2) *the colour*, τρέπεται χρώς, their colour changes, spoken of those who become pale from fear, Il. 13, 279. 17, 733. Od. 21, 412. 3) Poet. *the body*, 4, 137. 8, 43. 14, 170. 21, 568.

χυμένη, χύντο. see χέω.

χύσις, ιος, ἡ (χέω), *the act of pouring out*: that which is poured out, *a heap, a multitude*; φύλλων, the fall of leaves, *Od. 5, 483. 19, 443.

χυτλόω (χύτλον), aor. mid. optat. χυτλώσαιτο, *to purify, to wash, to bathe*. Mid. *to bathe oneself*; also *to anoint oneself* after bathing, Od. 6, 80.†

χυτός, ή, όν (χέω), *poured out*, spoken of things dry: χυτὴ γαῖα, cast-up earth, a mound, *6, 464. 14, 114. Od. 3, 258.

*χύτρη, ἡ, *an earthen pot*, Batr. 41.

χωλεύω (χωλός), *to be lame, to limp*, partcp. pres. *18, 411. 417. 20, 37.

χωλός, ή, όν, *lame, halting, limping*, πόδα, 2, 217. 9, 503. 18, 397. Od. 8, 308. 332.

χώομαι, Ep. depon. mid. aor. ἐχωσάμην and χωσάμην, subj. 3 sing. χώσεται for χώηται, 1, 80; the pres. always uncontr., *to be wroth, to be angry, to be displeased, to be grieved*, often with κῆρ, θυμόν, κατὰ θυμόν, etc. a) With dat. of the person with whom one is angry, 1, 80. 9, 555. 21, 306. b) With gen. of the person and thing on whose account one is angry, 1, 429. 2, 689. 13, 165. 14, 266; rarely περί τινι, h. Merc. 236. c) With accus. only with pron. μή μοι τόδε χώεο, be not angry with me on this account, Od. 5, 215. 23, 213. (An act. χώω is not to be found.)

χωρέω (χώρη), fut. ήσω, aor. ἐχώρησα, Ep. χώρησα, prop. *to give place*, i. e. *to make room, to yield, to retire*, γαῖα ὕπερθεν χώρησεν, the earth yielded from beneath, h. Cer. 430; esply spoken of persons: *to yield, to go away, to retire*. α) With gen. of place or thing, ἐπάλξιος, from the breast-work, 12, 406; νεῶν, 15, 655; also with prep. ἀπὸ νηῶν προτὶ Ἴλιον, 13, 724. b) With dat. of the person from whom one retires, Ἀχιλλῆϊ, *13, 324. 17, 101.

χώρη, ἡ (ΧΑΩ), 1) *the space* which any thing occupies, *a place*, 6, 516. Od. 16, 352. 2) *a region, a country*, χῶραι ἀνθρώπων, Od. 8, 573.

χωρίς, adv. (χῶρος), *separated, apart, separate, aside*, 7, 470. Od. 4. 130; χωρὶς μέν, χωρὶς δέ, Od. 9, 221, 222.

χῶρος, ὁ (ΧΑΩ) = χώρη, *space, place*, 3, 315. 4, 116. 8, 491. Od. 1, 426; see διω-

Ψαλιδόστομος. 440 Ψυχρός.

φαίνω. 2) *a region, a district*, ὑλήεις, Od. 14, 2.

Ψ.

Ψ, the twenty-third letter of the Greek alphabet; hence the sign of the twenty-third rhapsody.

*Ψαλιδόστομος, ον (στόμα), *having shears on the mouth, shear-jawed*, comic epith. of a crab, Batr. 297.

ψάμαθος, ἡ (ψάω)=ἄμαθος, *sand*, esply *the sand of the sea-shore, the sea-shore itself*, the 'dunes;' also in the plur. 7, 462. Od. 3, 38; as a periphrasis for a great number, 2, 800. 9, 385.

*ψαμαθώδης, ες (εἶδος), *sandy, abounding in sand*, h. Merc. 73, 347.

ψάμμος, ἡ (ψάω), *sand, dust, loose earth*, Od. 12, 243.†

ψάρ, ἀρός, ὁ, Ion. and Ep. ψήρ, *a starling (sturnus)*, ψαρῶν, 17, 755; ψῆρας, *16, 583.

ψαύω (ψάω), prop. ψάξω, with διχαμμα, imperf. without augm. ψαῦον, aor. 1 ἔψαυσα, subj. ψαύσῃ, *to touch, to graze, to glance upon*, with gen. ἐπισσώτρων, 23, 519. 806: αἴης, h. Ven. 125. ψαῦον ἱπποκόμοι κόρυθες λαμπροῖσι φάλοισι νευόντων, 13, 132. 16, 216. Construct with Damm: ψαῦον νευόντων, prop. a poet. brief expression for ψαῦον ἱπποκ. κόρ. νευόντων λαμπρ. φάλων νευόντων, the horse-hair helmets touched each other, as they nodded, with their glittering cones. [*The hairy crests of their resplendent casques Kiss'd close at every nod*. Cp.]. Passow joins (less well) ψαῦον φάλοισι, and translates, — helm struck on helm; although ψαύω with dat. occurs in later writers, Quint. Smyrn. 7, 349.

*ψαφαρότριχος, ον (θρίξ), *with dirty, rough hair*, μῆλα, h. 18, 32.

ψεδνός, ἤν, όν (ψέω), prop. scraped off, then *thin, scanty*, λάχνη, 2, 219.†

ψευδάγγελος, ον (ἄγγελος), *a faithless messenger, a false messenger*, 15, 159.†

ψευδής, ές, gen. έος (ψεύδω), *lying, false, deceptive*, οὐ γὰρ ἐπὶ ψευδέσσι πατήρ ἔσσετ' ἀρωγός, ed. Wolf after Aristarch, the father will not be an auxiliary to liars, 4, 235.† The earlier reading was ψευδέεσσι, as if from ψεῦδος, and is followed by Buthe and Voss: the father will not be an abettor of falsehoods.

ψεύδομαι, depon. mid. (ψεῦδος) fut. ψεύσομαι, aor. 1 partcp. ψευσάμενος, *to lie, to tell an untruth, to deceive*, 4, 404. 10, 534. Od. 4, 140. h. Merc. 369; In the partcp.. Il. 5, 635. 6, 163. *b*) With accus. *to cheat, to deceive*, ὅρκια, *to falsify a league*, 7, 352.

ψεῦδος, εος, τό, *a lie, untruth, deception, deceit*, 2. 81. 319. Od. 3, 20. οὔτι ψεῦδος ἄτας ἐμὰς κατέλεξας, no untruly (as a falsehood) hast thou related my offences, Il. 9, 115; often in the plur. 22, 576. Od. 11, 366.

ψευστέω (ψεύστης), fut. ψευστήσω, *to be a liar, to lie*, 19, 107.†

ψεύστης, ου (ψεύδω), *a liar, a deceiver*, 24, 261.†

ψηλαφάω (ψάω), Ep. partcp. ψηλαφόων, expanded for ψηλαφῶν, *to touch, to handle*, χερσί, Od. 9, 416.†

ψήρ, ηρός, ὁ, Ep. for ψάρ, q. v.

ψηφίς, ίδος, ἡ, dimin. of ψῆφος, *a little stone, a pebble*, fem. 21, 260.†

ψιάς, άδος, ἡ, poet. (ψίω) = ψακάς, *a drop*, in the plur. 16, 459.†

ψιλός, ἡ, όν (ψίω), prop. rubbed off, hence *bare, bald, naked, empty*, spoken of hair and other objects: δέρμα, a smooth hide, Od. 13, 437. ψιλὴ ἄροσις, a bare, i. e. an unplanted piece of ploughland, Il. 9, 580. ψιλὴ τρόπις, the bare keel (separated from the remaining timbers), Od. 12, 421, πόδας, Ep. 15.

Ψιχάρπαξ, αγος, ὁ (ψίξ, ἁρπάζω), that steals crumbs, *Crumb-thief*, a mouse's name, Batr. 24.

ψολόεις, εσσα, εν (ψόλος), prop. *sooty*, then *smoking, flaming, fiery, κεραυνός, *Od. 23, 330. 24, 539. h. Ven. 289.

*ψόφος, ὁ, *a sound, a noise*, h. Merc. 285.

Ψυρίη, ἡ (τὰ Ψύρα, Strab.), a little island between Lesbus and Chios, in the Ægæan sea, now Ιpsara, Od. 3. 172.

ψυχή, ἡ (ψύχω), prop. *the breath*, and because this is the index of life, it signifies also, 1) *life, the vital power, the soul, the spirit*, τὸν ἔλιπε ψυχή, the spirit left him, i. e. he swooned, 5, 695; but also the life, Od. 14, 426 (where it is used of animals); also often connected with μένος, Il. 5, 296. 8, 123: αἰών, 16, 453; with θυμός, 11, 334; also in the plur. ψυχὰς παρθέμενοι, staking their life, Od. 3, 74. Il. 1, 3, 13, 763. This vital principle was conceived of as a real substance: when the man died, it left the body through the mouth, 9, 409; or through a wound, 14, 518. 16, 503; hence 2) *the soul of the departed* in the underworld, *a spirit*, ψυχή Ἀγαμέμνονος, Διόστος, which was indeed destitute of a body, but still retained the form of the body, Od. 11, 207. Il. 23, 65; to this were wanting the φρένες, see φρήν. 23, 103; it was consequently only *a shade*, εἴδωλον, Od. 11, 601; hence also both together, ψυχὴ καὶ εἴδωλον, Il. 23, 103. Od. 24, 14; and in this sense ψυχή often stands opposed to the body, which the ancient Greks called *I*, Il. 1, 3. Od. 14, 32. (For states of mind it does not occur in Hom.) Worthy of note is the construct. κατὰ σύνεσιν. ψυχὴ Τειρεσίαο σκῆπτρον ἔχων, for ἔχουσα, Od. 11, 90: cf. Kühner, § 365. 2.

ψύχος, εος, τό (ψύχω), *coolness, cold*, Od. 10, 553.†

ψυχρός, ἡ, όν (ψύχω), *cold, cool, fresh*, ὕδωρ, Od. 9. 392; χαλκός, Il. 5, 75; χάλαζα, χιών, 15, 171. 22, 152.

Ψῦ'χω. 441 Ὠκεανός.

ψύχω, aor. 1 ἔψυξα, to breathe, to blow, ἦκα ψύξασα, 20, 440.†

ψωμός, ὁ (ψώω), a bit, a morsel, a mouthful, ψωμοὶ ἀνδρόμεοι, morsels of human flesh, Od. 9, 374.†

Ω.

Ω, the twenty-fourth letter of the Greek alphabet, and hence the sign of the twenty-fourth book.

ὦ and ὤ, Interj. O! 1) Simply to strengthen the address in the voc., in which case it is to be accented ὦ: ὦ Μενέλαε, 4, 189. 17, 716. 2) As an exclamation of astonishment or of lamentation it is accented ὤ: ὤ πόποι, 1, 254; often ὤ μοι, as an exclamation of lamentation with nom. following, ὤ μοι ἐγώ, ah me! 11, 404. 16, 433. Od. 5, 299.

Ὠγυγίη, ἡ, an island of mythic geography, the abode of Calypso, Od. 1, 85. 6, 172. 7, 244, seq. If the course of Hermês is connected with the voyage of Odysseus (Ulysses), and in this way an attempt is made to fix the situation of the island, it must be sought in the south-western sea. The ancients found it in the island Gaulus now Gozzo, near Malta, Strab. I. p. 26. Voss, Alte Weltkunde XV., places it in the great bay between Lybia and the Atlas, and Grotofend, Geograph. Ephem. 48. Bd. 3. St. p. 277, in the neighbourhood of Atlas; Völcker, Hom. Geog. 8. 120, seeks, on the other hand, to prove the north-western situation of the island.

ὧδε, adv. (from ὅς). 1) An adv. of manner: thus, so, in this way. a) Prim. referring to something following, 1, 181. 3, 297. 18, 266, and often; but also to something preceding, 7, 34. b) In complete sentences correlate: ὧδε—ὡς. so—as, 3, 300. Od. 19, 312; or ὡς—ὧδε, Il. 6, 177. c) Like αὕτως: ὧδε θέεις, thou runnest thus, i. e. in vain, 17, 75; thus, directly, upon the spot, just, 18, 392. Od. 1, 182. 2, 28 [see the close of the article]. 2) Adv. of place: hither, here, h. Ap. 471. In Hom., as the ancient Gramm. with Aristarch. maintain, ὧδε never has the local signif. (cf. Schol. Ven. ad Il. 3, 297. Apoll. Lex) There are however some passages which admit of no other easy explanation, as 18, 392. Od. 1, 182. 17, 545. Il. 12, 346. Od. 2, 28; in which it signifies hither; and Il. 2, 258. 24, 598, where it means here; cf. Buttm. Gr. Gram. § 1'6. Rem. 24. With the view of Aristarch. agree among the moderns critics Heyne, Hermann ad Orph. p. 692; Nitzsch ad Od. 1, 182; and Lehrs Aristarch. p. 84.

ᾤδει, see οἰδέω.

ᾠδή, ἡ, contract. from ἀοιδή (ἀείδω), a song, a hymn, h. Ap. 20. Cer. 494.

ὠδίνω, poet. (ὠδίς), only partcp. pres. to have the pangs of parturition, to bear, 11, 269. 2) Generally, to have violent pains. ὀδύνῃσιν, Od. 9, 415.

ὠδίς, ῖνος, ἡ, a pain of travail, mly in the plur. the pangs of parturition, 11, 271.† h. Ap. 92.

ὠδύσατο, see ὀδύσσομαι.

ὠθέω, Ep. iterat. imperf. ὤθεσκε, Od. 11, 596; aor. 1 ὦσα (ἔωσα, only 16, 410. h. Merc. 305); iterat. aor. ὤσασκε, Od. 11, 599; aor. 1 mid. ὠσάμην. Act. 1) to thrust, to press, to drive, and according to the relation indicated by the prep. to thrust away, to push forward, to drive along, τινά or τί, prim. spoken of men, mly in a hostile signif. τινὰ ἀφ' ἵππων, to thrust any one from the chariot, Il. 5, 19. 835. 11, 143. 320; τινὰ ἐκ Πύλου, to expel any one from Pylos, 2, 744; ἀπὸ σφείων, 4, 535. 5, 626; ἰθὺς τάφροιο, 8, 336. b) Without a hostile sense: ξίφος ἐς κουλεόν, to thrust the sword into the scabbard, 1, 220; λᾶαν ποτὶ λόφον, to thrust the stone up the hill, Od. 11, 596. Also for any one's benefit: δόρυ ὑπὲκ δίφροιο, to thrust away the spear from the chariot, Il. 5, 854; ἐκ μηροῦ δόρυ, 5, 194; ἀπ' ὀφθαλμῶν νέφος ἀχλύος, 15, 668. c) Spoken of the force of wind and waves. 13, 138. Od. 3, 295. Mid. 1) to thrust oneself forth, to press forwards, Il. 16, 592. 2) With accus. to thrust any thing, to push along, to drive away (away from oneself or apart), τινά, 5, 691; ἀπὸ ἕθεν, 6, 62; τινὰ ἀπὸ νεῶν, 11, 803; also with gen. alone τείχεος, 12, 420; τινὰ προτὶ Ἴλιον, to drive any one to Ilium, 8, 295. 16, 655.

ᾤετο, ὠΐσθην, see οἴομαι.

ὦκα, adv. Ep. (ὠκύς for ὠκέα). quickly, hastily, 1, 402. Od. 2, 8; and often.

Ὠκαλέη, ἡ, a village in Bœotia, between Haliartus and Alalcomenæ, 2, 501.

*Ὠκεανόνδε, adv. to the Ocean, h. Merc. 68.

Ὠκεανός, ὁ (according to the Schol. from ὠκύς and νάω, swift-flowing, according to Hermann, from ὠκύς and ἕειν, i. e. ἰέναι (ire), Celerivena: as Οὐρανός fm ὄρειν). 1) the mighty stream which encompasses the earth. It is always distinguished from the sea (θάλασσα, πόντος, ἅλς); Hom. calls it a river, ποταμός, 18, 607. 20, 7. ῥόος Ὠκεανοῖο, 16, 151. That it encompasses the whole earth appears from the epith. ἀψόρροος, and exply from the description of the shield of Achilles, where Hêphæstus so represents it, 18, 609. It is also mentioned in the four quarters of the world; in the east, Eôs (Aurora), Helios, and the constellations rise from it, 7, 422. 19, 1. Od. 22, 197; in the west they sink into it at their setting, Il. 8, 485. On its southern margin dwell the Pygmies, 3, 2—7; and of the northern bear it is said, that he alone is not immerged in the ocean, 18, 489. Od. 5

Ώκιμίδης.   442   Ώρετο.

475. It coincides also with the limits of the earth, Il. 14, 200. Od. 4, 563. Beyond the ocean in the west, is the gloomy Hades, Od. 10, 508; on this side, the blissful Elysium, Od. 4, 568. 2) As a god, he is inferior in power only to Zeus, Il. 20, 7. 14, 245. 21, 195. His wife is Tethys, and his daughters, Thetis. Eurynome, Perse, 14, 302. 18, 398. Od. 10, 139. He is the origin of all rivers and fountains, and indeed the father of all the gods, Il. 21, 196. 14, 201. 244. In Hes. Th. 133, he is the son of Uranus and Gæa [Cœlus and Terra], cf. Völcker, Hom. Geog. § 15, seq.

*Ώκιμίδης, ου, ὁ (from ὤκιμον, basil, ocimum basilicum), prop. name of a frog, basil-lover, Batr. 213.

ὤκιστος, η, ον, Ion. superl. from ὠκύς, q. v.

ὠκτειρα, see οἰκτείρω.

ὠκύαλος, ον, poet. (ἅλς), fleet in the sea, swift sailing, epith. of a ship, 15, 705. Od. 12, 182. [According to Ameis, ἅλς does not enter into the composit., but it is a mere paragogic form of ὠκύς, as εὐρύαλος for εὐρύς. So Schol. Bekk. ad Il. 15, 705; and Hesych.]

Ὠκύαλος, ὁ, a Phæacian, Od. 8, 111.

ὠκύμορος, ον, poet. (μόρος), superl. ὠκυμορώτατος, η, ον, 1, 505; of a quick fate or death, i. e. 1) Pass. dying a speedy death, dying early, 1, 417. 18, 95. Od. 1, 266. 2) Act.: bringing a speedy death, quick-slaying, ἰοί, Il. 15, 441. Od. 22, 35.

ὠκυπέτης, ου, ὁ, poet. (πέτομαι), quick-flying, fleet-rushing, epith. of horses, *8, 42. 13, 24.

ὠκύπορος, ον, poet. (πόρος), fleet-going, swift-sailing, epith. of ships, 1, 421. 2, 351. Od. 4, 708.

ὠκύπους, ὁ, ἡ, gen. ποδος (πούς), swift-footed, epith. of horses, 2, 383; often in the Il.; once Od. 18, 263. h. Ap. 265.

ὠκύπτερος, ον, poet. (πτερόν), having fleet pinions, swift-flying, ἱρηξ, 13, 62.†

*Ὠκυρόη, ἡ, daughter of Oceanus and Tethys, h. Cer. 420.

ὠκύροος, ον, Ep. for ὠκύρροος (ῥέω), swift-flowing, ποταμός, *5, 598. 7, 133.

ὠκύς, ὠκεία, ὠκύ, poet. and Ep. fem. ὠκέα, in the Il. always in connexion with Ἶρις, 2, 786; in Od. 12, 274, only with Lampetia. Superl. ὤκιστος, η, ον, also regular ὠκύτατος, Od. 8, 331; fleet, quick, active, hasty. 1) Spoken of animated beings: with accus. πόδας ὠκύς, Il. 1, 58. 84; without πόδας, Od. 8, 329; also ἱρηξ, Il. 15, 238; ἵπποι, 3, 263. 2) Of inanimate things: βέλος, ὀϊστός, 5, 112. 395. 11, 478; νόημα, h. Merc. 43; νέας, 8, 197. Od. 9, 101. The neut. plur. ὤκιστα, as adv., very quickly, Od. 22, 77. 133.

*ὠλένη, ἡ, the elbow, h. Merc. 388.

Ὠλενίη, ἡ, πέτρη, the Olenian rock, according to Strab. the summit of the mountain Scollis in Achaia, on the borders of Elis, 2, 617. 11, 756.

Ὤλενος, ἡ (ὁ, Strab. VIII. p. 386), a town in Ætolia, on the Aracynthus, even in antiquity destroyed, 2, 639. Strab. X. p. 386.

ὠλεσίκαρπος, ον (κάρπος), losing the fruit, epith. of pastures whose fruits fall before maturity, Od. 10. 510.†

ἆλξ, ἡ, only accus. sing. ἆλκα, poet. syncop. for ἆλαξ = αὔλαξ, a furrow, 3. 707. Od. 18, 375.

ὠμηστής, οῦ, ἡ (ὠμός, ἐσθίω), eating raw flesh, carnivorous (flesh-devouring; V.), οἰωνοί, κύνες. ἰχθῦς. 11, 454. 22, 67. 24, 78; hence blood-thirsty. inhuman, ἀνήρ, 24, 207 (not ὠμηστῆς according to Apion, cf. Spitzner ad Il. 11, 504).

ὠμογέρων, οντος, ὁ, ἡ (γέρων), a fresh, vigorous old man, whom age has not unstrung; one who enjoys a green old age. So Antilochus calls Odysseus (Ulysses), 23, 791.†

*Ὠμόδαμος. ὁ (δαμάω), that subdues rawness, a deity of the potters, Ep. 14, 10.

ὠμοθετέω, poet. (ὠμός, τίθημι), aor. 1 ὠμοθέτησα; mid. to place raw pieces of flesh), a part of the ceremony of sacrifice; pieces of flesh were cut from all the limbs and laid upon the thigh-bones enveloped in the caul (ἐπ' αὐτῶν): cf. Od. 14, 427; always ἐπ' αὐτῶν ὠμοθέτησαν, Il. 1, 461 [Which with crude slices thin they overspread, Cp.]. Od. 3, 458. 12, 361. Mid.=act. ὠμοθετεῖτο—ἐς πίονα δημόν, Od. 14, 427.

ὦμος, ὁ (οἴω=φέρω), a shoulder, the part of the body from the neck to the upper arm, νείατος ὦμος, 15, 341; πρυμνός, Od. 17, 504; often in the dual and plur.

ὠμός, ή, όν, 1) raw, uncooked, esply spoken of flesh, 22, 347. Od. 12, 346; ὠμὸν βεβρώθειν τινά, proverbial, spoken of the greatest cruelty, Il. 4, 35. Adv. ὠμὰ δάσασθαι, to swallow raw, 23, 21. Od. 18, 87. 2) unripe, untimely, spoken of fruits: metaph. γέρας, a too early age, Od. 15, 357.

ὠμοφάγος, ον (φαγεῖν), eating raw, esply eating raw flesh, epith. of wild beasts, *5, 782. 11, 479. h. Ven. 124.

ὤμωξα, see οἰμώζω.

ὠνάμην, ὤνησα, see ὀνίνημι.

ὠνητός, ή, όν, verb. adj. (ὠνέομαι), purchased, bought, Od. 14, 202.†

ὦνος, ὁ, purchase-money, the price of any thing, 21, 41. 23, 746; gain, Od. 14, 297. 15, 388. 2) the act of purchasing, ὦνος ὁδαίων, the procuring of a return freight [by exchange for the goods brought out]. Nitzsch, Od. 15, 445.

ὠνοσάμην, see ὄνομαι.

ὠνοχόει, see οἰνοχοέω.

ὤξε, see οἴγνυμι.

[ὤπασα, see ὀπάζω.]

ὤρ, ἡ, contr. for ὄαρ, of which the dat. plur. ὤρεσσιν, to the wives, 5, 486; see ὄαρ.

ὤρετο, see ὄρνυμι.

ὥρη, ἡ, Ion. for ὥρα, prop. *any definite time, a portion of time*, hence 1) *a season*, nly in the plur. to indicate the course of the year, ἐπήλυθον ὧραι, Od. 2, 107. 10, 469; eaply *spring*, Il. 2, 468. Od. 9, 51. Homer mentions four seasons: ἔαρ, or εἴαρος ὥρη, Il. 6, 148; or ὥρῃ εἰαρινῇ, Il. 2. 471. Od. 18, 367; θέρος, ὀπώρη, χειμών and ὥρη χειμερίη, Od. 5, 465. 2) *the time of the day, the hour*, νυκτὸς ἐν ὥρῃ, h. Merc. 65, 158 (not in the Il. and Od.) 3) Generally, *the proper time*, the time in which any thing is to be done, ὥρη κοίτοιο, Od. 3, 334 ; μύθων, ὕπνου, Od. 11, 379 ; δόρποιο, Od. 14, 407; with infin. ὥρη εὕδειν, Od. 11, 330. 373 ; and accus. with infin., Od. 21, 428 ; ἐν ὥρῃ, Od. 17, 176 ; εἰς ὥρας, Od. 14, 294.

Ὧραι, αἱ, *Horæ, the Hours*; in Homer, who mentions neither the number nor the names, they are the door-keepers of Olympus, whose cloudy gate they open and shut, i. e. they preside over the weather, giving rain and clear weather, 5, 749, seq., 8, 393. Because a regular change of weather marks the seasons of the year, they are the goddesses also of the seasons and their change, Od. 10, 469. With the change of time they bring many blessings, Il. 21, 430; in connexion with the Graces, h. in Apoll. 194. Also as handmaids of Hērê, they are named, 8, 433. According to Hes. Th. 901, they are the daughters of Zeus and of Themis, three in number, Eunomia, Dike, and Eirene, cf. Jacobi, Mythol. Wörterb. p. 465.

Ὠρείθυια, ἡ (θύουσα, ὄρος, *furens in monte*), daughter of Nereus and Doris, 18, 48.

ὠρηφόρος, ον (φέρω), *bringing the seasons of the year, bringing maturity*, epith. of Dêmêtêr, h. Cer. 54, 192.

ὠρίζεσκε, see ὀαρίζω.

ὥριος, ίη, ιον, poet. (ὥρη), that the season brings or ripens, hence *timely, ripe*, ὥρια πάντα, the fruits of each season, Od. 9, 131.†

ἄριστος, Ion. for ὁ ἄριστος, q. v.

Ὡρίων, ωνος, ὁ. son of Hyrieus of Hyria in Bœotia, of uncommon strength and beauty, and an excellent hunter, a lover of Ἠώs (Aurora), Od. 5, 121, seq., 11, 310. He was slain by Artĕmis in Delos; he preserved his love of the chase even in Hades, Od. 11, 572. We also find him as a constellation, Il. 18, 486. 488. 22, 29. Od. 5, 274. According to later writers, a son of Poseidôn and Euryale, daughter of Minos; he received from his father the power to go through the sea. Artĕmis slew him, because he challenged her to hurl the discus, or because he dishonoured Opis, her companion, Apd. 1, 403. (Strab. X. p. 416, derives the name from Ὠρεός, a town in Eubœa; according to another tradition, his name is prop. Οὐρίων, Palæph. 5, 4.)

ὦρορε, see ὄρνυμι.

Ὦρος, ὁ, a Greek, slain by Hector, 11, 303.

ὦρσε, ὦρτο, see ὄρνυμι.

ὠρώρει, see ὄρνυμι.

ὠρωρέχαται, see ὀρέγω.

ὥς, adv. of the demonstrat. pronoun (from the old demonstrat. ὅς), only poet., often in Hom. 1) *in this way, thus*; καὶ ὥς, even thus, i. e. still, nevertheless, 1, 116. 3, 159. οὐδ᾽ ὥς, μηδ᾽ ὥς, even thus not, i. e. still not, 7, 263. 9, 351. Od. 1, 6. ἀλλ᾽ οὐ μὰν οὐδ᾽ ὥς, not even thus indeed, Il. 23, 441. 2) In comparisons ; often ὥς—ὥς, *so—as*, or ὡς—ὥς, *as—so*, spoken not only of likeness in kind, but also of simultaneousness, ὡς ἥψατο γούνων, ὣς ἔχετ᾽ ἐμπεφυυῖα, 1, 512. cf. 14, 291. Often in wishes, 4, 319. 8, 538. Od. 3, 218. 3) *therefore, for that reason*, in assigning a reason, Od. 2, 137. 9, 306. 24, 93. Il. 9, 444; Nitzsch ad Od. 2, 137, prefers this to ὥς. 4) *thus*, i. e. for example, Od. 5, 121. 125. 129. h. Ven. 219. Herm. on the last passage, and Nitzsch ad Od. 5, 121, justly prefer ὥς, *as*. 5) ὣς for ὡς, *as*, when it stands after its substantive, cf. ὡς.

ὡς, adv. from the relative pronoun ὅς. A) adv. of *manner* and *comparison*. It stands, 1) With substantives, adjectives, adverbs, and participles: *as, just as, like*. a) With a subst. it stands in Hom. α) Before the subst.: ὡς κύματα θαλάσσης, 2, 144. cf. 19, 403. 21, 262. 23, 430. Od. 5, 371. 15, 479. β) After the subst., and is then accented ; θεὸς ὥς, like a god, Il. 5, 78. 10, 33 ; Buttm., Lex. p. 534, is mistaken in supposing that ὡς always follows the subst. except in elliptical cases, as Od. 14. 441. b) With adj. and adv. Il. 22, 425. 2, 344. c) With partcp. ὡς οὐκ ἀΐοντι ἐοικώς, 23, 430. II) In introducing entire clauses: 1) In relative clauses of the *manner* : *as, quomodo*, cf. on the construct. ὅπως. a) With indic. 1, 276. 2, 10. 409 ; ὡς ἴθυνεν, 23, 871, according to Bothe: as if he were taking aim ; Krause takes ὡς for ἕως: until he directed it; we find ἕως also in the Schol. The conjecture of Voss is however to be preferred: ὡς ἰθύνοι, that he might aim it. b) With the subjunct. only with ἄν, in the frequently recurring sentence : ἀλλ᾽ ἄγεθ᾽ ὡς ἂν ἐγὼν εἴπω, πειθώμεθα, as l (if ye will listen) shall say, 2, 139. 12, 75. c) With optat. after πειρᾶν, 9, 181. 2) In clauses of comparison, *as. like*, where ὥς, τώς, οὕτω often correlate to the ὡς. In comparisons it stands a) With indic. pres. when any thing is compared with that which is real or has taken place, 5, 499. 9, 4. β) Aorist, when it is taken as a single case from the past, for illustration, 2, 326. γ) The future, when it relates to an event which can always happen in the future, 10, 183. cf. δυσωρέω, Od. 5, 368. Still Nitzsch ad Od. l. c., and Thiersch, § 346. 10, require the

'Ως ἄν.

subjunct. in the passages quoted. *b*) With subjunct. pres. or aorist without ἄν, when the declaration is represented as something that can happen, Il. 5, 161. 10, 485. 22, 93. *c*) With optat. only after ὡσεί, q. v. Longer comparisons Homer often introduces with ὡς ὅτε; cf. ὅτε and Herm. ad Viger. p. 910, de Usu Modorum apud Homer. in Comparationibus, Thiersch, § 346. 8, 9. Kühner, § 690. 3) In independent clauses which contain an exclamation of interest or admiration: *how*: *a*) With adj. and adv. ὡς ἄνοον κραδίην ἔχες, how senseless a heart hast thou! 21, 441. cf. Od. 3, 196. 24, 194. *b*) In introducing whole clauses: *how*, ὡς μοι δέχεται κακὸν ἐκ κακοῦ αἰεί, how evil upon evil always follows me, 11. 19, 290. Thus 21, 273. 441. 17, 328. Od. 3, 196. *B*) Conj. 1) Of time: *as, when* (*ut*), always spoken of past things with indicat., Il. 1, 600. 2, 321. ὡς οὖν, 3, 21. ὡς τὰ πρῶτα, h. Cer. 80. 2) For ἕως, *until*, 23, 871, see Δ. II. *a*. II) Spoken of the cause: *as thus, because*, 1, 276. 10, 116. Od. 4, 373 (cf. Thiersch, § 317. 5). Il. 6, 109; *wherefore*, Od. 2, 137. 4, 93. cf. Nitzsch. III) In introducing explanatory clauses, ὅτι, *how, that*, ὡς δή, Il. 10, 110. 7, 402. 13, 204. Od. 1, 217. IV) In assigning the design or purpose : *so that, that, in order that*, cf. on the constr. ὅπως. 1) With subj. Il. 1, 558. 2, 3. 363; with which is joined ἄν or κέ, 1, 32. 16, 84. 2) With optat. 2, 281. 23, 361; also with κέ, Od. 8. 21. 13, 402. cf. Thiersch, § 341. 5. 6. Kühner, § 644, seq. V) In sentences which express a wish, and properly belong as elliptical clauses to sentences denoting design : *O that! would that!* (*utinam*). ὡς ἀπόλοιτο καὶ ἄλλος, would that another also might perish, Od. 1, 47. cf. Il. 18, 107; also with κέ: ὡς κέ οἱ αὖθι γαῖα χάνοι! O that the earth might yawn for him! 6, 282; also ὡς μὴ θάνοι, Od. 15, 359. 2) ὡς ὤφελον, see ὀφείλω. *c*) Prepos. with accus. *to* (*ad*), indicating only motion to persons, Od. 17, 218.†

ὡς ἄν, see ὡς.

ὡσαύτως, adv. (ὡς αὔτως), *just so, in the same way*, always separated by δέ: ὡς δ' αὔτως, 3, 339; in the Od. ὡς δ' αὔτως stands, Od. 6, 166. 9, 31; cf. αὔτως.

ὡσεί or ὡς εἰ, adv. *as if, as though*, with optat. 2, 780. 22, 410. *b*) With subjunct. 9, 481. cf. Thiersch, § 346 8 as ὥσπερ, *as, just as*, 16, 59. 23 5; with partcp. h. Cer. 238; also ὥστε ὥς εἴτε, Od. 10, 420; and ὡσεί περ, Cer. 215.

ὥς κε and ὥς κεν, see ὡς.

ὥσπερ, adv. (ὡς, πέρ), cf. ὅσπερ, *just as, even as*, often separated : ὡς τὸ πάρος περ, 5, 806; ὡς νύ περ ὧδε, 2, 258. Cer. 116. 2) Also in introducing enti clauses, 1, 211. Od. 21, 212.

ὥστε, adv. ὥς τέ, cf. ὅστε. 1) *as, just as, like*, rather Ep. 2, 289; and also *the quality of, as* (*οἷόν τε*), 3, 381; also separated, 17, 61. 3, 381. *b*) In introducing whole clauses: *a*) With indicat 2, 459. 17, 434. β) With subjunct. 2, 17 16, 428. cf. Thiersch, § 346. 8. Kühner § 690. 2) as conjunct. *so that, that*, to indicate an immediate consequence o effect from the preceding: with infin only twice, 9, 42. Od. 17, 21.

Ὦτος, ὁ. 1) son of Poseidon and Iphimedia, one of the Aloïdes, brother of Ephialtes, 5, 385; see Ἐφιάλτης. 2) a Cyllenian, a companion of Meges, 15, 518.

ὠτειλή, ἡ. (Dor. for οὐτειλή), *a wound*, esply an open wound: οὐταμένη ὠτειλή, 14, 518. 17, 86. Od. 19, 456.

ὠτώεις, εσσα, εν (οὖς), *eared, handled, furnished with handles*, τρίπους, *23, 264. 513.

αὐτός, Ion. and Ep. for ὁ αὐτός, 5, 396. cf. Buttm., § 27. N. 11; Rost, Dial. 13. p. 388; Kühner, § 15.

ὤφελλον and ὤφελον, see ὀφείλω.

ὠχράω (ὠχρός), fut. ήσω, *to become white* or *pale, to pale*, ὠχρήσαντα, Od. 11, 529.†

*ὠχρός, ή, όν, *pale, pallid*, esply a paleish green, spoken of a frog, Batr. 81. ὤχρος, ὁ, *paleness, pallour*, esply of the countenance, 3, 35.† (According to Buttm., Ausf. Spr. II. p. 325, prob. a neut. τὸ ὤχρος.)

ὤψ, ή, gen. ὠπός (ὄπτω), only accus. always εἰς ὦπα, *the eye, countenance, aspect*, εἰς ὦπα ἰδέσθαι τινί, to look at any one's face, 9, 373; also τινός, 15, 147; εἰς ὦπα ἔοικεν, she appears similar in countenance, 3, 158. cf. Od. 1, 411.

Ὤψ, ὦπος, ὁ, pr. n., son of Pisenor, father of Eurycleia, Od. 1, 429. 2, 347. On the accent, see Eustath. ad Od. 1, 429. Etym. Mag.

THE END.

www.ingramcontent.com/pod-product-compliance
Lightning Source LLC
Chambersburg PA
CBHW032007300426
44117CB00008B/931